W9-AGJ-678

GLENCOE LITERATURE

The Reader's Choice

The Reader's Choice

Program Consultants

Beverly Ann Chin
Denny Wolfe
Jeffrey Copeland
Mary Ann Dudzinski
William Ray
Jacqueline Jones Royster
Jeffrey Wilhelm

Course 3

New York, New York Columbus, Ohio Woodland Hills, California Peoria, Illinois

Acknowledgments

Grateful acknowledgment is given authors, publishers, photographers, museums, and agents for permission to reprint the following copyrighted material. Every effort has been made to determine copyright owners. In case of any omissions, the Publisher will be pleased to make suitable acknowledgments in future editions.

Acknowledgments continued on page R135.

The Standardized Test Practice pages in this book were written by The Princeton Review, the nation's leader in test preparation. Through its association with McGraw-Hill, The Princeton Review offers the best way to help students excel on standardized assessments.

The Princeton Review is not affiliated with Princeton University or Educational Testing Service.

Glencoe/McGraw-Hill

A Division of The ***McGraw·Hill*** *Companies*

Printed in the United States of America

Send all inquiries to:
Glencoe/McGraw-Hill
8787 Orion Place
Columbus, Ohio 43240

ISBN 0-02-635389-X
(Student Edition)

ISBN 0-02-635391-1
(Teacher's Wraparound Edition)

6 7 8 9 10 071/043 04 03 02 01

Senior Program Consultants

Beverly Ann Chin is Professor of English, Co-Director of the English Teaching Program, former Director of the Montana Writing Project, and former Director of Composition at the University of Montana in Missoula. In 1995–1996, Dr. Chin served as President of the National Council of Teachers of English. She currently serves as a Member of the Board of Directors of the National Board for Professional Teaching Standards. Dr. Chin is a nationally recognized leader in English language arts standards, curriculum, and assessment. Formerly a high school English teacher and adult education reading teacher, Dr. Chin has taught in English language arts education at several universities and has received awards for her teaching and service.

Denny Wolfe, a former high school English teacher and department chair, is Professor of English Education, Director of the Tidewater Virginia Writing Project, and Director of the Center for Urban Education at Old Dominion University in Norfolk, Virginia. For the National Council of Teachers of English, he has served as Chairperson of the Standing Committee on Teacher Preparation, President of the International Assembly, member of the Executive Committee of the Council on English Education, and editor of the SLATE Newsletter. Author of more than seventy-five articles and books on teaching English. Dr. Wolfe is a frequent consultant to schools and colleges on the teaching of English language arts.

Program Consultants

Jeffrey S. Copeland is Professor and Head of the Department of English Language and Literature at the University of Northern Iowa, where he teaches children's and young adult literature courses and a variety of courses in English education. A former public school teacher, he has published many articles in the professional journals in the language arts. The twelve books he has written or edited include *Speaking of Poets: Interviews with Poets Who Write for Children and Young Adults* and *Young Adult Literature: A Contemporary Reader.*

Mary Ann Dudzinski is a former high school English teacher and recipient of the Ross Perot Award for Teaching Excellence. She also has served as a member of the core faculty for the National Endowment for the Humanities Summer Institute for Teachers of Secondary School English and History at the University of North Texas. After fifteen years of classroom experience in grades 9–12, she currently is a language arts consultant.

William Ray has taught English in the Boston Public Schools; at Lowell University; University of Wroclaw, Poland; and, for the last fourteen years, at Lincoln-Sudbury Regional High School in Sudbury, Massachusetts. He specializes in world literature. He has worked on a variety of educational texts, as editor, consultant, and contributing writer.

Jacqueline Jones Royster is Associate Professor of English at The Ohio State University. She is also on the faculty of the Bread Loaf School of English at Middlebury College in Middlebury, Vermont. In addition to the teaching of writing, Dr. Royster's professional interests include the rhetorical history of African American women and the social and cultural implications of literate practices.

Jeffrey Wilhelm, a former English and reading teacher, is currently an assistant professor at the University of Maine where he teaches courses in middle and secondary level literacy. Author of several books and articles on the teaching of reading and the use of technology, he also works with local schools as part of the fledgling Adolescent Literacy Project and is the director of two annual summer institutes: the Maine Writing Project and Technology as a Learning Tool.

Teacher Reviewers

Bill Beyer
General Wayne Middle School
Malvern, Pennsylvania

Sister Marian Christi
St. Matthew School
Philadelphia, Pennsylvania

Christine Ferguson
North Buncombe Middle School
Asheville, North Carolina

Elizabeth Fischer
Tower Heights Middle School
Centerville, Ohio

Diane Gerrety
Bridgetown Junior High
Cincinnati, Ohio

Susan Giddings
Marble Falls Middle School
Marble Falls, Texas

Denise Goeckel
Magsig Middle School
Centerville, Ohio

Debbie Hampton
Central Davidson Middle School
Lexington, North Carolina

Tammy Harris
Walnut Springs Middle School
Columbus, Ohio

Marlene Henry
Northwood Elementary
Troy, Ohio

Brian Hinders
Tower Heights Middle School
Centerville, Ohio

Cheryl Keffer
Fayette County Schools Gifted Program
Oak Hill, West Virginia

Sheryl Kelso
Oldtown School
Oldtown, Maryland

Gail Kidd
Center Middle School
Azusa, California

Karen Mantia
Northmont City Schools
Clayton, Ohio

Nancy Mast
Hobart Middle School
Hobart, Indiana

Chiyo Masuda
Albany Middle School
Albany, California

Kim Mistler
Delhi Junior High School
Cincinnati, Ohio

Wilma Jean Nix
Baldwin Junior High School
Montgomery, Alabama

Joe Olague
Alder Junior High
Fontana, California

Bonita Rephann
Musselman Middle School
Bunker Hill, West Virginia

Marie Rinaudo
St. John Berchman's Cathedral School
Shreveport, Louisiana

Carol Schowalter
El Roble Intermediate School
Claremont, California

Karen Shannon
Davis Drive Middle School
Apex, North Carolina

Joan Slater
Strack Intermediate
Klein, Texas

Joyce Stakem
St. Catherine of Siena School
Wilmington, Delaware

Elizabeth Struckman
Bridgetown Junior High School
Centerville, Ohio

Debbie Trepanier
Jenkins Middle School
Chewelah, Washington

Sarah Vick
Central Davidson Middle School
Lexington, North Carolina

Erin Watts
Albright Middle School
Houston, Texas

Anne Welch
Huntsville Middle School
Huntsville, Alabama

James Zartler
Centennial Middle School
Portland, Oregon

Book Overview

Reference Section

Contents

THEME ONE

No Place Like Home

indicates world literature

THEME TWO

CONTENTS

THEME ❧ THREE

Which Way to Go?

THEME FOUR

Fantastic Capers and Mischief Makers

CONTENTS

THEME ❧ FIVE

Free to Be

THEME SIX

CONTENTS

THEME SEVEN

Faces of Dignity

THEME EIGHT

Hair-Raising Tales

Reference Section

Features

MEDIA Connection

COMPARING SELECTIONS

GENRE FOCUS

Active Reading Strategies

Interdisciplinary Connection

Writing WORKSHOP

Skills

Grammar Link

Listening, Speaking, and Viewing

Reading and Thinking Skills

Technology Skills

Vocabulary Skills

Writing Skills

Skill Minilessons

GRAMMAR AND LANGUAGE

READING AND THINKING

VOCABULARY

Selections by Genre

Short Story/Fiction

Nonfiction

Poetry

Myths, Legends, Folktales

Drama

Songs

Electronic Media

Comic Strip

No Place Like Home

> *“Home is the place where, when you have to go there, they have to take you in.”*
>
> —Robert Frost

Fire and Ice, 1993. Peter Menzel. From the book *Material World: A Global Family Portrait.*

THEME CONTENTS

GENRE FOCUS SHORT STORY

Exploring the Theme

No Place Like Home

What is home? To some, it is the place where we grew up. To others, it's the family members who shaped us. For still others, it's simply a place where we feel comfortable and loved. In this theme, you will explore how our homes influence us, and how one's understanding of home can change over time.

Starting Points

HUMOR AT HOME

Cartoonists often turn to families as a source of ideas for their work. What family situations can you think of that could make funny cartoons?

- Jot down ideas for cartoons about funny family situations.
- Choose one idea to sketch out. If needed, include dialogue or a caption.

FAMILY TIES

Relationships and events at home prepare us for life on our own. Think of a conversation, argument, or situation that changed the way you think about home.

- How did the experience affect you? Write a few paragraphs to explain what you learned about home, family, and yourself.

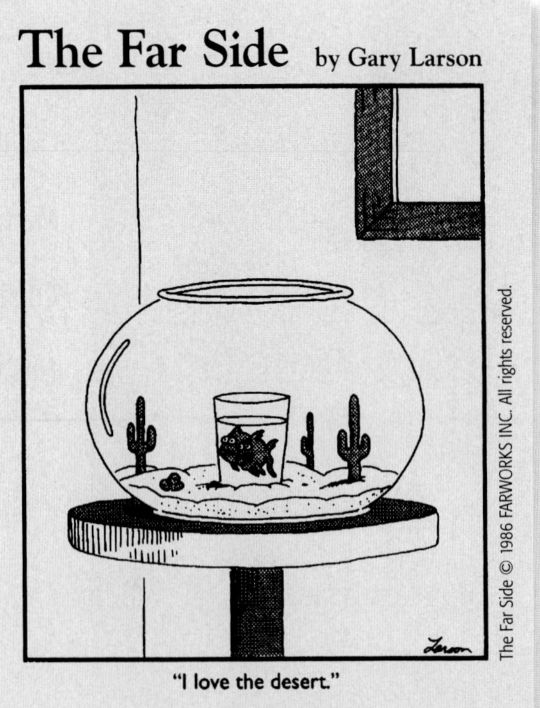

"I love the desert."

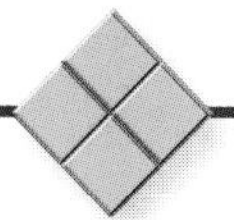

Theme Projects

Choose one of the projects below to complete as you read the selections in this theme. Work on your own, with a partner, or with a group.

CRITICAL VIEWING

Visions of Home

1. Create a collage to show what home means to you. Search through magazines, photographs, and newspapers for pictures that say "home."
2. Interview other people about their definitions of home. Write down their observations.
3. Paste your pictures and quotations onto poster board. Write a caption under each picture to explain its significance to you. Label each quote with the speaker's name.

MULTIMEDIA PROJECT

Create a Web Page

1. Collect favorite stories from relatives and close friends for a Web page. Use a Web publishing program that will allow you to create and edit text, graphics, and sound.
2. Gather souvenirs, family photographs, and tape recordings of stories. Write introductions, headings, and comments.
3. Follow the directions in the software to complete your page.

interNET CONNECTION

Visit lit.glencoe.com to get more project ideas or the titles of books related to the theme "No Place Like Home."

LEARNING FOR LIFE

Donate Your Time

1. Research homelessness in your community, and collect donations for a local homeless shelter. Try to get specific data, if possible. Ask what types of donations are needed (clothing, blankets, canned goods, household items).
2. Create posters inviting people to bring items to a central location. Use data from your research.
3. Have an adult help you deliver the items.
4. Report to the class about your experience.

Before You Read

The Treasure of Lemon Brown

MEET WALTER DEAN MYERS

Walter Dean Myers was ten years old when he started filling up notebooks with his stories and poems. Yet he never expected that his childhood hobby would blossom into a successful career. "I wrote for years without getting published," he remembers. "I never thought about having [anything] published outside of school publications." Myers later discovered that he could make a living at writing when he won a contest for picture book writers. Today he is an award-winning author, recognized especially for young-adult fiction.

Walter Dean Myers was born in 1937. This story was published in Boys' Life *in 1983.*

FOCUS ACTIVITY

Think of the objects you treasure most. Perhaps they include a letter, a ring, a picture, or a baseball.

Diagram It!

Using a word web like the one below, brainstorm several objects and personal belongings that you value.

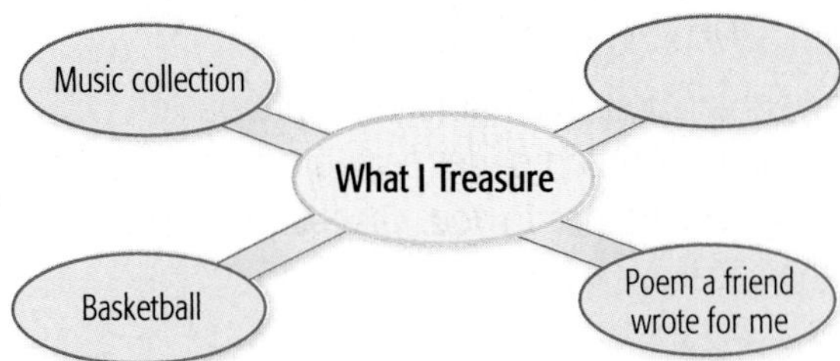

Setting a Purpose

Read to find out how one object can represent a person's life.

BACKGROUND

The Time and Place This contemporary story is set in an abandoned Harlem tenement in New York City.

Did You Know? The blues is a type of music that evolved from the experiences of African Americans over the last three centuries. More than just a beat or melody, the blues is a state of mind. The blues express sorrow and hardship.

VOCABULARY PREVIEW

impromptu (im promp′ to͞o) *adj.* made or done on the spur of the moment, without preparation; p. 6

tentatively (ten′ tə tiv lē) *adv.* hesitantly; uncertainly; p. 6

intently (in tent′ lē) *adv.* in a firmly focused way; with concentration; p. 8

involuntary (in vol′ ən ter′ ē) *adj.* not done willingly; p. 8

tremor (trem′ ər) *n.* a shaking or trembling movement; p. 8

commence (kə mens′) *v.* to begin; start; p. 9

eerie (ēr′ ē) *adj.* weird, especially in a frightening way; p. 10

ominous (om′ ə nəs) *adj.* threatening harm or evil; p. 11

The Treasure of Lemon Brown

Walter Dean Myers

The dark sky, filled with angry swirling clouds, reflected Greg Ridley's mood as he sat on the stoop[1] of his building. His father's voice came to him again, first reading the letter the principal had sent to the house, then lecturing endlessly about his poor efforts in math.

"I had to leave school when I was 13," his father had said, "that's a year younger than you are now. If I'd had half the chances that you have, I'd. . . ."

Greg had sat in the small, pale green kitchen listening, knowing the lecture would end with his father saying he couldn't play ball with the Scorpions. He had asked his father the week before, and his father had said it depended on his next report card. It wasn't often the Scorpions took on new players, especially 14-year-olds, and this was a chance of a lifetime for Greg. He hadn't been allowed to play high school ball, which he had really wanted to do, but playing for the Community Center team was the next best thing.

1. A *stoop* is one or more steps at the entrance of a building that lead up to a raised platform.

Report cards were due in a week, and Greg had been hoping for the best. But the principal had ended the suspense early when she sent that letter saying Greg would probably fail math if he didn't spend more time studying.

"And you want to play *basketball*?" His father's brows knitted over deep brown eyes. "That must be some kind of a joke. Now you just get into your room and hit those books."

That had been two nights before. His father's words, like the distant thunder that now echoed through the streets of Harlem,[2] still rumbled softly in his ears.

It was beginning to cool. Gusts of wind made bits of paper dance between the parked cars. There was a flash of nearby lightning, and soon large drops of rain splashed onto his jeans. He stood to go upstairs, thought of the lecture that probably awaited him if he did anything except shut himself in his room with his math book, and started walking down the street instead. Down the block there was an old tenement that had been abandoned for some months. Some of the guys had held an impromptu checker tournament there the week before, and Greg had noticed that the door, once boarded over, had been slightly ajar.

Pulling his collar up as high as he could, he checked for traffic and made a dash across the street. He reached the house just as another flash of lightning changed the night to day for an instant, then returned the graffiti-scarred building to the grim shadows. He vaulted[3] over the outer stairs and pushed tentatively on the door. It was open, and he let himself in.

The inside of the building was dark except for the dim light that filtered through the dirty windows from the streetlamps. There was a room a few feet from the door, and from where he stood at the entrance, Greg could see a squarish patch of light on the floor. He entered the room, frowning at the musty[4] smell. It was a large room that might have been someone's parlor at one time. Squinting, Greg could see an old table on its side against one wall, what looked like a pile of rags or a torn mattress in the corner, and a couch, with one side broken, in front of the window.

He went to the couch. The side that wasn't broken was comfortable enough, though a little creaky. From this spot he could see the blinking neon sign over the bodega[5] on the corner. He sat awhile, watching the sign blink first green then red, allowing his mind to drift to the Scorpions, then to his father. His father had been a postal worker for all Greg's life, and was proud of it, often telling Greg how hard he had worked to pass the test. Greg had heard the story too many times to be interested now.

For a moment Greg thought he heard something that sounded like a scraping

2. *Harlem* is a section of Manhattan in New York City inhabited mostly by Puerto Ricans and African Americans.

3. Here, as a verb, *vaulted* means "jumped."
4. A *musty* smell is stale or moldy.
5. The Spanish word *bodega* (bō dā′ gä) can refer to a bar, a restaurant, a shop, or a pantry.

Vocabulary

impromptu (im promp′ to͞o) *adj.* made or done on the spur of the moment, without preparation

tentatively (ten′ tə tiv lē) *adv.* hesitantly; uncertainly

Jim, 1930. William H. Johnson. Oil on canvas, 21⅝ x 18¼ in. National Museum of American Art, Washington, DC.
Viewing the painting: In what ways might the boy in the painting be similar to Greg?

against the wall. He listened carefully, but it was gone.

Outside the wind had picked up, sending the rain against the window with a force that shook the glass in its frame. A car passed, its tires hissing over the wet street and its red tail lights glowing in the darkness.

Greg thought he heard the noise again. His stomach tightened as he held himself still and listened intently. There weren't any more scraping noises, but he was sure he had heard something in the darkness—something breathing!

He tried to figure out just where the breathing was coming from; he knew it was in the room with him. Slowly he stood, tensing. As he turned, a flash of lightning lit up the room, frightening him with its sudden brilliance. He saw nothing, just the overturned table, the pile of rags and an old newspaper on the floor. Could he have been imagining the sounds? He continued listening, but heard nothing and thought that it might have just been rats. Still, he thought, as soon as the rain let up he would leave. He went to the window and was about to look out when he heard a voice behind him.

"Don't try nothin' 'cause I got a razor here sharp enough to cut a week into nine days!"

Greg, except for an involuntary tremor in his knees, stood stock still. The voice was high and brittle, like dry twigs being broken, surely not one he had ever heard before. There was a shuffling sound as the person who had been speaking moved a step closer. Greg turned, holding his breath, his eyes straining to see in the dark room.

The upper part of the figure before him was still in darkness. The lower half was in the dim rectangle of light that fell unevenly from the window. There were two feet, in cracked, dirty shoes from which rose legs that were wrapped in rags.

"Who are you?" Greg hardly recognized his own voice.

"I'm Lemon Brown," came the answer. "Who're you?"

"Greg Ridley."

"What you doing here?" The figure shuffled forward again, and Greg took a small step backward.

"It's raining," Greg said.

"I can see that," the figure said.

The person who called himself Lemon Brown peered forward, and Greg could see him clearly. He was an old man. His black, heavily wrinkled face was surrounded by a halo of crinkly white hair and whiskers that seemed to separate his head from the layers of dirty coats piled on his smallish frame. His pants were bagged to the knee, where they were met with rags that went down to the old shoes. The rags were held on with strings, and there was a rope around his middle. Greg relaxed. He had seen the man before, picking through the trash on the corner and pulling clothes out of a Salvation Army box. There was no sign of the razor that could "cut a week into nine days."

"What are you doing here?" Greg asked.

"This is where I'm staying," Lemon Brown said. "What you here for?"

Vocabulary

intently (in tent′ lē) *adv.* in a firmly focused way; with concentration
involuntary (in vol′ ən ter′ ē) *adj.* not done willingly
tremor (trem′ ər) *n.* a shaking or trembling movement

"Told you it was raining out," Greg said, leaning against the back of the couch until he felt it give slightly.

"Ain't you got no home?"

"I got a home," Greg answered.

"You ain't one of them bad boys looking for my treasure, is you?" Lemon Brown cocked his head to one side and squinted one eye. "Because I told you I got me a razor."

"I'm not looking for your treasure," Greg answered, smiling. "*If* you have one."

"What you mean, *if* I have one," Lemon Brown said. "Every man got a treasure. You don't know that, you must be a fool!"

"Sure," Greg said as he sat on the sofa and put one leg over the back. "What do you have, gold coins?"

"Don't worry none about what I got," Lemon Brown said. "You know who I am?"

"You told me your name was orange or lemon or something like that."

"Lemon Brown," the old man said, pulling back his shoulders as he did so, "they used to call me Sweet Lemon Brown."

"Sweet Lemon?" Greg asked.

"Yessir. Sweet Lemon Brown. They used to say I sung the blues so sweet that if I sang at a funeral, the dead would commence to rocking with the beat. Used to travel all over Mississippi and as far as Monroe, Louisiana, and east on over to Macon, Georgia. You mean you ain't never heard of Sweet Lemon Brown?"

"Afraid not," Greg said. "What . . . what happened to you?"

"Hard times, boy. Hard times always after a poor man. One day I got tired, sat down to rest a spell and felt a tap on my shoulder. Hard times caught up with me."

"Sorry about that."

"What you doing here? How come you didn't go home when the rain come. Rain don't bother you young folks none."

"Just didn't," Greg looked away.

"I used to have a knotty-headed boy just like you." Lemon Brown had half walked, half shuffled back to the corner and sat down against the wall. "Had them big eyes like you got. I used to call them moon eyes. Look into them moon eyes and see anything you want."

"How come you gave up singing the blues?" Greg asked.

"Didn't give it up," Lemon Brown said. "You don't give up the blues; they give you up. After a while you do good for yourself, and it ain't nothing but foolishness singing about how hard you got it. Ain't that right?"

"I guess so."

"What's that noise?" Lemon Brown asked, suddenly sitting upright.

Greg listened, and he heard a noise outside. He looked at Lemon Brown and saw the old man was pointing toward the window.

Greg went to the window and saw three men, neighborhood thugs, on the stoop. One was carrying a length of pipe. Greg looked back toward Lemon Brown, who moved quietly across the room to the window. The old man looked out, then beckoned frantically for Greg to follow him. For a moment Greg couldn't move. Then he found himself following Lemon Brown into the hallway and up darkened stairs. Greg followed as closely as he could. They

---

Vocabulary

commence (kə mens′) *v.* to begin; start

reached the top of the stairs, and Greg felt Lemon Brown's hand first lying on his shoulder, then probing down his arm until he finally took Greg's hand into his own as they crouched in the darkness.

"They's bad men," Lemon Brown whispered. His breath was warm against Greg's skin.

"Hey! Rag man!" A voice called. "We know you in here. What you got up under them rags? You got any money?"

Silence.

"We don't want to have to come in and hurt you, old man, but we don't mind if we have to."

Lemon Brown squeezed Greg's hand in his own hard, gnarled[6] fist.

There was a banging downstairs and a light as the men entered. They banged around noisily, calling for the rag man.

"We heard you talking about your treasure," the voice was slurred. "We just want to see it, that's all."

"You sure he's here?" One voice seemed to come from the room with the sofa.

"Yeah, he stays here every night."

"There's another room over there; I'm going to take a look. You got that flashlight?"

"Yeah, here, take the pipe too."

Greg opened his mouth to quiet the sound of his breath as he sucked it in uneasily. A beam of light hit the wall a few feet opposite him, then went out.

"Ain't nobody in that room," a voice said. "You think he's gone or something?"

"I don't know," came the answer. "All I know is that I heard him talking about some kind of treasure. You know they found that shopping bag lady with that money in her bags."

"Yeah. You think he's upstairs?"

"HEY, OLD MAN, ARE YOU UP THERE?"

Silence.

"Watch my back, I'm going up."

There was a footstep on the stairs, and the beam from the flashlight danced crazily along the peeling wallpaper. Greg held his breath. There was another step and a loud crashing noise as the man banged the pipe against the wooden banister. Greg could feel his temples throb as the man slowly neared them. Greg thought about the pipe, wondering what he would do when the man reached them—what he *could* do.

Then Lemon Brown released his hand and moved toward the top of the stairs. Greg looked around and saw stairs going up to the next floor. He tried waving to Lemon Brown, hoping the old man would see him in the dim light and follow him to the next floor. Maybe, Greg thought, the man wouldn't follow them up there. Suddenly, though, Lemon Brown stood at the top of the stairs, both arms raised high above his head.

"There he is!" A voice cried from below.

"Throw down your money, old man, so I won't have to bash your head in!"

Lemon Brown didn't move. Greg felt himself near panic. The steps came closer, and still Lemon Brown didn't move. He was an eerie sight, a bundle of rags standing at the top of the stairs, his shadow on

6. Lemon Brown's fist is rough, twisted, and knotted *(gnarled)*, like a tree branch. (And, as in most words that start with *gn*, such as *gnaw*, the *g* is silent.)

Vocabulary

eerie (ēr′ ē) *adj.* weird, especially in a frightening way came out. He swallowed hard, wet his lips once more and howled as evenly as he could.

"What's that?"

As Greg howled, the light moved away from Lemon Brown, but not before Greg saw him hurl his body down the stairs at the men who had come to take his treasure. There was a crashing noise, and then footsteps. A rush of warm air came in as the downstairs door opened, then there was only an ominous silence.

Greg stood on the landing. He listened, and after a while there was another sound on the staircase.

"Mr. Brown?" he called.

"Yeah, it's me," came the answer. "I got their flashlight."

Greg exhaled in relief as Lemon Brown made his way slowly back up the stairs.

"You O.K.?"

"Few bumps and bruises," Lemon Brown said.

"I think I'd better be going," Greg said, his breath returning to normal. "You'd better leave, too, before they come back."

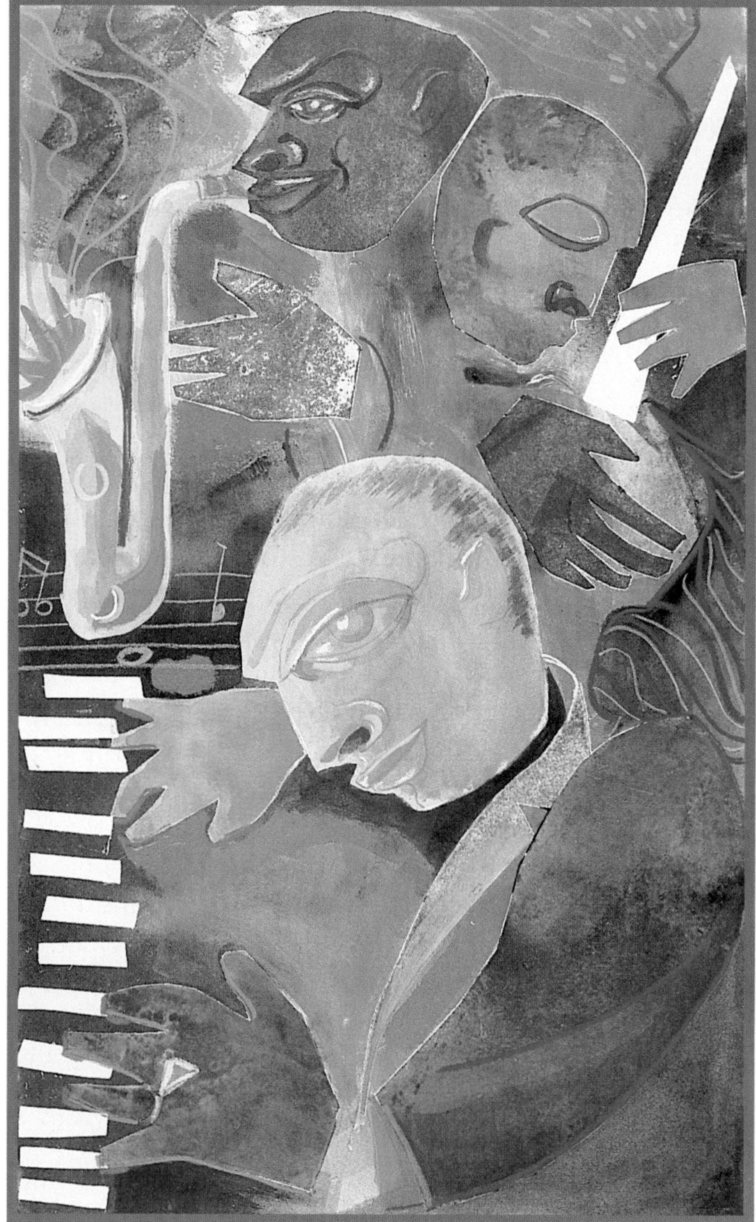

Jazz Messenger III, 1994. Gil Mayers. Mixed media, 16 x 10 in. Private collection.

Viewing the painting: **How do you think the painting might reflect Lemon Brown's experiences as a blues musician?**

the wall looming over him. Maybe, the thought came to Greg, the scene could be even eerier.

Greg wet his lips, put his hands to his mouth and tried to make a sound. Nothing

"They may hang around outside for a while," Lemon Brown said, "but they ain't getting their nerve up to come in here again. Not with crazy old rag men and howling spooks. Best you stay awhile till

Vocabulary

ominous (om′ ə nəs) *adj.* threatening harm or evil

the coast is clear. I'm heading out West tomorrow, out to east St. Louis."

"They were talking about treasures," Greg said. "You *really* have a treasure?"

"What I tell you? Didn't I tell you every man got a treasure?" Lemon Brown said. "You want to see mine?"

"If you want to show it to me," Greg shrugged.

"Let's look out the window first, see what them scoundrels be doing," Lemon Brown said.

They followed the oval beam of the flashlight into one of the rooms and looked out the window. They saw the men who had tried to take the treasure sitting on the curb near the corner. One of them had his pants leg up, looking at his knee.

"You sure you're not hurt?" Greg asked Lemon Brown.

"Nothing that ain't been hurt before," Lemon Brown said. When you get as old as me all you say when something hurts is, 'Howdy, Mr. Pain, sees you back again.' Then when Mr. Pain see he can't worry you none, he go on mess with somebody else."

Greg smiled.

"Here, you hold this." Lemon Brown gave Greg the flashlight.

He sat on the floor near Greg and carefully untied the strings that held the rags on his right leg. When he took the rags away, Greg saw a piece of plastic. The old man carefully took off the plastic and unfolded it. He revealed some yellowed newspaper clippings and a battered harmonica.

"There it be," he said, nodding his head. "There it be."

Greg looked at the old man, saw the distant look in his eye, then turned to the clippings. They told of Sweet Lemon Brown, a blues singer and harmonica player who was appearing at different theaters in the South. One of the clippings said he had been the hit of the show, although not the headliner. All of the clippings were reviews of shows Lemon Brown had been in more than 50 years ago. Greg looked at the harmonica. It was dented badly on one side, with the reed holes on one end nearly closed.

"I used to travel around and make money for to feed my wife and Jesse—that's my boy's name. Used to feed them good, too. Then his mama died, and he stayed with his mama's sister. He growed up to be a man, and when the war come he saw fit to go off and fight in it. I didn't have nothing to give him except these things that told him who I was, and what he come from. If you know your pappy did something, you know you can do something too.

"Anyway, he went off to war, and I went off still playing and singing. 'Course by then I wasn't as much as I used to be, not without somebody to make it worth the while. You know what I mean?"

"Yeah," Greg nodded, not quite really knowing.

"I traveled around, and one time I come home, and there was this letter saying Jesse got killed in the war. Broke my heart, it truly did.

"They sent back what he had with him over there, and what it was is this old mouth fiddle and these clippings. Him carrying it around with him like that told me it meant something to him. That was my treasure, and when I give it to him he treated it just like that, a treasure. Ain't that something?"

"Yeah, I guess so," Greg said.

"You *guess* so?" Lemon Brown's voice rose an octave as he started to put his treasure back into the plastic. "Well, you got to guess 'cause you sure don't know nothing. Don't know enough to get home when it's raining."

"I guess . . . I mean, you're right."

"You O.K. for a youngster," the old man said as he tied the strings around his leg, "better than those scalawags what come here looking for my treasure. That's for sure."

"You really think that treasure of yours was worth fighting for?" Greg asked. "Against a pipe?"

"What else a man got 'cepting what he can pass on to his son, or his daughter, if she be his oldest?" Lemon Brown said. "For a big-headed boy you sure do ask the foolishest questions."

Lemon Brown got up after patting his rags in place and looked out the window again.

"Looks like they're gone. You get on out of here and get yourself home. I'll be watching from the window so you'll be all right."

Lemon Brown went down the stairs behind Greg. When they reached the front door the old man looked out first, saw the street was clear and told Greg to scoot on home.

"You sure you'll be O.K.?" Greg asked.

"Now didn't I tell you I was going to east St. Louis in the morning?" Lemon Brown asked. "Don't that sound O.K. to you."

"Sure it does," Greg said. "Sure it does. And you take care of that treasure of yours."

"That I'll do," Lemon said, the wrinkles about his eyes suggesting a smile. "That I'll do."

The night had warmed and the rain had stopped, leaving puddles at the curbs. Greg didn't even want to think how late it was. He thought ahead of what his father would say and wondered if he should tell him about Lemon Brown. He thought about it until he reached his stoop, and decided against it. Lemon Brown would be O.K., Greg thought, with his memories and his treasure.

Greg pushed the button over the bell marked Ridley, thought of the lecture he knew his father would give him, and smiled.

❖

Responding to Literature

PERSONAL RESPONSE

Are you satisfied with the ending of the story? Why or why not? What other ending can you imagine?

Analyzing Literature

RECALL

1. Why is Greg upset at the beginning of the story?
2. Why did Lemon Brown stop singing the blues?
3. What does Lemon keep as his treasure?
4. Why doesn't Greg tell his father about Lemon?

INTERPRET

5. People "sing the blues" when they suffer difficult or sorrowful times. In your opinion, does Greg have a good reason to sing the blues? Support your answer with examples from the story.
6. In your opinion, does Lemon have good reason to sing the blues over his life? Explain.
7. How does the treasure reflect Lemon's life?
8. In your opinion, will Lemon be okay after Greg leaves him? Why or why not?

EVALUATE AND CONNECT

9. Lemon's treasure is a **symbol** in this story. It stands for things that have value beyond their physical attributes. What might the treasure symbolize to Lemon's son? to Lemon? to Greg?
10. Theme Connection When speaking of his treasure, Lemon says, "What else a man got 'cepting what he can pass on to his son, or his daughter, if she be his oldest?" Do you agree with this statement? Why or why not? Give examples to explain your position.

LITERARY ELEMENTS

Theme

The **theme** of a story is its central message. To find the theme you might ask, "What message is the author trying to tell the readers?" Sometimes a theme is stated directly by the narrator or by a character. Sometimes, however, the reader must figure it out by examining the characters, the plot, and literary devices such as symbolism and mood.

1. What, do you think, is the theme in "The Treasure of Lemon Brown"?
2. In your opinion, does the theme of this story apply to most people? Explain.

- See **Literary Terms Handbook,** p. R10.

Literature and Writing

Writing About Literature

Character Analysis When Greg questions whether Lemon really has a treasure, Lemon suggests that Greg might be a fool. Another time he tells Greg "you sure don't know nothing." Why might Lemon say this about Greg? What does Greg say or do that suggests Lemon might be right? In a paragraph, explain why you agree or disagree with Lemon.

Personal Writing

Family Treasure If you had to choose three possessions to pass on to a family member, what would they be? Look back over the items you brainstormed for the **Focus Activity** on page 4. Choose three items you value most. Then write a brief letter to the person who would inherit your three possessions and explain why you are passing them on.

Extending Your Response

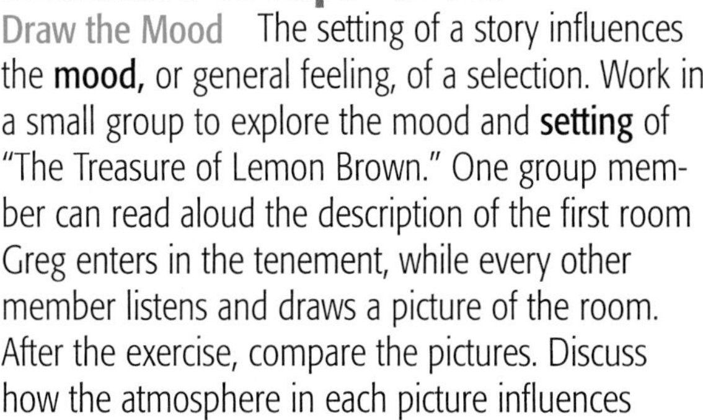

Literature Groups

Draw the Mood The setting of a story influences the **mood,** or general feeling, of a selection. Work in a small group to explore the mood and **setting** of "The Treasure of Lemon Brown." One group member can read aloud the description of the first room Greg enters in the tenement, while every other member listens and draws a picture of the room. After the exercise, compare the pictures. Discuss how the atmosphere in each picture influences your feelings about what takes place in the story.

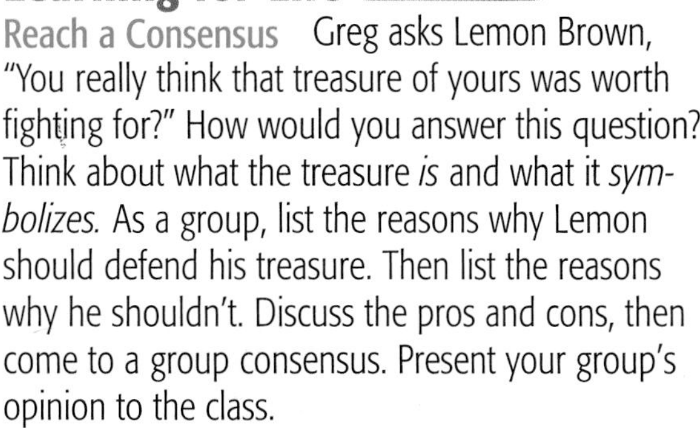

Learning for Life

Reach a Consensus Greg asks Lemon Brown, "You really think that treasure of yours was worth fighting for?" How would you answer this question? Think about what the treasure *is* and what it *symbolizes.* As a group, list the reasons why Lemon should defend his treasure. Then list the reasons why he shouldn't. Discuss the pros and cons, then come to a group consensus. Present your group's opinion to the class.

Interdisciplinary Activity

Music Create a musical presentation of a blues performer for your class. You might play audiotapes, show videotapes, or play an instrument yourself. Include a brief report describing the performer's career and contribution to the blues. Use the World Wide Web, the library, interviews, and other research sources.

The Jazz Singer, 1916. Charles Demuth. Pencil and watercolor, 12¾ x 7¾ in. Private collection.

Reading Further

For other stories of people who need a home and security, read:

Adam of the Road by Elizabeth Janet Gray

Amistad by Walter Dean Myers

Save your work for your portfolio.

Skill Minilessons

GRAMMAR AND LANGUAGE • PUNCTUATING DIALOGUE

Good writers follow these punctuation rules to make quotations and dialogue clear for readers:

- Quotation marks are used before and after the exact words of a speaker.
- A comma sets off the parts of a sentence that come before, between, or after a direct quotation. A comma at the end of a quotation goes inside the quotation marks.
- If a quotation ends with a question mark or an exclamation point, no comma is needed.

"What you mean, if *I have one," Lemon Brown said. "Every man got a treasure. You don't know that, you must be a fool!"*

PRACTICE Correct mistakes in the use of quotation marks and commas. Write *correct* if a sentence does not contain errors.

1. "Do you read a lot? I asked the boy sitting next to me on the bus.
2. "I read books about basketball", he said.
3. "Have you read any stories by Walter Dean Myers?," I asked him.
4. "Sure," he said, "and I liked them a lot."
5. I agreed. "I like his stories, too."

● For more about punctuating dialogue, see **Language Handbook,** p. R41.

READING AND THINKING • TEXT STRUCTURES

Writers structure their text in many different ways. One structure you may find when you read is problem/solution. In "The Treasure of Lemon Brown," Greg helped Lemon Brown solve a problem when he howled and scared away the thieves who wanted the old man's treasure.

● For more about text structures, see **Reading Handbook,** p. R87.

PRACTICE Answer these questions about another problem and solution in "The Treasure of Lemon Brown."

1. What problem does Greg have at the beginning of the story?
2. How does Lemon Brown help Greg look at this problem in a different way?
3. What solution does Greg come to at the end of the story?

VOCABULARY • ETYMOLOGY

Etymology is the study of word origins. Many English words come from other languages. For example, the word *impromptu* comes from a Latin phrase that means "ready now." An *impromptu* reply, party, or speech is one that isn't prepared ahead of time. The origins of some words, such as *impromptu,* are very clearly related to their present-day meaning. For other words, a little imagination is needed to make the connection.

PRACTICE Each word below appeared in the story "The Treasure of Lemon Brown." Explain how the origin of each word is tied to its present-day meaning.

1. tentative: from the Latin word *tentare,* meaning "to try."
2. intent: from the Latin word *intendere,* meaning "to aim at."
3. eerie: from the Old English word *earg,* meaning "timid."

Discovering the Blues

Listen to a blues song, and you're likely to tap a hand or foot to the music before you hum a tune. That's because blues music, which swept the southern United States in the late 1800s and early 1900s, focuses on rhythm instead of melody. Rhythm is a steady beat—a regular pattern of notes that is usually emphasized by drums or stringed instruments, such as guitars. The driving rhythm you hear in jazz and rock songs is borrowed from blues music.

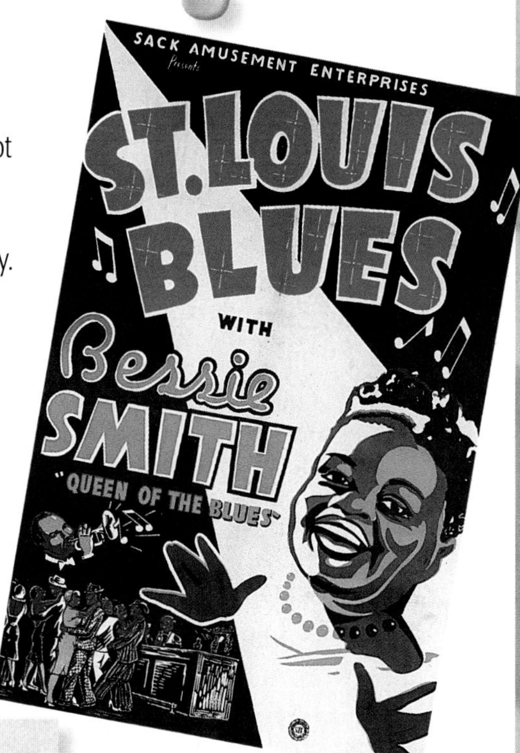

The Origin of Blues Blues music grew out of the "field hollers" that enslaved people used to call out while they labored in the fields. One worker would sing out a call, and the other workers would echo it. Blues musician Bessie Smith used the call-and-response form in these lines from her song "Back Water Blues":

> I woke up this mornin', can't even get out of my door
> I woke up this mornin', can't even get out of my door
> There's enough trouble to make a poor girl wonder
> where she wanna go.

The verse shown above is an example of the twelve-bar blues, a type of rhythm developed by Bessie Smith and other blues musicians. The verse has three lines of music. Each line is divided into four bars—groups of musical notes, rests, and lyrics. A song can have several verses, but each verse must follow the same rhythm.

Experiment With one hand, tap a steady rhythm of four beats. You've just counted out a bar, or measure, in 4/4 time, using four quarter notes. Just as in math, 4/4 can equal many combinations of fractions. So, for variety, a musician will fill a bar with combinations of fast notes, slow notes, and rests. Tap out your four-beat rhythm again, but substitute two quick notes (eighth notes) for one of the quarter notes.

ACTIVITY

Listen to a few blues recordings. Then write two or three verses for a blues song of your own, using the three-line call-and-response form. Work out a rhythm to accompany your lyrics.

Before You Read

My Two Dads

MEET
MARIE G. LEE

Marie G. Lee says that writing a book is a lot like maintaining a friendship: "It requires perseverance, it can have its ugly patches, but it is always ultimately fulfilling and worthwhile." Lee, who has written several books for young people, published her first essay in *Seventeen* magazine when she was sixteen years old. Besides writing, Lee enjoys in-line skating, skiing, and tae kwon do.

Marie G. Lee grew up in Minnesota and now lives in New York City. This essay was first published in 1989.

FOCUS ACTIVITY

How is your family's heritage evident? Is it difficult to maintain one's culture?

Round-robin

In a group, take turns describing a way in which each of you carries on your own culture.

Setting a Purpose

Read this selection to see how the author comes to understand her father and his culture.

BACKGROUND

The Time and Place A young Korean American woman joins her family as they visit her parents' birthplace—Korea.

Did You Know? North Korea is governed by a communist regime. South Korea, on the other hand, has a representative form of government. For three years in the 1950s, the two sides fought for control of the country, with the United States sending economic and military aid to South Korea. The war ended in a truce.

VOCABULARY PREVIEW

indifference (in dif′ ər əns) *n.* a lack of feeling, concern, or care; p. 20
smug (smug) *adj.* overly pleased with oneself; too self-satisfied; p. 20
simultaneously (sī′ məl tā′ nē əs lē) *adv.* at the same time; p. 20
blithely (blīth′ lē) *adv.* in a lighthearted way; cheerfully; p. 20
brazenly (brā′ zən lē) *adv.* in a boldly rude manner; p. 21
joviality (jō′ vē al′ ə tē) *n.* hearty, good-natured humor; p. 21
subsequently (sub′ sə kwənt lē) *adv.* at a later time; p. 21
aggression (ə gresh′ ən) *n.* the habit or practice of launching attacks; p. 21
discern (di surn′) *v.* to detect or recognize; identify; p. 21

두명의 내 아빠

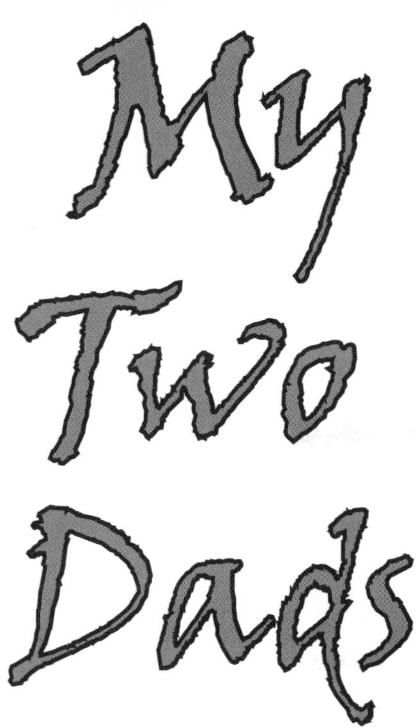

My Two Dads

Marie G. Lee

I am a first-generation Korean-American. On my first trip to Korea at age twenty-six, I found that I had two fathers. One was the Dad I'd always known, but the second was a Korean father I'd never seen before—one surprising and familiar at the same time, like my homeland.

I was born and raised in the Midwest, and to me, my Dad was like anyone else's. He taught my brothers to play baseball, fixed the garage door, and pushed the snowblower on chilly February mornings. If there was anything different about him, to my child's eyes, it was that he was a doctor.

Growing up, my siblings[1] and I rarely came into contact with our Korean heritage. Mom and Dad spoke Korean only when they didn't want us to know what they were saying. We didn't observe Korean customs, except for not wearing shoes in the house, which I always assumed was plain common sense. I'd once seen a photograph of Dad in a traditional Korean costume, and I remember thinking how odd those clothes made him look.

1. *Siblings* are brothers and sisters.

With my parents' tacit[2] encouragement, I "forgot" that I was Korean. I loved pizza and macaroni and cheese, but I had never so much as touched a slice of kimchi.[3] All my friends, including my boyfriend, were Caucasian.[4] And while I could explain in detail everything I thought was wrong with Ronald Reagan's policies, I had to strain to remember the name of Korea's president.

Attempting to learn the Korean language, *hangukmal*,[5] a few years ago was a first step in atoning[6] for my past indifference. I went into it feeling smug because of my fluency in French and German, but learning Korean knocked me for a loop. This was a language shaped by Confucian rules of reverence,[7] where the speaker states her position (humble, equal, superior) in relation to the person she is addressing. Simultaneously humbling myself and revering the person with whom I was speaking seemed like a painful game of verbal Twister. To further complicate the process, I found there are myriad[8] titles of reverence, starting with the highest, *sansengnim*, which loosely means "teacher/doctor," down to the ultra-specific, such as *waysukmo*,[9] "wife of mother's brother."

Armed, then, with a year's worth of extension-school classes, a list of polite phrases and titles, and a Berlitz tape in my Walkman, I was as ready as I'd ever be to travel with my family to Korea last year.

When we arrived at Kimpo Airport in Seoul, smiling relatives funneled us into the customs line for *wayguksalam*, "foreigners." I was almost jealous watching our Korean flight attendants breeze through the line for *hanguksalam*,[10] "Korean nationals." With whom did I identify more—the flight attendants or the retired white couple behind us, with their Bermuda shorts and Midwestern accents? My American passport stamped me as an alien in a land where everyone looked like me.

I got my first glimpse of my second father when we began trying to hail cabs in downtown Seoul. Because the government enforces low taxi fares, the drivers have developed their own system of picking up only individual passengers, then packing more in, to increase the per-trip profit. The streets are clogged not only with traffic but also with desperately gesticulating pedestrians and empty taxis.

Even my mother was stymied[11] by the cab-hailing competition. When Mom and I traveled alone, cabs zoomed blithely

2. *Tacit* means "understood without words or speech."
3. *Kimchi* is a Korean food made from pickled vegetables.
4. *Caucasian* refers to the group of people who make up what is loosely known as the white race.
5. *hangukmal* (hän gook mäl)
6. *Atoning* is making up for (something).
7. *Confucian* refers to Confucius (kən fū′ shəs), a Chinese teacher who taught that one could maintain peace, harmony, and justice by following certain rules of behavior. *Reverence* (rev′ ər əns) means "deep honor and affection."
8. *Myriad* means "a great number."
9. *sansengnim* (sun sông nēm); *waysukmo* (wā sook mō)
10. *wayguksalam* (wā gook sə läm); *hanguksalam* (hän gook sə läm)
11. To be *stymied* is to be defeated or blocked.

Vocabulary

indifference (in dif′ ər əns) *n.* a lack of feeling, concern, or care
smug (smug) *adj.* overly pleased with oneself; too self-satisfied
simultaneously (sī′ məl tā′ nē əs lē) *adv.* at the same time
blithely (blīth′ lē) *adv.* in a lighthearted way; cheerfully

past us. When we finally got one, the driver would shut off his meter, brazenly charge us triple the usual fare and ignominiously[12] dump us somewhere not very close to our destination.

But traveling with Dad was different. He would somehow stop a taxi with ease, chitchat with the driver (using very polite language), then shovel us all in. Not only would the cabbie take us where we wanted to go, but some of the usually taciturn drivers would turn into garrulous[13] philosophers.

I began to perceive[14] the transformation of my father from American dad to functioning urban Korean. When we met with relatives, I noticed how Dad's conversational Korean moved easily between the respect he gave his older sister to the joviality with which he addressed Mom's younger cousin. My brother Len and I and our Korean cousins, however, stared shyly and mutely at each other.

Keeping company with relatives eased my disorientation, but not my alienation. Korea is the world's most racially and culturally homogeneous country,[15] and although I was of the right race, I felt culturally shut out. It seemed to me that Koreans were pushy, even in church. When they ate, they slurped and inhaled their food so violently that at least once during every meal, someone would have a sputtering fit of coughing.

Watching my father "turn Korean" helped me as I tried to embrace the culture. Drinking *soju*[16] in a restaurant in the somewhat seedy Namdaemun area, he suddenly lit into a story of the time when Communists from North Korea confiscated his parents' a: ets.[17] Subsequently, he became a medical student in Seoul, where each day he ate a sparse breakfast at his sister's house, trekked across towering Namsan Mountain (visible from our room in the Hilton), and studied at Seoul National University until night, when he would grab a few hours of sleep in the borrowed bed of a friend who worked the night shift.

I have always lived in nice houses, gone on trips, and never lacked for pizza money. But as my father talked, I could almost taste the millet-and-water gruel[18] he subsisted on while hiding for months in cellars during the North Korean invasion of Seoul. Suddenly, I was able to feel the pain of the Korean people, enduring one hardship after another: Japanese colonial rule, North Korean aggression, and dependence on American military force. For a brief moment, I discerned the origins of the

12. *Ignominiously* means simply "shamefully; disgracefully."
13. *Taciturn* means "not inclined to speak much"; *garrulous* means "talking a lot, especially about unimportant matters."
14. When you *perceive* something, you notice it.
15. The writer's *disorientation* is a feeling of being lost. Her *alienation* is her sense of being different from her relatives. *Homogeneous* (hō′ mə jē′ nē əs) means "of the same kind."

16. *Soju* is a liquor made from rice.
17. The North Koreans seized *(confiscated)* his parents' property and valuables *(assets)*.
18. *Gruel* is a thin porridge.

Vocabulary

brazenly (brā′ zən lē) *adv.* in a boldly rude manner
joviality (jō′ vē al′ ə tē) *n.* hearty, good-natured humor
subsequently (sub′ sə kwənt lē) *adv.* at a later time
aggression (ə gresh′ ən) *n.* the habit or practice of launching attacks
discern (di surn′) *v.* to detect or recognize; identify

noble, sometimes harsh, Korean character. Those wizened[19] women who pushed past me at church were there only because they had fought their way to old age. The noises people made while eating began to sound more celebratory than rude.

And there were other things I saw and was proud of. When we visited a cemetery, I noticed that the headstones were small and unadorned,[20] except for a few with small, pagoda-shaped "hats" on them. The hats *(chinsa)*, Dad told me, were from a time when the country's leaders awarded "national Ph.D.'s,"[21] the highest civilian honor.

Did You Know?

A *pagoda* is a temple, two or more stories high. Each level has its own partial roof and is a little smaller than the level below it.

"Your great-grandfather has one of those on his grave," Dad mentioned casually. I began to admire a people who place such high value on hard work and scholarship. Even television commercials generally don't promote leisure pursuits, such as vacations or Nintendo, but instead proclaim[22] the merits of "super duper vitamin pills" to help you study longer and work harder.

After two weeks, as we prepared to return to the U.S., I still in many ways felt like a stranger in Korea. While I looked the part of a native, my textbook Korean was robotic, and the phrases I was taught—such as, "Don't take me for a five-won[23] plane ride"—were apparently very dated. I tried to tell my Korean cousins an amusing anecdote:[24] in the Lotte department store in Seoul, I asked for directions to the restroom and was directed instead to the stereo section. But the story, related once in English and once in halting Korean, became hopelessly lost in the translation.

Dad decided he would spend an extra week in Korea, savoring[25] a culture I would never fully know, even if I took every Berlitz course I could afford. When I said goodbye to him, I saw my Korean father; but I knew that come February, my American dad would be back out in our driveway, stirring up a froth of snow with his big yellow snowblower.

19. The *wizened* women were shriveled.
20. *Unadorned* means "not decorated."
21. The highest academic degree awarded to graduates in non-science areas of study is the Doctor of Philosophy, or *Ph.D.*
22. To *proclaim* means "to announce."
23. The *won* is a unit of money in both North and South Korea.
24. An *anecdote* is a short account of some incident or event.
25. *Savoring* means "taking great delight in."

Responding to Literature

PERSONAL RESPONSE

What do you think about the author's belief that she can never fully be a part of Korean culture?

Analyzing Literature

RECALL

1. Where did Marie G. Lee grow up?
2. What did she know about her father's past?
3. How did the author's childhood differ from her father's?
4. According to Lee, what has influenced the character of the South Korean people?

INTERPRET

5. Why might Lee's parents have encouraged her to forget her Korean background?
6. Why does the author emphasize the ease with which her father speaks Korean and his effective use of taxis?
7. How does Lee's growing knowledge of Korea affect the way she sees her father?
8. Theme Connection Explain why Lee feels she will never fully understand Korean culture.

Seoul, South Korea

EVALUATE AND CONNECT

9. This personal essay presents a **theme,** a main idea or message. What is this theme, and do you agree with it? Use examples to support your answer.
10. How might Lee's essay encourage others to learn more about the culture of their parents or grandparents?

LITERARY ELEMENTS

Character

A **character** is a person, animal, or other creature that appears in a literary work. Characters can be real or imaginary. Usually a story or other work is built around one **main character.** This character is often described in detail, and he or she may change as a result of events that occur. There are also **minor characters** who move the action along by interacting with the main character and providing background information.

1. Who is the main character in "My Two Dads"? How does the main character change or develop from the beginning of the selection to the end?
2. Who are the minor characters? How do they affect the main character?

• See **Literary Terms Handbook,** p. R2.

Extending Your Response

Creative Writing

Writing Home Imagine that you are Marie G. Lee and are just completing your Korean visit. Write to a friend comparing American culture with what you have learned about Korean culture.

interNET CONNECTION

Type the name *Korean Overseas Information Service* into a search engine to find information about Korean culture, language, art, or history.

Literature Groups

A Culture Debate Although her father embraces two cultures, the writer feels she will never be able to do the same. Debate whether people growing up outside of their ancestral culture can ever return to it and feel part of it. As you debate, consider your response to the **Focus Activity** on page 18.

Learning for Life

A Heritage Map Plan a trip to explore a heritage that interests you. You might focus on a group of Asian Americans, a specific Native American culture, a group of European settlers in the United States, or your own heritage. Create a map of the regions and cities to explore, as well as an itinerary that includes the people and specific places you would like to visit.

Save your work for your portfolio.

Skill Minilesson

VOCABULARY • ANALOGIES

An **analogy** is a type of comparison based on the relationships between things or ideas. An analogy is written this way:

virus : illness :: collision : injury

Notice that just as a *virus* can cause an *illness*, a *collision* can cause an *injury*. So, *virus* is to *illness* as *collision* is to *injury*. To understand an analogy, you must first figure out the relationship between the first pair of words.

PRACTICE Choose the word that best completes each analogy.

1. fist : violence :: dove :
   a. peace b. bird c. fear
2. wearily : trudge :: happily :
   a. plod b. skip c. stamp
3. friendly : unfriendly :: smug :
   a. mean b. insecure c. conceited
4. shrug : indifference :: nod :
   a. fear b. joy c. agreement

Previewing

Titles, headings, illustrations, and opening paragraphs–like "Coming Attractions" posters at the movies–alert you to what you are about to see. Using these features to learn about a reading selection is called **previewing.**

Preview this opening paragraph from "A Dictionary of Japanese-American Terms" by R. A. Sasaki.

> *Nihonjin* (nē′ hon′ jē-n′)
> At the age of six, I thought "Americans" and "English" meant the same thing—"white people." After all, Americans spoke English. You have to understand, this was at an age when I also wondered why "onion" was spelled with an "o." It seemed to me that it should be spelled with a "u," except that would make it "union," which was a different word altogether.

Note that the heading at the start of the paragraph looks like a dictionary entry. That heading and the title of the selection are clues that the writer may define *Nihonjin.* You learn that the author was confused about word meanings and that she wondered why English spelling was not logical. This information helps you predict the content and tone of the selection.

- For more about previewing, see **Reading Handbook,** p. R84.

ACTIVITY

Preview your next history, social studies, or science reading assignment, using the following suggestions.

1. List the title, headings, subheadings, illustrations, captions, charts, and photographs in the text.
2. Read the assignment. Write a sentence telling why you think previewing did or did not help you to understand the assignment.

Before You Read

A Dictionary of Japanese-American Terms

MEET R. A. SASAKI

According to R. A. Sasaki (sä sä′ kē), "History disappears if the stories are not told." As a child in the 1950s, Sasaki didn't study the history of Japanese people in America. It wasn't until the 1970s that she began to explore and understand her heritage. "Gradually I uncovered my world, buried like a treasure, or a lost civilization," she said. She began writing about the Japanese American experience, and one of her stories, "The Loom," won the American Japanese National Literary Award in 1983.

R. A. Sasaki was born in 1952. This selection was published in 1996.

FOCUS ACTIVITY

When you look into a mirror, what do you see? How would you describe yourself, inside and outside?

Reflect It!

Draw the outline of your head as it would appear in a mirror. Add pictures, words, and symbols to show the person you see reflected in the mirror.

Setting a Purpose

Read to meet a writer who discovers a new side of herself.

BACKGROUND

The Time and Place R. A. Sasaki writes about growing up in the 1950s as a third-generation Japanese American.

Did You Know? During World War II, some Americans feared that Japanese Americans might aid the armies of Japan that had bombed Hawaii. In 1942, about 110,000 Japanese and Japanese American residents were sent to live in internment camps in the western United States. At the same time, Japanese Americans were serving in the armed forces and many returned home to the United States as decorated war heroes. Not one case of espionage by Japanese Americans was reported.

VOCABULARY PREVIEW

emulate (em′ yə lāt′) *v.* to imitate; p. 28
convey (kən vā′) *v.* to express; communicate; p. 30
painstakingly (pānz′ tā′ king lē) *adv.* in a way requiring close, careful labor or attention; p. 30
incur (in kur′) *v.* to acquire (something undesirable); bring upon oneself; p. 31
intricate (in′ tri kit) *adj.* full of complicated detail; p. 31
humility (hū mil′ ə tē) *n.* the quality of being humble or modest; p. 32
naive (nä ēv′) *adj.* innocent to the ways of the world; p. 32
inflict (in flikt′) *v.* to force (something unwelcome) on someone; p. 33

A Dictionary of Japanese-American Terms

R. A. Sasaki

San Francisco Bay, 1936. Erle Loran. Watercolor and gouache on paper, 15 x 19 in.

Nihonjin (nē′ hon′ jē-n′)

At the age of six, I thought "Americans" and "English" meant the same thing—"white people." After all, Americans spoke English. You have to understand, this was at an age when I also wondered why "onion" was spelled with an "o." It seemed to me that it should be spelled with a "u," except that would make it "union," which was a different word altogether.

I never thought about what I was. My parents referred to us as "*Nihonjin*"—Japanese. "*Nihonjin*" meant us. "*Hakujin*" (white people) meant them. Being *Nihonjin* meant having straight black hair and a certain kind of last name. The Chinese kids looked like us, but had one-syllable last names.

When I was in the first grade I got into a fight with Lucinda Lee because she claimed that she was American. "You're Chinese," I accused her. She started to cry. Later, I told my mother about the disagreement, and, to my outrage, she sided with Lucinda. It had never occurred to me that Lucinda was American. That I, too, was American. Other kids never asked me if I was American. It was always, "Are you Chinese or Japanese?"

That's how I found out that I was American—one kind of American. I still wasn't sure how I could be both American and *Nihonjin* (was I English, too? I wondered).

I still wasn't sure how I could be both American and Nihonjin *(was I English, too? I wondered).*

Then a little girl who was REALLY *Nihonjin* moved in next door. Her father worked for a Japanese company, and the family had moved to San Francisco straight from Tokyo. Kimiko wore dresses all the time, even when she didn't have to. She covered her mouth with her hand when she laughed, and sounded like a little bird. When I stuck the nose of my wooden six-shooter in her back and called her a "low-down, dirty tinhorn," emulating my heroes on television westerns, my father, sitting in the next room, shot me a dark, warning look that made me quake in my boots. It was no good insulting Kimiko, anyway, because she wouldn't get mad and fight back. If Kimiko and I were both *Nihonjin*, well then, all I could say was that there must be different kinds of *Nihonjin*, too.

Jiichan (jē chăn)

I don't remember my grandfather. *Jiichan* died when I was too young to remember him, but old enough to be afraid of death. He haunted my childhood by appearing in a nightmare so disturbing that I used to force myself to recall it every night before going to sleep so that I wouldn't dream it again. I believed that terrors could only get you when you were least expecting them.

In my dream, there was a large pile of laundry, mainly sheets, on the floor of the dining room in our house on 23rd Avenue. I was sifting through it with my sister, playing in the mountainous folds suddenly dropped into the midst of the usually neat order of my mother's house. We climbed

Vocabulary
emulate (em′ yə lāt′) *v.* to imitate

the mountain; our feet sank into the soft mass. Suddenly I clutched a stiff hand. I screamed, and the dream ended abruptly; but I knew, without seeing the rest, that it was *Jiichan's* corpse in there.

My sisters, being older, had known *Jiichan* and did not have such dreams. They were not afraid of him. They remembered his quiet presence watching over them as they played in the backyard

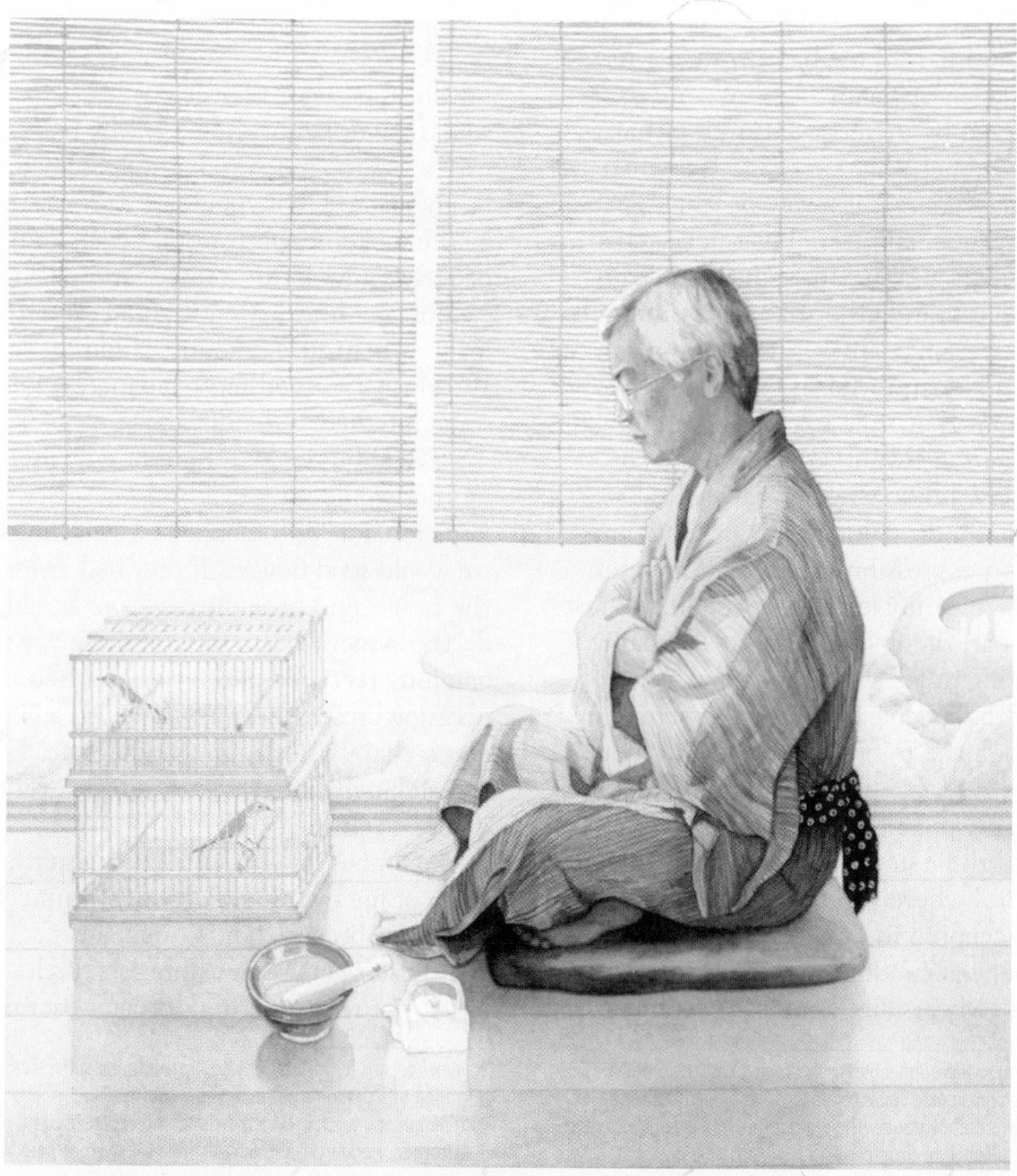

Elderly Japanese man with warblers and silvereyes. Courtesy Allen Say.

Viewing the painting: Do you think the man in the painting more closely resembles the narrator's or her sisters' memories of Jiichan?

of the house on Pine Street. They remembered him tending his beloved cherry tree. I was the only one who needed to reconstruct him. I tried to do it by collecting facts—his name, for example, where he was born, that he had left Japan and come to San Francisco sometime around 1897.

But a part of me has always distrusted language, especially facts. We are so often deceived by them into thinking that we know something. Language is applied after the fact. It is a way of labeling an experience, and if we have never been to Wakayama, Japan, it means nothing that our grandfather was born there. Or if we were not alive in 1897, how can we understand what it meant to leave Japan at that time to come to America?

In 1975 I went to Japan to teach English. I didn't really know why I was going. Finding one's roots at that time was an expression which had been rendered[1] meaningless by overuse. It was just that part of me that distrusts language, wanting to trade facts for knowing.

Other people don't seem to be haunted by the need to bring their grandfathers alive. Perhaps they remember their grandfathers, spoke the same language and heard their stories. If you know who you are and where you come from, or if you are accepted in American society at face value, you can forge ahead and never look back.[2] My Asian face doesn't let me forget my origins. Everytime I start to forget, I will come upon that stiff hand, which will remind me. And if I don't know who my grandfather was, who I am, I will scream with terror. But if I know, then I will know that it is my grandfather's hand that I hold; and I need not be afraid.

osewa ni natta (o-sĕ′ wă nē năt′ tă)

I decided early on that it was hopeless; I would never be Japanese, so why try? There was too much to know, too much to be understood that could not be conveyed by the spoken English word. I would rather be forward-looking—American.

But much as I tried, I could never leave it behind. Someone would die. We always seemed most Japanese when someone died.

"We should go to the funeral," my mother would say. "Iwashita-san[3] came to Pop's funeral." If someone had sent flowers, we would send flowers. If they had visited the house and brought food, we would do the same. *Koden*, funeral money, was carefully recorded and returned when the occasion arose. It seemed there was a giant ledger that existed in my mother's head that painstakingly noted every kindness ever rendered or received.[4] How could I ever know or remember its contents? I couldn't keep track of my own life. A friend of mine was hurt once because I didn't remember staying at his sister's house in Minnesota. I felt awful about not remembering. It seems that there

1. Here, *rendered* means simply "made; caused to be."
2. The phrase *face value* refers to value or significance based on outward appearance. The word *forge,* in this context, means "to advance or progress."
3. *Iwashita-san* (ē wäsh tä sän). In Japanese, the suffix *-san* is added to a person's name to show courtesy.
4. A *ledger* is a book in which income and expenses are recorded. *Rendered,* in this case, means "given or paid."

Vocabulary

convey (kən vā′) *v.* to express; communicate
painstakingly (pānz′ tā′ king lē) *adv.* in a way requiring close, careful labor or attention

are whole periods of my life that have simply dropped from memory. Sensory overload.[5] Am I busier than my mother was, or is there a Japanese gene that weakens in succeeding generations with increased Americanization?

Perhaps I was simply born too late. The youngest of four girls, I was the only one who didn't remember living in the old Victorian in Japantown[6] where my mother grew up and my grandparents lived until they died. I was the only one who couldn't understand what my grandmother was saying, even when she was speaking English. When someone talked about what a family acquaintance had done for us, I was the only one who didn't know who the person was.

This record-keeping and reciprocation[7] did not revolve only around death. My mother would tell me one day on the phone, "The Noguchis are coming up from Los Angeles. They want to take Kiyo and me out to lunch."

I had never heard of the Noguchis, but it turned out that sixty years before, *Bachan* (my grandmother) had let them stay at Pine for a month after Noguchi-san lost his job. Noguchi-san had recently undergone surgery for cancer. "*Osewa ni narimashita*,"[8] he had said. He had incurred debt. He wanted to repay it before it was too late.

The repayment of debt, then, apparently passes down from generation to generation. What will happen when my mother and my aunt Kiyo are no longer around? The ledger will be gone. How will I know to whom I am obligated, what debts to repay? One day in the future will I open the door to find a total stranger bringing me home-made sushi because of some kind act my grandmother did in 1946? Probably not. When I meet the grandsons and great-granddaughters of my grandparents' friends, who among us will know that our families were once connected? We will have lost the intricate web of obligation and reciprocation. The people who remember. This community.

Did You Know?
Many people of all nationalities have warmed to the taste of cold Japanese *sushi* (so͞o′ shē). Small cakes of rice wrapped in seaweed and topped with vinegar are garnished with raw or cooked fish, egg, or vegetables.

Japanese-American

(ja-pə-nēz′ ə-mĕ′-rĭ-kən)

A Japanese-American is someone who has been trained in the Japanese ways of ultimate courtesy, but who has a quite independent and secret American sensibility locked into that pleasant and self-effacing[9] exterior—like a *bonsai.* A tree trying to grow, but forced, through clipped roots and

5. The word *sensory* refers to the five senses, and the phrase *sensory overload* refers to being overwhelmed by too much information or experience.
6. *Victorian* is a style of architecture developed during the reign of Great Britain's Queen Victoria (1837–1901). *Japantown* is an area inhabited chiefly by people of Japanese descent.
7. When two people give each other gifts or trade favors, that's *reciprocation.*
8. *Osewa ni narimashita* (ō sē wä nē nä rē mäsh tä)
9. Here, *sensibility* refers to feelings of what is decent and proper. To *efface* is to make less obvious, and *self-effacing* means "tending to stay in the background."

Vocabulary

incur (in kur′) *v.* to acquire (something undesirable); bring upon oneself

intricate (in′ tri kit) *adj.* full of complicated detail

Did You Know?
Bonsai (bôn sī′) is the art of growing miniature trees in shallow pots or trays. Most bonsai trees are from two inches to three feet tall.

wired branches, into an expected shape. Like *bonsai*, a Japanese-American can be considered warped or deformed, or an object of uncanny[10] beauty.

A Japanese-American is someone who, after a lifetime of being asked if she's Japanese or Chinese, or how long she's been in the States, or where she learned her English, will laugh when some white guy who has taken two semesters of Beginning Japanese tells her that she's mispronouncing her own family name.

Being Japanese-American means being imbued with certain values treasured by Japanese culture—values such as consideration, loyalty, humility, restraint. Values which, when exercised by white Americans, seem civilized; but they make Japanese-Americans seem unassertive, not willing to take risks, lacking confidence and leadership qualities.

Some sansei are like brash young redwoods, so new and naive. It's so clear why the nisei[11] didn't talk. The nisei, whose psyches[12] were wired like Japanese baby pines by the internment. They wanted the third generation to grow up American, like redwoods. They wanted them to shoot for the sky, tall and straight, to walk ahead like gods. To free themselves of the past like a rocket that discards its used stages as it shoots into space. Let go of the past; if you carry your spent burden with you, you will never reach the moon.

the story of when I was born
(thə sto′ rē əv wĕn′ ī wəz born′)

When I was a little girl, and my mother put me to bed, she did not tell me stories about enchanted forests or beautiful princesses. I had seen "Sleeping Beauty." I knew "The Three Bears." These were not the stories I wanted to hear from my mother.

"Tell me the story of when I was born," I would say, mummified[13] up to my chin by bedcovers. There were no magic wands or fairy godmothers in this story. No poisoned apples or pumpkins that turned into coaches. It was a simple story, a sequence of mundane[14] events, barely connected and sparingly described, peopled not by bad wolves or evil stepmothers, but sisters, my father, my mother of course, and friends of the family. The reason I wanted to hear that story, the reason I liked it so much, was because I was in it. It was real.

Life for me began just eleven short years after the Japanese dropped bombs on Pearl Harbor, precipitating[15] events that would

10. If it's *uncanny,* it's so strange and extraordinary as to seem supernatural.
11. *Nisei* (nē sā′) are the U.S.-born children of Japanese immigrants, and *sansei* (sän′ sā) are the grandchildren.
12. The effect of internment on the *psyches* (sī′ kēz)—the souls or minds—of the *nisei* was to make them like bonsai trees, forced to grow into desired shapes and sizes.
13. Here, *mummified* means "covered up like a mummy."
14. Common, ordinary events are *mundane* ones.
15. In this context, *precipitating* means "causing or bringing on."

Vocabulary
humility (hū mil′ ə tē) *n.* the quality of being humble or modest
naive (nä ēv′) *adj.* innocent to the ways of the world

Richmond–San Rafael Ferry Arch, c. 1935. John Haley. Watercolor and gouache on paper, 15 x 22¾ in.

Viewing the painting: Do you think this view of Richmond corresponds to the narrator's thoughts about her old neighborhood? Explain.

inflict on my family a kind of willed amnesia that would last for forty years.

As soon as he could after the war, my father moved us out of Japantown, into an orderly and integrated neighborhood where we had an Armenian grocery, a Russian delicatessen, an Italian piano teacher, and kind *hakujin* neighbors named the Freemans. The Richmond District of San Francisco, where I grew up, was always foggy. The fog would come in off the Pacific during the night, and when I woke up, I would hear the mournful dialogue of fog horns warning ships in the Golden Gate. Sometimes the fog would burn off by noon, and we would get a glimpse of the blue sky that California is supposed to be so famous for. But often the fog remained all day, or came back in the afternoon, so thick and low that it seemed like a white smoke. If we went anywhere else in the city, we must have looked like foreigners, just come in from Siberia, in our sweaters and coats and knee-high socks. We probably had an intensity, too, that outside people, people who lived in the sun, lacked. A seriousness. An introspection,[16] come from too many days spent inside the house reading, or a range of options that did not include barbecues and lying on the beach.

In school we learned about the explorers, the *Mayflower*, the American Revolution.

16. An *introspection* is an examination of one's own thoughts and feelings.

Vocabulary

inflict (in flikt′) *v.* to force (something unwelcome) on someone

When we studied California history, we learned about Father Junipero Serra[17] and the California missions. History, it seemed, focused on the conquerors, never the conquered.

The first time I went to Japan, I was twenty-two. My plane lifted off from San Francisco International, gaining altitude as it banked over the Golden Gate. Down below I could see the Richmond District, the geometrical avenues where I had spent my childhood. Then the plane entered the fog, and for a few seconds there was nothing but whiteness outside my window. For a few seconds, there was no east or west, no time. No memory. Suddenly, we were through. Above the floor of clouds, the sky was blue. The wing of the plane reflected pure sunlight. It was like all the time I was growing up, I thought. We were down there, under the fog, going to school and church and piano lessons—and all that time there was this blue sky, this glorious sun. And suddenly I hated that fog. I'm out of it, I thought, my heart leaping. I'm on this side now.

We were down there, under the fog, going to school and church and piano lessons—and all that time there was this blue sky, this glorious sun.

Going to Japan was like that for me—like breaking through the fog and seeing, for the first time, in full light, where I had come from. What my grandparents had left behind. What they had intended to return to, until circumstances intervened and they ended up staying in America. Until I went to Japan, I was a person without a past; I looked into a mirror and saw no reflection. All I knew was the little white house on 23rd Avenue, in the Richmond District.

It wasn't until I was much older that I realized that the house my mother returned to from the hospital, after she had me, wasn't that house. The school where my sisters had a Halloween parade that day wasn't the school that was just up the hill from that house. All those years, I had imagined the story, my story, in the wrong place.

Living in that fog-shrouded[18] world perhaps made it easier for my mother and father to forget the past—America's lack of faith, the internment, the shame. To forget a heritage that cast suspicion on their loyalty. I didn't have to forget—I never knew.

In wartime, one must choose sides. But the price for doing so can be paid for generations.

17. *Serra* founded the first Spanish mission of the Roman Catholic Church in California, as well as eight others.

18. *Shrouded* means "covered or concealed."

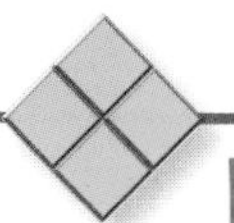

Responding to Literature

PERSONAL RESPONSE

What advice do you have for the narrator of this essay? Write a quick note to her explaining your ideas.

Analyzing Literature

RECALL

1. How did Sasaki learn she was both Japanese and American?
2. According to Sasaki, when can a person "forge ahead" without thinking of the past?
3. What does the ledger in her mother's head contain?
4. How does Sasaki define Japanese American?

INTERPRET

5. Why would the narrator wonder if she is English as well as Japanese and American?
6. Which of Sasaki's actions and words show that she is trying to "forge ahead"?
7. How does Sasaki's attitude toward paying off debt affect her life?
8. Why is the deformity and beauty of a bonsai tree a good image to represent the narrator's life?

EVALUATE AND CONNECT

9. Why does the author call this essay "A Dictionary of Japanese-American Terms"? How does the title relate to the structure of the selection?
10. How are Sasaki's concerns about being American like the concerns of other Americans? How are they different?

LITERARY ELEMENTS

Essay

An **essay** is a short piece of writing about a single subject. Essays are a type of **nonfiction,** writing that tells about real events and people. The writer of an essay uses facts, examples, and reasons to express an idea or an opinion. "A Dictionary of Japanese-American Terms" is a **personal essay,** an informal essay in which the writer reflects on his or her opinions and personal experiences. In contrast, a **formal essay** is a piece of writing that is serious, highly organized, and carefully researched.

1. What main idea or opinion does R. A. Sasaki express in her essay?
2. Find several facts, examples, or reasons that Sasaki uses to support her main idea.

• See **Literary Terms Handbook,** p. R3.

Literature and Writing

Writing About Literature

Analogy An **analogy** is a comparison between two things to show how one thing is like the other. Sasaki uses an analogy when she writes that visiting Japan was like "breaking through the fog." Think about the similarities between a fog that hangs over the ground and a fog that might cloud a person's mind. In your opinion, is Sasaki's analogy appropriate? Explain your answer in a paragraph or two, and support it with examples from the selection or your own experience.

Personal Writing

Reflection Sasaki says, "Until I went to Japan, I was a person without a past; I looked into a mirror and saw no reflection." Look back at the reflection you created for the **Focus Activity** on page 26. Write a letter to Sasaki, telling her what type of person you see reflected when you look into a mirror. You might also point out some similarities and differences between the two of you.

Extending Your Response

Literature Groups

Words for Your Life Sasaki defined several words and phrases in her essay. In your group, discuss why you think she chose each one. What has she learned about life and herself from each word? Then take turns describing words or phrases you might choose in writing a narration of your own life. Be prepared to explain your choices.

Listening and Speaking

Interview The *nisei* wanted their children to be confident and to "shoot for the sky." Interview someone who lived through World War II. Record the person's experience and his or her wishes for the children of today. Share your interview with the class.

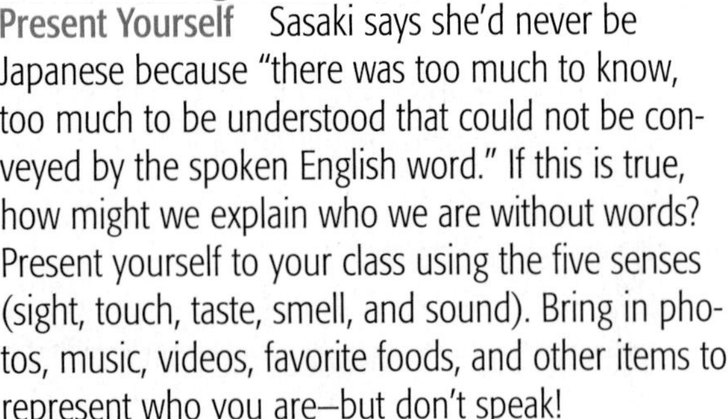

Performing

Present Yourself Sasaki says she'd never be Japanese because "there was too much to know, too much to be understood that could not be conveyed by the spoken English word." If this is true, how might we explain who we are without words? Present yourself to your class using the five senses (sight, touch, taste, smell, and sound). Bring in photos, music, videos, favorite foods, and other items to represent who you are—but don't speak!

Save your work for your portfolio.

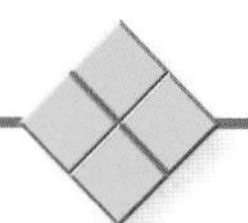

Skill Minilessons

GRAMMAR AND LANGUAGE • PERSONAL PRONOUNS

A **personal pronoun** names a person or thing. A personal pronoun may be the subject or the object of a sentence.

Subjects:	singular	I, you, he, she, it
	plural	we, you, they
Examples:	*I* accused her. *She* started to cry.	
Objects:	singular	me, you, him, her, it
	plural	us, you, them
Examples:	Other kids never asked *me*. I didn't talk to *them*.	

PRACTICE Choose the correct pronouns (subject or object) to complete each sentence.

1. Going to Japan was like that for (I, me).
2. My father moved (we, us) out of Japantown.
3. (She, Her) wore dresses all the time.
4. *Jiichan* died when (I, me) was too young to remember (he, him).
5. (They, them) remembered (he, him) tending his beloved cherry tree.

- For more about personal pronouns, see **Language Handbook,** p. R32.

READING AND THINKING • ELABORATING

Elaborating is adding details and examples to support a statement or idea. Most paragraphs contain a main idea backed up with elaboration that illustrates the idea for the reader. Sasaki says that her neighbor Kimiko is a *Nihonjin* and then elaborates with examples of Kimiko's *Nihonjin* background, habits, and appearance. Good readers learn to recognize main ideas, and the details that follow add to their understanding of the ideas.

PRACTICE Find examples and details in "A Dictionary of Japanese-American Terms" that elaborate on each sentence below.

1. At the age of six, I thought "Americans" and "English" meant the same thing–"white people."
2. *Jiichan* died when I was too young to remember him, but old enough to be afraid of death.
3. Perhaps I was simply born too late.
4. A Japanese American is . . . like a *bonsai.*

- For more about main idea and supporting details, see **Reading Handbook,** p. R88.

VOCABULARY • COMPOUND WORDS

Compound words are combinations of two words. The meaning of the new word combines the meanings of the original ones. If you see an unfamiliar word made from words you know, use your imagination to get at the meaning of the new word.

painstakingly

The words *pains* and *take* appear in the phrase "to take pains with" something, which means to give careful attention to doing it right. *Painstakingly* means "in a way requiring close, careful labor or attention."

PRACTICE Think about each compound word, then match it with the best definition on the right.

1. pacesetter	a. important or interesting
2. outdistance	b. leave behind; get ahead of
3. overseer	c. a result or consequence
4. newsworthy	d. one whose speed others must match
5. outgrowth	e. one who watches over and directs work

Before You Read

Homeless

MEET ANNA QUINDLEN

"Real life," says Anna Quindlen, "is in the dishes." Much of Quindlen's writing follows this belief that the best stories about the world focus on everyday activities and struggles. Quindlen began her writing career as a newspaper reporter, then went on to write columns for *The New York Times*, which at times dealt with politics, current events, and family life. Quindlen won a Pulitzer Prize for commentary in 1992. In addition, she has written a children's book, *The Tree That Came to Stay*, and two highly acclaimed novels about families.

Anna Quindlen was born in 1953. This essay was first published in 1989 in Living Out Loud.

FOCUS ACTIVITY

How many places have you called "home" in your life? Which "home" is most special to you, and why?

Sharing Ideas

With your group, discuss how your ideas, likes, and dislikes have been shaped by where you have lived.

Setting a Purpose

Read to discover how some people carry their "home" with them.

BACKGROUND

The Time and Place It is the mid- to late 1980s, and the writer is reflecting on her encounter with a homeless woman.

Did You Know? There may be as many as three million people in the United States who are homeless—that is, without a permanent address—according to estimates from the late 1990s. Some people are without a home for a short time. For others, being homeless is a way of life. Homeless people include families, patients released from psychiatric hospitals, and single men and women who are unemployed and poor. Many homeless people work but don't earn enough money to afford places to live.

The Homeless Families Foundation
It's Time To Reach Out

VOCABULARY PREVIEW

anonymous (ə non′ ə məs) *adj.* having no known name or origin; lacking qualities that make one different; p. 40

legacy (leg′ ə sē) *n.* anything handed down from an ancestor or from the past; p. 40

enfeebled (en fē′ bəld) *adj.* lacking force, strength, or effectiveness; weakened; p. 40

crux (kruks) *n.* the most important point or part; p. 41

Homeless

Anna Quindlen

Her name was Ann, and we met in the Port Authority[1] Bus Terminal several Januarys ago. I was doing a story on homeless people. She said I was wasting my time talking to her; she was just passing through, although she'd been passing through for more than two weeks. To prove to me that this was true, she rummaged through a tote bag and a manila envelope and finally unfolded a sheet of typing paper and brought out her photographs.

1. In the New York City area, the *Port Authority* operates all of the major bus and train terminals, airports, harbors, bridges, and tunnels.

Homeless

They were not pictures of family, or friends, or even a dog or cat, its eyes brown-red in the flashbulb's light. They were pictures of a house. It was like a thousand houses in a hundred towns, not suburb, not city, but somewhere in between, with aluminum siding and a chain-link fence, a narrow driveway running up to a one-car garage and a patch of backyard. The house was yellow. I looked on the back for a date or a name, but neither was there. There was no need for discussion. I knew what she was trying to tell me, for it was something I had often felt. She was not adrift, alone, anonymous, although her bags and her raincoat with the grime shadowing its creases had made me believe she was. She had a house, or at least once upon a time had had one. Inside were curtains, a couch, a stove, potholders. You are where you live. She was somebody.

I've never been very good at looking at the big picture, taking the global view, and I've always been a person with an overactive sense of place, the legacy of an Irish grandfather. So it is natural that the thing that seems most wrong with the world to me right now is that there are so many people with no homes. I'm not simply talking about shelter from the elements,[2] or three square meals a day or a mailing address to which the welfare people can send the check—although I know that all these are important for survival. I'm talking about a home, about precisely those kinds of feelings that have wound up in cross-stitch and French knots on samplers over the years.

Did You Know?
Cross-stitch is a needlework stitch that forms an *x*. A *sampler* is a piece of decorative needlework with embroidered letters in various stitches.

Home is where the heart is. There's no place like it. I love my home with a ferocity totally out of proportion to its appearance or location. I love dumb things about it: the hot-water heater, the plastic rack you drain dishes in, the roof over my head, which occasionally leaks. And yet it is precisely those dumb things that make it what it is—a place of certainty, stability, predictability, privacy, for me and for my family. It is where I live. What more can you say about a place than that? That is everything.

Yet it is something that we have been edging away from gradually during my lifetime and the lifetimes of my parents and grandparents. There was a time when where you lived often was where you worked and where you grew the food you ate and even where you were buried. When that era passed, where you lived at least was where your parents had lived and where you would live with your children when you became enfeebled. Then, suddenly, where you lived was where you lived for three years, until you could move on to something else and something else again.

And so we have come to something else again, to children who do not understand

2. Here, *elements* means "the forces of nature; weather."

Vocabulary

anonymous (ə non′ ə məs) *adj.* having no known name or origin; lacking qualities that make one different

legacy (leg′ ə sē) *n.* anything handed down from an ancestor or from the past

enfeebled (en fē′ bəld) *adj.* lacking force, strength, or effectiveness; weakened what it means to go to their rooms because they have never had a room, to men and women whose fantasy is a wall they can paint a color of their own choosing, to old people reduced to sitting on molded plastic chairs, their skin blue-white in the lights of a bus station, who pull pictures of houses out of their bags. Homes have stopped being homes. Now they are real estate.

People find it curious that those without homes would rather sleep sitting up on benches or huddled in doorways than go to shelters. Certainly some prefer to do so because they are emotionally ill, because they have been locked in before and they are damned if they will be locked in again. Others are afraid of the violence and trouble they may find there. But some seem to want something that is not available in shelters, and they will not compromise,[3] not for a cot, or oatmeal, or a shower with special soap that kills the bugs. "One room," a woman with a baby who was sleeping on her sister's floor, once told me, "painted blue." That was the crux of it; not size or location, but pride of ownership. Painted blue.

This is a difficult problem, and some wise and compassionate[4] people are working hard at it. But in the main I think we work around it, just as we walk around it when it is lying on the sidewalk or sitting in the bus terminal—the problem, that is. It has been customary to take people's pain and lessen our own participation in it by turning it into an issue, not a collection of human beings. We turn an adjective into a noun: the poor, not poor people; the homeless, not Ann or the man who lives in the box or the woman who sleeps on the subway grate.

Sometimes I think we would be better off if we forgot about the broad strokes and concentrated on the details. Here is a woman without a bureau. There is a man with no mirror, no wall to hang it on. They are not the homeless. They are people who have no homes. No drawer that holds the spoons. No window to look out upon the world. My God. That is everything.

3. In this context, *compromise* suggests being forced to make adjustments that might threaten one's independence or other personal interests.

4. A *compassionate* person sympathizes with the misfortune of others.

Vocabulary

crux (kruks) *n.* the most important point or part

Responding to Literature

PERSONAL RESPONSE

Think back to your discussion for the **Focus Activity** on page 38. In your opinion, how can not having a home affect a person's sense of identity?

Analyzing Literature

RECALL

1. Describe Ann, the woman in Quindlen's essay.
2. What was the subject of the picture that Ann showed the author?
3. What household objects does the author cherish?
4. According to the essay, what options for shelter exist for people without homes?

INTERPRET

5. Why, do you think, did Quindlen choose to open her essay with Ann's name?
6. What, in your opinion, was the significance of the picture for Ann?
7. Theme Connection Why, do you think, does the author describe the importance of household objects in her essay?
8. What conflict do some homeless people face when considering shelter options?

EVALUATE AND CONNECT

9. What images does Quindlen evoke in her essay? How do these images contribute to the effectiveness of the piece?
10. How does the essay reflect or enhance your understanding of the problem of homelessness?

LITERARY ELEMENTS

Stereotype

A **stereotype** is a generalization about a group of people in which individual differences are overlooked. Stereotypes might lead to unfair judgments because of a person's race, ethnic background, or physical appearance.

1. Quindlen's essay might be considered an attempt to break down the stereotype of "homeless people." What are some of the stereotypes Quindlen refers to?
2. What, according to the essay, is the effect of stereotyping on people without homes?

- See **Literary Terms Handbook**, p. R9.

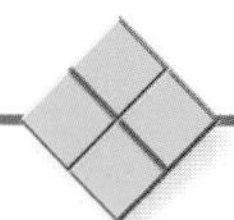

Extending Your Response

Writing About Literature

Analyze Details Quindlen's essay uses details about the ordinary contents of people's homes, including her own, to make her point. What details can you visualize about Quindlen's home? about Ann's former home? Write a paragraph that explains how Quindlen's imagery contributes to the effectiveness of her essay.

Interdisciplinary Activity

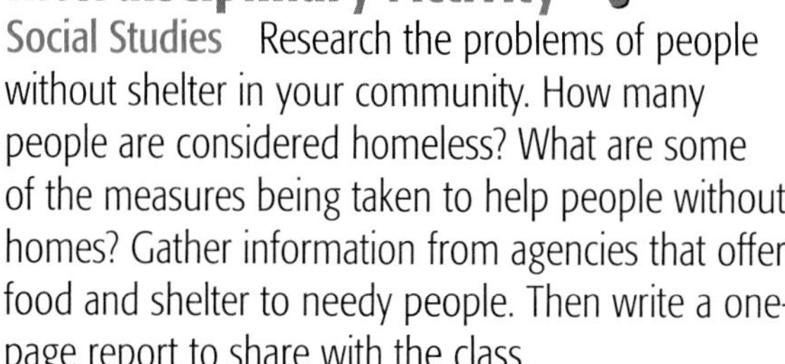

Social Studies Research the problems of people without shelter in your community. How many people are considered homeless? What are some of the measures being taken to help people without homes? Gather information from agencies that offer food and shelter to needy people. Then write a one-page report to share with the class.

Creative Writing

Interview Ann Quindlen wrote her essay after writing a newspaper article about homeless people. What interview questions do you suppose Quindlen asked Ann? Write ten questions you would ask Ann if you were to interview her.

Learning for Life

Create an Ad Campaign Use photographs and information from newspapers, magazines, and government agencies to create an advertising campaign to make people aware of homelessness in your community.

Literature Groups

Words to Think About The essay "Homeless" is full of thought-provoking quotations about home and family. In your group, pick the quotation that you think best summarizes Quindlen's point of view. List your reasons and share them with the class.

Reading Further

For a story about a family of homeless children, read:
Homecoming by Cynthia Voigt

Save your work for your portfolio.

Skill Minilesson

VOCABULARY • THE PREFIX *en-*

A common meaning of the prefix *en-* is "to make or cause to be." For example, to *enfeeble* someone is to cause that person to become feeble. The prefix *en-* is spelled *em-* when it comes in front of *p, b,* or *m.* So, if bad luck *embitters* you, it makes you bitter.

PRACTICE Match each word on the left with the correct meaning on the right.

1. embolden	a. to give physical form to
2. enfold	b. to give authority to
3. embody	c. to cause to be more energetic
4. enliven	d. to wrap up or to hug
5. empower	e. to make brave

MEDIA Connection

RADIO TRANSCRIPT

What can anyone do about homelessness? A group of teens enlisted help from an imaginary bear.

Homeless Children Write Book About Homelessness

From *Weekend Edition Saturday*–National Public Radio, December 25, 1993

STACEY BESS, Teacher [reading]: In the winter, the Wasatch Mountains above Salt Lake City are made of snow. In the city below, tall, glassy buildings reflect street lights and car headlights that shine like the Milky Way. From the mountains, signs and buildings look like clouds and rocky slopes. Even smart animals could get lost here. That's what happened to a bear cub named Frankie.

HOWARD BERKES, Reporter: "Even smart animals could get lost here. Anyone can become homeless." That's the first message sent by the forty-four young authors of *The Homeless Hibernating Bear,* a story they set here in Salt Lake City on busy downtown streets because this is where they were homeless and poor. Most of the kids lived for a time at the city's homeless shelter—a bright, brick, renovated building on a block framed by railroad tracks. Some were part of a peer support group made up of homeless and low-income kids.

BERKES [to students]: Does this book have a happy ending ? In your minds?

WHOLE GROUP: Yes, I think it does.

BERKES: Does it happen that way in real life?

ANNIE [one of the students]: Unfortunately not. I mean, if it did, there wouldn't be homelessness.

BERKES: Are you trying to get people to change the way they behave?

ANNIE: We want the pity stopped, you know, "all these little poor homeless people." You know, it's easy to say something like that, and give money, but it's a different thing to try to work at it, and get it so that it ends, you know.

BERKES: At the School With No Name, a dozen kids autograph their books. And there's talk of movie and cartoon deals, and network television appearances.

ANNIE: I feel like my voice is being heard, giving this message to people. I know it's working, because you're here asking these questions, and I mean, all these people. . . . It just kind of blows them away to think that kids can be thinking, you know, like this.

Respond

1. What did you learn about homelessness from this part of the NPR broadcast?
2. Do you agree with Annie when she says: "I know it's working, because you're here asking these questions"? Explain your answer.

Avoiding Sentence Fragments

A complete sentence contains a subject and a verb. A **sentence fragment** leaves out the subject or the verb. People often speak in sentence fragments, but writers must be more careful.

Problem 1 The subject is missing.
Was born in West Virginia but grew up in Harlem.

Solution Add a subject.
Myers was born in West Virginia but grew up in Harlem.

Problem 2 The subject and verb are missing.
As a child, he read comic books. Even during class.

Solution A Combine the fragment with another sentence.
As a child, he read comic books, even during class.

Solution B Rewrite the fragment as a complete sentence.
As a child, he read comic books. He even read them during class.

Problem 3 The verb is missing.
After high school, Myers faced a problem. No money for college.

Solution A *After high school, Myers faced a problem–no money for college.* [Combine the fragment with another sentence.]

Solution B *After high school, Myers faced a problem. No money was available for college.* [Add a verb to the fragment.]

- For more about sentence fragments, see **Language Handbook,** p. R11.

ACTIVITY

Rewrite the following paragraph to correct the sentence fragments.

When she was twenty-two. R. A. Sasaki flew to Japan. The fog of San Francisco became a symbol. For her confusion. And hidden truth about her roots.

SHORT STORY

Many of the selections in this book are short stories. Short stories are a type of prose fiction. **Prose** is any writing that is not poetry. **Fiction** is prose that is invented or imagined by the writer.

Each short story is unique, but most stories have the same basic features. The following examples from "The Farmer and His Sons," a fable by Aesop, explain how each feature works in a short story.

WHO IS THE STORY ABOUT?

CHARACTERS Characters are usually people. They move the action forward. The characters' words and actions reveal what their lives and personalities are like.

> **MODEL**
>
> In "The Farmer and His Sons," the characters are the father and several brothers.

WHAT HAPPENS TO THE CHARACTERS?

PLOT The plot is a series of events showing how a conflict, or problem is resolved. The conflict may be between characters; between a character and an idea (such as *right* or *wrong*); or between a character and a force, such as *nature.* A plot usually unfolds in these five steps:

1. **Exposition** introduces the story's setting and characters and sets up the conflict.
2. **Rising Action** develops the story's conflict or problem and builds suspense.
3. **Climax** is the moment of greatest suspense, emotion, and interest.
4. **Falling Action** reveals what happens to the characters after the climax and moves toward a conclusion.
5. **Resolution** completes the falling action and reveals the final outcome of the conflict.

> **MODEL**
>
> The conflict is between characters—the quarrelsome brothers who cannot succeed because they cannot get along.

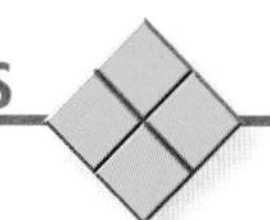

Most plots contain five steps.

The Farmer and His Sons

A certain farmer had several sons who were always quarreling with one another, and, try as he might, he could not get them to live together in harmony. So he made up his mind to convince them of their foolishness by the following means: First, he asked them to fetch a bundle of sticks, and challenged each in turn to break it across his knee. All tried and all failed.

Then he undid the bundle and handed them sticks one by one. This time they had no trouble at all in breaking them. "There, my sons," said he. "You can see that when you are united you will be more than a match for your enemies, but if you quarrel and separate, your weakness will put you at the mercy of those who would attack you."

Union is strength.

1 EXPOSITION
Introduces the problem: the quarreling between the farmer's sons.

2 RISING ACTION
The farmer devises a plan for helping his sons to get along.

3 CLIMAX
The farmer's plan is about to be revealed when he distributes the individual sticks.

4 FALLING ACTION
The sons break the sticks easily.

5 RESOLUTION
The farmer explains the lesson he has just taught his sons.

WHEN AND WHERE DOES THE STORY TAKE PLACE?

SETTING The setting is the time and place in which the story events occur.

MODEL

This fable takes place on a farm a long time ago.

WHAT IS THE MEANING OF THE STORY?

THEME The theme is the important message–or meaning–of the story. Sometimes the author states the theme directly, as in a fable. But often the reader has to figure it out.

MODEL

The theme of "The Farmer and His Sons" is that there is strength in unity.

ACTIVE READING MODEL

Active Reading Strategies

Active Reading Strategies for Short Story

Active readers of short stories talk back to writers. They ask questions and compare writers' ideas with their experiences. Use the strategies below as you discover ways several writers relate to the saying that there is "no place like home."

- For more about these and other reading strategies, see **Reading Handbook,** pp. R84–R103.

QUESTION

Questioning as you read helps you make sure you are getting to know the characters.

Ask Yourself . . .

- Why do characters behave as they do?
- Do people I know behave this way?
- Did I miss anything I need to know about the characters and the reasons for their actions?

CONNECT

Connecting helps you discover ways that stories reflect real lives.

Ask Yourself . . .

- What does "home" mean in this story?
- What does the setting have to do with the theme "No Place Like Home"?

PREDICT

Predicting helps you put details together logically and make educated guesses about what characters will do.

Ask Yourself . . .

- What do I think the characters may do next?
- How will their ideas about home affect the way they act and react to events in the story?

RESPOND

Respond to the characters and events. Think about how they make you feel.

Ask Yourself . . .

- What does this selection say to me?
- How do I feel about the way the plot wraps up?
- How does the selection fit my idea of "home"?

APPLYING THE STRATEGIES

As you read "Golden Glass," follow the Active Reading Model in the margins to get more out of the story.

ACTIVE READING MODEL

Before You Read

Golden Glass

MEET ALMA LUZ VILLANUEVA

What's the most important quality a writer should have? According to poet and fiction writer Alma Luz Villanueva, it's courage. "Writing takes all your courage—to stand by your work and see it through to publication—courage and luck (and discipline, discipline, discipline)," Villanueva says. Those qualities have helped Villanueva earn prizes for her poetry and novels, including a PEN award for fiction in 1994. Some of her work focuses on the search for personal identity, which Villanueva explores in the story "Golden Glass."

Alma Luz Villanueva was born in California in 1944. This story was first published in 1982.

FOCUS ACTIVITY

In what sort of place would you most like to spend a summer?

Web It!
Make a word web showing a kind of place where you would like to spend a summer.

Setting a Purpose
Read to find out how one teenager spends a summer away from home.

BACKGROUND

The Time and Place The setting of this contemporary story is the western part of the United States, but a similar story might be set anywhere there is a parent and a fourteen-year-old.

Did You Know? Many European churches constructed after the year A.D. 900 have magnificent windows of colorful stained glass. Smaller stained-glass objects, such as chandeliers and lamp shades, were introduced much later, in the nineteenth century.

VOCABULARY PREVIEW

angular (ang′ gyə lər) *adj.* bony and lean; p. 51
communion (kə mūn′ yən) *n.* closeness to, and sympathy with, another through sharing feelings or thoughts; p. 52
vividly (viv′ id lē) *adv.* clearly; intensely; p. 52
slither (slith′ ər) *v.* to move along with a sliding or gliding motion, as a snake; p. 52
concoct (kon kokt′) *v.* to make or put together, using skill and intelligence; p. 53
sheathe (shēth) *v.* to enclose in a case or covering; p. 54
hysteria (his ter′ ē ə) *n.* great, uncontrollable terror, panic, or other strong emotion; p. 54
meticulous (mi tik′ yə ləs) *adj.* showing great concern about details; p. 55

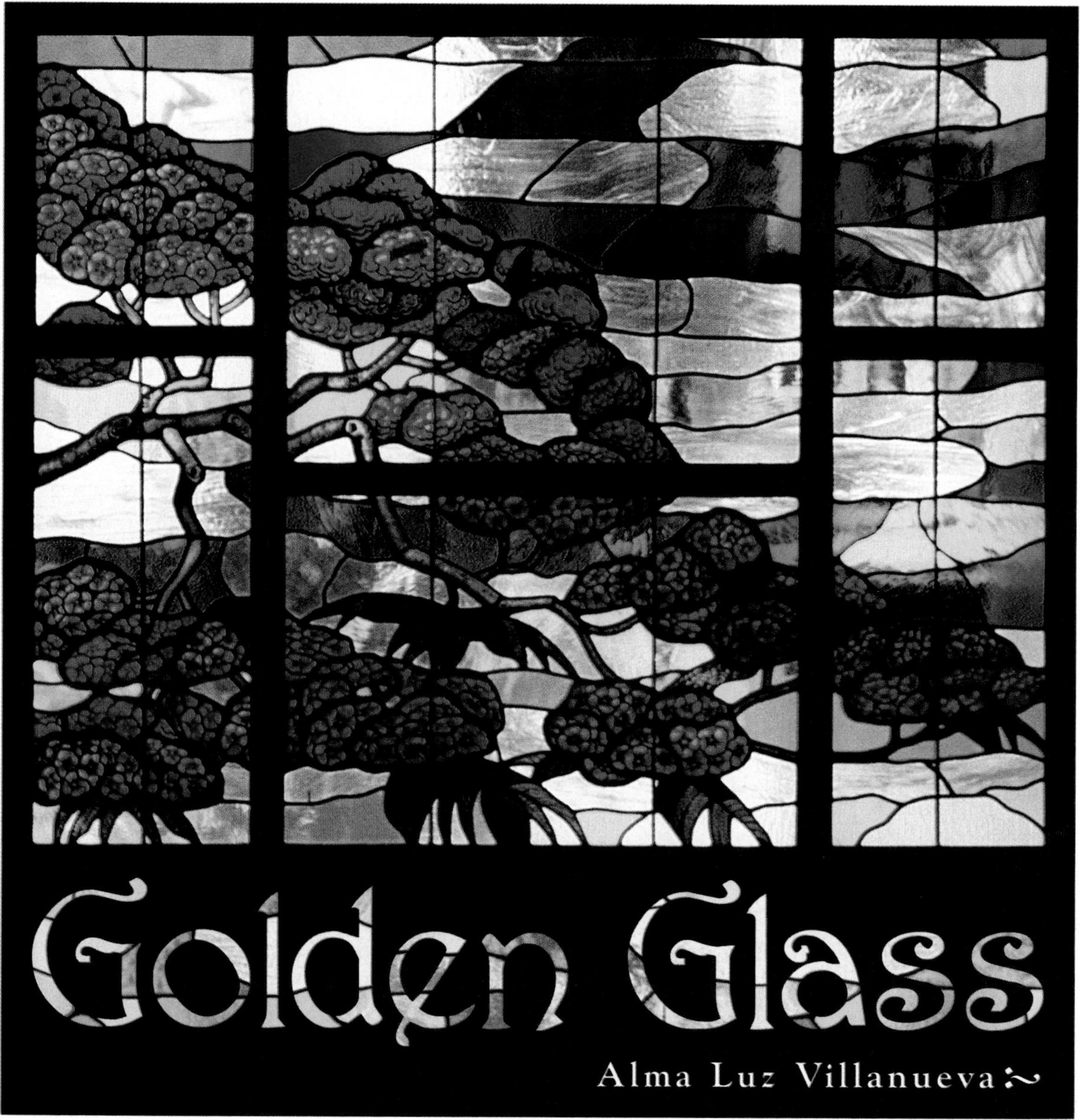

ACTIVE READING MODEL

It was his fourteenth summer. He was thinning out, becoming angular and clumsy, but the cautiousness, the old-man seriousness he'd had as a baby, kept him contained, ageless and safe. His humor, always dry and to the bone[1] since a small child, let you know he was watching everything.

1. Ted's humor is *dry and to the bone,* which means it is witty, but also sarcastic and sharp, as if it can cut through one's flesh.

Vocabulary

angular (ang′ gyə lər) *adj.* bony and lean

Golden Glass

QUESTION

What does it mean to be at the center of your own universe?

CONNECT

Is Ted's plan realistic? Could teens you know carry it out?

RESPOND

What do you think of Ted's plan so far?

He seemed always to be at the center of his own universe, so it was no surprise to his mother to hear Ted say: "I'm building a fort and sleeping out in it all summer, and I won't come in for anything, not even food. Okay?"

This had been their silent communion, the steady presence of love that flowed regularly, daily—food. The presence of his mother preparing it, his great appetite and obvious enjoyment of it—his nose smelling everything, seeing his mother more vividly than with his eyes.

He watched her now for signs of offense, alarm, and only saw interest. "Where will you put the fort?" Vida asked.

She trusted him to build well and not ruin things, but of course she had to know where. She looked at his dark, contained face and her eyes turned in and saw him when he was small, with curly golden hair, when he wrapped his arms around her neck. Their quiet times—undemanding—he could be let down, and a small toy could delight him for hours. She thought of the year he began kissing her elbow in passing, the way he preferred. Vida would touch his hair, his forehead, his shoulders—the body breathing out at the touch, his stillness. Then the explosion out the door told her he needed her touch, still.

"I'll build it by the redwoods, in the cypress trees. Okay?"

"Make sure you keep your nails together and don't dig into the trees. I'll be checking. If the trees get damaged, it'll have to come down."

"Jason already said he'd bring my food and stuff."

"Where do you plan to shower and go to the bathroom?" Vida wondered.

"With the hose when it's hot and I'll dig holes behind the barn," Ted said so quietly as to seem unspoken. He knew how to slither under her, smoothly, like silk.

"Sounds interesting, but it better stay clean—this place isn't that big. Also, on your dinner night, you can cook outdoors."

His eyes flashed, but he said, "Okay."

He began to gather wood from various stacks, drying it patiently from the long rains. He kept one of the hammers and a supply of nails that he bought in his room. It was early June and the seasonal creek was still running. It was pretty dark out there and he wondered if he'd meant what he'd said.

Ted hadn't seen his father in nearly four years, and he didn't miss him like you should a regular father, he thought. His father's image

Vocabulary

communion (kə mūn′ yən) *n.* closeness to, and sympathy with, another through sharing feelings or thoughts

vividly (viv′ id lē) *adv.* clearly; intensely

slither (sli*th*′ ər) *v.* to move along with a sliding or gliding motion, as a snake blurred with the memory of a football hitting him too hard, pointed (a bullet), right in the stomach, and the punishment for the penny candies—a test his father had set up for him to fail. His stomach hardened at the thought of his father, and he found he didn't miss him at all.

He began to look at the shapes of the trees, where the limbs were solid, where a space was provided (he knew his mother really would make him tear down the fort if he hurt the trees). The cypress was right next to the redwoods, making it seem very remote. Redwoods do that—they suck up sound and time and smell like another place. So he counted the footsteps, when no one was looking, from the fort to the house. He couldn't believe it was so close, it seemed so separate, alone—especially in the dark, when the only safe way of travel seemed flight (invisible at best).

The Dream Tree, 1993. Daniel Nevins. Oil & acrylic on wood, 48 x 40 in. Courtesy Williams Collection.

Viewing the painting: How might the boy in the painting feel about Ted's fort? How might Ted feel about this tree?

Ted had seen his mother walk out to the bridge at night with a glass of wine, looking into the water, listening to it. He knew she loved to see the moon's reflection in the water. She'd pointed it out to him once by a river where they camped, her face full of longing—too naked somehow, he thought. Then, she swam out into the water, at night, as though trying to touch the moon. He wouldn't look at her. He sat and glared at the fire and roasted another marshmallow the way he liked it: bubbly, soft and brown (maybe six if he could get away with it). Then she'd be back, chilled and bright, and he was glad she went. Maybe I like the moon too, he thought, involuntarily, as though the thought weren't his own—but it was.

RESPOND

When is a look "too naked"?

He built the ground floor directly on the earth, with a cover of old plywood, then scattered remnant rugs that he'd asked Vida to get for him. He concocted a latch and a door, with his hand ax over it, just in case.

Vocabulary

concoct (kon kokt′) *v.* to make or put together, using skill and intelligence

He brought his sleeping bag, some pillows, a transistor radio, some clothes, and moved in for the summer. The first week he slept with his buck knife open in his hand and his pellet gun loaded on the same side, his right. The second week Ted sheathed the knife and put it under his head, but kept the pellet gun loaded at all times. He missed no one in the house but the dog, so he brought him in the cramped little space, enduring dog breath because he missed *someone*.

PREDICT

Does Ted seem to be the type of person who will stick to his plans for the entire summer?

Ted thought of when his father left, when they lived in the city, with forty kids on one side of the block and forty on the other. He remembered that one little kid with the funny sores on his body who chose an apple over candy every time. He worried they would starve or something worse. That time he woke up screaming in his room (he forgot why), and his sister began crying at the same time, "Someone's in here," as though they were having the same terrible dream. Vida ran in with a chair in one hand and a kitchen knife in the other, which frightened them even more. But when their mother realized it was only their hysteria she became angry and left. Later they all laughed about this till they cried, including Vida, and things felt safer.

He began to build the top floor now but he had to prune some limbs out of the way. Well, that was okay as long as he was careful. So he stacked them to one side for kindling and began to brace things in place. It felt weird going up into the tree, not as safe as his small, contained place on the ground. He began to build it, thinking of light. He could bring his comic books, new ones, sit up straight, and eat snacks in the daytime. He would put in a side window facing the house to watch them, if he wanted, and a tunnel from the bottom floor to the top. Also, a ladder he'd found and repaired—he could pull it up and place it on hooks, out of reach. A hatch at the top of the ceiling for leaving or entering, tied down inside with a rope. He began to sleep up here, without the dog, with the tunnel closed off.

CONNECT

In what ways is Ted like you?

Vida noticed Ted had become cheerful and would stand next to her, to her left side, talking sometimes. But she realized she musn't face him or he'd become silent and wander away. So she stood listening, in the same even breath and heartbeat she kept when she spotted the wild pheasants with their long, lush tails trailing the grape arbor,[2]

2. An *arbor* is a shady area covered over and partly enclosed by trees, shrubs, or vines. Here, the arbor is formed by grape vines, probably growing on an arch-like wooden frame called a trellis.

Vocabulary

sheathe (shēth) *v.* to enclose in a case or covering
hysteria (his ter′ ē ə) *n.* great, uncontrollable terror, panic, or other strong emotion

picking delicately and greedily at the unpicked grapes in the early autumn light. So sharp, so perfect, so rare to see a wild thing at peace.

She knew he ate well—his brother brought out a half gallon of milk that never came back, waiting to be asked to join him, but never daring to ask. His sister made him an extra piece of ham for his four eggs; most always he ate cold cereal and fruit or got a hot chocolate on the way to summer school. They treated Ted somewhat like a stranger, because he was.

Ted was taking a make-up course and one in stained glass. There, he talked and acted relaxed, like a boy; no one expected any more or less. The colors of the stained glass were deep and beautiful, and special—you couldn't waste this glass. The sides were sharp, the cuts were slow and meticulous with a steady pressure. The design's plan had to be absolutely followed or the beautiful glass would go to waste, and he'd curse himself.

RESPOND

What do you think about Ted's attention to details?

It was late August and Ted hadn't gone inside the house once. He liked waking up, hearing nothing but birds—not his mother's voice or his sister's or his brother's. He could tell the various bird calls and liked the soft brown quail call the best. He imagined their taste and wondered if their flesh was as soft as their song. Quail would've been okay to kill, as long as he ate it, his mother said. Instead, he killed jays because they irritated him so much with their shrill cries. Besides, a neighbor paid Ted per bird because he didn't want them in his garden. But that was last summer and he didn't do that anymore, and the quail were proud and plump and swift, and Ted was glad.

The stained glass was finished and he decided to place it in his fort facing the back fields. In fact, it looked like the back fields—trees and the sun in a dark sky. During the day the glass sun shimmered a beautiful yellow, the blue a much better color than the sky outside: deeper, like night.

He was so used to sleeping outside now he didn't wake up during the night, just like in the house. One night, toward the end when he'd have to move back with everyone (school was starting, frost was coming and the rains), Ted woke up to see the stained glass full of light. The little sun was a golden moon and the inside glass sky and the outside sky matched.

RESPOND

What are the things about Ted's family that you like? What things don't you understand about his family?

In a few days he'd be inside, and he wouldn't mind at all.

Vocabulary

meticulous (mi tik′ yə ləs) *adj.* showing great concern about details

ACTIVE READING MODEL

Responding to Literature

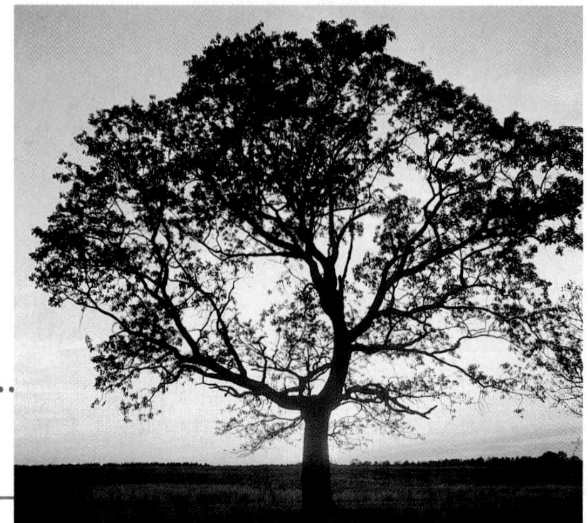

PERSONAL RESPONSE

Look back at the web you made for the **Focus Activity** on page 50. How do your ideas of a good place to be compare with Ted's plan?

Active Reading Response

Which of your **Active Reading** questions was most helpful in understanding Ted? Why?

Analyzing Literature

RECALL

1. What summer plan does Ted propose?
2. What demands does Vida make regarding Ted's plan?
3. What does Vida watch as she stands on the bridge? What emotion does Ted see in her face?
4. What object does Ted hang above the fort door?

INTERPRET

5. Do you think Vida is bothered by Ted's desire to separate himself from his family? Support your opinion with examples from the story.
6. In what ways does the author make clear the relationship between Vida and Ted?
7. Explain what the author means in the sentence, "Maybe I like the moon too, he thought, involuntarily, as though the thought weren't his own–but it was."
8. What objects do you see in the story that symbolize Ted's personality? What does each object tell the reader about Ted?

EVALUATE AND CONNECT

9. In some stories, the writer focuses on a **conflict,** or central problem. In others, characters and their development receive a strong emphasis. Which type of story do you prefer? In your opinion, which type of story is "Golden Glass"? Explain.
10. How does Villanueva use the stained glass to develop the character of Ted?

LITERARY ELEMENTS

Setting

The time and place in which a story takes place is its **setting.** The setting includes any elements in which the action occurs: the historical period; geographic region; season; weather; and spaces, such as buildings, rooms, and landscapes. The culture in which the characters develop is also part of the setting.

1. Which details describe the geographical setting of "Golden Glass"? In what way is this setting important to the story?
2. Are the spaces in which Ted lives important to him? How do you know?

• See **Literary Terms Handbook,** p. R9.

Extending Your Response

Writing About Literature

Character Analysis Alma Luz Villanueva characterizes Vida and Ted by letting them speak and act in ways that reveal their personalities. Select an important trait of one character. Describe a scene in which that trait is displayed.

Aren't sure exactly which setting you'd prefer to visit? Discover some of the possibilities by finding the home pages of the fifty states. Study the information, follow the links, and examine the many beautiful and interesting places you may someday see.

Personal Writing

Looking Back Think of a time when you felt a need for a change in your surroundings, or recall a story about someone who wanted such a change. Write a journal entry about the event. Explain how elements of the setting are important to you or the character about whom you are writing.

Literature Groups

Did Ted achieve real independence during his fourteenth summer? Are people interdependent? Look up the two words in a dictionary. Then, with a group, consider the meanings of *independence* and *interdependence.* Brainstorm names of characters you have met in other stories, in movies, and on television. How is each character dependent, independent, and interdependent?

Reading Further

These books are about other teens who find personal spaces:
The Island by Gary Paulsen
A Solitary Blue by Cynthia Voigt
My Side of the Mountain by Jean Craighead George

Save your work for your portfolio.

Skill Minilesson

VOCABULARY • LATIN ROOTS

If you describe something *vividly,* you provide such a clear picture of it that you bring it to life. The word *vivo* in Latin means "live" and *vita* means "life." *Viv* and *vit* are roots, or basic word parts, that have to do with life or liveliness.

PRACTICE Use what you know about the roots *vit* and *viv* to answer each question.

1. How might a *vivacious* person behave?
2. Name one *vital* need that people have.
3. Who needs to be *revived?*

Technology Skills

E-Mail: Mailing Lists

Mailing lists are like clubs whose members are brought together by a common interest and electronic mail. To join the "club," you subscribe to the E-mail list. It doesn't cost anything to subscribe to a mailing list, and you can find a list on just about any topic that interests you. Once you sign up for a list, you'll receive E-mail relating to its subject. For instance, suppose you enjoy science fiction, and you want to find out what others think of your favorite writers, movies, or TV shows. You can subscribe to a mailing list that features discussion about science fiction. As a subscriber, you can read what other subscribers write and add your own contributions.

Information Overload

When you subscribe to a mailing list, you may find yourself—and your hard drive—overwhelmed with messages. Much of it could be electronic junk mail, also known as *spam.* This junk E-mail is a lot like the advertising delivered by post office mail.

The most common form of spam is the ad that masquerades as a message. Often, the subject line gives away its true identity. For instance, suppose you've subscribed to a mailing list for skateboarders. You browse through messages and come across one with a subject line that reads "The best board available!" Chances are, you've run across an ad.

Other spam can be eliminated by skimming your E-mail. If the subject line doesn't tell you enough, just run your eye quickly over the first few paragraphs of the message to see what you can discover about it. If it looks like something that doesn't interest you, delete it and go on to the next message.

Digests are another tool to help you avoid information overload. Many mailing lists offer a digest option. Instead of sending you dozens of messages daily, they will send a single E-mail with a brief summary of each new message. If a summary of a message looks interesting, you can request the entire message. Mailing lists that offer a digest usually eliminate spam as well.

Practice

- Access a search engine on the World Wide Web and do a keyword search for "list of lists." The search should lead you to a number of sites with searchable databases of mailing lists.
- Select one of the sites and do a search for literature, a specific author, or other keywords relating to your study in this class. The site's search engine will sift through the database looking for the keywords you specified. If it finds a match, a subscription address will be displayed. Copy it.
- Open your E-mail software. Send a message to the subscription address you copied earlier. Leave the subject line blank. Generally, the format to follow for your message is: subscribe, mailing list name, your name—for example: *subscribe scifi linda sanchez.* In some cases, you may be asked to use a slightly different format or procedure to subscribe. Follow the directions.
- A day or two after you subscribe, you should receive a confirmation message in your electronic mailbox. This message includes important information about the mailing list, the availability of a digest, and instructions for unsubscribing if you want to stop receiving messages.

TECHNOLOGY TIP

The first site you visit may not contain the list you're looking for. Check out several sites and search their databases until you find a few lists that seem promising. Also, read the terms of agreement before you subscribe to a list. Look for lists that have strict policies limiting spam.

ACTIVITIES

1. Find and subscribe to two or three mailing lists that focus on a particular hobby or pastime. In your journal, evaluate each mailing list. Do you find the information helpful? Are the discussions relevant? How does participation on the mailing list add to or detract from your interest in the topic?
2. Create your own List of Lists for students at your school to use or for your school's Web site. Focus on lists that will interest other students.

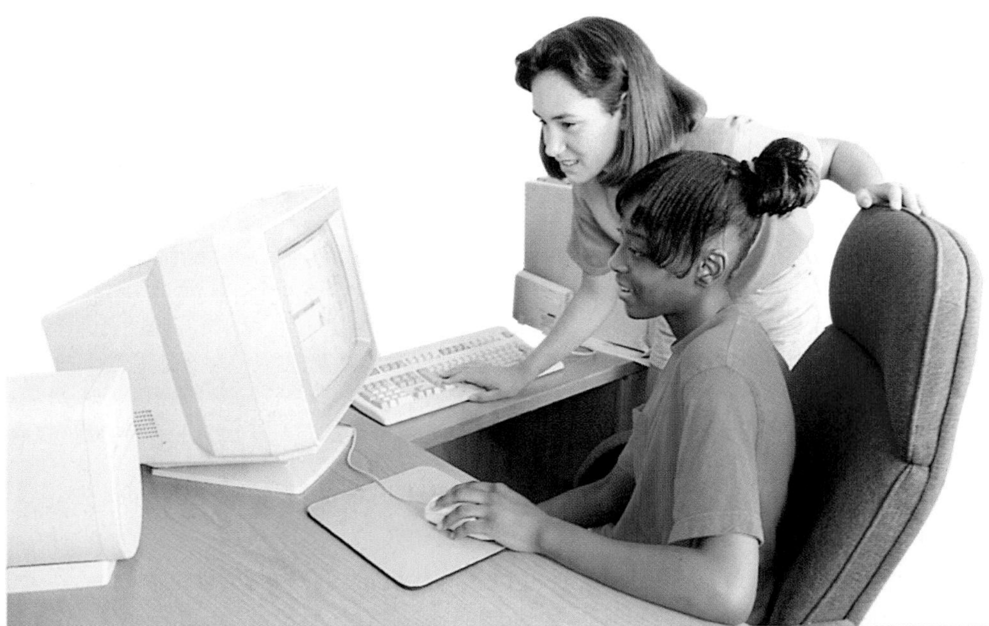

Writing Skills

Using Examples: Pictures, Sounds, and Action

Early in the story "Mother and Daughter," author Gary Soto says that Mrs. Moreno, Yollie's mother, has a strange sense of humor. Then he uses this **example**:

> "Mom, wake me up when the movie's over so I can go to bed," mumbled Yollie.
>
> "OK, Yollie, I wake you," said her mother through a mouthful of popcorn.
>
> But after the movie ended, instead of waking her daughter, Mrs. Moreno laughed under her breath, turned the TV and lights off, and tiptoed to bed. Yollie woke up in the middle of the night and didn't know where she was. . . . She blinked her sleepy eyes, looked around at the darkness, and called, "Mom? Mom, where are you?" But there was no answer, just the throbbing hum of the refrigerator.

The phrase "a strange sense of humor" gives a general description of Mrs. Moreno's personality. The example turns the description into pictures, sounds, and action.

When you add examples to your writing, you can create images in readers' minds.

General Statement	**Example**
I hate to dress up.	My fanciest clothes are a T-shirt and clean jeans with no holes.

ACTIVITIES

Use examples to illustrate and strengthen your own writing.

1. Write one or more examples to bring the following statement to life: *My favorite fast food place is terrific.*
2. Write a short paragraph about one of your personality traits. Include several examples of your habits or actions to illustrate the trait.

Before You Read

Mother and Daughter

MEET
GARY SOTO

Gary Soto grew up in a poor Mexican American neighborhood in California. His father died in a factory accident when Gary was only five. As a child, Soto didn't dream of being a writer, but his life changed in college when he came across a book titled *The New American Poetry*. "I discovered this poetry and thought, 'This is terrific: I'd like to do something like this.'" Soto is now the author of more than thirty books.

Gary Soto was born in 1952. This story was first published in 1990.

FOCUS ACTIVITY

Think of a time when you couldn't get something you needed.

FreeWrite
Write in your journal about how you reacted to the disappointment of not getting what you needed or wanted.

Setting a Purpose
Read to understand what two people mean by "need."

BACKGROUND

The Time and Place This story takes place in a Mexican American neighborhood after World War II.

Did You Know? Education makes a difference–inside or outside the classroom. High school graduates make more money than their peers who haven't graduated. College graduates earn even more. Many employers screen job applicants for reading and writing skills. Good readers learn a job more quickly than those who can't read well.

VOCABULARY PREVIEW

gloat (glōt) *v.* to feel or express pleasure or satisfaction in one's own success or achievement, especially in a triumphant or slightly nasty way; p. 63

meager (mē′ gər) *adj.* not enough in amount or quantity; insufficient; p. 64

taunt (tônt) *v.* to make fun of in a scornful, insulting way; p. 64

sophisticated (sə fis′ tə kā′ tid) *adj.* having or showing knowledge or experience of the world; p. 65

tirade (tī rād′) *n.* a long, angry or scolding speech; p. 67

lurch (lurch) *v.* to move suddenly in a jerky and uneven manner; p. 67

De la Corazón (From the Heart), 1973. Yreina D. Cervantes. Watercolor, 16 x 12 in. Collection of the artist.

Mother and Daughter

Gary Soto

Yollie's mother, Mrs. Moreno, was a large woman who wore a muumuu[1] and butterfly-shaped glasses. She liked to water her lawn in the evening and wave at low-riders, who would stare at her behind their smoky sunglasses and laugh. Now and then a low-rider from Belmont Avenue would make his car jump and shout "Mamacita!"[2] But most of the time they just stared and wondered how she got so large.

Mrs. Moreno had a strange sense of humor. Once, Yollie and her mother were watching a late-night movie called "They Came to Look." It was about creatures from the underworld who had climbed through molten lava to walk the earth. But Yollie, who had played soccer all day with the kids next door, was too tired to be scared. Her eyes closed but sprang open when her mother screamed, "Look, Yollie! Oh, you missed a scary part. The guy's face was all ugly!"

But Yollie couldn't keep her eyes open. They fell shut again and stayed shut, even when her mother screamed and slammed a heavy palm on the arm of her chair.

"Mom, wake me up when the movie's over so I can go to bed," mumbled Yollie.

"OK, Yollie, I wake you," said her mother through a mouthful of popcorn.

But after the movie ended, instead of waking her daughter, Mrs. Moreno laughed under her breath, turned the TV and lights off, and tiptoed to bed. Yollie woke up in the middle of the night and didn't know where she was. For a moment she thought she was dead. Maybe something from the underworld had lifted her from her house and carried her into the earth's belly. She blinked her sleepy eyes, looked around at the darkness, and called, "Mom? Mom, where are you?" But there was no answer, just the throbbing hum of the refrigerator.

Finally, Yollie's grogginess cleared and she realized her mother had gone to bed, leaving her on the couch. Another of her little jokes.

But Yollie wasn't laughing. She tiptoed into her mother's bedroom with a glass of water and set it on the nightstand next to the alarm clock. The next morning, Yollie woke to screams. When her mother reached to turn off the alarm, she had overturned the glass of water.

Yollie burned her mother's morning toast and gloated. "Ha! Ha! I got you

1. A *muumuu* (a Hawaiian word) is a long, loose dress, usually in a brightly colored pattern.
2. Here, the *low-riders* are the drivers of cars that have been customized so that they ride close to the ground. In Spanish, *Mamacita* (mä′ mä sē′ tä) means "little momma."

Vocabulary

gloat (glōt) *v.* to feel or express pleasure or satisfaction in one's own success or achievement, especially in a triumphant or slightly nasty way back. Why did you leave me on the couch when I told you to wake me up?"

Despite their jokes, mother and daughter usually got along. They watched bargain matinees together, and played croquet in the summer and checkers in the winter. Mrs. Moreno encouraged Yollie to study hard because she wanted her daughter to be a doctor. She bought Yollie a desk, a typewriter, and a lamp that cut glare so her eyes would not grow tired from hours of studying.

Yollie was slender as a tulip, pretty, and one of the smartest kids at Saint Theresa's. She was captain of crossing guards, an altar girl, and a whiz in the school's monthly spelling bees.

"*Tienes que estudiar mucho*,"[3] Mrs. Moreno said every time she propped her work-weary feet on the hassock. "You have to study a lot, then you can get a good job and take care of me."

"Yes, Mama," Yollie would respond, her face buried in a book. If she gave her mother any sympathy, she would begin her stories about how she had come with her family from Mexico with nothing on her back but a sack with three skirts, all of which were too large by the time she crossed the border because she had lost weight from not having enough to eat.

Everyone thought Yollie's mother was a riot. Even the nuns laughed at her antics. Her brother Raul, a nightclub owner, thought she was funny enough to go into show business.

But there was nothing funny about Yollie needing a new outfit for the eighth-grade fall dance. They couldn't afford one. It was late October, with Christmas around the corner, and their dented Chevy Nova had gobbled up almost one hundred dollars in repairs.

"We don't have the money," said her mother, genuinely sad because they couldn't buy the outfit, even though there was a little money stashed away for college. Mrs. Moreno remembered her teenage years and her hardworking parents, who picked grapes and oranges, and chopped beets and cotton for meager pay around Kerman. Those were the days when "new clothes" meant limp and out-of-style dresses from Saint Vincent de Paul.[4]

The best Mrs. Moreno could do was buy Yollie a pair of black shoes with velvet bows and fabric dye to color her white summer dress black.

"We can color your dress so it will look brand-new," her mother said brightly, shaking the bottle of dye as she ran hot water into a plastic dish tub. She poured the black liquid into the tub and stirred it with a pencil. Then, slowly and carefully, she lowered the dress into the tub.

Yollie couldn't stand to watch. She *knew* it wouldn't work. It would be like the time her mother stirred up a batch of molasses for candy apples on Yollie's birthday. She'd dipped the apples into the goo and swirled them and seemed to taunt Yollie by singing

3. *Tienes que estudiar mucho* (tye′ nes kā es too′ dē är moo′ chō)

4. The dresses come from a Catholic organization (named for Saint Vincent de Paul) that runs stores selling inexpensive secondhand goods.

Vocabulary

meager (mē′ gər) *adj.* not enough in amount or quantity; insufficient

taunt (tônt) *v.* to make fun of in a scornful, insulting way

"Las Mañanitas"[5] to her. When she was through, she set the apples on wax paper. They were hard as rocks and hurt the kids' teeth. Finally they had a contest to see who could break the apples open by throwing them against the side of the house. The apples shattered like grenades, sending the kids scurrying for cover, and in an odd way the birthday party turned out to be a success. At least everyone went home happy.

To Yollie's surprise, the dress came out shiny black. It looked brand-new and sophisticated, like what people in New York wear. She beamed at her mother, who hugged Yollie and said, "See, what did I tell you?"

The dance was important to Yollie because she was in love with Ernie Castillo, the third-best speller in the class. She bathed, dressed, did her hair and nails, and primped until her mother yelled, "All right already." Yollie sprayed her neck and wrists with Mrs. Moreno's Avon perfume and bounced into the car.

Mrs. Moreno let Yollie out in front of the school. She waved and told her to have a good time but behave herself, then roared off, blue smoke trailing from the tail pipe of the old Nova.

Yollie ran into her best friend, Janice. They didn't say it, but each thought the other was the most beautiful girl at the dance; the boys would fall over themselves asking them to dance.

The evening was warm but thick with clouds. Gusts of wind picked up the paper lanterns hanging in the trees and swung them, blurring the night with reds and yellows. The lanterns made the evening seem romantic, like a scene from a movie. Everyone danced, sipped punch, and stood in knots of threes and fours, talking. Sister Kelly got up and jitterbugged[6] with some kid's father. When the record ended, students broke into applause.

Janice had her eye on Frankie Ledesma, and Yollie, who kept smoothing her dress down when the wind picked up, had her eye on Ernie. It turned out that Ernie had his mind on Yollie, too. He ate a handful of cookies nervously, then asked her for a dance.

"Sure," she said, nearly throwing herself into his arms.

They danced two fast ones before they got a slow one. As they circled under the lanterns, rain began falling, lightly at first. Yollie loved the sound of the raindrops ticking against the leaves. She leaned her head on Ernie's shoulder, though his sweater was scratchy. He felt warm and tender. Yollie could tell that he was in love, and with her, of course. The dance continued successfully, romantically, until it began to pour.

"Everyone, let's go inside—and, boys, carry in the table and the record player," Sister Kelly commanded.

The girls and boys raced into the cafeteria. Inside, the girls, drenched to the bone, hurried to the restrooms to brush their hair and dry themselves. One girl cried because her velvet dress was ruined. Yollie felt sorry for her and helped her dry the dress off with paper towels, but it was no use. The dress was ruined.

5. *"Las Mañanitas"* (läs män′ yä nē′ täs) is a birthday song.

6. The *jitterbug* is a lively, acrobatic dance that was popular in the 1940s and 1950s.

Vocabulary

sophisticated (sə fis′ tə kā′ tid) *adj.* having or showing knowledge or experience of the world

Yollie went to a mirror. She looked a little gray now that her mother's makeup had washed away but not as bad as some of the other girls. She combed her damp hair, careful not to pull too hard. She couldn't wait to get back to Ernie.

Yollie bent over to pick up a bobby pin, and shame spread across her face. A black puddle was forming at her feet. Drip, black drip. Drip, black drip. The dye was falling from her dress like black tears. Yollie stood up. Her dress was now the color of ash. She looked around the room. The other girls, unaware of Yollie's problem, were busy grooming themselves. What could she do? Everyone would laugh. They would know she dyed an old dress because she couldn't afford a new one. She hurried from the restroom with her head down, across the cafeteria floor and out the door. She raced through the storm, crying as the rain mixed with her tears and ran into twig-choked gutters.

When she arrived home, her mother was on the couch eating cookies and watching TV.

"How was the dance, *m'ija?*[7] Come watch the show with me. It's really good."

Yollie stomped, head down, to her bedroom. She undressed and threw the dress on the floor.

Her mother came into the room. "What's going on? What's all the racket, baby?"

"The dress. It's cheap! It's no good!" Yollie kicked the dress at her mother and watched it land in her hands. Mrs. Moreno studied it closely but couldn't see what was wrong. "What's the matter? It's just a bit wet."

"The dye came out, that's what."

Mrs. Moreno looked at her hands and saw the grayish dye puddling in the shallow lines of her palms. Poor baby, she thought, her brow darkening as she made a sad face. She wanted to tell her daughter how sorry she was, but she knew it wouldn't help. She walked back to the living room and cried.

The next morning, mother and daughter stayed away from each other. Yollie sat in her room turning the pages of an old *Seventeen*, while her mother watered her plants with a Pepsi bottle.

Portrait, 1972. Eloy Blanco. Collection of El Museo del Barrio, New York.

Viewing the painting: What do you see in this young woman's face that reminds you of Yollie?

7. *M'ija* is a shortened form of *mi hija* (mē ē′ hä), meaning "my daughter."

"Drink, my children," she said loud enough for Yollie to hear. She let the water slurp into pots of coleus and cacti. "Water is all you need. My daughter needs clothes, but I don't have no money."

Yollie tossed her *Seventeen* on her bed. She was embarrassed at last night's tirade. It wasn't her mother's fault that they were poor.

When they sat down together for lunch, they felt awkward about the night before. But Mrs. Moreno had made a fresh stack of tortillas and cooked up a pan of *chile verde,*[8] and that broke the ice. She licked her thumb and smacked her lips.

"You know, honey, we gotta figure a way to make money," Yollie's mother said. "You and me. We don't have to be poor. Remember the Garcias. They made this stupid little tool that fixes cars. They moved away because they're rich. That's why we don't see them no more."

"What can we make?" asked Yollie. She took another tortilla and tore it in half.

"Maybe a screwdriver that works on both ends? Something like that." The mother looked around the room for ideas, but then shrugged. "Let's forget it. It's better to get an education. If you get a good job and have spare time then maybe you can invent something." She rolled her tongue over her lips and cleared her throat. "The county fair hires people. We can get a job there. It will be here next week."

Yollie hated the idea. What would Ernie say if he saw her pitching hay at the cows? How could she go to school smelling like an armful of chickens? "No, they wouldn't hire us," she said.

The phone rang. Yollie lurched from her chair to answer it, thinking it would be Janice wanting to know why she had left. But it was Ernie wondering the same thing. When he found out she wasn't mad at him, he asked if she would like to go to a movie.

"I'll ask," Yollie said, smiling. She covered the phone with her hand and counted to ten. She uncovered the receiver and said, "My mom says it's OK. What are we going to see?"

After Yollie hung up, her mother climbed, grunting, onto a chair to reach the top shelf in the hall closet. She wondered why she hadn't done it earlier. She reached behind a stack of towels and pushed her chubby hand into the cigar box where she kept her secret stash of money.

"I've been saving a little money every month," said Mrs. Moreno. "For you, *m'ija.*" Her mother held up five twenties, a blossom of green that smelled sweeter than flowers on that Saturday. They drove to Macy's and bought a blouse, shoes, and a skirt that would not bleed in rain or any other kind of weather.

8. *Tortillas* (tôr tē′ yäs) are made from corn or wheat meal and baked on a griddle so that they resemble very flat pancakes, and *chile verde* (chē′ lā vār′ dā) is a spicy sauce made with green chile peppers.

Vocabulary

tirade (tī rād′) *n.* a long, angry or scolding speech
lurch (lurch) *v.* to move suddenly in a jerky and uneven manner

Responding to Literature

PERSONAL RESPONSE

Look back at the notes you made for the **Focus Activity** on page 61. Compare your situation with Yollie's reaction to not being able to buy a new dress. How are the experiences similar and different?

Analyzing Literature

RECALL

1. Describe the tricks that Yollie and Mrs. Moreno play on each other after the late-night movie.
2. Why doesn't Mrs. Moreno let Yollie buy a new dress for the dance? What does she do for her instead?
3. What happens at the dance?
4. How do Yollie and her mother feel after the dance?

INTERPRET

5. What kind of mother is Mrs. Moreno? Does Yollie appreciate her? How can you tell?
6. What effect does being poor have on Yollie's life? How might her life be different if her mother had more money?
7. Were the things that happened at the dance humorous, sad, or both? Explain.
8. Describe the ongoing relationship between Yollie and Mrs. Moreno.

EVALUATE AND CONNECT

9. How important, in your opinion, is humor in the lives of the characters? Explain.
10. Theme Connection What helps Yollie to compensate for the difficult circumstances of her life?

LITERARY ELEMENTS

Tone

Tone is the attitude taken by a writer toward a subject. The tone can vary from gloomy and threatening to cheerful and hopeful. For example, when Gary Soto describes the tricks that Yollie and her mother play on each other in the story opening, his tone is humorous.

1. What is the author's tone when he describes what happens at the party?
2. In your opinion, is the overall tone of the story hopeful? Explain.
3. How might the author be using tone to suggest something about the characters' lives?

• See **Literary Terms Handbook,** p. R10.

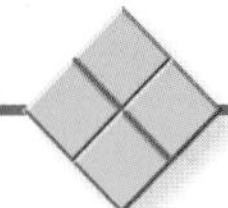

Extending Your Response

Writing About Literature

Like Mother, Like Daughter? Write one or two paragraphs in which you compare and contrast Yollie and Mrs. Moreno. Use the following questions to help you organize your ideas:

- What do you think is an outstanding characteristic of the mother and of the daughter?
- How does each character react to problems?
- What is the overall attitude of each toward life?

Creative Writing

Mom Award Suppose that Yollie wrote about her mother for a school assignment on "The Person I Admire Most." What would she say? Would she include anything negative? Write the assignment in Yollie's words.

Literature Groups

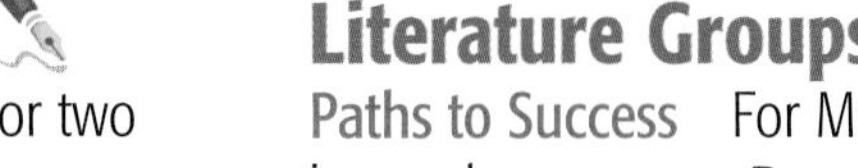

Paths to Success For Mrs. Moreno, studying hard is a path to success. Do you agree that education is the best way to prepare for a successful future? Why or why not? What other routes to success might Yollie consider? Are they equally likely to be effective? Explain. Be prepared to share your ideas with the class.

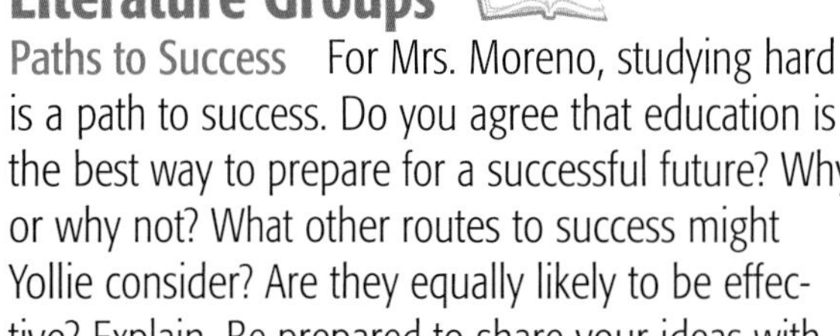

Learning for Life

Medical Careers Mrs. Moreno wanted Yollie to be a doctor one day. But she didn't specify what kind. Ophthalmologist? Pediatrician? Psychiatrist? Research a career in the field of medicine. Write a brief report. Include answers to the following questions: What is the specialty you chose? What kinds of problems does the specialist take care of? How many years of schooling are required to become such a specialist?

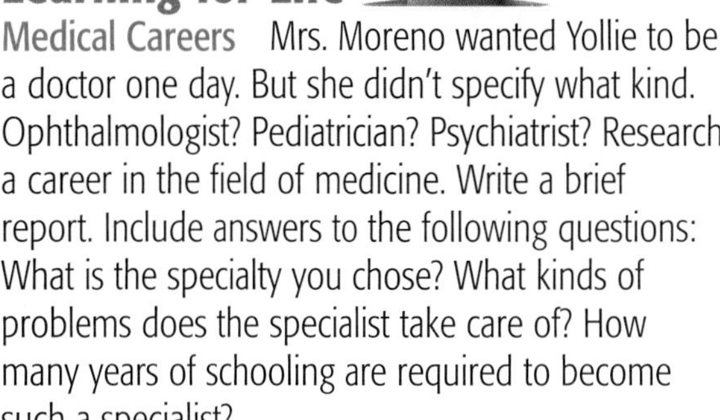

Save your work for your portfolio.

Skill Minilesson

VOCABULARY • SYNONYMS

Synonyms are words with nearly the same meaning. For example, *taunt* and *insult* are synonyms. However, you could *insult* someone accidentally, but you could not *taunt* someone accidentally. Taunting is a deliberate effort to make someone feel ashamed or ridiculous.

PRACTICE For each numbered word, write the letter of its synonym.

1. **gloat**
   a. praise b. boast c. scowl
2. **meager**
   a. scarce b. useless c. smart
3. **lurch**
   a. hurry b. stagger c. spin
4. **taunt**
   a. flirt b. criticize c. ridicule

Before You Read

Chanclas

MEET SANDRA CISNEROS

Sandra Cisneros (sis nā′ rōs′) is the only daughter in a family of seven children, and her brothers often made her feel like she had "seven fathers," she recalls. Her family was poor and moved frequently between the United States and Mexico, where her father's parents lived. Later, she wrote stories based on her early experiences "of third-floor flats, and fear of rats." As Cisneros put it, "They're all stories I lived, or witnessed, or heard; stories that were told to me." One of her best-known works is *The House on Mango Street*.

Sandra Cisneros was born in 1954. This story was published in 1983.

FOCUS ACTIVITY

Think about a time in the past when you felt awkward or embarrassed.

Sharing Ideas
Discuss things that you can do, or that friends can help you do, to feel more comfortable in an embarrassing situation.

Setting a Purpose
As you read, concentrate on the emotions of the characters.

BACKGROUND

The Time and Place This story takes place in a poor neighborhood where many Latinos live.

Did You Know? With a population of more than 22 million, Latinos are the fastest-growing minority in the United States. More than 60 percent of Latinos have roots in Mexico. Other places of origin include countries in South and Central America, Puerto Rico, and Cuba. Latinos work in virtually every sector of the U.S. economy.

VOCABULARY PREVIEW

baptism (bap′ tiz′ əm) *n.* a ceremony in which a person is cleansed of sin and becomes a member of a Christian religion; p. 71

tamale (tə mä′ lē) *n.* cornmeal, meat, and red peppers in corn husks, cooked by steaming or roasting; p. 71

Chanclas

Sandra Cisneros

It's me—Mama, Mama said. I open up and she's there with bags and big boxes, the new clothes and, yes, she's got the socks and a new slip with a little rose on it and a pink and white striped dress. What about the shoes? I forgot. Too late now. I'm tired. Whew!

Six-thirty already and my little cousin's baptism is over. All day waiting, the door locked, don't open up for nobody, and I don't till Mama gets back and buys everything except the shoes.

Now Uncle Nacho is coming in his car, and we have to hurry and get to Precious Blood Church quick because that's where the baptism party is, in the basement rented for today for dancing and tamales and everyone's kids running all over the place.

Vocabulary

baptism (bap′ tiz′ əm) *n.* a ceremony in which a person is cleansed of sin and becomes a member of a Christian religion

tamale (tə mä′ lē) *n.* cornmeal, meat, and red peppers in corn husks, cooked by steaming or roasting

Mama dances, laughs, dances. All of a sudden, Mama is sick. I fan her hot face with a paper plate. Too many tamales, but Uncle Nacho says too many this and tilts his thumb to his lips.

Everybody laughing except me, because I'm wearing the new dress, pink and white with stripes, and new underclothes and new socks and the old saddle shoes[1] I wear to school, brown and white, the kind I get every September because they last long and they do. My feet scuffed and round, and the heels all crooked that look dumb with this dress, so I just sit.

Meanwhile that boy who is my cousin by first communion[2] or something, asks me to dance and I can't. Just stuff my feet under the metal folding chair stamped Precious Blood and pick on a wad of brown gum that's stuck beneath the seat. I shake my head no. My feet growing bigger and bigger.

Then Uncle Nacho is pulling and pulling my arm and it doesn't matter how new the dress Mama bought is because my feet are ugly until my uncle who is a liar says, You are the prettiest girl here, will you dance, but I believe him, and yes, we are dancing, my Uncle Nacho and me, only I don't want to at first. My feet swell big and heavy like plungers, but I drag them across the linoleum floor straight center where Uncle wants to show off the new dance we learned. And Uncle spins me, and my skinny arms bend the way he taught me, and my mother watches, and my little cousins watch, and the boy who is my cousin by first communion watches, and everyone says, wow, who are those two who dance like in the movies, until I forget that I am wearing only ordinary shoes, brown and white, the kind my mother buys each year for school.

And all I hear is the clapping when the music stops. My uncle and me bow and he walks me back in my thick shoes to my mother who is proud to be my mother. All night the boy who is a man watches me dance. He watched me dance.

1. *Saddle shoes* tie with laces and rise to just below the ankle. What makes a saddle shoe unusual is the band, or "saddle," of color across the middle that contrasts with the color of the rest of the shoe.
2. In the Roman Catholic Church, children of a similar age often receive their first communion as a group. The writer's *cousin by first communion* is someone who was in the same group when she had her first communion.

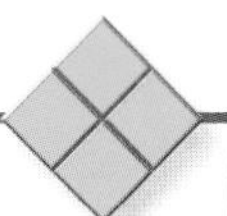

Responding to Literature

PERSONAL RESPONSE

- Do you sympathize with the narrator's self-consciousness about her shoes? Why or why not?
- Think back to your discussion for the **Focus Activity** on page 70. What might you say to make the girl feel better?

Analyzing Literature

RECALL AND INTERPRET

1. Describe the girl's shoes. Explain how the shoes add humor to the story.
2. Explain how Uncle Nacho "rescued" the girl, and tell why you think his tactics worked.
3. How do the narrator's emotions change during the course of the story? What causes these changes?

EVALUATE AND CONNECT

4. The title of the story, "Chanclas," means "old, worn-out shoes." In your opinion, is the title fitting? Explain.
5. How would the story be different if it had been told without humor?
6. Consider the importance of old shoes in the story. Explain why clothing is or is not important in a social setting today.

LITERARY ELEMENTS

Style

An author's **style** is the way he or she chooses and arranges words. In "Chanclas," Sandra Cisneros sometimes runs sentences together without punctuation. Her purpose is to quicken the pace of the story, build suspense, and make the words sound like spoken language.

1. Cisneros sometimes treats sentence fragments like complete sentences or leaves out part of a verb phrase. Find an example of this style.
2. What other rule of punctuation does the author break? What effect does she create?

- See **Literary Terms Handbook,** p. R9.

Extending Your Response

Literature Groups

Family Theme In a group, discuss how the idea of family closeness is important to the story "Chanclas." Address these questions: What details give the reader a feeling for the girl's family? What might the author be saying about the value of the family in Latino culture? What does *family* mean to the girl? Use a word web with *family* in the center to show your answers.

Writing About Literature

Secret Admirer The girl makes several allusions to a boy who watched her dance. What do you think the boy was like? How did he feel about the girl? Write an entry in the boy's diary from the night of the dance.

COMPARING SELECTIONS

Mother and Daughter and *Chanclas*

COMPARE **SOLUTIONS**

In both stories, a girl overcomes an embarrassing situation with the help of a family member. With a partner, think of other ways the girls are similar.

1. Each girl has a "cheerleader," someone who pushes her to set goals and to dream. How does each one boost the girl's self-confidence? Which character do you think makes the better cheerleader? Why?
2. What kind of friends do you think the girls from "Chanclas" and "Mother and Daughter" would be? Would you choose either one for a best friend? Why?

COMPARE **RESPONSES**

A dance party is crucial to the plots of both stories. With a partner, discuss the following questions about the dances.

1. How did each dance start and end?
2. On a scale of one to ten, with ten being the highest, how do you think each girl would rate the dance? Why?

Portrait, 1972. Eloy Blanco. Collection of El Museo del Barrio, New York.

COMPARE **EXPERIENCES**

The writers of both stories have messages to communicate, but they do so in different ways.

1. Write a few paragraphs comparing the humor and the serious messages of each story. Consider these questions: What contributed most to the humor of each story–the characters or the situations? How?
2. "Some things are more important than money." Do you agree or disagree with this statement? What would the main characters of each story say? What is most important to them, money or something else? Write a brief explanation.

Vo•cab•u•lar•y Skills

Using Context Clues

What do you think *obdurate* means in the following sentence?

Some people react in an obdurate way to certain situations but not to others.

The sentence provides no clues about the meaning of *obdurate,* except that the word is an adjective. Sometimes you can find information about an unfamiliar word by looking at its **context,** the sentence or group of sentences in which the word appears. The context often provides **context clues** that help readers figure out what an unfamiliar word means. There are many kinds of context clues, and the amount of help they provide varies. Study the examples below.

A. Our obdurate boss insisted that we finish the job on schedule, even though we were missing half our workers.

- This example provides only a little help. Being *obdurate* is a flaw of some kind, but what does it mean?

B. A stubborn person may become more obdurate if nagged.

- This example has several context clues. The words *stubborn* and *more* make it clear that *stubborn* and *obdurate* are synonyms.

C. Lisa was too obdurate to follow the coach's suggestions.

- Several clues are provided here. Lisa will not follow the advice of her coach, a more experienced person. She must be stubborn in a determined way.

D. It's hard to reason with an obdurate person—someone who simply won't give in.

- This example provides a definition.

EXERCISE

Use context clues to figure out what the underlined words mean. Write a synonym or a short definition for each word.

1. Yollie thinks the dyed dress will look ugly or tacky, but she is surprised when it comes out shiny black and sophisticated looking.
2. The black puddle at Yollie's feet is a conspicuous sign that her dress had been dyed.
3. In Korea, people follow rules of reverence and use titles of respect when they speak to others.
4. Lemon Brown seems to be a menacing figure at first, but he turns out to be a harmless old man who only wants to protect his memories.

MEDIA Connection

MAGAZINE ARTICLE

Where we come from shapes who we are. Or does it?

Real Indians Eat Jell-O and other things my Granny taught me

by Laurie Carlson—*Northern Lights*, Spring 1993

I don't get it. I've read every book about Indians that Mrs. Corigliano has in the school library, and they're all the same.

Indian kids are supposed to live in wide open spaces, in deserts or forests. They have horses and coyotes and wise grandparents. They get messages from nature and have visions.

I wait here, in our mobile home that has no axles, crowded next to other mobile homes without axles. I watch the television for messages, like everyone else. I wonder if I am the right kind of Indian.

My Granny doesn't have interesting tales about life and stuff. She only wants to talk about Esther Herbert's daughter, who she thinks is too wild.

Granny always makes Jell-O salads for fancy occasions, so I asked her, "What about fry bread?" She laughed and told me her fry bread could be used for shoulder pads.

"Granny," I ask, as she sits and strums her fingertips on the tabletop along with the radio's tune. Her "Primrose Passion" nail tips are the pride of Wanda's Nail Palace. "Aren't you supposed to be teaching me about beadwork and tales about coyotes? What about Indian wisdom? That's what Indian grandmothers in books and movies do."

My Granny snaps her gum and grins at me.

"Honey, be yourself."

She always says that.

That's all my Granny can give me.

I trust her.

"Want me to give you a perm?" she asks.

Respond

How do you think the narrator feels about her Native American roots? Do you agree with Granny's advice to "be yourself"? Write a brief explanation for each answer.

Before You Read

The Medicine Bag

MEET
VIRGINIA DRIVING HAWK SNEVE

The Rosebud Reservation in South Dakota was Virginia Driving Hawk Sneve's (snē′ vē) childhood home until she left to attend a boarding high school. She later went on to college and then began her work as a teacher. Sneve is a member of the Rosebud Sioux Tribe, and, as a writer, her goals are linked with her Native American roots. She says, "I try to present an accurate portrayal of American Indian life as I have known it. I also attempt to interpret history from the viewpoint of the American Indian."

Virginia Driving Hawk Sneve was born in 1933. This story was first published in 1975.

FOCUS ACTIVITY

Name an item you cherish because you received it from someone who means a lot to you.

QuickWrite
Make some notes about the item you cherish and its importance to you.

Setting a Purpose
As you read, think of why two characters have very different attitudes toward the same object.

BACKGROUND

The Time and Place This story takes place in a modern American neighborhood.

Did You Know?
"Sioux" is a name for groups of Native Americans also called *Ogallala, Dakota,* or *Lakota.* They farmed, hunted, and fished in the forests and lakes of the north-central part of what is now the United States between the Mississippi River and the Rocky Mountains.

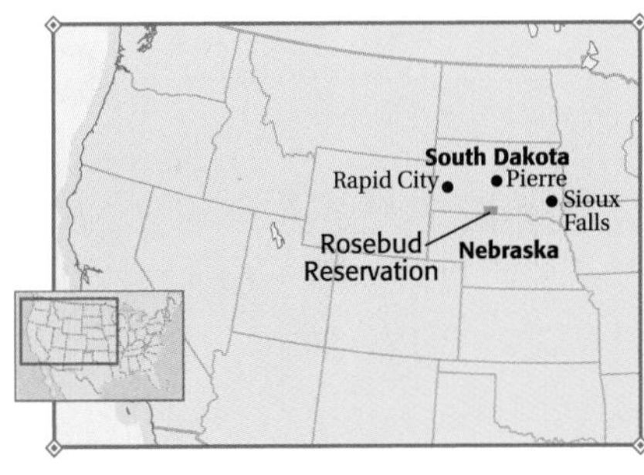

VOCABULARY PREVIEW

stately (stāt′ lē) *adv.* noble; dignified; majestic; p. 79
unseemly (un sēm′ lē) *adj.* not proper to the time or place; not in good taste; p. 80
sheepishly (shē′ pish lē) *adv.* in an awkwardly embarrassed way; bashfully; p. 81
awed (ôd) *adj.* filled with wonder combined with respect; p. 84
sacred (sā′ krid) *adj.* holy; deserving of great respect; p. 85

The Medicine Bag

Virginia Driving Hawk Sneve

My kid sister Cheryl and I always bragged about our Sioux grandpa, Joe Iron Shell. Our friends, who had always lived in the city and only knew about Indians from movies and TV, were impressed by our stories. Maybe we exaggerated and made Grandpa and the reservation sound glamorous, but when we'd return home to Iowa after our yearly summer visit to Grandpa we always had some exciting tale to tell.

We always had some authentic Sioux article to show our listeners. One year Cheryl had new moccasins that Grandpa had made. On another visit he gave me a small, round, flat, rawhide drum which was decorated with a painting of a warrior riding a horse. He taught me a real Sioux chant[1] to sing while I beat the drum with a leather-covered stick that had a feather on the end. Man, that really made an impression.

We never showed our friends Grandpa's picture. Not that we were ashamed of him, but because we knew that the glamorous tales we told didn't go with the real thing. Our friends would have laughed at the picture, because Grandpa wasn't tall and stately like TV Indians. His hair wasn't in braids, but hung in stringy, gray strands on his neck and he was old. He was our great-grandfather, and he didn't live in a tipi,[2] but all by himself in a part log, part tar-paper shack on the Rosebud Reservation in South Dakota. So when Grandpa came to visit us, I was so ashamed and embarrassed I could've died.

There are a lot of yippy poodles and other fancy little dogs in our neighborhood, but they usually barked singly at the mailman from the safety of their own yards. Now it sounded as if a whole pack of mutts were barking together in one place.

I got up and walked to the curb to see what the commotion was. About a block

Boy on Edge of Chasm, 1993 (detail). Kam Mak. Oil on panels, 14 x 10½ in. Collection of the artist.

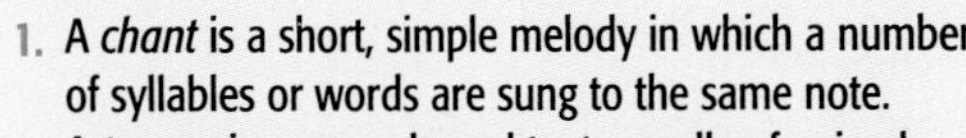

1. A *chant* is a short, simple melody in which a number of syllables or words are sung to the same note.
2. A *teepee* is a cone-shaped tent, usually of animal skins, used especially by the Plains Indians. The original Sioux word, *tipi,* is a combination of *ti,* "to dwell," and *pi,* "for use."

Vocabulary

stately (stāt′ lē) *adv.* noble; dignified; majestic

away I saw a crowd of little kids yelling, with the dogs yipping and growling around someone who was walking down the middle of the street.

I watched the group as it slowly came closer and saw that in the center of the strange procession was a man wearing a tall black hat. He'd pause now and then to peer at something in his hand and then at the houses on either side of the street. I felt cold and hot at the same time as I recognized the man. "Oh, no!" I whispered. "It's Grandpa!"

I stood on the curb, unable to move even though I wanted to run and hide. Then I got mad when I saw how the yippy dogs were growling and nipping at the old man's baggy pant legs and how wearily he poked them away with his cane. "Stupid mutts," I said as I ran to rescue Grandpa.

When I kicked and hollered at the dogs to get away, they put their tails between their legs and scattered. The kids ran to the curb where they watched me and the old man.

"Grandpa," I said and felt pretty dumb when my voice cracked. I reached for his beat-up old tin suitcase, which was tied shut with a rope. But he set it down right in the street and shook my hand.

"*Hau, Takoza,* Grandchild," he greeted me formally in Sioux.

All I could do was stand there with the whole neighborhood watching and shake the hand of the leather-brown old man. I saw how his gray hair straggled from under his big black hat, which had a drooping feather in its crown. His rumpled black suit hung like a sack over his stooped frame. As he shook my hand, his coat fell open to expose a bright-red, satin shirt with a beaded bolo tie[3] under the collar. His getup wasn't out of place on the reservation, but it sure was here, and I wanted to sink right through the pavement.

"Hi," I muttered with my head down. I tried to pull my hand away when I felt his bony hand trembling, and looked up to see fatigue in his face. I felt like crying. I couldn't think of anything to say so I picked up Grandpa's suitcase, took his arm, and guided him up the driveway to our house.

Mom was standing on the steps. I don't know how long she'd been watching, but her hand was over her mouth and she looked as if she couldn't believe what she saw. Then she ran to us.

"Grandpa," she gasped. "How in the world did you get here?"

She checked her move to embrace Grandpa and I remembered that such a display of affection is unseemly to the Sioux and would embarrass him.

"*Hau,* Marie," he said as he shook Mom's hand. She smiled and took his other arm.

As we supported him up the steps the door banged open and Cheryl came bursting out of the house. She was all smiles and was so obviously glad to see Grandpa that I was ashamed of how I felt.

"Grandpa!" she yelled happily. "You came to see us!"

3. A *bolo tie* is a piece of cord (often leather) fastened at the neck with an ornamental bar or clasp.

Vocabulary

unseemly (un sēm′ lē) *adj.* not proper to the time or place; not in good taste

Grandpa smiled and Mom and I let go of him as he stretched out his arms to my ten-year-old sister, who was still young enough to be hugged.

"*Wicincala,* little girl," he greeted her and then collapsed.

He had fainted. Mom and I carried him into her sewing room, where we had a spare bed.

After we had Grandpa on the bed Mom stood there helplessly patting his shoulder.

"Shouldn't we call the doctor, Mom?" I suggested, since she didn't seem to know what to do.

"Yes," she agreed with a sigh. "You make Grandpa comfortable, Martin."

I reluctantly moved to the bed. I knew Grandpa wouldn't want to have Mom undress him, but I didn't want to, either. He was so skinny and frail that his coat slipped off easily. When I loosened his tie and opened his shirt collar, I felt a small leather pouch that hung from a thong[4] around his neck. I left it alone and moved to remove his boots. The scuffed old cowboy boots were tight and he moaned as I put pressure on his legs to jerk them off.

I put the boots on the floor and saw why they fit so tight. Each one was stuffed with money. I looked at the bills that lined the boots and started to ask about them, but Grandpa's eyes were closed again.

Mom came back with a basin of water. "The doctor thinks Grandpa is suffering from heat exhaustion," she explained as she bathed Grandpa's face. Mom gave a big sigh, "*Oh hinh,* Martin. How do you suppose he got here?"

We found out after the doctor's visit. Grandpa was angrily sitting up in bed while Mom tried to feed him some soup.

"Tonight you let Marie feed you, Grandpa," spoke my dad, who had gotten home from work just as the doctor was leaving. "You're not really sick," he said as he gently pushed Grandpa back against the pillows. "The doctor said you just got too tired and hot after your long trip."

Grandpa relaxed, and between sips of soup he told us of his journey. Soon after our visit to him Grandpa decided that he would like to see where his only living descendants lived and what our home was like. Besides, he admitted sheepishly, he was lonesome after we left.

I knew everybody felt as guilty as I did—especially Mom. Mom was all Grandpa had left. So even after she married my dad, who's a white man and teaches in the college in our city, and after Cheryl and I were born, Mom made sure that every summer we spent a week with Grandpa.

I never thought that Grandpa would be lonely after our visits, and none of us noticed how old and weak he had become. But Grandpa knew and so he came to us. He had ridden on buses for two and a half days. When he arrived in the city, tired and stiff from sitting for so long, he set out, walking, to find us.

He had stopped to rest on the steps of some building downtown and a policeman found him. The cop, according to Grandpa, was a good man who took him

4. Here, a *thong* is a narrow strip of leather or similar material.

Vocabulary

sheepishly (shē′ pish lē) *adv.* in an awkwardly embarrassed way; bashfully

A Singing Indian. W. Ufer. Oil on canvas, 30 x 25¼ in.

Viewing the painting: What items in this painting reflect the man's Native American heritage? What details about Grandpa reveal his identity as a Sioux?

to the bus stop and waited until the bus came and told the driver to let Grandpa out at Bell View Drive. After Grandpa got off the bus, he started walking again. But he couldn't see the house numbers on the other side when he walked on the sidewalk so he walked in the middle of the street. That's when all the little kids and dogs followed him.

I knew everybody felt as bad as I did. Yet I was proud of this 86-year-old man, who had never been away from the reservation, having the courage to travel so far alone.

"You found the money in my boots?" he asked Mom.

"Martin did," she answered, and roused herself to scold. "Grandpa, you shouldn't have carried so much money. What if someone had stolen it from you?"

Grandpa laughed. "I would've known if anyone tried to take the boots off my feet. The money is what I've saved for a long time—a hundred dollars—for my funeral. But you take it now to buy groceries so that I won't be a burden to you while I am here."

"That won't be necessary, Grandpa," Dad said. "We are honored to have you with us and you will never be a burden. I am only sorry that we never thought to bring you home with us this summer and spare you the discomfort of a long trip."

Grandpa was pleased. "Thank you," he answered. "But do not feel bad that you didn't bring me with you for I would not have come then. It was not time." He said this in such a way that no one could argue with him. To Grandpa and the Sioux, he once told me, a thing would be done when it was the right time to do it and that's the way it was.

"Also," Grandpa went on, looking at me, "I have come because it is soon time for Martin to have the medicine bag."

We all knew what that meant. Grandpa thought he was going to die and he had to follow the tradition of his family to pass the medicine bag, along with its history, to the oldest male child.

"Even though the boy," he said still looking at me, "bears a white man's name, the medicine bag will be his."

I didn't know what to say. I had the same hot and cold feeling that I had when I first saw Grandpa in the street. The medicine bag was the dirty leather pouch I had found around his neck. "I could never wear such a thing," I almost said aloud. I thought of having my friends see it in gym class, at the swimming pool, and could imagine the smart things they would say. But I just swallowed hard and took a step toward the bed. I knew I would have to take it.

But Grandpa was tired. "Not now, Martin," he said, waving his hand in dismissal, "it is not time. Now I will sleep."

So that's how Grandpa came to be with us for two months. My friends kept asking to come see the old man, but I put them off. I told myself that I didn't want them laughing at Grandpa. But even as I made excuses I knew it wasn't Grandpa that I was afraid they'd laugh at.

Nothing bothered Cheryl about bringing her friends to see Grandpa. Every day after school started there'd be a crew of giggling little girls or round-eyed little boys crowded around the old man on the patio, where he'd gotten in the habit of sitting every afternoon.

Grandpa would smile in his gentle way and patiently answer their questions, or he'd tell them stories of brave warriors, ghosts, animals, and the kids listened in awed silence. Those little guys thought Grandpa was great.

Finally, one day after school, my friends came home with me because nothing I said stopped them. "We're going to see the great Indian of Bell View Drive," said Hank, who was supposed to be my best friend. "My brother has seen him three times so he oughta be well enough to see us."

Sioux vest, Plains Indian. British Museum, London.

When we got to my house Grandpa was sitting on the patio. He had on his red shirt, but today he also wore a fringed leather vest that was decorated with beads. Instead of his usual cowboy boots he had solidly beaded moccasins on his feet that stuck out of his black trousers. Of course, he had his old black hat on—he was seldom without it. But it had been brushed and the feather in the beaded headband was proudly erect, its tip a brighter white. His hair lay in silver strands over the red shirt collar.

I stared just as my friends did and I heard one of them murmur, "Wow!"

Grandpa looked up and when his eyes met mine they twinkled as if he were laughing inside. He nodded to me and my face got all hot. I could tell that he had known all along I was afraid he'd embarrass me in front of my friends.

"*Hau, hoksilas,* boys," he greeted and held out his hand.

My buddies passed in a single file and shook his hand as I introduced them. They were so polite I almost laughed. "How, there, Grandpa," and even a "How-do-you-do, sir."

"You look fine, Grandpa," I said as the guys sat on the lawn chairs or on the patio floor.

"*Hanh,* yes," he agreed. "When I woke up this morning it seemed the right time to dress in the good clothes. I knew that my grandson would be bringing his friends."

"You guys want some lemonade or something?" I offered. No one answered. They were listening to Grandpa as he started telling how he'd killed the deer from which his vest was made.

Grandpa did most of the talking while my friends were there. I was so proud of him and amazed at how respectfully quiet my buddies were. Mom had to chase them home at supper time. As they left they shook Grandpa's hand again and said to me:

"Martin, he's really great!"

"Yeah, man! Don't blame you for keeping him to yourself."

"Can we come back?"

But after they left, Mom said, "No more visitors for a while, Martin. Grandpa won't

Vocabulary

awed (ôd) *adj.* filled with wonder combined with respect admit it, but his strength hasn't returned. He likes having company, but it tires him."

That evening Grandpa called me to his room before he went to sleep. "Tomorrow," he said, "when you come home, it will be time to give you the medicine bag."

I felt a hard squeeze from where my heart is supposed to be and was scared, but I answered, "OK, Grandpa."

All night I had weird dreams about thunder and lightning on a high hill. From a distance I heard the slow beat of a drum. When I woke up in the morning I felt as if I hadn't slept at all. At school it seemed as if the day would never end and, when it finally did, I ran home.

Grandpa was in his room, sitting on the bed. The shades were down and the place was dim and cool. I sat on the floor in front of Grandpa, but he didn't even look at me. After what seemed a long time he spoke.

"I sent your mother and sister away. What you will hear today is only for a man's ears. What you will receive is only for a man's hands." He fell silent and I felt shivers down my back.

"My father in his early manhood," Grandpa began, "made a vision quest[5] to find a spirit guide for his life. You cannot understand how it was in that time, when the great Teton Sioux[6] were first made to stay on the reservation. There was a strong need for guidance from *Wakantanka,* the Great Spirit. But too many of the young men were filled with despair and hatred. They thought it was hopeless to search for a vision when the glorious life was gone and only the hated confines of a reservation lay ahead. But my father held to the old ways.

"He carefully prepared for his quest with a purifying sweat bath and then he went alone to a high butte top to fast and pray. After three days he received his sacred dream—in which he found, after long searching, the white man's iron. He did not understand his vision of finding something belonging to the white people, for in that time they were the enemy. When he came down from the butte to cleanse himself at the stream below, he found the remains of a campfire and the broken shell of an iron kettle. This was a sign which reinforced his dream. He took a piece of the iron for his medicine bag, which he had made of elk skin years before, to prepare for his quest.

Did You Know?
A *butte* (būt) is an isolated, flat-topped land formation created by the erosion of all but a portion of a hill or plateau.

"He returned to his village, where he told his dream to the wise old men of the tribe. They gave him the name *Iron Shell,* but neither did they understand the meaning of the dream. This first Iron Shell kept the piece of iron with him at all times and believed it gave him protection from the evils of those unhappy days.

5. Traditionally, a Sioux boy became a man by going on a *vision quest.* After purifying himself in a sweat lodge (a steam-heated hut), he stayed alone on a hilltop until he received a vision that showed him his purpose in life.
6. The *Teton* (tē′ ton) *Sioux* were the largest and westernmost group of the Sioux peoples; they're also known as the Lakota. In the 1860s, their hunting grounds in the western Dakotas and Nebraska were overrun by white settlers, and the Teton were forced onto reservations.

Vocabulary
sacred (sā′ krid) *adj.* holy; deserving of great respect

"Then a terrible thing happened to Iron Shell. He and several other young men were taken from their homes by the soldiers and sent far away to a white man's boarding school. He was angry and lonesome for his parents and the young girl he had wed before he was taken away. At first Iron Shell resisted the teachers' attempts to change him and he did not try to learn. One day it was his turn to work in the school's blacksmith shop. As he walked into the place he knew that his medicine had brought him there to learn and work with the white man's iron.

"Iron Shell became a blacksmith and worked at the trade when he returned to the reservation. All of his life he treasured the medicine bag. When he was old, and I was a man, he gave it to me, for no one made the vision quest any more."

Grandpa quit talking and I stared in disbelief as he covered his face with his hands. His shoulders were shaking with quiet sobs and I looked away until he began to speak again.

"I kept the bag until my son, your mother's father, was a man and had to leave us to fight in the war across the ocean. I gave him the bag, for I believed it would protect him in battle, but he did not take it with him. He was afraid that he would lose it. He died in a faraway place."

Again Grandpa was still and I felt his grief around me.

"My son," he went on after clearing his throat, "had only a daughter and it is not proper for her to know of these things."

He unbuttoned his shirt, pulled out the leather pouch, and lifted it over his head. He held it in his hand, turning it over and over as if memorizing how it looked.

"In the bag," he said as he opened it and removed two objects, "is the broken shell of the iron kettle, a pebble from the butte, and a piece of the sacred sage." He held the pouch upside down and dust drifted down.

"After the bag is yours you must put a piece of prairie sage within and never open it again until you pass it on to your son." He replaced the pebble and the piece of iron, and tied the bag.

I stood up, somehow knowing I should. Grandpa slowly rose from the bed and stood upright in front of me holding the bag before my face. I closed my eyes and waited for him to slip it over my head. But he spoke.

"No, you need not wear it." He placed the soft leather bag in my right hand and closed my other hand over it. "It would not be right to wear it in this time and place where no one will understand. Put it safely away until you are again on the reservation. Wear it then, when you replace the sacred sage."

Grandpa turned and sat again on the bed. Wearily he leaned his head against the pillow. "Go," he said, "I will sleep now."

"Thank you, Grandpa," I said softly and left with the bag in my hands.

That night Mom and Dad took Grandpa to the hospital. Two weeks later I stood alone on the lonely prairie of the reservation and put the sacred sage in my medicine bag.

Responding to Literature

PERSONAL RESPONSE

- Would your reaction to Grandpa have been different from Martin's? Explain.
- Look at the notes you made for the **Focus Activity** on page 77. How is Martin's response to receiving the medicine bag like your reaction to receiving a cherished gift? How is it different?

Analyzing Literature

RECALL

1. What happened during Grandpa's trip from the reservation to the door of his family's home?
2. Explain how Grandpa's appearance differs from that of "TV Indians."
3. What happens when Grandpa gives the medicine bag to Martin?
4. What does Grandpa understand about Martin without being told?

INTERPRET

5. What does Grandpa mean when he tells his family that he has come now, and not earlier, because now is the right time?
6. Why is Martin concerned about introducing his friends to Grandpa? Do his parents, in your opinion, share any of Martin's feelings? Explain.
7. Why do you think Grandpa cries after he tells Martin about how Iron Shell gave him the medicine bag?
8. Explain two or three ways that Martin changes during the story.

EVALUATE AND CONNECT

9. Theme Connection What, in your opinion, does the medicine bag mean to Martin? Does it have the same meaning to Grandpa?
10. At the end of the story, Martin puts the sacred sage–an aromatic plant–in his medicine bag. Explain why this is a strong or weak ending for the story.

LITERARY ELEMENTS

Symbol

A **symbol** is an object, person, place, or experience that stands for something more than what it is. For example, the medicine bag is a leather pouch that holds several items. It is also a symbol of Grandpa's and Martin's identity as Sioux.

1. What other meaning does the medicine bag have?
2. Identify another symbol used in the story.

- See **Literary Terms Handbook,** p. R10.

Literature and Writing

Writing About Literature

Narrator Write a paragraph or two explaining why having Martin as narrator makes the story meaningful for the reader. What special information or feelings does Martin bring to the story? Would the story touch the reader's feelings as much if Grandpa were the narrator?

Creative Writing

Journal Entry Write an entry from Martin's journal describing a visit he makes to the reservation after Grandpa's death.

Extending Your Response

Literature Groups

Journeys of Self-Discovery Compare the three journeys that are described in "The Medicine Bag." Consider the following questions: Which characters went on a journey? Did their experiences have anything in common? How is the vision quest a journey? What did each character learn or achieve from his journey? How did each journey help the character to move from one passage of life to the next? Would such a journey, in your opinion, be valuable to you and your friends? Explain.

Interdisciplinary Activity

Geography and Culture When European settlers arrived in America, about four million Native Americans lived in what is now the United States and Canada. What tribal groups lived in your area? Research to find out about these groups. Then create a booklet that covers the following topics: How did native people survive on the land? What was their diet? What kind of homes did they build? What were their beliefs about the land? What types of art and crafts are they known for? What happened to Native Americans once settlers arrived?

Reading Further

If you enjoyed this story by Virginia Driving Hawk Sneve, try these books:

High Elk's Treasure
When Thunders Spoke

Save your work for your portfolio.

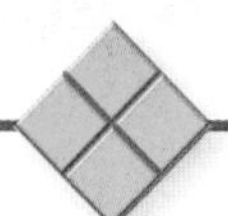

Skill Minilessons

GRAMMAR AND LANGUAGE • LEVELS OF USAGE

Levels of usage refers to the different ways that words are used in written and spoken language–from formal to informal. Formal is the strictest level of usage, and word definitions and grammar standards are carefully observed. By contrast, informal usage is more casual and conversational.

PRACTICE If a sentence below is formal, write *formal.* If it is informal, write *informal* and then rewrite it as a formal sentence.

1. "How-do-you-do, sir."
2. "You guys want some lemonade or something?"
3. "I . . . felt pretty dumb . . ."
4. "Martin, he's really great!"
5. "I will sleep now."

READING AND THINKING • AUTHOR'S PURPOSE

The **author's purpose** is his or her reason for writing the selection. The purpose might be to describe, to inform, to persuade, or simply to entertain. Identifying the author's purpose can help a reader to understand important story ideas.

PRACTICE Write a paragraph or two identifying the author's purpose in "The Medicine Bag." As you write, consider these questions: Is the story entertaining? What does the reader learn about Native Americans in this story? Does the author have more than one purpose?

- For more about the author's purpose, see **Reading Handbook,** p. R96.

VOCABULARY • WORD ORIGINS

The origin of the word *sheepish* is–you guessed it–*sheep.* Even though sheep are not particularly easy to embarrass, they are quite meek and mild, and so is a sheepish reaction. It is easy to see a connection for many words that come from names of animals. A path that *snakes* is one that twists. Other words are not as immediately clear because their meaning comes from a less obvious trait of an animal. To do something *doggedly* is to keep at it without giving up.

PRACTICE Each italicized word comes from the name of an animal. Think about the traits that people associate with the animal and use that knowledge to answer the question.

1. Is a person who behaves *mulishly* someone who is brave, mean, or stubborn?
2. If you *wolf* your food, do you eat it slowly, quickly and greedily, or in a picky way?
3. Is a *foxy* plan a sly and clever one, a dangerous one, or a careless and foolish one?
4. Is a *waspish* remark funny, bad-tempered, or highly intelligent?
5. If you *lionize* someone, do you treat that person as if he or she is worthless, amusing, or important and respectable?

Writing WORKSHOP

Descriptive Writing: Personal Essay

You've explored links between home and identity in this theme. Now think about your *own* identity. What makes you who you are? What likes and dislikes, habits, and hopes combine to make you unique?

Assignment: Write a personal essay describing yourself. Follow the process on these pages to create this "self-portrait in words."

- As you write your personal essay, refer to the **Writing Handbook,** pp. R50–R61.

The Writing Process

PREWRITING

PREWRITING TIP

Look through photos from your childhood, or jot down a few memories. The images and notes may reveal qualities about your personality.

Gather Details

You know yourself better than anyone else does, so you already have a wealth of material for this essay. To tap into it, try these strategies:

- Use a brainstorm board like the one below. Fill each section with as many details as possible.

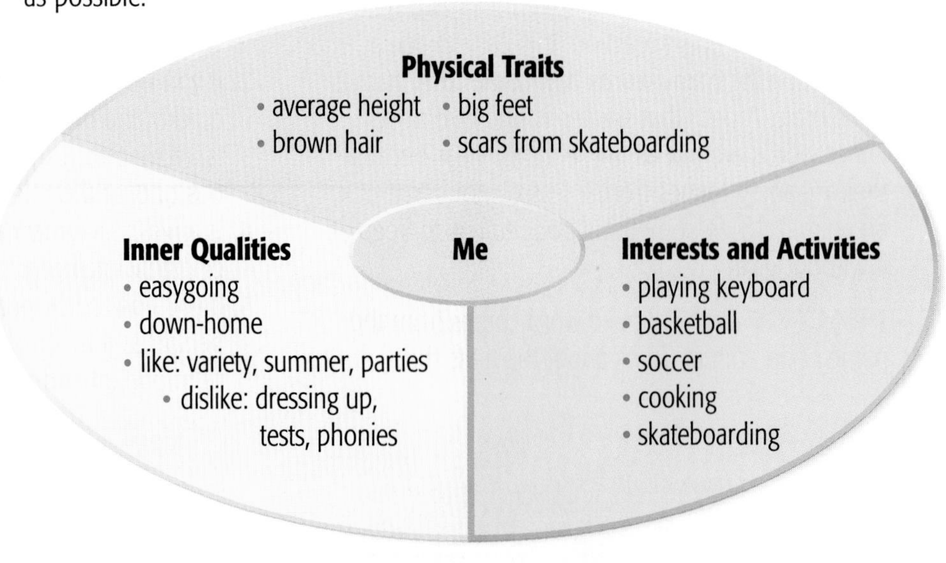

Physical Traits
- average height
- big feet
- brown hair
- scars from skateboarding

Me

Inner Qualities
- easygoing
- down-home
- like: variety, summer, parties
- dislike: dressing up, tests, phonies

Interests and Activities
- playing keyboard
- basketball
- soccer
- cooking
- skateboarding

- For a different approach to who you are, try completing sentences like these:

If I were an animal I'd be a(n) _____.

If I were a kind of music, I'd be _____.

If I were a food, I'd be _____.

If I were punctuation, I'd be a(n) _____.

If I were a machine, I'd be a(n) _____.

If I were a place, I'd be _____.

Choose Your Purpose and Audience

You can decide your own purpose and audience for this assignment. You might write to entertain classmates, to preserve memories for the future, or to inform someone who is interviewing or auditioning you.

Find a Focus

Your essay needs a **thesis**–a main idea–to tie it together. You might make a point about your identity. Or you might sum up the overall impression that you want to give your reader. State your thesis in a sentence or two to guide you as you draft.

Sketch Your Plan

A graphic can help you organize your essay. Will you plan one paragraph for physical traits, another for inner qualities, and another for activities and interests? Or will you blend types of characteristics in each paragraph, as you make points that illustrate your thesis?

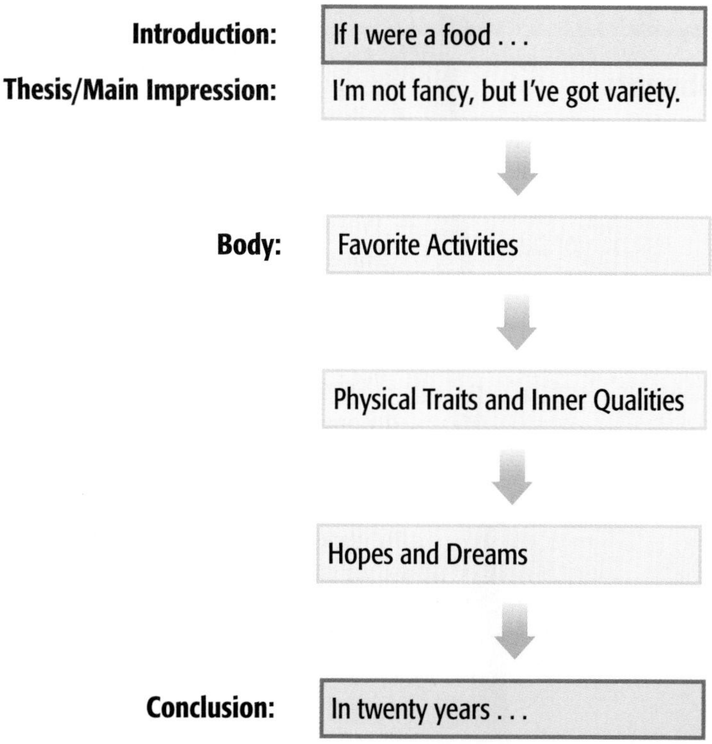

Introduction: If I were a food . . .

Thesis/Main Impression: I'm not fancy, but I've got variety.

↓

Body: Favorite Activities

↓

Physical Traits and Inner Qualities

↓

Hopes and Dreams

↓

Conclusion: In twenty years . . .

DRAFTING

DRAFTING TIP

For your personal essay, write in the first person, using the pronouns *I* and *me.* Offer your own views and observations.

Jump Right In

Your introduction needn't be long. A surprising statement to get readers interested and another sentence or two to state your thesis can do the trick. Then go on to your first body paragraph.

MODEL · DRAFTING

If I were a food, I'd be a homemade taco. I'm not fancy, but I've got variety.

Make Yourself Clear

Use details from your prewriting notes. For every inner quality you mention, include examples, as in the **Writing Skills** activity on page 60. In your concluding paragraph, you might look toward your future. In what ways do you expect to change as you grow older? Which parts of your identity will never change?

REVISING

REVISING TIP

Transitions such as *for instance, for example,* or *to show what I mean,* will help readers follow your essay.

Make Adjustments

The **Questions for Revising** can help you strengthen your draft. After your first revisions, you might have a classmate read your draft. Ask him or her which parts of it work best. Then go over the **Questions for Revising** once more with a classmate.

QUESTIONS FOR REVISING

- Where do I state my thesis or my main impression?
- Where do I mention physical traits, inner qualities, and favorite activities?
- Which parts might I rearrange to make my organization clearer?
- Where might I add more details and examples to help readers understand my ideas?
- Where could transitions make my essay smoother to read?

EDITING/PROOFREADING

For the final copy of your essay, use the **Proofreading Checklist** to spot and correct errors, especially sentence fragments, as shown in the **Grammar Link** on page 45.

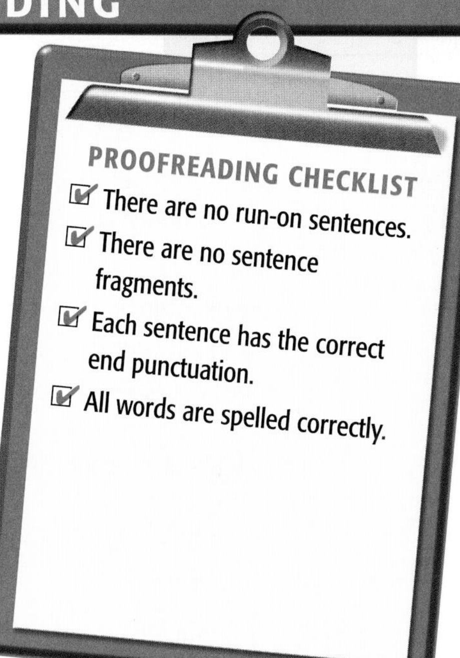

PROOFREADING CHECKLIST
There are no run-on sentences.
There are no sentence fragments.
Each sentence has the correct end punctuation.
All words are spelled correctly.

Grammar Hint

Check each sentence to be sure it has a subject and a verb. You might also want to be sure that every verb agrees in person and number with its subject.

MODEL · EDITING/PROOFREADING

I like to swim. And lie on the sand.

PUBLISHING/PRESENTING

If you wrote to entertain classmates, friends, or family, try delivering your essay as a monologue. If you wrote your essay as part of a letter of introduction or application, you might ask your teacher for suggestions about sending it.

Presenting Tip

For a monologue, practice your pacing. Ask a friend to help you decide when to pause and when to speed up.

Reflecting

Consider the following questions, and then answer them in writing:

- Which aspects of you does your essay show most accurately? Which aspects does your essay leave out?
- What other topics might you like to explore in personal essays?

Save your work for your portfolio.

Theme Wrap-Up

Personal Response

1. Which story, poem, or essay in the theme most helped you to understand the meaning of "No Place Like Home"?
2. What new ideas do you have about the following as a result of your reading this theme?
   - Memories of home can be joyful as well as tragic.
   - Family traditions help form the foundations of home life.
   - Home can be a place, a group of people, or a set of conditions.
3. Present your theme project to the class.

Analyzing Literature

In "Golden Glass" and "My Two Dads," Alma Luz Villanueva and Marie G. Lee describe characters who feel out of place in what some people might consider their homes. Choose these two stories or two others from the theme to compare and contrast how two different characters define home.

Evaluate and Set Goals

1. Which of the following was most enjoyable to you? Which was the most difficult?
   - reading and thinking about the stories
   - doing independent writing
   - analyzing the stories in discussions
   - making presentations
   - doing research
2. How would you assess your work in this theme, using the following scale? Give at least two reasons for your assessment.

   4 = outstanding
   3 = good
   2 = fair
   1 = weak
3. Based on what you found difficult in this theme, choose a goal to work toward in the next theme.
   - Write down your goal and three steps you will take to help you reach it.
   - Meet with your teacher to review your goal and your plan for achieving it.

Build Your Portfolio

SELECT

Choose two of your favorite pieces of work from this theme to include in your portfolio. The following questions can help you decide.

- ✦ Which pieces do you consider your best work?
- ✦ Which turned out to be more challenging than you thought?
- ✦ Which did you learn the most from?

REFLECT

Write some notes to accompany the pieces you selected. Use the following questions to guide you.

- ✦ What do you like best about the piece?
- ✦ What did you learn from creating it?
- ✦ What might you do differently if you were beginning this piece again?

Reading on Your Own

If you have enjoyed the literature in this theme, you might also be interested in the following books.

A Day No Pigs Would Die

by Robert Newton Peck A boy in rural Vermont, whose father slaughters pigs, develops a new understanding of family and home.

Walker of Time

by Helen Hughes Vick A fifteen-year-old Hopi boy and his funny, sympathetic Anglo friend travel seven hundred years back in time. Here they help a dying civilization to begin the move to a new home.

Tree by Leaf

by Cynthia Voigt Clothilde's family problems are multiplied when her father returns from World War I alive, but disfigured and depressed.

Missing May

by Cynthia Rylant Summer has had many homes, but when she joins her aunt and uncle, she is welcomed and shares in their deep love for one another. When Aunt May dies, Summer and Uncle Ob must come to terms with their loss.

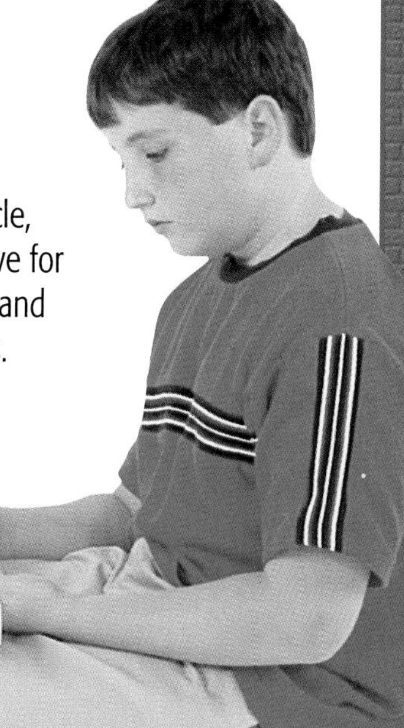

Standardized Test Practice

Read the following passages. Then read each question on page 97. Decide which is the best answer to each question. Mark the letter for that answer on your paper.

A New and Improved Smith Middle School

The *Windham Times* newspaper published an editorial opposing the construction of a new middle school. These letters to the editor were responses to that editorial.

LETTER 1

To the Editor:

I am writing about yesterday's editorial opposing a new middle school in Windham. I am dismayed that the *Times* opposes this project. It is time for Windham to take a step into the next millenium and give our children the type of educational institution that they deserve.

When was the last time this town spent a significant amount of money on education? If we want our children to compete with other students in the region and in the world, then we need to give them the tools they need. I strongly believe that 23.5 million dollars is a reasonable price to pay to build a school that will last for decades.

As the parent of a child who will be graduating from the current middle school, and also of a child entering the sixth grade next fall, I feel personally invested in this project. I hope that my eleven-year-old will have more opportunities in a brand new middle school than my fourteen-year-old had. The time is now, Windham. Say YES to a new middle school!

M. Woodrow

LETTER 2

To the Editor:

Thank you for your fair and well-written editorial about the proposed Windham Middle School. Clearly, the cost is <u>exorbitant</u>, especially for a small town. I strongly disagree with those who think that Windham needs such an extravagant new school.

My two children attended the middle school and they received fine educations. They did not have computers in every classroom, or an auditorium large enough to hold an entire school, but they had dedicated and caring teachers. If more money were spent on teachers' salaries, we would see vast improvements in the quality of education without having to spend nearly 23.5 million dollars.

Let's put more money into the existing school. By offering higher salaries, we can make sure that our talented teachers stay, and we can attract qualified new teachers. We can purchase supplies and textbooks and have more money for field trips. These suggestions are more practical and cost-efficient than the plan to build a new school.

T. Martinez

1 Compared with the writer of the second letter, the writer of the first letter —

A is less concerned with the amount of money needed to fund the new school

B has written more letters to the editor about this issue and plans to continue writing

C is more involved in the community

D does not believe that the teachers earn their salaries

2 The writer of the first letter claims that building the new school will do all of the following EXCEPT —

F improve tools available to the town's children

G bring the school system into the new millenium

H motivate the teachers to do a better job

J allow Windham students to compete with other students in the region and the world

3 Both letters give you reason to believe that —

A the newspaper's editorial was unfair to all readers

B it is old-fashioned to believe that schools should be remodeled

C building schools is more important than paying teachers well

D construction of a new school has not begun

4 The second letter writer states that building a new school is not really necessary because —

F the writer's kids don't want a new school to go to

G money should not be spent on supplies and materials or on a new building

H the middle school has excellent teachers

J the school budget doesn't have enough money

5 In this passage, the word exorbitant means —

A too small

B too important

C too great

D too clean

6 What is the main idea of the second letter?

F A new school and updated technology are needed and Windham should invest in them this year.

G A new school is unnecessary and the money could be better spent on teachers and supplies.

H The writer's children each received a fine education at the existing middle school.

J Many people agree that a new school is very important.

Lean on Me

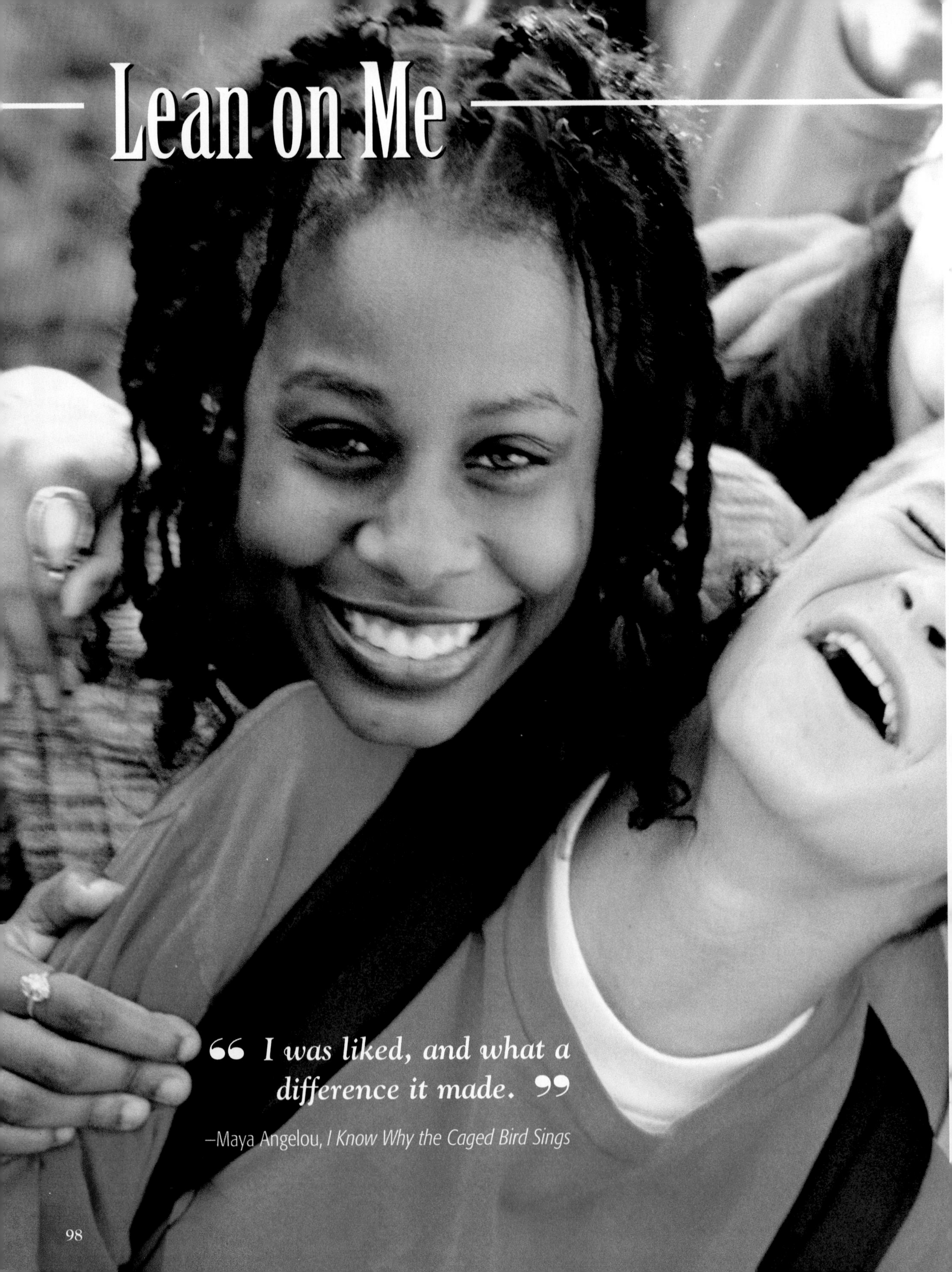

“I was liked, and what a difference it made.”

–Maya Angelou, *I Know Why the Caged Bird Sings*

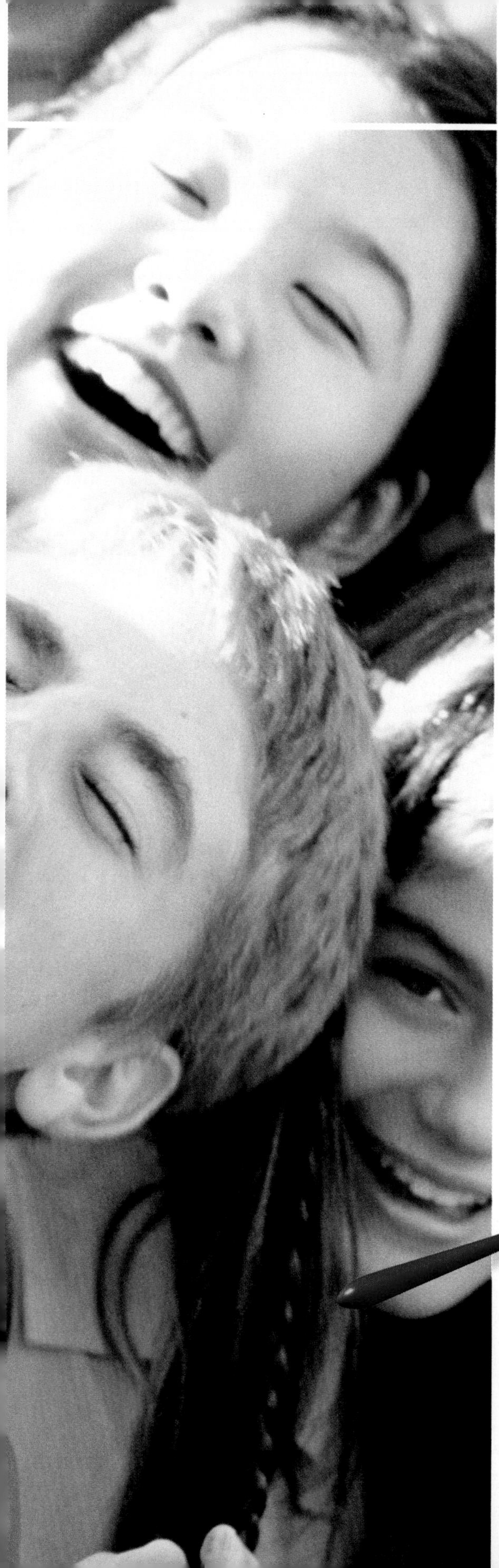

THEME CONTENTS

GENRE FOCUS *AUTOBIOGRAPHY*

Exploring the Theme

Lean on Me

What would the world be like without the people we depend on? In this theme, you will explore how we help–and sometimes hurt–others and what we learn from such experiences.

Starting Points

FOCUS ON FRIENDSHIP

One of the reasons Gary Larson started drawing cartoons was to make his friends laugh. His strip "The Far Side" has earned chuckles around the world for its absurd, offbeat, and sometimes disturbing ideas. What, do you think, is the point of the Larson cartoon shown here? Write a brief message about friendship based on the cartoon.

EXTENDING A HAND

Think about a time when a friend or family member did something special for you or helped you through a hard time.

- Now imagine the situation is reversed. Write a few notes on what you would do for this person in the same circumstances. Would you do the same thing for someone you knew less well? Explain.

The Far Side by Gary Larson

"Thanks for being my friend, Wayne."

Theme Projects

Look over the project ideas below. Then, as you read the selections, choose a project to complete. Work on your own, with a partner, or in a group.

LEARNING FOR LIFE

Lend a Hand

1. Volunteer to assist classes with younger children at your school or community center. Talk with your teacher to find out what you can do (teach a sport or craft, help with homework).
2. Keep a journal of your experiences as you work with the children.
3. After two weeks, report to the class on what you learned about yourself and others.

LISTENING AND SPEAKING

Interview

1. Interview someone who works with teenagers, such as a minister or a school counselor.
2. Ask questions like the ones that follow.
   - Why did you choose to work with teens?
   - What is the most important part of your work?
   - When a teenager is not accepted by a group, how do you help that person?
   - How do you encourage teens to help each other?
3. Type your interview questions and answers.

interNET CONNECTION

Visit lit.glencoe.com for additional project ideas and information about the writers and selections featured in "Lean on Me."

VISUAL LEARNING

Create a Support Web

1. Create a visual web of the influential people in your life: friends, teachers, family, and others. Use poster board or any family-tree software to create your web.
2. Group people in categories: friends in one, family in another. If possible, gather photos of the people in your web.
3. Under each name, jot down how long you have known the person. Also, briefly describe how the person has influenced you, and list the qualities you value in him or her.

Before You Read

from *All Things Bright and Beautiful*

MEET JAMES HERRIOT

For years, James Alfred Wight had told his wife that he was going to write a book about his life as a veterinarian. Finally one day she replied, "Who are you kidding? Vets of fifty don't write first books." Over the next twenty years, the British animal doctor answered his wife's challenge by writing and publishing more than twenty books. Wight used the pen name James Herriot because he didn't want it to seem that he was advertising his veterinary practice.

James Herriot was born in 1916 and died in 1995. All Things Bright and Beautiful *was first published in 1973.*

FOCUS ACTIVITY

What makes a visit to the doctor a pleasant or unpleasant experience for you?

List Ideas

Jot down some qualities you would want your pet's doctor to have. Share your ideas and experiences with a partner.

Setting a Purpose

Read to find out how one veterinarian gets along with the animals he takes care of—and their owners.

BACKGROUND

The Time and Place It is the 1940s in Yorkshire, a rural area in England.

Did You Know? A veterinarian is a doctor who treats animals. James Herriot cared for pets as well as large farm animals during his half century as a country veterinarian. It was a job, he once said, that was like "holidays with pay."

VOCABULARY PREVIEW

docile (dos′ əl) *adj.* easily managed, trained, or taught; p. 103
malice (mal′ is) *n.* a desire to harm another; ill will; p. 104
catastrophic (kat′ əs trof′ ik) *adj.* disastrous; p. 104
inhibition (in′ hə bish′ ən) *n.* a restraint on one's urges; p. 105
infinite (in′ fə nit) *adj.* boundless; limitless; extremely great; p. 105
uncomprehendingly (un kom′ pri hend′ ing lē) *adv.* without understanding; p. 106
alternative (ôl tur′ nə tiv) *n.* another choice; p. 106
placid (plas′ id) *adj.* calm or peaceful; p. 106
frustration (frus trā′ shən) *n.* disappointment or irritation at being kept from doing or achieving something; p. 107

from All Things Bright and Beautiful

James Herriot

Rhos Hilly Down. Sir Cedric Morris (1889–1982). Oil on canvas, 22 x 27 in.

"Move over, Bill!" Mr. Dacre cried some time later as he tweaked the big bull's tail.

Nearly every farmer kept a bull in those days and they were all called Billy or Bill. I suppose it was because this was a very mature animal that he received the adult version. Being a docile beast he responded to the touch on his tail by shuffling his great bulk to one side, leaving me enough space to push in between him and the wooden partition against which he was tied by a chain.

Vocabulary
docile (dos′ əl) *adj.* easily managed, trained, or taught

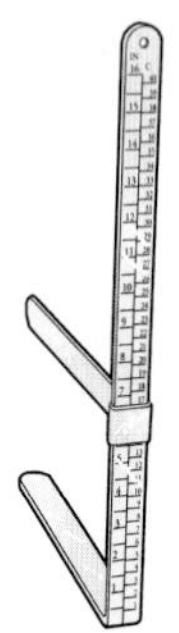

Did You Know?
A pair of *calipers* (kal′ ə pərz′) is a hinged instrument resembling a pair of tongs that is used to measure small objects.

I was reading a tuberculin test and all I wanted to do was to measure the intradermal reaction.[1] I had to open my calipers very wide to take in the thickness of the skin on the enormous neck.

"Thirty," I called out to the farmer.

He wrote the figure down on the testing book and laughed.

"By heck, he's got some pelt on 'im."

"Yes," I said, beginning to squeeze my way out. "But he's a big fellow, isn't he?"

Just how big he was was brought home to me immediately because the bull suddenly swung round, pinning me against the partition. Cows did this regularly and I moved them by bracing my back against whatever was behind me and pushing them away. But it was different with Bill.

Gasping, I pushed with all my strength against the rolls of fat which covered the vast roan-colored flank, but I might as well have tried to shift a house.

The farmer dropped his book and seized the tail again but this time the bull showed no response. There was no malice in his behavior—he was simply having a comfortable lean against the boards and I don't suppose he even noticed the morsel of puny humanity wriggling frantically against his rib cage.

Still, whether he meant it or not, the end result was the same; I was having the life crushed out of me. Pop-eyed, groaning, scarcely able to breathe, I struggled with everything I had, but I couldn't move an inch. And just when I thought things couldn't get any worse, Bill started to rub himself up and down against the partition. So that was what he had come round for; he had an itch and he just wanted to scratch it.

The effect on me was catastrophic. I was certain my internal organs were being steadily ground to pulp and as I thrashed about in complete panic the huge animal leaned even more heavily.

I don't like to think what would have happened if the wood behind me had not

1. The *tuberculin test* is used to diagnose the disease tuberculosis (TB). The narrator has injected the bull with a tiny amount of TB bacteria. An *intradermal* (or inside-the-skin) *reaction* is an allergic reaction that shows up as a thickening of the skin and can indicate whether a bull has TB.

Vocabulary

malice (mal′ is) *n.* a desire to harm another; ill will

catastrophic (kat′ əs trof′ ik) *adj.* disastrous

been old and rotten, but just as I felt my senses leaving me there was a cracking and splintering and I fell through into the next stall. Lying there like a stranded fish on a bed of shattered timbers I looked up at Mr. Dacre, waiting till my lungs started to work again.

The farmer, having got over his first alarm, was rubbing his upper lip vigorously in a polite attempt to stop himself laughing. His little girl who had watched the whole thing from her vantage point[2] in one of the hay racks had no such inhibitions. Screaming with delight, she pointed at me.

"Ooo, Dad, Dad, look at that man! Did you see him, Dad, did you see him? Ooo what a funny man!" She went into helpless convulsions. She was only about five but I had a feeling she would remember my performance all her life.

At length I picked myself up and managed to brush the matter off lightly, but after I had driven a mile or so from the farm I stopped the car and looked myself over. My ribs ached pretty uniformly as though a light road roller had passed over them and there was a tender area on my left buttock where I had landed on my calipers but otherwise I seemed to have escaped damage. I removed a few spicules[3] of wood from my trousers, got back into the car and consulted my list of visits.

And when I read my next call a gentle smile of relief spread over my face. "Mrs. Tompkin, 14, Jasmine Terrace. Clip budgie's beak."

Thank heaven for the infinite variety of veterinary practice. After that bull I needed something small and weak and harmless and really you can't ask for much better in that line than a budgie.

Number 14 was one of a row of small mean houses built of the cheap bricks so beloved of the jerry builders[4] after the first world war. I armed myself with a pair of clippers and stepped on to the narrow strip of pavement which separated the door from the road. A pleasant looking red haired woman answered my knock.

"I'm Mrs. Dodds from next door," she said. "I keep an eye on t'old lady. She's over eighty and lives alone. I've just been out gettin' her pension for her."

She led me into the cramped little room. "Here y'are, love," she said to the old woman who sat in a corner. She put the pension book and money on the mantelpiece. "And here's Mr. Herriot come to see Peter for you."

Mrs. Tompkin nodded and smiled. "Oh that's good. Poor little feller can't hardly eat with 'is long beak and I'm worried about him. He's me only companion, you know."

"Yes, I understand, Mrs. Tompkin." I looked at the cage by the window with the green budgie perched inside. "These little birds can be wonderful company when they start chattering."

2. A *vantage point* is a position that allows a clear view.
3. *Spicules* (spik′ ūlz) are small, needlelike points.

4. Here, the *mean* house is humble or modest in appearance. *Jerry builders* were construction companies that often used poor-quality materials to construct houses quickly for returning soldiers and their families after the war.

Vocabulary

inhibition (in′ hə bish′ ən) *n.* a restraint on one's urges
infinite (in′ fə nit) *adj.* boundless; limitless; extremely great

She laughed. "Aye, but it's a funny thing. Peter never has said owt much. I think he's lazy! But I just like havin' him with me."

"Of course you do," I said. "But he certainly needs attention now."

The beak was greatly overgrown, curving away down till it touched the feathers of the breast. I would be able to revolutionize his life with one quick snip from my clippers. The way I was feeling this job was right up my street.

I opened the cage door and slowly inserted my hand.

"Come on, Peter," I wheedled as the bird fluttered away from me. And I soon cornered him and enclosed him gently in my fingers. As I lifted him out I felt in my pocket with the other hand for the clippers, but as I poised them I stopped.

The tiny head was no longer poking cheekily from my fingers but had fallen loosely to one side. The eyes were closed. I stared at the bird uncomprehendingly for a moment then opened my hand. He lay quite motionless on my palm. He was dead.

Did You Know?
The bird's feathers *(plumage)* shimmer with shifting rainbow colors *(iridescence)*.

Dry mouthed, I continued to stare; at the beautiful iridescence of the plumage, the long beak which I didn't have to cut now, but mostly at the head dropping down over my forefinger. I hadn't squeezed him or been rough with him in any way but he was dead. It must have been sheer fright.

Mrs. Dodds and I looked at each other in horror and I hardly dared turn my head towards Mrs. Tompkin. When I did, I was surprised to see that she was still nodding and smiling.

I drew her neighbor to one side. "Mrs. Dodds, how much does she see?"

"Oh she's very shortsighted but she's right vain despite her age. Never would wear glasses. She's hard of hearin', too."

"Well look," I said. My heart was still pounding. "I just don't know what to do. If I tell her about this the shock will be terrible. Anything could happen."

Mrs. Dodds nodded, stricken-faced. "Aye, you're right. She's that attached to the little thing."

"I can only think of one alternative," I whispered. "Do you know where I can get another budgie?"

Mrs. Dodds thought for a moment. "You could try Jack Almond at t'town end. I think he keeps birds."

I cleared my throat but even then my voice came out in a dry croak. "Mrs. Tompkin, I'm just going to take Peter along to the surgery to do this job. I won't be long."

I left her still nodding and smiling and, cage in hand, fled into the street. I was at the town end and knocking at Jack Almond's door within three minutes.

"Mr. Almond?" I asked of the stout, shirt-sleeved man who answered.

"That's right, young man." He gave me a slow, placid smile.

Vocabulary

uncomprehendingly (un kom′ pri hend′ ing lē) *adv.* without understanding
alternative (ôl tur′ nə tiv) *n.* another choice
placid (plas′ id) *adj.* calm or peaceful

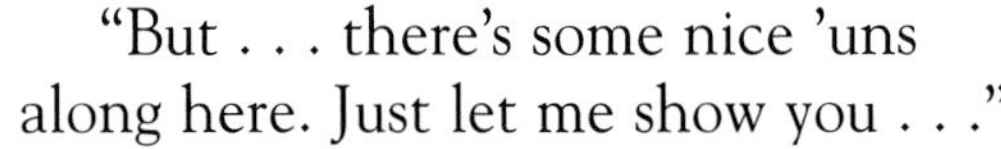

"Do you keep birds?"

He drew himself up with dignity. "I do, and I'm t'president of the Darrowby and Houlton Cage Bird Society."

"Fine," I said breathlessly. "Have you got a green budgie?"

"Ah've got Canaries, Budgies, Parrots, Parakeets. Cockatoos . . ."

"I just want a budgie."

"Well ah've got Albinos, Blue-greens, Barreds, Lutinos . . ."

"I just want a green one."

A slightly pained expression flitted across the man's face as though he found my attitude of haste somewhat unseemly.[5]

"Aye . . . well, we'll go and have a look," he said.

I followed him as he paced unhurriedly through the house into the back yard which was largely given over to a long shed containing a bewildering variety of birds.

Mr. Almond gazed at them with gentle pride and his mouth opened as though he was about to launch into a dissertation[6] then he seemed to remember that he had an impatient chap to deal with and dragged himself back to the job in hand.

"There's a nice little green 'un here. But he's a bit older than t'others. Matter of fact I've got 'im talkin'."

"All the better, just the thing. How much do you want for him?"

"But . . . there's some nice 'uns along here. Just let me show you . . ."

I put a hand on his arm. "I want that one. How much?"

He pursed his lips in frustration then shrugged his shoulders.

"Ten bob."[7]

"Right. Bung[8] him in this cage."

As I sped back up the road I looked in the driving mirror and could see the poor man regarding me sadly from his doorway.

Mrs. Dodds was waiting for me back at Jasmine Terrace.

"Do you think I'm doing the right thing?" I asked her in a whisper.

"I'm sure you are," she replied. "Poor awd thing, she hasn't much to think about and I'm sure she'd fret over Peter."

"That's what I thought." I made my way into the living room.

Mrs. Tompkin smiled at me as I went in. "That wasn't a long job, Mr. Herriot."

"No," I said, hanging the cage with the new bird up in its place by the window. "I think you'll find all is well now."

It was months before I had the courage to put my hand into a budgie's cage again. In fact to this day I prefer it if the owners will lift the birds out for me. People look at me strangely when I ask them to do this; I believe they think I am scared the little things might bite me.

---

5. Something *unseemly* is not proper or appropriate to the time or place.
6. Here, *dissertation* means "a long speech."
7. In informal British, a *bob* is a shilling, a coin formerly used in the United Kingdom, equal to about twenty cents.
8. *Bung* means "throw" or "toss."

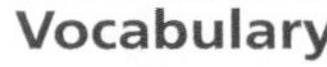

Vocabulary

frustration (frus trā′ shən) *n.* disappointment or irritation at being kept from doing or achieving something

It was a long time, too, before I dared go back to Mrs. Tompkin's but I was driving down Jasmine Terrace one day and on an impulse I stopped outside Number 14.

The old lady herself came to the door.

"How . . ." I said, "How is . . . er . . . ?"

She peered at me closely for a moment then laughed. "Oh I see who it is now. You mean Peter, don't you, Mr. Herriot. Oh 'e's just grand. Come in and see 'im."

In the little room the cage still hung by the window and Peter the Second took a quick look at me then put on a little act for my benefit; he hopped around the bars of the cage, ran up and down his ladder and rang his little bell a couple of times before returning to his perch.

His mistress reached up, tapped the metal and looked lovingly at him.

"You know, you wouldn't believe it," she said. "He's like a different bird."

I swallowed. "Is that so? In what way?"

"Well he's so active now. Lively as can be. You know 'e chatters to me all day long. It's wonderful what cuttin' a beak can do."

Responding to Literature

PERSONAL RESPONSE

What do you think about Mr. Herriot replacing the budgie? Would you have done the same thing in his position? Why or why not?

Analyzing Literature

RECALL

1. What happens to the veterinarian when he starts to leave the bull's pen?
2. Why is the veterinarian relieved when he realizes his next visit is to clip a budgie's beak?
3. How is the outcome of the veterinarian's visit to Mrs. Tompkin's home different from what he expected?
4. Describe what happens when the veterinarian returns to Mrs. Tompkin's home much later.

INTERPRET

5. What does the account of the narrator's accident with the bull show about the life of a veterinarian?
6. What does the author reveal about the veterinarian's character through each of his two visits?
7. How is the vet's visit with Mrs. Tompkin similar to his earlier visit with Mr. Dacre?
8. The story has a "happily ever after" ending. Or does it? What do you think? Explain.

EVALUATE

9. This story is based on Mr. Herriot's actual experience as a country veterinarian, but does the story seem realistic to you? Why or why not?
10. What part does humor play in the story? How would the story be different without humor?

LITERARY ELEMENTS

Imagery

Imagery is the use of words and phrases that appeal to our senses of sight, touch, hearing, smell, and taste. James Herriot uses imagery when he describes how the narrator struggles to push the bull away. ". . . I might as well have tried to shift a house," he writes. This image helps us feel the bull's power.

1. To what sense do these images appeal? Explain how each image adds humor to the situation.
   - "Lying there like a stranded fish on a bed of shattered timbers . . ."
   - "My ribs ached pretty uniformly as though a light road roller had passed over them."
2. To which sense does the following image appeal? What does the image tell you about Mr. Almond, who is described here? "His mouth opened as though he was about to launch into a dissertation."

See **Literary Terms Handbook,** p. R5.

Literature and Writing

Writing About Literature

Character Write a paragraph or two explaining how the author creates real, flesh-and-blood characters in very few lines. Focus on one of the characters *other than the narrator.* As you write, think about these questions: What do you learn about the character from what he or she says? What do the character's actions tell you about him or her? What does the character contribute to the story?

Creative Writing

Feature Story Suppose you write for a newspaper. You have followed Mr. Herriot, the veterinarian, for the day. Write a short newspaper story about at least one of the events in the selection from *All Things Bright and Beautiful.*

Extending Your Response

Literature Groups

A Perfect Pet Doctor Compare the list you made in the **Focus Activity** on page 102 with the lists of students in your group. Which qualities in a veterinarian do you agree are most important? Which skills does Mr. Herriot possess? Which does he lack? Does he have qualities that you'd like to add to your lists?

Performing

The Secret Is Out Suppose that Mrs. Tompkin discovers that Mr. Herriot has replaced her bird with another one. With a partner, discuss what might happen if she confronted Mr. Herriot about the deception. Consider the following questions: What factors did Mr. Herriot consider before making the decision? What other decisions could he have made? Then role-play a conversation between the two characters. Review the dialogue in the story, and try to mimic the characters' style of speaking.

Interdisciplinary Activity

Science The first Peter never said "owt much," but the second Peter is a talker. Investigate budgies, parrots, cockatoos, or other talking birds. Take notes on the natural habitat, eating habits, life expectancy, appearance, and other information about each type of bird. Then prepare a brief written report.

Reading Further

You might enjoy reading the rest of *All Things Bright and Beautiful* and these other works by James Herriot:

All Creatures Great and Small
All Things Wise and Wonderful
The Lord God Made Them All

Save your work for your portfolio.

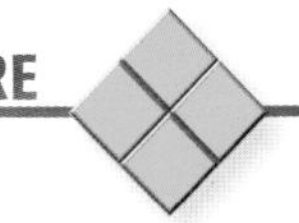

Skill Minilessons

GRAMMAR AND LANGUAGE • PRECISE VERBS

Good writers use precise, or exact, verbs to make their writing fresh and believable. Many verbs have synonyms, so writers must choose the verb that most precisely describes a particular character, setting, or action. For example, James Herriot writes, "I left [Mrs. Tompkin] still nodding and smiling and, cage in hand, fled into the street." *Fled* expresses the action and emotion better than *walked* or *ran* might.

- For more about verbs, see **Language Handbook,** pp. R33–R34.

PRACTICE Revise the following sentences by substituting a precise verb for each underlined word or phrase.

1. The bull pushed Mr. Herriot against the wood partition.
2. The bird moved away as Mr. Herriot reached for it.
3. Mr. Herriot left the house to get another bird.
4. Mr. Almond was frustrated with Mr. Herriot.
5. After a day of close calls, Mr. Herriot's head hurt.

READING AND THINKING • SEQUENCE

Several events occur in the selection from *All Things Bright and Beautiful.* The order in which events occur—first, next, and last—is called **sequence.** Author James Herriot maps the story sequence with words and phrases, such as *my next call, after that, within three minutes, back at Jasmine Terrace,* and *it was a long time.*

PRACTICE Write a paragraph that shows the sequence of four important events in the story. Use the author's word clues to help you. Include sequence words, such as *first, next,* and *last,* to clarify the order of events.

- For more about sequencing, see **Reading Handbook,** p. R89.

VOCABULARY • ANALOGIES

An **analogy** is a type of comparison that is based on the relationships between things or ideas. Some analogies, like the one below, are based on a relationship that could be called "degree of intensity."

warm : hot :: attractive : gorgeous

You could describe the degree of intensity in the example like this: "Something very warm is hot, just as something very attractive is gorgeous."

PRACTICE Figure out the relationship between the first pair of words. Then complete the analogy by choosing a second pair that has the same relationship.

1. unfortunate : catastrophic ::
   a. lucky : unlucky
   b. cheerful : pleasant
   c. afraid : terrified
   d. embarrassed : quiet
   e. large : heavy
2. vast : infinite ::
   a. good : perfect
   b. spacious : roomy
   c. tiny : huge
   d. necessary : sufficient
   e. old : wise

- For more about analogies, see **Communications Skills Handbook,** p. R67.

Before You Read

Flowers for Algernon

MEET
DANIEL KEYES

Daniel Keyes loves to explore the "complexities of the human mind." Writing allows him to ask questions about personality, intelligence, and the pros and cons of scientific progress. As a photographer, editor, teacher, and merchant seaman, Keyes has met and observed a wide range of people. This experience shows through in writings such as "Flowers for Algernon," which Keyes turned into a best-selling novel, a drama, and a movie, "Charly."

Daniel Keyes was born in 1927. "Flowers for Algernon" was first published in 1959 in The Magazine of Fantasy and Science Fiction.

FOCUS ACTIVITY

Imagine that one day you begin changing. You get smarter and more talented with each passing day.

QuickWrite

List three or four advantages of becoming smarter and more talented. What disadvantages do you see?

Setting a Purpose

Read to discover what happens when a simple person becomes a genius.

BACKGROUND

The Time and Place It is 1965 in New York City.

Did You Know? Several kinds of scientists study the brain and the mind:

- A neurosurgeon studies and operates on the brain.
- A psychiatrist studies the workings of the mind.
- A psychologist studies behavior, including thoughts, feelings, and learning abilities. There are many tests to measure human intelligence. The Intelligence Quotient, or I.Q., is one such measure. In recent years, scientists have come to think that people have "multiple intelligences"–special abilities for language, music, physical coordination, and other areas.

VOCABULARY PREVIEW

opportunist (op′ ər to͞o′ nist) *n.* one who takes advantage of every opportunity, regardless of consequences; p. 127

tangible (tan′ jə bəl) *adj.* able to be seen, touched, or felt; real; p. 129

intellectual (int′ əl ek′ cho͞o əl) *adj.* appealing to or involving intelligence or mental ability; p. 130

invariably (in vār′ ē ə blē) *adv.* constantly; always; p. 131

cower (kou′ ər) *v.* to shrink away, as in fear or shame; p. 131

obscure (əb skyoor′) *v.* to hide; p. 134

impaired (im pārd′) *adj.* lessened in quality; damaged; p. 134

stimulus (stim′ yə ləs) *n.* something that causes a response; p. 135

Flowers for Algernon

Daniel Keyes

progris riport 1—martch 5 1965

Dr. Strauss says I shud rite down what I think and evrey thing that happins to me from now on. I dont know why but he says its importint so they will see if they will use me. I hope they use me. Miss Kinnian says maybe they can make me smart. I want to be smart. My name is Charlie Gordon. I am 37 years old and 2 weeks ago was my birthday. I have nuthing more to rite now so I will close for today.

progris riport 2—martch 6

I had a test today. I think I faled it. and I think that maybe now they wont use me. What happind is a nice young man was in the room and he had some white cards with ink spillled all over them. He sed Charlie what do you see on this card. I was very skared even tho I had my rabits foot in my pockit because when I was a kid I always faled tests in school and I spillled ink to.

I told him I saw a inkblot. He said yes and it made me feel good. I thot that was all but when I got up to go he stopped me. He said now sit down Charlie we are not thru yet. Then I dont remember so good but he wantid me to say what was in the ink. I dint see nuthing in the ink but he said there was picturs there other pepul saw some picturs. I coudnt see any picturs. I reely tryed to see. I held the card close up and then far away. Then I said if I had my glases I coud see better I usally only ware my glases in the movies or TV but I said they are in the closit in the hall. I got them. Then I said let me see that card agen I bet Ill find it now.

I tryed hard but I still coudnt find the picturs I only saw the ink.

I tryed hard but I still coudnt find the picturs I only saw the ink. I told him maybe I need new glases. He rote somthing down on a paper and I got skared of faling the test. I told him it was a very nice inkblot with littel points al around the eges. He looked very sad so that wasnt it. I said please let me try agen. Ill get it in a few minits becaus Im not so fast somtimes. Im a slow reeder too in Miss Kinnians class for slow adults but I'm trying very hard.

He gave me a chance with another card that had 2 kinds of ink spillled on it red and blue.

He was very nice and talked slow like Miss Kinnian does and he explaned it to me that it was a *raw shok.*[1] He said pepul see things in the ink. I said show me where. He said think. I told him I think a inkblot but that wasnt rite eather. He said what does it remind you—pretend something. I closd my eyes for a long time to pretend. I told him I pretned a fowntan pen with ink leeking all over a table cloth. Then he got up and went out.

I dont think I passd the *raw shok* test.

progris report 3—martch 7

Dr Strauss and Dr Nemur say it dont matter about the inkblots. I told them I dint spill the ink on the cards and I coudnt see anything in the ink. They said that maybe they will still use me. I said Miss Kinnian never gave me tests like that one only spelling and reading. They said Miss Kinnian told that I was her bestist pupil in the adult nite scool becaus I tryed the hardist and I reely wantid to lern. They said how come you went to the adult nite scool all by yourself Charlie. How did you find it. I said I askd pepul and sumbody told me where I shud go to lern to read and spell good. They said why did you want to. I told them becaus all my life I wantid to be

1. When Charlie says *raw shok,* he is referring to the *Rorschach* (rôr′ shäk) test that gathers information about personality and intelligence from the images people see in inkblot designs.

smart and not dumb. But its very hard to be smart. They said you know it will probly be tempirery. I said yes. Miss Kinnian told me. I dont care if it herts.

Later I had more crazy tests today. The nice lady who gave it me told me the name and I asked her how do you spellit so I can rite it in my progris riport. THEMATIC APPERCEPTION TEST.[2] I dont know the frist 2 words but I know what *test* means. You got to pass it or you get bad marks. This test lookd easy becaus I coud see the picturs. Only this time she dint want me to tell her the picturs. That mixd me up. I said the man yesterday said I shoud tell him what I saw in the ink she said that dont make no difrence. She said make up storys about the pepul in the picturs.

I told her how can you tell storys about pepul you never met. I said why shud I make up lies. I never tell lies any more becaus I always get caut.

She told me this test and the other one the raw-shok was for getting personalty. I laffed so hard. I said how can you get that thing from inkblots and fotos. She got sore and put her picturs away. I dont care. It was sily. I gess I faled that test too.

Later some men in white coats took me to a difernt part of the hospitil and gave me a game to play. It was like a race with a white mouse. They called the mouse Algernon. Algernon was in a box with a lot of twists and turns like all kinds of walls and they gave me a pencil and a paper with lines and lots of boxes. On one side it said START and on the other end it said FINISH. They said it was *amazed*[3] and that Algernon and me had the same *amazed* to do. I dint see how we could have the same *amazed* if Algernon had a box and I had a paper but I dint say nothing. Anyway there wasnt time because the race started.

One of the men had a watch he was trying to hide so I woudnt see it so I tryed not to look and that made me nervus.

Anyway that test made me feel worser than all the others because they did it over 10 times with difernt *amazeds* and Algernon won every time. I dint know that mice were so smart. Maybe thats because Algernon is a white mouse. Maybe white mice are smarter then other mice.

progris riport 4—Mar 8

Their going to use me! Im so exited I can hardly write. Dr Nemur and Dr Strauss had a argament about it first. Dr Nemur was in the office when Dr Strauss brot me in. Dr Nemur was worryed about using me but Dr Strauss told him Miss Kinnian rekemmended me the best from all the people

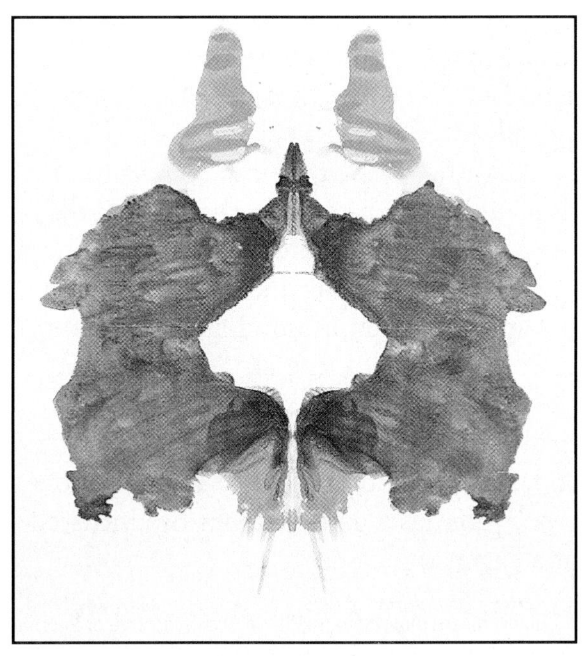

Inkblot design.

2. A ***Thematic Apperception*** (thē mat′ ik ap′ ər sep′ shən) ***Test*** **asks people to make up stories based on a series of pictures.**
3. **Charlie writes *amazed,* but he means to write *a maze.***

who she was teaching. I like Miss Kinnian becaus shes a very smart teacher. And she said Charlie your going to have a second chance. If you volenteer for this experament you mite get smart. They dont know if it will be perminint but theirs a chance. Thats why I said ok even when I was scared because she said it was an operashun. She said dont be scared Charlie you done so much with so little I think you deserv it most of all.

So I got scaird when Dr Nemur and Dr Strauss argud about it. Dr Strauss said I had something that was very good. He said I had a good *motor-vation.*[4] I never even knew I had that. I felt proud when he said that not every body with an eye-q[5] of 68 had that thing. I dont know what it is or where I got it but he said Algernon had it too. Algernons *motor-vation* is the cheese they put in his box. But it cant be that because I didnt eat any cheese this week.

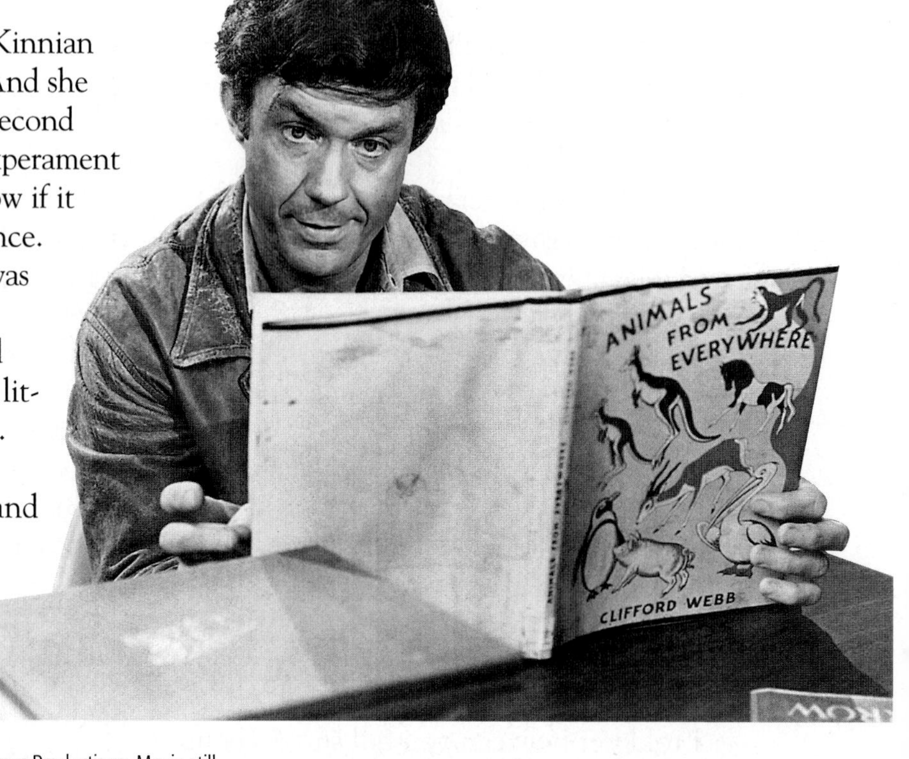

Charly, 1967. Selmur Productions. Movie still.

Viewing the photograph: How does this scene from the film show Charlie's attitude toward reading?

Then he told Dr Nemur something I dint understand so while they were talking I wrote down some of the words.

He said Dr Nemur I know Charlie is not what you had in mind as the first of your new brede of intelek** (coudnt get the word) superman. But most people of his low ment** are host** and uncoop** they are usualy dull apath** and hard to reach. He has a good natcher hes intristed and eager to please.

Dr Nemur said remember he will be the first human beeng ever to have his intelijence trippled by surgicle meens.

Dr Strauss said exakly. Look at how well hes lerned to read and write for his low mentel age its as grate an acheve** as you and I lerning einstines therey of **vity[6] without help. That shows the intenss motor-vation. Its comparat** a tremen** achev** I say we use Charlie.

I dint get all the words and they were talking to fast but it sounded like Dr Strauss was on my side and like the other one wasnt.

Then Dr Nemur nodded he said all right maybe your right. We will use Charlie. When he said that I got so exited

4. Charlie means *motivation* (mō′ tə vā′ shən), the urge or internal need to take action or to make an effort.
5. Charlie is referring to *IQ,* or Intelligence Quotient.
6. *[einstines therey of **vity]* Charlie is referring to the theory of relativity developed by the scientist Albert Einstein.

I jumped up and shook his hand for being so good to me. I told him thank you doc you wont be sorry for giving me a second chance. And I mean it like I told him. After the operashun Im gonna try to be smart. Im gonna try awful hard.

progris ript 5—Mar 10

Im skared. Lots of people who work here and the nurses and the people who gave me the tests came to bring me candy and wish me luck. I hope I have luck. I got my rabits foot and my lucky penny and my horse shoe. Only a black cat crossed me when I was comming to the hospitil. Dr Strauss says dont be supersitis Charlie this is sience. Anyway Im keeping my rabits foot with me.

I asked Dr Strauss if Ill beat Algernon in the race after the operashun and he said maybe. If the operashun works Ill show that mouse I can be as smart as he is. Maybe smarter. Then Ill be abel to read better and spell the words good and know lots of things and be like other people. I want to be smart like other people. If it works perminint they will make everybody smart all over the wurld.

They dint give me anything to eat this morning. I dont know what that eating has to do with getting smart. Im very hungry and Dr Nemur took away my box of candy. That Dr Nemur is a grouch. Dr Strauss says I can have it back after the operashun. You cant eat befor a operashun . . .

Progress Report 6—Mar 15

The operashun dint hurt. He did it while I was sleeping. They took off the bandijis from my eyes and my head today so I can make a PROGRESS REPORT. Dr Nemur who looked at some of my other ones says I spell PROGRESS wrong and he told me how to spell it and REPORT too. I got to try and remember that.

I have a very bad memary for spelling. Dr Strauss says its ok to tell about all the things that happin to me but he says I shoud tell more about what I feel and what I think. When I told him I dont know how to think he said try. All the time when the bandijis were on my eyes I tryed to think. Nothing happened. I dont know what to think about. Maybe if I ask him he will tell me how I can think now that Im suppose to get smart. What do smart people think about. Fancy things I suppose. I wish I knew some fancy things alredy.

Progress Report 7—mar 19

Nothing is happining. I had lots of tests and different kinds of races with Algernon. I hate that mouse. He always beats me. Dr Strauss said I got to play those games. And he said some time I got to take those tests over again. Thse inkblots are stupid. And those pictures are stupid too. I like to draw a picture of a man and a woman but I wont make up lies about people.

I got a headache from trying to think so much. I thot Dr Strauss was my frend but he dont help me. He dont tell me what to think or when Ill get smart. Miss Kinnian dint come to see me. I think writing these progress reports are stupid too.

Progress Report 8—Mar 23

Im going back to work at the factery. They said it was better I shud go back to work but I cant tell anyone what the operashun was for and I have to come to the hospitil for an hour evry night after work. They are gonna pay me mony every month for lerning to be smart.

Im glad Im going back to work because I miss my job and all my frends and all the fun we have there.

Dr Strauss says I shud keep writing things down but I dont have to do it every day just when I think of something or something speshul happins. He says dont get discoridged because it takes time and it happins slow. He says it took a long time with Algernon before he got 3 times smarter than he was before. Thats why Algernon beats me all the time because he had that operashun too. That makes me feel better. I coud probly do that *amazed* faster than a reglar mouse. Maybe some day Ill beat Algernon. Boy that would be something. So far Algernon looks like he mite be smart perminent.

Mar 25 (I dont have to write PROGRESS REPORT on top any more just when I hand it in once a week for Dr Nemur to read. I just have to put the date on. That saves time)

We had a lot of fun at the factery today. Joe Carp said hey look where Charlie had his operashun what did they do Charlie put some brains in. I was going to tell him but I remembered Dr Strauss said no. Then Frank Reilly said what did you do Charlie forget your key and open your door the hard way. That made me laff. Their really my friends and they like me.

Sometimes somebody will say hey look at Joe or Frank or George he really pulled a Charlie Gordon. I dont know why they say that but they always laff. This morning Amos Borg who is the 4 man at Donnegans used my name when he shouted at Ernie the office boy. Ernie lost a packige. He said Ernie for godsake what are you trying to be a Charlie Gordon. I dont understand why he said that. I never lost any packiges.

Mar 28 Dr Strauss came to my room tonight to see why I dint come in like I was suppose to. I told him I dont like to race with Algernon any more. He said I dont have to for a while but I shud come in. He had a present for me only it wasnt a present but just for lend. I thot it was a little television but it wasnt. He said I got to turn it on when I go to sleep. I said your kidding why shud I turn it on when Im going to sleep. Who ever herd of a thing like that. But he said if I want to get smart I got to do what he says. I told him I dint think I was going to get smart and he put his hand on my sholder and said Charlie you dont know it yet but your getting smarter all the time. You wont notice for a while. I think he was just being nice to make me feel good because I dont look any smarter.

Oh yes I almost forgot. I asked him when I can go back to the class at Miss Kinnians school. He said I wont go their. He said that soon Miss Kinnian will come to the hospitil to start and teach me speshul. I was mad at her for not comming to see me when I got the operashun but I like her so maybe we will be frends again.

Mar 29 That crazy TV kept me up all night. How can I sleep with something yelling crazy things all night in my ears. And the nutty pictures. Wow. I dont know what it says when Im up so how am I going to know when Im sleeping.

Dr Strauss says its ok. He says my brains are lerning when I sleep and that will help me when Miss Kinnian starts my lessons in the hospitl (only I found out it isnt a hospitil its a labatory). I think its all crazy. If you can get smart when your sleeping why do people go to school. That thing I dont think will work. I use to watch the late show and the late late show on TV all the time and it never made me smart. Maybe you have to sleep while you watch it.

PROGRESS REPORT 9—April 3

Dr Strauss showed me how to keep the TV turned low so now I can sleep. I dont hear a thing. And I still dont understand what it says. A few times I play it over in the morning to find out what I lerned when I was sleeping and I dont think so. Miss Kinnian says Maybe its another langwidge or something. But most times it sounds american. It talks so fast faster then even Miss Gold who was my teacher in 6 grade and I remember she talked so fast I coudnt understand her.

Charly, 1967, Selmur Productions. Movie still.

Viewing the photograph: What may Charlie be thinking as he arranges the puzzle pieces?

I told Dr Strauss what good is it to get smart in my sleep. I want to be smart when Im awake. He says its the same thing and I have two minds. Theres the *subconscious* and the *conscious* (thats how you spell it). And one dont tell the other one what its doing. They dont even talk to each other. Thats why I dream. And boy have I been having crazy dreams. Wow. Ever since that night TV. The late late late late late show.

I forgot to ask him if it was only me or if everybody had those two minds.

(I just looked up the word in the dictionary Dr Strauss gave me. The word is *subconscious. adj. Of the nature of mental operations yet not present in consciousness; as, subconscious conflict of desires.)* Theres more but I still don't know what it means. This isnt a very good dictionary for dumb people like me.

I think Ill be frends with Algernon.

Anyway the headache is from the party. My frends from the factery Joe Carp and Frank Reilly invited me to go with them to Muggsys Saloon for some drinks. I dont like to drink but they said we will have lots of fun. I had a good time.

Joe Carp said I shoud show the girls how I mop out the toilet in the factory and he got me a mop. I showed them and everyone laffed when I told that Mr Donnegan said I was the best janiter he ever had because I like my job and do it good and never come late or miss a day except for my operashun.

I said Miss Kinnian always said Charlie be proud of your job because you do it good.

Everybody laffed and we had a good time and they gave me lots of drinks and Joe said Charlie is a card when hes potted.[7] I dont know what that means but everybody likes me and we have fun. I cant wait to be smart like my best frends Joe Carp and Frank Reilly.

I dont remember how the party was over but I think I went out to buy a newspaper and coffe for Joe and Frank and when I came back there was no one their. I looked for them all over till late. Then I dont remember so good but I think I got sleepy or sick. A nice cop brot me back home. Thats what my landlady Mrs Flynn says.

But I got a headache and a big lump on my head and black and blue all over. I think maybe I fell but Joe Carp says it was the cop they beat up drunks some times. I don't think so. Miss Kinnian says cops are to help people. Anyway I got a bad headache and Im sick and hurt all over. I dont think Ill drink anymore.

April 6 I beat Algernon! I dint even know I beat him until Burt the tester told me. Then the second time I lost because I got so exited I fell off the chair before I finished. But after that I beat him 8 more times. I must be getting smart to beat a smart mouse like Algernon. But I dont *feel* smarter.

I wanted to race Algernon some more but Burt said thats enough for one day. They let me hold him for a minit. Hes not so bad.

7. *Charlie is a card when hes potted* means "Charlie is funny when he's had too much to drink."

Charly, 1967. Selmur Productions. Movie still.

Viewing the photograph: What does Charlie's smile reveal about his personality?

Hes soft like a ball of cotton. He blinks and when he opens his eyes their black and pink on the eges.

I said can I feed him because I felt bad to beat him and I wanted to be nice and make frends. Burt said no Algernon is a very spec-shul mouse with an operashun like mine, and he was the first of all the animals to stay smart so long. He told me Algernon is so smart that every day he has to solve a test to get his food. Its a thing like a lock on a door that changes every time Algernon goes in to eat so he has to lern something new to get his food. That made me sad because if he coudnt lern he woud be hungry.

I dont think its right to make you pass a test to eat. How woud Dr Nemur like it to have to pass a test every time he wants to eat. I think Ill be frends with Algernon.

April 9 Tonight after work Miss Kinnian was at the laboratory. She looked like she was glad to see me but scared. I told her dont worry Miss Kinnian Im not smart yet and she laffed. She said I have confidence in you Charlie the way you struggled so hard to read and right better than all the others. At werst you will have it for a littel wile and your doing somthing for sience.

We are reading a very hard book. I never read such a hard book before. Its called *Robinson Crusoe* about a man who gets merooned on a dessert Iland. Hes smart and figers out all kinds of things so he can have a house and food and hes a good swimmer. Only I feel sorry because hes all alone and has no frends. But I think their must be somebody else on the iland because theres a picture with his funny umbrella looking at footprints. I hope he gets a frend and not be lonly.

April 10 Miss Kinnian teaches me to spell better. She says look at a word and close your eyes and say it over and over until you remember. I have lots of truble with *through* that you say *threw* and *enough* and *tough* that you dont say *enew* and *tew*. You got to say *enuff* and *tuff*. Thats how

I use to write it before I started to get smart. Im confused but Miss Kinnian says theres no reason in spelling.

April 14 Finished *Robinson Crusoe*. I want to find out more about what happens to him but Miss Kinnian says thats all there is. *Why*

April 15 Miss Kinnian says Im lerning fast. She read some of the Progress Reports and she looked at me kind of funny. She says Im a fine person and Ill show them all. I asked her why. She said never mind but I shoudnt feel bad if I find out that everybody isnt nice like I think. She said for a person who god gave so little to you done more then a lot of people with brains they never even used. I said all my frends are smart people but there good. They like me and they never did anything that wasnt nice. Then she got something in her eye and she had to run out to the ladys room.

April 16 Today, I lerned, the *comma*, this is a comma (,) a period, with a tail, Miss Kinnian, says its importent, because, it makes writing, better, she said, sombeody, could lose, a lot of money, if a comma, isnt, in the, right place, I dont have, any money, and I dont see, how a comma, keeps you, from losing it,

But she says, everybody, uses commas, so Ill use, them too,

April 17 I used the comma wrong. Its punctuation. Miss Kinnian told me to look up long words in the dictionary to lern to spell them. I said whats the difference if you can read it anyway. She said its part of your education so now on Ill look up all the words Im not sure how to spell. It takes a long time to write that way but I think Im remembering. I only have to look up once and after that I get it right. Anyway thats how come I got the word *punctuation* right. (Its that way in the dictionary). Miss Kinnian says a period is punctuation too, and there are lots of other marks to lern. I told her I thot all the periods had to have tails but she said no.

You got to mix them up, she showed? me" how. to mix! them(up,. and now; I can! mix up all kinds" of punctuation, in! my writing? There, are lots! of rules? to lern; but Im gettin'g them in my head.

One thing I? like about, Dear Miss Kinnian: (thats the way it goes in a business letter if I ever go into business) is she, always gives me' a reason" when—I ask. She's a gen'ius! I wish! I cou'd be smart" like, her;

(Punctuation, is; fun!)

April 18 What a dope I am! I didn't even understand what she was talking about. I read the grammar book last night and it explanes the whole thing. Then I saw it was the same way as Miss Kinnian was trying to tell me, but I didn't get it. I got up in the middle of the night, and the whole thing straightened out in my mind.

Miss Kinnian said that the TV working in my sleep helped out. She said I reached a plateau. Thats like the flat top of a hill.

After I figgered out how punctuation worked, I read over all my old Progress Reports from the beginning. Boy, did I have crazy spelling and punctuation! I told Miss Kinnian I ought to go over the pages and fix all the mistakes but she said, "No, Charlie, Dr. Nemur wants them just as they are. That's why he let you keep them after they were photostated,[8] to see your own progress. You're coming along fast, Charlie."

That made me feel good. After the lesson I went down and played with Algernon. We don't race any more.

April 20 I feel sick inside. Not sick like for a doctor, but inside my chest it feels empty like getting punched and a heartburn at the same time.

I wasn't going to write about it, but I guess I got to, because it's important. Today was the first time I ever stayed home from work.

Last night Joe Carp and Frank Reilly invited me to a party. There were lots of girls and some men from the factory. I remembered how sick I got last time I drank too much, so I told Joe I didn't want anything to drink. He gave me a plain Coke instead. It tasted funny, but I thought it was just a bad taste in my mouth.

We had a lot of fun for a while. Joe said I should dance with Ellen and she would teach me the steps. I fell a few times and I couldn't understand why because no one else was dancing besides Ellen and me. And all the time I was tripping because somebody's foot was always sticking out.

Then when I got up I saw the look on Joe's face and it gave me a funny feeling in my stomack. "He's a scream," one of the girls said. Everybody was laughing.

Frank said, "I ain't laughed so much since we sent him off for the newspaper that night at Muggsy's and ditched him."

"Look at him. His face is red."

"He's blushing. Charlie is blushing."

"Hey, Ellen, what'd you do to Charlie? I never saw him act like that before."

I didn't know what to do or where to turn. Everyone was looking at me and laughing and I felt naked. I wanted to hide myself. I ran out into the street and I threw up. Then I walked home. It's a funny thing I never knew that Joe and Frank and the others liked to have me around all the time to make fun of me.

Now I know what it means when they say "to pull a Charlie Gordon."

I'm ashamed.

---

8. A *photostat* is a type of photocopy made on specially treated paper.

Responding to Literature

PERSONAL RESPONSE

- How did you react when Charlie discovered the truth about his friends?
- If you met Charlie before the operation, would you have chosen him as a friend? Why or why not?

Analyzing Literature

RECALL AND INTERPRET

1. What does Charlie think is the difference between himself and smart people? What does Charlie fail to see about the "smart" people around him? Explain.
2. Why is Charlie chosen for the project, even though he fails all the tests? Reread the information about intelligence on page 112. What types of intelligence might Charlie have? Explain.
3. What incidents in the first part of the story indicate Charlie is changing? When he realizes the meaning of "to pull a Charlie Gordon," what new understanding does Charlie have about himself and others?

EVALUATE AND CONNECT

4. The author presents "Flowers for Algernon" as a series of progress reports or journal entries. Is this style an effective way to tell the story? Why or why not? Support your opinion with examples.
5. **Internal conflict** is a struggle within a character. How does the writer show Charlie's internal conflict about the operation?
6. Suppose you wanted to change something about yourself. Someone offers you a risky operation to grant your wish, but the change will last only a few months. Describe the internal conflict you might have when faced with this decision.

LITERARY ELEMENTS

Irony

Irony is the difference between the way things seem to be and the way they really are. In a story like "Flowers for Algernon," the writer uses irony in two ways: In **dramatic irony,** readers have important knowledge that the character does not (Charlie thinks Frank and Joe like him a lot, but they are cruel to him). In **situational irony,** the outcome of a situation is the opposite of what the character expects (Charlie expects that being smart will help him fit in, but instead he sees how people laugh at him).

1. Reread the progress reports for March 6 to March 8. How does the writer use irony to show Charlie's personality and intelligence?
2. How would the story be different if the writer had simply reported Charlie's scores and not used irony?

- See **Literary Terms Handbook,** p. R5.

Flowers for Algernon (Continued)

PROGRESS REPORT 11

April 21 Still didn't go into the factory. I told Mrs. Flynn my landlady to call and tell Mr. Donnegan I was sick. Mrs. Flynn looks at me very funny lately like she's scared of me.

I think it's a good thing about finding out how everybody laughs at me. I thought about it a lot. It's because I'm so dumb and I don't even know when I'm doing something dumb. People think it's funny when a dumb person can't do things the same way they can.

Anyway, now I know I'm getting smarter every day. I know punctuation and I can spell good. I like to look up all the hard words in the dictionary and I remember them. I'm reading a lot now, and Miss Kinnian says I read very fast. Sometimes I even understand what I'm reading about, and it stays in my mind. There are times when I can close my eyes and think of a page and it all comes back like a picture.

Besides history, geography, and arithmetic, Miss Kinnian said I should start to learn a few foreign languages. Dr. Strauss gave me some more tapes to play while I sleep. I still don't understand how that conscious and unconscious mind works, but Dr. Strauss says not to worry yet. He asked me to promise that when I start learning college subjects next week I wouldn't read any books on psychology—that is, until he gives me permission.

I feel a lot better today, but I guess I'm still a little angry that all the time people were laughing and making fun of me because I wasn't so smart. When I become intelligent like Dr. Strauss says, with three times my I.Q. of 68, then maybe I'll be like everyone else and people will like me and be friendly.

I'm not sure what an I.Q. is. Dr. Nemur said it was something that measured how intelligent you were—like a scale in the drugstore weighs pounds. But Dr. Strauss had a big argument with him and said an I.Q. didn't weigh intelligence at all. He said an I.Q. showed how much intelligence you could get, like the numbers on the outside of a measuring cup. You still had to fill the cup up with stuff.

Then when I asked Burt, who gives me my intelligence tests and works with Algernon, he said that both of them were wrong (only I had to promise not to tell them he said so). Burt says that the I.Q. measures a lot of different things including some of the things you learned already, and it really isn't any good at all.

So I still don't know what I.Q. is except that mine is going to be over 200 soon. I didn't want to say anything, but I don't see how if they don't know *what* it is, or *where* it is—I don't see how they know *how much* of it you've got.

Dr. Nemur says I have to take a *Rorshach Test* tomorrow. I wonder what *that* is.

April 22 I found out what a *Rorshach* is. It's the test I took before the operation—the one with the inkblots on the pieces of cardboard. The man who gave me the test was the same one.

I was scared to death of those inkblots. I knew he was going to ask me to find the pictures and I knew I wouldn't be able to. I was thinking to myself, if only there was some way of knowing what kind of pictures were hidden there. Maybe there weren't any pictures at all. Maybe it was just a trick to see if I was dumb enough to look for something that wasn't there. Just thinking about that made me sore at him.

The test still doesn't make sense to me. It seems to me that anyone could make up lies about things that they didn't really see.

"All right, Charlie," he said, "you've seen these cards before, remember?"

"Of course I remember."

The way I said it, he knew I was angry, and he looked surprised. "Yes, of course. Now I want you to look at this one. What might this be? What do you see on this card? People see all sorts of things in these inkblots. Tell me what it might be for you—what it makes you think of."

I was shocked. That wasn't what I had expected him to say at all. "You mean there are no pictures hidden in those inkblots?"

He frowned and took off his glasses. "What?"

"Pictures. Hidden in the inkblots. Last time you told me that everyone could see them and you wanted me to find them too."

He explained to me that the last time he had used almost the exact same words he was using now.

I didn't believe it, and I still have the suspicion that he misled me at the time just for the fun of it. Unless—I don't know any more—could I have been *that* feebleminded?

We went through the cards slowly. One of them looked like a pair of bats tugging at something. Another one looked like two men fencing with swords. I imagined all sorts of things. I guess I got carried away. But I didn't trust him any more, and I kept turning them around and even looking on the back to see if there was anything there I was supposed to catch. While he was making his notes, I peeked out of the corner of my eye to read it. But it was all in code that looked like this:

WF+A DdF-Ad orig. WF-A SF+obj

The test still doesn't make sense to me. It seems to me that anyone could make up lies about things that they didn't really see. How could he know I wasn't making a fool of him by mentioning things that I didn't really imagine? Maybe I'll understand it when Dr. Strauss lets me read up on psychology.

April 25 I figured out a new way to line up the machines in the factory, and Mr. Donnegan says it will save him ten thousand dollars a year in labor and increased production. He gave me a twenty-five-dollar bonus.

I wanted to take Joe Carp and Frank Reilly out to lunch to celebrate, but Joe said he had to buy some things for his wife, and Frank said he was meeting his cousin for lunch. I guess it'll take a little time for them to get used to the changes in me. Everybody seems to be frightened of me. When I went over to Amos Borg and tapped him on the shoulder, he jumped up in the air.

People don't talk to me much any more or kid around the way they used to. It makes the job kind of lonely.

April 27 I got up the nerve today to ask Miss Kinnian to have dinner with me tomorrow night to celebrate my bonus.

At first she wasn't sure it was right, but I asked Dr. Strauss and he said it was okay. Dr. Strauss and Dr. Nemur don't seem to be getting along so well. They're arguing all the time. This evening when I came in to ask Dr. Strauss about having dinner with Miss Kinnian, I heard them shouting. Dr. Nemur was saying that it was *his* experiment and *his* research, and Dr. Strauss was shouting back that he contributed just as much, because he found me through Miss Kinnian and he performed the operation. Dr. Strauss said that someday thousands of neurosurgeons[9] might be using his technique all over the world.

Dr. Nemur wanted to publish the results of the experiment at the end of this month. Dr. Strauss wanted to wait a while longer to be sure. Dr. Strauss said that Dr. Nemur was more interested in the Chair of Psychology at Princeton[10] than he was in the experiment. Dr. Nemur said that Dr. Strauss was nothing but an opportunist who was trying to ride to glory on *his* coattails.

When I left afterwards, I found myself trembling. I don't know why for sure, but it was as if I'd seen both men clearly for the first time. I remember hearing Burt say that Dr. Nemur had a shrew[11] of a wife who was pushing him all the time to get things published so that he could become famous. Burt said that the dream of her life was to have a big-shot husband.

Was Dr. Strauss really trying to ride on his coattails?

April 28 I don't understand why I never noticed how beautiful Miss Kinnian really is. She has brown eyes and feathery brown hair that comes to the top of her neck. She's only thirty-four! I think from the

9. The prefix *neuro-* means "nerve," and a *neurosurgeon* (noor ō sur′ jən) performs surgery on part of the body's nervous system.
10. The *Chair of Psychology* is the chairperson of the Psychology Department. *Princeton* is a university in New Jersey.
11. Here, *shrew* means "a bad-tempered, nagging woman."

Vocabulary

opportunist (op′ ər tōō′ nist) *n.* one who takes advantage of every opportunity, regardless of consequences beginning I had the feeling that she was an unreachable genius—and very, very old. Now, every time I see her she grows younger and more lovely.

We had dinner and a long talk. When she said that I was coming along so fast that soon I'd be leaving her behind, I laughed.

"It's true, Charlie. You're already a better reader than I am. You can read a whole page at a glance while I can take in only a few lines at a time. And you remember every single thing you read. I'm lucky if I can recall the main thoughts and the general meaning."

"I don't feel intelligent. There are so many things I don't understand."

She took out a cigarette and I lit it for her. "You've got to be a *little* patient. You're accomplishing in days and weeks what it takes normal people to do in half a lifetime. That's what makes it so amazing. You're like a giant sponge now, soaking things in. Facts, figures, general knowledge. And soon you'll begin to connect them, too. You'll see how the different branches of learning are related. There are many levels, Charlie, like steps on a giant ladder that take you up higher and higher to see more and more of the world around you.

"I can see only a little bit of that, Charlie, and I won't go much higher than I am now, but you'll keep climbing up and up, and see more and more, and each step will open new worlds that you never even knew existed." She frowned. "I hope . . . I just hope to God—"

"What?"

"Never mind, Charles. I just hope I wasn't wrong to advise you to go into this in the first place."

I laughed. "How could that be? It worked, didn't it? Even Algernon is still smart."

We sat there silently for a while and I knew what she was thinking about as she watched me toying with the chain of my rabbit's foot and my keys. I didn't want to think of that possibility any more than elderly people want to think of death. I *knew* that this was only the beginning. I knew what she meant about levels because I'd seen some of them already. The thought of leaving her behind made me sad.

I'm in love with Miss Kinnian.

PROGRESS REPORT 12

April 30 I've quit my job with Donnegan's Plastic Box Company. Mr. Donnegan insisted that it would be better for all concerned if I left. What did I do to make them hate me so?

The first I knew of it was when Mr. Donnegan showed me the petition. Eight hundred and forty names, everyone connected with the factory, except Fanny Girden. Scanning the list quickly, I saw at once that hers was the only missing name. All the rest demanded that I be fired.

Joe Carp and Frank Reilly wouldn't talk to me about it. No one else would either, except Fanny. She was one of the few people I'd known who set her mind to something and believed it no matter what the rest of the world proved, said, or did—and Fanny did not believe that I should have been fired. She had been against the petition on principle and despite the pressure and threats she'd held out.

"Which don't mean to say," she remarked, "that I don't think there's something mighty strange about you, Charlie. Them changes. I don't know. You used to be a good, dependable, ordinary man—not too bright maybe, but honest. Who knows what you done to yourself to get so smart all of a sudden. Like everybody around here's been saying, Charlie, it's not right."

"But how can you say that, Fanny? What's wrong with a man becoming intelligent and wanting to acquire knowledge and understanding of the world around him?"

She stared down at her work and I turned to leave. Without looking at me, she said: "It was evil when Eve listened to the snake and ate from the tree of knowledge. It was evil when she saw that she was naked. If not for that none of us would ever have to grow old and sick, and die."

Once again now I have the feeling of shame burning inside me. This intelligence has driven a wedge between me and all the people I once knew and loved. Before, they laughed at me and despised me for my ignorance and dullness; now, they hate me for my knowledge and understanding. What in God's name do they want of me?

They've driven me out of the factory. Now I'm more alone than ever before . . .

May 15 Dr. Strauss is very angry at me for not having written any progress reports in two weeks. He's justified because the lab is now paying me a regular salary. I told him I was too busy thinking and reading. When I pointed out that writing was such a slow process that it made me impatient with my poor handwriting, he suggested that I learn to type. It's much easier to write now because I can type nearly seventy-five words a minute. Dr. Strauss continually reminds me of the need to speak and write simply so that people will be able to understand me.

I'll try to review all the things that happened to me during the last two weeks. Algernon and I were presented to the American Psychological Association sitting in convention with the World Psychological Association last Tuesday. We created quite a sensation. Dr. Nemur and Dr. Strauss were proud of us.

I suspect that Dr. Nemur, who is sixty—ten years older than Dr. Strauss—finds it necessary to see tangible results of his work. Undoubtedly the result of pressure by Mrs. Nemur.

Contrary to my earlier impressions of him, I realize that Dr. Nemur is not at all a genius. He has a very good mind, but it struggles under the spectre[12] of self-doubt. He

12. A *spectre* is anything that haunts or troubles the mind.

Vocabulary

tangible (tan′ jə bəl) *adj.* able to be seen, touched, or felt; real wants people to take him for a genius. Therefore, it is important for him to feel that his work is accepted by the world. I believe that Dr. Nemur was afraid of further delay because he worried that someone else might make a discovery along these lines and take the credit from him.

Dr. Strauss on the other hand might be called a genius, although I feel that his areas of knowledge are too limited. He was educated in the tradition of narrow specialization; the broader aspects of background were neglected far more than necessary—even for a neurosurgeon.

I was shocked to learn that the only ancient languages he could read were Latin, Greek, and Hebrew, and that he knows almost nothing of mathematics beyond the elementary levels of the calculus of variations.[13] When he admitted this to me, I found myself almost annoyed. It was as if he'd hidden this part of himself in order to deceive me, pretending—as do many people I've discovered—to be what he is not. No one I've ever known is what he appears to be on the surface.

Dr. Nemur appears to be uncomfortable around me. Sometimes when I try to talk to him, he just looks at me strangely and turns away. I was angry at first when Dr. Strauss told me I was giving Dr. Nemur an inferiority complex. I thought he was mocking me and I'm oversensitive at being made fun of.

How was I to know that a highly respected psychoexperimentalist like Nemur was unacquainted with Hindustani[14] and Chinese? It's absurd when you consider the work that is being done in India and China today in the very field of this study.

I asked Dr. Strauss how Nemur could refute[15] Rahajamati's attack on his method and results if Nemur couldn't even read them in the first place. That strange look on Dr. Strauss' face can mean only one of two things. Either he doesn't want to tell Nemur what they're saying in India, or else—and this worries me—Dr. Strauss doesn't know either. I must be careful to speak and write clearly and simply so that people won't laugh.

May 18 I am very disturbed. I saw Miss Kinnian last night for the first time in over a week. I tried to avoid all discussions of intellectual concepts and to keep the conversation on a simple, everyday level, but she just stared at me blankly and asked me what I meant about the mathematical variance equivalent in Dorbermann's *Fifth Concerto*.

When I tried to explain she stopped me and laughed. I guess I got angry, but I suspect I'm approaching her on the wrong level. No matter what I try to discuss with her, I am unable to communicate. I must review Vrostadt's equations on *Levels of Semantic Progression*. I find that I don't communicate with people much any more. Thank God for books and music and things I can think about. I am alone

13. The *calculus of variations* is an advanced mathematical system.

14. *Hindustani* is a language used in India.

15. To *refute* the attack would be to prove that the criticism is false or incorrect.

Vocabulary

intellectual (int′ əl ek′ cho͞o əl) *adj.* appealing to or involving intelligence or mental ability in my apartment at Mrs. Flynn's boardinghouse most of the time and seldom speak to anyone.

May 20 I would not have noticed the new dishwasher, a boy of about sixteen, at the corner diner where I take my evening meals if not for the incident of the broken dishes.

They crashed to the floor, shattering and sending bits of white china under the tables. The boy stood there, dazed and frightened, holding the empty tray in his hand. The whistles and catcalls from the customers (the cries of "hey, there go the profits!" . . . "*Mazeltov!*"[16] . . . and "well, *he* didn't work here very long . . ." which invariably seem to follow the breaking of glass or dishware in a public restaurant) all seemed to confuse him.

When the owner came to see what the excitement was about, the boy cowered as if he expected to be struck and threw up his arms as if to ward off the blow.

"All right! All right, you dope," shouted the owner, "don't just stand there! Get the broom and sweep that mess up. A broom . . . a broom, you idiot! It's in the kitchen. Sweep up all the pieces."

The boy saw that he was not going to be punished. His frightened expression disappeared and he smiled and hummed as he came back with the broom to sweep the floor. A few of the rowdier customers kept up the remarks, amusing themselves at his expense.

"Here, sonny, over here there's a nice piece behind you . . ."

"C'mon, do it again . . ."

"He's not so dumb. It's easier to break 'em than to wash 'em . . ."

As his vacant eyes moved across the crowd of amused onlookers, he slowly mirrored their smiles and finally broke into an uncertain grin at the joke which he obviously did not understand.

I felt sick inside as I looked at his dull, vacuous smile, the wide, bright eyes of a child, uncertain but eager to please. They were laughing at him because he was mentally retarded.

Charly, 1967. Selmur Productions. Movie still.

Viewing the photograph: How does the photo show that Charlie has changed?

16. *Mazeltov* (mäz′ əl tôf′) is a Hebrew word used to express congratulations or best wishes.

Vocabulary

invariably (in vār′ ē ə blē) *adv.* constantly; always

cower (kou′ ər) *v.* to shrink away, as in fear or shame

And I had been laughing at him too.

Suddenly, I was furious at myself and all those who were smirking at him. I jumped up and shouted, "Shut up! Leave him alone! It's not his fault he can't understand! He can't help what he is! But for God's sake . . . he's still a human being!"

The room grew silent. I cursed myself for losing control and creating a scene. I tried not to look at the boy as I paid my check and walked out without touching my food. I felt ashamed for both of us.

How strange it is that people of honest feelings and sensibility, who would not take advantage of a man born without arms or legs or eyes—how such people think nothing of abusing a man born with low intelligence. It infuriated me to think that not too long ago I, like this boy, had foolishly played the clown.

And I had almost forgotten.

It infuriated me to think that not too long ago I, like this boy, had foolishly played the clown.

I'd hidden the picture of the old Charlie Gordon from myself because now that I was intelligent it was something that had to be pushed out of my mind. But today in looking at that boy, for the first time I saw what I had been. *I was just like him!*

Only a short time ago, I learned that people laughed at me. Now I can see that unknowingly I joined with them in laughing at myself. That hurts most of all.

I have often reread my progress reports and seen the illiteracy, the childish naiveté,[17] the mind of low intelligence peering from a dark room, through the keyhole, at the dazzling light outside. I see that even in my dullness I knew that I was inferior, and that other people had something I lacked—something denied me. In my mental blindness, I thought that it was somehow connected with the ability to read and write, and I was sure that if I could get those skills I would automatically have intelligence too.

Even a feeble-minded man wants to be like other men.

A child may not know how to feed itself, or what to eat, yet it knows of hunger.

This then is what I was like, I never knew. Even with my gift of intellectual awareness, I never really knew.

This day was good for me. Seeing the past more clearly, I have decided to use my knowledge and skills to work in the field of increasing human intelligence levels. Who is better equipped for this work? Who else has lived in both worlds? These are my people. Let me use my gift to do something for them.

Tomorrow, I will discuss with Dr. Strauss the manner in which I can work in this area. I may be able to help him work out the problems of widespread use of the technique which was used on me. I have several good ideas of my own.

There is so much that might be done with this technique. If I could be made into a genius, what about thousands of others like myself? What fantastic levels

17. Here, *illiteracy* refers to Charlie's earlier inability to read and write well. *Naiveté* (nä ēv′ tā) is innocence, or lack of worldly knowledge and experience.

might be achieved by using this technique on normal people? On *geniuses?*

There are so many doors to open. I am impatient to begin.

PROGRESS REPORT 13

May 23 It happened today. Algernon bit me. I visited the lab to see him as I do occasionally, and when I took him out of his cage, he snapped at my hand. I put him back and watched him for a while. He was unusually disturbed and vicious.

May 24 Burt, who is in charge of the experimental animals, tells me that Algernon is changing. He is less cooperative; he refuses to run the maze any more; general motivation has decreased. And he hasn't been eating. Everyone is upset about what this may mean.

May 25 They've been feeding Algernon, who now refuses to work the shifting-lock problem. Everyone identifies me with Algernon. In a way we're both the first of our kind. They're all pretending that Algernon's behavior is not necessarily significant for me. But it's hard to hide the fact that some of the other animals who were used in this experiment are showing strange behavior.

Dr. Strauss and Dr. Nemur have asked me not to come to the lab any more. I know what they're thinking but I can't accept it. I am going ahead with my plans to carry their research forward. With all due respect to both of these fine scientists, I am well aware of their limitations. If there is an answer, I'll have to find it out for myself. Suddenly, time has become very important to me.

May 29 I have been given a lab of my own and permission to go ahead with the research. I'm on to something. Working day and night. I've had a cot moved into the lab. Most of my writing time is spent on the notes which I keep in a separate folder, but from time to time I feel it necessary to put down my moods and my thoughts out of sheer habit.

I find the *calculus of intelligence* to be a fascinating study. Here is the place for the application of all the knowledge I have acquired. In a sense it's the problem I've been concerned with all my life.

May 31 Dr. Strauss thinks I'm working too hard. Dr. Nemur says I'm trying to cram a lifetime of research and thought into a few weeks. I know I should rest, but I'm driven on by something inside that won't let me stop. I've got to find the reason for the sharp regression[18] in Algernon. I've got to know *if* and *when* it will happen to me.

June 4

LETTER TO DR. STRAUSS (*copy*)

Dear Dr. Strauss:

Under separate cover I am sending you a copy of my report entitled, "The Algernon-Gordon Effect: A Study of Structure and Function of Increased Intelligence," which I would like to have you read and have published.

As you see, my experiments are completed. I have included in my report all of my formulae, as well as mathematical analysis in the appendix. Of course, these should be verified.

---

18. *Regression* is a return to an earlier, less advanced condition or behavior pattern.

Because of its importance to both you and Dr. Nemur (and need I say to myself, too?) I have checked and rechecked my results a dozen times in the hope of finding an error. I am sorry to say the results must stand. Yet for the sake of science, I am grateful for the little bit that I here add to the knowledge of the function of the human mind and of the laws governing the artificial increase of human intelligence.

I recall your once saying to me that an experimental *failure* or the *disproving* of a theory was as important to the advancement of learning as a success would be. I know now that this is true. I am sorry, however, that my own contribution to the field must rest upon the ashes of the work of two men I regard so highly.

Yours truly,

Charles Gordon
encl.: rept.

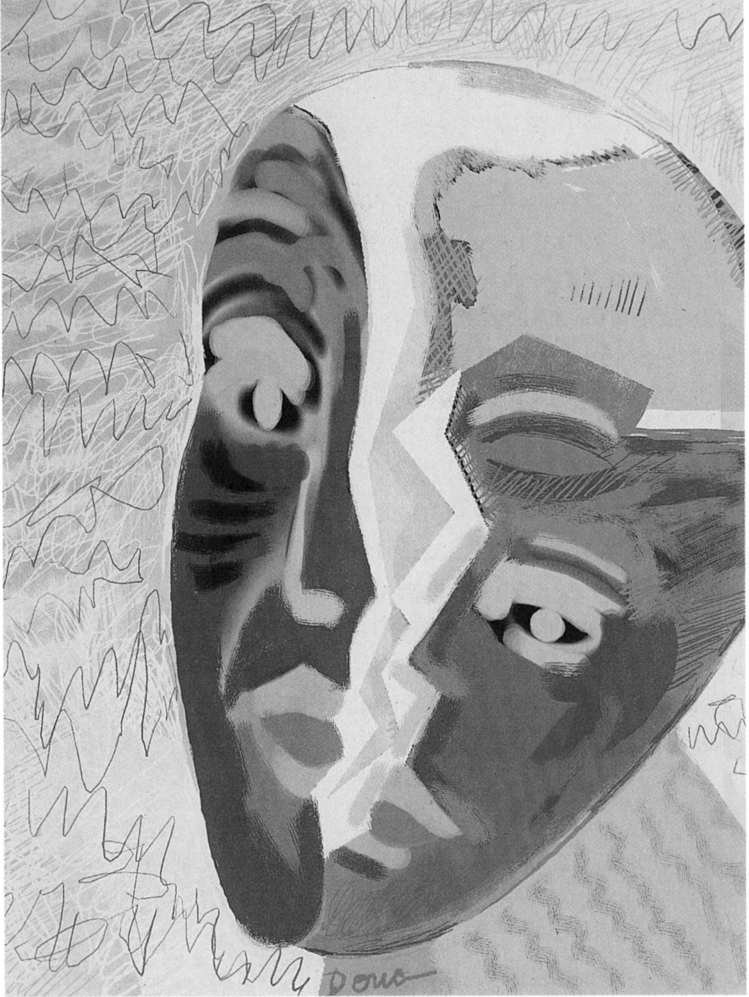

Conversion. Diana Ong. Computer Generated.

Viewing the art: In your opinion, how might this face show what is happening to Charlie?

June 5 I must not become emotional. The facts and the results of my experiments are clear, and the more sensational aspects of my own rapid climb cannot obscure the fact that the tripling of intelligence by the surgical technique developed by Drs. Strauss and Nemur must be viewed as having little or no practical applicability (at the present time) to the increase of human intelligence.

As I review the records and data on Algernon, I see that although he is still in his physical infancy, he has regressed mentally. Motor activity is impaired; there is a general reduction of glandular activity; there is an accelerated loss of co-ordination.

Vocabulary
obscure (əb skyoor′) *v.* to hide
impaired (im pārd′) *adj.* lessened in quality; damaged

There are also strong indications of progressive[19] amnesia.

As will be seen by my report, these and other physical and mental deterioration syndromes[20] can be predicted with statistically significant results by the application of my formula.

The surgical stimulus to which we were both subjected has resulted in an intensification and acceleration of all mental processes. The unforeseen development, which I have taken the liberty of calling the *Algernon-Gordon Effect,* is the logical extension of the entire intelligence speed-up. The hypothesis[21] here proven may be described simply in the following terms: Artificially increased intelligence deteriorates at a rate of time directly proportional to the quantity of the increase.

I feel that this, in itself, is an important discovery.

As long as I am able to write, I will continue to record my thoughts in these progress reports. It is one of my few pleasures. However, by all indications, my own mental deterioration will be very rapid.

I have already begun to notice signs of emotional instability and forgetfulness, the first symptoms of the burnout.

June 10 Deterioration progressing. I have become absentminded. Algernon died two days ago. Dissection shows my predictions were right. His brain had decreased in weight and there was a general smoothing out of cerebral convolutions as well as a deepening and broadening of brain fissures.

I guess the same thing is or will soon be happening to me. Now that it's definite, I don't want it to happen.

I put Algernon's body in a cheese box and buried him in the back yard. I cried.

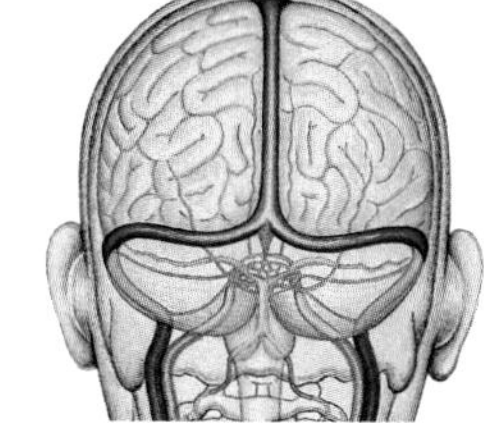

Did You Know?
Charlie has cut up Algernon's brain to study it. A healthy brain surface would have many irregular folds *(convolutions)* and cracks *(fissures)* that are long, narrow, and shallow.

June 15 Dr. Strauss came to see me again. I wouldn't open the door and I told him to go away. I want to be left to myself. I have become touchy and irritable. I feel the darkness closing in. It's hard to throw off thoughts of suicide. I keep telling myself how important this introspective[22] journal will be.

It's a strange sensation to pick up a book that you've read and enjoyed just a few months ago and discover that you don't remember it. I remembered how great I thought John Milton was, but when I picked up *Paradise Lost* I couldn't understand it at all. I got so angry I threw the book across the room.

I've got to try to hold on to some of it. Some of the things I've learned. Oh, God, please don't take it all away.

June 19 Sometimes, at night, I go out for a walk. Last night I couldn't remember where I lived. A policeman took me

19. In this context, *progressive* means "advancing steadily."
20. *Deterioration* means "a worsening," and a *syndrome* is a group of symptoms that, together, indicate a disease. The combined term refers to diseases that result in a lessening of some ability or strength.
21. A *hypothesis* (hī poth′ ə sis) is an unproven idea or theory.
22. *Introspective* means "looking into or examining one's own thoughts and feelings."

Vocabulary
stimulus (stim′ yə ləs) *n.* something that causes a response

home. I have the strange feeling that this has all happened to me before—a long time ago. I keep telling myself I'm the only person in the world who can describe what's happening to me.

June 21 Why can't I remember? I've got to fight. I lie in bed for days and I don't know who or where I am. Then it all comes back to me in a flash. Fugues of amnesia. Symptoms of senility[23]—second childhood. I can watch them coming on. It's so cruelly logical. I learned so much and so fast. Now my mind is deteriorating rapidly. I won't let it happen. I'll fight it. I can't help thinking of the boy in the restaurant, the blank expression, the silly smile, the people laughing at him. No—please—not that again . . .

June 22 I'm forgetting things that I learned recently. It seems to be following the classic pattern—the last things learned are the first things forgotten. Or is that the pattern? I'd better look it up again . . .

I reread my paper on the *Algernon-Gordon Effect* and I get the strange feeling that it was written by someone else. There are parts I don't even understand.

Motor activity impaired. I keep tripping over things, and it becomes increasingly difficult to type.

23. In psychiatry, a *fugue* (fūg) *of amnesia* is a condition during which a person seems to be aware of his or her actions but can't recall them later. *Senility* (si nil′ ə tē) refers to the loss of physical and mental abilities that can accompany old age.

June 23 I've given up using the typewriter completely. My coordination is bad. I feel that I'm moving slower and slower. Had a terrible shock today. I picked up a copy of an article I used in my research, Krueger's *Uber psychische Ganzheit,* to see if it would help me understand what I had done. First I thought there was something wrong with my eyes. Then I realized I could no longer read German. I tested myself in other languages. All gone.

I keep telling myself I must keep writing these reports so that somebody will know what is happening to me.

June 30 A week since I dared to write again. It's slipping away like sand through my fingers. Most of the books I have are too hard for me now. I get angry with them because I know that I read and understood them just a few weeks ago.

I keep telling myself I must keep writing these reports so that somebody will know what is happening to me. But it gets harder to form the words and remember spellings. I have to look up even simple words in the dictionary now and it makes me impatient with myself.

Dr. Strauss comes around almost every day, but I told him I wouldn't see or speak to anybody. He feels guilty. They all do. But I don't blame anyone. I knew what might happen. But how it hurts.

July 7 I don't know where the week went. Todays Sunday I know because I can see through my window people going to church. I think I stayed in bed all week but I remember Mrs. Flynn bringing food to me a few times. I keep saying over and over Ive got to do something but then I forget or maybe its just easier not to do what I say Im going to do.

I think of my mother and father a lot these days. I found a picture of them with me taken at a beach. My father has a big ball under his arm and my mother is holding me by the hand. I dont remember them the way they are in the picture. All I remember is my father drunk most of the time and arguing with mom about money.

He never shaved much and he used to scratch my face when he hugged me. My mother said he died but Cousin Miltie said he heard his mom and dad say that my father ran away with another woman. When I asked my mother she slapped my face and said my father was dead. I dont think I ever found out which was true but I don't care much. (He said he was going to take me to see cows on a farm once but he never did. He never kept his promises . . .)

July 10 My landlady Mrs Flynn is very worried about me. She says the way I lay around all day and dont do anything I remind her of her son before she threw him out of the house. She said she doesnt like loafers. If Im sick its one thing, but if Im a loafer thats another thing and she wont have it. I told her I think Im sick.

I try to read a little bit every day, mostly stories, but sometimes I have to read the same thing over and over again because I dont know what it means. And its hard to write. I know I should look up all the words in the dictionary but its so hard and Im so tired all the time.

Then I got the idea that I would only use the easy words instead of the long hard ones. That saves time. I put flowers on Algernons grave about once a week. Mrs Flynn thinks Im crazy to put flowers on a mouses grave but I told her that Algernon was special.

July 14 Its sunday again. I dont have anything to do to keep me busy now because my television set is broke and I dont have any money to get it fixed. (I think I lost this months check from the lab. I dont remember)

I get awful headaches and asperin doesnt help me much. Mrs Flynn knows Im really sick and she feels very sorry for me. Shes a wonderful woman whenever someone is sick.

July 22 Mrs Flynn called a strange doctor to see me. She was afraid I was going to die. I told the doctor I wasnt too sick and that I only forget sometimes. He asked me did I have any friends or relatives and I said no I dont have any. I told him I had a friend called Algernon once but he was a mouse and we used to run races together. He looked at me kind of funny like he thought I was crazy.

He smiled when I told him I used to be a genius. He talked to me like I was a baby and he winked at Mrs Flynn. I got mad and chased him out because he was making fun of me the way they all used to.

July 24 I have no more money and Mrs Flynn says I got to go to work somewhere and pay the rent because I havent paid for over two months. I dont know any work but the job I used to have at Donnegans Plastic Box Company. I dont want to go back there because they all knew me when I was smart and maybe theyll laugh at me. But I dont know what else to do to get money.

July 25 I was looking at some of my old progress reports and its very funny but I cant read what I wrote. I can make out some of the words but they dont make sense.

Miss Kinnian came to the door but I said go away I dont want to see you. She cried and I cried too but I wouldnt let her in because I didnt want her to laugh at me. I told her I didn't like her any more. I told her I didnt want to be smart any more. Thats not true. I still love her and I still want to be smart but I had to say that so shed go away. She gave Mrs Flynn money to pay the rent. I dont want that. I got to get a job.

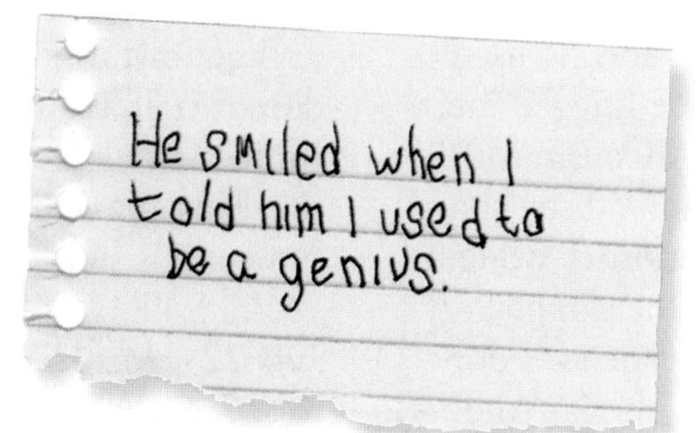
He smiled when I
told him I used to
be a genius.

Please . . . please let me not forget how to read and write . . .

July 27 Mr Donnegan was very nice when I came back and asked him for my old job of janitor. First he was very suspicious but I told him what happened to me then he looked very sad and put his hand on my shoulder and said Charlie Gordon you got guts.

Everybody looked at me when I came downstairs and started working in the toilet sweeping it out like I used to. I told myself Charlie if they make fun of you dont get sore because you remember their not so smart as you once thot they were. And besides they were once your friends and if they laughed at you that doesnt mean anything because they liked you too.

One of the new men who came to work there after I went away made a nasty crack he said hey Charlie I hear your a very smart fella a real quiz kid. Say something intelligent. I felt bad but Joe Carp came over and grabbed him by the shirt and said leave him alone you lousy cracker or Ill break your neck. I didnt expect Joe to take my part so I guess hes really my friend.

Later Frank Reilly came over and said Charlie if anybody bothers you or trys to take advantage you call me or Joe and we will set em straight. I said thanks Frank and I got choked up so I had to turn around and go into the supply room so he wouldnt see me cry. Its good to have friends.

July 28 I did a dumb thing today I forgot I wasnt in Miss Kinnians class at the adult center any more like I use to be. I went in and sat down in my old seat in the back of the room and she looked at me funny and she said Charles. I dint remember she ever called me that before only Charlie so I said hello Miss Kinnian Im redy for my lesin today only I lost my reader that we was using. She startid to cry and run out of the room and everybody looked at me and I saw they wasnt the same pepul who used to be in my class.

Then all of a suddin I rememberd some things about the operashun and me getting smart and I said holy smoke I reely pulled a Charlie Gordon that time. I went away before she come back to the room.

Thats why Im going away from New York for good. I dont want to do nothing

Tulips and an Iris, mid-17th century. Attributed to the Master of the Borders Mughal. Opaque watercolor on paper. Folio 12⅝ x 8 in. (26.4 x 16.1 cm.)

Viewing the painting: Why might this painting of three flowers be a symbol for Charlie's life?

like that agen. I dont want Miss Kinnian to feel sorry for me. Evry body feels sorry at the factery and I dont want that eather so Im going someplace where nobody knows that Charlie Gordon was once a genus and now he cant even reed a book or rite good.

Im taking a cuple of books along and even if I cant reed them Ill practise hard and maybe I wont forget every thing I lerned. If I try reel hard maybe Ill be a littel bit smarter than I was before the operashun. I got my rabits foot and my luky penny and maybe they will help me.

If you ever reed this Miss Kinnian dont be sorry for me Im glad I got a second chanse to be smart becaus I lerned a lot of things that I never even new were in this world and Im grateful that I saw it all for a littel bit. I dont know why Im dumb agen or what I did wrong maybe its becaus I dint try hard enuff. But if I try and practis very hard maybe Ill get a littl smarter and know what all the words are. I remember a littel bit how nice I had a feeling with the blue book that has the torn cover when I red it. Thats why Im gonna keep trying to get smart so I can have that feeling agen. Its a good feeling to know things and be smart. I wish I had it rite now if I did I would sit down and reed all the time. Anyway I bet Im the first dumb person in the world who ever found out something importent for sience. I remember I did somthing but I dont remember what. So I gess its like I did it for all the dumb pepul like me.

Good-by Miss Kinnian and Dr. Strauss and evreybody. And P.S. please tell Dr Nemur not to be such a grouch when pepul laff at him and he woud have more frends. Its easy to make frends if you let pepul laff at you. Im going to have lots of frends where I go.

P.P.S. Please if you get a chanse put some flowrs on Algernons grave in the bak yard . . .

Responding to Literature

PERSONAL RESPONSE

- If you could talk with Charlie before he leaves New York City, what would you want to say to him? Explain your answer.
- Think of a time when you felt like avoiding people after a failure. What helped you overcome your feelings?

Analyzing Literature

RECALL

1. In the entry dated May 20, what does Charlie realize about "smart" people and himself?
2. What are some of the first things Charlie loses when the experiment starts to fail? What does he fear losing the most?
3. List the people in Charlie's life. Explain briefly what each thinks about Charlie at the beginning of the story and at the end.
4. Why does Charlie decide to leave New York City?

INTERPRET

5. How does the author show Charlie's increasing intelligence? Provide examples from the story.
6. Do you think Charlie's other types of "intelligence" increase or decrease? Give examples to support your answer.
7. Theme Connection Charlie feels very cut off from other people. Consider how other people feel about Charlie at the end of the story. Do you think he should feel as lonesome as he does? Why or why not?
8. At the end, does Charlie have a better or worse view of himself? Support your opinion with examples.

EVALUATE AND CONNECT

9. Look back at the **Literary Element** on **irony** on page 124. How does Keyes use irony in the last part of the story? Find several examples.
10. Think of a time when someone you admired let you down. How would you talk about that person now? Explain.

LITERARY ELEMENTS

Foreshadowing

Foreshadowing is the planting of clues to prepare readers for events that will happen later. Daniel Keyes uses foreshadowing when he has Miss Kinnian say to Charlie,

> **". . . I just hope I wasn't wrong to advise you to go into this in the first place."**

Foreshadowing can add suspense. For example, it can be used to warn readers that the story may take an unexpected turn.

1. Look over the story and list some of the statements and actions that foreshadow the failure of the experiment.
2. Would the story have been better if the failure had come as a complete surprise? Explain.

- See **Literary Terms Handbook,** p. R4.

Literature and Writing

Writing About Literature 

Style In the story, Daniel Keyes uses a unique style of punctuation, spelling, and grammar to show the changes in Charlie's personality and mental development. Write a brief explanation of how these style elements work in the story. For example, did they help you understand the main character and the story better or did they interfere with reading? Give examples from the story to support your response.

Creative Writing 

Letter Writing Look over your notes from the **Focus Activity** on page 112 about what you would gain and lose by becoming smarter or more talented than your classmates. Write a letter to the "new" you from a best friend or family member. Address these questions: How do people feel about you as you change? What do they see you doing? Do they try to keep up with you? What happens in the end? If you wish, share your work with the class.

Extending Your Response

Literature Groups 

Fitting In–at What Price? Charlie's desire to be like everyone else motivates him to have an operation. In a group, discuss these questions: Why did Charlie have to change? Why didn't the other people change? Share your answers with other groups.

interNET CONNECTION

Animals On-line How much can animals learn? How much of their behavior is based on instinct? Find out by gathering information on the Internet. Hold a class discussion to talk about your findings.

Art Activity 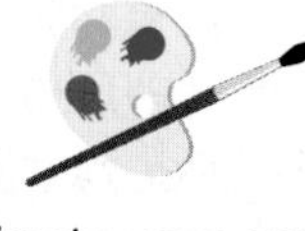

Seeing Spots Create your own Rorschach ink blot cards, using blank index cards, water color, ink, or acrylics. Dab some ink or paint on the center of a card. Fold the card in half with the ink on the inside. Open the card and let it dry. How many images do you see in each card? List the different images, and share your cards with the class to get more responses.

Reading Further 

You might enjoy these works about experiments and the characters involved in them.

Mary Shelley, *Frankenstein* (Learning Channel's Great Books)

Robert O'Brien, *Mrs. Frisby and the Rats of NIMH*

Benjamin Mikaelsen, *Rescue Josh McGuire*

Save your work for your portfolio.

Skill Minilessons

GRAMMAR AND LANGUAGE • SPELLING

Homophones are words that sound alike but are spelled differently and have different meanings. Examples are *threw* and *through, wrap* and *rap,* and *pier* and *peer.* Homophones are often misused. Notice that Charlie uses some homophones incorrectly in "Flowers for Algernon."

Avoid spelling errors by using the correct homophone.

PRACTICE Substitute the correct word for each boldfaced word.

1. He took **they're** tests and **red** the notes.
2. Dr. Nemur **herd** him come up the **stares.**
3. He said he **wood right** in his journal.
4. They used **plane** paper in **there** book.

• For more about spelling, see **Language Handbook,** pp. R21–R26.

READING AND THINKING • CAUSE AND EFFECT

Many events in stories are connected by cause-and-effect relationships. Each event causes other events to happen.

• For more about cause and effect, see **Reading Handbook,** p. R87.

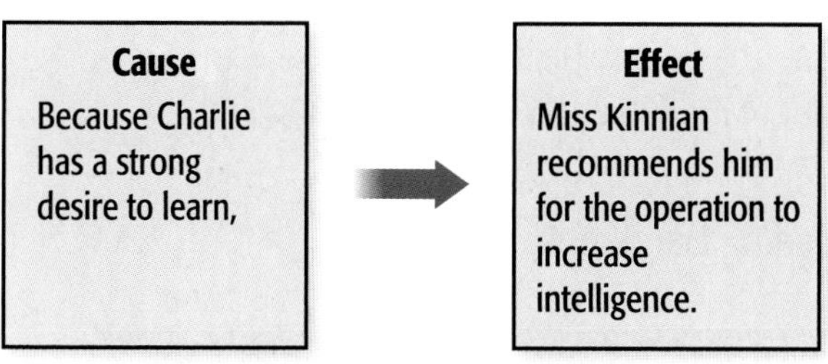

Cause		**Effect**
Because Charlie has a strong desire to learn,	→	Miss Kinnian recommends him for the operation to increase intelligence.

PRACTICE Copy and complete the following cause-and-effect chart.

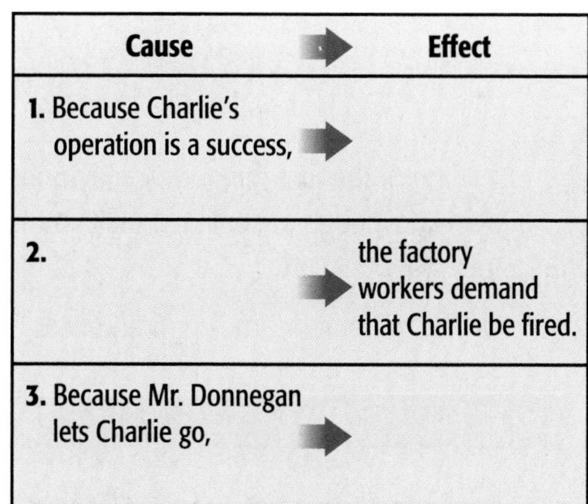

Cause	→	**Effect**
1. Because Charlie's operation is a success,	→	
2.	→	the factory workers demand that Charlie be fired.
3. Because Mr. Donnegan lets Charlie go,	→	

VOCABULARY • ETYMOLOGY

The history of a word is called its **etymology**. Some English words, such as *stimulus,* have simple and clear histories. Not only is *stimulus* spelled exactly like the original Latin word, but the Latin *stimulus* means "a sharp-pointed stick or spur."

It takes more thought to understand the etymologies of other words. *Intellectual* comes from Latin words that mean "choose" and "between." An intellectual person knows how to choose and is good at deciding which ideas to keep and which to reject.

PRACTICE Read the following etymologies. For each word, briefly explain how its historical meaning is tied to its current meaning.

obscure: from the Latin word *obscurus,* which means "covered over"

motivation: from the French *motif,* which comes from the Latin *movere,* meaning "to move"

tangible: from the Latin *tangibilis*, which means "to touch"

Making Inferences

An **inference** is an educated guess that a reader makes after connecting his or her own knowledge with information presented in a selection. Writers often use facts and events to imply, or hint at, an idea without saying it outright. Good readers can read between the lines and use what they know to figure out what the writer is hinting at. What idea about Charlie does the writer of "Flowers for Algernon" imply in the following passage from one of Charlie's progress reports?

> Dr Strauss says I shud rite down what I think and evrey thing that happins to me from now on. I dont know why but he says its importint so they will see if they will use me.

One of the first things you may notice is that Charlie misspells several words. Your own knowledge of spelling helps you figure out that Charlie has difficulty writing and may not be smart.

- For more about making inferences, see **Reading Handbook,** p. R91.

EXERCISE

Read the excerpt below from "Flowers for Algernon." Then answer the questions.

> We had a lot of fun at the factery today. Joe Carp said hey look where Charlie had his operashun what did they do Charlie put some brains in. I was going to tell him but I remembered Dr Strauss said no. Then Frank Reilly said what did you do Charlie forget your key and open your door the hard way. That made me laff. Their really my friends and they like me.

1. What inferences can you make about Charlie's appearance? What clues helped you to make those inferences?
2. What inference can you make about how Joe Carp and Frank Reilly feel about Charlie? How does your own experience help you make this inference?

Before You Read

The Kid Nobody Could Handle

MEET
KURT VONNEGUT

Kurt Vonnegut says that he can't stand to read what he writes. "I make my wife do that, then ask her to keep her opinions to herself," he says. Despite his own criticism, Vonnegut is one of the most popular authors of his generation. He is known for his fantasy and humor, as well as his beliefs in human dignity, hope, and free will. Vonnegut encourages young readers to think locally. "Write poetry for someone you like," he says. "Serve your community and be content with your success within it."

Kurt Vonnegut was born in 1922. This story was published in 1968 in Welcome to the Monkey House.

FOCUS ACTIVITY

Why do some people give up on a task while others never quit trying?

QuickWrite

List activities, people, or things in your life that take up your time but make you happy. Compare your list with a partner.

Setting a Purpose

Read to discover how one character works to help another find happiness.

BACKGROUND

The Time and Place This story is set in a small town and features a character who has just moved from Chicago to live with a relative.

Did You Know? John Philip Sousa is among the most famous names in band music and is appropriately called the March King for the 140 marches he composed in the late 1800s. Sousa is best known for his military music and for his years as leader of the U.S. Marine Band.

VOCABULARY PREVIEW

unnerving (un nurv′ ing) *adj.* causing nervousness or upset; disturbing; p. 147
arrogant (ar′ ə gənt) *adj.* full of self-importance; too proud; p. 147
diversion (di vur′ zhən) *n.* something that draws the attention away; distraction; p. 148
appalled (ə pôld′) *adj.* shocked; horrified; p. 148
quest (kwest) *n.* a search made to achieve a goal; p. 151
furtive (fur′ tiv) *adj.* secret; shifty; sly; p. 152
bravado (brə vä′ dō) *n.* a false show of bravery; pretended courage; p. 152
remorse (ri môrs′) *n.* a deep, painful feeling of guilt or sorrow for wrongdoing; p. 153
futility (fū til′ ə tē) *n.* uselessness; hopelessness; p. 155

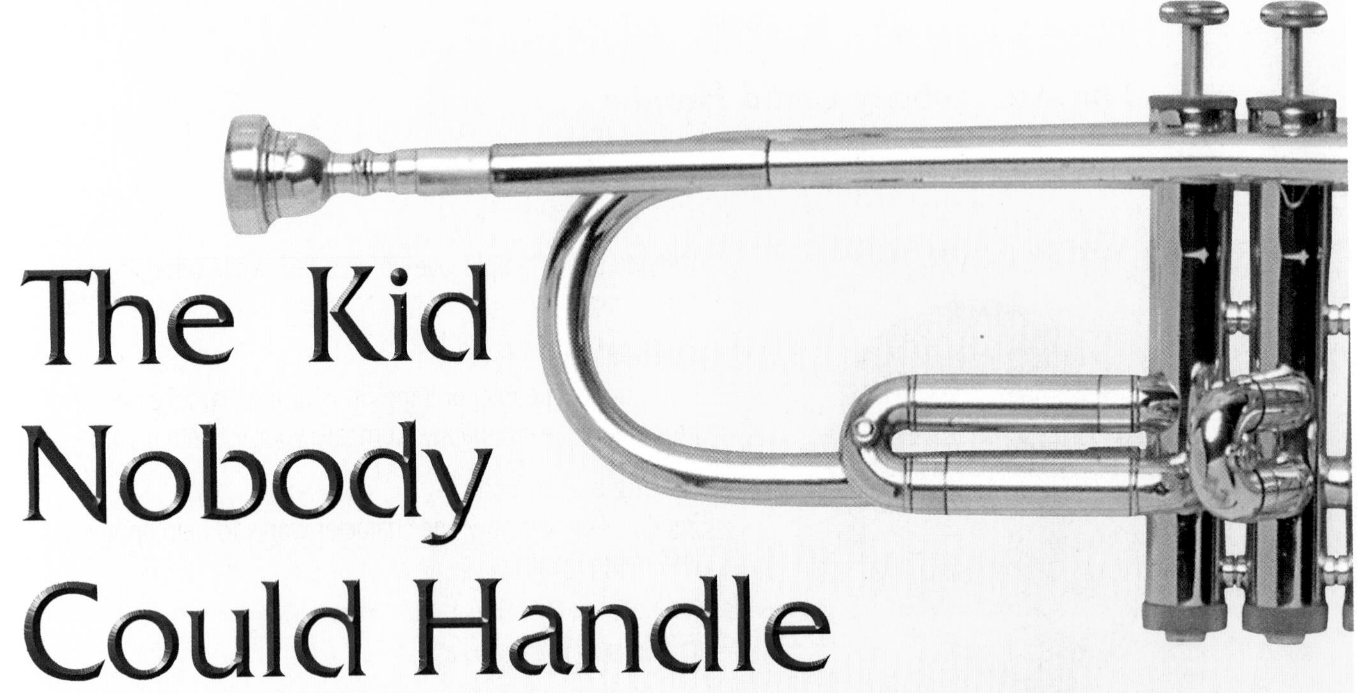

The Kid Nobody Could Handle

Kurt Vonnegut

It was seven-thirty in the morning. Waddling, clanking, muddy machines were tearing a hill to pieces behind a restaurant, and trucks were hauling the pieces away. Inside the restaurant, dishes rattled on their shelves. Tables quaked, and a very kind fat man with a headful of music looked down at the jiggling yolks of his breakfast eggs. His wife was visiting relatives out of town. He was on his own.

The kind fat man was George M. Helmholtz, a man of forty, head of the music department of Lincoln High School, and director of the band. Life had treated him well. Each year he dreamed the same big dream. He dreamed of leading as fine a band as there was on the face of the earth. And each year the dream came true.

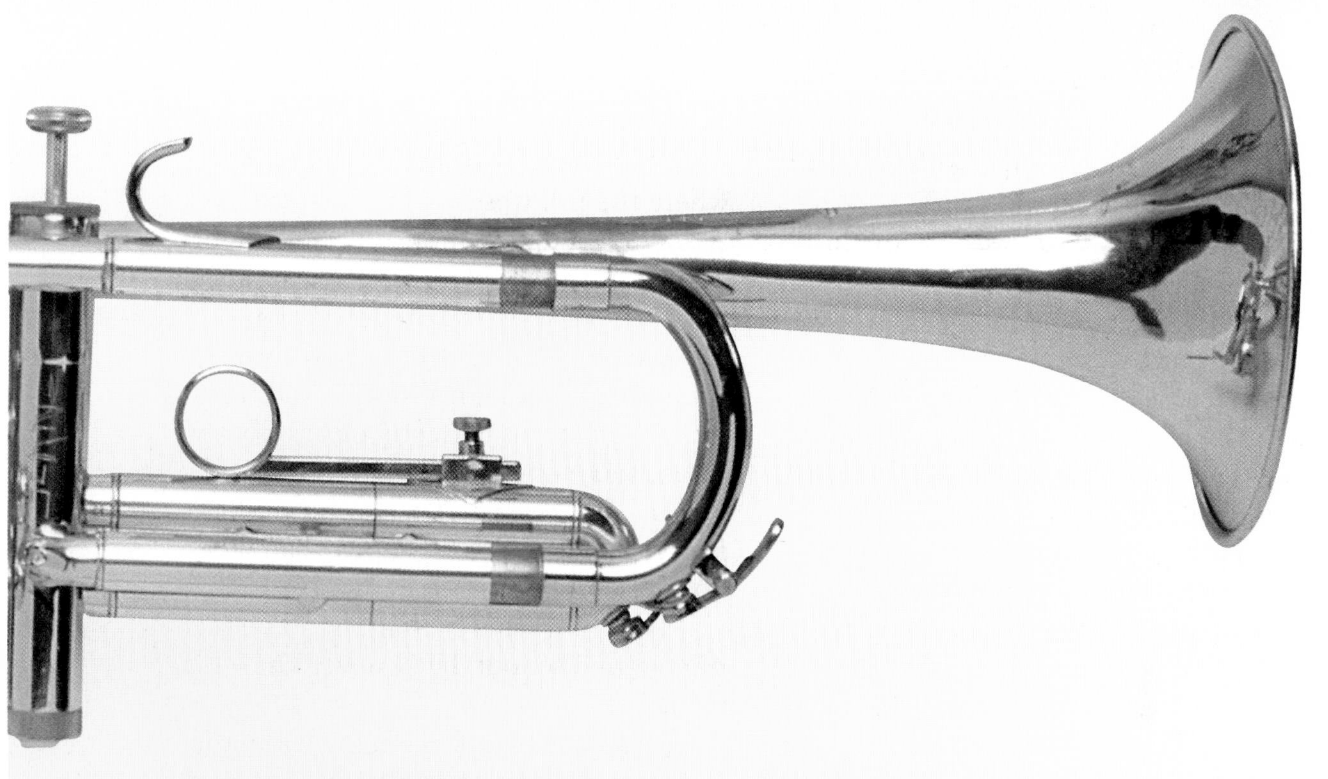

It came true because Helmholtz was sure that a man couldn't have a better dream than his. Faced by this unnerving sureness, Kiwanians, Rotarians, and Lions[1] paid for band uniforms that cost twice as much as their best suits, school administrators let Helmholtz raid the budget for expensive props, and youngsters played their hearts out for him. When youngsters had no talent, Helmholtz made them play on guts alone.

Everything was good about Helmholtz's life save his finances. He was so dazzled by his big dream that he was a child in the marketplace. Ten years before, he had sold the hill behind the restaurant to Bert Quinn, the restaurant owner, for one thousand dollars. It was now apparent, even to Helmholtz, that Helmholtz had been had.[2]

Quinn sat down in the booth with the bandmaster. He was a bachelor, a small, dark, humorless man. He wasn't a well man. He couldn't sleep, he couldn't stop working, he couldn't smile warmly. He had only two moods: one suspicious and self-pitying, the other arrogant and boastful. The first mood applied when he was losing money. The second mood applied when he was making it.

Quinn was in the arrogant and boastful mood when he sat down with Helmholtz.

1. The *Kiwanians, Rotarians, and Lions* are members of the Kiwanis, Rotary, and Lions clubs, groups of business and professional people who work to do good things for a community.

2. *[been had]* The expression *to be had* means "to be cheated or deceived."

Vocabulary

unnerving (un nurv′ ing) *adj.* causing nervousness or upset; disturbing

arrogant (ar′ ə gənt) *adj.* full of self-importance; too proud

He sucked whistlingly on a toothpick, and talked of vision—his own.

"I wonder how many eyes saw the hill before I did?" said Quinn. "Thousands and thousands, I'll bet—and not one saw what I saw. How many eyes?"

"Mine, at least," said Helmholtz. All the hill had meant to him was a panting climb, free blackberries, taxes, and a place for band picnics.

"You inherit the hill from your old man, and it's nothing but a pain in the neck to you," said Quinn. "So you figure you'll stick me with it."

"I didn't figure to stick you," Helmholtz protested. "The good Lord knows the price was more than fair."

"You say that now," said Quinn gleefully. "Sure, Helmholtz, you say that now. Now you see the shopping district's got to grow. Now you see what I saw."

"Yes," said Helmholtz. "Too late, too late." He looked around for some diversion, and saw a fifteen-year-old boy coming toward him, mopping the aisle between booths.

The boy was small but with tough, stringy muscles standing out on his neck and forearms. Childhood lingered in his features, but when he paused to rest, his fingers went hopefully to the silky beginnings of sideburns and a mustache. He mopped like a robot, jerkily, brainlessly, but took pains not to splash suds over the toes of his black boots.

"So what do I do when I get the hill?" said Quinn. "I tear it down, and it's like somebody pulled down a dam. All of a sudden everybody wants to build a store where the hill was."

"Um," said Helmholtz. He smiled genially at the boy. The boy looked through him without a twitch of recognition.

"We all got something," said Quinn. "You got music; I got vision." And he smiled, for it was perfectly clear to both where the money lay. "Think big!" said Quinn. "Dream big! That's what vision is. Keep your eyes wider open than anybody else's."

"That boy," said Helmholtz, "I've seen him around school, but I never knew his name."

Quinn laughed cheerlessly. "Billy the Kid? The storm trooper? Rudolph Valentino? Flash Gordon?"[3] He called the boy. . . . "Hey, Jim! Come here a minute."

Helmholtz was appalled to see that the boy's eyes were as expressionless as oysters.

"This is my brother-in-law's kid by another marriage—before he married my sister," said Quinn. "His name's Jim Donnini, and he's from the south side of Chicago, and he's very tough."

Jim Donnini's hands tightened on the mop handle.

"How do you do?" said Helmholtz.

"Hi," said Jim emptily.

"He's living with me now," said Quinn. "He's my baby now."

"You want a lift to school, Jim?"

3. *Billy the Kid* was a legendary Wild West gunslinger. A *storm trooper* was a member of a military organization in Nazi Germany known for its cruelty and savagery. *Rudolph Valentino* played the romantic hero in many early movies, and *Flash Gordon* is a comic book hero.

Vocabulary

diversion (di vur′ zhən) *n.* something that draws the attention away; distraction

appalled (ə pôld′) *adj.* shocked; horrified

Le Modèle Rouge (The Red Model), 1935. René Magritte.
Viewing the painting: How might these boots be a symbol for Jim?

"Not very funny, sometimes," said Helmholtz. He pushed his eggs away.

"Like some whole new race of people coming up," said Quinn wonderingly. "Nothing like the kids we got around here. Those boots, the black jacket—and he won't talk. He won't run around with the other kids. Won't study. I don't think he can even read and write very good."

"Does he like music at all? Or drawing? Or animals?" said Helmholtz. "Does he collect anything?"

"You know what he likes?" said Quinn. "He likes to polish those boots—get off by himself and polish those boots. And when he's really in heaven is when he can get off by himself, spread comic books all around him on the floor, polish his boots, and watch television." He smiled ruefully.[4] "Yeah, he had a collection too. And I took it away from him and threw it in the river."

"Threw it in the river?" said Helmholtz.

"Yeah," said Quinn. "Eight knives—some with blades as long as your hand."

Helmholtz paled. "Oh." A prickling sensation spread over the back of his neck. "This is a new problem at Lincoln High. I hardly know what to think about it." He swept spilled salt together in a neat little pile, just as he would have liked to sweep together his scattered thoughts. "It's a kind

"Yeah, he wants a lift to school," said Quinn. "See what you make of him. He won't talk to me." He turned to Jim. "Go on, kid, wash up and shave."

Robotlike, Jim marched away.

"Where are his parents?"

"His mother's dead. His old man married my sister, walked out on her, and stuck her with him. Then the court didn't like the way she was raising him, and put him in foster homes for a while. Then they decided to get him clear out of Chicago, so they stuck me with him." He shook his head. "Life's a funny thing, Helmholtz."

4. *Ruefully* means "regretfully."

of sickness, isn't it? That's the way to look at it?"

"Sick?" said Quinn. He slapped the table. "You can say that again!" He tapped his chest. "And Doctor Quinn is just the man to give him what's good for what ails him."

"What's that?" said Helmholtz.

"No more talk about the poor little sick boy," said Quinn grimly. "That's all he's heard from the social workers and the juvenile court, and God knows who all. From now on, he's the no-good bum of a man. I'll ride his tail till he straightens up and flies right or winds up in the can for life. One way or the other."

"I see," said Helmholtz.

"Like listening to music?" said Helmholtz to Jim brightly, as they rode to school in Helmholtz's car.

Jim said nothing. He was stroking his mustache and sideburns, which he had not shaved off.

"Ever drum with the fingers or keep time with your feet?" said Helmholtz. He had noticed that Jim's boots were decorated with chains that had no function but to jingle as he walked.

Jim sighed with ennui.[5]

"Or whistle?" said Helmholtz. "If you do any of those things, it's just like picking up the keys to a whole new world—a world as beautiful as any world can be."

Jim gave a soft Bronx cheer.[6]

"There!" said Helmholtz. "You've illustrated the basic principle of the family of brass wind instruments. The glorious voice of every one of them starts with a buzz on the lips."

5. *Ennui* (än wē') means "boredom."

6. A *Bronx cheer* is an expression of scorn or ridicule, not of good will or good wishes.

The seat springs of Helmholtz's old car creaked under Jim, as Jim shifted his weight. Helmholtz took this as a sign of interest, and he turned to smile in comradely fashion. But Jim had shifted his weight in order to get a cigarette from inside his tight leather jacket.

Helmholtz was too upset to comment at once. It was only at the end of the ride, as he turned into the teachers' parking lot, that he thought of something to say.

"Sometimes," said Helmholtz, "I get so lonely and disgusted, I don't see how I can stand it. I feel like doing all kinds of crazy things, just for the heck of it—things that might even be bad for me."

Jim blew a smoke ring expertly.

"And then!" said Helmholtz. He snapped his fingers and honked his horn. "And then, Jim, I remember I've got at least one tiny corner of the universe I can make just the way I want it! I can go to it and gloat over it until I'm brand-new and happy again."

"Aren't you the lucky one?" said Jim. He yawned.

"I am, for a fact," said Helmholtz. "My corner of the universe happens to be the air around my band. I can fill it with music. Mr. Beeler, in zoology, has his butterflies. Mr. Trottman, in physics, has his pendulum and tuning forks. Making sure everybody has a corner like that is about the biggest job we teachers have. I—"

The car door opened and slammed, and Jim was gone. Helmholtz stamped out Jim's cigarette and buried it under the gravel of the parking lot.

Helmholtz's first class of the morning was C Band, where beginners thumped and wheezed and tooted as best they could, and looked down the long, long, long road through B Band to A Band, the Lincoln High School Ten Square Band, the finest band in the world.

Helmholtz stepped onto the podium and raised his baton. "You are better than you think," he said. "A-one, a-two, a-three." Down came the baton.

C Band set out in its quest for beauty—set out like a rusty switch engine, with valves stuck, pipes clogged, unions leaking, bearings dry.

Helmholtz was still smiling at the end of the hour, because he'd heard in his mind the music as it was going to be someday. His throat was raw, for he had been singing with the band for the whole hour. He stepped into the hall for a drink from the fountain.

As he drank, he heard the jingling of chains. He looked up at Jim Donnini. Rivers of students flowed between classrooms, pausing in friendly eddies,[7] flowing on again. Jim was alone. When he paused, it wasn't to greet anyone, but to polish the toes of his boots on his trousers legs. He had the air of a spy in a melodrama, missing nothing, liking nothing, looking forward to the great day when everything would be turned upside down.

He had the air of a spy in a melodrama, missing nothing, liking nothing, looking forward to the great day when everything would be turned upside down.

"Hello, Jim," said Helmholtz. "Say, I was just thinking about you. We've got a lot of clubs and teams that meet after school. And that's a good way to get to know a lot of people."

Jim measured Helmholtz carefully with his eyes. "Maybe I don't want to know a lot of people," he said. "Ever think of that?" He set his feet down hard to make his chains jingle as he walked away.

When Helmholtz returned to the podium for a rehearsal of B Band, there was a note waiting for him, calling him to a special faculty meeting.

The meeting was about vandalism.

Someone had broken into the school and wrecked the office of Mr. Crane, head of the English Department. The poor man's treasures—books, diplomas, snapshots of England, the beginnings of eleven novels—had been ripped and crumpled, mixed, dumped and trampled, and drenched with ink.

Helmholtz was sickened. He couldn't believe it. He couldn't bring himself to think about it. It didn't become real to him until late that night, in a dream. In the dream Helmholtz saw a boy with barracuda teeth, with claws like baling hooks. The monster climbed into a window of the high school and dropped to

7. *Eddies* are circular currents of wind or water. The students were stopping to socialize in small groups and then moving on.

Vocabulary

quest (kwest) *n.* a search made to achieve a goal

the floor of the band rehearsal room. The monster clawed to shreds the heads of the biggest drum in the state. Helmholtz woke up howling. There was nothing to do but dress and go to school.

At two in the morning, Helmholtz caressed the drum heads in the band rehearsal room, with the night watchman looking on. He rolled the drum back and forth on its cart, and he turned the light inside on and off, on and off. The drum was unharmed. The night watchman left to make his rounds.

The band's treasure house was safe. With the contentment of a miser counting his money, Helmholtz fondled the rest of the instruments, one by one. And then he began to polish the sousaphones. As he polished, he could hear the great horns roaring, could see them flashing in the sunlight, with the Stars and Stripes and the banner of Lincoln High going before.

Did You Know?
A *sousaphone* (sōō′ zə fōn′), a large circular tuba with a wide bell that faces forward, is named for John Philip Sousa.

"Yump-yump, tiddle-tiddle, yump-yump, tiddle-tiddle!" sang Helmholtz happily. "Yump-yump-yump, ra-a-a-a-a, yump-yump, yump-yump—boom!"

As he paused to choose the next number for his imaginary band to play, he heard a furtive noise in the chemistry laboratory next door. Helmholtz sneaked into the hall, jerked open the laboratory door, and flashed on the lights. Jim Donnini had a bottle of acid in either hand. He was splashing acid over the periodic table of the elements, over the blackboards covered with formulas, over the bust of Lavoisier.[8] The scene was the most repulsive thing Helmholtz could have looked upon.

Jim smiled with thin bravado.

"Get out," said Helmholtz.

"What're you gonna do?" said Jim.

"Clean up. Save what I can," said Helmholtz dazedly. He picked up a wad of cotton waste and began wiping up the acid.

"You gonna call the cops?" said Jim.

"I—I don't know," said Helmholtz. "No thoughts come. If I'd caught you hurting the bass drum, I think I would have killed you with a single blow. But I wouldn't have had any intelligent thoughts about what you were—what you thought you were doing."

"It's about time this place got set on its ear," said Jim.

"Is it?" said Helmholtz. "That must be so, if one of our students wants to murder it."

"What good is it?" said Jim.

"Not much good, I guess," said Helmholtz. "It's just the best thing human beings ever managed to do." He was helpless, talking to himself. He had a bag of tricks for making boys behave like men—tricks that played on boyish fears

8. The *periodic table* is a chart showing all known chemical elements. The *bust of Lavoisier* (lä vwä zyā′) is a statue of the 18th-century French scientist known as the founder of modern chemistry, who lived during the 1700s.

Vocabulary

furtive (fur′ tiv) *adj.* secret; shifty; sly

bravado (brə vä′ dō) *n.* a false show of bravery; pretended courage and dreams and loves. But here was a boy without fear, without dreams, without love.

"If you smashed up all the schools," said Helmholtz, "we wouldn't have any hope left."

"What hope?" said Jim.

"The hope that everybody will be glad he's alive," said Helmholtz. "Even you."

"That's a laugh," said Jim. "All I ever got out of this dump was a hard time. So what're you gonna do?"

"I have to do something, don't I?" said Helmholtz.

"I don't care what you do," said Jim.

"I know," said Helmholtz. "I know." He marched Jim into his tiny office off the band rehearsal room. He dialed the telephone number of the principal's home. Numbly, he waited for the bell to get the old man from his bed.

Jim dusted his boots with a rag.

Helmholtz suddenly dropped the telephone into its cradle before the principal could answer. "Isn't there anything you care about but ripping, hacking, bending, rending, smashing, bashing?" he cried. "Anything? Anything but those boots?"

"Go on! Call up whoever you're gonna call," said Jim.

Helmholtz opened a locker and took a trumpet from it. He thrust the trumpet into Jim's arms. "There!" he said, puffing with emotion. "There's my treasure. It's the dearest thing I own. I give it to you to smash. I won't move a muscle to stop you. You can have the added pleasure of watching my heart break while you do it."

Jim looked at him oddly. He laid down the trumpet.

"Go on!" said Helmholtz. "If the world has treated you so badly, it deserves to have the trumpet smashed!"

"I—" said Jim. Helmholtz grabbed his belt, put a foot behind him, and dumped him on the floor.

Helmholtz pulled Jim's boots off and threw them into a corner. "There!" said Helmholtz savagely. He jerked the boy to his feet again and thrust the trumpet into his arms once more.

Jim Donnini was barefoot now. He had lost his socks with his boots. The boy looked down. The feet that had once seemed big black clubs were narrow as chicken wings now—bony and blue, and not quite clean.

The boy shivered, then quaked. Each quake seemed to shake something loose inside, until, at last, there was no boy left. No boy at all. Jim's head lolled, as though he waited only for death.

Helmholtz was overwhelmed by remorse. He threw his arms around the boy. "Jim! Jim—listen to me, boy!"

Jim stopped quaking.

"You know what you've got there—the trumpet?" said Helmholtz. "You know what's special about it?"

Jim only sighed.

"It belonged to John Philip Sousa!" said Helmholtz. He rocked and shook Jim gently, trying to bring him back to life. "I'll trade it to you, Jim—for your boots. It's yours, Jim! John Philip Sousa's trumpet is yours! It's worth hundreds of dollars, Jim—thousands!"

Jim laid his head on Helmholtz's breast.

"It's better than boots, Jim," said Helmholtz. "You can learn to play it.

Vocabulary

remorse (ri môrs′) *n.* a deep, painful feeling of guilt or sorrow for wrongdoing

You're somebody, Jim. You're the boy with John Philip Sousa's trumpet!"

Helmholtz released Jim slowly, sure the boy would topple. Jim didn't fall. He stood alone. The trumpet was still in his arms.

"I'll take you home, Jim," said Helmholtz. "Be a good boy and I won't say a word about tonight. Polish your trumpet, and learn to be a good boy."

"Can I have my boots?" said Jim dully.

"No," said Helmholtz. "I don't think they're good for you."

He drove Jim home. He opened the car windows and the air seemed to refresh the boy. He let him out at Quinn's restaurant. The soft pats of Jim's bare feet on the sidewalk echoed down the empty street. He climbed through a window, and into his bedroom behind the kitchen. And all was still.

The next morning the waddling, clanking, muddy machines were making the vision of Bert Quinn come true. They were smoothing off the place where the hill had been behind the restaurant. They were making it as level as a billiard table.

Helmholtz sat in a booth again. Quinn joined him again. Jim mopped again. Jim kept his eyes down, refusing to notice Helmholtz. And he didn't seem to care when a surf of suds broke over the toes of his small and narrow brown Oxfords.

"Eating out two mornings in a row?" said Quinn. "Something wrong at home?"

"My wife's still out of town," said Helmholtz.

"While the cat's away—" said Quinn. He winked.

"When the cat's away," said Helmholtz, "this mouse gets lonesome."

Quinn leaned forward. "Is that what got you out of bed in the middle of the night, Helmholtz? Loneliness?" He jerked his head at Jim. "Kid! Go get Mr. Helmholtz his horn."

Jim raised his head, and Helmholtz saw that his eyes were oysterlike again. He marched away to get the trumpet.

Quinn now showed that he was excited and angry. "You take away his boots and give him a horn, and I'm not supposed to get curious?" he said. "I'm not supposed to start asking questions? I'm not supposed to find out you caught him taking the school apart? You'd made a lousy crook, Helmholtz. You'd leave your baton, sheet music, and your driver's license at the scene of the crime."

"I don't think about hiding clues," said Helmholtz. "I just do what I do. I was going to tell you."

John Philip Sousa

Quinn's feet danced and his shoes squeaked like mice. "Yes?" he said. "Well, I've got some news for you too."

"What is that?" said Helmholtz uneasily.

"It's all over with Jim and me," said Quinn. "Last night was the payoff. I'm sending him back where he came from."

"To another string of foster homes?" said Helmholtz weakly.

"Whatever the experts figure out to do with a kid like that." Quinn sat back, exhaled noisily, and went limp with relief.

"You can't," said Helmholtz.

"I can," said Quinn.

"That will be the end of him," said Helmholtz. "He can't stand to be thrown away like that one more time."

"He can't feel anything," said Quinn. "I can't help him; I can't hurt him. Nobody can. There isn't a nerve in him."

"A bundle of scar tissue," said Helmholtz.

The bundle of scar tissue returned with the trumpet. Impassively,[9] he laid it on the table in front of Helmholtz.

Helmholtz forced a smile. "It's yours, Jim," he said. "I gave it to you."

"Take it while you got the chance, Helmholtz," said Quinn. "He doesn't want it. All he'll do is swap it for a knife or a pack of cigarettes."

"He doesn't know what it is, yet," said Helmholtz. "It takes a while to find out."

"It's all over with Jim and me," said Quinn. "Last night was the payoff."

"Is it any good?" said Quinn.

"Any good?" said Helmholtz, not believing his ears. "Any good?" He didn't see how anyone could look at the instrument and not be warmed and dazzled by it. "Any good?" he murmured. "It belonged to John Philip Sousa."

Quinn blinked stupidly. "Who?"

Helmholtz's hands fluttered on the table top like the wings of a dying bird. "Who was John Philip Sousa?" he piped. No more words came. The subject was too big for a tired man to cover. The dying bird expired and lay still.

After a long silence, Helmholtz picked up the trumpet. He kissed the cold mouthpiece and pumped the valves in a dream of a brilliant cadenza.[10] Over the bell of the instrument, Helmholtz saw Jim Donnini's face, seemingly floating in space—all but deaf and blind. Now Helmholtz saw the futility of men and their treasures. He had thought that his greatest treasure, the trumpet, could buy a soul for Jim. The trumpet was worthless.

Deliberately, Helmholtz hammered the trumpet against the table edge. He bent it around a coat tree. He handed the wreck to Quinn.

"Ya busted it," said Quinn, amazed. "Why'dja do that? What's that prove?"

9. To do something *impassively* is to do it without showing any emotion.

10. A *cadenza* is a difficult musical solo near the end of a musical composition.

Vocabulary

futility (fū til′ ə tē) *n.* uselessness; hopelessness

"I—I don't know," said Helmholtz. A terrible blasphemy[11] rumbled deep in him, like the warning of a volcano. And then, irresistibly, out it came. "Life is no damn good," said Helmholtz. His face twisted as he fought back tears and shame.

Helmholtz, the mountain that walked like a man, was falling apart. Jim Donnini's eyes filled with pity and alarm. They came alive. They became human. Helmholtz had got a message through. Quinn looked at Jim, and something like hope flickered for the first time in his bitterly lonely old face.

Drawing Music, 1997. Tam Van Tran. Ink on paper, 4¾ x 3⅝ in. Collection of the artist.

Viewing the art: If you were Jim, what message might this drawing have for you?

Two weeks later, a new semester began at Lincoln High.

In the band rehearsal room, the members of C Band were waiting for their leader—were waiting for their destinies as musicians to unfold.

Helmholtz stepped onto the podium, and rattled his baton against his music stand. "The Voices of Spring," he said. "Everybody hear that? The Voices of Spring?"

There were rustling sounds as the musicians put the music on their stands. In the pregnant silence[12] that followed their readiness, Helmholtz glanced at Jim Donnini, who sat on the last seat of the worst trumpet section of the worst band in school.

His trumpet, John Philip Sousa's trumpet, George M. Helmholtz's trumpet, had been repaired.

"Think of it this way," said Helmholtz. "Our aim is to make the world more beautiful than it was when we came into it. It can be done. You can do it."

A small cry of despair came from Jim Donnini. It was meant to be private, but it pierced every ear with its poignancy.[13]

"How?" said Jim.

"Love yourself," said Helmholtz, "and make your instrument sing about it. A-one, a-two, a-three." Down came his baton.

11. A *blasphemy* is an expression of scorn for anything considered sacred.

12. A *pregnant silence* is one filled with importance or meaning.

13. Here, *poignancy* (poin′ yən sē) means "sharply felt emotion or distress."

Responding to Literature

PERSONAL RESPONSE

- How did you react to George M. Helmholtz's repeated efforts to get through to Jim?
- What, in your opinion, might Helmholtz have done differently?

Analyzing Literature

RECALL

1. What do Helmholtz and Quinn say about their earlier business deal?
2. What is Helmholtz's big dream? When does it come true?
3. Name two or three ways Helmholtz tries to reach Jim.
4. What makes Jim's eyes fill "with pity and alarm"?

INTERPRET

5. What does their discussion of a business deal tell you about Helmholtz and Quinn?
6. What makes Helmholtz a successful teacher?
7. What do you learn about Helmholtz from the way he treats Jim?
8. The author writes that Helmholtz "had got a message through" to Jim. What is the message?

EVALUATE AND CONNECT

9. Does Helmholtz live up to his idea that "our aim is to make the world more beautiful than it was when we came into it"? Explain your answer.
10. Theme Connection Compare Quinn's and Helmholtz's ways of responding to Jim. Explain how each man is important in Jim's life.

LITERARY ELEMENTS

Dialogue

Dialogue is conversation between two or more characters. Dialogue reveals the personality of a character through the spoken words and descriptions of facial expressions and body language. Good dialogue sounds natural, like an overheard conversation. It can contain slang, sentence fragments, and contractions because that's how people talk.

1. What information about Quinn and Helmholtz is presented in their dialogue about the hill at the beginning of the story?
2. Find an example of natural dialogue from Helmholtz, from Quinn, and from Jim. What does each character's way of speaking reveal about his personality?

- See **Literary Terms Handbook,** p. R3.

Extending Your Response

Writing About Literature

Contrasting Characters Write a paragraph or two in which you contrast Helmholtz and Quinn. What was Quinn's approach to treating a troubled kid? What was Helmholtz's approach? What was the attitude of each toward the hill behind the restaurant? How does the author use Quinn to emphasize the kind of person that Helmholtz is?

Literature Groups

Public Problems A writer's job, Vonnegut believes, is to warn society about its problems so that people can work for change. What problems might Vonnegut be addressing in "The Kid Nobody Could Handle"? What solutions does he suggest? Are they, in your opinion, useful solutions? Discuss these questions with your group. Then compare your responses with those of other groups.

Learning for Life

Job Description What does it take to be a band leader? Write a job description that the principal of Helmholtz's school might write to look for a replacement when Helmholtz retires. As you write, think about the music skills a band leader like Helmholtz would need as well as the abilities required to reach different kinds of students.

Personal Writing

Journal Entry Look back at your list of things that make you happy from the **Focus Activity** on page 145. Write a journal entry to explain your feelings about one of these items. Be specific about what makes you happy and why. Support your ideas with details and examples.

 **Save your work for your portfolio.**

Skill Minilesson

VOCABULARY • ANTONYMS

An **antonym** is a word with a meaning that is opposite that of another word. Most words have antonyms, and writers often use antonyms to present contrast, as the example shows.

I used to think Lena was an honest person, but she has proved to me that she is untrustworthy.

PRACTICE Complete each sentence by writing an antonym for the word that is underlined.

1. Not all criminal behavior is furtive; some is quite _____.
2. How can two sisters be so different? One is so _____, the other so arrogant!
3. Dad thought his chatter from the bleachers would be _____; instead, it was unnerving.
4. You thought I'd be _____ by your behavior, but I was appalled.

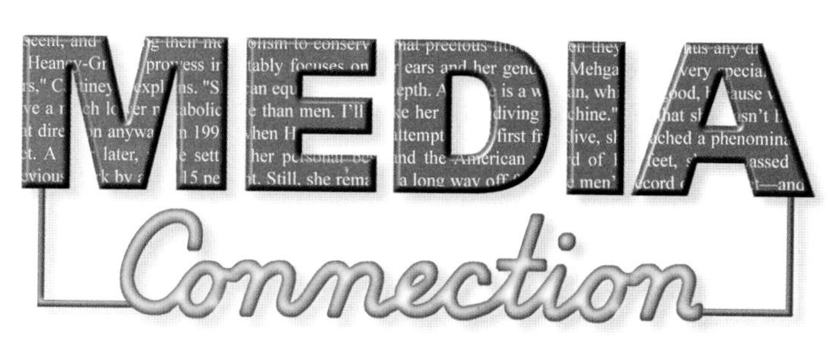

SONG LYRICS

What would you like to be? Loved? Free? Part of a crowd? Cool? Des'ree tells you to be many things!

You Gotta Be

By Des'ree and A. Ingram; Sony Music Entertainment, 1994

from Des'ree, *I Ain't Movin'*

Listen as your day unfolds
challenge what the future holds
Try to keep your head up to the sky
Lovers they may cause you tears
Go ahead release your fears
Stand up and be counted, don't be ashamed to cry
You gotta be

CHORUS:
You gotta be bad
You gotta be bold
You gotta be wiser
You gotta be hard
You gotta be tough
You gotta be stronger
You gotta be cool, you gotta be calm, you gotta stay
together
All I know, all I know, love will save the day

Herald what your mother said
Read the books your father read
Try to solve the puzzle in your own sweet time
Some may have more cash than you
Others take a different view
My oh my, you gotta be

CHORUS

Time asks no questions,
it goes on without
you
Leaving you behind if
you can't stand the
pace
The world keeps on
spinning, can't stop it
if you tried to
The best part is danger
staring you in the
face

Listen as your day
unfolds
challenge what the future holds
Try to keep your head up to the sky
Lovers they may cause you tears
Go ahead release your fears
Stand up and be counted, don't be ashamed to cry
You gotta be

CHORUS

Got to be bad
Got to be bold
Got to be wise
Don't ever be cold
Got to be hard
Not too, too hard
All I know is love will save the day.

Respond

1. What, according to the writer, will help you be everything named in the song?
2. Is everything listed in this song important to you? Explain your answer.

Before You Read

Thank You, M'am

MEET LANGSTON HUGHES

While working as a busboy in Washington, D.C., Langston Hughes showed some of his poems to a famous customer, the poet Vachel Lindsay. That night, Lindsay read the poems to an audience. In time, Hughes became known as the Poet Laureate of Black America. Hughes's subjects, he once said, are "people up today and down tomorrow, working this week and fired the next, beaten and baffled, but determined not to be wholly beaten." Hughes was one of the first African Americans to make a living as a writer and lecturer.

Langston Hughes was born in 1902 and died in 1967. This story was published in 1958.

FOCUS ACTIVITY

Think of someone you trust. Consider your reasons for trusting that person.

Chart It!
Copy the following chart, and list some qualities that you find in people you trust.

A trustworthy person is	

Setting a Purpose
Read to find out how two characters come to trust each other despite unlikely circumstances.

BACKGROUND

The Time and Place The setting of "Thank You, M'am" is a street scene and a rooming house, probably in a large city. The story, however, might take place in any city in the United States and at almost any time.

Did You Know? A rooming house is a place where people rent rooms to live in. Rooming houses are often found in urban areas, providing homes for people who cannot afford an apartment or a house of their own.

VOCABULARY PREVIEW

slung (slung) *adj.* hung or thrown loosely; p. 161
frail (frāl) *adj.* lacking in strength; weak; p. 162
barren (bar′ ən) *adj.* bare; empty; dull or uninteresting; p. 164

Thank You, M'am

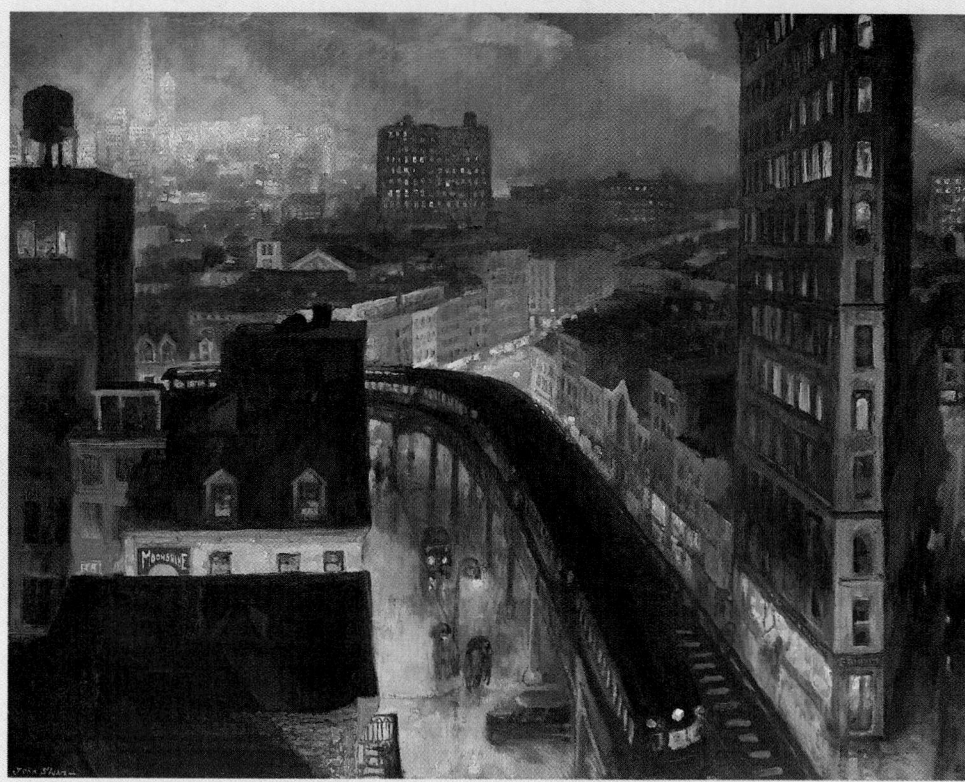

The City from Greenwich Village, 1922. John Sloan. Oil on canvas, 26 x 33¾ in. National Gallery of Art, Washington, DC.

Langston Hughes

She was a large woman with a large purse that had everything in it but hammer and nails. It had a long strap and she carried it slung across her shoulder. It was about eleven o'clock at night, and she was walking alone, when a boy ran up behind her and tried to snatch her purse. The strap broke with the single tug the boy gave it from behind. But the boy's weight, and the weight of the purse combined caused him to lose his balance so, instead of taking off full blast as he had hoped, the boy fell on his back on the sidewalk, and his legs flew up. The large woman simply turned around and kicked him right square in his blue jeaned sitter. Then she reached down, picked the boy up by his shirt front, and shook him until his teeth rattled.

Vocabulary

slung (slung) *adj.* hung or thrown loosely

Portrait of a Woman, 1932. John Wesley Hardrick. Oil on board, 30 x 24 in. Hampton University Museum, Hampton, VA. Indianapolis Museum of Art in cooperation with Indiana University Press.

Viewing the painting: How does the writer reveal Mrs. Jones's character? How does the painter reveal the character of his subject?

The woman said, "What did you want to do it for?"

The boy said, "I didn't aim to."

She said, "You a lie!"

By that time two or three people passed, stopped, turned to look, and some stood watching.

"If I turn you loose, will you run?" asked the woman.

"Yes'm," said the boy.

"Then I won't turn you loose," said the woman. She did not release him.

"I'm very sorry, lady, I'm sorry," whispered the boy.

"Um-hum! And your face is dirty. I got a great mind to wash your face for you. Ain't you got nobody home to tell you to wash your face?"

"No'm," said the boy.

"Then it will get washed this evening," said the large woman starting up the street, dragging the frightened boy behind her.

He looked as if he were fourteen or fifteen, frail and willow-wild, in tennis shoes and blue jeans.

The woman said, "You ought to be my son. I would teach you right from wrong. Least I can do right now is to wash your face. Are you hungry?"

After that the woman said, "Pick up my pocketbook, boy, and give it here."

She still held him. But she bent down enough to permit him to stoop and pick up her purse. Then she said, "Now ain't you ashamed of yourself?"

Firmly gripped by his shirt front, the boy said, "Yes'm."

Vocabulary

frail (frāl) *adj.* lacking in strength; weak

"No'm," said the being-dragged boy. "I just want you to turn me loose."

"Was I bothering *you* when I turned that corner?" asked the woman.

"No'm."

"But you put yourself in contact with *me*," said the woman. "If you think that that contact is not going to last awhile, you got another thought coming. When I get through with you, sir, you are going to remember Mrs. Luella Bates Washington Jones."

Sweat popped out on the boy's face and he began to struggle. Mrs. Jones stopped, jerked him around in front of her, put a half nelson[1] about his neck, and continued to drag him up the street. When she got to her door, she dragged the boy inside, down a hall, and into a large kitchenette-furnished room at the rear of the house. She switched on the light and left the door open. The boy could hear other roomers laughing and talking in the large house. Some of their doors were open, too, so he knew he and the woman were not alone. The woman still had him by the neck in the middle of her room.

She said, "What is your name?"

"Roger," answered the boy.

"Then, Roger, you go to that sink and wash your face," said the woman, whereupon she turned him loose—at last. Roger looked at the door—looked at the woman—looked at the door—*and went to the sink.*

"Let the water run until it gets warm," she said. "Here's a clean towel."

"You gonna take me to jail?" asked the boy, bending over the sink.

"Not with that face, I would not take you nowhere," said the woman. "Here I am trying to get home to cook me a bite to eat and you snatch my pocketbook! Maybe you ain't been to your supper either, late as it be. Have you?"

"There's nobody home at my house," said the boy.

"Then we'll eat," said the woman. "I believe you're hungry—or been hungry—to try to snatch my pocketbook."

"I wanted a pair of blue suede shoes,"[2] said the boy.

"Well, you didn't have to snatch *my* pocketbook to get some suede shoes," said Mrs. Luella Bates Washington Jones. "You could of asked me."

"M'am?"

The water dripping from his face, the boy looked at her. There was a long pause. A very long pause. After he had dried his face and not knowing what else to do dried it again, the boy turned around, wondering what next. The door was open. He could make a dash for it down the hall. He could run, run, run, run, *run*!

The woman was sitting on the daybed.[3] After a while she said, "I were young once and I wanted things I could not get."

There was another long pause. The boy's mouth opened. Then he frowned, but not knowing he frowned.

The woman said, "Um-hum! You thought I was going to say *but*, didn't you? You thought I was going to say, *but I didn't snatch people's pocketbooks*. Well, I wasn't going to say that." Pause. Silence. "I have done things, too, which I would not tell

1. A *half nelson* is a wrestling hold made from behind by hooking one arm under the opponent's arm and pressing the hand across the back of the opponent's neck.

2. *Blue suede shoes* are men's shoes made of velvety soft leather. These shoes became popular for a time in the late 1950s after Elvis Presley recorded a hit song called "Blue Suede Shoes."

3. A *daybed* is a sofa that can be converted into a bed.

you, son—neither tell God, if he didn't already know. So you set down while I fix us something to eat. You might run that comb through your hair so you will look presentable."

He did not trust the woman not to trust him. And he did not want to be mistrusted now.

In another corner of the room behind a screen was a gas plate and an icebox. Mrs. Jones got up and went behind the screen. The woman did not watch the boy to see if he was going to run now, nor did she watch her purse which she left behind her on the daybed. But the boy took care to sit on the far side of the room where he thought she could easily see him out of the corner of her eye, if she wanted to. He did not trust the woman *not* to trust him. And he did not want to be mistrusted now.

"Do you need somebody to go to the store," asked the boy, "maybe to get some milk or something?"

"Don't believe I do," said the woman, "unless you just want sweet milk yourself. I was going to make cocoa out of this canned milk I got here."

"That will be fine," said the boy.

She heated some lima beans and ham she had in the icebox, made the cocoa, and set the table. The woman did not ask the boy anything about where he lived, or his folks, or anything else that would embarrass him. Instead, as they ate, she told him about her job in a hotel beauty shop that stayed open late, what the work was like, and how all kinds of women came in and out, blondes, red-heads, and Spanish. Then she cut him a half of her ten-cent cake.

"Eat some more, son," she said.

When they were finished eating she got up and said, "Now, here, take this ten dollars and buy yourself some blue suede shoes. And next time, do not make the mistake of latching onto *my* pocketbook *nor nobody else's*—because shoes come by devilish like that will burn your feet. I got to get my rest now. But I wish you would behave yourself, son, from here on in."

She led him down the hall to the front door and opened it. "Goodnight! Behave yourself, boy!" she said, looking out into the street.

The boy wanted to say something else other than, "Thank you, m'am," to Mrs. Luella Bates Washington Jones, but he couldn't do so as he turned at the barren stoop and looked back at the large woman in the door. He barely managed to say, "Thank you," before she shut the door. And he never saw her again.

Vocabulary

barren (bar′ ən) *adj.* bare; empty; dull or uninteresting

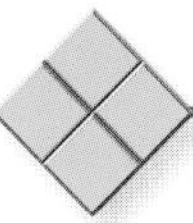

Responding to Literature

PERSONAL RESPONSE

- Were you surprised by the ending of this story? Why or why not?
- Which lines from the story will you remember? Why?

Analyzing Literature

RECALL AND INTERPRET

1. What does Mrs. Jones tell Roger he should have done to get the blue suede shoes he wants? Does Mrs. Jones seem to be a wealthy woman? Give details to support your answer.
2. How does Roger behave when he is in Mrs. Jones's room? Why, in your opinion, does Roger decide to stay there?
3. What does Mrs. Jones tell Roger when he leaves her building? How do you know that she has made an impression on Roger?

EVALUATE AND CONNECT

4. Which of the following adjectives describe Mrs. Jones: honest, generous, gullible, mean? Defend your choices.
5. After reading the story, would you say that Roger is trustworthy? Why or why not? Support your answer with examples and with information you wrote for the **Focus Activity** on page 160.
6. Do you find the characters in "Thank You, M'am" realistic? Explain your answer.

LITERARY ELEMENTS

Characterization

Characterization includes all the methods an author uses to develop a character. In "Thank You, M'am," Langston Hughes provides direct information about the characters. He also lets their words and actions reveal their personalities.

1. What traits does Mrs. Jones demonstrate when she drags Roger up the street?
2. Mrs. Jones says, "I were young once and I wanted things I could not get." What do these words reveal?
3. Find a quotation and an action that shows an important trait in Roger's personality.

● See **Literary Terms Handbook,** p. R2.

Extending Your Response

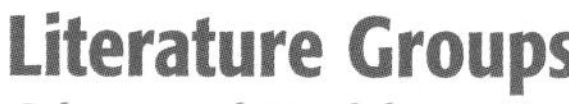

Literature Groups

Crime and Punishment Did Roger's punishment fit his crime? Debate the issue with your group. Consider these questions: Was Roger punished? If so, how? What did Mrs. Jones hope to accomplish when she brought him home? What effect did her actions have on him? Support your points with evidence from the story.

Writing About Literature

Setting Write a paragraph or two explaining the importance of setting to the story. Think about these questions as you write: What does Mrs. Jones's home reveal about her life? How would the story be different if the events had all taken place on the street?

COMPARING SELECTIONS

The Kid Nobody Could Handle **and** Thank You, M'am

COMPARE **SETTINGS**

"The Kid Nobody Could Handle" and "Thank You, M'am" take place in the mid-1900s.

1. How does the urban setting of "Thank You, M'am" help determine the action of the story? In what ways does the small-town setting of "The Kid Nobody Could Handle" make Jim Donnini stand out to the other characters?
2. How might the settings of both stories be different if they took place in the present? How might the new settings affect the characters and their actions?

The City from Greenwich Village, 1922 (detail).

COMPARE **SYMBOLS**

In "Thank You, M'am," Roger was willing to steal so that he could buy a pair of blue suede shoes. In "The Kid Nobody Could Handle," Jim's prized possession was a pair of big black boots. With a small group, compare the importance of the shoes in each story. Consider the following questions: What did the shoes mean to each boy? What did they mean to Mrs. Jones and George Helmholtz? What does "walking in another person's shoes" mean for each story?

COMPARE **CHARACTERS**

In both stories the main character faces a similar challenge or conflict–how to help a young person on the verge of serious trouble.

1. Compare the approaches of Mrs. Jones and George Helmholtz. How do you account for the success of each approach? Would you favor one approach over the other? Why? List the pros and cons for each approach. Then write a paragraph explaining which approach you think is most successful.
2. Suppose that George Helmholtz met Mrs. Jones. What might happen at their meeting? What advice or experiences might they share? Write a journal entry by one or the other, describing this encounter.

Avoiding Run-on Sentences

A **simple sentence** consists of a main clause–a group of words with both a subject and a verb. A r**un-on sentence** can occur when two or more main clauses are combined without correct punctuation.

Problem 1 Two main clauses with no punctuation between them
The boy grabbed the woman's purse the strap broke.

Solution A Separate the main clauses into two sentences.
The boy grabbed the woman's purse. The strap broke.

Solution B Separate the main clauses with a comma and a conjunction.
The boy grabbed the woman's purse, and the strap broke.

Solution C Separate the main clauses with a semicolon.
The boy grabbed the woman's purse; the strap broke.

Problem 2 Main clauses joined by only a comma
Mrs. Jones leaves the door open, Roger doesn't run away.

Solution Add a conjunction after the comma.
Mrs. Jones leaves the door open, but Roger doesn't run away.

Problem 3 Main clauses joined by only a conjunction
Roger wants blue suede shoes and Mrs. Jones seems to understand.

Solution Add a comma before the conjunction.
Roger wants blue suede shoes, and Mrs. Jones seems to understand.

- For more about run-on sentences, see **Language Handbook,** p. R12.

EXERCISE

Write *S* if the sentence is correct. If it is a run-on sentence, rewrite the sentence to correct it. (There is often more than one way to correct a run-on sentence.)

1. Helmholtz is a good-hearted man he tries to be kind to Jim.
2. Jim is unfriendly and rude, Helmholtz is determined to get through to him.
3. Helmholtz finds Jim destroying property and the sight makes him feel sick.
4. Jim's boots seem to represent his attitude; without them, he behaves differently.

Before You Read

The Journey

MEET PATRICIA PRECIADO MARTIN

Patricia Preciado Martin (prā sē ä′ dō mär tēn′) says her stories are "a verbal quilt of my mexicana life experiences sewn together with the fragile threads of love . . ." Instead of sewing bits of multicolored fabric, she pieces together her "personal and collective memories, impressions, observations, visions, inspirations, and *milagros* [miracles]." Martin has been a teacher in the Peace Corps, is active in the Mexican American community, and is the mother of two adult children.

Patricia Preciado Martin has been a resident of Tucson, Arizona, all her life. "The Journey" was first published in 1980 in La Confluencia.

FOCUS ACTIVITY

How do people in your family view the past and changes that have occurred since they were young?

Chart It!

Using a chart like the one below, write names of friends or family members and their ways of looking at the past.

Grandma Brennan	**Lives in Florida now, but she loves to tell stories about growing up in a bungalow in Chicago in the time of streetcars.**

Setting a Purpose

Read to discover how two different generations see the same city.

BACKGROUND

The Time and Place This contemporary story is set in Tucson, which has a large Hispanic population. There are many Spanish words and phrases in this story, and most are followed immediately by their English translations.

Did You Know? In the 1950s, many city residents moved to the suburbs, forcing downtown merchants out of business. Ten years later, businesses and residents returned to abandoned downtowns, giving these areas a new look. For many people, visiting the places where they grew up means looking at a garage or strip mall where homes once stood.

VOCABULARY PREVIEW

drone (drōn) *v.* to talk in a dull, monotonous tone or make a steady, low, humming sound; p. 170
primly (prim′ lē) *adv.* in a formal, proper way; p. 170
laboriously (lə bôr′ ē əs lē) *adv.* with great effort; p. 171
renovate (ren′ ə vāt′) *v.* to make like new; p. 173
patriarch (pā′ trē ärk′) *n.* the male head of a family; p. 173
laden (lād′ ən) *adj.* loaded; weighed down; burdened; p. 173
distinct (dis tingkt′) *adj.* clearly heard, seen, or felt; p. 173

The Journey

Patricia Preciado Martin

In the warm and sun-filled days
I remember in the haze
The happy sounds of children laughing,
The rustle of the cottonwoods.
Now all is old and cold and dark
Underneath Presidio Park.

The bell rings, the bus slows, and finally stops. I get off at the corner of Fifth and Congress. One North Fifth Avenue. The MARTIN LUTHER KING JR. APARTMENTS. LOW COST HOUSING FOR THE ELDERLY. Gray concrete walls five stories high. Honorable Mayor James M. Corbett, Jr. Honorable Councilmen Richard Kennedy, Kirk Storch, Conrad Joyner, Rudy Castro, and John Steiger. *Anno Domini*[1] 1969.

1. The Latin term *Anno Domini* (an′ ō dom′ i nī′), or its abbreviation A.D., means "year of the Lord," and refers to dates since the birth of Jesus Christ.

I go through the double-wide glass doors of the apartment building. (ENTER HERE ONLY.) Electronically operated. The high-ceilinged waiting room is painted bright yellow (to make it seem cheerful). The room is bare except for a few weatherbeaten chairs and scarred coffee tables cluttered with tattered magazines. GOOD HOUSEKEEPING—"Decorate A Bedroom With Sheets." U.S. NEWS AND WORLD REPORT—"The Effect of Arab Oil Prices on Wall Street." COSMOPOLITAN—"How To Tell If Your Husband Is Faithful." The black-and-white TV drones on, addressing no one in particular. The elevator clanks along noisily. (UP: DOWN: PRESS BUTTON ONLY ONCE.) A few viejitos[2] are coming and going with purpose. Some are waiting for the mail. Some are waiting for visitors. Some are just waiting.

And Tía[3] is there, as always. Every Saturday. Summer or winter, spring or fall, for the last two years. Except when the weather is too cold or too wet. It can never be too hot. Her small delicate figure is nearly lost in the big overstuffed chair (Donated by the Cochran Family; In Memory of Our Son, Lawrence, Jr.; Cochran Realty and Investments). Tía is waiting for me. Quietly, primly, regally, her hands folded in her lap. She is wearing a shawl and a small knit hat. A flowered print dress and black stockings and shoes.

"Ah, mihijita, ya llegaste."[4] I take her arm, and she rises to her feet, not without difficulty. On one arm she carries a straw bag, and on the other a worn black umbrella (just in case). We walk slowly out the wide glass doors (EXIT HERE ONLY) into the late morning sunshine.

"Qué bueno que llegaste temprano. Tengo mucho que hacer, y la tienda está lejos. It is good that you arrived early. I have a lot to do, and the store is far away."

We begin our walk; our journey. Every Saturday she insists on taking the same route. Across town. Down Congress Street. Past the Regal Cigar Store (MAGAZINES, CIGARS, NOVELTIES). Past the Discount Clothing City (GANGAS HOY! 60 DAYS TO PAY! SE HABLA ESPAÑOL). Past the empty store windows with the dusty, limbless mannequins.[5] We walk slowly, without talking. We turn on South Sixth Avenue and go south, past the numerous bars and liquor stores. A hippie plays a guitar for quarters in front of the O.K. Bar. We walk past Armory Park. Winter visitors are playing shuffleboard in the sunshine and winos are sleeping in the grass. On Ochoa Street we turn west again and walk toward the

2. In Spanish, *viejitos* (vē′ ə hē′ tōs) means "old people."
3. *Tía* (tē′ ə) is Spanish for "aunt."

4. Tía says, "*mihijita, ya llegaste*," or "My little girl, now you've arrived."
5. The sign reads, "BARGAINS TODAY! . . . SPANISH SPOKEN." *Mannequins* (man′ i kins) are dummies used to display clothes for sale.

Vocabulary

drone (drōn) *v.* to talk in a dull, monotonous tone or make a steady, low, humming sound
primly (prim′ lē) *adv.* in a formal, proper way

gleaming white towers of the Cathedral. San Agustín. The Dove of the Desert.[6] The pigeons flutter over our heads when the noon bells chime. Sr. Enríquez, the old bell chimer, died long ago. He climbed the rickety stairs to the bell tower three times a day for more years than anyone could remember. One day he climbed up and played the Noon Angelus[7] and never climbed down again. They found him with the bell rope still in his hands. Now the Angelus is a recorded announcement.

Tía laboriously climbs the concrete steps to the vestibule[8] of the Cathedral. I open the heavy carved doors for her and she makes her way into the cool darkness. The perfume of the incense from the early morning funeral Mass still lingers in the air.

(Sra. Juanita Mendoza. Born in Tucson of a Pioneer Family, Grandmother Eight Children. Twelve Grandchildren. Seven Great-Grandchildren.)

Down, down, the long corridor Tía walks until she reaches the side chapel of the Virgen de Guadalupe. La Madre de Nosotros. La Reina de Las Américas.[9] She lights a small vigil candle and prays for the souls of husbands and brothers and sons. The ones who have died or lost their souls in Los Angeles. Father Carrillo walks by, intent on something. Cuentas and almas. Bills and souls. El Padre.[10] Son of Barrio Anita. The pride of the people. "Y cómo estás, Doña Luz?"[11] He grasps her hand warmly.

We walk out once more into the brightness. Past an elegant old home that is now a funeral parlor. Down South Meyer and west on Cushing Street. Past a sign that says Barrio Histórico. THIS AREA HAS BEEN OFFICIALLY DESIGNATED AS AN HISTORICAL LANDMARK AND IS OFFICIALLY REGISTERED WITH THE NATIONAL REGISTER OF HISTORICAL PLACES. In bronze. Most of the houses in the Barrio Histórico are owned by Mr. Kelly Rollings, a local automobile dealer and millionaire and amateur anthropologist.[12] He owns the old Robles House. It is now the Cushing Street Bar. "EAT, DRINK AND BE MERRY IN AN AUTHENTIC RESTORED OLD ADOBE."

"That's where the Robles' lived," Tía tells me, in Spanish. "They had a piano. The Señora played beautifully. Everyone would come to listen. People would leave flowers on her doorstep." She continued. "On Sundays we would all walk down for

6. Saint Augustine (the English spelling) is sometimes called "Dove of the Desert" because he was born near the Sahara in northern Africa in A.D. 354.

7. In some churches, a bell is rung at morning, noon, and night to signal the time for saying a special prayer called, in Latin, the *Angelus* (an′ jə ləs).

8. A *vestibule* (ves′ tə būl′) is a small entrance hall.

9. These are names for Mary, the mother of Jesus Christ.

10. The people are proud of their priest (*El Padre*, "the Father") because he is from their neighborhood (*barrio*).

11. *Sr.* and *Sra.* are abbreviations for *Señor* (sen yôr′) and *Señora*, (sen yôr′ ə) like *Mr.* and *Mrs.* in English. *Don* (don) or *Doña* (dōn′ yə) before a person's first name is a title of respect for an acquaintance or employer.

12. An *anthropologist* studies humans and their cultures.

Vocabulary

laboriously (lə bôr′ ē əs lē) *adv.* with great effort

the Paseo[13] in the Plaza of the Cathedral. Sometimes we would walk down to the river. (It had water then! Can you believe that the Santa Cruz had water?!) In the summers we would picnic under the cool shade of the cottonwood trees. Everywhere there was music."

We continue south on Convent Street. Mr. Ortega is sitting on his porch. He pays his rent now to Coldwell and Banker, based in New York. "Buenas Tardes, Doña Luz." "Buenas Tardes, Don Felipe." We walk on slowly. Tía continues. "His father and his grandfather had tierras by the river. Everywhere it was green. They grew flowers and vegetables. And oh! The flowers! The perfume was everywhere in the summer breezes. His father, Don Raimundo, sold vegetables from a cart. All of us children would run after the cart. He gave us free sugar cane. Now the river is dry. The milpas[14] are gone and the people are gone. (The river had water then! Can you believe that the Santa Cruz had water?!)

13. Here, the *Paseo* (pə sā′ ō) is a stroll that many people took after church services.
14. *"Buenas Tardes"* (bwā′ nəs tär′ des) means "Good afternoon." *Tierras* (tyer′ əs) are gardens or small fields, and *milpas* (mēl′ pəs) are fields, usually of corn.

Comadre Rafaelita, 1934. Emil J. Bisttram. Oil on canvas, 72 x 44 in. The Anschutz Collection, Denver, CO.

Viewing the painting: What do the woman's pose and her setting tell you about her way of life? How does it compare with that of Tía?

The Freeway had cut the river from the people. The Freeway blocks the sunshine. The drone of the traffic buzzes like a giant unsleeping bee. A new music in the barrio.

On down South Convent. Past the old Padilla House. THIS HOUSE IS A REGISTERED HISTORICAL LANDMARK. In brass. It is being renovated. The sign has gone up. LOS ARCOS. ANTIQUES, PRIMITIVES,[15] AND COLLECTIBLES.

At last we arrive at our destination. Romero's Convent Street Market. Tía opens the screen door. RAINBOW BREAD IS GOOD. Rafael Romero. Patriarch of the Barrio. Mr. Rollings has offered him a good price. Mr. Romero has no price, but he has no sons either. "Buenas Tardes, Doña Luz." "Buenas Tardes, Don Rafael." Tía fills her bag. The ancient cash register rings and whirs metallically. Queso blanco. Salsa de tomate. Campbell's Chicken Noodle Soup. White bread. Tortillas de maíz. Tortillas de harina. Cheerios. Pan Mexicano. Coffee. Saladitos[16] for me. "Gracias Doña Luz. Hasta luego."

Then around the corner. Down South Main. I follow unquestioning. I know that the journey is not over. There is always one more destination. Toward the Tucson Community Center Complex. The Pride of Tucson. MUSIC HALL. LITTLE THEATRE, CONVENTION HALL. CONCERT ARENA. URBAN RENEWAL. Honorable Mayor James M. Corbett, Jr. Honorable Councilmen William Ruck, Ramon Castillo, Richard Kennedy, Robert Royal, and Conrad Joyner, *Anno Domini* 1971. Concrete walls, and steps, and fountains. Fountains, fountains, everywhere. (The river had water then! Can you believe that the Santa Cruz had water?!)

The pace of Tía quickens now. I follow her, carrying the straw bag laden with groceries. We walk past the Concert Hall to the vast parking lot of the Community Center Complex. A billboard reads: CONCERT TONIGHT. ALICE COOPER.[17] SOLD OUT. We stop in the middle of the parking lot. The winter sun is warm. The heat rises from the black asphalt. The roar of the Freeway is even more distinct. It is the end of the journey. I know what Tía will say.

"Aquí estaba mi casita. It was my father's house. And his father's house before that. They built it with their own hands with adobes made from the mud of the river. All their children were born here. I was born here. It was a good house, a strong house. When it rained, the adobes smelled like the good clean earth."

15. *Los Arcos*, or The Arches, is the shop name. *Primitives* are folk art, works of art with a simple style.

16. Tía's groceries include white cheese (*queso blanco*), tomato sauce (*salsa*), bread (*pan*), and little salted snacks (*saladitos*).

17. *Alice Cooper* was a rock performer popular in the late 1960s and early 1970s.

Vocabulary

renovate (ren′ ə vāt′) *v.* to make like new
patriarch (pā′ trē ärk′) *n.* the male head of a family
laden (lād′ ən) *adj.* loaded; weighed down; burdened
distinct (dis tingkt′) *adj.* clearly heard, seen, or felt

She pauses. She sees shadows I cannot see. She hears melodies I cannot hear. "See, here! I had a fig tree growing. In the summer I gave figs to the neighbors and the birds. And there—I hung a clay olla with water to sip from on the hot summer days. We always had a breeze from the river. I had a bougainvillea; it was so beautiful! Brilliant red. And I had roses and a little garden. Right here where I am standing my comadres[18] and I would sit and visit in the evenings. We would watch the children run and play in the streets. There was no traffic then. And there was laughter everywhere."

"Ah, well," she sighs. "Ya es tarde. It is time to go." I turn to follow her and then turn to look once more to the place where her casita once stood. I look across the parking lot. I look down. "Tía, Tía," I call. "Ven!" She turns and comes toward me. "Look!" I say excitedly. "There is a flower that has pushed its way through the asphalt! It is blooming!"

"Ah, mihijita," she says at last. Her eyes are shining. "You have found out the secret of our journeys."

"What secret, Tía?"

"Que las flores siempre ganan. The flowers always win."

We turn away from the sun that is beginning to drop in the West. I take her arm again. There is music everywhere.

Refrain

ABUELITA, ABUELITA,
ABUELITA, NO LLORES.
TE TRAIGO, TE TRAIGO,
 TE TRAIGO
UNA RAMITA DE FLORES.[19]

18. An *olla* (ō′ yə) is a pot with a handle. *Bougainvillea* (bo͞o′ gən vil′ ē ə) is a shrub or vine with brilliant purple or red flowers. Tía's *comadres* (kō mä′ drāz) were her close women friends.

19. *Abuelita* means "granny" or "old woman." *No llores* is "don't weep." *Te traigo* means "I bring you." And the last line is "A small bouquet of flowers." Pronunciations: *abuelita* (a′ bwə lē′ tə), *no llores* (nō yôr′ ās), *te traigo* (tā trī′ gō), *una ramita de flores* (o͞o′ nə rä mē′ tə dā flō′ rās)

❖

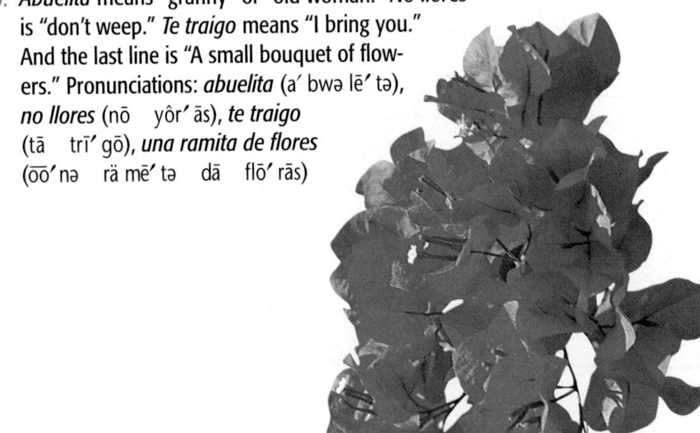

Bougainvillea

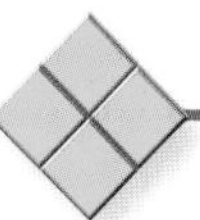

Responding to Literature

PERSONAL RESPONSE

What thoughts did you have about the narrator, her aunt, and their walk as you read the end of the story? Write a quick note to a classmate explaining why you thought this way.

Analyzing Literature

RECALL

1. What does the writer describe in the first four lines of the stanza that introduces "The Journey"? What is described in the last two lines?
2. Where does the narrator go to meet her aunt?
3. What has happened to the home of the Robles family?
4. How has the Santa Cruz River changed?

INTERPRET

5. Why might the writer have chosen to begin the story with a poem?
6. Why, in your opinion, does Tía follow the same route on her walks each week?
7. What is suggested about the ownership of land and buildings in the Barrio Histórico?
8. Why, do you think, does the narrator repeat her thoughts about the river?

EVALUATE AND CONNECT

9. How are the stops Tía makes on her weekly journey similar? How are they different?
10. Explain how the writer uses music and flowers to strengthen this story of change. In your opinion, is this **imagery** effective? Support your answer with examples.

Clay olla.

LITERARY ELEMENTS

Narration

Narration is storytelling, and writers use countless techniques to tell their stories. As you read "The Journey," you followed events through the eyes of a first-person narrator whose thoughts seem to leap from one thing to another as she considers every small detail, makes connections, and responds to her aunt's recollections.

1. Identify three or four details the narrator mentions, and tell how they help readers understand Tía's journey.
2. Which details make Tía's journey seem sad? Which add hope to the story?

● See **Literary Terms Handbook,** p. R6.

Literature and Writing

Writing About Literature

Setting Most of the scenes in this story take place on the streets of an old city. Why do you think the author has chosen this setting? Explain your answer in a paragraph. When writing, think about what the neighborhood means to the older woman.

Creative Writing

A Scene with Tía Imagine yourself as the narrator in "The Journey." What would you talk about with your aunt after your shopping trip? Write the dialogue for a short video set in Tía's apartment. Include camera directions and directions for the actors.

Extending Your Response

Literature Groups

Out of the Past Look over your response from the **Focus Activity** on page 168 and compare your chart with the situation in the story. With your group, discuss how characters in the story and in your chart are alike and different in their views of the past. Then summarize your comparisons and present your ideas to the class.

interNET CONNECTION

Use the Internet to research government policies on historic buildings or neighborhoods where you live. Type keywords such as "historic preservation" into a search engine. Share your findings with the class.

Learning for Life

Letter to the Editor Suppose that you are the narrator, and you've discovered that one more old building on Tía's journey is to be razed. Write a letter to the editor of a local Tucson newspaper stating your opinion about tearing down the building. Do you want it to be preserved, or is it a good idea to replace the building with something new? Give reasons for your opinion.

Reading Further

For other stories of how one generation helps another, try these books:

Patricia Preciado Martin, *Images and Conversations*
Margaret Rostkowski, *After the Dancing Days*
Richard E. Peck, *Something for Joey*
Robert Newton Peck, *A Day No Pigs Would Die*

Save your work for your portfolio.

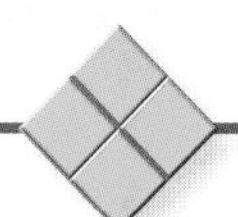

Skill Minilessons

GRAMMAR AND LANGUAGE • WORDS ENDING IN *-ly*

Many adjectives can be used as adverbs by adding *-ly.*

Tía is quiet, prim, *and* regal.

Tía is waiting for me. Quietly, primly, regally, *her hands are folded in her lap.*

- For more about adding suffixes, see **Language Handbook,** p. R48.

PRACTICE Write the adverbial form of each adjective listed below. Then use each adverb in a sentence of your own.

1. vigorous
2. reluctant
3. efficient
4. private
5. good-natured

READING AND THINKING • VISUALIZING

You will understand more of a story if you stop occasionally to visualize, or see in your mind, a person or place in the text. For example, it is easy to visualize Tía as she waits for her niece because the writer includes many details. In other scenes, the writer may include fewer details. An efficient reader will imagine the details that bring the story to life.

- For more about visualizing, see **Reading Handbook,** p. R86.

PRACTICE Read through "The Journey" to find a description of a place that interests you. Study the description and imagine you are there. Then sketch the scene. Include as many details as you can.

VOCABULARY • THE PREFIX *co-*

The prefixes *co-, col-, con-,* and *com-* often add the meaning "with" or "together" to a word or root. For example, a *coworker* is a person who "works with" another. If you *convoke* a meeting, you call people together, since the root *voke* is from the Latin *voc-,* meaning "call." Notice that many words beginning with *co-* are hyphenated.

PRACTICE Use each word below in a meaningful sentence.

1. costars
2. co-owners
3. cosponsors
4. coanchors
5. coexist
6. connect
7. cooperate
8. commute

Technology Skills

Word Processing: Working with Images

Pictures, graphs, maps, and charts are powerful communication tools. They can present a lot of information at a glance, and can spark readers' interest in the text that follows. Images work best when they support or enrich the meaning of the written text. They should strengthen your message, not just impress your readers.

In a small group, analyze the images in several magazines. How do the covers capture your attention? What do illustrations add to the meaning of articles? Do photographs look staged or candid? How are images used in ads? Discuss what you discover about how images are used for different purposes and audiences.

TECHNOLOGY TIP

Search the World Wide Web for photos and clip art you can add to your documents. To download an image, click the right mouse button (on the Mac, just click and hold). Select **Save As,** name the file, and save it to a specific location on your computer.

Inserting Pictures

You can add graphics (clip art, photos, graphs, and so on) to your word-processing documents. Here's how.

1. Open a new document. Pull down the **Insert** menu and select **Picture.**
2. A window will open asking you to select the folder where picture files are stored. Ask your teacher or lab instructor where to find the appropriate folder.
3. Browse through the picture files. Choose a picture you would like to insert into your document, then double click on it (or single click to select it and click on the **Insert** button). The picture will be copied onto your page.
4. To change the size of the picture, click on it. A border with eight "handles" will appear, as shown on the lower left. Resize the picture by clicking and dragging on the handles. To move the picture, click inside the border and drag it.

Use top or bottom handle to change height of picture.

Use any corner to change size of entire picture.

Use left or right handle to change width of picture.

Drawing Tools

Most word-processing programs have drawing features that allow you to create your own images. Follow the steps below to explore the drawing tool.

1. Open a new document. Find the **Drawing** icon on the standard toolbar. Click on it to open the drawing toolbar.

2. The drawing toolbar should contain icon buttons for several of the following tools. Click on each one, and try it out in your document. To delete an object you draw, select it and press the delete key.

The Drawing Toolbar

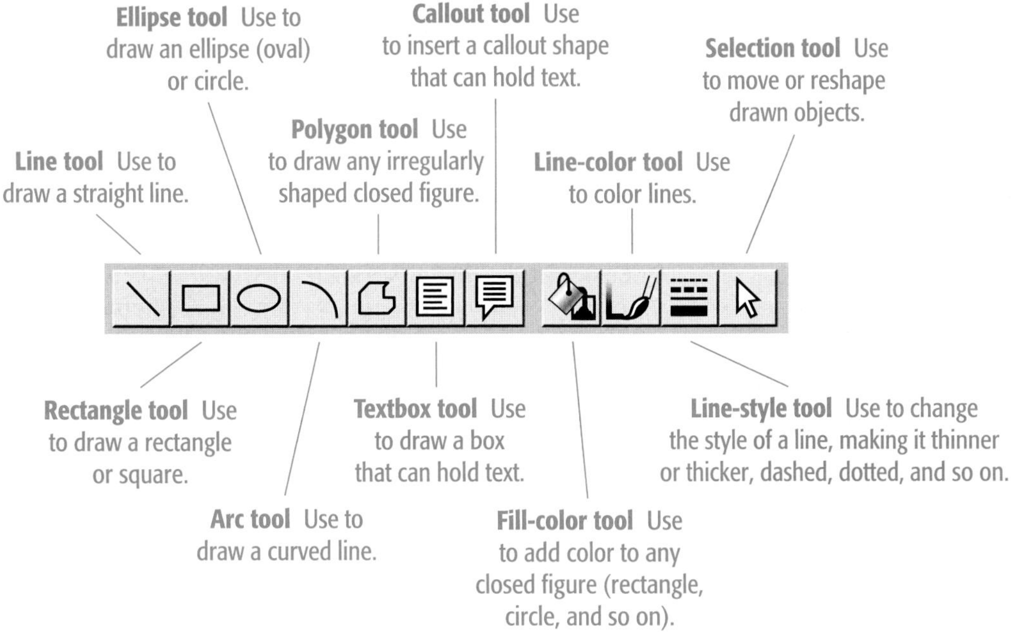
Ellipse tool Use to draw an ellipse (oval) or circle.
Callout tool Use to insert a callout shape that can hold text.
Selection tool Use to move or reshape drawn objects.
Polygon tool Use to draw any irregularly shaped closed figure.
Line tool Use to draw a straight line.
Line-color tool Use to color lines.
Rectangle tool Use to draw a rectangle or square.
Textbox tool Use to draw a box that can hold text.
Line-style tool Use to change the style of a line, making it thinner or thicker, dashed, dotted, and so on.
Arc tool Use to draw a curved line.
Fill-color tool Use to add color to any closed figure (rectangle, circle, and so on).

Your word processing software may also contain icon buttons that will allow you to:

- horizontally or vertically flip an object or picture
- group objects so that they will all move together (especially handy when you need to make up a drawing from several different lines and shapes)
- move an object in a many-layered group to the front or back

ACTIVITIES

1. Research the copyright laws relating to the use of images on the Internet. Use *copyright law* along with *images, clip art,* or *photos* as keywords on a search engine. Pay particular attention to the "fair use exemption" clause for schools.
2. If you have access to a scanner, scan pictures to accompany one of the selections in this theme. Import them into a word-processing document, along with a summary of the selection. Print the result for your classroom bulletin board.

Before You Read

Knoxville, Tennessee and *Legacies*

MEET NIKKI GIOVANNI

Although Nikki Giovanni grew up in Ohio, she spent many summers in Knoxville with her grandmother. Of "Knoxville, Tennessee," she says, "I simply tried to recall and capture . . . the summertime freedom. . . . The poem is fun to me because the experience was fun. And sometimes happiness is a good enough reason to write a poem." Like the child in "Legacies," Giovanni was close to her grandmother, from whom she learned pride and a sense of responsibility to her African American roots.

Nikki Giovanni was born Yolande Cornelia Giovanni in Knoxville in 1943. These poems were first published in 1968 and 1972.

FOCUS ACTIVITY

What makes your home special for you? Why are some people more important to you than others?

Sharing Ideas

Jot down your answers. Then share them with a partner. Do your partner's answers remind you of reasons you hadn't thought of?

Setting a Purpose

Read one person's thoughts and feelings about home.

BACKGROUND

Nikki Giovanni thinks of "Knoxville, Tennessee" as a "fun" poem, but she is known for writing poetry with strong themes of change and revolution. The ideas in her poetry come out of her background. She graduated from Fisk University in Nashville, Tennessee, in 1967, during the Civil Rights movement and became a strong voice in the struggle for equal treatment of African Americans. Since that time, she has published twelve books of poetry and become an English professor at Virginia Polytechnic University in Blacksburg, Virginia. Her poetry has earned her many awards, including the American Library Association commendation in 1973 for *My House,* one of the best books for young adult readers.

A Chat In the Road, 1991. Anna Belle Lee Washington. Oil on canvas, 20 x 30 in.

Knoxville, Tennessee

Nikki Giovanni

I always like summer
best
you can eat fresh corn
from daddy's garden
and okra
and greens
and cabbage
and lots of
barbecue
and buttermilk
and homemade ice-cream
at the church picnic
and listen to
gospel music
outside
at the church
homecoming
and go to the mountains with
your grandmother
and go barefooted
and be warm
all the time
not only when you go to bed
and sleep

Legacies

Nikki Giovanni

her grandmother called her from the playground
"yes, ma'am"
"i want chu to learn how to make rolls" said the old
woman proudly
but the little girl didn't want
to learn how because she knew
even if she couldn't say it that
that would mean when the old one died she would be less
dependent on her spirit so
she said
"i don't want to know how to make no rolls"
with her lips poked out
and the old woman wiped her hands on
her apron saying "lord
these children"
and neither of them ever
said what they meant
and i guess nobody ever does

Petite Fille, 1982. Loïs Mailou Jones. Watercolor, 30 x 24 in. Courtesy of the artist.

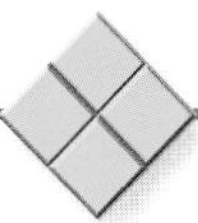

Responding to Literature

PERSONAL RESPONSE

What reactions do these poems stir in you? Make a web for each poem to record your response.

Analyzing Literature

RECALL AND INTERPRET

1. What is the main idea presented in "Knoxville, Tennessee"? How does the speaker feel about Knoxville? Explain.
2. Summarize what happens in "Legacies." How does the girl feel about her grandmother? What clue does the speaker give?

EVALUATE AND CONNECT

3. In which of the two poems can you place yourself more easily? Explain your reasons.
4. How would each of the young people in these poems define "home"? Which definition is closer to your thoughts about what "home" means?
5. How do the children's feelings about home in these two poems compare with your notes from the **Focus Activity** on page 180?
6. How are the grandmothers in the two poems alike? Cite lines from the poems to support your points.

LITERARY ELEMENTS

Mood

Mood is the emotional effect that a poem or story has on a reader. The author creates a mood through his or her choice of words and details to describe the setting, events, and objects. In "Knoxville, Tennessee," Nikki Giovanni creates a nostalgic mood by sharing her favorite childhood memories.

1. What other emotions describe the mood of "Knoxville, Tennessee"?
2. What mood did you find in "Legacies"? Did a second or third reading change that mood? Explain.

- See **Literary Terms Handbook,** p. R6.

Extending Your Response

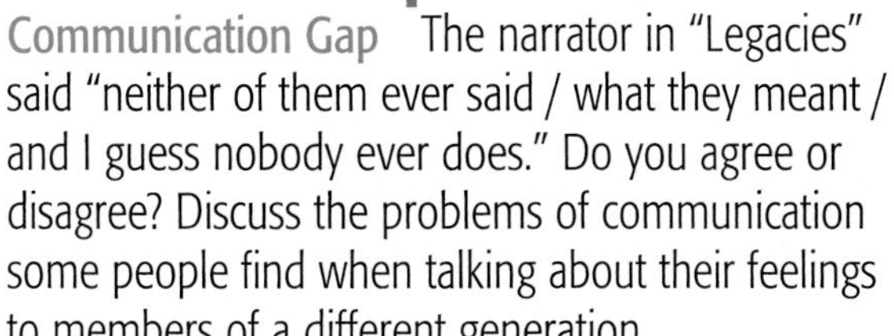

Literature Groups

Communication Gap The narrator in "Legacies" said "neither of them ever said / what they meant / and I guess nobody ever does." Do you agree or disagree? Discuss the problems of communication some people find when talking about their feelings to members of a different generation.

Performing

Reciting a Poem With a partner, practice reading "Knoxville, Tennessee" aloud. Show the rush of the speaker's recollections, while keeping your reading clear for your audience.

Before You Read

A Mother in Mannville

MEET MARJORIE KINNAN RAWLINGS

Marjorie Kinnan Rawlings produced her best work after moving in 1928 from New York City to a seventy-two-acre orange grove in Cross Creek, Florida. Rawlings found inspiration for her writing in the local scenery and likable neighbors. The area was the setting for her best-known novel, *The Yearling*, which won the Pulitzer Prize in 1939. "For myself, the Creek satisfies a thing that had gone hungry and unfed since childhood days," she said.

Marjorie Kinnan Rawlings was born in 1896 in Washington, D.C., and died in Florida in 1953. "A Mother in Mannville" was published in 1940.

FOCUS ACTIVITY

Have you ever thought you knew someone well, only to discover something that changed your impression of him or her?

Journal
Describe your experience in your journal. Is your relationship different now because of what you found out?

Setting a Purpose
Read about one person's impression and an important discovery.

BACKGROUND

The Time and Place This story takes place in the 1930s in North Carolina near an orphanage.

Did You Know? Orphanages were common in the 1930s. Such institutions cared for and protected children who were abandoned or had no guardian. The Great Depression occurred during this time, and parents sometimes sent children to orphanages because they were too poor to clothe and feed them.

VOCABULARY PREVIEW

suffused (sə fūzd′) *adj.* spread through or over, as with light, color, emotion, or quality; p. 186
integrity (in teg′ rə tē) *n.* moral uprightness; honesty; p. 187
subterfuge (sub′ tər fūj′) *n.* a trick or other method used to escape or conceal something; deception; p. 188
instinctive (in stingk′ tiv) *adj.* rising from an impulse or natural tendency; not learned; p. 189
intimate (in′ tə mit) *adj.* closely associated; p. 189
impel (im pel′) *v.* to drive to action; cause; p. 190
savor (sā′ vər) *v.* to take great delight in; p. 191
anomalous (ə nom′ ə ləs) *adj.* not following the usual or regular; abnormal; p. 192

A Mother in Mannville

Marjorie Kinnan Rawlings

The orphanage is high in the Carolina mountains. Sometimes in winter the snowdrifts are so deep that the institution is cut off from the village below, from all the world. Fog hides the mountain peaks, the snow swirls down the valleys, and a wind blows so bitterly that the orphanage boys who take the milk twice daily to the baby cottage reach the door with fingers stiff in an agony of numbness.

"Or when we carry trays from the cookhouse for the ones that are sick," Jerry said, "we get our faces frostbit, because we can't put our hands over them. I have gloves," he added. "Some of the boys don't have any."

He liked the late spring, he said. The rhododendron was in bloom, a carpet of color, across the mountainsides, soft as the May winds that stirred the hemlocks. He called it laurel.

"It's pretty when the laurel blooms," he said. "Some of it's pink and some of it's white."

I was there in the autumn. I wanted quiet, isolation, to do some troublesome writing. I wanted mountain air to blow out the malaria from too long a time in the subtropics. I was homesick, too, for the

Did You Know?
A *shock* is a bundle of corn or wheat, set upright in a field.

flaming of maples in October, and for corn shocks and pumpkins and black-walnut trees and the lift of hills. I found them all, living in a cabin that belonged to the orphanage, half a mile beyond the orphanage farm. When I took the cabin, I asked for a boy or man to come and chop wood for the fireplace. The first few days were warm, I found what wood I needed about the cabin, no one came, and I forgot the order.

I looked up from my typewriter one late afternoon, a little startled. A boy stood at the door, and my pointer dog, my companion, was at his side and had not barked to warn me. The boy was probably twelve years old, but undersized. He wore overalls and a torn shirt, and was barefooted.

He said, "I can chop some wood today."

I said, "But I have a boy coming from the orphanage."

"I'm the boy."

"You? But you're small."

"Size don't matter, chopping wood," he said. "Some of the big boys don't chop good. I've been chopping wood at the orphanage a long time."

I visualized mangled and inadequate branches for my fires. I was well into my work and not inclined to conversation. I was a little blunt.

"Very well. There's the ax. Go ahead and see what you can do."

I went back to work, closing the door. At first the sound of the boy dragging brush annoyed me. Then he began to chop. The blows were rhythmic and steady, and shortly I had forgotten him, the sound no more of an interruption than a consistent[1] rain. I suppose an hour and a half passed, for when I stopped and stretched, and heard the boy's steps on the cabin stoop,[2] the sun was dropping behind the farthest mountain, and the valleys were purple with something deeper than the asters.

The boy said, "I have to go to supper now. I can come again tomorrow evening."

I said, "I'll pay you now for what you've done," thinking I should probably have to insist on an older boy. "Ten cents an hour?"

"Anything is all right."

We went together back of the cabin. An astonishing amount of solid wood had been cut. There were cherry logs and heavy roots of rhododendron, and blocks from the waste pine and oak left from the building of the cabin.

"But you've done as much as a man," I said, "This is a splendid pile."

I looked at him, actually, for the first time. His hair was the color of the corn shocks and his eyes, very direct, were like the mountain sky when rain is pending—gray, with a shadowing of that miraculous blue. As I spoke, a light came over him, as though the setting sun had touched him with the same suffused glory with which it touched the mountains. I gave him a quarter.

1. Here, *consistent* means simply "steady."
2. A *stoop* is a small porch, platform, or staircase leading to the entrance of a house or building.

Vocabulary

suffused (sə fūzd′) *adj.* spread through or over, as with light, color, emotion, or quality

"You may come tomorrow," I said, "and thank you very much."

He looked at me, and at the coin, and seemed to want to speak, but could not, and turned away.

"I'll split kindling[3] tomorrow," he said over his thin ragged shoulder. "You'll need kindling and medium wood and logs and backlogs."

At daylight I was half wakened by the sound of chopping. Again it was so even in texture that I went back to sleep. When I left my bed in the cool morning, the boy had come and gone, and a stack of kindling was neat against the cabin wall. He came again after school in the afternoon and worked until time to return to the orphanage. His name was Jerry; he was twelve years old, and he had been at the orphanage since he was four. I could picture him at four, with the same grave gray-blue eyes and the same—independence? No, the word that comes to me is "integrity."

Boy Holding Logs, 1873. Winslow Homer. Oil on canvas, 12⅛ x 9¼ in.

Viewing the painting: Study the boy in this painting. What hopes and dreams do you imagine that he and Jerry may share?

The word means something very special to me, and the quality for which I use it is a rare one. My father had it—there is another of whom I am almost sure—but almost no man of my acquaintance possesses it with the clarity, the purity, the simplicity of a mountain stream. But the boy Jerry had it. It is bedded on courage, but it is more than brave. It is honest, but it is more than honesty. The ax handle

3. *Kindling* is material for starting a fire, especially small pieces of dry wood.

Vocabulary

integrity (in teg′ rə tē) *n.* moral uprightness; honesty

Springtime. Robert Vonnoh (1858–1933). Oil on canvas, 20 x 24 in. Private collection.
Viewing the painting: How does the mood of this painting reflect the mood of the story?

broke one day. Jerry said the woodshop at the orphanage would repair it. I brought money to pay for the job and he refused it.

"I'll pay for it," he said. "I broke it. I brought the ax down careless."

"But no one hits accurately every time," I told him. "The fault was in the wood of the handle. I'll see the man from whom I bought it."

It was only then that he would take the money. He was standing back of his own carelessness. He was a free-will agent and he chose to do careful work, and if he failed, he took the responsibility without subterfuge.

And he did for me the unnecessary thing, the gracious thing, that we find done only by the great of heart. Things no training can teach, for they are done

Vocabulary

subterfuge (sub′ tər fūj′) *n.* a trick or other method used to escape or conceal something; deception on the instant, with no predicated[4] experience. He found a cubbyhole beside the fireplace that I had not noticed. There, of his own accord, he put kindling and "medium" wood, so that I might always have dry fire material ready in case of sudden wet weather. A stone was loose in the rough walk to the cabin. He dug a deeper hole and steadied it, although he came, himself, by a short cut over the bank. I found that when I tried to return his thoughtfulness with such things as candy and apples, he was wordless. "Thank you" was, perhaps, an expression for which he had had no use, for his courtesy was instinctive. He only looked at the gift and at me, and a curtain lifted, so that I saw deep into the clear well of his eyes, and gratitude was there, and affection, soft over the firm granite of his character.

He made simple excuses to come and sit with me. I could no more have turned him away than if he had been physically hungry. I suggested once that the best time for us to visit was just before supper, when I left off my writing. After that, he waited always until my typewriter had been some time quiet. One day I worked until nearly dark. I went outside the cabin, having forgotten him. I saw him going up over the hill in the twilight toward the orphanage. When I sat down on my stoop, a place was warm from his body where he had been sitting.

He became intimate, of course, with my pointer, Pat. There is a strange communion between a boy and a dog. Perhaps they possess the same singleness of spirit, the same kind of wisdom. It is difficult to explain, but it exists. When I went across the state for a weekend, I left the dog in Jerry's charge. I gave him the dog whistle and the key to the cabin, and left sufficient food. He was to come two or three times a day and let out the dog, and feed and exercise him. I should return Sunday night, and Jerry would take out the dog for the last time Sunday afternoon and then leave the key under an agreed hiding place.

My return was belated and fog filled the mountain passes so treacherously that I dared not drive at night. The fog held the next morning, and it was Monday noon before I reached the cabin. The dog had been fed and cared for that morning. Jerry came early in the afternoon, anxious.

"The superintendent said nobody would drive in the fog," he said. "I came just before bedtime last night and you hadn't come. So I brought Pat some of my breakfast this morning. I wouldn't have let anything happen to him."

"I was sure of that. I didn't worry."

"When I heard about the fog, I thought you'd know."

He was needed for work at the orphanage and he had to return at once. I gave him a dollar in payment, and he looked at it and went away. But that night he came in the darkness and knocked at the door.

"Come in, Jerry," I said, "if you're allowed to be away this late."

"I told maybe a story," he said. "I told them I thought you would want to see me."

"That's true," I assured him, and I saw his relief. "I want to hear about how you managed with the dog."

4. Here, *predicated* means "established; basic."

Vocabulary

instinctive (in stingk′ tiv) *adj.* rising from an impulse or natural tendency; not learned
intimate (in′ tə mit) *adj.* closely associated

He sat by the fire with me, with no other light, and told me of their two days together. The dog lay close to him, and found a comfort there that I did not have for him. And it seemed to me that being with my dog, and caring for him, had brought the boy and me, too, together, so that he felt that he belonged to me as well as to the animal.

"He stayed right with me," he told me, "except when he ran in the laurel. He likes the laurel. I took him up over the hill and we both ran fast. There was a place where the grass was high and I lay down in it and hid. I could hear Pat hunting for me. He found my trail and he barked. When he found me, he acted crazy, and he ran around and around me, in circles."

We watched the flames.

"That's an apple log," he said. "It burns the prettiest of any wood."

We were very close.

He was suddenly impelled to speak of things he had not spoken of before, nor had I cared to ask him.

"You look a little bit like my mother," he said. "Especially in the dark, by the fire."

"But you were only four, Jerry, when you came here. You have remembered how she looked, all these years?"

"My mother lives in Mannville," he said.

For a moment, finding that he had a mother shocked me as greatly as anything in my life has ever done, and I did not know why it disturbed me. Then I understood my distress. I was filled with a passionate resentment that any woman should go away and leave her son. A fresh anger added itself. A son like this one—The orphanage was a wholesome place, the executives were kind, good people, the food was more than adequate, the boys were healthy, a ragged shirt was no hardship, nor the doing of clean labor. Granted, perhaps, that the boy felt no lack, what blood fed the bowels of a woman who did not yearn over this child's lean body that had come in parturition[5] out of her own? At four he would have looked the same as now. Nothing, I thought, nothing in life could change those eyes. His quality must be

5. *Parturition* (pär′ tə rish′ ən) is the act of giving birth.

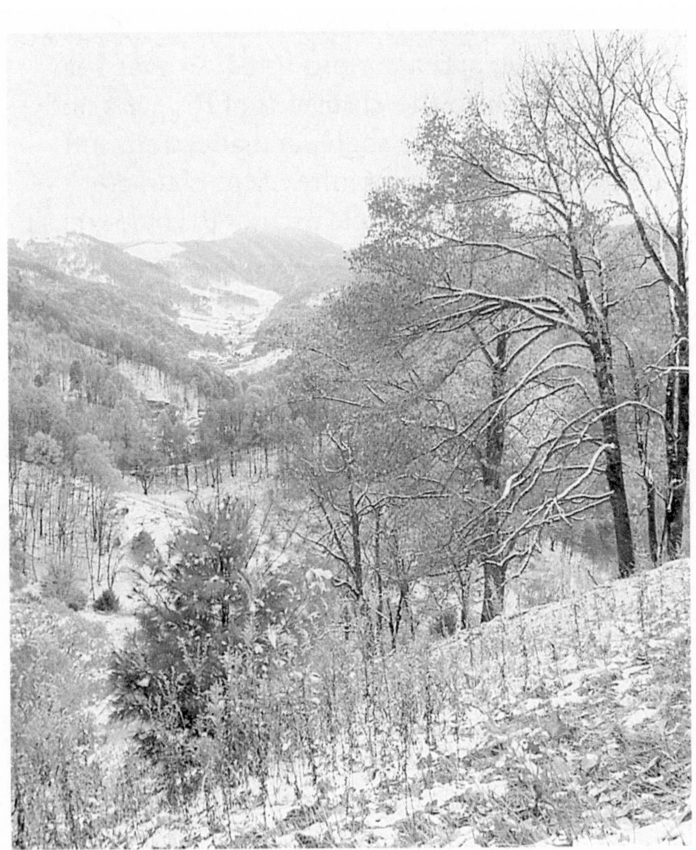

Viewing the photograph: How do you feel when you think of fall and winter? Why are these seasons important in the story?

Vocabulary
impel (im pel′) *v.* to drive to action; cause

apparent to an idiot, a fool. I burned with questions I could not ask. In any, I was afraid, there would be pain.

"Have you seen her, Jerry—lately?"

"I see her every summer. She sends for me."

I wanted to cry out, "Why are you not with her? How can she let you go away again?"

He said, "She comes up here from Mannville whenever she can. She doesn't have a job now."

His face shone in the firelight.

"She wanted to give me a puppy, but they can't let any one boy keep a puppy. You remember the suit I had on last Sunday?" He was plainly proud. "She sent me that for Christmas. The Christmas before that"—he drew a long breath, savoring the memory—"she sent me a pair of skates."

"Roller skates?"

My mind was busy, making pictures of her, trying to understand her. She had not, then, entirely deserted or forgotten him. But why, then— I thought, "I must not condemn her without knowing."

"Roller skates. I let the other boys use them. They're always borrowing them. But they're careful of them."

What circumstance other than poverty—

"I'm going to take the dollar you gave me for taking care of Pat," he said, "and buy her a pair of gloves."

I could only say, "That will be nice. Do you know her size?"

"I think it's 8½," he said.

He looked at my hands.

"Do you wear 8½?" he asked.

"No. I wear a smaller size, a 6."

"Oh! Then I guess her hands are bigger than yours."

I hated her. Poverty or no, there was other food than bread, and the soul could starve as quickly as the body. He was taking his dollar to buy gloves for her big stupid hands, and she lived away from him, in Mannville, and contented herself with sending him skates.

"She likes white gloves," he said. "Do you think I can get them for a dollar?"

"I think so," I said.

I decided that I should not leave the mountains without seeing her and knowing for myself why she had done this thing.

The human mind scatters its interests as though made of thistledown, and every wind stirs and moves it. I finished my work. It did not please me, and I gave my thoughts to another field. I should need some Mexican material.

Did You Know?
Thistledown is the soft, fluffy down on the flower head of a thistle.

I made arrangements to close my Florida place. Mexico immediately, and doing the writing there, if conditions were favorable. Then, Alaska with my brother. After that, heaven knew what or where.

I did not take time to go to Mannville to see Jerry's mother, nor even to talk with the orphanage officials about her. I was a trifle abstracted[6] about the boy, because of

6. Here, *abstracted* means "lost in thought"; preoccupied.

Vocabulary
savor (sā′ vər) *v.* to take great delight in

my work and plans. And after my first fury at her—we did not speak of her again—his having a mother, any sort at all, not far away, in Mannville, relieved me of the ache I had had about him. He did not question the anomalous relation. He was not lonely. It was none of my concern.

He came every day and cut my wood and did small helpful favors and stayed to talk. The days had become cold, and often I let him come inside the cabin. He would lie on the floor in front of the fire, with one arm across the pointer, and they would both doze and wait quietly for me. Other days they ran with a common ecstasy through the laurel, and since the asters were now gone, he brought me back vermilion maple leaves, and chestnut boughs dripping with imperial yellow. I was ready to go.

I said to him, "You have been my good friend, Jerry. I shall often think of you and miss you. Pat will miss you too. I am leaving tomorrow."

He did not answer. When he went away, I remember that a new moon hung over the mountains, and I watched him go in silence up the hill. I expected him the next day, but he did not come. The details of packing my personal belongings, loading my car, arranging the bed over the seat, where the dog would ride, occupied me until late in the day. I closed the cabin and started the car, noticing that the sun was in the west and I should do well to be out of the mountains by nightfall. I stopped by the orphanage and left the cabin key and money for my light bill with Miss Clark.

"And will you call Jerry for me to say good-bye to him?"

"I don't know where he is," she said. "I'm afraid he's not well. He didn't eat his dinner this noon. One of the other boys saw him going over the hill into the laurel. He was supposed to fire the boiler this afternoon. It's not like him; he's unusually reliable."

I was almost relieved, for I knew I should never see him again, and it would be easier not to say good-bye to him.

I said, "I wanted to talk with you about his mother—why he's here—but I'm in more of a hurry than I expected to be. It's out of the question for me to see her now too. But here's some money I'd like to leave with you to buy things for him at Christmas and on his birthday. It will be better than for me to try to send him things. I could so easily duplicate—skates, for instance."

She blinked her honest spinster's[7] eyes.

"There's not much use for skates here," she said.

Her stupidity annoyed me.

"What I mean," I said, "is that I don't want to duplicate things his mother sends him. I might have chosen skates if I didn't know she had already given them to him."

She stared at me.

"I don't understand," she said. "He has no mother. He has no skates."

7. *Spinster* usually refers to an older woman who has never been married.

Vocabulary

anomalous (ə nom′ ə ləs) *adj.* not following the usual or regular; abnormal

Responding to Literature

PERSONAL RESPONSE

What were your thoughts when you read the last sentence of this story? Write these thoughts in your journal.

Analyzing Literature

RECALL

1. How does the narrator's impression of Jerry change?
2. What does Jerry say about his mother?
3. How does the narrator react to what Jerry tells her about his mother?
4. Describe how Jerry spends his days at the narrator's cabin.

INTERPRET

5. What causes the narrator to believe that Jerry has integrity?
6. What does Jerry's description of his mother tell you about him?
7. Why do you think the narrator reacts as she does to Jerry's description of his mother and their relationship?
8. Why, do you think, does Jerry respond as he does to the narrator's news that she is leaving?

EVALUATE AND CONNECT

9. Theme Connection In what ways do Jerry and the narrator find closeness and strength in their relationship? Select details from the story to support your view.
10. Think about your response to the **Focus Activity** on page 184. How was your experience similar to the narrator's? How was it different?

LITERARY ELEMENTS

Narrator

A **narrator** is the person who tells a story. The narrator may be the author of a true story, such as R. A. Sasaki's "A Dictionary of Japanese-American Terms." In fiction, the narrator may be a voice outside the story or a character who participates in the story. A narrator outside the story uses the **third-person point of view.** A narrator who is a character in a story uses the **first-person point of view** to describe his or her experiences.

1. What type of narrator is this storyteller—an outside voice, a character, or the author? Explain.
2. Sometimes a narrator isn't knowledgeable or mature enough to fully explain a story. Suppose that Jerry were the narrator. How might he have told the story? Would he have been more or less reliable than the adult narrator? Explain.

● See **Literary Terms Handbook,** p. R6.

Literature and Writing

Writing About Literature

Definition The narrator tells us that the remarkable thing about Jerry is his "integrity." She defines the term and even gives an example (Jerry's wish to pay for the ax handle) to help the reader understand the concept. Write your own definition for a quality that you think the narrator possesses. Give examples or make comparisons to help clarify the word.

Personal Writing

Wanted: The Perfect Relative People sometimes wish for a relative they never had, such as a big brother; a healthy, energetic grandparent; or an aunt to take them to special places or to give them special things. In your journal, write a description of a relative you do not have or never knew, but wish you had. Tell how that person might fill a special need in your own life.

Extending Your Response

Literature Groups

Judging the Narrator Do you think the narrator was sensitive and kind, or was she self-absorbed and distant? What did she do for Jerry? What more might she have done? As a group, search for examples that show her concern for Jerry, as well as opportunities she missed for kindness. Also discuss the limits of her ability to help him. Conclude your discussion by writing a brief statement that rates the narrator's response to the boy. Compare your concluding statement with those of other groups.

Listening and Speaking

Between Friends With a small group, brainstorm some things Jerry might tell his friends about his time with the narrator. Without rehearsing, role-play the conversation they might have. The student playing Jerry should mention specific events and how they made him feel. The other students should ask questions or offer comments about what happened.

Learning for Life

Researching Community Resources "A Mother in Mannville" describes the orphanage where Jerry lives. Is there an institution in your town or city that offers help to needy people? Such institutions might include senior citizen homes or shelters for homeless families. Find out more about the institution through research and interviews, and report your findings to the class.

Reading Further

For stories about ways we rely on others, try these:
Marjorie Kinnan Rawlings, *The Yearling*
John Steinbeck, *The Red Pony*

Save your work for your portfolio.

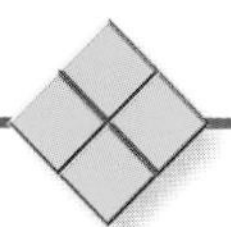

Skill Minilessons

GRAMMAR AND LANGUAGE • CAPITALIZATION

Good writers follow these basic rules for capitalization:

- Capitalize the first word of a direct quotation, a quotation that gives the speaker's exact words.
  I could only say, "That will be nice. Do you know her size?"
- Capitalize proper nouns (specific people, places, and things). Do not capitalize common nouns.
  He became intimate, of course, with my pointer, Pat.

PRACTICE Write each sentence, using capital letters as needed. If the sentence is correct, write *C.*

1. "come in jerry, if you're allowed to be away this late."
2. "I'll pay for it," he said.
3. He said, "she comes up here from mannville whenever she can."
4. his face shone in the firelight.
5. "oh! then I guess her hands are bigger than yours."

● For more about capitalization, see **Language Handbook,** p. R35.

READING AND THINKING • UNDERSTANDING DETAILS

Writers use details carefully. When Rawlings begins her story with details about dense fog, bitter winds, and swirling snow and deep drifts, she evokes the hardship and chill of orphanage life.

As you read, look for the details the writer uses to create a picture or to support an idea.

● For more about main idea and details, see **Reading Handbook,** p. R88.

PRACTICE Briefly explain what each detail tells about the character named in parentheses.

1. At first the sound of the boy dragging brush annoyed me. (the narrator)
2. "I have gloves," he added. "Some of the boys don't have any." (Jerry)
3. The dog lay close to him, and found a comfort there that I did not have for him. (Jerry and the narrator)

VOCABULARY • ANALOGIES

An **analogy** is a type of comparison that is based on relationships between things or ideas.

feathers : bird :: hair : mammal
Feathers cover birds; hair covers mammals.

You read the analogy in this way:

Feathers are to birds as hair is to mammals.

When one term is missing, you can finish an analogy by deciding what relationship exists between the first two things or ideas. Then apply that relationship to another pair of words.

PRACTICE Complete each analogy below.

1. avoid : dodge :: savor :
   a. relish b. taste c. swallow
2. happy : sad :: unusual :
   a. scary b. typical c. joyous
3. spurs : impel :: reins :
   a. halt b. measure c. mount
4. heat : cold :: evil :
   a. virtue b. bravery c. dishonesty
5. kindly : well-meaning :: intimate :
   a. distant b. similar c. familiar

AUTOBIOGRAPHY

An **autobiography** is the story of a person's life, written by that person. It is a type of **nonfiction**—writing that is based on fact, history, or personal opinion. Most autobiographies are **narrative nonfiction,** telling about the writer's life in story form. Many autobiographies are book length because they narrate the writer's entire life. However, some focus on one or two events or a brief period in the author's life.

When you read an autobiography, look for the following elements:

POINT OF VIEW An autobiography is always written from the first person point of view and uses the pronoun "I."

TURNING POINTS These are vivid and memorable experiences in the writer's life that affected him or her in some important way.

DESCRIPTION Writers carefully portray a person, place, thing, or event, using the five senses to help the reader experience the story.

INTERACTION BETWEEN CHARACTERS The action of the narrator with people and other creatures gives the reader insights into the personality of the autobiographer.

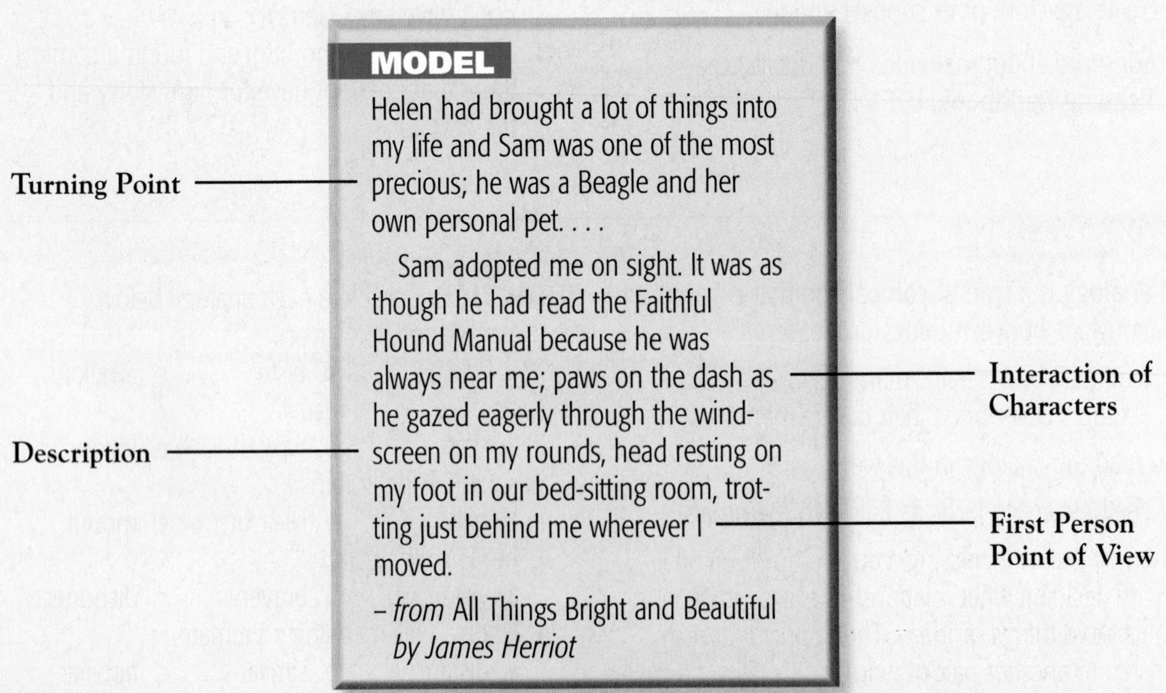

MODEL

Helen had brought a lot of things into my life and Sam was one of the most precious; he was a Beagle and her own personal pet. . . .

Sam adopted me on sight. It was as though he had read the Faithful Hound Manual because he was always near me; paws on the dash as he gazed eagerly through the windscreen on my rounds, head resting on my foot in our bed-sitting room, trotting just behind me wherever I moved.

– *from* All Things Bright and Beautiful *by James Herriot*

ACTIVE READING MODEL

Active Reading Strategies

Tips for Reading an Autobiography

Active readers talk to themselves and to the text as they read. Use the suggestions below to help you read autobiographies and other nonfiction narratives actively.

- For more about reading strategies, see **Reading Handbook,** pp. R84–R95.

PREVIEW

Look for dates and clue words that show sequence of events.

QUESTION

Follow the character's thoughts throughout the story. Ask yourself why the character interacts with other people and responds to events as he or she does. How does the character change? Why?

VISUALIZE

An autobiography involves actual places and events as the author remembers them. Try to see people and places, and consider why they were important to the writer.

RESPOND

Did the author want to share an experience, teach a lesson, or entertain? An effective reader will analyze and respond to the writer.

APPLYING THE STRATEGIES

Read the selection from Maya Angelou's autobiography, *I Know Why the Caged Bird Sings.* Use the **Active Reading** notes in the margins as you read. Write your responses on a separate sheet of paper to look over when you have finished reading.

ACTIVE READING MODEL

Before You Read

from *I Know Why the Caged Bird Sings*

MEET MAYA ANGELOU

"I love that there are other things I can put my hand to, but I am a Black American female writer," says Maya Angelou (mī′ yə an′ jə lō). Author of more than a dozen books, Angelou has written for Oprah Winfrey's TV company and read her poetry at President Bill Clinton's inauguration. She also has "put her hand to" acting, singing, and dancing. "I really wanted to be the person my grandmother wanted me to be," Angelou says. "And I'm still trying."

Maya Angelou was born in St. Louis, Missouri, in 1928. This selection is from I Know Why the Caged Bird Sings, *which was first published in 1969.*

FOCUS ACTIVITY

Think of a time you felt important or exceptional because someone gave you special attention.

QuickWrite
Jot down the details of this event. Describe the person, the setting, and your reaction to the situation.

Setting a Purpose
Read to discover how the right encouragement can help that person grow.

BACKGROUND

The Time and Place The story takes place during the 1930s in a small Arkansas town. The narrator has not spoken for a year because of a trauma experienced during a stay in St. Louis.

Did You Know? *A Tale of Two Cities,* a novel by Charles Dickens, is set during the French Revolution. Charles Darnay is in prison, condemned to death. Sidney Carton, a family friend, helps Darnay escape, then takes his place in jail. When Carton must face the guillotine, he says, "It is a far, far better thing that I do, than I have ever done."

VOCABULARY PREVIEW

taut (tôt) *adj.* tense; tight; p. 199
persistently (pər sis′ tənt lē) *adv.* repeatedly; p. 201
refined (ri fīnd′) *adj.* free from coarseness or crudeness; showing good taste and manners; p. 201
competently (kom′ pət ənt lē) *adv.* capably; p. 202
valid (val′ id) *adj.* well-supported by facts; true; p. 204
intolerant (in tol′ ər ənt) *adj.* unwilling to put up with; not accepting; p. 205
illiteracy (i lit′ ər ə sē) *n.* the inability to read or write; p. 205
collective (kə lek′ tiv) *adj.* having to do with a group of persons or things; common; shared; p. 205

from I Know Why the Caged Bird Sings

Maya Angelou

Pared Amarilla con Jaula (Yellow Wall with Birdcage), 1990. Elena Climent. Oil on canvas, 42 x 53 in. Mary-Anne Martin/Fine Art, New York.

ACTIVE READING MODEL

Mrs. Bertha Flowers was the aristocrat of Black Stamps. She had the grace of control to appear warm in the coldest weather, and on the Arkansas summer days it seemed she had a private breeze which swirled around, cooling her. She was thin without the taut look of wiry people, and her printed voile[1] dresses and flowered hats were as right for her as denim overalls for a farmer. She was our side's answer to the richest white woman in town.

Her skin was a rich black that would have peeled like a plum if snagged, but then no one would have thought of getting close enough to Mrs. Flowers to ruffle her dress, let alone snag her skin. She didn't encourage familiarity. She wore gloves too.

VISUALIZE

Take a moment to picture Mrs. Flowers in your mind.

1. *Voile* (voil) is a light cotton fabric.

Vocabulary

taut (tôt) *adj.* tense; tight

ACTIVE READING MODEL

I don't think I ever saw Mrs. Flowers laugh, but she smiled often. A slow widening of her thin black lips to show even, small white teeth, then the slow effortless closing. When she chose to smile on me, I always wanted to thank her. The action was so graceful and inclusively benign.[2]

The End of the Day, 1955. Hyacinth Manning-Carner. Pastel on paper, 29 x 22 in.

Viewing the painting: What characteristics of Mrs. Flowers do you see in the woman in this picture? In what ways is she different?

She was one of the few gentlewomen I have ever known, and has remained throughout my life the measure of what a human being can be.

QUESTION

What makes someone "the measure of what a human being can be"?

Momma had a strange relationship with her. Most often when she passed on the road in front of the Store, she spoke to Momma in that soft yet carrying voice, "Good day, Mrs. Henderson." Momma responded with "How you, Sister Flowers?"

Mrs. Flowers didn't belong to our church, nor was she Momma's familiar. Why on earth did she insist on calling her Sister Flowers? Shame made me want to hide my face. Mrs. Flowers deserved better than to be called Sister. Then, Momma left out the verb. Why not ask, "How *are* you, *Mrs.* Flowers?" With the unbalanced passion of the young, I hated her for showing her ignorance to Mrs. Flowers. It didn't occur to me for many years that they were as alike as sisters, separated only by formal education.

QUESTION

Why might two unrelated women seem as alike as sisters?

Although I was upset, neither of the women was in the least shaken by what I thought an unceremonious greeting. Mrs. Flowers would continue her easy gait up the hill to her little bungalow, and

2. *Benign* means "kindly and gentle." *Inclusively* means "in a way that includes everyone and everything."

Momma kept on shelling peas or doing whatever had brought her to the front porch.

Occasionally, though, Mrs. Flowers would drift off the road and down to the Store and Momma would say to me, "Sister, you go on and play." As I left I would hear the beginning of an intimate conversation. Momma persistently using the wrong verb, or none at all.

"Brother and Sister Wilcox is sho'ly the meanest—" "Is," Momma? "Is"? Oh, please, not "is," Momma, for two or more. But they talked, and from the side of the building where I waited for the ground to open up and swallow me, I heard the soft-voiced Mrs. Flowers and the textured voice of my grandmother merging and melting. They were interrupted from time to time by giggles that must have come from Mrs. Flowers (Momma never giggled in her life). Then she was gone.

She appealed to me because she was like people I had never met personally. Like women in English novels who walked the moors (whatever they were) with their loyal dogs racing at a respectful distance. Like the women who sat in front of roaring fireplaces, drinking tea incessantly from silver trays full of scones and crumpets.[3] Women who walked over the "heath" and read morocco-bound books[4] and had two last names divided by a hyphen. It would be safe to say that she made me proud to be Negro, just by being herself.

She acted just as refined as whitefolks in the movies and books and she was more beautiful, for none of them could have come near that warm color without looking gray by comparison.

It was fortunate that I never saw her in the company of powhitefolks. For since they tend to think of their whiteness as an evenizer, I'm certain that I would have had to hear her spoken to commonly as Bertha, and my image of her would have been shattered like the unmendable Humpty-Dumpty.

One summer afternoon, sweet-milk fresh in my memory, she stopped at the Store to buy provisions. Another Negro woman of her health and age would have been expected to carry the paper sacks home in one hand, but Momma said, "Sister Flowers, I'll send Bailey up to your house with these things."

ACTIVE READING MODEL

CONNECT

Does anyone you know make you proud to be who you are?

---

3. A *moor* is a stretch of open, rolling, wild land. *Incessantly* means "constantly." A *scone* is a sweet biscuit, and a *crumpet* is an English muffin.
4. Another word for moor is *heath*. A *morocco-bound book* is bound in leather made from goats raised in Morocco, a country in North Africa.

Vocabulary

persistently (pər sis′ tənt lē) *adv.* repeatedly

refined (ri fīnd′) *adj.* free from coarseness or crudeness; showing good taste and manners

ACTIVE READING MODEL

QUESTION

Why do Sister Flowers and Momma exchange "age-group looks"?

She smiled that slow dragging smile, "Thank you, Mrs. Henderson. I'd prefer Marguerite, though." My name was beautiful when she said it. "I've been meaning to talk to her, anyway." They gave each other age-group looks.

Momma said, "Well, that's all right then. Sister, go and change your dress. You going to Sister Flowers's."

Did You Know?
A *chifforobe* (shif′ə rōb) is a tall piece of furniture that has both drawers and space for hanging clothes.

The chifforobe was a maze. What on earth did one put on to go to Mrs. Flowers' house? I knew I shouldn't put on a Sunday dress. It might be sacrilegious.[5] Certainly not a house dress, since I was already wearing a fresh one. I chose a school dress, naturally. It was formal without suggesting that going to Mrs. Flowers' house was equivalent to attending church.

I trusted myself back into the Store.

"Now, don't you look nice." I had chosen the right thing, for once.

"Mrs. Henderson, you make most of the children's clothes, don't you?"

"Yes, ma'am. Sure do. Store-bought clothes ain't hardly worth the thread it take to stitch them."

"I'll say you do a lovely job, though, so neat. That dress looks professional."

RESPOND

Are you surprised that Mrs. Flowers does not sew?

Momma was enjoying the seldom-received compliments. Since everyone we knew (except Mrs. Flowers, of course) could sew competently, praise was rarely handed out for the commonly practiced craft.

"I try, with the help of the Lord, Sister Flowers, to finish the inside just like I does the outside. Come here, Sister."

I had buttoned up the collar and tied the belt, apronlike, in back. Momma told me to turn around. With one hand she pulled the strings and the belt fell free at both sides of my waist. Then her large hands were at my neck, opening the button loops. I was terrified. What was happening?

"Take it off, Sister." She had her hands on the hem of the dress.

QUESTION

Why does Momma want to explain her sewing techniques to Mrs. Flowers?

"I don't need to see the inside, Mrs. Henderson, I can tell . . ." But the dress was over my head and my arms were stuck in the sleeves. Momma said, "That'll do. See here, Sister Flowers, I French-seams around the armholes." Through the cloth film, I saw the shadow

5. *Sacrilegious* means "showing disrespect for something sacred or cherished."

Vocabulary
competently (kom′ pət ənt lē) *adv.* capably

Kept In, 1889. Edward Lamson Henry. Oil on canvas, 13½ x 18 in. © New York State Historical Association, Cooperstown. N-309.61. Photo by Richard Walker.

Viewing the painting: What about this girl reminds you of Marguerite?

approach. "That makes it last longer. Children these days would bust out of sheet-metal clothes. They so rough."

"That is a very good job, Mrs. Henderson. You should be proud. You can put your dress back on, Marguerite."

"No ma'am. Pride is a sin. And 'cording to the Good Book, it goeth before a fall."

"That's right. So the Bible says. It's a good thing to keep in mind."

I wouldn't look at either of them. Momma hadn't thought that taking off my dress in front of Mrs. Flowers would kill me stone dead. If I had refused, she would have thought I was trying to be "womanish" and might have remembered St. Louis. Mrs. Flowers had known that I would be embarrassed and that was even worse. I picked up the groceries and went out to wait in the hot sunshine. It would be fitting if I got a sunstroke and died before they came outside. Just dropped dead on the slanting porch.

RESPOND

How would you react to Momma?

There was a little path beside the rocky road, and Mrs. Flowers walked in front swinging her arms and picking her way over the stones.

She said, without turning her head, to me, "I hear you're doing very good school work, Marguerite, but that it's all written. The teachers report

that they have trouble getting you to talk in class." We passed the triangular farm on our left and the path widened to allow us to walk together. I hung back in the separate unasked and unanswerable questions.

"Come and walk along with me, Marguerite." I couldn't have refused even if I wanted to. She pronounced my name so nicely. Or more correctly, she spoke each word with such clarity that I was certain a foreigner who didn't understand English could have understood her.

"Now no one is going to make you talk—possibly no one can. But bear in mind, language is man's way of communicating with his fellow man and it is language alone which separates him from the lower animals." That was a totally new idea to me, and I would need time to think about it.

"Your grandmother says you read a lot. Every chance you get. That's good, but not good enough. Words mean more than what is set down on paper. It takes the human voice to infuse[6] them with the shades of deeper meaning."

QUESTION

What is Mrs. Flowers's attitude toward reading?

I memorized the part about the human voice infusing words. It seemed so valid and poetic.

She said she was going to give me some books and that I not only must read them, I must read them aloud. She suggested that I try to make a sentence sound in as many different ways as possible.

"I'll accept no excuse if you return a book to me that has been badly handled." My imagination boggled at the punishment I would deserve if in fact I did abuse a book of Mrs. Flowers'. Death would be too kind and brief.

The odors in the house surprised me. Somehow I had never connected Mrs. Flowers with food or eating or any other common experience of common people. There must have been an outhouse, too, but my mind never recorded it.

The sweet scent of vanilla had met us as she opened the door.

RESPOND

How would you feel in this scene?

"I made tea cookies this morning. You see, I had planned to invite you for cookies and lemonade so we could have this little chat. The lemonade is in the icebox."

It followed that Mrs. Flowers would have ice on an ordinary day, when most families in our town bought ice late on Saturdays only a few times during the summer to be used in the wooden ice-cream freezers.

She took the bags from me and disappeared through the kitchen door. I looked around the room that I had never in my wildest fantasies imagined I would see. Browned photographs leered or threatened from the walls and the white, freshly done curtains pushed

6. *Infuse* means "to introduce gradually or to soak up, as with principles or qualities."

Vocabulary

valid (val′ id) *adj.* well-supported by facts; true

against themselves and against the wind. I wanted to gobble up the room entire and take it to Bailey, who would help me analyze and enjoy it.

"Have a seat, Marguerite. Over there by the table." She carried a platter covered with a tea towel. Although she warned that she hadn't tried her hand at baking sweets for some time, I was certain that like everything else about her the cookies would be perfect.

They were flat round wafers, slightly browned on the edges and butter-yellow in the center. With the cold lemonade they were sufficient for childhood's lifelong diet. Remembering my manners, I took nice little lady-like bites off the edges. She said she had made them expressly for me and that she had a few in the kitchen that I could take home to my brother. So I jammed one whole cake in my mouth and the rough crumbs scratched the insides of my jaws, and if I hadn't had to swallow, it would have been a dream come true.

As I ate she began the first of what we later called "my lessons in living." She said that I must always be intolerant of ignorance but understanding of illiteracy. That some people, unable to go to school were more educated and even more intelligent than college professors. She encouraged me to listen carefully to what country people called mother wit. That in those homely sayings was couched[7] the collective wisdom of generations.

When I finished the cookies she brushed off the table and brought a thick, small book from the bookcase. I had read *A Tale of Two Cities*[8] and found it up to my standards as a romantic novel. She opened the first page and I heard poetry for the first time in my life.

"It was the best of times and the worst of times . . ." Her voice slid in and curved down through and over the words. She was nearly singing. I wanted to look at the pages. Were they the same that I had read? Or were there notes, music, lined on the pages, as in a hymn book? Her sounds began cascading gently. I knew from listening to a thousand preachers that she was nearing the end of her reading, and I hadn't really heard, heard to understand, a single word.

ACTIVE READING MODEL

VISUALIZE

What does Mrs. Flowers's house look like?

QUESTION

What does Mrs. Flowers teach Marguerite in her first "lesson in living"?

---

7. Here, *homely* means "simple; ordinary; everyday," and *couch,* as a verb, means "to express in words."
8. *A Tale of Two Cities,* a novel by Charles Dickens, describes English people who become caught up in the bloody French Revolution.

Vocabulary

intolerant (in tol′ ər ənt) *adj.* unwilling to put up with; not accepting
illiteracy (i lit′ ər ə sē) *n.* the inability to read or write
collective (kə lek′ tiv) *adj.* having to do with a group of persons or things; common; shared

"How do you like that?"

It occurred to me that she expected a response. The sweet vanilla flavor was still on my tongue and her reading was a wonder in my ears. I had to speak.

I said, "Yes, ma'am." It was the least I could do, but it was the most also.

"There's one more thing. Take this book of poems and memorize one for me. Next time you pay me a visit, I want you to recite."

Did You Know?
Wormwood is a sweet-smelling plant, but the word is often used to refer to something unpleasant.

I have tried often to search behind the sophistication of years for the enchantment I so easily found in those gifts. The essence escapes but its aura[9] remains. To be allowed, no, invited, into the private lives of strangers, and to share their joys and fears, was a chance to exchange the Southern bitter wormwood for a cup of mead with Beowulf or a hot cup of tea and milk with Oliver Twist.[10] When I said aloud, "It is a far, far better thing that I do, than I have ever done . . ." tears of love filled my eyes at my selflessness.

QUESTION

Why does Marguerite run down the hill?

On that first day, I ran down the hill and into the road (few cars ever came along it) and had the good sense to stop running before I reached the Store.

I was liked, and what a difference it made. I was respected not as Mrs. Henderson's grandchild or Bailey's sister but for just being Marguerite Johnson.

RESPOND

Does it matter *why* you are liked?

Childhood's logic never asks to be proved (all conclusions are absolute). I didn't question why Mrs. Flowers had singled me out for attention, nor did it occur to me that Momma might have asked her to give me a little talking to. All I cared about was that she had made tea cookies for *me* and read to *me* from her favorite book. It was enough to prove that she liked me.

9. The *essence* of a thing is its purest form or most basic nature. Its *aura* is the special feeling or mood that seems to surround it.
10. Beowulf, Oliver Twist, and the speaker of the quotation are all famous characters from literature.

ACTIVE READING MODEL

Responding to Literature

PERSONAL RESPONSE

How would you feel if Mrs. Flowers paid the same attention to you as she did to Marguerite? Why would you react this way?

Analyzing Literature

RECALL

1. What term does Marguerite use to summarize her opinion of Mrs. Flowers?
2. What decision must Marguerite make when Mrs. Flowers invites her to visit?
3. How does Momma prove to Mrs. Flowers that she sews her clothes in a professional manner?
4. Marguerite gives a detailed description of Mrs. Flowers's house. Summarize her description in two or three sentences.

INTERPRET

5. What details in the story support Marguerite's opinion of Mrs. Flowers?
6. In your opinion, why is Marguerite concerned about what she should wear?
7. What do you learn about Momma from her conversation with Mrs. Flowers about sewing clothes?
8. How does Marguerite react when she sees Mrs. Flowers's house? Why does she react this way?

EVALUATE AND CONNECT

9. Why does Maya Angelou write that Mrs. Flowers is "the measure of what a human being can be"? What do you think is the measure of what a person can be? Make a list of qualities such a person would have.
10. Theme Connection Why would a person like Mrs. Flowers pay special attention to a person like Marguerite? Is Mrs. Flowers typical of people you know? Explain.

LITERARY ELEMENTS

Dialect

A **dialect** is a way of speaking that is associated with a specific geographical area or a group of people. Authors use dialect to give their writing the flavor of a specific region and to reveal the economic or social class of a character. A dialect may have its own vocabulary, grammar, and system for pronunciation. Most countries and cultures have one principal dialect for writing and speaking. In the United States, it is Standard English, but several regional dialects also exist.

1. Momma uses a local dialect that is spoken by some people in the southeastern United States. Marguerite doesn't approve of this dialect. Why not?
2. What lesson about Momma and her dialect does Marguerite learn much later?

● See **Literary Terms Handbook,** p. R3.

Literature and Writing

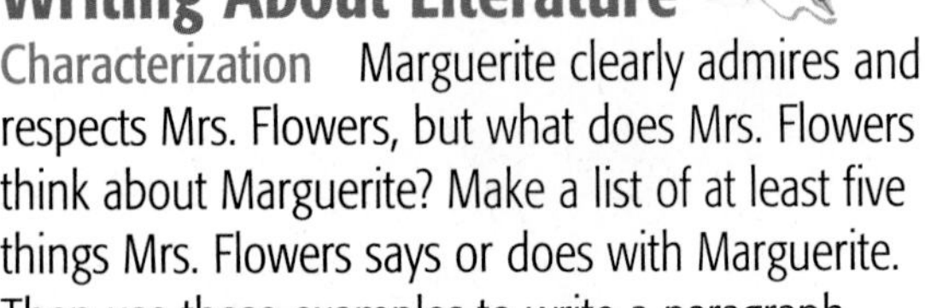

Writing About Literature

Characterization Marguerite clearly admires and respects Mrs. Flowers, but what does Mrs. Flowers think about Marguerite? Make a list of at least five things Mrs. Flowers says or does with Marguerite. Then use these examples to write a paragraph explaining her attitude toward Marguerite.

Personal Writing

Dear Friend Review the details you wrote in the **Focus Activity** on page 198. Write a letter to a friend describing a time when someone paid special attention to you. Be sure to tell your friend why you are writing the letter and why this incident is important to you. Include details and images that will capture your friend's attention. If you wish, read your finished letter to a classmate.

Extending Your Response

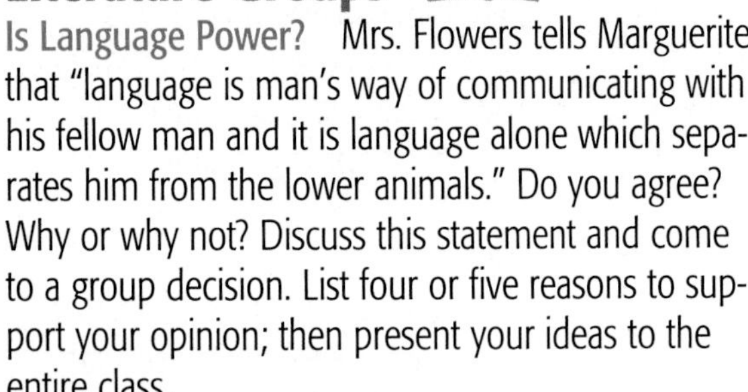

Literature Groups

Is Language Power? Mrs. Flowers tells Marguerite that "language is man's way of communicating with his fellow man and it is language alone which separates him from the lower animals." Do you agree? Why or why not? Discuss this statement and come to a group decision. List four or five reasons to support your opinion; then present your ideas to the entire class.

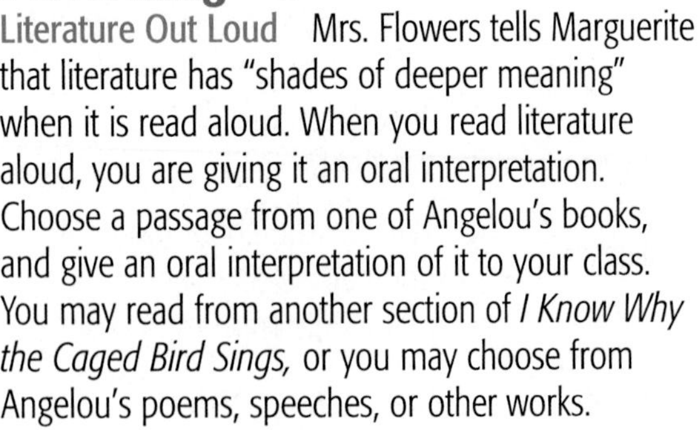

Performing

Literature Out Loud Mrs. Flowers tells Marguerite that literature has "shades of deeper meaning" when it is read aloud. When you read literature aloud, you are giving it an oral interpretation. Choose a passage from one of Angelou's books, and give an oral interpretation of it to your class. You may read from another section of *I Know Why the Caged Bird Sings,* or you may choose from Angelou's poems, speeches, or other works.

Learning for Life

Everyday Lessons Mrs. Flowers gives Marguerite a series of "lessons in living." What are some of these lessons? Discuss Mrs. Flowers's ideas. Do you agree with her ideas? Why or why not? Then make a list of three "lessons in living" of your own, and present them in a chart. You may want to use color, pictures, and graphic art in your design. Share your chart with the class.

Reading Further

If you enjoyed Maya Angelou's autobiographical sketch, try:

Steven Spielberg, Maya Angelou, Debbie Allen; *Amistad: 'Give Us Free'*

Audiocassette Maya Angelou, *And Still I Rise* (Maya Angelou reads her poems)

Save your work for your portfolio.

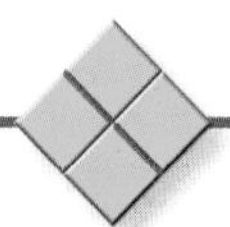

Skill Minilessons

GRAMMAR AND LANGUAGE • SUBJECT-VERB AGREEMENT

The verb of a sentence must agree with its subject in person (first, second, or third) and number (singular or plural).

first person singular:	I *know.*
first person plural:	We *know.*
second person singular:	You *know.*
second person plural:	You *know.*
third person singular:	He, she, it *knows.*
third person plural:	They *know.*

PRACTICE Rewrite the following sentences so the subjects and verbs agree in person and number.

1. She know Mrs. Flowers well.
2. They both understands that Marguerite is shy.
3. Marguerite is pleased because she knows someone respect her.
4. The writer hopes that you, the reader, understands the people in the story.
5. We all enjoys stories like this.

- For more about subject-verb agreement, see **Language Handbook,** p. R13.

READING AND THINKING • EVALUATING

Evaluating is making a judgment about the worth of something. Good readers evaluate what they read, judging the ways in which information and ideas are presented.

- For more about evaluating and literary response, see **Reading Handbook,** pp. R95–R98.

PRACTICE Maya Angelou presents Mrs. Flowers and Momma as important figures in Marguerite's life. In your opinion, which character is more memorable–Mrs. Flowers or Momma? Use examples from the story to support your answer.

VOCABULARY • NEGATING PREFIXES

The prefixes *in-, im-, ir-,* and *il-* add a negative meaning to many words. For example, *intolerant* means "not tolerant"; *impatience* means "without patience"; *illiteracy* is the opposite of *literacy;* and something *irresistible* cannot be resisted. However, these prefixes don't always add a negative meaning. (An *intense* person isn't calm. You don't *improve* something by showing it to be false.) When in doubt, look up the word in a dictionary.

PRACTICE Write the words in which the prefix *in-, im-, il-,* or *ir-* is a negating prefix.

a. impure
b. impulse
c. imitate
d. introduce
e. inconvenient
f. increase
g. independent
h. inflate
i. inform
j. insincere
k. injustice
l. illogical
m. illegal
n. iron
o. irregular
p. irritate

MEDIA Connection

NEWSPAPER ARTICLE

What kind of person would you expect Marguerite, the young Maya Angelou, to grow up to be?

Maya's Way: Maya Angelou's Zest for Life Continues to Fuel Her Creative Fire

by Patti Thorn—*Rocky Mountain News*, November 23, 1997

As a child, Maya Angelou knew how she'd carry herself when she was grown up: She'd be "friendly, but never gushing," she wrote in her acclaimed memoir *I Know Why the Caged Bird Sings*, "cool but not frigid or distant, distinguished without the awful stiffness."

Now she is nearly 70. And she has some other ideas about maturity:

"Maturity is seeing a young person and saying, 'Do it. Enjoy yourself. (Life's) about that long. Do it. Leave footprints on the sand and laugh as much as possible.'

"People sometimes look as if they've put airplane glue on the back of their hand." She mocks the melodramatic style of someone with their hand to their forehead in despair. Then she shakes her head. "I just can't bear it. I just can't bear it."

Angelou bursts into laughter, her big bear of a body shakes, and if there's any concern that she might have that awful stiffness she hoped to avoid as a child, that dissolves in an instant. Friendly? Indeed. Frigid or distant? Hardly. Distinguished? Check the resumé, which is only getting started with 32 honorary degrees and a Pulitzer Prize nomination.

Many of the essays in her latest collection, *Even the Stars Look Lonesome*, she notes, were written to help her come to grips with various situations. "If I really want to know how I feel about a thing, I write about it," she says. "I can't lie when I start to write. I can't fudge or hedge."

Thus, there's the story of her mother, hooked to an oxygen tank and fighting cancer, another about a visit to a folk museum, where slave cabins were so sanitized for viewing—wooden chairs, a "colorfully blanketed bed"—they aroused Angelou's ire. While the essays are unadorned and conversational, they didn't come easily, says the author. "Critics say 'Maya Angelou has a new book and of course it's good, she's a natural writer,'" she says. "That's like saying you're a natural open heart surgeon. For one page, it might take me five days, two weeks."

Respond

1. What impression do you have of Angelou after reading this article? Explain.
2. Do you agree with Angelou's comments about writing? Why or why not?

Writing Skills

Describing a Person

What makes you feel that you know a person you've only read about? What makes a character seem as familiar as a friend or the neighbor next door? Good writers use the following techniques to bring their readers into a story.

Gather Details When you describe a person, use details to help your readers see and hear that character. Use the most precise descriptive words you can.

Don't just *tell* readers about your subject. *Show* your readers what you're talking about. That's what Maya Angelou does when she describes Mrs. Flowers in *I Know Why the Caged Bird Sings.*

> She was thin without the taut look of wiry people, and her printed voile dresses and flowered hats were as right for her as denim overalls for a farmer.

Organize the Details Introduce your details in a logical order so that readers can easily picture the information. You can group details by order of importance or order of impression. Either way, the details should support a main idea, as shown in the example below.

> She pronounced my name so nicely. Or more correctly, she spoke each word with such clarity that I was certain a foreigner who didn't understand English could have understood her.

ACTIVITIES

1. Choose a character from this theme who seems real to you. Write a paragraph or two describing why you think the character is realistic, and include specific details.
2. Think of a person you admire. List details about the person's appearance, personality, and actions. Use your list of details to help you write a paragraph describing something about the person.

Before You Read

from *Sound-Shadows of the New World*

MEET VED MEHTA

Ved Mehta (ved mā′ tä) has never let his blindness stand in his way. Even as a child, he was determined to be active. He was miserable when his mother forbade him to play roughly with his cousins. Finally, his father assured Mehta that he had told everyone "to let you do whatever you wished." Thereafter, Mehta had a normal childhood. His persistence led him to the Arkansas School for the Blind, and eventually on to Oxford and Harvard.

Ved Mehta was born in India in 1934. This selection is from his autobiography Sound-Shadows of the New World, *which was first published in 1985.*

FOCUS ACTIVITY

Is a person who cannot see "disabled"? Think about what this word means to you.

QuickWrite
Make a quick list of personality characteristics that you think would be essential to anyone who faces the unfamiliar.

Setting a Purpose
Read to find out how a young blind man from India gets along on his first day in the United States.

BACKGROUND

The Time and Place In the 1940s many nations were unable to properly educate people with disabilities. Some of these people were able to come to the United States to study.

Did You Know?
Ved Mehta's religion, Hinduism, one of the world's oldest, is the major religion of India.

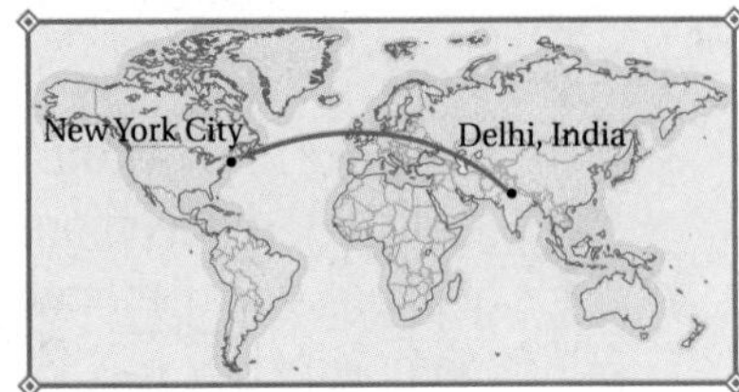

VOCABULARY PREVIEW

encounter (en koun′ tər) *v.* to meet unexpectedly or casually; p. 215
impulse (im′ puls) *n.* an internal force that causes one to act without thinking about it; p. 215
unrestrained (un′ ri strānd′) *adj.* not held in check or under control; p. 216
cringe (krinj) *v.* to draw back, as from fear or dislike; p. 217
servile (sur′ vil) *adj.* like a servant; too humble; p. 218
engulf (en gulf′) *v.* to swallow up; overwhelm; p. 219
resolutely (rez′ ə lo͞ot′ lē) *adv.* determinedly; p. 219
maladjustment (mal′ ə just′ mənt) *n.* poor adjustment to conditions or requirements; p. 220
obligingly (ə blī′ jing lē) *adv.* helpfully; agreeably; p. 220

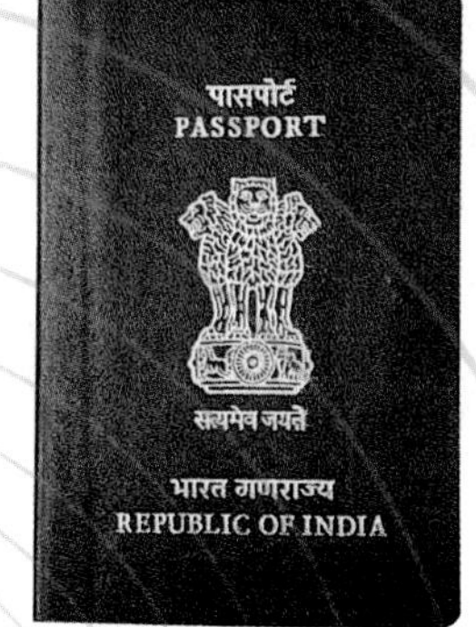

from Sound-Shadows of the New World

Ved Mehta

At the airport, I was questioned by an immigration official. "You're blind—totally blind—and they gave you a visa?[1] You say it's for your studies, but studies where?"

"At the Arkansas School for the Blind. It is in Little Rock, in Arkansas."

He shuffled through the pages of a book. Sleep was in my eyes. Drops of sweat were running down my back. My shirt and trousers felt dirty.

"Arkansas School is not on our list of approved schools for foreign students."

"I know," I said. "That is why the immigration officials in Delhi gave me only a visitor's visa. They said that when I got to the school I should tell the authorities to apply to be on your list of approved schools, so that I could get a student visa." I showed him a big manila envelope I was carrying; it contained my chest X rays, medical reports, and fingerprint charts, which were necessary for a student visa, and which I'd had prepared in advance.

"Why didn't you apply to an approved school in the first place and come here on a proper student visa?" he asked, looking through the material.

---

1. A *passport* identifies a traveler as a citizen of a particular country. To enter another country, a traveler must receive a *visa* from that country. Here, the narrator's passport is from India, and U.S. officials in Delhi gave him a visa.

My knowledge of English was limited. With difficulty, I explained to him that I had applied to some thirty schools but that, because I had been able to get little formal education in India, the Arkansas School was the only one that would accept me; that I had needed a letter of acceptance from an American school to get dollars sanctioned[2] by the Reserve Bank of India; and that now that I was in America I was sure I could change schools if the Arkansas School was not suitable or did not get the necessary approval.

Muttering to himself, the immigration official looked up at me, down at his book, and up at me again. He finally announced, "I think you'll have to go to Washington and apply to get your visa changed to a student visa before you can go to any school."

I recalled things that Daddyji[3] used to say as we were growing up: "In life, there is only fight or flight. You must always fight," and "America is God's own country. People there are the most hospitable and generous people in the world." I told myself I had nothing to worry about. Then I remembered that Daddyji had mentioned a Mr. and Mrs. Dickens in Washington—they were friends of friends of his—and told me that I could get in touch with them in case of emergency.

"I will do whatever is necessary," I now said to the immigration official. "I will go to Washington."

He hesitated, as if he were thinking something, and then stamped my passport and returned it to me. "We Mehtas carry our luck with us," Daddyji used to say. He is right, I thought.

The immigration official suddenly became helpful, as if he were a friend. "You shouldn't have any trouble with the immigration people in Washington," he said, and asked, "Is anybody meeting you here?"

"Mr. and Mrs. di Francesco," I said.

Mrs. di Francesco was a niece of Manmath Nath Chatterjee, whom Daddyji had known when he himself was a student, in London, in 1920. Daddyji had asked Mr. Chatterjee, who had a Scottish-American wife and was now settled in Yellow Springs, Ohio, if he could suggest anyone with whom I might stay in New York, so that I could get acclimatized[4] to America before proceeding to the Arkansas School, which was not due to open until the eleventh of September. Mr. Chatterjee had written back that, as it happened, his wife's niece was married to John di Francesco, a singer who was totally blind, and that Mr. and Mrs. di Francesco lived in New York, and would be delighted to meet me at the airport and keep me as a paying guest at fifteen dollars a week.

"How greedy of them to ask for money!" I had cried when I learned of the arrangement. "People come and stay with us for months and we never ask for an anna."[5]

Daddyji had said, "In the West, people do not, as a rule, stay with relatives and friends but put up in hotels, or in houses as paying guests. That is the custom there. Mr. and Mrs. di Francesco are probably a young, struggling couple who could do with a little extra money."

The immigration official now came from behind the counter, led me to an open area,

2. *Sanctioned* means "approved."

3. *[Daddyji]* In India, the suffix *-ji* is added to a name or title to show respect and affection.

4. *Acclimatized* (ə klī′ mə tīzd′) means "adjusted to a new environment or situation."

5. The *anna* is a former coin of India. Sixteen annas equaled one *rupee,* a unit of money still used in India and other countries.

and shouted, with increasing volume, "Francisco! . . . Franchesca! . . . De Franco!" I wasn't sure what the correct pronunciation was, but his shouting sounded really disrespectful. I asked him to call for Mr. and Mrs. di Francesco softly. He bellowed, "Di Fransesco!"

No one came. My mouth went dry. Mr. and Mrs. di Francesco had sent me such a warm invitation. I couldn't imagine why they would have let me down or what I should do next.

Then I heard the footsteps of someone running toward us. "Here I am. You must be Ved. I'm Muriel di Francesco. I'm sorry John couldn't come." I noted that the name was pronounced the way it was spelled, and that hers was a Yankee voice—the kind I had heard when I first encountered Americans at home, during the war[6]—but it had the sweetness of the voices of my sisters.

We shook hands; she had a nice firm grip. I had an impulse to call her Auntie Muriel—at home, an older person was always called by an honorific,[7] like "Auntie" or "Uncle"—but I greeted her as Daddyji had told me that Westerners liked to be greeted: "Mrs. di Francesco, I'm delighted to make your acquaintance."

"You had a terrible trip, you poor boy. What a terrible way to arrive!" Mrs. di Francesco said in the taxi. "Imagine, everything stolen from a bag!"

One bag had contained clothes. The other, a holdall, had contained (in addition to some extra shirts) a number of ivory curios—statues of Lord Krishna, "no evil" monkeys, brooches with a little pattern on them—which Daddyji had bought with the idea that I could sell them at great profit. "You can take the ivory curios to a shop in Little Rock and ask the shop to sell them for you—on commission, of course," he had said. "In America, a lot of people earn and learn. Who knows? Maybe we could start an ivory-export-import business in a year or so, when I retire from government service." He was deputy director general of health services in the Indian government. "I expect there is a great deal of demand over there for hand-carved things." The fact that neither of us had ever sold even a secondhand gramophone didn't stop us from dreaming.

Did You Know?
Curios are rare or unusual ornamental objects. *Lord Krishna* is one of the most important gods of Hinduism, the main religion in India. A *"no evil" monkey* is a good luck charm, and a *brooch* is a woman's ornamental pin.

I didn't want Mrs. di Francesco to feel bad, so I made light of the theft. "The other bag is still full," I said.

"The ivory things must have been really valuable," she said. She had helped me fill out the insurance-claim forms. "What a bad introduction to America!"

6. Here, *the war* was World War II, which ended in 1945.
7. An *honorific* is any title of honor or respect, such as "Auntie" or "Mrs."

Vocabulary

encounter (en koun′ tər) *v.* to meet unexpectedly or casually
impulse (im′ puls) *n.* an internal force that causes one to act without thinking about it

"But it could have happened in Delhi."

She regaled the taxi driver with the story, as if she and I were long-standing friends. "And we had to wait at the airport for two whole hours, filling out insurance forms. And he only knew the prices in rubles."

"Rupees," I said.

"Is that right?" the taxi driver said, from the front seat. "Well, it shouldn't have happened to you, son."

I leaned toward the half-open window and listened for the roar of street crowds, the cries of hawkers, the clatter of tonga wheels, the trot of tonga horses, the crackle of whips, the blasts of Klaxons, the trills of police whistles, the tinkling of bicycle bells—but all I heard was the steady hiss and rush of cars. "In America, you can really travel fast and get places," I said.

Did You Know?
The *hawkers* are people selling things; a *tonga* is a two-wheeled carriage; and *Klaxons* are loud electric horns.

Mrs. di Francesco took both my hands in hers and broke into open, unrestrained laughter. I have never heard a woman laugh quite like that, I thought.

"What are you laughing at?" I asked.

"I'd just noticed that all this time you had your hand in your breast pocket. Are you afraid of having your wallet stolen, too?"

I was embarrassed. I hadn't realized what I had been doing.

The taxi driver took a sharp turn.

"Where are we?" I asked.

"On Broadway," Mrs. di Francesco said.

"Is Broadway a wide road?" I asked.

She laughed. "A very wide avenue—it's the center of the universe."

At home, the center was a circle, but here the center, it seemed, was a straight line. At home, I often felt I was on a merry-go-round, circling activities that I couldn't join in. Here I would travel in taxis amid new friends and have adventures. I tried to voice my thoughts.

"Poor boy, you have difficulty with the language," Mrs. di Francesco said, gently pressing my hand.

"English is difficult," I said, and I tried to make a joke. "When I was small and first learning English, I was always confusing 'chicken' and 'kitchen.'"

"'Chicken' and 'kitchen,'" Mrs. di Francesco repeated, and laughed.

"I have enough trouble speaking English," the taxi driver said. "I could never learn to speak Hindu."[8]

"Hindi," I said, correcting him.

"You see?" the taxi driver said.

Mrs. di Francesco laughed, and the taxi driver joined in.

After a while, the taxi came to a stop. "Here we are at home, on a Hundred and Thirteenth Street between Broadway and Amsterdam," Mrs. di Francesco said.

Though I was carrying a bank draft for eighty dollars, I had only two dollars in cash, which a family friend had given me for good luck. I handed it to Mrs. di Francesco for the taxi.

---

8. *Hindu* refers to someone who practices Hinduism. *Hindi* is short for *Hindustani,* India's official language.

Vocabulary

unrestrained (un′ ri strānd′) *adj.* not held in check or under control

"That won't be enough," she said.

"But it is *seven rupees!*" I cried. "At home, one could hire a tonga for a whole day for that."

"This is New York," she said. She clicked open her purse and gave some money to the taxi driver.

The taxi driver put my bags on the curb, shook my hand, and said, "If I go to India, I will remember not to become a tonga driver." He drove away.

We picked up the luggage. Mrs. di Francesco tucked my free hand under her bare arm with a quick motion and started walking. A woman at home would probably have cringed at the touch of a stranger's hand under her arm, I thought, but thinking this did not stop me from making a mental note that the muscle of her arm was well developed.

We went into a house, and walked up to Mr. and Mrs. di Francesco's apartment, on the fourth floor. Mr. di Francesco opened the door and kissed Mrs. di Francesco loudly. Had a bomb exploded, I could not have been more surprised. They'll catch something, I thought. I had never heard any grownups kissing at home—not even in films.

Mr. di Francesco shook my hand. He had a powerful grip and a powerful voice. He took me by the shoulder and almost propelled me to a couch. "This is going to be your bed," he said. "I'm sorry I couldn't come to the airport. Anyway, I knew you wouldn't mind being greeted by a charming

Telephone Booths, 1968. Richard Estes. Oil on canvas, 48 x 69 in. Allan Stone Galleries, New York.

Viewing the painting: How might this painting symbolize Ved's first day in New York City?

Vocabulary

cringe (krinj) *v.* to draw back, as from fear or dislike lady." He doesn't have a trace of the timid, servile manner of music masters and blind people at home, I thought.

"We had a delightful ride from the airport," I said.

Mr. di Francesco wanted to know why we were so late, and Mrs. di Francesco told him about the theft.

"What bad luck!" he said.

"But I got here," I said.

"That's the spirit," he said, laughing.

"John, thank you for starting dinner," Mrs. di Francesco said from what I took to be the kitchen.

"Oh, you cook!" I exclaimed. I had never heard of a blind person who could cook.

"Yes, I help Muriel," he said. "We don't have servants here, as they do in your country. We have labor-saving devices." He then showed me around the apartment, casually tapping and explaining—or putting my hand on—various unfamiliar things: a stove that did not burn coal or give out smoke; an ice chest that stood on end and ran on electricity; a machine that toasted bread; a bed for two people; and a tub in which one could lie down. I was full of questions, and asked how natural gas from the ground was piped into individual apartments, and how people could have so much hot water that they could lie down in it. At home, a husband and wife never slept in one bed, but I didn't say anything about that, because I felt shy.

"Oh, you cook!" I exclaimed. I had never heard of a blind person who could cook.

"Do you eat meat?" Mrs. di Francesco asked me from the kitchen. "Aunt Rita—Mrs. Chatterjee—didn't know."

"Yes, I do eat meat," I called back to her. I started worrying about how I would cut it.

Mrs. di Francesco sighed with relief. "John and I hoped that you weren't a vegetarian. We're having spaghetti and meatballs, which are made of beef. Is that all right?"

I shuddered. As a Hindu, I had never eaten beef,[9] and the mere thought of it was revolting. But I recalled another of Daddyji's sayings, "When in Rome, do as the Romans do," and said, "I promised my father that I would eat anything and everything in America and gain some weight."

Mrs. di Francesco brought out the dinner and served it to us at a small table. "The peas are at twelve and the spaghetti and meatballs at six," she said. I must have looked puzzled, because she added, "John locates his food on a plate by the clock dial. I thought all blind people knew—"

"You forget that India has many primitive conditions," Mr. di Francesco interrupted. "Without a doubt, work for the blind there is very backward."

I bridled.[10] "There is nothing primitive or backward in India."

9. *[never eaten beef]* Hindus don't eat beef because they consider cows to be sacred animals.

10. In this context, to *bridle* means "to show anger or annoyance," as if by throwing back the head the way a horse might when a bridle is put on it.

Vocabulary

servile (sur′ vil) *adj.* like a servant; too humble

There was a silence, in which I could hear Mr. di Francesco swallowing water. I felt very much alone. I wished I were back home.

"I didn't mean it that way," Mr. di Francesco said.

"I'm sorry," I said, and then, rallying a little, confessed that Braille watches were unheard of in India—that I had first read about them a year or so earlier in a British Braille magazine, and then it had taken me several months to get the foreign exchange[11] and get a Braille pocket watch from Switzerland.

"Then how do blind people there know what time it is—whether it is day or night?" Mr. di Francesco asked.

"They have to ask someone, or learn to tell from the morning and night sounds. I suppose that things *are* a little backward there. That is why I had to leave my family and come here for education."

"The food is getting cold," Mrs. di Francesco said.

I picked up my fork and knife with trembling fingers and aimed for six. I suddenly wanted to cry.

"You look homesick," Mrs. di Francesco said.

I nodded, and tried to eat. A sense of relief engulfed me: we had mutton meatballs at home all the time, and they didn't require a knife. But the relief was short-lived: I had never had spaghetti, and the strands were long and tended to bunch together. They stretched from my mouth to my plate—a sign of my Indian backwardness, I thought. I longed for the kedgeree[12] at home, easily managed with a spoon.

Mrs. di Francesco reached over and showed me how to wrap the spaghetti around my fork, shake it, and pick it up. Even so, I took big bites when I thought that Mrs. di Francesco was not looking—when she was talking to Mr. di Francesco. Later in the meal, it occurred to me that I was eating the food that Daddyji had eaten when he was a student abroad. I resolutely bent my face over the plate and started eating in earnest.

Mrs. di Francesco took away our plates and served us something else, and I reached for my spoon.

"That's eaten with a fork," she said.

I attacked it with a fork. "It is a pudding with a crust!" I cried. "I have never eaten anything like it."

"It's not a pudding—it's apple pie," Mrs. di Francesco said. "By the way, we're having scrambled eggs for breakfast. Is that all right?"

I confessed that I didn't know what they were, and she described them to me.

"Oh, I know—rumble-tumble eggs!" I exclaimed. "I like them very much."

They both laughed. "British-Indian English is really much nicer than American English," Mr. di Francesco said. "You should keep it. In fact, I'll adopt 'rumble-tumble.'"

I felt sad that I had come to America for my studies instead of going to England

11. *Foreign exchange* refers to exchanging one country's money for another's.

12. *Kedgeree* is an Indian dish consisting of fish flakes, boiled rice, and eggs.

Vocabulary

engulf (en gulf′) *v.* to swallow up; overwhelm
resolutely (rez′ ə loot′ lē) *adv.* determinedly

first, as Daddyji had done. But no school in England had accepted me.

"We've heard so much about India from Uncle Manmath," Mrs. di Francesco said. "It must be a very exciting place."

"Yes, tell us about India," Mr. di Francesco said.

I felt confused. I couldn't think of what to say or how to say it.

"You look tired," Mrs. di Francesco said, patting me on the arm.

"I cannot think of the right English words sometimes," I said.

Mrs. di Francesco cleared some things off the table and said, "Don't worry. Now that you're here, your English will improve quickly."

She went to the kitchen and started washing the plates while Mr. di Francesco and I lingered at the table—much as we might at home.

I asked Mr. di Francesco how he had become self-supporting and independent, with a place of his own.

"You make it sound so romantic, but it's really very simple," he said. He spoke in a matter-of-fact way. "I spent twelve years at the Perkins Institution for the Blind, in Massachusetts. I entered when I was seven, and left when I was nineteen."

"Perkins!" I cried. "I have been trying to go there since I was seven. First, they would not have me because of the war. But after the war they would not have me, either—they said that I would end up a 'cultural misfit.'"

"What does that mean?"

"They said that bringing Eastern people to the West at a young age leads to 'cultural maladjustment'—and they said, 'Blindness is a maladjustment in itself.'"

"But now you're here. I'll call Perkins tomorrow and tell them that the damage is already done, and that your cultural maladjustment would be much worse if you were to end up in Arkansas." He laughed.

I was excited. "Perkins is said to be the best school for the blind anywhere. How did you like it? How was your life there?"

"Life at Perkins? It was probably no different from that of millions of other kids. We played and studied." He added obligingly, "It was a lot of fun."

Fun—so that's what it was, I thought. That is the difference between all the things he did at school and all the things I missed out on by not going to a good school.

"And after Perkins?"

"After Perkins, I studied voice at the New England Conservatory,[13] where Muriel and I met. Then I came to New York, started giving voice lessons, married Muriel, and here I am."

"There must be more to tell."

"There really isn't."

"Did Mrs. di Francesco's parents not object? She is sighted."

"I wasn't asking to marry Muriel's parents. She could do what she pleased. This is America."

13. Here, the *Conservatory* is a school for instruction in music.

Vocabulary

maladjustment (mal′ ə just′ mənt) *n.* poor adjustment to conditions or requirements
obligingly (ə blī′ jing lē) *adv.* helpfully; agreeably

Responding to Literature

PERSONAL RESPONSE

Why might the story of Ved Mehta make a difference in the lives of others? Who else would you like to have read this story? Why?

Analyzing Literature

RECALL

1. Describe the problem Ved has with the immigration official.
2. What does the merry-go-round symbolize to Ved?
3. Where does Mr. di Francesco want Ved to attend school?
4. What has Mr. di Francesco achieved?

INTERPRET

5. When Ved is dealing with the immigration official, he recalls his father saying, "In life, there is only fight or flight. You must always fight." Why does Ved remember this?
6. Why does Ved compare his life in India to being on the outside of a merry-go-round?
7. What does Mr. di Francesco mean when he says that the "damage is already done" in regard to Ved's "cultural maladjustment"?
8. Why is Ved so interested in Mr. di Francesco's success?

EVALUATE AND CONNECT

9. Theme Connection The quotes from Daddyji guided Ved. What have people told you to help you live your life?
10. Look back at the list you wrote for the **Focus Activity** on page 212. How do the items on your list compare with the author's personality?

Braillewriter

LITERARY ELEMENTS

Point of View

The selection from *Sound-Shadows of the New World* is a true story told from the **first-person point of view.** This means that the narrator, Ved, tells the story as he experienced it. A first-person narrator can tell about his own feelings. He can also reveal the feelings of other characters through their actions and dialogue.

1. How does the first-person narrator in this selection experience the world around him? Cite several examples.
2. Mehta could have told this story from a **third-person point of view,** using a voice outside the story to describe the characters and events. Do you think this would have been more effective than Mehta's own voice? Why or why not?

- See **Literary Terms Handbook,** p. R7.

Literature and Writing

Writing About Literature

Characterization Look at the descriptions of characters as they appear in this selection. Note that these observations are made by a blind person. Is Mehta, the author, effective in providing a mental image of the di Francescos for his readers? Write a paragraph evaluating how well he describes these two characters.

Creative Writing

Keeping Track Writers often keep journals that help them recall important events and vivid details. Write a journal entry that Ved Mehta might have written about his first day in the United States. Include details about the new things he heard, felt, tasted, and smelled, as well as his impressions of the people and places he encountered.

Extending Your Response

Learning for Life

Seeking Admission Letters of recommendation can occasionally make the difference between acceptance and rejection by a school. Mehta did not get accepted into the Perkins Institution for the Blind because of full enrollment. Write a letter to the school on Mehta's behalf. Ask them to reconsider him for admission.

interNET CONNECTION

Resources for the Blind Visit the National Federation of the Blind on the World Wide Web to identify resources Ved Mehta might use today as a blind adult writer.

Literature Groups

Culture Shock Ved Mehta was a shy teenager when he came to the United States in 1949. Who were the people he leaned on as a newcomer, and how did they help him? In a small group, discuss how each of the characters in the story helped Mehta adjust to his new surroundings. Consider these questions: How did his father's examples and advice help young Ved? What did Ved learn about sight-impaired people from Mr. and Mrs. di Francesco? What information about U.S. culture did Mehta learn from the other characters?

Reading Further

For other stories of life in India, you might try these:
Ved Mehta, *Portrait of India*
Rumer Goden, *An Episode of Sparrows*

Save your work for your portfolio.

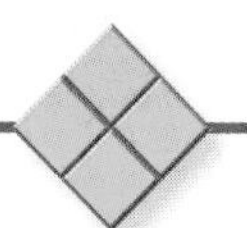

Skill Minilessons

GRAMMAR AND LANGUAGE • WORDS ENDING IN *-y*

When you add an ending to a word that ends with *-y*, you may have to change the *y* to *i*. Note the following rules.

CHANGE IT: When the *-y* is preceded by a consonant

happy happier

DON'T CHANGE IT: When the *-y* is preceded by a vowel

enjoy enjoyed

NEVER CHANGE IT: When you add *-ing*

study studying

PRACTICE Add the ending to each word. Write the new word.

1. funny + *-er*
2. cherry + *-es*
3. pray + *-ing*
4. apply + *-ed*
5. monkey + *-s*
6. loyalty + *-es*
7. toy + *-ed*
8. play + *-er*
9. cry + *-ing*
10. stay + *-s*

- For more about suffixes and final *-y*, see **Language Handbook,** p. R48.

READING AND THINKING • AVOIDING HASTY GENERALIZATIONS

A **generalization** is a broad statement that applies to many experiences or people. To make a generalization, you must first observe several specific experiences. If not, you could make a **hasty generalization,** one that is based on too little knowledge. Hasty generalizations may begin with words such as *all, always,* or *never.*

- For more about making generalizations, see **Reading Handbook,** pp. R97–R98.

PRACTICE Answer these questions about hasty generalizations from Ved Mehta's autobiography.

1. Explain whether the following statement is a hasty generalization: People in India do not eat spaghetti.
2. Find an example of a hasty generalization that Ved Mehta makes during his first meal with Mr. and Mrs. di Francesco.

VOCABULARY • PREFIXES AND SUFFIXES

The word *maladjustment* may look difficult until you take it apart. It is made from the base word *adjust* with *mal-* as a prefix and *-ment* as a suffix. *Mal-* means "bad or badly," and *-ment* (as in *argument* and *measurement*) is a common suffix. Prefixes and suffixes are often added to familiar words to make new words. When you find unfamiliar words, prefixes, or suffixes, look them up in a dictionary. Also, remember that a final *-e* may drop off a base word when a suffix is attached.

PRACTICE Use what you know about the prefixes, suffixes, and base words that form the numbered words on the left to match each with its meaning on the right.

1. fluidity	a. dissatisfied
2. irreversible	b. free
3. malcontent	c. unable to be undone
4. unenslaved	d. not giving in at all
5. uncompromising	e. the state of being liquid

Interdisciplinary Connection

SOCIAL STUDIES

Coming to America

When Ved Mehta emigrated from India in 1949, he was seeking an education not available to blind people at home. Alone in a strange country, fifteen-year-old Ved needed someone to lean on. His father's friend contacted a couple who took him in and helped him get acquainted with the United States.

As Ved began his studies in America in the decade following World War II, more than 2.5 million other immigrants came to the United States. Each arrival had a special reason for coming. Each needed support and encouragement. Among these immigrants was the family of young Madeleine Korbel. Her family was looking for freedom from a series of oppressive governments that had for decades controlled her native country of Czechoslovakia. Nearly fifty years later, Madeleine Korbel Albright became the first woman to be named U.S. Secretary of State, a member of the president's cabinet. "All I can offer," she said in an address, "is the benefit of my own experience as someone whose family was driven twice from its home—first by Hitler, then by Stalin—while I was still a girl."

ACTIVITY

Select a country from one of the charts on this page and prepare a report about people moving from that country to the United States. Answer the following questions:

- About how many immigrants come each year?
- Why do they come?
- How do they get here?
- Do they choose to settle in a special place or just anywhere in this country?
- To what people or institutions can they turn for support as they learn a new language and new ways?

Immigration, 1820–1996:	
Top Ten Countries of Last Residence	
All countries	**63,140,227**
Germany	7,142,393
Mexico	5,542,625
Italy	5,427,298
United Kingdom	5,225,701
Ireland	4,778,159
Canada	4,423,066
Soviet Union, former	3,752,811
Austria	1,841,068
Hungary	1,673,579
Philippines	1,379,403

Immigration, 1996:	
Top Ten Countries of Birth	
All countries	**915,900**
Mexico	163,572
Philippines	55,876
India	44,859
Vietnam	42,067
China	41,728
Dominican Republic	39,604
Cuba	26,466
Ukraine	21,079
Russia	19,668
Jamaica	19,089

Source: U.S. Immigration and Naturalization Service

Vo•cab•u•lar•y *Skills*

Using Familiar Words to Understand New Words

In the selection from *Sound-Shadows of the New World,* Mrs. di Francesco breaks into *unrestrained* laughter. What type of laughter is that?

Hint: What do *restrain* and *un-* mean?

By thinking about words you know, you can guess that Mrs. di Francesco bursts out in laughter that seems to be out of control.

As you read and listen to people speak, you will come across new words. Some of them will look like words you already know. For example, you may read a new word, such as *misinform,* and realize that it contains a familiar word *(inform)* and the prefix *mis-,* which means "not." Other words will have familiar suffixes attached. Still others will remind you of another word you know—perhaps because they share the same root.

EXERCISE

Each underlined word contains a familiar word. Use your knowledge to help you select the correct definition of the underlined word.

1. Mrs. Jones has no intention of being victimized by a purse snatcher.
   The meaning of *victim* indicates that *victimized* means
   a. stopped. **b.** forced to be cruel. **c.** made to suffer.
2. Mrs. Flowers teaches Marguerite to be intolerant of ignorance.
   The meaning of *tolerant* indicates that *intolerant* means
   a. unwilling to endure. **b.** doubtful. **c.** without intelligence.
3. Charlie feels obliged to continue with his journal.
   The meaning of *obligation* indicates that *obliged* means
   a. hardship. **b.** helpful. **c.** required by duty.
4. Roger sees that the door is open, and this emboldens him.
   The meaning of *bold* indicates that *emboldens* means
   a. amuses. **b.** gives courage to. **c.** causes hesitation in.
5. Mrs. Jones's question necessitates a response from Roger.
   The meaning of *necessary* indicates that *necessitates* means
   a. requires. **b.** discourages. **c.** suggests.

Writing WORKSHOP

Narrative Writing: Biographical Sketch

Whom do you lean on when you are troubled? You may rely on close friends, family members, teachers, or even famous people that you look up to. Whoever they are, these people have touched you through their actions, attitudes, or beliefs. Now you can try to touch others by sharing a story about one of these people.

Assignment: Follow the process explained in these pages to develop a biographical sketch: a brief, true story about a person. Write about an episode in the life of a person—an episode that illustrates the theme "Lean on Me."

- As you write your biographical sketch, refer to the **Writing Handbook,** pp. R50–R55.

The Writing Process

PREWRITING

PREWRITING TIP

When you freewrite, pour out all the ideas and details you can think of. Don't stop to read what you've written; keep your pen moving!

Explore Ideas

Spend about ten minutes freewriting about people who come to mind when you think of the words "Lean on Me." Think of people who have given you inspiration, comfort, advice, or a helping hand. Jot down what you remember.

Complete the **Writing Skills** activity on page 211 if you haven't done it already. Then go over your freewriting notes. Choose three people who stand out from the others, and think about what each person means to you. Ask yourself questions like these:

- What qualities does this person have that I admire? How do those qualities come through in the person's appearance, actions, and words?
- What has this person said or done to help me through a hard time? What details do I remember about that experience?

Research a Subject

Which person seems to have touched you more than the others? Select an experience with that person to be the subject of your biographical sketch. How much do you know about your subject? How well do you remember your experience with this person? If you need more information before you write:

- Conduct an interview with someone you can talk to who knows your subject well. Take careful notes, and be sure to include details.
- Visit the library if your subject is a contemporary or historical figure who has inspired you. Look for newspaper articles or books about this person. Did your subject leave a diary or letters that could tell you more about him or her?

Consider Your Purpose and Audience

Do you want to inspire your readers? Amuse them? Inform them? Set a purpose for your writing. Who will read your finished work? Choose words that they will respond to.

Organize Ideas

Before you start writing, organize your main ideas.

- Organize your writing around the personality traits you admire about your subject. Give examples and describe events to help the reader picture the person.
- Focus on the event or episode that shows why you can lean on your subject. Use a plan like the following:

Introduction:	**Introduce the subject and the major event.**
Body:	**Tell about the major event. Include details about your subject, other people, the action, and the result.**
Conclusion:	**Summarize the subject's life, qualities, or contribution.**

STUDENT MODEL

Neighbor, Dr. Donna Miller. Runs daily. Gave me tips about running faster and steadier.

Started running together for an hour every morning. Decided to enter race, with Donna coaching me.

Donna made me feel strong and good about helping other people.

DRAFTING

DRAFTING TIP

If you have trouble coming up with a good introduction, write the body first. The details may give you a good idea for the beginning.

Dig In to Your First Draft

Start with a strong introduction. You might point out a unique quality of your subject. You also could open with a question, a quotation, or an intriguing fact about your character or the major event.

Keep writing! Don't feel compelled to tell the person's entire life. Stick to the plan you made, describing your main ideas. Include interesting quotations and details to support your ideas.

MODEL · DRAFTING

I've never thought about running. Nobody in my family is athletic. But one morning I got up early and saw my neighbor, Doctor Miller, wave as she ran past. Amazing! She's kind of old for that, I thought. But then I apologized mentally. Old or not, she really could run!

REVISING

REVISING TIP

While you are working on your revision, think again about your audience. Have you provided all the information readers will need?

Review Your Work

Put your draft aside for a day or two, and then reread it. With a partner, go over the **Questions for Revising** to help you identify gaps in information and places that need improvement.

QUESTIONS FOR REVISING

- Does the opening make the reader want to know more about the subject or the event?
- Are there enough details about the subject to help the reader picture him or her?
- Is the main event explained clearly? Are there gaps you need to fill in?
- Is every event you include important to the story?
- Have you checked all your facts?
- Does your final paragraph summarize your main idea?

EDITING/PROOFREADING

After you have reviewed and revised your biographical sketch, use the **Proofreading Checklist** on the inside back cover to help you catch mistakes in grammar, usage, mechanics, and spelling. If you are unsure about how to punctuate dialogue, review the rules you learned in the **Grammar Link** on page 167.

PROOFREADING TIP

Make sure that dialogue, dates, and cities and states are punctuated properly.

Grammar Hint

Use commas to set off the day and year from the rest of the text. Also, use commas to set off the city and state and the state and country.

Lou Gehrig, a famous baseball player, was born June 19, 1903, in New York, New York. He died on June 2, 1941, of a neurological disorder.

MODEL · EDITING/PROOFREADING

It was September 12,1999, just three weeks before race day in Bellevue,Washington.

PUBLISHING/PRESENTING

In what medium will you present your final work? You might read your work aloud, videotape your reading of the biographical sketch, or work with other students to create a bulletin-board display or magazine about "People We Lean On."

PRESENTING TIP

Use photographs, maps, and diagrams or your own artwork to give your work visual impact.

Reflecting

In your journal, describe what you've learned about your relationship with your subject. Then, list things you would do differently for your next workshop.

Save your work for your portfolio.

Theme Wrap-Up

Responding to the Theme

1. Which selection in this theme helped you understand how people "lean" on each other? Explain your answer.
2. What new understanding do you have about the following after completing this theme?
   - the need to belong and fit in with others
   - the effect of self-esteem on relationships
   - the influence of friends and family members
3. Present your theme project to the class.

Analyzing Literature

LOOKING AT AUTOBIOGRAPHERS

This theme contains selections from the autobiographies of Maya Angelou, Ved Mehta, and James Herriot. Which author would you most like to meet? Write a list of questions you would ask about the selection, the theme, or the author's life. Discuss your questions with a partner.

Evaluate and Set Goals

1. Which of the following did you enjoy the most? Which would you like to improve?
   - reading and responding to the selections
   - doing research with a group
   - making presentations
   - doing independent writing
2. How would you assess your work in this theme, using the following scale? Give at least two reasons for your assessment.

   4 = outstanding   2 = fair
   3 = good   1 = weak
3. Based on your assessment, what skill would you like to improve in the next theme?
4. Write down your goal and two or three steps you will take to achieve it.
5. Review the goal and your plan with a partner or your teacher.

Build Your Portfolio

SELECT

Choose two of the best pieces of work you did in this theme, and include them in your portfolio. Use these questions to help you choose:

- ✦ Which did you enjoy doing the most?
- ✦ Which challenged you the most?
- ✦ Which did you learn the most from?
- ✦ Which expressed your ideas the best?

REFLECT

Write some notes to accompany the pieces you selected. Use these questions to guide you:

- ✦ What was the best feature about the piece?
- ✦ What did you learn from creating it?
- ✦ If you did it over again, what would you do differently?

Reading on Your Own

If you have enjoyed the literature in this theme, you might also be interested in the following books.

Cezanne Pinto

by Mary Stolz In this fictional memoir, an elderly man tells his story of being born into slavery, escaping to freedom, serving in the Civil War, and becoming a cowboy in Texas. As he nears his ninetieth birthday, Cezanne Pinto remembers his lifelong struggle for freedom and the friends who helped him along the way.

Timothy of the Cay

by Theodore Taylor This follow-up to the acclaimed novel *The Cay* traces the life of Timothy, who goes to sea as a boy and grows up to command a ship. It also tells of Philip, who hopes to regain his sight after being blinded in a shipwreck and rescued by Timothy.

Far North

by Will Hobbs Fifteen-year-old Gabe must rely on another teenager and an elderly Native American hunter after their plane crashes in the frozen Canadian wilderness. As they struggle to survive, Gabe develops a new appreciation for the world of the Far North and its inhabitants.

Walk Two Moons

by Sharon Creech What do you do when you need your mother, and your grandparents need *you?* In this story, thirteen-year-old Sal and her grandparents set out on a long drive to find Sal's missing mother and solve both problems. Along with a serious theme, there is humor in their search.

Standardized Test Practice

Read the following material. Then read each question on page 233. Decide which is the best answer to each question. Mark the letter for that answer on your paper.

Oliver's Office Supplies Central

Everything you need for your office, school, and home!

It's definitely worth your time to come to Oliver's Office Supplies Central Today! Located in Las Rosas, Oliver's has the largest selection of office supplies anywhere in the state, and our prices are unbeatable. Come in and compare our prices on these very popular items:

	Brenner's Offices	Supply City	Oliver's Office Supplies
Stargazer Nylon Binder	$11.49	$12.35	$ 7.48
Trails Backpack	10.60	12.21	9.99
Carl's Computer Paper	4.12	3.75	2.44
Super Stapler	3.89	3.99	3.19
Worldly Word Processor (Model 225)	159.40	179.66	132.11
Fabulous 3 Drawer File Cabinet	89.97	91.99	65.00

If you come in this week, Oliver's is offering an additional 10% off the everyday low discount price on these selected items. Come see our reduced prices on a multitude of other items. At Oliver's, you will find many name brands at the lowest prices around. We guarantee that you will be satisfied with what we have to offer. You'll never shop for supplies anywhere else!

Oliver's Supplies Central
83 Route 9
Las Rosas

1 In addition to mentioning a wide selection of supplies, the ad tries to persuade you to shop at Oliver's because of the —

A free parking

B 20% discount on all items

C low prices

D money-back guarantee

2 The last paragraph in the ad is included in order to convince you that —

A people who shop at Oliver's have a lot of money to spend

B Oliver's has more name brand merchandise than other stores

C Oliver's appeals to shoppers looking for great deals

D local office managers buy all of their supplies at Oliver's

3 In the passage, the word multitude means —

F large number

G warehouse

H short list

J small number

4 Based on the information in the ad, you can conclude that Supply City —

A does not carry name brand office supplies

B is more convenient than Oliver's

C has the highest prices on most supplies

D is larger than Brenner's Offices

5 If someone goes to Oliver's this week, that person will get —

F a free Stargazer Nylon Binder

G two Super Staplers for the price of one

H the largest selection of items Oliver's has ever had

J 10% off the price of some items

STOP

Which Way to Go?

> *Do not follow where the path may lead. Go instead where there is no path and leave a trail.*
>
> –*Muriel Strode*

THEME CONTENTS

GENRE FOCUS POETRY

Exploring the Theme

Which Way to Go?

Choices. Your life is full of them. Should you try out for the basketball team or the track team? Is it better to have a lot of casual friends or a handful of close ones? Some choices are difficult, like deciding to take a risk or selecting a difficult path over an easy one. In this theme, you will discover how the choices people make can help them grow.

Starting Points

DARING TO BE DIFFERENT

Sometimes people make choices based on what they think others expect them to do. They may be afraid to be different, or they may not realize that other options are available. How does Gary Larson show this idea with his cartoon?

BIG DECISIONS AND LESSONS LEARNED

Making difficult choices is a theme that comes up over and over in books, movies, and television shows. With a partner, make a list of books, movies, or TV shows you know that deal with choices. What, if anything, did you learn from them?

"Well, lemme think. ... You've stumped me, son. Most folks only wanna know how to go the other way."

Theme Projects

Choose one of the projects below to complete as you read the selections in this theme. Work on your own, with a partner, or with a group.

CRITICAL VIEWING

Art Ahead of Its Time

1. Many artists who are famous today were seen as unconventional, or even daring, during their day. Search through art history books for an artist whose work represented a unique approach in his or her day.
2. Find postcards showing some of the artist's work. Write captions explaining why the work was considered different.
3. Paste the pictures and text onto poster board.

Femme au Beret, 1938. Pablo Picasso. Oil on canvas, 18⅛ x 15 in. Private collection.

LEARNING FOR LIFE

Prepare a Feature Article

1. Interview an adult you respect about his or her life choices. Take a notebook and pen or a tape recorder to the interview. Ask if you can take pictures.
2. Ask questions such as the following:
   - What made you decide to become a . . . ?
   - Was there something else you once wanted to do with your life? Why did your goals change?
   - What was the best decision you've made?
3. Write a feature article about the person, using exact quotations and pictures.

MULTIMEDIA PROJECT

Campaign for Teens

1. Find an issue that faces teens today, such as deciding how to avoid smoking. Gather information and pictures about the possible physical and emotional effects of making that choice.
2. Use a Web publishing program to create and edit text, graphics, and sound.
3. Decide on a message to present to your audience. Choose the information that will best get your point across. Write introductions, headings, and comments.
4. Follow the directions in the software to complete your page.

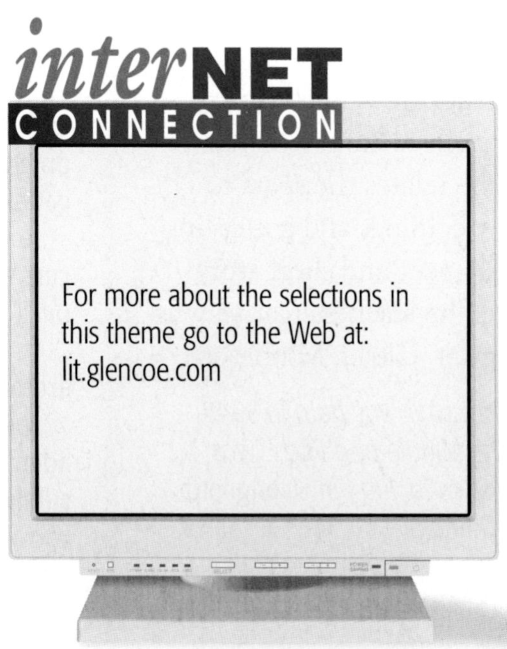

interNET
CONNECTION
For more about the selections in this theme go to the Web at: lit.glencoe.com

Before You Read

In the Middle of a Pitch

MEET
BILL MEISSNER

Bill Meissner says, "I know the meaning of the home run. It's the slow circling of the bases, and then the return. I know it well. My father was a traveling salesman with the highway wrapped around his wrist like a gray sweatband." Meissner grew up playing baseball in Iowa and Wisconsin, and he relates the sport to many comings and goings in life. A poet and short story writer, he teaches creative writing in St. Cloud, Minnesota.

Bill Meissner was born in 1948. "In the Middle of a Pitch" was published in 1994 in Hitting Into the Wind.

FOCUS ACTIVITY

What do you think athletes dream about or hope to achieve? What do you suppose they worry about?

Web It!
Share your ideas with a partner. Then make a web of words that you would use in answering the questions above.

Setting a Purpose
Read to find out how a former athlete deals with unfulfilled dreams.

BACKGROUND

The Time and Place This story is set in modern times and ordinary places in the United States.

Did You Know? Four million Americans under the age of fifteen suffer from sprains, strains, deep cuts, and fractures playing sports and other games each year. Injuries usually occur when an athlete plays to win instead of for fun. Even professional players suffer from injuries that can keep them away from the game or even end their careers.

VOCABULARY PREVIEW

elaborate (i lab′ ər it) *adj.* complicated and fancy; p. 240
potential (pə ten′ shəl) *n.* possibility of success; p. 241
gaudily (gô′ də lē) *adv.* in a way that is bright and showy to the point of being in bad taste; p. 241
curt (kurt) *adj.* so brief or short as to seem rude; p. 242
pitch (pich) *n.* an often high-pressure sales presentation; p. 242
aromatic (ar′ ə mat′ ik) *adj.* having a pleasant smell or special, delicate flavor; p. 242
adept (ə dept′) *adj.* highly skilled; masterful; p. 243
subtle (sut′ əl) *adj.* not open or direct; not obvious; p. 243
corroded (kə rōd′ əd) *adj.* eaten away by degrees, by gnawing or chemical action; p. 245
heft (heft) *v.* to lift up; p. 245

In the Middle of a Pitch

Bill Meissner

High and Outside–A Study, 1981. John Dobbs. Watercolor and chalk on paper, 4¾ x 4½ in. Courtesy John Dobbs and ACA Galleries, New York.

In the Middle of a Pitch

He wakes before his alarm to the far away song of an umpire calling a third strike. Standing in front of the bathroom mirror, he leans forward, narrowing his eyes at himself as if he were peering at the catcher for his sign. Then he stretches, his hands high, almost touches the plaster ceiling where the spiderweb cracks seem to lengthen a little each week. When he brings his right arm down in an imaginary pitch, a strike, he feels the old aching. Staring at the arm in the mirror, he wonders how the flesh got so flabby. *It didn't look that way yesterday, did it?* he thinks. Yesterday the tendons were taut[1] and ready like some finely tuned musical instrument; yesterday he was sure he could hear every muscle humming.

Everything happens so fast, he thinks, *everything happens in a day*. One day he's Dusty Sikarsky, starting pitcher for a major league team. The next day he's Dusty Sikarsky, used car salesman, tossing curves at the off-balance customers. As he dresses for work, his mind spans twenty years to the baseball days. He thinks about how you work your way up through the leagues: First it's town ball, where he pitched his team into the tournaments with his fastball. The photographer for the local paper could hardly catch that pitch with his flashbulb. Next the minor league scouts stood waiting for him after a game, their smiles like piano keys, and everything speeded up, as if someone had tilted the whole world and it started sliding toward him. A minor league coach watched him, chin on his hand, for three months in Class A, then, at midseason, the coach nodded at him once. The next day Dusty was moved up to Triple A, the bleachers bigger and more freshly painted, the fans louder. He kept moving up, faster and quicker. His life seemed to be rushing toward him and flying away from him at the same moment. His arm felt great, and the more he threw, the better it felt. The leather ball loved his fingertips. "The kid's so good he could pitch blindfolded and still strike out the side," a coach once remarked. On the mound, Dusty went through his motion: kicking, reaching way back in the still air with his right arm. Then he whirled down hard, and the ball was nestled in the catcher's mitt long before Dusty's cap, jolted from his head, had a chance to fall to the grass in front of the mound. The ball was like music that passed so fast you never really heard it.

He remembers the rush as he was called to the bigs: the flutter of a paper contract, the tingling static electricity as he slid a major league uniform over his head for the first time in the locker room, the click and spark of spikes on concrete as he jogged down the ramp to the dugout.

The next thing he knew, the game was starting, and the first batter stepped to the plate. Then, the funniest thing happened—everything slowed down. It took half an hour to reach up to adjust the bill of his cap. His windup[2] felt like an elaborate

1. *Tendons* are strong cords that attach muscles to bones; the tendons in the man's arm felt tense and tight *(taut)*.

2. A pitcher's *windup* is a series of regular and distinctive motions, such as swinging the arms, made before releasing a pitch.

Vocabulary

elaborate (i lab′ ər it) *adj.* complicated and fancy

dance performed underwater. When he threw that first pitch, the ball seemed to take a year to reach home plate, like some kind of satellite aimed for the moon, just rotating over and over slowly in the soft, endless vacuum of space.

Somehow, he made it through the first game and he did all right. He pitched six innings, gave up a couple of hits, but no runs. Not bad for a first outing. The guys patted him on the back after the game. The catcher congratulated him and told him later how his eyes always widened each time he delivered the ball. He had a great year, and the papers called him the Rookie Sensation. The sportswriters always used the word potential when they wrote about him; they predicted he'd be the best in the game.

The sportswriters always used the word *potential* when they wrote about him; they predicted he'd be the best in the game.

The seasons passed. One, two, three of them. He chalked up fifty wins. Then, one night in Chicago, too cool for June, when the bases were loaded in the late innings, he reached as far back as he could to fire a fastball and felt something snap in his arm. Not *snap*, exactly—it was more of a *ping*, like the off-key sound of a thin wire or guitar string being plucked. It didn't hurt at first, though he remembers shaking his arm a few times as if it had ants on it.

When he threw his next pitch, and the next, he knew something was wrong. The ball didn't quite go where it was aimed. Just an inch or two off target, but that's all it takes. He lost that game on a double. After that, the batters began hitting his curve, his slider. His fastball lost its jump, no longer appeared to be rising as it reached the batter, but instead drew a straight line to the sweet spot of their bats.

That's when the music slowed down, his career like a record clicked off in the middle of its playing, the needle dragging across the vinyl.

The team put him on the disabled list and he sat it out for a couple weeks. He worked with the trainer in the clubhouse, rotating the arm, wrapping it with heat, kneading the muscle as if it were bread dough about to rise. After he gave up six or seven runs in each of his next three starts, the manager shook his head and said the owners wanted him sent down to the minors.

"How long?" Dusty remembers asking the manager. He felt suddenly short of breath, unable to exhale a full sentence.

The manager stood chewing a toothpick, staring only at Dusty's arm. "Just a while. That's all. A month, maybe. You'll be back, kid."

"Yeah," he responded. "A month."

A month became the rest of the season. He struggled in the minors, too—even the rookies were hitting his best pitches, taking them to the gaudily painted wooden

Vocabulary

potential (pə ten′ shəl) *n.* possibility of success
gaudily (gô′ də lē) *adv.* in a way that is bright and showy to the point of being in bad taste

fences advertising CHEER and BRYLCREEM—A LITTLE DAB'LL DO YA, and COLGATE WITH GARDOL.

The next February, he got a letter from the club. He remembers staring at the outside of the long beige envelope that morning, not certain if he should open it or not. He set it down on the desk. He remembers watching TV for a while. The Colgate ad appeared—an announcer with a mike stood behind an invisible protective Gardol shield as a major league pitcher threw fastballs at him. The pitches bounced off the shield one by one. Dusty clicked the set off. After lunch, he picked the letter up again. As he tore it open, the ripping paper made the sound of crackling ice. The letter told him, in a few curt sentences, that his contract wouldn't be renewed. The last sentences read: *Thank you for your contribution to the club. Best wishes in the future*.

He remembers crumpling the letter in his fist, tossing it into the waste basket, and jogging out to the nearby sandlot field. Though it was cold outside and patches of ice still plastered themselves to the field, Dusty threw fastball after fastball toward the warped[3] black and white plate, none of them strikes. The pain in his arm seemed to make a noise that grew louder and louder, like a scream caught beneath the skin.

The shrill sound of his alarm clock brings him back to his apartment. He jogs into the bedroom, clicks off the ringing alarm. All that was years ago, he thinks as he brushes his teeth, combs his graying slicked-back hair, slides on his snappy brown striped tie and brown suit jacket, then slips out the front door for work. He's got a new career, and he's a different man now—he's Dusty Sikarsky, best damn car salesman in El Dorado, Kansas. He's got his sales pitch down perfect, and he's got plaques on the wall of his office at Edge Motors and citations[4] from the El Dorado Businessmen's Club to prove it. He's got a quick, bright smile on his face and the music in his voice; his boss once said he could sell any car on the lot blindfolded.

Dusty tastes the first warmth of April air as he walks through the town. It's a taste he's almost forgotten, a taste aromatic and rich that seems to come from deep inside the thawed earth and from deep inside himself at the same moment. By the time he reaches the low, tin-sided building at the car lot, he's puffing. He grins at his coworkers as he lopes toward his dark paneled office. Inside, as he waits for the first customer, he takes a wheezy drag from his cigarette, pours a mug of coffee, and, cupping a powdered sugar donut in his palm, stares beyond the hulls of the cars to the shimmering water mirage[5] beginning to form at the far end of the asphalt lot.

The whole town seems to know about his days in the majors. As he walks down

3. Something that is *warped* is bent or twisted in places where it once was flat.

4. Here, *citations* are awards for outstanding achievement.

5. Here, a *mirage* is an optical effect created by the reflection of light over hot pavement. Sikarsky sees a pool of water that doesn't exist on the asphalt lot.

Vocabulary

curt (kurt) *adj.* so brief or short as to seem rude

pitch (pich) *n.* an often high-pressure sales presentation

aromatic (ar′ ə mat′ ik) *adj.* having a pleasant smell or special, delicate flavor

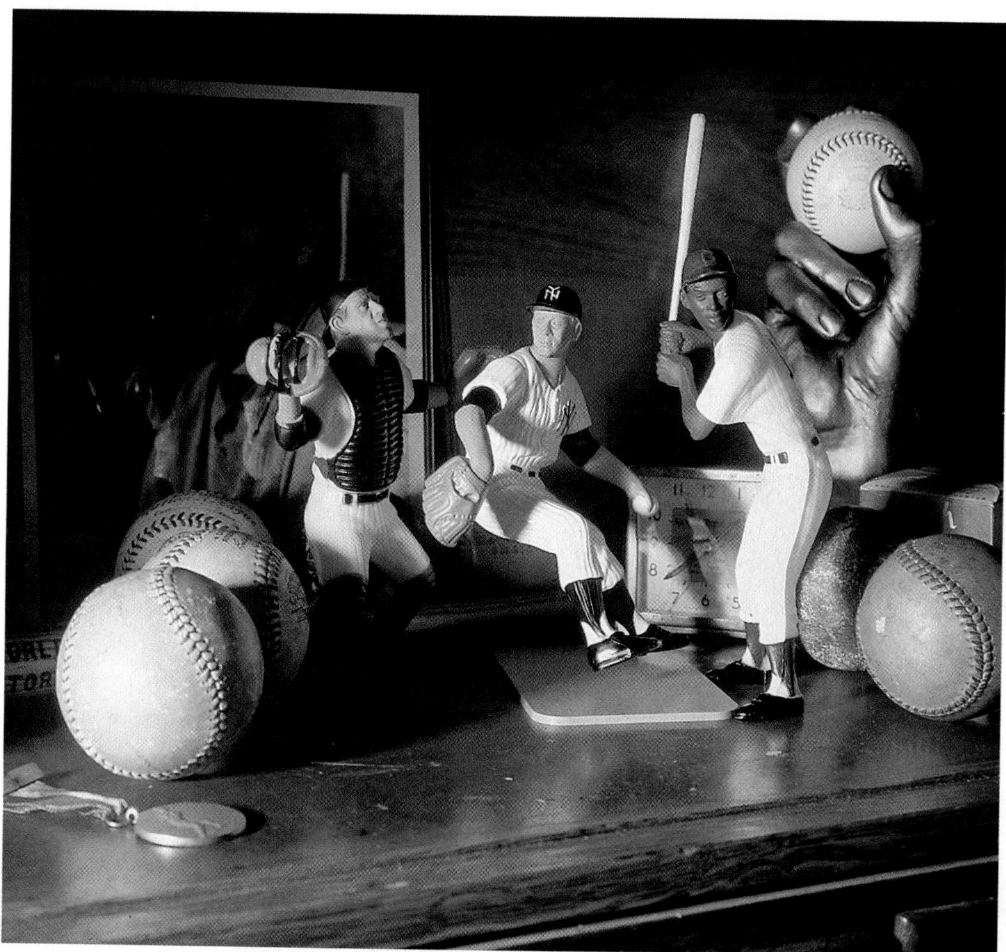

Untitled, 1993. Bret Willis. Color transparency, 4 x 5 in. Private collection.

Viewing the photograph: Which objects in this collection do you think would mean the most to Dusty Sikarsky? Why?

the big leagues?" Dusty usually just shakes his head. He wants to reply, *What's there to say? You just throw a ball at a glove.* But he doesn't want to sound flip[7] so he just says something pat like "Good. It was real good."

He never talks much about the big leagues, never mentions the injury. For years now, he's managed to avoid talking about it, has become adept at a subtle curve of conversation, a change of subject. *Gardol,* he thought once after he dodged a coworker's question about baseball, *an invisible protective shield.* He never goes to the town league baseball games on the weekends, though his buddies sometimes ask him to take in a game. Once in a while, as a gag, he'll ball up an old invoice, go into his wind-up, pitch it hard through the bright light of the open doorway, and the guys nod at him and know he remembers.

"You should pick up a baseball sometime, Dusty," the boss told him once.

Main in front of the crumbling two-story brick facades,[6] a little heavier and a little grayer, the kids open their eyes wide as they pass and then whisper behind him: "You know who *that* is? That's Dusty Sikarsky. He pitched in the majors." Some of the older guys at work smile and say, "Hey Dusty, what was it like, pitching in

6. A building's front is its *facade* (fə säd′), a word that comes from the Latin word for *face.*

7. *Flip* means "lacking proper respect or seriousness."

Vocabulary

adept (ə dept′) *adj.* highly skilled; masterful
subtle (sut′ əl) *adj.* not open or direct; not obvious

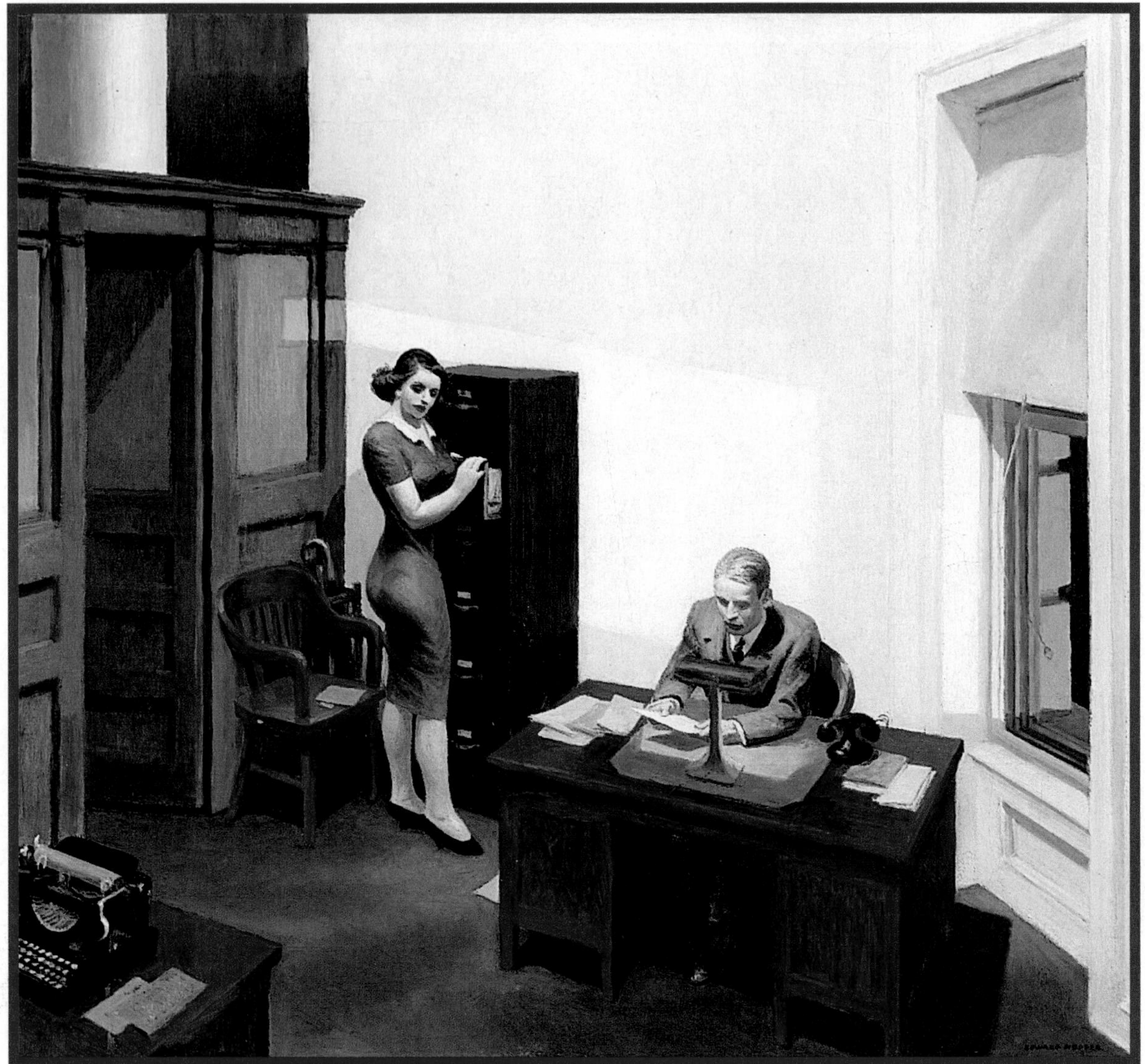

Office at Night, 1940. Edward Hopper. Oil on canvas, 22¾₁₆ x 25⅛ in. Walker Art Center, Minneapolis.

Viewing the painting: Describe the setting of Hopper's painting. What does it add to the description in the story of Sikarsky's life as a salesperson? Explain.

"Ever think of coaching or something?" Dusty just took a slurp of coffee, pretending not to hear. "Cripes, with no wife, no kids," the boss added, "you got all the time in the world."

His arm doesn't hurt like it used to the first couple years after he was cut from the team. It only aches a little once in a while as he lifts a pile of ledgers[8] or when he leans his weight the wrong way on the waxed fender of a Chevy while making a pitch about what a workhorse the V6 engine is, how fast this machine would be on the highway even though it's got a few miles on the ol' speedometer.

This April day passes with its usual blur of stats[9] and sales, printouts and

8. *Ledgers* are books containing financial records.

9. Here, *stats* (short for *statistics*) are numbers relating to car sales. *Stats* can also refer to baseball statistics.

receipts. Another day passes beneath his fingertips and it feels dry to the touch. In the late afternoon, an ad appears in the *El Dorado Weekly* proclaiming SHINY CLEAN USED CARS FOR SPRING. In the picture, Dusty, pudgy and not quite smiling, poses stiffly beside a Dodge, like he doesn't know what to do with his hands.

After work, on his way home, Dusty takes a detour to the town ball field. Shouldering through the creaking fence gate, he pulls off his wide striped tie, unbuttons the top button of his white shirt. He sits down on the front row of the bleachers, slips off his brown suit jacket, tosses it over a corroded railing. He can hear the whistle of the wind through the high backstop, a rusty music. He sits there a while, gazing at the empty sunlit field from behind the barrier of wires. Rolling up his sleeves, he massages the muscle of his right arm. Then he notices, directly behind the plate, widened gaps in the backstop wires. *A wild pitch could get caught in there easy*, Dusty thinks. *It could get caught for years between the bent wires.*

Another day passes beneath his fingertips and it feels dry to the touch.

Turning his head, Dusty notices two boys biking across the grass. He thinks at first that they're cutting across the field on their way to the video games at the arcade, but they stop in the middle of the infield. One skinny kid who looks about seven keeps trying to pitch from the gravelly mound sixty feet away, but can't quite get his throws to home plate. He hefts the ball like a shotput, and the ball skitters in the dirt a few feet from the plate where another boy, short and chunky, stands with a catcher's mitt that's too big for his hand. The boy who's pitching moves a few steps closer. An idea crosses Dusty's mind that he should go out there and give the kid a few tips. The kid brings his arm down pretty well, but he's bending all wrong at the elbow. *Naw*, he thinks. *Let the kids have their game*. The boy tosses another one, a rounded throw that skips in front of the catcher's mitt, rolls all the way to the backstop.

The skinny kid runs from the mound to retrieve it. By the time the boy reaches the backstop, Dusty is stretching his arm through the bent wires to pick up the baseball, snagging the sleeve of his white shirt on a sharp, loose wire.

"You stuck, mister?" the kid asks.

Dusty smiles up at the boy from his knees.

"Nope," Dusty blurts. "Yeah. I mean, I don't know."

A little embarrassed, Dusty manages a chuckle. Still clutching the baseball, he hears something in the sleeve tear as he pulls his arm back. *It's okay*, he thinks, *you*

Vocabulary

corroded (kə rōd′ əd) *adj.* eaten away by degrees, by gnawing or chemical action

heft (heft) *v.* to lift up

can replace a shirt. You can put a Band-Aid on a scratched arm.

He stands with the ball, faces the boy through the wires, and grins. The boy cups his hands as if expecting Dusty to toss the ball over, as if expecting a brief spring shower. But Dusty doesn't toss the ball. Instead, he finds himself stepping through a gate in the fence, hears his voice ask, "Wanna learn some pitches?" Instead, Dusty finds himself slipping off his polished shoes and brown dress socks, then climbing the small mountain of the pitcher's mound, all that gravel suddenly tender and welcoming beneath his bare feet.

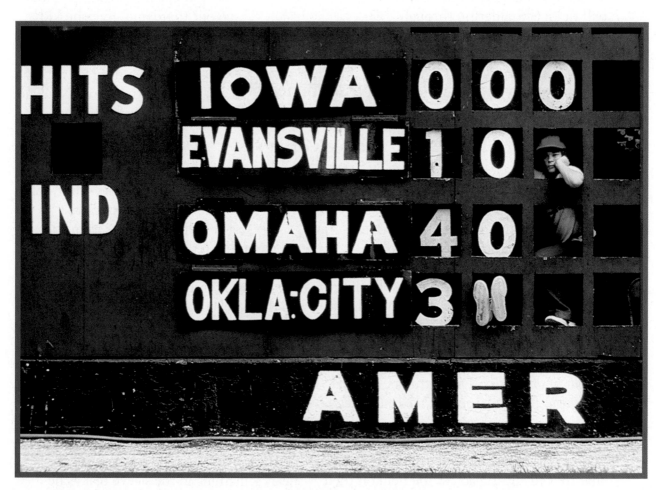

Triple A - 143, 1979. Gregory Thorp. Cibachrome photograph, 13 x 19½ in. Courtesy Carl Solway Gallery, Cincinnati, OH.

Viewing the photograph: What part of Sikarsky's life might this photograph represent? Explain your answer.

Responding to Literature

PERSONAL RESPONSE

Were you surprised by the ending of this story? Why or why not?

Analyzing Literature

RECALL

1. Why does Sikarsky remember his baseball career at the beginning of the story?
2. Describe how Sikarsky feels about his years as a pitcher. How did he deal with his injury?
3. What are some similarities and differences in Sikarsky's life as a ballplayer and his life as a salesperson?
4. What brings about a second change in Sikarsky's life?

INTERPRET

5. Why, do you suppose, does Sikarsky still think about his life as a ballplayer after twenty years? Give several reasons.
6. What qualities does Sikarsky show that may have a positive effect on his future? Explain.
7. In your opinion, does Sikarsky think of himself as a failure or as a success? Give examples to support your answer.
8. **Foreshadowing** is the planting of clues to prepare readers for what will happen later in a piece of literature. How does the writer foreshadow the end of the story? Explain.

EVALUATE AND CONNECT

9. Would the story be as effective if Sikarsky had become a famous actor or had recovered from his injury and played ball again? Explain your answer.
10. Theme Connection How do Sikarsky's choices affect his life? Support your answer with examples from the story.

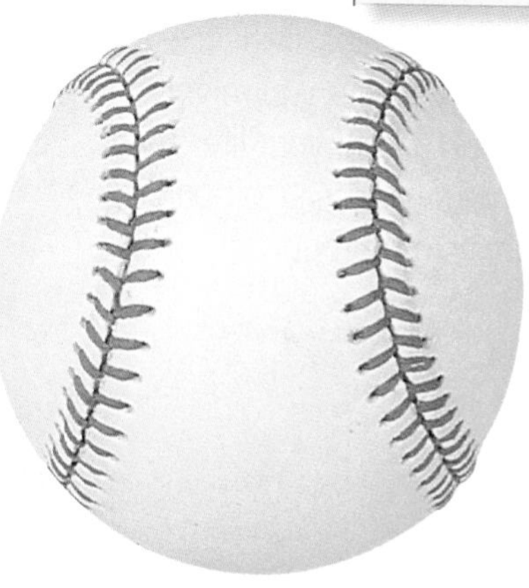

LITERARY ELEMENTS

Conflict

The tension that builds in a story is called **conflict.** The main character in this story has two kinds of conflict: external and internal. An **external conflict** is a struggle between a character and an outside force, such as nature or society. An **internal conflict** is a problem in a character's mind that is solved by the character's making choices among ideas or issues.

1. List an internal and an external conflict in the story.
2. Explain each conflict in the words that Sikarsky might have used if he were being interviewed by a sports reporter. Use examples from the story.

- See **Literary Terms Handbook,** p. R2.

Literature and Writing

Writing About Literature

Rich Language "In the Middle of a Pitch," contains several **similes**—comparisons using the word *like* or *as.* For example, the narrator says that a baseball thrown by the young Sikarsky was "like music that passed so fast you never really heard it." List other similes from the story. In your opinion, what do the similes add to the story? How do they help you understand or enjoy it more? Write your answer in a paragraph.

Creative Writing

From Prose to Poetry Use the similes you found in the story—or create some of your own—to write a poem about baseball. Will it be about your own passion for the sport, or your distaste for it? Will it be about baseball stadiums? the players? the fans? Consider using the words and phrases from your web in the **Focus Activity** on page 238.

Extending Your Response

Literature Groups

Baseball Forever What is it about baseball players that attracts fans? Do injuries to players change this passion? Why do some fans switch from one hero to another as the players they admire grow too old or become injured? Discuss these questions in your group and come to a consensus about why baseball is considered a national pastime.

Learning for Life

Comparing Ideas Bill Meissner compares his own father's comings and goings with the activity in a baseball game. List three or four ways you might compare a ball game to some part of your life. Then write a sentence in which you make that comparison. Share your ideas with a small group.

Interdisciplinary Activity

Mood Music Imagine that "In the Middle of a Pitch" is being made into a television drama. You are the music director and must show changes in Sikarsky's emotions and attitude. Select two scenes—one from the beginning of the story and one from the end. Choose music that you think would be appropriate and helpful to an audience. Play the music for your class as you read aloud the two parts of the story. Ask for a group evaluation.

Reading Further

If you enjoyed this story, read:
Shoeless Joe by W. P. Kinsella

Save your work for your portfolio.

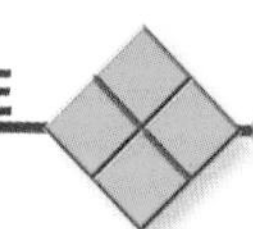

Skill Minilessons

GRAMMAR AND LANGUAGE • PARTICIPLES

A **participle** is a verb form that can function as an adjective. A **present participle** ends in *-ing.*

He was famous as the starting pitcher for a major league team.

A **past participle** usually ends in *-ed,* but irregular verbs may have different endings.

The old park once had freshly painted bleachers.

A **participial phrase** is a group of words that includes a participle and acts as an adjective.

Curving smoothly, the ball sped past.

PRACTICE List the participles and participial phrases in the following sentences. Tell if each is a present or a past participle, and if it is part of a participial phrase.

1. His windup was like a dance performed under water.
2. They placed his name on the disabled list.
3. Remembering his days as a pitcher, he watched as the boy threw the ball.
4. Caught in the fence and hidden behind bushes, the ball was not found for months.

- For more about participles, see **Language Handbook,** p. R31.

READING AND THINKING • CREATIVE THINKING

When you use **creative thinking** in your reading, you can look at characters and conflicts in new ways. For example, you might question why a character is involved in a conflict, what he or she is doing about it, and whether there are other ways that the character might handle the situation.

- For more about reading and thinking strategies, see **Reading Handbook,** pp. R84–R96.

PRACTICE Skim "In the Middle of a Pitch." List clues to Dusty Sikarsky's problem, and note the suggestions his friends make to help him solve his problem. Reread the ending, which tells about Dusty's meeting with the boys. Then write one or two paragraphs suggesting whether you think Dusty solved his problem and ways he might have found a solution earlier in the story.

VOCABULARY • CONNOTATION

The definition of a word is its **denotation.** However, a word may sometimes be used in a way that implies a special attitude or emotion. This is its **connotation.** For example, one of the definitions of *pitch* is "sales talk." But *pitch* is sometimes used in a negative way that implies that the speaker is using "pushy" language and may be making dishonest claims.

PRACTICE Write a sentence for each word, using the connotation shown in parentheses.

1. off balance (unpleasantly surprised)
2. nestled (snug and safe)
3. warped (twisted and ugly)
4. minor (unimportant, secondary)
5. facade (false front, a covering for the real surface)

- For more about connotation and denotation, see **Reading Handbook,** p. R83.

MEDIA Connection

COMIC STRIP

How do you feel about winning or losing a pick-up ball game? Cartoonist Bill Amend's friends have an attitude you may share.

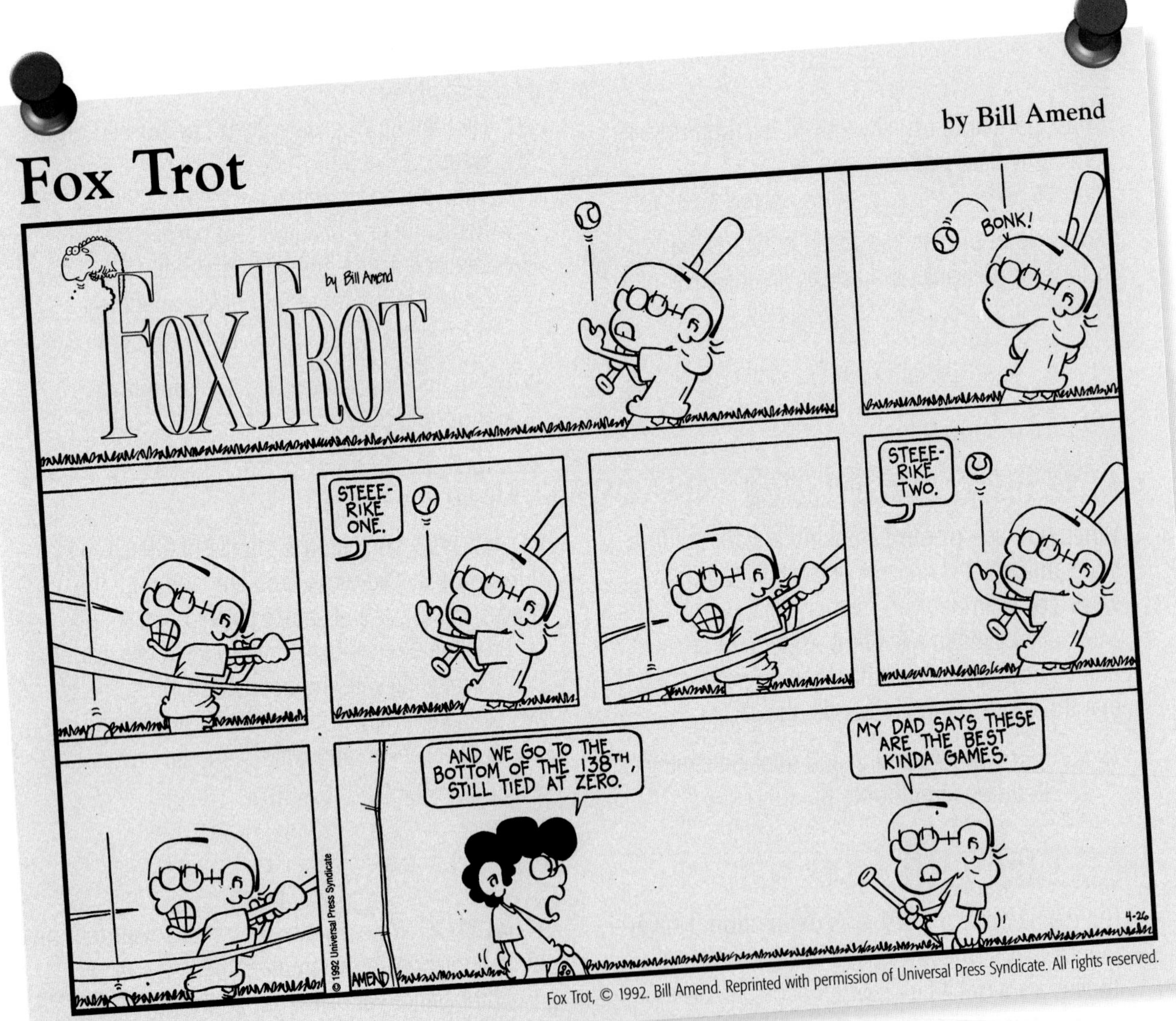

Respond

1. In your opinion, is a game of 138 innings "the best kind"? Explain your answer.
2. Describe the kind of player who would enjoy playing with these boys.

Before You Read

Casey at the Bat

MEET ERNEST LAWRENCE THAYER

Ernest Lawrence Thayer could have followed in his father's footsteps and run one of his family's woolen mills in Massachusetts. Instead, he surprised his family by taking a job as a humor columnist for the *San Francisco Examiner*. Thayer had a low opinion of his writing ability and once said, "I put out large quantities of nonsense . . . from advertisements to editorials." The ballad "Casey at the Bat" was one of Thayer's last contributions to the *Examiner*.

Ernest Lawrence Thayer was born in 1863 and died in 1940. "Casey at the Bat" was published in the San Francisco Examiner *in 1888.*

FOCUS ACTIVITY

What is your reaction as you watch an exciting moment in a ball game?

FreeWrite

How might you act if your team were relying on you to win a championship game? Write a brief answer.

Setting a Purpose

Read to enjoy a very tense moment for a group of baseball fans.

BACKGROUND

The Time and Place This poem was written about a fictitious baseball player. The action takes place before a hometown crowd of 5,000 spectators.

Did You Know? The national love affair with baseball was well under way when "Casey at the Bat" was first published. Abner Doubleday, a ballplayer from Cooperstown, New York, is often credited with forming the rules of baseball in 1839. Yet it was actually a group of businessmen who instituted the sport as we know it today. These men formed the New York Knickerbocker Base Ball Club in 1845. They changed the rules of a popular game called "town ball," in which the ball was thrown directly at players who ran haphazardly, often colliding. The Knickerbockers established bases and the "three strikes, you're out" rule, among other things.

Casey at the Bat

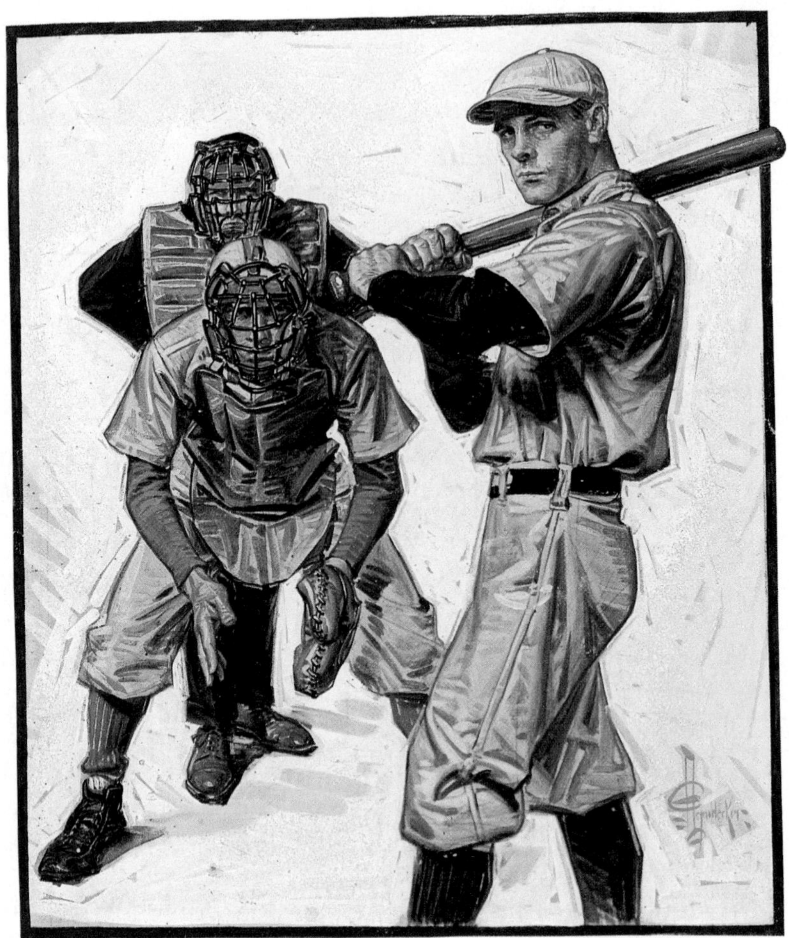

Baseball Scene of Batter, Catcher and Umpire, 1915. Joseph Christian Leyendecker. Oil on canvas, 31 x 22 in. Judy Goffman Fine Art, New York.

Ernest Lawrence Thayer

The outlook wasn't brilliant
   for the Mudville nine that day:
The score stood four to two
   with but one inning more to play.

And then when Cooney died at first,
   and Barrows did the same,
A sickly silence fell
   upon the patrons of the game.

A straggling few got up
   to go in deep despair. The rest
Clung to that hope which springs eternal
   in the human breast;

They thought if only Casey
could but get a whack at that—
We'd put up even money° now
with Casey at the bat.

But Flynn preceded° Casey,
as did also Jimmy Blake,
And the former° was a lulu
and the latter° was a cake;

So upon that stricken multitude
grim melancholy° sat,
For there seemed but little chance
of Casey's getting to the bat.

But Flynn let drive a single,
to the wonderment of all,
And Blake, the much despis-ed,
tore the cover off the ball;

And when the dust had lifted,
and the men saw what had occurred,
There was Jimmy safe at second
and Flynn a-hugging third.

Then from 5,000 throats and more
there rose a lusty yell;
It rumbled through the valley,
it rattled in the dell;

It knocked upon the mountain
and recoiled upon the flat,
For Casey, mighty Casey,
was advancing to the bat.

There was ease in Casey's manner
as he stepped into his place;
There was pride in Casey's bearing
and a smile on Casey's face.

And when, responding to the cheers,
he lightly doffed his hat,
No stranger in the crowd could doubt
'twas Casey at the bat.

Ten thousand eyes were on him
as he rubbed his hands with dirt;
Five thousand tongues applauded
when he wiped them on his shirt.

Then while the writhing pitcher
ground the ball into his hip,
Defiance gleamed in Casey's eye,
a sneer curled Casey's lip.

And now the leather-covered sphere
came hurtling through the air,
And Casey stood a-watching it
in haughty grandeur there.

Close by the sturdy batsman
the ball unheeded sped—
"That ain't my style," said Casey.
"Strike one," the umpire said.

From the benches, black with people,
there went up a muffled roar,
Like the beating of the storm-waves
on a stern and distant shore.

"Kill him! Kill the umpire!"
shouted someone on the stand;
And it's likely they'd have killed him
had not Casey raised his hand.

8 *Put up even money* means fans recognize that the teams have an even chance of winning.

9 *Preceded* means "came before."

10 *Former* refers to the first one mentioned, and *latter* to the last one mentioned. Both Flynn and Blake seem to be considered poor batters.

11 *Grim melancholy* describes the crowd's mood, which is serious and sadly thoughtful.

With a smile of Christian charity
great Casey's visage° shone;
He stilled the rising tumult;°
he bade the game go on;

He signaled to the pitcher,
and once more the spheroid° flew;
But Casey still ignored it,
and the umpire said, "Strike two."

"Fraud!" cried the maddened thousands,
and the echo answered fraud;
But one scornful look from Casey
and the audience was awed.

They saw his face grow stern and cold,
they saw his muscles strain,
And they knew that Casey
wouldn't let that ball go by again.

The sneer is gone from Casey's lips,
his teeth are clenched in hate;
He pounds with cruel violence
his bat upon the plate.

And now the pitcher holds the ball,
and now he lets it go,
And now the air is shattered
by the force of Casey's blow.

Oh, somewhere in this favored land
the sun is shining bright;
The band is playing somewhere,
and somewhere hearts are light,

And somewhere men are laughing,
and somewhere children shout;
But there is no joy in Mudville—
mighty Casey has struck out.

---

37 Casey's *visage* (viz′ ij) is his face.
38 *Tumult* (to͞o′ məlt) means "noisy uproar."
39 A *spheroid* is a round object–in this case, a baseball.

Crowd at the Polo Ground, 1895. Jay Hambidge. Four-color proof, 18⅞ x 14 in. Museum of the City of New York.

Viewing the painting: How do these fans seem to feel about the game they are watching?

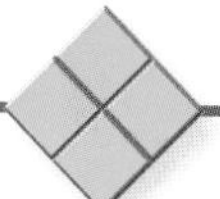

Responding to Literature

PERSONAL RESPONSE

What was your reaction when Casey struck out? How might your response compare to the reaction spectators may have had?

Analyzing Literature

RECALL AND INTERPRET

1. How does Casey behave at the plate during the first two pitches? the third pitch? What does Casey's behavior say about his personality?
2. Describe the action of the game through the third stanza. What would encourage the crowd to "put up even money"?
3. Why, do you think, does the poet have Casey strike out?

EVALUATE AND CONNECT

4. **Suspense** is a feeling of building excitement or uncertainty about what is going to happen next. How effective is the author's use of suspense in this poem? Use examples from the text in your answer.
5. Casey appears at first to be a hero. What other heroes do you know in literature? Do they ever fail?
6. Does Casey seem true to life? Why or why not?

LITERARY ELEMENTS

Narrative Poetry

Narrative poetry tells a story. A narrative poem has characters, a plot with a conflict, and a setting. Centuries ago, the stories of a tribe or village were passed along by a storyteller. To help people remember the tales, storytellers often used songs or poems. Today, narrative poems are usually printed or recorded.

1. What is the main conflict in "Casey at the Bat"?
2. In which line does the writer bring the story to a climax?
3. Where does the writer show how the conflict is resolved?

- See **Literary Terms Handbook,** p. R6.

Extending Your Response

Literature Groups

Spreading the Word "Casey at the Bat" became famous thanks to William De Wolf Hopper, an actor who popularized the poem by reciting it thousands of times before enthusiastic crowds and by making a recording in 1906. How might a modern-day audience differ from an audience in Hopper's time? Discuss ways to perform the poem that you think would appeal to a modern audience. Give a presentation of one of your ideas to the class.

Writing About Literature

The Return of Mighty Casey In 1906, Grantland Rice, a famous sportswriter, penned a poem he called "Casey's Revenge." It begins, "There were saddened hearts in Mudville for a week or even more; / There were muttered oaths and curses—every fan in town was sore." Provide a few more verses to this sequel. Will Casey strike out again or be a hero?

COMPARING SELECTIONS

In the Middle of a Pitch and **Casey at the Bat**

COMPARE **STORIES**

Both selections are about baseball, but that's not all they have in common.

1. What, other than playing the game, is an important topic in both "In the Middle of a Pitch" and "Casey at the Bat"?
2. In what ways do both selections appeal to readers who aren't baseball fans? Think of three reasons not related to baseball why readers may enjoy these two works.
3. How do Bill Meissner and Ernest Lawrence Thayer make their selections suspenseful and interesting? What techniques do both writers use?

Baseball Scene of Batter, Catcher and Umpire, 1915 (detail).

COMPARE **AUTHORS' PURPOSES**

Thayer later criticized his poem about Casey and his fans because he didn't think it deserved so much attention.

1. What might Thayer's purpose have been when he wrote the poem?
2. What do you think Meissner's purpose was for writing his story?

Discuss your answers with a small group, and give reasons to support your opinions.

COMPARE **FANS**

Fans are an important part of "Casey at the Bat" and "In the Middle of a Pitch."

- How do Casey's fans affect his behavior? How does the reader know that Sikarsky also has fans, even after his release from the ball club? Write a few paragraphs comparing the attitudes displayed by the fans of each player.
- With a group, discuss why someone may become a fan or supporter of a particular person or activity. What obligations do people and groups have toward their fans? What obligations do fans have toward the groups and people they admire? Write a letter to a fan or to one of the characters in these two selections. Explain why you support or do not support the person. Back up your opinions with reasons and examples from the selection.

Interdisciplinary Connection

The Evolution of America's Game

Picture a baseball game being played in the 1840s. The pitcher sails an underhand ball toward the catcher's thin leather glove. Players chase balls on uneven outfields, and balls bounce on infields strewn with pebbles. The ball, probably lopsided from too many hits with the bat, is changed only two or three times in an entire game. Only one umpire is present, so the players can–and do–trick him.

Today, pitchers fire overhand fastballs to catchers with padded mitts. Baseball fields are impeccably cared for. An average major league game uses between fifty and sixty baseballs, and six umpires govern the field.

Baseball has come a long way from its earlier versions, known as cricket and rounders, played by colonists in New England in the 1700s. The rules, playing fields, and players have changed, but the passion of fans hasn't waned. Jacques Barzun, a modern writer, educator, and baseball fan once said, "Whoever wants to know the heart and mind of America had better learn baseball." He speaks for millions of devoted fans who have been captivated by the sport through all of its changes. Here's a look at some of the major ones.

ACTIVITY

Invent a variation of a game you enjoy, such as kickball, checkers, or a card game. Revise the rules to make the game more fun, then rename the new version and teach your classmates to play.

The Knickerbocker Nine baseball club, 1864.

Early Baseball	Modern Baseball
The number of players on a side, the number of bases and distance between them, and other rules varied from place to place in the 1700s and early 1800s.	Alexander Cartwright, a New York sports enthusiast, laid out the present dimensions of the playing field in 1845 and wrote basic rules of the game.
Baseball was played mostly in New England until the Civil War, when Union soldiers spread its popularity across the country.	By 1903, sixteen teams played for one of two major leagues. Today, baseball is played enthusiastically around the globe, as far away as Japan. Players are stronger and faster than ever before.
African American ballplayers were not allowed to play in the major or minor leagues, so they started their own leagues in the 1920s and 1930s.	Jackie Robinson of the Brooklyn Dodgers became the first African American major league ballplayer in 1947.

Before You Read

The Wise Old Woman

MEET YOSHIKO UCHIDA

Yoshiko Uchida (yō shē′ kō ü′ chē dä) was among the many Japanese Americans sent to relocation centers during World War II. Uchida is renowned for her detailed narratives of life in such a center. Many of her other writings, however, are retellings of Japanese folktales. She hoped that the folktales would teach young Americans about Japanese culture and also entertain them. Uchida once expressed the hope that ". . . all children, in whatever country they may live, have the same love of fun and a good story."

Yoshiko Uchida was born in 1921 and died in 1992. This story was published in 1965.

FOCUS ACTIVITY

The number *three* often appears in folktales. What folktales can you recall that feature three main events, wishes, riddles, or characters?

List It!

With a partner, make a list of folktales in which the number *three* appears. Explain how *three* appears in each tale.

Setting a Purpose

Read to discover how three challenges affect a village.

BACKGROUND

The Time and Place This folktale is set in a Japanese village.

Did You Know? Folktales from around the world often follow a similar pattern. They begin with a dreamlike "once upon a time" or "in a land far away" that helps listeners or readers be carried away by the often fantastic events of the story. Characters are quickly introduced, and conflict appears early in the story. The characters are often in direct contrast to each other: one is very, very good and the other is terribly evil. Three events, riddles, or wishes often carry the plot along to the frequent conclusion of "happily ever after."

VOCABULARY PREVIEW

haughtily (hô′ tə lē) *adv.* in a way that shows too much pride in oneself and great scorn for others; p. 259

decree (di krē′) *v.* to set forth an official rule, order, or decision; dictate; p. 259

banish (ban′ ish) *v.* to force a person to leave a country or community; p. 259

bewilderment (bi wil′ dər mənt) *n.* deep confusion; p. 262

commend (kə mend′) *v.* to express approval of; p. 262

summon (sum′ ən) *v.* to send for or request the presence of, especially with authority; p. 263

The Wise Old Woman

Adapted by Yoshiko Uchida

Landscape, Mid-Edo. Ike Gyokuran. Hanging scroll; ink and colors on silk, 44⅛ x 19³⁄₁₆ in. Gift of the Asian Art Foundation of San Francisco, The Avery Brundage Collection. Asian Art Museum of San Francisco. B76 D3.

MANY LONG YEARS AGO, there lived an arrogant and cruel young lord who ruled over a small village in the western hills of Japan. "I have no use for old people in my village," he said haughtily. "They are neither useful nor able to work for a living. I therefore decree that anyone over seventy-one must be banished from the village and left in the mountains to die."

Vocabulary

haughtily (hô′ tə lē) *adv.* in a way that shows too much pride in oneself and great scorn for others

decree (di krē′) *v.* to set forth an official rule, order, or decision; dictate

banish (ban′ ish) *v.* to force a person to leave a country or community

"What a dreadful decree! What a cruel and unreasonable lord we have," the people of the village murmured. But the lord fearfully punished anyone who disobeyed him, and so villagers who turned seventy-one were tearfully carried into the mountains, never to return.

Gradually there were fewer and fewer old people in the village and soon they disappeared altogether. Then the young lord was pleased.

"What a fine village of young, healthy and hardworking people I have," he bragged. "Soon it will be the finest village in all of Japan."

Now there lived in this village a kind young farmer and his aged mother. They were poor, but the farmer was good to his mother, and the two of them lived happily together. However, as the years went by, the mother grew older, and before long she reached the terrible age of seventy-one.

"If only I could somehow deceive the cruel lord," the farmer thought. But there were records in the village books and everyone knew that his mother had turned seventy-one.

Each day the son put off telling his mother that he must take her into the mountains to die, but the people of the village began to talk. The farmer knew that if he did not take his mother away soon, the lord would send his soldiers and throw them both into a dark dungeon to die a terrible death.

"Mother—" he would begin, as he tried to tell her what he must do, but he could not go on.

Then one day the mother herself spoke of the lord's dread decree. "Well, my son," she said, "the time has come for you to take me to the mountains. We must hurry before the lord sends his soldiers for you." And she did not seem worried at all that she must go to the mountains to die.

"Forgive me, dear mother, for what I must do," the farmer said sadly, and the next morning he lifted his mother to his shoulders and set off on the steep path toward the mountains. Up and up he climbed, until the trees clustered close and the path was gone. There was no longer even the sound of birds, and they heard only the soft wail of the wind in the trees. The son walked slowly, for he could not bear to think of leaving his old mother in the mountains. On and on he climbed, not wanting to stop and leave her behind. Soon, he heard his mother breaking off small twigs from the trees that they passed.

"Mother, what are you doing?" he asked.

"Do not worry, my son," she answered gently. "I am just marking the way so you will not get lost returning to the village."

The son stopped. "Even now you are thinking of me?" he asked, wonderingly.

The mother nodded. "Of course, my son," she replied. "You will always be in my thoughts. How could it be otherwise?"

At that, the young farmer could bear it no longer. "Mother, I cannot leave you in the mountains to die all alone," he said. "We are going home and no matter what the lord does to punish me, I will never desert you again."

So they waited until the sun had set and a lone star crept into the silent sky. Then in the dark shadows of night, the farmer carried his mother down the hill and they returned quietly to their little house. The farmer dug a deep hole in the floor of his kitchen and made a small room where he could hide his mother. From that day, she spent all her time in the secret room and the farmer carried meals to her there. The rest of the time, he was careful to work in the fields and act as though he lived alone. In this way, for almost two years, he kept his mother safely hidden and no one in the village knew that she was there.

Standing Beauty, 1851. Ando Hiroshige. Hanging scroll, ink and color on paper, 91.5 x 27.7 cm. The British Museum, London.

Viewing the painting: Notice the woman's posture and expression. What qualities might she have in common with the old woman in this story?

Then one day there was a terrible commotion among the villagers for Lord Higa of the town beyond the hills threatened to conquer their village and make it his own.

"Only one thing can spare you," Lord Higa announced. "Bring me a box containing one thousand ropes of ash and I will spare your village."

The cruel young lord quickly gathered together all the wise men of his village. "You are men of wisdom," he said. "Surely you can tell me how to meet Lord Higa's demands so our village can be spared."

But the wise men shook their heads. "It is impossible to make even one rope of ash, sire," they answered. "How can we ever make one thousand?"

"Fools!" the lord cried angrily. "What good is your wisdom if you cannot help me now?"

And he posted a notice in the village square offering a great reward of gold to any villager who could help him save their village.

But all the people in the village whispered, "Surely, it is an impossible thing, for ash crumbles at the touch of the finger. How could anyone ever make a rope of ash?" They shook their heads and sighed, "Alas, alas, we must be conquered by yet another cruel lord."

The young farmer, too, supposed that this must be, and he wondered what would happen to his mother if a new lord even more terrible than their own came to rule over them.

When his mother saw the troubled look on his face, she asked, "Why are you so worried, my son?"

So the farmer told her of the impossible demand made by Lord Higa if the village was to be spared, but his mother did

not seem troubled at all. Instead she laughed softly and said, "Why, that is not such an impossible task. All one has to do is soak ordinary rope in salt water and dry it well. When it is burned, it will hold its shape and there is your rope of ash! Tell the villagers to hurry and find one thousand pieces of rope."

The farmer shook his head in amazement. "Mother, you are wonderfully wise," he said, and he rushed to tell the young lord what he must do.

"You are wiser than all the wise men of the village," the lord said when he heard the farmer's solution, and he rewarded him with many pieces of gold. The thousand ropes of ash were quickly made and the village was spared.

In a few days, however, there was another great commotion in the village as Lord Higa sent another threat. This time he sent a log with a small hole that curved and bent seven times through its length, and he demanded that a single piece of silk thread be threaded through the hole. "If you cannot perform this task," the lord threatened, "I shall come to conquer your village."

The young lord hurried once more to his wise men, but they all shook their heads in bewilderment. "A needle cannot bend its way through such curves," they moaned. "Again we are faced with an impossible demand."

"And again you are stupid fools!" the lord said, stamping his foot impatiently. He then posted a second notice in the village square asking the villagers for their help.

Once more the young farmer hurried with the problem to his mother in her secret room.

"Why, that is not so difficult," his mother said with a quick smile. "Put some sugar at one end of the hole. Then, tie an ant to a piece of silk thread and put it in at the other end. He will weave his way in and out of the curves to get to the sugar and he will take the silk thread with him."

"Mother, you are remarkable!" the son cried, and he hurried off to the lord with the solution to the second problem.

Once more the lord commended the young farmer and rewarded him with many pieces of gold. "You are a brilliant man and you have saved our village again," he said gratefully.

But the lord's troubles were not over even then, for a few days later Lord Higa sent still another demand. "This time you will undoubtedly fail and then I shall conquer your village," he threatened. "Bring me a drum that sounds without being beaten."

"But that is not possible," sighed the people of the village. "How can anyone make a drum sound without beating it?"

This time the wise men held their heads in their hands and moaned, "It is hopeless. It is hopeless. This time Lord Higa will conquer us all."

The young farmer hurried home breathlessly. "Mother, Mother, we must solve another terrible problem or Lord Higa will conquer our village!" And he quickly told his mother about the impossible drum.

His mother, however, smiled and answered, "Why, this is the easiest of them

Vocabulary

bewilderment (bi wil′ dər mənt) *n.* deep confusion

commend (kə mend′) *v.* to express approval of

all. Make a drum with sides of paper and put a bumblebee inside. As it tries to escape, it will buzz and beat itself against the paper and you will have a drum that sounds without being beaten."

The young farmer was amazed at his mother's wisdom. "You are far wiser than any of the wise men of the village," he said, and he hurried to tell the young lord how to meet Lord Higa's third demand.

When the lord heard the answer, he was greatly impressed. "Surely a young man like you cannot be wiser than all my wise men," he said. "Tell me honestly, who has helped you solve all these difficult problems?"

The young farmer could not lie. "My lord," he began slowly, "for the past two years I have broken the law of the land. I have kept my aged mother hidden beneath the floor of my house, and it is she who solved each of your problems and saved the village from Lord Higa."

He trembled as he spoke, for he feared the lord's displeasure and rage. Surely now the soldiers would be summoned to throw him into the dark dungeon. But when he glanced fearfully at the lord, he saw that the young ruler was not angry at all. Instead, he was silent and thoughtful, for at last he realized how much wisdom and knowledge old people possess.

He trembled as he spoke, for he feared the lord's displeasure and rage.

"I have been very wrong," he said finally. "And I must ask the forgiveness of your mother and of all my people. Never again will I demand that the old people of our village be sent to the mountains to die. Rather, they will be treated with the respect and honor they deserve and share with us the wisdom of their years."

And so it was. From that day, the villagers were no longer forced to abandon their parents in the mountains, and the village became once more a happy, cheerful place in which to live. The terrible Lord Higa stopped sending his impossible demands and no longer threatened to conquer them, for he too was impressed. "Even in such a small village there is much wisdom," he declared, "and its people should be allowed to live in peace."

And that is exactly what the farmer and his mother and all the people of the village did for all the years thereafter.

Vocabulary

summon (sum′ ən) *v.* to send for or request the presence of, especially with authority

Responding to Literature

PERSONAL RESPONSE

The lords in the story may remind you of some people in modern society. If so, who are these people? What do you think about such people?

LITERARY ELEMENTS

Climax

The **climax** of a story is the turning point, an exciting moment that all the earlier events lead up to. The climax is part of the plot, or story line. Nearly all folktales have a climax because they are built around a problem, puzzle, or conflict to solve.

1. Describe the climax of "The Wise Old Woman."
2. What makes the climax of this tale exciting?

- See **Literary Terms Handbook,** p. R2.

Analyzing Literature

RECALL

1. What does the young lord decree? Why does he make this demand?
2. What does the young farmer do when his mother, the wise old woman, turns seventy-one?
3. Name the three demands from Lord Higa and describe the wise old woman's solutions.
4. What does the young lord learn from the wise old woman?

INTERPRET

5. Why do the villagers go along with the lord's decree even though they don't want to?
6. Why does the young farmer disobey the decree?
7. Why does the author show that only the old woman can solve the problems and not the wise men of the village?
8. What point does this folktale make about people who have power over others?

EVALUATE AND CONNECT

9. What is the message, or theme, of the story? How important is this message for people today?
10. What is your impression of how modern American society treats older people? Explain your answer.

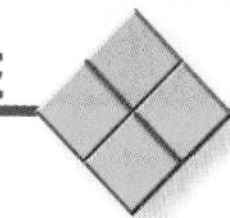

Extending Your Response

Writing About Literature

Compare Folktales Folktales have appealed to people since early times when they were sung or told by storytellers. Locate or recall a favorite folktale and compare its characters, setting, and plot to those of "The Wise Old Woman." Write a few paragraphs comparing the two folktales.

Creative Writing

Good Versus Evil Write a very short story following the folktale pattern described in the **Focus Activity** and **Background** sections on page 258. Begin with a good character and an evil character, a conflict that includes three main events, and a conclusion. Will good win over evil in your story?

Literature Groups

Abuse of Power Rulers throughout history have been known to abuse their power, as do the lords in "The Wise Old Woman." Discuss historical examples of people who were mistreated, such as the elderly in this story. What have people done, and what can people today do, to correct abuses of power?

Interdisciplinary Activity

Social Studies Japan has a history of feudal lords and their samurai warriors, shoguns (military governors), and emperors. Research Japanese rulers from ancient times through today. Learn more about several rulers, including their governmental power. Prepare a short written or oral presentation of your findings.

Save your work for your portfolio.

Skill Minilesson

VOCABULARY • SYNONYMS

Synonyms are words that have the same or nearly the same meanings. However, there are small but important differences between synonyms. For example, *bewilderment* and *confusion* are synonyms, but *bewilderment* is deep, hopeless confusion. Still, these two words are synonyms because they mean nearly the same thing.

PRACTICE Use your knowledge of the vocabulary words in the left column to match each to its synonym in the right column.

1. summon	a. proudly
2. decree	b. expel
3. haughtily	c. call
4. commend	d. command
5. banish	e. compliment

Technology Skills

Multimedia: Adding Sound and Video to Presentations

Almost any presentation can be improved by adding sound and video. For instance, if you're presenting a report on an actor, what better way to illustrate his style than with movie clips? You can videotape movie scenes on TV or download film clips from the Internet, but is it legal to use them without the studio's permission? A crash course on copyright law will help you find out.

Fair Use and Multimedia

In general, copyright law protects people who create and produce an original work. Consider for a minute how you would feel if you had written a short story just to have someone else publish it and get all the credit. Copyright law exists to protect you from such "piracy."

However, the law recognizes that students and teachers need to be able to access and share information with one another. To accommodate these needs, the 1976 Copyright Law includes a "fair use" clause allowing educators and students to use limited portions of copyrighted materials without permission and without paying a fee.

The box-office hit *Titanic,* released by Paramount in 1997, made actor Leonardo DiCaprio a household name. His character, Jack Dawson, and Rose DeWitt (played by Kate Winslet) fall in love aboard the ill-fated ship.

Get an Update

The 1976 law was passed years before students had access to the powerful multimedia tools of today. Fortunately, legislators have updated the law to include electronic material. To find out the latest on copyright and multimedia presentations, conduct a World Wide Web search for "Fair Use Guidelines for Educational Multimedia." Follow these guidelines when you use copyrighted materials in a multimedia presentation.

Practice

Work with a partner to access sound and movie files on the Internet. Check with your teacher or lab assistant to be sure you have the necessary software to play these files. This software (sometimes in demonstration versions) can usually be downloaded at no cost.

1. Using an Internet search engine, and type in the keywords *.wav + *.mid. The computer will find all sites with files that have *wav* or *mid* extensions. These two file endings indicate sound files.
2. You should be able to find music and other sound bites from movies, television shows, and other sources. Open and play a few files.
3. Select two files to download. Copy them into a folder where you can find them later.
4. Next search for *.avi + *.mov files. These are movie files. You'll find both live-action movies and animation. They may contain sound as well as moving pictures. Select two files that look interesting, and download them to the folder with your sound files. (Movie files can be huge. Select short ones to avoid long download times.)
5. Open your presentation software, and create a few blank slides. Then pull down the **Insert** menu and select **Movies and Sounds/from File.** Insert the sound and movie files from the folder containing your downloaded files.
6. To play your movies and sounds in a slide show, simply click (or double click) on the image or icon with your mouse. To change this default, click on the image, and select **Action Settings** from the **Slide Show** menu to see what other options are available to you.

TECHNOLOGY TIP

Extensions tell your computer what kind of file it's working with. PC extensions always have three letters; Macintosh files can have two, three, or four. The letters may be all lowercase or all capitals. Here are some common extensions that will help you identify files.

Sound files:
.aif, .au, .ram, .mid, .snd, .wav

Picture files:
.gif, .jpg or .jpeg, .tif or .tiff

Movie files:
.avi, .mov, .mpg or .mpeg, .qt

ACTIVITIES

1. Create a multimedia presentation that includes movies and sounds for one of your writing assignments in this theme. Present your work to your classmates.
2. If you have access to a digital video camera, work with a group to create some video files you can use, in addition to downloaded sounds or movies, in a multimedia slide show that relates to a theme or a selection in this book. Present your slide show to your school's PTA group or show it at an open house for parents.

Before You Read

Bagged Wolf

MEET CAROL KENDALL

By the fourth grade, Carol Kendall knew she would be a writer. She had already started her first novel. "It was a lurid tale of cruel stepfathers and pickpockets," she recalls. "I ran out of material after nineteen pages." Kendall's first novel was published in 1946. She is well known as a fantasy writer.

MEET YAO-WEN LI

Yao-wen Li (you wen lē) was a scientist, housewife, and mother before she became a writer. Born in Canton, China, she came to the United States in 1947. Years later, she began to write and translate.

This story was published in 1978 in Sweet and Sour: Tales from China.

FOCUS ACTIVITY

If someone were about to harm you, how might you protect yourself?

QuickWrite
Jot down your response. With a classmate, share responses.

Setting a Purpose
As you read, notice how various characters try to protect themselves.

BACKGROUND

The Time and Place This story dates back to the Ming dynasty, which ruled China from 1368 to 1644.

Did You Know? In the following tale, Tung Kuo is a student of the Chinese philosopher Mo-tzu, who lived from 479 to 381 B.C. Mo-tzu taught that it is what people do, not who they are, that makes them worthy of respect. Students of Mo-tzu lived simply, wore distinctive clothes, and followed his teachings of universal love and the consensus of the common good.

VOCABULARY PREVIEW

prowess (prou′ is) *n.* great ability or skill; p. 269
benevolence (bə nev′ ə ləns) *n.* kindliness; generosity; p. 271
loom (lo͞om) *v.* to appear or come into view in a way that seems very large and, often, threatening; p. 271
scavenger (skav′ in jər) *n.* an animal, such as a hyena or vulture, that feeds on dead, decaying plants or animals; p. 272
advocate (ad′ və kit) *n.* one who publicly supports or urges; p. 272
plight (plīt) *n.* an unfortunate or dangerous situation; p. 274
barter (bär′ tər) *v.* to trade goods for goods; p. 274
gravely (grāv′ lē) *adv.* very seriously; p. 275
sagely (sāj′ lē) *adv.* very wisely; p. 276
aghast (ə gast′) *adj.* filled with fear or horror; p. 276

Bagged Wolf

Retold by Carol Kendall and Yao-wen Li

One hard winter's day a lean, lank wolf was prowling the mountains in search of food. He was weak with hunger and had already missed two kills when suddenly he saw, munching unconcernedly on a patch of grass, the biggest, fattest, tastiest-looking rabbit he had seen all winter. His stomach fairly ached with longing, but he advanced carefully. In one more moment he would be sinking his teeth into the rabbit's soft neck . . . He went rigid at the rumbling sound of galloping horses. Looking over his shoulder, he saw Lord Chao himself bearing down upon him at the head of a hunting party. Lord Chao! Everyone knew of Lord Chao's prowess with bow and arrow. Where Lord Chao aimed, there Lord Chao struck!

Vocabulary

prowess (prou′ is) *n.* great ability or skill

Like an arrow himself, the wolf sprang into the air. He was too late; Lord Chao's arrow was already on its way. It caught him in his hind leg. With a yelp of pain the wolf faltered, but there was no time to nurse the wound. He gave himself a strong push with his good hind leg and shot off down the mountain path. Lord Chao raised a fierce cry, and the whole party came thundering after him.

At this very time there was on the mountain path a certain Tung Kuo on his way to the capital. With his book bag, which was his sole belonging, he rode on

Mongol Archer on Horseback. Ming dynasty drawing. By courtesy of The Board of Trustees of The Victoria & Albert Museum, London.

Viewing the painting: Notice the man's dress, posture, and horse. What characteristics does he seem to share with Lord Chao?

a tired skinny donkey, and love was in his mind—love for every human being under the sun. He belonged to a brotherhood that believed peace and happiness would come to the world if everyone would practice self-denial for the good of his fellow men. Tung Kuo, being a devoted disciple in this belief, positively ached to practice benevolence. When he saw clouds of dust rising from the ground far away, and heard noises like roaring drums, his first thought was that he might even now be put to the test of loving-kindness.

The wolf, an arrow dragging from his hind leg and blood tracing the dust behind him, came plump in front of him.

"O Merciful Sir!" the beast gasped, "please take pity on me. Save me from Lord Chao!" His chest heaved with the effort to get the words out. "Save me, and I shall repay you in my heart as long as I live!"

The sad sight of the suffering wolf would have unlocked a much stonier heart than Tung Kuo's. "Fear nothing, my good friend," he said. "Even though I myself should be killed by Lord Chao, I shall not deliver you into his bloody hands. I am a follower of the great philosopher[1] Mo-tzu and obey his teachings of love for all mankind, er, and wolfkind." He had climbed off his donkey and knelt beside the wolf. "Be patient and bear a little pain, my good fellow. I must first remove the arrow." Gently, he pulled the arrow from the beast's hind leg.

"Hurry! Hurry!" the wolf cried impatiently. "They are coming closer and closer. I must hide!" He looked about him with eyes of desperation, and then stared at the bag on the donkey's back. "There! Empty out that bag and I'll hide in it."

Obligingly Tung Kuo emptied all the books from his bag and, taking hold of the wolf's scruff, started stuffing him head first into the bag. Very shortly he had a bag full of wolf, except for the hind legs. They sprawled stubbornly out of the top. Hauling the wolf out, he stuffed the spindly hind legs in first, but then he ended with a pointed mouth and black nose jutting out. Head first, hind legs hanging out; legs first, nose showing—he tried and tried again, but he couldn't get everything belonging to the wolf inside the bag.

The distant cloud of dust was growing bigger and closer. Desperately, the wolf cried, "Tie my legs together, stupid! Anything! But hurry! Hurry!"

With the rope from round his waist, Tung Kuo tied up the wolf's legs, and tugging and shoving, managed finally to stuff all of him into the bag. Then he picked up the scattered books and crammed them in wherever he could find space—between the wolf's front and hind legs, under his nose, against his flanks, on top of his head. At last he got the bag closed and, with his remaining strength, heaved it up on the donkey's back. He was scarcely able to totter along the path from weakness, and had indeed moved only twenty footfalls when his way was blocked by Lord Chao himself, looming high on his horse.

1. A *philosopher* studies the meaning and purpose of life and the universe.

Vocabulary

benevolence (bə nev′ ə ləns) *n.* kindliness; generosity

loom (lo͞om) *v.* to appear or come into view in a way that seems very large and, often, threatening

"Have you seen a wolf?" Lord Chao demanded harshly. "A wounded wolf?"

Tung Kuo tried to keep his voice steady. "A wounded wolf, my Lord? A wolf is a very cunning animal. He would not run on an open way like this. Have you looked into the hidden paths in the woods?"

Lord Chao scowled down at him. "I know your kind," he said. "All melting heart and wet cheeks." Suddenly drawing his sword from its scabbard,[2] Lord Chao with a fearful stroke whipped it against a nearby sapling, which fell instantly to the ground. Then he pointed the tip of the sword at Tung Kuo's throat. "Such is the fate of anything that earns my displeasure. Should you find this wolf and aid him in any way to escape me, I shall be mightily displeased with you! Do you understand?"

Quaking, Tung Kuo tried to jerk his eyes from the glittering sword. "Oh, yes, my Lord, I understand very well. I should not like to suffer such a fate, you may depend on that!"

No sooner had the pounding of hooves died away than the wolf began a great noise. "Let me out, let me out! Hurry, will you! I am smothering to death!"

In the urgency of freeing the poor wolf, Tung Kuo let his own fear of Lord Chao slip from his mind. The wolf, however, with his feet squarely on the ground once more, looked up into Tung Kuo's face with a wicked grin.

"Dear Benevolent Sir, thank you for saving my life from Lord Chao. Unfortunately you have not saved it all the way. Not having eaten this entire day, I am perishing of hunger. If I do not have something to eat soon, I shall die and your effort at saving me will have been in vain. As a matter of fact," he went on cunningly, "I would rather be killed by Lord Chao and served on the table of a nobleman than be starved to death on the roadside and devoured by foul scavengers. As you are such a true advocate of universal love, you won't mind giving up your life to save mine!"

Tung Kuo had no time to reason. With mouth wide open and tongue slavering over his polished white teeth, the wolf charged right at him. The scholar leapt behind his donkey, and from that point dodged the wolf's assaults by jumping to the left or to the right as the animal lunged at him.

When the wolf stood still for a moment with lowered head and panting breath, Tung Kuo reproached[3] him. "When you begged me to save you, did you not say that you would be grateful and would repay me? Now you are safe and sound, you try to eat me. What an ungrateful wolf you are!"

"Not ungrateful," said the wolf craftily, "but a wolf, to be sure. Human beings are the natural enemies of wolves and must be eaten at every opportunity."

"I can scarcely agree with you there," said Tung Kuo. He was thinking furiously. The sun was no longer high. When it went down, and the wolves came in packs, he would surely be eaten. He cleared his

2. A *scabbard* is the case for the blade of a sword, bayonet, or similar weapon.

3. When Tung Kuo *reproached* the wolf, he scolded or blamed him for a fault.

Vocabulary

scavenger (skav′ in jər) *n.* an animal, such as a hyena or vulture, that feeds on dead, decaying plants or animals

advocate (ad′ və kit) *n.* one who publicly supports or urges

Blue Tree, 1909–1910. Piet Mondrian. Oil on composition board, 22⅜ x 29½ in. Dallas Museum of Art. Foundation for the Arts Collection. Gift of James H. and Lillian Clark Foundation.

Viewing the painting: **How is the subject of Mondrian's painting like the tree in this story?**

throat. "As we are both rather winded from all this dashing and dodging about, permit me to propose a solution. The old custom in the case of a dispute is to seek the wisdom of three elders. Let us do that. Their judgments will decide whether you should eat me or not. If they all say yes, I shall of course oblige."

"Very well," said the wolf, "and fair enough. I am weary of all this sparring[4] about. Let us go in search of three elders, then."

They trod on peacefully for a while, but the wolf quickly grew restless when they met nobody on the path. He came to a stop in front of an old tree with most of its branches chopped off.

"We'll ask this tree."

"Ask a tree! Whoever heard of—"

"I am HUNGRY," growled the wolf. "Go on and ask before I forget myself."

Tung Kuo hastily bowed to the tree and, from beginning to now, related the whole

4. Here, *sparring* refers to arguing in a cautious, restrained way, as if the two were testing one another's strength.

incident in all its details. "And so," he asked at the end of the recital, "is it your opinion that the wolf should eat me after all?"

A booming voice issued from the tree, and Tung Kuo stepped hastily back. "Now that you have told me what you think is a piteous tale, let me tell you about *me*. You could hardly guess that I am an apricot tree. The gardener planted me from a seed, and within a year I gave flowers; a few years later I gave fruit. In ten years my trunk was as big as the gardener's arms about me. The gardener sold my fruits, rested in my shade, and made a great profit. But now I am old and dying and can give no more fruit or thick shade. The only time the gardener comes to me is to cut off more of my limbs for firewood. I have repeatedly begged him to pity my old age and spare me the gashes of his axe and hatchet, but he turns a deaf ear. All my good services mean nothing to him! And you ask *me* whether this wolf in his desperate plight of starvation shouldn't eat you? I say yes! Eat, eat! And when he is finished, may he find the gardener and make a hearty meal of him too!"

Saliva drooling from his jaws, the wolf leapt up to attack Tung Kuo on the spot.

"Not just yet!" said Tung Kuo sternly. "You made an agreement, and you must stick by it. We have two more opinions to seek."

Unwillingly, the wolf swallowed back his saliva as best he could, and the two walked on again to the sound of the wolf's rumbling stomach. After a short time they saw a tired old cow leaning against a half-fallen wall.

"Go and ask that good dame," the wolf demanded. "She looks full of age and wisdom."

"But what is a cow's wisdom . . . ?"

The wolf growled threateningly. "I am about to start biting you!"

Tung Kuo hurriedly addressed himself to the old cow, who stared stonily at him, licked her cracked nose, and when the story finished with the apricot tree's verdict, fetched up a sigh that made her skinny flanks quiver. "The tree is certainly right. Listen to *my* story. The farmer bartered an old knife for me when I was but a calf. I soon got my strength and began to earn a living for him. I pulled his hunting cart while he tasted the joys of hunting; when he tilled the soil, I pulled the plow. I gave my strength freely. In those days, you should have seen how poor he was! In his kitchen there was never enough rice at one time to last three days, and his wine jug held only dust most of the year. If it weren't for me, his wife would still be wearing coarse drab clothes instead of silk and brocade and he would not be playing the country squire with his herds of cows and his fine horses. Every thread of silk, every grain of rice came from *my* efforts." She gave her head a weary toss. "Look at me, if you will. I am old and sick and can no longer work, so they send me out to the field where the sun burns me by day and the icy wind cuts into my skin by night. I heard the farmer's wife complain about wasting feed on me. 'There should be no waste in the whole cow,' she said. 'The skin can be turned into leather, the flesh

Vocabulary

plight (plīt) *n.* an unfortunate or dangerous situation
barter (bär′ tər) *v.* to trade goods for goods

sold as meat and the bones and horns sold for bone meal or even for carving!'

"And then," and the cow's voice sank lower, "just last night she came out here with the son and pointed her long finger at me. 'My son,' she said, 'you have been apprenticed to the butcher for three years now. It is time to sharpen your knife and practice your art.' Bought for a knife, and now slaughtered by one! That is my fate."

The cow drew another long breath. "You say the wolf is thankless and ungrateful. What right have you to demand his thanks? Have you given him your whole life as I did to the farmer? The apricot tree is right. The wolf should eat you. And I can think of some other morsels for his next meal."

With a joyous snarl, the wolf bared his pointed teeth and made to spring upon Tung Kuo, but the scholar stayed him with an upraised hand. "Not yet!" he said with all the sternness he could bring out of his quivering heart. "There is still more advice to seek, and I believe I see an elder approaching us even now. I shall speak to him."

Tung Kuo ran ahead of the wolf to meet the old man coming towards them. He had silvery white hair and a long silvery beard, and he carried a staff in his hand.

"O my Venerable[5] Sir," Tung Kuo cried out, "how glad I am to see a fellow man! Only a wise elder like yourself can save me."

"That is possible," said the old man gravely. "What is your trouble, my good friend?"

"It is like a nightmare," began Tung Kuo. "This morning when I was on my way to the capital I met this wolf who begged me to save him from Lord Chao's arrows and I did. Can you believe that when the wolf came out safe and sound, he demanded a meal of my body! I finally persuaded him to seek the wisdom of three elders before taking the first bite, but O Sir, that has been another nightmare until now. The wolf insisted that we ask an old apricot tree and an old cow. Both of them bear grudges against men, so of course they sided with the wolf. And now at last heaven is beginning to show pity on me. Only your great wisdom can save me from becoming wolf-fodder."[6]

The wise old man shook his head and pointed his staff at the wolf. "Tung Kuo saved your life, did he not? And you want to repay him by eating him up? Miserable creature who fears neither man nor God! Ungrateful and thankless beast! Scamp back to your den lest I kill you with this stick!"

"Oh, no, not yet, Venerable One," the wolf pleaded. "You have heard only half the story. Be fair and listen to my side as well. You see, Tung Kuo *pretended* to save me, but deep in his heart he planned to kill me all along by tying up my legs and crushing me into his bag with his books. To make certain, he closed the bag tight to suffocate me. Further, my stomach was doubled up and my back sprained with having to curve it. It is a surprise that I came out alive at all! Now tell me, wise old gentleman, does he not deserve to be eaten?"

5. A *venerable* (ven′ ər ə bəl) person deserves respect because of age, character, or rank.

6. Usually, *fodder* refers to the dried hay or grass fed to farm animals. Wolves prefer meat.

Vocabulary
gravely (grāv′ lē) *adv.* very seriously

The old man looked questioningly at Tung Kuo. "If this is the case, then you are also to blame."

Tung Kuo was alarmed by the old man's sudden change of attitude. "But good sir, you must see that the wolf—"

"Please be quiet," the wise man said sternly. "I am really confused and don't know whom to believe. I have got it firmly in mind as far as the wolf's being wounded by Lord Chao and seeking help from Tung Kuo, but after that I begin to get muddled. Would you be so kind as to reenact the scene for me so that I can see the whole thing for myself and make my fair judgment on who was saved or who was suffocated and beaten half to death by books."

Both the wolf and Tung Kuo were eager to oblige. Tung Kuo tied up the wolf's legs and shut him up tightly in the bag while the wise old man nodded his head sagely.

When the wolf was secure, the wise old man bent towards Tung Kuo. "Have you a dagger?" He made a stabbing motion towards the sack.

Tung Kuo stared at him aghast. "You don't mean that I should *kill* him!"

The wise old man gave a scornful snort. "Will you then release him to eat the both of us? No matter what my judgment is, do you think the wolf will let you reach the capital when you are the only meal in sight? Even if you leave him tied up here in your sack, how long before he eats through your precious books and the rope round his legs and is hot-tongued on your trail? Humane[7] you are—there is no question of that—but you are also worse than a fool. You would remove one humane soul from the world and leave in its place a devil-hearted fiend that preys on humanity."

Tung Kuo slowly drew his dagger from its sheath and looked from it to the humpy bookbag, still undecided. Were the years of teaching and learning to end in the thrust of a dagger into a living being's hide, or—and he smiled grimly—in the thrust of sharp claw and pointed fang into his own living hide? His hide and how many others after he had been gulped down? The bookbag stirred. There was a sound as of teeth gnawing on rope . . .

Tung Kuo killed the wolf.

Ming dynasty (1368–1644)

7. A person who is *humane* shows sympathy and kindness toward humans and animals.

Vocabulary

sagely (sāj′ lē) *adv.* very wisely

aghast (ə gast′) *adj.* filled with fear or horror

Responding to Literature

PERSONAL RESPONSE

Were you surprised by the ending? Why or why not?

Analyzing Literature

RECALL

1. What does Tung Kuo's brotherhood teach?
2. Why, according to the apricot tree and the cow, do the owners turn their backs on them?
3. After Tung Kuo tells the old man his side of the story, what story does the wolf tell?
4. What does Tung Kuo finally do to the wolf?

INTERPRET

5. A **stereotype** is a general statement about a group of people in which the individual differences are overlooked. Lord Chao stereotypes Tung Kuo when he says, "I know your kind. All melting heart and wet cheeks." What type of person does Lord Chao think Tung Kuo is? Why?
6. When Tung Kuo says the wolf is thankless, the cow replies, "What right have you to demand his thanks?" How might the cow answer her own question? Why?
7. After the wolf says Tung Kuo planned his murder, the old man acts confused, even though he is wise. How might you explain this apparent contradiction?
8. At the close, Tung Kuo asks, "Were the years of teaching and learning to end in the thrust of a dagger . . . ?" What might Tung Kuo answer? Why?

EVALUATE AND CONNECT

9. How dedicated is Tung Kuo to his brotherhood? Give three examples to support your answer.
10. Tung Kuo says, "The old custom in the case of a dispute is to seek the wisdom of three elders." Do you agree with this method? Give two reasons.

LITERARY ELEMENTS

Rising Action

Every good plot contains **rising action,** the point at which the action gets complicated and characters come into conflict with each other. Rising action begins with the events that set up a **conflict,** or central problem. As the conflict unfolds, a sense of excitement builds about what will happen next. Rising action leads up to the **climax,** the turning point in the story when the conflict is usually resolved. Review the action in "Bagged Wolf" to find the rising action.

1. When does the rising action begin?
2. When does it end? How do you know?

● See **Literary Terms Handbook,** p. R8.

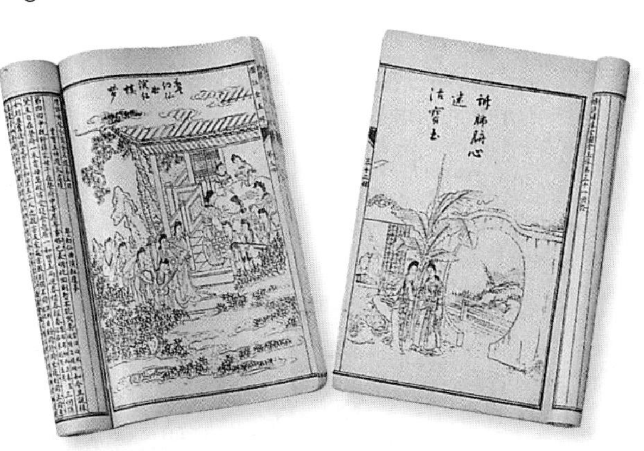

Literature and Writing

Writing About Literature

Symbolism What do you think the wolf symbolizes, or stands for? Intelligence? Weakness? Justice? Examine the wolf's characteristics. Look at what he says and how he treats people. What do other characters think of the wolf? Discuss these questions with a small group. Then, together, write a brief explanation of what the wolf symbolizes. Support your explanation with examples from the story.

Creative Writing

Scene from a Short Story Think about your response in the **Focus Activity** on page 268 and imagine that you are Tung Kuo. What will you do when the wolf informs you that you are about to become his dinner? Rewrite this scene from the story with yourself as the main character. Use dialogue, description, and action to increase reader interest. Read the scene to your classmates.

Extending Your Response

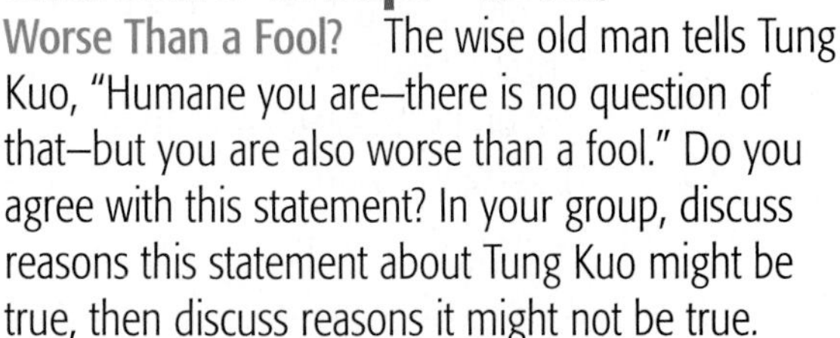

Literature Groups

Worse Than a Fool? The wise old man tells Tung Kuo, "Humane you are–there is no question of that–but you are also worse than a fool." Do you agree with this statement? In your group, discuss reasons this statement about Tung Kuo might be true, then discuss reasons it might not be true. Present your conclusions to the class.

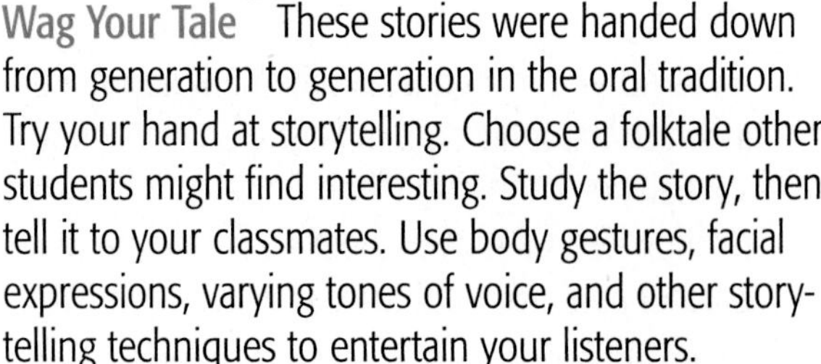

Performing

Wag Your Tale These stories were handed down from generation to generation in the oral tradition. Try your hand at storytelling. Choose a folktale other students might find interesting. Study the story, then tell it to your classmates. Use body gestures, facial expressions, varying tones of voice, and other storytelling techniques to entertain your listeners.

interNET CONNECTION

Investigate wolves throughout the world by keying the words *wolf* or *canid* into a search engine.

Interdisciplinary Activity

Life Science Is the wolf in this Chinese folktale true to life? Prepare a brief report on wolves and their behavior toward humans. Focus on one or two questions like these: Do wolves travel alone? Do they attack humans? Do people hunt wolves? Do wolves ever act sly or play tricks on people?

Save your work for your portfolio.

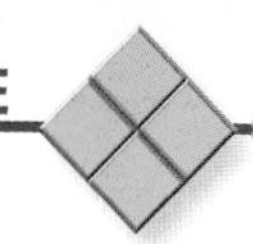

Skill Minilessons

GRAMMAR AND LANGUAGE • PUNCTUATING COMPOUND SENTENCES

An **independent clause** has a subject and predicate and can stand alone as a complete sentence. A **compound sentence** contains two or more independent clauses. The clauses usually are joined with a **coordinating conjunction** (*and, but, for, or, nor, so,* and *yet*) and are punctuated with a comma just before the conjunction.

Lord Chao raised a fierce cry, and the whole party came thundering after him.

PRACTICE Rewrite each pair of independent clauses as a compound sentence, using a comma and the coordinating conjunction that makes sense.

1. His stomach fairly ached with longing. He advanced carefully.
2. Save me. I shall repay you in my heart as long as I live!
3. He tried and tried again. He couldn't get everything belonging to the wolf inside the bag.

● For more about punctuation, see **Language Handbook,** p. R38.

READING AND THINKING • SUMMARIZING

Summarizing is restating what you read in your own words. A summary is a brief description of the main ideas in a longer work. Summarizing can help you better understand and remember the information in a story.

PRACTICE Practice your skill at summarizing with "Bagged Wolf." In one or two paragraphs, summarize the plot of this story. Stick to the major events and use transition words such as *next* and *then* so your reader can follow your ideas easily.

● For more about summarizing, see **Reading Handbook,** p. R90.

VOCABULARY • LATIN ROOTS

Many Latin words form roots for English words. For example, *advocate* contains the root *voc.* It comes from the Latin word *vocare,* which means "to call." The Latin prefix *ad-* means "to or toward"; therefore, an *advocate* is someone who is "called to" another person to help his or her cause. Your *advocate* in court is your lawyer. A *consumer advocate* is someone who stands up for consumers and cares about the safety and quality of products.

PRACTICE Use what you know about the root *voc* to answer the questions. (Note: *voc* is sometimes spelled *vok.*)

1. If you *provoke* laughter in someone, do you make the person start laughing or stop laughing? (Clue: *pro-* means "forth.")
2. If something *evokes* a memory, does it make you remember or make you forget? (Clue: *e-* means "out.")
3. If you *invoke* a law, do you break it, make it, or make use of it? (Clue: *in-* means "on.")

Reading and Thinking Skills

Monitoring Comprehension

Reading is a discussion between you and the writer. To get the most from your reading, you'll need to monitor your comprehension, or check your understanding of the information. Try these strategies as you read:

- Ask questions about things you don't understand. You may find the answers in the next paragraph or two.
- Jot down notes about what you *do* know. It may help you fill in gaps in your understanding.
- Read ahead to look for a main idea or to get an overview of a selection.
- Reread the passage or selection.

● For more about monitoring comprehension, see **Reading Handbook,** pp. R84–R96.

ACTIVITY

Read the following passage from "Bagged Wolf," and use one or more of the strategies above to monitor your comprehension. Then answer the questions.

At this very time there was on the mountain path a certain Tung Kuo on his way to the capital. With his book bag, which was his sole belonging, he rode on a tired skinny donkey, and love was in his mind—love for every human being under the sun. He belonged to a brotherhood that believed peace and happiness would come to the world if everyone would practice self-denial for the good of his fellow men. Tung Kuo, being a devoted disciple in this belief, positively ached to practice benevolence. When he saw clouds of dust rising from the ground far away, and heard noises like roaring drums, his first thought was that he might even now be put to the test of loving-kindness.

1. What do you learn about Tung Kuo from this passage?
2. What does the last sentence suggest about what may happen next?

Before You Read

The Moustache

MEET
ROBERT CORMIER

"I've aimed for the intelligent reader and have often found that that reader is fourteen years old," said Robert Cormier. He didn't write to make people feel good. He'd rather have readers say of his work, "I don't *like* what happened, but that's the way it *could* happen." Cormier was well known for writing about themes that often appeal to young adults. Some of Cormier's stories focus on ways people respond to abuses of power by institutions.

Robert Cormier was born in 1925 and died in 2000. "The Moustache" was published in 1980 in a collection of short stories called Eight Plus One.

FOCUS ACTIVITY

Why do you visit, phone, or write to grandparents or other older relatives? Have you visited relatives who live in a nursing home?

Discuss

Ask a partner to define "old." Discuss whether all older people have similar characteristics. Then share your observations with a larger group.

Setting a Purpose

Read to find out about a secret that a grandmother has kept to herself for many years.

BACKGROUND

The Time and Place This story takes place in a modern-day nursing home.

Did You Know? Nursing homes are not homes for old people. They are housing for people of any age who require nursing care on a regular or temporary basis.

VOCABULARY PREVIEW

chronic (kron′ ik) *adj.* lasting a long time or returning repeatedly; p. 284

complex (kom′ pleks) *n.* an exaggerated concern or fear; an overwhelming idea or feeling; p. 284

craggy (krag′ ē) *adj.* rugged, uneven, and worn; p. 285

lapse (laps) *v.* to slip, drift, or fall (into); p. 286

lucid (lo͞o′ sid) *adj.* mentally alert; clear-headed; p. 286

conspiratorial (kən spir′ ə tôr′ ē əl) *adj.* joining or acting together, especially to carry out some secret or evil deed or for a hidden or illegal purpose; p. 287

regally (rē′ gəl lē) *adv.* in a grand, dignified manner, as if done by a king or queen; royally; p. 287

pretense (prē′ tens) *n.* a false show or appearance, especially for the purpose of deceiving; falseness; p. 289

serene (sə rēn′) *adj.* calm; peaceful; undisturbed; p. 290

HAIR DRESSING
Professional
REGULAR FORMULA
for the hair
FOR REMOVING DANDRUFF SCALES
COOLING FOR HEAD AND FACE
ASSOCIATED BRANDS, Inc.

The Moustache

Robert Cormier

At the last minute Annie couldn't go. She was invaded by one of those twenty-four-hour flu bugs that sent her to bed with a fever, moaning about the fact that she'd also have to break her date with Handsome Harry Arnold that night. We call him Handsome Harry because he's actually handsome, but he's also a nice guy, cool, and he doesn't treat me like Annie's kid brother, which I am, but like a regular person. Anyway, I had to go to Lawnrest alone that afternoon. But first of all I had to stand inspection. My mother lined me up against the wall.

She stood there like a one-man firing squad, which is kind of funny because she's not like a man at all, she's very feminine, and we have this great relationship—I mean, I feel as if she really likes me. I realize that sounds strange, but I know guys whose mothers love them and cook special stuff for them and worry about them and all but there's something missing in their relationship.

Anyway. She frowned and started the routine.

"That hair," she said. Then admitted: "Well, at least you combed it."

I sighed. I have discovered that it's better to sigh than argue.

"And that moustache." She shook her head. "I still say a seventeen-year-old has no business wearing a moustache."

"It's an experiment," I said. "I just wanted to see if I could grow one." To tell the truth, I had proved my point about being able to grow a decent moustache, but I also had learned to like it.

"It's costing you money, Mike," she said.

"I know, I know."

The money was a reference to the movies. The Downtown Cinema has a special Friday night offer—half-price admission for high school couples, seventeen or younger. But the woman in the box office took one look at my moustache and charged me full price. Even when I showed her my driver's license. She charged full admission for Cindy's ticket, too, which left me practically broke and unable to take Cindy out for a hamburger with the crowd afterward. That didn't help matters, because Cindy has been getting impatient recently about things like the fact that I don't own my own car and have to concentrate on my studies if I want to win that college scholarship,[1] for instance. Cindy wasn't exactly crazy about the moustache, either.

Now it was my mother's turn to sigh.

"Look," I said, to cheer her up. "I'm thinking about shaving it off." Even though I wasn't. Another discovery: You can build a way of life on postponement.

1. A *scholarship* is money given to help a student continue his or her education. Scholarships are generally awarded for excellent work in high school and may also be based on financial need.

The Moustache

"Your grandmother probably won't even recognize you," she said. And I saw the shadow fall across her face.

Let me tell you what the visit to Lawnrest was all about. My grandmother is seventy-three years old. She is a resident—which is supposed to be a better word than *patient*—at the Lawnrest Nursing Home. She used to make the greatest turkey dressing in the world and was a nut about baseball and could even quote batting averages, for crying out loud. She always rooted for the losers. She was in love with the Mets until they started to win. Now she has arteriosclerosis, which the dictionary says is "a chronic disease characterized by abnormal thickening and hardening of the arterial walls." Which really means that she can't live at home anymore or even with us, and her memory has betrayed her as well as her body. She used to wander off and sometimes didn't recognize people. My mother visits her all the time, driving the thirty miles to Lawnrest almost every day. Because Annie was home for a semester break from college, we had decided to make a special Saturday visit. Now Annie was in bed, groaning theatrically[2]—she's a drama major—but I told my mother I'd go, anyway. I hadn't seen my grandmother since she'd been admitted to Lawnrest. Besides, the place is located on the Southwest Turnpike, which meant I could barrel along in my father's new Le Mans. My ambition was to see the speedometer hit seventy-five. Ordinarily, I used the old station wagon, which can barely stagger up to fifty.

Frankly, I wasn't too crazy about visiting a nursing home. They reminded me of hospitals and hospitals turn me off. I mean, the smell of ether makes me nauseous, and I feel faint at the sight of blood. And as I approached Lawnrest—which is a terrible cemetery kind of name, to begin with—I was sorry I hadn't avoided the trip. Then I felt guilty about it. I'm loaded with guilt complexes. Like driving like a madman after promising my father to be careful. Like sitting in the parking lot, looking at the nursing home with dread and thinking how I'd rather be with Cindy. Then I thought of all the Christmas and birthday gifts my grandmother had given me and I got out of the car, guilty, as usual.

Inside, I was surprised by the lack of hospital smell, although there was another odor or maybe the absence of an odor. The air was antiseptic, sterile. As if there was no atmosphere at all or I'd caught a cold suddenly and couldn't taste or smell.

A nurse at the reception desk gave me directions—my grandmother was in East Three. I made my way down the tiled corridor and was glad to see that the walls were painted with cheerful colors like yellow and pink. A wheelchair suddenly shot around a corner, self-propelled by an old man, white-haired and toothless, who cackled merrily as he barely missed me. I jumped aside—here I was, almost getting wiped out by a two-mile-an-hour wheelchair after doing seventy-five on the pike. As I walked through the corridor seeking East Three, I couldn't help glancing into the rooms, and it was like some kind of wax museum—all these figures in various

2. When Annie groans *theatrically,* she overdoes her groaning so that it suggests a performance by an actor.

Vocabulary

chronic (kron′ ik) *adj.* lasting a long time or returning repeatedly

complex (kom′ pleks) *n.* an exaggerated concern or fear; an overwhelming idea or feeling

Aunt Fanny (Old Lady in Black), 1920. George Wesley Bellows. Oil on canvas, 44¼ x 34¼ in. Purchased with funds from the Edmundson Art Foundation, Inc. Des Moines Art Center. 1942.1.

Viewing the painting: Mike admires certain features of his grandmother. What features are emphasized in this painting, and what do they suggest about the subject?

stances and attitudes, sitting in beds or chairs, standing at windows, as if they were frozen forever in these postures. To tell the truth, I began to hurry because I was getting depressed. Finally, I saw a beautiful girl approaching, dressed in white, a nurse or an attendant, and I was so happy to see someone young, someone walking and acting normally, that I gave her a wide smile and a big hello and I must have looked like a kind of nut. Anyway, she looked right through me as if I were a window, which is about par for the course[3] whenever I meet beautiful girls.

I finally found the room and saw my grandmother in bed. My grandmother looks like Ethel Barrymore. I never knew who Ethel Barrymore was until I saw a terrific movie, *None But the Lonely Heart,* on TV, starring Ethel Barrymore and Cary Grant.[4] Both my grandmother and Ethel Barrymore have these great craggy faces like the side of a mountain and wonderful voices like syrup being poured. Slowly. She was propped up in bed, pillows puffed behind her. Her hair had been combed out and fell upon her shoulders. For some reason, this flowing hair gave her an almost girlish appearance, despite its whiteness.

She saw me and smiled. Her eyes lit up and her eyebrows arched and she reached out her hands to me in greeting. "Mike, Mike," she said. And I breathed a sigh of relief. This was one of her good days. My

3. This expression means "average; normal." In golf, *par* is the number of strokes set as the standard for skillful play on one hole or all the holes of the course.
4. In this 1944 drama, *Barrymore* played the dying mother of *Grant's* character.

Vocabulary
craggy (krag′ ē) *adj.* rugged, uneven, and worn

mother had warned me that she might not know who I was at first.

I took her hands in mine. They were fragile. I could actually feel her bones, and it seemed as if they would break if I pressed too hard. Her skin was smooth, almost slippery, as if the years had worn away all the roughness the way the wind wears away the surfaces of stones.

"Mike, Mike, I didn't think you'd come," she said, so happy, and she was still Ethel Barrymore, that voice like a caress. "I've been waiting all this time." Before I could reply, she looked away, out the window. "See the birds? I've been watching them at the feeder. I love to see them come. Even the blue jays. The blue jays are like hawks—they take the food that the small birds should have. But the small birds, the chickadees, watch the blue jays and at least learn where the feeder is."

She lapsed into silence, and I looked out the window. There was no feeder. No birds. There was only the parking lot and the sun glinting on car windshields.

She turned to me again, eyes bright. Radiant, really. Or was it a medicine brightness? "Ah, Mike. You look so grand, so grand. Is that a new coat?"

"Not really," I said. I'd been wearing my Uncle Jerry's old army-fatigue jacket for months, practically living in it, my mother said. But she insisted that I wear my raincoat for the visit. It was about a year old but looked new because I didn't wear it much. Nobody was wearing raincoats lately.

"You always loved clothes, didn't you, Mike?" she said.

I was beginning to feel uneasy because she regarded me with such intensity. Those bright eyes. I wondered—are old people in places like this so lonesome, so abandoned that they go wild when someone visits? Or was she so happy because she was suddenly lucid and everything was sharp and clear? My mother had described those moments when my grandmother suddenly emerged from the fog that so often obscured her mind. I didn't know the answers, but it felt kind of spooky, getting such an emotional welcome from her.

"I remember the time you bought the new coat—the Chesterfield," she said, looking away again, as if watching the birds that weren't there. "That lovely coat with the velvet collar. Black, it was. Stylish. Remember that, Mike? It was hard times, but you could never resist the glitter."

Did You Know?
Named for a British earl, the *Chesterfield* is a type of overcoat with a velvet collar.

I was about to protest—I had never heard of a Chesterfield, for crying out loud. But I stopped. Be patient with her, my mother had said. Humor her. Be gentle.

We were interrupted by an attendant who pushed a wheeled cart into the room. "Time for juices, dear," the woman said.

Vocabulary
lapse (laps) *v.* to slip, drift, or fall (into)
lucid (lo͞o′ sid) *adj.* mentally alert; clear-headed

She was the standard forty- or fifty-year-old woman: glasses, nothing hair, plump cheeks. Her manner was cheerful but a businesslike kind of cheerfulness. I'd hate to be called "dear" by someone getting paid to do it. "Orange or grape or cranberry, dear? Cranberry is good for the bones, you know."

My grandmother ignored the interruption. She didn't even bother to answer, having turned away at the woman's arrival, as if angry about her appearance.

The woman looked at me and winked. A conspiratorial kind of wink. It was kind of horrible. I didn't think people winked like that anymore. In fact, I hadn't seen a wink in years.

"She doesn't care much for juices," the woman said, talking to me as if my grandmother weren't even there. "But she loves her coffee. With lots of cream and two lumps of sugar. But this is juice time, not coffee time." Addressing my grandmother again, she said, "Orange or grape or cranberry, dear?"

"Tell her I want no juices, Mike," my grandmother commanded regally, her eyes still watching invisible birds.

The woman smiled, patience like a label on her face. "That's all right, dear. I'll just leave some cranberry for you. Drink it at your leisure. It's good for the bones."

She wheeled herself out of the room. My grandmother was still absorbed in the view. Somewhere a toilet flushed. A wheelchair passed the doorway—probably that same old driver fleeing a hit-run accident. A television set exploded with sound somewhere, soap-opera voices filling the air. You can always tell soap-opera voices.

I turned back to find my grandmother staring at me. Her hands cupped her face, her index fingers curled around her cheeks like parenthesis marks.

"But you know, Mike, looking back, I think you were right," she said, continuing our conversation as if there had been no interruption. "You always said, 'It's the things of the spirit that count, Meg.' The spirit! And so you bought the baby-grand piano—a baby grand in the middle of the Depression.[5] A knock came on the door and it was the deliveryman. It took five of them to get it into the house." She leaned back, closing her eyes. "How I loved that piano, Mike. I was never that fine a player, but you loved to sit there in the parlor, on Sunday evenings, Ellie on your lap, listening to me play and sing." She hummed a bit, a fragment of melody I didn't recognize. Then she drifted into silence. Maybe she'd fallen asleep. My mother's name is Ellen, but everyone always calls her Ellie. "Take my hand, Mike," my grandmother said suddenly. Then I remembered—my grandfather's name was Michael. I had been named for him.

"Ah, Mike," she said, pressing my hands with all her feeble strength. "I thought I'd lost you forever. And here you are, back with me again. . . ."

5. Here, *Depression* refers to the period from 1929 to 1939, when the economy was extremely bad and many Americans lived in poverty or suffered severe hardships.

Vocabulary

conspiratorial (kən spir′ ə tôr′ ē əl) *adj.* joining or acting together, especially to carry out some secret or evil deed or for a hidden or illegal purpose

regally (rē′ gəl lē) *adv.* in a grand, dignified manner, as if done by a king or queen; royally

Open Window, 1993. Linda Fennimore. Colored pencil, 13¼ x 13¼ in. Artist's collection.

Viewing the art: How might this window and the view outside reflect the grandmother's state of mind?

Her expression scared me. I don't mean scared as if I were in danger but scared because of what could happen to her when she realized the mistake she had made. My mother always said I favored her side of the family. Thinking back to the pictures in the old family albums, I recalled my grandfather as tall and thin. Like me. But the resemblance ended there. He was thirty-five when he died, almost forty years ago. And he wore a moustache. I brought my hand to my face. I also wore a moustache now, of course.

"I sit here these days, Mike," she said, her voice a lullaby, her hand still holding mine, "and I drift and dream. The days are fuzzy sometimes, merging together. Sometimes it's like I'm not here at all but somewhere else altogether. And I always think of you. Those years we had. Not enough years, Mike, not enough. . . ."

Her voice was so sad, so mournful that I made sounds of sympathy, not words exactly but kind of soothings that mothers murmur to their children when they awaken from bad dreams.

"And I think of that terrible night, Mike, that terrible night. Have you ever really forgiven me for that night?"

"Listen . . ." I began. I wanted to say: "Nana, this is Mike your grandson, not Mike your husband."

"Sh . . . sh . . ." she whispered, placing a finger as long and cold as a candle against my lips. "Don't say anything. I've waited so long for this moment. To be here. With you. I wondered what I would say if suddenly you walked in that door like other people have done. I've thought and thought about it. And I finally made up my mind—I'd ask you to forgive me. I was too proud to ask before." Her fingers tried to mask her face. "But I'm not proud anymore, Mike." That great voice quivered and then grew strong again. "I hate you to see me this way—you always said I was beautiful. I didn't believe it. The Charity Ball when we led the grand march and you said I was the most beautiful girl there . . ."

"Nana," I said. I couldn't keep up the pretense any longer, adding one more burden to my load of guilt, leading her on this way, playing a pathetic game of make-believe with an old woman clinging to memories. She didn't seem to hear me.

"But that other night, Mike. The terrible one. The terrible accusations I made. Even Ellie woke up and began to cry. I went to her and rocked her in my arms and you came into the room and said I was wrong. You were whispering, an awful whisper, not wanting to upset little Ellie but wanting to make me see the truth. And I didn't answer you, Mike. I was too proud. I've even forgotten the name of the girl. I sit here, wondering now—was it Laura or Evelyn? I can't remember. Later, I learned that you were telling the truth all the time, Mike. That I'd been wrong . . ." Her eyes were brighter than ever as she looked at me now, but tear-bright, the tears gathering. "It was never the same after that night, was it, Mike? The glitter was gone. From you. From us. And then the accident . . . and I never had the chance to ask you to forgive me . . ."

My grandmother. My poor, poor grandmother. Old people aren't supposed to have those kinds of memories. You see their pictures in the family albums and that's what they are: pictures. They're not supposed to come to life. You drive out in your father's Le Mans doing seventy-five on the pike and all you're doing is visiting an old lady in a nursing home. A duty call. And then you find out that she's a person. She's *somebody*. She's my grandmother, all right, but she's also herself. Like my own mother and father. They exist outside of their relationship to me. I was scared again. I wanted to get out of there.

"Mike, Mike," my grandmother said. "Say it, Mike."

I felt as if my cheeks would crack if I uttered a word.

"Say you forgive me, Mike. I've waited all these years . . ."

I was surprised at how strong her fingers were.

"Say, '*I forgive you, Meg.*'"

I said it. My voice sounded funny, as if I were talking in a huge tunnel. "I forgive you, Meg."

Her eyes studied me. Her hands pressed mine. For the first time in my life, I saw love at work. Not movie love. Not Cindy's sparkling eyes when I tell her that we're going to the beach on a Sunday afternoon. But love like something alive and tender,

Vocabulary

pretense (prē′ tens) *n.* a false show or appearance, especially for the purpose of deceiving; falseness asking nothing in return. She raised her face, and I knew what she wanted me to do. I bent and brushed my lips against her cheek. Her flesh was like a leaf in autumn, crisp and dry.

She closed her eyes and I stood up. The sun wasn't glinting on the cars any longer. Somebody had turned on another television set, and the voices were the show-off voices of the panel shows. At the same time you could still hear the soap-opera dialogue on the other television set.

I waited awhile. She seemed to be sleeping, her breathing serene and regular. I buttoned my raincoat. Suddenly she opened her eyes again and looked at me. Her eyes were still bright, but they merely stared at me. Without recognition or curiosity. Empty eyes. I smiled at her, but she didn't smile back. She made a kind of moaning sound and turned away on the bed, pulling the blankets around her.

I counted to twenty-five and then to fifty and did it all over again. I cleared my throat and coughed tentatively. She didn't move; she didn't respond. I wanted to say, "Nana, it's me." But I didn't. I thought of saying, "Meg, it's me." But I couldn't.

Finally I left. Just like that. I didn't say goodbye or anything. I stalked through the corridors, looking neither to the right nor the left, not caring whether that wild old man with the wheelchair ran me down or not.

On the Southwest Turnpike I did seventy-five—no, eighty—most of the way. I turned the radio up as loud as it could go. Rock music—anything to fill the air. When I got home, my mother was vacuuming the living room rug. She shut off the cleaner, and the silence was deafening. "Well, how was your grandmother?" she asked.

I told her she was fine. I told her a lot of things. How great Nana looked and how she seemed happy and had called me Mike. I wanted to ask her—hey, Mom, you and Dad really love each other, don't you? I mean—there's nothing to forgive between you, is there? But I didn't.

Instead I went upstairs and took out the electric razor Annie had given me for Christmas and shaved off my moustache.

Vocabulary
serene (sə rēn′) *adj.* calm; peaceful; undisturbed

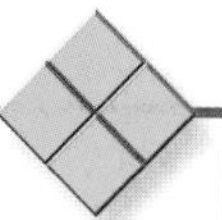

Responding to Literature

PERSONAL RESPONSE

- What was your reaction to the end of the story?
- What thoughts did you have about any elderly people you know while reading this short story?

Analyzing Literature

RECALL

1. Describe the medical condition of Mike's grandmother.
2. When talking to Mike, what does his grandmother reveal about her marriage?
3. What does Mike do when he realizes that his grandmother thinks he is someone else?
4. What does Mike do when he gets home?

INTERPRET

5. Why does the grandmother mistake Mike for his grandfather?
6. What does Mike mean when he says, "Old people aren't supposed to have those kinds of memories"?
7. After Mike kisses his grandmother's cheek, he sees "love at work." What does he mean? What has he learned from his grandmother?
8. Why doesn't Mike tell his mother everything that happened with his grandmother? Why does he shave off his moustache?

EVALUATE AND CONNECT

9. Theme Connection Mike makes decisions throughout this story. Do you agree with his decision not to tell his grandmother who he really is? Why does he make this choice?
10. Why is Mike's moustache so important to this story that the author uses it as the title?

LITERARY ELEMENTS

Characterization

Characterization is the way an author reveals information about characters through action, dialogue, and description. Robert Cormier does this by carefully choosing what Mike and his grandmother do, say, and think. Readers learn about the characters' appearance as well as their personalities.

1. Describe what you know about Mike's thoughts.
2. What conclusions can you draw about Mike's feelings? Cite the clues you found in the text.
3. Find dialogue that reveals the personality of Mike's grandmother.

- See **Literary Terms Handbook,** p. R2.

Literature and Writing

Writing About Literature

Comparison "The Moustache" is a story about relationships: Mike's relationship with his grandmother, with Cindy, and with his mother; and the relationship between Mike's grandparents. Choose one of these relationships. Explain the kinds of love each person shows and tell what the relationship reveals about the characters involved.

Personal Writing

Taking on a Role Look back at the observations about visiting a nursing home that you made in the **Focus Activity** on page 281. Now, imagine that you are eighty-five years old and living in a nursing home. Write a dialogue between yourself and your grandchild as you explain what life was like when you were a teenager.

Extending Your Response

Literature Groups

Reality Checks With your group, discuss books and stories you have read, television shows you have viewed, or movies you enjoyed in which several generations were portrayed. Discuss the various ways teens are shown in these media. Evaluate the ways adults, especially older adults, are depicted. Do these media portray all age groups with accuracy and sensitivity? Share your conclusions with other groups.

Learning for Life

At any age, exercise and diet are important means to maintaining health. Use books, Internet sites, and interviews with health professionals to investigate some of the ways teens, adults, and elderly adults can maintain good health.

Performing

On the Road! Student groups often entertain the residents of nursing homes and people who cannot leave their homes. Think of a poem, a story, or a song that others might enjoy. Prepare an act to perform at a hospital, a center for younger children, or a retirement home.

Reading Further

For other novels about teens and their elders, try:
Tunes for Bears to Dance To by Robert Cormier
Plain City by Virginia Hamilton

Save your work for your portfolio.

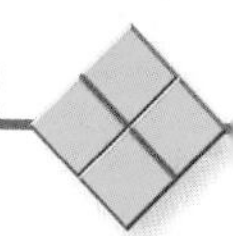

Skill Minilessons

GRAMMAR AND LANGUAGE • ADVERB PHRASES

An **adverb phrase** is a prepositional phrase that describes, or modifies, a verb, an adjective, or another adverb. Like an adverb, an adverb phrase tells *where, when, how, why,* or *to what extent* an action occurs.

Describes a verb	She reached out her hands to me **in greeting.** (this adverb phrase tells *how*)
Describes an adjective	I was surprised **by the lack of hospital smell.** (tells *why*)
Describes an adverb	She looked older **than I remembered.** (tells *to what extent*)

PRACTICE Write each adverb phrase below. Name the word each phrase modifies.

1. Robert Cormier's works can be found in libraries and bookstores.
2. Cormier says that his four children are proud of his success as a writer.
3. Cormier is pleased by the interest teenagers have in his writing.

- For more about adverb phrases, see **Language Handbook,** p. R31.

READING AND THINKING • CLARIFYING

Clarifying is stopping to make sure you understand what you've read. Good readers clarify information as they read along. They stop occasionally to review events and descriptions, ask themselves questions, and look for answers to their earlier questions.

PRACTICE Look back at "The Moustache" and find at least three points in the story when you had to clarify what was happening or being described.

- For more about clarifying, see **Reading Handbook,** pp. R80–R81.

VOCABULARY • GREEK ROOTS

English has developed by borrowing **roots,** or basic word parts, from other languages. The same root may appear in many different English words. For example, *chronos* is a Greek word that means "time." In English, *chron* is a root from which several words are made that have something to do with time. *Chronic* means "constant, lasting a long time," or "returning repeatedly." So, a *chronic* problem keeps occurring; a *chronic* liar lies frequently.

PRACTICE Complete each item below.

1. Write three months of the year in *chronological* order.
2. What do people do when they *synchronize* their watches? (Hint: *syn-* means "together.")
3. Which course usually has a textbook that is a *chronicle*–math, grammar, or history?
4. Which mistake in a carelessly made movie is an *anachronism?*
   a. A brontosaurus eats an animal.
   b. A brown dog runs after a ball, but a black dog brings it back.
   c. A motorboat passes by the Pilgrims landing at Plymouth Rock.

POETRY

A poem can have a dozen words or several thousand lines. It can leave you laughing or crying. It can rhyme or not. It can be hundreds of years old or a current rap. So how can you tell when a piece of writing is a poem? There are no firm rules, but most poems share two major characteristics: sound and language.

SOUND The sound of the words contributes to the overall effect of a poem. Poetry uses many techniques to create different sounds.

1. **Rhythm** Much like the beat of a song, the **rhythm** of a poem is a sound pattern. This pattern is often created by stressed and unstressed syllables in words. A stressed syllable is a word part that carries emphasis when it is read aloud; an unstressed syllable is read more softly. (Stressed syllables are marked with ´; unstressed syllables are marked with ˘.) Notice the different rhythms in the two lines below.

   bóuncĭng úp ănd dówn

   fár, fár frŏm thĕ sún's strŏng gláre

2. **Meter** The rhythm of stressed and unstressed syllables that is repeated throughout a poem is called **meter.** The poem by Emily Dickinson on this page, for example, uses **iambic meter**—almost every unstressed syllable is followed by a stressed one.

3. **Alliteration** The repetition of a sound at the beginning of words is called **alliteration,** as is heard in the rhyme "Peter Piper picked a peck of pickled peppers," and in "wantoned with" in line 4 of Emily Dickinson's poem.

4. **Rhyme** Repetition of ending sounds of words is **rhyme.** An example is "shone" and "Bone" (lines 2 and 4). Poems may use rhyming words within a single line of poetry or at the ends of different lines. Many poems use patterns of rhyme.

MODEL

Shĕ déalt hĕr préttў wórds lĭke
  Bládes—
Hŏw glíttĕrĭng thĕy shóne—
Ănd évĕry Óne ŭnbáred ă Nérve
Ŏr wántŏned wĭth ă Bóne—

—Emily Dickinson

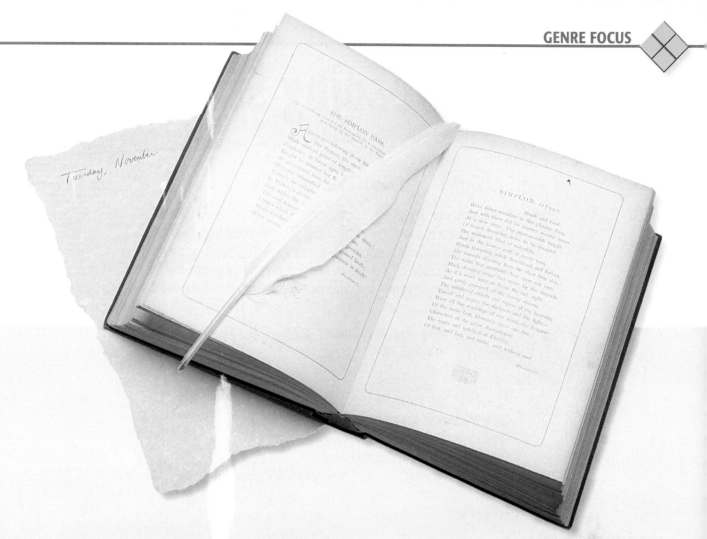

LANGUAGE Many poems have **imagery,** words that appeal to the five senses: touch, taste, smell, sight, and hearing. Poems also use **figures of speech,** language that describes ordinary things in new ways.

1. **Simile or Metaphor** A **simile** is a comparison of two different things using the word *like* or *as.* A simile points out a similarity between the two things. For example, the Dickinson poem uses the simile "words like Blades" to point out that both items can cut.

   A **metaphor** is a comparison of two unlike things without such clue words as *like* or *as.* For example, "words like Blades" is a simile; "words are blades" is a metaphor.

2. **Personification** In **personification,** a writer talks about an object or living thing as if it were a human. The wind, for example, might be described as a person banging on a window.

ACTIVE READING MODEL

Active Reading Strategies

Active Reading Strategies for Poetry

To get the most out of a poem, readers must put a good deal of themselves into it. Poets choose words not just for their meanings, but also for their sounds, the feelings they call up, the pictures they paint, and even, sometimes, how they look on a page. To really understand a poem, like the one below, you must use your mind, your ears, your eyes—or your mind's eye, and your emotions.

- For more about these and other reading strategies, see **Reading Handbook,** pp. R84–R96.

She dealt her pretty words like Blades—
How glittering they shone—
And every One unbared a Nerve
Or wantoned with a Bone—

—*Emily Dickinson*

QUESTION

If a word has more than one meaning, ask yourself which meaning the poet has in mind. If the poet uses a word in an unusual way, think about possible reasons for that usage. What is the poet getting at?

Say to Yourself . . .

- How can words be like blades? Blades cut. What can words cut? How?
- *Wanton* means "careless." Why is it used as a verb? What does the poet want me to understand about the character in the poem?

LISTEN

Read poems aloud, if possible, or say the words to yourself. Listen for words that call attention to themselves or to particular ideas.

Say to Yourself . . .

- The word *glittering* stands out to me. It's odd to think of words glittering. Why did the poet use this word?

VISUALIZE

Try to imagine the person or thing or scene described in the words. Build on any details the poet provides.

Say to Yourself . . .

- The word *blades* makes me think of sharp knives. It also makes me think of razor blades. Either way, a cruel scene comes to mind!

RESPOND

As you read a poem, or immediately afterward, take a moment to answer questions like these: How does the poem make you feel? What message, if any, did you get from the poem? Do you want to share the poem with friends?

Say to Yourself . . .

- The person described in this poem seems frightening. The poem describes a hateful person.

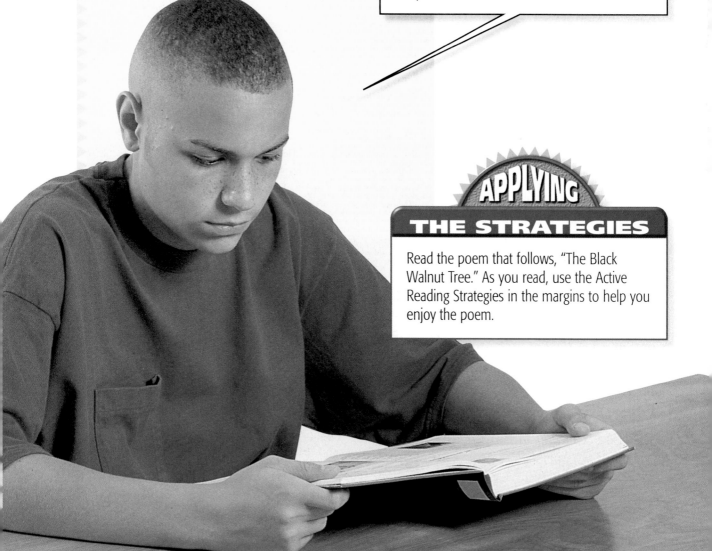

APPLYING THE STRATEGIES

Read the poem that follows, "The Black Walnut Tree." As you read, use the Active Reading Strategies in the margins to help you enjoy the poem.

ACTIVE READING MODEL

Before You Read

The Black Walnut Tree

MEET MARY OLIVER

Even the tables of contents in Mary Oliver's books reveal her love of the natural world. Oliver writes about everything from fish and wild geese to herons, rabbits, and moths. Her poems explore the light and dark sides of nature. Mary Oliver has lived a life away from cities: in Ohio, where she was raised, in Provincetown, Massachusetts, and in rural Virginia. She has received many awards for her poetry, including the Pulitzer Prize in 1984.

Mary Oliver was born in 1935. This poem was first published in 1979.

FOCUS ACTIVITY

Picture a beautiful or interesting scene or object that has impressed you. What shape, color, size, or other quality captured your attention?

FreeWrite

Jot down descriptive details or ideas that come to mind when you think of that object. How does it connect with your life?

Setting a Purpose

As you read, think about why a river, a tree, or a garden may be of special importance.

BACKGROUND

Mary Oliver carries on the American tradition of writing about our connections with nature that Henry David Thoreau started more than 100 years ago. A native of Concord, Massachusetts, Thoreau is the author of *Walden,* a description of his life near the pond during one span of seasons in the mid-1800s. New England poet Robert Frost continued in this tradition, describing the beauties and mysteries he experienced on his farm during the early 1900s.

The Great Heron, published in *The Birds of North America,* 1827–1838. John James Audubon. Aquatint plate, 973 x 635 mm.

The Black Walnut Tree

Mary Oliver

My mother and I debate:
we could sell
the black walnut tree
to the lumberman,
and pay off the mortgage.
Likely some storm anyway
will churn down its dark boughs,
smashing the house. We talk
slowly, two women trying
in a difficult time to be wise.
Roots in the cellar drains,
I say, and she replies
that the leaves are getting heavier
every year, and the fruit
harder to gather away.
But something brighter than money
moves in our blood—an edge
sharp and quick as a trowel
that wants us to dig and sow.
So we talk, but we don't do
anything. That night I dream
of my fathers out of Bohemia
filling the blue fields
of fresh and generous Ohio
with leaves and vines and orchards.
What my mother and I both know
is that we'd crawl with shame
in the emptiness we'd made
in our own and our fathers' backyard.
So the black walnut tree
swings through another year
of sun and leaping winds,
of leaves and bounding fruit,
and, month after month, the whip-
crack of the mortgage.

ACTIVE READING MODEL

QUESTION

What issue is being debated? What are the two choices the characters face?

QUESTION

What is this thing that is brighter than money?

PREDICT

Will they have the tree cut down?

LISTEN

What is usually meant by the crack of a whip? Why is it a good metaphor for the mortgage?

ACTIVE READING MODEL

Responding to Literature

PERSONAL RESPONSE

What do you think about the decision that the mother and daughter make?

Active Reading Response

Which strategies described on pages 296 and 297 did you use as you read this poem? Explain how the strategies helped you get more out of the poem.

Analyzing Literature

RECALL

1. Why are the mother and daughter debating?
2. What reasons do they have to justify selling the black walnut tree?
3. Describe the narrator's dream.

INTERPRET

4. What is the **conflict** in "The Black Walnut Tree?" How is this conflict resolved?
5. Why do the mother and daughter seem to need to justify selling the tree?
6. Explain the connection between the daughter's dream and her debate with her mother.

EVALUATE AND CONNECT

7. In your opinion, is the opening line of the poem **ironic?** (See page R5.) Are the mother and daughter really having a debate? Explain.
8. What attitude toward nature does the poem reflect?
9. What do you learn about the relationship between the mother and daughter in this poem? In what way are they alike? Are they different in any way? Explain.
10. Do you think dreams can affect a person's decisions or actions? Explain.

LITERARY ELEMENTS

Symbol

A **symbol** is an object, person, place, or event that stands for something else. The debate between the mother and daughter in "The Black Walnut Tree," for example, might be seen as a symbol of the conflict between commercial development and the preservation of nature.

1. What other symbol of conflict do you find in the poem?
2. Which two images imply a type of cutting? How are these symbols different?

- See **Literary Terms Handbook,** p. R10.

Extending Your Response

Writing About Literature

Story Structure "The Black Walnut Tree" is a narrative poem; that is, it has the structure of a story. It has characters, setting, theme, and plot. Write a paragraph or two describing the story told in the poem.

Literature Groups

Exploring Personal Connections The narrator of the poem describes important connections she has with nature, family, past generations, and home. What are those connections? How are they related to and different from the connections in your life? Compare and contrast the narrator's ideas with the ideas and experiences of others in your discussion group.

Creative Writing

Nature Poem Reread your notes from the **Focus Activity** on page 298. Use the notes to help you write a short poem about your connection with nature.

Performing

Oral Reading Work with a partner to present an oral reading of "The Black Walnut Tree" or your own poem about nature. Divide the poem in some meaningful way, for example, by alternating stanzas or by reading some lines together to help show character development.

Reading Further

If the connection between people and places interests you, try these other books:

Lessons from the Wolverine by Barry Lopez

Walking Up a Rainbow by Theodore Taylor

Save your work for your portfolio.

Skill Minilesson

GRAMMAR AND LANGUAGE • CONCRETE AND ABSTRACT NOUNS

A **concrete noun** names a person, place, or real thing, such as *mother, Ohio,* or *fruit.* An **abstract noun** names an idea, feeling, or quality, such as *happiness, conservation,* or *goodness.* "The Black Walnut Tree" has many concrete nouns, but only a few abstract nouns.

- For more about nouns, see **Language Handbook,** p. R30.

PRACTICE Complete each item.

1. List five concrete nouns in the poem that identify an element of nature.
2. List four concrete nouns that identify people in this poem.
3. Find two abstract nouns that help readers recognize emotions important to the poem.

Before You Read

A Time to Talk, Fire and Ice, and *Dust of Snow*

MEET ROBERT FROST

Robert Frost is one of America's best-loved poets. He wrote simply and directly about nature, including human nature. Frost once explained, "You learn first to know what you see and to put fresh words to it." Frost's poetry about the things he loved won him four Pulitzer Prizes.

Frost was born in San Francisco in 1874, but spent most of his life in New England, where he died in 1963.

FOCUS ACTIVITY

Do you prefer to be alone occasionally, or would you generally rather be with friends?

QuickWrite

Make two quick lists. First, list how you protect your solitude; then list how you reach out to others who may want your company.

Setting a Purpose

Read to explore Robert Frost's thoughts about nature and friendship.

BACKGROUND

Over his fifty-year career, Frost wrote about daily events and the out-of-doors. Many of his poems contain simple language, yet touch on complex themes, such as conflicting forces in life and human nature.

Robert Frost standing in front of his hen house, circa 1938.

The Sweep, 1967. Andrew Wyeth. Tempera, 23¾ x 35 in. Flint Institute of Art, Flint, MI.

A Time to Talk

Robert Frost

When a friend calls to me from the road
And slows his horse to a meaning walk,°
I don't stand still and look around
On all the hills I haven't hoed,
And shout from where I am, What is it?
No, not as there is a time to talk.
I thrust my hoe in the mellow ground,
Blade-end up and five feet tall,
And plod:° I go up to the stone wall
For a friendly visit.

---

2 Here, the *meaning walk* is a "meaningful or purposeful pace," with the friend slowing down to show that he wishes to talk with the speaker of the poem.

9 To *plod* is to trudge or walk along slowly and heavily.

A New England Winter. George Henry Durrie (1820–1863). Oil on board, 7 ft ¾ in x 12 ft ⅜ in. Santa Barbara Museum of Art.

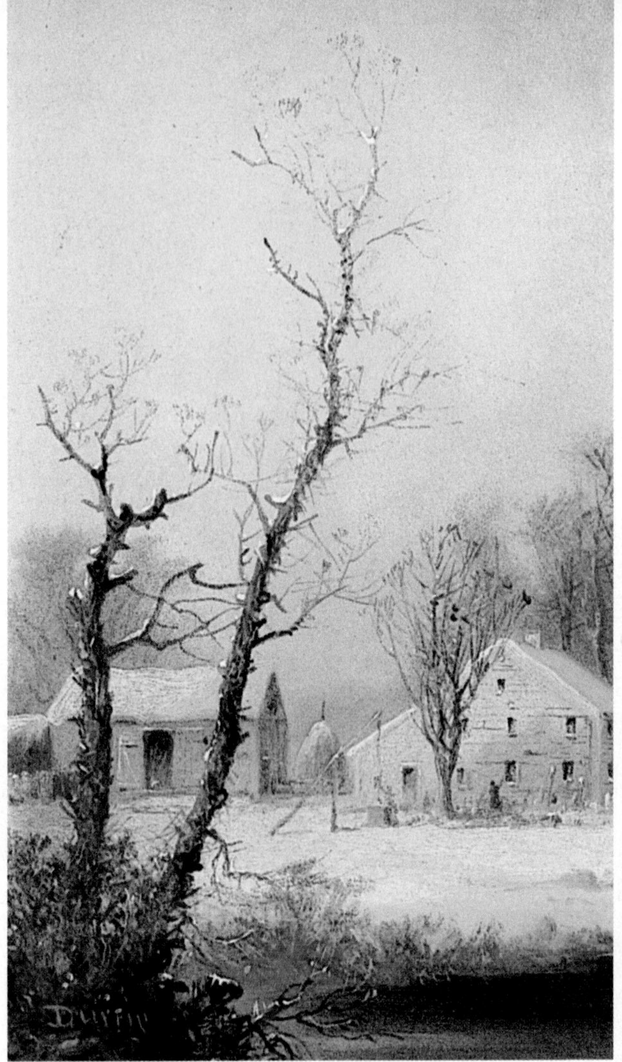

Fire and Ice

Robert Frost

Some say the world will end in fire,
Some say in ice.
From what I've tasted of desire
I hold with those who favor fire.
But if it had to perish twice,
I think I know enough of hate
To say that for destruction ice
Is also great
And would suffice.°

9 *Suffice* means "be enough."

Dust of Snow

Robert Frost

The way a crow
Shook down on me
The dust of snow
From a hemlock° tree

Has given my heart
A change of mood
And saved some part
Of a day I had rued.°

---

4 The *hemlock* is a kind of evergreen tree in the pine family.
8 To *rue* is to regret or be sorry for.

Responding to Literature

PERSONAL RESPONSE

Which of the poems impressed you most? Why?

Analyzing Literature

RECALL

1. What stands between the friend and the narrator in "A Time to Talk"?
2. Which poem focuses on the narrator's response to a single scene in nature?

INTERPRET

3. What does the stone wall in "A Time to Talk" suggest?
4. What causes the narrator's mood to change in "Dust of Snow"?

EVALUATE AND CONNECT

5. What message about modern life might Frost be expressing in "A Time to Talk"?
6. How do you respond to the narrator in "Fire and Ice"? Do you agree or disagree with him? Why?
7. Why do you think Frost selected ordinary scenes as he examined human behavior?
8. Which poem speaks to your experiences most directly? Why?
9. Theme Connection What types of choices does the narrator of each poem make? What values are reflected in the choices? How does each of the three poems relate to the theme "Which Way to Go"?
10. Frost once said he wrote poems that "begin in delight and end in wisdom." In your opinion, which of the poems follows this form?

LITERARY ELEMENTS

Lyric Poetry

Lyric poetry is poetry that expresses a mood, feeling, idea, or any other personal thought. Lyric poems do not tell stories, as narrative poems do. Originally, lyric poems were sung while accompanied by a lyre, a small stringed instrument. The word *lyric* means "with a lyre."

1. Explain how the narrator of each poem chooses between two moods or situations.
2. Briefly state the single thought the poet conveys in each of these poems.

- See **Literary Terms Handbook,** p. R5.

Extending Your Response

Writing About Literature

Poem to Poem Frost once wrote: "A poem is best read in the light of all the other poems ever written." List what you know about Frost's poetry that will help you read and understand other poems.

Creative Writing

Country Life Robert Frost spent several years as a farmer. Think about ways that working outdoors might have affected his poetry. Write a letter to a friend in which you use images from Frost's poems to convince the friend to give up city life and move to the country.

Interdisciplinary Activity

Art Robert Frost is known for writing directly and simply, using vivid imagery and symbolism. How could you illustrate one of his poems in a similar way? With a partner, create an artistic impression to illustrate one of the poems.

Literature Groups

Poetry Is Metaphor Robert Frost once said, "Education by poetry is education by metaphor." He defines metaphor as "saying one thing and meaning another." Each of the three poems is a metaphor about change and decisions about which way to go. Discuss the metaphor in each poem. What does each poem say, and what is the meaning behind each metaphor? What new ideas or meanings can you find in reading the poems? Discuss your answers with your group.

Reading Further

If you enjoyed Robert Frost's poems, try these other books by well-known poets:

Everywhere Faces Everywhere by James Berry
Classic Poems to Read Aloud edited by James Berry
Home on the Range: Cowboy Poetry by Paul B. Janeczko

Save your work for your portfolio.

Skill Minilesson

GRAMMAR AND LANGUAGE • ACTION VERBS

Words that express action and tell what a subject does are called **action verbs.** These verbs may describe physical actions, such as plowing, or mental actions, such as memorizing. Poets choose specific action verbs for the way they sound and for the images they paint in readers' minds.

PRACTICE Find at least four physical action verbs and four mental action verbs in the Frost poems. Then replace them with other verbs that have similar meanings. Reread the poems. How do the new verbs change the sound of the poems? How do they change the images in your mind?

- For more about using action verbs, see **Language Handbook,** p. R33.

Vo•cab•u•lar•y *Skills*

Dictionary Skills–Pronunciation

Does *gauge* sound like *page* or like *garage?* Pronouncing an unfamiliar word can be tricky, because vowels and some consonants, like *g* and *c,* have more than one pronunciation. When in doubt, check a dictionary for the correct pronunciation shown with letters and symbols. *Gauge* appears like this: gāj. The first *g* has the "hard" *g* sound; the second one has the "soft" *g* sound–the same sound that *j* has. In between, there is the sound of a long *a*. So *gauge* rhymes with *page.*

In a dictionary pronunciation, a vowel without a symbol has a "short" sound, like the vowels in *pat, pet, pit, hot,* and *hut.* Other vowel sounds are shown by symbols, such as a straight line above the vowel to show that it is a long vowel.

SYMBOL	MEANING	SYMBOL	MEANING
ä	an **ah** sound, as in **father**	ə	the unaccented vowel sound heard at the end of **pencil, lemon, taken**
ô	an **aw** sound, as in **coffee** and **law**	hw	**wh** as in **white**
oo	the vowel sound you hear in **wood**	th	**th** as in **thin**
o͞o	the vowel sound you hear in **fool**	t͟h	**th** as in **this**
oi	the vowel sound you hear in **toy**	zh	the sound heard in the middle of **treasure** or at the end of **garage**
ou	an **ow** sound, as in **cow** and **out**		

An **accent mark** points to the syllable you should stress. Stressing the correct syllable is extremely important in pronunciation. For example, the only difference in the sounds of *dessert* and *desert* is which syllable is stressed.

ACTIVITIES

1. Use the pronunciation given for each word to answer the question that follows it.
   a. *aghast* (ə gast′) Does this word rhyme with *fast* or *waste?*
   b. *psyche* (sī′ kē) Does this word rhyme with *like, spikey, itchy,* or *rich?*
   c. *scavenger* (skav′ in jər) Does the first syllable of this word rhyme with *have* or *save?*
2. Decide which word is represented by each dictionary pronunciation.
   a. ān′ jəl Is this word *angle* (corner) or *angel* (heavenly being)?
   b. buk′ it Is this word *bucket* or *bouquet?*
   c. pos′ ēz Is this word *possess* or *posse's?*

Before You Read

Between What I See and What I Say . . . / Entre Lo Que Veo y Digo . . .

MEET OCTAVIO PAZ

New isn't necessarily better, according to Mexican poet Octavio Paz (ok täv′ yō päz). In fact, he worried that his country was losing its rich literary heritage and culture to a modern society filled with action films, magazines, and "television but not vision." In his writing, Paz attempted to reach across cultural differences to speak from the human soul. Those efforts earned him the Nobel Prize in Literature in 1990.

Octavio Paz was born in 1914 and died in 1998. This poem was published in a collection of Paz's poems entitled A Tree Within.

FOCUS ACTIVITY

Do you find it difficult to express some emotions and ideas in words? How do poetry and the other arts encourage self-expression?

Define It!

Work with a partner to write a definition of poetry. Then share your definition with another pair of students.

Setting a Purpose

Read to explore the poet's definition of poetry.

BACKGROUND

This poem was written in 1982 for a memorial to Roman Jakobson, a Russian-born professor at Harvard University. Jakobson shared with Paz a love of language.

Throughout his writings, Paz posed questions and problems for the reader to ponder. His work appeals to young people because he understood the questions and problems of adolescents as they grow into who they are. Countries, he said, do the same. "Much the same thing happens to nations and peoples at a certain critical moment in their development. They ask themselves: 'What are we, and how can we fulfill our obligations to ourselves as we are?'"

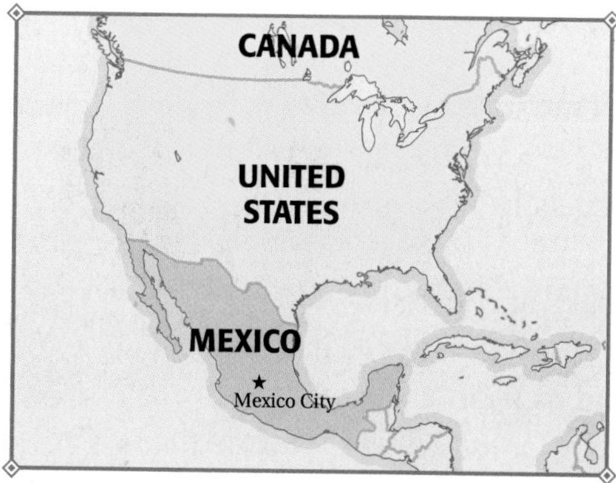

Between What I See and What I Say . . .

Octavio Paz
Translated by Eliot Weinberger

for Roman Jakobson

1

Between what I see and what I say,
between what I say and what I keep silent,
between what I keep silent and what I dream,
between what I dream and what I forget:
poetry.
It slips
between yes and no,
says
what I keep silent,
keeps silent
what I say,
dreams
what I forget.
It is not speech:
it is an act.
It is an act
of speech.
Poetry
speaks and listens:
it is real.
And as soon as I say
it is real,
it vanishes.
Is it then more real?

2

Tangible° idea,
intangible
word:
poetry
comes and goes
between what is
and what is not.
It weaves
and unweaves reflections.
Poetry
scatters eyes on a page,
scatters words on our eyes.
Eyes speak,
words look,
looks think.
To hear
thoughts,
see
what we say,
touch
the body of an idea.
Eyes close,
the words open.

25 A *tangible* idea is one that can be perceived, or almost perceived, by the senses, especially by the sense of touch.

Entre Lo Que Veo y Digo . . .

A Roman Jakobson

Octavio Paz

1

Entre lo que veo y digo,
entre lo que digo y callo,
entre lo que callo y sueño,
entre lo que sueño y olvido,
la poesía.
Se desliza
entre el sí y el no:
dice
lo que callo,
calla
lo que digo,
sueña
lo que olvido.
No es un decir:
es un hacer.
Es un hacer
que es un decir.
La poesía
se dice y se oye:
es real.
Y apenas digo
es real,
se disipa.
¿Así es más real?

2

Idea palpable,
palabra
impalpable:
la poesía
va y viene
entre lo que es
y lo que no es.
Teje reflejos
y los desteje.
La poesía
siembra ojos en la página,
siembra palabras en los ojos.
Los ojos hablan,
las palabras miran,
las miradas piensan.
Oír
los pensamientos,
ver
los que decimos,
tocar
el cuerpo de la idea.
Los ojos
se cierran,
las palabras se abren.

Presence of the Past, 1953 (details). Gunther Gerszo. Oil on Masonite. Museum of Fine Arts, Houston, TX.

Responding to Literature

PERSONAL RESPONSE

Does Paz's poem make you want to write a poem or read one?

Analyzing Literature

RECALL

1. What lies between the things the narrator sees and the things he says?
2. What image does Paz use to show that poetry puts things together to make something beautiful?
3. According to the poem, what happens when you close your eyes and think about a poem?

INTERPRET

4. Why does Paz describe poetry by telling what it is between, rather than what it is?
5. Why does Paz compare a poem to material that is woven?
6. How do the last two lines of the poem relate to the first line?

EVALUATE AND CONNECT

7. Does Paz's description of poetry emphasize the mystery of poetry or the rules of poetry? Explain your answer.
8. How does poetry affect your life? (Remember that the lyrics of songs are poems.)
9. What happens when you reread a poem many times? Does your interpretation change? Explain.
10. To whom would you recommend this poem? Give reasons for your answer.

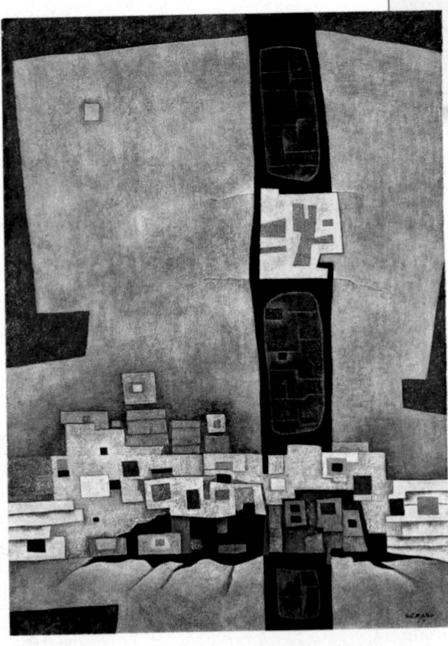

Presence of the Past, 1953. Gunther Gerszo. Oil on Masonite. Museum of Fine Arts, Houston, TX.

LITERARY ELEMENTS

Free Verse

Free verse is poetry that doesn't have a regular pattern of rhythm or rhyme. Free verse sounds like spoken language and contains modern words and phrases. The irregular line lengths and breaks of "Between What I See and What I Say" are characteristics of free verse. Read part of the poem aloud. Lines in free verse are often grouped to show meaning or create images.

1. Look at the form of the poem. How is the beginning different from the remaining lines?
2. How does this poem imitate conversation?

● See **Literary Terms Handbook,** p. R4.

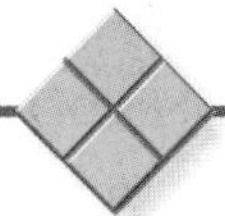

Extending Your Response

Writing About Literature

Reading Between the Lines This poem is about going beyond sight to find meaning. However, the poet has presented the poem in a visual format, breaking up sentences and putting fragments on single lines. Why might the author have written the poem in this way? What effect does this format achieve? How does it affect the way the poem is read? Write a paragraph to explain your thoughts.

Literature Groups

Poetry: Real or Unreal? In the poem, the narrator asks whether poetry is real. He writes: "And as soon as I say / *it is real,* / it vanishes." What makes words and ideas real to you? What poems or other forms of writing can you think of that seemed real or powerful when you read them? If possible, share these selections with your group and discuss your reasons for choosing them.

Personal Writing

You Are What You Write Paz's work was affected by his background, his Mexican nationality, and by his years of living in Asia as Mexico's ambassador to India, Pakistan, Nepal, and Ceylon (now Sri Lanka). Write an essay that explains how your writing is affected by your heritage, by where you live, and by your interests and activities.

Learning for Life

You As a Critic Think about Paz's concern for "television but not vision." Do you agree that there is a problem? If you do, write to your local newspaper. Share your concern and suggest ways to work against the bad effects of TV. If you think there is "vision" in the television shows you watch, write a letter explaining why you think as you do. Use examples from programs you consider worthwhile.

Reading Further

If you'd like to read more about choices and discoveries, try these novels:
Come a Stranger by Cynthia Voigt
Park's Quest by Katharine Paterson

Save your work for your portfolio.

Skill Minilesson

READING AND THINKING • AUTHOR'S PURPOSE

Poets have a **purpose,** or goal, for what they write, just as other writers do. Sometimes the purpose is to persuade, to inform, to entertain, or perhaps simply to express an idea or a feeling.

To better understand what you read, try to identify the author's purpose.

PRACTICE Reread the poem. What, do you think, was Paz's purpose for composing this poem for a memorial service to Roman Jakobson, a linguist? Explain your answer.

- For more about author's purpose, see **Reading Handbook,** p. R96.

Subject-Verb Agreement

A **subject** tells who or what is doing something. A **verb** tells what the subject is doing. A singular subject needs a singular verb, and a plural subject needs a plural verb. Making a subject agree with its verb is tricky sometimes, but the following problems and solutions can help you.

Problem 1 *My backpack, filled with poetry books, are heavy.*

Solution Make the verb agree with its subject, not with the closest noun.

My backpack, filled with poetry books, is heavy.

Problem 2 *Each of the poems contain similes.*

Few in the world is as observant as a poet.

Some of Paz's poetry focus on nature.

Solution If the subject is an indefinite pronoun, study the chart below to determine whether it is singular or plural. A few indefinite pronouns can be either singular or plural, depending on the object of the preposition that follows in the sentence.

Indefinite Pronouns		
Singular	**Plural**	**Either**
another, each, either, everybody, everything, much, neither, somebody, something	both, few, many, others, several	all, any, most, none, some

Each of the poems contains similes.

Few in the world are as observant as a poet.

Some of Paz's poetry focuses on nature.

EXERCISE

For each sentence, write the correct form of the verb in parentheses.

1. Some poems, such as "Casey at the Bat," (is, are) humorous.
2. Many poets (write, writes) poems in response to art.
3. Much of Frost's work (is, are) available on-line.
4. All of the local book stores (has, have) a section devoted to poetry.

LISTENING, SPEAKING, and VIEWING

Effective Listening Techniques

How can you get the most out of conversations, speeches, instructions, and everything you hear each day? Pay attention to more than words. Octavio Paz tells readers that listening involves eyes and minds, as well as ears:

> . . . To hear
> thoughts,
> see
> what we say,
> touch
> the body of an idea. . . .

Listening Tips

- **Focus** on the speaker's words. Zero in on main points. Are the main points supported by details and facts?
- **Watch** the speaker's posture, gestures, and facial expressions. What do they show about how the speaker feels?
- **Think** about ways the speaker's message relates to you. Will it help you learn? Understand? Enjoy?

The Listening Tips can help you answer questions like the following.

Questions for Effective Listening

1. What is the speaker's purpose? (To inform? To persuade? To share feelings?)
2. What are the speaker's main points?
3. What questions do I have after listening to this speaker?
4. What (if any) hidden messages or biases do I detect?

ACTIVITIES

1. With a partner, practice your listening skills. Take turns preparing and presenting a reading or speech. Then write your responses to the first two **Questions for Effective Listening.** Check your responses with your partner.
2. Listen to a short speech. It may be live, or it may be part of a film, a documentary, or a news broadcast. Write your responses to the **Questions for Effective Listening.** Discuss your responses with classmates.

Before You Read

Identity and *the lesson of the moth*

MEET JULIO NOBOA POLANCO

Julio Noboa Polanco (hōō lē′ ō nä bō′ ä pō lōn′ kō) was in the eighth grade when he wrote the poem "Identity." He got the idea for the poem during a long walk near his West Side home in Chicago after he and his girlfriend had broken up. Noboa now lives in San Antonio, Texas, where he writes a biweekly column for the *San Antonio Express-News* and works in the field of education.

MEET DON MARQUIS

Don Marquis (mär kē′) worked many years as a columnist with the *Evening Sun*, a New York newspaper. In his columns, Marquis created the characters of archy, a poetic cockroach, and his friend, mehitabel the cat. Marquis died in 1937, but his characters live on in poems such as "the lesson of the moth."

FOCUS ACTIVITY

Imagine that you could be a plant or an animal for just a day. What would you choose to be? A rose? A bear? What qualities would you possess?

Web It!

Use a word web to develop your ideas. Circle the word that states your choice and surround it with details and reasons supporting your choice.

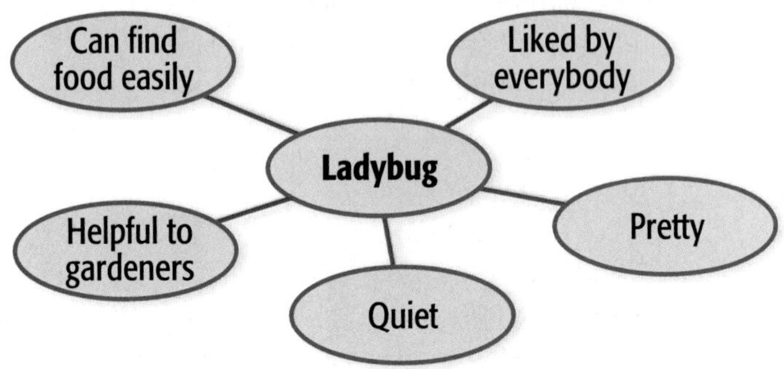

Setting a Purpose

Read to discover the comparisons in these poems.

BACKGROUND

Don Marquis's archy liked to write poetry. According to Marquis, archy composed poems like "the lesson of the moth" on a manual typewriter by hurling himself at each typewriter key. "After about an hour of this frightfully difficult literary labor he fell to the floor exhausted," Marquis said. Because archy couldn't reach the shift key, his writing (including his name) didn't include capitalization or punctuation.

Identity

Julio Noboa Polanco

Let them be as flowers,
always watered, fed, guarded, admired,
but harnessed to a pot of dirt.

I'd rather be a tall, ugly weed,
clinging on cliffs, like an eagle
wind-wavering above high, jagged rocks.

To have broken through the surface of stone
to live, to feel exposed to the madness
of the vast, eternal sky.
To be swayed by the breezes of an ancient sea,
carrying my soul, my seed beyond the mountains of time
or into the abyss° of the bizarre.°

I'd rather be unseen, and if,

then shunned° by everyone
than to be a pleasant-smelling flower,
growing in clusters in the fertile valley
where they're praised, handled, and plucked
by greedy, human hands.

I'd rather smell of musty, green stench
than of sweet, fragrant lilac.
If I could stand alone, strong and free,
I'd rather be a tall, ugly weed.

---

12 An *abyss* is an immeasurably deep hole or a vast emptiness. The *bizarre* (bi zär′) is something that is extremely strange.

14 A person who is being *shunned* is being avoided.

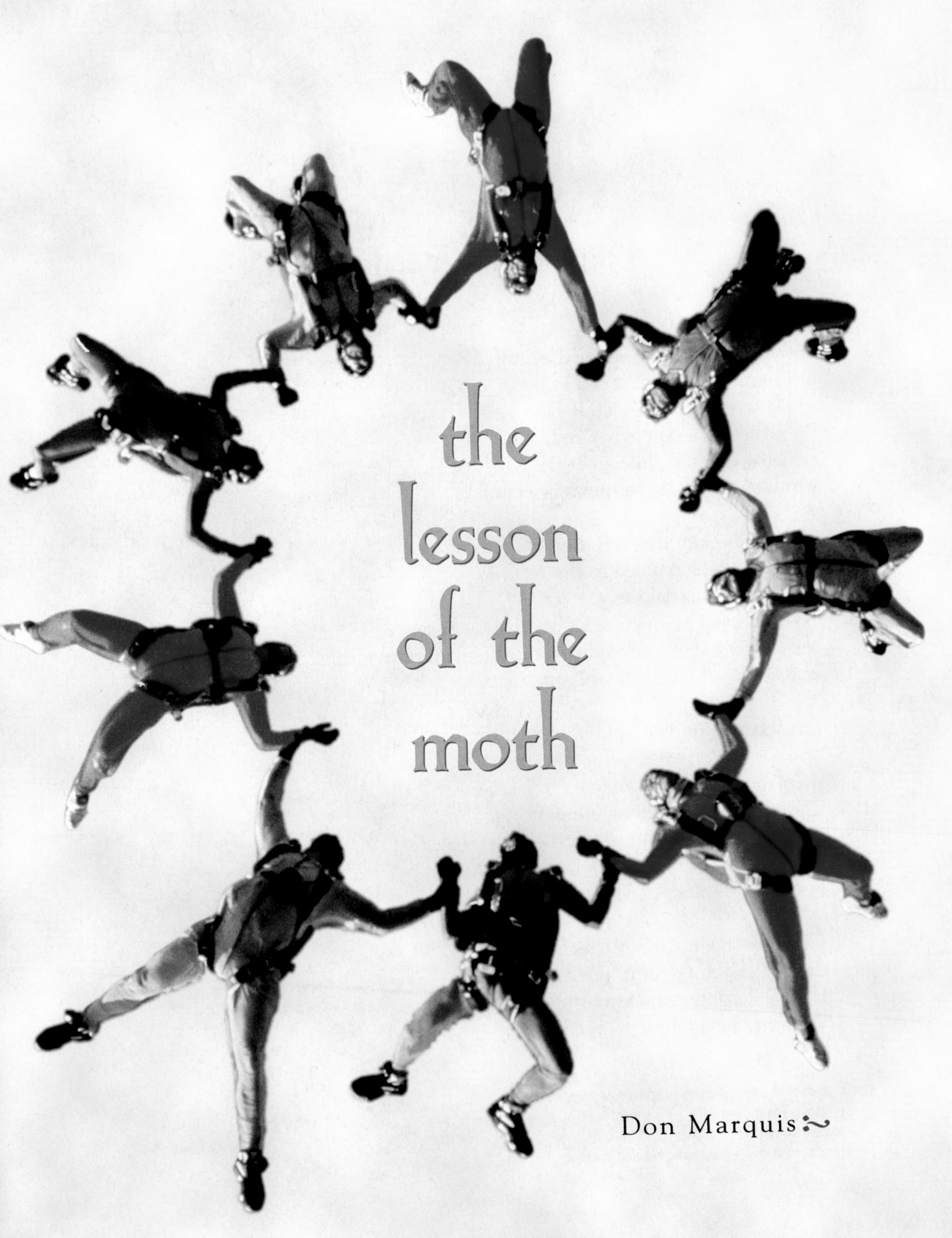

the lesson of the moth

Don Marquis

i was talking to a moth
the other evening
he was trying to break into
an electric light bulb
and fry himself on the wires

why do you fellows
pull this stunt i asked him
because it is the conventional°
thing for moths or why
if that had been an uncovered
candle instead of an electric
light bulb you would
now be a small unsightly cinder
have you no sense

plenty of it he answered
but at times we get tired
of using it
we get bored with the routine
and crave beauty
and excitement
fire is beautiful
and we know that if we get
too close it will kill us
but what does that matter
it is better to be happy
for a moment
and be burned up with beauty
than to live a long time
and be bored all the while
so we wad all our life up
into one little roll
and then we shoot the roll
that is what life is for
it is better to be a part of beauty
for one instant and then cease to
exist than to exist forever
and never be a part of beauty
our attitude toward life
is come easy go easy
we are like human beings
used to be before they became
too civilized to enjoy themselves

and before i could argue him
out of his philosophy°
he went and immolated° himself
on a patent cigar lighter
i do not agree with him
myself i would rather have
half the happiness and twice
the longevity°

but at the same time i wish
there was something i wanted
as badly as he wanted to fry himself

archy

8 *Conventional* describes what is usual, customary, or traditional.

44 Here, *philosophy* refers to the personal beliefs and principles that guide one's life.

45 The most common meaning of *immolate* is "to destroy by fire," but it can also mean "to offer in sacrifice."

50 *Longevity* (lon jev′ ə tē) means "long life."

Responding to Literature

PERSONAL RESPONSE

Which stands out most in your mind: the flower, the weed, the moth, or archy? Why?

Analyzing Literature

RECALL

1. What does the speaker in "Identity" choose to be? What are the reasons for the choice?
2. Summarize what happens in "the lesson of the moth."

INTERPRET

3. In your opinion, what kind of life does the weed in "Identity" live? Give three examples to support your claim.
4. What is archy's attitude toward life? Support your answer with examples from the poem.

EVALUATE AND CONNECT

5. Noboa uses a **simile,** which compares two things using *like* or *as.* In what ways might he think flowers are like people? What words or phrases in the poem show this idea?
6. Marquis uses **imagery** to create pictures that reinforce the ideas in the poem. List two images that show the type of life the moth leads.
7. According to lines 40–42 in "the lesson of the moth," what might the moth think about human beings? Do you agree? Why or why not?
8. In what ways might the speaker in "Identity" be like the moth? How is the flower like archy?
9. Describe archy's conflict in lines 48–53. What advice would you give archy to resolve this conflict?
10. Which image do you identify with the most: the flower, the weed, the moth, or archy? Why?

LITERARY ELEMENTS

Theme

The **theme,** or message, of a poem can often be stated in a simple sentence like "Live an honest life," or "Trust your instincts." Sometimes, the theme is not stated, and the reader must infer by looking at the thoughts and actions in the poem. Other times, a character or speaker states the theme directly.

1. State the theme of "Identity." What does the speaker say to reveal this theme?
2. Write a sentence that states the theme of "the lesson of the moth." What does the moth say that gives away the theme?

● See **Literary Terms Handbook,** p. R10.

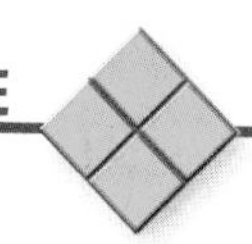

Extending Your Response

Writing About Literature

Style In his stories of archy and mehitabel, Marquis writes without capitalization and punctuation. Working with a partner, rewrite the first two stanzas of the poem, using standard punctuation and capitalization. Then discuss what is gained and what is lost by using standard conventions of punctuation and capitalization. Does lack of mechanics encourage you to read more about archy? Does it discourage you?

Literature Groups

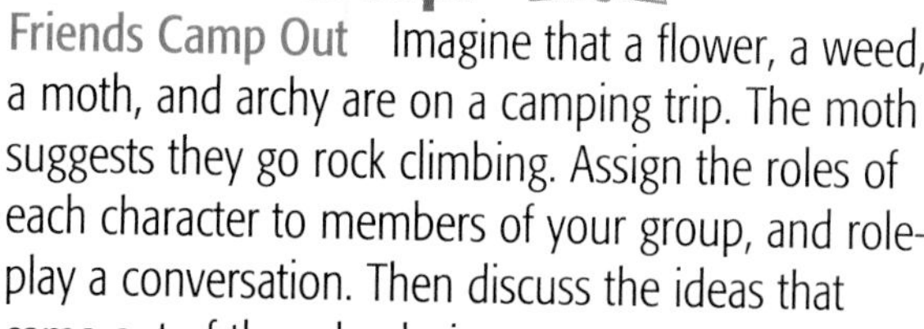

Friends Camp Out Imagine that a flower, a weed, a moth, and archy are on a camping trip. The moth suggests they go rock climbing. Assign the roles of each character to members of your group, and role-play a conversation. Then discuss the ideas that came out of the role-playing.

Interdisciplinary Activity

Art With a small group, construct a comic strip to show two advantages and two disadvantages of living as either a flower, a weed, a moth, or a cockroach. Before you draw the strip, consider the opinions of the authors and the ideas of each group member. Present the finished strip to the class.

Learning for Life

In Memory A **eulogy** is a speech given to honor a person who has died. Write a eulogy for the moth, flower, weed, or archy. Tell why the character was special and why he or she will be missed and mourned. Include an anecdote, a brief story that can be humorous or meaningful, to give insight into the character. Present your eulogy to the class.

Reading Further

For fiction about choosing a place in life, read:
The Prince and the Pauper by Mark Twain
The Call of the Wild by Jack London

Save your work for your portfolio.

Skill Minilesson

READING AND THINKING • COMPARE AND CONTRAST

When you **compare** two selections, you look at how they are similar. When you **contrast,** you study how two things are different. "Identity" and "the lesson of the moth" are good poems to compare because they are both about making life choices.

- For more about comparing and contrasting, see **Reading Handbook,** p. R91.

PRACTICE Compare and contrast the two poems by answering the following questions.

1. Compare the titles. What information does each give about the poem?
2. Compare the themes of the poems. How do they relate to the theme "Which Way to Go?"

MEDIA Connection

NEWSPAPER ARTICLE

For some athletes, baseball, soccer, and basketball aren't exciting enough. Such people have chosen to play new–and often dangerous–types of extreme sports.

Going to the EXTREME: Young daredevils zip into mainstream

by Karen Thomas—*USA Today*, August 13, 1997

EGG HARBOR TOWNSHIP, New Jersey— The skating-themed balloons are perfectly tethered. Happy Birthday streamers are strung. The guests have arrived.

We have a problem!

Matt Hunter, who's set to blow out the fourteen candles on the in-line skating cake, marches over to the piñata that his mother has just hung from a tree. It, too, is shaped like a skate, but it's not quite right.

Matt rips off the papier-mâché brake built into the heel and tosses it into the trash. His broad, self-assured smile says it all: He's hosting the perfect aggressive-skating birthday party. And aggressive means no brakes.

Aggressive or *extreme* sports—trick skating, skateboarding, and biking—are no longer exclusive to the progressive California dude. Driveways across the USA have become the breeding ground for youths as young as six and seven who are using two-, four-, and eight-wheeled toys to attempt flips, spins, jumps, and an array of airborne stunts.

The trend has transformed the curbs, stairways, and railings in communities into battlegrounds pitting pedestrians against daredevils with their wheeled weaponry while the medical community scurries to deal with potential injuries.

With extreme sports still in their infancy, it's too early for specific medical statistics. Unspecified in-line skating injuries treated in hospital emergency rooms have nearly tripled since 1993—from 36,986 to 102,819 last year—according to the Consumer Product Safety Commission. Participation in in-line skating among youths six to seventeen, though, has quadrupled.

Some experts will say at least the kids are moving. As youth participation in every traditional sport declines, in-line skating is the fastest-growing sport among youngsters. The Sporting Goods Manufacturers Association (SGMA) reports 7.9 million participants ages six to seventeen in 1996. Another study by Teenage Research Unlimited shows boys aged twelve to fifteen are more interested in extreme sports than professional basketball.

"You get a good workout, and it's a challenge," says in-line skater Matt Kreutzer, thirteen. He and Hunter are members of a neighborhood skating club, the 609 sk8 crew (609 is Egg Harbor's area code). "You have to have challenges in your life," he says, "or you'll get bored."

While participants, experts, and parents don't concur on safety measures, they do all agree that extreme sports are not a passing phase, and as the practice continues to grow among younger and younger children, it needs immediate attention.

"There's a valid reason for concern. The (extreme) formula has all the ingredients for a high injury rate," says Dr. Steven Anderson, who chairs the American Academy of Pediatrics' task force on sports medicine. The topic was first brought up at the group's May meeting when it received its first letter from a pediatrician asking what advice to give to parents. "We're going to have to formally look at it, so the academy may have some official position about whether this is a safe and reasonable activity for children," he says. "I'm trying to imagine a scenario where the benefits outweigh the risks."

"I doubt there has been a sport that has rivaled this ever," says the SGMA's Mike May, who says even basketball, traditionally the sport most played by kids, never reached skating's high mark. It's "surprising," he says, that raw data from 1996 shows a decline in kids' participation in nine of the top ten sports. Only in-line skating registered an increase. Extreme is for "your typically normal kid that likes to be on the

edge," says Gary Ream, president of Camp Woodward, a camp in Woodward, Pennsylvania, devoted to extreme sports and gymnastics. "I don't think they're any different than we were as kids."

The image: Another problem.

"People always think these are kids who smoke and do drugs and drop out of school," says Brenda Hunter at her son's birthday party. Matt and his brother, Jake, fifteen, attend Christian school and maintain high grades, she says. The 609 sk8 crew are all "good boys," she says, who come from good families.

But their clothes are over-sized (to fit pads underneath). Wallets dangle from chains attached at the belt (so you don't lose your money on aerial tricks). Some have spray painted their skates and helmets.

That image scares parents, Ream says. And the look is evolving in the early elementary years. "They're hip at nine in the '90s," says Kevin Thatcher, publisher of *Thrasher* magazine, devoted to skateboarding.

"It's the stereotype that skateboarding is so inherently dangerous," Thatcher says. "We're going to be in trouble if we don't give back to the youth by building skate parks."

Parents of his readers call for advice. He tells them, "Take them to the skate spot. Watch them. Listen." But don't stay so long as to embarrass your child. "Disappear when it's uncool."

Respond

1. Why do some people choose extreme sports over safer activities?
2. What is your opinion of these aggressive sports?

Writing WORKSHOP

Expository Writing: Writing an Evaluation

What's the hardest decision you've made this year? Were you happy with the decision you made? Do you still have doubts? Evaluating a decision takes a lot of thought, and writing about your thoughts is a good way to sort them out.

Assignment: For this workshop, **write an essay evaluating a decision.** Follow the process shown on these pages.

- As you write your evaluation, refer to **Writing Handbook,** pp. R50–R61.

The Writing Process

PREWRITING

PREWRITING TIP

Your thesis can be as simple as "I regret my decision to join the track team" or "I'm glad I joined the track team." In the body of your essay, you'll explain your thesis. You might discuss your criteria in **order of importance,** moving from least to most important.

Find a Topic

You may want to evaluate a real-life decision that you or someone else has made. You could also evaluate a decision made by a character in this theme. To find ideas, try freewriting about decisions that have meant something to you. Another strategy is to make an idea tree for the word *decisions.* For a strong essay, choose a decision that you have strong feelings about.

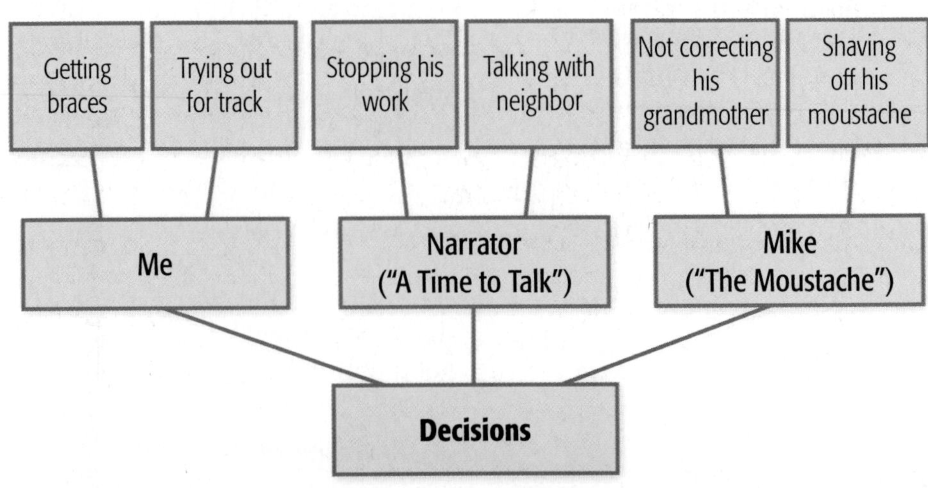

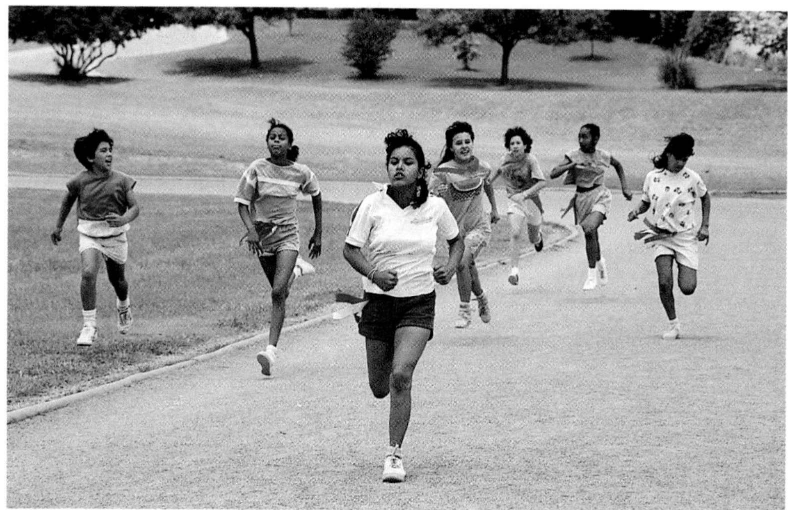

Set Your Standards

To evaluate, you need **criteria**–standards for judging. Your criteria reflect what's important to you. You might consider:

- personal happiness
- effects on others
- expense
- ethics

List your own criteria for evaluating the decision you have chosen.

Consider Audience and Purpose

Will you write mainly for yourself, exploring a decision in your life? If so, you might plan a personal essay. Will you evaluate the decision of a literary character? If so, you might plan your essay as a letter to that character, or as a more formal response to literature.

Get Organized

Your opinion of the decision is the **thesis**–the main idea–of your essay. Write your thesis now, as a sentence.

Least important criterion: pride	
Details:	I'm no star, but I do OK. In meets, I've placed second and third.
Second most important criterion: physical fitness	
Details:	Hate to run laps, but getting faster. New personal best: 7.9 sec. for 50 meters.
Most important criterion: pleasure	
Details:	When I run well, I'm happy. Feel like I'm flying. It's happening more often.

DRAFTING

DRAFTING TIP

You can state your thesis in your introduction, or you can build up to it, stating it in your conclusion.

TECHNOLOGY TIP

Use a computer's split screen or clipboard function to keep your prewriting notes handy as you draft.

Explain the Basics

You might "hook" your readers by opening with a question or with an action image. Then explain the decision that you will evaluate. Give just enough background for readers to understand the issues. For a decision in a literary selection, include the name of the author, the selection, and the character.

Draft Your Essay

For each criterion, write at least a paragraph, showing how the decision measures up. Transitional phrases, such as *for one thing, for another thing, more important,* and *most important,* will help readers follow your essay. To conclude, sum up your evaluation. You might bring readers full circle by referring again to your introduction: *For me, "to run" was definitely the best answer.*

MODEL • DRAFTING

To run or not to run? That was the question. I wanted to join the track team, but I wasn't sure. I was afraid the others would put me down, and I thought I'd hate the practices. Now I'm glad I decided to join.

REVISING

REVISING TIP

Perhaps your thesis is clearer to you now. If so, reword your thesis statement to reflect your new insights.

Improve Your Essay

Set your draft aside and take a break for at least a few minutes—longer, if possible. Then use the **Questions for Revising** as you go over your draft. You might work with a partner to plan revisions. Make changes that will strengthen your draft.

QUESTIONS FOR REVISING

- ☑ What background information do I provide for readers?
- ☑ Where is my thesis stated?
- ☑ What are my criteria, and where do I discuss each one?
- ☑ Where might I add transitions to help readers follow my essay?
- ☑ Where might more details make my points clearer?

EDITING/PROOFREADING

Before making a final copy of your essay, use the **Proofreading Checklist** on the inside back cover to help you find and correct errors in grammar and mechanics. The **Grammar Link** on page 314 can help you check your subject-verb agreement.

Grammar Hint

In a complex sentence, you can use *however* to join two clauses. Put a semicolon before it and a comma after it.

Mike is seventeen; however, his moustache makes him look older.

MODEL · EDITING/PROOFREADING

I hate to run laps, however, it builds up my endurance.

Editing Tip

Does your essay use time order to present a series of events? Reread your essay to make sure that the verb tenses are correct.

PUBLISHING/PRESENTING

Your essay can become a springboard for discussion. In a small group, read one another's essays. Then discuss the ideas in each essay. How would others in the group have evaluated the decision? Why? Explore one another's views and criteria.

Presenting Tip

If your topic is a literary character's decision, ask classmates to play the role of the character and respond to your essay.

Reflecting

Write your thoughts about the following questions.

- What new ideas about the decision occurred to you as you worked on your essay?
- Which was easier for you: evaluating the decision, or writing about your evaluation? Why?

Save your work for your portfolio.

Theme Wrap-Up

Responding to the Theme

1. Which of the choices made by the characters in this theme do you identify with the most? Why?
2. What new ideas do you have about each of the following statements as a result of reading the selections in this theme?
   - Sometimes, decisions have surprising results.
   - Choosing a more difficult path can help us in the long run.
   - Making no decision is worse than making the wrong decision.
3. Present your theme project to the class.

Analyzing Literature

In "Identity" and "the lesson of the moth," the speakers express their beliefs about choices and destiny. Reread these two poems, or choose two similar pieces from the theme. Compare and contrast attitudes toward making difficult choices.

Evaluate and Set Goals

1. Which of the activities below did you enjoy most? Which was the most difficult?
   - reading and thinking about the selections
   - writing independently
   - analyzing and discussing the selections
   - presenting ideas and projects
   - researching topics
2. How would you assess your work in this theme, using the following scale? Give at least two reasons for your assessment.

   4 = outstanding 2 = fair
   3 = good 1 = weak
3. Based on what you found difficult in this theme, choose a goal to work toward in the next theme.
   - Write down your goal and three steps you will take to help you reach it.
   - Meet with your teacher to review your goal and your plan for achieving it.

Build Your Portfolio

SELECT

Choose two of your favorite pieces of work from this theme to include in your portfolio. The following questions can help you choose.

- ✦ Which do you consider your best work?
- ✦ Which turned out to be more challenging than you thought?
- ✦ Which piece did you learn the most from?
- ✦ Which was the most interesting?

REFLECT

Write some notes to accompany the pieces you selected. Use these questions to guide you.

- ✦ What do you like best about the piece?
- ✦ What did you learn from creating it?
- ✦ What might you do differently if you were beginning this piece again?

Reading on Your Own

If you have enjoyed reading the selections about making choices and trusting your instincts, try these books.

Shabanu: Daughter of the Wind

by Suzanne Fisher Staples Shabanu is part of a family of nomads in Pakistan. She loves her life, but when she is faced with marriage to a man chosen for her, she tries to run away. The difficult life of the herders in a barren land is depicted realistically.

The Rain Catchers

by Jean Thesman Growing up in house of strong, funny, creative women, fourteen-year-old Grayling discovers the power of telling stories. She also learns how to make decisions of her own.

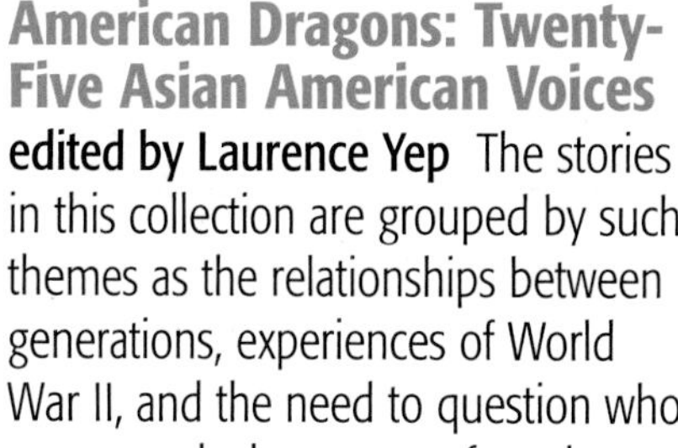

American Dragons: Twenty-Five Asian American Voices

edited by Laurence Yep The stories in this collection are grouped by such themes as the relationships between generations, experiences of World War II, and the need to question who we are and where we go from here.

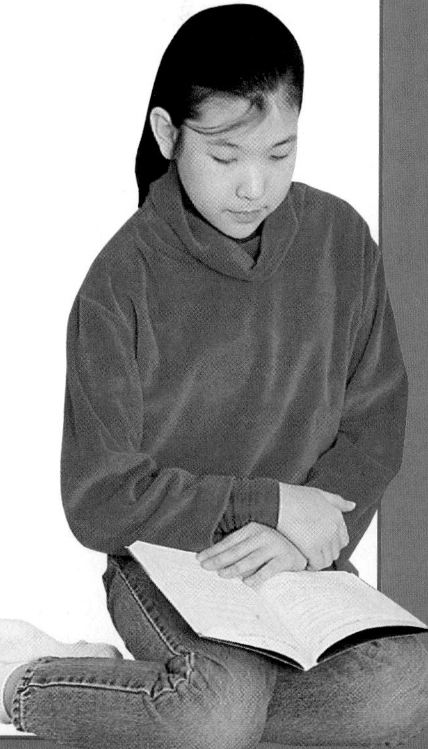

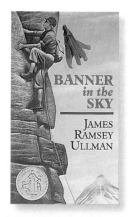

Banner in the Sky

by James Ramsey Ullman When Rudi's father dies in his attempt to scale a mountain in the Alps, Rudi decides that he must conquer the peak that killed his father. The author, an experienced climber, adds detailed information to a tense tale of courage and determination.

Standardized Test Practice

Read the passage. Some sections are underlined. The underlined sections may be one of the following:

- Incomplete sentences
- Run-on sentences
- Correctly written sentences that should be combined
- Correctly written sentences that do not need to be rewritten

Choose the best way to write each underlined section. Mark the letter for your answer on your paper. If the underlined section needs no change, mark the choice "Correct as is."

> If you've ever turned a rock over in a stream. You have probably seen planarians attached to its underside. (1) Planarians are flatworms. Most planarians live in freshwater and feed on small organisms or on the bodies of larger animals.
>
> Earthworms move through the soil. The worms digest the organic matter contained there. (2) Their waste, called casts, adds elements that fertilize the soil.

1 A If you've ever turned a rock over in a stream, you have probably seen planarians attached to its underside.

B Because you probably have seen planarians attached to its underside when you turned over a rock in a stream.

C If you've ever turned a rock over in a stream, but you probably have seen planarians attached to its underside.

D Turning a rock over in a stream probably seeing planarians attached to its underside.

2 F Earthworms move through the soil, digesting the organic matter contained there.

G Moving through the soil, digesting the organic matter contained there.

H Earthworms move through the soil they digest the organic matter contained there.

J Correct as is

Read the passage and decide which type of error, if any, appears in each underlined section. Mark the letter for your answer on your paper.

Dear Mom and Dad,

I am writing to let you know <u>that I am having a great time so far at camp this summr.</u> (1) The other girls in my cabin are from many different places around the world. I've learned how to play <u>soccer and field hockey but I'm not good at them yet.</u> (2)

<u>Yesterday, we had a Scavenger hunt.</u> (3) We had to capture a frog. <u>Since the frog had to be alive we crawled</u> (4) around slowly in the grass to get one. Finally, we found one and managed to put it in a bucket for safekeeping.

I hope you are having fun at home. I miss you!

Love,

Celeste

1 A Spelling error
B Capitalization error
C Punctuation error
D No error

2 F Spelling error
G Capitalization error
H Punctuation error
J No error

3 A Spelling error
B Capitalization error
C Punctuation error
D No error

4 F Spelling error
G Capitalization error
H Punctuation error
J No error

Fantastic Capers and Mischief Makers

> *"I know a trick worth two of that."*
>
> –*William Shakespeare*

Two of Clover Face Ace of Hearts, 1994 (detail). Maria Angelica Ruiz-Tagle. Oil on canvas, 76 x 46 cm. Private collection.

THEME CONTENTS

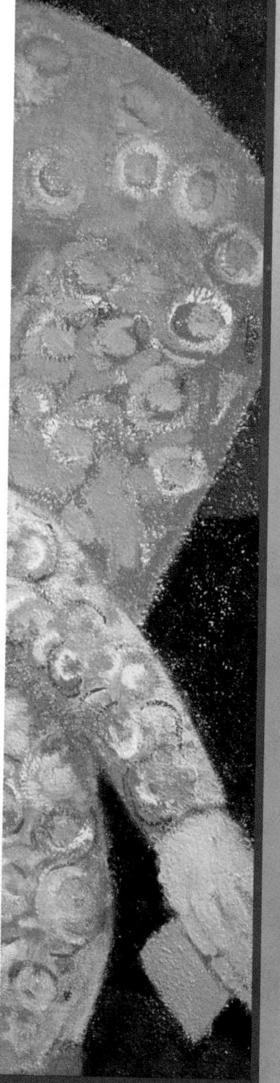

Exploring the Theme

Fantastic Capers and Mischief Makers

What can readers learn from tales of mischief, misfortune, and magical power? The selections in this theme will give you the opportunity to discuss and answer these questions. Try one of the following options to start your thinking about the theme.

Starting Points

MEMORIES OF MISCHIEF

Garfield the cat spends a lot of time causing mischief—whether he's persuading his owner to feed him cookies or tricking a bird into being his next meal. Have you or someone you know ever been tricked? Draw a cartoon showing how the incident turned out.

THE TRICK'S ON YOU

Think about a time you played a harmless trick on someone or made mischief of some kind. Put yourself in the place of the person on whom you played the trick or the person your mischief affected. Write a few notes about how you would have felt if you were the victim of the mischief.

Theme Projects

Complete one of the projects below as you read the selections in "Fantastic Capers and Mischief Makers." Work on your own, with a partner, or with a group.

CRITICAL VIEWING

Modern-Day Folk Heroes

1. Read comic books or watch television shows and films that feature the deeds of a super-hero, such as Superman or Wonder Woman.
2. Choose one character to study. What are his or her attributes? What amazing deeds does he or she perform? What message, if any, does his or her story convey?
3. Reflect on what you learned about folk heroes in this theme. What do these folk heroes have in common with modern-day superheroes?
4. Prepare an oral presentation that supports your main points with images of superheroes and folk heroes in action.

For more about "Fantastic Capers and Mischief Makers," visit lit.glencoe.com. You also might search the Internet for hoaxes and urban legends–outrageous stories about events that supposedly happened. Create a collection of your favorite stories.

MULTIMEDIA PROJECT

Create a Cyber Folk Hero

1. Gather information about a character featured in this theme or a character you discovered or created on your own. Use HyperStudio or similar software to create a multimedia presentation about the character.
2. Create visuals such as cartoons and drawings to show the amazing feats the character performed.
3. Write an introduction for the character, captions for the images, and a conclusion that wraps up your ideas.

LEARNING FOR LIFE

Legends Close to Home

1. Legends may be created when an ordinary person performs a heroic deed, overcomes a huge obstacle, or changes his or her family's fate. Ask your friends and relatives to recount stories of well-known or unusual people in their lives.
2. Choose one story to tell. If possible, plan to interview the subject of the story. Or, interview people who remember the story.
3. During the interview, gather as many details as possible about the story.
4. Put the story down on paper, organizing the events from start to finish.

MEDIA Connection

COMIC STRIP

Wouldn't you like to have a friend who could solve every problem? Cartoonist Bill Watterson gives young Calvin a perfect problem-solver.

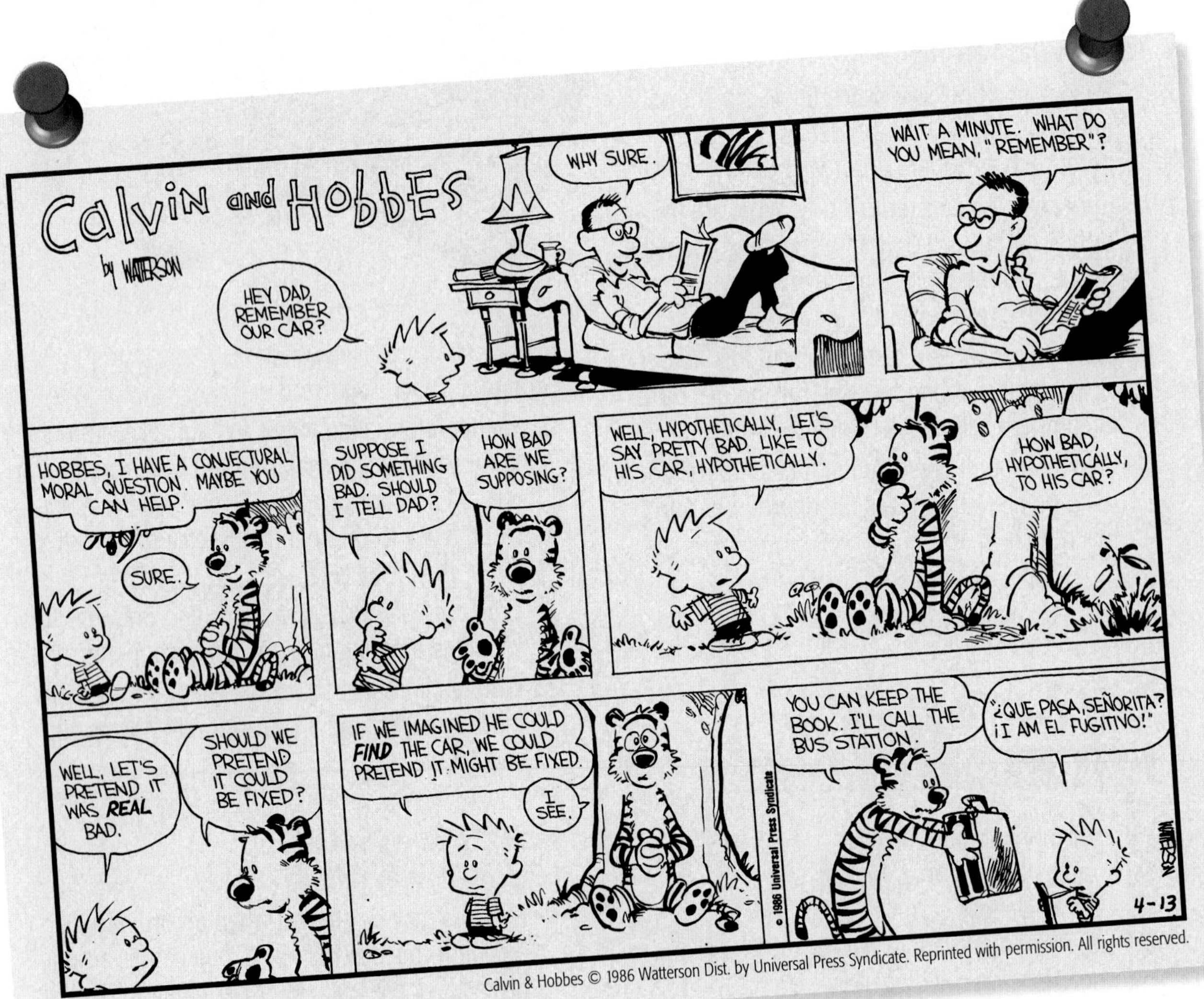

Respond

1. Find two examples in which Calvin uses the English language with great accuracy.
2. What other language does Calvin plan to use? Why might he need a second language?

Before You Read

The Ransom of Red Chief

MEET O. HENRY

The stories of O. Henry are as colorful as the man who wrote them: William Sydney Porter. He was a writer, a bank teller, and a convicted felon who spent three years in prison. While in jail, Porter adopted the name O. Henry and began a successful writing career. "I'll give you the whole secret of short-story writing," he wrote to his daughter. "Rule 1: Write stories that please yourself. There is no Rule 2."

William Sydney Porter (O. Henry) lived from 1862 to 1910. This story was published in 1918 in The Ransom of Red Chief and Other O. Henry Stories for Boys.

FOCUS ACTIVITY

Picture a nine- or ten-year-old boy you know. What does he look like? How does he speak and act?

QuickWrite

List some characteristics of a boy this age.

Setting a Purpose

Read to discover what happens when two "con men" and a mischievous young boy get together.

BACKGROUND

The Time and Place This story is set in Summit, Alabama, probably in the late 1800s.

Did You Know? O. Henry had firsthand knowledge of being on the wrong side of the law. He was convicted of embezzlement as a young bank teller when a $5,000 deposit was either unrecorded or stolen. He fled the country, only to return when his wife became ill. Friends wondered if he was covering up for a bank official, but the truth about his guilt or innocence was never revealed.

VOCABULARY PREVIEW

prominent (prom′ ə nənt) *adj.* widely known; p. 338
emit (i mit′) *v.* to utter; send forth or give out, as a sound; p. 341
dote (dōt) *v.* to show extreme affection; p. 341
peremptory (pə remp′ tər ē) *adj.* allowing no refusal; p. 342
decry (di krī′) *v.* to criticize openly; p. 343
comply (kəm plī′) *v.* to obey or go along with a request; p. 343
renegade (ren′ ə gād′) *n.* one who abandons or turns against a group, cause, or allegiance; traitor; p. 344
palatable (pal′ ə tə bəl) *adj.* agreeable to the taste, mind, or feelings; acceptable; p. 345
impudent (im′ pyə dənt) *adj.* boldly discourteous; p. 346

I t looked like a good thing: but wait till I tell you. We were down South, in Alabama—Bill Driscoll and myself—when this kidnapping idea struck us. It was, as Bill afterward expressed it, "during a moment of temporary mental apparition";[1] but we didn't find that out till later.

There was a town down there, as flat as a flannel cake, and called Summit, of course. It contained inhabitants of as undeleterious[2] and self-satisfied a class of peasantry as ever clustered around a maypole.

Bill and me had a joint capital of about six hundred dollars, and we needed just two thousand dollars more to pull off a fraudulent town-lot scheme in Western Illinois. We talked it over on the front steps of the hotel. Philoprogenitiveness,[3] says we, is strong in semi-rural communities; therefore, and for other reasons, a kidnapping project ought to do better there than in the radius of newspapers that send reporters out in plain clothes to stir up talk about such things. We knew that Summit couldn't get after us with anything stronger than constables and, maybe, some lackadaisical bloodhounds and a diatribe[4] or two in the *Weekly Farmers' Budget*. So, it looked good.

We selected for our victim the only child of a prominent citizen named Ebenezer Dorset. The father was respectable and tight, a mortgage fancier[5] and a stern, upright collection-plate passer and forecloser. The kid was a boy of ten, with bas-relief[6] freckles, and hair the color of the cover of the magazine you buy at the newsstand when you want to catch a train. Bill and me figured that Ebenezer would melt down for a ransom of two thousand dollars to a cent. But wait till I tell you.

About two miles from Summit was a little mountain, covered with a dense cedar

1. Sam (the narrator) and Bill seem to enjoy using big words, but they don't always choose the right ones. What Bill means here is *aberration* ("a slight mental weakness or disease"), not *apparition* ("a ghost or ghostly vision").
2. *Deleterious* means "causing harm or injury" and usually refers to one's health or well-being. Here, Sam is saying that the townspeople are harmless.
3. *Philoprogenitiveness* is an old, rarely used word meaning "love of one's children."
4. *Lackadaisical* means "showing little energy or interest." *Diatribes* are angry criticisms.
5. A *fancier* is one who has a fondness for a particular thing. Sam means to say that Dorset is a mortgage *financier* (fin′ an sēr′)—one who arranges mortgages.
6. *Bas-relief* (bä′ ri lēf′) is sculpture in which raised figures are carved on a flat background.

Vocabulary

prominent (prom′ ə nənt) *adj.* widely known

# of Red Chief

O. Henry

brake. On the rear elevation of this mountain was a cave. There we stored provisions.

One evening after sundown, we drove in a buggy past old Dorset's house. The kid was in the street, throwing rocks at a kitten on the opposite fence.

"Hey, little boy!" says Bill, "would you like to have a bag of candy and a nice ride?"

The boy catches Bill neatly in the eye with a piece of brick.

"That will cost the old man an extra five hundred dollars," says Bill, climbing over the wheel.

That boy put up a fight like a welterweight cinnamon bear; but, at last, we got him down in the bottom of the buggy and drove away. We took him up to the cave, and I hitched the horse in the cedar brake. After dark I drove the buggy to the little village, three miles away, where we had hired it, and walked back to the mountain.

Bill was pasting court-plaster[7] over the scratches and bruises on his features. There was a fire burning behind the big rock at the entrance of the cave, and the boy was watching a pot of boiling coffee, with two buzzard tail-feathers stuck in his red hair. He points a stick at me when I come up, and says:

"Ha! cursed paleface, do you dare to enter the camp of Red Chief, the terror of the plains?"

"He's all right now," says Bill, rolling up his trousers and examining some bruises on his shins. "We're playing Indian. We're making Buffalo Bill's show look like magic-lantern views of Palestine in the town hall.[8] I'm Old Hank, the Trapper, Red Chief's captive, and I'm to be scalped at daybreak. By Geronimo! that kid can kick hard."

Yes, sir, that boy seemed to be having the time of his life. The fun of camping out in a cave had made him forget that he was a captive himself. He immediately christened me Snake-eye, the Spy, and announced that, when his braves returned from the warpath, I was to be broiled at the stake at the rising of the sun.

Then we had supper; and he filled his mouth full of bacon and bread and gravy, and began to talk. He made a during-dinner speech something like this:

"I like this fine. I never camped out before; but I had a pet 'possum once, and

7. Like a modern adhesive bandage, *court-plaster* is cloth coated with a sticky substance and used to protect minor wounds.

8. Bill thinks the boy's rough role-playing makes a Wild West frontier show seem as tame and boring as a slide show about a foreign land.

I was nine last birthday. I hate to go to school. Rats ate up sixteen of Jimmy Talbot's aunt's speckled hen's eggs. Are there any real Indians in these woods? I want some more gravy. Does the trees moving make the wind blow? We had five puppies. What makes your nose so red, Hank? My father has lots of money. Are the stars hot? I whipped Ed Walker twice, Saturday. I don't like girls. You dassent catch toads unless with a string. Do oxen make any noise? Why are oranges round? Have you got beds to sleep on in this cave? Amos Murray has got six toes. A parrot can talk, but a monkey or a fish can't. How many does it take to make twelve?"

Every few minutes he would remember that he was a pesky redskin, and pick up his stick rifle and tiptoe to the mouth of the cave to rubber[9] for the scouts of the hated paleface. Now and then he would let out a war-whoop that made Old Hank the Trapper shiver. That boy had Bill terrorized from the start.

Part of the Game. Karl Witkowski (1860–1910). Oil on canvas, 24 x 20 in. Private collection.

Viewing the painting: Do you think the boy in this painting would get along with Red Chief? Why or why not?

"Red Chief," says I to the kid, "would you like to go home?"

"Aw, what for?" says he. "I don't have any fun at home. I hate to go to school. I like to camp out. You won't take me back home again, Snake-eye, will you?"

"Not right away," says I. "We'll stay here in the cave a while."

"All right!" says he. "That'll be fine. I never had such fun in all my life."

We went to bed about eleven o'clock. We spread down some wide blankets and quilts and put Red Chief between us. We weren't afraid he'd run away. He kept us awake for three hours, jumping up and reaching for his rifle and screeching: "Hist! pard," in mine and Bill's ears, as the fancied crackle of a twig or the rustle of a leaf revealed to his young imagination the stealthy approach of the outlaw band. At last, I fell into a troubled sleep, and dreamed that I had been kidnapped and chained to a tree by a ferocious pirate with red hair.

Just at daybreak, I was awakened by a series of awful screams from Bill. They

9. *Rubber* is short for *rubberneck,* which means "to look with exaggerated curiosity."

weren't yells, or howls, or shouts, or whoops, or yawps, such as you'd expect from a manly set of vocal organs—they were simply indecent, terrifying, humiliating screams, such as women emit when they see ghosts or caterpillars. It's an awful thing to hear a strong, desperate, fat man scream incontinently[10] in a cave at daybreak.

I jumped up to see what the matter was. Red Chief was sitting on Bill's chest, with one hand twined in Bill's hair. In the other he had the sharp case-knife we used for slicing bacon; and he was industriously and realistically trying to take Bill's scalp, according to the sentence that had been pronounced upon him the evening before.

I got the knife away from the kid and made him lie down again. But, from that moment, Bill's spirit was broken. He laid down on his side of the bed, but he never closed an eye again in sleep as long as that boy was with us. I dozed off for a while, but along toward sun-up I remembered that Red Chief had said I was to be burned at the stake at the rising of the sun. I wasn't nervous or afraid; but I sat up and lit my pipe and leaned against a rock.

"What you getting up so soon for, Sam?" asked Bill.

"Me?" says I. "Oh, I got a kind of a pain in my shoulder. I thought sitting up would rest it."

"You're a liar!" says Bill. "You're afraid. You was to be burned at sunrise, and you was afraid he'd do it. And he would, too, if he could find a match. Ain't it awful, Sam? Do you think anybody will pay out money to get a little imp like that back home?"

"Sure," said I. "A rowdy kid like that is just the kind that parents dote on. Now, you and the Chief get up and cook breakfast, while I go up on the top of this mountain and reconnoitre."

I went up on the peak of the little mountain and ran my eye over the contiguous vicinity. Over toward Summit I expected to see the sturdy yeomanry of the village armed with scythes and pitchforks beating the countryside for the dastardly[11] kidnappers. But what I saw was a peaceful landscape dotted with one man ploughing with a dun mule. Nobody was dragging the creek; no couriers dashed hither and yon, bringing tidings of no news to the distracted parents. There was a sylvan attitude of somnolent sleepiness pervading[12] that section of the external outward surface of Alabama that lay exposed to my view. "Perhaps," says I to myself, "it has not yet been discovered that the wolves have borne away the tender lambkin from the fold. Heaven help the wolves!" says I, and I went down the mountain to breakfast.

When I got to the cave I found Bill backed up against the side of it, breathing hard, and the boy threatening to smash him with a rock half as big as a coconut.

10. *Incontinently* means "uncontrollably."

11. When Sam *reconnoiters* the *contiguous vicinity,* he surveys the area. He expects to see farmers *(yeomanry)* pursuing the mean, sneaky, cowardly *(dastardly)* kidnappers.

12. What Sam sees are peaceful woods. *Sylvan* means "in or among trees." *Somnolent* means "sleepy," and *pervading* means "spreading throughout."

Vocabulary

emit (i mit′) *v.* to utter; send forth or give out, as a sound

dote (dōt) *v.* to show extreme affection

"He put a red-hot boiled potato down my back," explained Bill, "and then mashed it with his foot; and I boxed his ears. Have you got a gun about you, Sam?"

I took the rock away from the boy and kind of patched up the argument. "I'll fix you," says the kid to Bill. "No man ever yet struck the Red Chief but what he got paid for it. You better beware!"

After breakfast the kid takes a piece of leather with strings wrapped around it out of his pocket and goes outside the cave unwinding it.

"What's he up to now?" says Bill, anxiously. "You don't think he'll run away, do you, Sam?"

"No fear of it," says I. "He don't seem to be much of a homebody. But we've got to fix up some plan about the ransom. There don't seem to be much excitement around Summit on account of his disappearance; but maybe they haven't realized yet that he's gone. His folks may think he's spending the night with Aunt Jane or one of the neighbors. Anyhow, he'll be missed today. Tonight we must get a message to his father demanding the two thousand dollars for his return."

Just then we heard a kind of war whoop, such as David might have emitted when he knocked out the champion Goliath.[13] It was a sling that Red Chief had pulled out of his pocket, and he was whirling it around his head.

I dodged, and heard a heavy thud and a kind of a sigh from Bill, like a horse gives when you take his saddle off. A rock the size of an egg had caught Bill just behind his left ear. He loosened himself all over and fell in the fire across the frying pan of hot water for washing the dishes. I dragged him out and poured cold water on his head for half an hour.

By and by, Bill sits up and feels behind his ear and says: "Sam, do you know who my favorite Biblical character is?"

"Take it easy," says I. "You'll come to your senses presently."

"King Herod,"[14] says he. "You won't go away and leave me here alone, will you, Sam?"

I went out and caught that boy and shook him until his freckles rattled.

"If you don't behave," says I, "I'll take you straight home. Now, are you going to be good, or not?"

"I was only funning," says he sullenly. "I didn't mean to hurt Old Hank. But what did he hit me for? I'll behave, Snake-eye, if you won't send me home, and if you'll let me play the Black Scout today."

"I don't know the game," says I. "That's for you and Mr. Bill to decide. He's your playmate for the day. I'm going away for a while, on business. Now, you come in and make friends with him and say you are sorry for hurting him, or home you go, at once."

I made him and Bill shake hands, and then I took Bill aside and told him I was going to Poplar Cove, a little village three miles from the cave, and find out what I could about how the kidnapping had been regarded in Summit. Also, I thought it best to send a peremptory letter to old

13. In the Bible story, the boy *David* kills the giant *Goliath* with a stone shot from a sling.

14. In this Bible story, *King Herod* orders the murder of all Hebrew male infants in an effort to kill the child Jesus.

Vocabulary

peremptory (pə remp′ tər ē) *adj.* allowing no refusal

man Dorset that day, demanding the ransom and dictating how it should be paid.

"You know, Sam," says Bill, "I've stood by you without batting an eye in earthquakes, fire and flood—in poker games, dynamite outrages, police raids, train robberies, and cyclones. I never lost my nerve yet till we kidnapped that two-legged skyrocket of a kid. He's got me going. You won't leave me long with him, will you, Sam?"

"I'll be back some time this afternoon," says I. "You must keep the boy amused and quiet till I return. And now we'll write the letter to old Dorset."

Bill and I got paper and pencil and worked on the letter while Red Chief, with a blanket wrapped around him, strutted up and down, guarding the mouth of the cave. Bill begged me tearfully to make the ransom fifteen hundred dollars instead of two thousand. "I ain't attempting," says he, "to decry the celebrated moral aspect of parental affection, but we're dealing with humans, and it ain't human for anybody to give up two thousand dollars for that forty-pound chunk of freckled wildcat. I'm willing to take a chance at fifteen hundred dollars. You can charge the difference up to me."

So, to relieve Bill, I acceded, and we collaborated a letter that ran this way:

Ebenezer Dorset, Esq.:[15]

We have your boy concealed in a place far from Summit. It is useless for you or the most skillful detectives to attempt to find him. Absolutely, the only terms on which you can have him restored to you are these: We demand fifteen hundred dollars in large bills for his return; the money to be left at midnight tonight at the same spot and in the same box as your reply—as hereinafter described. If you agree to these terms, send your answer in writing by a solitary messenger tonight at half past eight o'clock. After crossing Owl Creek, on the road to Poplar Cove, there are three large trees about a hundred yards apart, close to the fence of the wheat field on the right-hand side. At the bottom of the fence post, opposite the third tree, will be found a small pasteboard box.

The messenger will place the answer in this box and return immediately to Summit.

If you attempt any treachery or fail to comply with our demand as stated, you will never see your boy again.

If you pay the money as demanded, he will be returned to you safe and well within three hours. These terms are final, and if you do not accede to them no further communication will be attempted.

Two Desperate Men.

I addressed this letter to Dorset, and put it in my pocket. As I was about to start, the kid comes up to me and says:

"Aw, Snake-eye, you said I could play the Black Scout while you was gone."

15. To *accede* (ak sēd′) is to yield and agree to. To *collaborate* (kə lab′ ə rāt′) is to work with another or others. The abbreviation *Esq.* is short for *esquire,* a title of respect or courtesy for a man.

Vocabulary

decry (di krī′) *v.* to criticize openly

comply (kəm plī′) *v.* to obey or go along with a request

"Play it, of course," says I. "Mr. Bill will play with you. What kind of a game is it?"

"I'm the Black Scout," says Red Chief, "and I have to ride to the stockade to warn the settlers that the Indians are coming. I'm tired of playing Indian myself. I want to be the Black Scout."

"All right," says I. "It sounds harmless to me. I guess Mr. Bill will help you foil the pesky savages."

"What am I to do?" asks Bill, looking at the kid suspiciously.

"You are the hoss," says Black Scout. "Get down on your hands and knees. How can I ride to the stockade without a hoss?"

"You'd better keep him interested," said I, "till we get the scheme going. Loosen up."

Bill gets down on his all fours, and a look comes in his eye like a rabbit's when you catch it in a trap.

"How far is it to the stockade, kid?" he asks, in a husky manner of voice.

"Ninety miles," says the Black Scout. "And you have to hump yourself to get there on time. Whoa, now!"

The Black Scout jumps on Bill's back and digs his heels in his side.

"For Heaven's sake," says Bill, "hurry back, Sam, as soon as you can. I wish we hadn't made the ransom more than a thousand. Say, you quit kicking me or I'll get up and warm you good."

I walked over to Poplar Cove and sat around the post office and store, talking with the chawbacons that came in to trade. One whiskerando[16] says that he hears Summit is all upset on account of Elder Ebenezer Dorset's boy having been lost or stolen. That was all I wanted to know. I bought some smoking tobacco, referred casually to the price of black-eyed peas, posted my letter surreptitiously and came away. The postmaster said the mail carrier would come by in an hour to take the mail on to Summit.

When I got back to the cave Bill and the boy were not to be found. I explored the vicinity of the cave, and risked a yodel or two, but there was no response.

So I lighted my pipe and sat down on a mossy bank to await developments.

In about half an hour I heard the bushes rustle, and Bill wabbled out into the little glade in front of the cave. Behind him was the kid, stepping softly like a scout, with a broad grin on his face. Bill stopped, took off his hat and wiped his face with a red handkerchief. The kid stopped about eight feet behind him.

"Sam," says Bill, "I suppose you'll think I'm a renegade, but I couldn't help it. I'm a grown person with masculine proclivities and habits of self-defense, but there is a time when all systems of egotism and predominance[17] fail. The boy is gone. I have sent him home. All is off. There was martyrs in old times," goes on Bill, "that suffered death rather than give up the particular graft they enjoyed. None of 'em ever was subjugated to such supernatural tortures as I have

16. *Chawbacons* are the men sitting around chewing tobacco. A *whiskerando* is an old-timer, especially one with whiskers.

17. Bill really shows off his vocabulary here. *Proclivities* are tendencies. *Egotism* is an exaggerated sense of self-importance. *Predominance* is using one's superior power or influence to control others.

Vocabulary

renegade (ren′ ə gād′) *n.* one who abandons or turns against a group, cause, or allegiance; traitor been. I tried to be faithful to our articles of depredation;[18] but there came a limit."

"What's the trouble, Bill?" I asks him.

"I was rode," says Bill, "the ninety miles to the stockade, not barring an inch. Then, when the settlers was rescued, I was given oats. Sand ain't a palatable substitute. And then, for an hour I had to try to explain to him why there was nothin' in holes, how a road can run both ways, and what makes the grass green. I tell you, Sam, a human can only stand so much. I takes him by the neck of his clothes and drags him down the mountain. On the way he kicks my legs black-and-blue from the knees down; and I've got to have two or three bites on my thumb and hand cauterized.

"But he's gone"—continues Bill—"gone home. I showed him the road to Summit and kicked him about eight feet nearer there at one kick. I'm sorry we lose the ransom; but it was either that or Bill Driscoll to the madhouse."

Bill is puffing and blowing, but there is a look of ineffable[19] peace and growing content on his rose-pink features.

"Bill," says I, "there isn't any heart disease in your family, is there?"

"No," says Bill, "nothing chronic except malaria and accidents. Why?"

"Then you might turn around," says I, "and have a look behind you."

Bill turns and sees the boy, and loses his complexion and sits down plump on the ground and begins to pluck aimlessly at grass and little sticks. For an hour I was afraid of his mind. And then I told him that my scheme was to put the whole job through immediately and that we would get the ransom and be off with it by midnight if old Dorset fell in with our proposition. So Bill braced up enough to give the kid a weak sort of a smile and a promise to play the Russian in a Japanese war[20] with him as soon as he felt a little better.

I had a scheme for collecting that ransom without danger of being caught by counterplots that ought to commend itself to professional kidnappers. The tree under which the answer was to be left—and the money later on—was close to the road fence with big, bare fields on all sides. If a gang of constables should be watching for any one to come for the note they could see him a long way off crossing the fields or in the road. But no, sirree! At half past eight I was up in that tree as well hidden as a tree toad, waiting for the messenger to arrive.

Exactly on time, a half-grown boy rides up the road on a bicycle, locates the pasteboard box at the foot of the fence post, slips a folded piece of paper into it and pedals away again back toward Summit.

I waited an hour and then concluded the thing was square. I slid down the tree, got the note, slipped along the fence till I struck the woods, and was back at the cave in another half an hour. I opened the note, got near the lantern and read it to Bill. It was written with a pen in a crabbed hand, and the sum and substance of it was this:

18. *Martyrs* are those who suffer or die for a cause. *Graft,* here, refers to money gained dishonestly. *Subjugated* means "forced to undergo an unpleasant experience." *Articles of depredation* are Sam and Bill's rules for robbing people.

19. *Ineffable* means "indescribable" or "unspeakable."

20. In 1905 mighty Russia suffered a humiliating defeat by the less-powerful Japan.

Vocabulary

palatable (pal′ ə tə bəl) *adj.* agreeable to the taste, mind, or feelings; acceptable

Two Desperate Men.

Gentlemen: I received your letter today by post, in regard to the ransom you ask for the return of my son. I think you are a little high in your demands, and I hereby make you a counter-proposition, which I am inclined to believe you will accept. You bring Johnny home and pay me two hundred and fifty dollars in cash, and I agree to take him off your hands. You had better come at night, for the neighbors believe he is lost, and I couldn't be responsible for what they would do to anybody they saw bringing him back. Very respectfully,

EBENEZER DORSET.

"Great pirates of Penzance!"[21] says I; "of all the impudent——"

But I glanced at Bill, and hesitated. He had the most appealing look in his eyes I ever saw on the face of a dumb or a talking brute.

"Sam," says he, "what's two hundred and fifty dollars, after all? We've got the money. One more night of this kid will send me to a bed in Bedlam. Besides being a thorough gentleman, I think Mr. Dorset is a spendthrift[22] for making us such a liberal offer. You ain't going to let the chance go, are you?"

"Tell you the truth, Bill," says I, "this little he ewe lamb has somewhat got on my nerves too. We'll take him home, pay the ransom, and make our getaway."

We took him home that night. We got him to go by telling him that his father had bought a silver-mounted rifle and a pair of moccasins for him, and we were going to hunt bears the next day.

It was just twelve o'clock when we knocked at Ebenezer's front door. Just at the moment when I should have been abstracting[23] the fifteen hundred dollars from the box under the tree, according to the original proposition, Bill was counting out two hundred and fifty dollars into Dorset's hand.

When the kid found out we were going to leave him at home he started up a howl like a calliope and fastened himself as tight as a leech to Bill's leg. His father peeled him away gradually, like a porous plaster.

"How long can you hold him?" asks Bill.

"I'm not as strong as I used to be," says old Dorset, "but I think I can promise you ten minutes."

"Enough," says Bill. "In ten minutes I shall cross the Central, Southern, and Middle Western States, and be legging it trippingly for the Canadian border."

And, as dark as it was, and as fat as Bill was, and as good a runner as I am, he was a good mile and a half out of Summit before I could catch up with him.

21. *The Pirates of Penzance* is an 1879 comic opera in which the pirates have a difficult and silly time trying to carry out a kidnapping.

22. *Bedlam* was an English hospital for the mentally ill. A *spendthrift* is one who spends money either generously or wastefully.

23. Here, *abstracting* means "removing or taking away secretly."

Vocabulary

impudent (im′ pyə dənt) *adj.* boldly discourteous

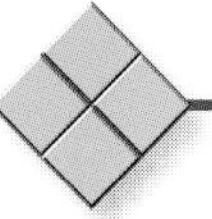

Responding to Literature

PERSONAL RESPONSE

How did your impression of the boy change from the beginning of the story to the end? Compare the boy with the list of characteristics you made in the **Focus Activity** on page 337.

Analyzing Literature

RECALL

1. Why do Bill and Sam decide to stage a kidnapping? Why do they choose Summit for their caper?
2. Describe the kidnapped boy.
3. When does Bill give up on the kidnapping plan? Why does he want to ask for less ransom money?
4. How does the boy's father respond to the ransom letter?

INTERPRET

5. Why does Bill say that the kidnapping plan struck them at a moment when they weren't thinking clearly?
6. Why don't the kidnappers worry that the boy might run away?
7. Why does the **narrator** say "Heaven help the wolves" after seeing no signs of anyone looking for the kidnapped boy?
8. Why do the men sign their ransom letter "Two Desperate Men"?

EVALUATE AND CONNECT

9. Theme Connection How many mischief makers are in this story? Which person do you think is the most mischievous? Explain.
10. How does O. Henry portray the crime of kidnapping in this story? What makes this treatment different from real-life kidnappings you know of or have read about?

LITERARY ELEMENTS

Suspense

Suspense is the growing anxiety and excitement that a reader feels as the plot of a story unfolds. Suspense draws readers toward the ending of a story. O. Henry uses suspense in an unusual way: he leads his readers to a likely climax, then presents them with a surprise outcome. O. Henry's fans read to see *how* the writer will use suspense to twist the ending, not *whether* he will come through with a surprise.

1. Find some examples of suspense in "The Ransom of Red Chief." How does O. Henry build interest in the upcoming events?
2. How does O. Henry use suspense to make his ending more of a surprise?

• See **Literary Terms Handbook,** p. R10.

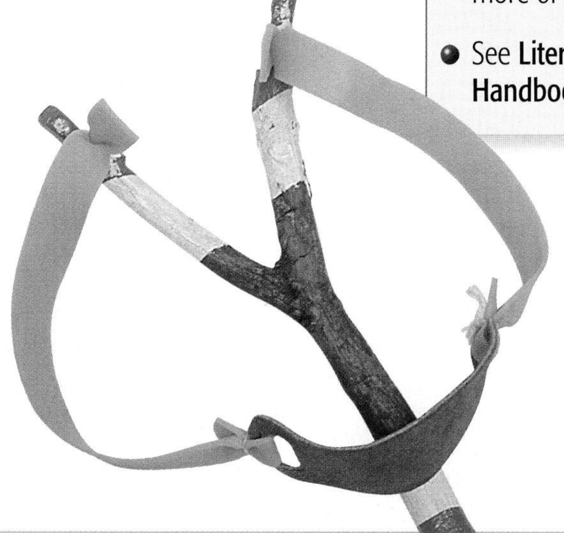

Literature and Writing

Writing About Literature

What's Funny? Find three humorous excerpts in "The Ransom of Red Chief," and write a short paragraph for each to explain the humor. Is the description of the event funny? Is the event itself humorous? Do the words, dialogue, or sentence structure tickle your funny bone?

Creative Writing

Surprise! Choose another short story, a fairy tale, or a young children's book that has a predictable ending. Compose an alternate ending that readers would find surprising. Include a notation of what might need to be added or changed in the first part of the story to make the new ending reasonable.

Extending Your Response

Learning for Life

Play Time! Many of O. Henry's stories were later produced as plays or movies. Plan a modern production of "The Ransom of Red Chief." Describe the setting and characters, and select actors to play each of the main roles.

interNET CONNECTION

To visit the O. Henry Museum, type "O. Henry Home and Museum" into a search engine. What interesting facts about O. Henry do you discover on the Internet? Compare the information you find with that of your classmates.

Literature Groups

What People Say O. Henry uses **dialogue** to characterize Bill and Sam. For example, Bill often confuses one big word for another, which makes him seem funny and somewhat foolish. Choose about ten lines of dialogue from the story to read aloud in your group.

Discuss the word choices and the tone O. Henry uses to show what kind of characters Bill and Sam are. Then, take turns role-playing a conversation that might take place between Bill and Sam after the boy goes home. Imitate the tone and types of word choices the men use.

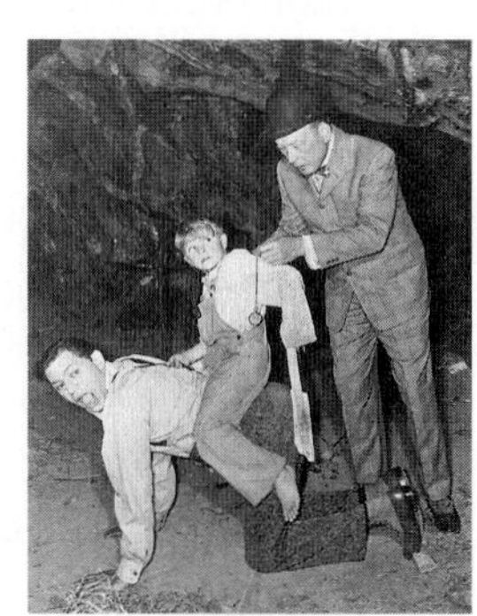

O'Henry's Full House. Twentieth Century Fox. Movie still.

Reading Further

For other stories of unusual situations, read:

Kidnapped by Robert Louis Stevenson

Crow and Weasel by Barry Holstun Lopez

Save your work for your portfolio.

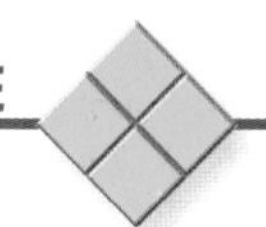

Skill Minilessons

GRAMMAR AND LANGUAGE • COLORFUL WORDS

O. Henry's ability to surprise the reader with just the right word–sometimes one he makes up–is unrivaled. This element of surprise is one technique the writer uses to create humor. In "The Ransom of Red Chief," the characters often use unusual adjectives and nouns or words–dialect the reader would not expect ordinary people to use.

PRACTICE Find the following words or phrases in the story, and explain their meaning. Suggest a more common word or phrase that might have been used.

1. "respectable and tight" (p. 338)
2. "dassent catch toads" (p. 340)
3. "imp like that" (p. 341)
4. "boxed his ears" (p. 342)

READING AND THINKING • VERIFYING PREDICTIONS

Readers often predict the subject and mood of a story based on the title, illustrations, or ideas they already have about a type of character. Readers also make predictions as they read, using clues in the story.

- For more about verifying predictions, see **Reading Handbook,** p. R85.

PRACTICE Look at the notes you made in the **Focus Activity** on page 337. Identify five places in "The Ransom of Red Chief" where you think the boy's appearance and behavior match the child you described. Then explain how the character differed from your idea of a nine- or ten-year-old.

VOCABULARY • DICTIONARY SKILLS: DEFINITIONS

If a word is unfamiliar to you, you can look it up in a dictionary. However, most words have several meanings, and the first definition in the dictionary may not be the one you need. Look for the meaning that relates to how the word was used in what you read or heard. Here is a typical set of meanings for the word *prominent.*

prom·i·nent *adj.* **1.** well-known or important: *a prominent politician.* **2.** very noticeable; obvious: *The tower is a prominent feature of the town.* **3.** sticking out or standing out from a surface: *a prominent chin.*

PRACTICE Decide which of the meanings of *prominent* is used in each sentence below, and write the number of the meaning.

1. Elvis Presley was a *prominent* musician.
2. Many prehistoric humans had *prominent* foreheads.
3. Uncle Fred is a *prominent* member of the golf club.
4. The picture was hung in a *prominent* place in the living room.
5. A tiger's stripes are less *prominent* than a zebra's.

Before You Read

John Henry and from *The People, Yes*

MEET CARL SANDBURG

Imagine a great American writer standing before an audience and singing folk songs. The writer, Carl Sandburg, was better known for his stories, biographies, and poems, but he also collected and sang folk music. His long poem "The People, Yes" celebrates the power of ordinary people to move forward in spite of hard times, just as folk heroes like John Henry did. Sandburg once said that all he wanted was "to eat regular, . . . to get what I write printed, . . . a little love at home . . . [and] to sing every day."

Carl Sandburg was born in 1878 and died in 1967. "The People, Yes" was first published in 1936.

FOCUS ACTIVITY

Think of a story you have heard about a person who accomplished something in spite of difficulties.

Plan It!
Jot down details from one or two of the stories you recall.

Setting a Purpose
Read to discover some colorful characters and stories that are part of American culture.

BACKGROUND

The Time and Place Many stories about the United States date back to the 1800s, when large numbers of Europeans and Americans from the East Coast began moving westward. Construction of railroads during this century brought new opportunities for some and the destruction of a way of life for others.

Did You Know? Many stories have been told about the crews that laid railroad tracks across the western United States. These workers, many of whom drove the steel spikes that held together the rails and ties, accomplished an amazing task. In the 1850s, track mileage in the United States increased by more than 20,000 miles. John Henry is the name of a hero said to be the greatest steel driver of all.

JOHN HENRY

Anonymous

"Big Bend — Tun-nel on the C. and O. — 'Road,

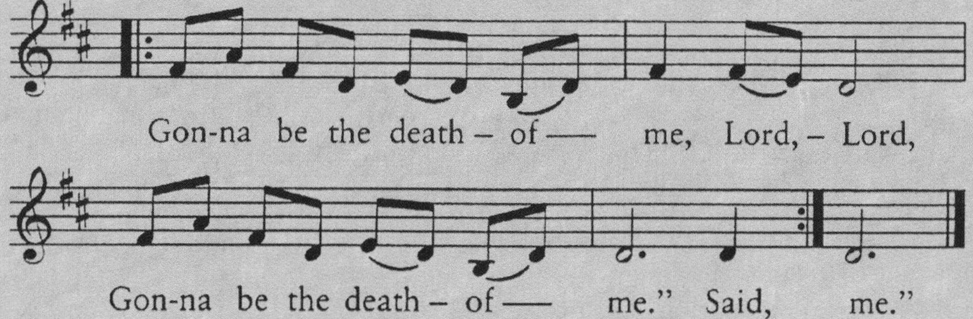
Gon-na be the death – of — me, Lord, – Lord,
Gon-na be the death – of — me." Said, me."

When John Henry was a little baby,
Settin' on his mammy's knee,
Said, "Big Bend Tunnel on the C. and O. 'Road,°
Gonna be the death of me, Lord, Lord,
Gonna be the death of me."

Now John Henry had a little woman,
Her name was Polly Ann,
When John Henry took sick and had to go to bed,
Polly Ann drove steel° like a man, Lord, Lord,
Polly Ann drove steel like a man!

The captain said to John Henry,
"I'm gonna bring that steel drill 'round,
I'm gonna bring that steel drill out on the job,
Gonna whop that steel on down, Lord, Lord,
Gonna whop that steel on down."

---

3 *C. and O. 'Road* is short for "Chesapeake and Ohio Railroad."

9 When John Henry and Polly Ann *drove steel,* they used a ten-pound hammer to pound a steel stake, called a drill, into rock to make holes for explosives.

Well, John Henry said to his captain,
"Lord, a man ain't nothin' but
a man,
But before I let your steam drill beat
me down,
I'll die with a hammer in my hand,
Lord, Lord,
I'll die with a hammer in my hand."

John Henry said to his shaker,°
"Shaker, you'd better pray,
If my hammer misses that little piece
of steel,
Tomorrow'll be your buryin' day,
Lord, Lord,
Tomorrow'll be your buryin' day."

Now the captain said to John Henry,
"I believe this mountain's sinkin' in."
John Henry just laughed at his
captain and he said,
"Ain't nothin' but my hammer
suckin' wind, Lord, Lord,
Ain't nothin' but my hammer suckin'
wind."

John Henry said to his shaker,
"Shaker, why don't you sing?
I'm throwin' twenty pounds from my
hips on down,
Just listen to that cold steel ring,
Lord, Lord,
Just listen to that cold steel ring."

Now the man that invented the
steam drill,
He thought he was mighty fine,
But John Henry drove fourteen feet,
And the steam drill only made nine,
Lord, Lord,
And the steam drill only made nine.

John Henry hammered on the
mountain,
And his hammer was striking fire,
But he drove so hard that he broke
his poor heart,
And he laid down his hammer and he
died, Lord, Lord,
He laid down his hammer and he
died.

John Henry had a little baby,
He could hold him in the palm of his
hand,
And the last words I heard that poor
boy say,
"My daddy was a steel-drivin' man,
Lord, Lord,
My daddy was a steel-drivin' man."

Well, they took John Henry to the
tunnel,
And they buried him in the sand,
Every locomotive comes rollin' by
Says, "There lies a steel-drivin' man,
Lord, Lord,
There lies a steel-drivin' man."

So every Monday morning,
When the bluebirds begin to sing,
You can hear those hammers a mile
or more,
You can hear John Henry's hammer
ring, Lord, Lord,
You can hear John Henry's hammer
ring.

21 A *shaker* held the steel drill steady while the steel driver hammered it and then shook the drill to free it from the rock.

Untitled, 1994. Illustration by Terry Small. From *The Legend of John Henry.*
Viewing the art: How does this image show John Henry's strength and endurance?

from

The People, Yes

Carl Sandburg

They have yarns
Of a skyscraper so tall they had to put hinges
On the two top stories so to let the moon go by,
Of one corn crop in Missouri when the roots
Went so deep and drew off so much water
The Mississippi riverbed that year was dry,
Of pancakes so thin they had only one side,
Of "a fog so thick we shingled the barn and six feet out on the fog,"
Of Pecos Pete straddling a cyclone in Texas and riding it to the west coast where "it rained out under him,"
Of the man who drove a swarm of bees across the Rocky Mountains and the Desert "and didn't lose a bee,"
Of a mountain railroad curve where the engineer in his cab can touch the caboose and spit in the conductor's eye,
Of the boy who climbed a cornstalk growing so fast he would have starved to death if they hadn't shot biscuits up to him,
Of the old man's whiskers: "When the wind was with him his whiskers arrived a day before he did,"
Of the hen laying a square egg and cackling, "Ouch!" and of hens laying eggs with the dates printed on them,
Of the ship captain's shadow: it froze to the deck one cold winter night,
Of mutineers° on that same ship put to chipping rust with rubber hammers,

16 The *mutineers* are sailors who have openly rebelled against their commanding officers. Their punishment is a nearly impossible task, something like being forced to remove all the paint from the side of a house, using only a sponge.

Of the sheep counter who was fast and accurate: "I just count their feet and divide by four,"
Of the man so tall he must climb a ladder to shave himself,
Of the runt so teeny-weeny it takes two men and a boy to see him,
Of mosquitoes: one can kill a dog, two of them a man,
Of a cyclone that sucked cookstoves out of the kitchen, up the chimney flue, and on to the next town,
Of the same cyclone picking up wagon-tracks in Nebraska and dropping them over in the Dakotas,
Of the hook-and-eye snake unlocking itself into forty pieces, each piece two inches long, then in nine seconds flat snapping itself together again,
Of the watch swallowed by the cow—when they butchered her a year later the watch was running and had the correct time,
Of horned snakes, hoop snakes that roll themselves where they want to go, and rattlesnakes carrying bells instead of rattles on their tails,
Of the herd of cattle in California getting lost in a giant redwood tree that had hollowed out,
Of the man who killed a snake by putting its tail in its mouth so it swallowed itself,
Of railroad trains whizzing along so fast they reach the station before the whistle,
Of pigs so thin the farmer had to tie knots in their tails to keep them from crawling through the cracks in their pens,
Of Paul Bunyan's big blue ox, Babe, measuring between the eyes forty-two ax-handles and a plug of Star tobacco exactly,
Of John Henry's hammer and the curve of its swing and his singing of it as "a rainbow round my shoulder."

Responding to Literature

PERSONAL RESPONSE

Did you find these poems funny, serious, or both? Explain.

Analyzing Literature

RECALL

1. Who was John Henry? What details in the poem tell about his life and death?
2. What kinds of yarns does Carl Sandburg tell in this excerpt from "The People, Yes"?

INTERPRET

3. What is the conflict, or challenge, that John Henry faces? Why does he choose to deal with the conflict in the way that he does?
4. What effect does Sandburg create by repeating one yarn after another?

EVALUATE AND CONNECT

5. Based on your reading of "John Henry," what might the "rainbow round my shoulder" from Sandburg's poem mean?
6. What do Pecos Pete, Paul Bunyan, and John Henry have in common? How are they different?
7. What, if anything, do you learn from "John Henry" about the life of frontier people who laid track in the wilderness?
8. Might Carl Sandburg, in your opinion, have enjoyed singing the ballad "John Henry"? Support your opinion with excerpts from Sandburg's poem.
9. How would you describe the picture Carl Sandburg creates of the United States?
10. How does the author of "John Henry" **foreshadow,** or give clues to the reader, that John Henry will die in the end?

LITERARY ELEMENTS

Ballad

A **ballad** is a narrative song, a song that tells a story. It may describe an important event or a hero. Ballads are passed from one generation to another, often in musical form. Because people learned the stories by listening to singers, ballads often are divided into short stanzas to make them easy to memorize. Many use repeated words and phrases and a regular rhyme scheme, or pattern. For example, in many ballads, the first and third lines rhyme, and the second and last lines rhyme.

1. Look at the first and final stanzas of "John Henry." Describe the rhyme scheme.
2. In "The People, Yes," Carl Sandburg refers to events and people who might appear in older ballads. List five such references.

● See **Literary Terms Handbook,** p. R1.

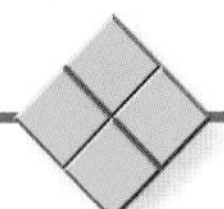

Extending Your Response

Writing About Literature

Describing the Plot Because a ballad tells a story, it must have a **plot,** or sequence of events. Write a paragraph or two summarizing the plot of "John Henry." Be sure to introduce the characters, the setting, and the conflict. Then describe the events. Explain how the conflict is resolved, and note what happens at the end of the story.

Creative Writing

Telling Your Story Carl Sandburg's ideas for "The People, Yes" came from observing and talking to people across the United States. Use your notes from the **Focus Activity** on page 350 to write several lines that Sandburg might have added to "The People, Yes" if he had spoken with you.

Literature Groups

Silly or Serious? The Sandburg poem has been characterized as "a series of one liners"–short, funny jokes–and as "a serious panorama of America." Which description do you think is more accurate? Discuss your opinion and reasons. Share your conclusions with the class.

Performing

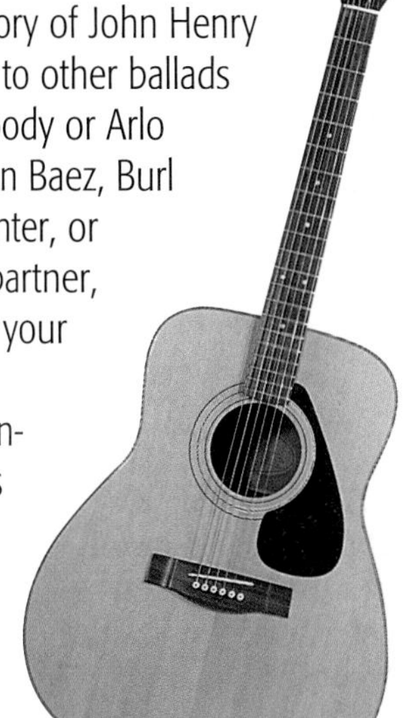

Song of a Hero The story of John Henry is told as a ballad. Listen to other ballads by such musicians as Woody or Arlo Guthrie, Pete Seeger, Joan Baez, Burl Ives, Mary Chapin Carpenter, or Michael Doucet. With a partner, choose a song you think your classmates should know about. Give a brief presentation about the song–its theme, place of origin, and musicians who have presented it. Then play a recording of the music or perform it for the class.

Reading Further

For another view of storytelling, try:
The Story Catcher by Mari Sandoz

Save your work for your portfolio.

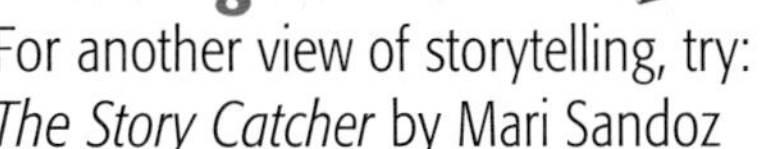

Skill Minilesson

GRAMMAR AND LANGUAGE • PROPER NOUNS

A **proper noun** is the name of a person, place, thing, or idea. Proper nouns always begin with a capital letter. The Sandburg poem contains many proper nouns, such as the names of states in the United States. The proper nouns in the poem help to establish it as an "all-American" work.

PRACTICE There are twelve proper nouns in the Sandburg poem. Find them, and identify the proper nouns as people, places, things, or ideas.

- For more about proper nouns, see **Language Handbook,** p. R30.

FOLKTALE

Long before caped crusaders and animated trouble-makers began entertaining audiences in the movies and on TV, people amused themselves by telling stories. They passed along **folktales,** anonymous stories meant to entertain listeners and to keep ideas and customs alive from generation to generation. Today you can find old tales and songs from many cultures retold in books, in the movies, and on television. Myths, tall tales, legends, fables, and fairy tales are kinds of folktales. In all of these you will find some of the following elements.

SETTING **The setting, if it is mentioned at all, is described quickly and without much detail. You learn only what you need to know to go on with the story. (In this folktale, there is a fast, wide river with a market on one side and a town on the other.)**

MODEL: from "Fox, Alligator, and Rabbit"

Once there was a fast, wide river. On one side stood a market and on the other a town. So to get to the market from the town, you had to cross the river. But—and this was a mighty big "but"—in the middle of the river was Alligator. Now, alligators have their own special way of letting you know they're around—they try and eat you. One day Fox and Rabbit wanted to cross the river to the market. Rabbit was working on some kind of a plan. "Say, Fox," he says, "Is it true you foxes are known for being just about the smartest, cleverest creatures around?"

"Yep," says Fox.

"Then hows about you taking me across the river?"

STYLE **The words and phrases in some folktales reflect the speaking style of the teller. The style, or manner of expression, is often conversational and informal. (This folktale has a breezy, informal style, reflecting how a good-natured storyteller would have told it.)**

THEME **The theme of a folktale is usually a lesson about human nature that all people can appreciate. (In the model, Rabbit wants to cross the river and tricks Fox into helping him. Later, Rabbit cannot get back because Fox won't be taken in twice. The theme: if you use others, you may not always get what you want.)**

CHARACTERS AND CONFLICT **Characters in folktales may be people or talking animals. They are usually simple folk with everyday problems or conflicts. (In the model, Rabbit needs help to get across a river.) Sometimes, however, they have exaggerated abilities or personality traits.**

ACTIVE READING MODEL

Active Reading Strategies

Tips for Reading Folktales

Each kind of reading requires slightly different skills. For example, when you read a bus schedule, you need to scan for data. With poetry, you need to listen to the sounds of the poem and take time to visualize the images. When you read a folktale, the following techniques will make you a better reader.

- For more about reading strategies, see **Reading Handbook,** pp. R84–R97.

QUESTION

As you read, focus on what you don't understand and what you want to know more about.

Ask Yourself . . . Do I understand what is happening so far? Why don't I trust this character?

PREDICT

Use clues to guess what might happen next.

Ask Yourself . . . Based on the style in the first paragraph, will this tale be humorous or serious? What will the character do to overcome this problem? Then check your predictions.

CONNECT

Folktales stay popular because readers see themselves in the stories.

Ask Yourself . . . Would I react as the character does? Keep track of your thoughts and feelings as you read.

Ask Yourself . . . Which characters do I like best? least? Do I agree with the message of this tale?

APPLYING THE STRATEGIES

Read the following selection, "Sally Ann Thunder Ann Whirlwind." Use the **Active Reading Model** notes in the margins to help you understand and enjoy the selection.

ACTIVE READING MODEL

Before You Read

Sally Ann Thunder Ann Whirlwind

MEET MARY POPE OSBORNE

Mary Pope Osborne spent most of her childhood on army posts in the southern United States. Today she acknowledges many influences on her work, including "my southern military background, my family, my editor, my work with runaway teenagers, and my interests in philosophy and mythology." Osborne began writing seriously in 1976, during a theater tour with her actor husband. Since then, she has published several novels, biographies, and collections of myths, fairy tales, and tall tales.

Mary Pope Osborne was born in 1949. This selection was first published in 1991 in American Tall Tales.

FOCUS ACTIVITY

Recall a time when you accomplished something you were really proud of.

Share It!
Make notes about your accomplishment. Share them with a partner.

Setting a Purpose
Read to learn about the accomplishments of a legendary person on the American frontier.

BACKGROUND

The Time and Place This story takes place on the frontier of Tennessee or Kentucky, probably in the early 1800s.

Did You Know? From 1835 to 1856, the *Davy Crockett Almanacks* helped spread the legends of women and men on the frontier. Their heroic exploits, real or imagined, were widely admired during that period. The most famous of these figures was Davy Crockett, a legendary American politician and frontiersman, known for bragging and spinning colorful yarns. Although an almanac is a book of interesting facts and statistics, the *Davy Crockett Almanacks* are probably not as factual as most. Crockett was born in 1786 in Tennessee and died in 1836 at the battle of the Alamo in San Antonio, Texas.

VOCABULARY PREVIEW

obliged (ə blījd′) *adj.* forced, bound, or required; p. 361
forage (fôr′ ij) *v.* to hunt or search about for food or needed supplies; p. 364

Sally Ann Thunder Ann Whirlwind

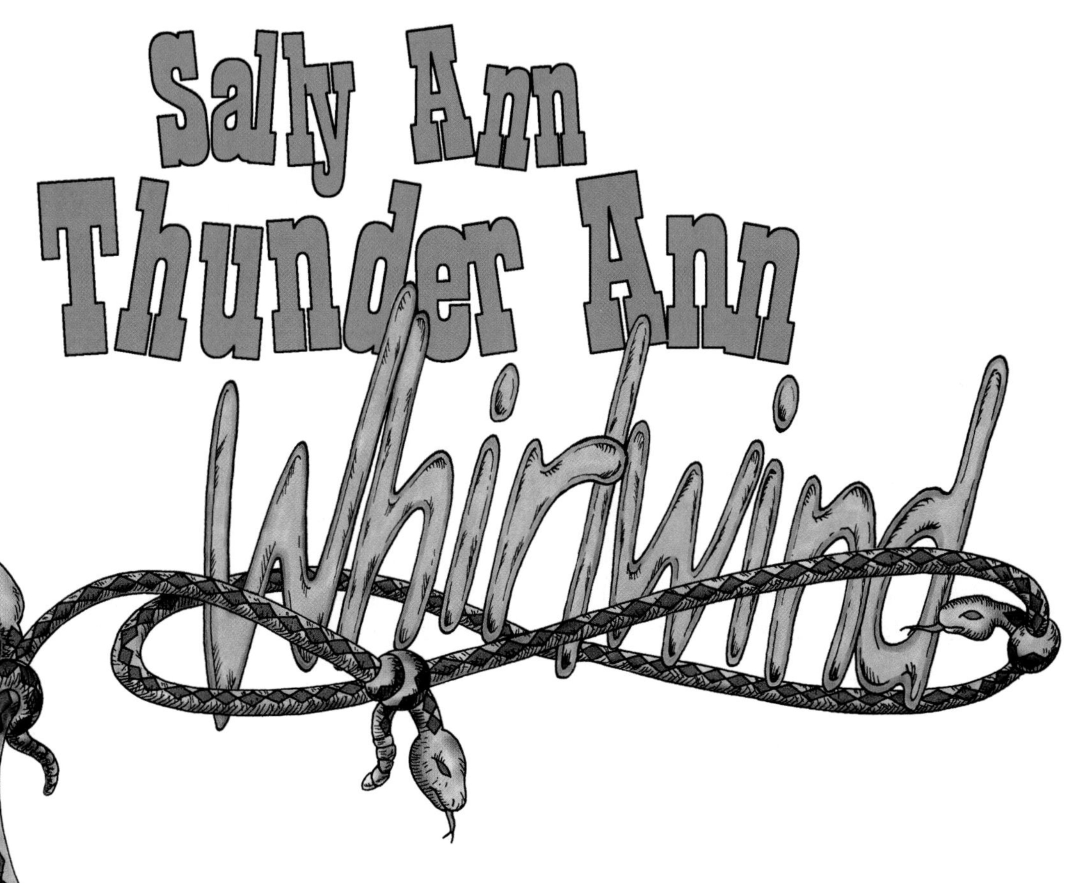

Mary Pope Osborne

ACTIVE READING MODEL

One early spring day, when the leaves of the white oaks were about as big as a mouse's ear, Davy Crockett set out alone through the forest to do some bear hunting. Suddenly it started raining real hard, and he felt obliged to stop for shelter under a tree. As he shook the rain out of his coonskin cap, he got sleepy, so he laid back into the crotch of the tree, and pretty soon he was snoring.

Vocabulary

obliged (ə blījd′) *adj.* forced, bound, or required

ACTIVE READING MODEL

VISUALIZE

Picture Davy trying to get out of this situation.

QUESTION

How would you characterize Sally Ann so far?

Davy slept so hard, he didn't wake up until nearly sundown. And when he did, he discovered that somehow or another in all that sleeping his head had gotten stuck in the crotch of the tree, and he couldn't get it out.

Well, Davy roared loud enough to make the tree lose all its little mouse-ear leaves. He twisted and turned and carried on for over an hour, but still that tree wouldn't let go. Just as he was about to give himself up for a goner, he heard a girl say, "What's the matter, stranger?"

Even from his awkward position, he could see that she was extraordinary—tall as a hickory sapling, with arms as big as a keelboat tiller's.[1]

"My head's stuck, sweetie," he said. "And if you help me get it free, I'll give you a pretty little comb."

"Don't call me sweetie," she said. "And don't worry about giving me no pretty little comb, neither. I'll free your old coconut, but just because I want to."

Then this extraordinary girl did something that made Davy's hair stand on end. She reached in a bag and took out a bunch of rattlesnakes. She tied all the wriggly critters together to make a long rope, and as she tied, she kept talking. "I'm not a shy little colt," she said. "And I'm not a little singing nightingale, neither. I can tote a steamboat on my back, outscream a panther, and jump over my own shadow. I can double up crocodiles any day, and I like to wear a hornets' nest for my Sunday bonnet."

As the girl looped the ends of her snake rope to the top of the branch that was trapping Davy, she kept bragging: "I'm a streak of lightning set up edgeways and buttered with quicksilver.[2] I can outgrin, outsnort, outrun, outlift, outsneeze, outsleep, outlie any varmint[3] from Maine to Louisiana. Furthermore, *sweetie,* I can blow out the moonlight and sing a wolf to sleep." Then she pulled on the other end of the snake rope so hard, it seemed as if she might tear the world apart.

The right-hand fork of that big tree bent just about double. Then Davy slid his head out as easy as you please. For a minute he was so dizzy, he couldn't tell up from down. But when he got everything going straight again, he took a good look at that girl. "What's your name, ma'am?"

"Sally Ann Thunder Ann Whirlwind," she said. "But if you mind your manners, you can call me Sally."

---

1. The lever used to steer a boat is the *tiller.* Here, a person who uses the tiller is referred to as a *tiller.*
2. *Quicksilver* is a name for mercury, a silver-colored metal that is liquid at room temperature. An old meaning of *quick* is "alive," and liquid mercury moves about as if it were alive.
3. A *varmint* is an informal word for *vermin,* which refers to insects, animals, or people that are troublesome, harmful, or destructive.

From then on Davy Crockett was crazy in love with Sally Ann Thunder Ann Whirlwind. He asked everyone he knew about her, and everything he heard caused another one of Cupid's arrows to jab him in the gizzard.

"Oh, I know Sally!" the preacher said. "She can dance a rock to pieces and ride a panther bareback!"

"Sally's a good ole friend of mine," the blacksmith said. "Once I seen her crack a walnut with her front teeth."

"Sally's so very special," said the schoolmarm. "She likes to whip across the Salt River, using her apron for a sail and her left leg for a rudder!"

Sally Ann Thunder Ann Whirlwind had a reputation for being funny, too. Her best friend, Lucy, told Davy, "Sally can laugh the bark off a pine tree. She likes to whistle out one side of her mouth while she eats with the other side and grins with the middle!"

According to her friends, Sally could tame about anything in the world, too. They all told Davy about the time she was churning butter and heard something scratching outside. Suddenly the door swung open, and in walked the Great King Bear of the Mud Forest. He'd come to steal one of her smoked hams. Well, before the King Bear could say boo, Sally grabbed a warm dumpling from the pot and stuffed it in his mouth.

The dumpling tasted so good, the King Bear's eyes winked with tears. But then he started to think that Sally might taste pretty good, too. So opening and closing his big old mouth, he backed her right into a corner.

Sally was plenty scared, with her knees a-knocking and her heart a-hammering. But just as the King Bear blew his hot breath in her face, she gathered the courage to say, "Would you like to dance?"

As everybody knows, no bear can resist an invitation to a square dance, so of course the old fellow forgot all about eating Sally and said, "Love to."

Then he bowed real pretty, and the two got to kicking and whooping and swinging each other through the air, as Sally sang:

We are on our way to Baltimore,
With two behind, and two before:
Around, around, around we go,
Where oats, peas, beans, and barley grow!

And while she was singing, Sally tied a string from the bear's ankle to her butter churn, so that all the time the old feller was kicking up his legs and dancing around the room, he was also churning her butter!

QUESTION

What is ironic, or unexpected, about someone like Davy falling for a person like Sally?

PREDICT

From what you know about Sally, what do you think she will do to the bear?

And folks loved to tell the story about Sally's encounter with another stinky varmint—only this one was a *human* varmint. It seems that Mike Fink, the riverboat man, decided to scare the toenails off Sally because he was sick and tired of hearing Davy Crockett talk about how great she was.

One evening Mike crept into an old alligator skin and met Sally just as she was taking off to forage in the woods for berries. He spread open his gigantic mouth and made such a howl that he nearly scared himself to death. But Sally paid no more attention to that fool than she would have to a barking puppy dog.

QUESTION

What does Sally reveal about herself when she gets angry with Mike?

However, when Mike put out his claws to embrace her, her anger rose higher than a Mississippi flood. She threw a flash of eye lightning at him, turning the dark to daylight. Then she pulled out a little toothpick and with a single swing sent the alligator head flying fifty feet! And then to finish him off good, she rolled up her sleeves and knocked Mike Fink clear across the woods and into a muddy swamp.

When the fool came to, Davy Crockett was standing over him. "What in the world happened to you, Mikey?" he asked.

"Well, I—I think I must-a been hit by some kind of wild alligator!" Mike stammered, rubbing his sore head.

REFLECT

Why does Davy smile when he knows Sally caused Mike's misfortune?

Davy smiled, knowing full well it was Sally Ann Thunder Ann Whirlwind just finished giving Mike Fink the only punishment he'd ever known.

That incident caused Cupid's final arrow to jab Davy's gizzard. "Sally's the whole steamboat," he said, meaning she was something great. The next day he put on his best raccoon hat and sallied forth[4] to see her.

When he got within three miles of her cabin, he began to holler her name. His voice was so loud, it whirled through the woods like a hurricane.

Sally looked out and saw the wind a-blowing and the trees a-bending. She heard her name a-thundering through the woods, and her heart began to thump. By now she'd begun to feel that Davy Crockett was the whole steamboat, too. So she put on her best hat—an eagle's nest with a wildcat's tail for a feather—and ran outside.

Just as she stepped out the door, Davy Crockett burst from the woods and jumped onto her porch as fast as a frog. "Sally, darlin'!" he cried. "I think my heart is bustin'! Want to be my wife?"

4. When Davy *sallied forth,* he went out briskly or energetically.

Vocabulary

forage (fôr′ ij) *v.* to hunt or search about for food or needed supplies

Untitled, 1991. Michael McCurdy. Wood engraving. From *American Tall Tales.*
Viewing the art: What does the wood engraving of Sally Ann add to your impression of her?

"Oh, my stars and possum dogs, why not?" she said.

From that day on, Davy Crockett had a hard time acting tough around Sally Ann Thunder Ann Whirlwind. His fightin' and hollerin' had no more effect on her than dropping feathers on a barn floor. At least that's what *she'd* tell you. *He* might say something else.

REFLECT

Think about why Sally and Davy might have different opinions about how Davy acts around Sally.

ACTIVE READING MODEL

Responding to Literature

PERSONAL RESPONSE

Which of Sally's escapades did you think was the most entertaining?

Active Reading Response

Find two or more ways to connect your life with the characters in this selection. If you need help, review the **Active Reading Strategies** on page 359.

Analyzing Literature

RECALL

1. Describe how Davy Crockett and Sally Ann Thunder Ann Whirlwind meet.
2. What stories does Davy Crockett hear about Sally from her friends?
3. Summarize what happens when Sally encounters the Great King Bear of the Mud Forest.
4. Why does Mike Fink want "to scare the toenails off Sally"? What happens when he tries to do this?

INTERPRET

5. How does Davy Crockett's attitude toward Sally change during their first meeting? Why does it change?
6. What effect do the stories Davy Crockett hears about Sally have on him? Explain.
7. What does Sally's encounter with the bear reveal about her?

EVALUATE AND CONNECT

8. In your opinion, does Mike Fink get what he deserves for trying to scare Sally? Does Sally get what she deserves? Explain.
9. Think about how people lived in the American wilderness during the 1800s. What true-to-life features of pioneer life does this selection reflect?
10. Do you think Sally's full name is a good one for her? Why or why not?

LITERARY ELEMENTS

Tall Tale

A **tall tale** is a story in which the exploits of a character are exaggerated extravagantly. When you read a tall tale, you expect to find ridiculous and unlikely situations narrated seriously, as if the events in the story were true. Tall tales rely on certain elements to be effective: a hero readers will like, deeds that are unbelievable, and character traits that are wildly exaggerated. For example, Sally Ann Thunder Ann Whirlwind ties rattlesnakes together to make a rope.

1. What, in your opinion, is Sally's most outstanding trait? Give one example of how that trait is exaggerated in the tall tale.
2. Why do you think Sally is an enjoyable heroine?

- See **Literary Terms Handbook,** p. R10.

Literature and Writing

Writing About Literature

Frontier Setting How important is the **setting** in this tall tale? Write your answer in a paragraph or two, and consider these questions: What details help the reader visualize the old frontier? How would the story be different if it happened in another time or place?

Creative Writing

Tall-Tale Wedding Suppose you were a guest at the wedding of Sally Ann Thunder Ann Whirlwind and Davy Crockett. Write a "tall tale" letter to relatives "back East" about this event. Include details about the setting and the characters. Try to follow the writing style the author uses in the tall tale.

Extending Your Response

Literature Groups

Sally Superhero How would Sally stack up against Superman, Batman, or another modern superhero? Compare her powers and abilities with those of contemporary male and female superheroes. What advantages and disadvantages does Sally have? Discuss them all, then come to an agreement in your group.

Interdisciplinary Activity

Social Studies Work with a partner to research the real story of the Alamo in San Antonio, Texas. Explain how sides were formed in the conflict over Texas and how the conflict was resolved. Prepare a brief oral, written, or visual report to share with the class.

Performing

Accomplishments on Stage How do Sally's accomplishments compare with those of real people? Look back at the notes about your own accomplishment from the **Focus Activity** on page 360. Dramatize your story, using the help of one or more students if you need additional actors. Present your dramatization to the class.

Reading Further

If you enjoyed this story, try:
Jackaroo by Cynthia Voigt
The Perilous Gard by Elizabeth Pope

Save your work for your portfolio.

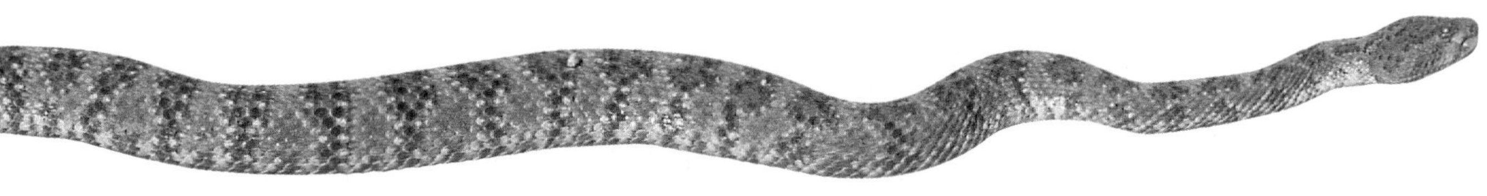

Skill Minilessons

GRAMMAR AND LANGUAGE • COMPOUND PREDICATES

A **compound predicate** is two or more verbs or verb phrases that have the same subject. The compound predicates are underlined in the sentences below.

Davy twisted and turned and carried on for over an hour.

Sally reached in a bag and took out a bunch of rattlesnakes.

- For more about predicates, see **Language Handbook,** p. R31.

PRACTICE Write the subject and the compound predicate in each of the following sentences.

1. Sally danced a rock to pieces and rode a panther bareback.
2. Sally pulled out a toothpick and sent the alligator's head flying.
3. Sally rolled up her sleeves and knocked Mike Fink across the woods.
4. Mike Fink put on an alligator skin and followed Sally.

READING AND THINKING • CHRONOLOGICAL ORDER

Chronological order is the grouping of events according to when they occurred. For example, the first and earliest event in Davy and Sally's romance is when Sally pulls Davy's head out of the tree.

- For more about text structures, see **Reading Handbook,** p. R87.

PRACTICE List the following events in chronological order.

a. Davy learns about many of Sally's amazing adventures.
b. Davy asks Sally to be his wife.
c. Sally helps Davy to get out of the tree.
d. Mike Fink tries to scare Sally.

VOCABULARY • SYNONYMS

Using vivid **synonyms** can keep your writing from becoming repetitive and boring. However, you should choose synonyms carefully. Most words have more than one meaning, and one synonym cannot always be substituted for another. A thesaurus is a useful reference book if you understand what each listed synonym means and suggests. For example, Sally is a *rugged* frontier woman. Good synonyms for *rugged* are *strong* and *sturdy.* However, *strong* coffee is neither *sturdy* nor *rugged.*

PRACTICE Choose the correct answer for each question.

1. In which sentence could *forage* be substituted for *search?*
   a. I will *search* through the pantry for a snack.
   b. I must *search* through the crowd for my friend.
2. In which sentence could *oblige* be substituted for *force?*
   a. Good manners *force* one to respond to invitations.
   b. Use a hammer to *force* the nail into the board.

Using Irregular Verbs Correctly

Most verbs have a past form that is made by adding *-ed* to the base form. The past participle form is usually the same as the past form and is always used with another verb, such as a form of *is, have,* or *did.*

Base form: ski; **Past form: skied**; **Past participle form:** has **skied**
Two common kinds of **irregular verbs** do not follow this pattern.

1. A single vowel changes to form the past and the past participle.

   Base form: K. C. and Marta **swim** almost every day.

   Past form: They **swam** yesterday afternoon.

   Past participle form: The girls have **swum** together on the team.

2. The present form changes significantly to form the past and past participle.

   Base form: Don't **bring** anything extra.

   Past form: We **brought** a good map.

   Past participle form: We have **brought** too much to carry.

Problem 1 an improperly formed irregular verb
Did you bring lunch? Yes, we ***brang*** *enough for everybody.*

Solution Yes, we **brought** enough for everybody.

Problem 2 misuse of the past and past participle forms
I thought he had ***sang*** *that song before.*

Solution I thought he had **sung** that song before.

● For more about verbs, see **Language Handbook,** pp. R33–R34.

EXERCISE

Rewrite the sentences. In each blank, use the correct form of the underlined verb.

1. I know that Davy Crockett ______ many famous people.
2. Do you understand that problem? I ______ not understand it at first.
3. The bears sleep now, just as they ______ through last winter's terrible cold.
4. She will buy more food than you would have ______.

Before You Read

Lazy Peter and His Three-Cornered Hat

MEET RICARDO E. ALEGRIA

Ricardo E. Alegria's (rē kär′ dō ä′ lā grē′ ə) life is proof of his interest in the folktales and customs of his native land of Puerto Rico. He is an anthropologist and historian, professions for people who study and preserve what they learn of the past. He has been director of an archaeological museum in Puerto Rico and a university professor. Alegria is the author of a book on the sculptures of the Tainos, a group of native people on the island, and he has collected folktales from the region.

Ricardo E. Alegria was born in Puerto Rico in 1921. This story was published in The Three Wishes *in 1968.*

FOCUS ACTIVITY

Think about different ways to earn a living. Could a person earn a living by tricking others? If so, how?

Journal

Would a person who makes a career out of tricking others be respected in your community? Why or why not? Write your answers in a journal entry.

Setting a Purpose

Read to discover what Lazy Peter, a Puerto Rican trickster, has up his sleeve.

BACKGROUND

The Time and Place

The story is set in a Puerto Rican village.

Did You Know? Lazy Peter lives in Puerto Rico, an island in the Caribbean. The Tainos and other Indian groups lived on the island when Spain established a colony there in 1508. Fewer than 100 years later, most of the native peoples were gone, either killed by the European explorers or exiled to other islands. The island became a commonwealth of the United States in 1917.

VOCABULARY PREVIEW

unsound (un sound′) *adj.* not accurate or sensible; p. 372

haggle (hag′ əl) *v.* to bargain, especially about price or the terms of an agreement; p. 373

revive (ri vīv′) *v.* to come back to consciousness; show new life, strength, or freshness; p. 373

priceless (prīs′ lis) *adj.* of greater value than can be measured; p. 373

Lazy Peter and His Three-Cornered Hat
(Pedro Animala y Su Sombrero de Tres Picos)

Adapted by Ricardo E. Alegria

Translated by Elizabeth Culbert

This is the story of Lazy Peter, a shameless rascal of a fellow who went from village to village making mischief.

One day Lazy Peter learned that a fair was being held in a certain village. He knew that a large crowd of country people would be there selling horses, cows, and other farm animals and that a large amount of money would change hands. Peter, as usual, needed money, but it was not his custom to work for it. So he set out for the village, wearing a red three-cornered hat.

The first thing he did was to stop at a stand and leave a big bag of money with the owner, asking him to keep it safely until he returned for it. Peter told the man that when he returned for the bag of money, one corner of his hat would be turned down, and that was how the owner of the stand would know him. The man promised to do this, and Peter thanked him. Then he went to the drugstore in the village and gave the druggist another bag of money, asking him to keep it until he returned with one corner of his hat turned up. The druggist agreed, and Peter left. He went to the church and asked the priest to keep another bag of money and to return it to him only when he came back with one corner of his hat twisted to the side. The priest said fine, that he would do this.

Having disposed of[1] three bags of money, Peter went to the edge of the village where the farmers were buying and selling horses and cattle. He stood and watched for a while until he decided that one of the farmers must be very rich indeed, for he had sold all of his horses and cows. Moreover, the man seemed to be a miser who was never satisfied but wanted always more and more money. This was Peter's man! He stopped beside him. It was raining; and instead of keeping his hat on to protect his head, he took it off and wrapped it carefully in his cape, as though it were very valuable. It puzzled the farmer to see Peter stand there with the rain falling on his head and his hat wrapped in his cape.

After a while he asked, "Why do you take better care of your hat than of your head?"

Peter saw that the farmer had swallowed the bait, and smiling to himself, he said that the hat was the most valuable thing in all the world and that was why he took care to protect it from the rain. The farmer's curiosity increased at this reply, and he asked Peter what was so valuable about a red three-cornered hat. Peter told him that the hat worked for him; thanks to it, he never had to work for a living because, whenever he put the hat on with one of the corners turned over, people just handed him any money he asked for.

The farmer was amazed and very interested in what Peter said. As money-getting was his greatest ambition, he told Peter that he couldn't believe a word of it until he saw the hat work with his own eyes. Peter assured him that he could do this, for he, Peter, was hungry, and the hat was about to start working since he had no money with which to buy food.

With this, Peter took out his three-cornered hat, turned one corner down, put it on his head, and told the farmer to come along and watch the hat work. Peter took the farmer to the stand. The minute the owner looked up, he handed over the bag of money Peter had left with him. The farmer stood with his mouth open in astonishment. He didn't know what to make of it. But of one thing he was sure—he had to have that hat!

Peter smiled and asked if he was satisfied, and the farmer said, yes, he was. Then he asked Peter if he would sell the hat. This was just what Lazy Peter wanted, but he said no, that he was not interested in selling the hat because, with it, he never had to work and he always had money. The farmer said he thought that was unsound reasoning because thieves could easily steal a hat, and wouldn't it be safer to invest in a farm with cattle? So they talked, and Peter pretended to be impressed with the farmer's arguments. Finally he said yes, that he saw the point, and if the farmer would make him a good offer, he would sell the hat. The farmer, who had made up his mind to have the hat at any price, offered a thousand pesos. Peter laughed aloud and said he could make as much as that by just putting his hat on two or three times.

1. The phrase *disposed of* means "dealt with; taken care of."

Vocabulary

unsound (un sound′) *adj.* not accurate or sensible

As they continued haggling over the price, the farmer grew more and more determined to have that hat until, finally, he offered all he had realized from the sale of his horses and cows—ten thousand pesos in gold. Peter still pretended not to be interested, but he chuckled to himself, thinking of the trick he was about to play on the farmer. All right, he said, it was a deal. Then the farmer grew cautious and told Peter that, before he handed over the ten thousand pesos, he would like to see the hat work again. Peter said that was fair enough. He put on the hat with one of the corners turned up and went with the farmer to the drugstore. The moment the druggist saw the turned-up corner, he handed over the money Peter had left with him. At this the farmer was convinced and very eager to set the hat to work for himself. He took out a bag containing ten thousand pesos in gold and was about to hand it to Peter when he had a change of heart and thought better of it. He asked Peter please to excuse him, but he had to see the hat work just once more before he could part with his gold. Peter said that that was fair enough, but now he would have to ask the farmer to give him the fine horse he was riding as well as the ten thousand pesos in gold. The farmer's interest in the hat revived, and he said it was a bargain!

Lazy Peter put on his hat again, doubled over one of the corners, and told the farmer that, since he still seemed to have doubts, this time he could watch the hat work in the church. The farmer was delighted with this, his doubts were stilled, and he fairly beamed thinking of all the money he was going to make once that hat was his.

They entered the church. The priest was hearing confession, but when he saw Peter with his hat, he said, "Wait here, my son," and he went to the sacristy[2] and returned with the bag of money Peter had left with him. Peter thanked the priest, then knelt and asked for a blessing before he left. The farmer had seen everything and was fully convinced of the hat's magic powers. As soon as they left the church, he gave Peter the ten thousand pesos in gold and told him to take the horse, also. Peter tied the bag of pesos to the saddle, gave the hat to the farmer, begging him to take good care of it, spurred his horse, and galloped out of town.

As soon as he was alone, the farmer burst out laughing at the thought of the trick he had played on Lazy Peter. A hat such as this was priceless! He couldn't wait to try it. He put it on with one corner turned up and entered the butcher shop. The butcher looked at the hat, which was very handsome, indeed, but said nothing. The farmer turned around, then walked up and down until the butcher asked him what he wanted. The farmer said he was waiting for the bag of money. The butcher laughed aloud and asked if he was crazy. The farmer thought that there must be something wrong with the way he had folded the hat. He took it off and doubled another corner down. But this had no effect on the butcher. So he

2. The *sacristy* is the room in a church where robes or objects used in ceremonies are kept.

Vocabulary

haggle (hag′ əl) *v.* to bargain, especially about price or the terms of an agreement
revive (ri vīv′) *v.* to come back to consciousness; show new life, strength, or freshness
priceless (prīs′ lis) *adj.* of greater value than can be measured

decided to try it out some other place. He went to the Mayor of the town.

The Mayor, to be sure, looked at the hat but did nothing. The farmer grew desperate and decided to go to the druggist who had given Peter a bag of money. He entered and stood with the hat on. The druggist looked at him but did nothing.

The farmer became very nervous. He began to suspect that there was something very wrong. He shouted at the druggist, "Stop looking at me and hand over the bag of money!"

The druggist said he owed him nothing, and what bag of money was he talking about, anyway? As the farmer continued to shout about a bag of money and a magic hat, the druggist called the police. When they arrived, he told them that the farmer had gone out of his mind and kept demanding a bag of money. The police questioned the farmer, and he told them about the magic hat he had bought from Lazy Peter. When he heard the story, the druggist explained that Peter had left a bag of money, asking that it be returned when he appeared with a corner of his hat turned up. The owner of the stand and the priest told the same story. And I am telling you the farmer was so angry that he tore the hat to shreds and walked home.

The Little Cemetery of Culebra, 1991. Mari Mater O'Neil. Oil on canvas, 48 x 60 in. Collection Ileana Font, Mirama, Puerto Rico.

Viewing the painting: What do the colors, shapes, and objects in this painting suggest to you about Puerto Rico and the setting of this story?

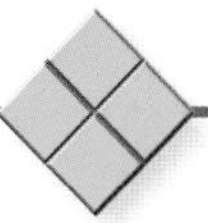

Responding to Literature

PERSONAL RESPONSE

If you were the farmer, what would you do after realizing that Peter tricked you?

Analyzing Literature

RECALL AND INTERPRET

1. What does Peter do for a living? How does he select people to trick?
2. When it rains, what does Peter do with his hat? Why?
3. What reason does Peter give the farmer for refusing to sell his hat? What is the true reason?

EVALUATE AND CONNECT

4. Peter tells the farmer that the three-cornered hat is "the most valuable thing in all the world." Evaluate this statement. How is it true and untrue?
5. An **idiom** is an expression that cannot be understood if taken literally, but that makes sense to most people who use the language. Alegria uses an idiom when he says the farmer "swallowed the bait." Looking at context clues, what might this idiom mean? How clear is its meaning?
6. Why does Peter choose a merchant, a druggist, and a priest to hold his money?

LITERARY ELEMENTS

Plot

To understand the **plot,** or action, of a story, readers must first recognize the traits of the main characters. In many stories, the struggle involves a central character, or **protagonist,** who usually has good traits. Opposing the protagonist is a person or force called an **antagonist,** who usually has bad traits.

1. State the plot of this folktale in one or two sentences, and identify the protagonist and the antagonist.
2. What characteristics do you see in Peter and the farmer that help you understand why they struggle?

- See **Literary Terms Handbook,** pp. R1, R7, and R8.

Extending Your Response

Writing About Literature

Theme A story's main message, called the **theme,** can often be stated in one sentence. For example, "Health is a valuable possession" and "Defend yourself against ignorance" could be themes. With a partner, identify the theme of this story. Write a paragraph supporting your statement.

Literature Groups

Is Peter a Liar? Did Peter lie to the farmer? Reexamine the story, looking at everything Peter said. Find three statements Peter made. Discuss whether the statements prove that Peter is a liar.

LISTENING, SPEAKING, and VIEWING

Storytelling

There's more to storytelling than simply repeating the words. Imagine Sam, the narrator of O. Henry's story, shaking his head over "The Ransom of Red Chief" or a jokester chuckling at "Lazy Peter and His Three-Cornered Hat." Skilled storytellers, like skilled moviemakers, blend sound, sight, and motion. They might mimic voices and actions; they might use props. Gifted storytellers also practice a story until they get the words and gestures just right.

Choose an episode from a short story or a real-life event. Practice telling it in front of a mirror, or ask a friend to listen, watch, and give you suggestions. The following guidelines can strengthen your storytelling skills:

- **Use your eyes.** Make eye contact. Don't look over your listeners' heads or at their feet. Move your eyes from one face to the next. Watch for listeners' reactions. When they meet your eyes, you have their attention. That's what you want!
- **Use your voice.** Make it loud or soft, fast or slow, depending on the action in your story. Change pitch and speaking style to fit your characters. If listeners whisper or fidget, it may be because they can't hear. Raise your voice.
- **Use your body.** Think posture. Your voice carries best when you stand tall. Changing your posture helps you "become" a character. Gestures work too: a character might "talk with his hands," shrug shyly, or peer sneakily about.
- **Use silence.** A well-timed pause is powerful. When your story's action peaks, pause for a beat. Let your listeners feel the suspense.

ACTIVITY

With a small group of listeners, use the guidelines to tell a story you have written. Ask each listener to comment, using these questions as guides: Which of your techniques are especially effective? What is one change that might improve your storytelling?

Before You Read

M'su Carencro and Mangeur de Poulet

MEET J. J. RENEAUX

As J. J. Reneaux (re nō′) was growing up in southeastern Texas and southern Louisiana, she listened to the Cajun stories told by her friends and family. Reneaux says that each folktale she retells today "contains a part of me—the beliefs, experiences, and people who have shaped my life." She hopes that "readers and listeners will discover the beauty and spirit of the Cajun people and—perhaps more importantly—of their own lives as well."

J. J. Reneaux was born in 1955. This story was first published in Cajun Folktales *in 1992.*

FOCUS ACTIVITY

How well do you know yourself? Why do you think it is important to know yourself?

Create It!

Create a banner, poster, or other display to tell about "the real you."

Setting a Purpose

As you read, discover what the characters seem to understand—or seem not to understand—about themselves.

BACKGROUND

The Time and Place This traditional tale is from the Cajun people of Louisiana. It is told partly in Cajun dialect, a speech based on French.

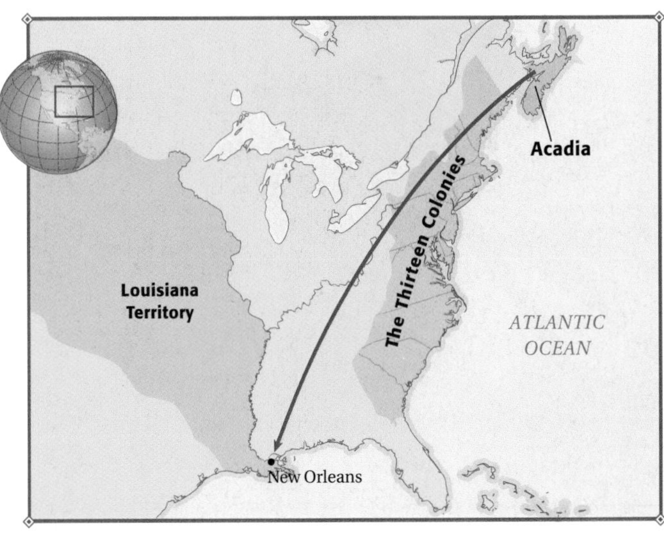

Did You Know? The word *Cajun* comes from *Acadian,* the name of French-speaking Canadians from the colony of Acadia, now Nova Scotia. British settlers captured the French colony in the mid-1700s, forcing the Acadians to move south. They eventually settled in Louisiana, where their French culture lives on today. Their painful experiences of being exiled and looked down upon can be found in Cajun literature.

M'su Carencro and Mangeur de Poulet

Retold by J. J. Reneaux

Crow on wire and papier mâché. Saulo Moreno. Height: 8⅝ in. Collection of the artist.

One day M'su Carencro,[1] the buzzard, was sitting on a fence post real patient-like, just waiting for something to drop dead so he could have his supper, when who should come flapping up but ol' Mangeur de Poulet,[2] the chicken hawk. Mangeur de Poulet calls out, "Hey, *ça va, mon padnat?*"[3]

M'su Carencro shook his head and sighed, "*Ça va mal!*[4] Not good at all! I am so hungry. I been waitin' for days for somethin' to drop dead so I can have my supper."

"What you talkin' 'bout?" says know-it-all Chicken Hawk. "If you're so hungry, why don'tcha get out there and hunt you some good fresh meat? You got eyes, you got wings, you got a beak. Go for it! You got to look out for Number One in this world, *mon ami*."[5]

"*Non, non, non,*" says Buzzard, "you don't understand. I'm s'posed to wait for somethin' to drop dead before I eat it. It's my job. That's just the way *le Bon Dieu*[6] made me."

"*Le Bon Dieu?* Aw, *non!* Don't waste your breath talkin' 'bout the Good God," says Chicken Hawk. "Besides, *mon ami*, even if there is a God, what makes you think he cares whether you get your supper? You gotta do like me, look out fo' yourself. Here, let ol' Chicken Hawk show you how to do that thang."

With that, Mangeur de Poulet leaped into the air and started wildly flapping about in daring loop-the-loops and crazy figure eights, showing off like you've never seen. All of a sudden, he spied a juicy little rabbit right down there next to Buzzard's fence post.

"Aw, this'll show Buzzard," he thought. Chicken Hawk took dead aim and down he zoomed after that rabbit, faster and faster. But Rabbit was smart-smart. She saw Chicken Hawk's shadow closing in on her, and she jumped down her hole just as the big show-off came zooming in. By this time, Chicken Hawk was speeding so fast that his brakes couldn't save him and he slammed smack dab into that fence post! And down he dropped—thunk!—deader than the post itself, right at Buzzard's feet.

Buzzard looked down at that dead chicken hawk. Then he looked up to heaven. He grins real big and says, "*Merci beaucoup, mon Grand Bon Dieu!*[7] Good God Almighty, thank you!" Then he jumps down off the fence post, smacks his lips, and says, "Suppertime!"

1. ***M'su Carencro*** (mə syo͞o′ kä ran′ krô) **means "Mr. Buzzard." (*M'su* is a short form of *Monsieur,* or "Mister.")**
2. ***Mangeur de Poulet*** (män zhur′ də po͞o lā′) **means "Chicken Eater," but Chicken Hawk makes a nicer-sounding name, doesn't it?**
3. ***Ça va, mon padnat?*** (sä vä′ môn päd nä′): **How's it going, partner?**
4. ***Ça va mal!*** (sä vä′ mäl′)
5. ***Mon ami*** (mô nä mē′) **means "my friend."**
6. ***Le Bon Dieu*** (lə bôn dyœ′) **is "the Good God."**
7. ***Merci beaucoup, mon Grand Bon Dieu!*** (mer sē′ bō ko͞o′ môn grän bôn dyœ′): **Thank you very much, my Great Good God!**

❖

Responding to Literature

PERSONAL RESPONSE

Do you feel sorry for Chicken Hawk? Why or why not?

Analyzing Literature

RECALL

1. Why is Buzzard waiting around? Why won't Buzzard kill something to eat?
2. How does Chicken Hawk look out for himself–whom he calls "Number One"?
3. How does Chicken Hawk show off? What happens to him?
4. What does Buzzard do when Chicken Hawk falls to the ground?

INTERPRET

5. What, in your opinion, does Buzzard think about who he is? Does he seem satisfied?
6. What is Chicken Hawk's motto? Why do you think the storyteller has Chicken Hawk die by this motto?
7. Why does Chicken Hawk taunt Buzzard?
8. Why doesn't Buzzard show sadness at Chicken Hawk's death?

EVALUATE AND CONNECT

9. How do you "look out for Number One"? Can you look out for yourself without harming others? Consider your answers to the **Focus Activity** on page 377 as you explain.
10. What characteristics do these two **characters** have that remind you of someone you know?

LITERARY ELEMENTS

Title

The words used to identify a literary work are called the **title.** The title an author chooses gives readers clues about what to expect in the story. Take "M'su Carencro and Mangeur de Poulet," for example. A reader who knows that folktales and fables often have animal characters might guess from this title that the story is a folktale or fable. A knowledgeable reader may also assume that the tale has a moral, as many folktales and fables do. In this story, the use of a French title is also a clue that the setting and characters probably speak French.

1. What is the first thing the reader must know to gain information from this title?
2. What clues does this selection title give about the characters or the story?

- See **Literary Terms Handbook,** p. R10.

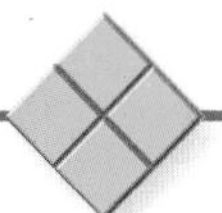

Literature and Writing

Writing About Literature

Talk the Talk Traditional folktales often tell about the way people in a culture think or act. J. J. Reneaux retold this tale using the Cajun dialect. Write a few sentences to describe how this dialect made the story interesting.

Personal Writing

Personal Best Compare yourself to Buzzard and Chicken Hawk. Which character are you most like? What situation could you explain that shows how your personality matches one of theirs? Write your comparison in two or three paragraphs.

Extending Your Response

Literature Groups

Wisdom Through Stories According to Reneaux, stories can be "as old as the hills, yet as new as each sunrise. When adults swap stories with children, new links are forged in a timeless chain of humanity." Discuss these questions about storytelling: What stories have been passed down in your family or community? What wisdom do these tales provide?

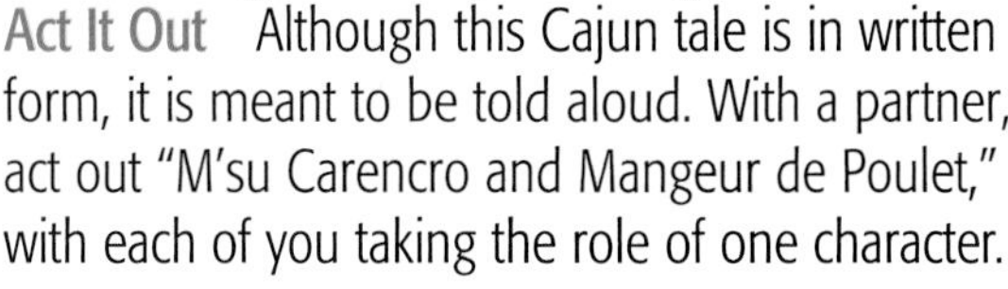

Listening and Speaking

Act It Out Although this Cajun tale is in written form, it is meant to be told aloud. With a partner, act out "M'su Carencro and Mangeur de Poulet," with each of you taking the role of one character.

Interdisciplinary Activity

Social Studies Research the history of the Cajun people, including why they were evicted from Acadia and how they lead their lives now. What challenges did their new homes present? Include information on the Cajun language, and discuss why the special style of Cajun cooking was developed and how it has had an impact on American cooking.

Save your work for your portfolio.

Skill Minilesson

READING AND THINKING • SETTING A PURPOSE FOR READING

Having a purpose for reading even a short selection can help you get more out of what you read. For example, when you know the origin of a folktale, you can read to learn something about the culture of the people who told the tale.

PRACTICE Reread "M'su Carencro and Mangeur de Poulet." Your purpose is to look for the theme, or main message, of the folktale. For help with themes in folktales, see the **Genre Focus** on page 358.

- For more about setting a purpose for reading, see **Reading Handbook,** p. R84.

Before You Read

Talk

MEET HAROLD COURLANDER

Harold Courlander traveled the world, collecting and editing folktales for forty years. He saw folktales as oral literature that contained information about human values and cultural heritage.

Harold Courlander was born in 1908 and died in 1996. "Talk" was first published in 1947 in The Cow-Tail Switch and Other West African Stories.

MEET GEORGE HERZOG

George Herzog was perhaps the world's first *ethnomusicologist*—a person who studies the relationship between music and culture. He recorded primitive and folk music from many cultures.

George Herzog was born in Hungary in 1901 and died in Indiana in 1983.

FOCUS ACTIVITY

Imagine that one day your breakfast cereal makes a comment (other than its normal crunch).

Note It!

What might your cereal or any other object say about you if it could? Write a brief note explaining your answer.

Setting a Purpose

Read this folktale to find out what happens when inanimate objects come to life.

BACKGROUND

The Time and Place

This tale is set in a small village near the city of Accra, the capital of Ghana.

Did You Know?

Ghana is an African country of grasslands and forests on the Gulf of Guinea.

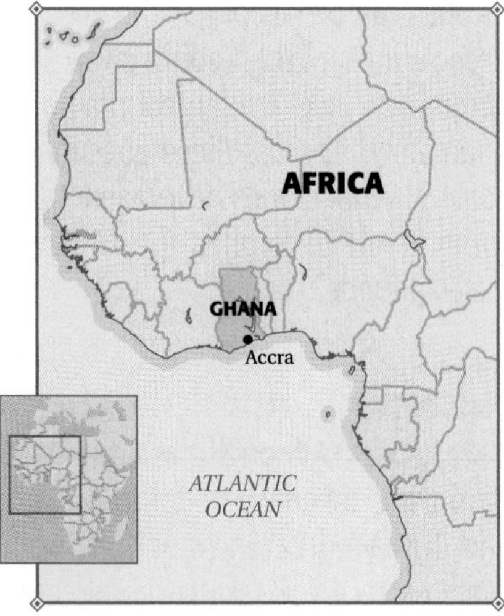

VOCABULARY PREVIEW

ford (fôrd) *n.* a shallow place where a river or stream may be crossed on foot; p. 384

refrain (ri frān′) *v.* to hold oneself back; restrain oneself; p. 384

scowling (skou′ ling) *n.* a facial expression of anger or disapproval; angry frown; p. 384

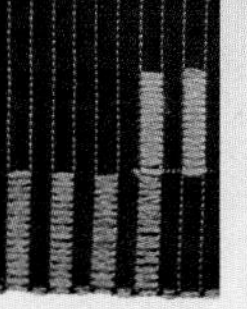

Told by Harold Courlander and George Herzog

Talk

Untitled, 1990. Agbagli Kossi. Painted wood, 37 x 12⅝ x 13⅜ in. Collection of Jean Pigozzi.

Once, not far from the city of Accra on the Gulf of Guinea, a country man went out to his garden to dig up some yams to take to market. While he was digging, one of the yams said to him:

"Well, at last you're here. You never weeded me, but now you come around with your digging stick. Go away and leave me alone!"

The farmer turned around and looked at his cow in amazement. The cow was chewing her cud and looking at him.

"Did you say something?" he asked.

The cow kept on chewing and said nothing, but the man's dog spoke up.

"It wasn't the cow who spoke to you," the dog said. "It was the yam. The yam says leave him alone."

The man became angry, because his dog had never talked before, and he didn't like his tone besides. So he took his knife and cut a branch from a palm tree to whip his dog. Just then the palm tree said:

"Put that branch down!"

The man was getting very upset about the way things were going, and he started to throw the palm branch away, but the palm branch said:

"Man, put me down softly!"

He put the branch down gently on a stone, and the stone said:

"Hey, take that thing off me!"

This was enough, and the frightened farmer started to run for his village. On the way he met a fisherman going the other way with a fish trap on his head.

"What's the hurry?" the fisherman asked.

"My yam said, 'Leave me alone!' Then the dog said, 'Listen to what the yam says!' When I went to whip the dog with a palm branch the tree said, 'Put that branch down!' Then the palm branch said, 'Do it softly!' Then the stone said, 'Take that thing off me!'"

"Is that all?" the man with the fish trap asked. "Is that so frightening?"

"Well," the man's fish trap said, "did he take it off the stone?"

"Wah!" the fisherman shouted. He threw the fish trap on the ground and began to run with the farmer, and on the trail they met a weaver with a bundle of cloth on his head.

"Where are you going in such a rush?" he asked them.

"My yam said, 'Leave me alone!'" the farmer said. "The dog said, 'Listen to what the yam says!' The tree said, 'Put that branch down!' The branch said, 'Do it softly!' And the stone said, 'Take that thing off me!'"

"And then," the fisherman continued, "the fish trap said, 'Did he take it off?'"

"That's nothing to get excited about," the weaver said, "no reason at all."

"Oh yes it is," his bundle of cloth said. "If it happened to you you'd run too!"

"Wah!" the weaver shouted. He threw his bundle on the trail and started running with the other men.

They came panting to the ford in the river and found a man bathing.

"Are you chasing a gazelle?"[1] he asked them.

The first man said breathlessly:

"My yam talked at me, and it said, 'Leave me alone!' And my dog said, 'Listen to your yam!' And when I cut myself a branch the tree said, 'Put that branch down!' And the branch said, 'Do it softly!' And the stone said, 'Take that thing off me!'"

The fisherman panted:

"And my trap said, 'Did he?'"

The weaver wheezed:

"And my bundle of cloth said, 'You'd run too!'"

"Is that why you're running?" the man in the river asked.

"Well, wouldn't you run if you were in their position?" the river said.

The man jumped out of the water and began to run with the others. They ran down the main street of the village to the house of the chief. The chief's servants brought his stool out, and he came and sat on it to listen to their complaints. The men began to recite their troubles.

"I went out to my garden to dig yams," the farmer said, waving his arms. "Then everything began to talk! My yam said, 'Leave me alone!' My dog said, 'Pay attention to your yam!' The tree said, 'Put that branch down!' The branch said, 'Do it softly!' And the stone said, 'Take it off me!'"

"And my fish trap said, 'Well, did he take it off?'" the fisherman said.

"And my cloth said, 'You'd run too!'" the weaver said.

"And the river said the same," the bather said hoarsely, his eyes bulging.

The chief listened to them patiently, but he couldn't refrain from scowling.

"Now this is really a wild story," he said at last. "You'd better all go back to your work before I punish you for disturbing the peace."

So the men went away, and the chief shook his head and mumbled to himself, "Nonsense like that upsets the community."

"Fantastic, isn't it?" his stool said. "Imagine, a talking yam!"

1. The *gazelle* is a kind of antelope native to hot, dry regions of Africa and Asia.

Vocabulary

ford (fôrd) *n.* a shallow place where a river or stream may be crossed on foot
refrain (ri frān′) *v.* to hold oneself back; restrain oneself
scowling (skou′ ling) *n.* a facial expression of anger or disapproval; angry frown

Responding to Literature

PERSONAL RESPONSE

Which character or characters have your sympathy? Why?

Analyzing Literature

RECALL AND INTERPRET

1. Which objects talk to the farmer? How are the comments of the objects alike?
2. How do the fisherman, the weaver, and the man in the river first react to the farmer's news? Why do they join him in his flight?
3. What does the chief say to the three men? What happens that may change the chief's mind about the incidents?

EVALUATE AND CONNECT

4. **Irony** occurs in a story when something happens contrary to what you expect. What is ironic about the ending of this story?
5. If you were the chief, how would you have responded to the men? Why?
6. In your opinion, is there an important message or theme in this story? Explain your answer.

A storyteller engages her audience.

LITERARY ELEMENTS

Repetition

When storytellers repeat sounds, words, phrases, and sentences, they are using **repetition.** This literary technique emphasizes events, ideas, and feelings by continually reminding readers of the author's point. Repetition also makes stories easier to remember and so is an important aspect of folklore because the stories are retold from memory. In "Talk," the men repeatedly explain their experience with the talking objects.

1. What do you think is the purpose of this story?
2. How does repetition help the storyteller achieve this purpose?

• See **Literary Terms Handbook,** p. R8.

Extending Your Response

Literature Groups

A Conversation Imagine what the objects from "Talk" might say to each other if they were the ones to tell this tale. What conversation might have been heard in the farmer's garden after he ran from his land? As you talk about the objects, also consider why the folktale ended as it did.

Writing About Literature

Personification Giving human characteristics to nonhuman objects is called **anthropomorphism.** This technique is often used in folktales. Write a brief explanation of the human attitudes attributed to each of the nonhuman characters in the story.

COMPARING SELECTIONS

M'su Carencro and Mangeur de Poulet and Talk

COMPARE **THEMES**

Crow on wire and papier mâché.

What, in your opinion, is the universal message, or **theme,** of "Talk"? Of "M'su Carencro and Mangeur de Poulet"?

- A universal theme is one that applies to people all around the world and in all periods of history. Which of the themes do you think is most important for people today to hear? Why?
- Think of a book, movie, or television program that had a message about being yourself woven into a funny story. Write a brief review in which you compare the message of the book, movie, or program with the message of one of these folktales.

COMPARE **CHARACTERS**

In both selections, the dialogue and action tell what the animal, person, or object thinks about its place in the world. Discuss the following questions about the characters.

- Compare the farmer with the chicken hawk. What view of the world might they share? How could they have avoided conflict with other characters?
- What do the yam, the tree, the stone, and the dog feel they are entitled to? What does M'su Carencro feel that he is entitled to?

COMPARE **ANIMAL TALES**

Although animals and objects cannot speak in real life, both of these folktales allow creatures to speak for themselves. Write a brief reaction to the presence of talking animals or objects in these tales. The following questions will help you organize your ideas.

- When can talking animals and objects make a story more interesting?
- Could the presence of talking creatures in a story ever mean you would not want to read it? Explain.
- Which characters in the two selections did you find most enjoyable? Why?

Vo•cab•u•lar•y Skills

Using Roots

A word's **root** is its basic part. It carries the meaning of the word and can usually be used to make other words. For example, the root of *careless* is *care.* Prefixes and suffixes can be added to *care* to get *careful, uncaring,* and *carefree.*

Some roots, such as *care,* can stand alone. These are called "base words." Other roots make no sense by themselves and need a prefix, suffix, or other combining form to make a word. For example, *viv* means "life" or "live," but it requires a suffix or prefix to make a word. If you know that the prefix *re-* means "again," you can figure out that *revive* means "live again," or "bring to life again."

The more roots you learn, the more likely you are to have a good idea of what an unfamiliar word means. The chart below shows some common roots.

Root	Meaning	Example	Root	Meaning	Example
anim	life	animal	**aud**	hear	auditorium
belli	war	rebellion	**cogn**	know	recognize
cred	believe	credit	**dom**	house	domestic

EXERCISE

Use the chart above as well as your own knowledge to complete each sentence.

1. If the man is not cognizant of the yam, he does not
   a. know about it.
   b. fear it.
   c. feel annoyed by it.
2. If a stone is audible, it can be
   a. seen.
   b. felt.
   c. heard.
3. Stones are inanimate objects, so they must be
   a. hard.
   b. not alive.
   c. not valuable.
4. If a man runs away from his domicile, he leaves his
   a. field.
   b. home.
   c. helpers.
5. If he tells his story to a credulous listener, the listener is
   a. dishonest.
   b. funny.
   c. believing.
6. If other objects rebel, they will
   a. celebrate.
   b. fight back.
   c. follow a different leader.

Before You Read

The People Could Fly

MEET VIRGINIA HAMILTON

Many of Virginia Hamilton's award-winning books celebrate her African American ancestry and culture. "In the background of much of my writing is the dream of freedom tantalizingly out of reach," she says. This dream and her lifelong interest in African folklore are the source of many folktales like "The People Could Fly." The tale, which grew out of hope in the midst of enslavement, had been told orally for two hundred years before Hamilton crafted it into a written story.

Virginia Hamilton was born in Ohio in 1936. The People Could Fly: American Black Folktales *was published in 1985.*

FOCUS ACTIVITY

Where does someone who is treated with great injustice turn for help?

FreeWrite

Spend a few minutes writing down ways people escape a bad situation.

Setting a Purpose

Read to discover how some people deal with injustice.

BACKGROUND

The Time and Place This story takes place on a plantation in North America during the 1700s. Folktales are not specific about time and place because their themes are universal.

Did You Know? When Europeans were struggling through the Dark Ages (A.D. 476 to 1000), Africa boasted civilizations of wealthy kingdoms and talented artists. Then, in 1619, the practice of kidnapping Africans and bringing them to North America for slave labor began. Slavery was allowed to continue in parts of the United States until the end of the Civil War in 1865, when all enslaved people were freed.

Give Me 2 Wings to Fly Away, 1970s. John Biggers.

The People Could Fly, 1985. Leo & Diana Dillon. Pastel and watercolor. Private collection.

The People Could Fly

Told by Virginia Hamilton

They say the people could fly. Say that long ago in Africa, some of the people knew magic. And they would walk up on the air like climbin up on a gate. And they flew like blackbirds over the fields. Black, shiny wings flappin against the blue up there.

Then, many of the people were captured for Slavery. The ones that could fly shed their wings. They couldn't take their wings across the water on the slave ships. Too crowded, don't you know.

The folks were full of misery, then. Got sick with the up and down of the sea. So they forgot about flyin when they could no longer breathe the sweet scent of Africa.

Say the people who could fly kept their power, although they shed their wings. They kept their secret magic in the land of slavery. They looked the same as the other people from Africa who had been coming over, who had dark skin. Say you couldn't tell anymore one who could fly from one who couldn't.

One such who could was an old man, call him Toby. And standin tall, yet afraid, was a young woman who once had wings. Call her Sarah. Now Sarah carried a babe tied to her back. She trembled to be so hard worked and scorned.

The slaves labored in the fields from sunup to sundown. The owner of the slaves callin himself their Master. Say he was a hard lump of clay. A hard, glinty coal. A hard rock pile, wouldn't be moved. His Overseer[1] on horseback pointed out the slaves who were slowin down. So the one called Driver cracked his whip over the slow ones to make them move faster. That whip was a slice-open cut of pain. So they did move faster. Had to.

Sarah hoed and chopped the row as the babe on her back slept.

Say the child grew hungry. That babe started up bawling too loud. Sarah couldn't stop to feed it. Couldn't stop to soothe and quiet it down. She let it cry. She didn't want to. She had no heart to croon[2] to it.

"Keep that thing quiet," called the Overseer. He pointed his finger at the babe. The woman scrunched low. The Driver cracked his whip across the babe anyhow. The babe hollered like any hurt child, and the woman fell to the earth.

The old man that was there, Toby, came and helped her to her feet.

"I must go soon," she told him.

"Soon," he said.

Sarah couldn't stand up straight any longer. She was too weak. The sun burned her face. The babe cried and cried, "Pity me, oh, pity me," say it sounded like.

Sarah was so sad and starvin, she sat down in the row.

"Get up, you black cow," called the Overseer. He pointed his hand, and the Driver's whip snarled around Sarah's legs. Her sack dress tore into rags. Her legs bled onto the earth. She couldn't get up.

Toby was there where there was no one to help her and the babe.

"Now, before it's too late," panted Sarah. "Now, Father!"

"Yes, Daughter, the time is come," Toby answered. "Go, as you know how to go!"

He raised his arms, holding them out to her. "*Kum . . . yali, kum buba tambe,*" and more magic words, said so quickly, they sounded like whispers and sighs.

The young woman lifted one foot on the air. Then the other. She flew clumsily at first, with the child now held tightly in her arms. Then she felt the magic, the African mystery. Say she rose just as free as a bird. As light as a feather.

The Overseer rode after her, hollerin. Sarah flew over the fences. She flew over the woods. Tall trees could not snag her. Nor could the Overseer. She flew like an eagle now, until she was gone from sight. No one dared speak about it. Couldn't believe it. But it was, because they that was there saw that it was.

Say the next day was dead hot in the fields. A young man slave fell from the heat. The Driver come and whipped him. Toby come over and spoke words to the fallen one. The words of ancient Africa once heard are never remembered completely. The young man forgot them as soon as he heard them. They went way inside him. He got up and rolled over on the air. He rode it awhile. And he flew away.

1. An *overseer* is the person who watches over and directs the work of laborers.
2. To sing or hum in a soft, low tone is to *croon.*

Alexander Chandler, 1955. Andrew Wyeth. Drybrush, 21¼ x 14½ in. Private collection. Photograph courtesy of the Wyeth Collection. © Andrew Wyeth.

Viewing the painting: Study the expression and pose of the man in this painting. What personal qualities might he have in common with Toby?

Another and another fell from the heat. Toby was there. He cried out to the fallen and reached his arms out to them. "*Kum kunka yali, kum . . . tambe!*" Whispers and sighs. And they too rose on the air. They rode the hot breezes. The ones flyin were black and shinin sticks, wheelin above the head of the Overseer. They crossed the rows, the fields, the fences, the streams, and were away.

"Seize the old man!" cried the Overseer. "I heard him say the magic *words*. Seize him!"

The one callin himself Master come runnin. The Driver got his whip ready to curl around old Toby and tie him up. The slaveowner took his hip gun from its place. He meant to kill old, black Toby.

But Toby just laughed. Say he threw back his head and said, "Hee, hee! Don't you know who I am? Don't you know some of us in this field?" He said it to their faces. "We are ones who fly!"

And he sighed the ancient words that were a dark promise. He said them all around to the others in the field under the whip, ". . . *buba yali* . . . *buba tambe*. . . ."

There was a great outcryin. The bent backs straighted up. Old and young who were called slaves and could fly joined hands. Say like they would ring-sing. But they didn't shuffle in a circle. They didn't sing. They rose on the air. They flew in a flock that was black against the heavenly blue. Black crows or black shadows. It didn't matter, they went so high. Way above the plantation, way over the slavery land. Say they flew away to *Free-dom*.

And the old man, old Toby, flew behind them, takin care of them. He wasn't cryin. He wasn't laughin. He was the seer. His gaze fell on the plantation where the slaves who could not fly waited.

"*Take us with you!*" Their looks spoke it but they were afraid to shout it. Toby couldn't take them with him. Hadn't the time to teach them to fly. They must wait for a chance to run.

"Goodie-bye!" The old man called Toby spoke to them, poor souls! And he was flyin gone.

So they say. The Overseer told it. The one called Master said it was a lie, a trick of the light. The Driver kept his mouth shut.

The slaves who could not fly told about the people who could fly to their children. When they were free. When they sat close before the fire in the free land, they told it. They did so love firelight and *Free-dom*, and tellin.

They say that the children of the ones who could not fly told their children. And now, me, I have told it to you.

Responding to Literature

PERSONAL RESPONSE

- ✦ With whom would you like to share this story? Why?
- ✦ Look back at your freewriting from the **Focus Activity** on page 388. Would your methods of escape work for any of the characters in this tale?

Analyzing Literature

RECALL

1. Why can't the people who were captured fly away from the ships?
2. What happens to the words of ancient Africa once they are heard?
3. How do those who cannot fly react to the amazing flight of their companions?
4. How has the story been passed down?

INTERPRET

5. What other sickness besides seasickness might the captured people have felt? Why?
6. Why does Toby choose to speak the magic words when he does?
7. When Toby speaks the words of Africa, the words go "way inside" a young enslaved man. What does this phrase mean?
8. What messages does this tale hold for people in the days of slavery and for people today?

EVALUATE AND CONNECT

9. In your opinion, does this story succeed in showing the evils of slavery?
10. Do you agree with Toby's decision not to speak the magic words earlier in the story? Explain your reasoning.

LITERARY ELEMENTS

Simile and Metaphor

The lively descriptions Virginia Hamilton uses in her writing are strengthened by a kind of figurative language in which she compares unlike things. A **simile** makes a comparison by using the words *as* or *like:* "They flew like blackbirds over the fields." Another type of comparison, a **metaphor,** does not use the words *as* or *like:* "He was a hard lump of clay." Figures of speech such as these help readers picture the characters, the action, or the setting of a story.

1. Why did the people who watched Sarah begin to fly think of her as "free as a bird, as light as a feather"?
2. List one additional simile and metaphor from "The People Could Fly." Explain what each adds to a reader's understanding of the characters, setting, or action.

- See **Literary Terms Handbook,** p. R9 and R6.

Extending Your Response

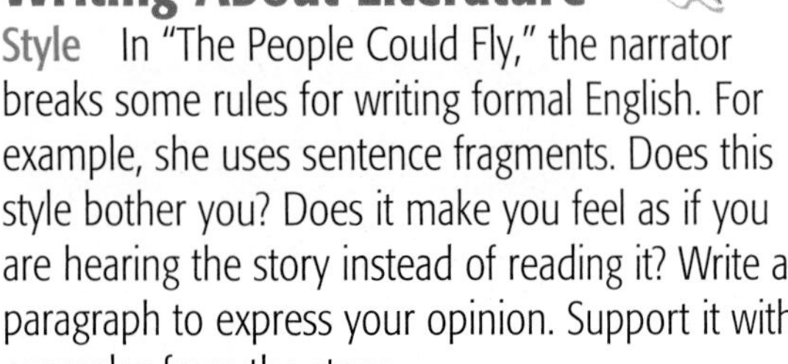

Writing About Literature

Style In "The People Could Fly," the narrator breaks some rules for writing formal English. For example, she uses sentence fragments. Does this style bother you? Does it make you feel as if you are hearing the story instead of reading it? Write a paragraph to express your opinion. Support it with examples from the story.

Learning for Life

Lights, Camera, Action! Imagine that you have been hired to make a movie of "The People Could Fly." Choose one scene and make a storyboard (a series of drawings that show what happens). If you can put together a cast of actors, you may make a photostory board. Present your plan to the class.

Creative Writing

First-person Account Imagine that you are present when Toby and the others fly. Write a short description of the event and of your reactions to it. How does it make you feel to watch them? What exactly do you see? What do you do next? What advice would you have for those left behind? Why do you think people may or may not believe your story?

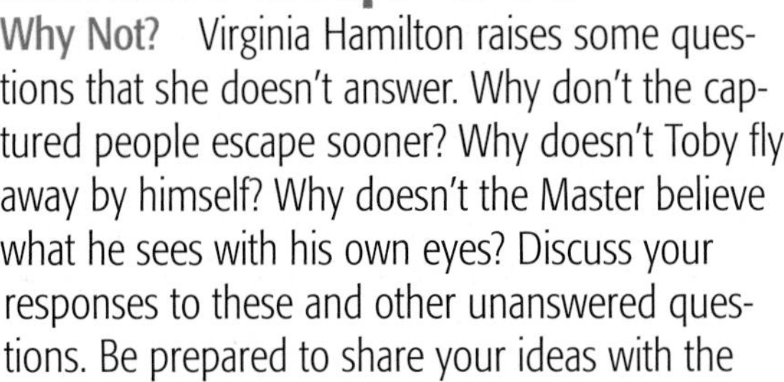

Literature Groups

Why Not? Virginia Hamilton raises some questions that she doesn't answer. Why don't the captured people escape sooner? Why doesn't Toby fly away by himself? Why doesn't the Master believe what he sees with his own eyes? Discuss your responses to these and other unanswered questions. Be prepared to share your ideas with the whole class.

Reading Further

For more by Virginia Hamilton, try these:

Justice and Her Brothers

Arilla Sun Down

Save your work for your portfolio.

Skill Minilesson

READING AND THINKING • QUESTIONING

"The People Could Fly" begins with the words, "They say." Perhaps you have questions about this story introduction. Who are "they" and what do they say? Other phrases and descriptions in the story may have caused you to stop and question how you should interpret their meanings.

PRACTICE Write three or four other questions that the language in this selection raises in your mind. Discuss the questions with classmates. See if you can discover the answers.

- For more about reading strategies, see **Reading Handbook,** pp. R84–R95.

Setting a Purpose for Reading

When you sit down to read an assignment, what is the first thing you do? Skillful readers take the time to preview the material and then **set a purpose for reading.** They look over the first few paragraphs and ask questions like the following:

- Is the selection fiction, poetry, or nonfiction?
- Do the title and opening images (pictures, charts, or graphs) give clues about the content of the selection?
- Is there dialogue in the selection? Are there clues to the setting?

Scan the opening paragraph from "Spotted Eagle and Black Crow." What purpose can you think of for reading the entire story?

> **This is a story of two warriors, of jealousy, and of eagles. This legend is supposed to have been a favorite of the great *Mahpiya Luta*—Chief Red Cloud of the Oglalas.**

The selection is a narrative, a Native American legend from the Oglala people. Your purpose for reading on may be to identify the other story elements–plot, theme, and setting. Because legends are written to entertain as well as to inform, you also may read to enjoy the story. You may want to read to find out what life was like then for these Native Americans.

- For more about setting a purpose, see **Reading Handbook,** p. R84.

ACTIVITY

Choose a selection from this book that you have already read, or select a chapter from a history or science book. Determine your purpose for reading by answering the bulleted questions above as well as the following ones.

1. Does this selection contain material that I need to know?
2. What in the selection will interest or entertain me?
3. What is my purpose for reading this selection?

Technology Skills

Photography: The Basics of Picture Taking

Today's technology has created cameras that do most of the work for you. Instead of worrying about shutter speeds and lens openings, you can concentrate on setting up shots or taking candid pictures that say what you want them to. The pictures you take can be scanned and inserted into word processing or Web documents to complement the text and make your work more visually interesting.

Steps to Taking Better Pictures

Try to remember the following points when you take photos.

STEP	REASON
Get close!	If your subject is the Grand Canyon, you'll want a distant shot, but if you're photographing people, get close. Failing to get close enough to a subject is a major reason for ineffective photographs. Focus on the key elements. For instance, if you're taking a head-and-shoulders shot, make sure you can see your subject's eyes.
Keep it simple.	Try to focus on only one or two subjects per photograph. A cluttered background detracts from the overall picture.
Keep it steady!	If you're getting fuzzy pictures, you might be shaking the camera. Try tilting your head forward a bit to balance the camera against your forehead, or use a tripod.
Go off-center.	Put the subject of your picture a little to the left or right of the frame to add variety and a sense of movement.
Experiment!	Try taking pictures from a variety of angles. If you take a photograph from above, the subject is minimized. If you take it from below, it is emphasized. Tilting the camera so your shots are on an angle lends a sense of unease.
Pose with action.	Most posed photographs feature a subject staring at the camera, arms hanging down awkwardly. Try to capture your subjects doing something that expresses who they are, whether it's playing a saxophone or shooting a basketball.
Extreme close-up!	Try the extreme close-up to focus on a specific element. For instance, if you're looking for a shot to accompany a love poem, you can take a picture of two people holding hands, or you can take an extreme close-up of just their hands.

Getting Started with Photography

1. The first thing to do is familiarize yourself with your camera. Different cameras have different features. You can get acquainted with them by reading the manual or looking through the photography section at your local library.
2. Study the work of the pros. You can find books of photos by great photographers at the library. The World Wide Web is another good source. Try the Library of Congress site (http://lcweb.loc.gov). Use a search engine and the keywords *photography* and *museums* to find other sources. As you examine an image, ask yourself, What makes this a great photograph?
3. Next, go out and take pictures. Take them at night, outdoors, indoors, of groups, of individuals, with flash, and without flash. Experiment. If you have an instant camera, you can view your work immediately and adjust accordingly.
4. Don't be afraid of black and white. Most of the greatest photographers of the past worked with black-and-white film and so do many of today's photographers. You can do things with light and shadow in black and white that color cannot duplicate.
5. The most important aspect of photography is fun. With a little skill and a lot of practice, you can create real art.

TECHNOLOGY TIP

More and more photographers are turning to digital cameras. With a digital camera, a memory card replaces film. You can see your pictures almost instantly on the camera's small screen. If you don't like a picture, you can delete it from memory and try again. The digital picture files can be transferred directly into your computer, where you can use them in word processing documents or put them into an E-mail message.

ACTIVITIES

1. Choose one or two selections from this theme and take photographs that relate to the literature in some way. For instance, your photos could illustrate the plot of a story, represent the theme, or capture a personal quality of one of the characters.
2. Include photographs with your next written assignment by scanning them into your computer and inserting them into your word processed document.
3. Volunteer to take pictures for the yearbook or school newspaper.

This classic photo of a migrant mother was taken by Dorothea Lange in 1936. It has been reprinted and exhibited countless times since then. What do you think makes it a great photo?

Before You Read

The Souls in Purgatory

MEET GUADALUPE BACA-VAUGHN

Guadalupe Baca-Vaughn (gwä dä lo͞o′ pā bä′ kä vôn) has been interested in storytelling since she was a little girl in New Mexico, where her aunt told her stories from old Mexico. Baca-Vaughn later became a teacher, and she shared her love of stories with others. Setting aside Fridays as storytelling time, Baca-Vaughn told stories and invited students to tell their stories. Among the children's favorites, she remembers, were tales of the supernatural, including "The Souls in Purgatory."

Guadalupe Baca-Vaughn was born in 1905. This story was published in 1987 in Voces: An Anthology of Nuevo Mexicano Writers.

FOCUS ACTIVITY

Have you ever exaggerated your abilities or performed a difficult task to impress another person? What was the result?

Journal

In your journal, list some times you think impressing someone may be important and times when it is not a good idea to try.

Setting a Purpose

Read to find out what happens when a young woman is expected to perform impossible feats.

BACKGROUND

The Time and Place Like most folktales, this story does not have a specific setting. It probably originated in Mexico or New Mexico.

Did You Know? The Roman Catholic Church has taught that the souls of those who die without sin go directly to heaven. The souls of those who die with mortal—very serious—sin go to hell. However, the souls of those who die with less serious sin enter a state of purgatory. In purgatory, these souls wait to be purified from sin in order to enter heaven. The living can help purify these souls by praying and doing good deeds on the souls' behalf.

VOCABULARY PREVIEW

intercession (in′ tər sesh′ ən) *n.* a request, appeal, or prayer in the interest of another or others; p. 400

dumbfounded (dum′ found′ əd) *adj.* made speechless with amazement; astonished; p. 400

reproach (ri prōch′) *v.* to scold or blame; p. 401

vibrant (vī′ brənt) *adj.* full of life and energy; p. 402

The Souls in Purgatory

Retold by
Guadalupe Baca-Vaughn

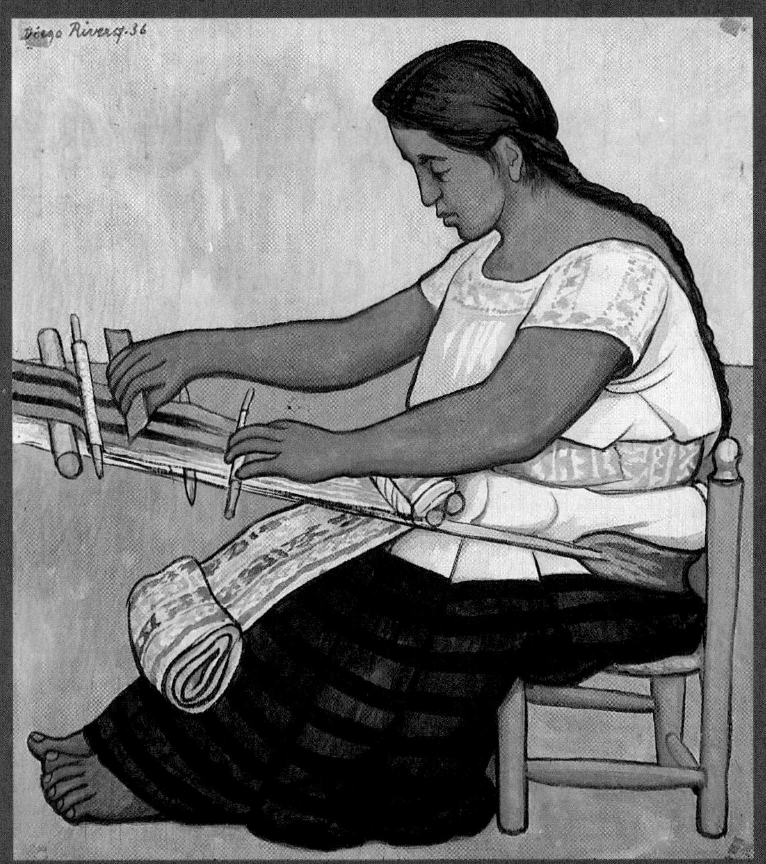

Tejedora (Weaver), 1936. Diego Rivera. Watercolor on rice paper, 22½ x 20⅝. Private collection.

Si es verdad, allá va,
Si es mentira, queda urdida.

(If it be true, so it is.
If it be false, so be it.)

There was once an old lady who had raised a niece since she was a tiny baby. She had taught the girl to be good, obedient, and industrious, but the girl was very shy and timid, and spent much time praying, especially to the Souls in Purgatory.

The Souls in Purgatory

As the girl grew older and very beautiful, the old woman began to worry that when she died her niece would be left all alone in the world, a world which her niece saw only through innocent eyes. The old lady prayed daily to all the saints in heaven for their intercession to Our Lord that He might send some good man who would fall in love with her niece and marry her . . . then she could die in peace.

As it happens, the old woman did chores for a *comadre*[1] who had a rooming house. Among her tenants there was a seemingly rich merchant who one day said that he would like to get married if he could find a nice quiet girl who knew how to keep house, and be a good wife and mother to his children when they came.

The old lady opened her ears and began to smile and scheme in her mind, for she could imagine her niece married to the nice gentleman. She told the merchant that he could find all that he was looking for in her niece, who was a jewel, a piece of gold, and so gifted that she could even catch birds while they were flying!

The gentleman became interested and said that he would like to meet the girl, and would go to her house the next day.

The old woman ran home as fast as she could, she appeared to be flying. When she got home all out of breath, she called her niece and told her to straighten up the house and get herself ready for the next day, as there was a gentleman who would be calling. She told her to be sure to wash her hair and brush it until it shone like the sun, and to put on her best dress, for in this meeting her future was at stake.

The poor timid girl was dumbfounded. She went to her room and knelt before her favorite *retablo* of the Souls in Purgatory. "Please," she prayed, "don't let my aunt do something rash to embarrass us both."

Did You Know?
A *retablo* (rə tä′ blō) is a wooden panel painted or carved with a religious picture.

The next day she obediently prepared herself for the meeting. When the merchant arrived, he asked her if she could spin. "Spin?" answered the old woman, while the poor embarrassed girl stood by with bowed head. "Spin! The hanks[2] disappear so fast you would think she was drinking them like water."

The merchant left three hanks of linen to be spun by the following day. "What have you done Tía?"[3] the poor girl asked. "You know I can't spin!" "Don't sell yourself short," the old lady replied with twinkling eyes. "Where is your faith in God, the Souls in Purgatory? You pray to them every day. They will help you. Just wait and see!" Sobbing, the girl ran to her room and knelt down beside her bed and began to pray,

1. The Spanish word *comadre* (kō mä′ drā) may refer to a godmother or to any female friend.

2. Here, the *hanks* are bundles of fibers that are spun into yarn or thread.

3. *Tía* (tē′ ə) means "aunt."

Vocabulary

intercession (in′ tər sesh′ ən) *n.* a request, appeal, or prayer in the interest of another or others

dumbfounded (dum′ found′ əd) *adj.* made speechless with amazement; astonished often raising her head to the *retablo* of the Souls in Purgatory which hung on the wall beside her bed. After she quieted down, she thought she heard a soft sound behind her. She turned and saw three beautiful ghosts dressed in white, smiling at her. "Do not be concerned," they said, "we will help you in gratitude for all the good you have done for us." Saying this, each one took a hank of linen and in a wink spun the linen into thread as fine as hair.

The following day when the merchant came, he was astonished to see the beautiful linen, and was very pleased. "Didn't I tell you, Sir?" said the old lady with pride and joy. The gentleman asked the girl if she could sew. Before the surprised girl could answer, the old aunt cried. "Sew? Of course she can sew. Her sewing is like ripe cherries in the mouth of a dragon." The merchant then left a piece of the finest linen to be made into three shirts. The poor girl cried bitterly, but her aunt told her not to worry, that her devotion to the Poor Souls would get her out of this one too, as they had shown how much they loved her on the previous day.

The three ghosts were waiting for the girl beside her bed when she went into her room, crying miserably. "Don't cry, little girl," they said. "We will help you again, for we know your aunt, and she knows what she is doing and why."

The ghosts went to work cutting and snipping and sewing. In a flash they had three beautiful shirts finished with the finest stitches and the tiniest seams.

The next morning when the gentleman came to see if the girl had finished the shirts, he could not believe his eyes. "They are lovely, they seem to have been made in heaven," he said.

This time the merchant left a vest of rare satin to be embroidered. He thought he would try this girl for the third and last time. The girl cried desperately, and could not even reproach her aunt. She had decided that she would not ask any more favors of the Souls. She went to her room and lay across the bed and cried and cried. When she finally sat up and dried her tears, she saw the three ghosts smiling at her. "We will help you again, but this time we have a condition, and that is that you will invite us to your wedding." "Wedding? Am I going to get married?" she asked in surprise. "Yes," they said, "and very soon."

Vocabulary

reproach (ri prōch′) *v.* to scold or blame

Mujeres, La Cama Azul, 1910–1913. José Clemente Orozco. Oil. Private collection.

Viewing the painting: How do the figures in this painting compare with the descriptions of the souls in this story?

The next day a very happy gentleman came for his vest, for he was sure that the lovely girl would have it ready for him. But he was not prepared for the beauty of the vest. The colors were vibrant and beautifully matched. The embroidery looked like a painting. It took his breath away. Without hesitation, he asked the old lady for her niece's hand in marriage. "For," he said, "this vest looks as if it was not touched by human hands, but by angels!"

The old woman danced with joy, and could hardly contain her happiness. She gave her consent at once. The merchant left to arrange for the wedding. Wringing her hands, the poor girl cried, "But Tía, what am I going to do when he finds out that I can't do any of those things?" "Don't worry, my *Palomita,*[4] the Blessed Souls will get you out of this trouble too. You wait and see!"

Almost at once the old woman went to her *comadre* to tell her the good news, and to ask her to help get ready for the wedding. Soon everything was ready.

4. Used here as an affectionate term, *Palomita* (päl′ ō mē′ tə) means "little dove."

Vocabulary

vibrant (vī′ brənt) *adj.* full of life and energy

The poor girl did not know how to invite the Souls to her wedding. She timidly went and stood beside her bed and asked the *retablo* to come to her wedding.

The great day finally arrived. The girl looked beautiful in the gown which the merchant had brought as part of her *donas*.[5] Everyone in the village had been invited to the wedding.

During the fiesta when everyone was drinking *brindes* to the bride and groom, and the music was playing, three ugly hags came to the *sala*[6] and stood waiting for the groom to come and welcome them in. One of the hags had an arm that reached to the floor and dragged; the other arm was short. The second hag was bent almost double, and had to turn her head sideways to look up. The third hag had bulging, bloodshot eyes like a lobster. "Jesús María," cried the groom. "Who are those ugly creatures?" "They are aunts of my father, whom I invited to my wedding," answered the bride, knowing quite well who they might be. The groom, being well bred, went at once to greet the ugly hags. He took them to their seats and brought them refreshments. Very casually, he asked the first hag, "Tell me, Señora,[7] why is one of your arms so long and the other one short?" "My son," she answered, "my arms are like that because I spin so much."

The groom went to his wife and said, "Go at once and tell the servants to burn your spinning wheel, and never let me see a spinning wheel in my house, never let me see you spinning ever!"

The groom went to the second hag and asked her why she was so humped over. "My son," she replied, "I am that way from embroidering on a frame so much." The groom went to his wife and whispered, "Burn your embroidery frame at once, and never let me see you embroider another thing."

Next, the groom went to the third hag and asked, "Why are your eyes so bloodshot and bulging?" "My son, it is because I sew so much and bend over while sewing." She had hardly finished speaking when the groom went to his wife and said, "Take your needles and thread and bury them. I never want to see you sewing, never! If I see you sewing, I will divorce you and send you far away, for the wise man learns from others' painful experiences."

Well . . . so the Souls, in spite of being holy, can also be rascals.

Colorín, colorado,
ya mi cuento se ha acabado.
(Scarlet or ruby red,
my story has been said.)

5. The gifts a groom gives to his bride upon their marriage are called *donas* (dō′ nəs).
6. *Brindes* (brēn′ dās) are toasts—drinks in honor of a person or thing. A *sala* (sä′ lə) is a parlor or other large room used for entertaining.
7. *Señora* (sen yôr′ ə) can mean either "Mrs." or, as here, "Madam."

Responding to Literature

PERSONAL RESPONSE

- ✦ Did you find this story humorous? Why or why not?
- ✦ If you were in a challenging situation, would you want the Souls to help you? Explain.

Analyzing Literature

RECALL

1. Briefly describe the girl and her aunt. How are they alike and different?
2. List the three tests that the merchant wants the girl to perform. How does she pass each test?
3. What does the girl say when the merchant questions the presence of the Souls at the fiesta?
4. How do the Souls solve the girl's problem?

INTERPRET

5. The Souls tell the girl: "We know your aunt, and she knows what she is doing and why." What do you think the Souls mean by this statement?
6. The merchant says how much he likes his new garments. How does this **dialogue** add to the humor of the story?
7. Is the girl less shy by the end of the story? Explain.
8. "The Souls, in spite of being holy, can also be rascals." Why is this a suitable line to end the story?

EVALUATE AND CONNECT

9. What qualities does the merchant appreciate in his bride? What qualities does he dislike in the Souls? How does the storyteller use this information to **characterize** the merchant?
10. In what ways does this story remind you of other folktales you know? In what ways is it different?

LITERARY ELEMENTS

Climax and Falling Action

The **climax** is the turning point of a story. The climax in "The Souls in Purgatory" occurs when the three hags come to the wedding. Readers wait in suspense to see if their arrival will cause a good or bad outcome for the girl. The falling action of a story follows the climax and leads to the resolution of the problem or plot. In this story, the **falling action** occurs when the groom greets the hags and asks each one to explain her appearance.

1. What positive or negative outcomes could result from the climax of "The Souls in Purgatory"?
2. At what point in the falling action is it clear that the hags will solve the girl's problem?
3. Look back at one other folktale from this theme and identify its climax.

- See **Literary Terms Handbook,** p. R2 and R3.

Mexican Shawl (Rebozo), c. 1790. Silk fabric, silver and gold thread, 28½ x 87 in. Parham Park, West Sussex, Great Britain.

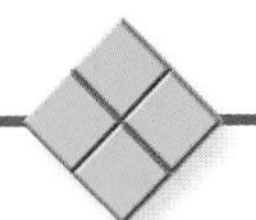

Literature and Writing

Writing About Literature

Analyze an Epigraph An **epigraph** is a quotation at the beginning of a story that gives a clue about the writer's intention. Read the epigraph at the beginning of "The Souls in Purgatory." What does it tell you about the writer's intention? Is it an effective way to begin the story? Why or why not?

Creative Writing

A Character's Journal Read over your journal entry from the **Focus Activity** on page 398. Imagine that you are the girl in "The Souls in Purgatory." Write a journal entry describing the wedding day. How does she feel when the Souls appear? How does she feel at the end of the story?

Extending Your Response

Literature Groups

Talk About the Three Souls Read over the information about purgatory on page 398. Discuss these questions: Why are the three Souls in purgatory in the first place? Is it surprising that they behave as "rascals" in the story? Why or why not? Finally, discuss possible ways the story would be different if, in the folktale, three angels came to the girl's aid instead of three Souls.

Art Activity

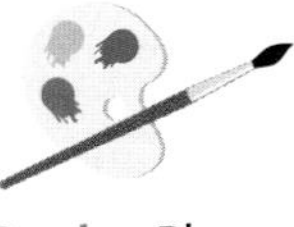

Design a Picture Book Plan a children's picture book to illustrate "The Souls in Purgatory." Reread the folktale and identify the most important images from the story. Be sure to include the different appearances of the Souls, both as ghosts and as hags, in your plan. Make rough sketches of the illustrations and write captions to go with them.

Interdisciplinary Activity

Social Studies What do people around the world believe about life after death? With a partner, research two or three major world religions and compare their views of the afterlife with the view suggested in this story. Conduct your research on the Internet and in encyclopedias and other books. Share your findings with the class.

Reading Further

For stories about girls who had to rely on their wits to escape unwanted suitors, try these novels:
A Girl Named Disaster by Nancy Farmer
Catherine, Called Birdy by Karen Cushman

Save your work for your portfolio.

Skill Minilessons

GRAMMAR AND LANGUAGE • ACTIVE AND PASSIVE VOICE

A verb is in the **active voice** when the subject performs the action of the verb. A verb is in the **passive voice** when the subject receives the action of the verb.

. . . the old woman began to worry. . . .

The verb *began* is active because the woman (the subject of the clause) is performing the action.

. . . her niece would be left all alone. . . .

The verb phrase *would be left* is passive because the niece (the subject of the clause) receives the action of the verb.

PRACTICE Tell if the underlined verb or verb phrase is in the active or passive voice.

1. The old lady opened her ears.
2. This vest looks as if it was not touched by human hands.
3. Bury your needles and thread.
4. My story has been said.

- For more about active and passive voice, see **Language Handbook,** p. R34.

READING AND THINKING • SUMMARIZING

A **summary** is a short statement that tells the important events and ideas in a story. Summarizing can help you understand and remember a story. It is also a good way to share the story's plot with others.

- For more about summarizing, see **Reading Handbook,** p. R90.

PRACTICE Summarize "The Souls in Purgatory" for someone who has not read it. Be sure to include the most important events, in the correct order, as well as the important details about characters and setting. However, keep in mind that a summary is a *short* statement. Be sure to select only important elements as you share the story.

VOCABULARY • THE PREFIX *inter-*

Intercession combines the prefix *inter-,* meaning "between" or "among," with the root *cede,* which means "to go." If you try to help one person by making a request of another, you intercede, or "go between" the two people. The request or effort you make is an *intercession.* Sometimes, the prefix *inter-* is attached to a whole word instead of to a root.

PRACTICE Choose the word that fits each phrase.

intercollegiate	interplanetary
interdependence	interstate
interlock	intertwine

1. what the pieces of a jigsaw puzzle do
2. a game between two universities
3. a highway between Ohio and Iowa
4. what vines do when they twist
5. people's need for each other
6. type of travel between Earth and Mars

Celebrating Life and Death, Mexican Style

People often think of death as a sad part of life, but once a year in Mexico, it is cause for celebration. *El Día de los Muertos* (the Day of the Dead) is a uniquely Mexican holiday in which families try to tempt dead loved ones back to earth for a visit. Food, flowers, music, and dancing are all part of this three-day fiesta, which begins on October 31.

At the heart of this celebration are *ofrendas,* or offerings, for deceased relatives. Families often create an altar in their homes to prepare for the arrival of their dead loved ones. Around the altar, they carefully spread out their *ofrenda.* This offering may contain the deceased's favorite foods–such as hot chocolate, tamales, and *mole* (a spicy chocolate-based sauce served over meat)–as well as loaves of *pan de muertos* (bread of the dead), flowers, candles, and old photographs. You might even see some favorite belongings, such as a pair of cowboy boots. Outdoors, orange and yellow flowers line gravestones and pathways to illuminate the way home for the dead.

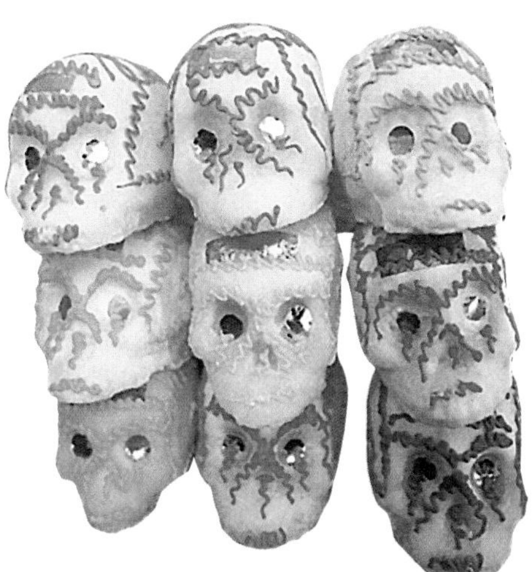
Candy skulls

Meanwhile, the living take special care to enjoy life. Children exchange candy skulls with friends. Families visit each other and share food left over from the altars. All-night picnics with dancing and singing take place in the cemeteries. In some regions, people even write special poems and songs or perform skits that often focus on humorous memories. One type of poem, the *calavera,* is a humorous obituary for a well-known person who is still alive.

The Day of the Dead fiesta originated hundreds of years ago when Spanish and Aztec cultures integrated in Mexico. (The Spanish, like many of their American neighbors to the north, celebrated All Hallows' Eve on October 31 and All Saints' Day on November 1.) Today, many Mexican American communities blend Halloween with traditional activities for Día de los Muertos.

Young people say the celebration helps them feel close to the memory of their grandparents and other relatives by bringing the spirits of their loved ones back to life with stories and art. By nightfall on November 2, the living and the dead part ways again, at peace with one another.

ACTIVITY

Choose a famous person who is no longer alive and whose life you would like to celebrate with an *ofrenda.* You might want to write a *calavera* (a rhyming poem written in the form of an obituary) for the person too. Make the *ofrenda* a colorful, artistic symbol of the good qualities you remember about that person.

Before You Read

Spotted Eagle and Black Crow and *The Siege of Courthouse Rock*

MEET JENNY LEADING CLOUD

Storyteller Jenny Leading Cloud recounted many legends from her Sioux heritage to artist and writer Richard Erdoes in the late 1960s. Erdoes transcribed the stories and published them in his collections of Native American tales. In describing the storyteller, Erdoes said, "She was a very bright, very active, very in-your-face lady. . . . She liked to tell stories." Leading Cloud spent her life in White River, a town on the Rosebud Reservation in South Dakota.

Jenny Leading Cloud was born in South Dakota in the late 1800s and died sometime around 1980.

FOCUS ACTIVITY

Why do people seek revenge? Think of several reasons.

Share and Write

With a classmate, discuss reasons why people get revenge and how they go about getting revenge. Then write a definition for revenge. Share your definition with the entire class.

Setting a Purpose

As you read, discover how the characters take revenge on their enemies.

BACKGROUND

The Time and Place These legends, told from the Sioux point of view, focus on centuries-old competition between the Sioux and the Pahani, or Pawnee, who lived in modern-day Nebraska. The Sioux lived and hunted in what are now Nebraska, Minnesota, Montana, and North and South Dakota.

Did You Know? In Sioux tradition, most young men belonged to a warrior society. They were invited to join or were sponsored by an older warrior. Warriors gained honor and prestige by performing brave acts during battle.

VOCABULARY PREVIEW

sheer (shēr) *adj.* very steep; straight up or down; p. 410
abyss (ə bis′) *n.* an extremely deep hole; p. 411
enmity (en′ mə tē) *n.* the bitter hatred between enemies; ill will; p. 412
alight (ə līt′) *v.* to come down after flight; land; p. 413
pact (pakt) *n.* an agreement; deal; pledge; p. 413
summit (sum′ it) *n.* the highest point or part; peak; p. 415
jut (jut) *v.* to extend outward or upward from a surface; bulge; p. 415

When the Eagle Spoke to Me, 1979. Jerry Ingram. Watercolor on paper, 18 x 24 in. Collection of the artist.

Spotted Eagle and Black Crow

Told by Jenny Leading Cloud

This is a story of two warriors, of jealousy, and of eagles. This legend is supposed to have been a favorite of the great *Mahpiya Luta*—Chief Red Cloud of the Oglalas.[1]

1. The *Oglalas* (ō glä′ ləs) are a Teton (tē′ ton), or Western Sioux, people. Red Cloud was a chief during the 1860s, when Sioux hunting grounds were overrun by white settlers.

Many lifetimes ago, there lived two brave warriors. One was named *Wanblee Gleska*—Spotted Eagle. The other's name was *Kangi Sapa*—Black Crow. They were friends but, as it happened, they both loved the same girl, *Zintkala Luta Win*—Red Bird. She was beautiful, a fine tanner and quill-worker,[2] and she liked Spotted Eagle best, which made Black Crow very jealous. Black Crow went to his friend and said, "Let us, you and I, go on a war party against the Pahani. Let us get ourselves some fine horses and earn eagle feathers." Spotted Eagle thought this a good idea. The two young men purified themselves in a sweat bath. They got out their war medicine[3] and their war shields. They painted their faces. They did all that warriors should do before a raid. Then they went against the Pahani.

Their raid was not a success. The Pahani were watchful. The young warriors got nowhere near the Pahani horse herd. Not only did they capture no ponies, but they even lost their own mounts, because while they were trying to creep up to their enemies' herd, the Pahani found their horses. The two young men had a hard time getting away on foot because the enemy were searching for them everywhere. At one time they had to hide themselves in a lake, under the water, breathing through long, hollow reeds which were sticking up above the surface. They were so clever at hiding themselves that the Pahani finally gave up searching for them.

The young men had to travel home on foot. It was a long way. Their moccasins were tattered, their feet bleeding. At last they came to a high cliff. "Let us go up there," said Black Crow, "and see whether the enemy is following us." They climbed up. They could see no one following them; but on a ledge far below them, halfway up the cliff, they spied a nest with two young eagles in it. "Let us at least get those eagles," Black Crow proposed. There was no way one could climb down the sheer rock wall, but Black Crow took his rawhide lariat, made a loop in it, put the rope around Spotted Eagle's chest under his armpits, and lowered him down. When his friend was on the ledge with the nest, Black Crow said to himself, "I will leave him there to die. I will come home alone and then Red Bird will marry me." And he threw his end of the rawhide thong down and left without looking back and without listening to Spotted Eagle's cries of what had happened to the lariat and to Black Crow.

Spotted Eagle cried in vain. He got no answer, only silence. At last it dawned

2. As a *tanner,* Red Bird made animal skins into leather. As a *quill-worker,* she made decorations using porcupine quills.
3. In reward for acts of bravery, warriors were given *eagle feathers* to wear in their headdresses. Among Native Americans, *medicine* refers to objects or ceremonies thought to have special powers.

Vocabulary
sheer (shēr) *adj.* very steep; straight up or down

on him that his companion had betrayed him, that he had been left to die. The lariat was much too short for him to lower himself to the ground; there was an abyss of two hundred feet yawning beneath him. He was left with the two young eagles screeching at him, angered that this strange, two-legged creature had invaded their home.

Black Crow came back to his village. "Spotted Eagle died a warrior's death," he told the people. "The Pahani killed him." There was loud wailing throughout the village because everybody had liked Spotted Eagle. Red Bird grieved more than the others. She slashed her arms with a sharp knife and cut her hair to make plain her sorrow to all. But in the end she became Black Crow's wife, because life must go on.

But Spotted Eagle did not die on his lonely ledge. The eagles got used to him. The old eagles brought plenty of food—rabbits, prairie dogs, or sage hens—and Spotted Eagle shared this raw meat with the two chicks. Maybe it was the eagle medicine in his bundle which he carried on his chest that made the eagles accept him. Still, he had a very hard time on that ledge. It was so narrow that, when he wanted to rest, he had to tie himself with the rawhide thong to a little rock sticking out of the cliff, for fear of falling off the ledge in his sleep. In this way he spent a few very uncomfortable weeks; after all, he was a human being and not a bird to whom such a crack in the rock face is home.

At last the young eagles were big enough to practice flying. "What will become of me now?" thought the young warrior. "Once these fledglings[4] have flown the nest for good, the old birds won't be bringing any more food up here." Then he had an inspiration. "Perhaps I will die. Very likely I will die. But I will try it. I will not just sit here and give up." He took his little pipe out of the medicine bundle and lifted it to the sky and prayed, "*Wakan Tanka, onshimala ye.*

4. *Fledglings* are young birds that haven't yet grown the feathers needed to fly.

Vocabulary
abyss (ə bis′) *n.* an extremely deep hole

Great Spirit, pity me. You have created man and his cousin, the eagle. You have given me the eagle's name. I have decided to try to let the eagles carry me to the ground. Let the eagles help me, let me succeed."

He smoked and felt a surge of confidence. He grabbed hold of the legs of the two young eagles. "Brothers," he told them, "you have accepted me as one of your own. Now we will live together, or die together. *Hokahay*." And he jumped off the ledge. He expected to be shattered on the ground below, but with a mighty flapping of wings the two young eagles broke his fall and all landed safely. Spotted Eagle said a prayer of thanks to the Ones Above. He thanked the eagles, telling them that one day he would be back with gifts and have a giveaway in their honor.

Spotted Eagle returned to his village. The excitement was great. He had been dead and had come back to life. Everybody asked him how it happened that he was not dead, but he would not tell them. "I escaped," he said, "and that is all." He saw his love married to his treacherous friend, but bore it in silence. He was not one to bring enmity to his people, to set one family against the other. Besides, what happened could not be changed. Thus he accepted his fate.

A year or so later, a great war party of Pahani attacked his village. The enemy outnumbered them tenfold, and there was no chance of victory for Spotted Eagle's band. All the warriors could do was to fight a slow rear-guard action, which would give the helpless ones—the women, children, and old folks—a chance to escape across the river. Guarding their people this way, the few warriors at hand fought bravely, charging the enemy again and again, making them halt and regroup. Each time, the warriors retreated a little, taking up a new position on a hill, or across a gully. In this way they could save their families.

Showing the greatest courage, exposing their bodies freely, were Spotted Eagle and Black Crow. In the end they alone faced the enemy. Then, suddenly, Black Crow's horse was hit by several arrows in succession and collapsed under him. "Brother, forgive me for what I have done," he cried to Spotted Eagle. "Let me jump up on your horse behind you."

Spotted Eagle answered, "You are a Fox. Pin yourself and fight. Then, if you survive, I will forgive you; and if you die, I will forgive you also."

What Spotted Eagle meant was this: Black Crow was a member of the Fox Warrior Society. The braves who belong to it sing this song:

I am a Fox.
If there is anything daring,
If there is anything dangerous to do,
That is a task for me to perform.
Let it be done by me.

Foxes wear a long, trailing sash, decorated with quillwork, which reaches all the way to the ground even when the warrior is on horseback. In the midst of battle, a Fox will sometimes defy death by pinning his sash to the earth with a special wooden pin, or with a knife or arrow. This means: I will stay here, rooted to this spot, facing my foes, until someone comes to release

Vocabulary

enmity (en′ mə tē) *n.* the bitter hatred between enemies; ill will the pin, or until the enemies flee, or until I die.

Black Crow pinned his sash to the ground. There was no one to release him, and the enemy did not flee. Black Crow sang his death song. He was hit by lances and arrows and died a warrior's death. Many Pahani died with him.

Spotted Eagle had been the only one to see this. He finally joined his people, safe across the river. The Pahani had lost all taste to follow them there. "Your husband died well," Spotted Eagle told Red Bird. After some time had passed, Spotted Eagle married Red Bird. And much, much later he told his parents, and no one else, how Black Crow had betrayed him. "I forgive him now," he said, "because once he was my friend, and because he died like a warrior should, fighting for his people, and also because Red Bird and I are happy now."

After a long winter, when spring came again, Spotted Eagle told his wife, "I must go away for a few days to fulfill a promise. I must go alone." He rode off by himself to that cliff. Again he stood at its foot, below the ledge where the eagles' nest had been. He pointed his sacred pipe to the four directions, down to Grandmother Earth and up to the Grandfather, letting the smoke ascend to the sky, calling out: "*Wanblee, misunkala*. Little eagle brothers, hear me."

High above him in the clouds appeared two black dots, circling. These were the eagles who had saved his life. They came at his call, their huge wings spread majestically, uttering a shrill cry of joy and recognition. Swooping down, they alighted at his feet. He stroked them with a feather fan, and thanked them many times, and fed them choice morsels of buffalo meat, and fastened small medicine bundles around their legs as a sign of friendship, and spread sacred tobacco offerings around the foot of the cliff. Thus he made a pact of friendship and brotherhood between *Wanblee Oyate*—the Eagle Nation—and his own people. After he had done all this, the stately birds soared up again into the sky, circling motionless, carried by the wind, disappearing into the clouds. Spotted Eagle turned his horse's head homeward, going happily back to Red Bird.

Bow Case and Quiver. Sioux. Beaded hide, length: 41 in. Private collection. Christie's Images.

Vocabulary

alight (ə līt′) *v.* to come down after flight; land

pact (pakt) *n.* an agreement; deal; pledge

The Siege of Courthouse Rock

Told by Jenny Leading Cloud

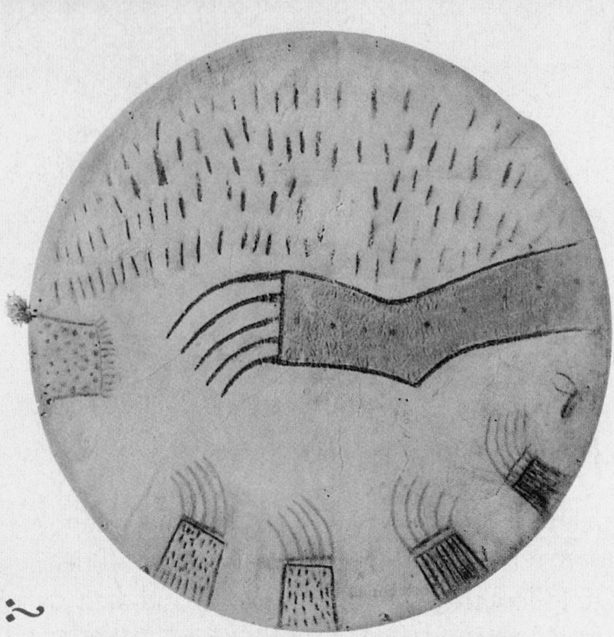

Shield Cover, c. 1820. Upper Missouri. Smithsonian Instituion.

Nebraska is green and flat, a part of the vast corn belt. There are farms everywhere, and silos, and the land does not look like the West at all. But as you travel on toward the setting sun, you find three great, wild rocks which rise out of the plains. First you come to Chimney Rock, towering like a giant needle on the prairie. It was a famous landmark for the settlers in their covered wagons as they traveled west on the Oregon trail or took the more southerly route to the Colorado goldfields.

Then you come to the twins—Courthouse Rock and Jailhouse Rock. Formed of yellowish stone, they are covered with yucca plants and sagebrush. Mud swallows nest in the rock faces. If you climb one of the twins, there is a wonderful view of the plains all around. And westward beyond the plains rise the chalk cliffs and the sandhills of Nebraska, home of many western Sioux.

Did You Know?
Yucca (yuk′ ə) *plants* have woody stems and clusters of white, bell-shaped, drooping flowers. They grow mainly in desert areas of western and southwestern North America.

A long time ago a Sioux war party surprised a war party of Pahani near Courthouse Rock. We Sioux had been fighting many battles with the Pahani. The whites had pushed nations like ours, whose homeland was further east near the Great Lakes, westward into the prairie and the hunting grounds of other tribes. Maybe the Pahani were there before us; who knows? At any rate, now we were hunting the same herds in the same place, and naturally we fought.

I guess there must have been more of us than of the Pahani, and they retreated to the top of Courthouse Rock to save themselves. Three sides of Courthouse Rock go straight up and down like the sides of a skyscraper. No one can climb them. Only the fourth side had a path to the top, and it could be easily defended by a few brave men.

Thus the Pahani were on the top and the Sioux at the foot of Courthouse Rock. The Sioux chief told his warriors: "It's no use trying to storm it. Only three or four men can go up that path abreast,[1] so even women and children could defend it. But the Pahani have no water, and soon they'll run out of food. They can stay up there and starve or die of thirst, or they can come and fight us on the plain. When they climb down, we can kill them and count many coups[2] on them." The Sioux settled down to wait at the foot of the rock.

On the summit, as the Sioux chief expected, the Pahani suffered from hunger and thirst. They grew weak. Though there was little hope for them, they had a brave leader who could use his head. He knew that three sides of the rock were unguarded but that one would have to be a bird to climb down them. On one of the three steep sides, however, there was a round bulge jutting out from the rock face. "If we could fasten a rope to it, we could let ourselves down," he thought. But the outcropping was too smooth, round, and wide to hold a lasso.

Then the Pahani leader tried his knife on the rock bulge. He found that the stone was soft enough for the knife to bite easily into, and he began patiently whittling a groove around the bulge. He and his men worked only at night so that the Sioux wouldn't see what they were up to. After two nights they had carved the groove deep enough. When they tied all their rawhide ropes together, they found that the line would reach to the ground.

On the third night the Pahani leader tied one end of the rope around the bulge in the rock. He himself tested it by climbing all the way down and then up again, which took most of the night.

On the next and fourth night, he told his men: "Now we do it. Let the youngest go first." The Pahani climbed down one by one, the youngest and least accomplished first, so that a large group could belay[3] them, and the older and more experienced warriors later. The leader came down last. The Sioux did not notice them at all, and the whole party stole away.

The Sioux stayed at the foot of the rock for many days. They themselves grew hungry, because they had hunted out all the game. At last a young, brave warrior said: "They must be all dead up there. I'm fed up with waiting; I'll go up and see." He climbed the path to the top and shouted down that nobody was up there.

That time the joke was on us Sioux. It's always good to tell a story honoring a brave enemy, especially when the story is true. Are there any Pahani listening?

1. *Abreast* means "side by side."
2. Among some Native American peoples, to *count coups* (ko͞oz) meant touching a live enemy and then getting away safely—an act that required skill and courage. This phrase can also refer to telling the stories of such deeds.
3. In mountain climbing, to *belay* is to connect the climbers to one another with a rope. Here, each person probably loops the rope under his arms and around his back for security as he climbs down. The more experienced men stay at the top to hold the rope steady for less skilled climbers.

Vocabulary

summit (sum′ it) *n.* the highest point or part; peak
jut (jut) *v.* to extend outward or upward from a surface; bulge

Responding to Literature

PERSONAL RESPONSE

Whose side did you take in each of these stories?

Analyzing Literature

RECALL

1. How does Red Bird react to word of Spotted Eagle's death?
2. What happens when Spotted Eagle trusts the young eagles to help him?
3. Why does Spotted Eagle finally forgive Black Crow?
4. How do the Pahani escape the Sioux in "The Siege of Courthouse Rock"?

INTERPRET

5. How does Red Bird's reaction affect the events that follow?
6. How might the last paragraph in "Spotted Eagle and Black Crow" increase the significance of the story?
7. What three values does Spotted Eagle possess that allow him to forgive Black Crow?
8. What does the **narrator** of "The Siege of Courthouse Rock" admire more than success in battle?

EVALUATE AND CONNECT

9. A quality held or displayed by a person is a **character trait.** What character traits do Spotted Eagle and Black Crow display? What traits do the Sioux and the Pahani show in "The Siege of Courthouse Rock"?
10. Do you think Spotted Eagle's behavior at the end of the story was appropriate? Explain.

LITERARY ELEMENTS

Legend

A **legend** is a story handed down in a society from several generations. Legends are generally considered to be based loosely on a historical event, but are so old that they cannot be proven true or false. In a legend, a character performs deeds that the society values.

1. Why do you think the story of Spotted Eagle and Black Crow became a legend? Explain your answer.
2. What deed, in your opinion, turned the story of Courthouse Rock into a legend?

- See **Literary Terms Handbook,** p. R5.

Courthouse Rock, c. 1860. Albert Bierstadt. Oil on board, 13 x 18 15/16 in. University of Nebraska, Lincoln, NE. Great Plains Art Collection.

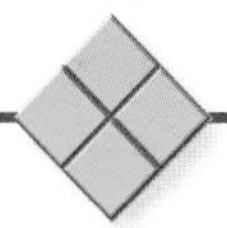

Extending Your Response

Writing About Literature

Setting The events in "The Siege of Courthouse Rock" occurred long ago. What details indicate that Jenny Leading Cloud's version of the story occurred in modern times? Write a paragraph that lists details and explains why you chose those details.

Creative Writing

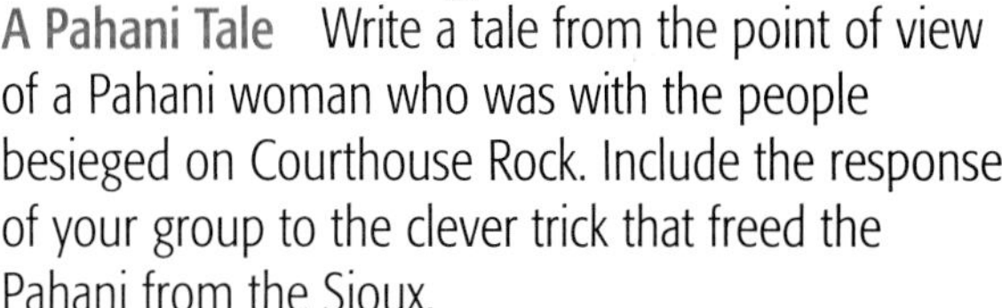

A Pahani Tale Write a tale from the point of view of a Pahani woman who was with the people besieged on Courthouse Rock. Include the response of your group to the clever trick that freed the Pahani from the Sioux.

Literature Groups

Tales of Honor Behaving in an honorable way is an important element in "Spotted Eagle and Black Crow." With a group, analyze the actions of both warriors. Which actions were honorable? Which ones were not, and why? Consider your ideas from the **Focus Activity** on page 408 as you discuss your answers. Share your responses with the class.

Interdisciplinary Activity

Social Studies Use the Internet, the library, or other appropriate sources to research a topic related to these two selections. For example, you might focus on Chief Red Cloud, the Sioux, the history of South Dakota, or contemporary Native American writers. Prepare a brief report to present in your class. If you wish, include drawings, pictures, or audiotapes.

Reading Further

For information about native peoples of the Midwest, try:

These Were the Sioux by Mari Sandoz

The Life and Death of Crazy Horse by Russell Freeman, with photographs by Amos Bad Heart Bull

Save your work for your portfolio.

Skill Minilesson

VOCABULARY • MULTIPLE-MEANING WORDS

Most words have more than one meaning. These meanings are often related, but sometimes they are very different. For example, the rock wall behind Spotted Eagle's ledge is *sheer,* or very steep. However, *sheer* can also mean "very thin and fine," as in *sheer fabric.* And it can mean "complete or absolute," as in *sheer boredom.* There is yet another *sheer* that comes from a different root altogether and means "to swerve."

PRACTICE For each pair of phrases, write two sentences using the word, one with each meaning. Use a dictionary as needed.

1. a. a rude remark
   b. a rude cabin
2. a. dinner reservations
   b. reservations about cheating
3. a. a copy of the picture
   b. the copy in the ad

Before You Read

Chicoria and *Coyote and Wasichu*

MEET JOSÉ GRIEGO Y MAESTAS

José Griego y Maestas (hō zā′ grē ā′ gō ē mī es′ täs) included "Chicoria" in a collection of stories that represent the culture and history of the Hispanic southwest. He is director of the Guadalupe Historic Foundation in Santa Fe, New Mexico.

José Griego y Maestas was born in 1949. "Chicoria" was first published in Cuentos: Tales from the Hispanic Southwest *in 1980.*

MEET RUDOLFO A. ANAYA

Rudolfo Anaya (rōō dôl′ fō ä nī′ yä), who retells "Chicoria" in English, uses folk stories and myths in his novels about modern life in the Southwest.

Rudolfo Anaya was born in New Mexico in 1937. He is a professor of languages and literature at the University of New Mexico.

FOCUS ACTIVITY

Is getting even the same thing as seeking revenge? Think about your answer.

Think/Pair/Share
When is getting even dangerous? When is it just a harmless trick? Write a sentence explaining your reactions to these questions. With a partner, discuss your answers, and examine where you agree and disagree. Then share your questions and explanations with a larger group.

Setting a Purpose
Read the next two folktales to discover how different characters use their wits to suit their purposes.

BACKGROUND

The Time and Place Both of these tales of mischief come from the recent past. Look for clues that tell the reader these stories are not ancient ones.

Did You Know?
A coyote is more than just an animal in the stories of many civilizations. In Native American literature, the coyote is a trickster. He can appear as a hunter, a thief, or a friend—and he usually gets away with his mischief. Even today, wily coyotes defy the efforts of those who try to destroy them.

Coyote Song, 1997. Mindy Dwyer. Watercolor and colored pencil, 10½ x 8⅝ in. Private collection.

The World of Don Francisco, 1934. Theoden Van Soelen. Oil on canvas.

Chicoria

Adapted in Spanish
by José Griego y Maestas
Retold in English by Rudolfo A. Anaya

There were once many big ranches in California, and many New Mexicans went to work there. One day one of the big ranch owners asked his workers if there were any poets in New Mexico.

"Of course, we have many fine poets," they replied. "We have old Vilmas, Chicoria, Cinfuegos, to say nothing of the poets of Cebolleta[1] and the Black Poet."

"Well, when you return next season, why don't you bring one of your poets to compete with Gracia[2]—here none can compare with him!"

When the harvest was done the New Mexicans returned home. The following season when they returned to California they took with them

1. ***Cebolleta*** **is the name of a town. Pronunciations:** ***Vilmas*** (vēl′ mäs), ***Chicoria*** (chē′ kō rē′ ä), ***Cinfuegos*** (sēn fwā′ gōs), ***Cebolleta*** (sā′ bō yā′ tä)
2. ***Gracia*** (grä′ syä)

the poet Chicoria, knowing well that in spinning a rhyme or in weaving wit there was no *Californio*[3] who could beat him.

As soon as the rancher found out that the workers had brought Chicoria with them, he sent his servant to invite his good neighbor and friend to come and hear the new poet. Meanwhile, the cooks set about preparing a big meal. When the maids began to dish up the plates of food, Chicoria turned to one of the servers and said, "Ah, my friends, it looks like they are going to feed us well tonight!"

The servant was surprised. "No, my friend," he explained, "the food is for *them*. We don't eat at the master's table. It is not permitted. We eat in the kitchen."

"Well, I'll bet I can sit down and eat with them," Chicoria boasted.

"If you beg or if you ask, perhaps, but if you don't ask they won't invite you," replied the servant.

"I never beg," the New Mexican answered. "The master will invite me of his own accord,[4] and I'll bet you twenty dollars he will!"

So they made a twenty dollar bet and they instructed the serving maid to watch if this self-confident New Mexican had to ask the master for a place at the table. Then the maid took Chicoria into the dining room. Chicoria greeted the rancher cordially, but the rancher appeared haughty and did not invite Chicoria to sit with him and his guest at the table. Instead, he asked that a chair be brought and placed by the wall where Chicoria was to sit. The rich ranchers began to eat without inviting Chicoria.

So it is just as the servant predicted, Chicoria thought. The poor are not invited to share the rich man's food!

Then the master spoke: "Tell us about the country where you live. What are some of the customs of New Mexico?"

"Well, in New Mexico when a family sits down to eat each member uses one spoon for each biteful of food," Chicoria said with a twinkle in his eyes.

The ranchers were amazed that the New Mexicans ate in that manner, but what Chicoria hadn't told them was that each spoon was a piece of tortilla: one fold and it became a spoon with which to scoop up the meal.

"Furthermore," he continued, "our goats are not like yours."

"How are they different?" the rancher asked.

"Here your nannies give birth to two kids, in New Mexico they give birth to three!"

"What a strange thing!" the master said. "But tell us, how can the female nurse three kids?"

"Well, they do it exactly as you're doing it now: While two of them are eating the third one looks on."

The rancher then realized his lack of manners and took Chicoria's hint. He apologized and invited his New Mexican guest to dine at the table. After dinner, Chicoria sang and recited his poetry, putting Gracia to shame. And he won his bet as well.

3. Someone who lives in or is from California is called, in Spanish, a *Californio* (ka lē for′ nyō).
4. The phrase *of his own accord* means "voluntarily; without being asked."

Coyote and Wasichu

Cowboy, c. 1930s. Aurelio Flores. Earthenware, gesso, paint and varnish, 5½ x 3 x 5¾ in. San Antonio Museum of Art.

Sioux legend

There was a white man who was such a sharp trader that nobody ever got the better of him. Or so people said, until one day a man told this *wasichu:* "There's somebody who can outcheat you anytime, anywhere."

"That's not possible," said the *wasichu.* "I've had a trading post for many years, and I've cheated all the Indians around here."

"Even so, Coyote can beat you in any deal."

"Let's see whether he can. Where is Coyote?"

"Over there, that tricky-looking guy."

"Okay, all right, I'll try him."

The *wasichu* trader went over to Coyote. "Hey, let's see you outsmart me."

"I'm sorry," said Coyote, "I'd like to help you out, but I can't do it without my cheating medicine."

"Cheating medicine, hah! Go get it."

"I live miles from here and I'm on foot. But if you'd lend me your fast horse?"

"Well, all right, you can borrow it. Go on home and get your cheating medicine!"

"Well, friend, I'm a poor rider. Your horse is afraid of me, and I'm afraid of him. Lend me your clothes; then your horse will think that I am you."

"Well, all right. Here are my clothes; now you can ride him. Go get that medicine. I'm sure I can beat it!"

So Coyote rode off with the *wasichu's* fast horse and his fine clothes, while the *wasichu* stood there bare.

Sioux legend told at Grass Mountain,
Rosebud Indian Reservation,
South Dakota, 1974.

Responding to Literature

PERSONAL RESPONSE

Which story do you find most interesting? Why?

Analyzing Literature

RECALL

1. In "Chicoria," who suggests the competition between poets? Why?
2. What is the subject of the bet made between the New Mexicans and Chicoria?
3. In "Coyote and Wasichu," who began the competition between the two main characters?
4. What is the first excuse Coyote offers when he refuses to try to cheat the *wasichu?*

INTERPRET

5. How does the reason for Chicoria's visit change?
6. What does Chicoria win in this tale?
7. Why do you think the onlookers encourage the contest between Coyote and *wasichu?*
8. Why is Coyote's original refusal to cheat important to the story?

EVALUATE AND CONNECT

9. In each of these stories, you find winners other than the **main characters.** Name these other winners and explain what they win.
10. Have you any sympathy for the *wasichu?* for the landowner in "Chicoria"? Explain.

LITERARY ELEMENTS

Hero

The term **hero** is often used in modern literature to refer to the main character in a work of fiction. However, in folktales, legends, and other older forms of writing, a hero often has superhuman abilities, represents the traits most admired by a society, and faces great odds in adventures or battles.

1. Explain why Chicoria may be considered a hero.
2. What characteristics of Coyote are admired by others in the story? Explain why you and your friends would admire these characteristics or would disapprove of them.

- See **Literary Terms Handbook,** p. R4.

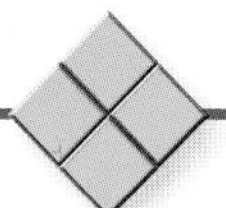

Literature and Writing

Writing About Literature

Dialogue and Narration Skim the two stories and note how the writers use both **dialogue** and **narrative passages** to tell each story. Is the conversation between characters more important in one tale than in the other? Does one story have more narrative paragraphs than the other? Write a brief analysis of each story, explaining how each writer chose to tell the tale.

Creative Writing

Getting Even Even today, some people feel that getting the better of another person is a fun thing to do. Look at the writing you did for the **Focus Activity** on page 418. With a partner, think of a situation in which a trickster must be dealt with. Write a short story or play in which one character gets the better of an annoying pest. Read your story or dramatize your play for the class.

Extending Your Response

Literature Groups

Adventure Tales Tales of adventure have been told since storytelling began. Discuss modern stories that rely on adventures for their plots. Why do you think these stories are popular? Brainstorm a list of reasons with your group, then share them with the class.

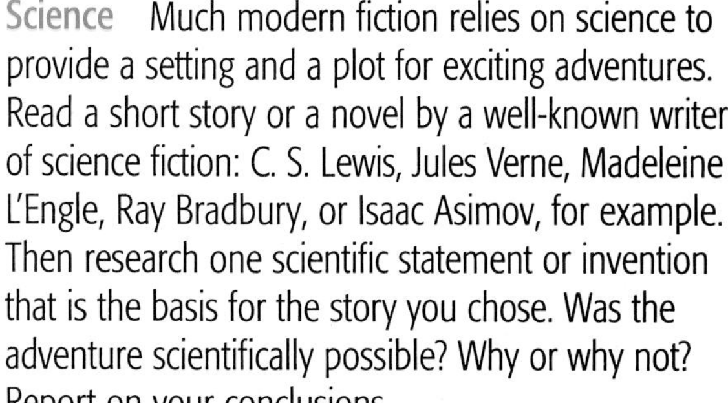

Interdisciplinary Activity

Science Much modern fiction relies on science to provide a setting and a plot for exciting adventures. Read a short story or a novel by a well-known writer of science fiction: C. S. Lewis, Jules Verne, Madeleine L'Engle, Ray Bradbury, or Isaac Asimov, for example. Then research one scientific statement or invention that is the basis for the story you chose. Was the adventure scientifically possible? Why or why not? Report on your conclusions.

Learning for Life

Catch a Cheater The people who watch the cheating match between Coyote and the *wasichu* would probably handle the situation differently today. Imagine that you are upset with the man at the trading post who brags about cheating his customers. Decide how to publicize his bad behavior in order to change it. Would you notify an investigative reporter at a television station? tell your friends and classmates? suggest the newspaper send a reporter? In a small group, discuss the best modern method for getting justice. Record your suggestion and share it with the class.

Reading Further

For modern tales of trickery, try:
The Maestro by Tim Wynne-Jones
The Westing Game by Ellen Raskin

Save your work for your portfolio.

Skill Minilessons

GRAMMAR AND LANGUAGE • VERB TENSES

You know that the **present tense** of a verb names an action that is taking place at the time of the narrative. The **past tense** names an action that is finished. The **future tense** names an action not yet occurring. A good storyteller uses verb tenses carefully to help listeners keep track of the time in which actions take place.

- For more about verb tense, see **Language Handbook,** p. R34.

PRACTICE Rewrite the following sentences by substituting the tense shown in brackets for each verb in the sentence. Be sure the completed sentence will be clear to a reader.

1. [past] There is a white man who is such a sharp trader that nobody will ever get the better of him.
2. [future] Every autumn he goes to New Mexico.
3. [present] This was a story of a clever storyteller who used his wits to win a bet.

READING AND THINKING • FINDING CLUES

A folktale is usually brief, with little room for explanation of why characters behave as they do. As you read these stories, you may wonder why characters are trying to trick one another. There are clues to help you understand their actions. Descriptions, dialogue, and background information may contain clues, but you must read carefully to find them.

PRACTICE With a partner, select one of the two folktales you just finished reading. Look for words and phrases that explain the behavior of the trickster character. Examine what motivates the person against whom the trick is directed. Finally, read to see how the narrator tells you whose side other characters in the story are supporting and why.

- For more about reading strategies, see **Reading Handbook,** pp. R84–R97.

VOCABULARY • THE PREFIX *re-*

When the prefix *re-* is added to a word or root, it changes the meaning in one of two ways. *Re-* can mean either "again" or "back." If you *reread* a book, you read it again, but if you *repay* a loan, you pay it back, not again. Many words join the prefix *re-* to a root rather than to a whole word. In *refrain, re-,* meaning "back," is joined to a Latin root meaning "rein." So, if you *refrain* from an action, you keep yourself from doing it. In a sense, you pull back on the reins. There is also another meaning for *refrain*—a part of a song that is repeated. Here, *re-* has the "again" meaning.

PRACTICE Use your familiarity with the underlined words and the context clues to decide whether the prefix *re-* in each sentence means "again" or "back."

1. When the harvest was done the New Mexicans returned home.
2. The *wasichu* did not recover his clothes or his horse from the clever coyote.
3. The rancher reclined in a comfortable chair and listened to Chicoria's stories.
4. After the *wasichu* reviewed what happened, he knew that he had been tricked.

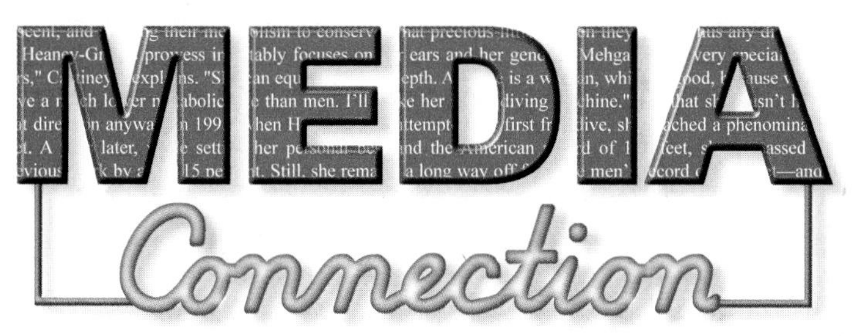

NEWSPAPER ARTICLE

Are coyotes mischief makers, or are they dangerous creatures? Some people fear this cunning relative of the wolf.

Plucky Poodle Returns Alive After Dog-Napping by Coyotes

by Guy Kelly—*The Rocky Mountain News*, November 24, 1997

If only Henri could talk, what a tale he could tell. Henri, a 13-year-old toy poodle, was carried away last week by a pack of coyotes at Cherry Creek State Recreation Area.

John Turner says he was running in the park Wednesday morning when a half-dozen coyotes attacked Henri and dragged the poodle to what seemed a certain death. But Thursday afternoon, when Susan Turner pulled into the driveway of their Piney Creek home about three miles from the park, there was Henri, bloodied but unbowed.

"It's such a miracle this little dog could escape," Susan Turner said Sunday. "We were absolutely amazed he was able to get away and that he managed to find his way home, because he was really chewed up."

The Turners raced Henri to the Parker Center Animal Clinic, where the 13-pound, 8-ounce dog underwent surgery for three hours, emerging with 40 stitches, nine tubes sticking out of him to drain toxins, and a badly mangled coiffure.

But by Saturday, Henri was well enough to have some chow, and Sunday the petite but proud poodle seemed to have regained his attitude. He strutted about, his tiny torso criss-crossed with black stitches.

Henri probably will go home today, much to the relief of the Turners' two daughters, Freyja and Malaina, who have grown up with the dog.

"This is really one of those times when you wish the dog could talk," said veterinarian Kimberly Roberts. "He's a lucky dog." And plucky.

"He's always been around big dogs and he gets a lot of exercise," John Turner said. "He thinks he's a big dog. He's got an attitude."

Turner said he was running in the southeast corner of the park with Henri and his other two dogs—a Weimaraner and a Labrador retriever-Weimaraner mix—just before dawn Wednesday when the jogger behind him started yelling. One of about six coyotes had snatched Henri.

"We gave chase, but it wasn't quite light and they just went away so quickly all we could hear was the howls as they disappeared," Turner said.

The Turners, who moved to Colorado from Scotland two years ago, returned to the park several times Wednesday and Thursday, hoping to find some sign of Henri.

It's not unusual to see coyotes in the vast open spaces that make up much of the 3,900-acre park, Ranger Jason Trujillo said.

Respond

1. Why do you think Henri was able to come home alive?
2. How does this article relate to "Coyote and Wasichu"?

Writing WORKSHOP

Narrative Writing: Trickster Tale

Look out! You never know what might happen when a trickster is around. Now that you have met such characters as Lazy Peter and Coyote, try your hand at creating a trickster of your own.

Assignment: Follow the process in this Workshop to write an original trickster tale.

- As you write your trickster tale, refer to **Writing Handbook,** pp. R50–R55.

The Writing Process

PREWRITING

PREWRITING TIP
For more ideas, read or listen to tales about such classic tricksters as Brer Rabbit, Grandmother Spider, Anansi, or Tortoise.

Sketch Your Trickster

Your trickster might be a relative of a character you have read about, or your unique creation. Sketching can help you find ideas. You might also try freewriting or brainstorming with friends. Think about your trickster's personality and appearance (human? animal? robot? computer? a little of each?).

Get Set

Every tale needs a setting–a specific time and place for the action. You might set your tale in the past, present, or future; in your school, a nearby town, a faraway country, or an imaginary galaxy. A chart will help you plan your setting in detail.

Time: 1700s	Place: Gambia River, West Africa			
sights	sounds	smells	feelings	tastes
green, lush jungle murky river mud-colored cave walls slave trader's greedy eyes	river running mosquito whining	campfire smoke musty river smell	humid heat itchy mosquito bites	

Plan Your Audience and Purpose

Will you write for people your own age, for people of all ages, or perhaps for young children? Will your goal be to entertain, or will your tale teach a lesson? Plan how to reach your audience and achieve your purpose. Children need simple words and sentences; older people might not understand current slang. Fast action and humor will help you entertain readers. To teach, you might add a moral at the end.

Devise a Plot

All good trickster tales involve a problem. Lazy Peter wants easy money. Coyote wants to get even with an arrogant person. Think of a problem that your trickster might solve. The problem and its outcome will form the plot of your tale. Put together your characters, setting, and plot to create a framework for drafting.

framework for drafting

Characters
Mosquito—trickster
Slave trader—greedy
Villagers—Mosquito's friends
Setting
Gambia River, 1700s, jungle and cave near the villagers' home
Plot
First: Slave trader plans to ambush villagers. Mosquito tells trader that villagers will hide in cave.
Next: Trader leads troops into cave. Many are lost in twisting passages.
Last: Villagers, hiding in jungle, escape.

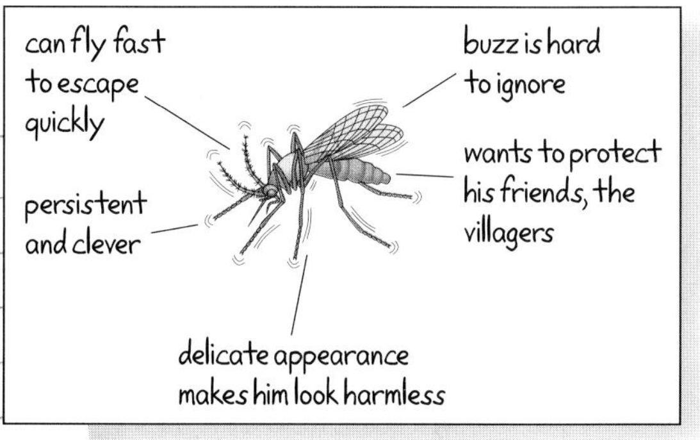

can fly fast to escape quickly
buzz is hard to ignore
wants to protect his friends, the villagers
persistent and clever
delicate appearance makes him look harmless

DRAFTING

DRAFTING TIP

Possible openers for your tale: an intriguing line of dialogue • a tense or funny scene • a classic phrase, such as "Once upon a time" or "Long ago and far away."

Use Time Order

Write what happens first, next, and last in your tale. Include details from your prewriting notes so that readers can picture what you mean. Start a new paragraph whenever the time or place of the action changes. Transitions such as *after an hour, in the morning, near the river,* and so on, will keep your tale on track.

Work with Dialogue

Dialogue reveals characters' traits through their own words. It also keeps your writing from getting bogged down in explanations. If you have your trickster snap, "Slow down! Look out for water snakes!" you can give clues about the setting and the action, as well as your character, through dialogue.

MODEL • DRAFTING

"Friend, want advice?" whined a voice in the dark. The trader woke with a start. "Lie still!" warned the voice. "Just listen. You know the cave by the river?" The trader nodded, eyes darting about. "It's full of passages," the voice hummed. "Villagers hide there."

REVISING

REVISING TIP

With dialogue, don't overuse the vague word *said.* Use a thesaurus to find synonyms richer in sensory detail, such as *whispered, thundered, mumbled,* or *croaked.*

Look Again at Your Tale

After a break, read your draft. Use the **Questions for Revising** to plan changes that will improve your tale. Working with a partner can make revising easier.

You might jot your changes in the margins of your first draft. Or you might put aside your first draft, write a completely new second draft, and then compare the two.

QUESTIONS FOR REVISING

- ☑ Where might transitions or paragraph breaks make the order of events clearer?
- ☑ Where might I add dialogue to show more about my trickster's personality?
- ☑ Where might I add sensory details to help readers imagine the setting?
- ☑ How might I shorten or lengthen the ending to make it more effective?

EDITING/PROOFREADING

Go over your revised tale once more to correct errors in grammar, usage, and mechanics. The **Grammar Link** on page 369 can help you make sure you are using irregular verbs correctly. When you proofread, use the **Proofreading Checklist** on the inside back cover of this book to look for one kind of error at a time.

Grammar Hint

To make sure you have used an irregular verb correctly, ask yourself which tense is needed in the sentence. Then look up the present tense of the verb in the dictionary. It will list all irregular tenses, as shown in the example below.

take (tāk) took, taken, taking

MODEL • EDITING/PROOFREADING

The trader ~~taken~~ took the mosquito's advice and ~~gone~~ went to the cave.

PROOFREADING TIP

Scan your trickster tale to make sure that punctuation marks—especially quotation marks and commas for dialogue—are in the right places.

TECHNOLOGY TIP

Check your spelling by scrolling backwards on your computer, so that reading your tale doesn't distract you.

PUBLISHING/PRESENTING

If possible, read your trickster tale aloud to your intended audience. Practice several times first, so that you know your tale almost by heart. Use the storytelling guidelines in the **Listening, Speaking, and Viewing** feature on page 376.

PRESENTING TIP

Simple props can help you tell your tale. A square of cloth or a stick could represent several objects from your story.

Reflecting

Think about the following questions, and then write responses.

- How did you come up with the idea for your character?
- How is your tale like other trickster tales? How is it unique?

Save your work for your portfolio.

Theme Wrap-Up

Responding to the Theme

1. Which story, poem, or folktale in this theme most helped you understand the meaning of "Fantastic Capers and Mischief Makers"?
2. What new thoughts do you have about the following ideas as a result of your reading this theme?
   - Folktales about fantastic creatures or mythical powers can motivate and inspire as well as entertain.
   - Greed can put people at the mercy of dishonest people.
   - Sometimes pranks can backfire.
3. Present your theme project to the class.

Analyzing Literature

CONSIDER THE AUTHOR'S PURPOSE
Some folktales teach lessons about human behavior. Others reveal the values of the society in which they originated; still others simply entertain. Choose two folktales from this theme. Compare and contrast the author's purpose for each.

Evaluate and Set Goals

1. Which of the following activities did you enjoy the most? Which did you find the most difficult?
   - reading and thinking about the selections
   - writing independently
   - analyzing and discussing the selections
   - presenting ideas and projects
   - researching topics
2. How would you assess your work in this theme, using the following scale? Give at least two reasons for your assessment.

   4 = outstanding 2 = fair
   3 = good 1 = weak
3. Based on what you found difficult in this theme, choose a goal to work toward in the next theme.
   - Write down your goal and three steps you will take to help you reach it.
   - Meet with your teacher to review your goal and your plan for achieving it.

Build Your Portfolio

SELECT

Choose two favorite pieces of work from this theme to include in your portfolio. The following questions can help you choose.

- ✦ Which turned out to be more challenging than you expected?
- ✦ Which did you learn the most from?

REFLECT

Write notes to accompany the pieces you selected. Use these questions to guide you.

- ✦ What do you like best about the piece?
- ✦ What did you learn from creating it?
- ✦ What might you do differently if you were beginning this piece again?

Reading on Your Own

If you enjoy tales of mischief and fantasy, you will also enjoy the following books.

When the Legends Die

by Hal Borland Left alone in the wilderness when his parents die, Thomas Black Bull uses the survival skills his mother has taught him. He eventually learns how to make his way in the world, facing mischief as well as suffering.

A String in the Harp

by Nancy Bond When Peter Morgan finds an ancient harp key, he enters a frightening world, moving between two historical periods and between the practical and the magical. Peter and his sisters must find the source of the mischief as they are threatened by the key, the past, and modern laws.

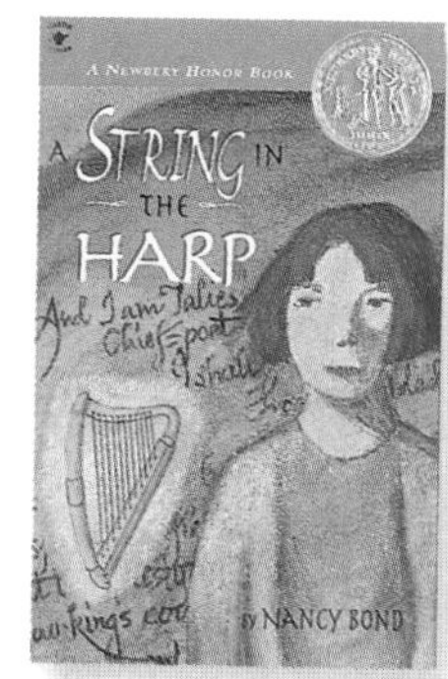

Nothing but the Truth: A Documentary Novel

by Avi Philip Malloy discovers how a single act of mischief can change his life and the lives of innocent people. Told through written announcements, journal entries, and newspaper articles—the story shows how lies and mistakes can pile up until few really know the truth.

The Thirteen Clocks

by James Thurber This funny tale of mischief combines unusual language, a fantastic plot, and an intriguing cast of characters, including a princess and an evil duke.

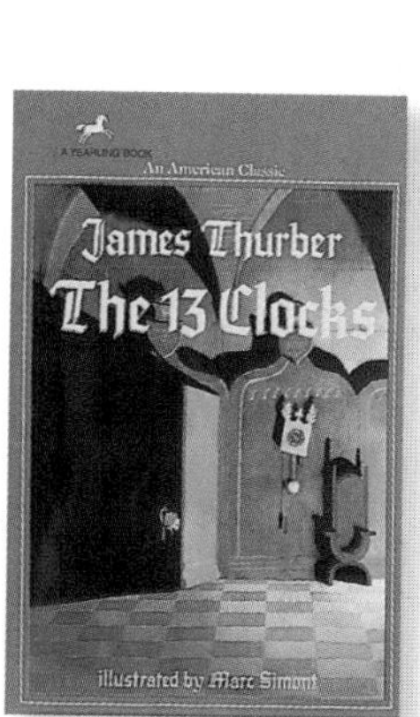

Standardized Test Practice

Read the following passage. Then read each question on page 433. Decide which is the best answer to each question. Mark the letter for that answer on your paper.

Anything But That

I knew from my first hour in school that this would not be one of my best days. But I had no idea how bad it would be. To begin with, I was embarrassed in history class when Ms. Samek called on me. Of course I didn't know the answer. I'd forgotten to read the assignment.

After class, she warned me. "Mark, you are not doing well this quarter and your progress report will reflect that. You aren't even doing enough to pass this class. Think about it and let's discuss the problem." She left me standing there, seriously worried.

Then, of course, I was thirty seconds late for English class. Mr. Parker glared. That was the third time in a week he had given me his famous "look." Could I help it if I had been late a few times?

"Robinson, get out!" he barked, and I headed for the office.

I settled into a chair to wait for Mr. Stolt, the assistant principal. As I sat there, Mr. C, the basketball coach, came in and gave me a small smile. I smiled back and tried to look as though I were in there for a great and noble reason, like winning a geography prize or something.

"What did you do?" he asked.

"Nothing!" I answered. He smiled again.

"Well, make sure you're rested for tomorrow night's game. We're counting on you for big points."

Just then, I was summoned into Mr. Stolt's office. "Good luck," said Mr. C.

I'd been in this room before, so I knew the drill. Mr. Stolt would make me go and apologize to Mr. Parker after school. I'd take a zero on any work I missed. I'd be given after-school detention. I'd promise that this would never happen again. Then I'd be on my way.

But it didn't go that way! "Mark, your grades have been slipping," were Mr. Stolt's first words. "Your careless attitude is affecting your school performance. I'm not going to give you a detention this time. But I'm going to forbid you to play in the last two regular-season basketball games. You've been warned and you need to learn that your actions have consequences."

I wanted to say that I was needed at the games. That these games would determine whether or not we would go to the playoffs. That I'd take any other punishment. But I couldn't get a word out.

"You may go back to class now," Mr. Stolt told me while I was still hunting for words that would make him change his mind. I left the office and stood in the hall, stunned. This was definitely not one of my best days.

1 Why did Mr. C, the basketball coach, wish Mark luck?

A Mark was studying for a big test the next day.

B The team had a big game the next day.

C He knew Mark was about to see the assistant principal for punishment.

D Mr. C was a nice person and he wished everyone he saw good luck.

2 What is the main idea of the fifth paragraph?

F Mark sat in a classroom with Mrs. Samek.

G The basketball coach and the gym teacher stopped and had a conversation with Mr. Stolt.

H Mark was going to be tested on his geography knowledge.

J Mark was waiting to see Mr. Stolt when the coach saw him.

3 You can tell from this passage that the punishment Mr. Stolt assigned —

A was exactly what Mark expected

B was worse than Mark expected

C gave Mark a choice between a detention and not playing basketball

D left Mark feeling lucky that he had a harsh, yet friendly assistant principal

4 What is a FACT in the passage?

F During sixth period, Mark was dismissed from the office.

G Ms. Samek teaches history.

H Mark is an excellent student.

J Mark is the most important player on the basketball team.

5 The author probably uses the phrase "Mr. C, the basketball coach, came in and gave me a small smile" to show you that —

A Mr. C doesn't recognize Mark

B Mr. C is angry with Mark

C Mr. C is interested in finding out why Mark was sent to the office

D Mr. C admires Mark

6 What is the main idea of the passage?

F A student who doesn't do all of his work will be rewarded.

G Mark is a good example of how a poor student can turn into a star athlete.

H A student learns a lesson about consequences.

J A coach figures out how to motivate a team to make it to the playoffs.

7 What word best describes how Mark will feel for the rest of the day?

A Hopeful

B Thrilled

C Contented

D Disappointed

Free to Be

“Freedom’s not bought with dust.”

–Ann Petry, from *Harriet Tubman: Conductor on the Underground Railroad*

We the People, 1986. Dane Tilghman. Watercolor and pencil, 30 x 60 in. Courtesy of the artist.

THEME CONTENTS

GENRE FOCUS *HISTORICAL FICTION*

Exploring the Theme

Free to Be

The pursuit of freedom can be a source of conflict and satisfaction. It may involve groups of people, such as American colonists fighting for independence from England. It also can be personal, as in the freedom to pursue one's dreams. The selections in "Free to Be" touch on both aspects of freedom. Choose an activity below to begin thinking about what freedom means to different people in different situations.

Starting Points

ONE PERSON'S FREEDOM . . .

In the comic strip "Calvin and Hobbes," Calvin thinks that his "rights" will free him from doing schoolwork. Sometimes, one person's pursuit of freedom may conflict with rules of society or the rights of others.

- Think of a time when the pursuit of freedom by one person or a group of people caused problems for others. Describe the situation.

INDEPENDENCE DAY

Recall a time when you achieved some independence, such as the first time you were allowed to buy your own clothes.

- Was your feeling of independence accompanied by a feeling of responsibility? Create a piece of art that expresses your feelings about the experience.

Calvin and Hobbes by Bill Watterson

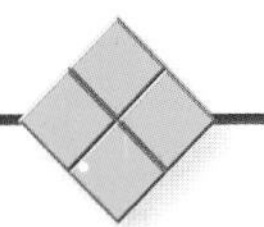

Theme Projects

Choose one of the projects below and complete it as you read the selections in this theme. Work on your own, with a partner, or with a group.

CRITICAL VIEWING

Signs of the Times

1. Gather books and newspaper articles about a war or other conflict involving the United States.
2. Find images, such as posters, political cartoons, and signs, that express support for–or objection to–the conflict.
3. Discuss these questions: Can both sides of a conflict seek or represent freedom? How did the opposing groups in the conflict use ideas about freedom to appeal to their audience?
4. Plan a presentation that describes the conflict and the ideas that both sides had about freedom.

Visit lit.glencoe.com for more project ideas and to find out more about the selections in this theme.

LEARNING FOR LIFE

A Right or a Privilege?

1. Discuss the difference between a right and a privilege. Then, with a group, list some of the rights that U.S. teenagers enjoy. Divide your list into various topics, such as education, recreation, and employment.
2. Now make a list of privileges that young people in the United States enjoy.
3. Research another country, such as Russia or China. What rights and privileges do teenagers from this country have?
4. Share your conclusions with the class. Include visuals, such as a chart that compares and contrasts rights for teenagers in both countries.

MULTIMEDIA PROJECT

A Case for the First Amendment

1. With a group, read the First Amendment to the U.S. Constitution from a social studies book. Discuss the wording of this law, which grants citizens the freedom of speech and expression.
2. Gather video clips, audiotapes, and photos that show people exercising their right of free speech in an inoffensive way.
3. For each item you gather, write a few sentences explaining its importance and why it shows the need for the First Amendment.
4. Organize your work, and then use HyperStudio or similar software to create a multimedia presentation.

Before You Read

The Drummer Boy of Shiloh

MEET RAY BRADBURY

Ray Bradbury is often referred to as the greatest living science fiction writer, but he has written about all sorts of subjects—most of which express his flair for revealing human nature. Whether writing about the past or the future, Bradbury says, "Everything's play. If you work at it, it turns into rocks and dust. Everything must be approached happily, for having a lot of fun—even the most serious thing."

Ray Bradbury was born in 1920. "The Drummer Boy of Shiloh" was first published in the Saturday Evening Post *in 1960.*

FOCUS ACTIVITY

What feelings do you think a soldier may experience before a battle?

QuickWrite

Think of a time when you were afraid of a coming event or awaited an event with great impatience. Write about how you coped with your feelings as you waited.

Setting a Purpose

Read to discover how two very different soldiers deal with fear.

BACKGROUND

The Time and Place A significant battle of the U.S. Civil War took place in April of 1862 near Shiloh, Tennessee, a town on the Tennessee River. The Union Army, led by General Ulysses S. Grant, won the encounter, but at the cost of thousands of lives. This battle is recorded as one of the fiercest battles in history, and with it began the legend of a drummer boy.

Did You Know? Most drummers in the Civil War were boys, some as young as twelve. The beat of drums and the blare of bugles, heard above the cannon and rifle booms, alerted soldiers to change formations during battle.

VOCABULARY PREVIEW

solemn (sol′ əm) *adj.* serious; p. 439
askew (ə skū′) *adv.* in a twisted way; crookedly; p. 439
benediction (ben′ ə dik′ shən) *n.* a divine blessing or the condition of being blessed; p. 440
immortality (im′ ôr tal′ ə tē) *n.* the state of living or lasting forever; p. 440
legitimately (li jit′ ə mit lē) *adv.* in a way that follows the rules; legally; p. 441
mutely (mūt′ lē) *adv.* without speaking; silently; p. 443

The Drummer Boy of Shiloh

Ray Bradbury

Union drummer boy at Shiloh.

In the April night, more than once, blossoms fell from the orchard trees and lit with rustling taps on the drumskin. At midnight a peach stone left miraculously on a branch through winter, flicked by a bird, fell swift and unseen, struck once, like panic, which jerked the boy upright. In silence he listened to his own heart ruffle away, away, at last gone from his ears and back in his chest again.

After that, he turned the drum on its side, where its great lunar face peered at him whenever he opened his eyes.

His face, alert or at rest, was solemn. It was indeed a solemn time and a solemn night for a boy just turned fourteen in the peach field near the Owl Creek not far from the church at Shiloh.

". . . thirty-one, thirty-two, thirty-three . . ."

Unable to see, he stopped counting.

Beyond the thirty-three familiar shadows, forty thousand men, exhausted by nervous expectation, unable to sleep for romantic dreams of battles yet unfought, lay crazily askew in their uniforms. A mile yet farther on, another army was strewn helter-skelter,[1] turning slow, basting

1. Both armies were scattered *(strewn)* in a disorganized way *(helter-skelter)*.

Vocabulary

solemn (sol′ əm) *adj.* serious

askew (ə skū′) *adv.* in a twisted way; crookedly

themselves with the thought of what they would do when the time came: a leap, a yell, a blind plunge their strategy, raw youth their protection and benediction.

Now and again the boy heard a vast wind come up, that gently stirred the air. But he knew what it was, the army here, the army there, whispering to itself in the dark. Some men talking to others, others murmuring to themselves, and all so quiet it was like a natural element arisen from south or north with the motion of the earth toward dawn.

What the men whispered the boy could only guess, and he guessed that it was: Me, I'm the one, I'm the one of all the rest won't die. I'll live through it. I'll go home. The band will play. And I'll be there to hear it.

Yes, thought the boy, that's all very well for them, they can give as good as they get!

For with the careless bones of the young men harvested by night and bindled[2] around campfires were the similarly strewn steel bones of their rifles, with bayonets fixed like eternal lightning lost in the orchard grass.

Me, thought the boy, I got only a drum, two sticks to beat it, and no shield.

There wasn't a man-boy on this ground tonight did not have a shield[3] he cast, riveted or carved himself on his way to his first attack, compounded of remote but nonetheless firm and fiery family devotion, flag-blown patriotism and cocksure immortality strengthened by the touchstone of very real gunpowder, ramrod, minnieball and flint.[4] But without these last the boy felt his family move yet farther off away in the dark, as if one of those great prairie-burning trains had chanted them away never to return, leaving him with this drum which was worse than a toy in the game to be played tomorrow or some day much too soon.

The boy turned on his side. A moth brushed his face, but it was peach blossom. A peach blossom flicked him, but it was a moth. Nothing stayed put. Nothing had a name. Nothing was as it once was.

If he lay very still, when the dawn came up and the soldiers put on their bravery with their caps, perhaps they might go away, the war with them, and not notice him lying small here, no more than a toy himself.

"Well, by God, now," said a voice.

The boy shut up his eyes, to hide inside himself, but it was too late. Someone, walking by in the night, stood over him.

"Well," said the voice quietly, "here's a soldier crying *before* the fight. Good. Get it over. Won't be time once it all starts."

And the voice was about to move on when the boy, startled, touched the drum at his elbow. The man above, hearing this, stopped. The boy could feel his eyes,

2. *Bindled* means "bedded" or "bundled." A *bindle* is a bed roll.
3. Civil War soldiers didn't carry *shields* of armor. The narrator is referring to ways the men prepared themselves for battle mentally and emotionally.
4. A *touchstone* is anything used to test for quality or genuineness. In the mid-1800s, a rifle had to be loaded for each shot. The *ramrod* forced gunpowder down the rifle barrel. The *minnieball* was a kind of bullet. *Flint* ignited the powder that shot the bullet.

Vocabulary

benediction (ben′ ə dik′ shən) *n.* a divine blessing or the condition of being blessed
immortality (im′ ôr tal′ ə tē) *n.* the state of living or lasting forever

sense him slowly bending near. A hand must have come down out of the night, for there was a little rat-tat as the fingernails brushed and the man's breath fanned his face.

"Why, it's the drummer boy, isn't it?"

The boy nodded, not knowing if his nod was seen. "Sir, is that *you*?" he said.

"I assume it is." The man's knees cracked as he bent still closer.

He smelled as all fathers should smell, of salt sweat, ginger tobacco, horse and boot leather, and the earth he walked upon. He had many eyes. No, not eyes, brass buttons that watched the boy.

He could only be, and was, the General.

"What's your name, boy?" he asked.

"Joby," whispered the boy, starting to sit up.

"All right, Joby, don't stir." A hand pressed his chest gently, and the boy relaxed. "How long you been with us, Joby?"

"Three weeks, sir."

"Run off from home or joined legitimately, boy?"

Silence.

"Fool question," said the General. "Do you shave yet, boy? Even more of a fool. There's your cheek, fell right off the tree overhead. And the others here not much older. Raw, raw, the lot of you. You ready for tomorrow or the next day, Joby?"

"I think so, sir."

"You want to cry some more, go on ahead. I did the same last night."

"*You*, sir?"

"God's truth. Thinking of everything ahead. Both sides figuring the other side will just give up, and soon, and the war done in weeks, and us all home. Well, that's not how it's going to be. And maybe that's why I cried."

"Yes, sir," said Joby.

The General must have taken out a cigar now, for the dark was suddenly filled with the Indian smell of tobacco unlit as yet, but chewed as the man thought what next to say.

"It's going to be a crazy time," said the General. "Counting both sides, there's a hundred thousand men, give or take a few thousand out there tonight, not one as can spit a sparrow off a tree, or knows a horse clod from a minnieball. Stand up, bare the breast, ask to be a target, thank them and sit down, that's us, that's them. We should turn tail and train four months, they should do the

Eagle drum from the 27th Massachusetts Infantry.

Vocabulary

legitimately (li jit′ ə mit lē) *adv.* in a way that follows the rules; legally same. But here we are, taken with spring fever and thinking it blood lust, taking our sulphur[5] with cannons instead of with molasses as it should be, going to be a hero, going to live forever. And I can see all of them over there nodding agreement, save the other way around. It's wrong, boy, it's wrong as a head put on hind side front and a man marching backward through life. It will be a double massacre if one of their itchy generals decides to picnic his lads on our grass. More innocents will get shot out of pure Cherokee enthusiasm than ever got shot before. Owl Creek was full of boys splashing around in the noonday sun just a few hours ago. I fear it will be full of boys again, just floating, at sundown tomorrow, not caring where the tide takes them."

The General stopped and made a little pile of winter leaves and twigs in the darkness, as if he might at any moment strike fire to them to see his way through the coming days when the sun might not show its face because of what was happening here and just beyond.

The boy watched the hand stirring the leaves and opened his lips to say something, but did not say it. The General heard the boy's breath and spoke himself.

"Why am I telling you this? That's what you want to ask, eh? Well, when you got a bunch of wild horses on a loose rein somewhere, somehow you got to bring order, rein them in. These lads, fresh out of the milkshed, don't know what I know, and I can't tell them: men actually die, in war. So each is his own army. I got to make *one* army of them. And for that, boy, I need you."

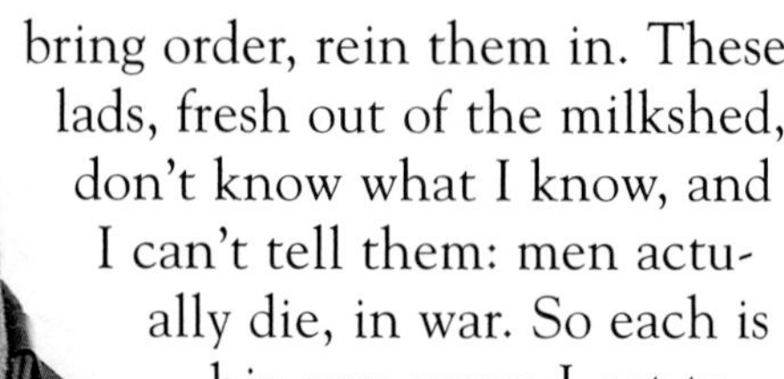

Confederate soldier's hat.

"Me!" The boy's lips barely twitched.

"Now, boy," said the General quietly, "you are the heart of the army. Think of that. You're the heart of the army. Listen, now."

And, lying there, Joby listened.

And the General spoke on.

If he, Joby, beat slow tomorrow, the heart would beat slow in the men. They would lag by the wayside. They would drowse in the fields on their muskets. They would sleep forever, after that, in those same fields, their hearts slowed by a drummer boy and stopped by enemy lead.

But if he beat a sure, steady, ever faster rhythm, then, then their knees would come up in a long line down over that hill, one knee after the other, like a wave on the ocean shore! Had he seen the ocean ever? Seen the waves rolling in like a well-ordered cavalry charge to the sand? Well, that was it, that's what he wanted, that's what was needed! Joby was his right hand and his left. He gave the orders, but Joby set the pace!

So bring the right knee up and the right foot out and the left knee up and the left foot out. One following the other in good time, in brisk time. Move the blood up the body and make the head proud and the spine stiff and the jaw resolute. Focus the eye and set the teeth, flare the nostrils and tighten the hands, put steel armor all

5. ***Blood lust*** means "a desire for bloodshed." ***Sulphur*** (now usually spelled *sulfur*) is a chemical once used as an ingredient of gunpowder; also, when combined with molasses, it was drunk as a medicine.

over the men, for blood moving fast in them does indeed make men feel as if they'd put on steel. He must keep at it, at it! Long and steady, steady and long! Then, even though shot or torn, those wounds got in hot blood—in blood he'd helped stir—would feel less pain. If their blood was cold, it would be more than slaughter, it would be murderous nightmare and pain best not told and no one to guess.

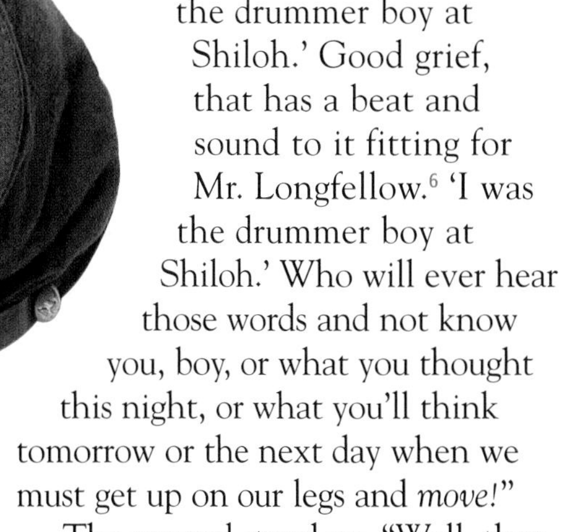
Union soldier's hat.

The General spoke and stopped, letting his breath slack off. Then, after a moment, he said, "So there you are, that's it. Will you do that, boy? Do you know now you're general of the army when the General's left behind?"

The boy nodded mutely.

"You'll run them through for me then, boy?"

"Yes, sir."

"Good. And, God willing, many nights from tonight, many years from now, when you're as old or far much older than me, when they ask you what you did in this awful time, you will tell them—one part humble and one part proud—'I was the drummer boy at the battle of Owl Creek,' or the Tennessee River, or maybe they'll just name it after the church there. 'I was the drummer boy at Shiloh.' Good grief, that has a beat and sound to it fitting for Mr. Longfellow.[6] 'I was the drummer boy at Shiloh.' Who will ever hear those words and not know you, boy, or what you thought this night, or what you'll think tomorrow or the next day when we must get up on our legs and *move!*"

The general stood up. "Well, then. God bless you, boy. Good night."

"Good night, sir."

And, tobacco, brass, boot polish, salt sweat and leather, the man moved away through the grass.

Joby lay for a moment, staring but unable to see where the man had gone.

He swallowed. He wiped his eyes. He cleared his throat. He settled himself. Then, at last, very slowly and firmly, he turned the drum so that it faced up toward the sky.

He lay next to it, his arm around it, feeling the tremor, the touch, the muted thunder as, all the rest of the April night in the year 1862, near the Tennessee River, not far from the Owl Creek, very close to the church named Shiloh, the peach blossoms fell on the drum.

6. Henry Wadsworth *Longfellow* (1807–1882), an American poet, was very popular and highly respected during his lifetime.

Vocabulary
mutely (mūt′ lē) *adv.* without speaking; silently

Responding to Literature

PERSONAL RESPONSE

Would you have been encouraged or more fearful after listening to the General's words? As you think about your answer, consider what you wrote for the **Focus Activity** on page 438.

Analyzing Literature

RECALL

1. Where is the drummer boy when the story begins? What is he waiting for?
2. According to the boy, what is his only defense?
3. Describe the General. What does he say to help the drummer boy, Joby, understand his own importance?
4. What does Joby do to his drum at the end of the story?

INTERPRET

5. How does the drummer boy feel about his situation? Why does he consider remaining behind when the fighting begins?
6. How are Joby and the General alike?
7. What is **ironic,** or unexpected, in the dialogue between the General and the drummer boy? How is the boy the "heart of the army"?
8. Why do you think Joby turns his drum to face the sky?

EVALUATE AND CONNECT

9. Why, in your opinion, does the General say what he does to the drummer boy? Do you think it was wise for the General to speak so frankly to the boy?
10. Theme Connection Joby is fourteen years old. Why do you think he and other soldiers enlisted to fight in the Civil War? Why do people enlist in the armed services today?

LITERARY ELEMENTS

Description

Description is language that creates a vivid picture of a person, situation, or mood. It brings a reader into the story. In historical fiction, as in "The Drummer Boy of Shiloh," clear description can help readers experience the past.

1. How does the description of the April night in the first three paragraphs set the mood for the story? Explain.
2. What information about setting does the reader get from the descriptions in the next three paragraphs?

- See **Literary Terms Handbook,** p. R2.

Union recruitment poster.

Literature and Writing

Writing About Literature

Legend Has It! A play about the legendary drummer boy of Shiloh, written in 1870 by Samuel Muscroft, was popular in the North for nearly forty years after the Civil War. What might have been Muscroft's purpose for writing this play? How might you account for the popularity of this legend, especially in the 1870s? Explain your answers in one or two paragraphs.

Personal Writing

Letter Home Suppose that you are a fourteen-year-old in 1862. Write a letter to a friend who is considering running away to join one of the armies. Explain why you cannot join him or her and why your friend should stay home.

Extending Your Response

Literature Groups

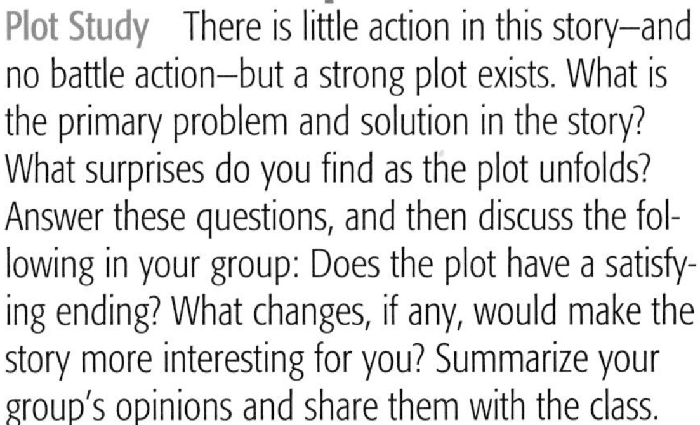

Plot Study There is little action in this story—and no battle action—but a strong plot exists. What is the primary problem and solution in the story? What surprises do you find as the plot unfolds? Answer these questions, and then discuss the following in your group: Does the plot have a satisfying ending? What changes, if any, would make the story more interesting for you? Summarize your group's opinions and share them with the class.

Interdisciplinary Activity 

History With a group, research one of the following Civil War topics: the Union forces, the Confederate forces, the issues that sparked the war, or the effects of the war on the North and the South. Present your findings in a report accompanied by visuals, such as a map of battles or a mural of major events. If you wish, you might write a story set during the Civil War and read it or act it out for the class.

Learning for Life 

News Broadcast With a partner, research the Battle of Shiloh to find out how long it lasted, what weapons and tactics were used, and how many soldiers died, among other information. Prepare a detailed news report about the battle, as if it just happened. Include charts, maps, profiles of the generals, or photographs, if available. Present the news report to your class.

Reading Further 

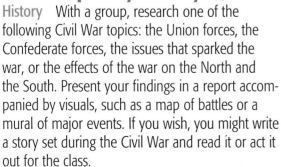

For more stories about young people and war, try these books:

The Bomb by Theodore Taylor

The Forty-Third War by Louise Moeri

Save your work for your portfolio.

Skill Minilessons

GRAMMAR AND LANGUAGE • ADJECTIVES

Writers strengthen descriptions with adjectives–words that describe people, places, things, or ideas. When Ray Bradbury writes of "the **careless** bones of young men" and the "**steel** bones of their rifles," he chooses the adjectives *careless* and *steel* to make his description easier for readers to imagine.

- For more about using adjectives, see **Language Handbook,** p. R27.

PRACTICE Look back at "The Drummer Boy of Shiloh" to find one or more adjectives that describe each of the following people, places, things, or ideas.

1. face of the drum
2. patriotism
3. leather
4. generals
5. cavalry charge

READING AND THINKING • VISUALIZING

When you **visualize** a person, place, object, or event, you see it in your mind. Bradbury uses details effectively to help his readers visualize what is happening during a brief episode in the Civil War.

- For more about visualizing, see **Reading Handbook,** p. R86.

PRACTICE Choose a passage from the story. Think about how the scene would look if you were to draw it or stage it. What backdrop, or background scenery, can you imagine? Who is present? Are they standing or sitting? What is the weather like? Write a paragraph describing your view of the scene.

VOCABULARY • THE SUFFIX *-ity*

The suffix *-ity* means "state or condition." It is similar to the suffix *-ness.* Before the Battle of Shiloh, the soldiers have a feeling of *immortality,* the condition of being *immortal.* Something that is *solid* is in a state of *solidity;* something that is *acid* has *acidity.* Attaching a suffix, especially one that begins with a vowel, may change the spelling of a base word. For example, *possible* becomes *possibility* and *fragile* becomes *fragility.*

PRACTICE Use your knowledge of vocabulary to match each word ending in *–ity* with its synonym.

1. authenticity	a. politeness
2. civility	b. phoniness
3. essentiality	c. cruelty
4. durability	d. genuineness
5. artificiality	e. permanence
6. totality	f. importance
7. inhumanity	g. completeness

Vo•cab•u•lar•y *Skills*

Using Homophones

The word *homophone* comes from *homo,* meaning "same," and *phone,* meaning "sound." Therefore, **homophones** are words that sound the same. However, homophones have different meanings and spellings. For example, to *pedal* a bike is to ride it; to *peddle* a bike is to try to sell it. Not recognizing a homophone can result in spelling errors. Even a computer can't fix your mistake if you wrote *flower* when you should have written *flour,* because both of those are correctly spelled words.

The English language includes many homophones. Those who have watched a short play have *seen* a *scene.* A baby antelope is a *new gnu.* If only one thing is borrowed, it is a *lone loan.* Some homophones are only slightly different in meaning, such as *who's* and *whose,* and you might have to give some thought to choose the correct one. Usually, however, using the wrong homophone is simply a result of being careless.

EXERCISES

1. If the underlined word in the selection below is the correct homophone, write *Correct.* If it is the wrong word, write the correct form.

   The soldiers were not week [1]; they were only young and inexperienced. Death awaited many at the break [2] of day, soon after the sun [3] rows [4] in the sky. The general knew [5] that training could lesson [6] the hardships his men would [7] face, but their [8] was no time for that. All he could due [9] was to [10] walk among them, stop, hear [11], and speak to those he found awake. He new [12] that many young hearts were to be stopped by led [13]. How heavily his responsibilities must have wade [14] upon him.

2. Complete each sentence by using two homophones. An example is provided.
   Example: The cake baked by a female servant is a cake that the maid made.
   a. If you form your letters correctly, you ______.
   b. I blistered the back of my foot, but new shoes helped my ______.
   c. A just, honest, and proper price for a taxi ride is a ______.
   d. We called the sixty minutes we spent together ______.
   e. Our team lost fourteen out of fifteen games; we only ______.

Before You Read

Paul Revere's Ride

MEET HENRY WADSWORTH LONGFELLOW

Henry Wadsworth Longfellow's father wanted his son to become a lawyer, but the young Longfellow had other ideas. In 1824 he wrote to his father from college: "If I can ever rise in the world, it must be by the exercise of my talent in the wide field of literature." A popular author during his time, Longfellow was known for poems that were gentle, sweet, simple, and romantic. His best-known works include *The Song of Hiawatha*, *Evangeline*, and "Paul Revere's Ride."

Henry Wadsworth Longfellow was born in 1807 and died in 1882. "Paul Revere's Ride" was first published in 1863 in Tales of a Wayside Inn.

FOCUS ACTIVITY

Imagine that you are an American colonist during 1775. You pay heavy taxes to England, but you are denied a voice in its government. Your neighbors are talking about fighting for independence from England. Weigh the pros and cons of a revolution. What might you contribute to this struggle?

Share It!

Is war a good solution when freedom is denied? Discuss your response with a partner. Then share with the class the points on which you and your partner agree.

Setting a Purpose

Read the story of one person whose contribution to freedom became a legend.

BACKGROUND

The Time and Place This poem celebrates the historic ride of Paul Revere, one of the men who rode from Boston to Lexington, Massachusetts, just before the American Revolution. Revere's mission was to warn Samuel Adams and John Hancock, two prominent rebel colonists, that British troops had arrived in Boston and were marching to arrest the two men.

Did You Know? Before and after the ride that made him famous, Paul Revere was well known as a craftsman. He cast musket balls and cannons during the war and church bells after the war. He also made beautiful silverware and copper goods.

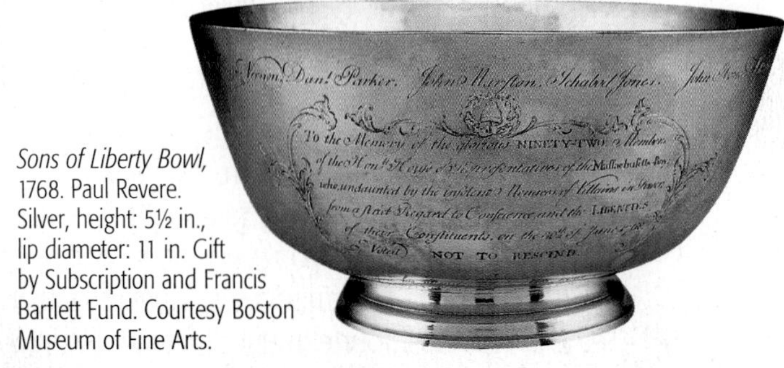

Sons of Liberty Bowl, 1768. Paul Revere. Silver, height: 5½ in., lip diameter: 11 in. Gift by Subscription and Francis Bartlett Fund. Courtesy Boston Museum of Fine Arts.

Midnight Ride of Paul Revere, 1931. Grant Wood. Oil on composition board, 30 x 40 in. The Metropolitan Museum of Art, NY.

Paul Revere's Ride

Henry Wadsworth Longfellow

Listen, my children, and you shall hear
Of the midnight ride of Paul Revere,
On the eighteenth of April, in Seventy-five;
Hardly a man is now alive
Who remembers that famous day and year.

He said to his friend, "If the British march
By land or sea from the town to-night,
Hang a lantern aloft in the belfry° arch
Of the North Church tower as a signal light,—
One, if by land, and two, if by sea;
And I on the opposite shore will be,
Ready to ride and spread the alarm
Through every Middlesex° village and farm,
For the country folk to be up and to arm."

Then he said, "Good night!" and with muffled oar
Silently rowed to the Charlestown shore,
Just as the moon rose over the bay,
Where swinging wide at her moorings° lay
The Somerset, British man-of-war;°
A phantom ship, with each mast and spar°
Across the moon like a prison bar,
And a huge black hulk, that was magnified
By its own reflection in the tide.

Meanwhile, his friend, through alley and street,
Wanders and watches with eager ears,
Till in the silence around him he hears
The muster of men at the barrack door,
The sound of arms, and the tramp of feet,
And the measured tread° of the grenadiers,°
Marching down to their boats on the shore.

Then he climbed the tower of the Old North Church,
By the wooden stairs, with stealthy tread,°

---

8 A *belfry* (bel′ frē) is the bell tower of a church or another building.

13 The county of *Middlesex,* Massachusetts, includes the town of Concord, where the first shots of the Revolutionary War were fired on April 19, 1775.

18 The place where a ship is docked is called its *moorings.*

19 A *man-of-war* is a warship.

20 On a sailing ship, a *spar* is any of the poles used to fasten or support the sails.

29 The *measured tread* is a steady march or walk. In the British army, *grenadiers* (gren′ ə dērz′) were foot soldiers.

32 The *stealthy tread* is the man's secret or sneaky steps.

To the belfry-chamber overhead,
And startled the pigeons from their perch
On the somber° rafters, that round him made
Masses and moving shapes of shade,—
By the trembling ladder, steep and tall,
To the highest window in the wall,
Where he paused to listen and look down
A moment on the roofs of the town,
And the moonlight flowing over all.

Beneath, in the churchyard, lay the dead,
In their night-encampment on the hill,
Wrapped in silence so deep and still
That he could hear, like a sentinel's° tread,
The watchful night-wind, as it went
Creeping along from tent to tent,
And seeming to whisper, "All is well!"
A moment only he feels the spell
Of the place and the hour, and the secret dread
Of the lonely belfry and the dead;
For suddenly all his thoughts are bent
On a shadowy something far away,
Where the river widens to meet the bay,—
A line of black that bends and floats
On the rising tide, like a bridge of boats.

Meanwhile, impatient to mount and ride,
Booted and spurred, with a heavy stride
On the opposite shore walked Paul Revere.
Now he patted his horse's side,
Now gazed at the landscape far and near,
Then, impetuous,° stamped the earth,
And turned and tightened his saddlegirth;
But mostly he watched with eager search

---

35 *Somber* means "dark and gloomy."
45 A *sentinel* is a guard.
62 Here, *impetuous* means "acting suddenly."

Paul Revere's Midnight Ride. Artist unknown.

Viewing the painting: **In what ways does this painting capture the drama of Revere's late-night ride?**

The belfry-tower of the Old North Church,
As it rose above the graves on the hill,
Lonely and spectral° and somber and still.
And lo! as he looks, on the belfry's height
A glimmer, and then a gleam of light!
He springs to the saddle, the bridle he turns,
But lingers and gazes, till full on his sight
A second lamp in the belfry burns!

67 Something *spectral* is ghost-like.

A hurry of hoofs in a village street,
A shape in the moonlight, a bulk in the dark,
And beneath, from the pebbles, in passing, a spark
Struck out by a steed flying fearless and fleet:°
That was all! And yet, through the gloom and the light,
The fate of a nation was riding that night;
And the spark struck out by that steed, in his flight,
Kindled the land into flame with its heat.

He has left the village and mounted the steep,°
And beneath him, tranquil and broad and deep,
Is the Mystic,° meeting the ocean tides;
And under the alders° that skirt its edge,
Now soft on the sand, now loud on the ledge,
Is heard the tramp of his steed as he rides.

It was twelve by the village clock,
When he crossed the bridge into Medford town.
He heard the crowing of the cock,
And the barking of the farmer's dog,
And felt the damp of the river fog,
That rises after the sun goes down.

It was one by the village clock,
When he galloped into Lexington.
He saw the gilded° weathercock
Swim in the moonlight as he passed,
And the meeting-house windows, blank and bare,
Gaze at him with a spectral glare,
As if they already stood aghast
At the bloody work they would look upon.

---

76 Here, *fleet* means "very fast."
81 As a noun, *steep* means "a steep slope."
83 The *Mystic* is a short river that flows into Boston Harbor.
84 *Alders* are trees in the birch family.
95 A *gilded* object has, or seems to have, a thin coating of gold.

It was two by the village clock,
When he came to the bridge in Concord town.
He heard the bleating of the flock,
And the twitter of birds among the trees,
And felt the breath of the morning breeze
Blowing over the meadows brown.
And one was safe and asleep in his bed
Who at the bridge would be first to fall,
Who that day would be lying dead,
Pierced by a British musket-ball.

You know the rest. In the books you have read,
How the British Regulars° fired and fled,—
How the farmers gave them ball for ball,
From behind each fence and farm-yard wall,
Chasing the red-coats down the lane,
Then crossing the fields to emerge° again
Under the trees at the turn of the road,
And only pausing to fire and load.

So through the night rode Paul Revere;
And so through the night went his cry of alarm
To every Middlesex village and farm,—
A cry of defiance and not of fear,
A voice in the darkness, a knock at the door,
And a word that shall echo forevermore!
For, borne on the night-wind of the Past,
Through all our history, to the last,
In the hour of darkness and peril° and need,
The people will waken and listen to hear
The hurrying hoof-beats of that steed,
And the midnight message of Paul Revere.

112 *Regulars* are soldiers and officers belonging to a permanent, professional army. *Irregulars* are those who are drafted for a short time.

116 To *emerge* is to come out.

127 *Peril* means "danger."

Responding to Literature

PERSONAL RESPONSE

How does this poem make you feel about the United States and the people who helped found it? Explain.

Analyzing Literature

RECALL

1. How will the friend signal Revere when the British march?
2. What methods of transportation do the British troops use?
3. Summarize the events in lines 87–106.
4. What happens when the British and the farmers meet?

INTERPRET

5. How might the friend feel waiting in the church? Why?
6. How does Revere seem to feel waiting for the signal? What actions reveal his feelings?
7. The meeting-house windows look at Paul Revere "as if they already stood aghast / At the bloody work they would look upon." What might "the bloody work" refer to?

EVALUATE AND CONNECT

8. Theme Connection What types of people make up the American militia? What do you learn from this poem about their desire for freedom? Support your answers with details from the poem.
9. **Imagery** is the use of words and phrases to create images in the minds of readers. What words and phrases does Longfellow use to describe the British ship *Somerset?* Why, do you think, would Longfellow want to create these images of the ship?
10. Where might a situation like the one in the poem occur in the world today? How would you like the problem to be resolved? For ideas, look at what you wrote for the **Focus Activity** on page 448.

LITERARY ELEMENTS

Meter

Meter is a regular pattern, or beat, of stressed and unstressed syllables in a line of poetry. If you read a poem aloud, you can hear the pattern. For example, the meter in "Paul Revere's Ride" sounds like the hoof beats of a galloping horse. To show the meter, mark each stressed syllable with the symbol ´, like this:

Lísten my chíldren and yóu shall heár

1. Copy the first stanza of the poem, and mark the four stressed syllables in each line.
2. Choose another poem or nursery rhyme. Mark the stressed syllables in the first few lines.

- See **Literary Terms Handbook,** p. R6.

The Old North Church, Boston.

Extending Your Response

Writing About Literature

Setting Suppose that Paul Revere's ride took place in your neighborhood in the year 2010. With a partner, retell a few stanzas of the poem, using this new setting. How will the different setting affect the action?

Creative Writing

Children's Book Write and illustrate a children's book based on Paul Revere. Include details, dialogue, and vivid language that young readers can understand. Illustrate your storybook, then share it with a child, a family member, or a classmate.

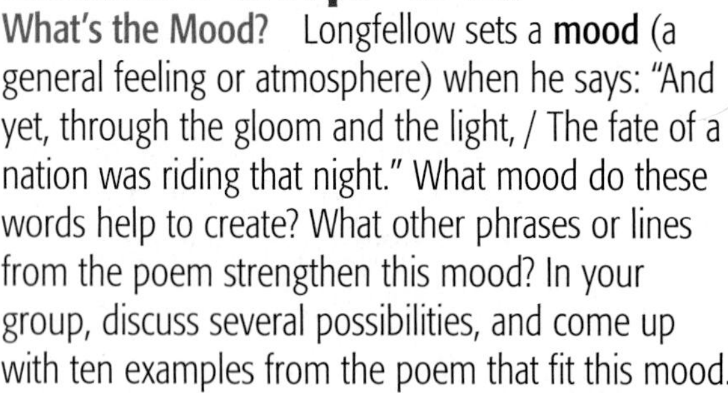

Literature Groups

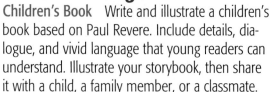

What's the Mood? Longfellow sets a **mood** (a general feeling or atmosphere) when he says: "And yet, through the gloom and the light, / The fate of a nation was riding that night." What mood do these words help to create? What other phrases or lines from the poem strengthen this mood? In your group, discuss several possibilities, and come up with ten examples from the poem that fit this mood.

interNET CONNECTION

Use the Internet to learn more about Paul Revere's ride, his life, and other events in the American Revolution. Type keywords into a search engine. Use the information you find to write a report you can share with your class.

Reading Further

If you enjoyed "Paul Revere's Ride," try these other poems that Longfellow wrote about historical events:

The Courtship of Miles Standish
The Song of Hiawatha

Save your work for your portfolio.

Skill Minilesson

GRAMMAR AND LANGUAGE • USING CAPITAL LETTERS IN POETRY

A capital letter usually begins a new line of a poem. Poetry written in the twentieth century doesn't always follow this rule. Capital letters also are used for proper nouns–including specific names of people, places, and things–and for proper adjectives.

PRACTICE Find three mistakes in capitalization.

Listen, my classmates, until I am done
With the tale of a patriot's ride to jackson.
He had traveled the black-tarred roads of mississippi,
in a white sports car that was quite zippy.

- For more about capitalization, see **Language Handbook,** pp. R35–R37.

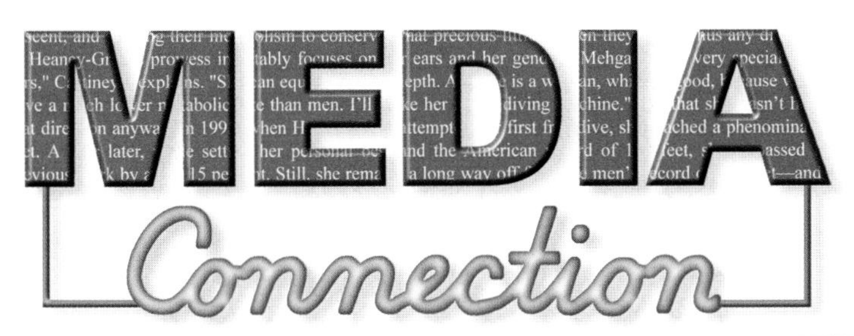

RADIO TRANSCRIPT

Is everything you read about a hero true? Can a person still be a hero if you discover that person's story was used by others to get a point across?

Author Says Revere's Midnight Ride Not a Solitary One

from *All Things Considered*, National Public Radio, April 18, 1994

Robert Siegel, Host: On April 18, in 1775, a fabled event occurred in the American Revolution. The version that came down to most of us was the poem by Henry Wadsworth Longfellow, the one that begins, "Listen my children and you shall hear of the midnight ride of Paul Revere." Revere emerges from a new book by historian David Hackett Fischer as a far more complex and interesting figure. Fischer says the most famous rendering of Revere's story, the Longfellow poem, was crafted for a purpose.

Fischer: Longfellow published the poem in 1861, and it was meant to be a contribution to the Union war effort. Paul Revere becomes a historical loner who does almost everything by himself. The point was that one man, acting alone, could turn the course of history, and this was an appeal to individuals in the North to do it again in another crisis.

Siegel: The ride that emerged from your history is, above all, not a solitary act.

Fischer: No, quite the reverse. We found something like sixty other riders who were out that same night while he was on the road, and all of this doesn't in any way take away from Paul Revere. He, more than anybody, set those other people in motion. Joseph Warren, who was the other major leader, caught wind of it as well and had a secret informer whose identity he never revealed.

The circumstantial evidence is very strong to suggest that it was probably General Gage's American wife, who was deeply divided, who once said that she hoped her husband would never be the instrument of punishing her own people.

Siegel: Why wouldn't Revere tell how many people were involved and how it had all been planned?

Fischer: They wanted to present the idea that they were the innocent victims of British tyranny, and they were very careful to play down any sort of active role on their own part. Paul Revere was asked to write two depositions just after the battle as part of a campaign to prove that the British fired first. What he did was also to tell the story of the midnight ride, and these depositions were both suppressed and remained unpublished for more than a hundred years.

Siegel: Historian David Hackett Fischer of Brandeis University is the author of *Paul Revere's Ride*, published in April 1994 by Oxford University Press.

Respond

1. Why do you think Paul Revere's statements about April 18 were unpublished for more than a hundred years?
2. If Mrs. Gage *was* the secret informer, was she a hero?

Before You Read

Barbara Frietchie

MEET JOHN GREENLEAF WHITTIER

John Greenleaf Whittier was eighteen years old when his sister secretly sent one of his poems to a local paper in Newburyport, Massachusetts. Not only did the editor of the paper print the poem, but he also encouraged the shy farmer's son to educate himself and develop his talent. After two terms of high school, Whittier went on to work as a journalist, writer, and opponent of slavery. He published more than eight volumes of poetry, numerous articles and reviews, and one novel. He wrote for forty years before achieving financial success with his poetry.

John Greenleaf Whittier was born in Haverhill, Massachusetts, in 1807 and died in 1892. "Barbara Frietchie" was first published in 1863.

FOCUS ACTIVITY

What makes some people more courageous than others?

Web It!

What characteristics do most brave people share? Make a word web to explore your ideas.

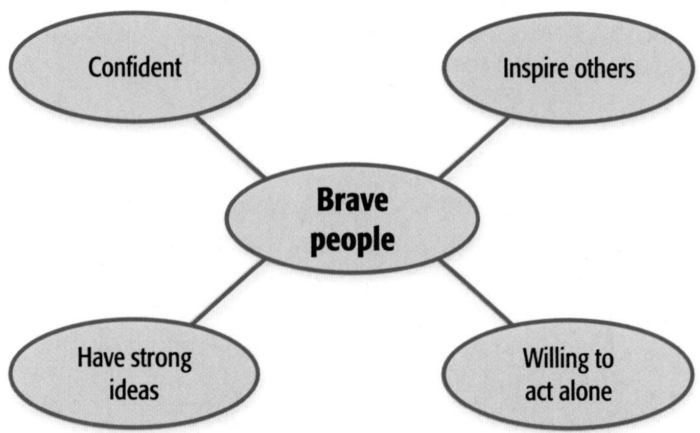

Setting a Purpose

Read to discover how one woman's act of courage became a legend.

BACKGROUND

The Time and Place It is September 6, 1862, in Frederick, Maryland. The United States is involved in the Civil War.

Did You Know? The poem you are about to read celebrates the courage of Barbara Frietchie, an elderly woman who reportedly stood up to the Confederate soldiers as they marched through her town. The poem turned Frietchie into a legend. However, like most legends, the story is part truth and part fiction. Many people think that John Greenleaf Whittier gave credit to the wrong woman. It may be that Mary S. Quantrill is the person who waved flags at the Confederates as they marched through Frederick.

Barbara Frietchie

John Greenleaf Whittier

Barbara Frietchie, 1876.
Dennis Malone Carter.
Oil on canvas, 36¼ x 46¼.
Kirby Collection of Historical Painting, Lafayette College, Easton, PA.

Up from the meadows rich with corn,
Clear in the cool September morn,

The clustered spires of Frederick stand
Green-walled by the hills of Maryland.

Round about them orchards sweep,
Apple and peach tree fruited deep,

Fair as the garden of the Lord
To the eyes of the famished rebel horde,°

On that pleasant morn of the early fall
When Lee marched over the mountain wall;

8 A *horde* is a large group.

Barbara Frietchie

Over the mountains winding down,
Horse and foot, into Frederick town.

Forty flags with their silver stars,
Forty flags with their crimson bars,

Flapped in the morning wind: the sun
Of noon looked down, and saw not one.

Up rose old Barbara Frietchie then,
Bowed with her fourscore° years and ten;

Bravest of all in Frederick town,
She took up the flag the men hauled down

In her attic window the staff she set,
To show that one heart was loyal yet.

Up the street came the rebel tread,
Stonewall° Jackson riding ahead.

Under his slouched hat left and right
He glanced; the old flag met his sight.

"Halt!"—the dust-brown ranks stood fast.
"Fire!"—out blazed the rifle-blast.

It shivered the window, pane and sash;
It rent the banner with seam and gash.

Quick, as it fell, from the broken staff
Dame° Barbara snatched the silken scarf.

She leaned far out on the window-sill,
And shook it forth with a royal will.

---

18 One *score* is twenty, so *fourscore* is eighty.

24 Confederate General Thomas J. Jackson got this nickname after the Battle of Bull Run in 1861. Another general urged his troops to follow the example of Jackson and his men, exclaiming, "They stand like a *stone wall.*"

32 *Dame* is a title formerly used for the woman in charge of a household.

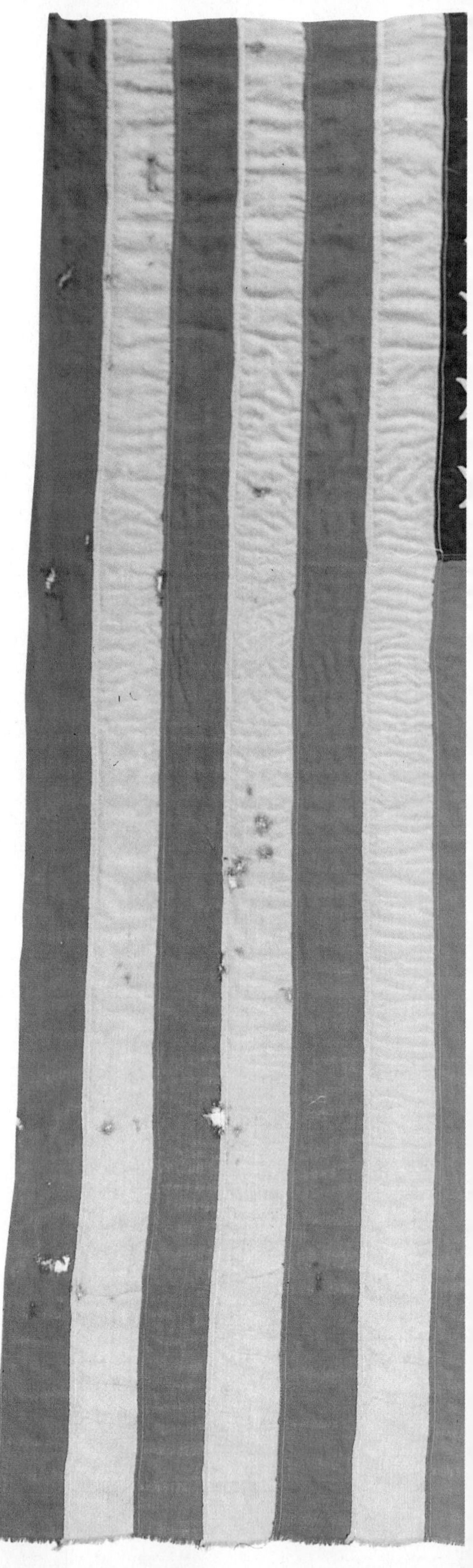

First Maryland Infantry battle flag.

"Shoot, if you must, this old gray head,
But spare your country's flag," she said.

A shade of sadness, a blush of shame,
Over the face of the leader came;

The nobler nature within him stirred
To life at that woman's deed and word;

"Who touches a hair of yon gray head
Dies like a dog! March on!" he said.

All day long through Frederick street
Sounded the tread of marching feet:

All day long that free flag tost°
Over the heads of the rebel host.°

Ever its torn folds rose and fell
On the loyal winds that loved it well;

And through the hill-gaps sunset light
Shone over it with a warm good-night.

Barbara Frietchie's work is o'er,
And the Rebel rides on his raids no more.

Honor to her! and let a tear
Fall, for her sake, on Stonewall's bier.°

Over Barbara Frietchie's grave,
Flag of Freedom and Union, wave!

Peace and order and beauty draw
Round thy symbol of light and law;

And ever the stars above look down
On thy stars below in Frederick town!

---

45 *Tost* is an old spelling of *tossed.*
46 *Host,* here, has the old meaning of "army."
54 A *bier* (bēr) is a stand on which a coffin is placed before burial.

Responding to Literature

PERSONAL RESPONSE

Which of the qualities from the **Focus Activity** on page 458 does Barbara Frietchie display?

Analyzing Literature

RECALL AND INTERPRET

1. The first sixteen lines of the poem establish the **setting.** (See page R9.) Describe the setting in a few sentences. Why, in your opinion, does Whittier begin the poem in this way?
2. How does the narrator describe Stonewall Jackson, the leader of the troops who invaded Frederick? Does the narrator condemn Jackson? Cite lines from the poem to support your answer.
3. How does Jackson react when Barbara Frietchie tells him to spare the flag? What does Jackson's reaction tell you about his character? Explain.

EVALUATE AND CONNECT

4. In lines 20–22 of the poem, what is the speaker's attitude toward all of the townspeople except Barbara Frietchie? Do you agree with the narrator's attitude? Explain.
5. If you were Jackson, how would you have wanted your troops to deal with Frietchie? Explain.
6. Is this poem about a battle? Explain.

LITERARY ELEMENTS

Rhyme

Words that end with the same stressed vowel and consonant pattern are words that **rhyme.** Often, the words at the ends of lines of poetry rhyme. The pattern of end rhyme is called a **rhyme scheme.** In the first stanza of "Paul Revere's Ride," the last words in the first, second, and fifth lines rhyme: *hear, Revere,* and *year.* Call this rhyme *a.* The third and fourth lines also rhyme: *five* and *alive.* Call this rhyme *b.* The rhyme scheme for this stanza is *aabba.*

1. What is the rhyme scheme for the first stanza of "Barbara Frietchie"?
2. Which two stanzas in "Barbara Frietchie" do not have end rhyme?

● See **Literary Terms Handbook,** p. R8.

Extending Your Response

Literature Groups

Turning the Tables John Greenleaf Whittier supported the Union. How might Barbara Frietchie have been portrayed differently if a Confederate soldier had written the poem? Discuss your answers in a group, and then share them with the class.

Writing About Literature

Celebrate Your History Mary S. Quantrill may have been the woman who taunted Jackson. Research her life, and then write a poem as a late tribute to her. Use rhyme and imagery. Present your poem to the class.

COMPARING SELECTIONS

Paul Revere's Ride and Barbara Frietchie

COMPARE CHARACTERS

Both poems are named after famous people from U.S. history. Think about how Paul Revere and Barbara Frietchie are alike and different.

- How are the situations facing the two characters alike? Name at least two important similarities they share.
- What personal traits do Paul Revere and Barbara Frietchie have in common? What personal traits set them apart from each other?
- Fill in a chart like the one below to finish your comparison.

Person	Traits	Date	War	Purpose
Paul Revere				
Barbara Frietchie				

COMPARE LEGENDS

The stories of Paul Revere and Barbara Frietchie are **legends.** They combine historical fact and oral history.

- What single deed is celebrated in each poem?
- What might that deed represent for other people who lived during the historical period?
- Which story do you find more inspiring? Why?

COMPARE SYMBOLS

"Paul Revere's Ride" and "Barbara Frietchie" are poems about freedom and courage. Both poems use symbols to stand for these patriotic ideas.

- Find two symbols in each poem that stand for the ideas of courage, danger, or freedom.
- Sketch the symbols you find in the poems. Then, add symbols for freedom or bravery that come from your own life and times. Create a collection or a collage of these symbols to share with the class. When you present your finished work, be sure to explain what each symbol means to you.

Uncle Sam's hat.

Database: Organizing and Grouping Data

A database is a handy tool for organizing information. It allows you to sort and group data that you have collected in different ways. Using a database may help you discover relationships between groups of data. Best of all, it's quicker and more accurate than using paper and pencil.

Gather Data

Research a period in U.S. history, such as World War II or the Civil Rights movement. Consult print resources as well as the Internet, then choose a group of about twelve sources that you would recommend to other students. Create categories of information that are common to your sources, such as the title, author, and location of the source.

Using a Database

Database software programs differ, but they all have similar functions. The following table, which contains only a few records, will help you understand some of the terms used in database programs. These terms are defined on the next page.

Fields

Records

Title of Source	Author	Type of Source	Genre	Location
Laborers for Liberty: American Women 1865–1890	Sigerman, Harriet	Book	Nonfiction	School library
Women's Rights National Historic Park, Seneca Falls, NY	National Park Service	Web site	Nonfiction	www.cr.nps.gov
"Anthony, Susan Brownell," *Notable American Women,* Vol. 1	Alma Lute	Biographical dictionary	Biography	Public library

Field Each field in a database contains only one kind of information. The top row of a database usually contains the names of the fields.

Field type The most common type of field contains text, as in the table on page 464. You can also define fields to hold numbers, dates, times, yes/no options, and, on some programs, pictures.

Record A record holds information for a single person or item. It includes one piece of information from each of the fields.

Sorting Once your information is in a database, you can sort it in a variety of ways for different purposes. For example, the items in an address book could be sorted alphabetically by persons' names.

Search In the database program's search mode, you can define a search from any field. In the pictured example, for instance, you could use the Type of Source field and ask to see only items from Web sites.

Viewing Options You can see your information in different ways. The table on page 464 shows a layout view. The browse view (below) shows only one record at a time.

TECHNOLOGY TIP

Names of views and other functions differ from one database program to another. The locations of items on menus may also differ. Check with your teacher or lab instructor or use the program's Help button to learn the names and locations in your database program.

Practice

Using your notes on materials about a period in American history, enter the items into a database. If you need help getting started, use your database program's tutorial or Help function or talk to your instructor.

1. Begin by defining your fields. You can use or adapt those shown in the example on page 464. Define them as text fields.
2. Enter each item into a record in your database.
3. After you have entered all your records, sort them in at least two different ways.
4. Look at your completed database in both the layout and browse views.
5. Try a few searches—for example, for all the books in your database or all items from Web sites.

Title of Source	*Laborers for Liberty: American Women 1865–1890*
Author	Sigerman, Harriet
Type of Source	Book
Genre	Nonfiction
Location	School library

ACTIVITIES

1. In your journal, brainstorm three ways in which you could use a database, whether for personal or academic reasons.
2. Build a membership database for a school club or team to which you belong.

Before You Read

The Pinta, the Nina and the Santa Maria; and many other cargoes of Light and *The Other Pioneers*

MEET JOHN TAGLIABUE

There's no doubt that John Tagliabue loves poetry: he's been a poet for more than fifty years. "Poetry," he says, "is all a matter of design, play, ritual, decorations, symbolism, and like our life it is always changing."

John Tagliabue was born in Italy in 1923 and lives in Maine. The poem you are about to read was first published in 1963.

MEET ROBERTO FÉLIX SALAZAR

A native of Laredo, Texas, Roberto Félix Salazar (rō ber′ tō fā′ lēs sä lä zär′) wrote "The Other Pioneers" to remind Americans that the first pioneers in the Southwest had Spanish names and that their descendants—American citizens—still do.

Roberto Félix Salazar was born in 1921. "The Other Pioneers" was first published in 1939.

FOCUS ACTIVITY

What are some symbols of the United States of America? Jot down any symbols that come to mind.

QuickWrite
Share your ideas in a note to a partner.

Setting a Purpose
Read the poems to see how two individuals view their places in U.S. history.

BACKGROUND

The Time and Place Two poets, writing in the twentieth century, respond to events from earlier times that built the United States.

Did You Know? Until 1848 present-day Texas, California, Nevada, Utah, most of Arizona and New Mexico, and parts of Colorado and Wyoming were Mexican territory. After a two-year war, the area became part of the United States. Many people from the region had been Mexican citizens and they feared that their freedom to live in a Spanish-speaking culture would be challenged.

Lone Star flag of the Republic of Texas, 1839. Collection of the Star of the Republic Museum, Washington, TX.

The Pinta, the Nina and the Santa Maria; and many other cargoes of Light

John Tagliabue

America
I
carry
you
around
with
me
the
way
Buddha°
carried
a
grain
of
sand
the
way
Columbus
carried
a
compass
the
way
Whitman°
carried
a
poem
growing
expanding
like
a
galaxy
the
way
a
firefly
carries
a
galaxy
the
way
Faulkner°
carries
eloquence°
the
way
eloquence
carries
hope,
faith,
and
the
4th
of
July.

Ivory compass, c. 1580. Maker unknown. National Maritime Museum Picture Library.

---

10 *Buddha* (563?–483? B.C.) was the founder of Buddhism, one of the world's major religions. He believed that all things are connected, so that one might see the world in a grain of sand.

24 Walt *Whitman* (1819–1892) is considered one of America's greatest poets.

42 William *Faulkner* (1897–1962) was an American novelist and short-story writer.

44 *Eloquence* is speech or writing that is effective and stirring.

The Other Pioneers

Roberto Félix Salazar

Jose Herrera, 1938. Peter Hurd. Tempera on panel, 48 x 46⅝ in. The Nelson Atkins Museum of Art, Kansas City, MO. Gift of Mr. and Mrs. Robert B. Fizzell through the Friends of Art.

Now I must write
Of those of mine who rode these plains
Long years before the Saxon° and the Irish came.
Of those who plowed the land and built the towns
And gave the towns soft-woven Spanish names.
Of those who moved across the Rio Grande
Toward the hiss of Texas snake and Indian yell.
Of men who from the earth made thick-walled homes
And from the earth raised churches to their God.
And of the wives who bore them sons
And smiled with knowing joy.

They saw the Texas sun rise golden-red with promised wealth
And saw the Texas sun sink golden yet, with wealth unspent.
"Here," they said. "Here to live and here to love."
"Here is the land for our sons and the sons of our sons."
And they sang the songs of ancient Spain
And they made new songs to fit new needs.
They cleared the brush and planted the corn
And saw green stalks turn black from lack of rain.
They roamed the plains behind the herds
And stood the Indian's cruel attacks.
There was dust and there was sweat.
And there were tears and the women prayed.

And the years moved on.
Those who were first placed in graves
Beside the broad mesquite° and the tall nopal.°
Gentle mothers left their graces and their arts
And stalwart° fathers pride and manly strength.
Salinas, de la Garza, Sánchez, García,
Uribe, Gonzálaz, Martinez, de León:
Such were the names of the fathers.
Salinas, de la Garza, Sánchez, García,
Uribe, Gonzálaz, Martinez, de León:
Such are the names of the sons.

---

3 Here, *Saxon* means "English."

26 *Mesquite* (mes kēt′) is a small thorny tree, and *nopal* (nō′ päl) is a kind of cactus. Both plants grow in desert regions of the Americas.

28 To be *stalwart* is to be morally or physically strong.

Responding to Literature

PERSONAL RESPONSE

What images came to mind as you read these poems?

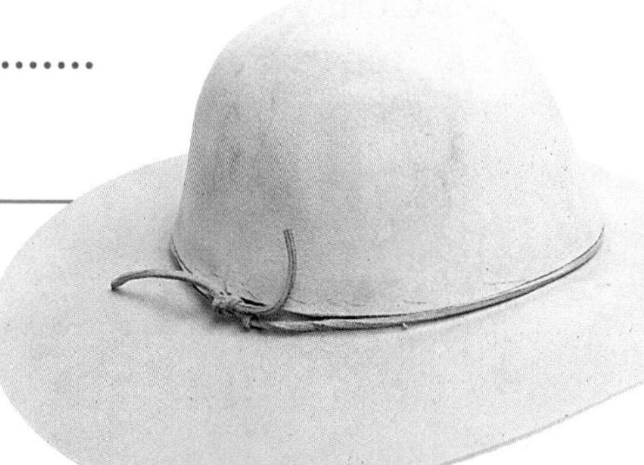

Analyzing Literature

RECALL

1. What does the speaker in Tagliabue's poem do with America? Why?
2. Who are the "other pioneers" in Salazar's poem, and from which country did they come?

INTERPRET

3. What might the sand, compass, poem, and galaxy in Tagliabue's poem all have in common?
4. In your opinion, what is the speaker's opinion of the "other pioneers"? Cite lines from the poem to support your answer.

EVALUATE AND CONNECT

5. Could these two poems exchange titles? Why or why not?
6. Salazar repeats the names of the fathers and sons in the last lines of his poem. What purpose might this **repetition** serve?
7. Salazar uses standard punctuation in his poem, but Tagliabue writes in a **style** (see page R9) that uses very little punctuation. What effect does each style have on the poems?
8. Both poems speak about America. Which poem has more meaning for you? Why?
9. Do you carry a pioneer or an American spirit with you as the people in these poems do? Explain.
10. "The Other Pioneers" opens with "Now I must write . . ." What, do you think, is urging the speaker to write? What might motivate the speaker in Tagliabue's poem?

LITERARY ELEMENTS

Speaker

The **speaker** is the voice of a poem. The speaker is either the poet, a fictional person, or even a thing. The speaker's words communicate a particular **tone,** or attitude, toward the subject of the poem. To understand the speaker's feelings, it is important to look at what the speaker says and study how it is said.

1. Describe the tone used by the speaker in "The Pinta, the Nina and the Santa Maria; and many other cargoes of Light."
2. What do you know about the speaker in "The Other Pioneers"?

- See **Literary Terms Handbook,** p. R9.

Extending Your Response

Writing About Literature

Symbolism Both poets use symbols in their poems. In "The Other Pioneers," the Texas sun may represent wealth that is to come. What do the symbols in the poems say about each poet's attitude toward the United States? Which symbol do you think is most powerful or effective, and why? What do the symbols you listed in the **Focus Activity** on page 466 say about your view of the United States? Write a paragraph to answer one of these questions.

Creative Writing

Poem Write a poem about how you carry America with you. You might begin with Tagliabue's first nine lines, and then add five or six lines of your own. You also might start with Salazar's first line and tell of what you must write. If you prefer, write the poem using your own style.

Literature Groups

Title A poet usually chooses a title that gives readers a greater understanding of the poem. Discuss the titles of the two poems you have read. In what ways do the titles help you understand the poems?

Interdisciplinary Activity

Social Studies Compare and contrast your family history with that of Salazar's pioneers. Use a Venn diagram like the one below, and list similarities in the area where the circles overlap.

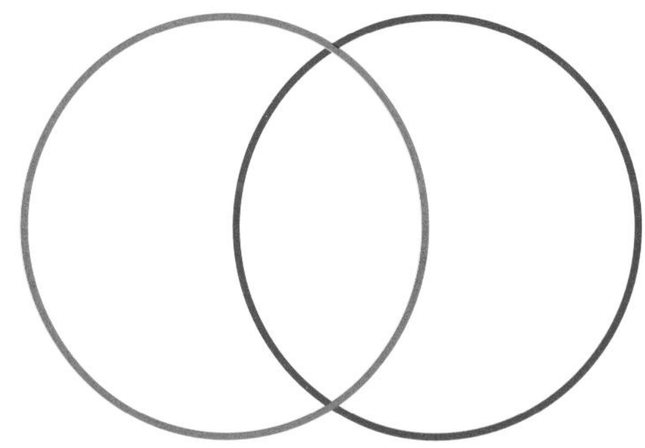

Reading Further

For other stories about Americans, read:
Letters from a Slave Girl by Mary E. Lyons
Dragon's Gate by Laurence Yep

Save your work for your portfolio.

Skill Minilesson

READING AND THINKING • ELABORATION

Elaboration is the use of details to expand on an idea or situation. In the third stanza of "The Other Pioneers," the speaker tells of "those who were first placed in graves." Then the speaker elaborates by identifying those in the graves as "the gentle mothers" and "stalwart fathers," and tells the family names of those buried there.

PRACTICE With a small group, find five or six additional examples of elaboration in the poems. Identify the initial statement and list the elaborating details.

- For more about main idea and details, see **Reading Handbook,** p. R88.

Before You Read

The Gettysburg Address and *O Captain! My Captain!*

MEET ABRAHAM LINCOLN

During his public life, Abraham Lincoln became known as an eloquent speaker. His ability to state an important truth in a few memorable words kept his messages alive in the minds of his audiences—and in the minds of readers today.

Abraham Lincoln was born in 1809 and was assassinated in 1865, while he was president.

MEET WALT WHITMAN

Walt Whitman is among the most respected and studied poets in U.S. literature today. Whitman, who attended to wounded and dying soldiers during the Civil War, greatly admired Abraham Lincoln and wrote several poems about him.

Walt Whitman was born in New York in 1819 and died in 1892 in New Jersey.

FOCUS ACTIVITY

For what is Abraham Lincoln best known?

QuickWrite
Write for three minutes, listing as many qualities as you can to describe Abraham Lincoln.

Setting a Purpose
Read the following selections to increase your understanding of a president who led the nation through the Civil War.

BACKGROUND

The Time and Place
More than 40,000 Confederate and Union soldiers were killed or wounded at the Battle of Gettysburg in Pennsylvania in July 1863. In November of that year, the National Cemetery was dedicated at Gettysburg, and President Lincoln gave the now-famous Gettysburg Address honoring the Union dead.

Gettysburg National Military Park.

Did You Know? Walt Whitman was greatly affected by the Civil War, in which his brother George was wounded. Lincoln's assassination also deeply saddened him.

VOCABULARY PREVIEW

conceive (kən sēv′) *v.* to form; imagine; p. 473
proposition (prop′ ə zish′ ən) *n.* a suggestion or plan; proposal; p. 473
consecrate (kon′ sə krāt′) *v.* to make, declare, or honor as holy; p. 474
detract (di trakt′) *v.* to take something away; lessen; p. 474

The Gettysburg Address

Abraham Lincoln

Four score[1] and seven years ago our fathers brought forth on this continent a new nation, conceived in Liberty, and dedicated to the proposition that all men are created equal.

Now we are engaged in a great civil war, testing whether that nation, or any nation so conceived and so dedicated, can long endure. We are met on a great battlefield of that war. We have come to dedicate a portion of that field, as a final resting place for those who here gave their lives that that nation might live. It is altogether fitting and proper that we should do this.

1. A *score* is twenty.

Vocabulary

conceive (kən sēv′) *v.* to form; imagine

proposition (prop′ ə zish′ ən) *n.* a suggestion or plan; proposal

The Angle, Gettysburg, Pennsylvania, July 3, 1863, 1988. Mort Künstler. Oil on canvas, 18 x 24 in. Collection of Mr. and Mrs. Robert L. Sharpe.

Viewing the painting: What lines or ideas in the Gettysburg Address does this painting bring to mind? Explain.

But, in a larger sense, we can not dedicate—we can not consecrate—we can not hallow[2]—this ground. The brave men, living and dead, who struggled here, have consecrated it, far above our poor power to add or detract. The world will little note, nor long remember what we say here, but it can never forget what they did here. It is for us the living, rather, to be dedicated here to the unfinished work which they who fought here have thus far so nobly advanced. It is rather for us to be here dedicated to the great task remaining before us—that from these honored dead we take increased devotion to that cause for which they gave the last full measure of devotion—that we here highly resolve that these dead shall not have died in vain[3]—that this nation, under God, shall have a new birth of freedom—and that government of the people, by the people, for the people, shall not perish from the earth.

November 19, 1863

2. *Hallow* is a synonym for *consecrate.*

3. Here, the phrase *in vain* means "for no good purpose; uselessly."

Vocabulary

consecrate (kon′ sə krāt′) *v.* to make, declare, or honor as holy
detract (di trakt′) *v.* to take something away; lessen

O Captain! My Captain!

Walt Whitman

O Captain! my Captain! our fearful trip is done;
The ship has weather'd every rack,° the prize we sought is won;
The port is near, the bells I hear, the people all exulting,°
While follow eyes the steady keel,° the vessel grim and daring:
  But O heart! heart! heart!
    O the bleeding drops of red,
      Where on the deck my Captain lies,
        Fallen cold and dead.

O Captain! my Captain! rise up and hear the bells;
Rise up—for you the flag is flung—for you the bugle trills;
For you bouquets and ribbon'd wreaths—for you the shores
  a-crowding;
For you they call, the swaying mass, their eager faces turning:
  Here, Captain! dear father!
    This arm beneath your head;
      It is some dream that on the deck,
        You've fallen cold and dead.

My Captain does not answer, his lips are pale and still;
My father does not feel my arm, he has no pulse nor will;
The ship is anchor'd safe and sound, its voyage closed and
  done;
From fearful trip, the victor ship comes in with object won:
    Exult, O shores, and ring, O bells!
      But I, with mournful tread,
        Walk the deck my Captain lies,
          Fallen cold and dead.

---

2 Here, *rack* means "storm" or "jolt."
3 People *exulting* are rejoicing greatly.
4 The keel is the main timber that runs the length of a boat's bottom; so, *a steady keel* is a straight, even course.

Flying Cloud, 1852. Currier and Ives. Private collection.

Responding to Literature

PERSONAL RESPONSE

What impression do you have of Lincoln after reading these selections? How does it compare with what you wrote for the **Focus Activity** on page 472?

Analyzing Literature

RECALL

1. What does Lincoln say will be most remembered about Gettysburg? What will be forgotten?
2. In Whitman's poem, at what stage in the ship's journey does its captain die?

Gettysburg grave of unidentified soldiers.

INTERPRET

3. What irony do you find in Lincoln's comments about what the world will forget and remember?
4. Why does the speaker in the poem find the time of the captain's death to be **ironic** and particularly sad?

EVALUATE AND CONNECT

5. What feelings about death do these selections convey?
6. What does Lincoln say in his address that you find relevant to your life? Explain.
7. Whitman uses the terms *Captain* and *father* to refer to Lincoln. What terms, in your opinion, might a modern writer use in mourning a great leader? Explain your choices.
8. The term "ship of state" was often used in earlier times to represent a nation. Contrast and compare a ship and the United States. How are they alike? different?
9. Would you care if a leader you respect were a great or a poor speaker? Explain.
10. **Theme Connection** What have these selections added to your understanding of the theme "Free to Be"?

LITERARY ELEMENTS

Author's Purpose

Historical events may trigger strong emotions. Authors and poets, speechwriters and journalists—many of them attempt to capture the emotion and significance of a world event through words. They might have another purpose for writing, such as to educate the public, build support for a cause, honor a group of people, or simply tell a story. Lincoln and Whitman each based their writing on a very recent historical event about which they felt strongly.

1. In your opinion, for what purpose did Lincoln write the Gettysburg Address? What did he want his words to accomplish?
2. For what reasons might Whitman have been moved by Lincoln's assassination? How does he honor Lincoln in the poem?

● See **Literary Terms Handbook,** p. R1.

Extending Your Response

Writing About Literature

Symbols in Poetry What does the captain stand for in the poem "O Captain! My Captain!"? What do the ship and the journey symbolize, or stand for? How do these **symbols** compare with those in the poems on pages 449 and 459? Choose the symbol that you identify with most closely, and write a paragraph explaining what it means to you.

Creative Writing

Honoring a Leader With a group, choose an important historical figure, and write a poem or essay to honor him or her. First, brainstorm a list of the person's accomplishments. List words to describe that person. Then, as you write, be sure your feelings about the individual come through.

Literature Groups

Pick a Modern-day Patriot Whitman and Lincoln shared an intense love for their country. Discuss other American figures, political or literary, that you consider to be patriotic. How do they express their patriotism? How does their ability to speak or write contribute to their importance?

Reading Further

For more books about Lincoln and his times, try these:
Till Victory Is Won by Zak Mettger
Lincoln, a Photobiography by Russell Freedman

Save your work for your portfolio.

Skill Minilesson

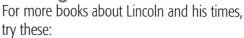

VOCABULARY • THE LATIN ROOT *TRACT*

The word *detract* comes from the Latin prefix *de-*, meaning "down," and the root *tract,* meaning "to drag, draw, or pull." Lincoln said that the soldiers of Gettysburg had accomplished something beyond our powers to *detract*–drag down, or lessen–what they had done.

PRACTICE Match each word with its meaning. Use these prefixes to help you.

ex- "out" *pro-* "forward"
in- "not" *con-* "together"
re- "back"

1. contraction *(n.)*
2. extraction *(n.)*
3. intractable *(adj.)*
4. retraction *(n.)*
5. protracted *(adj.)*

a. long and drawn out
b. something pulled out of something else
c. a withdrawal, as of a promise or statement
d. something shortened or made smaller
e. unable to be guided or led; stubborn

MEDIA Connection

MAGAZINE ARTICLE

Anthony Cohen tried to understand what freedom meant to enslaved Henry Brown by following the journey Brown undertook to find freedom in 1848.

Traveling the Long Road to Freedom, One Step at a Time

by Donovan Webster—*Smithsonian*, October 1996

When historian Anthony Cohen set out to retrace a route on the Underground Railroad, he recovered a piece of American history.

In Spencerport, New York, the school cafeteria is packed with kids. Cohen is onstage at the room's far end. He has just started telling the story of Henry (Box) Brown. "He was a slave in Richmond, Virginia, and sometime in 1848 he had himself shipped to freedom in Philadelphia," Cohen says. "He did it in a wooden box measuring three feet by two feet by twenty-six inches. He was in there for twenty-six hours!" The students gasp. "I decided to try the same thing, only I'd ship myself from Philly to New York City."

He sits on the floor, curled tight, knees at his chest. "With the help of a few friends," Cohen says, "we measured around me. My box's dimensions were twenty-four inches by twenty-eight by thirty. We built a trapdoor into one side, so the only person able to open it was me. We drilled one-inch air holes in the box, so I could breathe. Then we figured out that people would be able to see me, so we covered most of the holes over with stickers.

"All I had in the box with me was my telephone, a bottle of water, a small quilt, a pillow, and a pocket-knife," he continues. "The trip was

Anthony Cohen

supposed to take two hours, but the train was late. It took more than five hours. Inside the box, the temperature rose to more than 100 degrees. My glasses fogged over. I could see sweat forming on the box's hinges: they were dripping. It was so hot I had to shift around and pull out my pocketknife. I cut the legs off my pants."

I kept thinking: 'Come on, Tony, you can do this; Box Brown did it for twenty-six hours.' Then, when I got to New York, they almost didn't take me off the train. My box had been marked to go farther on, to Long Island, but some friends found me and pulled me off."

Respond

1. In what ways was Cohen's journey different from that of Box Brown?
2. Cohen suffered greatly. Why, in your opinion, was Brown able to undertake a much longer journey and survive?

Before You Read

from *Harriet Tubman: Conductor on the Underground Railroad*

MEET ANN PETRY

When Ann Petry was growing up in the early 1900s, textbooks didn't have much to say about the history of slavery. So, she decided to write historical novels that would give an accurate picture of slavery in the United States. Her novel, *The Street*, published in 1946, was the first book by an African American woman to sell more than one million copies. Petry has spent much of her life in Old Saybrook, Connecticut, surrounded by historic sites and antiques that make the past come alive.

Ann Petry was born in 1908. Harriet Tubman: Conductor on the Underground Railroad *was published in 1955.*

FOCUS ACTIVITY

Would you consider camping outdoors for a month in cold weather? Why or why not?

Journal

In your journal, list reasons someone might have for winter camping and equipment they would need to be comfortable.

Setting a Purpose

Read to understand the hardships that Harriet Tubman–and those she led to freedom–endured during one winter.

BACKGROUND

Time and Place The story takes place in December 1851, nine years before the Civil War began. The setting ranges from Maryland to Canada.

Did You Know? Those who used slave labor usually believed that the best way to keep enslaved people powerless was to keep them uneducated. Several states passed laws making it illegal to teach a slave to read or write.

VOCABULARY PREVIEW

incomprehensible (in′ kom prē hen′ sə bəl) *adj.* not understandable; p. 483

incentive (in sen′ tiv) *n.* that which urges to action, especially a promised reward for working harder; p. 483

disheveled (di shev′ əld) *adj.* untidy or rumpled; p. 483

serenity (sə ren′ ə tē) *n.* calmness; peacefulness; p. 485

sullen (sul′ ən) *adj.* stubbornly withdrawn or gloomy because of bad humor; sulky; p. 485

eloquence (el′ ə kwəns) *n.* speech or writing that is expressive, effective, and stirring; p. 485

vain (vān) *adj.* unsuccessful; useless; p. 485

disclose (dis klōz′) *v.* to make known; reveal; p. 486

cajole (kə jōl′) *v.* to persuade, especially by soothing words; coax; p. 486

bleak (blēk) *adj.* cheerless; depressing; p. 488

Harriet Tubman, c. 1945. William H. Johnson. Oil on paperboard, 29⅜ x 23⅜ in. Gift of the Harmon Foundation. National Museum of American Art, Washington, DC.

from Harriet Tubman:

Conductor on the Underground Railroad

Ann Petry

Along the Eastern Shore of Maryland, in Dorchester County, in Caroline County, the masters kept hearing whispers about the man named Moses, who was running off slaves. At first they did not believe in his existence. The stories about him were fantastic, unbelievable. Yet they watched for him. They offered rewards for his capture.

They never saw him. Now and then they heard whispered rumors to the effect that he was in the neighborhood. The woods were searched. The roads were watched. There was never anything to indicate his whereabouts. But a few days afterward, a goodly number of slaves would be gone from the plantation. Neither the master nor the overseer had heard or seen anything unusual in the quarter. Sometimes one or the other would vaguely remember having heard a whippoorwill[1] call somewhere in the woods, close by, late at night. Though it was the wrong season for whippoorwills.

Sometimes the masters thought they had heard the cry of a hoot owl, repeated, and would remember having thought that the intervals between the low moaning cry were wrong, that it had been repeated four times in succession instead of three. There was never anything more than that to suggest that all was not well in the quarter. Yet when morning came, they invariably discovered that a group of the finest slaves had taken to their heels.

1. Here, *quarter* refers to the area in which the enslaved people lived. The *whippoorwill,* a North American bird, is active mainly at night; its name imitates the sound of its call.

Harriet Tubman (left) poses with a group of unidentified people she helped to escape from slavery.

Viewing the photograph: What may these people have in common with the eleven people Harriet Tubman conducted to freedom in this selection?

Unfortunately, the discovery was almost always made on a Sunday. Thus a whole day was lost before the machinery of pursuit could be set in motion. The posters offering rewards for the fugitives could not be printed until Monday. The men who made a living hunting for runaway slaves were out of reach, off in the woods with their dogs and their guns, in pursuit of four-footed game, or they were in camp meetings[2] saying their prayers with their wives and families beside them.

Harriet Tubman could have told them that there was far more involved in this matter of running off slaves than signaling the would-be runaways by imitating the call of a whippoorwill, or a hoot owl, far more involved than a matter of waiting for a clear night when the North Star was visible.

In December, 1851, when she started out with the band of fugitives that she planned to take to Canada, she had been in the vicinity of the plantation for days, planning the trip, carefully selecting the slaves that she would take with her.

She had announced her arrival in the quarter by singing the forbidden spiritual—"Go down, Moses, 'way down to Egypt Land"[3]—singing it softly outside the door of a slave cabin, late at night. The husky voice was beautiful even when it was barely more than a murmur borne[4] on the wind.

Once she had made her presence known, word of her coming spread from cabin to cabin. The slaves whispered to each other, ear to mouth, mouth to ear, "Moses is here." "Moses has come." "Get ready. Moses is back again." The ones who had agreed to go North with her put ashcake[5] and salt herring in an old bandanna, hastily tied it into a bundle, and then waited patiently for the signal that meant it was time to start.

There were eleven in this party, including one of her brothers and his wife. It was the largest group that she had ever conducted, but she was determined that more and more slaves should know what freedom was like.

She had to take them all the way to Canada. The Fugitive Slave Law[6] was no

2. *Camp meetings* are religious services held in a tent or outdoors.
3. *["Go down . . . Egypt Land"]* is a line from an African American folk song based on a Bible story about Moses leading the Israelites out of slavery in Egypt. Certain songs were forbidden for fear that they might inspire enslaved people to escape or rebel.
4. *Borne* is the past participle of *to bear* and, here, means "carried; transported."
5. *Ashcake* is a cornmeal bread that's baked among the ashes at the back of a fireplace.
6. The 1850 *Fugitive Slave Law* allowed owners of escaped enslaved people to get those people back, even if the people fleeing slavery had reached free states.

longer a great many incomprehensible words written down on the country's lawbooks. The new law had become a reality. It was Thomas Sims, a boy, picked up on the streets of Boston at night and shipped back to Georgia. It was Jerry and Shadrach, arrested and jailed with no warning.

She had never been in Canada. The route beyond Philadelphia was strange to her. But she could not let the runaways who accompanied her know this. As they walked along she told them stories of her own first flight, she kept painting vivid word pictures of what it would be like to be free.

But there were so many of them this time. She knew moments of doubt when she was half-afraid, and kept looking back over her shoulder, imagining that she heard the sound of pursuit. They would certainly be pursued. Eleven of them. Eleven thousand dollars' worth of flesh and bone and muscle that belonged to Maryland planters. If they were caught, the eleven runaways would be whipped and sold South, but she—she would probably be hanged.

They tried to sleep during the day but they never could wholly relax into sleep. She could tell by the positions they assumed, by their restless movements. And they walked at night. Their progress was slow. It took them three nights of walking to reach the first stop. She had told them about the place where they would stay, promising warmth and good food, holding these things out to them as an incentive to keep going.

When she knocked on the door of a farmhouse, a place where she and her parties of runaways had always been welcome, always been given shelter and plenty to eat, there was no answer. She knocked again, softly. A voice from within said, "Who is it?" There was fear in the voice.

She knew instantly from the sound of the voice that there was something wrong. She said, "A friend with friends," the password on the Underground Railroad.

The door opened, slowly. The man who stood in the doorway looked at her coldly, looked with unconcealed astonishment and fear at the eleven disheveled runaways who were standing near her. Then he shouted, "Too many, too many. It's not safe. My place was searched last week. It's not safe!" and slammed the door in her face.

She turned away from the house, frowning. She had promised her passengers food and rest and warmth, and instead of that, there would be hunger and cold and more walking over the frozen ground. Somehow she would have to instill[7] courage into these eleven people, most of them strangers, would have to feed them on hope and bright dreams of freedom instead of the fried pork and corn bread and milk she had promised them.

They stumbled along behind her, half-dead for sleep, and she urged them on, though she was as tired and as discouraged as they were. She had never been in Canada but she kept painting wondrous

7. To *instill* something is to put it in gradually, little by little.

Vocabulary

incomprehensible (in′ kom prē hen′ sə bəl) *adj.* not understandable

incentive (in sen′ tiv) *n.* that which urges to action, especially a promised reward for working harder

disheveled (di shev′ əld) *adj.* untidy or rumpled

word pictures of what it would be like. She managed to dispel[8] their fear of pursuit, so that they would not become hysterical, panic-stricken. Then she had to bring some of the fear back, so that they would stay awake and keep walking though they drooped with sleep.

Yet during the day, when they lay down deep in a thicket, they never really slept, because if a twig snapped or the wind sighed in the branches of a pine tree, they jumped to their feet, afraid of their own shadows, shivering and shaking. It was very cold, but they dared not make fires because someone would see the smoke and wonder about it.

She kept thinking, eleven of them. Eleven thousand dollars' worth of slaves. And she had to take them all the way to Canada. Sometimes she told them about Thomas Garrett, in Wilmington. She said he was their friend even though he did not know them. He was the friend of all fugitives. He called them God's poor. He was a Quaker and his speech was a little different from that of other people. His clothing was different, too. He wore the wide-brimmed hat that the Quakers wear.

She said that he had thick white hair, soft, almost like a baby's, and the kindest eyes she had ever seen. He was a big man and strong, but he had never used his strength to harm anyone, always to help people. He would give all of them a new pair of shoes. Everybody. He always did. Once they reached his house in Wilmington, they would be safe. He would see to it that they were.

She described the house where he lived, told them about the store where he sold shoes. She said he kept a pail of milk and a loaf of bread in the drawer of his desk so that he would have food ready at hand for any of God's poor who should suddenly appear before him, fainting with hunger. There was a hidden room in the store. A whole wall swung open, and behind it was a room where he could hide fugitives. On the wall there were shelves filled with small boxes—boxes of shoes—so that you would never guess that the wall actually opened.

While she talked, she kept watching them. They did not believe her. She could tell by their expressions. They were thinking, New shoes, Thomas Garrett, Quaker, Wilmington—what foolishness was this? Who knew if she told the truth? Where was she taking them anyway?

That night they reached the next stop—a farm that belonged to a German. She made the runaways take shelter behind trees at the edge of the fields before she knocked at the door. She hesitated before she approached the door, thinking, suppose that he, too, should refuse shelter, suppose—Then she thought, Lord, I'm going to hold steady on to You and You've got to see me through—and knocked softly.

She heard the familiar guttural[9] voice say, "Who's there?"

She answered quickly, "A friend with friends."

He opened the door and greeted her warmly. "How many this time?" he asked.

"Eleven," she said and waited, doubting, wondering.

He said, "Good. Bring them in."

He and his wife fed them in the lamplit kitchen, their faces glowing, as they offered food and more food, urging them to eat, saying there was plenty for everybody,

8. To *dispel* something is to make it go away or disappear.

9. A *guttural* voice has a rough, harsh sound.

have more milk, have more bread, have more meat.

They spent the night in the warm kitchen. They really slept, all that night and until dusk the next day. When they left, it was with reluctance. They had all been warm and safe and well-fed. It was hard to exchange the security offered by that clean warm kitchen for the darkness and the cold of a December night.

Harriet had found it hard to leave the warmth and friendliness, too. But she urged them on. For a while, as they walked, they seemed to carry in them a measure of contentment; some of the serenity and the cleanliness of that big warm kitchen lingered on inside them. But as they walked farther and farther away from the warmth and the light, the cold and the darkness entered into them. They fell silent, sullen, suspicious. She waited for the moment when some one of them would turn mutinous.[10] It did not happen that night.

Two nights later she was aware that the feet behind her were moving slower and slower. She heard the irritability in their voices, knew that soon someone would refuse to go on.

She started talking about William Still and the Philadelphia Vigilance Committee.[11] No one commented. No one asked any questions. She told them the story of William and Ellen Craft and how they escaped from Georgia. Ellen was so fair that she looked as though she were white, and so she dressed up in a man's clothing and she looked like a wealthy young planter. Her husband, William, who was dark, played the role of her slave. Thus they traveled from Macon, Georgia, to Philadelphia, riding on the trains, staying at the finest hotels. Ellen pretended to be very ill—her right arm was in a sling, and her right hand was bandaged, because she was supposed to have rheumatism. Thus she avoided having to sign the register at the hotels for she could not read or write. They finally arrived safely in Philadelphia, and then went on to Boston.

No one said anything. Not one of them seemed to have heard her.

She told them about Frederick Douglass, the most famous of the escaped slaves, of his eloquence, of his magnificent appearance. Then she told them of her own first vain effort at running away, evoking[12] the memory of that miserable life she had led as a child, reliving it for a moment in the telling.

But they had been tired too long, hungry too long, afraid too long, footsore too long. One of them suddenly cried out in despair, "Let me go back. It is better to be a slave than to suffer like this in order to be free."

She carried a gun with her on these trips. She had never used it—except as a threat. Now as she aimed it, she experienced a feeling of guilt, remembering that

10. To turn *mutinous* (mūt′ ən əs) is to become openly rebellious.
11. Before the Civil War, this organization raised money to help escaping slaves. *Vigilance* means "the state of being watchful and alert to danger or trouble."
12. Harriet is calling up *(evoking)* this memory.

Vocabulary

serenity (sə ren′ ə tē) *n.* calmness; peacefulness
sullen (sul′ ən) *adj.* stubbornly withdrawn or gloomy because of bad humor; sulky
eloquence (el′ ə kwəns) *n.* speech or writing that is expressive, effective, and stirring
vain (vān) *adj.* unsuccessful; useless

time, years ago, when she had prayed for the death of Edward Brodas, the Master, and then not too long afterward had heard that great wailing cry that came from the throats of the field hands, and knew from the sound that the Master was dead.

One of the runaways said, again, "Let me go back. Let me go back," and stood still, and then turned around and said, over his shoulder, "I am going back."

She lifted the gun, aimed it at the despairing slave. She said, "Go on with us or die." The husky low-pitched voice was grim.

He hesitated for a moment and then he joined the others. They started walking again. She tried to explain to them why none of them could go back to the plantation. If a runaway returned, he would turn traitor, the master and the overseer would force him to turn traitor. The returned slave would disclose the stopping places, the hiding places, the cornstacks they had used with the full knowledge of the owner of the farm, the name of the German farmer who had fed them and sheltered them. These people who had risked their own security to help runaways would be ruined, fined, imprisoned.

She said, "We got to go free or die. And freedom's not bought with dust."

This time she told them about the long agony of the Middle Passage[13] on the old slave ships, about the black horror of the holds, about the chains and the whips. They too knew these stories. But she wanted to remind them of the long hard way they had come, about the long hard way they had yet to go. She told them about Thomas Sims, the boy picked up on the streets of Boston and sent back to Georgia. She said when they got him back to Savannah, got him in prison there, they whipped him until a doctor who was standing by watching said, "You will kill him if you strike him again!" His master said, "Let him die!"

Thus she forced them to go on. Sometimes she thought she had become nothing but a voice speaking in the darkness, cajoling, urging, threatening. Sometimes she told them things to make them laugh, sometimes she sang to them, and heard the eleven voices behind her blending softly with hers, and then she knew that for the moment all was well with them.

She gave the impression of being a short, muscular, indomitable[14] woman who could never be defeated. Yet at any moment she was liable to be seized by one of those curious fits of sleep,[15] which might last for a few minutes or for hours.

Even on this trip, she suddenly fell asleep in the woods. The runaways, ragged, dirty, hungry, cold, did not steal the gun as they might have, and set off by themselves, or turn back. They sat on the ground near her and waited patiently until she awakened. They had come to trust her implicitly,[16] totally. They, too, had come to believe her repeated statement, "We got to go

13. The *Middle Passage* was the sea route followed by slave traders between Africa and the Americas.

14. *Indomitable* (in dom′ ə tə bəl) means "that cannot be conquered; unbeatable."

15. Harriet's *curious fits of sleep* were occasional unexplained spells of dizziness or unconsciousness.

16. To trust *implicitly* (im plis′ it lē) is to have complete faith—no questions, doubts, or hesitations.

Vocabulary

disclose (dis klōz′) *v.* to make known; reveal

cajole (kə jōl′) *v.* to persuade, especially by soothing words; coax free or die." She was leading them into freedom, and so they waited until she was ready to go on.

Finally, they reached Thomas Garrett's house in Wilmington, Delaware. Just as Harriet had promised, Garret gave them all new shoes, and provided carriages to take them on to the next stop.

By slow stages they reached Philadelphia, where William Still hastily recorded their names, and the plantations whence they had come, and something of the life they had led in slavery. Then he carefully hid what he had written, for fear it might be discovered. In 1872 he published this record in book form and called it *The Underground Railroad*. In the foreword to his book he said: "While I knew the danger of keeping strict records, and while I did not then dream that in my day slavery would be blotted out, or that the time would come when I could publish these records, it used to afford me great satisfaction to take them down, fresh from the lips of fugitives on the way to freedom, and to preserve them as they had given them."

William Still, who was familiar with all the station stops on the Underground Railroad, supplied Harriet with money and sent her and her eleven fugitives on to Burlington, New Jersey.

Harriet felt safer now, though there were danger spots ahead. But the biggest part of her job was over. As they went farther and farther north, it grew colder; she was aware of the wind on the Jersey ferry and aware of the cold damp in New York. From New York they went on to Syracuse, where the temperature was even lower.

In Syracuse she met the Reverend J. W. Loguen, known as "Jarm" Loguen. This was the beginning of a lifelong friendship. Both Harriet and Jarm Loguen were to become friends and supporters of Old John Brown.

Did You Know?
John Brown was a leader of the American antislavery movement. In 1859 he led an unsuccessful raid of a federal weapons storehouse in Virginia, hoping to inspire a slave rebellion.

From Syracuse they went north again, into a colder, snowier city—Rochester. Here they almost certainly stayed with Frederick Douglass, for he wrote in his autobiography:

"On one occasion I had eleven fugitives at the same time under my roof, and it was necessary for them to remain with me until I could collect sufficient money to get them to Canada. It was the largest number I ever had at any one time, and I had some difficulty in providing so many with food and shelter, but, as may well be imagined, they were not very fastidious[17] in either direction, and were well content with very plain food, and a strip of carpet on the floor for a bed, or a place on the straw in the barnloft."

Late in December, 1851, Harriet arrived in St. Catharines, Canada West (now Ontario), with the eleven fugitives. It had taken almost a month to complete this journey; most of the time had been spent getting out of Maryland.

That first winter in St. Catharines was a terrible one. Canada was a strange frozen land, snow everywhere, ice everywhere, and a bone-biting cold the like of which none of them had ever experienced before. Harriet rented a small frame house in the

17. If they had been *fastidious* (fas tid′ ē əs), they would have been difficult to please or satisfy.

Underground Railroad, c. 1945. William H. Johnson. Oil on paperboard, 33⅜ x 36⅜ in. National Museum of American Art, Washington, DC.

Viewing the painting: In what ways does this painting reflect the concept of the Underground Railroad?

town and set to work to make a home. The fugitives boarded with her. They worked in the forests, felling trees, and so did she. Sometimes she took other jobs, cooking or cleaning house for people in the town. She cheered on these newly arrived fugitives, working herself, finding work for them, finding food for them, praying for them, sometimes begging for them.

Often she found herself thinking of the beauty of Maryland, the mellowness of the soil, the richness of the plant life there. The climate itself made for an ease of living that could never be duplicated in this bleak, barren countryside.

In spite of the severe cold, the hard work, she came to love St. Catharines, and the other towns and cities in Canada where black men lived. She discovered that freedom meant more than the right to change jobs at will, more than the right to keep the money that one earned. It was the right to vote and to sit on juries. It was the right to be elected to office. In Canada there were black men who were county officials and members of school boards. St. Catharines had a large colony of ex-slaves, and they owned their own homes, kept them neat and clean and in good repair. They lived in whatever part of town they chose and sent their children to the schools.

When spring came she decided that she would make this small Canadian city her home—as much as any place could be said to be home to a woman who traveled from Canada to the Eastern Shore of Maryland as often as she did.

In the spring of 1852, she went back to Cape May, New Jersey. She spent the summer there, cooking in a hotel. That fall she returned, as usual, to Dorchester County, and brought out nine more slaves, conducting them all the way to St. Catharines, in Canada West, to the bone-biting cold, the snow-covered forests—and freedom.

She continued to live in this fashion, spending the winter in Canada, and the spring and summer working in Cape May, New Jersey, or in Philadelphia. She made two trips a year into slave territory, one in the fall and another in the spring. She now had a definite crystallized[18] purpose, and in carrying it out, her life fell into a pattern which remained unchanged for the next six years.

18. Here, *crystallized* means "having a clear, specific form."

Vocabulary

bleak (blēk) *adj.* cheerless; depressing

Responding to Literature

PERSONAL RESPONSE

Could you have completed a journey like the one Tubman and the fugitives endured? As you think about your answer, review your journal entry from the **Focus Activity** on page 479.

Analyzing Literature

RECALL

1. What was the Fugitive Slave Law?
2. What does Harriet Tubman tell the fugitives about Garrett?
3. How does Harriet use her gun?
4. What is life like for the formerly enslaved people who make it to Canada?

INTERPRET

5. Why does Harriet take her group all the way to Canada?
6. How does Harriet use words to keep the runaways going?
7. Why does Harriet refuse to let any of the fugitives return to their former homes?
8. What does Harriet learn about freedom in Canada?

EVALUATE AND CONNECT

9. **Situational irony** exists when the actual outcome of a situation is the opposite of what is expected. What is ironic about the reason many of the fugitive-slave hunters are not available on Sundays?
10. Theme Connection Harriet says, "We got to go free or die." Do you think she is right? Is freedom more important than food or shelter or safety? Give reasons for your opinion.

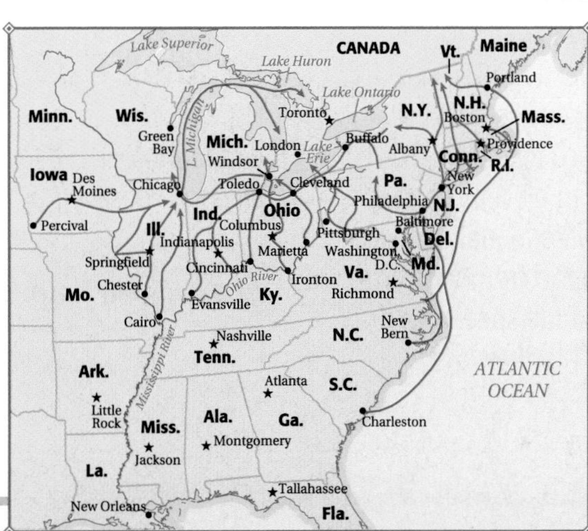

Underground Railroad routes traveled by people escaping slavery during the 1800s.

LITERARY ELEMENTS

Point of View

Point of view is the relationship of the narrator, or storyteller, to the story. In this selection, Petry uses an **omniscient third-person point of view.** The narrator is outside of the story and reveals the thoughts of several characters. We learn not only what Harriet Tubman, the main character, is thinking, but also what various other characters think—slave masters, fugitives, and some of the people who assist them.

1. Look over the story and list some of the things the slave masters think.
2. Would the story have been more interesting told in the first person—that is, as if Tubman were telling her story? Why or why not?

- See **Literary Terms Handbook,** p. R7.

Literature and Writing

Writing About Literature 

Analyzing Emotional Appeal Ann Petry's goal is to make readers understand the situation faced by people escaping slavery. She wants readers to feel the injustice, fear, hunger, cold, and ultimately, the hope of freedom that kept the fugitives going. Write a paragraph analyzing whether, in your opinion, Petry succeeds in her goal. Give examples from the story and describe your emotional response.

Creative Writing 

Dialogue Reread the last part of the selection that begins: "Late in December, 1851, Harriet arrived in St. Catharines. . . ." Tubman and the escaped enslaved people have made it to Canada. They are free but homesick in this harsh, cold environment. With a partner, write dialogue for a scene between Tubman and two fugitives discussing their new lives. You could make one character sorry she came north, while the other has decided to run for county office.

Extending Your Response

Literature Groups 

Harriet or Moses After escaping slavery herself, Tubman returned to the South nineteen times to rescue three hundred people. In your group, discuss these questions about Tubman: Why was Tubman widely known as "Moses"? If Tubman were alive today, would she suffer from the effects of racism? Would she suffer from the effects of sexism? Which *ism,* in your opinion, might cause her the most trouble?

Interdisciplinary Activity 

Communication Imagine that it is 1851 and that radio and social service agencies exist in this time. You work for one such agency in St. Catharines. Tubman arrives with eleven refugees. How will you help them? Prepare a public service announcement asking for support from the community. Rehearse your one-minute speech with a tape recorder. Then deliver it to the class.

Performing 

Weather Report The men and women who escaped to Canada were shocked by the bitter weather there. They were used to mild winters in the South. In pairs, research the winter weather in the southern United States and southern Canada. Locate helpful photographs and meteorological data from which you can create charts, graphs, and posters that compare and contrast the two environments. Present your information to the class.

Reading Further 

For a view of other strong women, try these books:
Grand Mothers edited by Nikki Giovanni
Eleanor Roosevelt by Russell Freedman

Save your work for your portfolio.

Skill Minilessons

GRAMMAR AND LANGUAGE • PROPER AND COMMON NOUNS

A **noun** is a word that names a person, place, thing, or idea. A **proper noun** names a specific person, place, or thing and is capitalized. A **common noun** is not capitalized.

PRACTICE Correct the errors in capitalization.

1. harriet tubman smuggled 300 Fugitives to freedom, leading her people from maryland to Canada.
2. During the civil war, harriet commanded a raid that freed more than 750 Slaves.
3. Her military Campaign was the first in united states history to be led by a Woman.

- For more about proper and common nouns, see **Language Handbook,** pp. R35–R37.

READING AND THINKING • USING A TIME LINE

A **time line** is a graphic aid that shows events over a given period of time. A time line may show a few years or a few thousand years, and it may include captions and images.

Enslaved People in Virginia

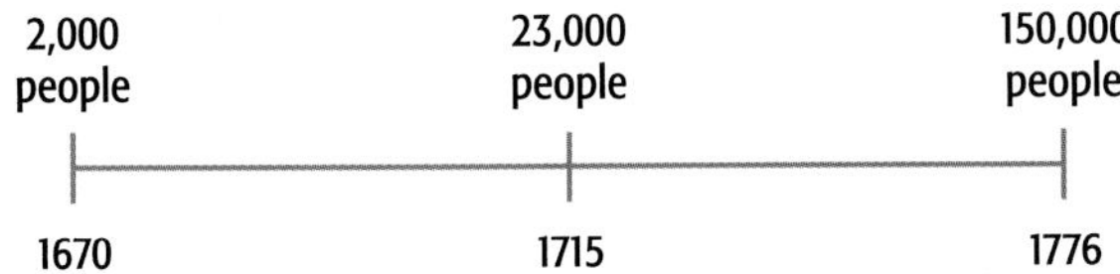

PRACTICE List five or six important events in the story of Harriet Tubman. Construct a time line to show these events. Illustrate your time line. For example, draw a whippoorwill at the start, and a symbol of Canada at the end.

- For more about graphic organizers, see **Reading Handbook,** p. R86.

VOCABULARY • MULTIPLE-MEANING WORDS

Multiple-meaning words can be confusing, especially if a familiar word has another meaning that you don't know. If you read about a nation *forging* a Bill of Rights, you might think the document is a fake. However, *forging* also means "shaping, forming, or creating." In the selection from *Harriet Tubman, vain* means "useless." However, it can also mean "conceited." When you come across a word you know, but that does not make sense in the sentence, look up the word in a dictionary. It may have a second meaning.

PRACTICE Choose the underlined word whose meaning is *different from* the definition given.

1. *corner: the area within an angle*
   He sat in the corner [a] planning how to get a corner [b] on the wheat market.
2. *hard: firm to the touch; resistant to pressure*
   We need hard [a] facts about how hard [b] the metal is.
3. *minute: very tiny*
   Her minute [a] cassette tape held a two-minute [b] account of the events.
4. *prone: having a natural tendency*
   I am prone [a] to fall asleep while prone [b].

Interdisciplinary Connection

SOCIAL STUDIES

The Fight for Civil Rights

Frances Foster

Frances Foster was barely fourteen years old when she walked into a store one day in Birmingham, Alabama, knowing that she might be arrested. It was the late 1950s, when segregation was still common in much of the country. African Americans, especially in the South, were familiar with signs reading "No Coloreds" and sometimes couldn't check out books from the public library.

However, African American leaders, such as Birmingham minister Dr. Martin Luther King Jr., gave powerful speeches that inspired people to fight legal segregation. With the help of Dr. King and others, students learned how to organize nonviolent protests, such as sit-ins, marches, and boycotts.

Frances Foster knew that because she was African American, no one would wait on her at the store's luncheonette that afternoon. But each time Frances was told to leave, she politely requested the same service white patrons received. A television news crew arrived to film her sit-in. The police eventually took Frances to a juvenile detention center, where she watched herself on the evening news.

In 1964 Dr. King won the Nobel Peace Prize for his work. The same year, President Lyndon Johnson signed the Civil Rights Act, making public segregation illegal.

Before 1960 was over, more than 50,000 people had participated in sit-ins at segregated movie theaters, parks, swimming pools, beaches, churches, and hotels. The protesters were arrested, attacked, and sometimes even killed, but support for Civil Rights kept growing. In 1963 Dr. King gave one of the most inspirational speeches of the Civil Rights movement, "I Have a Dream," to 250,000 people at the March on Washington.

Today, the law supports Frances Foster's right to eat at any restaurant she chooses. "I feel that the movement carries on with me today," she says. "I can do anything I want to do."

ACTIVITIES

1. Mahatma Gandhi led a fight against discrimination in India beginning in the 1920s. Dr. King and other civil rights leaders studied Gandhi's ideas to help them organize the Civil Rights movement in the United States. Research Ghandi's work, and prepare a short report on his teachings.
2. Research key events in the Civil Rights movement to make a time line of the movement. Write captions and include visuals for each item on the time line.

Before You Read

I Have a Dream

MEET MARTIN LUTHER KING JR.

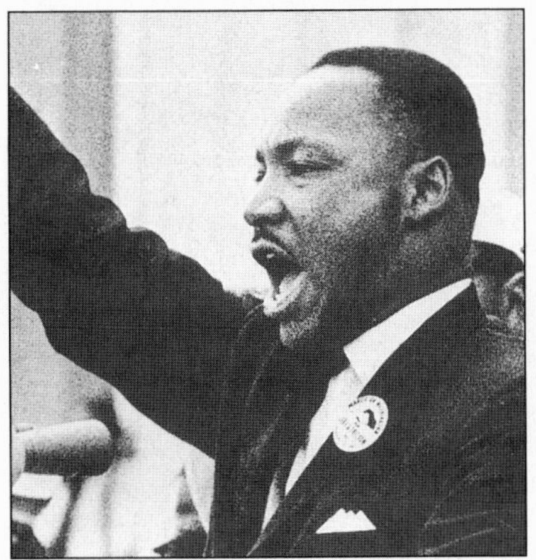

Growing up in the segregated South during the Great Depression of the 1930s, Dr. Martin Luther King Jr. saw the effects of prejudice and recognized the need to combat it. "Nonviolence is a powerful and just weapon," said Dr. King, who became a Baptist minister. "It . . . cuts without wounding and ennobles the man who wields it." Dr. King won the Nobel Peace Prize in 1964. He was assassinated when he was only thirty-nine years old.

Martin Luther King Jr. was born in 1929 and was killed in 1968.

FOCUS ACTIVITY

What dreams and plans do you have for the future? Could anything interfere with those dreams?

FreeWrite

Jot down your thoughts, hopes, or dreams for the future.

Setting a Purpose

Read to learn more about the dream that one man had for himself and the entire nation.

Nobel Peace Prize medal.

BACKGROUND

The Time and Place This most famous of Dr. King's speeches was delivered at a Civil Rights rally in Washington, D.C., on August 28, 1963.

Did You Know? After the U.S. Civil War, African Americans were allowed to own land and hold political office. Then laws were passed that made discrimination legal. There were separate schools, separate jobs, even separate water fountains for black and white people. Not until 1954 did the U.S. Supreme Court say that separate but equal treatment was in fact *unequal*–and illegal.

VOCABULARY PREVIEW

discrimination (dis krim′ ə nā′ shən) *n.* unfair treatment, especially as a result of policies directed against minority groups; p. 495

default (di fôlt′) *v.* to fail to do as required; p. 495

desolate (des′ ə lit) *adj.* without comfort; p. 495

inextricably (in eks′ tri kə blē) *adv.* in a way that cannot be separated; p. 496

tribulation (trib′ yə lā′ shən) *n.* great misery or distress; p. 496

wallow (wol′ ō) *v.* to become or remain helpless; p. 497

exalt (ig zôlt′) *v.* to raise in status, dignity, power; glorify; p. 498

discord (dis′ kôrd) *n.* disagreement; conflict; p. 498

prodigious (prə dij′ əs) *adj.* enormous; p. 498

King Mural, 1986. Don Miller. District of Columbia Public Library.

I Have a Dream

Martin Luther King Jr.

I am happy to join with you today in what will go down in history as the greatest demonstration for freedom in the history of our nation.

Fivescore years ago, a great American, in whose symbolic shadow we stand today, signed the Emancipation Proclamation. This momentous[1] decree came as a great beacon light of hope to millions of Negro slaves who had been seared in the flames of withering injustice. It came as a joyous daybreak to end the long night of their captivity.

But one hundred years later, the Negro still is not free; one hundred years later, the life of the Negro is still sadly crippled by the manacles[2] of segregation and the chains of discrimination; one hundred years later, the Negro lives on a lonely island of poverty in the midst of a vast ocean of material prosperity; one hundred years later, the Negro is still languished[3] in the corners of American society and finds himself in exile in his own land.

So we've come here today to dramatize a shameful condition. In a sense we've come to our nation's capital to cash a check. When the architects of our republic wrote the magnificent words of the Constitution and the Declaration of Independence, they were signing a promissory note[4] to which every American was to fall heir. This note was the promise that all men, yes, black men as well as white men, would be guaranteed the unalienable[5] rights of life, liberty, and the pursuit of happiness.

It is obvious today that America has defaulted on this promissory note in so far as her citizens of color are concerned. Instead of honoring this sacred obligation, America has given the Negro people a bad check; a check which has come back marked "insufficient funds." We refuse to believe that there are insufficient funds in the great vaults of opportunity of this nation. And so we've come to cash this check, a check that will give us upon demand the riches of freedom and the security of justice.

We have also come to this hallowed spot to remind America of the fierce urgency of now. This is no time to engage in the luxury of cooling off or to take the tranquilizing drug of gradualism.[6] Now is the time to make real the promises of democracy; now is the time to rise from the dark and desolate valley of segregation to the sunlit path of racial justice; now is the time to lift our nation from the quicksands of racial injustice to the solid rock of brotherhood; now is the time to make justice a reality for all God's children. It would be fatal for the nation

1. *Momentous* (mō men′ təs) means "very important."
2. Handcuffs and other physical restraints are *manacles* (man′ ə kəlz).
3. Here, *languished* refers to living under distressing conditions.
4. A *promissory note* is a written promise to pay a certain sum of money to someone at a future date.
5. *Unalienable* rights, according to the Declaration of Independence, are rights that may not be taken away.
6. Dr. King was speaking at the Lincoln Memorial, a place many people consider holy *(hallowed). Gradualism* is trying to bring about social or political change gradually or slowly.

Vocabulary

discrimination (dis krim′ ə nā′ shən) *n.* unfair treatment, especially as a result of policies directed against minority groups
default (di fôlt′) *v.* to fail to do as required
desolate (des′ ə lit) *adj.* without comfort

to overlook the urgency of the moment. This sweltering summer of the Negro's legitimate discontent will not pass until there is an invigorating[7] autumn of freedom and equality.

Nineteen sixty-three is not an end, but a beginning. And those who hope that the Negro needed to blow off steam and will now be content, will have a rude awakening if the nation returns to business as usual. There will be neither rest nor tranquility in America until the Negro is granted his citizenship rights. The whirlwinds of the revolt will continue to shake the foundations of our nation until the bright day of justice emerges.

But there is something that I must say to my people, who stand on the warm threshold which leads into the palace of justice. In the process of gaining our rightful place, we must not be guilty of wrongful deeds. Let us not seek to satisfy our thirst for freedom by drinking from the cup of bitterness and hatred. We must forever conduct our struggle on the high plain of dignity and discipline. We must not allow our creative protest to generate into physical violence. Again and again we must rise to the majestic heights of meeting physical force with soul force; and the marvelous new militancy,[8] which has engulfed the Negro community, must not lead us to a distrust of all white people. For many of our white brothers, as evidenced by their presence here today, have come to realize that their destiny is tied up with our destiny. And they have come to realize that their freedom is inextricably bound to our freedom. We cannot walk alone. And as we talk, we must make the pledge that we shall always march ahead. We cannot turn back.

There are those who are asking the devotees of Civil Rights, "When will you be satisfied?" We can never be satisfied as long as the Negro is the victim of the unspeakable horrors of police brutality; we can never be satisfied as long as our bodies, heavy with the fatigue of travel, cannot gain lodging in the motels of the highways and the hotels of the cities; we cannot be satisfied as long as the Negro's basic mobility is from a smaller ghetto to a larger one; we can never be satisfied as long as our children are stripped of their selfhood and robbed of their dignity by signs stating "For Whites Only"; we cannot be satisfied as long as the Negro in Mississippi cannot vote and a Negro in New York believes he has nothing for which to vote. No! no, we are not satisfied, and we will not be satisfied until "justice rolls down like waters and righteousness like a mighty stream."[9]

I am not unmindful that some of you have come here out of great trials and tribulations. Some of you have come fresh from narrow jail cells. Some of you have come from areas where your quest for freedom left you battered by the storms of persecution and staggered by the winds of police

7. *Sweltering* means "very hot and humid," and *invigorating* means "bringing new life and energy." However, Dr. King is talking about more than just seasonal changes.

8. Dr. King uses *generate into* to mean "produce or cause." *Militancy* is a readiness to fight for a cause.

9. This line is from the Old Testament's Book of Amos.

Vocabulary

inextricably (in eks′ tri kə blē) *adv.* in a way that cannot be separated

tribulation (trib′ yə lā′ shən) *n.* great misery or distress brutality. You have been the veterans of creative suffering. Continue to work with the faith that unearned suffering is redemptive.[10] Go back to Mississippi. Go back to Alabama. Go back to South Carolina. Go back to Georgia. Go back to Louisiana. Go back to the slums and ghettos of our Northern cities, knowing that somehow this situation can and will be changed. Let us not wallow in the valley of despair.

I say to you today, my friends, so even though we face the difficulties of today and tomorrow, I still have a dream. It is a dream deeply rooted in the American dream. I have a dream that one day this nation will rise up and live out the true meaning of its creed, "We hold these truths to be self-evident, that all men are created equal." I have a dream that one day on the red hills of Georgia, sons of former slaves and the sons of former slave owners will be able to sit down together at the table of brotherhood. I have a dream that one day even the state of Mississippi, a state sweltering with the heat of injustice, sweltering with the heat of oppression, will be transformed into an oasis of freedom and justice. I have a dream that my four little children will one day live in a nation where they will not be judged by the color of their skin, but by the content of their character.

I have a dream today!

I have a dream that one day down in Alabama—with its vicious racists, with its Governor having his lips dripping with the

Crowd at Lincoln Memorial listening to King's "I Have a Dream" speech.

10. If something is *redemptive,* it brings rescue or freedom. Christians believe that Jesus Christ's suffering and death brought *redemption* from sin and punishment.

Vocabulary

wallow (wol′ ō) *v.* to become or remain helpless

words of interposition and nullification[11]—one day right there in Alabama, little black boys and black girls will be able to join hands with little white boys and white girls as sisters and brothers.

I have a dream today!

I have a dream that one day "every valley shall be exalted and every hill and mountain shall be made low. The rough places will be made plain and the crooked places will be made straight, and the glory of the Lord shall be revealed, and all flesh shall see it together."[12]

This is our hope. This is the faith that I go back to the South with. With this faith we shall be able to transform the jangling discords of our nation into a beautiful symphony of brotherhood. With this faith we will be able to work together, to pray together, to struggle together, to go to jail together, to stand up for freedom together, knowing that we will be free one day. And this will be the day. This will be the day when all of God's children will be able to sing with new meaning, "My country 'tis of thee, sweet land of liberty, of thee I sing. Land where my fathers died, land of the pilgrim's pride, from every mountain side, let freedom ring." And if America is to be a great nation, this must become true.

So let freedom ring from the prodigious hilltops of New Hampshire; let freedom ring from the mighty mountains of New York; let freedom ring from the heightening Alleghenies of Pennsylvania; let freedom ring from the snowcapped Rockies of Colorado; let freedom ring from the curvaceous slopes of California. But not only that. Let freedom ring from Stone Mountain of Georgia; let freedom ring from Lookout Mountain of Tennessee; let freedom ring from every hill and molehill of Mississippi. From every mountainside, let freedom ring.

And when this happens, and when we allow freedom to ring, when we let it ring from every village and every hamlet, from every state and every city; we will be able to speed up that day when all God's children, black men and white men, Jews and gentiles,[13] Protestants and Catholics, will be able to join hands and sing in the words of the old Negro spiritual: "Free at last. Free at last. Thank God Almighty, we are free at last."

11. George Wallace, Alabama's then-*Governor,* opposed all efforts to end official segregation in his state. *Interposition* and *nullification* are legal arguments that have to do with a state's right to reject and refuse to enforce federal laws.
12. This passage comes from the Old Testament's Book of Isaiah.

13. People who are not Jews are *gentiles.* (The original Latin root word means "clan.")

Vocabulary

exalt (ig zôlt′) *v.* to raise in status, dignity, power; glorify
discord (dis′ kôrd) *n.* disagreement; conflict
prodigious (prə dij′ əs) *adj.* enormous

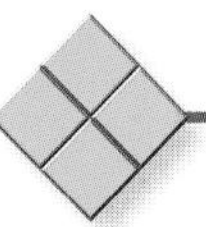

Responding to Literature

PERSONAL RESPONSE

How does Dr. King's dream compare with the hopes and dreams you wrote about in the **Focus Activity** on page 493?

In CONGRESS, July 4, 1776.
A DECLARATION
By the REPRESENTATIVES of the
UNITED STATES OF AMERICA,
In GENERAL CONGRESS assembled.

Analyzing Literature

RECALL

1. What document in the United States guarantees the rights of life, liberty, and the pursuit of happiness?
2. How does Dr. King respond to those who "hope that the Negro needed to blow off steam and will now be content"?
3. How does Dr. King feel about the use of violence against white people? Explain.
4. What does Dr. King want his children to be judged by?

INTERPRET

5. Why does Dr. King quote from the Declaration of Independence?
6. To whom is Dr. King talking when he says "this is no time to engage in the luxury of cooling off"? How do you know?
7. Why does Dr. King caution against distrusting all white people?
8. Is Dr. King's dream the American dream? Why or why not?

EVALUATE AND CONNECT

9. **Figurative language** (see page R3) often states a truth beyond the literal meaning. What do you understand by such phrases as "the sunlit path of racial justice" and "a beautiful symphony of brotherhood"?
10. Theme Connection What does *equality* mean? Is equality necessary for you to have a happy life? Is it the most important thing?

LITERARY ELEMENTS

Repetition

Repetition is the recurrence of sounds, words, phrases, or lines. Repetition in a speech may strengthen the message by reminding the audience over and over again of the theme. Repetition can also build a speech to a climax that raises emotions or moves the audience to action.

1. Find three examples of repetition in Dr. King's speech.
2. What effects do you think Dr. King aims for with the repetition of "let freedom ring"?
3. Think of a song you like that uses repetition. What phrase is repeated? What effect does it have?

- See **Literary Terms Handbook,** p. R8.

Literature and Writing

Writing About Literature

Summary of a Speech Imagine that you have been assigned to write a summary of Dr. King's speech for a special issue of your school newspaper celebrating Black History Month. Start by listing the main ideas from Dr. King's speech. Then write a summary in one or two paragraphs.

Personal Writing

Getting Along After Dr. King's Time How far do you think we have come in the struggle for racial equality? Write an addition to Dr. King's speech that might be read to people today. Your writing should address these questions: Are Dr. King's words true for people of all races? How big of a problem is racism today? Who are the victims of this racism? Can racism be fought without violence?

Extending Your Response

Literature Groups

Group Reactions Dr. King's speech is both emotional and patriotic. What overall effect does his speech have on you? Which points have the most impact on you? What, if anything, does the speech make you want to do? Share your responses with those in your group. Then make a large word web to record your group's responses.

interNET CONNECTION

With a partner, use the Internet to find out more about Dr. King's life, work, or family. To begin, type Dr. King's name into a search engine. Gather images, articles, and other information for a brief presentation to the class.

Interdisciplinary Activity

Music Many protesters in the Civil Rights movement sang songs about their determination to become free. These freedom songs were based on spirituals, hymns, rhythm and blues, and even football chants. Research freedom songs such as "We Shall Overcome" to create a booklet of song lyrics. Or, gather recordings of the songs and create a collection of music.

Reading Further

If you would like to read more about civil rights, try:
They Had a Dream by Jules Archer

Save your work for your portfolio.

Skill Minilessons

GRAMMAR AND LANGUAGE • PUNCTUATING QUOTATIONS

Direct quotes, or the exact words of a speaker, are enclosed in quotation marks. For example, Martin Luther King said, "So we've come here today to dramatize a shameful condition." Note that the quote is preceded by a comma. If the quote were divided, both parts would be set off with commas and enclosed in quotation marks: "So we've come here today," Dr. King said, "to dramatize a shameful condition." The period and first comma are inside the closing quotation marks.

PRACTICE Rewrite each sentence using the proper punctuation for each quote.

1. Dr. King said Now is the time to make real the promises of democracy.
2. In the process of gaining our rightful place, he warned we must not be guilty of wrongful deeds.
3. I have a dream today! he said.
4. This is our hope said Dr. King. This is the faith that I go back to the South with.

● For more about punctuating quotations, see **Language Handbook,** p. R41.

READING AND THINKING • ANALYZING ARGUMENTS

Persuasive writing argues for a certain point of view, aiming to make someone feel a certain way or do something. Persuasive arguments often slant the facts and appeal to readers' emotions. Advertising, editorials, and political speeches, like Dr. King's, are all forms of persuasive writing.

PRACTICE Analyze the argument in Dr. King's speech, asking yourself these questions: Is Dr. King's position clear? Does he present enough evidence? Can the facts he cites be proven? Which statements are opinions rather than facts? What emotions does he appeal to?

● For more about analyzing reasonings, see **Reading Handbook,** p. R97.

VOCABULARY • ANTONYMS

One technique that Dr. Martin Luther King Jr. used to communicate strongly and clearly was the presentation of contrasts. Dr. King used antonyms to contrast two situations, ideas, or things. He pointed out that "Nineteen sixty-three is not an *end,* but a *beginning.*" He dreamed that we would "transform the jangling *discords* of our nation into a beautiful *symphony* of brotherhood."

PRACTICE Fill in the blank with an antonym for the underlined word.

1. Everyone has the right to be treated with ____, but many people face <u>discrimination</u> instead.
2. When you face a difficult situation, do your best qualities <u>emerge</u>, or do they ____?
3. Do you say, "What can I, only one ____ person, do against the <u>prodigious</u> forces against me?"
4. The failure to try can never <u>exalt</u> us; instead it will only ____ us.

LISTENING, SPEAKING, and VIEWING

Reaching Your Audience

A good speaker captures the attention of the audience. The speaker takes a stand on an issue, aiming to make listeners respond intellectually, emotionally, or through action. To get this response, the speaker must give details, examples, and reasons that will persuade listeners. In addition, a successful speaker will hold the attention of listeners, encourage their interest, and convince them with strong evidence.

Many people have read the moving "I Have a Dream" speech delivered by Dr. Martin Luther King Jr. His use of words, strong feelings, and examples of injustice have impressed readers of the speech. However, only those who have heard Dr. King deliver his speech will understand his message fully. Martin Luther King was a powerful, persuasive speaker.

Guidelines for Public Speaking

Here are some techniques that powerful speakers use. Think about how you can incorporate them into your own speaking style when you give a speech.

- To engage your listeners from the outset, meet their eyes. Eye contact is an unbeatable way to reach people.
- Aim your voice at the last row of your audience. Look often to be sure people in that row are paying attention.
- After each important point, pause. A brief pause calls attention to your words, giving them a chance to sink in. Remember that your words must encourage your audience to feel, think, or act in a certain way.
- Shift position from time to time, as you normally would. If you stand stiffly, your voice can stiffen too.

ACTIVITY

1. Plan to deliver a speech that is about four or five minutes long. You may choose a speech that you have written or one that you have read–a passage from "I Have a Dream" or "The Gettysburg Address," for example.
2. With a partner, take turns practicing your speech. Follow the guidelines above, and give each other feedback and suggestions for improvement.
3. Deliver your speech to a small group or to the class.

Before You Read

Sorrow Home and *Sit-ins*

MEET MARGARET WALKER

"I have lived most of my life in the segregated South," said Margaret Walker, who grew up in New Orleans and became a legend in African American literature. "My adjustment . . . to this South—whether real or imagined, violent or non-violent—is the subject and source of all my poetry." Walker experienced the Civil Rights movement firsthand and knew most of the movement's leaders. She also served as head of the Black Studies Program at Jackson State College in Jackson, Mississippi.

Margaret Walker was born in 1915 in Alabama and died in 1998. "Sorrow Home" and "Sit-ins" are from her collection of poetry This Is My Century, *published in 1989.*

FOCUS ACTIVITY

Where would you like to live when you are an adult? For example, would you prefer a city, a rural area, or a small town?

List It!

Make a list of influences that may help determine where you live throughout your life.

Setting a Purpose

Read the poems to understand the speaker's love of a particular place.

BACKGROUND

The Time and Place In "Sorrow Home," the speaker reflects on the South she knew as a child. "Sit-ins" is also set in the South, but later, in the 1960s.

Did You Know? Until the 1960s, a policy of segregation separated African Americans from other people in schools, restaurants, and other public places. On February 1, 1960, four African American college freshmen sat down at a Woolworth's lunch counter in Greensboro, North Carolina, and ordered coffee. The waitress refused to serve them. They stayed. Word spread, and daily sit-ins followed at stores in fifteen cities. Protesters were arrested by the carloads, but others took their places. Today, prejudice may still exist in some places, but segregation is against the law.

Two protestors carry a banner during a Civil Rights march.

Sorrow Home

Margaret Walker

My roots are deep in southern life; deeper than John Brown°
or Nat Turner° or Robert Lee.° I was sired and weaned°
in a tropic world. The palm tree and banana leaf,
mango and coconut, breadfruit and rubber trees know
me.

Warm skies and gulf blue streams are in my blood. I belong
with the smell of fresh pine, with the trail of coon, and
the spring growth of wild onion.

I am no hothouse bulb° to be reared in steam-heated flats
with the music of El and subway in my ears, walled in
by steel and wood and brick far from the sky.

I want the cotton fields, tobacco and the cane. I want to
walk along with sacks of seed to drop in fallow° ground.
Restless music is in my heart and I am eager to be
gone.

O Southland, sorrow home, melody beating in my bone and
blood! How long will the Klan° of hate, the hounds and
the chain gangs° keep me from my own?

1–2 *John Brown* raided a federal weapons storehouse. *Nat Turner* led an unsuccessful slave rebellion. General *Robert E. Lee* led the Confederate forces during the Civil War. *Sired and weaned* means "born and raised."

9 A *hothouse bulb* is a plant grown in a greenhouse.

13 *Fallow* ground is left unseeded for one season to improve it agriculturally.

17 The Ku Klux *Klan* opposes the influence of certain minority groups.

18 A *chain gang* is a group of convicts, chained together and forced to do hard labor.

Sit-ins

Margaret Walker

Greensboro, North Carolina, in the Spring of 1960

You were our first brave ones to defy their dissonance° of hate
With your silence
With your willingness to suffer
Without violence
Those first bright young to fling your names across pages
Of new southern history
With courage and faith, convictions, and intelligence
The first to blaze a flaming path for justice
And awaken consciences
Of these stony ones.

Come, Lord Jesus, Bold Young Galilean°
Sit Beside this Counter,° Lord, with Me!

---

1 *Dissonance* can mean both "harsh, unpleasant sounds" and "sharp disagreement."
11 *Jesus* grew up in Galilee, a region of what is now Israel.
12 This sit-in took place at a lunch *counter.*

A sit-in at Woolworth's lunch counter in Greensboro, North Carolina.

Responding to Literature

PERSONAL RESPONSE

How did reading each poem make you feel? Jot down your reactions.

Analyzing Literature

RECALL

1. In the final stanza of "Sorrow Home," to whom is the narrator speaking?
2. In "Sit-ins," Margaret Walker addresses a person or persons using the words "you" and "your." Whom is she addressing?

INTERPRET

3. How does the narrator use contrast to describe the South in "Sorrow Home"?
4. In "Sit-ins," how might the people that Walker is speaking to "awaken consciences"?

EVALUATE AND CONNECT

5. In your opinion, does the narrator of "Sorrow Home" have enough reasons to feel such deep sorrow? Explain.
6. Do you agree with the speaker that the young participants at the sit-in show "courage and faith, convictions, and intelligence"? Support your answer.
7. What do the sensory images in "Sorrow Home" add to the poem? Explain.
8. Theme Connection Why do you think these two poems are in the theme "Free to Be"? In your opinion, are they good choices for this theme? Explain.
9. "Sit-ins" celebrates nonviolent resistance. Do you agree that the students should be honored? If you had been at the lunch counter with the men, how might you have behaved?
10. Which of the two poems do you find more appealing? Why?

LITERARY ELEMENTS

Assonance, Consonance, and Alliteration

Writers use several techniques to create interesting sound patterns in poetry. **Assonance** is the repetition of vowel sounds in stressed syllables: ***Awe*** *was the* ***auto****matic response of us* ***all.*** (It is the sound, not the spelling, that creates assonance.) **Consonance** is the repetition of a single consonant sound: *Dee****p*** *o****p****en s****p****aces s****p****read far.* If the repeated consonant sound comes at the beginning of each word, the element is called **alliteration:** *The* ***t****errible,* ***t****reeless* ***t****undra faced us.*

1. Find one example of consonance and one of alliteration in "Sorrow Home."
2. Where in "Sorrow Home" does the poet use assonance?

• See **Literary Terms Handbook,** pp. R1 and R2.

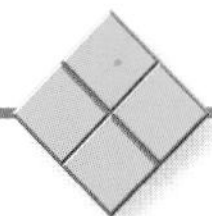

Extending Your Response

Writing About Literature

Sensory Images A poet uses images as if they cost money—every image must be useful and support the message or theme of the poem. For example, Margaret Walker says that the men at the sit-ins are the first ones to "blaze a flaming path." Readers can see the light of the blaze and feel its heat. Find another image in either of Walker's poems that you think is very effective. Explain in a paragraph why you selected that image.

Personal Writing

Remembering The poet William Wordsworth said poetry is "emotion recollected in tranquillity." Readers can sense the emotions of the speaker who recalls past sights and events in "Sorrow Home." What place or event in your past matters that much to you? In your journal, jot down words that describe the object or event. Next to the words, write the emotions that you felt at the time. If you prefer, refer to your notes from the **Focus Activity** on page 503 and describe your feelings about the place where you want to live as an adult.

Literature Groups

Scenes from a Poem Imagine that you are planning a book that will contain these two poems. How will you illustrate each poem? What images communicate the main message of each poem? Support the images you suggest by referring to specific lines from the poems. When you agree on two or three possible images for each poem, share your ideas with the class.

Listening and Speaking

Poetry Reading Find a poem you like that fits the theme "Free to Be." Take turns reading or reciting poems aloud. Pay attention to others as they read, and offer feedback. When it is your turn, read your poem slowly, clearly, and with emotion.

Reading Further

For a view of home fought for in another land, read:
O Jerusalem! by Jane Yolen

Save your work for your portfolio.

Skill Minilesson

READING AND THINKING • QUESTIONING

The words a writer chooses can tell you something about his or her attitude about a subject. To understand and respond to a selection, you must ask yourself questions about the words used and the attitudes they may reveal.

- For more about related comprehension strategies, see **Reading Handbook,** pp. R84–R96.

PRACTICE For each group of words, identify one of the following attitudes that the words may reveal.

approval, fear, suspicion, celebration, pride

1. triumph, joy, remembering
2. kindness, honor, courage
3. masked, vague, watchful
4. power, hate, bias
5. achievement, work, triumph

HISTORICAL FICTION

Some types of fiction are so realistic that it's hard to believe they aren't true. In **historical fiction,** a story is set in the past—often in a real place—and the action revolves around an actual event or historical period. However, the characters may exist only in the author's mind. Here are some special features of historical fiction.

Civil War drummer boy.

ACCURATE SETTING Each item or action described in historical fiction must belong in the life of the period–every chair, shoe, meal, game, or tool. Although the writer may invent some characters, their lives must be like those of the people of the time.

ATTITUDES OF CHARACTERS The attitudes and beliefs of people change over time. Characters in a story set many years ago probably will have some attitudes and beliefs different from ours.

MODEL

Having little boys serve as drummers was common during the Civil War. So, in "The Drummer Boy of Shiloh," the general is not surprised to see a boy in the camp. His approving attitude, so wrong today, was judged to be right in 1862.

THE ERA AND THE PLOT In historical fiction, the problems that characters face, and their reactions to the problems, are affected by the attitudes and events of their time. If the events of a story could happen any time, the story is simply fiction.

MODEL

The drummer boy's fear of battle is a problem of any era. However, the Civil War marked the last time that young American boys served in a war. The general, sad but determined, is most likely patterned after Ulysses Grant, the Union commander at Shiloh. The events of the story could occur only during the Civil War.

ACTIVE READING MODEL

Active Reading Strategies

Tips for Reading Historical Fiction

In historical fiction, you can't count on characters to live, think, or act as people do today. To understand the story, you must build bridges between the present and the past. Here are some strategies that will help.

• For more about reading strategies, see **Reading Handbook,** pp. R84–R96.

QUESTION

As you read, compare and contrast the lives of the characters with your own life. Ask yourself how the times affected the events about which you are reading.

INFER

The writer may not always explain conditions fully. Instead, small clues can lead readers to facts that are important in the story.

VISUALIZE

In historical fiction, trying to imagine the homes, the towns, even the clothing of the period can give you a feeling of being part of the story.

RESPOND

What do you think is the writer's purpose in creating this story? What is your response to that purpose?

APPLYING THE STRATEGIES

The next selection is an example of historical fiction. As you read "The Battleground," use the strategies in the margins to help you enjoy the short story.

ACTIVE READING MODEL

Before You Read

The Battleground

MEET ELSIE SINGMASTER

Elsie Singmaster was born in Gettysburg, Pennsylvania, grew up not far from there, and moved back after her young husband died. Singmaster spent the rest of her life writing historical fiction, short stories, and novels for children and young adults. The setting for most of her writing was the region around Gettysburg. The local color of the town inspired her early writing. In Gettysburg, Singmaster was surrounded by reminders of the Civil War, which also influenced her work.

Elsie Singmaster was born in 1879 and died in 1958. "The Battleground" was published in 1930 in her book Gettysburg.

FOCUS ACTIVITY

How do you think the Civil War may have affected civilians?

Brainstorm

In a small group, brainstorm details of how the Civil War was fought. Share your information with the class.

Setting a Purpose

Read to discover how one young mother responds to events in the Civil War.

BACKGROUND

The Time and Place This selection is set in Gettysburg, Pennsylvania, on the day Lincoln delivered the Gettysburg Address.

Did You Know? The Battle of Gettysburg was the turning point in the Civil War. The Union forces led by General George Meade defeated General Robert E. Lee's Confederate army in July of 1863. More than 6,000 soldiers died in battle; another 40,000 were wounded or missing.

General George Meade

VOCABULARY PREVIEW

covet (kuv′ it) *v.* to desire strongly; wish for longingly; p. 513

diligence (dil′ ə jəns) *n.* great attention, care, and effort; p. 513

repress (ri pres′) *v.* to hold back or keep under control; restrain; p. 514

lunacy (lo͞o′ nə sē) *n.* insanity; senseless conduct; folly; p. 514

doggedly (dô′ gid lē) *adv.* stubbornly; firmly; p. 514

wan (won) *adj.* pale or weak, indicating illness or weariness; p. 515

interminable (in tur′ mi nə bəl) *adj.* lasting, or seeming to last, forever; endless; p. 518

righteousness (rī′ chəs nəs) *n.* the condition of being right, moral, just, or legal; p. 519

wretchedness (rech′ id nəs) *n.* great unhappiness or deep distress; p. 521

The Battleground

Elsie Singmaster

The Leister farmhouse in Gettysburg, PA, on July 6, 1863, three days after the Battle of Gettysburg ended. Photograph by Alexander Gardner.

Mercifully, Mary Bowman, a widow, whose husband had been missing since the battle of Gettysburg,[1] had been warned, together with other citizens of Gettysburg, that on Thursday the nineteenth of November, 1863, she would be awakened from sleep by a bugler's reveillé,[2] and that during that great day she would hear again the dread sound of cannon.

Nevertheless, hearing again the reveillé, she sat up in bed with a scream and put her hands over her ears. Then, gasping, groping about in her confusion and terror, she rose and began to dress. She put on a dress which had been once a bright plaid, but which now, having lost both its color and the stiff, outstanding quality of the skirts of '63, hung about her in straight and dingy folds. It was clean, but it had upon it certain ineradicable[3] brown stains on which soap and water seemed to have no effect. She was thin and pale, and her eyes had a set look, as though they saw other sights than those directly about her.

ACTIVE READING MODEL

QUESTION

What happened at Gettysburg in the summer of 1863?

RESPOND

What state of mind would you be in if you had lived through the battle?

1. The *Battle of Gettysburg* was fought from July 1 through July 3, 1863.
2. *Reveillé* (rev′ ə lē) is the signal used each morning to call soldiers to roll-call formation.
3. Stains that are *ineradicable* (in′ i rad′ i kə bəl) cannot be removed completely.

The Battleground

ACTIVE READING MODEL

In the bed from which she had risen lay her little daughter; in a trundle bed nearby, her two sons, one about ten years old, the other about four. They slept heavily, lying deep in their beds, as though they would never move. Their mother looked at them with her strange, absent gaze; then she barred a little more closely the broken shutters, and went down the stairs. The shutters were broken in a curious fashion. Here and there they were pierced by round holes, and one hung from a single hinge. The window frames were without glass, the floor was without carpet, the bed without pillows.

In her kitchen Mary Bowman looked about her as though still seeing other sights. Here, too, the floor was carpetless. Above the stove a patch of fresh plaster on the wall showed where a great rent had been filled in; in the doors were the same little round holes as in the shutters of the room above. But there was food and fuel, which was more than one might have expected from the aspect[4] of the house and its mistress. She opened the shattered door of the cupboard, and, having made the fire, began to prepare breakfast.

QUESTION

How does the description of Mary's house help you understand her situation?

Outside the house there was already, at six o'clock, noise and confusion. Last evening a train from Washington had brought to the village Abraham Lincoln; for several days other trains had been bringing less

4. Here, the *rent* is a hole. An *aspect* is how a person or thing looks.

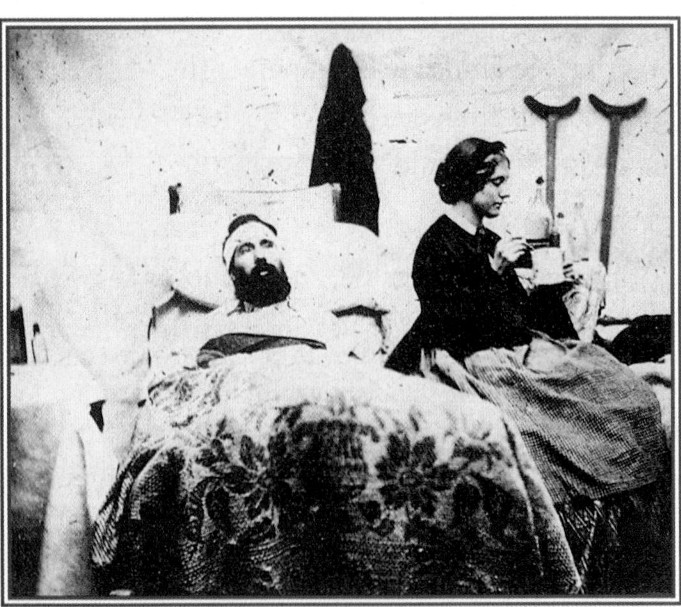

A nurse tends to a wounded soldier at a federal hospital in Nashville, TN, during the Civil War.

Viewing the photograph: In what ways might this woman's experiences as a nurse be similar to Mary Bowman's?

distinguished guests, until thousands thronged[5] the little town. This morning the tract of land between Mary Bowman's house and the village cemetery was to be dedicated for the burial of the Union dead, who were to be laid there in sweeping semicircles round a center on which a great monument was to rise.

ACTIVE READING MODEL

But of the dedication, of the President of the United States, of his distinguished associates, of the great crowds, of the soldiers, of the crape-banded banners, Mary Bowman and her children would see nothing. Mary Bowman would sit in her little wrecked kitchen with her children. For to her the President of the United States and others in high places who prosecuted war or who tolerated war, who called for young men to fight, were hateful. To Mary Bowman the crowds of curious persons who coveted a sight of the great battlefields were ghouls; their eyes wished to gloat upon ruin, upon fragments of the weapons of war, upon torn bits of the habiliments[6] of soldiers; their feet longed to sink into the loose ground of hastily made graves; the discovery of a partially covered body was precious to them.

REVIEW

Think about Mary's reasons for not wanting to take her children to hear President Lincoln speak.

Mary Bowman knew that field! From Culp's Hill to the McPherson farm, from Big Round Top to the poorhouse, she had traveled it, searching, searching, with frantic, insane disregard of positions or of possibility. Her husband could not have fallen here among the Eleventh Corps, he could not lie here among the unburied dead of the Louisiana Tigers! If he was in the battle at all, it was at the Angle that he fell.

She had not been able to begin her search immediately after the battle because there were forty wounded men in her little house; she could not prosecute it with diligence even later, when the soldiers had been carried to the hospitals, in the Presbyterian Church, the Catholic Church, the two Lutheran churches, the Seminary, the College, the Courthouse, and the great tented hospital on the York road. Nurses were here, Sisters of Mercy[7] were here, compassionate women were here by the score; but still she was needed, with all the other women of the village, to nurse, to bandage, to comfort, to pray with those who must die. Little Mary Bowman had assisted at the amputation of limbs, she had helped to control strong

5. To *throng* is to gather in large numbers; a *throng* is a large crowd.
6. *Crape,* also spelled *crepe* (krāp), is a light, crinkled cloth; black crepe is a traditional symbol of mourning. Those who *prosecuted* war actively supported it, while those who *tolerated* war accepted or put up with it. *Ghouls* are people who enjoy things that disgust and upset most people. *Habiliments* are garments.
7. A *seminary* is a school that trains ministers or priests. The *Sisters of Mercy* are Catholic nuns.

Vocabulary

covet (kuv′ it) *v.* to desire strongly; wish for longingly

diligence (dil′ ə jəns) *n.* great attention, care, and effort

ACTIVE READING MODEL

RESPOND

Do you think that seeing movies or news reports about war would prepare you to experience a real battle?

QUESTION

Why is Hannah comparing herself to Barbara Frietchie and Molly Pitcher?

EVALUATE

What do you make of the narrator's comment on people of "this generation"?

men torn by the frenzy of delirium,[8] she had tended poor bodies which had almost lost all semblance to humanity. Neither she nor any of the other women of the villages counted themselves especially heroic; the delicate wife of the judge, the petted daughter of the doctor, the gently bred wife of the preacher forgot that fainting at the sight of blood was one of the distinguishing qualities of their sex; they turned back their sleeves and repressed their tears, and shoulder to shoulder with Mary Bowman and her Irish neighbor, Hannah Casey, they fed the hungry and healed the sick and clothed the naked. If Mary Bowman had been herself, she might have laughed at the sight of her dresses cobbled into trousers, her skirts wrapped round the shoulders of sick men. But neither then nor ever after did Mary laugh at any incident of that summer.

Hannah Casey laughed, and by and by she began to boast. Meade, Hancock, Slocum, were noncombatants beside her. She had fought whole companies of Confederates, she had wielded bayonets, she had assisted at the spiking of a gun, she was Barbara Frietchie and Molly Pitcher[9] combined. But all her lunacy could not make Mary Bowman smile.

Of John Bowman no trace could be found. No one could tell her anything about him, to her frantic letters no one responded. Her old friend, the village judge, wrote letters also, but could get no reply. Her husband was missing; it was probable that he lay somewhere upon this field, the field upon which they had wandered as lovers.

In midsummer a few trenches were opened, and Mary, unknown to her friends, saw them opened. At the uncovering of the first great pit, she actually helped with her own hands. For those of this generation who know nothing of war, that fact may be written down, to be passed over lightly. The soldiers, having been on other battlefields, accepted her presence without comment. She did not cry, she only helped doggedly, and looked at what they found. That, too, may be written down for a generation which has not known war.

Immediately, an order went forth that no graves, large or small, were to be opened before cold weather. The citizens were panic-stricken with fear

8. Men in a *frenzy of delirium* would be greatly disturbed and upset.
9. *Meade, Hancock,* and *Slocum* commanded Union troops at Gettysburg. *Noncombatants* are people who do not fight. The gun mentioned here would have been a Confederate cannon; *spiking* was a way of disabling a cannon. If you aren't familiar with *Barbara Frietchie,* see page 459. During the Revolutionary War, *Molly Pitcher* fired her wounded husband's cannon until the end of a battle.

Vocabulary

repress (ri pres′) *v.* to hold back or keep under control; restrain
lunacy (lo͞o′ nə sē) *n.* insanity; senseless conduct; folly
doggedly (dô′ gid lē) *adv.* stubbornly; firmly

A crowd of people in Gettysburg watch President Abraham Lincoln on his way to dedicate the National Cemetery, where he gave the Gettysburg Address on November 19, 1863.

of an epidemic; already there were many cases of dysentery and typhoid. Now that the necessity for daily work for the wounded was past, the village became nervous, excited, irritable. Several men and boys were killed while trying to open unexploded shells; their deaths added to the general horror. There were constant visitors who sought husbands, brothers, sweethearts; with these the Gettysburg women were still able to weep, for them they were still able to care; but the constant demand for entertainment for the curious annoyed those who wished to be left alone to recover from the shock of battle. Gettysburg was prostrate, bereft[10] of many of its worldly possessions, drained to the bottom of its well of sympathy. Its schools must be opened, its poor must be helped. Cold weather was coming and there were many, like Mary Bowman, who owned no longer any quilts or blankets, who had given away their clothes, their linen, even the precious sheets which their grandmothers had spun. Gettysburg grudged nothing, wished nothing back, it asked only to be left in peace.

CONNECT

Consider how the people of Gettysburg changed after the battle.

When the order was given to postpone the opening of graves till fall, Mary began to go about the battlefield searching alone. Her good, obedient children stayed at home in the house or in the little field. They were beginning to grow thin and wan, they were shivering in the hot August weather, but their mother did not see. She gave them a great deal more to eat than she had herself, and they had far better clothes than her bloodstained motley.[11]

10. Here, *prostrate* means "made weak and helpless," and *bereft* means "robbed of."
11. Mary's mismatched clothing is her *motley*.

Vocabulary

wan (won) *adj.* pale or weak, indicating illness or weariness

The Battleground

An unidentified woman from the 1860s.

RESPOND

How might you have felt after wandering the battlefields? Would you cry, or would you respond the way that Mary did?

She went about the battlefield with her eyes on the ground, her feet treading gently, anticipating loose soil or some sudden obstacle. Sometimes she stooped suddenly. To fragments of shells, to bits of blue or gray cloth, to cartridge belts or broken muskets, she paid no heed; at sight of pitiful bits of human bodies she shuddered. But there lay also upon that field little pocket Testaments, letters, trinkets, photographs. John had had her photograph and the children's, and surely he must have had some of the letters she had written!

But poor Mary found nothing.

One morning, late in August, she sat beside her kitchen table with her head on her arm. The first of the scarlet gum leaves had begun to drift down from the shattered trees; it would not be long before the ground would be covered, and those depressed[12] spots, those tiny wooden headstones, those fragments of blue and gray be hidden. The thought smothered her. She did not cry, she had not cried at all. Her soul seemed hardened, stiff, like the terrible wounds for which she had helped to care.

Suddenly, hearing a sound, Mary had looked up. The judge stood in the doorway; he had known all about her since she was a little girl; something in his face told her that he knew also of her terrible search. She could not ask him to sit down, she said nothing at all. She had been a loquacious[13] person, she had become an abnormally silent one. Speech hurt her.

The judge looked round the little kitchen. The rent in the wall was still unmended, the chairs were broken; there was nothing else to be seen but the table and the rusty stove and the thin, friendless-looking children standing by the door. It was the house not only of poverty and woe, but of neglect.

"Mary," said the judge, "how do you mean to live?"

Mary's thin, sunburned hand stirred a little as it lay on the table.

"I do not know."

CONNECT

Who in your life might play a role similar to the one played by the judge in Mary's life?

"You have these children to feed and clothe and you must furnish your house again. Mary—" The judge hesitated for a moment. John Bowman had been a schoolteacher, a thrifty, ambitious soul, who would have thought it a disgrace for his wife to earn her living. The judge laid his hand on the thin hand beside him. "Your children must have food, Mary. Come down to my house, and my wife will give you work. Come now."

---

12. The *depressed* spots are the tops of graves that have sunk slightly.
13. A *loquacious* person is a talkative one.

ACTIVE READING MODEL

Slowly Mary had risen from her chair, and smoothed down her dress and obeyed him. Down the street they went together, seeing fences still prone, seeing walls torn by shells, past the houses where the shock of battle had hastened the deaths of old persons and little children, and had disappointed the hearts of those who longed for a child, to the judge's house in the square. There wagons stood about, loaded with wheels of cannon, fragments of burst caissons, or with long, narrow pine boxes, brought from the railroad, to be stored against the day of exhumation.[14] Men were laughing and shouting to one another, the driver of the wagon on which the long boxes were piled cracked his whip as he urged his horses.

Hannah Casey congratulated her neighbor heartily upon her finding work.

"That'll fix you up," she assured her.

She visited Mary constantly, she reported to her the news of the war, she talked at length of the coming of the President.

"I'm going to see him," she announced. "I'm going to shake him by the hand. I'm going to say, 'Hello, Abe, you old rail splitter, God bless you!' Then the bands'll play, and the people will march, and the Johnny Rebs[15] will hear 'em in their graves."

Mary Bowman put her hands over her ears.

"I believe in my soul you'd let 'em all rise from the dead!"

"I would!" said Mary Bowman hoarsely. "I would!"

"Well, not so Hannah Casey! Look at me garden tore to bits! Look at me beds, stripped to the ropes!"

And Hannah Casey departed to her house.

CONNECT

Read Mary and Hannah's dialogue. Whose reactions are more similar to what your own might be?

Details of the coming celebration penetrated to the ears of Mary Bowman whether she wished it or not, and the gathering crowds made themselves known. They stood upon her porch, they examined the broken shutters, they wished to question her. But Mary Bowman would answer no questions, would not let herself be seen. To her the thing was horrible. She saw the battling hosts,[16] she heard once more the roar of artillery, she smelled the smoke of battle, she was torn by its confusion. Besides, she seemed to feel in the ground beneath her a feebly stirring, suffering, ghastly host. They had begun again to open the trenches, and she looked into them.

14. *Caissons* were two-wheeled wagons for hauling ammunition. *Exhumation* (eks′ hū mā′ shən) is the digging up of a corpse. After the battle, the dead were buried quickly to prevent the spread of disease. Later, the bodies would be reburied in coffins in the newly dedicated cemetery.

15. *Johnny Rebs* were Confederate soldiers.

16. Here, *hosts* means "armies."

The Battleground

Now, on the morning of Thursday, the nineteenth of November, her children dressed themselves and came down the steps. They had begun to have a little plumpness and color, but the dreadful light in their mother's eyes was still reflected in theirs. On the lower step they hesitated, looking at the door. Outside stood the judge, who had found time in the multiplicity of his cares, to come to the little house.

He spoke with kind but firm command.

"Mary," said he, "you must take these children to hear President Lincoln."

"What!" cried Mary.

"You must take these children to the exercises."

"I cannot!" cried Mary. "I cannot! I cannot!"

"You must!" The judge came into the room. "Let me hear no more of this going about. You are a Christian, your husband was a Christian. Do you want your children to think it is a wicked thing to die for their country? Do as I tell you, Mary."

QUESTION

Why does Mary respond so strongly to the judge's suggestion?

Mary got up from her chair, and put on her children all the clothes they had, and wrapped about her own shoulders a little black coat which the judge's wife had given her. Then, as one who steps into an unfriendly sea, she started out with them into the great crowd. Once more, poor Mary said to herself, she would obey. She had seen the platform; by going round through the citizen's cemetery she could get close to it.

The November day was bright and warm, but Mary and her children shivered. Slowly she made her way close to the platform, patiently she stood and waited. Sometimes she stood with shut eyes, swaying a little. On the moonlit night of the third day of battle she had ventured from her house down toward the square to try to find some brandy for the dying men about her, and as in a dream she had seen a tall general, mounted upon a white horse with muffled hoofs, ride down the street. Bending from his saddle he had spoken, apparently to the empty air.

"Up, boys, up!"

There had risen at his command thousands of men lying asleep on pavement and street, and quietly, in an interminable line, they had stolen out like dead men toward the Seminary, to join their comrades and begin the long, long march to Hagerstown.[17] It seemed to her that

17. At the battle's end, Confederate General Robert E. Lee had led his defeated troops back to Virginia by way of *Hagerstown,* Maryland, about thirty miles southeast of Gettysburg.

Vocabulary

interminable (in tur′ mi nə bəl) *adj.* lasting, or seeming to last, forever; endless

ACTIVE READING MODEL

all about her dead men might rise now to look with reproach upon these strangers who disturbed their rest.

The procession was late, the orator of the day was delayed, but still Mary waited, swaying a little in her place. Presently the great guns roared forth a welcome, the bands played, the procession approached. On horseback, erect, gauntleted,[18] the President of the United States drew rein beside the platform, and, with the orator and the other famous men, dismounted. There were great cheers, there were deep silences, there were fresh volleys of artillery, there was new music.

Of it all, Mary Bowman heard but little. Remembering the judge, whom she saw now near the President, she tried to obey the spirit as well as the letter of his command; she directed her children to look, she turned their heads toward the platform.

Men spoke and prayed and sang, and Mary stood still in her place. The orator of the day described the battle, he eulogized[19] the dead, he proved the righteousness of this great war; his words fell upon Mary's ears unheard. If she had been asked who he was, she might have said vaguely that he was Mr. Lincoln. When he ended, she was ready to go home. There was singing; now she could slip away, through the gaps in the cemetery fence. She had done as the judge commanded and now she would go back to her house.

With her arms about her children, she started away. Then someone who stood near by took her by the hand.

"Madam," said he, "the President is going to speak!"

Half turning, Mary looked back. The thunder of applause made her shiver, made her even scream, it was so like that other thunderous sound which she would hear forever. She leaned upon her little children heavily, trying to get her breath, gasping, trying to keep her consciousness. She fixed her eyes upon the rising figure before her, she clung to the sight of him as a drowning swimmer in deep waters, she struggled to fix her thoughts upon him. Exhaustion, grief, misery threatened to engulf her, she hung upon him in desperation.

Slowly, as one who is old or tired or sick at heart, he rose to his feet, the President of the United States, the Commander in Chief of the Army and Navy, the hope of his country. Then he stood waiting. In great waves of sound the applause rose and died and rose again. He

CONNECT

Think of a time you did something because another person thought it would be good for you to do.

18. An *orator* is a speaker. When President Lincoln arrives, he is sitting upright *(erect)* and wearing long, formal gloves *(gauntlets)*.
19. To *eulogize* (ū′ lə jīz′) the dead is to make a speech praising and honoring them.

Vocabulary
righteousness (rī′ chəs nəs) *n.* the condition of being right, moral, just, or legal

The Gettysburg Address, 1987. Mort Künstler. Oil on canvas, 30 x 30 in. Private collection.

Viewing the painting: How does this painting of Lincoln compare with the narrator's description of him as he rises to give the address?

waited quietly. The winner of debate, the great champion of a great cause, the veteran in argument, the master of men, he looked down upon the throng. The clear, simple things he had to say were ready in his mind, he had thought them out, written out a first draft of them in Washington, copied it here in Gettysburg. It is probable that now, as he waited to speak, his mind traveled to other things, to the misery, the wretchedness, the slaughter of this field, to the tears of mothers, the grief of widows, the orphaning of little children.

Slowly, in his clear voice, he said what little he had to say. To the weary crowd, settling itself into position once more, the speech seemed short; to the cultivated[20] who had been listening to the elaborate periods of great oratory, it seemed commonplace, it seemed a speech which anyone might have made. But it was not so with Mary Bowman, nor with many other unlearned persons. Mary Bowman's soul seemed to smooth itself out like a scroll, her hands lightened their clutch on her children, the beating of her heart slackened, she gasped no more.

She could not have told exactly what he said, though later she read it and learned it and taught it to her children and her children's children. She only saw him, felt him, breathed him in, this great, common, kindly man. His gaze seemed to rest upon her; it was not impossible, it was even probable, that during the hours that passed he had singled out that little group so near him, that desolate woman in her motley dress, with her children clinging about her. He said that the world would not forget this field, these martyrs;[21] he said it in words which Mary Bowman could understand, he pointed to a future for which there was a new task.

"Daughter!" he seemed to say to her from the depths of trouble, of responsibility, of care greater than her own. "Daughter, be of good comfort!"

Unhindered[22] now, amid the cheers, across ground which seemed no longer to stir beneath her feet, Mary Bowman went back to her house. There, opening the shutters, she bent and solemnly kissed her little children, saying to herself that henceforth they must have more than food and raiment;[23] they must be given some joy in life.

ACTIVE READING MODEL

QUESTION

How does Lincoln's speech compare with that of the person who spoke before him?

CONNECT

Have you ever felt a speaker who was addressing a large group was actually speaking directly to you? Why did you feel that way?

20. Here, the *cultivated* are those who are (or think they are) better educated and more refined than most other people.
21. Those who suffer or die for a cause are *martyrs* (mär′ tərz).
22. To *hinder* is to hold back; so, *unhindered* means "not held back."
23. *Raiment* (rā′ mənt) means "clothing."

Vocabulary

wretchedness (rech′ id nəs) *n.* great unhappiness or deep distress

ACTIVE READING MODEL

Responding to Literature

PERSONAL RESPONSE

What emotions about war do you share with Mary Bowman?

Active Reading Response

Review the strategy for questioning described on page 509. Identify two or three places in the story where questioning helped you to understand a character, place, or event.

Analyzing Literature

RECALL

1. In your own words, describe Mary Bowman and her house as both are described in the first four paragraphs of the story.
2. How long after the Battle of Gettysburg does the story begin? What search has Mary undertaken in that time?
3. How does Mary feel about Lincoln's upcoming visit and the dedication ceremonies?
4. How does Mary Bowman respond to the president's speech?

INTERPRET

5. Why is Mary unable to refurbish her household and care for her children as others in Gettysburg have done?
6. What events or actions, in your opinion, contribute to the slow change in Mary Bowman?
7. Given Mary's determination to avoid the ceremony, why does she take her children to hear Lincoln's speech? Explain.
8. Why, do you think, does Mary memorize Lincoln's speech and teach it to her children?

EVALUATE AND CONNECT

9. Do you identify more with Mary Bowman's reactions to the battle or with Hannah Casey's? Explain, using your response to the **Focus Activity** on page 510 to help you.
10. What attitudes toward their country do Mary Bowman, the people caring for the wounded and dead, and President Lincoln share?

LITERARY ELEMENTS

Exposition

Exposition is the part of a story plot in which the writer presents the information readers will need to follow the story. In "The Battleground," the results of the terrible fighting in and near a small town are described for readers. This information helps readers to understand the characters and the action.

1. How does learning about Mary's connection with the fighting affect the way you respond to her character?
2. Explain how having a battle fought around them may have contributed to towns-people's appreciation of Lincoln's words.

- See **Literary Terms Handbook,** p. R3.

Literature and Writing

Writing About Literature

Fiction from Facts "The Battleground" is fiction, but it is based on historical events. List important characters, events, and places in the story. Which, in your opinion, are fictional? Which are historical facts? How can you tell?

Creative Writing

You Are There This story was written from the third-person point of view. How would it be different if it were a first-person narrative? As Mary Bowman, write three journal entries: one written during the battle, one after searching for your husband, and one after hearing Lincoln's dedication speech.

Extending Your Response

Literature Groups

Building Character Where in the story does Elsie Singmaster use actions and description to reveal Mary's character? Choose a scene from the story to read aloud. With your group, identify the emotions Mary feels at that point. Why, do you think, did Singmaster use so little dialogue to reveal Mary's character?

Learning for Life

Read All About It! Work in a group to create a newspaper front page that might have been published just after the Battle of Gettysburg or just before the dedication ceremony for the Gettysburg National Cemetery. Include a feature story, an interview, and a personal profile of a real or fictional character of the times.

Interdisciplinary Activity

Art There are many memorials throughout the United States to honor those who fought in Civil War battles. Sketch or design plans for a memorial that would commemorate the contributions of civilians like Mary Bowman.

New York State Memorial at Gettysburg National Cemetery.

Reading Further

For more stories about the effects of the Civil War, try these books:

The Dreams of Mairhe Mehan by Jennifer Armstrong

Mine Eyes Have Seen the Glory by Ann Rinaldi

Save your work for your portfolio.

Skill Minilessons

GRAMMAR AND LANGUAGE • NUMBERS

When writing about history, you use numbers to present data, the sequence of events, and dates. Some numbers should be represented by words; others should be written as numerals.

1. Spell out numbers that you can write in one or two words *(twenty-two)*.
2. Use numerals for numbers of more than two words *(220)*.
3. Spell ordinal numbers *(first, second, third)*.
4. Spell out any number that begins a sentence, or reword the sentence.
5. Always use numerals to express dates *(June 1)*.

PRACTICE Copy the following paragraph, writing all numbers correctly.

50 people moved from our town in eighteen sixty-six, the 1st year after the war. For 100 miles around, the land had been ruined. I was 14 years old that year on May thirtieth.

- For more about numbers, see **Language Handbook,** p. R45.

READING AND THINKING • ACTIVATING PRIOR KNOWLEDGE

The beginning of "The Battleground" does not state that the setting is the Civil War. Readers must use information they already have, their **prior knowledge,** to connect Gettysburg with the Civil War. To activate prior knowledge, notice clues that jog your memory. Then ask yourself questions to relate those clues with what you already know about a setting or a person.

PRACTICE List four or five clues that you noticed or questions that you asked yourself when you read "The Battleground." Explain how your prior knowledge helped you understand the clues and answer your questions.

- For more about activating prior knowledge, see **Reading Handbook,** p. R84.

VOCABULARY • BASE WORDS

An unfamiliar word is sometimes just a familiar base word with a suffix or prefix (or both) attached to it. You can often get a good idea of what the new word means by looking for a base word within it. For example, Gettysburg's women *repressed* tears while nursing wounded soldiers, and Mary Bowman knew that leaves would hide the *depressed* spots that marked graves. Both *repressed* and *depressed* contain the base word *press. Re-* adds the meaning of "back," so to *repress* tears is to press, or steadily push, them back. *De-* adds the meaning of "down."

PRACTICE Use your knowledge of base words to answer the questions.

1. The cautionary advice that the judge gives Mary about her children is meant to
   a. warn her. b. encourage her. c. inform her.
2. What Mary presupposes is what she
   a. sees and hears. b. remembers. c. assumes beforehand.
3. To say that Mary becomes uncustomarily silent means that her silence is
   a. rude. b. forced on her. c. unusual for her.

Identifying Persuasive Techniques

Writers often write with a single purpose: to convince their readers to think, feel, or act in a certain way. This type of writing is called **persuasive writing.** Persuasive writing may be about unimportant things, such as which toothpaste you should use or which jeans will look best on you. However, many writers also speak out about important topics, such as those that prevent people from feeling "free to be."

Most writers of persuasive articles or speeches do the following:

- take a stand on a topic
- support that stand with examples, details, or background information

A skillful reader must be able to understand what the writer is doing and decide whether to think, feel, or behave in the way the writer suggests. The reader can do these things by asking questions like these:

1. Is the writer's stand clear?
2. Does the writer know enough about the topic to make decisions about it?
3. Do I know why the writer believes as he or she does?
4. Does the writer give enough information to show that the stand he or she has taken is a reasonable one?
5. Do I know enough about the topic to make a decision?

● For more about author's purpose, see **Reading Handbook,** p. R96.

ACTIVITY

Read the following example of persuasive writing. Then, using the questions above to organize your ideas, write three or four paragraphs explaining whether the writer influenced the way you may act, feel, or think about the topic.

> Women have always struggled with their men-folk for the abolition of slavery, the liberation of countries from colonialism, the dismantling of apartheid and the attainment of peace. It is now the turn of men to join women in their struggle for equality.
>
> —*Gertrude Mongella of Tanzania*
> *Secretary General of U.S. Fourth Conference*
> *on the World's Women, 1995*

Before You Read

from *Letters from Rifka*

MEET KAREN HESSE

Karen Hesse (**hes**) was a lonely child growing up in Baltimore, Maryland. Then, when she was about eleven years old, she read a book on Hiroshima that affected her strongly. "If more books for children had existed at that time with real issues . . . I don't think I would have felt so lonely, so isolated," she says. Now she writes for children to show them that they are not alone in the world. "My hope is to help [young people] through hard times, to present characters who survive ordeals and grow as a result of them," she says.

Karen Hesse was born in 1952. Letters from Rifka *was published in 1992. The book won several awards and was named an American Library Association Best Book for Young Adults.*

FOCUS ACTIVITY

Do you agree with Karen Hesse that reading helps people feel less isolated?

List It!

With a partner, list five books that you think do a good job of telling young people about others who share their concerns and problems. Include the title, author, and a one-sentence statement of the main conflict.

Setting a Purpose

Read to discover how the ability to read gives one young boy a special kind of freedom.

BACKGROUND

The Time and Place Between 1892 and 1943, millions of people emigrated to the United States. The first stop for most European immigrants at that time was Ellis Island in the harbor of New York City, within sight of the Statue of Liberty. Here the immigrants remained until they had received a clean bill of health and official permission to enter the United States.

Did You Know? Immigrants brought with them a knowledge and love of writing, music, and art from their countries of origin. The immigrants in the story you are about to read enjoy the work of Alexander Pushkin (1799–1837), one of Russia's greatest poets. Pushkin often earned the disapproval of his government for writing from the point of view of those who fought oppression.

VOCABULARY PREVIEW

minimal (min′ ə məl) *adj.* smallest or least possible; very small; p. 529

tempest (tem′ pist) *n.* a violent windstorm, usually accompanied by rain, hail, snow, or thunder; p. 530

modest (mod′ ist) *adj.* tending to avoid praise or credit; humble; bashful; p. 532

from

Letters from Rifka

Karen Hesse

> ... The heavy-hanging chains will fall,
> The walls will crumble at a word;
> And Freedom greet you in the light,
> And brothers give you back the sword.
>
> —*Pushkin*

October 22, 1920
Ellis Island

Dear Tovah,

This is the last letter I will ever write you from Ellis Island. It is almost impossible to believe what has happened today. I don't know where to start.

I woke up feeling like a lump of wool had caught in my throat. I let Ilya sleep in bed beside me last night. I knew it was probably our last night together, whatever happened.

We whispered for a long time in the dark. I told him not to be afraid of America. That he would make friends here. That his uncle would love him and take care of him.

An immigrant family waits at Ellis Island.

Viewing the photograph: Do the people in the photograph seem to share Rifka's attitude toward Ellis Island? Explain.

I told him that in Russia, he would always be a peasant. That would never change. He would die young just as his father had and maybe leave a little boy just as his father had left him. I told him in America, he could grow up to be anything he wanted. He could have a wife and children and live to be an old man and see his grandchildren born.

He said he would stay, if he could marry me.

That made me smile. I'm glad it was dark so he couldn't see. I didn't want him to think I was making fun.

I have learned so much about America in these three weeks. It is hard to believe I got so upset over Ilya and the toilet paper just a few days ago. I laugh about it now. I understand so much more.

Yet as I woke this morning, with Ilya curled up beside me, I wondered what good would come from my understanding. What chance did I have of staying? Not only did I have no hair, but the ringworm[1] had returned. Every second I had to remind myself not to scratch at the ringworm.

Ilya had America within his grasp, but me, I held nothing. I held only Russia.

Mr. Fargate, the man who makes these decisions, came into the little office beside the ward. He called Ilya in first.

Ilya gripped my hand and pulled me into the office with him. Mr. Fargate and Doctor Askin discussed Ilya, examined him. Mr. Fargate noticed that Ilya had gained weight.

Ilya's uncle sat in a chair nearby. He was such a little man, with thin blond hair and stormy eyes, just like Ilya's.

1. *Ringworm* is a skin disease that is caused by a tiny fungus (not a worm).

My family, my whole beautiful family, Papa and Mama and Saul, and Nathan and Asher and Reuben, and Isaac and Sadie and the little baby, Aaron, they were all there too. How I longed to be with them. I looked at each of them, memorizing their faces. My brothers Reuben and Asher and Isaac, I would have known them anywhere. Isaac and Asher look just like Papa, and Reuben, he looks like me. When they first arrived, I hugged and kissed them all.

I whispered to Saul, "Did you get the candlesticks?"

He said, "Yes, Rifka. But I have not given them to Mama yet."

"What are you waiting for?" I asked.

Saul shrugged.

Now I could only look at my family from a distance. Ilya needed me.

Ilya's uncle cowered under the giant shadow of my family. When Nurse Bowen passed him, his hair lifted off his high forehead in the little breeze that she made. He held his hat in his hand, his fingers inching around the brim over and over again, his shoulders hunched. It looked to me like he needed Ilya as much as Ilya needed him.

Mr. Fargate said, "This boy shows minimal intelligence. He doesn't feed himself, he doesn't speak. Has there been any change since his last review, Doctor Askin?"

The doctor said many things, but the more he talked the more clear it became he didn't know Ilya at all.

He believed Ilya *was* a simpleton.

Ilya could read Pushkin. He was smart enough to figure out if he starved himself, he'd get shipped back home. That's not a simpleton. They couldn't send him back for being a simpleton.

Mr. Fargate pushed his glasses up on his nose and leaned over his desk to peer at Ilya.

"Can you speak?" he asked in English.

Ilya stared straight into Mr. Fargate's eyes, but he said nothing.

"He doesn't understand English," Nurse Bowen said.

Mr. Fargate nodded. "Find someone who can translate."

"I can," I offered.

Mr. Fargate looked over his glasses at me. "Ask the boy if he can talk," said Mr. Fargate.

"Talk," I told Ilya in Russian.

Ilya glared at me.

"Ilya, talk!"

Ilya slowly shook his head.

"Go get my Pushkin," I told Ilya.

He looked up at me and brushed his blond hair out of his eyes. His uncle looked up at me too, startled.

"Go on, get the book," I repeated.

Ilya was being as stubborn as ever. He stood in his place and refused to move.

"Ilya," I commanded. "Go over there and get the book of Pushkin. Now!"

I pointed toward my cot.

Ilya stared at me with those stormy green eyes. Then he lowered his chin, brushed past his uncle, and got the book.

"Ilya is a smart boy," I told Mr. Fargate in English.

I looked down at Ilya. "Read to them," I ordered in Russian. "Show them that you are smart enough to live in America. I

Vocabulary

minimal (min′ ə məl) *adj.* smallest or least possible; very small know how clever you are, Ilya. But Mr. Fargate needs to know. Your uncle needs to know too."

I looked back to where the uncle sat with his hat in his lap. The man's eyes never left Ilya. He drank in the sight of his nephew the way a thirsty man pulls at a dipper of water.

Still, Ilya remained silent.

Mr. Fargate lifted the stamp, the deportation[2] stamp.

"Please," I begged Ilya's uncle in Russian. "You are losing him. He must prove to them that he is not a simpleton or they will send him away."

I tried to get the uncle to understand.

"He is afraid of you. He thinks you don't want him."

"He is my sister's son," Ilya's uncle said in Russian. "Of course I want him. He is my flesh and blood. I sent for him to give him a better life here in America. I work day and night so he can have a good life."

"Do you hear, Ilya?" I said. "Do you hear?"

Ilya turned his eyes for the first time on his uncle.

"Doctor Askin," I said in English. "Ilya is not a simpleton. I know he won't talk to you. But he *can* talk. He can read, too. He is only seven years, but he can read."

I gave Ilya the book. "Now read," I commanded in Russian.

Ilya's uncle got up out of his seat and came over. He put his hat down on the edge of Mr. Fargate's desk and knelt before his nephew. "Please, Ilya," he said. "Do what your friend says."

Ilya brushed the blond hair up onto his forehead. Then he began to read.

> *"Storm-clouds dim the sky; the tempest*
> *Weaves the snow in patterns wild . . ."*

Ilya's voice shook, but he was reading.

> *"Like a beast the gale is howling,*
> *And now wailing like a child . . ."*

Tears filled the eyes of Ilya's uncle.

"Is he reading?" Mr. Fargate asked. "Is that Russian?"

Ilya's uncle nodded. "Pushkin."

"Let me see the book a moment," Mr. Fargate said. He reached for the Pushkin. Ilya pulled it back, clasping the book to his chest.

"Show Mr. Fargate the book," I said in Russian. "Go on, Ilya."

Ilya's hands trembled as he handed the book to Mr. Fargate. Mr. Fargate opened our Pushkin to another page. "Read this."

> *". . . I like the grapes whose clusters ripen*
> *Upon the hillside in the sun . . ."*

Ilya's finger dragged across the page as he read the words.

I smiled. Doctor Askin smiled. Nurse Bowen smiled too.

"He understands this?" Mr. Fargate said. "At the age of seven?"

"Yes, sir," I said. "He understands."

Mr. Fargate lifted the stamp that permitted Ilya to enter the country and thumped it down on Ilya's papers. Ilya was going to stay in America.

2. *Deportation* is the act of forcing a noncitizen to leave a country because the person is considered undesirable for some reason.

Vocabulary

tempest (tem′ pist) *n.* a violent windstorm, usually accompanied by rain, hail, snow, or thunder

"Did I do it right, Rifka?" he asked in Russian.

"Yes, Ilya," I said. "You did it just right."

Ilya's uncle still knelt on the floor beside us. His arms opened up to take Ilya in. Oh, Tovah. You should have seen the way Ilya and his uncle embraced. In all the times he clung to me, Ilya never held me in such a way. Never.

Ilya had attracted a lot of attention on the ward. No one but myself had ever heard his voice. Now there he was, reading Pushkin. Other nurses and doctors came over. They stood around in wonder at Ilya, now jabbering in Russian as he led his uncle back to his cot.

I could not listen to what they were saying. The time had come for my review. My family waited tensely, some sitting, some standing, waiting for a decision about me. If only I could melt into their tight strong circle, but now, as I had so often over the last year, I stood alone.

Mr. Fargate was talking with Doctor Askin about me. He wanted to know about the ringworm.

"She arrived fully cured," Doctor Askin said. "They made sure she was clean in Belgium before they sent her."

Please, I prayed. Don't let them check for the ringworm now.

They hadn't checked in over a week. I'd shown no sign of being infectious for so long, they believed the ringworm was gone.

I bit the insides of my cheeks to keep from scratching my itchy scalp. In my head, I repeated Sister Mary Katherine's prayer; I repeated a few Hebrew prayers too.

Mr. Fargate turned to Doctor Askin. "What about her hair? Is there any sign of growth?"

I slipped my hand up to my kerchief and gave a quick scratch. I tried not to, but I couldn't keep my hand away from it. It itched so badly. It had been itching all morning.

"Here, Rifka," Doctor Askin said kindly, starting to unknot my kerchief. "Let me look once more to see if there is any sign of hair."

I pulled away.

Oh, Tovah, if ever I needed to be clever, it was now.

An Ellis Island doctor checks the health of immigrants.

"You know," I said. "What does it matter if my hair grows? A girl can not depend on her looks. It is better to be clever. I learned to speak English in three weeks, you know."

"Yes, I know," Mr. Fargate replied.

"I help here too," I said. "I am a good worker."

Mr. Fargate's eyeglasses slid down to the tip of his nose and he stared over them at me. "Not very modest, is she?"

They all laughed.

"It is true!" I cried. "I *am* a good worker!"

"You are, Rifka," Doctor Askin agreed. He turned to Mr. Fargate. "With the right opportunity, the girl could study medicine. She has skill and talent."

"In your opinion, then," Mr. Fargate said, "she would not end up a ward of the state?"[3]

"Who can tell?" said the doctor. "But the opposite is more likely. I have seen her care for the patients. Compassion is a part of medicine you can't teach, Mr. Fargate. Compassion is a quality I have often seen in Rifka. Look what she did for the boy."

"I still worry about her hair," Mr. Fargate said.

I looked Mr. Fargate right in the eye. "I do not need hair to get a good life," I said.

"Maybe right now you don't," Mr. Fargate answered. "But what about when you wish to marry?"

"If I wish to marry, Mr. Fargate," I said—can you believe I spoke like this to an American official, Tovah?— "if I wish to marry, I will do so with hair or without hair."

I heard Mama gasp. This much English she understood.

Mr. Fargate leaned forward to study me. He stared at me through the glasses balanced at the bottom of his nose.

"Read to them your poetry," Saul said.

"You have plenty to say, young lady," Mr. Fargate said.

"Yes," I agreed, "I do."

"Oy, Rifka," Mama whispered.

I turned toward Mama. What I saw, though, was my brother Saul kneeling beside Ilya. Ilya and Saul were looking at the book of Pushkin together. Then Saul stood and took Ilya's hand and they approached Mr. Fargate.

"Yes?" Mr. Fargate asked.

Ilya looked up at me. "Read to them," he commanded in Russian.

"Ilya, that will not work for me," I told him in his own language. "They already know I can read. My case is not the same as yours."

"Read to them your poetry," Saul said. "The words you have written in the back of this book."

I looked hard at Ilya. "You had no right to show that to anyone," I said. "Those are my words."

3. For Rifka to become a *ward of the state,* a judge would have to decide that she cannot take care of herself. A guardian would be appointed to look after her.

Vocabulary

modest (mod′ ist) *adj.* tending to avoid praise or credit; humble; bashful

"They are good words, Rifka," Saul said.

"They are nothing," I answered. "Simple little poems. They don't even rhyme. What good would it do to read such things aloud? Leave it be."

Ilya would not leave it.

He took the Pushkin and elbowed in front of me to stand under the stern eye of Mr. Fargate.

"This," he said, speaking English with a very thick accent. "This Rifka write."

I'd never heard him speak anything but Russian before.

He took a deep breath and let it out. He swallowed once, hard. Then he began reciting my latest poem in English. How I had struggled with the words. Ilya had made me repeat them to him each time I stopped or changed something. Now he remembered it perfectly. He didn't look at the book. He just held it in front of him and said the poem from memory.

"I leave to you the low and leaning room,
where once we drank the honey-sweetened tea,
and bowed our heads in prayer and waited there,
for cossacks[4] *with their boots and bayonets."*

They were all listening, even Ilya's uncle.

"I leave behind my cousins, young and dear;
They'll never know the freedom I have known,
Or learn as I have learned, that kindness dwells,
In hearts that have no fear."

"You wrote these words?" Mr. Fargate asked.

I nodded, embarrassed.

"Rifka Nebrot," Mr. Fargate said. "This is a very nice poem."

"You think?" I asked. "That is just one poem." I took the book from Ilya and started turning pages. "I have more, Mr. Fargate, many more. I can read to you. Do you have time? Here is one you will like, I think . . ."

Mr. Fargate looked at his watch. Then he looked at Doctor Askin. "No wonder the boy never talked. She talks enough for both of them."

Now, I thought, it would be clever to keep quiet.

"Well, Miss Nebrot," Mr. Fargate said. "After giving the matter some consideration, I think you are correct. Whether you wish to marry or not is no business of mine." He turned to Doctor Askin. "Heaven help the man she does marry."

Turning back to me, he said, "I have no doubt that if you wish to marry, you will manage to do so, whether you have hair or not."

Then he looked over to Mama and Papa. "Mr. and Mrs. Nebrot. These are your daughter's papers. With this stamp I give permission for her to enter the United States of America."

My heart thundered in my chest.

Mr. Fargate stamped my entrance papers and handed them to me. "Here, Rifka Nebrot," he said. "Welcome to America."

The nurses and doctors swept over me. Ilya, too. Best of all my family, my beloved family, Saul, Nathan, Reuben, Asher, Isaac, Mama, Papa, Sadie, and little Aaron. There was such a commotion

4. In the 1800s (when Pushkin wrote), the *cossacks* were members of special military units. Their cruel treatment of Jews, other minorities, and peasants made the cossacks greatly feared and hated.

with all the kissing and the hugging I could hardly breathe.

Then I felt something that made me stiffen with fear. In all the kissing and hugging, someone had loosened the kerchief covering my head. I felt it slipping off.

I tried to get my hand up to hold on to it, but Doctor Askin held my arms. He enfolded me in a crushing hug, and I felt the kerchief sliding down, inching away from the sores it covered, to betray me. The kerchief, as Doctor Askin let go, dropped around my neck, settling on my shoulders like a heavy weight.

With my head exposed to the air, it itched worse than ever.

Quickly my hands flew up to replace the kerchief. I swept it back up in a matter of seconds, trying to cover my head before anyone had a chance to see my scalp.

I wasn't fast enough. Towering over me as he did, Saul had seen it. Doctor Askin had seen it too. They stared down at me.

"Rifka, your head," Saul said.

I pulled the kerchief tightly over my scalp.

Not now, I prayed. They've stamped the papers. Don't let them find out now.

"But Rifka," Saul said. "There's something on your head."

"Take off your kerchief," Doctor Askin ordered.

"Please," I begged in a whisper. "Don't make me take it off."

"Take it off, Rifka," Doctor Askin insisted.

My hands shook as I lifted them to the knot under my chin. I had difficulty untying it. Everyone stared at me, at my trembling hands, at my disloyal kerchief.

"Whatever it is," I said, trying to talk my way out of it, "I'm certain it will go away."

I could delay no longer. The kerchief dropped to my shoulders.

"This isn't going away," said Nurse Bowen. "Here, feel for yourself."

She took my hand and guided it up to the top of my head. I stretched my hand out, expecting to feel the ringworm sores under my fingertips.

Everyone stared at me, at my trembling hands, at my disloyal kerchief.

But I didn't feel ringworm.

I felt hair!

Not very much. But it was hair. My hair! And it was growing.

* * *

Mama and Papa are sitting beside me on a bench at Ellis Island. We are waiting for my brother Isaac. I am writing on the paper Nurse Bowen gave to me.

Saul says at home there is a notebook full of paper, a whole empty notebook for me to write in. He bought it for me himself, with his own money. And at home is a pair of brass candlesticks, he said. A pair just like the ones Mama used to own. Tonight, Saul said, tonight I would give them to her.

On my head is the black velvet hat with the shirring[5] and the light blue lining. My head still itches, but Nurse

5. Here, the *shirring* is a stitched gathering of the velvet.

Italian Girl at Ellis Island Finds Her First Penny, 1926. Lewis Hine. The New York Public Library. Gift of the Russell Sage Foundation Library.

Viewing the photograph: What qualities do you think the girl in this photograph may share with Rifka?

Bowen said that is normal. That often the scalp prickles when new hair grows in.

Mama's gold locket lies softly between her breasts again, where it belongs. Around my neck is a small Star of David on a silver chain, a gift from Mama and Papa.

"Saul said this is what you would like the most," Mama had said when she gave it to me.

"Saul was right," I said, and I kissed Mama and Papa on their hands, first one and then the other.

My brother Isaac has gone home to Borough Park to bring his car. He said, "Never mind the trouble, my sister Rifka is going to enter America in style."

A clever girl like me, Tovah, how else should I enter America?

I will write you tonight a real letter, a letter I can send. I will wrap up our precious book and send it to you too, so you will know of my journey. I hope you can read all the tiny words squeezed onto the worn pages. I hope they bring to you the comfort they have brought to me. I send you my love, Tovah. At last I send you my love from America.

Shalom,[6] *my dear cousin,*
Rifka

6. Used both as a greeting and a farewell, *shalom* (shə lōm′) is a Hebrew word meaning "peace."

Responding to Literature

PERSONAL RESPONSE

What three words do you think best describe this story?

Analyzing Literature

RECALL

1. What is Mr. Fargate's impression of Ilya?
2. How does Rifka distract the doctor from examining her head?
3. What does Ilya do to help Rifka pass inspection?
4. What gifts do Rifka's family members give her when she finally receives permission to enter the country?

INTERPRET

5. Why does Rifka tell Ilya that he must show his uncle that he is not a simpleton?
6. Do you think Rifka is frightened? Support your answer with examples from the story.
7. Why does Rifka's poem impress the American officials?
8. How do you know that Rifka is Jewish? Give several reasons.

EVALUATE AND CONNECT

9. **Characterization** is the method a writer uses to develop a character's personality. How does the author let you know what kind of person Rifka is? List three adjectives that fit Rifka, and then list details from the story that support those adjectives.
10. Have you ever had to wait for someone's approval the way Rifka waits to have her papers stamped? How was your experience like or different from Rifka's?

LITERARY ELEMENTS

Narration

Narration is the telling of a story. The author of *Letters from Rifka* chose to tell this story through a series of letters written by the main character. Rifka is the narrator, and everything that happens is told from her perspective.

1. What are some advantages of telling a story in the form of letters?
2. What effect does telling the story through Rifka's eyes have on the ringworm episode?
3. How does Rifka tailor, or put together, her story so that her cousin Tovah will know what is important and will understand an unfamiliar situation? How does the author tailor the story for her audience, you?

● See **Literary Terms Handbook,** p. R6.

Literature and Writing

Writing About Literature

Conflict There are several conflicts in this story, both **external** (a character's struggle against some outside force) and **internal** (a struggle within a character's own mind). Write a paragraph identifying and analyzing one conflict of each type. To identify conflicts, begin by asking yourself what the character wants. Look over your list from the **Focus Activity** on page 526. Which of those conflicts are similar to the ones in this story?

Personal Writing

Your Heritage If you know how someone in your family came to America, write about the experience in narrative form. Use description and dialogue to bring your story to life. You might ask your parents, grandparents, or elderly friends if they have immigration stories. If you wish, you may make up a story and write it as historical fiction. (For help with historical fiction, see the **Genre Focus** on page 508.)

Extending Your Response

Literature Groups

Jump-Start Memories With a group, brainstorm a list of questions you can ask family members or older friends to help them think about their past. Use your list to start a conversation about adjusting to a new culture or place.

Today, technology has made communication easier than it was for Rifka. Gather the E-mail addresses of friends or relatives who use the Internet. Begin a correspondence with one person, sending one E-mail per week for a month.

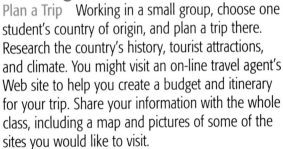

Learning for Life

Plan a Trip Working in a small group, choose one student's country of origin, and plan a trip there. Research the country's history, tourist attractions, and climate. You might visit an on-line travel agent's Web site to help you create a budget and itinerary for your trip. Share your information with the whole class, including a map and pictures of some of the sites you would like to visit.

Reading Further

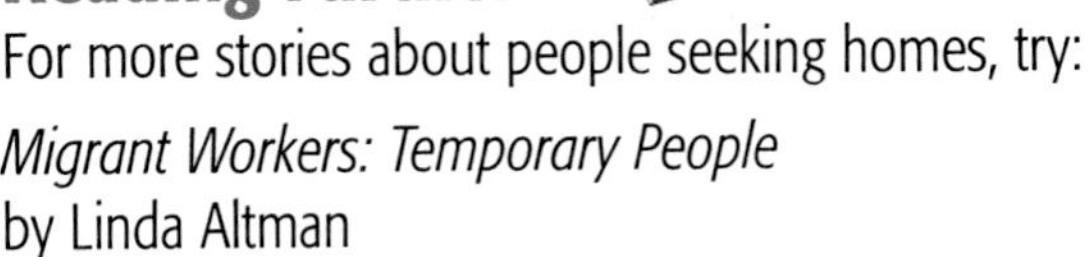

For more stories about people seeking homes, try:

Migrant Workers: Temporary People
by Linda Altman

Save your work for your portfolio.

Skill Minilessons

GRAMMAR AND LANGUAGE • USING APOSTROPHES

An **apostrophe** may indicate missing letters in a contraction (as in *cannot* → *can't*). An apostrophe plus *s* forms the possessive of the following items:

- a singular noun *(Rifka's)*
- a plural noun that doesn't end in *s (women's)*
- an indefinite pronoun *(somebody's).*

Use an apostrophe alone to form the possessive of a plural noun that ends in *s (ships').*

For more about using apostrophes, see **Language Handbook,** p. R42.

PRACTICE Rewrite each underlined plural, possessive, or contraction, adding apostrophes if they are needed. (*Note:* One of the underlined words is correct.)

1. Rifkas family was waiting for her.
2. The mens concern was with Ilyas intelligence.
3. Its anyones guess whether Rifka will keep writing poetry.
4. Pushkin was a favorite author of hers.
5. "Theres a lot youre going to have to learn," Mr. Fargate said.

READING AND THINKING • PARAPHRASING

Paraphrasing means restating a text, passage, or conversation. You often paraphrase when you summarize or when you need to simplify an idea for someone. Paraphrasing usually involves changing direct quotes to indirect quotes or making a passage clearer, perhaps by replacing large words with smaller ones and eliminating trivial details.

PRACTICE In a few sentences, paraphrase the conversation between Rifka, Dr. Askin, and Mr. Fargate about Rifka's hair.

For more about paraphrasing, see **Reading Handbook,** p. R90.

VOCABULARY • WORD PARTS THAT EXPRESS SIZE

Some word parts are used to express size. Mr. Fargate says that Ilya has *minimal* intelligence, the least possible intelligence. The word part *mini-* carries the meaning of "small." *Maxi-* has the opposite meaning, so *maximal* intelligence would be the greatest possible intelligence.

Here are some examples of common word parts that express size:

micro-	small	*-et*	small
-let	small	*macro-*	large, enlarged
mega-	large, powerful	*-ette*	small

PRACTICE Use the list of word parts at the left to figure out what the underlined words mean, and then answer the questions.

1. Is an owlet a baby owl or an old owl?
2. Why would it be difficult to lift a stone that was a megalith?
3. Which is a field of science that studies tiny living things–macrobiotics or microbiology?
4. Where would you be likely to find a statuette–on a shelf or on a huge pedestal?
5. Which will fill a pail first–a ceiling that is leaking droplets or a ceiling that is leaking drops?

Using Pronouns Correctly

Pronouns are substitutes for nouns. Sentences without pronouns would be clumsy.

Rifka told Rifka's brother that Rifka's poetry was private to Rifka.

Rifka told *her* brother that *her* poetry was private to *her.*

A pronoun refers to a noun or another pronoun, called its **antecedent.** It must be clear *which* antecedent a pronoun refers to, and the correct pronoun must be used.

Problem 1 A pronoun with an unclear antecedent

While Mr. Fargate was dealing with Ilya, he said nothing. [*He* could refer to *Mr. Fargate* or to *Ilya.*]

Solution *While Mr. Fargate was dealing with Ilya, the boy said nothing.* [Use a noun instead of the pronoun.]

Problem 2 Using an object pronoun as a subject

Rifka and him both faced problems during their interviews.

Solution *Rifka and he both faced problems during their interviews.* [In the subject part of a sentence, use a subject pronoun.]

Problem 3 Using a subject pronoun as an object

Rifka's determination helped both Ilya and she.

Solution *Rifka's determination helped both Ilya and her.* [Use an object pronoun as the object of a verb or a preposition.]

- For more about pronoun use, see **Language Handbook,** p. R16.

EXERCISES

1. Revise each sentence to make it clear.
   - **a.** Mr. Fargate wanted to talk with Ilya, but he didn't say a word.
   - **b.** Rifka told Tovah that she had become a more understanding person.
   - **c.** The officials' experience with Rifka and Ilya showed that they did not understand.
   - **d.** Ilya's uncle told Ilya that he could live to be an old man.
2. Choose the correct pronoun.
   - **a.** Emma and (I, me) were the last students to finish.
   - **b.** The teacher asked (she, her) and (I, me) what took us so long.
   - **c.** It turned out that the same thing was true for both Emma and (I, me).
   - **d.** Both (she, her) and (I, me) had been so interested in Rifka's poem that we had read it over and over again.

Writing WORKSHOP

Persuasive Writing: Speech

Which freedoms mean the most to you? Which controversies concern you? By speaking out, you can rally people behind ideas and issues that you care about. Speaking out involves **persuasion**—the art of convincing others. The language of persuasion is powerful. With it, you can inspire people to see things in a new light and you can motivate them to take action.

Assignment: Follow the process in this workshop to write a persuasive speech that will inspire and motivate your listeners.

- As you write your persuasive speech, see **Writing Handbook,** pp. R50–R61.

The Writing Process

PREWRITING

PREWRITING TIP

For more topic ideas, check the Internet. Many newspapers have Web sites with in-depth looks at current issues. Add new topics to your list.

TECHNOLOGY TIP

To freewrite on a computer, darken the screen on your monitor. Then type, letting your thoughts flow without visual distractions.

Choose a Topic

List selections you have read recently that remind you of freedoms you cherish or situations you'd like to change. Check newspapers and television news programs for issues and ideas that affect your world. Jot down one or two topics that you feel strongly about.

Examine Your Views

Freewrite about each of your topics, one at a time. Explore the reasons each topic is important to you. Examine how the topic touches your life and the lives of those you care about. Then, read your freewriting. Underline key ideas and circle well-worded statements or phrases that you could use in your speech. Finally, select the topic you want to pursue.

Consider Your Purpose and Audience

Will you take a straightforward approach? Should you use humor, statistics, and stories to persuade? Your answers depend on your subject and your audience. Consider the attitudes and concerns of those who will hear your speech. Also, consider the background information they will need to understand your topic.

Build Your Framework

When preparing your speech, focus on a single important point–your **position statement.** This may be one of the key ideas from your freewriting activity. Support your position statement by listing several **reasons.** To persuade, you need strong evidence for each reason, so gather facts, examples, quotations, or statistics, depending on your subject. Be sure your reasoning makes sense. If you jump to conclusions, ignore important factors, or accept unreliable opinions, you will lose your listeners' trust.

Position Statement: **We must work to wipe out hunger in our country.**

Reason 1	**Hunger is a serious and often hidden problem in this country.**
Evidence	Newspaper article: statistics on city, suburban, or rural poor Survey: local people's awareness of the problem

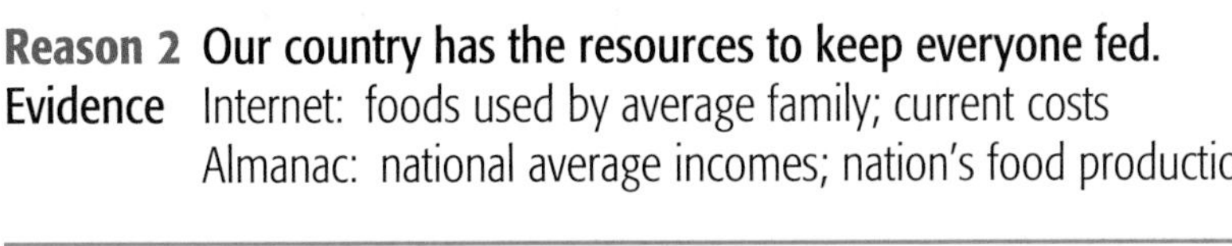

Reason 2	**Our country has the resources to keep everyone fed.**
Evidence	Internet: foods used by average family; current costs Almanac: national average incomes; nation's food production

Reason 3	**Hunger leads to worse problems.**
Evidence	Encyclopedia: nutrition links to health, intellectual development

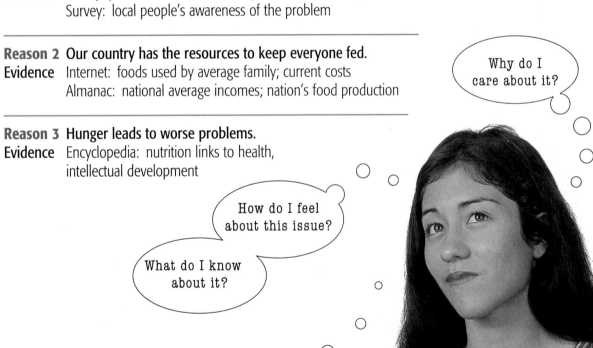

Why do I care about it?

How do I feel about this issue?

What do I know about it?

How long has it been important to me?

DRAFTING

Drafting Tip

Your word choices affect listeners' emotions. Are listeners more likely to accept an *old* theory or a *proven* theory? a *cheap* plan or a *reasonably priced* plan?

Make a Strong Start

Capture your listeners' attention with your first words. Try using a surprising fact, an intriguing question, a meaningful quotation, or a brief story to lead into your position statement. Make your views clear from the beginning.

Follow Your Thoughts

Write about each of your reasons, citing evidence and building toward your conclusion. Include effective wording from your freewriting. Transitions such as *one important reason, another reason, the most important reason, finally,* and *because of this* will keep the links between your ideas clear. Conclude with a strong restatement of your position: a call for awareness or for action.

MODEL • DRAFTING

If you think hunger is someone else's problem, think again. According to the *Daily News*, 8 percent of the children in our city go without food one day a week. This figure may seem small—until you realize how big our country is.

REVISING

Revising Tip

Watch out for the adverb *very.* Used too often, it can weaken your statements instead of adding emphasis.

Look and Listen

Don't just look over your speech; listen to it too. Read it aloud to yourself or to a partner. Listen for meaning, using the **Questions for Revising.** Then listen again for sound and rhythm. Try repeating one key phrase. Rhythm and repetition will help your listeners remember your words.

QUESTIONS FOR REVISING

- How do my opening words grab my listeners?
- Where might I add transitions to help listeners follow the flow of my ideas?
- How might I change the order of my reasons to lead more effectively to my conclusion?
- Which words might I change to affect listeners' emotions more strongly?
- How does my conclusion call for action or increased awareness?

EDITING/PROOFREADING

Go over your revised draft, using the **Proofreading Checklist** on the right as a guide. Correct errors in grammar, usage, and mechanics. Be sure that you use pronouns correctly, as shown in the **Grammar Link** on page 539.

Grammar Hint

Sure is an adjective used to modify nouns only. To modify verbs, adjectives, or other adverbs, use the adverb *surely*.

As a volunteer, you will *surely* be doing your community a favor.

PROOFREADING CHECKLIST

- ☑ Modifiers are correctly used (double-check *sure* and *surely*).
- ☑ Sentences are complete; there are no sentence fragments or run-ons.
- ☑ All verbs agree with their subjects.
- ☑ Pronouns are in the proper forms and agree with their antecedents.
- ☑ Spelling, punctuation, and capitalization are correct.

MODEL • EDITING/PROOFREADING

Hunger is everyone's problem, and it sure [surely] won't go away on its own.

PUBLISHING/PRESENTING

Record your speech on note cards, and then present it to a small group, to your class, or to a larger group at school or in the community. For guidelines on public speaking, see the **Listening, Speaking, and Viewing** feature on page 502.

PRESENTING TIP

Record your speech word for word or in outline form on note cards. Use double spacing–it will be easier on your eyes as you deliver the speech.

Reflecting

Think about the following questions, and then write responses.

- Which part(s) of your speech do you consider strongest? Why?
- Write one suggestion that could help another student write a persuasive speech. Explain the benefits of your advice.

Save your work for your portfolio.

Theme Wrap-Up

Responding to the Theme

1. Which selection most helped you to understand the theme "Free to Be"?
2. What new thoughts do you have about the following ideas as a result of reading the literature in this theme?
   - Many people in the past made great sacrifices for the freedoms we enjoy today.
   - Religious or political freedom does not come easily.
   - The struggle for freedom continues today.
3. Present your theme project to the class.

Analyzing Literature

ANALYZE THE THEME

Many of the selections in this theme express the dangers and joys that come with the struggle for freedom. Choose two poems or other pieces from this theme that express how you feel about "Free to Be." Write a few paragraphs explaining your ideas. Include quotations from the selections.

Evaluate and Set Goals

1. Which of the following activities did you enjoy the most? Which did you find most difficult?
   - reading and thinking about the selections
   - writing on your own
   - analyzing and discussing the selections
   - presenting ideas and projects
   - researching topics
2. How would you assess your work in this theme, using the scale below? Give at least two reasons for your assessment.

   4 = outstanding 2 = fair
   3 = good 1 = weak
3. Based on what you found challenging in this theme, choose a goal to work toward in the next theme.
   - In your notebook, record your goal and three steps you will take to help you reach it.
   - Meet with your teacher to review your goal and your plan for achieving it.

Build Your Portfolio

SELECT

Choose two of your favorite pieces of work from this theme to include in your portfolio. The following questions can help you choose.

- ✦ Which do you consider your best work?
- ✦ Which turned out to be more challenging than you thought? Why?
- ✦ Which was the most interesting?

REFLECT

Write some notes to accompany the pieces you selected. Use these questions to guide you.

- ✦ What do you like best about the piece?
- ✦ What did you learn from creating it?
- ✦ What might you do differently if you were beginning this piece again?

Reading on Your Own

If you have enjoyed the literature in this theme, you might also be interested in the following books.

Across Five Aprils

by Irene Hunt Jethrow Creighton fights for freedom in his own way as he is left with the responsibility of maintaining his family's farm when the men and older boys join the army.

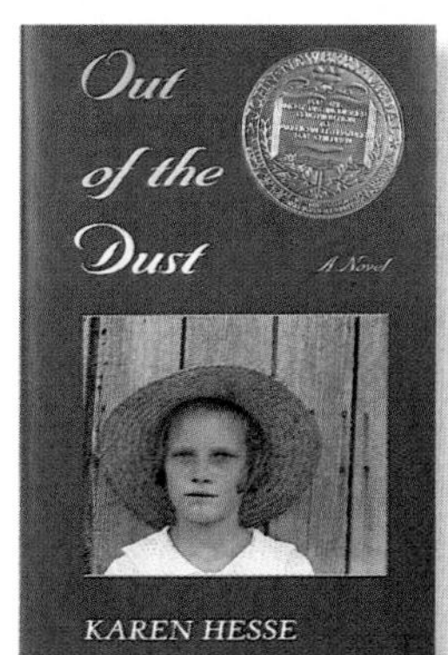

Out of the Dust

by Karen Hesse Fourteen-year-old Billie Jo lost her mother in an accident for which Billie Jo blames her father and herself. In her journal, she records her life in the Oklahoma dust bowl during the Great Depression.

Laborers for Liberty: American Women 1865–1890

by Harriet Sigerman This is the story of American women from New England to New Mexico as they meet new freedoms and challenges, new work opportunities and falling barriers.

I Thought My Soul Would Rise and Fly: The Diary of Patsy, a Freed Girl

by Joyce Hansen In this fictional account, Patsy keeps a diary of her life during the important year of 1865, as slavery ends and the South adjusts to new circumstances.

Standardized Test Practice

Read the passage and decide which type of error, if any, appears in each underlined section. Mark the letter for your answer on your paper.

I once saw a famous musician play my favorite insturment, the piano. (1) He gave an exciting concert at Radio City music Hall in New York. (2) I can honestly say that I've never heard someone play the piano so beautifully before. (3) He seemed to massage music from the keys and the audience thrilled to every note that he played. (4)

The magnificent performance did not come from tallent alone. (5) The musician paid for his success by a lifetime of hard work diligent study, and willpower. (6)

1 A Spelling error
B Capitalization error
C Punctuation error
D No error

2 F Spelling error
G Capitalization error
H Punctuation error
J No error

3 A Spelling error
B Capitalization error
C Punctuation error
D No error

4 F Spelling error
G Capitalization error
H Punctuation error
J No error

5 A Spelling error
B Capitalization error
C Punctuation error
D No error

6 F Spelling error
G Capitalization error
H Punctuation error
J No error

Read the passage and choose the word or group of words that belongs in each space. Mark the letter for your answer on your paper.

Perhaps the __(1)__ modern example of women doing work normally performed by men occurred in America during World War II. With so many American men __(2)__ overseas, many industries lacked the workforce necessary to produce goods for military and domestic use. So manufacturers __(3)__ women to operate the machines. Thus the legend of Rosie the Riveter was born! Rosie was a symbol of the __(4)__ woman of the forties. She __(5)__ a shop outfit like those worn by male workers and performed a job formerly held by a man on an airplane assembly line. The likeness of Rosie the Riveter __(6)__ on posters all over America. She became one of the images American citizens rallied around during the upheaval of a world torn by conflict.

1 **A** more famous
B famouser
C famed
D most famous

2 **F** fighting
G to have fought
H are fighting
J were fighting

3 **A** will hire
B hires
C hired
D was hiring

4 **F** strength
G strong
H strongly
J strengthened

5 **A** weared
B wore
C had been wearing
D will be wearing

6 **F** was seen
G seen
H saw
J have been seen

Flashes of Insight

Miracle of Life, 1996. Christian Pierre. Acrylic on Masonite, 48 x 48 in. Private collection.

> “A moment's insight is sometimes worth a life's experience.”
>
> –Oliver Wendell Holmes Sr., *The Professor at the Breakfast Table*

THEME CONTENTS

GENRE FOCUS PERSONAL ESSAY

Exploring the Theme

Flashes of Insight

The way you look at the world is constantly being shaped by your experiences. Occasionally, you learn something that turns on a lightbulb in your head. In an instant, thoughts come together in a way that changes your understanding. Selections in this theme describe such moments. Choose one of the activities below to start your thinking about "Flashes of Insight."

Starting Points

TAKE A NEW VIEW

Ziggy has a flash of insight! He plays with a word, *present,* and it changes from an ordinary word that means *now* to a word that means *gift.* Ziggy realizes that the time we call *now* is a gift–a chance to enjoy today and tomorrow and all the other tomorrows.

- When you look at a person, an experience, a time, a story, or a word in a new way, you, too, can experience a flash of insight into something you have never understood before. When might such an experience be helpful?

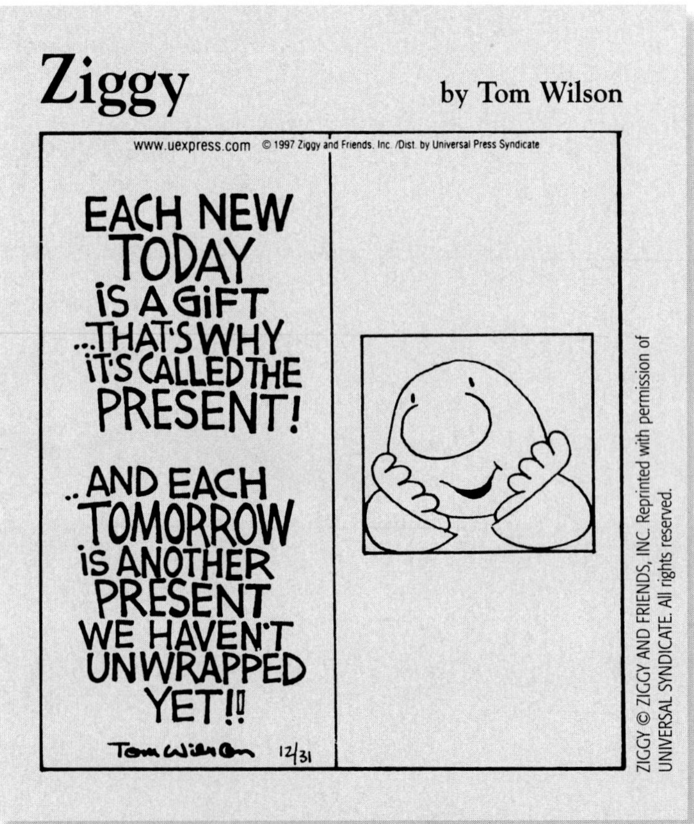

Ziggy
by Tom Wilson
www.uexpress.com © 1997 Ziggy and Friends, Inc. /Dist. by Universal Press Syndicate
EACH NEW TODAY IS A GIFT ...THAT'S WHY IT'S CALLED THE PRESENT!
..AND EACH TOMORROW IS ANOTHER PRESENT WE HAVEN'T UNWRAPPED YET!!
Tom Wilson 12/31

AWAKENING TO PEOPLE

Everyone has moments when they awaken to a new understanding of a familiar person.

- Recall a moment when you suddenly understood something important about a family member, friend, or acquaintance. Think of a title for a story you could write to describe your new understanding.

Theme Projects

Choose one of the projects below to work on as you read the selections in "Flashes of Insight." Work with a partner or a small group.

CRITICAL VIEWING

Examining Both Sides

1. Gather books, photographs, and other materials about a conflict—a war or other serious disagreement—involving the United States. Examine arguments for and against the issue.
2. Discuss how learning arguments for both sides of any issue can give you a flash of insight.

Autumn. Giuseppe Arcimboldo, 1530–1593. Brescia, Pinacoteca, Civica.

LEARNING FOR LIFE

Who Thought of That?

1. With a partner or a group, search several books of art to find unexpected ways in which artists view common objects.
2. Select an ordinary classroom object, such as an eraser, a computer mouse, or a student's desk or chair. Draw, sculpt, or describe in writing a new way to use or show the object.

Visit lit.glencoe.com for more ideas and projects relating to this theme. Select a topic that interests you, such as women in sports, jobs for teens, or helping the environment. Join a chat group or visit Web sites devoted to your topic.

MULTIMEDIA PROJECT

Why Do They Do That?

1. Select an author from those listed in the **Theme Contents** on page 549, or another writer you like but know little about. Gather information about the author. If possible, include a quotation about why he or she writes.
2. Use HyperStudio or similar software to create a multimedia presentation.

Before You Read

Raymond's Run

MEET TONI CADE BAMBARA

Toni Cade Bambara (kād bäm bä′ rä) wrote to make a difference in the lives of women and African Americans. "I write because I really think I've got hold of something, that if I share it, [it] might save somebody else some time, might lift someone's spirits, or might enable someone to see more clearly," she said. Bambara's works, which include short stories, a novel, and several films, are known for their rich portrayals of ordinary African American life. Bambara was also a respected professor of English and African American studies and a civil rights activist.

Toni Cade Bambara was born in 1939 and died in 1995. "Raymond's Run" was first published in 1972 in Gorilla, My Love.

FOCUS ACTIVITY

How do you feel when people recognize you for being good at something?

Cluster

Create a cluster to express these feelings.

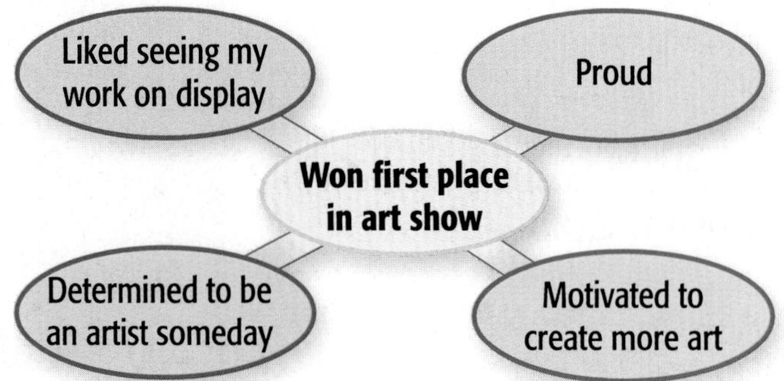

Setting a Purpose

Read to experience a flash of insight that one young person has about her favorite pastime: running.

BACKGROUND

The Time and Place This modern story takes place in Harlem, a section of New York City.

Did You Know? A fast runner might earn the nickname "Mercury" after the Roman god who is known for speed. Statues show Mercury with a winged hat and winged sandals.

VOCABULARY PREVIEW

prodigy (prod′ ə jē) *n.* an extraordinarily gifted or talented person, especially a child; p. 555

liable (lī′ ə bəl) *adj.* likely; apt; p. 555

reputation (rep′ yə tā′ shən) *n.* what people generally think about the character of a person or thing; good name; p. 555

crouch (krouch) *v.* to stoop or bend, especially with knees bent; p. 558

obviously (ob′ vē əs lē) *adv.* in a way that is easily seen or understood; clearly; p. 560

Raymond's Run

Toni Cade Bambara

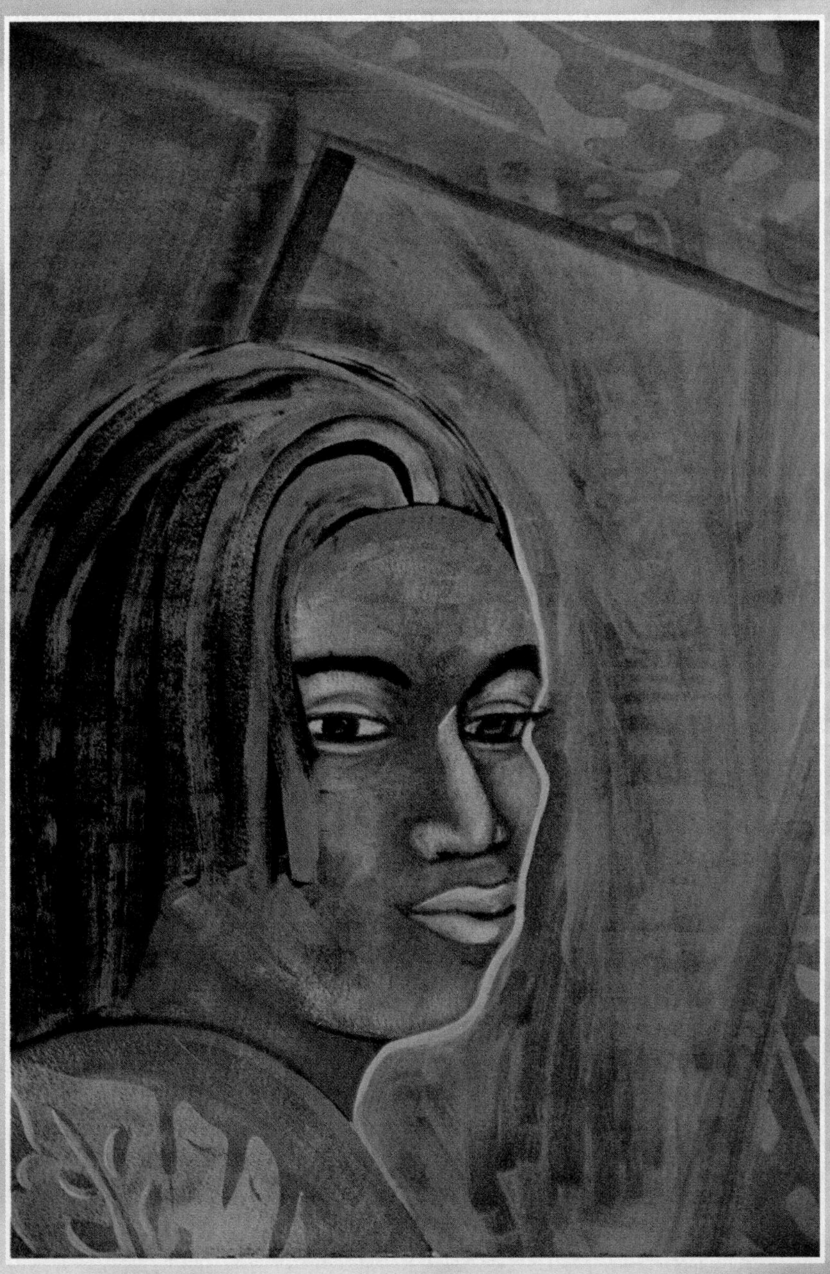

La Miranda 2, 1995. Robin Holder. Monotype with stencils and photo silkscreen, 18 x 14 in. Courtesy of the artist.

I don't have much work to do around the house like some girls. My mother does that. And I don't have to earn my pocket money by hustling; George runs errands for the big boys and sells Christmas cards. And anything else that's got to get done, my father does. All I have to do in life is mind my brother Raymond, which is enough.

Sometimes I slip and say my little brother Raymond. But as any fool can see he's much bigger and he's older too. But a lot of people call him my little brother cause he needs looking after cause he's not quite right. And a lot of smart mouths got lots to say

about that too, especially when George was minding him. But now, if anybody has anything to say to Raymond, anything to say about his big head,[1] they have to come by me. And I don't play the dozens[2] or believe in standing around with somebody in my face doing a lot of talking. I much rather just knock you down and take my chances even if I am a little girl with skinny arms and a squeaky voice, which is how I got the name Squeaky. And if things get too rough, I run. And as anybody can tell you, I'm the fastest thing on two feet.

There is no track meet that I don't win the first place medal. I used to win the twenty-yard dash when I was a little kid in kindergarten. Nowadays, it's the fifty-yard dash. And tomorrow I'm subject to run the quarter-meter relay all by myself and come in first, second, and third. The big kids call me Mercury cause I'm the swiftest thing in the neighborhood. Everybody knows that—except two people who know better, my father and me. He can beat me to Amsterdam Avenue with me having a two fire-hydrant head-start and him running with his hands in his pockets and whistling. But that's private information. Cause can you imagine some thirty-five-year-old man stuffing himself into PAL shorts to race little kids? So as far as everyone's concerned, I'm the fastest and that goes for Gretchen, too, who has put out the tale that she is going to win the first-place medal this year. Ridiculous. In the second place, she's got short legs. In the third place, she's got freckles. In the first place, no one can beat me and that's all there is to it.

I'm standing on the corner admiring the weather and about to take a stroll down Broadway so I can practice my breathing exercises, and I've got Raymond walking on the inside close to the buildings, cause he's subject to fits of fantasy and starts thinking he's a circus performer and that the curb is a tightrope strung high in the air. And sometimes after a rain he likes to step down off his tightrope right into the gutter and slosh around getting his shoes and cuffs wet. Then I get hit when I get home. Or sometimes if you don't watch him he'll dash across traffic to the island in the middle of Broadway and give the pigeons a fit. Then I have to go behind him apologizing to all the old people sitting around trying to get some sun and getting all upset with the pigeons fluttering around them, scattering their newspapers and upsetting the waxpaper lunches in their laps. So I keep Raymond on the inside of me, and he plays like he's driving a stage coach which is O.K. by me so long as he doesn't run me over or interrupt my breathing exercises, which I have to do on account of I'm serious about my running, and I don't care who knows it.

Now some people like to act like things come easy to them, won't let on that they practice. Not me. I'll high-prance down 34th Street like a rodeo pony to keep my knees strong even if it does get my mother uptight so that she walks ahead like she's not with me, don't know me, is all by herself on a shopping trip, and I am somebody else's crazy child. Now you take Cynthia Procter for instance. She's just

1. Raymond's *big head* may be the result of *hydrocephaly* (hī′ drə sef′ ə lē), a condition in which fluid is trapped around the brain, damaging the brain and enlarging the skull.
2. *Play the dozens* refers to an exchange of insulting remarks.

the opposite. If there's a test tomorrow, she'll say something like, "Oh, I guess I'll play handball this afternoon and watch television tonight," just to let you know she ain't thinking about the test. Or like last week when she won the spelling bee for the millionth time, "A good thing you got 'receive,' Squeaky, cause I would have got it wrong. I completely forgot about the spelling bee." And she'll clutch the lace on her blouse like it was a narrow escape. Oh, brother. But of course when I pass her house on my early morning trots around the block, she is practicing the scales on the piano over and over and over and over. Then in music class she always lets herself get bumped around so she falls accidently on purpose onto the piano stool and is so surprised to find herself sitting there that she decides just for fun to try out the ole keys. And what do you know—Chopin's[3] waltzes just spring out of her fingertips and she's the most surprised thing in the world. A regular prodigy. I could kill people like that. I stay up all night studying the words for the spelling bee. And you can see me any time of day practicing running. I never walk if I can trot, and shame on Raymond if he can't keep up. But of course he does, cause if he hangs back someone's liable to walk up to him and get smart, or take his allowance from him, or ask him where he got that great big pumpkin head. People are so stupid sometimes.

So I'm strolling down Broadway breathing out and breathing in on counts of seven, which is my lucky number, and here comes Gretchen and her sidekicks: Mary Louise, who used to be a friend of mine when she first moved to Harlem from Baltimore and got beat up by everybody till I took up for her on account of her mother and my mother used to sing in the same choir when they were young girls, but people ain't grateful, so now she hangs out with the new girl Gretchen, and talks about me like a dog; and Rosie, who is as fat as I am skinny and has a big mouth where Raymond is concerned and is too stupid to know that there is not a big deal of difference between herself and Raymond and that she can't afford to throw stones.[4] So they are steady coming up Broadway and I see right away that it's going to be one of those Dodge City scenes cause the street ain't that big and they're close to the buildings just as we are. First I think I'll step into the candy store and look over the new comics and let them pass. But that's chicken and I've got a reputation to consider. So then I think I'll just walk straight on through them or even over them if necessary. But as they get to me, they slow down. I'm ready to fight, cause like I said I don't feature a whole lot of chit-chat, I much prefer to just

3. *Chopin* (shō′ pan) was a nineteenth-century Polish composer famous for his beautiful but difficult piano pieces.

4. The narrator is referring to the saying, "People who live in glass houses shouldn't *throw stones.*" It warns people not to criticize others for something that they themselves might also be criticized for.

Vocabulary

prodigy (prod′ ə jē) *n.* an extraordinarily gifted or talented person, especially a child
liable (lī′ ə bəl) *adj.* likely; apt
reputation (rep′ yə tā′ shən) *n.* what people generally think about the character of a person or thing; good name

knock you down right from the jump and save everybody a lotta precious time.

"You signing up for the May Day races?" smiles Mary Louise, only it's not a smile at all. A dumb question like that doesn't deserve an answer. Besides, there's just me and Gretchen standing there really, so no use wasting my breath talking to shadows.

"I don't think you're going to win this time," says Rosie, trying to signify with her hands on her hips all salty,[5] completely forgetting that I have whupped her behind many times for less salt than that.

"I always win cause I'm the best," I say straight at Gretchen who is, as far as I'm concerned, the only one talking in this ventriloquist-dummy routine. Gretchen smiles, but it's not a smile, and I'm thinking that girls never really smile at each other because they don't know how and don't want to know how and there's probably no one to teach us how, cause grown-up girls don't know either. Then they all look at Raymond who has just brought his mule team to a standstill. And they're about to see what trouble they can get into through him.

"What grade you in now, Raymond?"

"You got anything to say to my brother, you say it to me, Mary Louise Williams of Raggedy Town, Baltimore."

"What are you, his mother?" sasses Rosie.

"That's right, Fatso. And the next word out of anybody and I'll be *their* mother too." So they just stand there and Gretchen shifts from one leg to the other and so do they. Then Gretchen puts her hands on her hips and is about to say something with her freckle-face self but doesn't. Then she walks around me looking me up and down but keeps walking up Broadway, and her sidekicks follow her. So me and Raymond smile at each other and he says, "Gidyap" to his team and I continue with my breathing exercises, strolling down Broadway toward the ice man on 145th with not a care in the world cause I am Miss Quicksilver[6] herself.

I take my time getting to the park on May Day because the track meet is the last thing on the program. The biggest thing on the program is the May Pole dancing, which I can do without, thank you, even if my mother thinks it's a shame I don't take part and act like a girl for a change. You'd think my mother'd be grateful not to have to make me a white organdy[7] dress with a big satin sash and buy me new white baby-doll shoes that can't be taken out of the box till the big day. You'd think she'd be glad her daughter ain't out there prancing around a May Pole getting the new clothes all dirty and sweaty and trying to act like a fairy or a flower or whatever you're supposed to be when you should be trying to be yourself, whatever that is, which is, as far as I am concerned, a poor Black girl who really can't afford to buy shoes and a new dress you only wear once a lifetime cause it won't fit next year.

I was once a strawberry in a Hansel and Gretel pageant when I was in nursery school and didn't have no better sense than to dance on tiptoe with my arms in a circle over my head doing umbrella steps and being a perfect fool just so my

5. Here, *signify* is slang for "to stir things up; cause trouble for fun." This is what Rosie is trying to do by being *salty,* or critical and sarcastic.

6. The narrator is comparing herself to Mercury again. Actually, *quicksilver* is another name for the metal mercury, which was named for the swift Roman god. At room temperature, the silver-colored metal is a liquid that flows rapidly.

7. *Organdy* is a lightweight fabric, usually made of cotton.

mother and father could come dressed up and clap. You'd think they'd know better than to encourage that kind of nonsense. I am not a strawberry. I do not dance on my toes. I run. That is what I am all about. So I always come late to the May Day program, just in time to get my number pinned on and lay in the grass till they announce the fifty-yard dash.

I put Raymond in the little swings, which is a tight squeeze this year and will be impossible next year. Then I look around for Mr. Pearson, who pins the numbers on. I'm really looking for Gretchen if you want to know the truth, but she's not around. The park is jam-packed. Parents in hats and corsages and breast-pocket handkerchiefs peeking up. Kids in white dresses and light-blue suits. The parkees[8] unfolding chairs and chasing the rowdy kids from Lenox[9] as if they had no right to be there. The big guys with their caps on backwards, leaning against the fence swirling the basketballs on the tips of their fingers, waiting for all these crazy people to clear out the park so they can play. Most of the kids in my class are carrying bass drums and glockenspiels and flutes. You'd think they'd put in a few bongos or something for real like that.

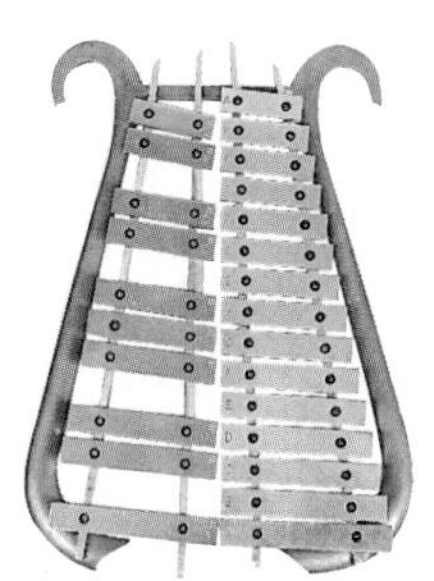

Did You Know?
The *glockenspiel* (glok′ ən spēl′) is a musical instrument that has a series of metal bars mounted in a frame. It is played by striking the bars with two small hammers.

Then here comes Mr. Pearson with his clipboard and his cards and pencils and whistles and safety pins and fifty million other things he's always dropping all over the place with his clumsy self. He sticks out in a crowd because he's on stilts. We used to call him Jack and the Beanstalk to get him mad. But I'm the only one that can outrun him and get away, and I'm too grown for that silliness now.

"Well, Squeaky," he says, checking my name off the list and handing me number seven and two pins. And I'm thinking he's got no right to call me Squeaky, if I can't call him Beanstalk.

"Hazel Elizabeth Deborah Parker," I correct him and tell him to write it down on his board.

"Well, Hazel Elizabeth Deborah Parker, going to give someone else a break this year?" I squint at him real hard to see if he is seriously thinking I should lose the race on purpose just to give someone else a break. "Only six girls running this time," he continues, shaking his head sadly like it's my fault all of New York didn't turn out in sneakers. "That new girl should give you a run for your money." He looks around the park for Gretchen like a periscope in a submarine movie. "Wouldn't it be a nice gesture if you were . . . to ahhh . . ."

I give him such a look he couldn't finish putting that idea into words. Grownups got a lot of nerve sometimes. I pin number seven to myself and stomp away, I'm so burnt. And I go straight for the track and stretch out on the grass while the band winds up with "Oh, the Monkey Wrapped His Tail Around the Flag Pole," which my teacher calls by some other name. The man on the loudspeaker is calling everyone over

8. The city's park employees are the *parkees.*
9. *Lenox* is a street that runs through Harlem.

to the track and I'm on my back looking at the sky, trying to pretend I'm in the country, but I can't, because even grass in the city feels hard as sidewalk, and there's just no pretending you are anywhere but in a "concrete jungle" as my grandfather says.

The twenty-yard dash takes all of two minutes cause most of the little kids don't know no better than to run off the track or run the wrong way or run smack into the fence and fall down and cry. One little kid, though, has got the good sense to run straight for the white ribbon up ahead so he wins. Then the second-graders line up for the thirty-yard dash and I don't even bother to turn my head to watch cause Raphael Perez always wins. He wins before he even begins by psyching[10] the runners, telling them they're going to trip on their shoelaces and fall on their faces or lose their shorts or something, which he doesn't really have to do since he is very fast, almost as fast as I am. After that is the forty-yard dash which I used to run when I was in first grade. Raymond is hollering from the swings cause he knows I'm about to do my thing cause the man on the loudspeaker has just announced the fifty-yard dash, although he might just as well be giving a recipe for angel food cake cause you can hardly make out what he's sayin for the static. I get up and slip off my sweat pants and then I see Gretchen standing at the starting line, kicking her legs out like a pro. Then as I get into place I see that ole Raymond is on line on the other side of the fence, bending down with his fingers on the ground just like he knew what he was doing. I was going to yell at him but then I didn't. It burns up your energy to holler.

Every time, just before I take off in a race, I always feel like I'm in a dream, the kind of dream you have when you're sick with fever and feel all hot and weightless. I dream I'm flying over a sandy beach in the early morning sun, kissing the leaves of the trees as I fly by. And there's always the smell of apples, just like in the country when I was little and used to think I was a choo-choo train, running through the fields of corn and chugging up the hill to the orchard. And all the time I'm dreaming this, I get lighter and lighter until I'm flying over the beach again, getting blown through the sky like a feather that weighs nothing at all. But once I spread my fingers in the dirt and crouch over the Get on Your Mark, the dream goes and I am solid again and am telling myself, Squeaky you must win, you must win, you are the fastest thing in the world, you can even beat your father up Amsterdam if you really try. And then I feel my weight coming back just behind my knees then down to my feet then into the earth and the pistol shot explodes in my blood and I am off and weightless again, flying past the other runners, my arms pumping up and down and the whole world is quiet except for the crunch as I zoom over the gravel in the track. I glance to my left and there is no one. To the right, a blurred Gretchen, who's got her chin jutting out as if it would win the race all by itself. And on the other side of the fence is Raymond with

10. *Psyching* the runners means scaring or intimidating them.

Vocabulary

crouch (krouch) *v.* to stoop or bend, especially with knees bent

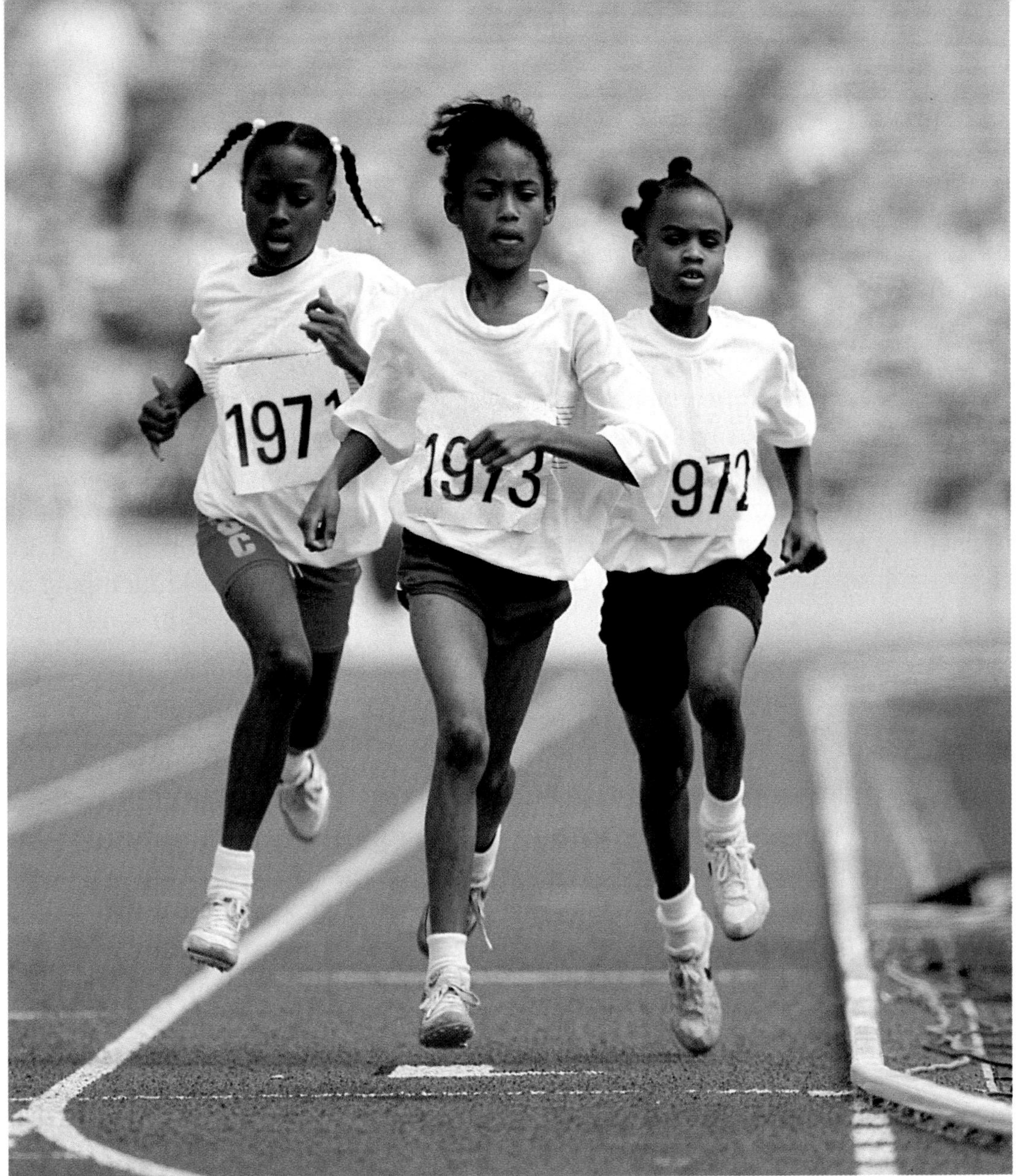

Viewing the photograph: Which runner reminds you of Squeaky? Why?

his arms down to his side and the palms tucked up behind him, running in his very own style, and it's the first time I ever saw that and I almost stop to watch my brother Raymond on his first run. But the white ribbon is bouncing toward me and I tear past it, racing into the distance till my feet with a mind of their own start digging up footfuls of dirt and brake me short. Then all the kids standing on the side pile on me, banging me on the back and slapping my head with their May Day programs, for I have won again and everybody on 151st Street can walk tall for another year.

"In the first place . . ." the man on the loudspeaker is clear as a bell now. But then he pauses and the loudspeaker starts to whine. Then static. And I lean down to catch my breath and here comes Gretchen walking back, for she's overshot the finish line too, huffing and puffing with her hands on her hips taking it slow, breathing in steady time like a real pro and I sort of like her a little for the first time. "In first place . . ." and then three or four voices get all mixed up on the loudspeaker and I dig my sneaker into the grass and stare at Gretchen who's staring back, we both wondering just who did win. I can hear old Beanstalk arguing with the man on the loudspeaker and then a few others running their mouths about what the stopwatches say. Then I hear Raymond yanking at the fence to call me and I wave to shush him, but he keeps rattling the fence like a gorilla in a cage like in them gorilla movies, but then like a dancer or something he starts climbing up nice and easy but very fast. And it occurs to me, watching how smoothly he climbs hand over hand and remembering how he looked running with his arms down to his side and with the wind pulling his mouth back and his teeth showing and all, it occurred to me that Raymond would make a very fine runner. Doesn't he always keep up with me on my trots? And he surely knows how to breathe in counts of seven cause he's always doing it at the dinner table, which drives my brother George up the wall. And I'm smiling to beat the band cause if I've lost this race, or if me and Gretchen tied, or even if I've won, I can always retire as a runner and begin a whole new career as a coach with Raymond as my champion. After all, with a little more study I can beat Cynthia and her phony self at the spelling bee. And if I bugged my mother, I could get piano lessons and become a star. And I have a big rep as the baddest thing around. And I've got a roomful of ribbons and medals and awards. But what has Raymond got to call his own?

So I stand there with my new plans, laughing out loud by this time as Raymond jumps down from the fence and runs over with his teeth showing and his arms down to the side, which no one before him has quite mastered as a running style. And by the time he comes over I'm jumping up and down so glad to see him—my brother Raymond, a great runner in the family tradition. But of course everyone thinks I'm jumping up and down because the men on the loudspeaker have finally gotten themselves together and compared notes and are announcing "In first place—Miss Hazel Elizabeth Deborah Parker." (Dig that.) "In second place—Miss Gretchen P. Lewis." And I look over at Gretchen wondering what the "P" stands for. And I smile. Cause she's good, no doubt about it. Maybe she'd like to help me coach Raymond; she obviously is serious about running, as any fool can see. And she nods to congratulate me and then she smiles. And I smile. We stand there with this big smile of respect between us. It's about as real a smile as girls can do for each other, considering we don't practice real smiling every day, you know, cause maybe we too busy being flowers or fairies or strawberries instead of something honest and worthy of respect . . . you know . . . like being people.

Vocabulary

obviously (ob′ vē əs lē) *adv.* in a way that is easily seen or understood; clearly

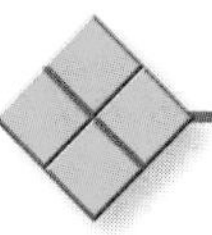

Responding to Literature

PERSONAL RESPONSE

Are you satisfied with the ending to this story? In a short note to a classmate, explain why or why not.

Analyzing Literature

RECALL

1. Why does Raymond need to be looked after?
2. To which girl—Gretchen, Mary Louise, or Rosie—does Squeaky address her remarks?
3. Describe Raymond's behavior while Squeaky runs the race.
4. After Squeaky wins the race, how does her attitude toward Gretchen change?

INTERPRET

5. How does Squeaky appear to feel about her responsibility for Raymond? Explain.
6. What does Squeaky mean by "this ventriloquist-dummy routine"?
7. Why, in your opinion, did the author name the story after Raymond?
8. How does Squeaky's attitude toward running change at the end of the race? Use details from the story to support your answer.

EVALUATE AND CONNECT

9. Bambara uses a **metaphor** to compare two incidents (see page R6). How is meeting Gretchen and her friends "one of those Dodge City scenes"? In your opinion, is this metaphor appropriate for the story? Why or why not?
10. Recalling your thoughts from the **Focus Activity** on page 552, would you have reacted differently than Squeaky did to winning the race? Explain.

LITERARY ELEMENTS

External Conflict

The **conflict** in a story is a struggle between opposing forces. In an **internal conflict,** a character struggles with his or her emotions or convictions. An **external conflict** is present when the problem or struggle is between characters, or between a character and another force, such as an animal or a storm.

1. Describe two examples in which Squeaky faces an external conflict.
2. Would you enjoy this story if there were no external conflicts? Why or why not?

- See **Literary Terms Handbook,** p. R2.

Literature and Writing

Writing About Literature

Understanding Tone The language used by a writer may reveal an attitude toward characters and events. This way of using language is called **tone.** Write a paragraph describing the tone used by the author of "Raymond's Run." Does it seem mocking? respectful? understanding? Tell which words and phrases make the author's attitude clear for you.

Creative Writing

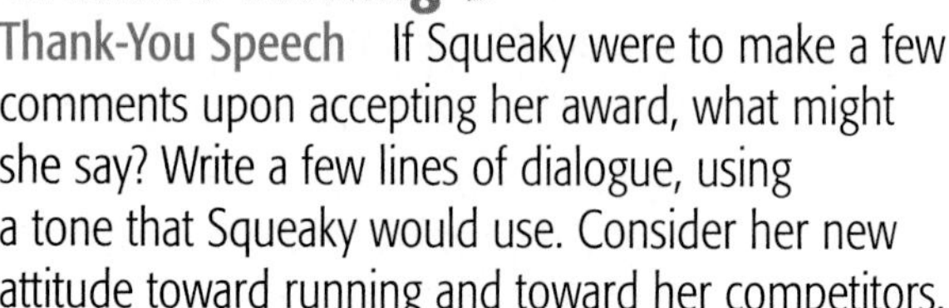

Thank-You Speech If Squeaky were to make a few comments upon accepting her award, what might she say? Write a few lines of dialogue, using a tone that Squeaky would use. Consider her new attitude toward running and toward her competitors.

Extending Your Response

Literature Groups

A New Outlook What does Squeaky come to realize about her abilities and the abilities of others at the end of the story? With your group, discuss these new insights. Consider the following questions: How has Squeaky changed? How will these changes affect her relationships with other people? How will Squeaky's realizations make her a better person?

Listening and Speaking

Interview the Winner Imagine that Squeaky's race has just ended and a TV reporter wants the winner's immediate reaction. With a partner, role-play a sportscaster's interview with Squeaky. Perform your interview live before your class. Use the style and attitude you have observed in this type of interview.

Learning for Life

Promote the Race Imagine that you are an artist designing a poster to advertise an annual race or another major event in your school or community. Examine ads for similar events, and list the elements your poster should include. Finally, create the poster. Consider including a short statement about Squeaky and what her participation will mean for the meet.

Reading Further

For other stories about responsibility, try these books:

Flour Babies by Anne Fine

There's a Girl in My Hammerlock by Jerry Spinelli

Save your work for your portfolio.

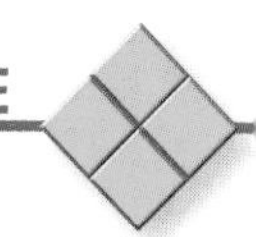

Skill Minilessons

GRAMMAR AND LANGUAGE • TROUBLESOME WORDS

Compound words are often troublesome because they can be written several ways—as open compounds, closed compounds, or hyphenated compounds.

For compound modifiers, like *light-blue* and *first-place,* use a hyphen in the following situations:

1. If the compound modifier comes before the noun.
2. When the first word modifies the second word.
3. If a hyphen is needed to make the meaning clearer.

- For more about troublesome words, see **Language Handbook,** pp. R21–R26.

PRACTICE Rewrite the following sentences correctly. If you wish, use a dictionary.

1. I used to win the (twenty-yard, twentyyard, twenty yard) dash when I was a little kid.
2. Tomorrow I will run the (quarter-meter, quartermeter, quarter meter) relay.
3. Oh, I guess I'll play (hand-ball, handball, hand ball) this afternoon.
4. I accidentally pushed the sheet music off the (piano-stool, pianostool, piano stool).
5. The students are in white dresses and (light-blue, lightblue, light blue) suits.

READING AND THINKING • PREDICTING

If you want to get more involved in a story and improve your reading at the same time, try **predicting** while you read. Predicting means making an educated guess about what's going to happen next. To predict well, you must pay attention to details as you read. If you were predicting while reading "Raymond's Run," you probably foresaw the outcome of the race.

PRACTICE Answer these questions about predicting events in "Raymond's Run."

1. In predicting who would win the race, which details or clues would you use from the story?
2. Why, do you think, might predicting make a reader more involved in a story?
3. Does predicting make the story more interesting for you? Why or why not?

- For more about predicting, see **Reading Handbook,** p. R85.

VOCABULARY • ANALOGIES

An **analogy** is a type of comparison that is based on the relationships between things or ideas. Two kinds of analogies deal with synonyms and antonyms.

Synonyms—rapid : quick :: slippery : slick
Antonyms—spend : save :: respond : ignore

To finish an analogy, decide what relationship exists between the first pair of words and apply it to the second pair of words. For example, if the first pair of words are synonyms, the second pair must be synonyms.

PRACTICE Choose the pair of words that best completes each analogy.

1. crouch : bend ::
   a. stoop : stretch
   b. stumble : fall
   c. fear : frighten
   d. leap : jump
   e. race : win
2. obviously : unclearly ::
   a. well : poorly
   b. slightly : mildly
   c. luckily : fortunately
   d. dimly : slowly
   e. quickly : carelessly

- For more about analogies, see **Communications Skills Handbook,** p. R67.

MEDIA Connection

MAGAZINE ARTICLE

Who are winners in sports events? Who are losers? Joe Henderson knows from personal experience the best answer to these questions.

Fast Finisher

by Joe Henderson—*Runner's World,* October 1996

My daughter Leslie was a slow starter in life. She arrived late, on Labor Day 1982, and was late leaving the hospital because of a blood disorder. In her first six months, Leslie gained only two pounds, then nearly died during heart surgery. Her recovery was complicated by anemia so severe she required several transfusions.

Oh, yes, Leslie also has Down's syndrome and is deaf. She didn't sit up until she was two years old and didn't walk until she was almost four. She'll never talk.

But don't feel sorry for Leslie. She's fourteen and healthy now.

If you picture Down's syndrome kids as slow moving, forget it. If you think of deaf kids as wordless, forget that, too. Neither description fits Leslie.

From the day she stood up and took her first steps, she's been making up for lost time. And for what Leslie lacks in voice, she compensates with sign language.

Leslie Henderson

So, when the opportunity arose, it seemed only natural that Leslie would choose to enter the Special Olympics. We went to a meet this spring.

Leslie lined up, with two other runners, in the eighth heat of the 50 meters. She knew about the starting line and about running in lanes. Some other things, she didn't comprehend so well.

She signed an "8" to me, indicating this was her favorite lane. Fine, but the other two runners were in lanes 1 and 2. This left her all alone on the outside of the track. I had to coax her over to lane 3.

Leslie didn't understand about starts, either. The other two runners took off when signaled. Leslie held her ground. She didn't start after them until they were about ten meters down the track.

Even with the delayed start, Leslie caught one of the others. After finishing, she flopped dramatically onto her back, arms spread wide, eyes closed, tongue hanging out. (She and I like to watch televised track meets together; no doubt she was mimicking the runners she'd seen on TV.)

She knew just what to do on the victory stand. After having the medal draped around her neck, she pumped both arms for ten seconds of triumph.

Respond

1. Why was Leslie's medal such a triumph for her?
2. Why didn't the writer think you should feel sorry for his daughter? Did this surprise you? Why or why not?

Identifying Main Ideas and Supporting Details

Active readers look for the **main idea** in a paragraph. This idea often is stated in a **topic sentence.** Other sentences add **supporting details.** Consider this example from "Raymond's Run."

> I don't have much work to do around the house like some girls. My mother does that. And I don't have to earn my pocket money by hustling; George runs errands for the big boys and sells Christmas cards. And anything else that's got to get done, my father does. All I have to do in life is mind my brother Raymond, which is enough.

Can you find the main idea in the paragraph? It is in the final sentence.

Sometimes, the main idea in a paragraph is implied, not stated in a topic sentence. In this case, reread the supporting details and then state the implied main idea in your own words.

- For more about main ideas and details, see **Reading Handbook,** p. R88.

EXERCISE

Read the following paragraph. What is the main idea? Is it implied or stated directly? List three details that support the main idea.

> Now some people like to act like things come easy to them, won't let on that they practice. Not me. I'll high-prance down 34th Street like a rodeo pony to keep my knees strong even if it does get my mother uptight so that she walks ahead like she's not with me, don't know me, is all by herself on a shopping trip, and I am somebody else's crazy child. Now you take Cynthia Procter for instance. She's just the opposite. If there's a test tomorrow, she'll say something like, "Oh, I guess I'll play handball this afternoon and watch television tonight," just to let you know she ain't thinking about the test.

Before You Read

Forgotten Language and *New World*

MEET SHEL SILVERSTEIN

Shel Silverstein wrote and illustrated witty books of children's poetry, but his quirky take on ordinary things appealed to adults as well. He hoped that a person of any age could pick up one of his books and have "a personal sense of discovery."

Shel Silverstein was born in 1932 and died in 1999. "Forgotten Language" was published in Where the Sidewalk Ends.

MEET N. SCOTT MOMADAY

N. Scott Momaday (mō′ mä dā) is a Pulitzer Prize–winning novelist, as well as a poet, painter, playwright, storyteller, and English professor. He won the Native American Prize for Literature in 1990.

N. Scott Momaday was born in 1934. "New World" was published in The Gourd Dancer.

FOCUS ACTIVITY

Think about something natural that was once important to you but that you haven't thought about lately—the name of something, a dandelion, or a lady bug, for example. Why are things that once were important to you sometimes forgotten?

QuickWrite

Search your memory and list two or three additional things you once treasured.

Setting a Purpose

Read to find out about two lost pleasures.

BACKGROUND

Shel Silverstein and N. Scott Momaday, like all good poets, describe the world in ways that make their readers see it in a new light. For example, when Momaday brings his Kiowa background to a story or poem, he helps readers make connections between themselves and nature. In a different way, Silverstein may ask a question that can be answered only after the reader's understanding has changed.

FORGOTTEN LANGUAGE

Shel Silverstein

Once I spoke the language of the flowers,
Once I understood each word the caterpillar said,
Once I smiled in secret at the gossip of the starlings,
And shared a conversation with the housefly
in my bed.
Once I heard and answered all the questions
of the crickets,
And joined the crying of each falling dying
flake of snow,
Once I spoke the language of the flowers. . . .
How did it go?
How did it go?

NEW WORLD

N. Scott Momaday

1

First Man,
behold:
the earth
glitters
with leaves;
the sky
glistens
with rain.
Pollen
is borne
on winds
that low
and lean
upon
mountains.
Cedars
blacken
the slopes—
and pines.

2

At dawn
eagles
hie° and
hover°
above
the plain
where light
gathers
in pools.
Grasses
shimmer
and shine.
Shadows
withdraw
and lie
away
like smoke.

3

At noon
turtles
enter
slowly
into
the warm
dark loam.°
Bees hold
the swarm.
Meadows
recede
through planes
of heat
and pure
distance.

4

At dusk
the gray
foxes
stiffen
in cold;
blackbirds
are fixed
in the
branches.
Rivers
follow
the moon,
the long
white track
of the
full moon.

---

22 To *hie* is to move quickly.
23 To *hover* is to remain as if suspended in the air over a particular spot.

43 *Loam* is a type of soil.

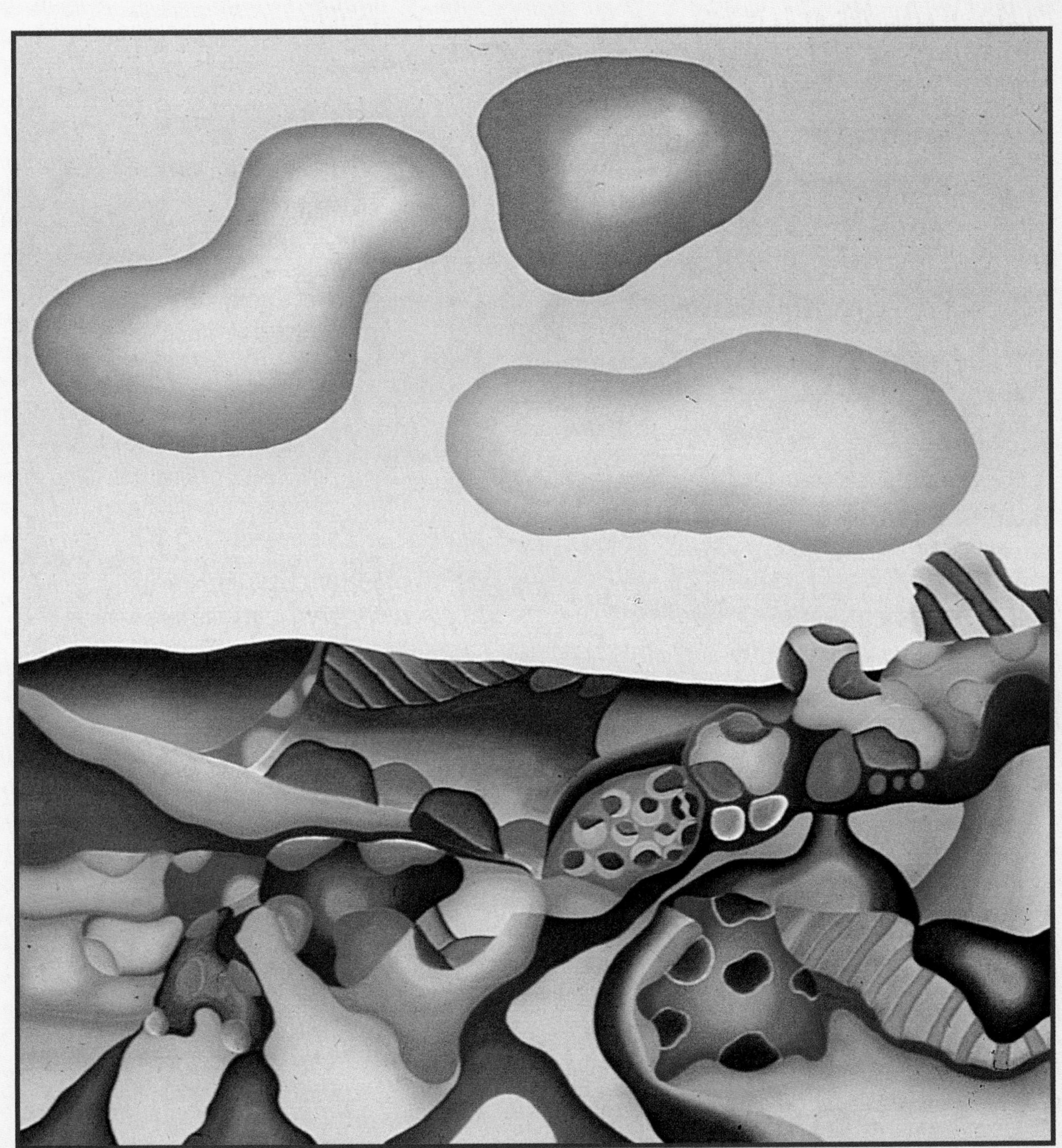

Pink Clouds and Desert, 1970. Linda Lomahaftewa. Oil on canvas, 60 x 60 in. Courtesy of the artist.

Responding to Literature

PERSONAL RESPONSE

What specific words or phrases from these poems remind you to treasure the natural world?

Analyzing Literature

RECALL

1. What does the speaker in "Forgotten Language" say about the ability to speak "the language of the flowers"?
2. In what time period is "New World" set?

INTERPRET

3. Why is Silverstein's poem called "Forgotten Language"?
4. Why, do you think, did Momaday divide his poem into four parts?

EVALUATE AND CONNECT

5. How is the subject matter of the two poems alike? How is it different?
6. Theme Connection How does Momaday's poem offer you an opportunity to develop a new insight into the natural world?
7. In your opinion, which element described in "New World" has changed most over time? Which element, do you think, will change the most in the next hundred years?
8. Which of the poems, in your opinion, refers to experiences common to most people? Explain.
9. Briefly describe your thoughts about one of the poems. Explain how the poem's language creates that response in you.
10. Imagine that you are an artist. Reread one of the poems. What colors would you use in a painting to go with the poem? Name details from the poem that suggest these colors.

LITERARY ELEMENTS

Stanza

A **stanza** is a group of lines arranged together in a poem. The lines may be arranged to show a rhyming pattern or to create the form of a poem. You can recognize stanzas by the spaces that divide them.

1. Look at the form created by the stanzas in "New World." How does this form help strengthen the effect of the poem?
2. Why, do you think, did Silverstein write his poem in one stanza?

● See **Literary Terms Handbook,** p. R9.

Vocal Fabric of the Singer Rosa Silber (Das Vokaltuch der Kammersangerin Rosa Silber), 1922. Paul Klee. Watercolor and plaster on muslin, mounted on cardboard, 24½ x 20½ in. The Museum of Modern Art, New York.

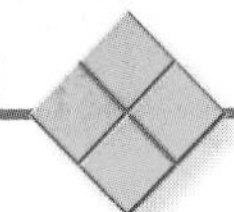

Extending Your Response

Writing About Literature

Nature Images Both poems are about nature and how views of nature may change. Write a paragraph comparing the images of nature that each poet uses. Why do some images appear in both poems? Which images do you think are most effective, and why?

Creative Writing

Natural Reflections Write a short poem that expresses your ideas about nature or something you once treasured. You might write a one-stanza poem that rhymes or a three-stanza poem that doesn't rhyme. Use your notes from the **Focus Activity** on page 566 as a starting place.

Listening and Speaking

Sharing Poems When poetry is read aloud, the reader often adds new meaning with gestures and **inflection**–the change in volume of a person's voice. In a group, take turns reading the poems aloud with expression and inflection, emphasizing the words that you think are important. Then discuss each reader's interpretation.

Literature Groups

Remembering the Earth Momaday, who is half Kiowa, often writes to express his respect and love for the earth, as he does in "New World." What can we learn from this attitude? How could it affect your own everyday thoughts and behavior?

Formal Mask, 1989. N. Scott Momaday.

Reading Further

If you enjoyed these poems about nature, try *In a Sacred Manner I Live* edited by Neil Philip.

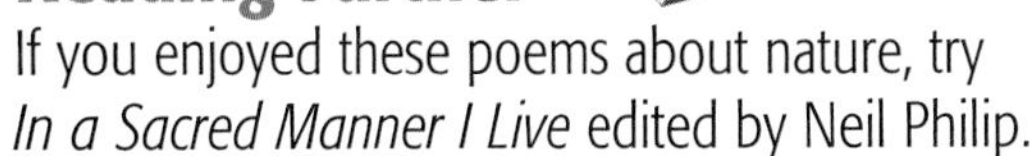

Save your work for your portfolio.

Skill Minilesson

READING AND THINKING • PREVIEWING

A reader may get an idea of a poem's subject and style by previewing the title and first line. What connections might a reader make when reading the title "New World"? What is a "Forgotten Language"?

PRACTICE Think back to when you were previewing the two poems. Try to recall conclusions you drew. Select one of the poems. What were your expectations of the poem based on the title and first line? Explain why you were or were not surprised by what followed.

- For more about previewing, see **Reading Handbook,** p. R84.

Using Adjectives Correctly

When you use an adjective to compare two things, use the **comparative** form of the adjective. Add *-er* to short adjectives and the word *more* to adjectives with at least two syllables.

We live ***longer*** *than our ancestors did. Are we* ***more*** *satisfied with our world?*

To compare more than two things, use the **superlative** form. Add *-est* to short adjectives; add *most* to adjectives with two or more syllables.

Squeaky is the ***fastest*** *thing on two feet. Raymond seems the* ***most awkward.***

Some adjectives are irregular and do not follow these patterns.

Many *teens are on track teams.* ***More*** *teens run for fun.* ***Most*** *teens enjoy sports.*

Problem 1 *Squeaky is a gooder runner than her friend.*
Her friend is the baddest runner in school.

Solution *Good* and *bad* are irregular adjectives. The comparative form of *good* is *better;* the superlative form is *best.* For the adjective *bad,* the comparative form is *worse;* the superlative form is *worst.*

Squeaky is a better runner than her friend who is the worst runner in school.

Problem 2 *Being herself is more importanter than acting like a girl.*

Solution Never use both *-er* and *more* or *-est* and *most.*

Being herself is more important than acting like a girl.

- For more about using adjectives correctly, see **Language Handbook,** p. R17.

EXERCISE

Write the correct comparative or superlative form of the adjective in parentheses.

1. Raymond isn't Squeaky's little brother because he's (old) than she is.
2. Squeaky thinks Mary Louise should be (grateful) to her than she is.
3. Squeaky says she is the (good) runner in the neighborhood.
4. The idea that Gretchen will win is the (ridiculous) thing Squeaky has ever heard.
5. Squeaky is (honest) about needing to practice her skills than Cynthia is.

Before You Read

Thank You in Arabic

MEET NAOMI SHIHAB NYE

Writing has been an insightful experience for Naomi Shihab Nye (nā ō′ mē shi häb nī). In 1992, soon after the Persian Gulf War, she published *This Same Sky: A Collection of Poetry from Around the World*. Nye, an Arab American, hoped to bring the war to a more human level. "So I found some poems by Iraqi poets and had the kids read them and let them see that these people were no different than we were," she said. "They had the same daily needs, the same inner lives."

Naomi Shihab Nye was born in Missouri in 1952. This memoir was first published in Going Where I'm Coming From *in 1995.*

FOCUS ACTIVITY

Imagine a situation in which you can't make people understand you, or you can't understand others.

Discuss

With a group, discuss why such situations can be upsetting.

Setting a Purpose

Read to find out how a teenage girl deals with situations she doesn't fully understand.

BACKGROUND

The Time and Place The author is fourteen years old and is moving to Jerusalem with her family.

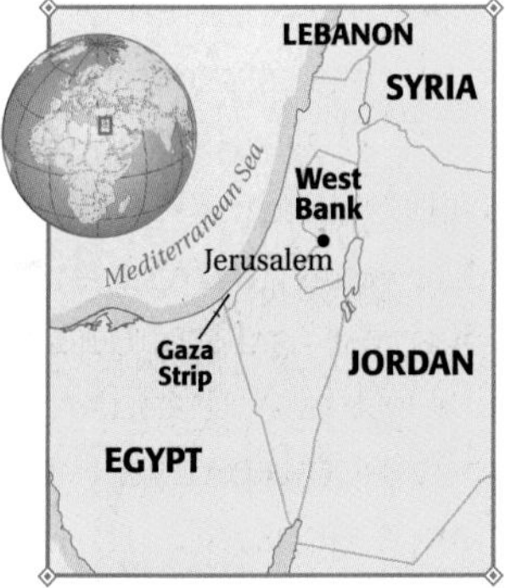

Did You Know? Jerusalem is a sacred city to the religions of Judaism, Christianity, and Islam. For centuries, people of these faiths have disputed borders in the Middle East and especially in Jerusalem. When Israel was established in 1948, Jerusalem was divided into an Israeli section and an Arab section. Since 1967, the city has been united under Israeli rule—a source of conflict between Israel and its Arab neighbors.

VOCABULARY PREVIEW

crevice (krev′ is) *n.* a narrow crack; p. 574
transition (tran zish′ ən) *n.* passage from one position, condition, or activity to another; change; shift; p. 576
insolence (in′ sə ləns) *n.* deliberate rudeness; disrespect; p. 578
valiant (val′ yənt) *adj.* brave; courageous; p. 582
pious (pī′ əs) *adj.* having either genuine or pretended religious devotion; p. 583
skirmish (skur′ mish) *n.* a brief or minor conflict; p. 583
virtue (vur′ cho͞o) *n.* a good quality or admirable trait; p. 584

Thank You in Arabic

Naomi Shihab Nye

Shortly after my mother discovered my brother had been pitching his vitamin C tablets behind the stove for years, we left the country. Her sharp alert, "Now the truth be known!" startled us at the breakfast table as she poked into the dim crevice with the nozzle of her vacuum. We could hear the pills go click, click, up the long tube.

My brother, an obedient child, a bright-eyed, dark-skinned charmer who scored high on all his tests and trilled a boy's sweet soprano, stared down at his oatmeal. Four years younger than I, he was also the youngest and smallest in his class. Somehow he maintained an intelligence and dignity more notable than those of his older, larger companions, and the pills episode was really a pleasant surprise to me.

Companions in mischief are not to be underestimated, especially when everything else in your life is about to change.

We sold everything we had and left the country. The move had been brewing for months. We took a few suitcases each. My mother cried when the piano went. I wished we could have saved it. My brother and I had sung so many classics over its keyboard— "Look for the Silver Lining" and "Angels We Have Heard on High"—that it would have been nice to return to a year later, when we came straggling back. I sold my life-size doll and my toy sewing machine. I begged my mother to save her red stove for me, so I could have it when I grew up—no one else we knew had a red stove. So my mother asked some friends to save it for me in their barn.

Our parents had closed their imported-gifts stores. Our mother ran a little shop in our neighborhood in St. Louis and our father ran a bigger one in a Sheraton Hotel downtown. For years my brother and I had been sitting with them behind the counters after school, guessing if people who walked through the door would buy something or only browse. We curled up with our library books on Moroccan hassocks and Egyptian camel saddles. I loved the stacks of waiting white paper bags as they lay together, and the reams of new tissue. I'd crease the folds as our smooth father in dark suit and daily drench of cologne counted change. Our mother rearranged shelves and penned the perfect tags with calligrapher's ink. My brother and I helped unpack the crates: nested Russian dolls, glossy mother-of-pearl earrings from Bethlehem, a family of sandalwood fans nestled in shredded packaging. Something wonderful was always on its way.

Vocabulary

crevice (krev′ is) *n.* a narrow crack

But there were problems too. Sometimes whole days passed and nobody came in. It seemed so strange to wait for people to give you money for what you had. But that's what stores did everywhere. Then the stockroom filled with pre-Christmas inventory caught on fire and burned up, right when our father was between insurance policies. We could hear our parents in the living room, worrying and debating after we went to bed at night. Finally they had to give the business up. What seemed like such a good idea in the beginning—presents from around the world—turned into the sad sound of a broom sweeping out an empty space.

Our father had also been attending the Unity School for Christianity for a few years, but decided not to become a minister after all. We were relieved, having felt like imposters the whole time he was enrolled. He wasn't even a Christian, to begin with, but a gently nonpracticing Muslim. He didn't do anything like fasting or getting down on his knees five times a day. Our mother had given up the stern glare of her Lutheran ancestors, raising my brother and me in the Vedanta Society of St. Louis. When anyone asked what we were, I said, "Hindu." We had a swami,[1] and sandalwood incense. It was over our heads, but we liked it and didn't feel very attracted to the idea of churches and collection baskets and chatty parish good will.

Now and then, just to keep things balanced, we attended the Unity Sunday School. My teacher said I was lucky my father came from the same place Jesus came from. It was a passport to notoriety. She invited me to bring artifacts for Show and Tell. I wrapped a red and white *keffiyah* around my friend Jimmy's curly blond head while the girls in lacy socks giggled behind their hands. I told about my father coming to America from Palestine on the boat and throwing his old country clothes overboard before docking at Ellis Island.[2] I felt relieved he'd kept a few things, like the *keffiyah* and its black braided band. Secretly it made me mad to have lost the blue pants from Jericho with the wide cuffs he told us about.

Did You Know?
A *keffiyah* (usually spelled *kaffiyah*) is a type of Arab headdress consisting of folded cloth and a cord.

1. *Vedanta* is a branch of Hinduism, one of the major religions of India. A *swami* is a Hindu religious teacher.

2. *Notoriety* usually refers to being known for something bad, but the author uses it to mean simply "fame." *Artifacts* are objects, such as pots, used in the daily life of an ancient civilization. *Ellis Island,* near New York City, was the main U.S. immigration reception center from 1892 to 1943.

I liked standing in front of the group, talking about my father's homeland. Stories felt like elastic bands that could stretch and stretch. Big fans purred inside their metal shells. I held up a string of olivewood camels. I didn't tell our teacher about the Vedanta Society. We were growing up ecumenical,[3] though I wouldn't know that word till a long time later in college. One night I heard my father say to my mother in the next room, "Do you think they'll be confused when they grow up?" and knew he was talking about us. My mother, bless her, knew we wouldn't be. She said, "At least we're giving them a choice." I didn't know then that more clearly than all the stories of Jesus, I'd remember the way our Hindu swami said a single word three times, "*Shantih, shantih, shantih*"—peace, peace, peace.

Our father was an excellent speaker—he stood behind pulpits and podiums easily, delivering gracious lectures on "The Holy Land" and "The Palestinian Question." He was much in demand during the Christmas season. I think that's how he had fallen into the ministerial swoon.[4] While he spoke, my brother and I moved toward the backs of gathering halls, hovering over and eyeing the tables of canapes and tiny tarts, slipping a few into our mouths or pockets.

What next? Our lives were entering a new chapter, but I didn't know its title yet.

We had never met our Palestinian grandmother, Sitti Khadra, or seen Jerusalem, where our father had grown up, or followed the rocky, narrow alleyways of the Via Dolorosa,[5] or eaten an olive in its own neighborhood. Our mother hadn't either. The Arabic customs we knew had been filtered through the fine net of folktales. We did not speak Arabic, though the lilt of the language was familiar to us—our father's endearments,[6] his musical blessings before meals. But that language had never lived in our mouths.

And that's where we were going, to Jerusalem. We shipped our car, a wide golden Impala, over on a boat. We would meet up with it later.

The first plane flight of my whole life was the night flight out of New York City across the ocean. I was fourteen years old. Every glittering light in every skyscraper looked like a period at the end of the sentence. Good-bye, our lives.

We stopped in Portugal for a few weeks. We were making a gradual transition. We stopped in Spain and Italy and Egypt, where the pyramids shocked me by sitting right on the edge of the giant city of Cairo, not way out in the desert as I had imagined them. While we waited for our baggage to clear customs, I stared at six tall African men in brilliantly patterned dashikis negotiating

Did You Know?
The *dashiki* is a loose, brightly colored African garment.

3. The writer uses *ecumenical* to mean that she was exposed to several different religions.
4. The *ministerial swoon* refers to the narrator's father falling in love with the idea of becoming a minister.
5. The *Via Dolorosa* (vē′ ə dō′ lə rō′ sə), or "Way of Sorrow," is the route by which Jesus was led to his execution.
6. *Endearments* are expressions of affection.

Vocabulary
transition (tran zish′ ən) *n.* passage from one position, condition, or activity to another; change; shift

with an Egyptian customs agent[7] and realized I did not even know how to say "thank you" in Arabic. How was this possible? The most elemental[8] and important of human phrases in my father's own tongue had evaded me till now. I tugged on his sleeve, but he was busy with visas and passports.[9] "Daddy," I said. "Daddy, I have to know. Daddy, tell me. Daddy, why didn't we ever *learn*?" An African man adjusted his turban. Always thereafter, the word *shookrun*, so simple, with a little roll in the middle, would conjure up[10] the vast African baggage, the brown boxes looped and looped in African twine.

We stayed one or two nights at the old Shepheard's Hotel downtown but couldn't sleep due to the heat and honking traffic beneath our windows. So our father moved us to the famous Mena House Hotel next to the pyramids. We rode camels for the first time, and our mother received a dozen blood-red roses at her hotel room from a rug vendor who apparently liked her pale brown ponytail. The belly dancer at the hotel restaurant twined a gauzy pink scarf around my brother's astonished ten-year-old head as he tapped his knee in time to her music.

Back in our rooms, we laughed until we fell asleep. Later that night, my brother and I both awakened burning with fever and deeply nauseated, though nobody ever threw up. We were so sick that a doctor hung a Quarantine sign in Arabic and English on our hotel room door the next day. Did he know something we didn't know? I kept waiting to hear that we had malaria or typhoid, but no dramatic disease was ever mentioned. We lay in bed for a week. The aged doctor tripped over my suitcase every time he entered to take our temperatures. We smothered our laughter. "*Shookrun*," I would say. But as soon as he left, to my brother, "I feel bad. How do you feel?"

"I feel really, really bad."

"I think I'm dying."

"I think I'm already dead."

At night we heard the sound and lights show from the pyramids drifting across the desert air to our windows. We felt our lives stretching out across a thousand miles. The pharaohs stomped noisily through my head and churning belly. We had eaten spaghetti in the restaurant. I would not be able to eat spaghetti again for years.

Finally, finally, we appeared in the restaurant, thin and weakly smiling, and ordered the famous Mena House *shorraba*, lentil[11] soup, as my brother nervously scanned the room for the belly dancer. Maybe she wouldn't recognize him now.

In those days Jerusalem, which was then a divided city, had an operating airport on the Jordanian side. My brother and I remember flying in upside down, or in a plane dramatically tipped, but it may have been the effect of our medicine. The land reminded us of a dropped canvas, graceful brown hillocks and green patches. Small and provincial,[12] the airport had just two runways, and the first thing I observed as we climbed down slowly from the stuffy plane was all my underwear strewn across

7. A government's *customs agent* inspects imported goods and collects taxes on them.
8. Here, the writer uses *elemental* to mean "basic."
9. Her father's language had escaped her. A *visa* is written permission for a traveler to enter a country, whereas a *passport* identifies the traveler as a citizen of the country that issued it.
10. *Shookrun* is Arabic for "thank you." To *conjure up* something is to call it to mind.
11. The *lentil* is a vegetable related to peas.
12. A *provincial* airport is a local one used for short flights within a region.

one of them. There were my flowered cotton briefs and my pink panties and my slightly embarrassing raggedy ones and my extra training bra, alive and visible in the breeze. Somehow my suitcase had popped open in the hold and dropped its contents the minute the men pried open the cargo door. So the first thing I did on the home soil of my father was re-collect my underwear, down on my knees, the posture of prayer over that ancient holy land.

Our relatives came to see us at a hotel. Our grandmother was very short. She wore a long, thickly embroidered Palestinian dress, had a musical, high-pitched voice and a low, guttural[13] laugh. She kept touching our heads and faces as if she couldn't believe we were there. I had not yet fallen in love with her. Sometimes you don't fall in love with people immediately, even if they're your own grandmother. Everyone seemed to think we were all too thin.

We moved into a second-story flat in a stone house eight miles north of the city, among fields and white stones and wandering sheep. My brother was enrolled in the Friends Girls School and I was enrolled in the Friends Boys School in the town of Ramallah a few miles farther north—it all was a little confused. But the Girls School offered grades one through eight in English and high school continued at the Boys School. Most local girls went to Arabic-speaking schools after eighth grade.

I was a freshman, one of seven girl students among two hundred boys, which would cause me problems a month later. I was called in from the schoolyard at lunchtime, to the office of our counselor who wore shoes so pointed and tight her feet bulged out pinkly on top.

"You will not be talking to them anymore," she said. She rapped on the desk with a pencil for emphasis.

"To whom?"

"All the boy students at this institution. It is inappropriate behavior. From now on, you will speak only with the girls."

"But there are only six other girls! And I like only one of them!" My friend was Anna, from Italy, whose father ran a small factory that made matches. I'd visited it once with her. It felt risky to walk the aisles among a million filled matchboxes. Later we visited the factory that made olive oil soaps and stacked them in giant pyramids to dry.

"No, thank you," I said. "It's ridiculous to say that girls should only talk to girls. Did I say anything bad to a boy? Did anyone say anything bad to me? They're my friends. They're like my brothers. I won't do it, that's all."

The counselor conferred with the headmaster and they called a taxi. I was sent home with a little paper requesting that I transfer to a different school. The charge: insolence. My mother, startled to see me home early and on my own, stared out the window when I told her.

My brother came home from his school as usual, full of whistling and notebooks. "Did anyone tell you not to talk to girls?" I asked him. He looked at me as if I'd gone goofy. He was too young to know

13. A *guttural* laugh would have a rough, harsh sound.

Vocabulary

insolence (in′ sə ləns) *n.* deliberate rudeness; disrespect the troubles of the world. He couldn't even imagine them.

"You know what I've been thinking about?" he said. "A piece of cake. That puffy white layered cake with icing like they have at birthday parties in the United States. Wouldn't that taste good right now?" Our mother said she was thinking about mayonnaise. You couldn't get it in Jerusalem. She'd tried to make it and it didn't work. I felt too gloomy to talk about food.

My brother said, "Let's go let Abu Miriam's chickens out." That's what we always did when we felt sad. We let our fussy landlord's red-and-white chickens loose to flap around the yard happily, puffing their wings. Even when Abu Miriam shouted and waggled his cane and his wife waved a dishtowel, we knew the chickens were thanking us.

My father went with me to the St. Tarkmanchatz Armenian[14] School, a solemnly ancient stone school tucked deep into the Armenian Quarter of the Old City of Jerusalem. It was another world in there. He had already called the school officials on the telephone and

14. *Armenia* is a small country east of Turkey. In the late 1800s and early 1900s, Armenians fled Turkish rule, and some settled in Jerusalem.

Old City, Jerusalem.
Viewing the photograph: What facts about Jerusalem does this photograph present?

tried to enroll me, though they didn't want to. Their school was for Armenian students only, kindergarten through twelfth grade. Classes were taught in three languages: Armenian, Arabic and English, which was why I needed to go there. Although most Arab students at other schools were learning English, I needed a school where classes were actually taught in English—otherwise I would have been staring out the windows triple the usual amount.

I felt I had left my old life entirely.

The head priest wore a long robe and a tall cone-shaped hat. He said, "Excuse me, please, but your daughter, she is not an Armenian, even a small amount?"

"Not at all," said my father. "But in case you didn't know, there is a stipulation[15] in the educational code books of this city that says no student may be rejected solely on the basis of ethnic background, and if you don't accept her, we will alert the proper authorities."

They took me. But the principal wasn't happy about it. The students, however, seemed glad to have a new face to look at. Everyone's name ended in *-ian*, the beautiful, musical Armenian ending—Boghossian, Minassian, Kevorkian, Rostomian. My new classmates started calling me Shihabian. We wore uniforms, navy blue pleated skirts for the girls, white shirts, and navy sweaters. I waited during the lessons for the English to come around, as if it were a channel on television. While other students were on the other channels, I scribbled poems in the margins of my pages, read library books, and wrote a lot of letters filled with exclamation points. All the other students knew all three languages with three entirely different alphabets. How could they carry so much in their heads? I felt humbled by my ignorance. One day I felt so frustrated in our physics class—still another language—that I pitched my book out the open window. The professor made me go collect it. All the pages had let loose at the seams and were flapping free into the gutters along with the white wrappers of sandwiches.

Every week the girls had a hands-and-fingernails check. We had to keep our nails clean and trim, and couldn't wear any rings. Some of my new friends would invite me home for lunch with them, since we had an hour-and-a-half break and I lived too far to go to my own house.

Their houses were a thousand years old, clustered bee-hive-fashion behind ancient walls, stacked and curled and tilting and dark, filled with pictures of unsmiling relatives and small white cloths dangling crocheted edges. We ate spinach pies and white cheese. We dipped our bread in olive oil, as the Arabs did. We ate small sesame cakes, our mouths full of crumbles. They taught me to say "I love you" in Armenian, which sounded like *yes-kay-see-goo-see-rem*. I felt I had left my old life entirely.

Every afternoon I went down to the basement of the school where the kindergarten class was having an Arabic lesson.

15. A *stipulation* is a condition or restriction.

Their desks were pint-sized, their full white smocks tied around their necks. I stuffed my fourteen-year-old self in beside them. They had rosy cheeks and shy smiles. They must have thought I was a very slow learner.

More than any of the lessons, I remember the way the teacher rapped the backs of their hands with his ruler when they made a mistake. Their little faces puffed up with quiet tears. This pained me so terribly I forgot all my words. When it was my turn to go to the blackboard and write in Arabic, my hand shook. The kindergarten students whispered hints to me from the front row, but I couldn't understand them. We learned horribly useless phrases: "Please hand me the bellows for my fire." I wanted words simple as tools, simple as *food* and *yesterday* and *dreams*. The teacher never rapped my hand, especially after I wrote a letter to the city newspaper, which my father edited, protesting such harsh treatment of young learners. I wish I had known how to talk to those little ones, but they were just beginning their English studies and didn't speak much yet. They were at the same place in their English that I was in my Arabic.

From the high windows of St. Tarkmanchatz, we could look out over the Old City, the roofs and flapping laundry and television antennas, the pilgrims and churches and mosques, the olivewood prayer beads and fragrant *falafel*[16] lunch stands, the intricate interweaving of cultures and prayers and songs and holidays.

We saw the barbed wire separating Jordan from Israel then, the bleak, uninhabited strip of no-man's land reminding me how little education saved us after all. People who had differing ideas still came to blows, imagining fighting could solve things. Staring out over the quiet roofs of afternoon, I thought it so foolish. I asked my friends what they thought about it and they shrugged.

"It doesn't matter what we think about it. It just keeps happening. It happened in Armenia too, you know. Really, really bad in Armenia. And who talks about it in the world news now? It happens everywhere. It happens in *your* country one by one, yes? Murders and guns. What can we do?"

Sometimes after school, my brother and I walked up the road that led past the crowded refugee camp of Palestinians who owned even less than our modest relatives did in the village. The little kids were stacking stones in empty tin cans and shaking them. We waved our hands and they covered their mouths and laughed. We wore our beat-up American tennis shoes and our old sweatshirts and talked about everything we wanted to do and everywhere else we wished we could go.

"I want to go back to Egypt," my brother said. "I sort of feel like I missed it. Spending all that time in bed instead of exploring—what a waste."

"I want to go to Greece," I said. "I want to play a violin in a symphony orchestra in Austria." We made up things. I wanted to go back to the United States most of all. Suddenly I felt like a patriotic citizen. One of my friends, Sylvie Markarian, had just been shipped off to Damascus, Syria, to marry a man who was fifty years old, a widower. Sylvie was exactly my age—we

16. The most ancient section of Jerusalem is called the *Old City.* The *pilgrims* are travelers of all faiths who come to visit, or worship at, the city's holy places. *Mosques* are Muslim places of worship, and *falafel* is an Arab food consisting of ground, spiced vegetables shaped into balls and fried.

had turned fifteen two days apart. She had never met her future husband before. I thought this was the most revolting thing I had ever heard of. "Tell your parents no thank you," I urged her. "Tell them you *refuse*."

Sylvie's eyes were liquid, swirling brown. I could not see clearly to the bottom of them.

"You don't understand," she told me. "In United States you say no. We don't say no. We have to follow someone's wishes. This is the wish of my father. Me, I am scared. I never slept away from my mother before. But I have no choice. I am going because they tell me to go." She was sobbing, sobbing on my shoulder. And I was stroking her long, soft hair. After that, I carried two fists inside, one for Sylvie and one for me.

Most weekends my family went to the village to sit with the relatives. We sat and sat and sat. We sat in big rooms and little rooms, in circles, on chairs or on woven mats or brightly covered mattresses piled on the floor. People came in and out to greet my family. Sometimes even donkeys and chickens came in and out. We were like movie stars or dignitaries. They never seemed to get tired of us.

My father translated the more interesting tidbits of conversation, the funny stories my grandmother told. She talked about angels and food and money and people and politics and gossip and old memories from my father's childhood, before he emigrated away from her. She wanted to make sure we were going to stick around forever, which made me feel very nervous. We ate from mountains of rice and eggplant on large silver trays—they gave us little plates of our own since it was not our custom to eat from the same plate as other people. We ripped the giant wheels of bread into triangles. Shepherds passed through town with their flocks of sheep and goats, their long canes and cloaks, straight out of the Bible. My brother and I trailed them to the edge of the village, past the lentil fields to the green meadows studded with stones, while the shepherds pretended we weren't there. I think they liked to be alone, unnoticed. The sheep had differently colored dyed bottoms, so shepherds could tell their flocks apart.

During these long, slow, smoke-stained weekends—the men still smoked cigarettes a lot in those days, and the old *taboon*, my family's mounded bread-oven, puffed billowy clouds outside the door—my crying jags began. I cried without any warning, even in the middle of a meal. My crying was usually noiseless but dramatically wet—streams of tears pouring down my cheeks, onto my collar or the back of my hand.

Everything grew quiet.

Someone always asked in Arabic, "What is wrong? Are you sick? Do you wish to lie down?"

My father made valiant excuses in the beginning. "She's overtired," he said. "She has a headache. She is missing her friend who moved to Syria. She is homesick just now."

My brother stared at me as if I had just landed from Planet X.

Vocabulary

valiant (val′ yənt) *adj.* brave; courageous

Worst of all was our drive to school every morning, when our car came over the rise in the highway and all Jerusalem lay sprawled before us in its golden, stony splendor pockmarked with olive trees and automobiles. Even the air above the city had a thick, religious texture, as if it were a shining brocade[17] filled with broody incense. I cried hardest then. All those hours tied up in school lay just ahead. My father pulled over and talked to me. He sighed. He kept his hands on the steering wheel even when the car was stopped and said, "Someday, I promise you, you will look back on this period in your life and have no idea what made you so unhappy here."

"I want to go home." It became my anthem. "This place depresses me. It weighs too much. I hate all these old stones that everybody keeps kissing. I'm sick of pilgrims. They act so pious and pure. And I hate the way people stare at me here." Already I'd been involved in two street skirmishes with boys who stared a little too hard and long. I'd socked one in the jaw and he socked me back. I hit the other one straight in the face with my purse.

"You could be happy here if you tried just a little harder," my father said. "Don't compare it to the United States all the time. Don't pretend the United States is perfect. And look at your brother—he's not having any problems!"

"My brother is eleven years old."

I had crossed the boundary from uncomplicated childhood when happiness was a good ball and a hoard[18] of candy-coated Jordan almonds.

One problem was that I had fallen in love with four different boys who all played in the same band. Two of them were even twins. I never quite described it to my parents, but I wrote reams and reams of notes about it on loose-leaf paper that I kept under my sweaters in my closet.

Such new energy made me feel reckless. I gave things away. I gave away my necklace and a whole box of shortbread cookies that my mother had been saving. I gave my extra shoes away to the gypsies. One night when the gypsies camped in a field down the road from our house, I thought about their mounds of white goat cheese lined up on skins in front of their tents, and the wild *oud*[19] music they played deep into the black belly of the night, and I wanted to go sit around their fire. Maybe they could use some shoes.

I packed a sack of old loafers that I rarely wore and walked with my family down the road. The gypsy mothers stared into my shoes curiously. They took them into their tent. Maybe they would use them as vases or drawers. We sat with small glasses of hot, sweet tea until a girl bellowed from deep in her throat, threw back her head, and began dancing. A long bow thrummed across the strings. The girl circled the fire, tapping and clicking, trilling a long musical wail from deep in her throat. My brother looked

17. *Brocade* is a heavy cloth woven with raised designs.

18. A *hoard* is a quantity of something stored up for future use.

19. The *oud* (o͞od) is a stringed instrument of southwest Asia and northern Africa.

Vocabulary

pious (pī′ əs) *adj.* having either genuine or pretended religious devotion

skirmish (skur′ mish) *n.* a brief or minor conflict

nervous. He was remembering the belly dancer in Egypt, and her scarf. I felt invisible. I was pretending to be a gypsy. My father stared at me. Didn't I recognize the exquisite oddity of my own life when I sat right in the middle of it? Didn't I feel lucky to be here? Well, yes I did. But sometimes it was hard to be lucky.

In the barbed-wire no-man's land visible from the windows of our house, guns cracked loudly in the middle of the night.

When we left Jerusalem, we left quickly. Left our beds in our rooms and our car in the driveway. Left in a plane, not sure where we were going. The rumbles of fighting with Israel had been growing louder and louder. In the barbed-wire no-man's land visible from the windows of our house, guns cracked loudly in the middle of the night. We lived right near the edge. My father heard disturbing rumors at the newspaper that would soon grow into the infamous Six Day War[20] of 1967. We were in England by then, drinking tea from thin china cups and scanning the newspapers. Bombs were blowing up in Jerusalem. We worried about the village. We worried about my grandmother's dreams, which had been getting worse and worse, she'd told us. We worried about the house we'd left, and the chickens, and the children at the refugee camp. But there was nothing we could do except keep talking about it all.

My parents didn't want to go back to Missouri because they'd already said goodbye to everyone there. They thought we might try a different part of the country. They weighed the virtues of different states. Texas was big and warm. After a chilly year crowded around the small gas heaters we used in Jerusalem, a warm place sounded appealing. In roomy Texas, my parents bought the first house they looked at. My father walked into the city newspaper and said, "Any jobs open around here?"

I burst out crying when I entered a grocery store—so many different kinds of bread.

A letter on thin blue airmail paper reached me months later, written by my classmate, the bass player in my favorite Jerusalem band. "Since you left," he said, "your empty desk reminds me of a snake ready to strike. I am afraid to look at it. I hope you are having a better time than we are."

Of course I was, and I wasn't. *Home* had grown different forever. *Home* had doubled. Back *home* again in my own country, it seemed impossible to forget the place we had just left: the piercing call of the *muezzin*[21] from the mosque at

20. *Infamous* means "having a reputation for evil or criminal acts." The *Six Day War* between Israel and the Arab countries of Egypt, Syria, and Jordan resulted in Israel expanding its boundaries and taking control of Jerusalem.

21. The *muezzin* (mōō′ zən), or crier, calls the time for Muslims to pray five times daily.

Vocabulary

virtue (vur′ chōō) *n.* a good quality or admirable trait

Untitled. Illustration by Nancy Carpenter. From *Sitta's Secret.*
Viewing the painting: Imagine this meeting. What may be happening?

prayer time, the dusky green tint of the olive groves, the sharp, cold air that smelled as deep and old as my grandmother's white sheets flapping from the line on her roof. What story hadn't she finished?

Our father used to tell us that when he was little, the sky over Jerusalem crackled with meteors and shooting stars almost every night. They streaked and flashed, igniting the dark. Some had long golden tails. For a few seconds, you could see their whole swooping trail lit up. Our father and his brothers slept on the roof to watch the sky. "There were so many of them, we didn't even call out every time we saw one."

During our year in Jerusalem, my brother and I kept our eyes cast upwards whenever we were outside at night, but the stars were different since our father was a boy. Now the sky seemed too orderly, stuck in place. The stars had learned where they belonged. Only people on the ground kept changing.

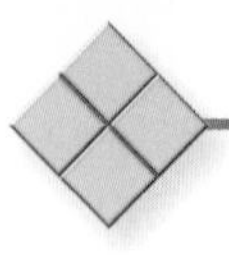

Responding to Literature

PERSONAL RESPONSE

Which incidents or images from this selection stay in your mind? Jot them down in your journal and tell why they affected you.

Analyzing Literature

RECALL

1. Why do the Shihabs close their business and move to Jerusalem?
2. How do you say *thank you* in Arabic?
3. What does the barbed wire separating Jordan from Israel make young Naomi think about?
4. What reason does Naomi give for her brother's not being homesick?

INTERPRET

5. In your opinion, how does the narrator feel about her parents' decision to move?
6. Why is Naomi upset about not being able to say *thank you* in Arabic?
7. How does Naomi feel about the prospect of her father's people going to war with Israel?
8. Why, in your opinion, does Naomi cry so much while she is in Jerusalem?

EVALUATE AND CONNECT

9. Theme Connection What insight does Naomi gain from her experience in Jerusalem?
10. In your opinion, how might Naomi's year in Jerusalem have affected her life after she returned to the United States? Explain.

LITERARY ELEMENTS

Setting

The time and place in which the events of a story occur are its **setting.** In "Thank You in Arabic," Nye uses sensory images to portray her home near Jerusalem. For example, on the drive to school, "all Jerusalem lay sprawled before us in its golden, stony splendor pockmarked with olive trees and automobiles. Even the air above the city had a thick, religious texture, as if it were a shining brocade filled with broody incense."

1. Why is the time an important element in the setting of this selection?
2. In your opinion, which place was most important in the narrator's life? How did the writer show this? Explain your choice.

• See **Literary Terms Handbook,** p. R9.

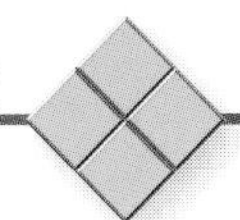

Literature and Writing

Personal Writing

Your Own Awakening Think back to your discussion from the **Focus Activity** on page 573. What situation have you experienced that led to some sort of an awakening, or flash of insight? It might be a new way of understanding your family or geographic heritage. In a few paragraphs, describe the experience, including your thoughts and reactions.

Writing About Literature

Close Characters In this memoir, Naomi Shihab Nye describes her childhood experiences in her father's homeland. What do you learn about the relationship between Naomi and her father from this memoir? Look at descriptions of Naomi and her father, as well as their actions and dialogue. Write a brief analysis of her changing relationship with her father.

Extending Your Response

Literature Groups

Friendly Advice When Naomi's friend Sylvie learns that her parents want her to marry a man she has never met, Naomi urges her to refuse. What would you advise Sylvie to do? What would you do if you were in her position? Discuss possible solutions to Sylvie's situation.

Interdisciplinary Activity

Social Studies With a partner, research the history of the Middle East since 1948 (when the present state of Israel was founded). Draw maps of the changing borders at four points in time: 1949, 1968, 1991, and the present.

Learning for Life

Rules of Conduct Naomi gets into trouble in the Friends Boys School because she talks to the boys. What are some of the rules of your school or group of friends–written rules or generally accepted ways to behave–that someone from another place might not know? Write a list of these rules so that a newcomer might fit in. Discuss with the class how the newcomer might view your rules.

Reading Further

To discover places important to other people, read

Madeleine L'Engle's Time Quartet by Madeleine L'Engle

Dandelion Wine by Ray Bradbury

Save your work for your portfolio.

Skill Minilessons

GRAMMAR AND LANGUAGE • PUNCTUATION IN COMPOUND SENTENCES

Follow these rules when punctuating compound sentences.

- When the clauses of a compound sentence are joined by a conjunction, use a comma before the conjunction.
- When there is no conjunction joining two clauses of a compound sentence, use a semicolon before, and a comma after, the conjunctive adverb that joins the clauses. Some common conjunctive adverbs are *therefore, however, then, nevertheless, consequently,* and *besides.*

For more about punctuation in a compound sentence, see **Language Handbook,** p. R12.

PRACTICE Punctuate the following sentences.

1. We worried about the children at the refugee camp however there was nothing we could do except keep talking about it.
2. I wish I had known how to talk to those little ones but they were just beginning their English studies and didn't speak much yet.
3. They took me however, the principal wasn't happy about it.
4. Our father had also been attending the Unity School for Christianity for a few years but he decided not to become a minister after all.
5. Something wonderful was always on its way but there were problems too.

READING AND THINKING • PROBLEM AND SOLUTION

Most stories revolve around a main character facing a **problem** and attempting to find a **solution** for the problem. During Naomi's year-long stay in Jerusalem, she faces many problems, from finding a suitable school to dealing with what she considers harsh treatment of students.

PRACTICE Reread the memoir to see how Nye has organized the text using problems and solutions. Create a chart showing several examples.

For more about problems and solutions, see **Reading Handbook,** pp. R96–R97.

VOCABULARY • CONNOTATION

When you want to create a mood or influence your readers' attitude, you can sometimes use words in a way that adds to their meaning. This added meaning is the word's **connotation.** For example, Nye uses three descriptive synonyms–*bulge, puff,* and *stuff.* Nye uses the words in contexts that give them connotations that influence the reader's attitude or mood.

PRACTICE Tell if each underlined word has no connotation, a pleasant connotation, or an unpleasant connotation.

1. I was called in from the schoolyard at lunchtime, to the office of our counselor who wore shoes so pointed and tight her feet <u>bulged</u> out pinkly on top.
2. That <u>puffy</u> white layered cake with icing like they have at birthday parties in the United States.
3. We let our fussy landlord's red-and-white chickens loose to flap around the yard happily, <u>puffing</u> their wings.
4. Their little faces <u>puffed</u> up with quiet tears.
5. I <u>stuffed</u> my fourteen-year-old self in beside them.

For more about connotation, see **Reading Handbook,** p. R83.

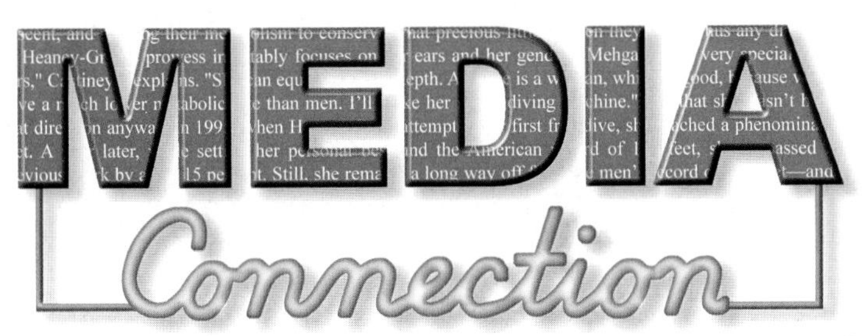

OPINION POLL

Who are more concerned about the environment–teens or their parents? A poll offers some insights.

EarthView Poll Highlights

In March 1998, a thousand teenagers and a thousand "baby boomers" (adults then forty to fifty-five years old) took part in a national poll about the environment. Below are some highlights of the survey, sponsored by the National 4-H Council and Honda.

Future of the Environment

1. Boomers and teens agree that we are running out of time to save the world's environment from permanent damage.
   - Teens: 77%
   - Boomers: 67%

Sources of Environmental Damage

2. Greatest barriers to improving environmental conditions in the United States:
   - "Lack of individual concern": teens: 45%, boomers: 32%
   - Corporations: teens: 20%, boomers: 32%
   - Government leaders: teens: 19%, boomers: 22%

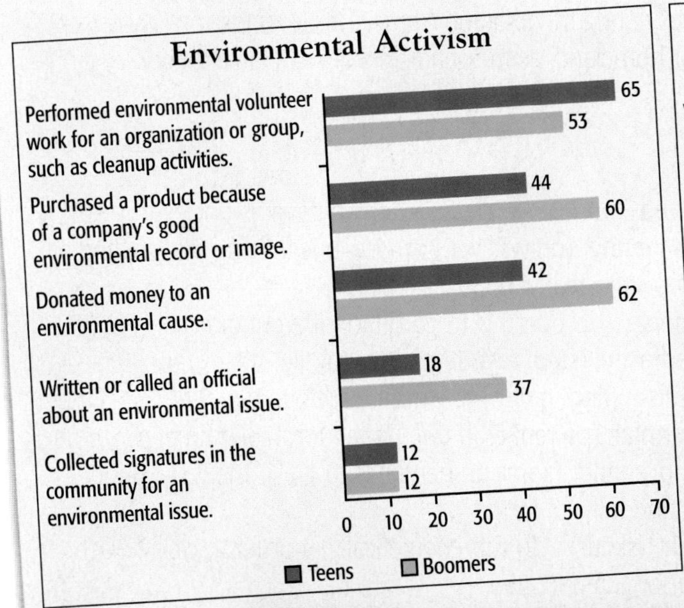

Steps Willing to Take to Improve the Environment

Step	Group	Very Willing	Willing	Total
Walk, use a bike, car pool, or use public transportation when possible instead of a car.	Teens	28	60	88
	Boomers	22	58	80
Pay an extra fifty cents when purchasing a CD or cassette tape to fund a plastic recycling program.	Teens	21	66	87
	Boomers	19	58	77
Limit the number and length of showers you take to conserve energy and water.	Teens	13	67	80
	Boomers	17	62	79
Cut back on your use of the TV, radio, stereo, or home computer by one hour per day to conserve electricity.	Teens	13	65	78
	Boomers	21	58	79

0 20 40 60 80 100

■ Very Willing □ Willing

Respond

1. With a group, summarize the information on each graph. What do these graphs tell you about the concerns of teens and parents for the environment?
2. What programs or ideas to protect the environment do you think are most effective?

Before You Read

"If I Forget Thee, Oh Earth . . ."

MEET
ARTHUR C. CLARKE

Arthur C. Clarke has been a fan of futuristic fiction since he was twelve years old. "Science fiction is virtually the only kind of writing that's dealing with real problems and possibilities; it's a concerned fiction," Clarke says. He was a successful author when he moved to Sri Lanka in 1956 to set up an underwater exploration business. Clarke is a native of England who has written more than fifty books, including *2001: A Space Odyssey*.

Arthur C. Clarke was born in 1917. He wrote "If I Forget Thee, Oh Earth . . ." in 1950.

FOCUS ACTIVITY

Where do you think the human race will be in 500 years?

Freewrite
Take a few moments to write your prediction of life in the distant future.

Setting a Purpose
Read to discover the connection between a distant past and a fictional future.

BACKGROUND

The Time and Place The story takes place somewhere in our solar system in the distant future.

Did You Know? The title of this story is taken from the Book of Psalms in the Bible. The original psalm begins "If I forget thee, O Jerusalem" and was sung by the Jewish captives in Egypt during the pharaohs' time. The Jews felt torn away from their homeland, as the characters are in Clarke's story.

VOCABULARY PREVIEW

purged (purjd) *adj.* cleansed of whatever is unclean; p. 591
unwavering (un wā′ vər ing) *adj.* unchanging; not shifting or moving; steady; p. 592
disperse (dis purs′) *v.* to go off in different directions; p. 592
steadfastly (sted′ fast′ lē) *adv.* faithfully; steadily; p. 593
anguish (ang′ gwish) *n.* extreme suffering; p. 594
perennial (pə ren′ ē əl) *adj.* lasting for a long time; p. 595
comprehend (kom′ pri hend′) *v.* to grasp mentally; understand fully; p. 595
scour (skour) *v.* to rub energetically in order to clean, wash, or brighten; p. 595
insight (in′ sīt) *n.* an understanding of the inner character or hidden nature of something; p. 595

"IF I FORGET THEE, OH EARTH..."

Arthur C. Clarke

When Marvin was ten years old, his father took him through the long, echoing corridors that led up through Administration and Power, until at last they came to the uppermost levels of all and were among the swiftly growing vegetation of the Farmlands. Marvin liked it here: it was fun watching the great, slender plants creeping with almost visible eagerness toward the sunlight as it filtered down through the plastic domes to meet them. The smell of life was everywhere, awakening inexpressible longings in his heart: no longer was he breathing the dry, cool air of the residential levels, purged of all smells but the faint tang of ozone.[1] He wished he could stay here for a little while, but Father would not let him. They went onward until they had reached the entrance to the Observatory, which he had never visited: but they did not stop, and Marvin knew with a sense of rising excitement that there could be only one goal left. For the first time in his life, he was going Outside.

1. *Ozone* is a gas that has a sharp odor and is sometimes used as a disinfectant. Ozone is present in the earth's atmosphere.

Vocabulary

purged (purjd) *adj.* cleansed of whatever is unclean

There were a dozen of the surface vehicles, with their wide balloon tires and pressurized cabins, in the great servicing chamber. His father must have been expected, for they were led at once to the little scout car waiting by the huge circular door of the airlock. Tense with expectancy, Marvin settled himself down in the cramped cabin while his father started the motor and checked the controls. The inner door of the lock slid open and then closed behind them: he heard the roar of the great air pumps fade slowly away as the pressure dropped to zero. Then the "Vacuum" sign flashed on, the outer door parted, and before Marvin lay the land which he had never yet entered.

He had seen it in photographs, of course: he had watched it imaged on television screens a hundred times. But now it was lying all around him, burning beneath the fierce sun that crawled so slowly across the jet-black sky. He stared into the west, away from the blinding splendor of the sun—and there were the stars, as he had been told but had never quite believed. He gazed at them for a long time, marveling that anything could be so bright and yet so tiny. They were intense unscintillating[2] points, and suddenly he remembered a rhyme he had once read in one of his father's books:

Twinkle, twinkle, little star,
How I wonder what you are.

Well, *he* knew what the stars were. Whoever asked that question must have been very stupid. And what did they mean by "twinkle"? You could see at a glance that all the stars shone with the same steady, unwavering light. He abandoned the puzzle and turned his attention to the landscape around him.

They were racing across a level plain at almost a hundred miles an hour, the great balloon tires sending up little spurts of dust behind them. There was no sign of the Colony: in the few minutes while he had been gazing at the stars, its domes and radio towers had fallen below the horizon. Yet there were other indications of man's presence, for about a mile ahead Marvin could see the curiously shaped structures clustering round the head of a mine. Now and then a puff of vapor would emerge from a squat smokestack and would instantly disperse.

They were past the mine in a moment: Father was driving with a reckless and exhilarating[3] skill as if—it was a strange thought to come into a child's mind—he were trying to escape from something. In a few minutes they had reached the edge of the plateau on which the Colony had been built. The ground fell sharply away beneath them in a dizzying slope whose lower stretches were lost in shadow. Ahead, as far as the eye could reach, was a jumbled wasteland of craters, mountain ranges, and ravines. The crests of the mountains, catching the low sun, burned like islands

2. Stars seem to be twinkling, *scintillating* (sint′ əl ā′ ting), when seen through Earth's atmosphere. These stars are *unscintillating;* they do not twinkle.

3. Father drives with skill, but the recklessness makes the ride exciting, or *exhilarating* (ig zil′ ə rāt ing).

Vocabulary

unwavering (un wā′ vər ing) *adj.* unchanging; not shifting or moving; steady
disperse (dis purs′) *v.* to go off in different directions

of fire in a sea of darkness: and above them the stars still shone as steadfastly as ever.

There could be no way forward—yet there was. Marvin clenched his fists as the car edged over the slope and started the long descent. Then he saw the barely visible track leading down the mountain-side, and relaxed a little. Other men, it seemed, had gone this way before.

Night fell with a shocking abruptness as they crossed the shadow line and the sun dropped below the crest of the plateau. The twin searchlights sprang into life, casting blue-white bands on the rocks ahead, so that there was scarcely need to check their speed. For hours they drove through valleys and past the foot of mountains whose peaks seemed to comb the stars, and sometimes they emerged for a moment into the sunlight as they climbed over higher ground.

And now on the right was a wrinkled, dusty plain, and on the left, its ramparts and terraces[4] rising mile after mile into the sky, was a wall of mountains that marched into the distance until its peaks sank from sight below the rim of the world. There was no sign that men had ever explored this land, but once they passed the skeleton of a crashed rocket, and beside it a stone cairn surmounted[5] by a metal cross.

It seemed to Marvin that the mountains stretched on forever: but at last, many hours later, the range ended in a towering, precipitous[6] headland that rose steeply from a cluster of little hills. They drove down into a shallow valley that curved in a great arc toward the far side of the mountains: and as they did so, Marvin slowly realized that something very strange was happening in the land ahead.

The sun was now low behind the hills on the right: the valley before them should be in total darkness. Yet it was awash with a cold white radiance that came spilling over the crags beneath which they were driving. Then, suddenly, they were out in the open plain, and the source of the light lay before them in all its glory.

It was very quiet in the little cabin now that the motors had stopped. The only sound was the faint whisper of the oxygen

6. *Precipitous* means "very steep."

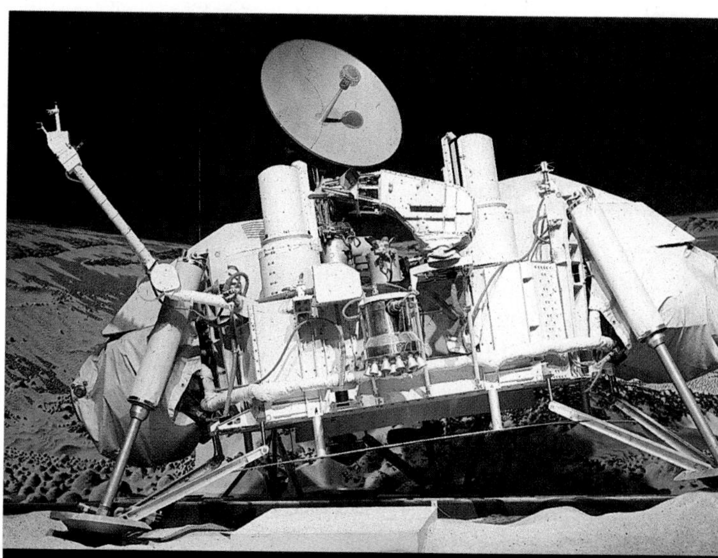

NASA photograph of the moon.

Viewing the photograph: In what ways is this vehicle like the one Marvin and his father travel in? In what ways is it different?

4. Here, the *ramparts* are high, steep banks or cliffs, and *terraces* are level strips of land.
5. A *cairn* is a mound of stones piled up as a memorial. This one is topped, or *surmounted,* with a cross.

Vocabulary

steadfastly (sted′ fast′ lē) *adv.* faithfully; steadily feed and an occasional metallic crepitation[7] as the outer walls of the vehicle radiated away their heat. For no warmth at all came from the great silver crescent that floated low above the far horizon and flooded all this land with pearly light. It was so brilliant that minutes passed before Marvin could accept its challenge and look steadfastly into its glare, but at last he could discern the outlines of continents, the hazy border of the atmosphere, and the white islands of cloud. And even at this distance, he could see the glitter of sunlight on the polar ice.

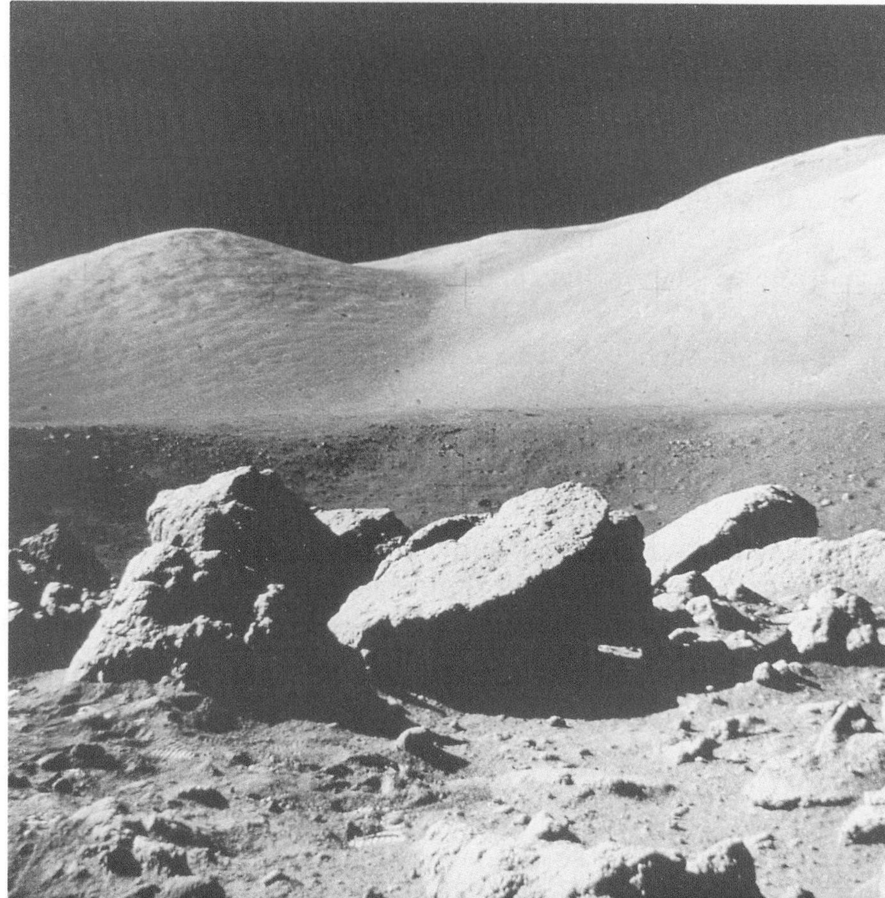

The moon.
Viewing the photograph: What scientific statement does the photo make?

It was beautiful, and it called to his heart across the abyss of space. There in that shining crescent were all the wonders that he had never known—the hues of sunset skies, the moaning of the sea on pebbled shores, the patter of falling rain, the unhurried benison[8] of snow. These and a thousand others should have been his rightful heritage, but he knew them only from the books and ancient records, and the thought filled him with the anguish of exile.

Why could they not return? It seemed so peaceful beneath those lines of marching cloud. Then Marvin, his eyes no longer blinded by the glare, saw that the portion of the disk that should have been in darkness was gleaming faintly with an evil phosphorescence: and he remembered. He was looking upon the funeral pyre of a world—upon the radioactive aftermath of Armageddon.[9] Across a quarter of a million miles of space, the glow of dying

7. A series of repeated crackles, rattles, or similar sounds is called *crepitation.*
8. *Benison* means "a blessing."

9. The *phosphorescence* (fos′ fə res′ əns) is a glow; a *pyre* (pīr) is a pile of wood used for burning a dead body; and *Armageddon* (är′ mə ged′ ən), here, refers to nuclear war. A Bible prophecy connects Armageddon, a place in Israel, with the world's great and final battle between good and evil.

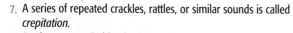

Vocabulary
anguish (ang′ gwish) *n.* extreme suffering

atoms was still visible, a perennial reminder of the ruinous past. It would be centuries yet before that deadly glow died from the rocks and life could return again to fill that silent, empty world.

And now Father began to speak, telling Marvin the story which until this moment had meant no more to him than the fairy tales he had once been told. There were many things he could not understand: it was impossible for him to picture the glowing, multicolored pattern of life on the planet he had never seen. Nor could he comprehend the forces that had destroyed it in the end, leaving the Colony, preserved by its isolation, as the sole survivor. Yet he could share the agony of those final days, when the Colony had learned at last that never again would the supply ships come flaming down through the stars with gifts from home. One by one the radio stations had ceased to call: on the shadowed globe the lights of the cities had dimmed and died, and they were alone at last, as no men had ever been alone before, carrying in their hands the future of the race.

Then had followed the years of despair, and the long-drawn battle for survival in this fierce and hostile world. That battle had been won, though barely: this little oasis of life was safe against the worst that Nature could do. But unless there was a goal, a future toward which it could work, the Colony would lose the will to live, and neither machines nor skill nor science could save it then.

So, at last, Marvin understood the purpose of this pilgrimage. He would never walk beside the rivers of that lost and legendary world, or listen to the thunder raging above its softly rounded hills. Yet one day—how far ahead?—his children's children would return to claim their heritage. The winds and the rains would scour the poisons from the burning lands and carry them to the sea, and in the depths of the sea they would waste their venom[10] until they could harm no living things. Then the great ships that were still waiting here on the silent, dusty plains could lift once more into space, along the road that led to home.

That was the dream: and one day, Marvin knew with a sudden flash of insight, he would pass it on to his own son, here at this same spot with the mountains behind him and the silver light from the sky streaming into his face.

He did not look back as they began the homeward journey. He could not bear to see the cold glory of the crescent Earth fade from the rocks around him, as he went to rejoin his people in their long exile.

10. *Venom* is the poison released by some animals, but here the word refers to deadly, radioactive pollution.

Vocabulary

perennial (pə ren′ ē əl) *adj.* lasting for a long time
comprehend (kom′ pri hend′) *v.* to grasp mentally; understand fully
scour (skour) *v.* to rub energetically in order to clean, wash, or brighten
insight (in′ sīt) *n.* an understanding of the inner character or hidden nature of something

Responding to Literature

PERSONAL RESPONSE

Do you think Clarke's story is hopeful or discouraging about the future? How does his prediction compare with your own from the **Focus Activity** on page 590? Explain.

Analyzing Literature

RECALL AND INTERPRET

1. Describe the vehicle that Marvin's father uses. How does this description help you to understand the setting of the story?
2. When the vehicle stops, what does Marvin see "low above the far horizon"? Why, in your opinion, has it "called to his heart across the abyss of space"?
3. What does Marvin see that prevents him from visiting the disk? What is the name of this disk, and what, do you think, is the reason for what he sees?

EVALUATE AND CONNECT

4. How does the author's description of technology affect your understanding of the story? Give examples. Do you think this effect is intentional?
5. What message might Clarke be sending to readers? What things are happening on our planet today that may have inspired him to write this story?
6. Who else would you like to have read this selection? Explain.

LITERARY ELEMENTS

Science Fiction

Science fiction is a type of literature in which the events and situations are scientifically possible. Critics debate the difference between science fiction and **fantasy.** Some say science fiction must follow the laws of science, while fantasy may contain unexplainable events. Others lump the two together and call the literature **speculative fiction.**

1. How does the author use facts as he describes life in the Colony? List three examples.
2. If this story were fantasy, how might the description of the Colony change? If you could break the laws of science, how would you change the ending?

- See **Literary Terms Handbook,** p. R9.

Extending Your Response

Literature Groups

Images from Earth Focus on Clarke's descriptions of Earth. What ideas or impressions do these images give you? How might they change your thinking about Earth? Discuss how these images add to your understanding of the story.

Listening and Speaking

Politics of the Future Should residents spend resources to improve life in the Colony or prepare for a return to Earth? Write and deliver a speech to persuade others to agree with your position.

COMPARING SELECTIONS

Thank You in Arabic and "If I Forget Thee, Oh Earth . . ."

COMPARE SETTINGS

Tire tracks on the moon.

Both Naomi and Marvin find themselves in settings that awaken them to the meaning of the word "home." Arthur C. Clarke and Naomi Shihab Nye use precise details to show these settings. Reread descriptions of the Colony and of Jerusalem. Briefly explain which of the two places is most real to you, and give examples from the story to support your choice.

COMPARE SITUATIONS

Naomi journeys to a foreign land, learns about herself and others, and returns home. Marvin journeys to a barren landscape and experiences a new feeling about the place that should have been his home. Think of some experiences of exile or homecoming that you know about personally or have learned about.

1. List these situations, noting the details.
2. Describe one of these situations to a small group.
3. Answer any questions the group may have.
4. Practice telling the story again and then share it with the class.

COMPARE ATTITUDES

Both of these stories raise questions about war. Naomi Shihab Nye expresses her opinions on the fighting in the Middle East, but the results of war are only implied in Arthur C. Clarke's story. Make a Venn diagram comparing and contrasting how the stories treat war.

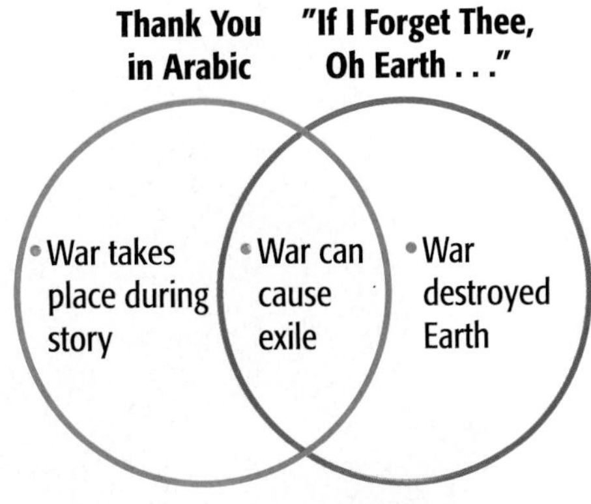

Before You Read

I like to see it lap the miles* and *Southbound on the Freeway

MEET EMILY DICKINSON

Emily Dickinson did well in school, went to parties, and was considered clever, but she eventually withdrew from the world around her. As a writer, she is known for her passion and wit. "If I read a book and it makes my whole body so cold that no fire can ever warm me, I know *that* is poetry," she said.

Emily Dickinson lived from 1830 to 1886.

MEET MAY SWENSON

May Swenson worked as a journalist, secretary, and editor, but above all she was a poet. She said that her poetry came from "a craving to get through the curtains of things as they *appear*, to things as they *are*, and then into the larger, wilder space of things as they *are becoming*."

May Swenson was born in 1913 and died in 1989.

FOCUS ACTIVITY

Are people and machines alike in any way? How are they different?

Diagram It!

Use a Venn diagram to show your answers to the questions above. Include ideas about action, appearance, and function.

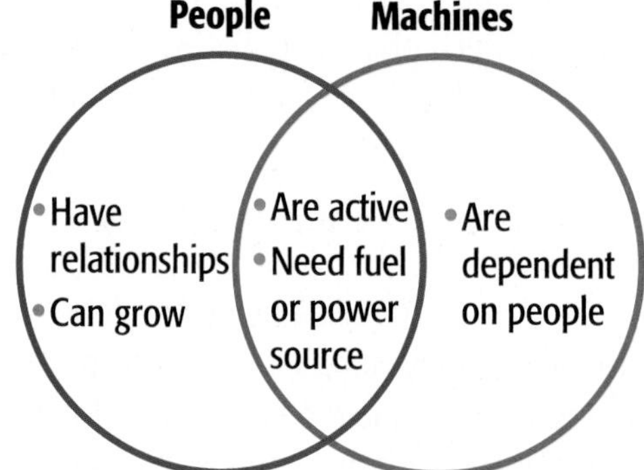

Setting a Purpose

Read to discover the unusual ways in which two poets look at certain objects.

BACKGROUND

Emily Dickinson wrote "I like to see it lap the miles" in response to seeing a steam locomotive for the first time. Steam-powered trains were introduced in 1830 and earned the nickname "iron horses" because they replaced horse-drawn cars.

I like to see it lap the miles

Emily Dickinson

I like to see it lap the miles,
And lick the valleys up,
And stop to feed itself at tanks;
And then, prodigious,° step

Around a pile of mountains,
And, supercilious,° peer
In shanties° by the sides of roads;
And then a quarry° pare°

To fit its sides, and crawl between,
Complaining all the while
In horrid, hooting stanza;°
Then chase itself down hill

And neigh like Boanerges;°
Then, punctual as a star,
Stop—docile and omnipotent°—
At its own stable door.

4 *Prodigious,* here, means "enormous."
6 *Supercilious* means "having excessive pride or scorn."
7 *Shanties* are crude huts or cabins.
8 A *quarry* is a pit from which stone is cut or blasted. To *pare* is to shave off the outer layer.
11 A *stanza* is a group of lines; this poem has four stanzas.
13 In the Bible, Jesus calls two of his followers *Boanerges,* or "sons of thunder," because of their fiery tempers.
15 *Omnipotent* means "having unlimited power."

Through to the Pacific, 1870. Currier and Ives. 12 x 15¼ in. Museum of the City of New York.

Southbound on

May Swenson

A tourist came in from Orbitville,
parked in the air, and said:

The creatures of this star
are made of metal and glass.

Through the transparent parts
you can see their guts.

Their feet are round and roll
on diagrams or long

measuring tapes, dark
with white lines.

They have four eyes.
The two in the back are red.

Sometimes you can see a five-eyed
one, with a red eye turning

on the top of his head.
He must be special—

the others respect him
and go slow

when he passes, winding
among them from behind.

They all hiss as they glide,
like inches, down the marked

tapes. Those soft shapes,
shadowy inside

the hard bodies—are they
their guts or their brains?

the Freeway

Landscape in Forward Motion, 1989. Stephen Fox. Oil on linen, 42 x 58 in. O.K. Harris Works of Art, New York.

Responding to Literature

PERSONAL RESPONSE

Describe your reactions to the poems. Did you find them humorous? strange? both?

Analyzing Literature

RECALL

1. What settings are identified in Emily Dickinson's poem?
2. Where does the tourist in May Swenson's poem come from?

INTERPRET

3. What two things are compared in Dickinson's poem? How do you know?
4. What is the tourist in "Southbound on the Freeway" looking at? Who are "the creatures of this star"? How do you know?

EVALUATE AND CONNECT

5. How might Dickinson write about a car? How might Swenson describe a train? Think of details and examples each poet might use.
6. In "Southbound on the Freeway," Swenson uses **free verse.** The sentences have the rhythm of everyday speech. Why, in your opinion, might she have chosen free verse?
7. In your opinion, how accurate is the tourist in describing the creatures? Consider your response to the **Focus Activity** on page 598 as you answer this question.
8. Why, in your opinion, is the title of each poem appropriate–or inappropriate?
9. Which poem, in your opinion, made the most intriguing comparison? Why do you think so?
10. **Theme Connection** Which poem do you think is most likely to give readers a flash of insight–a new understanding of a common object? Explain.

LITERARY ELEMENTS

Metaphor

A **metaphor** is a comparison that doesn't use the words *like* or *as.* The two things being compared are usually not similar. For example, a train and an animal are different, but the poet sees some similarities between them. Since the comparison in Dickinson's poem is used throughout the entire poem, it is an **extended metaphor.**

1. What characteristics of a train might be noted in a comparison with an animal?
2. What is the metaphor in Swenson's poem? What other metaphor might be used to describe the creatures on the highway?

• See **Literary Terms Handbook,** p. R6.

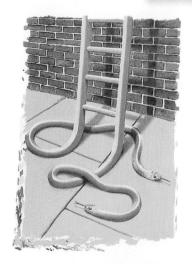

Ladder to Success, 1994. John Holcroft. Oil on canvas, 420 x 295 mm. Private collection.

Extending Your Response

Writing About Literature

Making Metaphors May Swenson's tourist sees strange creatures rolling along a measuring tape. Imagine you are one of the "soft shapes" inside the creatures. What do you see when you view the tourist from Orbitville parked in the air? Write a brief description in which you use a metaphor to compare the tourist with something familiar.

Creative Writing

Interview With a partner, present an interview for a local TV station. The subject of your interview can be a visitor from Orbitville or an artist who illustrates books about transportation. Assign the roles of reporter and interviewee. Be prepared with thoughtful questions and answers that give insights into the future of transportation.

Literature Groups

Guts or Brains? The speaker of "Southbound on the Freeway" asks if the soft bodies are "their guts or their brains." Discuss this question among yourselves. List reasons why the bodies might be the guts. Then list reasons why they might be the brains. Present your group's ideas to the class.

Art Activity

Visual Metaphors Create a drawing or collage using images that work like metaphors; for example, a train with hooves and a tail, or a row of cars with eyes and mouths. Create a display of class images.

Reading Further

If you enjoyed these poems, you might want to try the following collections:

The Complete Poems to Solve by May Swenson

I Wouldn't Thank You for a Valentine: Poems for Young Feminists by Carol Ann Duffy

Save your work for your portfolio.

Skill Minilesson

GRAMMAR AND LANGUAGE • SENTENCE PATTERNS

Poets often use unusual sentence patterns. Dickinson separates the adjective *prodigious* from the pronoun it modifies:

I like to see it lap the miles . . .
And then, prodigious, *step*
Around a pile of mountains

• For more about sentences, see **Language Handbook,** pp. R32–R33.

Swenson places the adjective *dark* after the noun it modifies:

Their feet are round and roll
on diagrams or long
measuring tapes, dark
with white lines.

PRACTICE Write two sentences imitating each of the patterns shown above.

Interdisciplinary Connection

The Vietnam War

It was a war that pitted U.S. soldiers against a Communist army called the Vietcong. It was a country little known to the Americans who went to battle on beaches, in jungles, and in rice paddies. It was the longest war the United States ever fought—and the only one it never won. It was the Vietnam War.

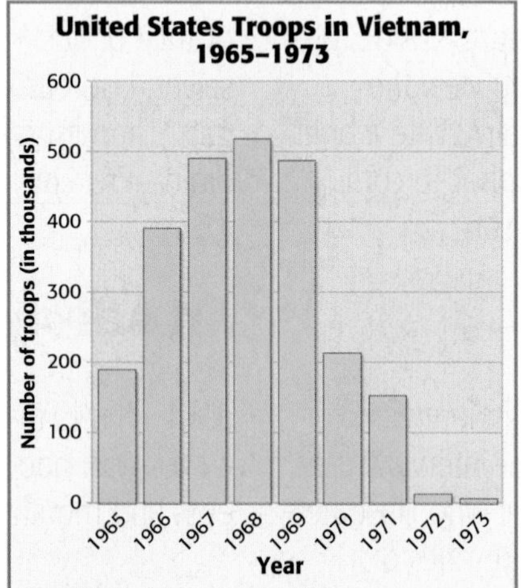

In the 1950s the Vietcong of North Vietnam attempted to invade South Vietnam and create a Communist country. The United States came to the aid of South Vietnam, sending more than 2.5 million U.S. military personnel from the mid-1950s until 1975.

As American soldiers marched with heavy equipment through thick, dark jungles, they knew one wrong step could set off a Vietcong land mine. The relentless enemy attacks and the constant heat, rain, and insects left the U.S. soldiers miserable. They struggled to cope with discomfort, illness, fear, and the deaths that took place every day, including massacres of Vietnamese civilians.

When the United States withdrew from Vietnam in 1975, some 58,000 Americans had been declared killed or missing. More than 300,000 others had been injured.

The war never had complete public support in the United States. As a result, returning soldiers felt that few understood what it had been like to serve in Vietnam. The war left many Vietnam veterans at odds with themselves and with their country.

"... all of a sudden, you're back on this airplane, with ... people who are laughing and happy—and you're coming out of this freaky atmosphere, and you land back in the United States of America. And nobody cares, and nobody wants you to be in uniform. You get in a taxi and off you go! You try to go home."

—*John Kerry, U.S. senator from Massachusetts who served in Vietnam in the U.S. Navy*

ACTIVITIES

1. What is life like for the people of Vietnam today? How has the United States recognized its citizens who served in the war? Research answers to one or more questions you have about Vietnam. Prepare a brief report.
2. Study the chart showing the number of troops sent to Vietnam each year. What story does the chart tell? Write a paragraph describing the information and any patterns you see in the chart.

Vo•cab•u•lar•y *Skills*

Using Idioms

A word or phrase that has a meaning other than its literal meaning is an **idiom.** Saying that a *dog* is tied up in the backyard probably means that the dog is literally tied up. But saying that a *person* is tied up in the backyard probably means that the person is busy there. Some idioms, such as "Get off my back," and "Cut it out!" are familiar. Unfamiliar idioms, however, can cause confusion.

- One way to figure out the meaning of an unfamiliar idiom is to think about what the ordinary meanings of the words suggest.

  Naomi and her brother attended a talk by a swami about the use of incense. The talk was over their heads, but they liked it.

  If something were literally over their heads, it would be above them and, therefore, hard to reach. In this case, the talk was beyond the reach of their understanding. The idiom means "beyond their understanding."

- Context clues are also useful in dealing with unfamiliar idioms.

  Although she is famous today, Emily Dickinson chose to live a private life, and published little of her poetry. As a result, Dickinson never saw her star rise.

  Context clues suggest that being private and publishing few poems kept Dickinson from "seeing her star rise." They contrast her current fame with her situation during her lifetime. These clues suggest that when a person's "star rises," he or she is becoming famous.

● For more about idioms, see **Reading Handbook,** p. R81.

EXERCISE

Use the ordinary meanings of the underlined words and context clues to figure out the meaning of each underlined idiom. Then write a short definition of the idiom.

1. There was nothing stale or ordinary about Emily Dickinson's poetry. Her work broke new ground with originality and skill.
2. For most of her life, she refused to leave her home to go shopping or to attend social gatherings, choosing to remain out of the mainstream.
3. She withdrew from social relationships. On the other hand, she wrote letters constantly to her friends.
4. Dickinson buried herself in her work, completing hundreds of brilliant poems before her death at the age of fifty-six.

Before You Read

Stop the Sun

MEET GARY PAULSEN

Gary Paulsen, an award-winning author of survival stories, has an unlikely hero: a librarian. "There's nothing that has happened to me that would have happened if she hadn't got me to read," he says. That's quite a statement from a former dog sledder who ran his dogs in the Iditarod race, rode a motorcycle to Alaska, and ate raw turtle eggs as research for a book. Paulsen writes and reads from 5:30 A.M. until he goes to bed at midnight. "You really have to be able to read to learn things," he says. "You try to learn to grow to be more."

Gary Paulsen was born in 1939. "Stop the Sun" was first published in Boy's Life *in 1986.*

FOCUS ACTIVITY

When might someone your age have trouble communicating with a family member?

List It!

With a partner, make a list of problems that can cause poor communication among family members. Next to each problem, list your advice for trying to solve each problem.

Setting a Purpose

Read to find out what happens when a teenage boy digs into his father's battle-scarred past.

BACKGROUND

The Time and Place

This story takes place in an American city sometime in the 1980s.

Did You Know?

From 1965 to 1973, U.S. troops fought alongside the South Vietnamese in their struggle against Communist North Vietnam.

Chopper Pickup (detail), 1969. Brian H. Clark. Acrylic, 40 x 40 in. United States Army Center of Military History, Washington, DC.

VOCABULARY PREVIEW

syndrome (sin′ drōm′) *n.* a group of symptoms that, together, indicate a certain disease; p. 608

dry (drī) *adj.* not interesting; dull; boring; p. 608

specific (spi sif′ ik) *adj.* entirely clear and definite; p. 608

founder (foun′ dər) *v.* to break down, collapse, or fail; p. 611

inert (i nurt′) *adj.* without power to move or act; lifeless; p. 613

Stop the Sun

Gary Paulsen

Con Thien Run, 1967. H. Avery Chenowith. Acrylic, 3½ x 2½ ft. United States Marine Corps Art Collection, Washington, DC.

Terry Erickson was a tall boy, 13, starting to fill out with muscle but still a little awkward. He was on the edge of being a good athlete, which meant a lot to him. He felt it coming too slowly, though, and that bothered him.

But what bothered him even more was when his father's eyes went away.

Usually it happened when it didn't cause any particular trouble. Sometimes during a meal his father's fork would stop halfway to his mouth, just stop, and there would be a long pause while the eyes went away, far away.

After several minutes his mother would reach over and take the fork and put it gently down on his plate, and they would go back to eating—or try to go back to eating—normally.

They knew what caused it. When it first started, Terry had asked his mother in private what it was, what was causing the strange behavior.

"It's from the war," his mother had said. "The doctors at the veterans' hospital call it the Vietnam syndrome."[1]

"Will it go away?"

"They don't know. Sometimes it goes away. Sometimes it doesn't. They are trying to help him."

"But what happened? What actually caused it?"

"I told you. Vietnam."

"But there had to be something," Terry persisted. "Something made him like that. Not just Vietnam. Billy's father was there, and he doesn't act that way."

"That's enough questions," his mother said sternly. "He doesn't talk about it, and I don't ask. Neither will you. Do you understand?"

"But, Mom."

"That's enough."

And he stopped pushing it. But it bothered him whenever it happened. When something bothered him, he liked to stay with it until he understood it, and he understood no part of this.

Words. His father had trouble, and they gave him words like Vietnam syndrome. He knew almost nothing of the war, and when he tried to find out about it, he kept hitting walls. Once he went to the school library and asked for anything they might have that could help him understand the war and how it affected his father. They gave him a dry history that described French involvement, Communist involvement, American involvement. But it told him nothing of the war. It was all numbers, cold numbers, and nothing of what had *happened.* There just didn't seem to be anything that could help him.

Another time he stayed after class and tried to talk to Mr. Carlson, who taught history. But some part of Terry was embarrassed. He didn't want to say why he wanted to know about Vietnam, so he couldn't be specific.

"What do you want to know about Vietnam, Terry?" Mr. Carlson had asked. "It was a big war."

Terry had looked at him, and something had started up in his mind, but he didn't let it out. He shrugged. "I just want to know what it was like. I know somebody who was in it."

"A friend?"

"Yessir. A good friend."

1. *Vietnam syndrome* refers to the lasting psychological problems suffered by many Vietnam veterans. Some of the symptoms are anger, nervousness, and nightmares.

Vocabulary

syndrome (sin′ drōm′) *n.* a group of symptoms that, together, indicate a certain disease
dry (drī) *adj.* not interesting; dull; boring
specific (spi sif′ ik) *adj.* entirely clear and definite

Mr. Carlson had studied him, looking into his eyes, but didn't ask any other questions. Instead he mentioned a couple of books Terry had not seen. They turned out to be pretty good. They told about how it felt to be in combat. Still, he couldn't make his father be one of the men he read about.

And it may have gone on and on like that, with Terry never really knowing any more about it except that his father's eyes started going away more and more often. It might have just gone the rest of his life that way except for the shopping mall.

It was easily the most embarrassing thing that ever happened to him.

It started as a normal shopping trip. His father had to go to the hardware store, and he asked Terry to go along.

When they got to the mall they split up. His father went to the hardware store, Terry to a record store to look at albums.

War & Peace, 1990. Tsing-Fang Chen. Acrylic on canvas, 66 x 96 in. Lucia Gallery, New York.

Viewing the painting: How does the artist reflect opposite ideas—war and peace—in this painting?

Terry browsed so long that he was late meeting his father at the mall's front door. But his father wasn't there, and Terry looked out to the car to make sure it was still in the parking lot. It was, and he supposed his father had just gotten busy, so he waited.

Still his father didn't come, and he was about to go the hardware store to find him when he noticed the commotion. Or not a commotion so much as a sudden movement of people.

He couldn't remember when the feeling first came to him that there was something wrong.

Later, he thought of it and couldn't remember when the feeling first came to him that there was something wrong. The people were moving toward the hardware store and that might have been what made Terry suspicious.

There was a crowd blocking the entry to the store, and he couldn't see what they were looking at. Some of them were laughing small, nervous laughs that made no sense.

Terry squeezed through the crowd until he got near the front. At first he saw nothing unusual. There were still some people in front of him, so he pushed a crack between them. Then he saw it: His father was squirming along the floor on his stomach. He was crying, looking terrified, his breath coming in short, hot pants like some kind of hurt animal.

It burned into Terry's mind, the picture of his father down on the floor. It burned in and in, and he wanted to walk away, but something made his feet move forward. He knelt next to his father and helped the owner of the store get him up on his feet. His father didn't speak at all but continued to make little whimpering sounds, and they led him back into the owner's office and put him in a chair. Then Terry called his mother and she came in a taxi to take them home.

Waiting, Terry sat in a chair next to his father, looking at the floor, wanting only for the earth to open and let him drop in a deep hole. He wanted to disappear.

Words. They gave him words like Vietnam syndrome, and his father was crawling through a hardware store on his stomach.

When the embarrassment became so bad that he would cross the street when he saw his father coming, when it ate into him as he went to sleep, Terry realized he had to do something. He had to know this thing, had to understand what was wrong with his father.

When it came, it was simple enough at the start. It had taken some courage, more than Terry thought he could find. His father was sitting in the kitchen at the table and his mother had gone shopping. Terry wanted it that way; he wanted his father alone. His mother seemed to try to protect him, as if his father could break.

Terry got a soda out of the refrigerator and popped it open. As an afterthought, he handed it to his father and got another for himself. Then he sat at the table.

His father smiled. "You look serious."

"Well . . ."

It went nowhere for a moment, and Terry was just about to drop it altogether. It may be the wrong time, he thought, but there might never be a better one. He tightened his back, took a sip of pop.

"I was wondering if we could talk about something, Dad," Terry said.

His father shrugged. "We already did the bit about girls. Some time ago, as I remember it."

"No. Not that." It was a standing joke[2] between them. When his father finally got around to explaining things to him, they'd already covered it in school. "It's something else."

"Something pretty heavy, judging by your face."

"Yes."

"Well?"

I still can't do it, Terry thought. Things are bad, but maybe not as bad as they could get. I can still drop this thing.

"Vietnam," Terry blurted out. And he thought, there, it's out. It's out and gone.

"No!" his father said sharply. It was as if he had been struck a blow. A body blow.

"But, Dad."

"No. That's another part of my life. A bad part. A rotten part. It was before I met your mother, long before you. It has nothing to do with this family, nothing. No."

2. A *standing joke* is one that continues to be told or shared over time.

So, Terry thought, so I tried. But it wasn't over yet. It wasn't started yet.

"It just seems to bother you so much," Terry said, "and I thought if I could help or maybe understand it better. . . ." His words ran until he foundered, until he could say no more. He looked at the table, then out the window. It was all wrong to bring it up, he thought. I blew it. I blew it all up. "I'm sorry."

But now his father didn't hear him. Now his father's eyes were gone again, and a shaft of something horrible went through Terry's heart as he thought he had done this thing to this father, caused his eyes to go away.

"You can't know," his father said after a time. "You can't know this thing."

Terry said nothing. He felt he had said too much.

"This thing that you want to know—there is so much of it that you cannot know it all, and to know only a part is . . . is too awful. I can't tell you. I can't tell anybody what it was really like."

It was more than he'd ever said about Vietnam, and his voice was breaking. Terry hated himself and felt he would hate himself until he was an old man. In one second he had caused such ruin. And all because he had been embarrassed. What difference did it make? Now he had done this, and he wanted to hide, to leave. But he sat, waiting, knowing that it wasn't done.

His father looked to him, through him, somewhere into and out of Terry. He wasn't in the kitchen anymore. He wasn't in the house. He was back in the green places, back in the hot places, the wet-hot places.

Vocabulary

founder (foun′ dər) *v.* to break down, collapse, or fail

"You think that because I act strange, that we can talk and it will be all right," his father said. "That we can talk and it will just go away. That's what you think, isn't it?"

Terry started to shake his head, but he knew it wasn't expected.

"That's what the shrinks say," his father continued. "The psychiatrists tell me that if I talk about it, the whole thing will go away. But they don't know. They weren't there. You weren't there. Nobody was there but me and some other dead people, and they can't talk because they couldn't stop the morning."

Terry pushed his soda can back and forth, looking down, frightened at what was happening. *The other dead people*, he'd said, as if he were dead as well. *Couldn't stop the morning*.

"I don't understand, Dad."

"No. You don't." His voice hardened, then softened again, and broke at the edges. "But see, see how it was. . . ." He

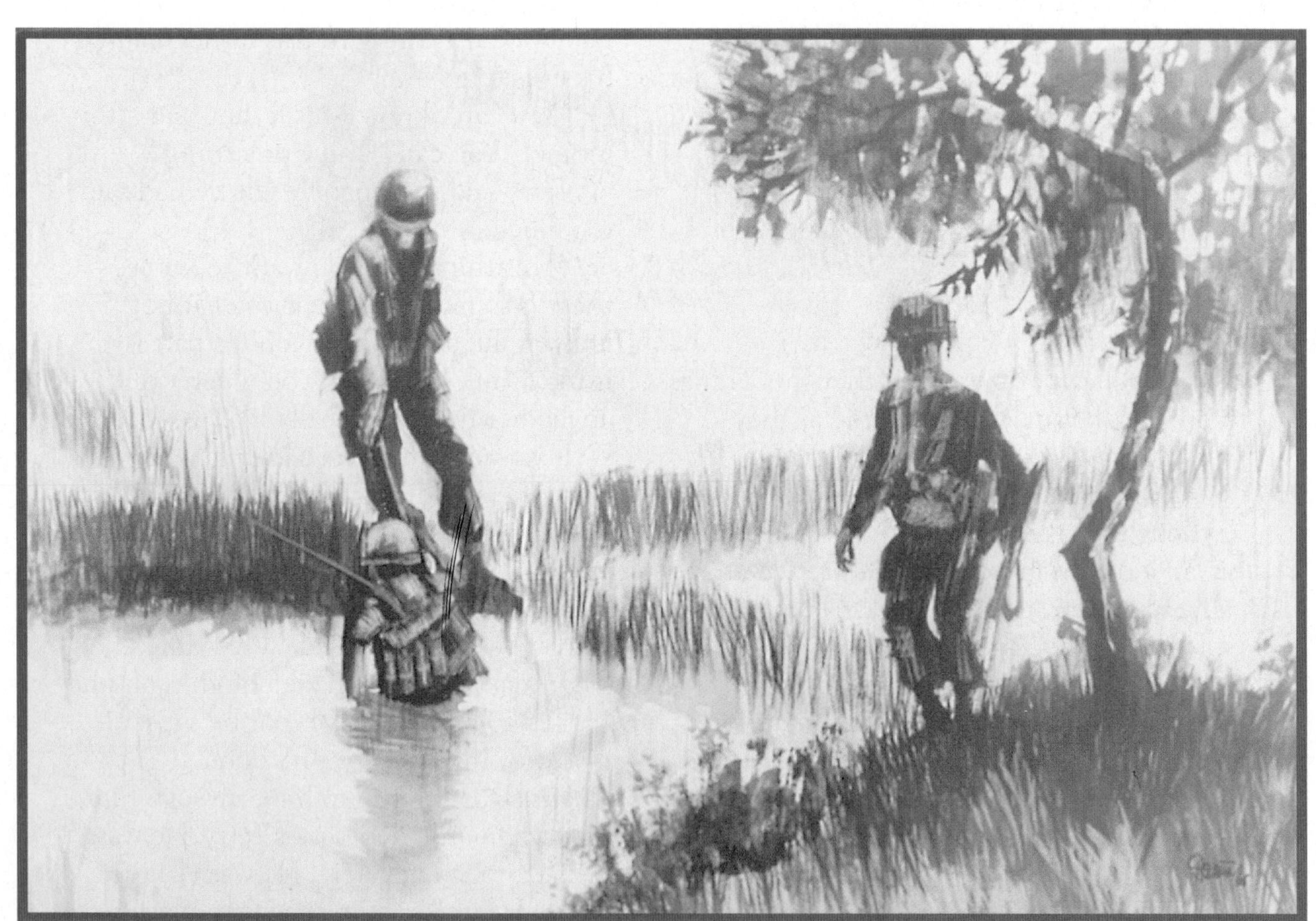

Rice Paddies–Vietnam, 1966. Augustine Acuna. Watercolor, 18 x 28 in. United States Army Center of Military History, Washington, DC.

Viewing the painting: How does this scene call forth a response from the viewer?

trailed off, and Terry thought he was done. His father looked back down to the table, at the can of soda he hadn't touched, at the tablecloth, at his hands, which were folded, inert on the table.

"We were crossing a rice paddy in the dark," he said, and suddenly his voice flowed like a river breaking loose. "We were crossing the paddy, and it was dark, still dark, so black you couldn't see the end of your nose. There was a light rain, a mist, and I was thinking that during the next break I would whisper and tell Petey Kressler how nice the rain felt, but of course I didn't know there wouldn't be a Petey Kressler."

He took a deep, ragged breath. At that moment Terry felt his brain swirl, a kind of whirlpool pulling, and he felt the darkness and the light rain because it was in his father's eyes, in his voice.

"So we were crossing the paddy, and it was a straight sweep, and then we caught it. We began taking fire from three sides, automatic weapons, and everybody went down and tried to get low, but we couldn't. We couldn't get low enough. We could never get low enough, and you could hear the rounds hitting people. It was just a short time before they brought in the mortars[3] and we should have moved, should have run, but nobody got up, and after a time nobody *could* get up. The fire just kept coming and coming, and then incoming mortars, and I heard screams as they hit, but there was nothing to do. Nothing to do."

"Dad?" Terry said. He thought, maybe I can stop him. Maybe I can stop him before . . . before it gets to be too much. Before he breaks.

"Mortars," his father went on, "I hated mortars. You just heard them *wump* as they fired, and you didn't know where they would hit, and you always felt like they would hit your back. They swept back and forth with the mortars, and the automatic weapons kept coming in, and there was no radio, no way to call for artillery. Just the dark to hide in. So I crawled to the side and found Jackson, only he wasn't there, just part of his body, the top part, and I hid under it and waited, and waited, and waited.

"Finally the firing quit. But see, see how it was in the dark with nobody alive but me? I yelled once, but that brought fire again, so I shut up and there was nothing, not even the screams."

His father cried, and Terry tried to understand, and he thought he could feel part of it. But it was so much, so much and so strange to him.

"You cannot know this," his father repeated. It was almost a chant. "You cannot know the fear. It was almost dark, and I was the only one left alive out of 54 men, all dead but me, and I knew that the Vietcong were just waiting for light. When the dawn came, 'Charley'[4] would come out and finish everybody off, the way they always did. And I thought if I could stop the dawn, just stop the sun from coming up, I could make it."

3. *Mortars* are small, portable cannons that fire explosive shells, also sometimes called mortars.

4. The *Vietcong* were the Communist forces whom American soldiers often referred to as *Charley.*

Vocabulary

inert (i nurt′) *adj.* without power to move or act; lifeless

Terry felt the fear, and he also felt the tears coming down his cheeks. His hand went out across the table, and he took his father's hand and held it. It was shaking.

"I mean I actually thought that if I could stop the sun from coming up, I could live. I made my brain work on that because it was all I had. Through the rest of the night in the rain in the paddy, I thought I could do it. I could stop the dawn." He took a deep breath. "But you can't, you know. You can't stop it from coming, and when I saw the gray light, I knew I was dead. It would just be minutes, and the light would be full, and I just settled under Jackson's body, and hid."

I actually thought that if I could stop the sun from coming up, I could live.

He stopped, and his face came down into his hands. Terry stood and went around the table to stand in back of him, his hands on his shoulders, rubbing gently.

"They didn't shoot me. They came, one of them poked Jackson's body and went on and they left me. But I was dead. I'm still dead, don't you see? I died because I couldn't stop the sun. I died. Inside where I am—I died."

Terry was still in back of him, and he nodded, but he didn't see. Not that. He understood only that he didn't understand, and that he would probably never understand what had truly happened.

And maybe his father would never be truly normal.

But Terry also knew that it didn't matter. He would try to understand, and the trying would have to be enough. He would try hard from now on, and he would not be embarrassed when his father's eyes went away. He would not be embarrassed no matter what his father did. Terry had knowledge now. Maybe not enough and maybe not all that he would need.

But it was a start.

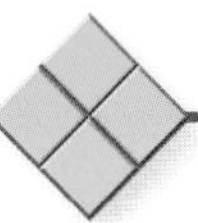

Responding to Literature

PERSONAL RESPONSE

What images in this story are most vivid for you? Why?

Analyzing Literature

RECALL

1. When do Terry's father's eyes "go away"?
2. Why is Terry interested in the Vietnam War?
3. What causes Terry's father to crawl on the floor of the hardware store?
4. What reason does Terry's father have for wanting to "stop the sun"?

INTERPRET

5. What might Terry's father's eyes **symbolize** in this story?
6. In your opinion, why does Terry's father insist that Vietnam has "nothing to do with this family"?
7. Why is Terry so bothered by his father's behavior?
8. Theme Connection What does Terry understand, and not understand, about his father by the end of the story?

EVALUATE AND CONNECT

9. How might knowing about a family member's past affect how others feel about that person?
10. Theme Connection What have you learned about the ways in which world events can affect ordinary families?

LITERARY ELEMENTS

Climax

The **climax** of a story is the highest point of action in the plot. All of the earlier events in the story build up to the climax. The ending of the story depends on what happens at the climax.

1. At what point in "Stop the Sun" does the climax occur?
2. How does the action of the characters at the climax affect the outcome of the story?

- See **Literary Terms Handbook,** p. R2.

Literature and Writing

Writing About Literature

Characterization Gary Paulsen develops characters by sharing their thoughts and feelings with the reader. In a paragraph, explain how Paulsen shows the changes in Terry's feelings for his father. Use examples from Terry's thoughts and his words.

Creative Writing

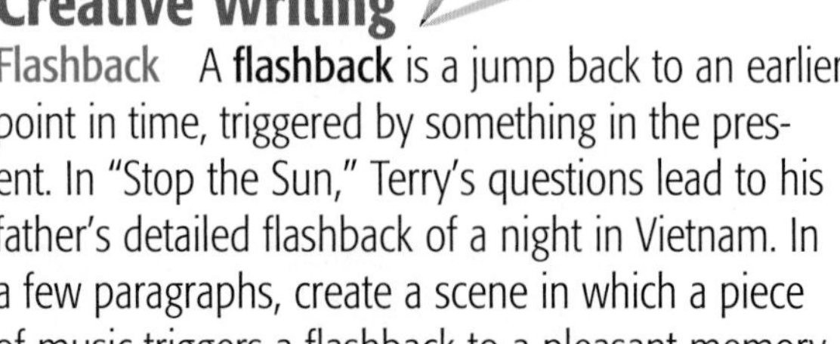

Flashback A **flashback** is a jump back to an earlier point in time, triggered by something in the present. In "Stop the Sun," Terry's questions lead to his father's detailed flashback of a night in Vietnam. In a few paragraphs, create a scene in which a piece of music triggers a flashback to a pleasant memory. Describe both the trigger and the original event.

Extending Your Response

Literature Groups

Communication Gap Look back at your list from the **Focus Activity** on page 606, and add new ideas that you have after reading "Stop the Sun." Share lists in your group and identify similarities. Discuss ways to avoid or solve breakdowns in communication within a family or another group.

interNET CONNECTION

Use the World Wide Web to find examples of songs about war sung during the Vietnam War. An example is Pete Seeger's circular song, "Where Have All the Flowers Gone." Discuss the lyrics with a group.

Interdisciplinary Activity

Social Studies: History What types of international conflicts has the United States been involved in since 1950? What forces or events led up to these tensions, and what were the results? Use reference materials to help you create a time line of U.S. military involvement overseas. If you wish, work with a group to build a time line that you can post in the classroom.

Reading Further

For more Newbery Honor Books by Gary Paulsen, try these:
Dogsong
Canyons

Save your work for your portfolio.

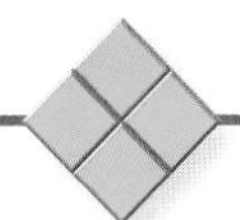

Skill Minilessons

GRAMMAR AND LANGUAGE • SUBJECT-VERB AGREEMENT

A verb must agree with its subject in person and number, even when words or phrases separate the subject from the verb.

Terry, after hearing about his father's experiences, knows more about him.

The subject, *Terry,* is a third-person, singular noun. The third-person, singular form of the verb is *knows.*

- For more about subject-verb agreement, see **Language Handbook,** pp. R13–R14.

PRACTICE Copy and complete each sentence, choosing the correct verb in parentheses.

1. Terry and his father (were, was) planning to meet at the front door of the mall.
2. The troops in the night patrol (crosses, cross) the jungle together.
3. The enemy soldiers, the Vietcong, expectantly (await, awaits) dawn.
4. Terry's father, when his eyes go away, (seem, seems) to be in Vietnam.

READING AND THINKING • CAUSE AND EFFECT

Authors may connect ideas by showing a cause-and-effect relationship. In "Stop the Sun," Terry worries that he might be causing his father's illness until he learns that war experiences are the real cause.

- For more about cause and effect, see **Reading Handbook,** p. R87.

PRACTICE Use each pair of words in a sentence that shows a cause-and-effect relationship.

1. war, fear
2. joke, laughter
3. conversation, awakening

VOCABULARY • MULTIPLE-MEANING WORDS

Many words have more than one meaning. For example, the noun *founder* means "a person who founds, or establishes." William Penn was the *founder* of Pennsylvania. The verb *founder* means "to break down, collapse, or fail." Terry *foundered* when he ran out of words. Context clues usually help when a familiar word looks strange. When they fail, use a dictionary.

- For more about multiple-meaning words, see **Reading Handbook,** pp. R80–R81.

PRACTICE Write an original sentence for each underlined word. Pay careful attention to the contexts. Consult a dictionary as needed.

1. a tale with <u>humor</u>
   <u>humor</u> your guest
2. <u>pitch</u> the ball
   the <u>pitch</u> of the slope
3. a doe and <u>fawn</u>
   <u>fawn</u> over the child
4. a <u>loud</u> noise
   a <u>loud</u> tie
5. <u>master</u> a skill
   <u>master</u> of the house

PERSONAL ESSAY

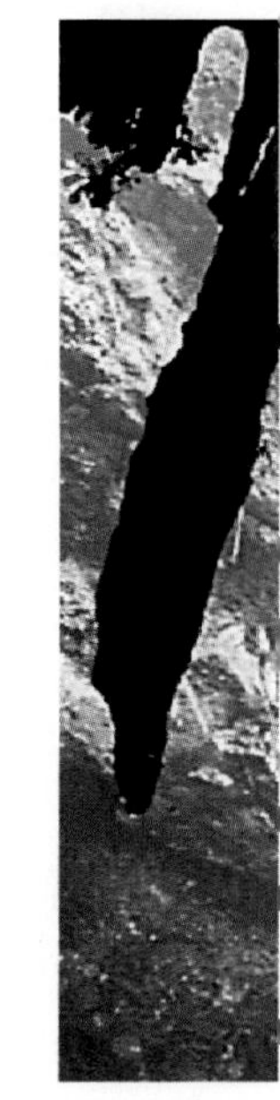

Many types of nonfiction are meant to inform or to relate experiences based on fact. For example, biographies, textbooks, and news articles are packed with factual information. One type of nonfiction, the **personal essay,** is meant to let the writer express himself or herself.

Most personal essays share the characteristics explained and illustrated on these two pages.

1 PERSONAL OPINIONS AND EXPERIENCE In a personal essay, the writer shares his or her own beliefs and experiences. Even when pointing out a universal truth, the essayist builds up to it by sharing personal experiences.

2 INFORMAL LANGUAGE The author of a personal essay writes as he or she might speak in normal conversation, using familiar words, even slang. The writing may include fragments and run-on sentences that ramble on, jumping from idea to idea in a loose, conversational way.

3 TONE The writer of a personal essay often speaks to readers as directly as friends speak to each other. This direct informal approach can make it easy to identify the author's tone, or attitude, about a topic.

4 IMAGERY Like a poet, an essayist wants to share with readers his or her view of things and reactions to them. To do so, the writer uses sensory details that combine ideas forcefully.

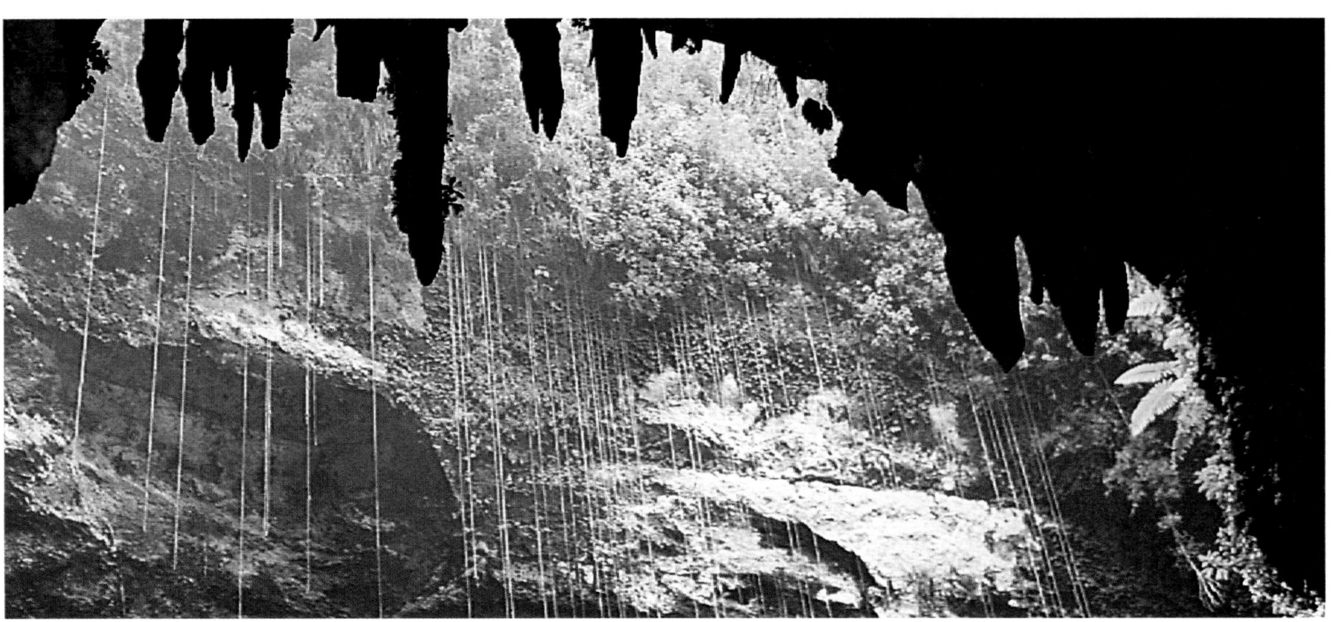

1 PERSONAL OPINIONS AND EXPERIENCE
In this passage, the writer describes his experience in a deep mountain cave. To do this, he shares what he sees, smells, and touches.

2 INFORMAL LANGUAGE
Lopez's casual observation is startling in its contrasts. Notice how he contrasts light and dark.

MODEL

Inside the mountains are old creeks that run in circles over the floors of low-ceilinged caves. The fish in these waters are white and translucent; you can see a pink haze of organs beneath the skin. Where there should be eyes there are bulges that do not move. On the walls are white spiders like grey tight buttons of surgical cotton suspended on long hairy legs. There are white beetles, too, scurrying through the hills of black bat dung.

I have always been suspicious of these caves because walls crumble easily under your fingertips; there is no moisture in the air and it smells like balloons. The water smells like oranges but has no taste. Nothing you do here makes any sound.

–Barry Holstun Lopez,
from *Desert Notes: Reflections in the Eye of the Raven*

3 TONE
While Lopez seems to marvel at what he finds in the caves, their otherworldly nature fosters in him a sense of distrust, which he shares with the reader.

4 IMAGERY
Lopez uses sensory details to make the reader feel as if he or she is in the cave with him.

ACTIVE READING MODEL

Active Reading Strategies

Tips for Reading a Personal Essay

Reading a personal essay can be a lot like listening to a friend talk. However, in a personal essay, organized thoughts and carefully worded choices can make the message more powerful than normal conversation.

- For more about comprehension and sustained silent reading, see **Reading Handbook,** pp. R78–R95.

PREVIEW

As you read the first few paragraphs, identify the general topic and listen for the writer's tone, or attitude. Is the writer amused or angered by the subject? Does he or she expect you to laugh, cry, or listen thoughtfully?

Ask Yourself . . .

- What do the writer's style and word choices tell me about this essay?
- Why might a friend start a conversation this way? What would he or she expect from me?

CLARIFY

Does the writer make points clear by using examples readers can understand? What larger idea do these examples show?

Ask Yourself . . .

- Do I understand every word and sentence in this passage?
- Is the writer making a more important point in this paragraph than in other paragraphs? Can I state the main point in my own words?

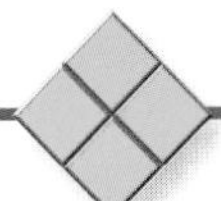

QUESTION

Put yourself in the place of the writer. Ask yourself if you can understand his or her feelings and ideas. If you don't understand, go back and reread.

Ask Yourself . . .

- Do I understand the point the writer is trying to make?
- What details provide clues to the purpose of this essay?

EVALUATE

As you read, think about your reaction to the writer's words. Have your opinions and understanding of the topic changed? Were thoughts presented logically, or was the reasoning biased or faulty?

Ask Yourself . . .

- Do I understand the subject better now?
- Were the writer's opinions adequately supported?
- Does the writer succeed in his or her purpose?

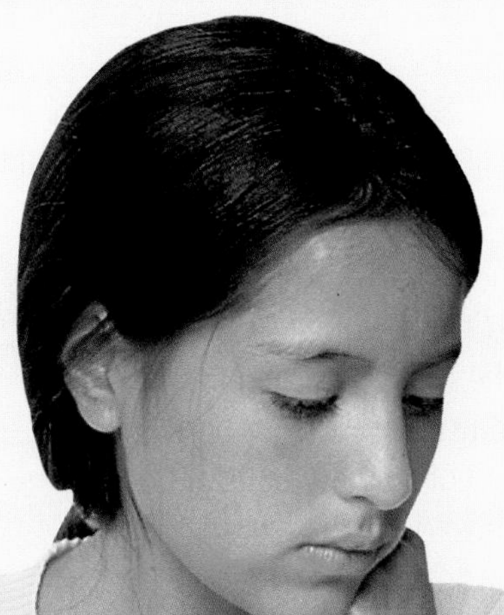

APPLYING THE STRATEGIES

Read the following personal essay, "The Summer of Vietnam." Use the **Active Reading Model** notes in the margins as you read. Write your responses on a separate piece of paper, and review them when you have finished reading.

ACTIVE READING MODEL

Before You Read

The Summer of Vietnam

MEET BARBARA RENAUD GONZÁLEZ

Barbara Renaud González describes herself this way: "I am the daughter of an illegal immigrant. My mother is a Mexican. . . . I am visibly Mexican and an invisible American." González grew up in Texas and graduated from college with a degree in social work. She is a regular contributor to the *Dallas Morning News* and a local public radio station.

Barbara Renaud González was born in 1953. "The Summer of Vietnam" was published in 1992 in New Chicana/Chicano Writing.

FOCUS ACTIVITY

You have read about Vietnam. Have you ever talked about this war with someone who experienced it in some way?

Journal

Using what you know from what people have said or written, jot down some thoughts about war in general or about Vietnam.

Setting a Purpose

Read to experience the thoughts and feelings of a writer who saw many people go to Vietnam—and never come back.

BACKGROUND

The Time and Place Barbara Renaud González wrote the following essay in the 1990s, more than twenty years after the Vietnam War.

Did You Know? The Medal of Honor, the Distinguished Service Cross, and the Bronze Star are awarded by the U.S. government to men and women who risk their lives or perform extraordinary, heroic actions during battle. The Purple Heart may be awarded to those wounded or killed in action.

Purple Heart

VOCABULARY PREVIEW

adolescence (ad′ əl es′ əns) *n.* the period or process of growing from youth to adulthood; teenage years; p. 624

extinguish (iks ting′ gwish) *v.* to put out; end; destroy; p. 624

constitute (kon′ stə to͞ot′) *v.* to form; make up; compose; p. 625

prestigious (pre sti′ jəs) *adj.* having widely recognized importance and influence; impressive; p. 625

agonize (ag′ ə nīz′) *v.* to suffer greatly; struggle painfully; p. 625

redeemed (ri dēmd′) *adj.* gotten or won back; recovered; p. 625

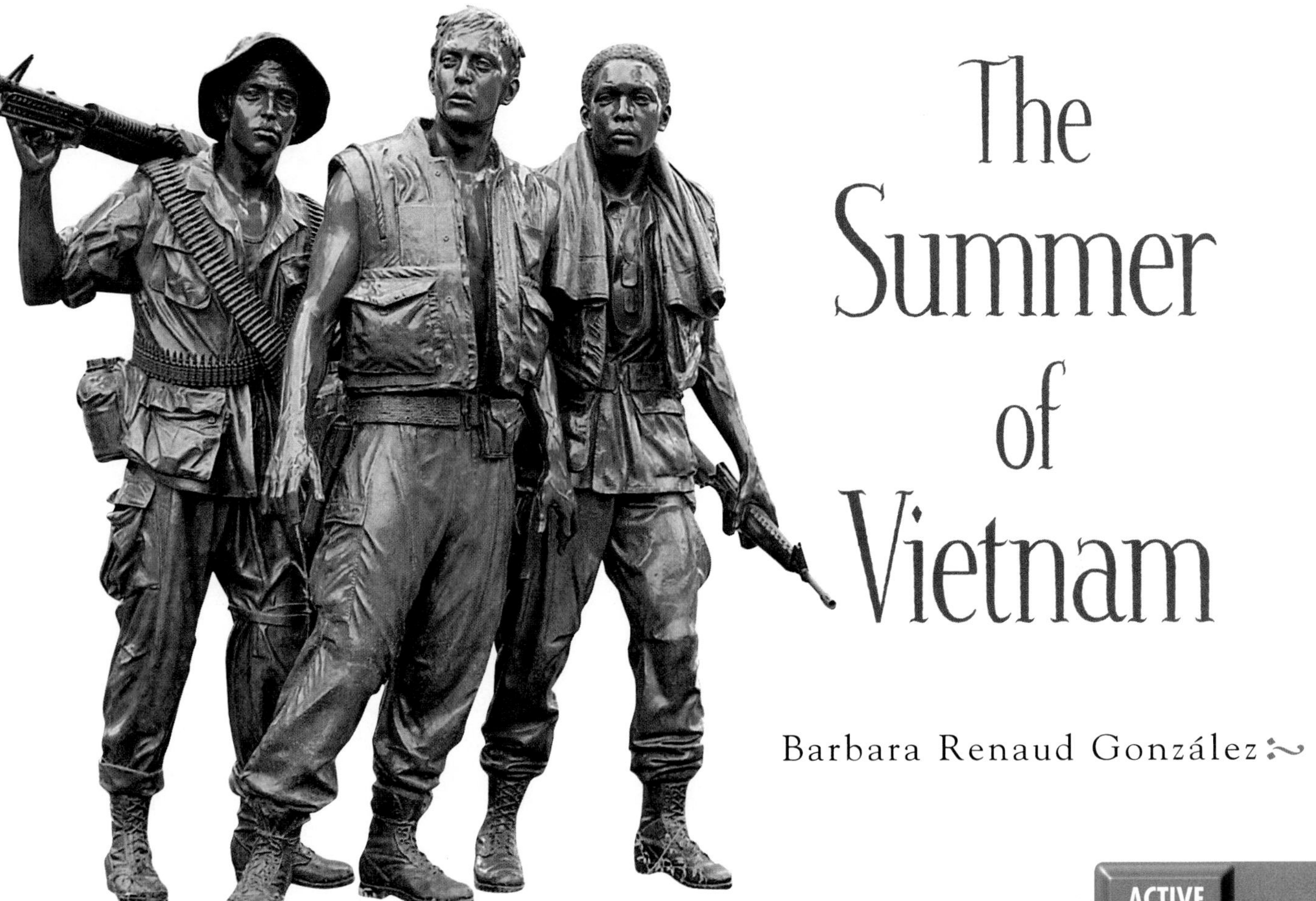

The Summer of Vietnam

Barbara Renaud González

Three Servicemen, 1984. Frederick Hart. Cast bronze, height: 7 ft. National Park Service, Washington, DC.

ACTIVE READING MODEL

So, what are you writing about? I ask Bill Broyles, the former *Newsweek Magazine* goldenboy.[1] He's the Texas man who can write *anything* and get it published. Unlike me.

PREDICT

Can you guess from the first two paragraphs what the writer's attitude about Vietnam might be?

"Vietnam," he says. The worst answer. The only answer that can make me cry.

Instead, at night I remember.

Ernesto Sánchez is Vietnam to me. Born July 9, 1947. In a place called Kennedy, Texas. Died in the summer of 1967, somewhere in Vietnam. Somewhere in my 13th summer.

This is my Vietnam.

1. Anyone referred to as a *goldenboy* (or *goldengirl*) is seen as having a promising future.

I sang love songs to them. Made up Ken dolls after them. Imagined kissing them. I still do. Marine-boys. Boys in dress green with stiff brass buttons that would catch your breaking heart when they gave you the biggest *abrazo*[2] of your life. Then they died in Vietnam.

Always teasing me. "This last dance is for you, Barbara," they'd say. Taught me to dance those skip-steps of adolescence. Told me they'd wait for me. And they never came back from Vietnam to see how I'd grown up for them.

Vietnam Veterans Memorial, 1982. Maya Lin. Washington, DC.

Viewing the photograph: Why, in your view, has this memorial wall become such a powerful monument?

CONNECT

What do I know about the people who died in Vietnam and those who survived?

I knew they would not die. Heroes don't die in the movies, after all. The good guys always win. Who would dare extinguish the crooked smiles, football hands and Aqua Velva[3] faces I knew so well? My brothers-at-war.

Of the 3,427 Texas men who died in Vietnam, 22 percent were Latinos. And another 12 percent of the dead were African-American. The minorities were *not* a minority in the platoons, but a majority of the frightened faces. And one-third of the body bags.[4]

2. An *abrazo* (ə brä′ zō) is a hug or embrace.
3. *Aqua Velva* is the brand name of a popular after-shave lotion.
4. In the U.S. Army, a *platoon* consists of four squads having ten soldiers each. *Body bags* are zippered bags, usually made of rubber, for transporting human corpses.

Vocabulary

adolescence (ad′ əl es′ əns) *n.* the period or process of growing from youth to adulthood; teenage years

extinguish (iks ting′ gwish) *v.* to put out; end; destroy

This at a time when Latinos constituted 12 percent of the population.

But the machismo goes a long way in war. We Latinos received more medals, thirteen of the prestigious Medal of Honor,[5] than any other group.

We can count soldiers in the American Revolution (as Spaniards), the Roosevelt Rough Riders,[6] both sides of the Civil War, and plenty of fathers and abuelitos[7] in the world wars. Soldiering doesn't require U.S. citizenship, and no one cares how you crossed the border if you're willing to fight on our side.

We lost our best men in Vietnam. Isaac Camacho died first in 1963. Everett Alvarez was the first American pilot shot down, spending eight-and-a-half years as a POW.[8] Juan Valdez was in the last helicopter leaving Vietnam. First in, and last out. They didn't go to Canada or Mexico.[9] They went directly to Vietnam.

But from Oliver Stone, you would think that all our boys looked like Tom Cruise. Or agonized at China Beach.[10] No. They were my brothers, uncles, cousins, my heroes.

Sometimes it looks as if they died for nothing. Impossible. It cannot be. Blood lost is blood redeemed, they say. What is the boy worth? If he died for all of us, then we must gain in proportion to the sacrifice. A Medal of Honor for the neighborhood school. Some Distinguished Service Crosses for family housing. Maybe the Bronze Stars for the judge or councilman. Flying Crosses for a good job. And a Purple Heart for a mother who still cries in Spanish.

EVALUATE

What information is based on fact, and what is the author's opinion?

CLARIFY

What does González mean by "no one cares how you crossed the border" and "they didn't go to Canada or Mexico"?

QUESTION

How does the author seem to feel about the recognition of Latino soldiers in Vietnam?

EVALUATE

Does it serve the writer's purpose to end the essay with a listing of military awards?

5. *Machismo* (mä chēz′ mō) is the idea that males are (or should be) masculine and superior to females. (Men who are seen as having these qualities are described as being *macho.*) The *Medal of Honor* is the highest U.S. military decoration.
6. The *Rough Riders* were members of a cavalry unit, led by Theodore *Roosevelt,* that fought in Cuba during the Spanish-American War.
7. *Abuelitos* (ä′ bwə lē′ tōs) are grandfathers or old men.
8. Alvarez was a prisoner of war, or *POW.*
9. Some young men fled to *Canada* or *Mexico* to avoid military service in Vietnam.
10. Oliver Stone directed the 1989 movie *Born on the Fourth of July,* starring Tom Cruise. *China Beach* was a 1980s television drama about Vietnam.

Vocabulary

constitute (kon′ stə to͞ot′) *v.* to form; make up; compose

prestigious (pre sti′ jəs) *adj.* having widely recognized importance and influence; impressive

agonize (ag′ ə nīz′) *v.* to suffer greatly; struggle painfully

redeemed (ri dēmd′) *adj.* gotten or won back; recovered

ACTIVE READING MODEL

Responding to Literature

PERSONAL RESPONSE

How has this essay changed or affected your attitude toward war?

Active Reading Response

Which of the **Active Reading Strategies** on pages 620–621 did you find most useful in reading this essay?

Analyzing Literature

RECALL

1. What is the subject of the article Bill Broyles is writing?
2. Describe the boys González admired when she was thirteen.
3. What percentage of the U.S. population was Hispanic during the Vietnam War? What percentage of the soldiers from Texas who died were Hispanic?
4. What kinds of comments are made by people who think the fighting in Vietnam was worth the sacrifice?

INTERPRET

5. What seems to be the writer's attitude toward Broyles? toward Broyles's subject?
6. How does González feel about the danger to her friends as they leave for Vietnam? Why, do you think, does she have this attitude?
7. What does González mean by "this is my Vietnam"?
8. In your opinion, does González agree with those who think the men in Vietnam died for nothing? Does she side with those who believe "that we must gain in proportion to the sacrifice"? Explain.

EVALUATE AND CONNECT

9. What stand do you think González takes on the war? Do you agree with her position? Support your answers with examples. Look at your response in the **Focus Activity** on page 622.
10. Theme Connection What new insight might readers of this essay gain? Why?

LITERARY ELEMENTS

Irony

Irony is the use of language to show the contrast between what things may seem to be and what they really are. For example, thirteen-year-old Barbara admires the young Marines, their uniforms, and their stiff brass buttons. She knows from the movies that they will win and will not die. The irony is that these uniforms and brass buttons put them in a place where they do, in fact, die.

1. How does the writer use irony to contrast attitudes toward illegal aliens and attitudes toward those who enlist in the military?
2. Find and explain another example of irony in the essay.

• See **Literary Terms Handbook,** p. R5.

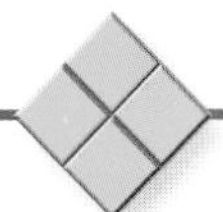

Extending Your Response

Writing About Literature

Point of View In this essay, González recalls childhood memories and retells them from a **first-person point of view,** using the pronouns *I* and *me.* Write a paragraph or two explaining how González's use of a personal experience strengthens or weakens the effect of her essay.

Creative Writing

Celebrate Your Heritage González is a Mexican American who writes about Mexican Americans. Write a poem in which you celebrate your own heritage and the contributions that Americans of your ethnic background have made to the country. If possible, include imagery–language that describes what you see, hear, feel, smell, or taste–in your poem.

Literature Groups

Hollywood vs. the Real World González writes that "from [the movie director] Oliver Stone, you would think that all our boys looked like Tom Cruise." With a group, discuss various movies and television programs that succeed or fail in showing realistic views of life in the United States. Be prepared to summarize your group's ideas for the class.

Interdisciplinary Activity

Math Numbers tell a story. With a partner, research the number of U.S. soldiers from various ethnic backgrounds who died in Vietnam. Create a chart that shows which ethnic group lost the highest percentage of soldiers. With your class, discuss and explain your reactions to these numbers. What story do they seem to tell?

Reading Further

For a girl's experience of a different war, read *Summer of My German Soldier* by Bette Greene.

Save your work for your portfolio.

Skill Minilesson

VOCABULARY • THE SUFFIX *-ize*

A **suffix** is a word part added to the end of a word. Suffixes change the meaning of a word, but only slightly. For example, the suffix *-ize* means "to cause to be or become." Adding this suffix to the noun *fertile* simply changes the noun into a verb, *fertilize.* Think of *capitalize.* When you *capitalize* a letter, you cause it to become a capital. When you *agonize,* you cause yourself to be in agony.

- For more about suffixes, see **Language Handbook,** pp. R47–R48.

PRACTICE Match each word in the left column with its meaning. Use what you know about the suffix *-ize* to help you.

1. humanize
2. socialize
3. economize
4. localize
5. personalize

a. able to get along well with others
b. thrifty, not wasteful
c. clearly intended for a particular individual
d. like a person instead of an animal
e. limited or confined to a particular place

Before You Read

Finding America

MEET A. C. GREENE

When A. C. Greene sits down to write, he asks himself what he can say that readers will care about. As a journalist and university instructor, he has developed this philosophy: "You have to think that you're saying something or revealing one little point in life that never has quite been revealed in quite this fashion about quite this type of situation. And then you write."

Alvin Carl Greene was born in 1923 in Abilene, Texas. This selection was taken from a transcript of the MacNeil/Lehrer NewsHour *on June 30, 1986.*

FOCUS ACTIVITY

Imagine that you are watching leaders in the American colonies as they walk up to sign the Declaration of Independence.

Quickwrite

In a few sentences, describe your feelings at this historic moment.

Setting a Purpose

Read to find out how a World War II soldier discovers the meaning of the Fourth of July.

BACKGROUND

The Time and Place The following selection is set in Philadelphia, Pennsylvania, during World War II.

Did You Know? Most Americans today think of the founding fathers as heroes, but many people of their time saw them as traitors to England. Treason was punishable by death; yet the patriots showed great courage. John Hancock signed his name to the Declaration of Independence in large letters so that England's King George could see it easily. Benjamin Franklin said, "We must all hang together, or assuredly we shall all hang separately."

John Hancock

VOCABULARY PREVIEW

diverse (di vurs′) *adj.* noticeably different; varied; p. 630

compelling (kəm pel′ ing) *adj.* impressive and forceful; p. 630

paramount (par′ ə mount′) *adj.* above all others in influence or importance; supreme; p. 630

lurk (lurk) *v.* to lie hidden or move about in a sneaky way; p. 631

resolve (ri zolv′) *n.* steady determination; firmness of purpose; p. 631

Finding America

A. C. Greene

One summer evening in the middle of World War II, I found myself wandering the streets of Philadelphia—a little lost, and more than a little lonesome. I had arrived in town only a few days before—a sailor from Texas who had never been any further east than Chicago.

The Fourth of July, 1917. Childe Hassam. Oil on canvas, 36 x 26 in. Private collection.

Finding America

It was my first liberty[1] in the city of brotherly love. I left the naval station alone without a plan or a phone number to my name and rode the Broad Street subway to Center Square where city hall towered over downtown, with William Penn at its tiptop, hands outstretched, blessing his city. I passed some wonderfully attractive restaurants with red roses on snowy tables, but when I looked at the menu posted in the window, the prices took away my hunger. My navy salary was $64 a month. I settled for a bowl of clam chowder at the Reading Terminal Oyster Bar.

Emerging at dusk, I walked down Market Street feeling even more lonesome—the least important sailor in the U.S. Navy. Turning into a side street and walking a few more blocks, I realized I had no idea where I was. The sidewalks were empty. I stopped and looked around, glancing at the doorway of the red brick building where I had halted. A plaque was mounted there, and the words brought me to tears as I read them. "The Birthplace of the United States of America." Looking upward, following the lines of the familiar spire, I recognized this was Independence Hall, where the Declaration of Independence was signed July 4, 1776. It happened here. That diverse group of heroes gathered on this very spot to make that final, awesome decision. Thomas Jefferson, who wrote the document; Benjamin Franklin, age 70; John Adams, who would one day be President of the United States; Francis Hopkinson, author and songwriter; Benjamin Rush, physician. They touched these bricks that morning, taking those decisive steps, turning their back on the safety of concession. Cautiously, with a sort of metaphysical[2] expectation, I placed my foot in that stone footprint. I put my foot in the Fourth of July.

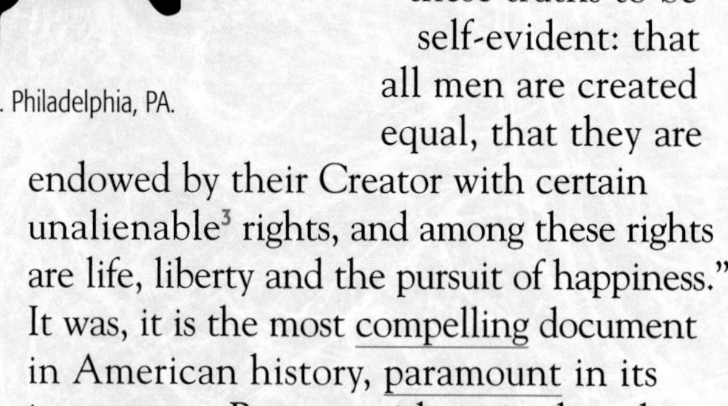

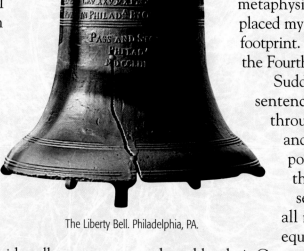

The Liberty Bell. Philadelphia, PA.

Suddenly, the bold sentences thundered through me with new and immediate power. "We hold these truths to be self-evident: that all men are created equal, that they are endowed by their Creator with certain unalienable[3] rights, and among these rights are life, liberty and the pursuit of happiness." It was, it is the most compelling document in American history, paramount in its importance. Because without it, the other

1. In the navy, *liberty* is time off granted to a sailor to go ashore.

2. *Concession,* here, is an act of giving something up. These men chose to stand up for their beliefs rather than to keep giving in to the British. *Metaphysical* refers to what is beyond the limits of the physical world. Walking where these men walked carries the author, in mind and spirit, into their presence.

3. Rights given *(endowed)* by God may not be taken away *(are unalienable).*

Vocabulary

diverse (di vurs′) *adj.* noticeably different; varied

compelling (kəm pel′ ing) *adj.* impressive and forceful

paramount (par′ ə mount′) *adj.* above all others in influence or importance; supreme documents and amendments remain locked in the hearts and minds of those who conceived them.

These men who put their names to that declaration put their lives on the line—the firing line or the lines to the gallows.[4] If the colonies lost the revolution, there was no place for them to hide, no shelter from the wrath of King George, no Bill of Rights to call on for protection. Their names were on this treasonable paper. There was no denial.

I could hear voices. John Hancock, president of Congress and first in line, penning that now familiar signature and exclaiming, we are told, "King George will have no trouble reading that." None of them acknowledging the fear that must have lurked beneath the consciousness of them all. They were not just signing a petition; they were demanding the noose.

And yet there was surely an even stronger fear lurking: would it work? Even if the battles and political struggles were successful, what terrible creature might they be loosing on mankind? What price independence at a time in history when it had never before been defined? Even the taste for human freedom was uncertain. They were writing the original recipe. That to secure these rights governments were instituted among men deriving[5] their just powers from the consent of the governed.

And there I was that darkening evening in Philadelphia, waiting to be sent into a war which, in a sense, was being fought because of what they did here on that long before July 4—a war from which I had no assurance of returning. A war that would cost me years of time and the death of friends and take me where I, like millions of others, would ask, "What am I doing here?"

But where might I have been had they hesitated, had they divided and lacked resolve? With all the flaws and failings of the creature they created, where would the world be? Would I have chosen otherwise? Of course not. No, all these thoughts didn't find me that one night. Over the years I have believed, then changed my mind; have taken stands, then deserted them; have raged and wondered and prayed. But no matter what I've discovered about my country or myself, I've not forgotten that evening more than 40 years ago when I put my foot in the Fourth of July.

4. *Gallows* refers to the frame from which condemned criminals were hanged.

5. To *derive* is to get from a source.

Vocabulary

lurk (lurk) *v.* to lie hidden or move about in a sneaky way

resolve (ri zolv′) *n.* steady determination; firmness of purpose

Responding to Literature

PERSONAL RESPONSE

Visualize the many scenes from this story. Quickly sketch the one you found most vivid.

Analyzing Literature

RECALL

1. At first, how does the speaker feel in Philadelphia?
2. What is the red brick building that the speaker calls "The Birthplace of the United States of America"? What once occurred there?
3. What two fears do the signers of the Declaration have?
4. What feelings and observations does the speaker express as he considers being sent into war?

INTERPRET

5. In your opinion, why have the speaker's feelings changed by the end of the story?
6. What might the speaker mean when he says that without the Declaration, "the other documents and amendments remain locked in the hearts and minds of those who conceived them"?
7. What might the "terrible creature" be that the signers were "loosing on mankind"? Why might it be terrible?
8. What might the speaker mean when he says the war (World War II) "was being fought because of what they did here"?

EVALUATE AND CONNECT

9. The **title** of a selection often gives important information about people and their ideas. Why might this story be called "Finding America"?
10. Do you think the Declaration and the freedom it created have "flaws and failings," as the writer suggests? Explain.

LITERARY ELEMENTS

Speaker

The **speaker** is the voice in a poem. In nonfiction and fiction, this term can also refer to the **narrator,** the person or character who tells a story. A speaker may reveal his or her own attitudes and opinions. For example, the speaker of "Finding America" shares his deepest thoughts with readers.

1. How would you tell this true story differently if you were the speaker?
2. How might a person who lost a loved one in World War II tell this story differently? Explain.
3. How might the speaker react to a student who didn't know the history of the Declaration of Independence?

- See **Literary Terms Handbook,** p. R9.

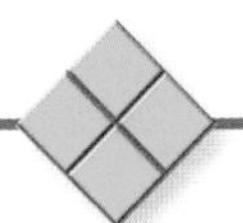

Extending Your Response

Writing About Literature

Setting In "Finding America," A. C. Greene shares a flash of insight that he experienced during World War II. Join with a small group of students, and list the effects that the setting–both time and place–might have had on Greene's attitude. You may find it helpful to reread parts of the selection and try to visualize the setting as Greene saw it.

Creative Writing

Letter from Philadelphia Imagine that you are seeing Independence Hall for the first time. Describe your thoughts and feelings in a letter to a friend back home. If you need help getting started, review what you wrote for the **Focus Activity** on page 628. Consider using a narrative form, including setting, dialogue, and quotations.

Literature Groups

What If? A. C. Greene asks, "But where might I have been had they hesitated, had they divided and lacked resolve?" In a small group, discuss possible answers to this question. Then agree on the two most likely ones. Be prepared to share your responses with the class.

Interdisciplinary Activity

Art Draw, sketch, or paint a picture to accompany Greene's story. If you prefer, find a photograph or painting that captures the thoughts and emotions of the speaker. Remember that the setting you choose will create an atmosphere for the story.

Reading Further

For other ways to find America, read:
Paperquake: A Puzzle by Kathryn Reiss

Save your work for your portfolio.

Skill Minilesson

VOCABULARY • ANALOGIES

An **analogy** is a type of comparison that is based on the relationships between things or ideas.

stomp : walk :: shout : talk

To *stomp* is to *walk* loudly; to *shout* is to *talk* loudly.

If an analogy uses words with similar meanings, try to make up a sentence that uses both words plus a descriptive word. For example, "to *slurp* is to *drink* noisily." Then see if the same descriptive word can also be used to describe the relationship between another pair of words.

PRACTICE Choose the pair of words that best completes each analogy.

1. lurk : wait ::
   a. spy : watch
   b. study : cheat
   c. skip : run
   d. gulp : drink
   e. tease : criticize
2. diverse : similar ::
   a. small : heavy
   b. sad : cheerful
   c. familiar : dangerous
   d. important : serious
   e. thankful : apologetic

For more about analogies, see **Communications Skills Handbook,** p. R67.

Before You Read

from *On the Road with Charles Kuralt*

MEET CHARLES KURALT

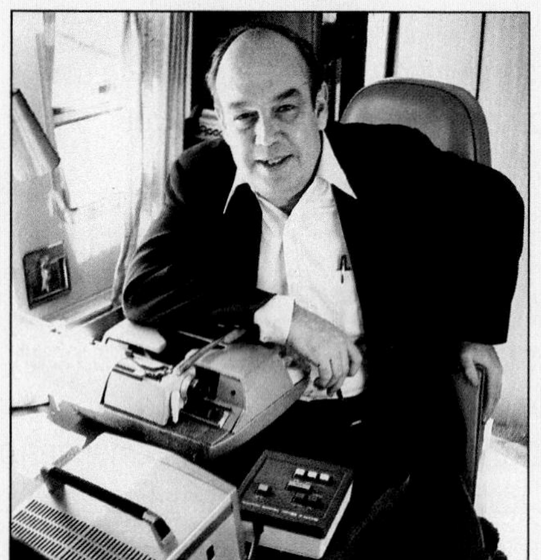

Charles Kuralt was already entertaining crowds at thirteen, when he recited "Casey at the Bat" for fans at a Charlotte Hornets minor-league baseball game. He continued for the rest of his life to share his interest in ordinary people with extraordinary stories to tell—as a newspaper journalist, a television personality, and a writer.

Charles Kuralt was born in 1934 and died in 1997. On the Road with Charles Kuralt *was first published in 1985.*

FOCUS ACTIVITY

How did your city or town get its name?

Brainstorm
Think of other names that would suit the place you live, and discuss why you think these names would be appropriate.

Setting a Purpose
Read to discover some of the stories behind the unusual names of towns across the United States.

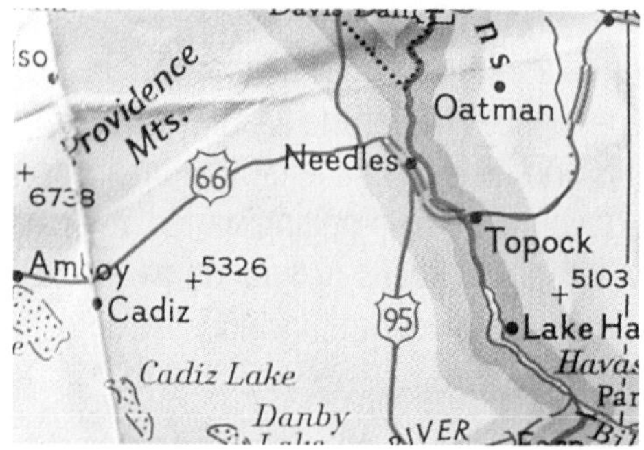

BACKGROUND

The Time and Place From 1967 to 1980, author and journalist Charles Kuralt traveled across the United States with a three-person television crew, looking for the "unimportant and irrelevant and insignificant." His reports profiling uncelebrated people in often obscure places were broadcast during CBS news programs.

Did You Know? During the years Kuralt traveled around the United States, he received twelve Emmy awards for outstanding work in television.

VOCABULARY PREVIEW

vain (vān) *adj.* overly concerned with or proud of one's appearance, abilities, or accomplishments; conceited; p. 636

pauper (pô′ pər) *n.* a very poor person, especially one supported by public charity; p. 638

quaint (kwānt) *adj.* charming in an old-fashioned way; pleasingly unusual or odd; p. 638

from On the Road with Charles Kuralt

Charles Kuralt

We spend a lot of time in bus stations. When every place else in town is closed, you can still get a cup of coffee in a bus station. I don't know how long it's been since you've been in a bus station, but if you are in love with American names, you could be happy just sitting here all day and listening.

BUS ANNOUNCER: This will be the first call for the eastbound bus for Junction City, Harrisburg, Halsey, Brownsville, Crawfordsville, Holley, Sweet Home, Hoodoo, Sisters, Bend,—

Did you hear what that man said? Sweet Home, Hoodoo, Sisters, and Bend? I suppose the names of Paris and London and Rome make some people's hearts beat faster. As for me, give me Sweet Home, Hoodoo, Sisters, and Bend.

BUS ANNOUNCER: Cheyenne, Denver, Dallas, Oklahoma City, Wichita, Kansas City, St. Louis.

"I have fallen in love with American names," Stephen Vincent Benét[1] wrote. "The sharp names that never get fat. The snakeskin titles of mining claims. The plumed war bonnet of Medicine Hat, Tucson and Deadwood and Lost Mule Flat." Oh, we know what you mean, Mr. Benét, we have been there too, to Bug Tussle and Granny's Neck and Hell-for-Certain, and we have learned that America's names tell stories if you will listen to them. Stories of hard times on the frontier.

Times couldn't have been very easy in Gnaw Bone, Indiana. Life must have been a little chancy in Cut and Shoot, Texas. And probably not much better for the settlers who named Hardscrabble Creek in Oregon. But more common are the satisfied names like Humansville or New Deal or Fair Play or Enough. Or outright Chamber of Commerce names like Frostproof, Florida, which of course isn't really. Likewise, we found little competition in Competition, Missouri. And no excessive opportunity in Opportunity, Washington. But their founders *hoped* there'd be, you see. The Chamber of Commerce instinct is strong, but sometimes vain. One night we passed through what must be the smallest town in America, about three families, and named, of course, Jumbo.

Americans have always loved the names of faraway places. I mean, why name a town Stony Lonesome when you can name it Valparaiso? It's a safe bet that the namers of Palestine and Warsaw had never been to either place; they just thought those names sounded nice. And if those folks in Ohio who named their towns for Cairo and Lima had ever been there, they wouldn't call them "Cay-ro" and "Lie-ma." The same goes

1. *Benét* (bə nā′) was an American who wrote poems, novels, and short stories in the first part of the twentieth century.

Vocabulary

vain (vān) *adj.* overly concerned with or proud of one's appearance, abilities, or accomplishments; conceited for "CAL-lus," Maine, and "MAD-rid," Iowa, and "Vi-EE-na," Georgia. Faraway places with strange sounding names, which sound even stranger coming out of American mouths. And if Odysseus, that old Greek traveler, could have come as we did to this intersection in North Carolina [*sign pointing in different directions to Carthage and Troy,*[2] N.C.], which way would he turn?

On we drove to Grubville, Missouri, where a traveler could always get a little grub. We had a Pepsi and a pack of Nabs there ourselves. And on to Limberlost Landing, Indiana, where limber Jim McDowell got lost in the swamps one day.

Some town names are just obviously the result of indecision or desperation. When they were trying to think of a name for one pleasant North Carolina community, somebody suggested why not call it this? Somebody else, why not call it that? Until one wise man said, why not call it Whynot? And indeed, why not?

"I have fallen in love with American names." So have we, Mr. Benét. All those places named out of patriotism, some of them, or convenience, or humor, or hope; all those places, all those lovely names. Sweet Home and Hoodoo and Sisters and Bend.

People travel far too fast to read milestones nowadays. And whenever you find one, you can be sure it's a very unimportant road. But when one particular milestone was planted 150 years ago, it was on the most important road in America. The road started one mile back in Cumberland, Maryland. And it went—west.

The road was a dream of Washington and Jefferson's; and John C. Calhoun made a great speech in favor of it. He said, "Let us conquer space." The space he meant was not from here to the moon. But in 1817, it might as well have been. It was from Cumberland, Maryland, clear to the Illinois frontier. And they built it with mattocks and axes and paving stones. They actually built the thing west to the river

Did You Know?
The *mattock* is a tool consisting of a handle and a two-bladed head, used for loosening soil and cutting roots.

2. The adventures of *Odysseus* (ō dis′ ē əs) are described in two works written around 800 B.C. The original *Carthage* was founded around 700 B.C. in northern Africa, and *Troy* was first built more than 4,000 years ago in what is now western

town of Wheeling, and west to Zanesville, and west to the prairie village of Columbus, Ohio, and west across the Wabash. It was the longest, straightest road in history and a marvel of the world. They called it the National Road.

We stumbled upon a few miles of the old roadbed in Ohio; a few cobblestones, a few massive old abandoned bridges. And we thought we better show you these things now, because before long there might be nothing left to show you.

Already the road is a nearly forgotten part of the American romance. This incredible road, which carried so many peddlers and paupers and preachers and politicians west to the new America; and carried so many poor families in battered wagons from worn-out farms west to a second chance. Ideas went west, mail and newspapers; and in fancy stagecoaches, Jenny Lind and P. T. Barnum;[3] and in groaning Conestoga freight wagons, calico and iron and whiskey and gunpowder—all the things it took to build a country. The National Road brought Henry Clay east from Kentucky and Abraham Lincoln from Illinois.

You mustn't imagine that it was just a road. It was an Appian Way,[4] sixty-six feet wide for six hundred miles. "A finer road," an English traveler said, "than the highway from London to Bath." It must have been impossible for travelers on this highroad through the wilderness to imagine that anything would ever take its place. In places, the route of the National Road is now called U.S. 40. In places, it is called Interstate 70, our new National Road, on which the thunder of the big diesels drowns out the creaking echo of the Conestoga wagons.

But in quieter places, the vacant windows of shuttered general stores still reflect the pathway of the original road. A handful of the fine old taverns—which once watered the horses and brandied the gentlemen—still stand. The one on Mount Washington in Pennsylvania is remembered as unusual: its landlady was civil and her husband was sober.

Nobody reads the mileposts anymore; great green signs have taken their place. And the traffic roars up the hills past the old tollhouses with their quaint list of charges: "For every chariot, coach, coachee, stage, phaeton or chaise[5] with two horses and four wheels, 12 cents." Today's chariots pass without reading or paying.

We just wanted to show you this much before it's too late. If you go slow enough and look hard enough, you can still find traces in the weeds, the last faint traces of the road that made us a nation.

3. *Lind* was a Swedish opera singer. *Barnum,* an American showman, brought Lind to the United States and managed her very successful nationwide concert tour in the 1850s.

4. The *Appian Way* was the first and best of the great roadways built by the ancient Romans. Construction began in 312 B.C., eventually extending the road to 366 miles. The road is still in use today.

5. The *coachee* is a carriage shaped like a coach, but longer and open in the front. The *phaeton* (fā′ ət ən) is a light, low, open four-wheeled carriage. And the *chaise* is a light two-wheeled carriage, often with a hood or folding top.

Vocabulary

pauper (pô′ pər) *n.* a very poor person, especially one supported by public charity

quaint (kwānt) *adj.* charming in an old-fashioned way; pleasingly unusual or odd

Responding to Literature

PERSONAL RESPONSE

What do you think Charles Kuralt might have said about the region in which you live?

Analyzing Literature

RECALL

1. Who, in Kuralt's opinion, should spend some time in a bus station?
2. What are some of the "faraway places" Americans have used as names for their towns?
3. What was the National Road?
4. What is a *milestone?*

INTERPRET

5. What are some of the reasons, in your opinion, that Kuralt enjoys place names?
6. Why, do you think, might settlers name a town Lima or Warsaw?
7. Why, do you think, does Kuralt want readers to know about the National Road?
8. Why does America have lots of "great green signs"?

EVALUATE AND CONNECT

9. Theme Connection In your view, what can give Americans new insights about their country's value besides visiting places with interesting names?
10. Would you enjoy traveling with someone like Charles Kuralt? Explain why or why not.

LITERARY ELEMENTS

Style

Some authors write in such a distinctive way that readers can guess who they are by reading a short paragraph. **Style** is the distinctive way in which a writer uses words, constructs sentences, and creates meaning. Charles Kuralt developed a style of writing in which he used a conversational tone and often addressed the reader directly.

1. List some questions Kuralt liked to ask the reader.
2. Point out places where it seems as though Kuralt could be speaking directly to you.

- See **Literary Terms Handbook,** p. R9.

Charles Kuralt (far right) and his traveling crew.

Extending Your Response

Writing About Literature

Names, American Style Kuralt based "American Names" on poet Stephen Vincent Benét's remark, "I have fallen in love with American names." Reread Benét's words carefully. Then, analyze why Kuralt may have chosen this quote, and explain how well he supported Benét's idea.

Interdisciplinary Activity

History Charles Kuralt was interested in finding out about the lives of ordinary people. Conduct your own investigation of a specific time period and location in the United States. Find out what life was like for ordinary people in that place and time. Then, write a description from the point of view of one of those people. Include the most interesting details from your research.

Personal Writing

"Quote Me!" Use a book of quotations, Internet sources, or periodicals to find a quote that expresses an idea you would like to share. Write a short essay based on and including the quote. You might use it in the title of the essay to emphasize your point.

Literature Groups

Hurry Up! Discuss why many people in the United States seem to be in such a hurry. Name stories, poems, songs, movies, or television programs that show this characteristic of many Americans at different periods in U.S. history.

Reading Further

If you enjoy traveling in books, read:
The Car by Gary Paulsen

Save your work for your portfolio.

Skill Minilesson

VOCABULARY • MULTIPLE-MEANING WORDS

Many multiple-meaning words, such as the *bark* of a dog and the *bark* of a tree, are different parts of speech and have different meanings. However, some words, such as *vain,* have different meanings for the same part of speech, which can be confusing.

Vain can mean "conceited" or "worthless" or "having little or no effect." By paying attention to context clues, you can tell which meaning is correct in a sentence.

PRACTICE Use context clues to help you decide which would be the best synonym for *vain* in each example.

1. She is untrustworthy and makes vain promises.
   a. conceited b. worthless c. unsuccessful
2. I made a vain effort to eat my soup with a fork.
   a. conceited b. worthless c. unsuccessful
3. His vain comments showed how high an opinion he had of himself.
   a. conceited b. worthless c. unsuccessful

- For more about multiple-meaning words, see **Reading Handbook,** pp. R80–R81.

Writing Skills

Writing an Effective Introduction

You and your remote control are exploring the possibilities as a new hour of television is starting. What makes you stop clicking that button and stay with a show? An interesting beginning! In the same way, a good introduction can make you sit up and pay close attention in school when someone begins to speak. Good writers and good speakers know that a strong introduction will attract and hold an audience.

Off to a Good Start! Whether you are planning an essay or a speech, you want to focus on a strong beginning. One way to do this is by surprising your reader. Consider the first sentence of the selection from *On the Road with Charles Kuralt:* "We spend a lot of time in bus stations." This statement is unusual and helps Kuralt catch the reader's attention. Then he moves right into the main idea of his essay by telling his readers why he is in bus stations.

> We spend a lot of time in bus stations. When every place else in town is closed, you can still get a cup of coffee in a bus station. I don't know how long it's been since you've been in a bus station, but if you are in love with American names, you could be happy just sitting here all day and listening.

Statement of Purpose Always plan to introduce a topic in an interesting way. Then use your introduction to lead your audience to the main idea of your essay or speech. You may want to be serious or funny, entertaining or persuasive, but you always want to be interesting. The list below may help you think of other introductory techniques that will guarantee an attentive audience for your ideas.

- Begin with a vivid story, a joke, or a funny story.
- Let your first sentence be an unexpected, interesting statement or question.

● For more about the writing process, see **Writing Handbook,** pp. R50–R53.

ACTIVITIES

1. Choose a selection you have read that has a strong introduction. Write a paragraph or two giving reasons and examples to support your choice.
2. Think of an awakening that you have experienced or that someone has told you about. List details that you might include in an introduction to an essay about the experience. Explain how each detail would help you write a strong introduction.

Before You Read

Americans All

MEET MICHAEL DORRIS

Michael Dorris's life changed when a neighbor repaid him for some yard work by giving him a book. He recalled, "I was stunned by the undiluted power a novel could contain." Reading helped lead him to a career as an anthropologist—a scientist who studies the development of human cultures—and as a professor of Native American studies at Dartmouth College. Dorris, who was Irish, French, and Modoc, also gained fame as a writer of poetry, essays, and novels.

Michael Dorris was born in 1945 and died in 1997. "Americans All" was first printed by Newsday *in 1992.*

FOCUS ACTIVITY

Do all Americans share the same music? language? values? Is there anything that all Americans have in common?

List It!
With a partner, list objects and beliefs that you think most Americans share.

Setting a Purpose
Read to find out how one writer describes his fellow Americans.

BACKGROUND

The Time and Place In this essay, Michael Dorris shares some thoughts about the people of the United States in modern times.

VOCABULARY PREVIEW

emphatically (em fat′ i kəl ē) *adv.* very definitely; clearly; p. 643
proximity (prok sim′ ə tē) *n.* closeness in space, time, order, or degree; nearness; p. 644
manifest (man′ ə fest′) *adj.* obvious; clear; plain; evident; p. 644
incompatible (in′ kəm pat′ ə bəl) *adj.* not capable of existing or working together in harmony; conflicting; p. 644
disembark (dis′ im bärk′) *v.* to get off of a train, airplane, ship, or other vehicle; p. 644
revel (rev′ əl) *v.* to take great pleasure; p. 644

Americans All

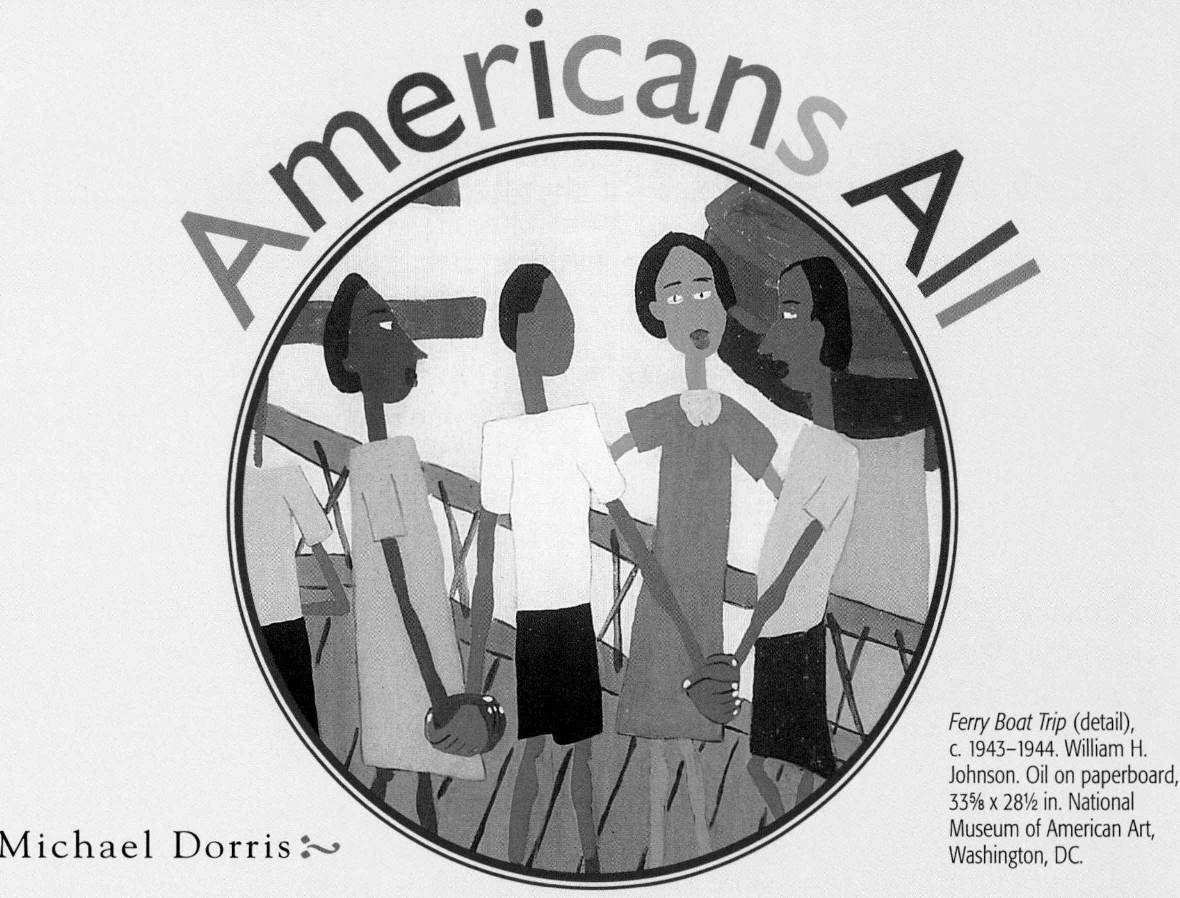

Ferry Boat Trip (detail), c. 1943–1944. William H. Johnson. Oil on paperboard, 33⅝ x 28½ in. National Museum of American Art, Washington, DC.

Michael Dorris

I recognize them instantly abroad: on the street, in crowded rooms, on airplanes, at restaurants—but how? It's emphatically not skin color, not clothing, not little red-white-and-blues stitched to their breast pockets. They don't have to say anything, to show a passport, or to sing the "Star Spangled Banner," but nevertheless they're unmistakable in any foreign setting.

Americans. We come in all varieties of size, age, and style. We travel singly and in groups. We're alternately loud and disapproving or humble and apologetic. We seek each other out or self-consciously avoid each other's company. We pack our gear in Gucci bags or stuff it into Patagonia backpacks, travel first class or on Eurorail passes, stay in youth hostels[1] or in luxury hotels, but none of that matters.

1. *Eurorail passes* are inexpensive train tickets that allow purchasers to travel throughout Europe within a limited period of time. *Hostels* are inexpensive lodging places.

Vocabulary

emphatically (em fat′ i kəl ē) *adv.* very definitely; clearly

It's as though we're individually implanted with some invisible beeper, some national homing device, that's activated by the proximity of similar equipment.

This common denominator is manifest in shared knowledge (we all know who Mary Tyler Moore[2] is), topics of mutual interest or dispute (guns, the environment, choice), and popular culture (do we or do we not deserve a thousand-calorie break today?). In other words, we take the same things seriously or not seriously, are capable of speaking, when we choose to, not merely a common language but a common idiom,[3] and know the melodies, if not all the words, to many of the same songs.

Why, then, doesn't any of this count when we're *not* overseas? Why, at home, do we seem so different from each other, so mutually incompatible, so strange and forbidding? Do we have to recognize each other in Tokyo or Cairo in order to see through the distinctions and into the commonalities?[4] How does that "we," so obvious anywhere else in the world, get split into "us" and "them" when we're stuck within our own borders?

The answer is clear: to be Americans means to be not the clone of the people next door. I fly back from any homogeneous country, from a place where every person I see is blond, or black, or belongs to only one religion, and then disembark at JFK. I revel in the cadence[5] of many accents, catch a ride to the city with a Nigerian-American or Russian-American cab driver. Eat Thai food at a Greek restaurant next to a table of Chinese-American conventioneers[6] from Alabama. Get directions from an Iranian-American cop and drink a cup of Turkish coffee served by a Navajo student at Fordham who's majoring in Japanese literature. Argue with everybody about everything. I'm home.

from *Newsday*
October 1992

2. *Mary Tyler Moore* is an actress who had a popular television show during the 1970s.
3. *Common idiom* refers to the way words are put together to express thoughts so that most people with the same background understand them. An *idiom* is an expression whose meaning cannot always be determined from the literal meaning of its words.
4. *Distinctions* are differences, and *commonalities* are similarities.
5. A *clone* is an exact copy, and *homogeneous* (hō′ mə jē′ nē əs) means "having a similar character or similar parts throughout." *JFK* refers to the New York City airport named for President John F. Kennedy. The rhythmic flow, or rising and falling sound, of speech is its *cadence.*
6. *Conventioneers* are people who attend conventions, large meetings of state or national organizations.

Vocabulary

proximity (prok sim′ ə tē) *n.* closeness in space, time, order, or degree; nearness
manifest (man′ ə fest′) *adj.* obvious; clear; plain; evident
incompatible (in′ kəm pat′ ə bəl) *adj.* not capable of existing or working together in harmony; conflicting
disembark (dis′ im bärk′) *v.* to get off of a train, airplane, ship, or other vehicle
revel (rev′ əl) *v.* to take great pleasure

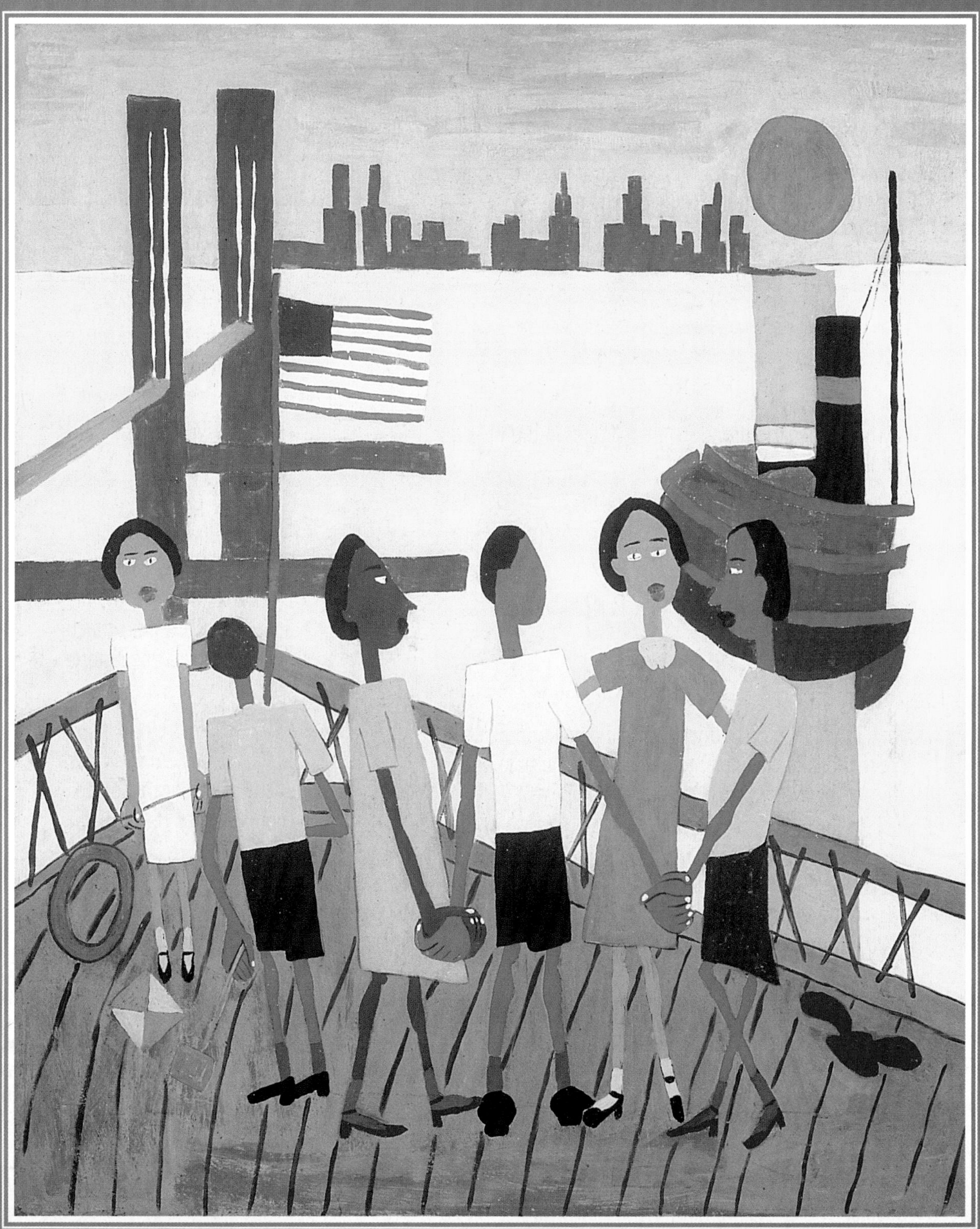

Ferry Boat Trip, c. 1943–1944.

Viewing the painting: Would you, like Michael Dorris, "recognize them instantly abroad"? Why or why not?

Responding to Literature

PERSONAL RESPONSE

If you were in a foreign country, do you think you would recognize other Americans? Why or why not?

Analyzing Literature

RECALL

1. To whom does the pronoun "them" refer in the opening sentence?
2. What, according to Dorris, do Americans have in common?
3. When do the things Americans have in common seem not to count?
4. Does Dorris think that all Americans should try to be alike? Explain.

INTERPRET

5. What, in your opinion, does Dorris mean when he says, "We're individually implanted with some invisible beeper . . . activated by the proximity of similar equipment"?
6. How do the references to Mary Tyler Moore, a thousand-calorie break, and the environment support Dorris's main idea?
7. What might Dorris want readers to consider when he asks, "How does that 'we' . . . get split into 'us' and 'them' when we're stuck within our own borders?"
8. Why does the writer "revel" in what he experiences when he arrives home after foreign travel?

EVALUATE AND CONNECT

9. In the second paragraph, Dorris repeatedly begins a sentence with "we" to drive his point home. Does his use of **repetition** convince you to believe him? Why or why not?
10. Are you a "clone of the people next door"? Give three reasons why or why not.

LITERARY ELEMENTS

Author's Purpose

The **author's purpose** is the reason a piece of literature was written: to entertain, inform, persuade, or explain. The main purpose of an essay like "Americans All" is to persuade readers to see a situation the way the writer sees it.

1. State briefly the situation described by Michael Dorris.
2. How does Dorris show his attitude toward the situation? Give examples to support your answer.
3. In your opinion, how successful is Michael Dorris in persuading Americans to see themselves as he does?

- See **Literary Terms Handbook,** p. R1.

Extending Your Response

Personal Writing

Dear Editor Write a letter to the editor of your newspaper. State one of Dorris's ideas, and explain why you agree or disagree with him. Give examples based on personal experience to back up your opinion. Look at your response to the **Focus Activity** on page 642.

Literature Groups

Why? Dorris asks four questions in his fourth paragraph. Join with your group and answer his four questions. Give two reasons or examples to support each answer.

Learning for Life

Examining Popular Culture Dorris wrote, "We all know who Mary Tyler Moore is," referring to the power of television to spread popular culture. Imagine that you are a person from another country seeing a popular U.S. show for the first time. Write an evaluation of the show, drawing conclusions about American culture from it.

Writing About Literature

Idioms When Dorris says Americans speak a common idiom, he means we understand the same buzz words, slang, and jargon. An **idiom** is a word or phrase that has a meaning other than that shown by its parts. For example, if a coach tells a runner, "You're wasting time! Here's where I draw the line," the runner doesn't expect the coach to bend over and draw a line on the floor. With a partner, list some idioms common to you and your classmates.

Reading Further

If you enjoyed this essay, try these books about Americans who are like and unlike others.

Eleanor Roosevelt: A Life of Discovery by Russell Freedman

And One for All by Theresa Nelson

Save your work for your portfolio.

Skill Minilesson

VOCABULARY • UNLOCKING MEANING

You can often unlock the meaning of a word by analyzing parts of the word that are familiar. For example, if you know that *emphatically* means "very definitely" or "clearly," you may be able to guess that *emphasis* means "a special stress or importance given to something."

- For more on unlocking word meanings, see **Reading Handbook,** pp. R80–R81.

PRACTICE Use your knowledge of the vocabulary words from this selection to write a definition for each underlined word.

1. Their laughter was a manifestation of their shared memory.
2. The revelry continued all day.
3. Every traveler found a compatible partner.
4. The cities are approximately forty miles apart.

Technology Skills

Internet: Evaluating On-line Sources

"The number of UFO sightings worldwide proves that extraterrestrial beings are visiting Earth regularly."
"UFOs are a sign that the end of the world is at hand. We cannot identify these objects; they are beyond our understanding."
"UFOs are simply unidentified flying objects. They could be balloons or airplanes or even meteors. The existence of UFOs does not prove that life exists on other planets."

Each statement above presents a different point of view on the subject of UFOs. As you explore the Internet, you will find that many topics can be interpreted in a number of ways. Because the Net provides a voice to so many people on such a variety of topics, you will need to sort through the information to determine for yourself what you can believe and which point of view you can accept.

TECHNOLOGY TIP

You can often use the Internet to check on a person's reliability as a source of information. If a writer claims to teach at a university, check the list of faculty names at the university's Web site. The American Medical Association may be able to help you find out whether the person offering medical opinions is a licensed physician. Most professions have organizations that keep records of their members, and these organizations usually have Web sites. A search engine will help you find these sites.

Before You Get Started

Take a few minutes and consider how you form your own opinions. What influences your thinking? How, exactly, do you determine what you believe? Do you consider all the facts? Do you go with a gut feeling or a hunch? Do you ask for the opinions of others and then weigh the strengths of their arguments? Jot down in your journal several sentences that sum up how you arrive at your own conclusions.

Point of View: How Can You Tell?

A statement that represents only one point of view often includes context clues to let the reader know that the assertion is just an opinion. Such hints include: *in my opinion, I submit, I assert, I believe, we feel, I surmise, we infer that,* and *the speculation is.* A reader who is alert to such clues will not be led into thinking that a point of view is a statement of fact.

You may have more trouble when the person does not use such hints. The above statements about UFOs, for example, simply state opinions as though they were facts. When you come across such statements—as you are likely to do often on the Internet—you will need to analyze what the writers say.

- Is the evidence from a reliable source? Anyone can operate a Web site. Doing so does not necessarily make the person an authority on a topic.

- Is the source someone commonly known and accepted as an expert in the field under discussion? For example, a professor who teaches American literature at a major university is probably a more reliable source of information about Mark Twain than a television personality or a surgeon would be.
- Has the source convincingly argued his or her case?
- What evidence does the source offer to support her or his arguments?
- Can information presented as factual be confirmed by other sources?
- Are there other points of view that present equally convincing arguments?

Practice

With a partner, decide on a topic that interests both of you. Try to choose a topic on which people are likely to have different points of view.

1. Log on to the World Wide Web. Open a search engine, and type in keywords that describe the topic you are researching. For example, if you were searching for sites about UFOs, *UFO* and *theories* might be useful keywords.
2. Browse through the hits to locate examples of differing points of view. For each opinion you come across, record the name and URL (Web address) of the site on which it is found and a brief summary of the point of view. When you have found and documented at least two different points of view, log off.
3. Together, determine the criteria by which you will evaluate these points of view. On what will you base the credibility of the opinions? Factual evidence? Strength of persuasive arguments? Attractiveness of Web site? Your personal opinions?
4. Cooperatively, write a brief report in which you:
   - **a.** compare and contrast the points of view expressed.
   - **b.** evaluate the opinions and explain the criteria you used in your evaluation.
   - **c.** decide which point of view, if any, you and your partner agree with.
5. Share your report with your class.

ACTIVITIES

1. Do a World Wide Web search on an issue in the news, such as pollution or the destruction of the world's rain forests. Find at least two different points of view on the subject. In your journal, compare your own opinion with those you find on the Net.
2. Create a site on your school's Intranet where students can argue their points of view on particular topics of interest to your community.

Writing WORKSHOP

Expository Writing: Public Service Announcement

"And now, this message . . ." Public service messages are wake-up calls. On television and radio, in the newspaper, and on bulletin boards, these nuggets of information alert us to up-to-the-minute activities and ideas. What subject do you think people should know about?

Assignment: Follow the process on these pages to write your own public service message.

- As you write your public service announcement, refer to the **Writing Handbook, pp. R50–R55.**

The Writing Process

PREWRITING

PREWRITING TIP

Find a subject or event that you want to get involved with. If *you* feel enthusiastic, you can spark enthusiasm in your audience.

Launch an Idea Search

You may already know what you want to write about: a walk-a-thon for a charity or a homework help line, for instance. The following sources may help you think of other events that are interesting and worthwhile.

- school, church, club, or community newsletters
- public library bulletin boards and information desks
- your local newspaper or its Web site
- Chamber of Commerce booths and Web sites

Know Your Audience and Purpose

Is your message for people your age or for people of all ages who share a concern or interest? Your purpose is to spread the word, so know your audience. If you know what your audience cares about, you can plan ways to make people take notice.

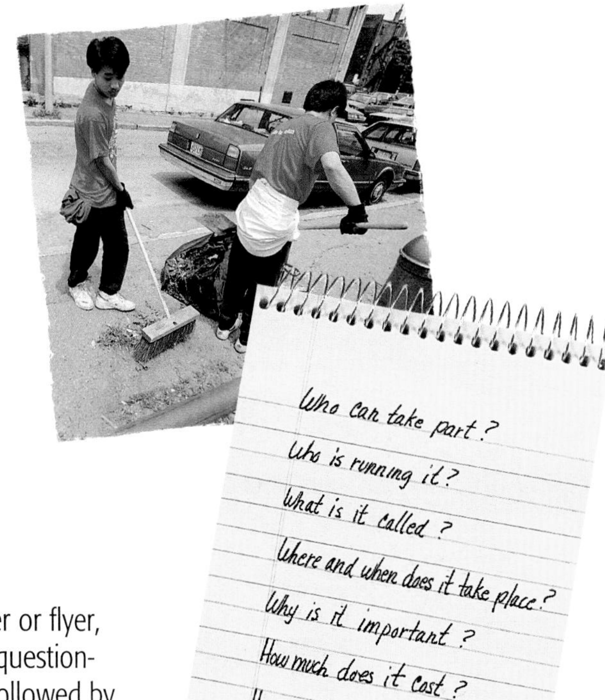

Who can take part?
Who is running it?
What is it called?
Where and when does it take place?
Why is it important?
How much does it cost?
How can people get more information?

Get the Facts

Your message may be in the form of a flier, a television announcement, or a radio bulletin. The six news writing questions—*who, what, where, when, why,* and *how*—will help you gather facts to make your message thorough and effective.

Pull It Together

If you want to write an announcement or design a poster or flyer, plan your message to fit on one page. You might use a question-and-answer format, a bulleted list, or a set of headings followed by short paragraphs. Planning where each item will be on the page can help you organize your ideas.

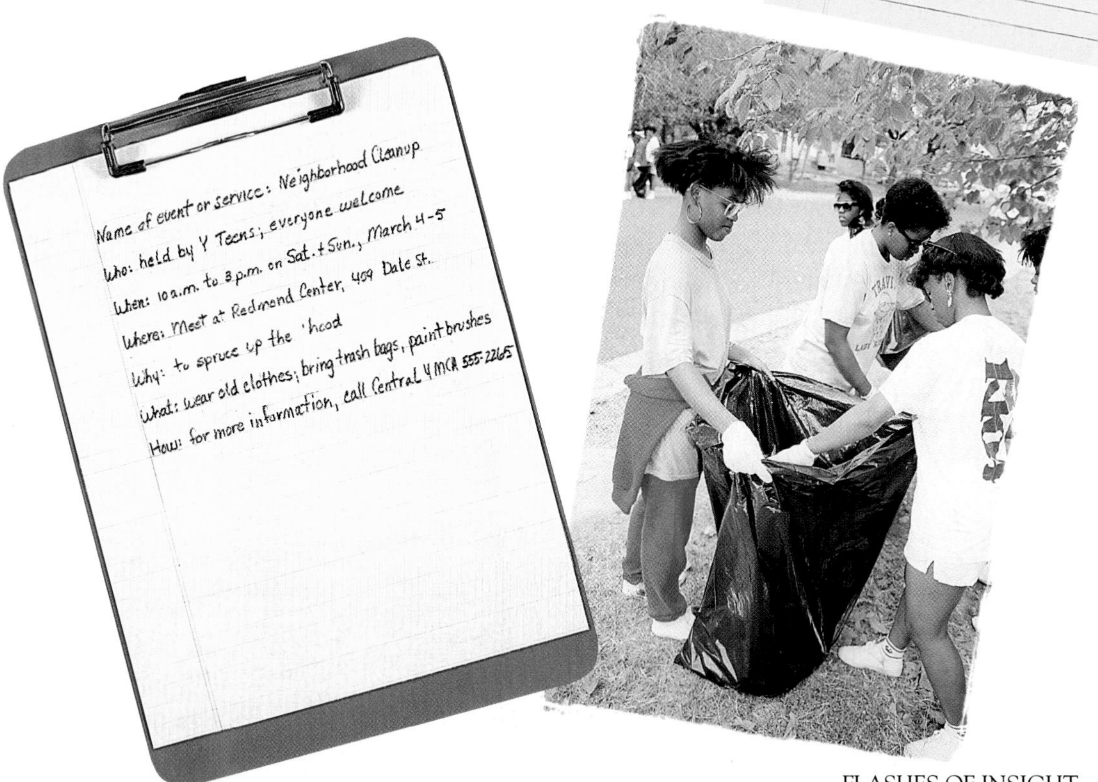

Name of event or service: Neighborhood Cleanup
Who: held by Y Teens; everyone welcome
When: 10 a.m. to 3 p.m. on Sat. + Sun., March 4-5
Where: Meet at Redmond Center, 409 Dale St.
Why: to spruce up the 'hood
What: wear old clothes; bring trash bags, paint brushes
How: for more information, call Central YMCA 555-2265

DRAFTING

DRAFTING TIP

Be clear about your facts. Write to inform more than to persuade. A public service message isn't a commercial.

Get Down to Basics

A catchy opening line is a strong way to start–but don't worry if you can't think of one. Just begin writing the basics. The introduction may occur to you as you write, and it is often the last part a professional writer drafts. For help with introductions, see the **Writing Skills** feature on page 641.

Follow Through

Keep writing, turning your prewriting notes into clear phrases, sentences, or paragraphs. Effective public service announcements are brief and straightforward, so steer clear of long explanations and complicated language.

MODEL • DRAFTING

Want to spruce up your neighborhood? Here's your chance. Join the Y Teens' neighborhood cleanup!
WHEN? March 4-5, from 10 A.M. to 3 P.M.
WHERE? Redmond Center, 409 Dale St.

REVISING

REVISING TIP

Listen as a partner reads your draft aloud. Catch tongue-twisters and straighten them out.

TECHNOLOGY TIP

Check your school computer lab for software to help you generate posters.

Relax and Reconsider

If you can, take a break from your draft. Then return to it, and use the **Questions for Revising** to plan changes that will improve your message. For a flier, consider visual elements too. For an announcement, consider sound. A partner can help you see–and hear–your work objectively.

QUESTIONS FOR REVISING

- How can I be sure I have my audience's attention at the beginning?
- What, if any, important information is missing?
- Which parts seem wordy? How can I make them simple?
- How might I change the order of my facts to make the message more effective?
- Where might a change in words or design make my message clearer?

EDITING/PROOFREADING

When your announcement reads exactly the way you want it to, it's time to proofread for errors in grammar, usage, and mechanics. The **Proofreading Checklist** at the right can help. Pay special attention to adjectives. The **Grammar Link** on page 572 shows you how to use regular and irregular adjectives correctly.

Grammar Hint

Use the comparative adjective *better* for comparing two things. For comparing three or more things, use *best*.

That was the best day of the whole year!

PROOFREADING CHECKLIST

- ☑ Adjectives are used correctly. (Double-check adjectives in comparisons.)
- ☑ Sentences are complete; there are no fragments or run-ons.
- ☑ Verbs agree with subjects.
- ☑ Pronouns are in the correct forms and agree with their antecedents.
- ☑ Spelling, capitalization, and punctuation are correct.

MODEL • EDITING/PROOFREADING

It is ~~best~~ better to help solve problems in your community than to pretend they don't exist.

PUBLISHING/PRESENTING

Decide on the best way to deliver your public service message. Then put out the word! If you plan to deliver the message orally, you might review the guidelines in the **Listening, Speaking, and Viewing** feature on page 502.

PRESENTING TIP

If listeners ask a question you can't answer, don't panic. Tell them you'll find out and get back to them—then do.

Reflecting

Write your thoughts about this project in your journal.

- Was it difficult to keep your message short and complete? Explain.
- Might you enjoy creating public service messages? Why or why not?

Save your work for your portfolio.

Theme Wrap-Up

Responding to the Theme

1. Based on your reading in this theme, explain the following statements about "Flashes of Insight."
   - Reading about a new way of looking at the world can lead to personal growth.
   - Understanding an event may change the way a reader thinks.
2. Which selection in the theme helped you to gain a new insight? Explain.
3. Present your theme project to the class.

Analyzing Literature

FIND THE FOIL

A **foil** is a character who draws attention to traits of a main character by showing contrasting traits. For example, a very selfish character will contrast with the generosity of the main character. Identify a foil somewhere in this theme, and describe how the foil helps you understand the main character.

Evaluate and Set Goals

1. Which of the following activities did you enjoy the most in this theme? Which was most difficult?
   - reading and understanding the selections
   - writing on your own
   - analyzing and discussing the selections
   - presenting ideas and projects
   - researching topics
2. How would you assess your work in this theme, using the following scale? Give at least two reasons for your assessment.

   4 = outstanding   2 = fair
   3 = good   1 = weak
3. Think about what you found challenging in this theme and choose a goal to work toward in the next theme.
   - Record your goal and three steps you will take to help you reach it.
   - Meet with your teacher to review your plan for achieving your goal.

Build Your Portfolio

SELECT

Choose two of your favorite pieces of work from this theme to include in your portfolio. The following questions can help you choose.

- Which did you learn the most from?
- Which was more challenging than you expected?
- Which was the most interesting to others?

REFLECT

Write some notes to accompany the pieces you selected. Use these questions to guide you.

- What do you like best about the piece?
- What did others like best?
- What did you learn from creating it?

Reading on Your Own

If you enjoyed the literature in this theme, you might also be interested in the following books.

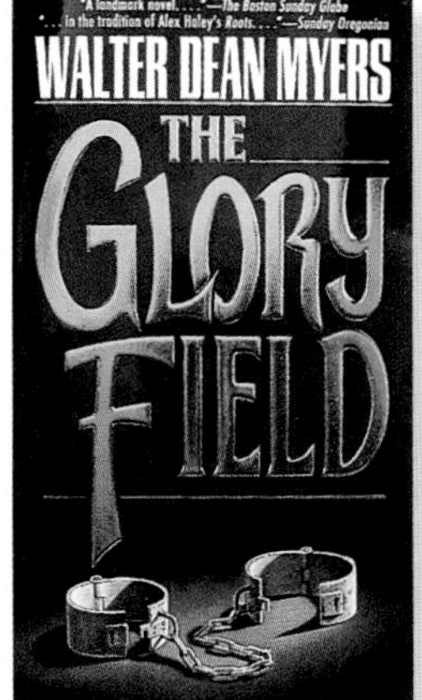

The Glory Field

by Walter Dean Myers This is a story of the Lewis family, beginning in their African homeland and ending in contemporary America. Throughout the decades, they manage to maintain continuous ownership of a piece of land, the Glory Field. The author focuses on a strong teenage character in each generation as he tells their story.

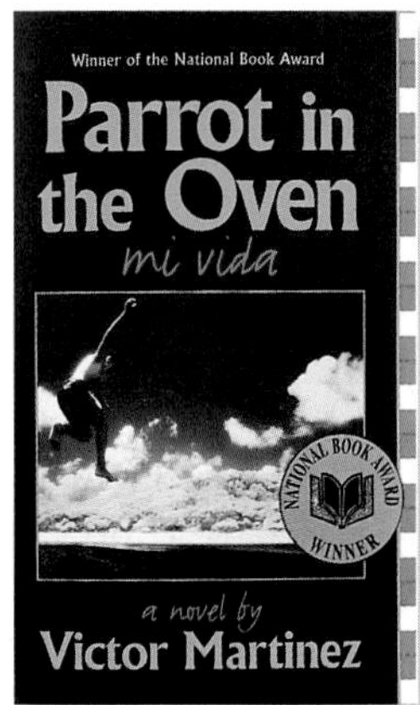

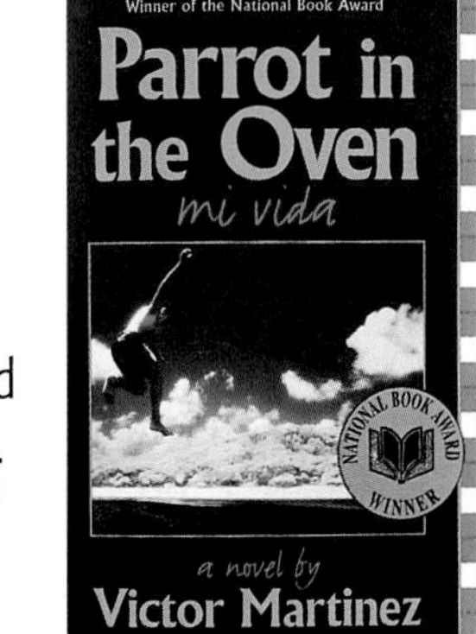

Parrot in the Oven: *mi vida*

by Victor Martinez Manny Hernandez is fourteen, and his father has him convinced that he is "just a penny"–not worth much. One way to be worth a lot is to be part of a gang, and Manny must decide.

SOS Titanic

by Eve Bunting
As the *Titanic* sinks, Irish immigrants trapped in cabins below deck awaken to new values and extend help to old enemies, as well as to family members.

Lupita Mañana

by Patricia Beatty Lupita Torres is thirteen when she and her older brother enter the United States to find work and support their widowed mother and younger siblings. The two must weigh the need to find jobs with the dangers and difficulties of crossing a border illegally.

Standardized Test Practice

Read the following passage. Then read each question on page 657. Decide which is the best answer to each question. Mark the letter for that answer on your paper.

Langston Hughes: A Poet's Journey

Langston Hughes was one of the most influential poets in a movement known as the Harlem Renaissance. Hughes was born on February 1, 1902, in Joplin, Missouri. In 1914, he moved to Illinois to live with his father and stepmother. While in grade school in Illinois, Hughes developed an interest in poetry, and before he had finished high school, he had read the works of many famous thinkers and poets.

In 1919, Hughes moved to Mexico, where his father had become a prosperous businessman. However, Hughes did not agree with his father's plans for him to attend college and study engineering. He returned to New York, where he studied for a year at Columbia University. He then began two years of travel, working at odd jobs in several countries.

When Hughes returned to the United States, he rejoined his mother in Washington, D.C., and took a job as a hotel busboy. In the restaurant, he saw Vachel Lindsay, a noted poet. Hughes was too shy to approach and introduce himself, but while Lindsay dined, Hughes managed to slide several of his own poems under Lindsay's plate. As he read the poems, Lindsay noticed that Hughes was using structural qualities he himself aimed for. That night he read Hughes's poems to an audience of selected guests, and overnight Hughes became a respected local figure.

With Lindsay's guidance, Hughes submitted several of his pieces to magazines for publication. One poem, "The Weary Blues," won a prize from *Opportunity*, a leading periodical that featured African American writing. This poem became the title piece for Hughes's first volume of verse, published in 1926.

Hughes received his college degree in 1929. That same year, he completed his first novel, *Not Without Laughter*. His career skyrocketed from this point, and Hughes suddenly found himself to be a writer of national fame. He was particularly well known for his readings of his own pieces.

Until his death in 1967, Hughes continued to break new ground in poetry by creating verse that dealt with life as an African American man. He created several fictitious characters, such as Jesse Simple, a wise and humorous black laborer. With Simple, he explored America through the eyes of a minority figure. In addition, Hughes contributed a weekly column to the *New York Post* that began to express to a growing nation the experiences of its African American citizens. With his writing, Hughes helped to bridge the gap between people of different ethnic backgrounds.

1 The author of the passage seems to believe that Langston Hughes was —

A unlucky

B talented

C impatient

D quiet

2 According to the passage, which of the following events happened first?

F Hughes met Vachel Lindsay.

G Hughes worked at odd jobs and traveled.

H Hughes developed an interest in poetry.

J Hughes wrote for the *New York Post*.

3 The author of this passage seems to provide evidence that —

A diligence and a love for your work are necessary for an artist's success

B poets need to live hard lives if they have any hope of becoming famous

C artists must set aside their families and friends in order to work

D a religious upbringing is essential to writing good poetry

4 Which is the best summary of the passage?

F Travel is good for aspiring young poets.

G Langston Hughes's background influenced his career as a writer.

H Hughes held many different jobs during his life.

J Hughes never got along well with his father, and they had particularly bad times in 1919.

5 Why did Vachel Lindsay find Hughes's poems impressive?

A He liked reading poems with his dinner.

B He, too, had traveled and understood Hughes's work.

C He thought Hughes was very motivated.

D The poems had a structure similar to that in his own work.

6 What is the main idea of the last paragraph?

F Hughes had traveled widely and could speak for people everywhere.

G Simple was Hughes's favorite character.

H Hughes's writing influenced and characterized the black experience of his era.

J The *New York Post* column was profitable for Hughes.

Faces of Dignity

"Think of all the beauty still left around you and be happy."

—Anne Frank, from *Anne Frank: The Diary of a Young Girl*

Korczak and the Children of the Ghetto. Boris Saktsier.

THEME 7

THEME CONTENTS

GENRE FOCUS *DRAMA*

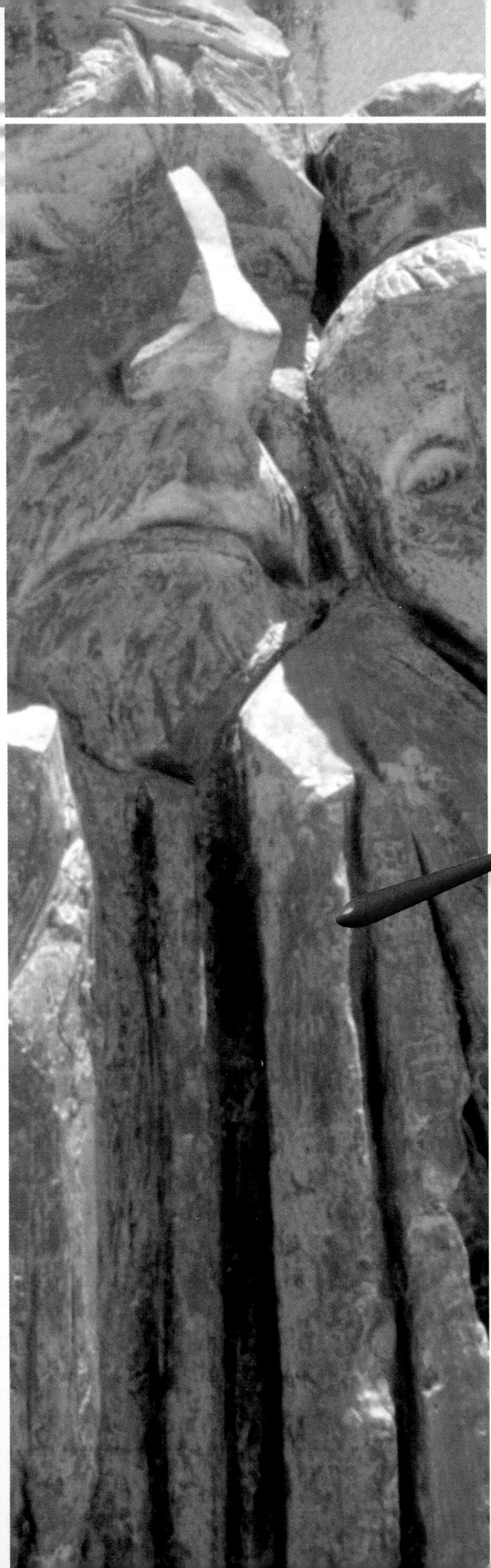

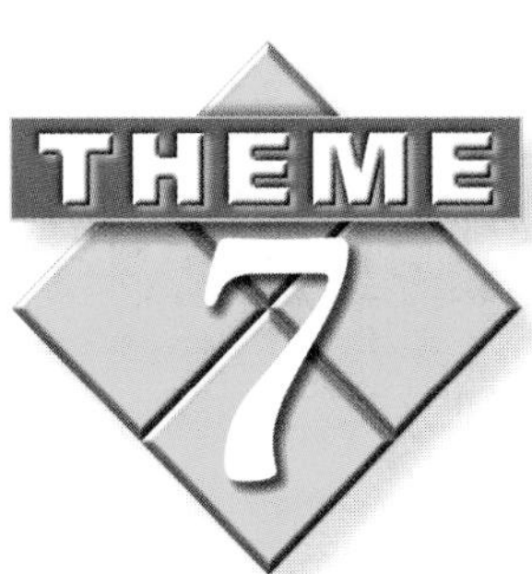

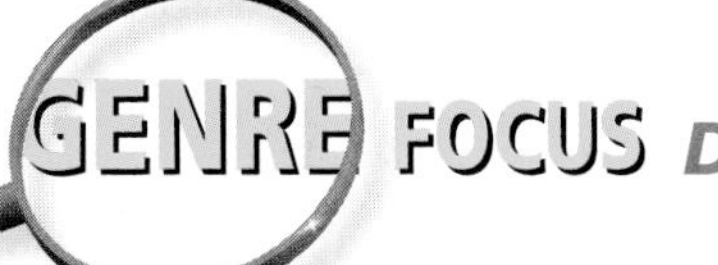

Exploring the Theme

Faces of Dignity

What is it that helps a person to endure a crisis with immense courage and dignity? Some people cope with difficult situations by focusing on a guiding principle, such as religious faith or a belief in the goodness of people. Others focus on whatever beauty and goodness they can find in a situation. In this theme, you will learn about people who endured the Holocaust with inner strength and self-respect.

Starting Points

MEETING WITH DIGNITY

The people in the photograph are about to regain the freedom long denied them by the Nazis in World War II. Put yourself in the place of one of the American soldiers who has just arrived to free those who were imprisoned. What will you say to the first person you meet? How will you respond to these survivors who have lost everything except their lives and their human dignity?

Young and old survivors of the Dachau concentration camp in Germany cheer approaching U.S. troops in 1945. Courtesy of U.S. Holocaust Memorial Museum.

DIGNIFIED MOMENTS

Difficult times often bring out the best in people. Volunteers work to help flood victims, or a neighbor takes food to someone who has lost a loved one.

- In the newspaper or on TV, find an example of a person who has shown heroism or compassion in an emergency. Write a note to that person expressing your admiration for the act.

Theme Projects

Choose one of the projects below to work on as you read the selections in "Faces of Dignity." Work on your own, with a partner, or with a group.

CRITICAL VIEWING

Gallery of Hope

1. Look through photography books, newspapers and magazines, and history books for images of people enduring crises or difficult times with dignity. You might focus on an historical period–such as the Depression or World War II–or on a contemporary topic.
2. Create a collage, computer slide show, or photo album using the images you've found.
3. Write a caption or paragraph describing the significance of each image and why you think it shows dignity.

LEARNING FOR LIFE

Change Makers

1. Research a contemporary problem or crisis that is in the news and is important to you, such as disease, injustice, poverty, hunger, or war.
2. Find one person–an activist, educator, victim, ordinary citizen, or professional–who has worked to help the victims of this crisis.
3. Write a poem or an essay about the person you have selected.

MULTIMEDIA PROJECT

Exhibit of Heroes

1. Create an exhibit about people who have faced crises with dignity. Subjects might include Rosa Parks, Mahatma Gandhi, Dolores Huerta, a friend, a relative, or a neighbor.
2. Find or create pictures of the people and write brief biographies that show the qualities that allowed the person to behave as he or she did.
3. Include quotes or speeches by the people in your exhibit.

interNET CONNECTION

For more about this theme, visit Glencoe's Web site at lit.glencoe.com.

To learn more about the Holocaust, type *Holocaust* or *Anne Frank* into a search engine.

Before You Read

from *All but My Life*

MEET GERDA WEISSMANN KLEIN

Gerda Weissmann was just eighteen when the Nazis sent her to the first of a series of labor camps in Poland and Germany. Three years later, in early 1945, she was forced on a freezing three-hundred-mile march into the former Czechoslovakia. American soldiers freed Gerda in May of that year, and she eventually married one of the soldiers, Kurt Klein. Her story was the focus of the film *One Survivor Remembers*, which won an Academy Award in 1996.

Gerda Weissmann Klein was born in Poland in 1924. This selection is from her memoir All but My Life, *published in 1957 and updated in 1995.*

FOCUS ACTIVITY

In your experience, how do people respond to the suffering of others? to their own suffering?

Journal
Write your ideas in your journal.

Setting a Purpose
Read to find out how the author responds to both her suffering and her new-found freedom.

BACKGROUND

The Time and Place
It is May 1945 in Volary, Czechoslovakia. American soldiers have just freed the author and her fellow prisoners.

VOCABULARY PREVIEW

grimace (grim′ əs) *n.* a twisting of the face, as in pain or displeasure; p. 664

embodiment (em bod′ ē mənt) *n.* the bodily form of an idea or quality; visible form; p. 664

demean (di mēn′) *v.* to degrade; disgrace; p. 664

invigorating (in vig′ ə rāt ing) *adj.* energizing; refreshing; p. 665

capitulate (kə pich′ ə lāt′) *v.* to stop resisting; surrender; p. 666

bedraggled (bi drag′ əld) *adj.* wet, dirty, and rumpled; untidy; p. 666

inevitably (i nev′ ə tə blē) *adv.* in a way that cannot be avoided or prevented; p. 667

revert (ri vurt′) *v.* to return to an earlier condition, behavior, or belief; p. 667

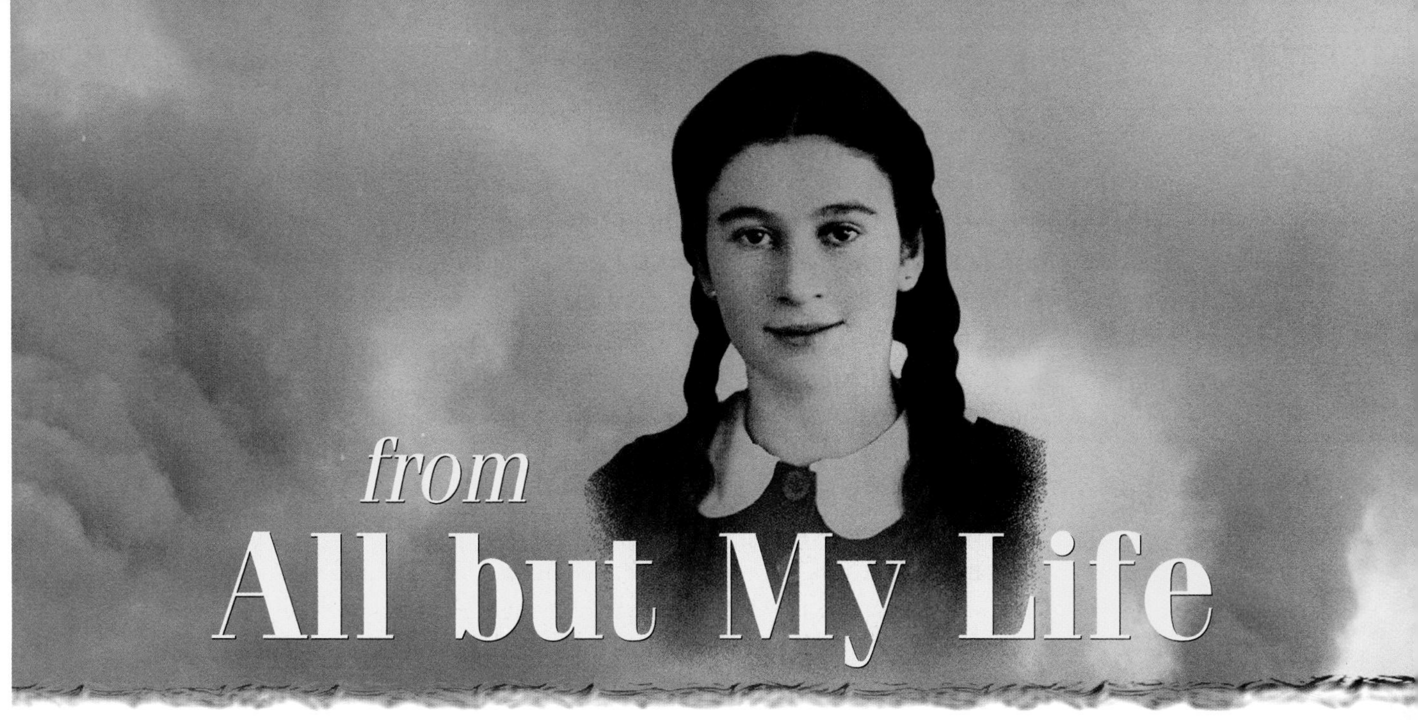

from All but My Life

Gerda Weissmann Klein

As I look back now, trying to recall my feelings during those first hours, I actually think that there were none. My mind was so dull, my nerves so worn from waiting, that only an emotionless vacuum remained. Like many of the other girls I just sat and waited for whatever would happen next.

In the afternoon a strange vehicle drove up. In it were two soldiers in strange uniforms, one of whom spoke German.

The German mayor of the town was with them. He was trying to tell the two soldiers that he really was not anti-Semitic.[1] The soldiers were Americans; I knew as soon as I heard them speak to one another. Arthur[2] had spoken their language a little.

Tears welled from my eyes as they approached us. The German-speaking soldier patted me with his clean hand. "Don't cry, my child," he said with compassion, "it is all over now."

"We must return to headquarters," said the other one in German. "Can you girls wait until morning? We shall return."

I remember nothing else happening that day. The next thing I remember was waking up, wrapped snugly and warm in a coat which the SS[3] had

1. To be *anti-Semitic* (an′ tē sə mit′ ik) is to be anti-Jewish.
2. *Arthur* was the author's brother.
3. The *SS* were the German soldiers in charge of killing prisoners in countries conquered by Germany during World War II.

left behind, waking up with what I thought was a smile, which must have seemed more like a grimace in my pitifully thin face.

The austere[4] hall was bathed in sunshine, and I woke up with the knowledge that I was free. I was eager to go outside, to move about freely. Perhaps I would meet the Americans again. I swayed as I started to walk. My skin was hot and dry. As I reached the door, the first thing I saw was that strange vehicle bouncing toward us through the brilliant May sunshine. I was overcome with joy.

I called to the other girls that some Americans were coming. The soldier on the left made a motion to the driver who stopped the vehicle across the yard from where I was standing. The soldier jumped out and walked toward me. He wasn't the one who had come the day before. Shaking my head, I stared at this man who was to me the embodiment of all heroism and liberty. He greeted me. I must tell him from the start, I resolved, so that he has no illusions[5] about us. Perhaps I had acquired a feeling of shame. After all, for six long years the Nazis had tried to demean us.

"May I see the other ladies?" he asked.

"Ladies!" my brain repeated. He probably doesn't know, I thought. I must tell him.

"We are Jews," I said in a small voice.

"So am I," he answered. Was there a catch[6] in his voice, or did I imagine it?

I could have embraced him but I was aware how dirty and repulsive I must be.

4. *Austere* means "plain" and "lacking in luxuries."

5. Here, *illusions* means "false ideas."

6. Here, a *catch* is a break, or shakiness, resulting from emotion.

"Won't you come with me?" he asked. He held the door open. I didn't understand at first. I looked at him questioningly but not a muscle in his face moved. He wanted me to feel that he had not seen the dirt or the lice. He saw a lady and I shall be forever grateful to him for his graciousness.

"I want you to see a friend of mine," I remember telling the American, and we started to walk toward Liesel.[7] On the dirty, straw-littered floor Lilli was lying, covered with rags. As we tried to reach Liesel, she looked up, her eyes enormous, burning in their sockets. She looked at my companion and her face lit up with a strange fire. I heard her say something in English, and saw how the American bent down closer and answered her. Her hands were shaking as she gently, unbelievingly touched the sleeve of his jacket. In the exchange that followed, I made out the word "happy." I understood that word. Then she sighed, released his hand and, looking at him, shook her head and whispered, "Too late."

We moved on to Liesel. Liesel just smiled, and said nothing. She didn't seem to care much. I looked back at Lilli; her eyes were fixed on the American, a solitary tear ran down her cheek. An ant was crawling over her chin. Shortly afterward, Lilli died.

I heard the American give commands in English. He seemed furious that things weren't moving fast enough. He explained

7. *Liesel* (lē′ sel)

Vocabulary

grimace (grim′ əs) *n.* a twisting of the face, as in pain or displeasure
embodiment (em bod′ ē mənt) *n.* the bodily form of an idea or quality; visible form
demean (di mēn′) *v.* to degrade; disgrace

to me in German that a hospital was being set up for us. Then he asked me:

"Is there anything I can do for you in particular?"

"Yes, there is," I said. "If you would be kind enough, and could find the time. You see, I have an uncle in Turkey. Could you write to him, let him know that I am alive, and that I hope he has news from my parents and my brother?"

He took out a notebook, and removed the sunglasses he had been wearing. I saw tears in his eyes. He wore battle gear with a net over his helmet. And as he wrote, I looked at him and couldn't absorb enough of the wonder that he had fought for my freedom.

He snapped his book shut.

"I would like to ask you a question," he said softly. "But please don't answer if you don't want to. We are aware of what has happened. Tell me, were you girls sterilized?"[8]

I did not answer at once. I was too full of emotion. Why should he, of all people, who looked to me like a young god, inquire about the deepest treasure that I, who must have looked like an animal to him, carried still within me?

"We were spared," I managed to say.

A few moments later, joined by his companion and the mayor, he drove off. Before I had even asked his name—he vanished!

Within an hour, Red Cross trucks arrived. Litter[9] bearers gently but swiftly loaded the ill. Other soldiers carried girls in their arms like babies, speaking to them soothingly in words the girls did not understand. But the gestures of warmth and help were unmistakable. In a trance I walked to a truck and got in. On the soldiers' sleeves was a red diamond, the insignia of the Fifth U.S. Infantry Division. Their uniforms, their language, their kindness and concern made it true: we were finally free!

Did You Know?
Military *insignia* (in sig′ nē ə) are the badges sewn or pinned to uniforms to show rank, division, assignment, and so on.

The hospital we were taken to was a converted school. Wounded German soldiers had been moved to the third floor so that we could be installed in the first two floors. How strange—in a matter of one day, the world had changed: Germans were put out to make room for us.

We were taken to a room where huge caldrons of water were being heated on a stove. Round wooden tubs stood steaming on the floor.

A woman in a white coat motioned me to undress.

Doing so, I stepped into one of the tubs. The warm water, reaching to my neck, felt strange: it had been at least three years since last I sat in a tub. Bidding me stand, the nurse soaped my body with quick, invigorating pressure. It was pleasantly painful to sit back in the tub again and let the warm water engulf me.

A young peasant girl came in, her cheeks rosy and shining, her colorful peasant skirt

8. When a woman is *sterilized,* an operation is performed that makes her unable to reproduce.
9. A *litter* is a stretcher for carrying a sick or injured person.

Vocabulary
invigorating (in vig′ ə rāt ing) *adj.* energizing; refreshing

reaching to her ankles, her deep-cut blouse revealing her full bosom. I felt slight and thin. When I saw the girl gather up my clothes in a basket, I looked at the nurse with a questioning glance.

"They will be burned," she said.

Only one thought remained. With my wet hand I reached for my ski boots, took the left one and reached under the lining. There was the dirty shapeless package containing the pictures I wanted to save. I pulled the pictures out and laid them on the dry towel beside the tub. And the other packet—the poison I had bought in Grünberg[10]—I gratefully let go to the fire.

I stepped out of the tub; the nurse dried my body and hair. As I stood, before a clean blue and white checkered man's shirt was put on me, I realized abruptly that I possessed nothing, not even a stitch of clothing that I could call my own. I owned only the pictures of Papa, Mama, Arthur, and Abek that I had carried for three years.

A blanket was thrown over my shoulders as I was led to a bunk. The sheets were fresh and white. A nurse brought me a drink of milk. Milk!—I hadn't had any in three years. As I drank it something tremendous and uncontrollable broke loose within me. My body shook convulsively.[11] I wanted to stop it but I couldn't. I heard my voice and could do nothing about it.

A nurse hurried up; then a doctor. I heard him say, "No, let her cry it out."

Long pent-up[12] emotions finally burst out. I cried for Ilse, for Suse,[13] for other friends, and finally for my family too. Deep in my heart I had known they were dead, but dreams about happy reunions with them had kept me going.

When I opened my eyes a night had passed. A nurse was approaching with a breakfast tray. This is the life of a fairy princess, I thought.

As I lay daydreaming after breakfast there was a sudden commotion. Nurses hurried in.

"Germany has capitulated!" they told us. "The war in Europe is over!"

For me, the war had ended with my liberation. I had not realized that the fighting had continued after that.

I looked out the window. Coming down the hilly, winding road was a company of unarmed and bedraggled German soldiers. As they passed my window, I could see their unshaven faces and hollow cheeks. Proud, handsome American soldiers guarded them.

A doctor and a nurse came in. They stopped at each bed. After asking my name and birthplace, the doctor asked for my date of birth.

"May 8, 1924."

"May 8!" the doctor exclaimed. "Why, today is the eighth."

"Happy birthday!" the nurse chanted.

After they left, I repeated to myself, "It's my birthday, my twenty-first birthday, and Germany capitulated!"

10. *Grünberg* (grōō′ burg) was, at the time, a city in eastern Germany. (In 1950 it became part of Poland and was given a Polish name.)
11. *Convulsively* means "suddenly and violently."
12. *Pent-up* emotions have been held in and not expressed or released.
13. *Ilse* (il′ sə), *Suse* (sōō′ sə)

Vocabulary

capitulate (kə pich′ ə lāt′) *v.* to stop resisting; surrender
bedraggled (bi drag′ əld) *adj.* wet, dirty, and rumpled; untidy

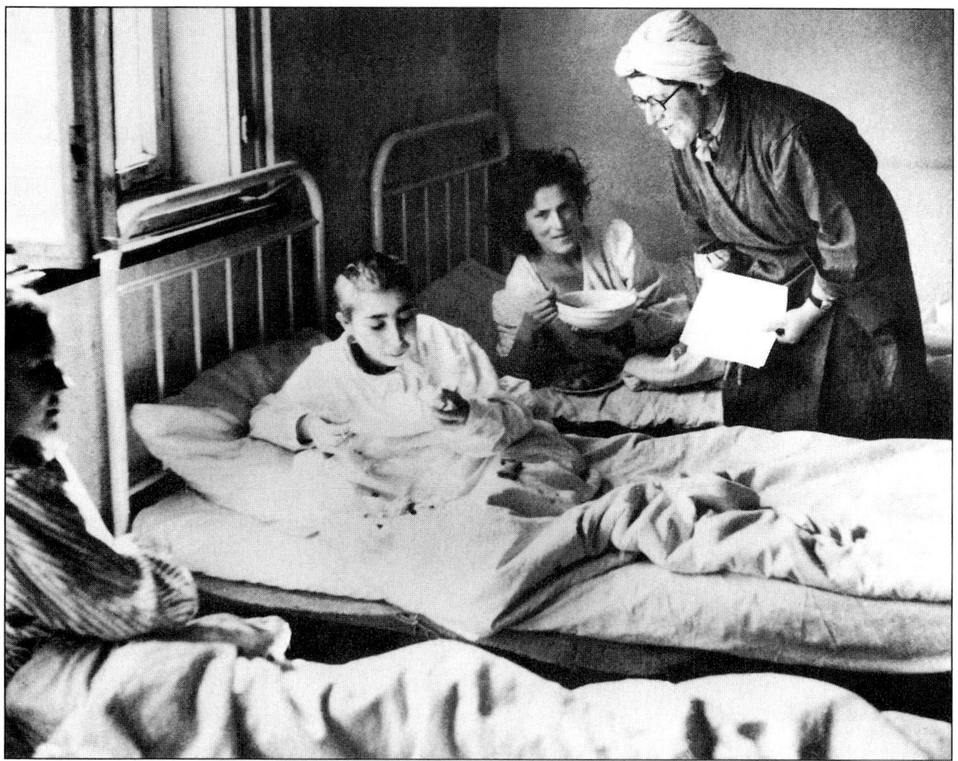

A French Relief Service worker tends to survivors of the Bergen-Belsen concentration camp. May 2, 1945.

Viewing the photograph: Bergen-Belsen was one of several former Nazi concentration camps that were converted into refugee camps and hospitals for victims of the Holocaust. How does this photo compare with the hospital Gerda describes?

I thought of Tusia,[14] who had so desperately wanted my assurance that we would both be free on this day. I remembered her lying dead in the snow. Why am I here? I wondered. I am no better.

As I lay back on my white clean pillow, lost in thought, I heard someone approach. It was the doctor again. He put something in my hand.

"For your birthday," he said, smiling.

It was a piece of chocolate.

Inevitably, we all revert to the core of our existence in moments of crisis and look for our lodestar.[15] I have tried to follow mine ever since I left my parents and my childhood home. I know full well what saw me through those unspeakable years. It was the powerful memory of an evening at home. The living room of my childhood. My father smoking his pipe and reading the evening paper; my mother working on her needlepoint; my brother and I doing our homework; the lamps throwing a soft glow around the room as my cat, stretched out on the green-patterned carpet, purred softly. An evening at home. How many

14. *Tusia* (too͞′ sē ə)

15. A *lodestar* is a star that guides. Here, it is the beliefs that guide one through life.

Vocabulary

inevitably (i nev′ ə tə blē) *adv.* in a way that cannot be avoided or prevented

revert (ri vurt′) *v.* to return to an earlier condition, behavior, or belief times I saw that picture—from my bunk in the camps, looking down on the barbed wire, during the bitterness of bone-chilling nights during the death march. Those evenings at home that I had thought dull and boring! The desire to know them once more became a driving force leading to survival. I never saw my childhood home again nor any member of my family. But their images at times merge into those of my husband, and are recreated in my children. I am home again.

Gerda Weissmann Klein

After nearly a half century, the opportunity presented itself for my return to the scene of the last chapter of that dark past. My husband, my children, and my friends made a pilgrimage[16] to Volary, Czechoslovakia, the place where I was liberated—the site where the curtain closed on the tragedy, where the stirring of love and hope blossomed again in the springtime of my life.

We went back in the autumn and, for Kurt and me, in the autumn of our lives. Although everything had changed for me, nothing there seemed to have changed. As if frozen in time and memory, I stood again in the doorway of the abandoned factory where I first greeted the freedom I had dreamed about for so many years. I paused at the graves of my beloved friends who were never privileged to know the joy of freedom, the security of a loaf of bread, or the supreme happiness of holding a child in their arms. I listened to the gentle wind in the trees, to the screech of a bird, and I looked at the flickering memorial candles on the headstones of their graves. It brought up the unanswerable question that has haunted me ever since the day I left them there: Why?

I lingered at the window of what used to be the American field hospital, now a furniture factory, where I lay in critical condition for many months. It was the window next to my double-decker bunk, in which I awoke on my first day of freedom to ask myself, "Why am I here? . . . I am no better!"

Standing there, I prayed, in the hope that perhaps through my life's work I might have provided a fragment of the answer and given back a small part of what I have received.

Gerda Weissmann Klein
Arizona, August 1994

16. A *pilgrimage* is a long journey, especially to a holy place or for a religious purpose.

Responding to Literature

PERSONAL RESPONSE

What moment in this memoir do you think is most powerful? Why?

Analyzing Literature

RECALL

1. Who accompanies the U.S. soldiers when they first visit Gerda and the other survivors?
2. What are Gerda's feelings when the U.S. soldiers first arrive?
3. When an American soldier comes back to help the freed prisoners, what questions does he ask Gerda? How does she answer?
4. What is the "unanswerable question" that has haunted the author? How does she deal with the question?

INTERPRET

5. Why, in your opinion, does the mayor tell the soldiers that he "really was not anti-Semitic"?
6. On the first day of her liberation, why do you think Gerda just waits for "whatever would happen next"?
7. What do the soldier's questions and Gerda's responses reveal about the suffering she has endured?
8. How might the writing of this memoir represent one answer to the author's "unanswerable question"?

EVALUATE AND CONNECT

9. When the first soldier arrives, the author feels that she must reveal that she is a Jew. Are you surprised by this action? Explain.
10. What new ideas do you have about the ways in which people respond to suffering? How do your new ideas compare with those you wrote for the **Focus Activity** on page 662?

LITERARY ELEMENTS

Memoir

A **memoir** is a type of writing that tells about a significant time or event in a writer's life. Memoirs are told in the first person, from the narrator's point of view. A memoir can be very personal and revealing, much like a journal. Sometimes the journals of people are published as memoirs.

1. What significant time in the writer's life is presented in this selection from Klein's memoir?
2. To what other time periods does the memoir refer? Why are these other times significant?

- See **Literary Terms Handbook,** p. R6.

Literature and Writing

Writing About Literature

Title Write a paragraph or two explaining the meaning of the title that Klein chose for her memoir: *All but My Life.* Think about these questions as you write: What did the author lose during the war? How was she able to keep her dignity? How does the title relate to her unanswerable question, "Why am I here?" What alternative title might you suggest? Be prepared to explain your choice.

Creative Writing

Letter Home Imagine that you are the doctor who gave Gerda Weissmann Klein a piece of chocolate for her birthday. As the doctor, write a letter home, describing the events in the hospital and in Europe. If you wish, read about World War II, the Nazis, and their concentration camps so that you can include additional facts and details in your letter.

Extending Your Response

Literature Groups

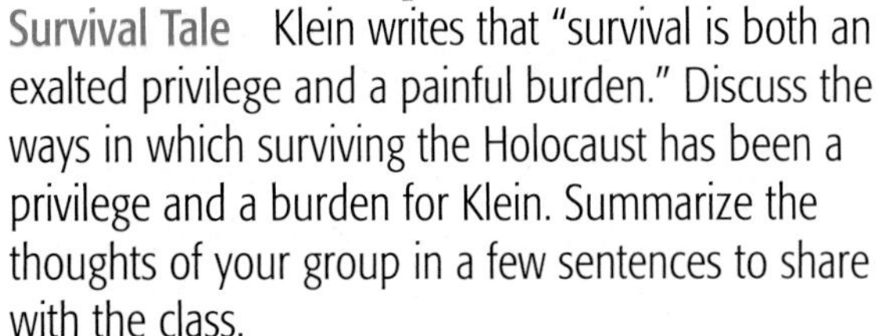

Survival Tale Klein writes that "survival is both an exalted privilege and a painful burden." Discuss the ways in which surviving the Holocaust has been a privilege and a burden for Klein. Summarize the thoughts of your group in a few sentences to share with the class.

The Nazis mistreated and killed millions of civilians who opposed them or of whom they did not approve. Among them were handicapped people, political opponents, and Gypsies. Use the Internet to search for information about such a group.

Interdisciplinary Activity

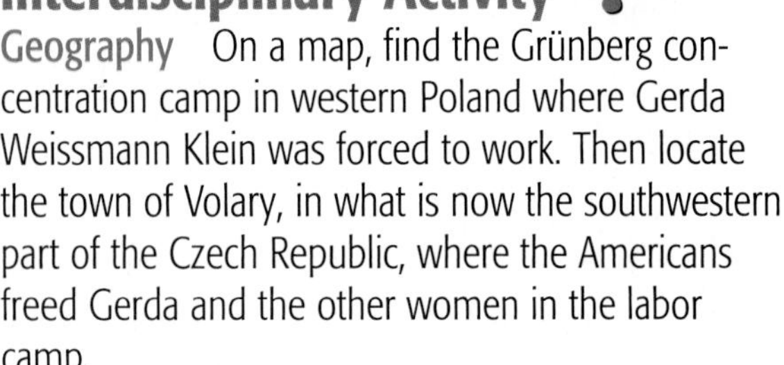

Geography On a map, find the Grünberg concentration camp in western Poland where Gerda Weissmann Klein was forced to work. Then locate the town of Volary, in what is now the southwestern part of the Czech Republic, where the Americans freed Gerda and the other women in the labor camp.

Reading Further

If you would like to read other accounts of young people during the war, try these books:

Farewell to Manzanar by Jeanne Wakatsuki Houston

The Devil in Vienna by Doris Orgel

Save your work for your portfolio.

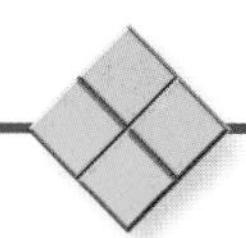

Skill Minilessons

GRAMMAR AND LANGUAGE • WRITING DATES

When you write dates, keep these rules in mind:

- You can write a century or a decade in one of two ways: *twentieth century* or *20th century.*
- Write the name of a decade in numerals and add *-s: 1940s* or *40s.* You also can spell out the decade: *the forties.*
- Dates usually begin with the month (spelled out with the first letter capitalized), the day (numeral and comma), and the year (numeral): *January 2, 1944.* However, European writers reverse the day and month, and eliminate the comma: *2 January 1944.*

PRACTICE Rewrite the three sentences in which dates have been written incorrectly.

1. The Dutch boy's diary was dated May second 1942.
2. What will the thirtieth century be like?
3. Trouble began in the early 19 thirties.
4. They came to the United States Aug, 3, 1939.

- For more about commas, see **Language Handbook,** pp. R38–R40.

READING AND THINKING • IDENTIFYING ASSUMPTIONS

An **assumption** is a belief, taken for granted, based on opinion or experience; it may or may not be true. Identifying the assumptions characters make can help you better understand their behavior. In *All but My Life,* Gerda Weissmann Klein doesn't understand that the soldier is holding the door *for her;* she assumes that she is not worthy of such courtesy. This false assumption shows how worthless the Nazis must have made her feel.

PRACTICE Identify three other assumptions made by characters in *All but My Life* and describe the beliefs on which they are based. Write a few sentences for each assumption, telling whether it is true or false. Explain what you learn about the author or the situation by identifying the assumption.

VOCABULARY • THE LATIN ROOT *vert*

Revert comes from two word parts: the prefix *re-,* meaning "back," and the root *vert,* meaning "to turn." Someone who *reverts* "turns back" to an earlier way of behaving. Words containing the root *vert* have to do with turning. To *invert* something is to turn it upside down. An *advertisement* turns people's attention toward a product. The root may drop the *t,* as in *reverse,* which means "turned backwards."

PRACTICE Use the prefixes below to match each word with its meaning.

di- "aside"
con- "together"
extra- "outside"
contra- "against"

1. divert
2. converge
3. extrovert
4. controversy

a. to move toward each other
b. one whose personality is unreserved and outgoing
c. to change the direction of
d. a quarrel or debate

Interdisciplinary Connection

Europe: Fifty Years of Change

Germany had an unstoppable war machine from 1939 to 1942. The German army invaded nation after nation across Europe, bringing much of the continent under its control. Finally, in 1945, the Nazi government surrendered to the combined forces of England, France, the Soviet Union, and the United States.

Following the war, Germany was reduced in size and divided. First, it was divided into four parts, with each part occupied and governed by England, France, the United States, or the Soviet Union. The Soviet zone eventually became East Germany, a communist country. The other zones joined to form West Germany.

In the fifty years following World War II, the boundaries and governments of many European nations changed. The two parts of Germany were reunified in 1990. The Soviet Union was disbanded in 1991.

ACTIVITY

With a group, compare the two maps. List the nations on the 1997 map that are not shown on the earlier map. Where were they in the 1940s? Describe the changes that you see.

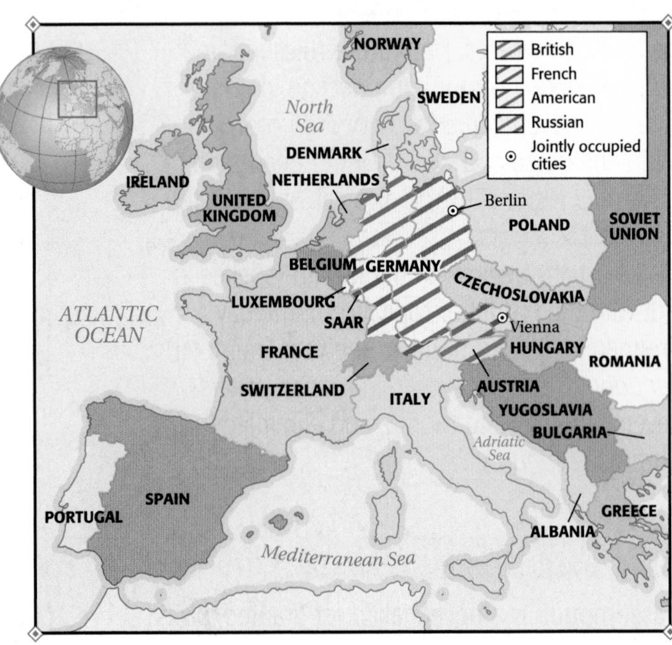

Europe After World War II

Europe in 1997

Activating Prior Knowledge

What you already know about any topic you are preparing to study or read is called *prior knowledge.* Besides facts, prior knowledge includes personal experiences that can be related to your reading. Activating, or tapping into, your prior knowledge helps you understand what is happening in a piece of writing. It also can help you identify questions to ask as you read.

Reread the following passage from *All but My Life.* Think about what readers might already know that will help them understand this scene.

> In the afternoon a strange vehicle drove up. In it were two soldiers in strange uniforms, one of whom spoke German.
>
> The German mayor of the town was with them. He was trying to tell the two soldiers that he really was not anti-Semitic. The soldiers were Americans; I knew as soon as I heard them speak to one another.

The scene takes place in Czechoslovakia in 1945. What do you know about the events in Europe at this time? Why is it significant that a soldier speaks German? What does *anti-Semitic* mean? Why do you suppose the mayor is claiming that he is not anti-Semitic?

- For more about activating prior knowledge, see **Reading Handbook,** p. R84.

ACTIVITY

Before you read the next selection, from *Anne Frank: The Diary of a Young Girl,* list what you already know about the times, places, and attitudes that were important to World War II. If you already know details about Anne Frank's life, include them in your list. Then share your prior knowledge in a discussion with your class.

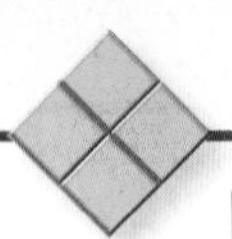

Before You Read

from *Anne Frank: The Diary of a Young Girl*

MEET ANNE FRANK

Anne Frank's world changed in 1940, when the Nazis began persecuting Jewish people in the Netherlands. Two years later, the teenager's family went into hiding on the top floor of the warehouse where her father had run his business. Despite her confinement, Anne had many hopes and dreams for herself and a strong desire to be a writer. She kept a diary, and in it she wrote: "I want to be useful or bring enjoyment to all people, even those I've never met. I want to go on living even after my death!"

Anne Frank was born in 1929 and died in early 1945. Anne Frank: The Diary of a Young Girl *was first published in Dutch in 1947.*

FOCUS ACTIVITY

Why do you think many teenagers keep diaries?

Quick List
Make a list of people, ideas, or thoughts you might write about in a private diary.

Setting a Purpose
Read to explore the hopes and dreams of one teenager.

BACKGROUND

The Time and Place Anne Frank recorded her daily life in a diary from June 1942 to July 1944. This selection contains two passages from her diary—one from before she went into hiding, and another just one month before the Nazis found her family.

Did You Know? During the Holocaust, two million Jewish children died. Both Anne and her sister Margot died of typhoid fever in the Bergen-Belsen concentration camp.

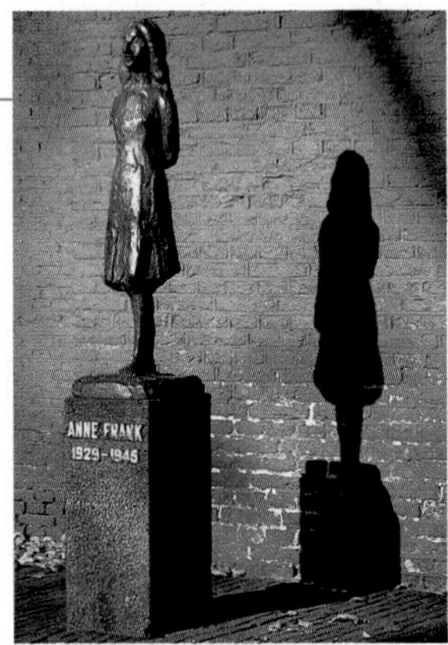

Statue of Anne Frank. Mari Andriessen. Westermarkt, Amsterdam.

VOCABULARY PREVIEW

melancholy (mel′ ən kol′ ē) *adj.* sadly thoughtful; p. 676
enhance (en hans′) *v.* to make greater; p. 676
ban (ban) *v.* to forbid; outlaw; prohibit; p. 677
superficial (sōō′ pər fish′ əl) *adj.* lacking deep meaning; shallow; unimportant or unnecessary; p. 677
prejudice (prej′ ə dis) *n.* an opinion formed without considering all sides of a question; p. 679
perturb (pər turb′) *v.* to disturb greatly; p. 680
ponder (pon′ dər) *v.* to think over carefully; p. 680
waver (wā′ vər) *v.* to become uncertain; falter; p. 681
tranquillity (trang kwil′ ə tē) *n.* the state or quality of being calm and free from disturbance; quietness; p. 681

from

Anne Frank: The Diary of a Young Girl

Anne Frank

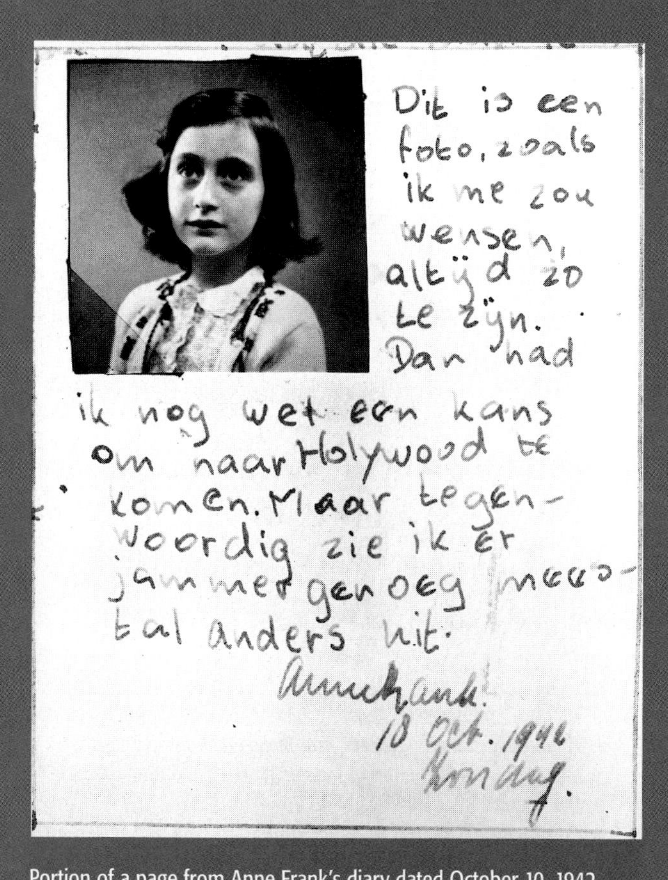
Dit is een
foto, zoals
ik me zou
wensen,
altijd zo
te zijn.
Dan had
ik nog wel een kans
om naar Holywood te
komen. Maar tegen-
woordig zie ik er
jammer genoeg meest-
tal anders uit.
Annefrank.
10 Oct. 1942
Zondag.

Portion of a page from Anne Frank's diary dated October 10, 1942.

Saturday, 20 June, 1942

I haven't written for a few days, because I wanted first of all to think about my diary. It's an odd idea for someone like me to keep a diary; not only because I have never done so before, but because it seems to me that neither I—nor for that matter anyone else—will be interested in the unbosomings[1] of a thirteen-year-old schoolgirl. Still, what does that matter? I want to write, but more than that, I want to bring out all kinds of things that lie buried deep in my heart.

1. *Unbosomings* are Anne's expressions, in her diary, of her most personal thoughts and feelings; in these writings, she "gets things off her chest."

Anne in 1935.

There is a saying that "paper is more patient than man"; it came back to me on one of my slightly melancholy days, while I sat chin in hand, feeling too bored and limp even to make up my mind whether to go out or stay at home. Yes, there is no doubt that paper is patient and as I don't intend to show this cardboard-covered notebook, bearing the proud name of "diary," to anyone, unless I find a real friend, boy or girl, probably nobody cares. And now I come to the root of the matter, the reason for my starting a diary: it is that I have no such real friend.

Let me put it more clearly, since no one will believe that a girl of thirteen feels herself quite alone in the world, nor is it so. I have darling parents and a sister of sixteen. I know about thirty people whom one might call friends—I have strings of boy friends, anxious to catch a glimpse of me and who, failing that, peep at me through mirrors in class. I have relations, aunts and uncles, who are darlings too, a good home, no—I don't seem to lack anything. But it's the same with all my friends, just fun and joking, nothing more. I can never bring myself to talk of anything outside the common round. We don't seem to be able to get any closer, that is the root of the trouble. Perhaps I lack confidence, but anyway, there it is, a stubborn fact and I don't seem to be able to do anything about it.

Hence, this diary. In order to enhance in my mind's eye the picture of the friend for whom I have waited so long, I don't want to set down a series of bald facts in a diary like most people do, but I want this diary itself to be my friend, and I shall call my friend Kitty. No one will grasp what I'm talking about if I begin my letters to Kitty just out of the blue, so, albeit[2] unwillingly, I will start by sketching in brief the story of my life.

My father was thirty-six when he married my mother, who was then twenty-five. My sister Margot was born in 1926 in Frankfort-on-Main, I followed on June 12, 1929, and, as we are Jewish, we emigrated to Holland in 1933, where my father was appointed Managing Director of Travies N.V. This firm is in close relationship with the firm of Kolen & Co. in the same building, of which my father is a partner.

The rest of our family, however, felt the full impact of Hitler's anti-Jewish laws,[3] so life was filled with anxiety. In 1938 after the pogroms,[4] my two uncles (my mother's brothers) escaped to the U.S.A.

Anne in December 1935.

2. *Albeit* is another way of saying "although" or "even if."
3. An *impact* is a strong effect. Anti-Jewish feelings increased sharply in Germany during the early 1930s, and many Jews left the country after Hitler came to power in 1933.
4. *Pogroms* (pō gromz′) were organized efforts to persecute and kill Jews. The Netherlands tried to stay neutral early in the war, but Germany invaded the nation.

Vocabulary

melancholy (mel′ ən kol′ ē) *adj.* sadly thoughtful
enhance (en hans′) *v.* to make greater

My old grandmother came to us, she was then seventy-three. After May 1940 good times rapidly fled: first the war, then the capitulation,[5] followed by the arrival of the Germans, which is when the sufferings of us Jews really began. Anti-Jewish decrees followed each other in quick succession. Jews must wear a yellow star, Jews must hand in their bicycles, Jews are banned from trams and are forbidden to drive. Jews are only allowed to do their shopping between three and five o'clock and then only in shops which bear the placard "Jewish shop." Jews must be indoors by eight o'clock and cannot even sit in their own gardens after that hour. Jews are forbidden to visit theaters, cinemas, and other places of entertainment. Jews may not take part in public sports. Swimming baths, tennis courts, hockey fields, and other sports grounds are all prohibited to them. Jews may not visit Christians. Jews must go to Jewish schools, and many more restrictions of a similar kind.

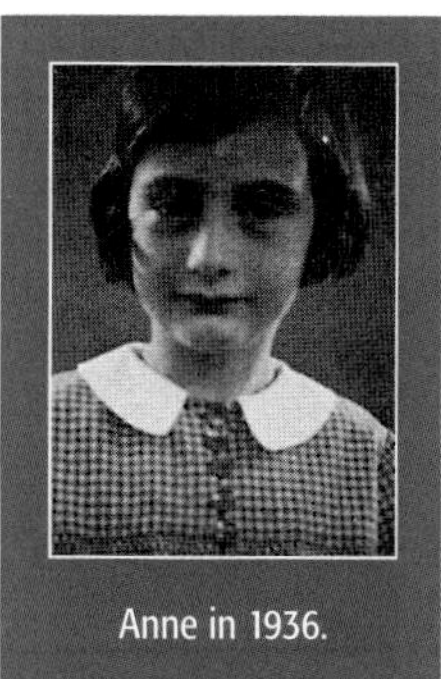
Anne in 1936.

So we could not do this and were forbidden to do that. But life went on in spite of it all. Jopie[6] used to say to me, "You're scared to do anything, because it may be forbidden." Our freedom was strictly limited. Yet things were still bearable.

Granny died in January 1942; no one will ever know how much she is present in my thoughts and how much I love her still.

In 1934 I went to school at the Montessori[7] Kindergarten and continued there. It was at the end of the school year, I was in form 6B, when I had to say good-bye to Mrs. K. We both wept, it was very sad. In 1941 I went, with my sister Margot, to the Jewish Secondary School, she into the fourth form and I into the first.

So far everything is all right with the four of us and here I come to the present day.

Saturday, 15 July, 1944

Dear Kitty,

We have had a book from the library with the challenging title of: *What Do You Think of the Modern Young Girl?* I want to talk about this subject today.

The author of this book criticizes "the youth of today" from top to toe, without, however, condemning the whole of the young brigade as "incapable of anything good." On the contrary, she is rather of the opinion that if young people wished, they have it in their hands to make a bigger, more beautiful and better world, but that they occupy themselves with superficial things, without giving a thought to real beauty.

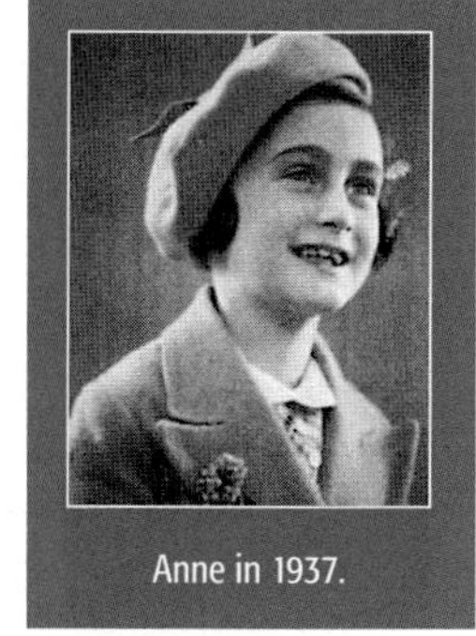
Anne in 1937.

5. The surrender, or *capitulation* (kə pich′ ə lā′ shən), of the Dutch army came on May 14, 1940.
6. Anne's best friend was *Jopie* deWaal (yo′ pē də väl′).
7. A *Montessori* (mon′ tə sôr′ ē) school is a type of private school that encourages students to act, think, and speak freely.

Vocabulary

ban (ban) *v.* to forbid; outlaw; prohibit

superficial (so͞o′ pər fish′ əl) *adj.* lacking deep meaning; shallow; unimportant or unnecessary

Margot and Anne Frank

In some passages the writer gave me very much the feeling she was directing her criticism at me, and that's why I want to lay myself completely bare to you for once and defend myself against this attack.

I have one outstanding trait in my character, which must strike anyone who knows me for any length of time, and that is my knowledge of myself. I can watch myself and my actions, just like an outsider. The Anne of every day I can face entirely without prejudice, without making excuses for her, and watch what's good and what's bad about her. This "self-consciousness" haunts me, and every time I open my mouth I know as soon as I've spoken whether "that ought to have been different" or "that was right as it was." There are so many things about myself that I condemn; I couldn't begin to name them all. I understand more and more how true Daddy's words were when he said: "All children must look after their own upbringing." Parents can only give good advice or put them on the right paths, but the final forming of a person's character lies in their own hands.

In addition to this, I have lots of courage, I always feel so strong and as if I can bear a great deal, I feel so free and so young! I was glad when I first realized it, because I don't think I shall easily bow down before the blows that inevitably come to everyone.

Anne in 1938.

But I've talked about these things so often before. Now I want to come to the chapter of "Daddy and Mummy don't understand me." Daddy and Mummy have always thoroughly spoiled me, were sweet to me, defended me, and have done all that parents could do. And yet I've felt so terribly lonely for a long time, so left out, neglected, and misunderstood. Daddy tried all he could to check my rebellious spirit, but it was no use, I have cured myself, by seeing for myself what was wrong in my behavior and keeping it before my eyes.

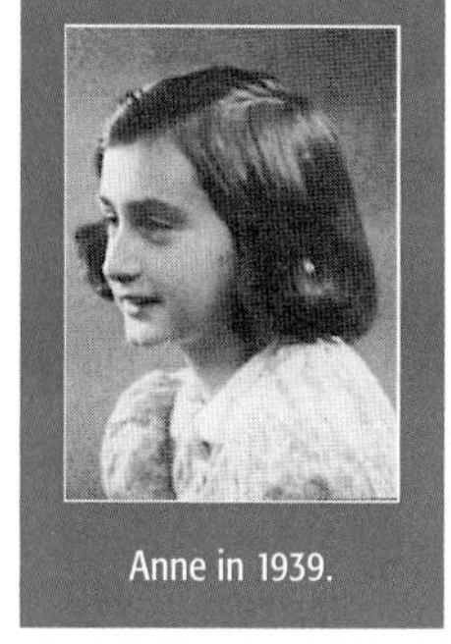
Anne in 1939.

How is it that Daddy was never any support to me in my struggle, why did he completely miss the mark when he wanted to offer me a helping hand? Daddy tried the wrong methods, he always talked to me as a child who was going through difficult phases. It sounds crazy, because Daddy's the only one who has always taken me into his confidence, and no one but Daddy has given me the feeling that I'm sensible. But there's one thing he's omitted: you see, he hasn't realized that for me the fight to get on top was more important than all else. I didn't want to hear about "symptoms of your age," or "other girls," or "it wears off by itself"; I didn't want to be treated as a girl-like-all-others, but as Anne-on-her-own-merits. Pim[8] didn't understand that. For that matter, I can't confide in anyone, unless they tell me a lot about themselves, and as I know very little about Pim, I don't feel that I can tread upon more intimate ground with him. Pim

8. *Pim* was a nickname Anne gave her father.

Vocabulary

prejudice (prej′ ə dis) *n.* an opinion formed without considering all sides of a question

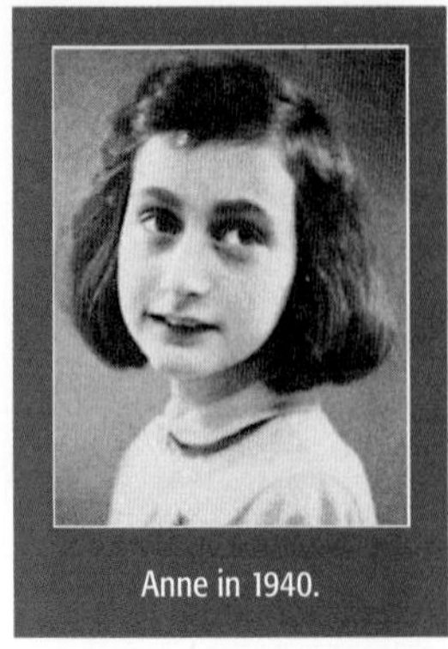
Anne in 1940.

always takes up the older, fatherly attitude, tells me that he too has had similar passing tendencies. But still he's not able to feel with me like a friend, however hard he tries. These things have made me never mention my views on life nor my well-considered theories to anyone but my diary and, occasionally, to Margot. I concealed from Daddy everything that perturbed me; I never shared my ideals[9] with him. I was aware of the fact that I was pushing him away from me.

I couldn't do anything else. I have acted entirely according to my feelings, but I have acted in the way that was best for my peace of mind. Because I should completely lose my repose[10] and self-confidence, which I have built up so shakily, if, at this stage, I were to accept criticisms of my half-completed task. And I can't do that even from Pim, although it sounds very hard, for not only have I not shared my secret thoughts with Pim but I have often pushed him even further from me, by my irritability.

This is a point that I think a lot about: why is it that Pim annoys me? So much so that I can hardly bear him teaching me, that his affectionate ways strike me as being put on, that I want to be left in peace and would really prefer it if he dropped me a bit, until I felt more certain in my attitude towards him. Because I still have a gnawing feeling of guilt over that horrible letter that I dared to write him when I was so wound up. Oh, how hard it is to be really strong and brave in every way!

Yet this was not my greatest disappointment; no, I ponder far more over Peter[11] than Daddy. I know very well that I conquered him instead of he conquering me. I created an image of him in my mind, pictured him as a quiet, sensitive, lovable boy, who needed affection and friendship. I needed a living person to whom I could pour out my heart; I wanted a friend who'd help to put me on the right road. I achieved what I wanted, and slowly but surely, I drew him towards me. Finally, when I had made him feel friendly, it automatically developed into an intimacy which, on second thought, I don't think I ought to have allowed.

Anne in 1941.

We talked about the most private things, and yet up till now we have never touched on those things that filled, and still fill, my heart and soul. I still don't know quite what to make of Peter, is he superficial, or does he still feel shy, even of me? But dropping that, I committed one error in my desire to make a real friendship: I switched over and tried to get at him by developing it into a more intimate relation, whereas I should have explored all

9. People's *ideals* involve what they believe to be standards of excellence or perfection.
10. Anne's *repose* was her calm, relaxed manner.
11. *Peter* Van Daan (fän dän) and his parents lived in hiding with the Franks. Peter and Margot were closer in age, but Peter and Anne became closer friends.

Vocabulary
perturb (pər turb′) *v.* to disturb greatly
ponder (pon′ dər) *v.* to think over carefully

other possibilities. He longs to be loved and I can see that he's beginning to be more and more in love with me. He gets satisfaction out of our meetings, whereas they just have the effect of making me want to try it out with him again. And yet I don't seem able to touch on the subjects that I'm so longing to bring out into the daylight. I drew Peter towards me, far more than he realizes. Now he clings to me, and for the time being, I don't see any way of shaking him off and putting him on his own feet. When I realized that he could not be a friend for my understanding, I thought I would at least try to lift him up out of his narrow-mindedness and make him do something with his youth.

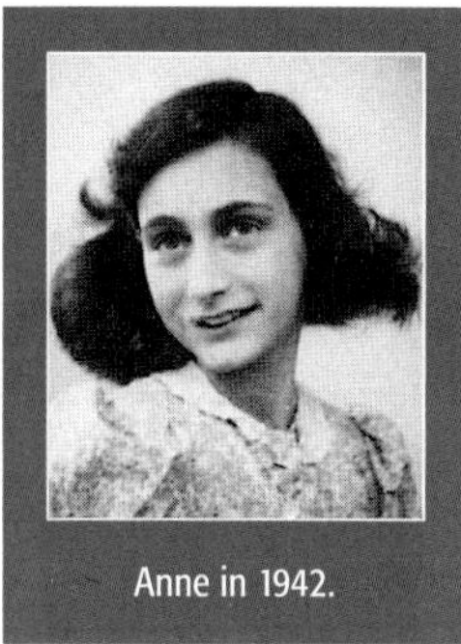
Anne in 1942.

"For in its innermost depths youth is lonelier than old age." I read this saying in some book and I've always remembered it, and found it to be true. Is it true then that grown-ups have a more difficult time here than we do? No. I know it isn't. Older people have formed their opinions about everything, and don't waver before they act. It's twice as hard for us young ones to hold our ground, and maintain our opinions, in a time when all ideals are being shattered and destroyed, when people are showing their worst side, and do not know whether to believe in truth and right and God.

Anyone who claims that the older ones have a more difficult time here certainly doesn't realize to what extent our problems weigh down on us, problems for which we are probably much too young, but which thrust themselves upon us continually, until, after a long time, we think we've found a solution, but the solution doesn't seem able to resist the facts which reduce it to nothing again. That's the difficulty in these times: ideals, dreams, and cherished hopes rise within us, only to meet the horrible truth and be shattered.

It's really a wonder that I haven't dropped all my ideals, because they seem so absurd[12] and impossible to carry out. Yet I keep them, because in spite of everything I still believe that people are really good at heart. I simply can't build up my hopes on a foundation consisting of confusion, misery, and death. I see the world gradually being turned into a wilderness, I hear the ever approaching thunder, which will destroy us too, I can feel the sufferings of millions and yet, if I look up into the heavens, I think that it will all come right, that this cruelty too will end, and that peace and tranquillity will return again.

In the meantime, I must uphold my ideals, for perhaps the time will come when I shall be able to carry them out.

Yours, Anne

12. *Absurd* means "silly" or "ridiculous."

Vocabulary

waver (wā′ vər) *v.* to become uncertain; falter

tranquillity (trang kwil′ ə tē) *n.* the state or quality of being calm and free from disturbance; quietness

Responding to Literature

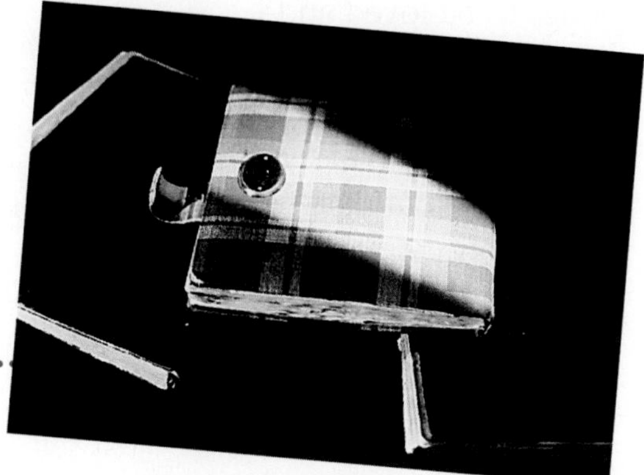

PERSONAL RESPONSE

How do Anne's relationship with her parents, her view of freedom, and her ideas about friendship compare with your own? Look back at your notes from the **Focus Activity** on page 674 as you answer this question.

Analyzing Literature

RECALL

1. Why does Anne plan to keep a diary?
2. What outstanding character trait does Anne claim to have?
3. Why is youth lonelier than old age, according to Anne?
4. What does Anne believe happens to the ideals, dreams, and hopes of young people?

INTERPRET

5. What does Anne's faithfulness to her decision to keep a diary tell you about her?
6. Why, in your opinion, does Anne say that "There are so many things about myself that I condemn"?
7. What factors in her life probably influence Anne's belief that youth is a lonely time?
8. What, in your opinion, gives Anne the ability to hope regarding her plans and dreams?

EVALUATE AND CONNECT

9. How is reading Anne's diary different from reading a short story about a girl like her?
10. How does your knowledge of Anne's death affect your experience of reading her diary?

LITERARY ELEMENTS

Journal

A **journal,** or **diary,** is an account of day-to-day events or a record of experiences, thoughts, or ideas. Journals are updated regularly and are usually only for private use, although some are made public, usually after the death of the writer. Journal writing is a type of nonfiction because it records actual events.

1. What historical events are recorded in this selection from *Anne Frank: The Diary of a Young Girl*?
2. Anne wrote for herself. What benefit have we received from Anne's diary being made public?

- See **Literary Terms Handbook,** p. R5.

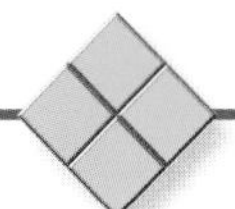

Extending Your Response

Writing About Literature

Characterization Anne writes about the people who share the small living space above the factory. Describe one of these people and your attitude toward him or her. Give details about the person's appearance, self-image, and opinions of the other occupants. Explain which of Anne's words and descriptions help to shape your attitude.

Personal Writing

Reflections on Prejudice Imagine that you are a non-Jewish student in Europe during the Nazi regime. What are your reactions as you see restrictions placed on Jewish friends or acquaintances? Knowing that the Nazis kill or jail their opponents, will you protest? Why or why not? Explain your answers in a few paragraphs.

Learning for Life

Interview with Anne Write three questions that you would like to ask Anne if she were alive today. Exchange questions with a partner and write answers you think Anne might give, keeping in mind what you know about her. Discuss the questions and answers with your partner.

Literature Groups

Age-old Questions Do you agree that "youth is lonelier than old age"? How would you define "lonely"? How do circumstances influence a person's sense of loneliness? Debate the question.

Reading Further

To know more about Anne Frank, read the rest of *Anne Frank: The Diary of a Young Girl.*

Save your work for your portfolio.

Skill Minilesson

VOCABULARY • ANTONYMS

Antonyms are words with opposite meanings. *Whisper* and *scream* are antonyms because their meanings are opposite.

Not all words have antonyms, but some words have several. *Whisper,* for example, has many: *scream, yell, holler, bellow, whoop,* and *howl* are a few. When choosing an antonym for a word, read all of the choices and choose the word that expresses your exact meaning.

PRACTICE Choose the antonym for each word.

1. ban
   a. cause b. require c. discourage
2. perturb
   a. soothe b. excite c. annoy
3. melancholy
   a. joyful b. interested c. determined
4. tranquillity
   a. ugliness b. happiness c. excitement
5. enhance
   a. conquer b. injure c. decrease

MEDIA Connection

WEB SITE

Some people who keep diaries imagine that their writings may be widely read someday. This portion of a Web site describes how Anne Frank's diary made her one of the most famous teenagers and well-known writers in the world.

from the Anne Frank House Web site

Address: www.annefrank.nl

The Story Behind the Diary

While in hiding Anne Frank keeps a diary. In more than two years she fills several notebooks.

Anne would have liked to correspond with someone from the outside world, but that would have been far too dangerous. Therefore, she makes up imaginary friends to whom she writes the letters in her diary. After about a year Anne singles out one of these imaginary friends to address the letters in her diary to; this friend is called Kitty.

Anne tries to describe daily life in the Annex and the news from the outside world, too. Sometimes there are exciting events to report, for example a bombing or a break-in in the middle of the night. In her pursuit Anne Frank succeeds in describing the ups and downs of those living in hiding in an honest and also, at times, comic way.

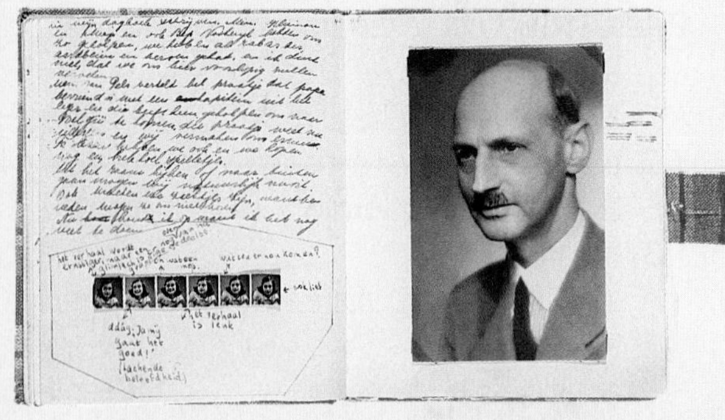

On a Dutch Free Radio Oranje broadcast from England in March of 1944, there is a call-up for ordinary citizens to provide their diaries for collection after the war for historical purposes. It is then that Anne realizes that her diary could actually be of interest to others. She makes a plan to rework her diary into a real book.

In the ten weeks from May 20th until August 4, 1944, Anne rewrites a big portion of her diary. Especially the beginning is greatly improved. In the meantime she continues writing her daily entries. Her rewrite is still not completed when the Secret Annex is raided by police on August 4, 1944. Anne is taken away; the diary is left behind. By then Anne has filled 321 pages with her words.

After the arrest of those in hiding, Miep Gies and Bep Voskuijl, the company secretaries, remain behind.

from the Anne Frank House Web site

Address: www.annefrank.nl

Together they discover Anne's notebooks lying scattered on the floor of the empty hiding place. Miep saves the diaries with the hope that she will see Anne again. After the war has ended, when she learns that Anne has died, she gives the notebooks and loose pages to Otto Frank, recently returned from the concentration camp, with the words: "Here is your daughter Anne's legacy to you."

Through the urging of friends, Otto Frank decides to publish his daughter's work. He compiles one book made up of the original diary and Anne's rewritten version. Anne Frank had already chosen the title "The Secret Annex" herself, and in June 1947 the book is published in the Netherlands.

After the initial release of 1,500 copies, *The Secret Annex* is translated and published in more than fifty-five languages. The diary of Anne Frank is one of the most widely read books in the world.

"It took a very long time to read it and I must say I was very surprised about the deep thoughts Anne had, her seriousness, especially her self-criticism. It was quite a different girl than I had known as my daughter. She never showed these kind of inner feelings."

—Otto Frank

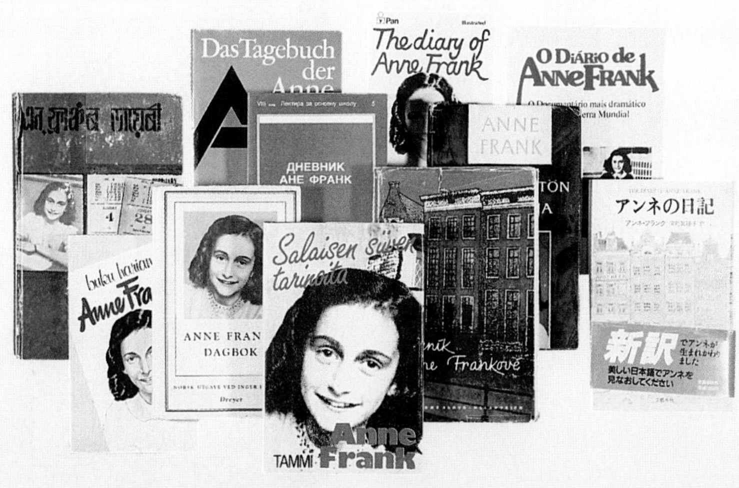

Respond

1. What new facts about Anne's diary did you learn from this Web site?
2. How do you think Anne might react to her diary's popularity?

Before You Read

The Anne Frank House: Amsterdam

MEET JOAN LABOMBARD

Poet Joan LaBombard (lä bōm′ bärd) was on a trip to Europe with her husband when she visited the Anne Frank house—the place Anne lived in hiding from the Germans. LaBombard was surprised by the small size of the Franks' living quarters and by how little privacy the family would have had. When LaBombard left, she started to cry. "I felt her [Anne's] presence really strongly," she says. Later, back at her home in Los Angeles, she was inspired to write this poem, "The Anne Frank House."

Joan LaBombard was born in 1920. Her poem "The Anne Frank House: Amsterdam," first appeared in Yankee *magazine in 1988.*

FOCUS ACTIVITY

Why do certain places, sounds, or items remind you of other people?

QuickWrite

List five places or things that remind you of a special person.

Setting a Purpose

Read to explore the thoughts and feelings that one poet had after visiting the hiding place of Anne Frank.

BACKGROUND

The Time and Place This poem is set in Amsterdam, the Netherlands, in and near the restored building where Anne and her family were once in hiding.

Did You Know? Since the Anne Frank House opened to the public in 1960, about 600,000 people have visited it each year. The visitors can see Anne's diary and the rooms where she and the others lived in hiding. Anne's photos of movie stars remain on the walls. The building also has exhibits on hate crimes and on the history of the Nazis and the Netherlands during World War II.

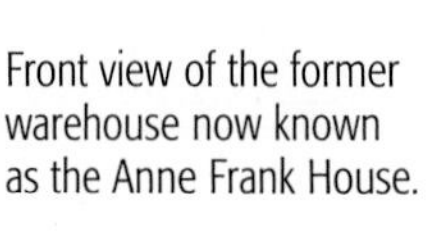

Front view of the former warehouse now known as the Anne Frank House.

The Anne Frank House: Amsterdam

Joan LaBombard

Wasn't that you in the Flower Market
holding the fresh-cut blooms,
dahlias, yellow chrysanthemums
like suns that would never fade?
Were you the one who hovered°
by the fruit stalls
and the trays of slithery eels
in Albert Cuypstraat° market,
your arms thin in the raveled sweater?
I think I passed you on Mozes en Aåronstraat°
teaching yourself the faces, the faces
to the next generation.
Anne, each day, strangers file
soberly through your room.
Your schoolgirl pictures are still there
pasted to the raw wall—
the postcard of Venice, Norma Shearer.°
The window you dared not peer from
looks out on a yard overgrown
with leggy geraniums.
Guinea hens scratch in the dirt.
When I came from your house,
I swear I saw you framed
in the sunset's red apocalypse,°
the sun roaring down behind you
and the sky in flames,
through which you walked, most womanly,
into the pages of your testament°
and did not burn.

5 Here, *hovered* means "lingered or remained nearby."

8–10 The market is on a street, or *straat* (strät), named for an eighteenth-century Dutch painter, Aelbert Cuyp (ko͞op). Line 10 refers to a street, *Mozes en Aåronstraat* (mō′ zəs en är′ ôn strät′), named for two early Jewish leaders.

17 *Venice* (ven′ is) is the Italian city that has canals for streets. *Shearer* was a popular movie star of the 1930s and 1940s.

24 An *apocalypse* (ə pok′ ə lips′) can be either a remarkable revelation or terrible doom and destruction.

28 Here, Anne's diary is the *testament,* a statement of beliefs or opinions offered as evidence of the truth.

Responding to Literature

PERSONAL RESPONSE

What impressions do you have about Anne Frank after reading this poem?

Analyzing Literature

RECALL AND INTERPRET

1. In what settings besides the Anne Frank House does the narrator picture Anne? Why, in your opinion, does she select these places?
2. What information does the narrator share with Anne about the house as it is now? Why, do you think, might she want to tell Anne about these things?
3. What do lines 22–29 mean? Why are the apocalypse, flames, and burning appropriate images?

EVALUATE AND CONNECT

4. The narrator addresses Anne as if she were an old friend. What effect might that have on a reader?
5. Why might the narrator feel that she knows Anne like an old friend? Do you feel that way? Explain.
6. *Testament* has several meanings. Which one, do you think, does the poet have in mind in line 28? Why?

LITERARY ELEMENTS

Rhythm

Rhythm is the pattern of stressed and unstressed syllables in a poem. The pattern gives each line a kind of beat. In the first line of "The Anne Frank House," you might read the pattern of beats like this, using the symbol (′) to indicate a stressed syllable:

Wásn't that yóu
in the Flówer Márket

1. Choose another line from the poem and show the pattern of stressed syllables.
2. Do all lines have the same rhythm? How does the pattern of stress give this poem a conversational tone?

- See **Literary Terms Handbook,** p. R8.

Extending Your Response

Writing About Literature

Seeing Anne Frank Where might you connect with or "see" Anne Frank, as the poet did when she visited Anne's hiding place? What might you say to Anne? Refer to your notes from the **Focus Activity** on page 686 to help you write your answer.

Literature Groups

Stanzas The poem is written in one stanza. Discuss other ways the poem might have been presented—as a rhyming poem or a narrative poem, for example. Consider different settings and themes. Why might the poet have chosen to write a single stanza?

COMPARING SELECTIONS

from **Anne Frank: The Diary of a Young Girl** and **The Anne Frank House: Amsterdam**

COMPARE CONTENT

A reader often needs background information to fully understand a literature selection.

1. How much would you understand about Anne's situation if you had read the poem before learning anything else about her life?
2. Does Anne's diary include enough background information for readers today to understand what is happening to her without additional reading? Explain how, and why, Anne provides information about her situation.
3. How does reading Anne's diary affect your understanding of the poem?
4. How does reading the poem add to your appreciation of Anne's diary?

COMPARE EXPERIENCES

Think about your experiences with some of the elements that make up the story of Anne Frank. You, or people you know or have read about, have experienced fear, prejudice, injustice, loneliness, hatred, and all of the normal problems faced by young people as they grow.

- Jot down some common experiences that help you understand the tragedy of Anne's life.
- List phrases from Anne's diary and from LaBombard's poem that help you understand the tragedy.
- Share your notes with a small group.

COMPARE RESPONSES

Both selections focus the reader's thoughts on Anne Frank's life. As she talks to her diary, Anne shares her feelings about her own life. In the poem, the writer speaks to Anne and expresses her feelings about Anne's life. Compare the Anne of Joan LaBombard's poem with the Anne who wrote the diary.

1. Which selection brought you closer to Anne Frank? Explain your answer.
2. Which selection best brings out the theme "Faces of Dignity"?
3. Which selection do you think you will remember longer? Why?

Using Commas Correctly

Some rules about using commas require more thought than others. Two examples are the rules about using commas with appositives and with adjective clauses. An **appositive** is a noun or pronoun (and its modifiers, if any) that renames or explains another noun or pronoun. An **adjective clause** is a clause used as an adjective.

If the clause or appositive is **essential,** or necessary, to the meaning of the sentence, no commas are used to set it off. If it is **nonessential,** not necessary to the meaning, it *is* set off by commas. An easy way to decide if information is essential or if it is "extra" is to think about whether it could be omitted.

Essential appositive: *The writer Anne Frank lives on through her work.*
Nonessential appositive: *Margot Frank, Anne's older sister, was close to her.*

Essential adjective clause: *People who hid the Jews showed courage.*
Nonessential adjective clause: *Margot, who hid with Anne, was a sweet girl.*

Problem 1 Missing commas with a nonessential appositive
Anne Frank a young victim of the Nazis kept a diary.

Solution Set off a nonessential appositive with commas.
Anne Frank, a young victim of the Nazis, kept a diary.

Problem 2 Missing commas with a nonessential adjective clause
Anne's father who survived the Holocaust later published her diary.

Solution Set off a nonessential adjective clause with commas.
Anne's father, who survived the Holocaust, later published her diary.

- For more about commas, see **Language Handbook,** pp. R38–R40.

EXERCISE

Rewrite each sentence, adding necessary commas. If the sentence is correct as written, write *Correct.*

1. The Nazis treated people who were Jewish very badly.
2. The hiding place which was in a warehouse was very crowded.
3. The Van Daan family who also feared the Nazis hid with the Franks.
4. Anne a thirteen-year-old kept a detailed record of her experiences in hiding.

Writing Skills

Using Transitions in Cause-Effect Relationships

Anne Frank muses about why she is keeping a diary: "I want to write, but more than that, I want to bring out all kinds of things that lie buried deep in my heart. . . . And now I come to the root of the matter, the reason for my starting a diary: it is that I have no such real friend."

Her musings show that several reasons, or **causes,** can lead to one event. In the same way, several results, or **effects,** can arise from one cause. When you write, choose appropriate transitions to make cause-and-effect relationships clear.

Transitions for Cause and Effect				
since for	so therefore	if hence	that's why as a result	because then

Anne Frank's thoughts often explore causes and effects. In the quotations from her diary, below, notice the underlined transitions that show cause and effect.

"Let me put it more clearly, since no one will believe that a girl of thirteen feels herself quite alone in the world. . . ."

"The rest of our family, however, felt the full impact of Hitler's anti-Jewish laws, so life was filled with anxiety."

". . . the writer gave me very much the feeling that she was directing her criticism at me, and that's why I want to lay myself completely bare to you for once and defend myself against this attack."

"It's really a wonder that I haven't dropped all my ideals, because they seem so absurd and impossible to carry out."

"I must uphold my ideals, for perhaps the time will come when I shall be able to carry them out."

ACTIVITIES

1. Write three sentences giving reasons why you follow a particular holiday tradition. In each sentence, correctly use a different transition from the boxed list.
2. Write a paragraph explaining the causes or effects of an historical event. Use transitions from the boxed list to make the cause-effect relationships clear.

DRAMA

The first time you acted out a scene from your favorite TV show or imitated a conversation to make someone laugh, you were creating a drama. A **drama,** or play, is a story performed for an audience. It is a type of entertainment that people have been performing and viewing since ancient times. Understanding the elements of drama will help you appreciate plays.

The main character in Washington Irving's story *Rip Van Winkle* falls asleep one day and doesn't wake up for eighteen years. This scene is from the beginning of a play based on the story.

- For more about drama, see **Literary Terms Handbook,** p. R3.

MODEL: "Rip Van Winkle"

SCENE 1

TIME: *Early autumn, a few years before the Revolutionary War.*

SETTING: *A village in the Catskill Mountains. At left, there is an inn with a sign, King George Tavern, and a picture of King George III. A British Union Jack hangs on flagpole. At right are a tree and a well.*

AT RISE: *NICHOLAS VEDDER, DERRICK VAN BUMMEL, BROM DUTCHER, and PETER VANDERDONK are seated outside the tavern. VEDDER is sprawled back in his chair. DUTCHER and VANDERDONK are at table, playing checkers. VAN BUMMEL is reading aloud from paper. From time to time, a rumble of thunder can be heard in the distance. . . .*

1 SETTING AND MOOD
Dramas usually begin by describing the time and place of the action and giving information about the opening scene. The names of the characters are included here, as are the sounds and sights that the audience will experience when the curtain rises. This information helps actors develop their roles, and it allows readers to get into the mood, or atmosphere, of the play.

Rip Van Winkle awakens to peculiar surroundings in Seattle Children's Theater's 1989 production of *Rip Van Winkle and the Legend of Sleepy Hollow: A Tribute to Washington Irving.*

2 PLAY FORMAT
In a play, each character's name is printed in the center or on the left-hand side of the page, followed by his or her words, or lines. In this way, actors reading the script can easily see where each speaker's lines begin.

3 STAGE DIRECTIONS
Stage directions describe the appearance of the stage; the sounds to be heard; and the clothing, movements, and expressions of the actors. Without stage directions, it would be difficult for directors and actors to understand what the playwright had in mind. People who are reading the play instead of watching it use stage directions to visualize the action.

4 DIALOGUE AND CHARACTERIZATION
A play's action moves forward because of the words of the characters. Dialogue, the words spoken in a play, tells the story while revealing the personalities of its characters. What does the dialogue between Rip and Dame Van Winkle tell the audience about these two characters?

VEDDER. [*Pointing off right as a merry whistle is heard.*] Well, here comes one man who is not troubled by these problems—Rip Van Winkle. [*RIP VAN WINKLE enters, holding bucket and gun. He props gun against tree at right, then crosses to men.*] . . .

VEDDER. Sit down, Rip. Derrick is reading us the news.

VANDERDONK. How about a game of checkers, Rip?

RIP. [*Hesitating.*] I don't know. Dame Van Winkle sent me for a bucket of water, but—maybe *one* game. [*Sets down bucket and draws stool up to table. Suddenly DAME VAN WINKLE's voice is heard.*]

DAME VAN WINKLE. [*Calling from off right.*] Rip! R-i-p! Rip Van Winkle!

RIP. Oh, my galligaskins! It's my wife! [*DAME VAN WINKLE enters with a broom and crosses directly to RIP.*]

DAME VAN WINKLE. So this is how you draw water from the well! Sitting around with a lot of lazy, good-for-nothing loafers. [*Tries to hit RIP with broom.*] Pick up that bucket, you dawdling Dutchman, and fill it with water!

ACTIVE READING MODEL

Active Reading Strategies

Tips for Reading Drama

Playwrights usually plan their work for people in a theater audience. Active readers, however, can also enjoy drama.

- For more strategies for reading fluently, see **Reading Handbook,** pp. R75–R77.

VISUALIZE

As you read, take time to understand stage directions. The details you find in these directions will help you visualize the setting and imagine the actors as if they were performing the play in front of you.

Ask Yourself . . .

- Which characters are onstage now? Where are they standing?
- What does this character look like? How is he or she dressed? What is the expression on his or her face?
- What should I remember about the setting of the scene? How does this setting affect or reveal the plot?

PREDICT

In a drama, events occur in logical sequence. As you read, try to predict what will happen next in the play. Base your prediction on what has happened so far and what the characters have revealed about their personalities.

Ask Yourself . . .

- Has the playwright included hints of what might happen next?
- What do I hope will happen to these characters? Are those events likely?
- How will this character react to good or bad news?
- Will the play end happily or unhappily?

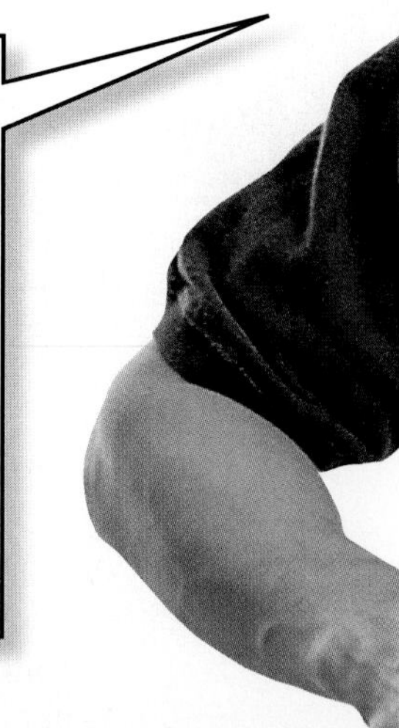

QUESTION

As you read a play, ask yourself questions about the dialogue, action, and the setting to check your understanding.

Ask Yourself . . .

- Do I follow what is happening in this scene?
- What details about the setting help me understand this play?
- What behavior can I expect from this character?

RESPOND

As a reader or a member of the audience, you will respond to the characters and the situations they face. Getting involved with the characters and their problems will help you get more out of the drama and determine its **theme,** or main message.

Ask Yourself . . .

- What are my feelings about each of the characters?
- Why am I interested in what will happen to them?
- With which of the characters do I feel a particular connection? Do these characters and their problems remind me of anyone I know?

APPLYING THE STRATEGIES

Read the play that follows, *The Diary of Anne Frank.* As you read, use the **Active Reading Model** in the margins of act 1, scene 1, to help you enjoy the play.

ACTIVE READING MODEL

Before You Read

The Diary of Anne Frank, Act 1

MEET FRANCES GOODRICH AND ALBERT HACKETT

"Think of this thirteen-year-old child writing this diary. The vitality of it is amazing," Frances Goodrich has said. Inspired by *Anne Frank: The Diary of a Young Girl*, the authors, a husband-and-wife team, spent two years writing a play about Anne. They met with Anne's father, Otto Frank, the only family member to survive the war, and also visited the building in which the Franks had hidden. The play, *The Diary of Anne Frank*, has won many awards, including the Pulitzer Prize.

The Diary of Anne Frank *was first published in 1956.*

FOCUS ACTIVITY

Imagine sharing a small living space with several people. What are some of the difficulties you might face in getting along?

Journal

Jot down your ideas about why some people desire more time alone than others do.

Setting a Purpose

Read to find out how several people cope when they are forced to live in a crowded, and very dangerous, situation.

BACKGROUND

The Time and Place It is July of 1942 in German-controlled Holland. World War II has been going on for three years.

Did You Know?

During World War II, Jews in Europe were forced into hiding to avoid German labor and death camps. Most hideouts were tiny and uncomfortable: a barn, an attic, a basement, or even the space under a floorboard.

VOCABULARY PREVIEW

conspicuous (kən spik′ ū əs) *adj.* easily seen; apparent; p. 701

unabashed (un′ ə basht′) *adj.* not ashamed or self-conscious; bold; p. 706

loathe (lōth) *v.* to regard with extreme disgust; hate; p. 709

vile (vīl) *adj.* very bad; unpleasant; foul; p. 715

indignantly (in dig′ nənt lē) *adv.* with dignified anger in response to an insult or injustice; p. 718

aggravating (ag′ rə vāt′ ing) *adj.* irritating; annoying; p. 718

subdued (səb do͞od′) *adj.* quiet and downcast; p. 725

jubilation (jo͞o′ bə lā′ shən) *n.* great joy and excitement; p. 736

The Diary of Anne Frank

Frances Goodrich and Albert Hackett

The Diary of Anne Frank, 1959. 20th Century Fox. Movie still.

CHARACTERS

MR. FRANK
MIEP
MRS. VAN DAAN
MR. VAN DAAN
PETER VAN DAAN
MRS. FRANK
MARGOT FRANK
ANNE FRANK
MR. KRALER
MR. DUSSEL

ACTIVE READING MODEL

ACT 1

SCENE

VISUALIZE

What would the stage look like if you were part of an audience for this drama?

[The scene remains the same throughout the play. It is the top floor of a warehouse and office building in Amsterdam, Holland. The sharply peaked roof of the building is outlined against a sea of other rooftops, stretching away into the distance. Nearby is the belfry of a church tower, the Westertoren, whose carillon[1] *rings out the hours. Occasionally faint sounds float up from below: the voices of children playing in the street, the tramp of marching feet, a boat whistle from the canal.*

The three rooms of the top floor and a small attic space above are exposed to our view. The largest of the rooms is in the center, with two small rooms, slightly raised, on either side. On the right is a bathroom, out of sight. A narrow steep flight of stairs at the back leads up to the attic. The rooms are sparsely furnished with a few chairs, cots, a table or two. The windows are painted over, or covered with makeshift blackout curtains.[2] *In the main room there is a sink, a gas ring for cooking and a wood-burning stove for warmth.*

The room on the left is hardly more than a closet. There is a skylight in the sloping ceiling. Directly under this room is a small steep stairwell, with steps leading down to a door. This is the only entrance from the building below. When the door is opened we see that it has been concealed on the outer side by a bookcase attached to it.

The curtain rises on an empty stage. It is late afternoon, November, 1945.

The rooms are dusty, the curtains in rags. Chairs and tables are overturned.

The door at the foot of the small stairwell swings open. MR. FRANK *comes up the steps into view. He is a gentle, cultured European in his middle years. There is still a trace of a German accent in his speech.*

He stands looking slowly around, making a supreme effort at self-control. He is weak, ill. His clothes are threadbare.

After a second he drops his rucksack on the couch and moves slowly about. He opens the door to one of the smaller rooms, and then abruptly closes it again, turning away. He goes to the window at the back, looking off at the Westertoren as its carillon strikes the hour of six, then he moves restlessly on.

From the street below we hear the sound of a barrel organ and children's voices at play. There is a many-colored scarf hanging from a nail. MR. FRANK *takes*

1. The *carillon* (kar′ ə lon′) is a set of bells sounded by machinery, rather than rung manually.
2. *Blackout curtains* were used to hide room lights from enemy bombers.

it, putting it around his neck. As he starts back for his rucksack, his eye is caught by something lying on the floor. It is a woman's white glove. He holds it in his hand and suddenly all of his self-control is gone. He breaks down, crying.
We hear footsteps on the stairs. MIEP GIES[3] *comes up, looking for* MR. FRANK. MIEP *is a Dutch girl of about twenty-two. She wears a coat and hat, ready to go home. She is pregnant. Her attitude toward* MR. FRANK *is protective, compassionate.*]

MIEP. Are you all right, Mr. Frank?

MR. FRANK. [*Quickly controlling himself.*] Yes, Miep, yes.

MIEP. Everyone in the office has gone home . . . It's after six. [*Then pleading.*] Don't stay up here, Mr. Frank. What's the use of torturing yourself like this?

MR. FRANK. I've come to say good-bye . . . I'm leaving here, Miep.

MIEP. What do you mean? Where are you going? Where?

MR. FRANK. I don't know yet. I haven't decided.

MIEP. Mr. Frank, you can't leave here! This is your home! Amsterdam is your home. Your business is here, waiting for you . . . You're needed here . . . Now that the war is over, there are things that . . .

MR. FRANK. I can't stay in Amsterdam, Miep. It has too many memories for me. Everywhere there's something . . . the house we lived in . . . the school . . . that street organ playing out there . . . I'm not the person you used to know, Miep. I'm a bitter old man. [*Breaking off.*] Forgive me. I shouldn't speak to you like this . . . after all that you did for us . . . the suffering . . .

MIEP. No. No. It wasn't suffering. You can't say we suffered.

[*As she speaks, she straightens a chair which is overturned.*]

MR. FRANK. I know what you went through, you and Mr. Kraler.[4] I'll remember it as long as I live. [*He gives one last look around.*] Come, Miep.

[*He starts for the steps, then remembers his rucksack, going back to get it.*]

MIEP. [*Hurrying up to a cupboard.*] Mr. Frank, did you see? There are some of your papers here. [*She brings a bundle of papers to him.*] We found them in a heap of rubbish on the floor after . . . after you left.

MR. FRANK. Burn them.

[*He opens his rucksack to put the glove in it.*]

MIEP. But, Mr. Frank, there are letters, notes . . .

RESPOND

How does this opening scene make you feel about Mr. Frank?

QUESTION

What do you think Mr. Frank might be referring to when he says "after all that you did for us"?

QUESTION

Why does Mr. Frank want to burn the bundle of papers that Miep shows him?

---

3. ***Miep Gies*** (mēp gēs)
4. ***Kraler*** (krä′ lər)

MR. FRANK. Burn them. All of them.

MIEP. Burn *this?*

[*She hands him a paperbound notebook.*]

MR. FRANK. [*Quietly.*] Anne's diary. [*He opens the diary and begins to read.*] "Monday, the sixth of July, nineteen forty-two." [*To* MIEP.] Nineteen forty-two. Is it possible, Miep? . . . Only three years ago. [*As he continues his reading, he sits down on the couch.*] "Dear Diary, since you and I are going to be great friends, I will start by telling you about myself. My name is Anne Frank. I am thirteen years old. I was born in Germany the twelfth of June, nineteen twenty-nine. As my family is Jewish, we emigrated to Holland when Hitler[5] came to power."

[*As* MR. FRANK *reads on, another voice joins his, as if coming from the air. It is* ANNE'S VOICE.]

QUESTION

Why does Anne's voice begin to read along with Mr. Frank?

MR. FRANK AND ANNE. "My father started a business, importing spice and herbs. Things went well for us until nineteen forty. Then the war came, and the Dutch capitulation,[6] followed by the arrival of the Germans. Then things got very bad for the Jews."

[MR. FRANK'S VOICE *dies out.* ANNE'S VOICE *continues alone. The lights dim slowly to darkness. The curtain falls on the scene.*]

PREDICT

What do you think Anne's diary will reveal?

ANNE'S VOICE. You could not do this and you could not do that. They forced Father out of his business. We had to wear yellow stars.[7] I had to turn in my bike. I couldn't go to a Dutch school any more. I couldn't go to the movies, or ride in an automobile, or even on a streetcar, and a million other things. But somehow we children still managed to have fun. Yesterday Father told me we were going into hiding. Where, he wouldn't say. At five o'clock this morning Mother woke me and told me to hurry and get dressed. I was to put on as many clothes as I could. It would look too suspicious if we walked along carrying suitcases. It wasn't until we were on our way that I learned where we were going. Our hiding place was to be upstairs in the building where Father used to have his business. Three other people were coming in with us . . . the Van Daans and their son Peter . . . Father knew the Van Daans but we had never met them . . .

RESPOND

What is your first impression of *this* Anne Frank?

[*During the last lines the curtain rises on the scene. The lights dim on.* ANNE'S VOICE *fades out.*]

---

5. Thousands of German Jews left the country after *Hitler* became the head of the government in 1933.
6. Germany began its invasion of the Netherlands on May 10, 1940, and forced the surrender, or *capitulation* (kə pich′ ə lā′ shən), of the Dutch army a few days later.
7. The Nazis ordered Jews to wear *yellow stars* at all times for easy identification. The six-pointed Star of David is a religious symbol of the Jewish people.

SCENE

[It is early morning, July, 1942. The rooms are bare, as before, but they are now clean and orderly.

MR. VAN DAAN, a tall, portly man in his late forties, is in the main room, pacing up and down, nervously smoking a cigarette. His clothes and overcoat are expensive and well cut.

MRS. VAN DAAN sits on the couch, clutching her possessions, a hatbox, bags, etc. She is a pretty woman in her early forties. She wears a fur coat over her other clothes.

PETER VAN DAAN is standing at the window of the room on the right, looking down at the street below. He is a shy, awkward boy of sixteen. He wears a cap, a raincoat, and long Dutch trousers,[8] like "plus fours." At his feet is a black case, a carrier for his cat. The yellow Star of David is conspicuous *on all of their clothes.]*

MRS. VAN DAAN. [*Rising, nervous, excited.*] Something's happened to them! I know it!

MR. VAN DAAN. Now, Kerli!

MRS. VAN DAAN. Mr. Frank said they'd be here at seven o'clock. He said . . .

MR. VAN DAAN. They have two miles to walk. You can't expect . . .

MRS. VAN DAAN. They've been picked up. That's what's happened. They've been taken . . .

[MR. VAN DAAN indicates that he hears someone coming.]

MR. VAN DAAN. You see?

[PETER takes up his carrier and his schoolbag, etc., and goes into the main room as MR. FRANK comes up the stairwell from below. MR. FRANK looks much younger now. His movements are brisk, his manner confident. He wears an overcoat and carries his hat and a small cardboard box. He crosses to the VAN DAANS, shaking hands with each of them.]

MR. FRANK. Mrs. Van Daan, Mr. Van Daan, Peter. [*Then, in explanation of their lateness.*] There were too many of the Green Police[9] on the streets . . . we had to take the long way around.

[Up the steps come MARGOT FRANK, MRS. FRANK, MIEP (not pregnant now), and MR. KRALER. All of them carry bags, packages, and so forth. The Star of David is conspicuous on all of the FRANKS' clothing. MARGOT is eighteen, beautiful, quiet, shy. MRS. FRANK is a young mother, gently bred, reserved. She, like MR. FRANK, has a slight German accent. MR. KRALER is a Dutchman, dependable, kindly.

As MR. KRALER and MIEP go upstage[10] to put down their parcels, MRS. FRANK turns back to call ANNE.]

MRS. FRANK. Anne?

[ANNE comes running up the stairs. She is thirteen, quick in her movements, interested

8. *Dutch trousers* are loose pants gathered a few inches below the knees.

9. One branch of the Nazi police force was called the *Green Police* because its members wore green uniforms.

10. *Upstage* refers to the back of the stage; *downstage* is the front, near the audience.

Vocabulary

conspicuous (kən spik′ ū əs) *adj.* easily seen; apparent

The Diary of Anne Frank, 1959. 20th Century Fox. Movie still.

Viewing the photograph: What mood, or emotional atmosphere, does this scene suggest to you?

in everything, mercurial[11] *in her emotions. She wears a cape, long wool socks and carries a schoolbag.*]

MR. FRANK. [*Introducing them.*] My wife, Edith. Mr. and Mrs. Van Daan [*MRS. FRANK hurries over, shaking hands with them.*] . . . their son, Peter . . . my daughters, Margot and Anne.

[*ANNE gives a polite little curtsy as she shakes MR. VAN DAAN's hand. Then she immediately starts off on a tour of investigation of her new home, going upstairs to the attic room.*
MIEP and MR. KRALER are putting the various things they have brought on the shelves.]

MR. KRALER. I'm sorry there is still so much confusion.

MR. FRANK. Please. Don't think of it. After all, we'll have plenty of leisure to arrange everything ourselves.

MIEP. [*To MRS. FRANK.*] We put the stores of food you sent in here. Your drugs are here . . . soap, linen here.

MRS. FRANK. Thank you, Miep.

MIEP. I made up the beds . . . the way Mr. Frank and Mr. Kraler said. [*She starts out.*] Forgive me. I have to hurry. I've got to go to the other side of town to get some ration books[12] for you.

MRS. VAN DAAN. Ration books? If they see our names on ration books, they'll know we're here.

---

11. Anne is *mercurial* (mər kyoor′ ē əl) in that her emotions change quickly and unpredictably.
12. *Ration books* contain coupons that people use to buy a limited amount of food and supplies.

MR. KRALER. There isn't anything . . .

MIEP. Don't worry. Your names won't be on them. [*As she hurries out.*] I'll be up later.

} *Together*

MR. FRANK. Thank you, Miep.

MRS. FRANK. [*To* MR. KRALER.] It's illegal, then, the ration books? We've never done anything illegal.

MR. FRANK. We won't be living here exactly according to regulations.

[*As* MR. KRALER *reassures* MRS. FRANK, *he takes various small things, such as matches, soap, etc., from his pockets, handing them to her.*]

MR. KRALER. This isn't the black market, Mrs. Frank. This is what we call the white market[13] . . . helping all of the hundreds and hundreds who are hiding out in Amsterdam.

[*The carillon is heard playing the quarter-hour before eight.* MR. KRALER *looks at his watch.* ANNE *stops at the window as she comes down the stairs.*]

ANNE. It's the Westertoren!

MR. KRALER. I must go. I must be out of here and downstairs in the office before the workmen get here. [*He starts for the stairs leading out.*] Miep or I, or both of us, will be up each day to bring you food and news and find out what your needs are. Tomorrow I'll get you a better bolt for the door at the foot of the stairs. It needs a bolt that you can throw yourself and open only at our signal. [*To* MR. FRANK.] Oh . . . You'll tell them about the noise?

MR. FRANK. I'll tell them.

MR. KRALER. Good-bye then for the moment. I'll come up again, after the workmen leave.

MR. FRANK. Good-bye, Mr. Kraler.

MRS. FRANK. [*Shaking his hand.*] How can we thank you?

[*The others murmur their good-byes.*]

MR. KRALER. I never thought I'd live to see the day when a man like Mr. Frank would have to go into hiding. When you think—

[*He breaks off, going out.* MR. FRANK *follows him down the steps, bolting the door after him. In the interval before he returns,* PETER *goes over to* MARGOT, *shaking hands with her. As* MR. FRANK *comes back up the steps,* MRS. FRANK *questions him anxiously.*]

MRS. FRANK. What did he mean, about the noise?

MR. FRANK. First let us take off some of these clothes.

[*They all start to take off garment after garment. On each of their coats, sweaters, blouses, suits, dresses, is another yellow Star of David.* MR. *and* MRS. FRANK *are underdressed quite simply. The others wear several things, sweaters, extra dresses, bathrobes, aprons, nightgowns, etc.*]

MR. VAN DAAN. It's a wonder we weren't arrested, walking along the streets . . . Petronella with a fur coat in July . . . and that cat of Peter's crying all the way.

ANNE. [*As she is removing a pair of panties.*] A cat?

MRS. FRANK. [*Shocked.*] Anne, please!

ANNE. It's all right. I've got on three more.

13. In the *black market,* goods were sold illegally, usually at very high prices. In the *white market,* which also violated Nazi laws, goods were donated by people who wanted to help the Jews.

[*She pulls off two more. Finally, as they have all removed their surplus clothes, they look to* MR. FRANK, *waiting for him to speak.*]

MR. FRANK. Now. About the noise. While the men are in the building below, we must have complete quiet. Every sound can be heard down there, not only in the workrooms, but in the offices too. The men come at about eight-thirty, and leave at about five-thirty. So, to be perfectly safe, from eight in the morning until six in the evening we must move only when it is necessary, and then in stockinged feet. We must not speak above a whisper. We must not run any water. We cannot use the sink, or even, forgive me, the w.c.[14] The pipes go down through the workrooms. It would be heard. No trash . . . [MR. FRANK *stops abruptly as he hears the sound of marching feet from the street below. Everyone is motionless, paralyzed with fear.* MR. FRANK *goes quietly into the room on the right to look down out of the window.* ANNE *runs after him, peering out with him. The tramping feet pass without stopping. The tension is relieved.* MR. FRANK, *followed by* ANNE, *returns to the main room and resumes his instructions to the group.*] . . . No trash must ever be thrown out which might reveal that someone is living up here . . . not even a potato paring. We must burn everything in the stove at night. This is the way we must live until it is over, if we are to survive.

[*There is silence for a second.*]

MRS. FRANK. Until it is over.

MR. FRANK. [*Reassuringly.*] After six we can move about . . . we can talk and laugh and have our supper and read and play games . . . just as we would at home. [*He looks at his watch.*] And now I think it would be wise if we all went to our rooms, and were settled before eight o'clock. Mrs. Van Daan, you and your husband will be upstairs. I regret that there's no place up there for Peter. But he will be here, near us. This will be our common room, where we'll meet to talk and eat and read, like one family.

MR. VAN DAAN. And where do you and Mrs. Frank sleep?

MR. FRANK. This room is also our bedroom.

MRS. VAN DAAN. That isn't right. We'll sleep here and you take the room upstairs.

MR. VAN DAAN. It's your place.

} *Together*

MR. FRANK. Please. I've thought this out for weeks. It's the best arrangement. The only arrangement.

MRS. VAN DAAN. [*To* MR. FRANK.] Never, never can we thank you. [*Then to* MRS. FRANK.] I don't know what would have happened to us, if it hadn't been for Mr. Frank.

MR. FRANK. You don't know how your husband helped me when I came to this country . . . knowing no one . . . not able to speak the language. I can never repay him for that. [*Going to* VAN DAAN.] May I help you with your things?

MR. VAN DAAN. No. No. [*To* MRS. VAN DAAN.] Come along, *liefje*.[15]

MRS. VAN DAAN. You'll be all right, Peter? You're not afraid?

PETER. [*Embarrassed.*] Please, Mother.

---

14. Short for "water closet," the *w.c.* is a bathroom.

15. *Liefje* (lēf′ hyə) or (lēf yə) is Dutch for "darling."

The Diary of Anne Frank, 1959. 20th Century Fox. Movie still.
Viewing the photograph: What do the expressions on Anne's and Peter's faces reveal about their attitudes toward each other?

[*They start up the stairs to the attic room above.* MR. FRANK *turns to* MRS. FRANK.]

MR. FRANK. You too must have some rest, Edith. You didn't close your eyes last night. Nor you, Margot.

ANNE. I slept, Father. Wasn't that funny? I knew it was the last night in my own bed, and yet I slept soundly.

MR. FRANK. I'm glad, Anne. Now you'll be able to help me straighten things in here. [*To* MRS. FRANK *and* MARGOT.] Come with me . . . You and Margot rest in this room for the time being.

[*He picks up their clothes, starting for the room on the right.*]

MRS. FRANK. You're sure . . . ? I could help . . . And Anne hasn't had her milk . . .

MR. FRANK. I'll give it to her. [*To* ANNE *and* PETER.] Anne, Peter . . . it's best that you take off your shoes now, before you forget.

[*He leads the way to the room, followed by* MARGOT.]

MRS. FRANK. You're sure you're not tired, Anne?

ANNE. I feel fine. I'm going to help Father.

MRS. FRANK. Peter, I'm glad you are to be with us.

PETER. Yes, Mrs. Frank.

[MRS. FRANK *goes to join* MR. FRANK *and* MARGOT.

During the following scene MR. FRANK *helps* MARGOT *and* MRS. FRANK *to hang up their clothes. Then he persuades them both to lie down and rest. The* VAN DAANS *in their room above settle themselves. In the main room* ANNE *and* PETER *remove their shoes.* PETER *takes his cat out of the carrier.*]

ANNE. What's your cat's name?

PETER. Mouschi.[16]

ANNE. Mouschi! Mouschi! Mouschi! [*She picks up the cat, walking away with it. To* PETER.] I love cats. I have one . . . a darling little cat. But they made me leave her behind. I left some food and a note for the neighbors to take care of her . . . I'm going to miss her terribly. What is yours? A him or a her?

PETER. He's a tom. He doesn't like strangers.

[*He takes the cat from her, putting it back in its carrier.*]

---

16. ***Mouschi*** (mōōs′ kē)

ANNE. [*Unabashed*.] Then I'll have to stop being a stranger, won't I? Is he fixed?

PETER. [*Startled*.] Huh?

ANNE. Did you have him fixed?

PETER. No.

ANNE. Oh, you ought to have him fixed—to keep him from—you know, fighting. Where did you go to school?

PETER. Jewish Secondary.

ANNE. But that's where Margot and I go! I never saw you around.

PETER. I used to see you . . . sometimes . . .

ANNE. You did?

PETER. . . . in the school yard. You were always in the middle of a bunch of kids.

[He takes a penknife from his pocket.]

ANNE. Why didn't you ever come over?

PETER. I'm sort of a lone wolf.

[He starts to rip off his Star of David.]

ANNE. What are you doing?

PETER. Taking it off.

ANNE. But you can't do that. They'll arrest you if you go out without your star.

[He tosses his knife on the table.]

PETER. Who's going out?

ANNE. Why, of course! You're right! Of course we don't need them any more. [*She picks up his knife and starts to take her star off*.] I wonder what our friends will think when we don't show up today?

PETER. I didn't have any dates with anyone.

ANNE. Oh, I did. I had a date with Jopie to go and play ping-pong at her house. Do you know Jopie de Waal?

PETER. No.

ANNE. Jopie's my best friend. I wonder what she'll think when she telephones and there's no answer? . . . Probably she'll go over to the house . . . I wonder what she'll think . . . we left everything as if we'd suddenly been called away . . . breakfast dishes in the sink . . . beds not made . . . [*As she pulls off her star, the cloth underneath shows clearly the color and form of the star*.] Look! It's still there! [*PETER goes over to the stove with his star*.] What're you going to do with yours?

PETER. Burn it.

ANNE. [*She starts to throw hers in, and cannot*.] It's funny, I can't throw mine away. I don't know why.

PETER. You can't throw . . . ? Something they branded you with . . . ? That they made you wear so they could spit on you?

ANNE. I know. I know. But after all, it *is* the Star of David, isn't it?

[In the bedroom, right, MARGOT and MRS. FRANK are lying down. MR. FRANK starts quietly out.]

PETER. Maybe it's different for a girl.

[MR. FRANK comes into the main room.]

MR. FRANK. Forgive me, Peter. Now let me see. We must find a bed for your cat. [*He goes to a cupboard*.] I'm glad you brought your cat. Anne was feeling so badly about hers. [*Getting a used small washtub*.] Here we are. Will it be comfortable in that?

PETER. [*Gathering up his things*.] Thanks.

MR. FRANK. [*Opening the door of the room on the left*.] And here is your room. But I warn you, Peter, you can't grow any more. Not an inch, or you'll have to sleep with

Vocabulary

unabashed (un′ ə basht′) *adj.* not ashamed or self-conscious; bold your feet out of the skylight. Are you hungry?

PETER. No.

MR. FRANK. We have some bread and butter.

PETER. No, thank you.

MR. FRANK. You can have it for luncheon then. And tonight we will have a real supper . . . our first supper together.

PETER. Thanks. Thanks.

[*He goes into his room. During the following scene he arranges his possessions in his new room.*]

MR. FRANK. That's a nice boy, Peter.

ANNE. He's awfully shy, isn't he?

MR. FRANK. You'll like him, I know.

ANNE. I certainly hope so, since he's the only boy I'm likely to see for months and months.

[MR. FRANK *sits down, taking off his shoes.*]

MR. FRANK. Annele,[17] there's a box there. Will you open it?

[*He indicates a carton on the couch.* ANNE *brings it to the center table. In the street below there is the sound of children playing.*]

ANNE. [*As she opens the carton.*] You know the way I'm going to think of it here? I'm going to think of it as a boarding house. A very peculiar summer boarding house, like the one that we—[*She breaks off as she pulls out some photographs.*] Father! My movie stars! I was wondering where they were! I was looking for them this morning . . . and Queen Wilhelmina![18] How wonderful!

MR. FRANK. There's something more. Go on. Look further.

[*He goes over to the sink, pouring a glass of milk from a thermos bottle.*]

ANNE. [*Pulling out a pasteboard-bound book.*] A diary! [*She throws her arms around her father.*] I've never had a diary. And I've always longed for one. [*She looks around the room.*] Pencil, pencil, pencil, pencil. [*She starts down the stairs.*] I'm going down to the office to get a pencil.

MR. FRANK. Anne! No!

[*He goes after her, catching her by the arm and pulling her back.*]

ANNE. [*Startled.*] But there's no one in the building now.

MR. FRANK. It doesn't matter. I don't want you ever to go beyond that door.

ANNE. [*Sobered.*] Never . . . ? Not even at nighttime, when everyone is gone? Or on Sundays? Can't I go down to listen to the radio?

MR. FRANK. Never. I am sorry, Anneke. It isn't safe. No, you must never go beyond that door.

[*For the first time* ANNE *realizes what "going into hiding" means.*]

ANNE. I see.

MR. FRANK. It'll be hard, I know. But always remember this, Anneke. There are no walls, there are no bolts, no locks that anyone can put on your mind. Miep will bring us books. We will read history, poetry, mythology. [*He gives her the glass of milk.*] Here's your milk. [*With his arm about her, they go over to the couch, sitting down side by side.*] As a matter of fact, between us, Anne, being here has certain advantages for you. For instance, you remember the battle you had with your

17. Both ***Annele*** (än′ ə lə) and ***Anneke,*** which is used later, are terms of affection.

18. ***Wilhelmina*** (wil′ hel mē′ nə) was queen of the Netherlands from 1890 to 1948. She and her family escaped to England at the time of the German invasion.

The Diary of Anne Frank, 1959. 20th Century Fox. Movie still.

Viewing the photograph: What does this scene tell you about the relationship between Anne and her father?

mother the other day on the subject of overshoes? You said you'd rather die than wear overshoes? But in the end you had to wear them? Well now, you see, for as long as we are here you will never have to wear overshoes! Isn't that good? And the coat that you inherited from Margot, you won't have to wear that any more. And the piano! You won't have to practice on the piano. I tell you, this is going to be a fine life for you!

[*ANNE's panic is gone. PETER appears in the doorway of his room, with a saucer in his hand. He is carrying his cat.*]

PETER. I . . . I . . . I thought I'd better get some water for Mouschi before . . .

MR. FRANK. Of course.

[*As he starts toward the sink the carillon begins to chime the hour of eight. He tiptoes to the window at the back and looks down at the street below. He turns to PETER, indicating in pantomime that it is too late. PETER starts back for his room. He steps on a creaking board. The three of them are frozen for a minute in fear. As PETER starts away again, ANNE tiptoes over to him and pours some of the milk from her glass into the saucer for the cat. PETER squats on the floor, putting the milk before the cat. MR. FRANK gives ANNE his fountain pen, and then goes into the room at the right. For a second ANNE watches the cat, then she goes over to the center table, and opens her diary.*

In the room at the right, MRS. FRANK has sat up quickly at the sound of the carillon. MR. FRANK comes in and sits down beside her on the settee, his arm comfortingly around her.

Upstairs, in the attic room, MR. and MRS. VAN DAAN have hung their clothes in the closet and are now seated on the iron bed. MRS. VAN DAAN leans back exhausted. MR. VAN DAAN fans her with a newspaper. ANNE starts to write in her diary. The lights dim out, the curtain falls.

In the darkness ANNE'S VOICE comes to us again, faintly at first, and then with growing strength.]

ANNE'S VOICE. I expect I should be describing what it feels like to go into hiding. But I really don't know yet myself. I only know it's funny never to be able to go outdoors . . . never to breathe fresh air . . . never to run and shout and jump. It's the silence in the nights that frightens me most. Every time I hear a creak in the house, or a step on the street outside, I'm sure they're coming for us. The days aren't so bad. At least we know that Miep and Mr. Kraler are down there below us in the office. Our protectors, we call them. I asked Father what would happen to them if the Nazis found out they were hiding us. Pim said that they would suffer the same fate that we would . . . Imagine! They know this, and yet when they come up here, they're always cheerful and gay as if there were nothing in the world to bother them . . . Friday, the twenty-first of August, nineteen forty-two. Today I'm going to tell you our general news. Mother is unbearable. She insists on treating me like a baby, which I loathe. Otherwise things are going better. The weather is . . .

[*As ANNE'S VOICE is fading out, the curtain rises on the scene.*]

Vocabulary

loathe (lōth) *v.* to regard with extreme disgust or hatred; hate

ACTIVE READING MODEL

Responding to Literature

PERSONAL RESPONSE

Which two characters do you find most interesting so far? Why?

Active Reading Response

Which Active Reading notes did you find most helpful? Why?

Analyzing Literature

RECALL AND INTERPRET

1. Why is Mr. Frank in the warehouse in scene 1, and what occurs that he does not expect? Why do you think the play opens with this scene?
2. What is worrying Mrs. Van Daan as scene 2 begins? Does she understand the seriousness of the situation? Explain.
3. Why is Mr. Frank grateful to Mr. Van Daan? What do Mr. Frank's actions toward the Van Daans reveal about him?

EVALUATE AND CONNECT

4. Compare the attitudes of Anne and Peter toward their yellow stars as they remove them from their clothes. Which character behaves the way you might have acted? Explain.
5. How does the first conversation between Anne and Peter introduce the problems in store for the people in the annex?
6. Compare Anne's talk with her father and her diary entry about her mother. How might these events indicate future problems in the annex? Review what you wrote for the **Focus Activity** on page 696 to help you answer this question.

LITERARY ELEMENTS

Acts and Scenes

In a play, an **act** covers a significant part of the plot. Acts are divided into **scenes,** which are comparable to the chapters of a book. A change in scene often indicates a change in time or place. Act 1, scene 1 of *The Diary of Anne Frank* takes place in the Secret Annex in November of 1945.

1. Where and when does act 1, scene 2 take place?
2. What changes take place between scene 1 and scene 2?

- See **Literary Terms Handbook,** pp. R1 and R9.

Extending Your Response

Literature Groups

Words of Comfort Mr. Frank tells Anne: "There are no walls, there are no bolts, no locks that anyone can put on your mind." Do you agree that it is a reassuring concept? Discuss your thoughts.

Personal Writing

Reflections on a Diary How is Anne adjusting as scene 2 ends? What frustrations would you share with her if you were living under similar circumstances? Respond in a journal entry of your own.

The Diary of Anne Frank (Continued)

SCENE

[It is a little after six o'clock in the evening, two months later.
MARGOT is in the bedroom at the right, studying. MR. VAN DAAN is lying down in the attic room above.
The rest of the "family" is in the main room. ANNE and PETER sit opposite each other at the center table, where they have been doing their lessons. MRS. FRANK is on the couch. MRS. VAN DAAN is seated with her fur coat, on which she has been sewing, in her lap. None of them are wearing their shoes.
Their eyes are on MR. FRANK, waiting for him to give them the signal which will release them from their day-long quiet. MR. FRANK, his shoes in his hand, stands looking down out of the window at the back, watching to be sure that all of the workmen have left the building below.
After a few seconds of motionless silence, MR. FRANK turns from the window.]

MR. FRANK. [*Quietly, to the group.*] It's safe now. The last workman has left.

[There is an immediate stir of relief.]

ANNE. [*Her pent-up energy explodes.*] WHEE!

MRS. FRANK. [*Startled, amused.*] Anne!

MRS. VAN DAAN. I'm first for the w.c.

[She hurries off to the bathroom. MRS. FRANK puts on her shoes and starts up to the sink to prepare supper. ANNE sneaks PETER's shoes from under the table and hides them behind her back. MR. FRANK goes into MARGOT's room.]

MR. FRANK. [*To MARGOT.*] Six o'clock. School's over.

[MARGOT gets up, stretching. MR. FRANK sits down to put on his shoes. In the main room PETER tries to find his.]

PETER. [*To ANNE.*] Have you seen my shoes?

ANNE. [*Innocently.*] Your shoes?

PETER. You've taken them, haven't you?

ANNE. I don't know what you're talking about.

PETER. You're going to be sorry!

ANNE. Am I?

[PETER goes after her. ANNE, with his shoes in her hand, runs from him, dodging behind her mother.]

MRS. FRANK. [*Protesting.*] Anne, dear!

PETER. Wait till I get you!

ANNE. I'm waiting! [*PETER makes a lunge for her. They both fall to the floor. PETER pins her down, wrestling with her to get the shoes.*] Don't! Don't! Peter, stop it. Ouch!

MRS. FRANK. Anne! . . . Peter!

[Suddenly PETER becomes self-conscious. He grabs his shoes roughly and starts for his room.]

ANNE. [*Following him.*] Peter, where are you going? Come dance with me.

PETER. I tell you I don't know how.

ANNE. I'll teach you.

PETER. I'm going to give Mouschi his dinner.

ANNE. Can I watch?

PETER. He doesn't like people around while he eats.

The Diary of Anne Frank, 1959. 20th Century Fox. Movie still.

Viewing the photograph: Notice the facial expressions of the adults in this scene. How does each person seem to respond to Anne?

ANNE. Peter, please.

PETER. No!

[*He goes into his room.* ANNE *slams his door after him.*]

MRS. FRANK. Anne, dear, I think you shouldn't play like that with Peter. It's not dignified.

ANNE. Who cares if it's dignified? I don't want to be dignified.

[MR. FRANK *and* MARGOT *come from the room on the right.* MARGOT *goes to help her mother.* MR. FRANK *starts for the center table to correct* MARGOT's *school papers.*]

MRS. FRANK. [*To* ANNE.] You complain that I don't treat you like a grown-up. But when I do, you resent it.

ANNE. I only want some fun . . . someone to laugh and clown with . . . After you've sat still all day and hardly moved, you've got to have some fun. I don't know what's the matter with that boy.

MR. FRANK. He isn't used to girls. Give him a little time.

ANNE. Time? Isn't two months time? I could cry. [*Catching hold of* MARGOT.] Come on, Margot . . . dance with me. Come on, please.

MARGOT. I have to help with supper.

ANNE. You know we're going to forget how to dance . . . When we get out we won't remember a thing.

[*She starts to sing and dance by herself.* MR. FRANK *takes her in his arms, waltzing with her.* MRS. VAN DAAN *comes in from the bathroom.*]

MRS. VAN DAAN. Next? [*She looks around as she starts putting on her shoes.*] Where's Peter?

ANNE. [*As they are dancing.*] Where would he be!

MRS. VAN DAAN. He hasn't finished his lessons, has he? His father'll kill him if he catches him in there with that cat and his work not done. [MR. FRANK *and* ANNE *finish their dance. They bow to each other with extravagant formality.*] Anne, get him out of there, will you?

ANNE. [*At* PETER's *door.*] Peter? Peter?

PETER. [*Opening the door a crack.*] What is it?

ANNE. Your mother says to come out.

PETER. I'm giving Mouschi his dinner.

MRS. VAN DAAN. You know what your father says.

[*She sits on the couch, sewing on the lining of her fur coat.*]

PETER. For heaven's sake, I haven't even looked at him since lunch.

MRS. VAN DAAN. I'm just telling you, that's all.

ANNE. I'll feed him.

PETER. I don't want you in there.

MRS. VAN DAAN. Peter!

PETER. [*To* ANNE.] Then give him his dinner and come right out, you hear?

[*He comes back to the table.* ANNE *shuts the door of* PETER's *room after her and disappears behind the curtain covering his closet.*]

MRS. VAN DAAN. [*To* PETER.] Now is that any way to talk to your little girlfriend?

PETER. Mother . . . for heaven's sake . . . will you please stop saying that?

MRS. VAN DAAN. Look at him blush! Look at him!

PETER. Please! I'm not . . . anyway . . . let me alone, will you?

MRS. VAN DAAN. He acts like it was something to be ashamed of. It's nothing to be ashamed of, to have a little girlfriend.

PETER. You're crazy. She's only thirteen.

MRS. VAN DAAN. So what? And you're sixteen. Just perfect. Your father's ten years older than I am. [*To* MR. FRANK.] I warn you, Mr. Frank, if this war lasts much longer, we're going to be related and then . . .

MR. FRANK. *Mazeltov!*[19]

MRS. FRANK. [*Deliberately changing the conversation.*] I wonder where Miep is. She's usually so prompt.

[*Suddenly everything else is forgotten as they hear the sound of an automobile coming to a screeching stop in the street below. They are tense, motionless in their terror. The car starts away. A wave of relief sweeps over them. They pick up their occupations again.* ANNE *flings open the door of* PETER'S *room, making a dramatic entrance. She is dressed in* PETER'S *clothes.* PETER *looks at her in fury. The others are amused.*]

ANNE. Good evening, everyone. Forgive me if I don't stay. [*She jumps up on a chair.*] I have a friend waiting for me in there. My friend Tom. Tom Cat. Some people say that we look alike. But Tom has the most beautiful whiskers, and I have only a little fuzz. I am hoping . . . in time . . .

PETER. All right, Mrs. Quack Quack!

ANNE. [*Outraged—jumping down.*] Peter!

PETER. I heard about you . . . How you talked so much in class they called you Mrs. Quack Quack. How Mr. Smitter made you write a composition . . . "'Quack, quack,' said Mrs. Quack Quack."

ANNE. Well, go on. Tell them the rest. How it was so good he read it out loud to the class and then read it to all his other classes!

PETER. Quack! Quack! Quack . . . Quack . . . Quack . . .

[ANNE *pulls off the coat and trousers.*]

ANNE. You are the most intolerable, insufferable[20] boy I've ever met!

[*She throws the clothes down the stairwell.* PETER *goes down after them.*]

PETER. Quack, quack, quack!

MRS. VAN DAAN. [*To* ANNE.] That's right, Anneke! Give it to him!

ANNE. With all the boys in the world . . . Why I had to get locked up with one like you! . . .

PETER. Quack, quack, quack, and from now on stay out of my room!

[*As* PETER *passes her,* ANNE *puts out her foot, tripping him. He picks himself up, and goes on into his room.*]

MRS. FRANK. [*Quietly.*] Anne, dear . . . your hair. [*She feels* ANNE'S *forehead.*] You're warm. Are you feeling all right?

ANNE. Please, Mother.

[*She goes over to the center table, slipping into her shoes.*]

MRS. FRANK. [*Following her.*] You haven't a fever, have you?

ANNE. [*Pulling away.*] No. No.

MRS. FRANK. You know we can't call a doctor here, ever. There's only one thing to do . . . watch carefully. Prevent an illness before it comes. Let me see your tongue.

ANNE. Mother, this is perfectly absurd.

MRS. FRANK. Anne, dear, don't be such a baby. Let me see your tongue. [*As* ANNE

---

19. ***Mazeltov*** (mä′ zəl tof) or (mä zəl tōv′) is a Hebrew word used to express congratulations or best wishes.

20. Both *intolerable* and *insufferable* mean "unbearable."

refuses, MRS. FRANK *appeals to* MR. FRANK.] Otto . . . ?

MR. FRANK. You hear your mother, Anne.

[ANNE *flicks out her tongue for a second, then turns away.*]

MRS. FRANK. Come on—open up! [*As* ANNE *opens her mouth very wide.*] You seem all right . . . but perhaps an aspirin . . .

MRS. VAN DAAN. For heaven's sake, don't give that child any pills. I waited for fifteen minutes this morning for her to come out of the w.c.

ANNE. I was washing my hair!

MR. FRANK. I think there's nothing the matter with our Anne that a ride on her bike, or a visit with her friend Jopie de Waal wouldn't cure. Isn't that so, Anne?

[MR. VAN DAAN *comes down into the room. From outside we hear faint sounds of bombers going over and a burst of ack-ack.*][21]

MR. VAN DAAN. Miep not come yet?

MRS. VAN DAAN. The workmen just left, a little while ago.

MR. VAN DAAN. What's for dinner tonight?

MRS. VAN DAAN. Beans.

MR. VAN DAAN. Not again!

MRS. VAN DAAN. Poor Putti! I know. But what can we do? That's all that Miep brought us.

[MR. VAN DAAN *starts to pace, his hands behind his back.* ANNE *follows behind him, imitating him.*]

ANNE. We are now in what is known as the "bean cycle." Beans boiled, beans *en casserole,* beans with strings, beans without strings . . .

[PETER *has come out of his room. He slides into his place at the table, becoming immediately absorbed in his studies.*]

MR. VAN DAAN. [*To* PETER.] I saw you . . . in there, playing with your cat.

MRS. VAN DAAN. He just went in for a second, putting his coat away. He's been out here all the time, doing his lessons.

MR. FRANK. [*Looking up from the papers.*] Anne, you got an excellent in your history paper today . . . and very good in Latin.

ANNE. [*Sitting beside him.*] How about algebra?

MR. FRANK. I'll have to make a confession. Up until now I've managed to stay ahead of you in algebra. Today you caught up with me. We'll leave it to Margot to correct.

ANNE. Isn't algebra vile, Pim!

MR. FRANK. Vile!

MARGOT. [*To* MR. FRANK.] How did I do?

ANNE. [*Getting up.*] Excellent, excellent, excellent, excellent!

MR. FRANK. [*To* MARGOT.] You should have used the subjunctive[22] here . . .

MARGOT. Should I? . . . I thought . . . look here . . . I didn't use it here . . .

[*The two become absorbed in the papers.*]

ANNE. Mrs. Van Daan, may I try on your coat?

MRS. FRANK. No, Anne.

---

21. *Ack-ack* was the slang name for antiaircraft gunfire. It was the Allies who were bombing Nazi-controlled Netherlands.

22. The *subjunctive* is a verb form used to express wishes, possibilities, or things that are opposed to fact. In the sentence, "If I were you, I wouldn't go," *were* is the subjunctive.

Vocabulary
vile (vīl) *adj.* very bad; unpleasant; foul

MRS. VAN DAAN. [*Giving it to* ANNE.] It's all right . . . but careful with it. [ANNE *puts it on and struts with it.*] My father gave me that the year before he died. He always bought the best that money could buy.

ANNE. Mrs. Van Daan, did you have a lot of boyfriends before you were married?

MRS. FRANK. Anne, that's a personal question. It's not courteous to ask personal questions.

MRS. VAN DAAN. Oh I don't mind. [*To* ANNE.] Our house was always swarming with boys. When I was a girl we had . . .

MR. VAN DAAN. Oh, God. Not again!

MRS. VAN DAAN. [*Good-humored.*] Shut up! [*Without a pause, to* ANNE. MR. VAN DAAN *mimics* MRS. VAN DAAN, *speaking the first few words in unison with her.*] One summer we had a big house in Hilversum. The boys came buzzing round like bees around a jam pot. And when I was sixteen! . . . We were wearing our skirts very short those days and I had good-looking legs. [*She pulls up her skirt, going to* MR. FRANK.] I still have 'em. I may not be as pretty as I used to be, but I still have my legs. How about it, Mr. Frank?

MR. VAN DAAN. All right. All right. We see them.

MRS. VAN DAAN. I'm not asking you. I'm asking Mr. Frank.

PETER. Mother, for heaven's sake.

MRS. VAN DAAN. Oh, I embarrass you, do I? Well, I just hope the girl you marry has as good. [*Then to* ANNE.] My father used to worry about me, with so many boys hanging round. He told me, if any of them gets fresh, you say to him . . . "Remember, Mr. So-and-So, remember I'm a lady."

ANNE. "Remember, Mr. So-and-So, remember I'm a lady."

[*She gives* MRS. VAN DAAN *her coat.*]

MR. VAN DAAN. Look at you, talking that way in front of her! Don't you know she puts it all down in that diary?

MRS. VAN DAAN. So, if she does? I'm only telling the truth!

[ANNE *stretches out, putting her ear to the floor, listening to what is going on below. The sound of the bombers fades away.*]

MRS. FRANK. [*Setting the table.*] Would you mind, Peter, if I moved you over to the couch?

ANNE. [*Listening.*] Miep must have the radio on.

[PETER *picks up his papers, going over to the couch beside* MRS. VAN DAAN.]

MR. VAN DAAN. [*Accusingly, to* PETER.] Haven't you finished yet?

PETER. No.

MR. VAN DAAN. You ought to be ashamed of yourself.

PETER. All right. All right. I'm a dunce. I'm a hopeless case. Why do I go on?

MRS. VAN DAAN. You're not hopeless. Don't talk that way. It's just that you haven't anyone to help you, like the girls have. [*To* MR. FRANK.] Maybe you could help him, Mr. Frank?

MR. FRANK. I'm sure that his father . . . ?

MR. VAN DAAN. Not me. I can't do anything with him. He won't listen to me. You go ahead . . . if you want.

MR. FRANK. [*Going to* PETER.] What about it, Peter? Shall we make our school coeducational?[23]

MRS. VAN DAAN. [*Kissing* MR. FRANK.] You're an angel, Mr. Frank. An angel. I don't know

23. A *coeducational* school has both male and female students.

The Diary of Anne Frank, 1959. 20th Century Fox. Movie still.
Viewing the photograph: How does this scene illustrate a typical day in hiding for the Franks?

why I didn't meet you before I met that one there. Here, sit down, Mr. Frank . . . [*She forces him down on the couch beside* PETER.] Now, Peter, you listen to Mr. Frank.

MR. FRANK. It might be better for us to go into Peter's room.

[PETER *jumps up eagerly, leading the way.*]

MRS. VAN DAAN. That's right. You go in there, Peter. You listen to Mr. Frank. Mr. Frank is a highly educated man.

[*As* MR. FRANK *is about to follow* PETER *into his room,* MRS. FRANK *stops him and wipes the lipstick from his lips. Then she closes the door after them.*]

ANNE. [*On the floor, listening.*] Shh! I can hear a man's voice talking.

MR. VAN DAAN. [*To* ANNE.] Isn't it bad enough here without your sprawling all over the place?

[ANNE *sits up.*]

MRS. VAN DAAN. [*To* MR. VAN DAAN.] If you didn't smoke so much, you wouldn't be so bad-tempered.

MR. VAN DAAN. Am I smoking? Do you see me smoking?

MRS. VAN DAAN. Don't tell me you've used up all those cigarettes.

MR. VAN DAAN. One package. Miep only brought me one package.

MRS. VAN DAAN. It's a filthy habit anyway. It's a good time to break yourself.

MR. VAN DAAN. Oh, stop it, please.

MRS. VAN DAAN. You're smoking up all our money. You know that, don't you?

MR. VAN DAAN. Will you shut up? [*During this,* MRS. FRANK *and* MARGOT *have studiously kept their eyes down. But* ANNE*, seated on the floor, has been following the discussion interestedly.* MR. VAN DAAN *turns to see her staring up at him.*] And what are you staring at?

ANNE. I never heard grown-ups quarrel before. I thought only children quarreled.

MR. VAN DAAN. This isn't a quarrel! It's a discussion. And I never heard children so rude before.

ANNE. [*Rising, indignantly.*] *I*, rude!

MR. VAN DAAN. Yes!

MRS. FRANK. [*Quickly.*] Anne, will you get me my knitting? [*ANNE goes to get it.*] I must remember, when Miep comes, to ask her to bring me some more wool.

MARGOT. [*Going to her room.*] I need some hairpins and some soap. I made a list.

[*She goes into her bedroom to get the list.*]

MRS. FRANK. [*To ANNE.*] Have you some library books for Miep when she comes?

ANNE. It's a wonder that Miep has a life of her own, the way we make her run errands for us. Please, Miep, get me some starch. Please take my hair out and have it cut. Tell me all the latest news, Miep. [*She goes over, kneeling on the couch beside MRS. VAN DAAN.*] Did you know she was engaged? His name is Dirk, and Miep's afraid the Nazis will ship him off to Germany to work in one of their war plants. That's what they're doing with some of the young Dutchmen . . . they pick them up off the streets—

MR. VAN DAAN. [*Interrupting.*] Don't you ever get tired of talking? Suppose you try keeping still for five minutes. Just five minutes.

[*He starts to pace again. Again ANNE follows him, mimicking him. MRS. FRANK jumps up and takes her by the arm up to the sink, and gives her a glass of milk.*]

MRS. FRANK. Come here, Anne. It's time for your glass of milk.

MR. VAN DAAN. Talk, talk, talk. I never heard such a child. Where is my . . . ? Every evening it's the same, talk, talk, talk. [*He looks around.*] Where is my . . . ?

MRS. VAN DAAN. What're you looking for?

MR. VAN DAAN. My pipe. Have you seen my pipe?

MRS. VAN DAAN. What good's a pipe? You haven't got any tobacco.

MR. VAN DAAN. At least I'll have something to hold in my mouth! [*Opening MARGOT's bedroom door.*] Margot, have you seen my pipe?

MARGOT. It was on the table last night.

[*ANNE puts her glass of milk on the table and picks up his pipe, hiding it behind her back.*]

MR. VAN DAAN. I know. I know. Anne, did you see my pipe? . . . Anne!

MRS. FRANK. Anne, Mr. Van Daan is speaking to you.

ANNE. Am I allowed to talk now?

MR. VAN DAAN. You're the most aggravating . . . The trouble with you is, you've been spoiled. What you need is a good old-fashioned spanking.

ANNE. [*Mimicking MRS. VAN DAAN.*] "Remember, Mr. So-and-So, remember I'm a lady."

[*She thrusts the pipe into his mouth, then picks up her glass of milk.*]

Vocabulary

indignantly (in dig′ nənt lē) *adv.* with dignified anger in response to an insult or injustice

aggravating (ag′ rə vāt ing) *adj.* irritating; annoying

MR. VAN DAAN. [*Restraining himself with difficulty.*] Why aren't you nice and quiet like your sister Margot? Why do you have to show off all the time? Let me give you a little advice, young lady. Men don't like that kind of thing in a girl. You know that? A man likes a girl who'll listen to him once in a while . . . a domestic girl, who'll keep her house shining for her husband . . . who loves to cook and sew and . . .

ANNE. I'd cut my throat first! I'd open my veins! I'm going to be remarkable! I'm going to Paris . . .

MR. VAN DAAN. [*Scoffingly.*] Paris!

ANNE. . . . to study music and art.

MR. VAN DAAN. Yeah! Yeah!

ANNE. I'm going to be a famous dancer or singer . . . or something wonderful.

[*She makes a wide gesture, spilling the glass of milk on the fur coat in* MRS. VAN DAAN's *lap.* MARGOT *rushes quickly over with a towel.* ANNE *tries to brush the milk off with her skirt.*]

MRS. VAN DAAN. Now look what you've done . . . you clumsy little fool! My beautiful fur coat my father gave me . . .

ANNE. I'm so sorry.

MRS. VAN DAAN. What do you care? It isn't yours . . . So go on, ruin it! Do you know what that coat cost? Do you? And now look at it! Look at it!

ANNE. I'm very, very sorry.

MRS. VAN DAAN. I could kill you for this. I could just kill you!

[MRS. VAN DAAN *goes up the stairs, clutching the coat.* MR. VAN DAAN *starts after her.*]

MR. VAN DAAN. Petronella . . . *liefje! Liefje!* . . . Come back . . . the supper . . . come back!

MRS. FRANK. Anne, you must not behave in that way.

ANNE. It was an accident. Anyone can have an accident.

MRS. FRANK. I don't mean that. I mean the answering back. You must not answer back. They are our guests. We must always show the greatest courtesy to them. We're all living under terrible tension. [*She stops as* MARGOT *indicates that* VAN DAAN *can hear. When he is gone, she continues.*] That's why we must control ourselves . . . You don't hear Margot getting into arguments with them, do you? Watch Margot. She's always courteous with them. Never familiar. She keeps her distance. And they respect her for it. Try to be like Margot.

ANNE. And have them walk all over me, the way they do her? No, thanks!

MRS. FRANK. I'm not afraid that anyone is going to walk all over you, Anne. I'm afraid for other people, that you'll walk on them. I don't know what happens to you, Anne. You are wild, self-willed. If I had ever talked to my mother as you talk to me . . .

ANNE. Things have changed. People aren't like that any more. "Yes, Mother." "No, Mother." "Anything you say, Mother." I've got to fight things out for myself! Make something of myself!

MRS. FRANK. It isn't necessary to fight to do it. Margot doesn't fight, and isn't she . . . ?

ANNE. [*Violently rebellious.*] Margot! Margot! Margot! That's all I hear from everyone . . . how wonderful Margot is . . . "Why aren't you like Margot?"

MARGOT. [*Protesting.*] Oh, come on, Anne, don't be so . . .

ANNE. [*Paying no attention.*] Everything she does is right, and everything I do is wrong!

I'm the goat[24] around here! . . . You're all against me! . . . And you worst of all!

[She rushes off into her room and throws herself down on the settee, stifling her sobs. MRS. FRANK sighs and starts toward the stove.]

MRS. FRANK. [*To MARGOT.*] Let's put the soup on the stove . . . if there's anyone who cares to eat. Margot, will you take the bread out? [*MARGOT gets the bread from the cupboard.*] I don't know how we can go on living this way . . . I can't say a word to Anne . . . she flies at me . . .

MARGOT. You know Anne. In half an hour she'll be out here, laughing and joking.

MRS. FRANK. And . . . [*She makes a motion upwards, indicating the VAN DAANS.*] . . . I told your father it wouldn't work . . . but no . . . no . . . he had to ask them, he said . . . he owed it to him, he said. Well, he knows now that I was right! These quarrels! . . . This bickering!

MARGOT. [*With a warning look.*] Shush. Shush.

[The buzzer for the door sounds. MRS. FRANK gasps, startled.]

MRS. FRANK. Every time I hear that sound, my heart stops!

MARGOT. [*Starting for PETER's door.*] It's Miep. [*She knocks at the door.*] Father?

[MR. FRANK comes quickly from PETER's room.]

MR. FRANK. Thank you, Margot. [*As he goes down the steps to open the outer door.*] Has everyone his list?

MARGOT. I'll get my books. [*Giving her mother a list.*] Here's your list. [*MARGOT goes into her and ANNE's bedroom on the right. ANNE sits up, hiding her tears, as MARGOT comes in.*] Miep's here.

[MARGOT picks up her books and goes back. ANNE hurries over to the mirror, smoothing her hair.]

MR. VAN DAAN. [*Coming down the stairs.*] Is it Miep?

MARGOT. Yes. Father's gone down to let her in.

MR. VAN DAAN. At last I'll have some cigarettes!

MRS. FRANK. [*To MR. VAN DAAN.*] I can't tell you how unhappy I am about Mrs. Van Daan's coat. Anne should never have touched it.

MR. VAN DAAN. She'll be all right.

MRS. FRANK. Is there anything I can do?

MR. VAN DAAN. Don't worry.

[He turns to meet MIEP. But it is not MIEP who comes up the steps. It is MR. KRALER, followed by MR. FRANK. Their faces are grave. ANNE comes from the bedroom. PETER comes from his room.]

MRS. FRANK. Mr. Kraler!

MR. VAN DAAN. How are you, Mr. Kraler?

MARGOT. This is a surprise.

MRS. FRANK. When Mr. Kraler comes, the sun begins to shine.

MR. VAN DAAN. Miep is coming?

MR. KRALER. Not tonight.

[KRALER goes to MARGOT and MRS. FRANK and ANNE, shaking hands with them.]

MRS. FRANK. Wouldn't you like a cup of coffee? . . . Or, better still, will you have supper with us?

---

24. A *goat* or *scapegoat* is one who is blamed or punished for other people's mistakes. In the Bible, the high priest Aaron symbolically placed the Jews' sins on the head of a goat that was then driven into the wilderness.

MR. FRANK. Mr. Kraler has something to talk over with us. Something has happened, he says, which demands an immediate decision.

MRS. FRANK. [*Fearful.*] What is it?

[MR. KRALER *sits down on the couch. As he talks he takes bread, cabbages, milk, etc., from his briefcase, giving them to* MARGOT *and* ANNE *to put away.*]

MR. KRALER. Usually, when I come up here, I try to bring you some bit of good news. What's the use of telling you the bad news when there's nothing that you can do about it? But today something has happened . . . Dirk . . . Miep's Dirk, you know, came to me just now. He tells me that he has a Jewish friend living near him. A dentist. He says he's in trouble. He begged me, could I do anything for this man? Could I find him a hiding place? . . . So I've come to you . . . I know it's a terrible thing to ask of you, living as you are, but would you take him in with you?

MR. FRANK. Of course we will.

MR. KRALER. [*Rising.*] It'll be just for a night or two . . . until I find some other place. This happened so suddenly that I didn't know where to turn.

MR. FRANK. Where is he?

MR. KRALER. Downstairs in the office.

MR. FRANK. Good. Bring him up.

MR. KRALER. His name is Dussel . . . Jan Dussel.[25]

MR. FRANK. Dussel . . . I think I know him.

MR. KRALER. I'll get him.

[*He goes quickly down the steps and out.* MR. FRANK *suddenly becomes conscious of the others.*]

25. ***Jan Dussel*** (yän dōōs′ əl)

MR. FRANK. Forgive me. I spoke without consulting you. But I knew you'd feel as I do.

MR. VAN DAAN. There's no reason for you to consult anyone. This is your place. You have a right to do exactly as you please. The only thing I feel . . . there's so little food as it is . . . and to take in another person . . .

[PETER *turns away, ashamed of his father.*]

MR. FRANK. We can stretch the food a little. It's only for a few days.

MR. VAN DAAN. You want to make a bet?

MRS. FRANK. I think it's fine to have him. But, Otto, where are you going to put him? Where?

PETER. He can have my bed. I can sleep on the floor. I wouldn't mind.

MR. FRANK. That's good of you, Peter. But your room's too small . . . even for *you.*

ANNE. I have a much better idea. I'll come in here with you and Mother, and Margot can take Peter's room and Peter can go in our room with Mr. Dussel.

MARGOT. That's right. We could do that.

MR. FRANK. No, Margot. You mustn't sleep in that room . . . neither you nor Anne. Mouschi has caught some rats in there. Peter's brave. He doesn't mind.

ANNE. Then how about *this?* I'll come in here with you and Mother, and Mr. Dussel can have my bed.

MRS. FRANK. No. No. *No!* Margot will come in here with us and he can have her bed. It's the only way. Margot, bring your things in here. Help her, Anne.

[MARGOT *hurries into her room to get her things.*]

ANNE. [*To her mother.*] Why Margot? Why can't I come in here?

MRS. FRANK. Because it wouldn't be proper for Margot to sleep with a . . . Please, Anne. Don't argue. Please.

[*ANNE starts slowly away.*]

MR. FRANK. [*To ANNE.*] You don't mind sharing your room with Mr. Dussel, do you, Anne?

ANNE. No. No, of course not.

MR. FRANK. Good. [*ANNE goes off into her bedroom, helping MARGOT. MR. FRANK starts to search in the cupboards.*] Where's the cognac?[26]

MRS. FRANK. It's there. But, Otto, I was saving it in case of illness.

MR. FRANK. I think we couldn't find a better time to use it. Peter, will you get five glasses for me?

[*PETER goes for the glasses. MARGOT comes out of her bedroom, carrying her possessions, which she hangs behind a curtain in the main room. MR. FRANK finds the cognac and pours it into the five glasses that PETER brings him. MR. VAN DAAN stands looking on sourly. MRS. VAN DAAN comes downstairs and looks around at all the bustle.*]

MRS. VAN DAAN. What's happening? What's going on?

MR. VAN DAAN. Someone's moving in with us.

MRS. VAN DAAN. In here? You're joking.

26. *Cognac* (kōn′ yak) is a brandy.

The Diary of Anne Frank, 1959. 20th Century Fox. Movie still.

Viewing the photograph: Notice how Anne and Margot interact with their mother. What does this scene tell you about the personality of each girl?

MARGOT. It's only for a night or two . . . until Mr. Kraler finds him another place.

MR. VAN DAAN. Yeah! Yeah!

[*MR. FRANK hurries over as MR. KRALER and DUSSEL come up. DUSSEL is a man in his late fifties, meticulous, finicky . . . bewildered now. He wears a raincoat. He carries a briefcase, stuffed full, and a small medicine case.*]

MR. FRANK. Come in, Mr. Dussel.

MR. KRALER. This is Mr. Frank.

DUSSEL. Mr. Otto Frank?

MR. FRANK. Yes. Let me take your things. [*He takes the hat and briefcase, but DUSSEL clings to his medicine case.*] This is my wife Edith . . . Mr. and Mrs. Van Daan . . . their son, Peter . . . and my daughters, Margot and Anne.

[*DUSSEL shakes hands with everyone.*]

MR. KRALER. Thank you, Mr. Frank. Thank you all. Mr. Dussel, I leave you in good hands. Oh . . . Dirk's coat.

[*DUSSEL hurriedly takes off the raincoat, giving it to MR. KRALER. Underneath is his white dentist's jacket, with a yellow Star of David on it.*]

DUSSEL. [*To MR. KRALER.*] What can I say to thank you . . . ?

MRS. FRANK. [*To DUSSEL.*] Mr. Kraler and Miep . . . They're our life line. Without them we couldn't live.

MR. KRALER. Please. Please. You make us seem very heroic. It isn't that at all. We simply don't like the Nazis. [*To MR. FRANK, who offers him a drink.*] No, thanks. [*Then going on.*] We don't like their methods. We don't like . . .

MR. FRANK. [*Smiling.*] I know. I know. "No one's going to tell us Dutchmen what to do with our damn Jews!"

MR. KRALER. [*To DUSSEL.*] Pay no attention to Mr. Frank. I'll be up tomorrow to see that they're treating you right. [*To MR. FRANK.*] Don't trouble to come down again. Peter will bolt the door after me, won't you, Peter?

PETER. Yes, sir.

MR. FRANK. Thank you, Peter. I'll do it.

MR. KRALER. Good night. Good night.

GROUP. Good night, Mr. Kraler.

We'll see you tomorrow, *etc., etc.*

[*MR. KRALER goes out with MR. FRANK. MRS. FRANK gives each one of the "grown-ups" a glass of cognac.*]

MRS. FRANK. Please, Mr. Dussel, sit down.

[*MR. DUSSEL sinks into a chair. MRS. FRANK gives him a glass of cognac.*]

DUSSEL. I'm dreaming. I know it. I can't believe my eyes. Mr. Otto Frank here! [*To MRS. FRANK.*] You're not in Switzerland then? A woman told me . . . She said she'd gone to your house . . . the door was open, everything was in disorder, dishes in the sink. She said she found a piece of paper in the wastebasket with an address scribbled on it . . . an address in Zurich.[27] She said you must have escaped to Zurich.

ANNE. Father put that there purposely . . . just so people would think that very thing!

DUSSEL. And you've been *here* all the time?

MRS. FRANK. All the time . . . ever since July.

[*ANNE speaks to her father as he comes back.*]

ANNE. It worked, Pim . . . the address you left! Mr. Dussel says that people believe we escaped to Switzerland.

27. ***Zurich*** (zoor′ ik)

MR. FRANK. I'm glad. . . . And now let's have a little drink to welcome Mr. Dussel. [*Before they can drink,* MR. DUSSEL *bolts his drink.* MR. FRANK *smiles and raises his glass.*] To Mr. Dussel. Welcome. We're very honored to have you with us.

MRS. FRANK. To Mr. Dussel, welcome.

[*The* VAN DAANS *murmur a welcome. The "grown-ups" drink.*]

MRS. VAN DAAN. Um. That was good.

MR. VAN DAAN. Did Mr. Kraler warn you that you won't get much to eat here? You can imagine . . . three ration books among the seven of us . . . and now you make eight.

[PETER *walks away, humiliated. Outside a street organ is heard dimly.*]

DUSSEL. [*Rising.*] Mr. Van Daan, you don't realize what is happening outside that you should warn me of a thing like that. You don't realize what's going on . . . [*As* MR. VAN DAAN *starts his characteristic pacing,* DUSSEL *turns to speak to the others.*] Right here in Amsterdam every day hundreds of Jews disappear . . . They surround a block and search house by house. Children come home from school to find their parents gone. Hundreds are being deported . . . people that you and I know . . . the Hallensteins . . . the Wessels . . .

MRS. FRANK. [*In tears.*] Oh, no. No!

DUSSEL. They get their call-up notice . . . come to the Jewish theater on such and such a day and hour . . . bring only what you can carry in a rucksack. And if you refuse the call-up notice, then they come and drag you from your home and ship you off to Mauthausen.[28] The death camp!

MRS. FRANK. We didn't know that things had got so much worse.

DUSSEL. Forgive me for speaking so.

ANNE. [*Coming to* DUSSEL.] Do you know the de Waals? . . . What's become of them? Their daughter Jopie and I are in the same class. Jopie's my best friend.

DUSSEL. They are gone.

ANNE. Gone?

DUSSEL. With all the others.

ANNE. Oh, no. Not Jopie!

[*She turns away, in tears.* MRS. FRANK *motions to* MARGOT *to comfort her.* MARGOT *goes to* ANNE, *putting her arms comfortingly around her.*]

MRS. VAN DAAN. There were some people called Wagner. They lived near us . . . ?

MR. FRANK. [*Interrupting, with a glance at* ANNE.] I think we should put this off until later. We all have many questions we want to ask . . . But I'm sure that Mr. Dussel would like to get settled before supper.

DUSSEL. Thank you. I would. I brought very little with me.

MR. FRANK. [*Giving him his hat and briefcase.*] I'm sorry we can't give you a room alone. But I hope you won't be too uncomfortable. We've had to make strict rules here . . . a schedule of hours . . . We'll tell you after supper. Anne, would you like to take Mr. Dussel to his room?

ANNE. [*Controlling her tears.*] If you'll come with me, Mr. Dussel?

[*She starts for her room.*]

DUSSEL. [*Shaking hands with each in turn.*] Forgive me if I haven't really expressed my gratitude to all of you. This has been such

28. Located in Austria, *Mauthausen* (mout′ hou′ zən) was a Nazi concentration camp.

a shock to me. I'd always thought of myself as Dutch. I was born in Holland. My father was born in Holland, and my grandfather. And now . . . after all these years . . . [*He breaks off.*] If you'll excuse me.

[*DUSSEL gives a little bow and hurries off after ANNE. MR. FRANK and the others are subdued.*]

ANNE. [*Turning on the light.*] Well, here we are.

[*DUSSEL looks around the room. In the main room MARGOT speaks to her mother.*]

MARGOT. The news sounds pretty bad, doesn't it? It's so different from what Mr. Kraler tells us. Mr. Kraler says things are improving.

MR. VAN DAAN. I like it better the way Kraler tells it.

[*They resume their occupations, quietly. PETER goes off into his room. In ANNE's room, ANNE turns to DUSSEL.*]

ANNE. You're going to share the room with me.

DUSSEL. I'm a man who's always lived alone. I haven't had to adjust myself to others. I hope you'll bear with me until I learn.

ANNE. Let me help you. [*She takes his briefcase.*] Do you always live all alone? Have you no family at all?

DUSSEL. No one.

[*He opens his medicine case and spreads his bottles on the dressing table.*]

ANNE. How dreadful. You must be terribly lonely.

DUSSEL. I'm used to it.

ANNE. I don't think I could ever get used to it. Didn't you even have a pet? A cat, or a dog?

DUSSEL. I have an allergy for fur-bearing animals. They give me asthma.

ANNE. Oh, dear. Peter has a cat.

DUSSEL. Here? He has it here?

ANNE. Yes. But we hardly ever see it. He keeps it in his room all the time. I'm sure it will be all right.

DUSSEL. Let us hope so.

[*He takes some pills to fortify himself.*]

ANNE. That's Margot's bed, where you're going to sleep. I sleep on the sofa there. [*Indicating the clothes hooks on the wall.*] We cleared these off for your things. [*She goes over to the window.*] The best part about this room . . . you can look down and see a bit of the street and the canal. There's a houseboat . . . you can see the end of it . . . a bargeman lives there with his family . . . They have a baby and he's just beginning to walk and I'm so afraid he's going to fall into the canal some day. I watch him. . . .

DUSSEL. [*Interrupting.*] Your father spoke of a schedule.

ANNE. [*Coming away from the window.*] Oh, yes. It's mostly about the times we have to be quiet. And times for the w.c. You can use it now if you like.

DUSSEL. [*Stiffly.*] No, thank you.

ANNE. I suppose you think it's awful, my talking about a thing like that. But you don't know how important it can get to be, especially when you're frightened . . . About this room, the way Margot and I did

Vocabulary

subdued (səb do͞od′) *adj.* quiet and downcast

. . . she had it to herself in the afternoons for studying, reading . . . lessons, you know . . . and I took the mornings. Would that be all right with you?

DUSSEL. I'm not at my best in the morning.

ANNE. You stay here in the mornings then. I'll take the room in the afternoons.

DUSSEL. Tell me, when you're in here, what happens to me? Where am I spending my time? In there, with all the people?

ANNE. Yes.

DUSSEL. I see. I see.

ANNE. We have supper at half past six.

DUSSEL. [*Going over to the sofa.*] Then, if you don't mind . . . I like to lie down quietly for ten minutes before eating. I find it helps the digestion.

ANNE. Of course. I hope I'm not going to be too much of a bother to you. I seem to be able to get everyone's back up.

[*DUSSEL lies down on the sofa, curled up, his back to her.*]

DUSSEL. I always get along very well with children. My patients all bring their children to me, because they know I get on well with them. So don't you worry about that.

[*ANNE leans over him, taking his hand and shaking it gratefully.*]

ANNE. Thank you. Thank you, Mr. Dussel.

[*The lights dim to darkness. The curtain falls on the scene. ANNE'S VOICE comes to us faintly at first, and then with increasing power.*]

ANNE'S VOICE. . . . And yesterday I finished Cissy Van Marxvelt's latest book. I think she is a first-class writer. I shall definitely let my children read her. Monday the twenty-first of September, nineteen forty-two. Mr. Dussel and I had another battle yesterday. Yes, Mr. Dussel! According to him, nothing, I repeat . . . nothing, is right about me . . . my appearance, my character, my manners. While he was going on at me I thought . . . sometime I'll give you such a smack that you'll fly right up to the ceiling! Why is it that every grown-up thinks he knows the way to bring up children? Particularly the grown-ups that never had any. I keep wishing that Peter was a girl instead of a boy. Then I would have someone to talk to. Margot's a darling, but she takes everything too seriously. To pause for a moment on the subject of Mrs. Van Daan. I must tell you that her attempts to flirt with father are getting her nowhere. Pim, thank goodness, won't play.

[*As she is saying the last lines, the curtain rises on the darkened scene. ANNE'S VOICE fades out.*]

The Diary of Anne Frank, 1959. 20th Century Fox. Movie still.

Viewing the photograph: What might Anne and Mr. Dussel be discussing in this scene?

Responding to Literature

PERSONAL RESPONSE

Have your first impressions of the members of the Secret Annex changed? Why or why not?

Analyzing Literature

RECALL AND INTERPRET

1. Who is Mrs. Quack Quack? What does the audience learn about Anne and Peter from their teasing each other?
2. What are the young people studying? What does their parents' insistence that they study tell you about the parents?
3. Why does Mr. Kraler arrive unexpectedly? What do the responses of the Van Daans and the Franks show about each character?

EVALUATE AND CONNECT

4. In your opinion, is Mr. and Mrs. Van Daan's criticism of Anne justified? Is their attitude unusual for adults? Explain.
5. What is Anne's relationship with her mother? with her father? How does her attitude toward her parents seem different from, or typical of, the ways young people today relate to their parents?
6. Mr. Kraler tells the group, "You make us seem very heroic. It isn't that at all. We simply don't like the Nazis." Do you believe this statement is the complete truth? Why or why not?

LITERARY ELEMENTS

Dialogue

Dialogue is conversation between characters. In a play, the words of each character are *not* set off in quotes as they would be in a narrative. Instead, the name of the character is printed in front of the words that he or she speaks. Notice that, in some cases, a brief description follows the name of the person speaking.

MR. KRALER. Good-bye then for the moment. I'll come up again, after the workmen leave.
MR. FRANK. Good-bye, Mr. Kraler.
MRS. FRANK. [*Shaking his hand.*] How can we thank you?

1. Who are the three characters in the example above?
2. Which character speaks first?

• See **Literary Terms Handbook,** p. R3.

Extending Your Response

Literature Groups

Anne's "Family" The characters in the annex are frequently referred to as a "family." In your opinion, is this an accurate term? How would you define *family?* Share your group's thoughts with the rest of the class.

Creative Writing

A New Hiding Place Suppose Mr. Dussel were keeping a journal. Write an entry for his first night at the Secret Annex. Keep in mind that he is aware of the brutality going on outside. How would this knowledge affect his impression of the people and the place?

The Diary of Anne Frank (Continued)

SCENE

[*It is the middle of the night, several months later. The stage is dark except for a little light which comes through the skylight in* PETER*'s room.*
Everyone is in bed. MR. *and* MRS. FRANK *lie on the couch in the main room, which has been pulled out to serve as a makeshift double bed.* MARGOT *is sleeping on a mattress on the floor in the main room, behind a curtain stretched across for privacy. The others are all in their accustomed rooms.*
From outside we hear two drunken soldiers singing "Lili Marlene." *A girl's high giggle is heard. The sound of running feet is heard coming closer and then fading in the distance. Throughout the scene there is the distant sound of airplanes passing overhead.*
A match suddenly flares up in the attic. We dimly see MR. VAN DAAN. *He is getting his bearings.*[29] *He comes quickly down the stairs, and goes to the cupboard where the food is stored. Again the match flares up, and is as quickly blown out. The dim figure is seen to steal back up the stairs.*
There is quiet for a second or two, broken only by the sound of airplanes, and running feet on the street below.
Suddenly, out of the silence and the dark, we hear ANNE *scream.*]

ANNE. [*Screaming.*] No! No! Don't . . . don't take me!

29. When Mr. Van Daan is *getting his bearings,* he is figuring out his position in the dimly lit room and deciding where to go.

[*She moans, tossing and crying in her sleep. The other people wake, terrified.* DUSSEL *sits up in bed, furious.*]

DUSSEL. Shush! Anne! Anne, for God's sake, shush!

ANNE. [*Still in her nightmare.*] Save me! Save me!

[*She screams and screams.* DUSSEL *gets out of bed, going over to her, trying to wake her.*]

DUSSEL. For God's sake! Quiet! Quiet! You want someone to hear?

[*In the main room* MRS. FRANK *grabs a shawl and pulls it around her. She rushes in to* ANNE*, taking her in her arms.* MR. FRANK *hurriedly gets up, putting on his overcoat.* MARGOT *sits up, terrified.* PETER*'s light goes on in his room.*]

MRS. FRANK. [*To* ANNE*, in her room.*] Hush, darling, hush. It's all right. It's all right. [*Over her shoulder to* DUSSEL.] Will you be kind enough to turn on the light, Mr. Dussel? [*Back to* ANNE.] It's nothing, my darling. It was just a dream.

[DUSSEL *turns on the light in the bedroom.* MRS. FRANK *holds* ANNE *in her arms. Gradually* ANNE *comes out of her nightmare, still trembling with horror.* MR. FRANK *comes into the room, and goes quickly to the window, looking out to be sure that no one outside has heard* ANNE*'s screams.* MRS. FRANK *holds* ANNE*, talking softly to her. In the main room* MARGOT *stands on a chair, turning on the center hanging lamp. A light goes on in the* VAN DAANS' *room overhead.* PETER *puts his robe on, coming out of his room.*]

DUSSEL. [*To* MRS. FRANK, *blowing his nose.*] Something must be done about that child, Mrs. Frank. Yelling like that! Who knows but there's somebody on the streets? She's endangering all our lives.

MRS. FRANK. Anne, darling.

DUSSEL. Every night she twists and turns. I don't sleep. I spend half my night shushing her. And now it's nightmares!

[MARGOT *comes to the door of* ANNE'*s room, followed by* PETER. MR. FRANK *goes to them, indicating that everything is all right.* PETER *takes* MARGOT *back.*]

MRS. FRANK. [*To* ANNE.] You're here, safe, you see? Nothing has happened. [*To* DUSSEL.] Please, Mr. Dussel, go back to bed. She'll be herself in a minute or two. Won't you, Anne?

DUSSEL. [*Picking up a book and a pillow.*] Thank you, but I'm going to the w.c. The one place where there's peace!

[*He stalks out.* MR. VAN DAAN, *in underwear and trousers, comes down the stairs.*]

MR. VAN DAAN. [*To* DUSSEL.] What is it? What happened?

DUSSEL. A nightmare. She was having a nightmare!

MR. VAN DAAN. I thought someone was murdering her.

DUSSEL. Unfortunately, no.

[*He goes into the bathroom.* MR. VAN DAAN *goes back up the stairs.* MR. FRANK, *in the main room, sends* PETER *back to his own bedroom.*]

MR. FRANK. Thank you, Peter. Go back to bed.

[PETER *goes back to his room.* MR. FRANK *follows him, turning out the light and looking out the window. Then he goes back to the main room, and gets up on a chair, turning out the center hanging lamp.*]

MRS. FRANK. [*To* ANNE.] Would you like some water? [ANNE *shakes her head.*] Was it a very bad dream? Perhaps if you told me . . . ?

ANNE. I'd rather not talk about it.

MRS. FRANK. Poor darling. Try to sleep then. I'll sit right here beside you until you fall asleep.

[*She brings a stool over, sitting there.*]

ANNE. You don't have to.

MRS. FRANK. But I'd like to stay with you . . . very much. Really.

ANNE. I'd rather you didn't.

MRS. FRANK. Good night, then. [*She leans down to kiss* ANNE. ANNE *throws her arm up over her face, turning away.* MRS. FRANK, *hiding her hurt, kisses* ANNE'*s arm.*] You'll be all right? There's nothing that you want?

ANNE. Will you please ask Father to come.

MRS. FRANK. [*After a second.*] Of course, Anne dear. [*She hurries out into the other room.* MR. FRANK *comes to her as she comes in.*] *Sie verlangt nach Dir!*

MR. FRANK. [*Sensing her hurt.*] Edith, *Liebe, schau . . .*

MRS. FRANK. *Es macht nichts! Ich danke dem lieben Herrgott, dass sie sich wenigstens an Dich wendet, wenn sie Trost braucht! Geh hinein, Otto, sie ist ganz hysterisch vor Angst.* [*As* MR. FRANK *hesitates.*] *Geh zu ihr.*[30] [*He looks at her for a second and then goes to get a cup of water for* ANNE. MRS. FRANK *sinks down on the bed,*

30. The Franks' conversation in German beginning *"Sie verlangt . . ."* translates as follows: MRS. FRANK. "She wants to see you." MR. FRANK. "Edith, dear, look . . ." MRS. FRANK. "It's all right. Thank God that at least she turns to you when she is in need of comfort. Go in, Otto, she is hysterical with fear. Go to her."

her face in her hands, trying to keep from sobbing aloud. MARGOT *comes over to her, putting her arms around her.*] She wants nothing of me. She pulled away when I leaned down to kiss her.

MARGOT. It's a phase . . . You heard Father . . . Most girls go through it . . . they turn to their fathers at this age . . . they give all their love to their fathers.

MRS. FRANK. You weren't like this. You didn't shut me out.

MARGOT. She'll get over it . . .

[*She smooths the bed for* MRS. FRANK *and sits beside her a moment as* MRS. FRANK *lies down. In* ANNE*'s room* MR. FRANK *comes in, sitting down by* ANNE. ANNE *flings her arms around him, clinging to him. In the distance we hear the sound of ack-ack.*]

ANNE. Oh, Pim. I dreamed that they came to get us! The Green Police! They broke down the door and grabbed me and started to drag me out the way they did Jopie.

MR. FRANK. I want you to take this pill.

ANNE. What is it?

MR. FRANK. Something to quiet you.

[*She takes it and drinks the water. In the main room* MARGOT *turns out the light and goes back to her bed.*]

MR. FRANK. [*To* ANNE.] Do you want me to read to you for a while?

ANNE. No. Just sit with me for a minute. Was I awful? Did I yell terribly loud? Do you think anyone outside could have heard?

MR. FRANK. No. No. Lie quietly now. Try to sleep.

ANNE. I'm a terrible coward. I'm so disappointed in myself. I think I've conquered my fear . . . I think I'm really grown-up . . . and then something happens . . . and I run to you like a baby . . . I love you, Father. I don't love anyone but you.

MR. FRANK. [*Reproachfully.*] Annele!

ANNE. It's true. I've been thinking about it for a long time. You're the only one I love.

MR. FRANK. It's fine to hear you tell me that you love me. But I'd be happier if you said you loved your mother as well . . . She needs your help so much . . . your love . . .

ANNE. We have nothing in common. She doesn't understand me. Whenever I try to explain my views on life to her she asks me if I'm constipated.

MR. FRANK. You hurt her very much just now. She's crying. She's in there crying.

ANNE. I can't help it. I only told the truth. I didn't want her here . . . [*Then, with sudden change.*] Oh, Pim, I was horrible, wasn't I? And the worst of it is, I can stand off and look at myself doing it and know it's cruel and yet I can't stop doing it. What's the matter with me? Tell me. Don't say it's just a phase! Help me.

MR. FRANK. There is so little that we parents can do to help our children. We can only try to set a good example . . . point the way. The rest you must do yourself. You must build your own character.

ANNE. I'm trying. Really I am. Every night I think back over all of the things I did that day that were wrong . . . like putting the wet mop in Mr. Dussel's bed . . . and this thing now with Mother. I say to myself, that was wrong. I make up my mind, I'm never going to do that again. Never! Of course I may do something worse . . . but at least I'll never do *that* again! . . . I have a nicer side, Father . . . a sweeter, nicer side. But I'm scared to show it. I'm afraid that people are going to laugh at me if I'm serious. So the mean Anne comes to the outside and the good Anne stays on the inside, and I keep on trying to switch them around and have the good Anne outside and the bad Anne inside and be what I'd like to be . . . and might be . . . if only . . . only . . .

[*She is asleep.* MR. FRANK *watches her for a moment and then turns off the light, and starts out. The lights dim out. The curtain falls on the scene.* ANNE'S VOICE *is heard dimly at first, and then with growing strength.*]

ANNE'S VOICE. . . . The air raids are getting worse. They come over day and night. The noise is terrifying. Pim says it should be music to our ears. The more planes, the sooner will come the end of the war. Mrs. Van Daan pretends to be a fatalist.[31] What will be, will be. But when the planes come over, who is the most frightened? No one else but Petronella! . . . Monday, the ninth of November, nineteen forty-two. Wonderful news! The Allies have landed in Africa. Pim says that we can look for an early finish to the war. Just for fun he asked each of us what was the first thing we wanted to do when we got out of here. Mrs. Van Daan longs to be home with her own things, her needle-point chairs, the Beckstein piano her father gave her . . .

31. A *fatalist* is someone who believes that fate controls everything that happens.

The Diary of Anne Frank, 1959. 20th Century Fox. Movie still.

Viewing the photograph: Why is the group standing by the window? In your opinion, is this scene frightening or hopeful?

the best that money could buy. Peter would like to go to a movie. Mr. Dussel wants to get back to his dentist's drill. He's afraid he is losing his touch. For myself, there are so many things . . . to ride a bike again . . . to laugh till my belly aches . . . to have new clothes from the skin out . . . to have a hot tub filled to overflowing and wallow in it for hours . . . to be back in school with my friends . . .

[*As the last lines are being said, the curtain rises on the scene. The lights dim on as* ANNE'S VOICE *fades away.*]

SCENE

[*It is the first night of the Hanukkah*[32] *celebration.* MR. FRANK *is standing at the head of the table on which is the Menorah. He lights the Shamos, or servant candle,*[33] *and holds it as he says the blessing. Seated listening is all of the "family," dressed in their best. The men wear hats,* PETER *wears his cap.*]

MR. FRANK. [*Reading from a prayer book.*] "Praised be Thou, oh Lord our God, Ruler of the universe, who has sanctified us with Thy commandments and bidden us kindle the Hanukkah lights. Praised be Thou, oh Lord our God, Ruler of the universe, who has wrought wondrous deliverances for our fathers in days of old. Praised be Thou, oh Lord our God, Ruler of the universe, that Thou has given us life and sustenance[34] and brought us to this happy season." [MR. FRANK *lights the one candle of the Menorah as he continues.*] "We kindle this Hanukkah light to celebrate the great and wonderful deeds wrought through the zeal with which God filled the hearts of the heroic Maccabees, two thousand years ago. They fought against indifference, against tyranny and oppression,[35] and they restored our Temple to us. May these lights remind us that we should ever look to God, whence cometh our help." Amen. [Pronounced O-mayn.]

ALL. Amen.

[MR. FRANK *hands* MRS. FRANK *the prayer book.*]

MRS. FRANK. [*Reading.*] "I lift up mine eyes unto the mountains, from whence cometh my help. My help cometh from the Lord who made heaven and earth. He will not suffer thy foot to be moved. He that keepeth thee will not slumber. He that keepeth Israel doth neither slumber nor sleep. The Lord is thy keeper. The Lord is thy shade upon thy right hand. The sun shall not smite thee by day, nor the moon by night. The Lord shall keep thee from all evil. He shall keep thy soul. The Lord shall guard thy going out and thy coming in, from this time forth and forevermore." Amen.

ALL. Amen.

[MRS. FRANK *puts down the prayer book and goes to get the food and wine.* MARGOT

---

32. The eight-day Jewish holiday *Hanukkah* (hä′ nə kə) is celebrated in December. It honors a victory in 165 B.C. over Syrian enemies.
33. The *Menorah* (mə nôr′ ə) is a candlestick with nine branches. On the first day of Hanukkah, one candle is lit, and an additional candle is lit on each of the following days. The *Shamos* (shäm′ əs) or (shä′ mäs), *or servant candle,* is used to light the others.
34. Here, *sanctified* means "set apart as holy." *Wrought* is an old form of the word *worked. Sustenance* is food and other necessities of life.
35. *Zeal* means "great devotion." It was the *Maccabees,* a family of Jewish patriots, who led the Jews to victory. They fought the Syrians' cruel and unjust use of power (*tyranny* and *oppression*).

helps her. MR. FRANK *takes the men's hats and puts them aside.*]

DUSSEL. [*Rising.*] That was very moving.

ANNE. [*Pulling him back.*] It isn't over yet!

MRS. VAN DAAN. Sit down! Sit down!

ANNE. There's a lot more, songs and presents.

DUSSEL. Presents?

MRS. FRANK. Not this year, unfortunately.

MRS. VAN DAAN. But always on Hanukkah everyone gives presents . . . everyone!

DUSSEL. Like our St. Nicholas'[36] Day.

[*There is a chorus of "no's" from the group.*]

MRS. VAN DAAN. No! Not like St. Nicholas! What kind of a Jew are you that you don't know Hanukkah?

MRS. FRANK. [*As she brings the food.*] I remember particularly the candles . . . First one, as we have tonight. Then the second night you light two candles, the next night three . . . and so on until you have eight candles burning. When there are eight candles it is truly beautiful.

MRS. VAN DAAN. And the potato pancakes.

MR. VAN DAAN. Don't talk about them!

MRS. VAN DAAN. I make the best *latkes*[37] you ever tasted!

MRS. FRANK. Invite us all next year . . . in your own home.

MR. FRANK. God willing!

MRS. VAN DAAN. God willing.

MARGOT. What I remember best is the presents we used to get when we were little . . . eight days of presents . . . and each day they got better and better.

MRS. FRANK. [*Sitting down.*] We are all here, alive. That is present enough.

ANNE. No, it isn't. I've got something . . .

[*She rushes into her room, hurriedly puts on a little hat improvised from the lamp shade, grabs a satchel bulging with parcels and comes running back.*]

MRS. FRANK. What is it?

ANNE. Presents!

MRS. VAN DAAN. Presents!

DUSSEL. Look!

MR. VAN DAAN. What's she got on her head?

PETER. A lamp shade!

ANNE. [*She picks out one at random.*] This is for Margot. [*She hands it to* MARGOT, *pulling her to her feet.*] Read it out loud.

MARGOT. [*Reading.*]

"You have never lost your temper.
You never will, I fear,
You are so good.
But if you should,
Put all your cross words here."

[*She tears open the package.*] A new crossword puzzle book! Where did you get it?

ANNE. It isn't new. It's one that you've done. But I rubbed it all out, and if you wait a little and forget, you can do it all over again.

MARGOT. [*Sitting.*] It's wonderful, Anne. Thank you. You'd never know it wasn't new.

[*From outside we hear the sound of a streetcar passing.*]

ANNE. [*With another gift.*] Mrs. Van Daan.

MRS. VAN DAAN. [*Taking it.*] This is awful . . . I haven't anything for anyone . . . I never thought . . .

---

36. In the Netherlands, Christian children receive gifts from *St. Nicholas* on December 6.
37. *Latkes* (lät′ kəz) are potato pancakes.

MR. FRANK. This is all Anne's idea.

MRS. VAN DAAN. [*Holding up a bottle.*] What is it?

ANNE. It's hair shampoo. I took all the odds and ends of soap and mixed them with the last of my toilet water.

MRS. VAN DAAN. Oh, Anneke!

ANNE. I wanted to write a poem for all of them, but I didn't have time. [*Offering a large box to* MR. VAN DAAN.] Yours, Mr. Van Daan, is *really* something . . . something you want more than anything. [*As she waits for him to open it.*] Look! Cigarettes!

MR. VAN DAAN. Cigarettes!

ANNE. Two of them! Pim found some old pipe tobacco in the pocket lining of his coat . . . and we made them . . . or rather, Pim did.

MRS. VAN DAAN. Let me see . . . Well, look at that! Light it, Putti! Light it.

[MR. VAN DAAN *hesitates.*]

ANNE. It's tobacco, really it is! There's a little fluff in it, but not much.

[*Everyone watches intently as* MR. VAN DAAN *cautiously lights it. The cigarette flares up. Everyone laughs.*]

PETER. It works!

MRS. VAN DAAN. Look at him.

MR. VAN DAAN. [*Spluttering.*] Thank you, Anne. Thank you.

[ANNE *rushes back to her satchel for another present.*]

ANNE. [*Handing her mother a piece of paper.*] For Mother, Hanukkah greeting.

[*She pulls her mother to her feet.*]

MRS. FRANK. [*She reads.*] "Here's an I.O.U. that I promise to pay. Ten hours of doing whatever you say. Signed, Anne Frank."

[MRS. FRANK, *touched, takes* ANNE *in her arms, holding her close.*]

DUSSEL. [*To* ANNE.] Ten hours of doing what you're told? *Anything* you're told?

ANNE. That's right.

DUSSEL. You wouldn't want to sell that, Mrs. Frank?

MRS. FRANK. Never! This is the most precious gift I've ever had!

[*She sits, showing her present to the others.* ANNE *hurries back to the satchel and pulls out a scarf, the scarf that* MR. FRANK *found in the first scene.*]

ANNE. [*Offering it to her father.*] For Pim.

MR. FRANK. Anneke . . . I wasn't supposed to have a present!

[*He takes it, unfolding it and showing it to the others.*]

ANNE. It's a muffler . . . to put round your neck . . . like an ascot, you know. I made it myself out of odds and ends . . . I knitted it in the dark each night, after I'd gone to bed. I'm afraid it looks better in the dark!

MR. FRANK. [*Putting it on.*] It's fine. It fits me perfectly. Thank you, Annele.

[ANNE *hands* PETER *a ball of paper, with a string attached to it.*]

ANNE. That's for Mouschi.

PETER. [*Rising to bow.*] On behalf of Mouschi, I thank you.

ANNE. [*Hesitant, handing him a gift.*] And . . . this is yours . . . from Mrs. Quack Quack. [*As he holds it gingerly in his hands.*] Well . . . open it . . . Aren't you going to open it?

PETER. I'm scared to. I know something's going to jump out and hit me.

ANNE. No. It's nothing like that, really.

MRS. VAN DAAN. [*As he is opening it.*] What is it, Peter? Go on. Show it.

ANNE. [*Excitedly.*] It's a safety razor!

DUSSEL. A what?

ANNE. A razor!

MRS. VAN DAAN. [*Looking at it.*] You didn't make that out of odds and ends.

ANNE. [*To PETER.*] Miep got it for me. It's not new. It's second-hand. But you really do need a razor now.

DUSSEL. For what?

ANNE. Look on his upper lip . . . you can see the beginning of a mustache.

DUSSEL. He wants to get rid of that? Put a little milk on it and let the cat lick it off.

PETER. [*Starting for his room.*] Think you're funny, don't you?

DUSSEL. Look! He can't wait! He's going in to try it!

PETER. I'm going to give Mouschi his present!

[*He goes into his room, slamming the door behind him.*]

MR. VAN DAAN. [*Disgustedly.*] Mouschi, Mouschi, Mouschi.

[*In the distance we hear a dog persistently barking. ANNE brings a gift to DUSSEL.*]

ANNE. And last but never least, my roommate, Mr. Dussel.

DUSSEL. For me? You have something for me?

[*He opens the small box she gives him.*]

ANNE. I made them myself.

DUSSEL. [*Puzzled.*] Capsules! Two capsules!

ANNE. They're ear-plugs!

DUSSEL. Ear-plugs?

ANNE. To put in your ears so you won't hear me when I thrash around at night. I saw them advertised in a magazine. They're not real ones . . . I made them out of cotton and candle wax. Try them . . . See if they don't work . . . see if you can hear me talk . . .

DUSSEL. [*Putting them in his ears.*] Wait now until I get them in . . . so.

ANNE. Are you ready?

DUSSEL. Huh?

ANNE. Are you ready?

DUSSEL. Good God! They've gone inside! I can't get them out! [*They laugh as MR. DUSSEL jumps about, trying to shake the plugs out of his ears. Finally he gets them out. Putting them away.*] Thank you, Anne! Thank you!

Together:

MR. VAN DAAN. A real Hanukkah!

MRS. VAN DAAN. Wasn't it cute of her?

MRS. FRANK. I don't know when she did it.

MARGOT. I love my present.

ANNE. [*Sitting at the table.*] And now let's have the song, Father . . . please . . . [*To DUSSEL.*] Have you heard the Hanukkah song, Mr. Dussel? The song is the whole thing! [*She sings.*] "Oh, Hanukkah! Oh Hanukkah! The sweet celebration . . ."

MR. FRANK. [*Quieting her.*] I'm afraid, Anne, we shouldn't sing that song tonight. [*To DUSSEL.*] It's a song of jubilation, of rejoicing. One is apt to become too enthusiastic.

Vocabulary

jubilation (jōō′ bə lā′ shən) *n.* great joy and excitement

ANNE. Oh, please, please. Let's sing the song. I promise not to shout!

MR. FRANK. Very well. But quietly now . . . I'll keep an eye on you and when . . .

[As ANNE starts to sing, she is interrupted by DUSSEL, who is snorting and wheezing.]

DUSSEL. [*Pointing to PETER.*] You . . . You! [*PETER is coming from his bedroom, ostentatiously[38] holding a bulge in his coat as if he were holding his cat, and dangling ANNE's present before it.*] How many times . . . I told you . . . Out! Out!

MR. VAN DAAN. [*Going to PETER.*] What's the matter with you? Haven't you any sense? Get that cat out of here.

PETER. [*Innocently.*] Cat?

MR. VAN DAAN. You heard me. Get it out of here!

PETER. I have no cat.

[Delighted with his joke, he opens his coat and pulls out a bath towel. The group at the table laugh, enjoying the joke.]

DUSSEL. [*Still wheezing.*] It doesn't need to be the cat . . . his clothes are enough . . . when he comes out of that room . . .

MR. VAN DAAN. Don't worry. You won't be bothered any more. We're getting rid of it.

DUSSEL. At last you listen to me.

[He goes off into his bedroom.]

MR. VAN DAAN. [*Calling after him.*] I'm not doing it for you. That's all in your mind . . . all of it! [*He starts back to his place at the table.*] I'm doing it because I'm sick of seeing that cat eat all our food.

PETER. That's not true! I only give him bones . . . scraps . . .

38. Peter holds the bulge in a showy way that is meant to attract notice *(ostentatiously).*

MR. VAN DAAN. Don't tell me! He gets fatter every day! Damn cat looks better than any of us. Out he goes tonight!

PETER. No! No!

ANNE. Mr. Van Daan, you can't do that! That's Peter's cat. Peter loves that cat.

MRS. FRANK. [*Quietly.*] Anne.

PETER. [*To MR. VAN DAAN.*] If he goes, I go.

MR. VAN DAAN. Go! Go!

MRS. VAN DAAN. You're not going and the cat's not going! Now please . . . this is Hanukkah . . . Hanukkah . . . this is the time to celebrate . . . What's the matter with all of you? Come on, Anne. Let's have the song.

ANNE. [*Singing.*] "Oh, Hanukkah! Oh, Hanukkah! The sweet celebration."

MR. FRANK. [*Rising.*] I think we should first blow out the candle . . . then we'll have something for tomorrow night.

MARGOT. But, Father, you're supposed to let it burn itself out.

MR. FRANK. I'm sure that God understands shortages. [*Before blowing it out.*] "Praised be Thou, oh Lord our God, who hast sustained us and permitted us to celebrate this joyous festival."

[He is about to blow out the candle when suddenly there is a crash of something falling below. They all freeze in horror, motionless. For a few seconds there is complete silence. MR. FRANK slips off his shoes. The others noiselessly follow his example. MR. FRANK turns out a light near him. He motions to PETER to turn off the center lamp. PETER tries to reach it, realizes he cannot and gets up on a chair. Just as he is touching the lamp he loses his balance. The chair goes out from under him. He falls. The iron lamp

The Diary of Anne Frank, 1959. 20th Century Fox. Movie still.

Viewing the photograph: Why might a noise under the Secret Annex alarm the occupants? How do you think they will respond to the noise?

shade crashes to the floor. There is a sound of feet below, running down the stairs.]

MR. VAN DAAN. [*Under his breath.*] God Almighty! [*The only light left comes from the Hanukkah candle.* DUSSEL *comes from his room.* MR. FRANK *creeps over to the stairwell and stands listening. The dog is heard barking excitedly.*] Do you hear anything?

MR. FRANK. [*In a whisper.*] No. I think they've gone.

MRS. VAN DAAN. It's the Green Police. They've found us.

MR. FRANK. If they had, they wouldn't have left. They'd be up here by now.

MRS. VAN DAAN. I know it's the Green Police. They've gone to get help. That's all. They'll be back!

MR. VAN DAAN. Or it may have been the Gestapo,[39] looking for papers . . .

MR. FRANK. [*Interrupting.*] Or a thief, looking for money.

MRS. VAN DAAN. We've got to do something . . . Quick! Quick! Before they come back.

MR. VAN DAAN. There isn't anything to do. Just wait.

[MR. FRANK *holds up his hand for them to be quiet. He is listening intently. There is complete silence as they all strain to hear any sound from below. Suddenly* ANNE *begins to sway. With a low cry she falls to the floor in a faint.* MRS. FRANK *goes to her quickly, sitting beside her on the floor and taking her in her arms.*]

MRS. FRANK. Get some water, please! Get some water!

[MARGOT *starts for the sink.*]

MR. VAN DAAN. [*Grabbing* MARGOT.] No! No! No one's going to run water!

MR. FRANK. If they've found us, they've found us. Get the water. [MARGOT *starts*

39. The *Gestapo* (gə stä′ pō) were the Nazi secret police.

again for the sink. MR. FRANK, *getting a flashlight.*] I'm going down.

[MARGOT *rushes to him, clinging to him.* ANNE *struggles to consciousness.*]

MARGOT. No, Father, no! There may be someone there, waiting . . . It may be a trap!

MR. FRANK. This is Saturday. There is no way for us to know what has happened until Miep or Mr. Kraler comes on Monday morning. We cannot live with this uncertainty.

MARGOT. Don't go, Father!

MRS. FRANK. Hush, darling, hush. [MR. FRANK *slips quietly out, down the steps, and out through the door below.*] Margot! Stay close to me.

[MARGOT *goes to her mother.*]

MR. VAN DAAN. Shush! Shush!

[MRS. FRANK *whispers to* MARGOT *to get the water.* MARGOT *goes for it.*]

MRS. VAN DAAN. Putti, where's our money? Get our money. I hear you can buy the Green Police off, so much a head. Go upstairs quick! Get the money!

MR. VAN DAAN. Keep still!

MRS. VAN DAAN. [*Kneeling before him, pleading.*] Do you want to be dragged off to a concentration camp? Are you going to stand there and wait for them to come up and get you? Do something, I tell you!

MR. VAN DAAN. [*Pushing her aside.*] Will you keep still!

[*He goes over to the stairwell to listen.* PETER *goes to his mother, helping her up onto the sofa. There is a second of silence, then* ANNE *can stand it no longer.*]

ANNE. Someone go after Father! Make Father come back!

PETER. [*Starting for the door.*] I'll go.

MR. VAN DAAN. Haven't you done enough?

[*He pushes* PETER *roughly away. In his anger against his father* PETER *grabs a chair as if to hit him with it, then puts it down, burying his face in his hands.* MRS. FRANK *begins to pray softly.*]

ANNE. Please, please, Mr. Van Daan. Get Father.

MR. VAN DAAN. Quiet! Quiet!

[ANNE *is shocked into silence.* MRS. FRANK *pulls her closer, holding her protectively in her arms.*]

MRS. FRANK. [*Softly, praying.*] "I lift up mine eyes unto the mountains, from whence cometh my help. My help cometh from the Lord who made heaven and earth. He will not suffer thy foot to be moved . . . He that keepeth thee will not slumber . . ."

[*She stops as she hears someone coming. They all watch the door tensely.* MR. FRANK *comes quietly in.* ANNE *rushes to him, holding him tight.*]

MR. FRANK. It was a thief. That noise must have scared him away.

MRS. VAN DAAN. Thank God.

MR. FRANK. He took the cash box. And the radio. He ran away in such a hurry that he didn't stop to shut the street door. It was swinging wide open. [*A breath of relief sweeps over them.*] I think it would be good to have some light.

MARGOT. Are you sure it's all right?

MR. FRANK. The danger has passed. [MARGOT *goes to light the small lamp.*] Don't be so terrified, Anne. We're safe.

DUSSEL. Who says the danger has passed? Don't you realize we are in greater danger than ever?

MR. FRANK. Mr. Dussel, will you be still!

[MR. FRANK *takes* ANNE *back to the table, making her sit down with him, trying to calm her.*]

DUSSEL. [*Pointing to* PETER.] Thanks to this clumsy fool, there's someone now who knows we're up here! Someone now knows we're up here, hiding!

MRS. VAN DAAN. [*Going to* DUSSEL.] Someone knows we're here, yes. But who is the someone? A thief! A thief! You think a thief is going to go to the Green Police and say . . . I was robbing a place the other night and I heard a noise up over my head? You think a thief is going to do that?

DUSSEL. Yes. I think he will.

MRS. VAN DAAN. [*Hysterically.*] You're crazy!

[*She stumbles back to her seat at the table.* PETER *follows protectively, pushing* DUSSEL *aside.*]

DUSSEL. I think some day he'll be caught and then he'll make a bargain with the Green Police . . . if they'll let him off, he'll tell them where some Jews are hiding!

[*He goes off into the bedroom. There is a second of appalled silence.*]

MR. VAN DAAN. He's right.

ANNE. Father, let's get out of here! We can't stay here now . . . Let's go . . .

MR. VAN DAAN. Go! Where?

MRS. FRANK. [*Sinking into her chair at the table.*] Yes. Where?

MR. FRANK. [*Rising, to them all.*] Have we lost all faith? All courage? A moment ago we thought that they'd come for us. We were sure it was the end. But it wasn't the end. We're alive, safe. [MR. VAN DAAN *goes to the table and sits.* MR. FRANK *prays.*] "We thank Thee, oh Lord our God, that in Thy infinite mercy Thou hast again seen fit to spare us." [*He blows out the candle, then turns to* ANNE.] Come on, Anne. The song! Let's have the song! [*He starts to sing.* ANNE *finally starts falteringly to sing, as* MR. FRANK *urges her on. Her voice is hardly audible at first.*]

ANNE. [*Singing.*]

"Oh, Hanukkah! Oh, Hanukkah!
The sweet . . . celebration . . ."

[*As she goes on singing, the others gradually join in, their voices still shaking with fear.* MRS. VAN DAAN *sobs as she sings.*]

GROUP. "Around the feast . . . we . . . gather
In complete . . . jubilation . . .
Happiest of sea . . . sons
Now is here.
Many are the reasons for good cheer."

[DUSSEL *comes from the bedroom. He comes over to the table, standing beside* MARGOT, *listening to them as they sing.*]

"Together
We'll weather
Whatever tomorrow may bring."

[*As they sing on with growing courage, the lights start to dim.*]

"So hear us rejoicing
And merrily voicing
The Hanukkah song that we sing.
Hoy!"

[*The lights are out. The curtain starts slowly to fall.*]

"Hear us rejoicing
And merrily voicing
The Hanukkah song that we sing."

[*They are still singing, as the curtain falls.*]

Curtain

The Diary of Anne Frank, 1959. 20th Century Fox. Movie still.

Viewing the photograph: What contrast is shown in this scene with Margot, Mrs. Frank, and Anne?

Responding to Literature

PERSONAL RESPONSE

How did you respond to the scares in scenes 4 and 5? What were your first thoughts when Anne screamed?

Analyzing Literature

RECALL AND INTERPRET

1. What nightmare wakes Anne? What do you learn about Dussel and Anne from this episode?
2. What surprise does Anne plan for Hanukkah, and what does the surprise show about her? Why do you think Mrs. Frank is moved by Anne's actions?
3. What effect does the noise downstairs have on the celebration? Of what is it a reminder?

EVALUATE AND CONNECT

4. Hanukkah is a Jewish celebration of freedom from oppression. How does this add to the meaning of the play?
5. What do you learn about the family members from their reactions to the intruder downstairs? Were the various reactions surprising to you? Explain.
6. How are the crises that arise between group members similar, in a small way, to the crisis in Europe?

LITERARY ELEMENTS

Stage Directions

Stage directions are instructions in a play that give important information about characters and setting. Stage directions may give details about a character's appearance or actions. These directions are meant to help an actress or an actor to understand how to play a role, or to help a director set up the stage, but they are also useful for readers.

- Choose eight or ten lines of dialogue that do not have specific stage directions. Visualize the scene. Then write directions for the actors to follow as they speak.

See **Literary Terms Handbook,** p. R9.

Extending Your Response

Literature Groups

Holes in the Story The audiences for *The Diary of Anne Frank* know how the play will end. What may they not know as they watch the play? Discuss how dramatizing Anne's nightmare at this point in the story strengthens the suspense for the audience. What other events in the play add to the suspense?

Personal Writing

Looking at Both Sides Anne talks to her father about the two sides of herself: the good Anne and the mean Anne. Does everyone have a good side and a mean side? Under what circumstances might people show a good side? a bad side? Write your ideas in your journal.

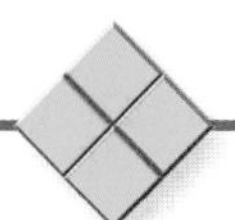

Skill Minilessons

VOCABULARY • SYNONYMS

Some words, such as *happiness,* have many levels of meaning. For instance, *happiness* can mean "mild contentment" or "intense joy." To make clear a particular level of happiness, a writer may choose a synonym that is more precise. *Jubilation,* for example, means "great, joyful happiness."

PRACTICE Choose a synonym to answer each question.

1. Is a person who screams over a disappointment behaving indignantly or furiously?
2. Are the voices of people discussing a tragedy calm or subdued?
3. Does the winning side in a championship game show delight or jubilation?

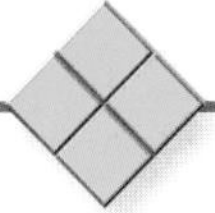

Before You Read

The Diary of Anne Frank, Act 2

BACKGROUND

The Time and Place More than one year has passed since the end of act 1.

Did You Know? During Anne's first year in hiding, the Germans continued their conquest of Europe and North Africa. At the same time, Hitler crafted a plan to kill all Jewish people in German-controlled Europe.

By 1944, when act 2 of the play begins, the war has taken a turn in favor of the Allied forces–the United States, Great Britain, and the Soviet Union. In 1943 Soviet troops attacked German forces from the east, pushing them out of the Soviet Union. Meanwhile, American, British, and Canadian troops approached from the south, driving the Germans out of North Africa and eventually invading Southern Europe. By the summer of 1944, Italy (an ally of Germany) and France were free from Nazi rule.

VOCABULARY PREVIEW

disgruntled (dis grunt′ əld) *adj.* displeased; p. 744

onslaught (ôn′ slôt′) *n.* a forceful or destructive attack; assault; p. 747

foreboding (fôr bō′ ding) *n.* a feeling that something evil is going to happen; p. 748

apprehension (ap′ ri hen′ shən) *n.* fear of what may happen; dread; p. 749

intuition (in′ to͞o ish′ ən) *n.* an ability to know things without having to reason them out; p. 755

poise (poiz) *n.* relaxed and self-controlled dignity in manner; p. 760

stealthily (stel′ thə lē) *adv.* in a secret or sneaky manner; p. 762

frenzy (fren′ zē) *n.* a state of great excitement or deep disturbance; p. 762

pandemonium (pan′ də mō′ nē əm) *n.* wild disorder and uproar; p. 765

The Diary of Anne Frank (Continued)

ACT 2

SCENE

[*In the darkness we hear* ANNE'S VOICE, *again reading from the diary.*]

ANNE'S VOICE. Saturday, the first of January, nineteen forty-four. Another new year has begun and we find ourselves still in our hiding place. We have been here now for one year, five months, and twenty-five days. It seems that our life is at a standstill.

[*The curtain rises on the scene. It is late afternoon. Everyone is bundled up against the cold. In the main room* MRS. FRANK *is taking down the laundry which is hung across the back.* MR. FRANK *sits in the chair down left, reading.* MARGOT *is lying on the couch with a blanket over her and the many-colored knitted scarf around her throat.* ANNE *is seated at the center table, writing in her diary.* PETER, MR. *and* MRS. VAN DAAN, *and* DUSSEL *are all in their own rooms, reading or lying down.*
As the lights dim on, ANNE'S VOICE *continues, without a break.*]

ANNE'S VOICE. We are all a little thinner. The Van Daans' "discussions" are as violent as ever. Mother still does not understand me. But then I don't understand her either. There is one great change, however. A change in myself. I read somewhere that girls of my age don't feel quite certain of themselves. That they become quiet within and begin to think of the miracle that is taking place in their bodies. I think that what is happening to me is so wonderful . . . not only what can be seen, but what is taking place inside. Each time it has happened I have a feeling that I have a sweet secret. [*We hear the chimes and then a hymn being played on the carillon outside.*] And in spite of any pain, I long for the time when I shall feel that secret within me again.

[*The buzzer of the door below suddenly sounds. Everyone is startled,* MR. FRANK *tiptoes cautiously to the top of the steps and listens. Again the buzzer sounds, in* MIEP'S *V-for-Victory*[40] *signal.*]

MR. FRANK. It's Miep!

[*He goes quickly down the steps to unbolt the door.* MRS. FRANK *calls upstairs to the* VAN DAANS *and then to* PETER.]

MRS. FRANK. Wake up, everyone! Miep is here! [ANNE *quickly puts her diary away.* MARGOT *sits up, pulling the blanket around her shoulders.* MR. DUSSEL *sits on the edge of his bed, listening, disgruntled.* MIEP *comes up the steps, followed by* MR. KRALER. *They bring flowers, books, newspapers, etc.* ANNE *rushes to* MIEP, *throwing her arms affectionately around her.*] Miep . . . *and* Mr. Kraler . . . What a delightful surprise!

40. *V-for-Victory* was three short buzzes followed by a long one, based on Morse Code for the letter *v.*

Vocabulary
disgruntled (dis grunt′ əld) *adj.* displeased

The Diary of Anne Frank, 1959. 20th Century Fox. Movie still.

Viewing the photograph: What effect do Miep's visits have on Anne and the other occupants of the Secret Annex?

MR. KRALER. We came to bring you New Year's greetings.

MRS. FRANK. You shouldn't . . . you should have at least one day to yourselves.

[*She goes quickly to the stove and brings down teacups and tea for all of them.*]

ANNE. Don't say that, it's so wonderful to see them! [*Sniffing at* MIEP's *coat.*] I can smell the wind and the cold on your clothes.

MIEP. [*Giving her the flowers.*] There you are. [*Then to* MARGOT, *feeling her forehead.*] How are you, Margot? . . . Feeling any better?

MARGOT. I'm all right.

ANNE. We filled her full of every kind of pill so she won't cough and make a noise.

[*She runs into her room to put the flowers in water.* MR. *and* MRS. VAN DAAN *come from upstairs. Outside there is the sound of a band playing.*]

MRS. VAN DAAN. Well, hello, Miep. Mr. Kraler.

MR. KRALER. [*Giving a bouquet of flowers to* MRS. VAN DAAN.] With my hope for peace in the New Year.

PETER. [*Anxiously.*] Miep, have you seen Mouschi? Have you seen him anywhere around?

MIEP. I'm sorry, Peter. I asked everyone in the neighborhood had they seen a gray cat. But they said no.

[MRS. FRANK *gives* MIEP *a cup of tea.* MR. FRANK *comes up the steps, carrying a small cake on a plate.*]

MR. FRANK. Look what Miep's brought for us!

MRS. FRANK. [*Taking it.*] A cake!

MR. VAN DAAN. A cake! [*He pinches* MIEP's *cheeks gaily and hurries up to the cupboard.*] I'll get some plates.

[DUSSEL, *in his room, hastily puts a coat on and starts out to join the others.*]

MRS. FRANK. Thank you, Miepia. You shouldn't have done it. You must have used all of your sugar ration for weeks. [*Giving it to* MRS. VAN DAAN.] It's beautiful, isn't it?

MRS. VAN DAAN. It's been ages since I even saw a cake. Not since you brought us one last year. [*Without looking at the cake, to* MIEP.] Remember? Don't you remember, you gave us one on New Year's Day? Just this time last year? I'll never forget it because you had "Peace in nineteen forty-three" on it. [*She looks at the cake and reads.*] "Peace in nineteen forty-four!"

MIEP. Well, it has to come sometime, you know. [*As* DUSSEL *comes from his room.*] Hello, Mr. Dussel.

MR. KRALER. How are you?

MR. VAN DAAN. [*Bringing plates and a knife.*] Here's the knife, *liefje*. Now, how many of us are there?

MIEP. None for me, thank you.

MR. FRANK. Oh, please. You must.

MIEP. I couldn't.

MR. VAN DAAN. Good! That leaves one . . . two . . . three . . . seven of us.

DUSSEL. Eight! Eight! It's the same number as it always is!

MR. VAN DAAN. I left Margot out. I take it for granted Margot won't eat any.

ANNE. Why wouldn't she!

MRS. FRANK. I think it won't harm her.

MR. VAN DAAN. All right! All right! I just didn't want her to start coughing again, that's all.

DUSSEL. And please, Mrs. Frank should cut the cake.

MR. VAN DAAN. What's the difference?

MRS. VAN DAAN. It's not Mrs. Frank's cake, is it, Miep? It's for all of us.

Together

DUSSEL. Mrs. Frank divides things better.

MRS. VAN DAAN. [*Going to* DUSSEL.] What are you trying to say?

MR. VAN DAAN. Oh, come on! Stop wasting time!

Together

MRS. VAN DAAN. [*To* DUSSEL.] Don't I always give everybody exactly the same? Don't I?

MR. VAN DAAN. Forget it, Kerli.

MRS. VAN DAAN. No. I want an answer! Don't I?

DUSSEL. Yes. Yes. Everybody gets exactly the same . . . except Mr. Van Daan always gets a little bit more.

[VAN DAAN *advances on* DUSSEL, *the knife still in his hand.*]

MR. VAN DAAN. That's a lie!

[DUSSEL *retreats before the onslaught of the* VAN DAANS.]

MR. FRANK. Please, please! [*Then to* MIEP.] You see what a little sugar cake does to us? It goes right to our heads!

MR. VAN DAAN. [*Handing* MRS. FRANK *the knife.*] Here you are, Mrs. Frank.

MRS. FRANK. Thank you. [*Then to* MIEP *as she goes to the table to cut the cake.*] Are you sure you won't have some?

MIEP. [*Drinking her tea.*] No, really, I have to go in a minute.

[*The sound of the band fades out in the distance.*]

PETER. [*To* MIEP.] Maybe Mouschi went back to our house . . . they say that cats . . . Do you ever get over there . . . ? I mean . . . do you suppose you could . . . ?

MIEP. I'll try, Peter. The first minute I get I'll try. But I'm afraid, with him gone a week . . .

DUSSEL. Make up your mind, already someone has had a nice big dinner from that cat!

[PETER *is furious, inarticulate.*[41] *He starts toward* DUSSEL *as if to hit him.* MR. FRANK *stops him.* MRS. FRANK *speaks quickly to ease the situation.*]

MRS. FRANK. [*To* MIEP.] This is delicious, Miep!

MRS. VAN DAAN. [*Eating hers.*] Delicious!

MR. VAN DAAN. [*Finishing it in one gulp.*] Dirk's in luck to get a girl who can bake like this!

MIEP. [*Putting down her empty teacup.*] I have to run. Dirk's taking me to a party tonight.

ANNE. How heavenly! Remember now what everyone is wearing, and what you have to eat and everything, so you can tell us tomorrow.

MIEP. I'll give you a full report! Good-bye, everyone!

MR. VAN DAAN. [*To* MIEP.] Just a minute. There's something I'd like you to do for me.

[*He hurries off up the stairs to his room.*]

41. Peter is so angry that he becomes unable to speak *(inarticulate).*

Vocabulary

onslaught (ôn′ slôt′) *n.* a forceful or destructive attack; assault

MRS. VAN DAAN. [*Sharply.*] Putti, where are you going? [*She rushes up the stairs after him, calling hysterically.*] What do you want? Putti, what are you going to do?

MIEP. [*To* PETER.] What's wrong?

PETER. [*His sympathy is with his mother.*] Father says he's going to sell her fur coat. She's crazy about that old fur coat.

DUSSEL. Is it possible? Is it possible that anyone is so silly as to worry about a fur coat in times like this?

PETER. It's none of your darn business . . . and if you say one more thing . . . I'll, I'll take you and I'll . . . I mean it . . . I'll . . .

[*There is a piercing scream from* MRS. VAN DAAN *above. She grabs at the fur coat as* MR. VAN DAAN *is starting downstairs with it.*]

MRS. VAN DAAN. No! No! No! Don't you dare take that! You hear? It's mine! [*Downstairs* PETER *turns away, embarrassed, miserable.*] My father gave me that! You didn't give it to me. You have no right. Let go of it . . . you hear?

[MR. VAN DAAN *pulls the coat from her hands and hurries downstairs.* MRS. VAN DAAN *sinks to the floor, sobbing. As* MR. VAN DAAN *comes into the main room the others look away, embarrassed for him.*]

MR. VAN DAAN. [*To* MR. KRALER.] Just a little—discussion over the advisability[42] of selling this coat. As I have often reminded Mrs. Van Daan, it's very selfish of her to keep it when people outside are in such desperate need of clothing . . . [*He gives the coat to* MIEP.] So if you will please to sell it for us? It should fetch a good price. And by the way, will you get me cigarettes. I don't care what kind they are . . . get all you can.

MIEP. It's terribly difficult to get them, Mr. Van Daan. But I'll try. Good-bye.

[*She goes.* MR. FRANK *follows her down the steps to bolt the door after her.* MRS. FRANK *gives* MR. KRALER *a cup of tea.*]

MRS. FRANK. Are you sure you won't have some cake, Mr. Kraler?

MR. KRALER. I'd better not.

MR. VAN DAAN. You're still feeling badly? What does your doctor say?

MR. KRALER. I haven't been to him.

MRS. FRANK. Now, Mr. Kraler! . . .

MR. KRALER. [*Sitting at the table.*] Oh, I tried. But you can't get near a doctor these days . . . they're so busy. After weeks I finally managed to get one on the telephone. I told him I'd like an appointment . . . I wasn't feeling very well. You know what he answers . . . over the telephone . . . Stick out your tongue! [*They laugh. He turns to* MR. FRANK *as* MR. FRANK *comes back.*] I have some contracts here . . . I wonder if you'd look over them with me . . .

MR. FRANK. [*Putting out his hand.*] Of course.

MR. KRALER. [*He rises.*] If we could go downstairs . . . [MR. FRANK *starts ahead,* MR. KRALER *speaks to the others.*] Will you forgive us? I won't keep him but a minute.

[*He starts to follow* MR. FRANK *down the steps.*]

MARGOT. [*With sudden foreboding.*] What's happened? Something's happened! Hasn't it, Mr. Kraler?

42. *Advisability* means "suitability" or "the quality of being wise, fitting, or proper."

Vocabulary

foreboding (fôr bō′ ding) *n.* a feeling that something evil is going to happen

[*MR. KRALER stops and comes back, trying to reassure MARGOT with a pretense of casualness.*]

MR. KRALER. No, really. I want your father's advice . . .

MARGOT. Something's gone wrong! I know it!

MR. FRANK. [*Coming back, to MR. KRALER.*] If it's something that concerns us here, it's better that we all hear it.

MR. KRALER. [*Turning to him, quietly.*] But . . . the children . . . ?

MR. FRANK. What they'd imagine would be worse than any reality.

[*As MR. KRALER speaks, they all listen with intense apprehension. MRS. VAN DAAN comes down the stairs and sits on the bottom step.*]

MR. KRALER. It's a man in the storeroom . . . I don't know whether or not you remember him . . . Carl, about fifty, heavy-set, near-sighted . . . He came with us just before you left.

MR. FRANK. He was from Utrecht?[43]

MR. KRALER. That's the man. A couple of weeks ago, when I was in the storeroom, he closed the door and asked me . . . how's Mr. Frank? What do you hear from Mr. Frank? I told him I only knew there was a rumor that you were in Switzerland. He said he'd heard that rumor too, but he thought I might know something more. I didn't pay any attention to it . . . but then a thing happened yesterday . . . He'd brought some invoices to the office for me to sign. As I was going through them, I looked up. He was standing staring at the bookcase . . . your bookcase. He said he thought he remembered a door there . . . Wasn't there a door that used to go up to the loft? Then he told me he wanted more money. Twenty guilders[44] more a week.

MR. VAN DAAN. Blackmail!

MR. FRANK. Twenty guilders? Very modest blackmail.

MR. VAN DAAN. That's just the beginning.

DUSSEL. [*Coming to MR. FRANK.*] You know what I think? He was the thief who was down there that night. That's how he knows we're here.

MR. FRANK. [*To MR. KRALER.*] How was it left? What did you tell him?

MR. KRALER. I said I had to think about it. What shall I do? Pay him the money? . . . Take a chance on firing him . . . or what? I don't know.

DUSSEL. [*Frantic.*] For God's sake don't fire him! Pay him what he asks . . . keep him here where you can have your eye on him.

MR. FRANK. Is it so much what he's asking? What are they paying nowadays?

MR. KRALER. He could get it in a war plant. But this isn't a war plant. Mind you, I don't know if he really knows . . . or if he doesn't know.

MR. FRANK. Offer him half. Then we'll soon find out if it's blackmail or not.

DUSSEL. And if it is? We've got to pay it, haven't we? Anything he asks we've got to pay!

---

43. *Utrecht* (ū′ trekt) is a city in the central Netherlands.

44. The *guilder* is the basic monetary unit of the Netherlands. Twenty guilders is about ten dollars in American money.

Vocabulary

apprehension (ap′ ri hen′ shən) *n.* fear of what may happen; dread

The Diary of Anne Frank, 1959. 20th Century Fox. Movie still.

Viewing the photograph: Compare this image with the one on page 705. How have both characters changed since they came to the Secret Annex?

MR. FRANK. Let's decide that when the time comes.

MR. KRALER. This may be all my imagination. You get to a point, these days, where you suspect everyone and everything. Again and again . . . on some simple look or word, I've found myself . . .

[The telephone rings in the office below.]

MRS. VAN DAAN. *[Hurrying to* MR. KRALER.*]* There's the telephone! What does that mean, the telephone ringing on a holiday?

MR. KRALER. That's my wife. I told her I had to go over some papers in my office . . . to call me there when she got out of church. *[He starts out.]* I'll offer him half then. Goodbye . . . we'll hope for the best!

[The group call their good-bye's half-heartedly. MR. FRANK *follows* MR. KRALER*, to bolt the door below. During the following scene,* MR. FRANK *comes back up and stands listening, disturbed.]*

DUSSEL. *[To* MR. VAN DAAN.*]* You can thank your son for this . . . smashing the light! I tell you, it's just a question of time now.

[He goes to the window at the back and stands looking out.]

MARGOT. Sometimes I wish the end would come . . . whatever it is.

MRS. FRANK. *[Shocked.]* Margot!

*[*ANNE *goes to* MARGOT*, sitting beside her on the couch with her arms around her.]*

MARGOT. Then at least we'd know where we were.

MRS. FRANK. You should be ashamed of yourself! Talking that way! Think how lucky we are! Think of the thousands dying in the war, every day. Think of the people in concentration camps.

ANNE. *[Interrupting.]* What's the good of that? What's the good of thinking of misery when you're already miserable? That's stupid!

MRS. FRANK. Anne!

[As ANNE *goes on raging at her mother,* MRS. FRANK *tries to break in, in an effort to quiet her.]*

ANNE. We're young, Margot and Peter and I! You grown-ups have had your chance! But look at us . . . If we begin thinking of all the horror in the world, we're lost! We're trying to hold onto some kind of ideals . . . when everything . . . ideals, hopes . . . everything, are being destroyed! It isn't our fault that the world is in such a mess! We weren't around when all this started! So don't try to take it out on us!

[She rushes off to her room, slamming the door after her. She picks up a brush from the chest and hurls it to the floor. Then she sits on the settee, trying to control her anger.]

MR. VAN DAAN. She talks as if we started the war! Did we start the war?

[He spots ANNE*'s cake. As he starts to take it,* PETER *anticipates him.]*

PETER. She left her cake. *[He starts for* ANNE*'s room with the cake. There is silence in the main room.* MRS. VAN DAAN *goes up to her room, followed by* MR. VAN DAAN. DUSSEL *stays looking out the window.* MR. FRANK *brings* MRS. FRANK *her cake. She eats it slowly, without relish.* MR. FRANK *takes his cake to* MARGOT *and sits quietly on the sofa beside her.* PETER *stands in the doorway of* ANNE*'s darkened room, looking at her, then makes a little movement to let her know he is there.* ANNE *sits up, quickly, trying to hide the signs of her tears.* PETER *holds out the cake to her.]* You left this.

ANNE. *[Dully.]* Thanks.

[*PETER starts to go out, then comes back.*]

PETER. I thought you were fine just now. You know just how to talk to them. You know just how to say it. I'm no good . . . I never can think . . . especially when I'm mad . . . That Dussel . . . when he said that about Mouschi . . . someone eating him . . . all I could think is . . . I wanted to hit him. I wanted to give him such a . . . a . . . that he'd . . . That's what I used to do when there was an argument at school . . . That's the way I . . . but here . . . And an old man like that . . . it wouldn't be so good.

ANNE. You're making a big mistake about me. I do it all wrong. I say too much. I go too far. I hurt people's feelings . . .

[*DUSSEL leaves the window, going to his room.*]

PETER. I think you're just fine . . . What I want to say . . . if it wasn't for you around here, I don't know. What I mean . . .

[*PETER is interrupted by DUSSEL's turning on the light. DUSSEL stands in the doorway, startled to see PETER. PETER advances toward him forbiddingly. DUSSEL backs out of the room. PETER closes the door on him.*]

ANNE. Do you mean it, Peter? Do you really mean it?

PETER. I said it, didn't I?

ANNE. Thank you, Peter!

[*In the main room MR. and MRS. FRANK collect the dishes and take them to the sink, washing them. MARGOT lies down again on the couch. DUSSEL, lost, wanders into PETER's room and takes up a book, starting to read.*]

PETER. [*Looking at the photographs on the wall.*] You've got quite a collection.

ANNE. Wouldn't you like some in your room? I could give you some. Heaven knows you spend enough time in there . . . doing heaven knows what . . .

PETER. It's easier. A fight starts, or an argument . . . I duck in there.

ANNE. You're lucky, having a room to go to. His lordship is always here . . . I hardly ever get a minute alone. When they start in on me, I can't duck away. I have to stand there and take it.

PETER. You gave some of it back just now.

ANNE. I get so mad. They've formed their opinions . . . about everything . . . but we . . . we're still trying to find out . . . We have problems here that no other people our age have ever had. And just as you think you've solved them, something comes along and bang! You have to start all over again.

PETER. At least you've got someone you can talk to.

ANNE. Not really. Mother . . . I never discuss anything serious with her. She doesn't understand. Father's all right. We can talk about everything . . . everything but one thing. Mother. He simply won't talk about her. I don't think you can be really intimate with anyone if he holds something back, do you?

PETER. I think your father's fine.

ANNE. Oh, he is, Peter! He is! He's the only one who's ever given me the feeling that I have any sense. But anyway, nothing can take the place of school and play and friends of your own age . . . or near your age . . . can it?

PETER. I suppose you miss your friends and all.

ANNE. It isn't just . . . [*She breaks off, staring up at him for a second.*] Isn't it funny, you and I? Here we've been seeing each other every minute for almost a year and a half, and this is the first time we've ever really talked. It helps a lot to have someone to talk to, don't you think? It helps you to let off steam.

PETER. [*Going to the door.*] Well, any time you want to let off steam, you can come into my room.

ANNE. [*Following him.*] I can get up an awful lot of steam. You'll have to be careful how you say that.

PETER. It's all right with me.

ANNE. Do you mean it?

PETER. I said it, didn't I?

[*He goes out.* ANNE *stands in her doorway looking after him. As* PETER *gets to his door he stands for a minute looking back at her. Then he goes into his room.* DUSSEL *rises as he comes in, and quickly passes him, going out. He starts across for his room.* ANNE *sees him coming, and pulls her door shut.* DUSSEL *turns back toward* PETER*'s room.* PETER *pulls his door shut.* DUSSEL *stands there, bewildered, forlorn.*
The scene slowly dims out. The curtain falls on the scene. ANNE'S VOICE *comes over in the darkness . . . faintly at first, and then with growing strength.*]

ANNE'S VOICE. We've had bad news. The people from whom Miep got our ration books have been arrested. So we have had to cut down on our food. Our stomachs are so empty that they rumble and make strange noises, all in different keys. Mr. Van Daan's is deep and low, like a bass fiddle. Mine is high, whistling like a flute. As we all sit around waiting for supper, it's like an orchestra tuning up. It only needs Toscanini to raise his baton and we'd be off in the Ride of the Valkyries. Monday, the sixth of March, nineteen forty-four. Mr. Kraler is in the hospital. It seems he has ulcers.[45] Pim says we are his ulcers. Miep has to run the business and us too. The Americans have landed on the southern tip of Italy. Father looks for a quick finish to the war. Mr. Dussel is waiting every day for the warehouse man to demand more money. Have I been skipping too much from one subject to another? I can't help it. I feel that spring is coming. I feel it in my whole body and soul. I feel utterly confused. I am longing . . . so longing . . . for everything . . . for friends . . . for someone to talk to . . . someone who understands . . . someone young, who feels as I do . . .

[*As these last lines are being said, the curtain rises on the scene. The lights dim on.* ANNE'S VOICE *fades out.*]

SCENE

[*It is evening, after supper. From outside we hear the sound of children playing. The "grown-ups," with the exception of* MR. VAN DAAN, *are all in the main room.* MRS. FRANK *is doing some mending,* MRS. VAN DAAN *is reading a fashion magazine.* MR. FRANK *is going over business accounts.* DUSSEL, *in his dentist's jacket, is pacing up and down, impatient to get into his bedroom.* MR. VAN DAAN *is upstairs working on a piece of embroidery in an embroidery frame. In his room* PETER *is sitting before the mirror, smoothing his hair. As the scene goes on, he*

45. Arturo *Toscanini* (täs′ kə nē′ nē) was an Italian orchestra conductor. *Ride of the Valkyries* is a passage from an opera by Richard Wagner, a German composer. Mr. Kraler's *ulcers* are sores on the lining of his stomach.

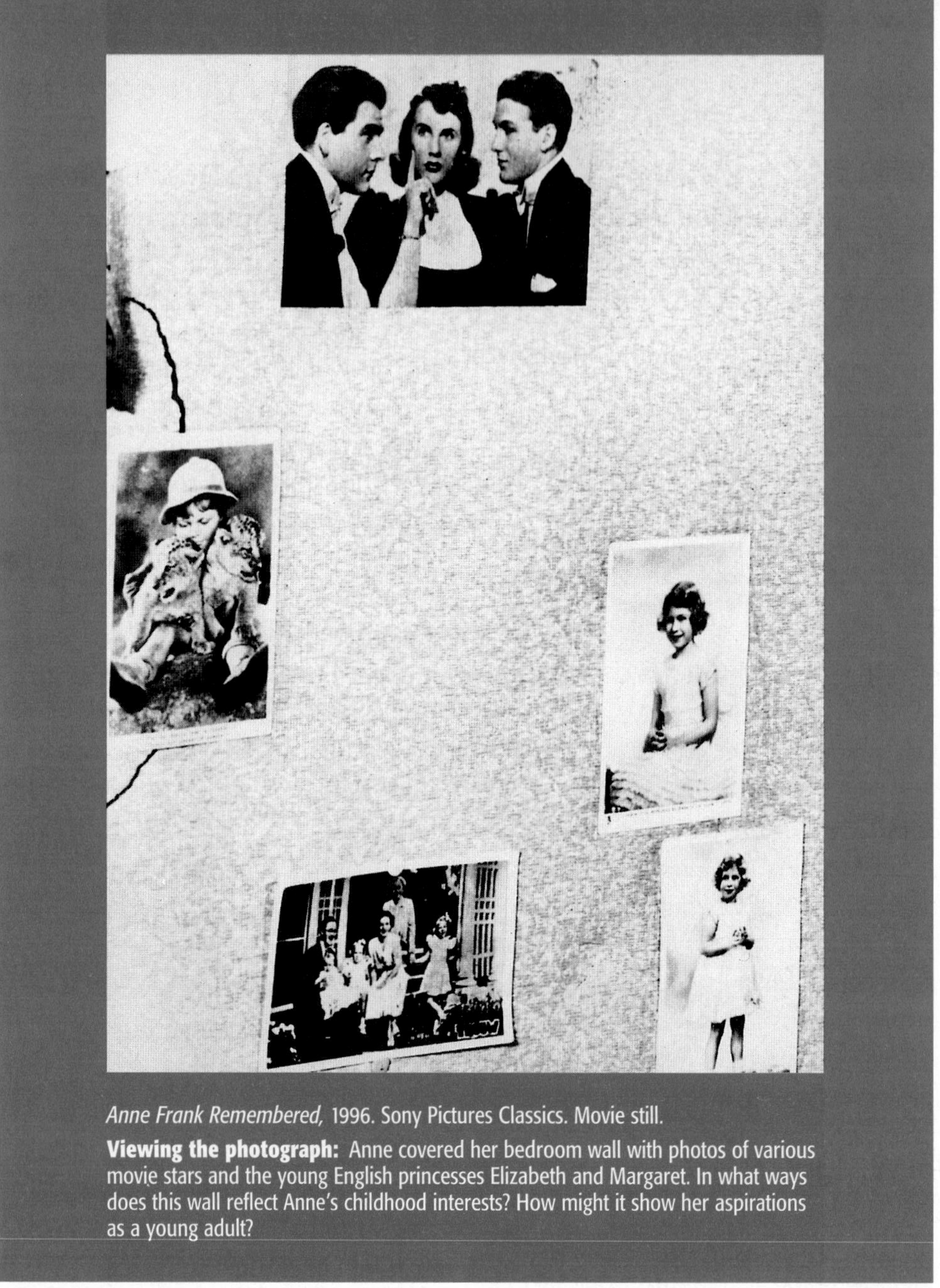

Anne Frank Remembered, 1996. Sony Pictures Classics. Movie still.

Viewing the photograph: Anne covered her bedroom wall with photos of various movie stars and the young English princesses Elizabeth and Margaret. In what ways does this wall reflect Anne's childhood interests? How might it show her aspirations as a young adult?

puts on his tie, brushes his coat and puts it on, preparing himself meticulously for a visit from ANNE*. On his wall are now hung some of* ANNE*'s motion picture stars.*

In her room ANNE *too is getting dressed. She stands before the mirror in her slip, trying various ways of dressing her hair.* MARGOT *is seated on the sofa, hemming a skirt for* ANNE *to wear.*

In the main room DUSSEL *can stand it no longer. He comes over, rapping sharply on the door of his and* ANNE*'s bedroom.*]

ANNE. [*Calling to him.*] No, no, Mr. Dussel! I am not dressed yet. [DUSSEL *walks away, furious, sitting down and burying his head in his hands.* ANNE *turns to* MARGOT.] How is that? How does that look?

MARGOT. [*Glancing at her briefly.*] Fine.

ANNE. You didn't even look.

MARGOT. Of course I did. It's fine.

ANNE. Margot, tell me, am I terribly ugly?

MARGOT. Oh, stop fishing.

ANNE. No. No. Tell me.

MARGOT. Of course you're not. You've got nice eyes . . . and a lot of animation,[46] and . . .

ANNE. A little vague, aren't you?

[She reaches over and takes a brassière out of MARGOT's sewing basket. She holds it up to herself, studying the effect in the mirror. Outside, MRS. FRANK, feeling sorry for DUSSEL, comes over, knocking at the girls' door.]

MRS. FRANK. [*Outside.*] May I come in?

MARGOT. Come in, Mother.

MRS. FRANK. [*Shutting the door behind her.*] Mr. Dussel's impatient to get in here.

ANNE. [*Still with the brassière.*] Heavens, he takes the room for himself the entire day.

MRS. FRANK. [*Gently.*] Anne, dear, you're not going in again tonight to see Peter?

ANNE. [*Dignified.*] That is my intention.

MRS. FRANK. But you've already spent a great deal of time in there today.

ANNE. I was in there exactly twice. Once to get the dictionary, and then three-quarters of an hour before supper.

MRS. FRANK. Aren't you afraid you're disturbing him?

ANNE. Mother, I have some intuition.

MRS. FRANK. Then may I ask you this much, Anne. Please don't shut the door when you go in.

ANNE. You sound like Mrs. Van Daan!

[She throws the brassière back in MARGOT's sewing basket and picks up her blouse, putting it on.]

MRS. FRANK. No. No. I don't mean to suggest anything wrong. I only wish that you wouldn't expose yourself to criticism . . . that you wouldn't give Mrs. Van Daan the opportunity to be unpleasant.

ANNE. Mrs. Van Daan doesn't need an opportunity to be unpleasant!

MRS. FRANK. Everyone's on edge, worried about Mr. Kraler. This is one more thing . . .

ANNE. I'm sorry, Mother. I'm going to Peter's room. I'm not going to let Petronella Van Daan spoil our friendship.

[MRS. FRANK hesitates for a second, then goes out, closing the door after her. She gets a pack of playing cards and sits at the center table, playing solitaire. In ANNE's room MARGOT hands the finished skirt to ANNE. As ANNE is putting it on, MARGOT takes off her high-heeled shoes and stuffs paper in the toes so that ANNE can wear them.]

MARGOT. [*To ANNE.*] Why don't you two talk in the main room? It'd save a lot of trouble. It's hard on Mother, having to listen to those remarks from Mrs. Van Daan and not say a word.

ANNE. Why doesn't she say a word? I think it's ridiculous to take it and take it.

MARGOT. You don't understand Mother at all, do you? She can't talk back. She's not like you. It's just not in her nature to fight back.

ANNE. Anyway . . . the only one I worry about is you. I feel awfully guilty about you.

46. Here, *animation* means "liveliness; spiritedness."

Vocabulary

intuition (in′ to͞o ish′ ən) *n.* an ability to know things without having to reason them out

[*She sits on the stool near* MARGOT, *putting on* MARGOT*'s high-heeled shoes.*]

MARGOT. What about?

ANNE. I mean, every time I go into Peter's room, I have a feeling I may be hurting you. [MARGOT *shakes her head.*] I know if it were me, I'd be wild. I'd be desperately jealous, if it were me.

MARGOT. Well, I'm not.

ANNE. You don't feel badly? Really? Truly? You're not jealous?

MARGOT. Of course I'm jealous . . . jealous that you've got something to get up in the morning for . . . But jealous of you and Peter? No.

[ANNE *goes back to the mirror.*]

ANNE. Maybe there's nothing to be jealous of. Maybe he doesn't really like me. Maybe I'm just taking the place of his cat . . . [*She picks up a pair of short white gloves, putting them on.*] Wouldn't you like to come in with us?

MARGOT. I have a book.

[*The sound of the children playing outside fades out. In the main room* DUSSEL *can stand it no longer. He jumps up, going to the bedroom door and knocking sharply.*]

DUSSEL. Will you please let me in my room!

ANNE. Just a minute, dear, dear Mr. Dussel. [*She picks up her Mother's pink stole and adjusts it elegantly over her shoulders, then gives a last look in the mirror.*] Well, here I go . . . to run the gauntlet.[47]

[*She starts out, followed by* MARGOT.]

DUSSEL. [*As she appears—sarcastic.*] Thank you so much.

[DUSSEL *goes into his room.* ANNE *goes toward* PETER*'s room, passing* MRS. VAN DAAN *and her parents at the center table.*]

MRS. VAN DAAN. My God, look at her! [ANNE *pays no attention. She knocks at* PETER*'s door.*] I don't know what good it is to have a son. I never see him. He wouldn't care if I killed myself. [PETER *opens the door and stands aside for* ANNE *to come in.*] Just a minute, Anne. [*She goes to them at the door.*] I'd like to say a few words to my son. Do you mind? [PETER *and* ANNE *stand waiting.*] Peter, I don't want you staying up till all hours tonight. You've got to have your sleep. You're a growing boy. You hear?

MRS. FRANK. Anne won't stay late. She's going to bed promptly at nine. Aren't you, Anne?

ANNE. Yes, Mother . . . [*To* MRS. VAN DAAN.] May we go now?

MRS. VAN DAAN. Are you asking me? I didn't know I had anything to say about it.

MRS. FRANK. Listen for the chimes, Anne dear.

[*The two young people go off into* PETER*'s room, shutting the door after them.*]

MRS. VAN DAAN. [*To* MRS. FRANK.] In my day it was the boys who called on the girls. Not the girls on the boys.

MRS. FRANK. You know how young people like to feel that they have secrets. Peter's room is the only place where they can talk.

MRS. VAN DAAN. Talk! That's not what they called it when I was young.

[MRS. VAN DAAN *goes off to the bathroom.* MARGOT *settles down to read her book.* MR. FRANK *puts his papers away and brings a chess game to the center table. He and* MRS. FRANK *start to play. In*

47. To *run the gauntlet* is to endure opposition or difficulties.

PETER's room, ANNE speaks to PETER, indignant, humiliated.]

ANNE. Aren't they awful? Aren't they impossible? Treating us as if we were still in the nursery.

[*She sits on the cot. PETER gets a bottle of pop and two glasses.*]

PETER. Don't let it bother you. It doesn't bother me.

ANNE. I suppose you can't really blame them . . . they think back to what *they* were like at our age. They don't realize how much more advanced we are . . . When you think what wonderful discussions we've had! . . . Oh, I forgot. I was going to bring you some more pictures.

PETER. Oh, these are fine, thanks.

ANNE. Don't you want some more? Miep just brought me some new ones.

PETER. Maybe later.

[*He gives her a glass of pop and, taking some for himself, sits down facing her.*]

ANNE. [*Looking up at one of the photographs.*] I remember when I got that . . . I won it. I bet Jopie that I could eat five ice-cream cones. We'd all been playing ping-pong . . . We used to have heavenly times . . . we'd finish up with ice cream at the Delphi, or the Oasis, where Jews were allowed . . . there'd always be a lot of boys . . . we'd laugh and joke . . . I'd like to go back to it for a few days or a week. But after that I know I'd be bored to death. I think more seriously about life now. I want to be a journalist . . . or something. I love to write. What do you want to do?

PETER. I thought I might go off some place . . . work on a farm or something . . . some job that doesn't take much brains.

ANNE. You shouldn't talk that way. You've got the most awful inferiority complex.

PETER. I know I'm not smart.

ANNE. That isn't true. You're much better than I am in dozens of things . . . arithmetic and algebra and . . . well, you're a million times better than I am in algebra. [*With sudden directness.*] You like Margot, don't you? Right from the start you liked her, liked her much better than me.

PETER. [*Uncomfortably.*] Oh, I don't know.

[*In the main room MRS. VAN DAAN comes from the bathroom and goes over to the sink, polishing a coffee pot.*]

ANNE. It's all right. Everyone feels that way. Margot's so good. She's sweet and bright and beautiful and I'm not.

PETER. I wouldn't say that.

ANNE. Oh, no, I'm not. I know that. I know quite well that I'm not a beauty. I never have been and never shall be.

PETER. I don't agree at all. I think you're pretty.

ANNE. That's not true!

PETER. And another thing. You've changed . . . from at first, I mean.

ANNE. I have?

PETER. I used to think you were awful noisy.

ANNE. And what do you think now, Peter? How have I changed?

PETER. Well . . . er . . . you're . . . quieter.

[*In his room DUSSEL takes his pajamas and toilet articles and goes into the bathroom to change.*]

ANNE. I'm glad you don't just hate me.

PETER. I never said that.

ANNE. I bet when you get out of here you'll never think of me again.

PETER. That's crazy.

ANNE. When you get back with all of your friends, you're going to say . . . now what did I ever see in that Mrs. Quack Quack.

PETER. I haven't got any friends.

ANNE. Oh, Peter, of course you have. Everyone has friends.

PETER. Not me. I don't want any. I get along all right without them.

ANNE. Does that mean you can get along without me? I think of myself as your friend.

PETER. No. If they were all like you, it'd be different.

[*He takes the glasses and the bottle and puts them away. There is a second's silence and then* ANNE *speaks, hesitantly, shyly.*]

ANNE. Peter, did you ever kiss a girl?

PETER. Yes. Once.

ANNE. [*To cover her feelings.*] That picture's crooked. [PETER *goes over, straightening the photograph.*] Was she pretty?

PETER. Huh?

ANNE. The girl that you kissed.

PETER. I don't know. I was blindfolded. [*He comes back and sits down again.*] It was at a party. One of those kissing games.

ANNE. [*Relieved.*] Oh. I don't suppose that really counts, does it?

PETER. It didn't with me.

ANNE. I've been kissed twice. Once a man I'd never seen before kissed me on the cheek when he picked me up off the ice and I was crying. And the other was Mr. Koophuis,[48] a friend of Father's who kissed my hand. You wouldn't say those counted, would you?

PETER. I wouldn't say so.

ANNE. I know almost for certain that Margot would never kiss anyone unless she was engaged to them. And I'm sure too that Mother never touched a man before Pim. But I don't know . . . things are so different now . . . What do you think? Do you think a girl shouldn't kiss anyone except if she's engaged or something? It's so hard to try to think what to do, when here we are with the whole world falling around our ears and you think . . . well . . . you don't know what's going to happen tomorrow and . . . What do you think?

PETER. I suppose it'd depend on the girl. Some girls, anything they do's wrong. But others . . . well . . . it wouldn't necessarily be wrong with them. [*The carillon starts to strike nine o'clock.*] I've always thought that when two people . . .

ANNE. Nine o'clock. I have to go.

PETER. That's right.

ANNE. [*Without moving.*] Good night.

[*There is a second's pause, then* PETER *gets up and moves toward the door.*]

PETER. You won't let them stop you coming?

ANNE. No. [*She rises and starts for the door.*] Sometime I might bring my diary. There are so many things in it that I want to talk over with you. There's a lot about you.

PETER. What kind of things?

ANNE. I wouldn't want you to see some of it. I thought you were a nothing, just the way you thought about me.

PETER. Did you change your mind, the way I changed my mind about you?

48. ***Koophuis*** (koip′ hœs)

The Diary of Anne Frank, 1959. 20th Century Fox. Movie still.

Viewing the photograph: How do you think Anne might feel at this moment?

ANNE. Well . . . You'll see . . .

[*For a second* ANNE *stands looking up at* PETER, *longing for him to kiss her. As he makes no move she turns away. Then suddenly* PETER *grabs her awkwardly in his arms, kissing her on the cheek.* ANNE *walks out dazed. She stands for a minute, her back to the people in the main room. As she regains her poise she goes to her mother and father and* MARGOT, *silently kissing them. They murmur their good nights to her. As she is about to open her bedroom door, she catches sight of* MRS. VAN DAAN. *She goes quickly to her, taking her face in her hands and kissing her first on one cheek and then on the other. Then she hurries off into her room.* MRS. VAN DAAN *looks after her, and then looks over at* PETER's *room. Her suspicions are confirmed.*]

MRS. VAN DAAN. [*She knows.*] Ah hah!

[*The lights dim out. The curtain falls on the scene. In the darkness* ANNE'S VOICE *comes faintly at first and then with growing strength.*]

ANNE'S VOICE. By this time we all know each other so well that if anyone starts to tell a story, the rest can finish it for him. We're having to cut down still further on our meals. What makes it worse, the rats have been at work again. They've carried off some of our precious food. Even Mr. Dussel wishes now that Mouschi was here. Thursday, the twentieth of April, nineteen forty-four. Invasion fever[49] is mounting every day. Miep tells us that people outside talk of nothing else. For myself, life has become much more pleasant. I often go to Peter's room after supper. Oh, don't think I'm in love, because I'm not. But it does make life more bearable to have someone with whom you can exchange views. No more tonight. P.S. . . . I must be honest. I must confess that I actually live for the next meeting. Is there anything lovelier than to sit under the skylight and feel the sun on your cheeks and have a darling boy in your arms? I admit now that I'm glad the Van Daans had a son and not a daughter. I've outgrown another dress. That's the third. I'm having to wear Margot's clothes after all. I'm working hard on my French and am now reading *La Belle Nivernaise*.[50]

[*As she is saying the last lines—the curtain rises on the scene. The lights dim on, as* ANNE'S VOICE *fades out.*]

49. *Invasion fever* refers to the widely held expectation that the Allies would soon invade areas of Europe occupied by German forces.

50. *La Belle Nivernaise* (lä bel′ nē′ ver näz′) was a work by a nineteenth-century French novelist.

Vocabulary

poise (poiz) *n.* relaxed and self-controlled dignity in manner

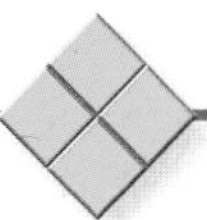

Responding to Literature

PERSONAL RESPONSE

How did you react to the change in Anne's relationship with Peter? Does the change surprise you? Explain.

LITERARY ELEMENTS

Monologue

A **monologue** is a long, uninterrupted speech by one character in a play. A monologue may provide important information about character and plot. In the opening of act 2, for example, Anne reads from her diary, describing the situation at the start of 1944.

- Identify and describe two other monologues in the play. For each example, explain what you learn about the character who is speaking or about the plot.

See **Literary Terms Handbook,** p. R6.

Analyzing Literature

RECALL AND INTERPRET

1. As a new year begins, Anne recognizes that she has changed. How does she describe those changes, and how does she feel about them? What other changes in Anne do her Hanukkah gifts (from the end of act 1) show?
2. How does each family member react to Miep's gift of a cake? What do these reactions reveal about each person? about their situation?
3. Why is Anne dressing up? How do the family members feel about this? Why?

EVALUATE AND CONNECT

4. What does Anne mean when she says, "We have problems that no other people our age have ever had"? Does Anne fully understand the problems she has? Explain.
5. How is Mr. Kraler's news of the blackmail a kind of turning point for the members of the Secret Annex? What does it mean for them?
6. What two sides of life in the Secret Annex are shown in act 2, scene 1 and scene 2? Is one side more important than the other? Explain.

Extending Your Response

Literature Groups

A Precious Object Mrs. Van Daan's fur coat appears in the story several times. How does its importance change? Why might it have such deep meaning for Mrs. Van Daan? for Mr. Van Daan? for other members of the Secret Annex?

Creative Writing

Pen Pals Anne and Margot sometimes wrote letters to each other during their stay in the Secret Annex. Write a letter from Margot to Anne about Anne's growing friendship with Peter. As you write, keep in mind what she says to Anne in the play.

The Diary of Anne Frank (Continued)

SCENE

[*It is night, a few weeks later. Everyone is in bed. There is complete quiet. In the* VAN DAANS' *room a match flares up for a moment and then is quickly put out.* MR. VAN DAAN, *in bare feet, dressed in underwear and trousers, is dimly seen coming stealthily down the stairs and into the main room, where* MR. *and* MRS. FRANK *and* MARGOT *are sleeping. He goes to the food safe and again lights a match. Then he cautiously opens the safe, taking out a half-loaf of bread. As he closes the safe, it creaks. He stands rigid.* MRS. FRANK *sits up in bed. She sees him.*]

MRS. FRANK. [*Screaming.*] Otto! Otto! *Komme schnell!*

[*The rest of the people wake, hurriedly getting up.*]

MR. FRANK. *Was ist los? Was ist passiert?*

[DUSSEL, *followed by* ANNE, *comes from his room.*]

MRS. FRANK. [*As she rushes over to* MR. VAN DAAN.] *Er stiehlt das Essen!*[51]

DUSSEL. [*Grabbing* MR. VAN DAAN.] You! You! Give me that.

MRS. VAN DAAN. [*Coming down the stairs.*] Putti . . . Putti . . . what is it?

51. MRS. FRANK. "Come quickly!" MR. FRANK. "What's the matter? What has happened?" MRS. FRANK. "He is stealing food!"

DUSSEL. [*His hands on* VAN DAAN's *neck.*] You dirty thief . . . stealing food . . . you good-for-nothing . . .

MR. FRANK. Mr. Dussel! For God's sake! Help me, Peter!

[PETER *comes over, trying, with* MR. FRANK, *to separate the two struggling men.*]

PETER. Let him go! Let go!

[DUSSEL *drops* MR. VAN DAAN, *pushing him away. He shows them the end of a loaf of bread that he has taken from* VAN DAAN.]

DUSSEL. You greedy, selfish . . . !

[MARGOT *turns on the lights.*]

MRS. VAN DAAN. Putti . . . what is it?

[*All of* MRS. FRANK's *gentleness, her self-control, is gone. She is outraged, in a frenzy of indignation.*]

MRS. FRANK. The bread! He was stealing the bread!

DUSSEL. It was you, and all the time we thought it was the rats!

MR. FRANK. Mr. Van Daan, how could you!

MR. VAN DAAN. I'm hungry.

MRS. FRANK. We're all of us hungry! I see the children getting thinner and thinner. Your own son Peter . . . I've heard him moan in his sleep, he's so hungry. And you come in the night and steal food that should go to them . . . to the children!

MRS. VAN DAAN. [*Going to* MR. VAN DAAN *protectively.*] He needs more food than the rest of us. He's used to more. He's a big man.

Vocabulary

stealthily (stel′ thə lē) *adv.* in a secret or sneaky manner

frenzy (fren′ zē) *n.* a state of great excitement or deep disturbance

[*MR. VAN DAAN breaks away, going over and sitting on the couch.*]

MRS. FRANK. [*Turning on MRS. VAN DAAN.*] And you . . . you're worse than he is! You're a mother, and yet you sacrifice your child to this man . . . this . . . this . . .

MR. FRANK. Edith! Edith!

[*MARGOT picks up the pink woolen stole, putting it over her mother's shoulders.*]

MRS. FRANK. [*Paying no attention, going on to MRS. VAN DAAN.*] Don't think I haven't seen you! Always saving the choicest bits for him! I've watched you day after day and I've held my tongue. But not any longer! Not after this! Now I want him to go! I want him to get out of here!

MR. FRANK. Edith!

MR. VAN DAAN. Get out of here?

} *Together*

MRS. VAN DAAN. What do you mean?

MRS. FRANK. Just that! Take your things and get out!

MR. FRANK. [*To MRS. FRANK.*] You're speaking in anger. You cannot mean what you are saying.

MRS. FRANK. I mean exactly that!

[*MRS. VAN DAAN takes a cover from the FRANKS' bed, pulling it about her.*]

MR. FRANK. For two long years we have lived here, side by side. We have respected each other's rights . . . we have managed to live in peace. Are we now going to throw it all away? I know this will never happen again, will it, Mr. Van Daan?

MR. VAN DAAN. No. No.

MRS. FRANK. He steals once! He'll steal again!

[*MR. VAN DAAN, holding his stomach, starts for the bathroom. ANNE puts her arms around him, helping him up the step.*]

MR. FRANK. Edith, please. Let us be calm. We'll all go to our rooms . . . and afterwards we'll sit down quietly and talk this out . . . we'll find some way . . .

MRS. FRANK. No! No! No more talk! I want them to leave!

MRS. VAN DAAN. You'd put us out, on the streets?

MRS. FRANK. There are other hiding places.

MRS. VAN DAAN. A cellar . . . a closet. I know. And we have no money left even to pay for that.

MRS. FRANK. I'll give you money. Out of my own pocket I'll give it gladly.

[*She gets her purse from a shelf and comes back with it.*]

MRS. VAN DAAN. Mr. Frank, you told Putti you'd never forget what he'd done for you when you came to Amsterdam. You said you could never repay him, that you . . .

MRS. FRANK. [*Counting out money.*] If my husband had any obligation to you, he's paid it, over and over.

MR. FRANK. Edith, I've never seen you like this before. I don't know you.

MRS. FRANK. I should have spoken out long ago.

DUSSEL. You can't be nice to some people.

MRS. VAN DAAN. [*Turning on DUSSEL.*] There would have been plenty for all of us, if *you* hadn't come in here!

MR. FRANK. We don't need the Nazis to destroy us. We're destroying ourselves.

[*He sits down, with his head in his hands. MRS. FRANK goes to MRS. VAN DAAN.*]

MRS. FRANK. [*Giving* MRS. VAN DAAN *some money.*] Give this to Miep. She'll find you a place.

ANNE. Mother, you're not putting *Peter* out. Peter hasn't done anything.

MRS. FRANK. He'll stay, of course. When I say I must protect the children, I mean Peter too.

[PETER *rises from the steps where he has been sitting.*]

PETER. I'd have to go if Father goes.

[MR. VAN DAAN *comes from the bathroom.* MRS. VAN DAAN *hurries to him and takes him to the couch. Then she gets water from the sink to bathe his face.*]

MRS. FRANK. [*While this is going on.*] He's no father to you . . . that man! He doesn't know what it is to be a father!

PETER. [*Starting for his room.*] I wouldn't feel right. I couldn't stay.

MRS. FRANK. Very well, then. I'm sorry.

ANNE. [*Rushing over to* PETER.] No, Peter! No! [PETER *goes into his room, closing the door after him.* ANNE *turns back to her mother, crying.*] I don't care about the food. They can have mine! I don't want it! Only don't send them away. It'll be daylight soon. They'll be caught . . .

MARGOT. [*Putting her arms comfortingly around* ANNE.] Please, Mother!

MRS. FRANK. They're not going now. They'll stay here until Miep finds them a place. [*To* MRS. VAN DAAN.] But one thing I insist on! He must never come down here again! He must never come to this room where the food is stored! We'll divide what we have . . . an equal share for each! [DUSSEL *hurries over to get a sack of potatoes from the food safe.* MRS. FRANK *goes on, to* MRS. VAN DAAN.] You can cook it here and take it up to him.

[DUSSEL *brings the sack of potatoes back to the center table.*]

MARGOT. Oh, no. No. We haven't sunk so far that we're going to fight over a handful of rotten potatoes.

DUSSEL. [*Dividing the potatoes into piles.*] Mrs. Frank, Mr. Frank, Margot, Anne, Peter, Mrs. Van Daan, Mr. Van Daan, myself . . . Mrs. Frank . . .

[*The buzzer sounds in* MIEP'S *signal.*]

MR. FRANK. It's Miep!

[*He hurries over, getting his overcoat and putting it on.*]

MARGOT. At this hour?

MRS. FRANK. It is trouble.

MR. FRANK. [*As he starts down to unbolt the door.*] I beg you, don't let her see a thing like this!

MR. DUSSEL. [*Counting without stopping.*] . . . Anne, Peter, Mrs. Van Daan, Mr. Van Daan, myself . . .

MARGOT. [*To* DUSSEL.] Stop it! Stop it!

DUSSEL. . . . Mr. Frank, Margot, Anne, Peter, Mrs. Van Daan, Mr. Van Daan, myself, Mrs. Frank . . .

MRS. VAN DAAN. You're keeping the big ones for yourself! All the big ones . . . Look at the size of that! . . . And that! . . .

[DUSSEL *continues on with his dividing.* PETER, *with his shirt and trousers on, comes from his room.*]

MARGOT. Stop it! Stop it!

[*We hear* MIEP'S *excited voice speaking to* MR. FRANK *below.*]

MIEP. Mr. Frank . . . the most wonderful news! . . . The invasion has begun!

MR. FRANK. Go on, tell them! Tell them!

[MIEP comes running up the steps, ahead of MR. FRANK. She has a man's raincoat on over her nightclothes and a bunch of orange-colored flowers in her hand.]

MIEP. Did you hear that, everybody? Did you hear what I said? The invasion has begun! The invasion!

[They all stare at MIEP, unable to grasp what she is telling them. PETER is the first to recover his wits.]

PETER. Where?

MRS. VAN DAAN. When? When, Miep?

MIEP. It began early this morning . . .

[As she talks on, the realization of what she has said begins to dawn on them. Everyone goes crazy. A wild demonstration takes place. MRS. FRANK hugs MR. VAN DAAN.]

MRS. FRANK. Oh, Mr. Van Daan, did you hear that?

[DUSSEL embraces MRS. VAN DAAN. PETER grabs a frying pan and parades around the room, beating on it, singing the Dutch National Anthem. ANNE and MARGOT follow him, singing, weaving in and out among the excited grown-ups. MARGOT breaks away to take the flowers from MIEP and distribute them to everyone. While this pandemonium is going on MRS. FRANK tries to make herself heard above the excitement.]

MRS. FRANK. *[To MIEP.]* How do you know?

MIEP. The radio . . . The B.B.C.! They said they landed on the coast of Normandy![52]

PETER. The British?

MIEP. British, Americans, French, Dutch, Poles, Norwegians . . . all of them! More than four thousand ships! Churchill spoke, and General Eisenhower![53] D-Day they call it!

MR. FRANK. Thank God, it's come!

MRS. VAN DAAN. At last!

MIEP. *[Starting out.]* I'm going to tell Mr. Kraler. This'll be better than any blood transfusion.

MR. FRANK. *[Stopping her.]* What part of Normandy did they land, did they say?

MIEP. Normandy . . . that's all I know now . . . I'll be up the minute I hear some more!

[She goes hurriedly out.]

MR. FRANK. *[To MRS. FRANK.]* What did I tell you? What did I tell you?

[MRS. FRANK indicates that he has forgotten to bolt the door after MIEP. He hurries down the steps. MR. VAN DAAN, sitting on the couch, suddenly breaks into a convulsive sob. Everybody looks at him, bewildered.]

MRS. VAN DAAN. *[Hurrying to him.]* Putti! Putti! What is it? What happened?

MR. VAN DAAN. Please. I'm so ashamed.

[MR. FRANK comes back up the steps.]

DUSSEL. Oh, for God's sake!

MRS. VAN DAAN. Don't, Putti.

MARGOT. It doesn't matter now!

MR. FRANK. *[Going to MR. VAN DAAN.]* Didn't you hear what Miep said? The

52. *B.B.C.* stands for "British Broadcasting Corporation." *Normandy* is a region of northwestern France, across the English Channel from the southern coast of England.

53. Winston *Churchill* was the prime minister of England, and Dwight D. *Eisenhower* commanded the Allied forces in Europe.

Vocabulary

pandemonium (pan′ də mō′ nē əm) *n.* wild disorder and uproar invasion has come! We're going to be liberated! This is a time to celebrate!

[*He embraces* MRS. FRANK *and then hurries to the cupboard and gets the cognac and a glass.*]

MR. VAN DAAN. To steal bread from children!

MRS. FRANK. We've all done things that we're ashamed of.

ANNE. Look at me, the way I've treated Mother . . . so mean and horrid to her.

MRS. FRANK. No, Anneke, no.

[ANNE *runs to her mother, putting her arms around her.*]

ANNE. Oh, Mother, I was. I was awful.

MR. VAN DAAN. Not like me. No one is as bad as me!

DUSSEL. [*To* MR. VAN DAAN.] Stop it now! Let's be happy!

MR. FRANK. [*Giving* MR. VAN DAAN *a glass of cognac.*] Here! Here! *Schnapps! Locheim!*[54]

[VAN DAAN *takes the cognac. They all watch him. He gives them a feeble smile.* ANNE *puts up her fingers in a V-for-Victory sign. As* VAN DAAN *gives an answering V-sign, they are startled to hear a loud sob from behind them. It is* MRS. FRANK, *stricken with remorse. She is sitting on the other side of the room.*]

MRS. FRANK. [*Through her sobs.*] When I think of the terrible things I said . . .

[MR. FRANK, ANNE *and* MARGOT *hurry to her, trying to comfort her.* MR. VAN DAAN *brings her his glass of cognac.*]

MR. VAN DAAN. No! No! You were right!

MRS. FRANK. That I should speak that way to you! . . . Our friends! . . . Our guests!

[*She starts to cry again.*]

DUSSEL. Stop it, you're spoiling the whole invasion!

[*As they are comforting her, the lights dim out. The curtain falls.*]

ANNE'S VOICE. [*Faintly at first and then with growing strength.*] We're all in much better spirits these days. There's still excellent news of the invasion. The best part about it is that I have a feeling that friends are coming. Who knows? Maybe I'll be back in school by fall. Ha, ha! The joke is on us! The warehouse man doesn't know a thing and we are paying him all that money! . . . Wednesday, the second of July, nineteen forty-four. The invasion seems temporarily to be bogged down. Mr. Kraler has to have an operation, which looks bad. The Gestapo have found the radio that was stolen. Mr. Dussel says they'll trace it back and back to the thief, and then, it's just a matter of time till they get to us. Everyone is low. Even poor Pim can't raise their spirits. I have often been downcast myself . . . but never in despair. I can shake off everything if I write. But . . . and that is the great question . . . will I ever be able to write well? I want to so much. I want to go on living even after my death. Another birthday has gone by, so now I am fifteen. Already I know what I want. I have a goal, an opinion.

[*As this is being said—the curtain rises on the scene, the lights dim on, and* ANNE'S VOICE *fades out.*]

54. ***Schnapps*** (schnäps) is the cognac, or brandy. ***Locheim!*** (lə KHĪʹ əm) or (lə khäʹ yim) means "To Life!"

SCENE

[It is an afternoon a few weeks later . . . Everyone but Margot is in the main room. There is a sense of great tension. Both MRS. FRANK *and* MR. VAN DAAN *are nervously pacing back and forth,* DUSSEL *is standing at the window, looking down fixedly at the street below.* PETER *is at the center table, trying to do his lessons.* ANNE *sits opposite him, writing in her diary.* MRS. VAN DAAN *is seated on the couch, her eyes on* MR. FRANK *as he sits reading. The sound of a telephone ringing comes from the office below. They all are rigid, listening tensely.* MR. DUSSEL *rushes down to* MR. FRANK.*]*

DUSSEL. There it goes again, the telephone! Mr. Frank, do you hear?

MR. FRANK. [*Quietly.*] Yes. I hear.

DUSSEL. [*Pleading, insistent.*] But this is the third time, Mr. Frank! The third time in quick succession! It's a signal! I tell you it's Miep, trying to get us! For some reason she can't come to us and she's trying to warn us of something!

MR. FRANK. Please. Please.

MR. VAN DAAN. [*To* DUSSEL.] You're wasting your breath.

DUSSEL. Something has happened, Mr. Frank. For three days now Miep hasn't been to see us! And today not a man has come to work. There hasn't been a sound in the building!

MRS. FRANK. Perhaps it's Sunday. We may have lost track of the days.

MR. VAN DAAN. [*To* ANNE.] You with the diary there. What day is it?

DUSSEL. [*Going to* MRS. FRANK.] I don't lose track of the days! I know exactly what day it is! It's Friday, the fourth of August. Friday,

The Diary of Anne Frank, 1959. 20th Century Fox. Movie still.

Viewing the photograph: Describe the expression on Mr. Van Daan's face. How do you think he feels about himself and his situation?

and not a man at work. [*He rushes back to* MR. FRANK, *pleading with him, almost in tears.*] I tell you Mr. Kraler's dead. That's the only explanation. He's dead and they've closed down the building, and Miep's trying to tell us!

MR. FRANK. She'd never telephone us.

DUSSEL. [*Frantic.*] Mr. Frank, answer that! I beg you, answer it!

MR. FRANK. No.

MR. VAN DAAN. Just pick it up and listen. You don't have to speak. Just listen and see if it's Miep.

DUSSEL. [*Speaking at the same time.*] For God's sake . . . I ask you.

MR. FRANK. No. I've told you, no. I'll do nothing that might let anyone know we're in the building.

The Diary of Anne Frank, 1959. 20th Century Fox. Movie still.

Viewing the photograph: How has Peter dealt with being in hiding up to this point? What does his expression suggest about what the future might hold?

PETER. Mr. Frank's right.

MR. VAN DAAN. There's no need to tell us what side you're on.

MR. FRANK. If we wait patiently, quietly, I believe that help will come.

[*There is silence for a minute as they all listen to the telephone ringing.*]

DUSSEL. I'm going down. [*He rushes down the steps.* MR. FRANK *tries ineffectually*[55] *to hold him.* DUSSEL *runs to the lower door, unbolting it. The telephone stops ringing.* DUSSEL *bolts the door and comes slowly back up the steps.*] Too late. [MR. FRANK *goes to* MARGOT *in* ANNE's *bedroom.*]

MR. VAN DAAN. So we just wait here until we die.

MRS. VAN DAAN. [*Hysterically.*] I can't stand it! I'll kill myself! I'll kill myself!

MR. VAN DAAN. For God's sake, stop it!

[*In the distance, a German military band is heard playing a Viennese waltz.*]

MRS. VAN DAAN. I think you'd be glad if I did! I think you want me to die!

MR. VAN DAAN. Whose fault is it we're here? [MRS. VAN DAAN *starts for her room. He follows, talking at her.*] We could've been safe somewhere . . . in America or Switzerland. But no! No! You wouldn't leave when I wanted to. You couldn't

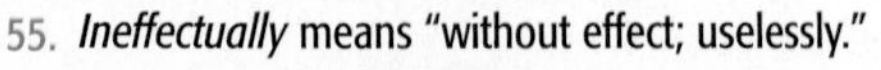

55. ***Ineffectually*** means "without effect; uselessly."

leave your things. You couldn't leave your precious furniture.

MRS. VAN DAAN. Don't touch me!

[*She hurries up the stairs, followed by* MR. VAN DAAN. PETER, *unable to bear it, goes to his room.* ANNE *looks after him, deeply concerned.* DUSSEL *returns to his post at the window.* MR. FRANK *comes back into the main room and takes a book, trying to read.* MRS. FRANK *sits near the sink, starting to peel some potatoes.* ANNE *quietly goes to* PETER'S *room, closing the door after her.* PETER *is lying face down on the cot.* ANNE *leans over him, holding him in her arms, trying to bring him out of his despair.*]

ANNE. Look, Peter, the sky. [*She looks up through the skylight.*] What a lovely, lovely day! Aren't the clouds beautiful? You know what I do when it seems as if I couldn't stand being cooped up for one more minute? I *think* myself out. I think myself on a walk in the park where I used to go with Pim. Where the jonquils and the crocus and the violets grow down the slopes. You know the most wonderful part about *thinking* yourself out? You can have it any way you like. You can have roses and violets and chrysanthemums all blooming at the same time . . . It's funny . . . I used to take it all for granted . . . and now I've gone crazy about everything to do with nature. Haven't you?

PETER. I've just gone crazy. I think if something doesn't happen soon . . . if we don't get out of here . . . I can't stand much more of it!

ANNE. [*Softly.*] I wish you had a religion, Peter.

PETER. No, thanks! Not me!

ANNE. Oh, I don't mean you have to be Orthodox . . . or believe in heaven and hell and purgatory[56] and things . . . I just mean some religion . . . it doesn't matter what. Just to believe in something! When I think of all that's out there . . . the trees . . . and flowers . . . and seagulls . . . when I think of the dearness of you, Peter . . . and the goodness of the people we know . . . Mr. Kraler, Miep, Dirk, the vegetable man, all risking their lives for us every day . . . When I think of these good things, I'm not afraid any more . . . I find myself, and God, and I . . .

[PETER *interrupts, getting up and walking away.*]

PETER. That's fine! But when I begin to think, I get mad! Look at us, hiding out for two years. Not able to move! Caught here like . . . waiting for them to come and get us . . . and all for what?

ANNE. We're not the only people that've had to suffer. There've always been people that've had to . . . sometimes one race . . . sometimes another . . . and yet . . .

PETER. That doesn't make me feel any better!

ANNE. [*Going to him.*] I know it's terrible, trying to have any faith . . . when people are doing such horrible . . . But you know what I sometimes think? I think the world may be going through a phase, the way I was with Mother. It'll pass, maybe not for hundreds of years, but someday . . . I still believe, in spite of everything, that people are really good at heart.

PETER. I want to see something now . . . Not a thousand years from now!

[*He goes over, sitting down again on the cot.*]

56. Jews in the *Orthodox* branch of Judaism are the most traditional, strictly observing the ancient laws and customs. *Purgatory* is the Roman Catholic belief in a place of temporary punishment for the souls of the dead.

ANNE. But, Peter, if you'd only look at it as part of a great pattern . . . that we're just a little minute in the life . . . [*She breaks off.*] Listen to us, going at each other like a couple of stupid grown-ups! Look at the sky now. Isn't it lovely? [*She holds out her hand to him.* PETER *takes it and rises, standing with her at the window looking out, his arms around her.*] Someday, when we're outside again, I'm going to . . .

[*She breaks off as she hears the sound of a car, its brakes squealing as it comes to a sudden stop. The people in the other rooms also become aware of the sound. They listen tensely. Another car roars up to a screeching stop.* ANNE *and* PETER *come from* PETER's *room.* MR. *and* MRS. VAN DAAN *creep down the stairs.* DUSSEL *comes out from his room. Everyone is listening, hardly breathing. A doorbell clangs again and again in the building below.* MR. FRANK *starts quietly down the steps to the door.* DUSSEL *and* PETER *follow him. The others stand rigid, waiting, terrified. In a few seconds* DUSSEL *comes stumbling back up the steps. He shakes off* PETER's *help and goes to his room.* MR. FRANK *bolts the door below, and comes slowly back up the steps. Their eyes are all on him as he stands there for a minute. They realize that what they feared has happened.* MRS. VAN DAAN *starts to whimper.* MR. VAN DAAN *puts her gently in a chair, and then hurries off up the stairs to their room to collect their things.* PETER *goes to comfort his mother. There is a sound of violent pounding on a door below.*]

MR. FRANK. [*Quietly.*] For the past two years we have lived in fear. Now we can live in hope.

[*The pounding below becomes more insistent. There are muffled sounds of voices, shouting commands.*]

MEN'S VOICES. *Auf machen! Da drinnen! Auf machen! Schnell! Schnell! Schnell!*[57] etc., etc.

[*The street door below is forced open. We hear the heavy tread of footsteps coming up.* MR. FRANK *gets two school bags from the shelves, and gives one to* ANNE *and the other to* MARGOT. *He goes to get a bag for* MRS. FRANK. *The sound of feet coming up grows louder.* PETER *comes to* ANNE, *kissing her good-bye, then he goes to his room to collect his things. The buzzer of their door starts to ring.* MR. FRANK *brings* MRS. FRANK *a bag. They stand together, waiting. We hear the thud of gun butts on the door, trying to break it down.*

ANNE *stands, holding her school satchel, looking over at her father and mother with a soft, reassuring smile. She is no longer a child, but a woman with courage to meet whatever lies ahead.*

The lights dim out. The curtain falls on the scene. We hear a mighty crash as the door is shattered. After a second ANNE'S VOICE *is heard.*]

ANNE'S VOICE. And so it seems our stay here is over. They are waiting for us now. They've allowed us five minutes to get our things. We can each take a bag and whatever it will hold of clothing. Nothing else. So, dear Diary, that means I must leave you behind. Good-bye for a while. P.S. Please, please, Miep, or Mr. Kraler, or anyone else. If you should find this diary, will you please keep it safe for me, because some day I hope . . .

[*Her voice stops abruptly. There is silence. After a second the curtain rises.*]

---

57. **"Open up! Inside there! Open up! Quick! Quick! Quick!" Pronunciation: *Auf machen!* (ouf mäkн′ ən) *Da drinnen!* (dä drin′ ən) *Schnell!* (shnel)**

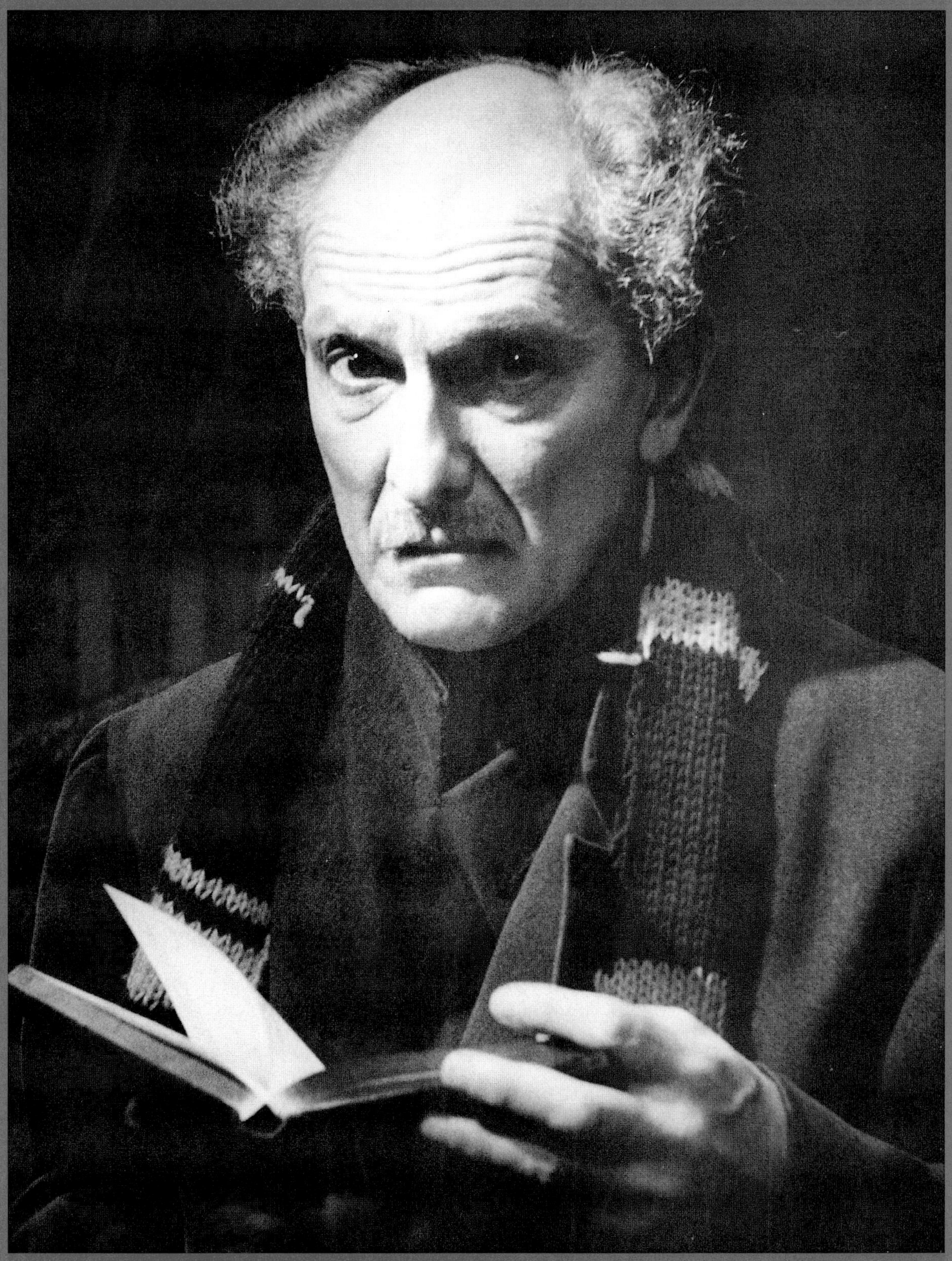

The Diary of Anne Frank, 1959. 20th Century Fox. Movie still.

Viewing the photograph: How does this image illustrate Mr. Frank's closing words about Anne?

SCENE

[*It is again the afternoon in November, 1945. The rooms are as we saw them in the first scene.* MR. KRALER *has joined* MIEP *and* MR. FRANK. *There are coffee cups on the table. We see a great change in* MR. FRANK. *He is calm now. His bitterness is gone. He slowly turns a few pages of the diary. They are blank.*]

MR. FRANK. No more.

[*He closes the diary and puts it down on the couch beside him.*]

MIEP. I'd gone to the country to find food. When I got back the block was surrounded by police . . .

MR. KRALER. We made it our business to learn how they knew. It was the thief . . . the thief who told them.

[MIEP *goes up to the gas burner, bringing back a pot of coffee.*]

MR. FRANK. [*After a pause.*] It seems strange to say this, that anyone could be happy in a concentration camp. But Anne was happy in the camp in Holland where they first took us. After two years of being shut up in these rooms, she could be out . . . out in the sunshine and the fresh air that she loved.

MIEP. [*Offering the coffee to* MR. FRANK.] A little more?

MR. FRANK. [*Holding out his cup to her.*] The news of the war was good. The British and Americans were sweeping through France. We felt sure that they would get to us in time. In September we were told that we were to be shipped to Poland . . . The men to one camp. The women to another. I was sent to Auschwitz. They went to Belsen. In January we were freed, the few of us who were left. The war wasn't yet over, so it took us a long time to get home. We'd be sent here and there behind the lines where we'd be safe. Each time our train would stop . . . at a siding, or a crossing . . . we'd all get out and go from group to group . . . Where were you? Were you at Belsen? At Buchenwald?[58] At Mauthausen? Is it possible that you knew my wife? Did you ever see my husband? My son? My daughter? That's how I found out about my wife's death . . . of Margot, the Van Daans . . . Dussel. But Anne . . . I still hoped . . . Yesterday I went to Rotterdam.[59] I'd heard of a woman there . . . She'd been in Belsen with Anne . . . I know now.

[*He picks up the diary again, and turns the pages back to find a certain passage. As he finds it we hear* ANNE'S VOICE.]

ANNE'S VOICE. In spite of everything, I still believe that people are really good at heart.

[MR. FRANK *slowly closes the diary.*]

MR. FRANK. She puts me to shame.

[*They are silent.*]

The Curtain Falls

---

58. *Auschwitz* (oush′ vits), *Belsen* (bel′ zən), and *Buchenwald* (bo͞o′ KHən vält′) or (bo͞o′ k'n wôld′) were the sites of Nazi concentration camps in Poland and Germany that specialized in exterminating prisoners.
59. *Rotterdam* is a city in the southwestern Netherlands.

Responding to Literature

PERSONAL RESPONSE

Did the ending of the play surprise you in any way? Why or why not?

Analyzing Literature

RECALL

1. How do Mr. and Mrs. Frank react to Mr. Van Daan's stealing the bread? How does his family react?
2. What news does Miep bring?
3. Anne and Peter each view their situation differently. Explain their points of view.
4. What are Mr. Frank's last words of encouragement to the group?

INTERPRET

5. What does the audience learn about each character from the uproar over the stolen bread?
6. What do you learn about the characters from their reactions to Miep's news?
7. How do you account for the difference in the way Peter and Anne view their situation?
8. What does Mr. Frank mean by his final words of encouragement?

EVALUATE AND CONNECT

9. Who, in your opinion, behaves better during the scene with the stolen bread, the young people or the adults? Explain.
10. Why do you think the playwrights end the play with these five words: *She puts me to shame?* Do you agree with Mr. Frank's self-criticism? Is the criticism meant for anyone else? Explain your answer.

LITERARY ELEMENTS

Tragedy

In a **tragedy,** the main character, a dignified or heroic person, suffers a downfall, or death. This downfall may be the result of a personal weakness, such as pride, or it may result from outside forces over which the character has no control. In this play, Anne Frank is the main character.

1. In what ways is Anne heroic?
2. Are there other heroes in the story?
3. What causes Anne's "downfall"?

• See **Literary Terms Handbook,** p. R10.

Literature and Writing

Writing About Literature 

Analyzing Characters The Holocaust Museum in Israel honors rescuers like Miep and Kraler as the "Righteous Among Nations of the World." Examine how Miep and Kraler interact with the group hiding in their building–the way they speak to each person, their comments about the dangers to themselves, and the attitude each group member shows to them. Then write a paragraph or two explaining how the playwrights show that Miep and Kraler are righteous.

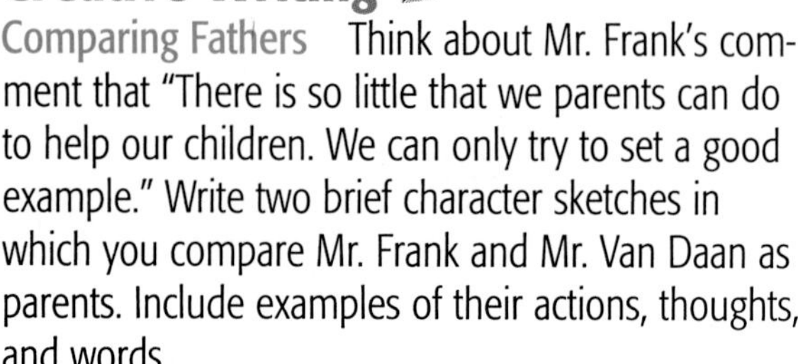

Creative Writing

Comparing Fathers Think about Mr. Frank's comment that "There is so little that we parents can do to help our children. We can only try to set a good example." Write two brief character sketches in which you compare Mr. Frank and Mr. Van Daan as parents. Include examples of their actions, thoughts, and words.

Extending Your Response

Literature Groups 

Anne's Famous Words In her diary, Anne Frank wrote this famous sentence: "In spite of everything, I still believe that people are really good at heart." What does Anne mean by *in spite of everything?* Using examples from the play and your knowledge of what happened to Anne after leaving the annex, discuss her words. Would she, in your opinion, have made the same statement near the end of her life?

Performing 

Readers Theater Work with another student or a small group to prepare a readers theater presentation of an episode from the play that you find very significant. As part of your presentation, explain your reasons for choosing that episode.

Interdisciplinary Activity 

History In every European country courageous people risked their lives to rescue Jews from Nazi persecution. With a group, research some of the rescuers, such as Miep Gies, Raoul Wallenberg, Oskar Schindler, and the villagers of Le Chambon-sur-Lignon. Share with the class the motives and the actions of each person or group.

Miep Gies

Reading Further 

If you would like to read about Anne Frank from another point of view, try one of these books:

Anne Frank Remembered: The Story of the Woman Who Helped to Hide the Frank Family by Miep Gies and Alison Leslie Gold

The Last Seven Months of Anne Frank by Willy Lindwer

 **Save your work for your portfolio.**

Skill Minilessons

GRAMMAR AND LANGUAGE • ITALICS AND QUOTATION MARKS

The following rules for using type treatments can help you understand materials you are reading.

- Quotation marks set off the title of a short story, essay, song, poem, news or feature article, or chapter from a book. ("The Anne Frank House" is a poem about a building in Amsterdam.)
- Italics or underlining set off the title of a book, play, film, television series, magazine, newspaper, or work of art. (*The Diary of Anne Frank* is a story of hope.)
- Italics or underlining identify a word being defined or being used as a word. Definitions are placed in quotation marks. (The word *diary* comes from a Latin word meaning "daily.")

PRACTICE Rewrite the following sentences and correct the mistakes in type treatments.

1. In 1947 Otto Frank published his daughter's diary under the title "The Diary of a Young Girl."
2. While in hiding, Anne Frank wrote a number of short stories, including *The Best Little Table.*
3. "Mazeltov" is a Hebrew word meaning *congratulations.*
4. The word Holocaust refers to the mass killing of millions of people, especially Jews, during World War II.

For more about italics and quotation marks, see **Language Handbook,** p. R41.

READING AND THINKING • FOCUSING ON A QUESTION

Focusing on a question at the beginning of a story, chapter, act, or scene is a good way to read for meaning. At the beginning of act 1, for example, you could focus on the question *What is Anne's relationship with her father (or mother)?* Look for details that help you to understand Anne's relationships.

PRACTICE Think of questions that will help a friend read the play for the first time. Write one question to be considered before reading each scene in act 2.

For more about questioning strategies, see **Reading Handbook,** p. R84.

VOCABULARY • ETYMOLOGY

The **etymology,** or history, of a word may be quite straightforward. *Onslaught* comes from an Old English word that means "to strike." *Stealthily* comes from an Old English word meaning "to steal." Sometimes, however, a word's history is like a story. *Pandemonium* was made up by John Milton to be the name of the capital of hell in his famous poem *Paradise Lost.* He created the word by combining Greek words meaning "all" and "demons."

PRACTICE Use the information about word histories to answer these questions.

1. *Frenzy* comes from the Greek word *phrenesis,* which means "insanity." Which word do you think probably has the same history–*frantic, friend,* or *French?*
2. *Apprehension* comes from the Latin word *apprehendere,* which means "to take hold of." If a criminal was *apprehended,* was the criminal wounded, arrested, or put on trial?
3. *Foreboding* comes from the Old English *fore,* meaning "before," and *bode,* meaning "messenger." If you *forestall* an action, do you encourage it, prevent it, or react to it?

MEDIA Connection

SONG LYRICS

How would you cope with being forced to stay inside for two years? Lyricist Enid Futterman wrote these words to describe how Anne Frank would "think herself out" of the Secret Annex during her period of hiding.

I Think Myself Out

I'm facing the night.
I think myself stars.
I think myself free.
I'm bathing in moonlight.
I'm breathing the sea.

The night faces me
and takes me away
to walk on the wind
to ride on the rain
to come to the day.

It's morning.
It's evening.
It's raining.
It's snowing.
There are roses and lilies
and crocuses growing.
Sunlight is shining.
Breezes are blowing.
I'm running.
I'm leaping.
I'm flying
I'm going,
I'm going outside.

I think myself rain,
rain in my hair
I think myself air,
air on myself.
I think myself out.

from "I Am Anne Frank"
Copyright © 1985 by Enid Futterman and Michael Cohen

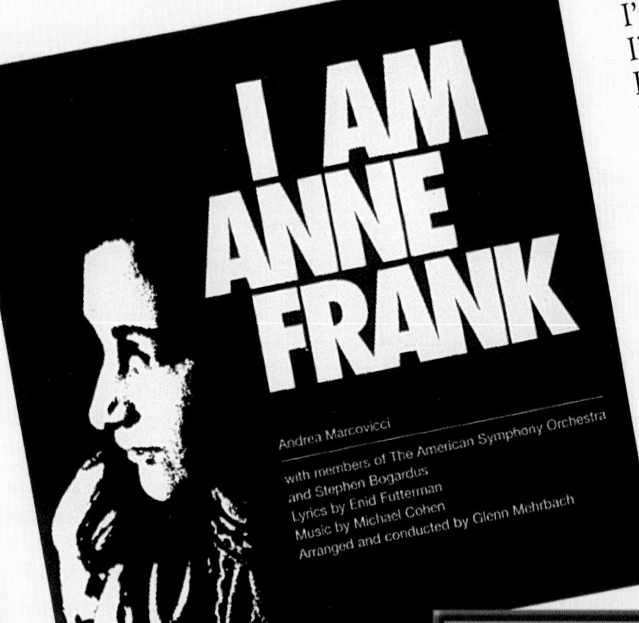

I AM ANNE FRANK
Andrea Marcovicci
with members of The American Symphony Orchestra
and Stephen Bogardus
Lyrics by Enid Futterman
Music by Michael Cohen
Arranged and conducted by Glenn Mehrbach

Respond

1. Why is "I Think Myself Out" an appropriate title for this song?
2. How would visualizing the images in the song help you if you couldn't see them firsthand?

Vo•cab•u•lar•y *Skills*

Analyzing Words

Context clues may not always provide the meaning of an unfamiliar word. Before turning to a dictionary, break the word into pieces, and look carefully to see if its parts are familiar.

The harm done to the Franks was irreversible.

This sentence provides no clue to the meaning of *irreversible.* However, the word parts are helpful. The base word *reverse* is familiar. Also, the prefix *ir-* is familiar to anyone who knows other words with the same prefix–*irregular,* for example. It is likely that you know that the suffix *-ible* means "able." Putting the clues together reveals that *irreversible* means "not able to be reversed." In the sentence, the harm done to the Franks cannot be undone.

Another kind of analysis is needed if an unfamiliar word is not built on a base word you know. However, it may have a root you recognize.

It is sad to think about the brevity of Anne Frank's life.

The root *brev* is in the word *abbreviation,* so you may realize that *brevity* has something to do with shortness. In the sentence, it is sad to think that Anne Frank's life was so short.

EXERCISE

Analyze the underlined words on the left and match each one to its meaning on the right.

1. an instinctive reaction
2. a nondescript house
3. a preexisting condition
4. disclose the facts
5. count the fatalities
6. to feel rejuvenated
7. provide a curative
8. difficult to quantify
9. a state of quietude
10. solidify her support

a. remedy
b. deaths
c. reveal
d. measure
e. stillness
f. already present
g. natural; unlearned
h. made young again
i. make strong or firm
j. hard to describe in words

Writing WORKSHOP

Expository Writing: Historical Research Report

Past events still touch people all over the world. By examining the past, you may know and understand the present. One way to examine history is to write about it.

Assignment: Use the process on these pages to write a report about a past event.

- As you write your research report, refer to **Writing Handbook,** pp. R56–R59.

The Writing Process

PREWRITING

PREWRITING TIP

Need more ideas? Ask yourself what life was like during times of peace since the war. List questions about interesting people or events from a more recent era.

TECHNOLOGY TIP

Check your word processing program: it may have an outlining feature to help you plan your report.

Find Ideas

What more would you like to know about events described in the selections in "Faces of Dignity"? On your own or with a partner, choose one or two people or events that you would like to know more about. Brainstorm a list of questions about the topics you select.

- What went on in the United States during World War II?
- How did the war touch members of my family?
- How do wars affect young people?

Shape Your Topic

Choose one of the questions you wrote and explore it further, using a general reference book. Narrow your topic until you find a focus that you can cover thoroughly in a short report.

Far too broad
America in WWII

Still too broad
Texas people in World War II

Good-size—narrow enough
How WWII changed one Texan's life

Consider Your Audience and Purpose

For a report, your purpose is to present information in an interesting way. Your audience will be your teacher and classmates—and perhaps others. You might make a copy for your family, your library, or your local historical society.

Source Card

Source number (1)

Author: Phillips, Cabell.
Book title: The 1940's: Decade of Triumph and Trouble.
New York: Macmillan, 1975.
City of Publication/Publisher/Copyright date
Location of Source: Public Library
Library call number E806.P5

Search Out the Facts

Look for information in a variety of sources. Since you are reporting on modern historical events, you will probably be able to talk with people who remember the period you select. An interview—or even informal conversation—can be a valuable source of information. Ask about family members and close friends whom you can interview. Use at least three sources from the list below. Make note cards for the information you want to include in your report, and record your sources on source cards.

Note Card

Source number (1)

Main idea: Home Front, WWII - Background on plane spotters

The U.S. Army expected enemy air raids on American cities. The War Dept. trained volunteer air raid wardens and plane spotters.

(Summary)
Type of note

Page numbers 342–344

family photos	encyclopedias
videos	history books
the Internet	autobiographies
magazines	interviews
newspapers	biographies and diaries
museums	

Outline a Plan

This is the time to choose a focus for your report. Look over your notes, and see what main idea they suggest. State this idea in one or two sentences. This will be your **thesis,** and it should tell clearly what you have chosen as the focus of your topic. It also may answer the question that started your research.

Create an outline to guide you as you draft. List the main points that you will make and the details explaining each point. Plan to show causes and effects.

Thesis: My Grandma is proud of the contribution she and other teens made during World War II.

I. Her life before the war
  A. Home life comfortable
  B. High school and a part-time job
  C. Dances and parties with friends

II. Her life during the war
  A. Rationing and shortages
  B. Volunteered to be an "airplane spotter"
  C. Some friends died in battles

III. Her life after the war
  A. Understood more about the world and its problems
  B. Was accustomed to responsibility

DRAFTING

DRAFTING TIP

One way to show cause-and-effect relationships is to use transitions. For help with transitions, see the **Writing Skills** feature on page 691.

Craft a Working Opener

Your first paragraph should not only catch readers' interest, but also provide background information they will need. You might start with an intriguing sentence, then add facts about the people, events, or time period. If you end your opener with your thesis, readers will find your report easier to follow.

MODEL • DRAFTING

My grandma says that she'll never forget her seventeenth birthday in 1942. She had just started a volunteer job, scanning the night sky for enemy planes. America was at war, and she was determined to help her country.

Write On

As you continue your writing, be sure you develop your main points by using details, quotes, and examples. Make causes and effects clear. Be sure to credit your sources. Your outline will help you stay organized, but if a new point occurs to you, try it out. You might conclude with a personal reflection on the information you've presented.

REVISING

REVISING TIP

Check your prewriting notes to be sure you have correctly matched information and sources.

Consider Changes

Take a break before you begin revising. You might ask a classmate to help. Using the **Questions for Revising** as guidelines, plan your changes.

QUESTIONS FOR REVISING

- How might I change my first paragraph to better grab readers' attention?
- Where might I use more information?
- Where might transitions clarify the relationships among my sentences?
- What changes might I need in the way I credit my sources?
- How might I strengthen my conclusion?

EDITING/PROOFREADING

After revising your report, go over it once more to catch errors in grammar, usage, and mechanics. The **Proofreading Checklist** on the inside back cover offers guidelines. Double-check your use of commas, as shown in the **Grammar Link** on page 690.

Grammar Hint

When you use commas to set off a phrase, don't forget the second comma:
Niels Bohr, the brilliant Danish physicist, spoke out against atomic warfare.

MODEL · EDITING/PROOFREADING

June, the youngest in the group, was one of the fastest learners.

PUBLISHING/PRESENTING

You can add an extra dimension to your report with photos, charts or other visuals, or with relevant audiotaped material. If your report involves people you know, send them a copy. If it is about community figures or events, you might give a copy to your local historical society or library.

PRESENTING TIP

For an oral presentation, try accompanying your report with audiotaped music of the period.

Reflecting

Think about the following questions before writing your responses.

- Which did you find easier, doing your research or writing it? Explain.
- What are the two most useful pieces of advice you could give to another student who is about to write a research report?

Save your work for your portfolio.

Theme Wrap-Up

Responding to the Theme

1. In which selection were the main character's experiences most moving to you? Why?
2. As a result of your reading this theme, what new thoughts do you have about these ideas?
   - Crises can bring out the best and the worst in people.
   - It is important to seek the good in even the worst situations.
   - Ordinary people can be heroes.
3. Present your theme project to the class.

Analyzing Literature

FLASHBACK

In *The Diary of Anne Frank,* a long flashback is used to show the Frank family's experiences while hiding from the Nazis. Why, do you think, did the author choose to begin and end the play with events that occurred much later than the main narrative? What does the use of flashback in this play accomplish? Explain your answers using examples from the play.

Evaluate and Set Goals

1. Which of the following activities were the most enjoyable? Which were the most challenging?
   - reading and understanding the selections
   - writing on your own
   - analyzing and discussing selections
   - presenting ideas and projects
   - researching topics
2. How would you assess the work you've completed in this theme, using the following scale? Give two or more reasons for your assessment.

   4 = outstanding   2 = fair
   3 = good   1 = weak
3. Think of an aspect of this theme that you found difficult. Choose a goal to work toward in the next theme.
   - Record your goal and three steps you will take to help you reach it.
   - Meet with your teacher to review your plan for achieving your goal.

Build Your Portfolio

SELECT

Choose two of your favorite pieces of work from this theme to include in your portfolio. The following questions can help you choose.

- Which do you consider your best work?
- Which did you learn the most from?
- Which was the most interesting?

REFLECT

Write some notes to accompany the pieces you selected. Use these questions to guide you:

- What do you like best about the piece?
- What did you learn from creating it?
- What might you do differently if you were beginning this piece again?

Reading on Your Own

If you have enjoyed the literature in this theme, you might also be interested in these books, which show the dignity of many kinds of people during a time when the world was at war.

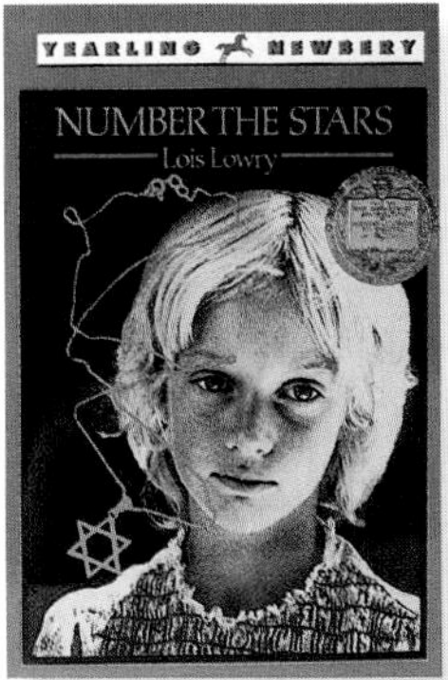

Number the Stars

by Lois Lowry Annemarie Johansen and her best friend Ellen Rosen live in Copenhagen, Denmark, a city of shortages and Nazi soldiers. When the Germans begin to "relocate" Copenhagen's Jews in 1943, Ellen moves in with Annemarie's family. Soon Annemarie must risk her own life to save her friend.

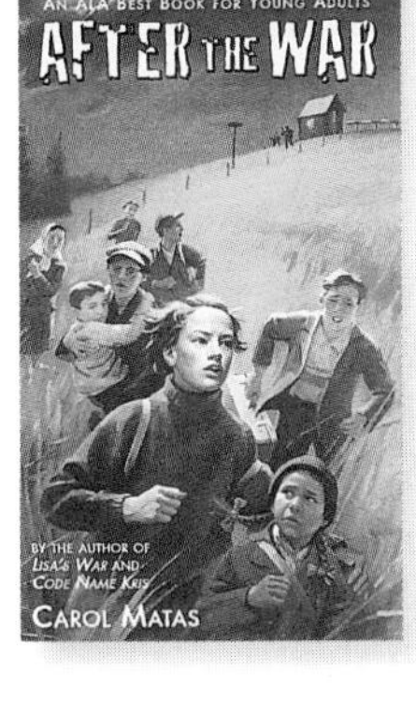

After the War

by Carol Matas Ruth is fifteen when she is freed from a Nazi concentration camp and fears that she is the only surviving member of her family. She joins an underground organization to make a dangerous and illegal journey to Palestine. Along the way, she rediscovers her inner strength and finds reasons for hope.

The Island on Bird Street

by Uri Orlev A Jewish boy, left on his own for months during World War II, learns to survive in a ruined house in the Warsaw Ghetto of Poland. He learns how to find food, contact others, and live amid constant danger.

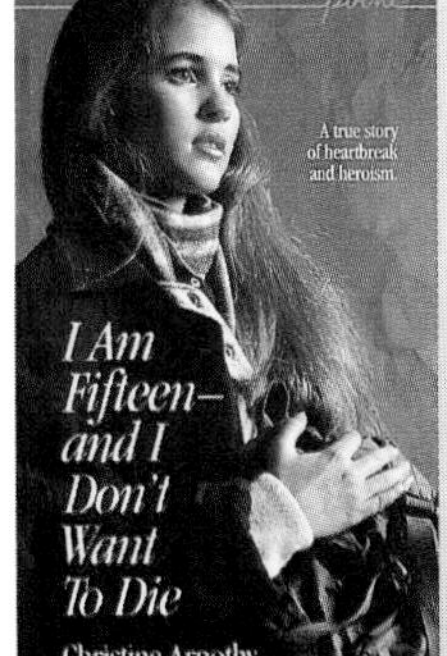

I Am Fifteen—and I Don't Want to Die

by Christine Arnothy The autobiography of Christine Arnothy focuses on one terrifying year during World War II when the author's family hid in the cellars of Budapest as German and Russian armies battled for control of Hungary.

Standardized Test Practice

Read the passage. Some sections are underlined. The underlined sections may be one of the following:

- Incomplete sentences
- Run-on sentences
- Correctly written sentences that should be combined
- Correctly written sentences that do not need to be rewritten

Choose the best way to write each underlined section. Mark the letter for your answer on your paper . If the underlined section needs no change, mark the choice "Correct as is."

> Franklin Delano Roosevelt was the thirty-second President of the United States. <u>Following an attack on Pearl Harbor, Roosevelt declared war on Japan, marking the United States' entry into World War II.</u> (1) <u>Roosevelt was a skilled negotiator he was instrumental in brokering the terms of peace that ended World War II.</u> (2)

1 A Marking the United States' entry into World War II, Roosevelt's declaring war on Japan following an attack on Pearl Harbor.

B Following an attack on Pearl Harbor. Roosevelt declared war on Japan, marking the United States' entry into World War II.

C Marking the United States' entry into World War II, Roosevelt declared war on Japan. Following an attack on Pearl Harbor.

D Correct as is.

2 F Roosevelt was a skilled negotiator, he was instrumental in brokering the terms of peace that ended World War II.

G A skilled negotiator, Roosevelt was instrumental in brokering the terms of peace that ended World War II.

H Roosevelt was a skilled negotiator. Brokering the terms of peace that ended World War II.

J Correct as is.

Read the passage and decide which type of error, if any, appears in each underlined section. Mark the letter for your answer on your paper.

"Whos next, please?" (1) The tired cashier frowned at the line of shoppers. A customer steped forward and handed the cashier a pile of coupons. (2) The cashier stared at the coupons. (3) "I can't take these," He said. (4) "This is an express line. We only accept cash checks and credit cards." (5)

The next shopper in the line asked the cashier, "Can't you make an exception just this once." (6) When several other people spoke up in agreement, the cashier accepted the coupons and began checking out the purchases.

1 A Spelling error
B Capitalization error
C Punctuation error
D No error

2 F Spelling error
G Capitalization error
H Punctuation error
J No error

3 A Spelling error
B Capitalization error
C Punctuation error
D No error

4 F Spelling error
G Capitalization error
H Punctuation error
J No error

5 A Spelling error
B Capitalization error
C Punctuation error
D No error

6 F Spelling error
G Capitalization error
H Punctuation error
J No error

Hair-Raising Tales

“We like the bad dreams because . . . we know [when] we wake up everything is going to be all right.”

—Stephen King

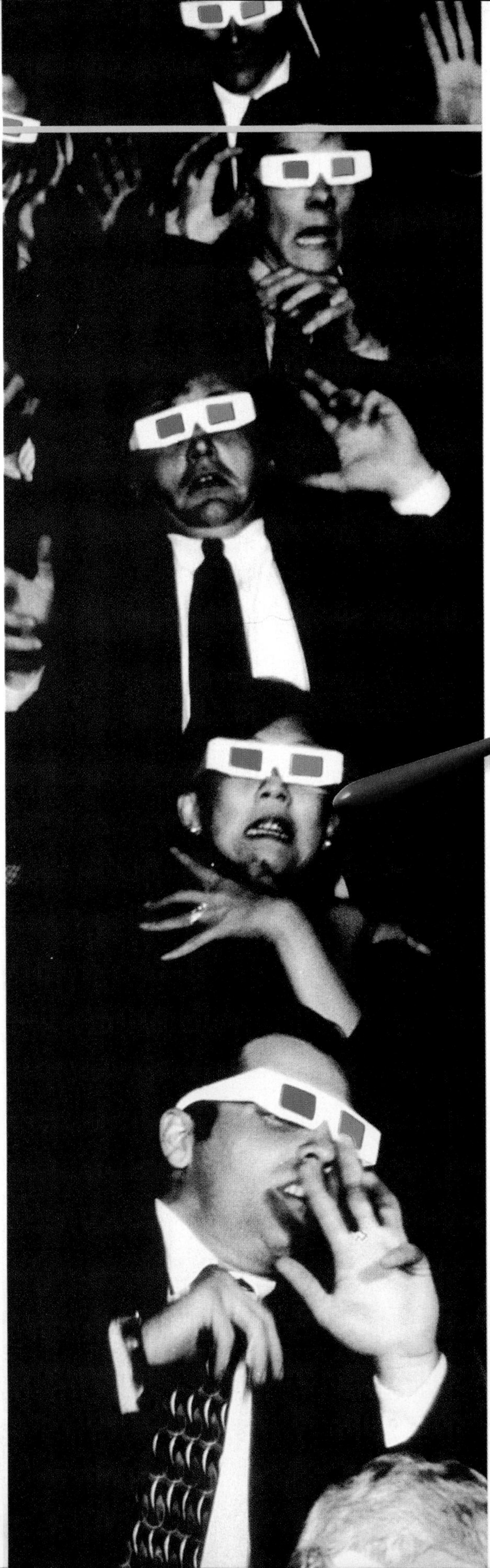

THEME CONTENTS

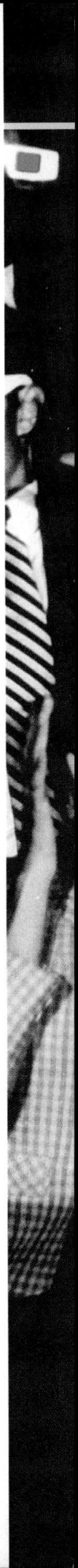

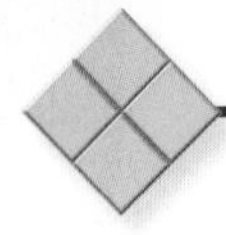

Exploring the Theme

Hair-Raising Tales

It's night. You're alone with a book. The words fill your head with scary music, although the room is silent. Shadows on the wall move each time you turn the page. Your heart pounds. You race, reluctantly, to the end of the story. You are scared and thrilled. Like an intense thriller or tale of horror, the selections in "Hair-Raising Tales" will make your spine tingle and pulse quicken. Choose one of the activities below to begin your thinking about the theme.

Starting Points

GHOULISH HUMOR

Humor and horror may seem to be unlikely partners. However, many scary stories heighten the suspense by putting funny surprises together with frightful moments. Other stories simply poke fun at traditional horror plots.

- Create a comic strip that either turns a scary situation into a funny one or pokes fun at a popular scary story you've read recently.

HEART-STOPPING MOMENTS

Every now and then, our imaginations get the best of us. In the dark, the lamp's shadow on the wall becomes a lunging monster. The rustle of the trees becomes a haunting voice.

- Remember a time when your imagination went into overdrive and scared you silly. Write two or three paragraphs describing the scene that set off your imagination.

The Quigmans

by Buddy Hickerson

"Pine box or plastic?"

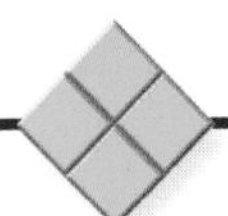

Theme Projects

Choose one of the projects below to work on as you read the selections in this theme. Work on your own, with a partner, or with a group.

LEARNING FOR LIFE

Critic's Corner

1. Read a movie or book review of your favorite horror, thriller, or mystery story.
2. Compare your own thoughts and feelings about the book or film with those in the review. On what do you and the critic agree? On what do you disagree? In your opinion, is the review a fair one? Explain.
3. Write a letter to the critic describing your reactions to the review. Cite reasons and examples to explain why you think the review was on target or unfair.

inter NET CONNECTION

For more about "Hair-Raising Tales," visit Glencoe's Web site at lit.glencoe.com

You can learn more about your favorite horror writer on-line. Many authors have their own Web sites. Check them out, or visit the site of the Biography Channel.

Dracula, starring Bela Lugosi, 1931. Movie still.

CRITICAL VIEWING

Book vs. Movie

1. Find a scary story or novel that has been produced in a movie version. Read the story and then watch the movie.
2. Compare the written story with the film version. How much do they have in common? What elements appear in the film but not in the story, and vice versa? Which version do you prefer, and why?
3. Write a brief report comparing and contrasting the written story with the film. Be sure to explain which form you enjoyed most.

MULTIMEDIA PROJECT

Build a Fright Site

1. Choose four or five of your favorite villains from literature. Write descriptions of their evil deeds and physical appearances, collect or draw pictures of them, and create audio clips of yourself reading the scary dialogue.
2. Use drawing software to create a multimedia presentation that invites people to vote on their favorite villain.
3. Organize and present your work.

Before You Read

Sorry, Right Number

MEET STEPHEN KING

Stephen King has this advice for talented writers: "If you work out with weights for fifteen minutes a day over a course of ten years, you're gonna get muscles. If you write for an hour and a half a day for ten years, you're gonna turn into a good writer." King, a writer who seems constantly to have a book on the best-seller list, should know. He has published more than thirty horror novels.

Stephen King was born in Maine in 1947. Sorry, Right Number *was first published in 1993 in* Nightmares and Dreamscapes.

FOCUS ACTIVITY

What kinds of things scare you? Is it ever fun to be scared?

Web It!
Make a word web to record the kinds of things that frighten you or the things that you enjoy in a scary movie or story.

Setting a Purpose
As you read, consider what you find frightening in this play.

BACKGROUND

The Time and Place *Sorry, Right Number* is a modern drama about an ordinary American family. It is written as a screenplay.

Did You Know? Some critics think that horror is popular today because it is *cathartic.* That is, it frightens people but then lets them relax at the end. They project their fears onto the monster and stop worrying about their own problems, which look small by comparison.

Phantom of the Opera, starring Lon Chaney, 1925. Movie still.

VOCABULARY PREVIEW

dejected (di jek′ tid) *adj.* sad; depressed; in low spirits; p. 793
strenuous (stren′ ū əs) *adj.* very active; energetic; p. 800
amiable (ā′ mē ə bəl) *adj.* friendly, good-natured; p. 801
interim (in′ tər im) *n.* the time between events; meantime; p. 804
presumably (pri zo͞o′ mə blē) *adv.* supposedly; probably; p. 804
impending (im pen′ ding) *adj.* about to occur; p. 805
chasm (kaz′ əm) *n.* a deep hole or crack, as in the earth's surface; p. 807
bland (bland) *adj.* dull and uninteresting; p. 808

SORRY, RIGHT NUMBER

Stephen King

CHARACTERS

KATIE WEIDERMAN	**BILL WEIDERMAN**	**MINISTER**
JEFF WEIDERMAN	**POLLY WEIDERMAN**	**GROUNDSKEEPER**
CONNIE WEIDERMAN	**OPERATOR**	**HANK**
DENNIS WEIDERMAN	**DAWN**	

AUTHOR'S NOTE: *Screenplay abbreviations are simple and exist, in this author's opinion, mostly to make those who write screenplays feel like lodge brothers.*[1] *In any case, you should be aware that* CU *means* close-up; ECU *means* extreme close-up; INT. *means* interior; EXT. *means* exterior; B.G. *means* background; POV *means* point of view. *Probably most of you knew all that stuff to begin with, right?*

ACT 1

[*FADE IN ON: KATIE WEIDERMAN'S MOUTH, ECU.*
She's speaking into the telephone. Pretty mouth; in a few seconds we'll see that the rest of her is just as pretty.]

KATIE. Bill? Oh, he says he doesn't feel very well, but he's always like that between books . . . can't sleep, thinks every headache is the first symptom of a brain tumor . . . once he gets going on something new, he'll be fine.

[*SOUND, B.G.: THE TELEVISION. THE CAMERA DRAWS BACK. KATIE is sitting in the kitchen phone nook, having a good gab with her sister while she idles through some catalogues. We should notice one not-quite-ordinary thing about the phone she's on: it's the sort with two lines. There are LIGHTED BUTTONS to show which ones are engaged. Right now only one—KATIE's—is. As KATIE CONTINUES HER CONVERSATION, THE CAMERA SWINGS AWAY FROM HER, TRACKS*[2] *ACROSS THE KITCHEN, and through the arched doorway that leads into the family room.*]

KATIE. [*Voice, fading.*] Oh, I saw Janie Charlton today . . . yes! Big as a *house!* . . .

[*She fades. The TV gets louder. There are three kids: JEFF, eight, CONNIE, ten, and DENNIS, thirteen.* Wheel of Fortune *is on, but they're not watching. Instead they're engaged in that great pastime, Fighting About What Comes On Later.*]

JEFF. Come *onnn!* It was his first *book!*

CONNIE. His first *gross* book.

DENNIS. We're gonna watch *Cheers* and *Wings*, just like we do every week, Jeff.

[*DENNIS speaks with the utter finality*[3] *only a big brother can manage. "Wanna talk about it some more and see how much pain I can inflict on your scrawny body, Jeff?" his face says.*]

JEFF. Could we at least tape it?

1. *Lodge brothers* are men who belong to the same social club. Lodges sometimes have special ceremonies that seem mysterious to outsiders.

2. When a movie camera *tracks,* it moves smoothly. Often, it's mounted on a little wheeled platform that moves along a set of tracks.

3. Dennis speaks with complete *(utter)* decisiveness *(finality)*.

CONNIE. We're taping CNN[4] for Mom. She said she might be on the phone with Aunt Lois for quite awhile.

JEFF. How can you tape CNN? It *never stops!*

DENNIS. That's what she likes about it.

[*JEFF gets up, walks to the window, and looks out into the dark. He's really upset. DENNIS and CONNIE, in the grand tradition of older brothers and sisters, are delighted to see it.*]

DENNIS. Poor Jeffie.

JEFF. [*Turns to them.*] It was his *first* book! Don't you guys even *care?*

CONNIE. Rent it down at the Video Stop tomorrow, if you want to see it so bad.

JEFF. They don't rent R-rated pictures to little kids and you know it!

CONNIE. [*Dreamily.*] Shut up, it's Vanna! I *love* Vanna!

JEFF. Dennis—

DENNIS. Go ask Dad to tape it on the VCR in his office and quit being such a totally annoying little kid.

[*JEFF crosses the room, poking his tongue out at Vanna White as he goes. THE CAMERA FOLLOWS as he goes into the kitchen.*]

KATIE. . . . so when he asked me if *Polly* had tested strep positive, I had to remind him she's away at prep school . . .[5] and Lois, I miss her . . .

[*JEFF is just passing through, on his way to the stairs.*]

KATIE. Will you kids *please* be quiet?

JEFF. [*Glum.*] They'll be quiet. *Now.*

[*He goes up the stairs, a little dejected. KATIE looks after him for a moment, loving and worried.*]

KATIE. They're squabbling again. Polly used to keep them in line, but now that she's away at school . . . I don't know . . . maybe sending her to Bolton wasn't such a hot idea. Sometimes when she calls home she sounds so *unhappy* . . .

[*INT. BELA LUGOSI[6] AS DRACULA, CU. Drac's standing at the door of his Transylvanian castle. Someone has pasted a comic-balloon coming out of his mouth which reads: "Listen! My children of the night! What music they make!" The poster is on a door, but we only see this as JEFF opens it and goes into his father's study. INT. A PHOTOGRAPH OF KATIE, CU. THE CAMERA HOLDS, THEN PANS[7] SLOWLY RIGHT. We pass another photo, this one of POLLY, the daughter away at school. She's a lovely girl of sixteen or so. Past POLLY is DENNIS . . . then CONNIE . . . then JEFF. THE CAMERA CONTINUES TO PAN AND ALSO WIDENS OUT so we can see BILL WEIDERMAN, a man of about forty-four.*]

4. *CNN* stands for Cable News Network.
5. *Strep,* or strep throat infection, is caused by the streptococcus bacteria. A *prep school* is a private high school that prepares students for college; Polly's school, Bolton, is also a boarding school.
6. Following this horrifyingly successful 1931 film, *Bela Lugosi* (bel′ ə lo͞o gō′ sē) went on to play other movie monsters and mad scientists, as well as ordinary people.
7. When a movie camera *pans,* it makes a slow, sweeping movement to capture a series of images that represent one continuous scene.

Vocabulary

dejected (di jek′ tid) *adj.* sad; depressed; in low spirits

He looks tired. He's peering into the word-processor on his desk, but his mental crystal ball must be taking the night off, because the screen is blank. On the walls we see framed book-covers. All of them are spooky. One of the titles is Ghost Kiss.

JEFF comes up quietly behind his dad. The carpet muffles his feet. BILL sighs and shuts off the word-cruncher. A moment later JEFF claps his hands on his father's shoulders.]

JEFF. *BOOGA-BOOGA!*

BILL. Hi, Jeffie.

[*He turns in his chair to look at his son, who is disappointed.*]

JEFF. How come you didn't get scared?

BILL. Scaring is my business. I'm case-hardened.[8] Something wrong?

JEFF. Daddy, can I watch the first hour of *Ghost Kiss* and you tape the rest? Dennis and Connie are hogging *everything*.

[*BILL swivels to look at the book-jacket, bemused.*]

BILL. You sure you want to watch *that*, champ? It's pretty—

JEFF. *Yes!*

[*INT. KATIE, IN THE PHONE NOOK.*

In this shot, we clearly see the stairs leading to her husband's study behind her.]

BILL. Scaring is my business.

KATIE. I *really* think Jeff needs the orthodontic[9] work but you know Bill—

[*The other line rings. The other light stutters.*]

KATIE. That's just the other line, Bill will—

[*But now we see BILL and JEFF coming downstairs behind her.*]

BILL. Honey, where're the blank video-tapes? I can't find any in the study and—

KATIE. [*To BILL.*] *Wait!* [*To LOIS.*] Gonna put you on hold a sec, Lo.

[*She does. Now both lines are blinking. She pushes the top one, where the new call has just come in.*]

KATIE. Hello, Weiderman residence.

[*SOUND: DESPERATE SOBBING.*]

SOBBING VOICE. [*Filter.*][10] Take . . . please take . . . t-t-

KATIE. Polly? Is that you? What's wrong?

[*SOUND: SOBBING. It's awful, heartbreaking.*]

SOBBING VOICE. [*Filter.*] *Please—quick—*

[*SOUND: SOBBING . . . Then, CLICK! A broken connection.*]

KATIE. Polly, calm down! Whatever it is can't be that b—

[*HUM OF AN OPEN LINE.*

JEFF has wandered toward the TV room, hoping to find a blank tape.]

8. *Case-hardened* means "made callous or insensitive." Bill's business is scaring people through his writing, so he is used to all the scary tricks.

9. *Orthodontic* work refers to a type of dentistry involving irregularities of the teeth. Jeff may need braces to straighten his teeth.

10. An electronic *filter* makes the actor's voice sound as if it is coming over the telephone line. The actor has to do the sobbing.

BILL. Who was that?

[*Without looking at her husband or answering him,* KATIE *slams the lower button in again.*]

KATIE. Lois? Listen, I'll call you back. That was Polly, and she sounded very upset. No . . . she hung up. Yes. I will. Thanks.

[*She hangs up.*]

BILL. [*Concerned.*] It was Polly?

KATIE. Crying her head off. It sounded like she was trying to say "Please take me home" . . . I knew that school was bumming her out . . . Why I ever let you talk me into it . . .

[*She's rummaging frantically on her little phone desk. Catalogues go slithering to the floor around her stool.*]

KATIE. *Connie did you take my address book?*

CONNIE. [*Voice.*] No, Mom.

[BILL *pulls a battered book out of his back pocket and pages through it.*]

BILL. I got it. Except—

KATIE. I know, that dorm phone is always busy. Give it to me.

BILL. Honey, calm down.

KATIE. I'll calm down after I talk to her. She is sixteen, Bill. Sixteen-year-old girls are prone to depressive interludes.[11] Sometimes they even k . . . just give me the number!

BILL. 617-555-8641.

[*As she punches the numbers,* THE CAMERA SLIDES IN TO CU.]

KATIE. Come on, come on . . . don't be busy . . . just this once . . .

[SOUND: CLICKS. *A pause. Then . . . the phone starts ringing.*]

KATIE. [*Eyes closed.*] Thank You, God.

VOICE. [*Filter.*] Hartshorn Hall, this is Frieda. If you want Christine, she's still in the shower, Arnie.

KATIE. Could you call Polly to the phone? Polly Weiderman? This is Kate Weiderman. Her mother.

VOICE. [*Filter.*] Oh! sorry. I thought—hang on, please, Mrs. Weiderman.

[SOUND: THE PHONE CLUNKS DOWN.]

VOICE. [*Filter, and very faint.*] Polly? Pol? . . . Phone call! . . . It's your mother!

[INT. A WIDER ANGLE ON THE PHONE NOOK, WITH BILL.]

BILL. Well?

KATIE. Somebody's getting her. I hope.

[JEFF *comes back in with a tape.*]

JEFF. I found one, Dad. Dennis hid 'em. As usual.

BILL. In a minute, Jeff. Go watch the tube.

JEFF. But—

BILL. I won't forget. Now go *on.*

[JEFF *goes.*]

KATIE. Come on, come on, come on . . .

BILL. Calm down, Katie.

KATIE. [*Snaps.*] If you'd heard her, you wouldn't tell me to calm down! She sounded—

POLLY. [*Filter, cheery voice.*] Hi, mom!

KATIE. Pol? Honey? Are you all right?

POLLY. [*Happy, bubbling voice.*] Am I *all right?* I aced my bio exam, got a B on my French Conversational Essay, and Ronnie Hansen asked me to the Harvest Ball. I'm

11. People who are *prone to depressive interludes* get depressed occasionally.

so all right that if one more good thing happens to me today, I'll probably blow up like the *Hindenburg*.[12]

KATIE. You didn't just call me up, crying your head off?

[*We see by* KATIE*'s face that she already knows the answer to this question.*]

POLLY. [*Filter.*] Heck no!

KATIE. I'm glad about your test and your date, honey. I guess it was someone else. I'll call you back, okay?

POLLY. [*Filter.*] 'Kay. Say hi to Dad!

KATIE. I will.

[*INT. THE PHONE NOOK, WIDER.*]

BILL. She okay?

KATIE. Fine. I could have *sworn* it was Polly, but . . . *she's* walking on air.

BILL. So it was a prank. Or someone who was crying so hard she dialed a wrong number . . . "through a shimmering film of tears," as we veteran hacks[13] like to say.

KATIE. It was not a prank and it was not a wrong number! It was someone in *my family!*

BILL. Honey, you can't know that.

KATIE. No? If Jeffie called up, just crying, would you know it was him?

BILL. [*Struck by this.*] Yeah, maybe. I guess I might.

[*She's not listening. She's punching numbers, fast.*]

BILL. Who you calling?

[*She doesn't answer him.* SOUND: PHONE RINGS TWICE. *Then:*]

OLDER FEMALE VOICE. [*Filter.*] Hello?

KATIE. Mom? Are you . . . [*She pauses.*] Did you call just a few seconds ago?

VOICE. [*Filter.*] No, dear . . . why?

KATIE. Oh . . . you know these phones. I was talking to Lois and I lost the other call.

VOICE. [*Filter.*] Well, it wasn't me. Kate, I saw the *prettiest* dress in La Boutique today, and—

KATIE. We'll talk about it later, Mom, okay?

VOICE. [*Filter.*] Kate, are you all right?

KATIE. I have . . . Mom, I have to go. 'Bye. [*She hangs up. Then, to Bill:*] *I tell you it was someone in my family and she sounded*—oh, you don't understand. I *knew* that voice.

BILL. But if Polly's okay and your mom's okay . . .

KATIE. [*Positive.*] It's Dawn.

BILL. Come on, hon, a minute ago you were sure it was Polly.

KATIE. It *had* to be Dawn. I was on the phone with Lois and Mom's okay so Dawn's the only other one it *could* have been. She's the youngest . . . I could have mistaken her for Polly . . . and she's out there in that farmhouse alone with the baby!

BILL. [*Startled.*] What do you mean, alone?

KATIE. Jerry's in Burlington! It's Dawn! *Something's happened to Dawn!*

[CONNIE *comes into the kitchen, worried.*]

CONNIE. Mom? Is Aunt Dawn okay?

BILL. So far as we know, she's fine. Take it easy, doll. Bad to buy trouble before you know it's on sale.

12. In 1937 the airship *Hindenburg* exploded in midair and crashed to the ground.

13. Bill is poking fun at himself. *Hacks* are authors whose books sell well even though the writing is dull and unimaginative, like the overused phrase Bill gives as an example.

[KATIE punches numbers and listens. SOUND: The DAH-DAH-DAH of a busy signal. KATIE hangs up. BILL looks a question at her with raised eyebrows.]

KATIE. Busy.

BILL. Katie, are you sure—

KATIE. She's the only one left—it had to be her. Bill, I'm scared. Will you drive me out there?

[BILL takes the phone from her.]

BILL. What's her number?

KATIE. 555-6169.

[BILL dials. Gets a busy. Hangs up and punches 0.]

OPERATOR. *[Filter.]* Operator.

BILL. I'm trying to reach my sister-in-law, operator. The line is busy. I suspect there may be a problem. Can you break into the call, please?

Housecall, 1995. Diana Ong. Computer graphic. Private collection.

Viewing the art: What might the woman's expression tell the viewer about the topic of this call?

[INT. THE DOOR TO THE TV ROOM. All three kids are standing there, silent and worried. INT. THE PHONE NOOK, WITH BILL AND KATIE.]

OPERATOR. *[Filter.]* What is your name, sir?

BILL. William Weiderman. My number is—

OPERATOR. *[Filter.]* Not the William Weiderman that wrote *Spider Doom?!*

BILL. Yes, that was mine. If—

OPERATOR. *[Filter.]* Oh, I just *loved* that book! I love *all* your books! I—

BILL. I'm delighted you do. But right now my wife is very worried about her sister. If it's possible for you to—

OPERATOR. *[Filter.]* Yes, I can do that. Please give me your number, Mr. Weiderman, for the records. *[She GIGGLES.]* I *promise* not to give it out.

BILL. It's 555-4408.

OPERATOR. [*Filter.*] And the call number?

BILL. [*Looks at* KATIE.] Uh . . .

KATIE. 555-6169.

BILL. 555-6169.

OPERATOR. [*Filter.*] Just a moment, Mr. Weiderman . . . *Night of the Beast* was also great, by the way. Hold on.

[*SOUND: TELEPHONIC CLICKS AND CLACKS.*]

KATIE. Is she—

BILL. Yes. Just . . .

[*There's one final* CLICK.]

OPERATOR. [*Filter.*] I'm sorry, Mr. Weiderman, but that line is not busy. It's off the hook. I wonder if I sent you my copy of *Spider Doom*—

[*BILL hangs up the phone.*]

KATIE. Why did you hang up?

BILL. She can't break in. Phone's not busy. It's off the hook.

[*They stare at each other bleakly.*
EXT. A LOW-SLUNG SPORTS CAR PASSES THE CAMERA. NIGHT.
INT. THE CAR, WITH KATIE AND BILL.
KATIE's scared. BILL, at the wheel, doesn't look exactly calm.]

KATIE. Hey, Bill—tell me she's all right.

BILL. She's all right.

KATIE. Now tell me what you really think.

BILL. Jeff snuck up behind me tonight and put the old booga-booga on me. He was disappointed when I didn't jump. I told him I was case-hardened. [*Pause.*] I lied.

KATIE. Why did Jerry have to move out there when he's gone half the time? Just her and that little tiny baby? *Why?*

BILL. Shh, Kate. We're almost there.

KATIE. Go faster.

[*EXT. THE CAR.*
He does. That car is smokin'.
INT. THE WEIDERMAN TV ROOM.
The tube's still on and the kids are still there, but the horsing around has stopped.]

CONNIE. Dennis, do you think Aunt Dawn's okay?

DENNIS. [*Thinks she's dead, decapitated*[14] *by a maniac.*] Yeah. Sure she is.

[*INT. THE PHONE, POV FROM THE TV ROOM.*
Just sitting there on the wall in the phone nook, lights dark, looking like a snake ready to strike.
FADE OUT.]

ACT 2

[*EXT. AN ISOLATED FARMHOUSE.*
A long driveway leads up to it. There's one light on in the living room. Car lights sweep up the driveway. The WEIDERMAN car pulls up close to the garage and stops.
INT. THE CAR, WITH BILL AND KATIE.]

KATIE. I'm scared.

[*BILL bends down, reaches under his seat, and brings out a pistol.*]

BILL. [*Solemnly.*] Booga-booga.

KATIE. [*Total surprise.*] How long have you had that?

BILL. Since last year. I didn't want to scare you or the kids. I've got a license to carry. Come on.

[*EXT. BILL AND KATIE.*

14. While he tries to reassure Connie, Dennis actually fears that Dawn has had her head chopped off—that she has been *decapitated*.

They get out. KATIE *stands by the front of the car while* BILL *goes to the garage and peers in.*]

BILL. Her car's here.

[THE CAMERA TRACKS WITH THEM *to the front door. Now we can hear the TV,* PLAYING LOUD. BILL *pushes the doorbell. We hear it inside. They wait.* KATIE *pushes it. Still no answer. She pushes it again and doesn't take her finger off.* BILL *looks down at:*

EXT. THE LOCK, BILL'S POV.

Big scratches on it.

EXT. BILL AND KATIE.]

BILL. [*Low.*] The lock's been tampered with.

[KATIE *looks, and whimpers.* BILL *tries the door. It opens. The TV is louder.*]

BILL. Stay behind me. Be ready to run if something happens. Gosh, I wish I'd left you home, Kate.

[*He starts in.* KATIE *comes after him, terrified, near tears.*

INT. DAWN AND JERRY'S LIVING ROOM.

From this angle we see only a small section of the room. The TV is much louder. BILL *enters the room, gun up. He looks to the right . . . and suddenly all the tension goes out of him. He lowers the gun.*]

KATIE. [*Draws up beside him.*] Bill . . . what . . .

[*He points.*

INT. THE LIVING ROOM, WIDE, BILL AND KATIE'S POV.

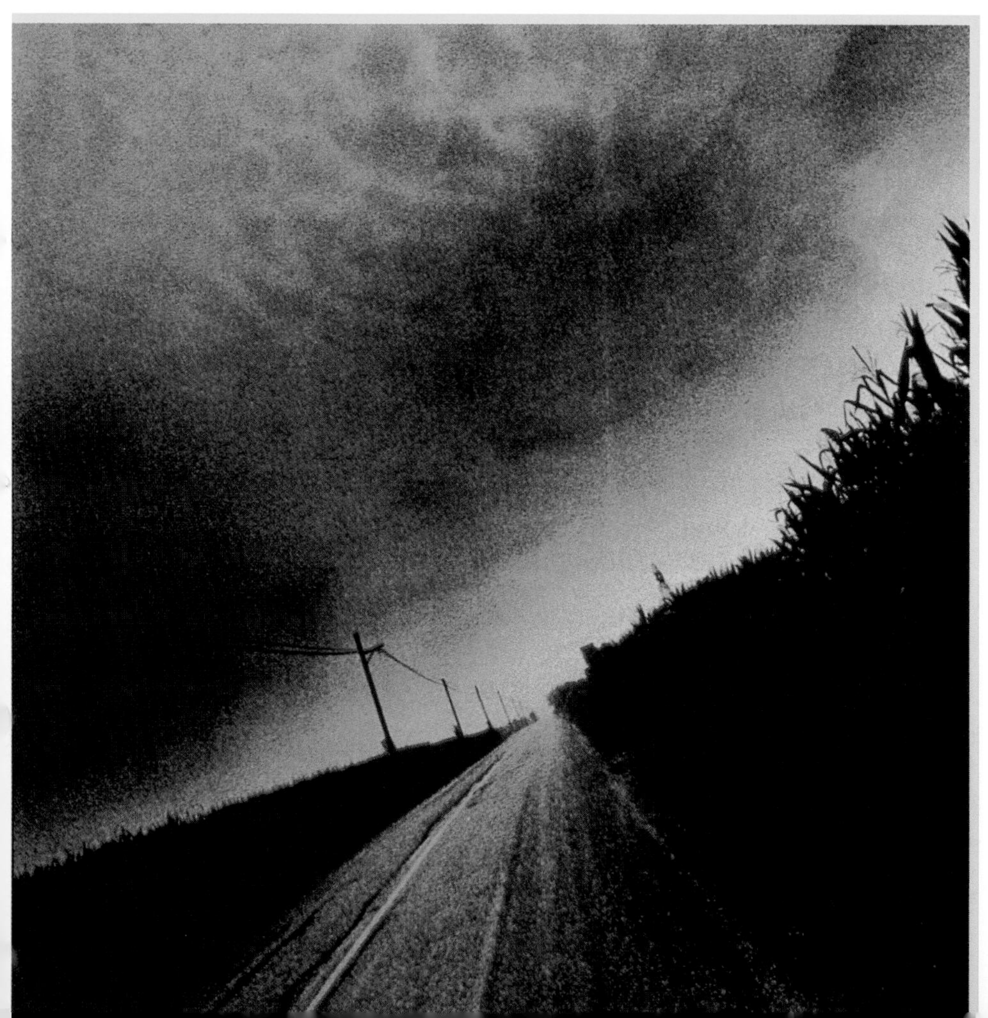

Viewing the photograph: What mood in the screenplay does this picture reflect? How do you think the photographer achieved the mood?

The place looks like a cyclone hit it . . . but it wasn't robbery and murder that caused this mess; only a healthy eighteen-month-old baby. After a strenuous *day of trashing the living room, Baby got tired and Mommy got tired and they fell asleep on the couch together. The baby is in* DAWN's *lap. There is a pair of Walkman earphones on her head. There are toys—tough plastic Sesame Street and PlaySkool stuff, for the most part—scattered all over. The baby has also pulled most of the books out of the bookcase. Had a good munch on one of them, too, by the look.* BILL *goes over and picks it up. It is* Ghost Kiss.]

BILL. I've had people say they just eat my books up, but this is ridiculous.

[*He's amused.* KATIE *isn't. She walks over to her sister, ready to be mad . . . but she sees how really exhausted* DAWN *looks and softens.*

INT. DAWN AND THE BABY, KATIE'S POV.

Fast asleep and breathing easily, like a Raphael painting of Madonna and Child. THE CAMERA PANS DOWN TO: *the Walkman. We can hear the faint strains of Huey Lewis and the News.*[15] THE CAMERA PANS A BIT FURTHER TO *a Princess telephone on the table by the chair. It's off the cradle. Not much; just enough to break the connection and scare people to death.*

INT. KATIE.

She sighs, bends down, and replaces the phone. Then she pushes the STOP *button on the Walkman.*

INT. DAWN, BILL, AND KATIE.

DAWN *wakes up when the music stops. Looks at* BILL *and* KATIE, *puzzled.*]

DAWN. [*Fuzzed out.*] Well . . . hi.

[*She realizes she's got the Walkman phones on and removes them.*]

BILL. Hi, Dawn.

DAWN. [*Still half asleep.*] Shoulda called, guys. Place is a mess.

[*She smiles. She's radiant when she smiles.*]

KATIE. We *tried.* The operator told Bill the phone was off the hook. I thought something was wrong. How can you sleep with that music blasting?

DAWN. It's restful. [*Sees the gnawed book* BILL's *holding.*] Oh, Bill, I'm sorry! Justin's teething and—

BILL. There are critics who'd say he picked just the right thing to teethe on. I don't want to scare you, beautiful, but somebody's been at your front door lock with a screwdriver or something. Whoever it was forced it.

DAWN. Gosh, no! That was Jerry, last week. I locked us out by mistake and he didn't have his key and the spare wasn't over the door like it's supposed to be. So he took the screwdriver to it. It didn't work, either—that's one tough lock.

BILL. If it wasn't forced, how come I could just open the door and walk in?

DAWN. [*Guiltily.*] Well . . . sometimes I forget to lock it.

KATIE. You didn't call me tonight, Dawn?

DAWN. Gee, no! I didn't call *anyone!* I was too busy chasing Justin around! He kept

15. ***Raphael's*** famous painting shows the infant Jesus on his mother's lap, and *Huey Lewis and the News* was a popular rock band, not a news program.

Vocabulary
strenuous (stren′ ū əs) *adj.* very active; energetic

wanting to eat the fabric softener! Then he got sleepy and I sat down here and thought I'd listen to some tunes while I waited for your movie to come on, Bill, and I fell asleep—

[*At the mention of the movie* BILL *starts visibly and looks at the book. Then he glances at his watch.*]

BILL. I promised to tape it for Jeff. Come on, Katie, we've got time to get back.

KATIE. Just a second.

[*She picks up the phone and dials.*]

DAWN. Gee, Bill, do you think Jeffie's old enough to watch something like that?

BILL. It's network. They take out the blood-bags.

DAWN. [*Confused but amiable.*] Oh. That's good.

[*INT.* KATIE, CU.]

DENNIS. [*Filter.*] Hello?

KATIE. Just thought you'd like to know your Aunt Dawn's fine.

DENNIS. [*Filter.*] Oh! Cool. Thanks, Mom.

[*INT.* THE PHONE NOOK, WITH DENNIS AND THE OTHERS. *He looks* very *relieved.*]

DENNIS. Aunt Dawn's okay.

[*INT.* THE CAR, WITH BILL AND KATIE. *They drive in silence for awhile.*]

KATIE. You think I'm a hysterical idiot, don't you?

BILL. [*Genuinely surprised.*] No! I was scared, too.

KATIE. You sure you're not mad?

BILL. I'm too relieved. [*Laughs.*] She's sort of a scatterbrain, old Dawn, but I love her.

KATIE. [*Leans over and kisses him.*] I love *you*. You're a sweet man.

BILL. I'm the *boogeyman!*

KATIE. I am not fooled, sweetheart.

[*EXT.* THE CAR. PASSES THE CAMERA *and we* DISSOLVE[16] TO:

INT. JEFF, IN BED. *His room is dark. The covers are pulled up to his chin.*]

JEFF. You *promise* to tape the rest?

[CAMERA WIDENS OUT *so we can see* BILL, *sitting on the bed.*]

BILL. I promise.

JEFF. I especially liked the part where the dead guy ripped off the punk rocker's head.

BILL. Well . . . they *used* to take out all the blood-bags.

JEFF. What, Dad?

BILL. Nothing. I love you, Jeffie.

BILL. I was scared, too.

16. In film, to *dissolve* is to fade out on one scene while the next scene fades in and becomes clearer.

Vocabulary
amiable (ā′ mē ə bəl) *adj.* friendly, good-natured

JEFF. I love you, too. So does Rambo.

[JEFF holds up a stuffed dragon of decidedly unmilitant aspect.[17] *BILL kisses the dragon, then JEFF.]*

BILL. 'Night.

JEFF. 'Night. [*As BILL reaches his door.*] Glad Aunt Dawn was okay.

BILL. Me too.

[He goes out.
INT. TV, CU.
A guy who looks like he died in a car crash about two weeks prior to filming (and has since been subjected to a lot of hot weather) is staggering out of a crypt.[18] *THE CAMERA WIDENS to show BILL, releasing the VCR PAUSE button.]*

KATIE. [*Voice.*] Booga-booga.

[BILL looks around companionably. THE CAMERA WIDENS OUT MORE to show KATIE, wearing a nightgown.]

BILL. Same to you. I missed the first forty seconds or so after the break. I had to kiss Rambo.

KATIE. You sure you're not mad at me, Bill?

[He goes to her and kisses her.]

BILL. Not even a smidge.

KATIE. It's just that I could have sworn it was one of mine. You know what I mean? One of mine?

BILL. Yes.

KATIE. I can still hear those sobs. So lost . . . so heartbroken.

BILL. Kate, have you ever thought you recognized someone on the street, and called her, and when she finally turned around it was a total stranger?

KATIE. Yes, once. In Seattle. I was in a mall and I thought I saw my old roommate. I . . . oh. I see what you're saying.

BILL. Sure. There are sound-alikes as well as look-alikes.

KATIE. But . . . *you know your own.* At least I thought so until tonight.

[She puts her cheek on his shoulder, looking troubled.]

KATIE. I was so *positive* it was Polly . . .

BILL. Because you've been worried about her getting her feet under her at the new school . . . but judging from the stuff she told you tonight, I'd say she's doing just fine in that department. Wouldn't you?

KATIE. Yes . . . I guess I would.

BILL. Let it go, hon.

KATIE. [*Looks at him closely.*] I hate to see you looking so tired. Hurry up and have an idea, you.

BILL. Well, I'm trying.

KATIE. You coming to bed?

BILL. Soon as I finish taping this for Jeff.

KATIE. [*Amused.*] Bill, that machine was made by Japanese technicians who think of everything. It'll run on its own.

BILL. Yeah, but it's been a long time since I've seen this one, and . . .

KATIE. Okay. Enjoy. I think I'll be awake for a little while. [*Pause.*] I've got a few ideas of my own.

BILL. [*Smiles.*] Yeah?

KATIE. Yeah.

[She starts out, then turns in the doorway as something else strikes her.]

KATIE. If they show that part where the punk's head gets—

---

17. The toy's *unmilitant aspect* is a nonthreatening appearance.
18. A *crypt* is a burial chamber.

BILL. [*Guiltily.*] I'll edit it.

KATIE. 'Night. And thanks again. For everything.

[*She leaves. BILL sits in his chair.*
INT. TV, CU.
A couple is necking in a car. Suddenly the passenger door is ripped open by the dead guy and we DISSOLVE TO:
INT. KATIE, IN BED.
It's dark. She's asleep. She wakes up . . . sort of.

KATIE. [*Sleepy.*] Hey, big guy—

[*She feels for him, but his side of the bed is empty, the coverlet still pulled up. She sits up. Looks at:*
INT. A CLOCK ON THE NIGHT-TABLE, KATIE'S POV.
It says 2:03 A.M. Then it flashes to 2:04.
INT. KATIE.
Fully awake now. And concerned. She gets up, puts on her robe, and leaves the bedroom.
INT. THE TV SCREEN, CU.
Snow.]

KATIE. [*Voice, approaching.*] Bill? Honey? You okay? Bill? Bi—

[*INT. KATIE, IN BILL'S STUDY.*
She's frozen, wide-eyed with horror.
INT. BILL, IN HIS CHAIR.
He's slumped to one side, eyes closed, hand inside his shirt. DAWN was sleeping. BILL is not.
EXT. A COFFIN, BEING LOWERED INTO A GRAVE.]

MINISTER. [*Voice.*] And so we commit the earthly remains of William Weiderman to the ground, confident of his spirit and soul. "Be ye not cast down, brethren . . ."

[*EXT. GRAVESIDE.*
All the WEIDERMANS are ranged here. KATIE and POLLY wear identical black dresses and veils. CONNIE wears a black skirt and white blouse. DENNIS and JEFF wear black suits. JEFF is crying. He has Rambo the Dragon under his arm for a little extra comfort.
CAMERA MOVES IN ON KATIE. Tears course slowly down her cheeks. She bends and gets a handful of earth. Tosses it into the grave.

KATIE. Love you, big guy.

[*EXT. JEFF.*
Weeping.
EXT. LOOKING DOWN INTO THE GRAVE.
Scattered earth on top of the coffin.
DISSOLVE TO:
EXT. THE GRAVE.
A GROUNDSKEEPER pats the last sod into place.]

GROUNDSKEEPER. My wife says she wishes you'd written a couple more before you had your heart attack, mister. [*Pause.*] I like Westerns, m'self.

[*THE GROUNDSKEEPER walks away, whistling.*
DISSOLVE TO:
EXT. A CHURCH. DAY.
TITLE CARD: FIVE YEARS LATER.
THE WEDDING MARCH is playing. POLLY, older and radiant with joy, emerges into a pelting shower of rice. She's in a wedding gown, her new husband by her side. Celebrants throwing rice line either side of the path. From behind the bride and groom come others. Among them are KATIE, DENNIS, CONNIE, and JEFF . . . all five

years older. With KATIE is another man. This is HANK. In the interim, KATIE has also taken a husband.
POLLY turns and her mother is there.]

POLLY. Thank you, Mom.

KATIE. [*Crying.*] Oh doll, you're so welcome.

[*They embrace. After a moment POLLY draws away and looks at HANK. There is a brief moment of tension, and then POLLY embraces HANK, too.*]

POLLY. Thank you too, Hank. I'm sorry I was such a creep for so long . . .

HANK. [*Easily.*] You were never a creep, Pol. A girl only has one father.

CONNIE. Throw it! Throw it!

[*After a moment, POLLY throws her bouquet.*
EXT. THE BOUQUET, CU, SLOW MOTION. Turning and turning through the air.
DISSOLVES TO:
INT. THE STUDY, WITH KATIE. NIGHT. The word-processor has been replaced by a wide lamp looming over a stack of blueprints. The book jackets have been replaced by photos of buildings. Ones that have first been built in HANK's mind, presumably. KATIE is looking at the desk, thoughtful and a little sad.]

HANK. [*Voice.*] Coming to bed, Kate?

Vocabulary
interim (in′ tər im) *n.* the time between events; meantime
presumably (pri zo͞o′ mə blē) *adv.* supposedly; probably

Viewing the photograph: Why is a bouquet important in this play? What does it symbolize?

[*She turns and* THE CAMERA WIDENS OUT *to give us* HANK. *He's wearing a robe over pajamas. She comes to him and gives him a little hug, smiling. Maybe we notice a few streaks of gray in her hair; her pretty pony has done its fair share of running*[19] *since* BILL *died.*]

KATIE. In a little while. A woman doesn't see her first one get married every day, you know.

HANK. I know.

[THE CAMERA FOLLOWS *as they walk from the work area of the study to the more informal area. This is much the same as it was in the old days, with a coffee table, stereo, TV, couch, and* BILL*'s old easy-chair. She looks at this.*]

HANK. You still miss him, don't you?

KATIE. Some days more than others. You didn't know, and Polly didn't remember.

HANK. [*Gently.*] Remember what, doll?

KATIE. Polly got married on the five-year anniversary of Bill's death.

HANK. [*Hugs her.*] Come on to bed, why don't you?

KATIE. In a little while.

19. *[her pretty . . . running]* The passage of time has left Katie looking and feeling older.

HANK. Okay. Maybe I'll still be awake.

[*He kisses her, then leaves, closing the door behind him.* KATIE *sits in* BILL*'s old chair. Close by, on the coffee table, is a remote control for the TV and an extension phone.* KATIE *looks at the blank TV, and* THE CAMERA MOVES IN *on her face. One tear rims one eye, sparkling like a sapphire.*]

KATIE. I *do* still miss you, big guy. Lots and lots. Every day. And you know what? It hurts.

[*The tear falls. She picks up the TV remote and pushes the* ON *button.*

INT. TV, KATIE'S POV.

An ad for Ginsu Knives comes to an end and is replaced by a STAR LOGO.

ANNOUNCER. [*Voice.*] Now back to Channel 63's Thursday night Star Time Movie . . . *Ghost Kiss.*

[*The logo* DISSOLVES INTO *a guy who looks like he died in a car crash about two weeks ago and has since been subjected to a lot of hot weather. He comes staggering out of the same old crypt.*

INT. KATIE.

Terribly startled—almost horrified. She hits the OFF *button on the remote control. The TV blinks off.*

KATIE*'s face begins to work. She struggles against the impending emotional storm, but the coincidence of the movie is just one thing too many on what must have*

HANK. You still miss him, don't you?

Vocabulary

impending (im pen′ ding) *adj.* about to occur

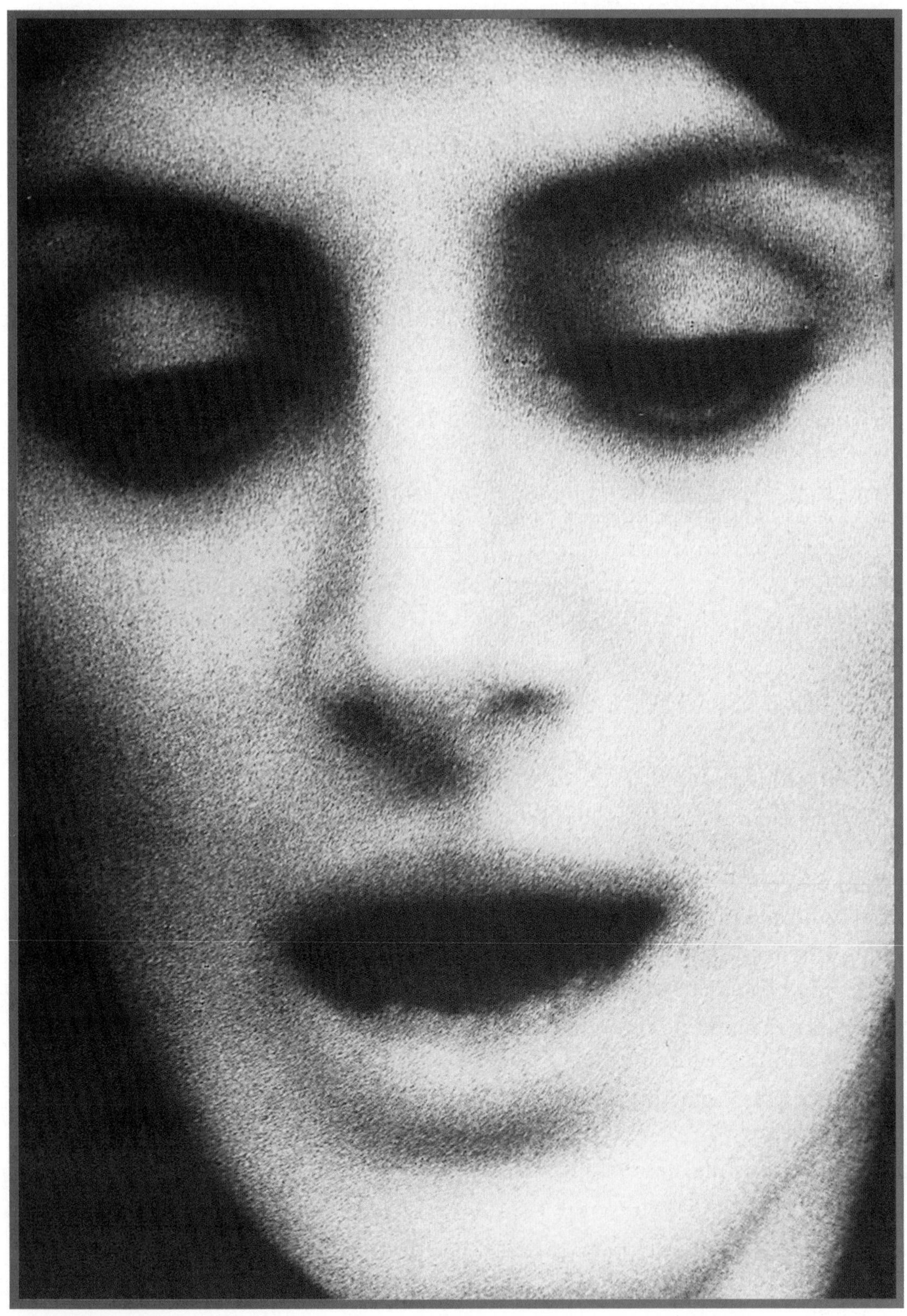

Viewing the photograph: How do the emotions shown in this photograph compare with Katie's feelings and her state of mind?

already been one of the most emotionally trying days of her life. The dam breaks and she begins to sob . . . terrible heart-broken sobs. She reaches out for the little table by the chair, meaning to put the remote control on it, and knocks the phone onto the floor.
SOUND: The HUM OF AN OPEN LINE.
Her tear-stained face grows suddenly still as she looks at the telephone. Something begins to fill it . . . an idea? an intuition? Hard to tell. And maybe it doesn't matter.
INT. THE TELEPHONE, KATIE'S POV.
THE CAMERA MOVES IN TO ECU . . .
MOVES IN until the dots in the off-the-hook receiver look like chasms.
SOUND OF OPEN-LINE BUZZ UP TO LOUD.
WE GO INTO THE BLACK . . . and hear:]

BILL. [*Voice.*] Who are you calling? Who do you *want* to call? Who *would* you call, if it wasn't too late?

[*INT. KATIE.*
There is now a strange hypnotized look on her face. She reaches down, scoops the telephone up, and punches in numbers, seemingly at random.
SOUND: RINGING PHONE.
KATIE continues to look hypnotized. The look holds until the phone is answered . . . and she hears herself *on the other end of the line.*]

KATIE. [*Voice; filter.*] Hello, Weiderman residence.

[*KATIE—our present-day KATIE with the streaks of gray in her hair—goes on sobbing, yet an expression of desperate hope is trying to be born on her face. On some level she understands that the depth of her grief has allowed a kind of telephonic time-travel. She's trying to talk, to force the words out.*]

KATIE. [*Sobbing.*] Take . . . please take . . . t-t-

[*INT. KATIE, IN THE PHONE NOOK, REPRISE.*[20]
It's five years ago. BILL is standing beside her, looking concerned. JEFF is wandering off to look for a blank tape in the other room.]

KATIE. Polly? What's wrong?

[*INT. KATIE, IN THE STUDY.*]

KATIE. [*Sobbing.*] *Please—quick—*

[*SOUND: CLICK OF A BROKEN CONNECTION.*]

KATIE. [*Screaming.*] *Take him to the hospital! If you want him to live, take him to the hospital! He's going to have a heart attack! He—*

[*SOUND: HUM OF AN OPEN LINE.*
Slowly, very slowly, KATIE hangs up the telephone. Then after a moment, she picks it up again. She speaks aloud with no self-consciousness whatever. Probably doesn't even know she's doing it.]

KATIE. I dialed the old number. I dialed—

[*SLAM CUT*[21] *TO:*
INT. BILL, IN THE PHONE NOOK WITH KATIE BESIDE HIM.
He's just taken the phone from KATIE and is speaking to the operator.]

OPERATOR. [*Filter,* GIGGLES.] I *promise* not to give it out.

BILL. It's 555-

[*SLAM CUT TO:*
INT. KATIE, IN BILL' S OLD CHAIR, CU.]

---

20. The repetition of an earlier scene or part of a scene is a *reprise* (ri prēz′).
21. A *slam cut* is a sudden shift to another scene, with no fade-out or dissolve.

Vocabulary
chasm (kaz′ əm) *n.* a deep hole or crack, as in the earth's surface

KATIE. [*Finishes.*] -4408.

[*INT. THE PHONE, CU.*
KATIE's trembling finger carefully picks out the number, and we hear the corresponding tones: 555-4408.
INT. KATIE, IN BILL'S OLD CHAIR, CU.
She closes her eyes as the PHONE BEGINS TO RING. Her face is filled with an agonizing mixture of hope and fear. If only she can have one more chance to pass the vital message on, it says . . . just one more chance.]

KATIE. [*Low.*] Please . . . please . . .

RECORDED VOICE. [*Filter.*] You have reached a non-working number. Please hang up and dial again. If you need assistance—

[*KATIE hangs up again. Tears stream down her cheeks. THE CAMERA PANS AWAY AND DOWN to the telephone.*
INT. THE PHONE NOOK, WITH KATIE AND BILL, REPRISE.]

BILL. So it was a prank. Or someone who was crying so hard she dialed a wrong number . . . "through a shimmering film of tears," as we veteran hacks like to say.

KATIE. It was not a prank and it was not a wrong number! It was someone in *my family!*

[*INT. KATIE (PRESENT DAY) IN BILL'S STUDY.*]

KATIE. Yes. Someone in my family. Someone very close. [*Pause.*] Me.

[*She suddenly throws the phone across the room. Then she begins to SOB AGAIN and puts her hands over her face. THE CAMERA HOLDS on her for a moment, then DOLLIES*[22] *ACROSS TO:*
INT. THE PHONE.
It lies on the carpet, looking both bland and somehow ominous. CAMERA MOVES IN TO ECU—the holes in the receiver once more look like huge dark chasms. We HOLD, then
FADE TO BLACK.]

22. When a movie camera *dollies,* it moves smoothly, either on tracks or wheels.

Vocabulary
bland (bland) *adj.* dull and uninteresting

Responding to Literature

PERSONAL RESPONSE

Did the ending of this play surprise you? Why or why not?

Analyzing Literature

RECALL

1. What is Katie saying about Bill as the play begins?
2. Who does Katie think is sobbing at the other end of the phone line?
3. Why do the Weidermans drive to Dawn's house?
4. Why is the date of Polly's wedding important to Katie?

INTERPRET

5. What do the stage directions tell the audience about Katie's attitude toward Bill's headache?
6. Why do you think Katie draws the conclusion she does about the phone call?
7. Why is Bill's gun important in act 2?
8. After Polly's wedding, whom does Katie call, and why is she able to make the phone call?

EVALUATE AND CONNECT

9. Theme Connection Many of Stephen King's stories have normal, everyday settings and characters. Do you think this makes the horror part more or less frightening when it comes?
10. *Sorry, Right Number* is a horror story with very little blood or gore. The character Bill Weiderman writes stories with lots of gore. Which kind of story appeals to you? List several reasons for your answer.

LITERARY ELEMENTS

Screenplay

A **screenplay** is the script of a film, which contains dialogue, stage directions, and instructions about camera shots and angles. A screenplay is very much like the script for a stage play.

Dialogue is preceded by the name of the speaker, just as it is in a stage play script. A screenplay also includes stage directions in brackets and italic type. These directions are written for directors, actors, and camera operators. For example, when Connie asks if Dawn is okay, Dennis replies, "Yeah. Sure she is." However, readers know from the stage direction that he really thinks she's been decapitated by a maniac. An actor must show by expression, tone, and gestures what Dennis really thinks.

1. How do the stage directions that describe Bill's office add to your understanding of the character?
2. Would you prefer to *see* this story as a movie instead of reading the screenplay? Why or why not?

- See **Literary Terms Handbook,** p. R9.

Literature and Writing

Writing About Literature

For the Role of the Dead Writer . . . Imagine you work for a film producer. *Sorry, Right Number* is one of a dozen screenplays you're assigned to evaluate. Write a few paragraphs telling the producer your opinion of the story. Would it make a good movie? Should your boss invest several million dollars in it? Why or why not? What actors would you recommend to play the characters?

Creative Writing

Fill in the Blanks The play jumps from Bill's funeral to Polly's wedding five years later. Write a page of a screenplay from Polly's point of view, filling in some of the blanks in those five years. What happens when she learns of her father's death? How does she feel about Hank, her mother's new husband? Use the screenplay format, with dialogue and stage directions.

Extending Your Response

Interdisciplinary Activity

Music Before a movie is released, a composer scores it–adds music to heighten the emotional impact. Look through CDs or tapes and identify music that would enhance *Sorry, Right Number.* Make a list of the titles and musicians, and determine where in the movie they should be played. If you own the CDs, bring them to class and play the tracks you've chosen.

Literature Groups

Boo! Bill spends his career trying to scare his readers. Jeff tries unsuccessfully to scare him. Katie is afraid the movie version of *Ghost Kiss* will scare the kids, but in fact, Jeff's favorite part is the goriest. Review your notes from the **Focus Activity** on page 790. In a group, discuss scaring people: What's the point? Is it better to be the scarer or the scared?

Performing

Acting Up With a group of three students, act out the scene in which Jeff, Connie, and Dennis first appear. Remember to follow the stage directions regarding your voice inflections and movements.

Reading Further

Other novels that use time shifts and suspense are:
Tangerine by Edward Bloor
Alien Game by Catherine Dexter

Save your work for your portfolio.

Skill Minilessons

GRAMMAR AND LANGUAGE • END PUNCTUATION

The three types of punctuation used to end a sentence are the period, the question mark, and the exclamation point. A period ends a declarative statement: "He'll be fine." or a mild imperative: "Then don't call me Jeffie." A question mark ends an interrogative sentence: "Could we at least tape it?" An exclamation point shouts: "It never stops!"

PRACTICE Rewrite each sentence, using correct end punctuation.

1. What's your name
2. I promised to tape the movie for Jeff
3. It was not a wrong number
4. I suspect there may be a problem
5. Are you sure you want to watch that movie

- For more about punctuation, see **Language Handbook,** pp. R38–R43.

READING AND THINKING • TEXT STRUCTURE: SEQUENCE OF EVENTS

Authors organize their writing in different ways depending on their purpose and topic. The pattern of organization that a writer uses is called **text structure.** One important type of text structure is chronological order, which presents events in the sequence in which they occur. In *Sorry, Right Number,* Stephen King uses chronological order and also **flashback,** which interrupts the sequence and moves the action back in time. The end of the play flashes back and forth between the older Katie making the phone call and the younger Katie receiving it. This flashback creates an intense mood and brings the play to its conclusion.

PRACTICE Reread the last few pages of the play. List the places where the time order changes. The first flashback occurs when Katie hears her own voice answer, "Hello, Weiderman residence." Where does the action flash forward again? back again? How do you know? What does the flashback tell you about Katie and her feelings? What do you think was King's purpose in using flashback in this play? Explain.

- For more about text structures and sequencing, see **Reading Handbook,** pp. R87–R89.

VOCABULARY • LATIN ROOT *JECT*

The word *dejected* comes from the Latin prefix *de-*, meaning "down," and the root *ject,* meaning "to throw." A *dejected* person feels "thrown down." If you *reject* something, you "throw" it back. If you *inject* a comment, you "throw" it in. The prefix *ob-*, meaning "against," is used in *object.* When you *object* to an idea, you "throw" something "against" it. Below are some of the prefixes that have been attached to *ject* to create words:

inter-: between   *pro-*: forward   *e-*: out

PRACTICE Use the meaning of *ject* and the prefixes on the left to answer the questions.

1. If someone *interjects* a comment, does the person interrupt, shout, or repeat something?
2. Which of the following is most useful to an *ejected* pilot—a windshield, a parachute, or radar?
3. Which weapon is designed to be used as a *projectile*—an arrow, a sword, or a battering ram?

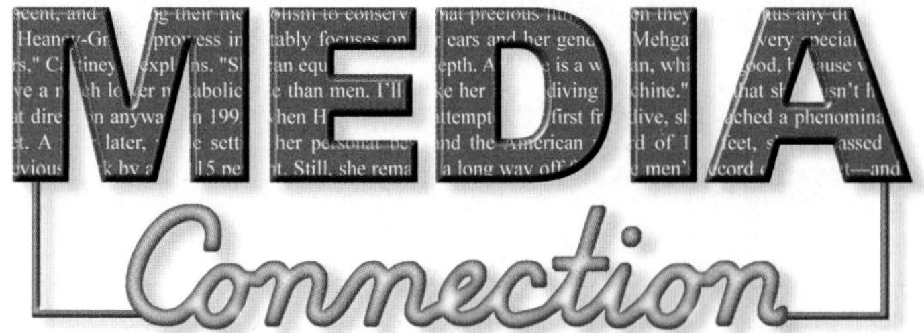

TELEVISION TRANSCRIPT

Do you enjoy horror stories? Reporters Cokie Roberts and Jeff Greenfield lead a discussion of America's "obsession with the dark side."

American Gothic

from *ABC Nightline*, December 10, 1997

COKIE ROBERTS

It's safe to say that kids have always been fascinated by scary stuff—terrifying fairy tales, ghost stories on camping trips, horror movies so popular they have sequels in the double digits, not to mention the delight over slimy substances and artificial bugs and snakes. But now grownups seem to be getting in on the fun, celebrating Halloween in a big way, watching TV shows and movies that can't be called cheery by any description and reading millions and millions of books by authors like Anne Rice and Stephen King. King has sold one book for every American, over 250 million of them.

JEFF GREENFIELD

These are the good times, right? The cold war is over, the economy is booming, unemployment is dropping, inflation is gone, the budget is almost balanced, even the crime rate is falling. So here's something to puzzle over. If the reality is so sunny, why are the stories we're drawn to so dark? If it is morning in America, why is so much of our fact and fiction coming from round midnight?

COKIE ROBERTS

Mr. King, your books have certainly been incredibly popular. You've heard this discussion about all of the meaningfulness in this. Are we reading too much into this or are people just having fun reading your books?

STEPHEN KING

Yeah, I think you probably are reading a little bit too much into it. . . . We like to be scared, we like to pretend, we like to make believe.

COKIE ROBERTS

But haven't children liked to be scared from time out of mind? I mean the Brothers Grimm and Hans Christian Andersen did a pretty good job of scaring them.

STEPHEN KING

Sure, and the inheritors of the Brothers Grimm and Hans Christian Andersen are people like R. L. Stine. . . . Being scared for fun is something that's always appealed to young people. It's not much different than the roller coaster thing or, you know, the loop-de-loop thing, only it's at the movie theater where you can get dark, put your arm around your girlfriend or your boyfriend and enjoy being scared.

Respond

1. What is your answer to the question "Why are the stories we're drawn to so dark?"
2. How are modern-day horror stories similar to old fairy tales?

LISTENING, SPEAKING, and VIEWING

Critical Viewing

"Seeing is believing," people used to say–but that was before the era of special effects. Today, you know that what you see, whether on television, in films, or on the Internet, can't always be taken at face value. A smart viewer is a critical viewer: not necessarily one who finds fault, but one who thinks carefully about what he or she sees. The following questions can help you evaluate what you find on the screen.

Questions for Critical Viewing

What's the purpose?

- Are you viewing something made to entertain, to inform, or to persuade? Purpose affects accuracy. If a film is made to entertain, it may not be accurate in every detail, even when based on real-life events. If an infomercial has two purposes–to inform viewers and to sell a product–it may omit facts that would decrease sales.

Are statements supported by facts?

- Do you detect a bias–a "slant" that reflects personal views? Watch for manipulation of statistics and for opinions presented as facts.

Is the subject presented fairly?

- Are there "loaded" images or words–ones designed to trigger emotions? Appeals to emotion shouldn't lead viewers to ignore the voice of reason.

What's the source?

- Who created the material you're viewing? Is the creator known for artistry, accuracy, or independent thinking–or for sensationalism or bias? (A librarian can help you find out.)

What are the details?

- When, where, and how was the material produced? How might these conditions affect its content?

ACTIVITIES

1. With a partner or on your own, view a televised news show. Use the **Questions for Critical Viewing** to evaluate it, and share your evaluation with your class.
2. Use the **Questions for Critical Viewing** to evaluate a mysterious or chilling event that you've seen on film or on television. Write a paragraph explaining your evaluation.

Vo•cab•u•lar•y Skills

Using Base Words

In *Sorry, Right Number,* the stage directions describe the office of Bill Weiderman five years after his death: "The book jackets have been replaced by photos of buildings. Ones that have first been built in Hank's mind, *presumably.*"

If you don't know what *presumably* means, how can you figure it out? The base word, *presume,* may be a familiar word that can help you guess at the meaning. A **base word** can stand alone or it can be the basis of other words. Suffixes or prefixes or both can be attached to a base word to make new words.

Prefixes often change the meaning of a word, as when *applicable* becomes *inapplicable.* Suffixes, on the other hand, often merely change the part of speech, as when *apply* becomes *applicable.* (An exception to this is *-less;* clearly, *hope* and *hopeless* have very different meanings.)

The spelling of the end of a base word often changes when a suffix is added. The *y* in *apply* disappears when *applicable* is formed. The *e* in *suppose* changes to an *i* to make *supposition.* Even so, base words are usually obvious if you look for them.

If you come across an unfamiliar word, look at it carefully to see if it has a base word you know. A familiar base word can help you understand a new word.

- For more about spelling base words, see **Language Handbook,** pp. R46–R49.

EXERCISES

1. Write the base word from which each word below was formed. (Remember, a vowel at the end of a base word may disappear when a suffix is added.)
   a. punster
   b. begrime
   c. finery
   d. presuppose
   e. finality
   f. accredited
   g. pressurized
   h. generalization
   i. accusatory
   j. disembodied
2. Use your knowledge of the base words and familiar prefixes and suffixes in the underlined words to answer each question.
   a. If Katie has a feeling of <u>disquietude</u>, is she relieved, tired, or upset?
   b. Is a <u>prophetic</u> phone call one that tells about danger, the future, or the past?
   c. If an event of the past is <u>irreversible</u>, is it unknown, unchangeable, or unimportant?
   d. If a fear is <u>inexpressible</u>, is it one that cannot be said, explained, or relieved?
   e. If Katie <u>theorizes</u> about who has called, does that mean she is guessing who it was, describing the voice, or becoming frightened?

Before You Read

The Legend of Sleepy Hollow

MEET WASHINGTON IRVING

The Hudson River Valley in New York is the setting of Washington Irving's eerie and popular short story, "The Legend of Sleepy Hollow." Irving lived and traveled in the region. Then, while traveling in Europe, he was encouraged by the famous writer Sir Walter Scott to publish stories and essays based on his travels. As a result, Irving published *The Sketch Book of Geoffrey Crayon, Gent* in 1820. "The Legend of Sleepy Hollow" and "Rip Van Winkle," another tale from *The Sketch Book*, are considered by many to be the first American short stories.

Washington Irving was born in 1783 and died in 1859. "The Legend of Sleepy Hollow" was first published in The Sketch Book *in 1820.*

FOCUS ACTIVITY

What stories about scary or unexplainable events have you heard in your community?

Share It!

Share a scary story or ghost story with a partner, and then listen to your partner tell you one. What do your two stories have in common?

Setting a Purpose

Read to discover what makes "The Legend of Sleepy Hollow" a scary tale.

BACKGROUND

The Time and Place Irving based "The Legend of Sleepy Hollow" on an old German legend. However, he Americanized it, placing it in New York's Hudson River Valley near the village of Tarrytown, sometime in the 1800s. Some of the characters in this story are of Dutch descent. Many Dutch people settled in what is now New York.

VOCABULARY PREVIEW

dominant (dom′ ə nənt) *adj.* having the greatest power or force; controlling; p. 817

apparition (ap′ ə rish′ ən) *n.* ghostly vision; p. 817

conscientious (kon′ shē en′ shəs) *adj.* guided by one's conscience; showing careful attention to what is right and wrong; p. 818

speculation (spek′ yə lā′ shən) *n.* an opinion or conclusion based on guesswork; p. 819

perceive (pər sēv′) *v.* to take in or grasp mentally; notice; p. 820

renown (ri noun′) *n.* widespread reputation; fame; p. 821

wary (wār′ ē) *adj.* cautious; on the alert; p. 822

pensive (pen′ siv) *adj.* thinking deeply, often about something sad; p. 822

aloof (ə lo͞of′) *adj.* emotionally distant; uninvolved; standoffish; p. 826

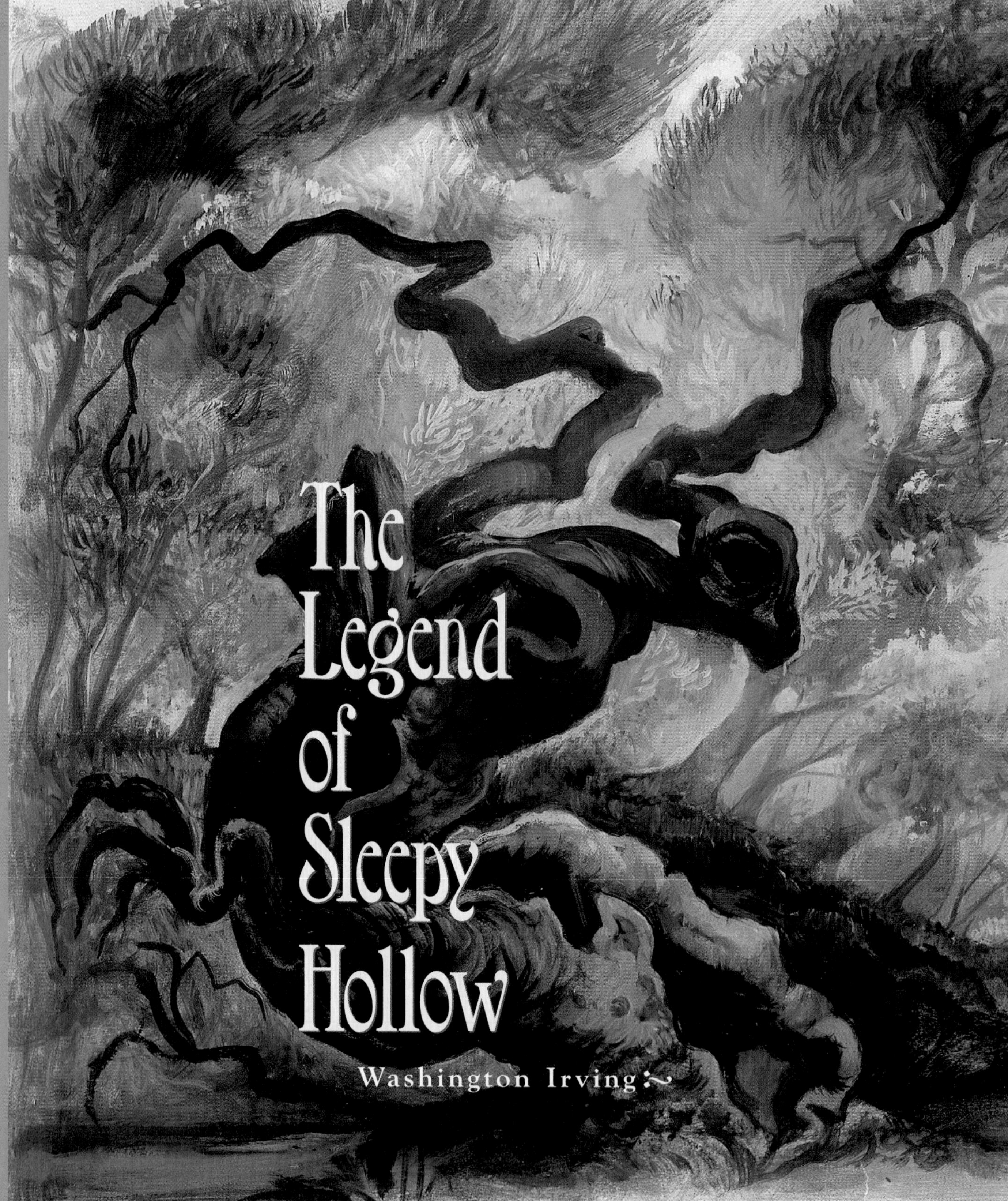

Illustration © 1990 by Russ Flint from *The Legend of Sleepy Hollow.*

In the bosom of one of those spacious coves which indent the eastern shore of the Hudson, there lies a small market town, which by some is called Greensburgh, but which is more generally and properly known by the name of Tarrytown. This name was given by the good housewives of the adjacent[1] country, from the tendency of their husbands to linger about the village tavern on market days. Not far from this village, perhaps about two miles, there is a little valley among high hills, which is one of the quietest places in the whole world. A small brook glides through it, with just murmur enough to lull one to repose, and the occasional whistle of a quail, or tapping of a woodpecker, is almost the only sound that ever breaks in upon the uniform tranquility.[2] This glen has long been known by the name of Sleepy Hollow.

A drowsy, dreamy influence seems to hang over the land. The whole neighborhood abounds with local tales, haunted spots, and twilight superstitions. The dominant spirit, however, that haunts this enchanted region is the apparition of a figure on horseback without a head. It is said by some to be the ghost of a Hessian trooper[3] whose head had been carried

1. *Adjacent* (ə jā′ sənt) means "surrounding" or "nearby."
2. *Tranquility* (trang kwil′ ə tē) means "peacefulness."
3. A *Hessian* (hesh′ ən) *trooper* is a German soldier who fought with the British during the American Revolution.

Vocabulary

dominant (dom′ ə nənt) *adj.* having the greatest power or force; controlling

apparition (ap′ ə rish′ ən) *n.* ghostly vision

away by a cannonball, in some nameless battle during the Revolutionary War. His haunts are not confined to the valley, but extend at times to the adjacent roads, and especially to the vicinity of a church at no great distance. Certain historians of those parts claim that the body of the trooper having been buried in the churchyard, the ghost rides forth to the scene of battle in nightly quest of his head; and that the rushing speed with which he sometimes passes along the Hollow is owing to his being late, and in a hurry to get back to the churchyard before daybreak. The specter[4] is known, at all the country firesides, by the name of the Headless Horseman of Sleepy Hollow.

In this by-place of nature, there abode, some thirty years since, a worthy fellow of the name of Ichabod Crane, who sojourned[5] in Sleepy Hollow for the purpose of instructing the children of the vicinity. The name of Crane was not inapplicable to his person.[6] He was tall, but exceedingly lank, with narrow shoulders, long arms and legs, hands that dangled a mile out of his sleeves, feet that might have served for shovels, and his whole frame most loosely hung together. To see him striding along the profile of a hill on a windy day, with his clothes bagging and fluttering about him, one might have mistaken him for the spirit of famine descending upon the earth, or some scarecrow eloped[7] from a cornfield.

4. A *specter* is a ghost.
5. Here, *abode* means "lived." *Ichabod* (ik′ ə bod). Someone who has *sojourned* has traveled.
6. The name *Crane* fit the man because he resembled a long-legged, long-necked bird.
7. Here, *eloped* means "run off" or "escaped."

His schoolhouse was a low building of one large room, rudely constructed of logs. From here the low murmur of his pupils' voices might be heard in a drowsy summer's day, like the hum of a beehive; interrupted now and then by the authoritative voice of the master, in the tone of menace or command; or, perhaps, by the appalling sound of the birch, as he urged some tardy loiterer along the flowery path of knowledge. Truth to say, he was a conscientious man, and ever bore in mind the golden maxim,[8] "Spare the rod and spoil the child."—Ichabod Crane's scholars certainly were not spoiled.

The revenue arising from his school was small, and would have been scarcely sufficient to furnish him with daily bread, for he was a huge feeder. To help out his maintenance, he was, according to country custom in those parts, boarded and lodged at the houses of the farmers whose children he instructed. With these he lived successively a week at a time, thus going the rounds of the neighborhood, with all his worldly effects tied up in a cotton handkerchief. In addition, he was the singing master of the neighborhood, and picked up many bright shillings by instructing the young folks in psalmody.[9] Thus, by various little makeshifts, the worthy pedagogue[10] got on tolerably enough, and was thought, by all who understood nothing of the labor of headwork, to have a wonderfully easy life of it.

8. A *maxim* is a saying.
9. *Psalmody* is the singing of hymns.
10. *Makeshifts* are things done in place of the proper or desired things. A *pedagogue* (ped′ ə gog′) is a teacher.

Vocabulary

conscientious (kon′ shē en′ shəs) *adj.* guided by one's conscience; showing careful attention to what is right and wrong

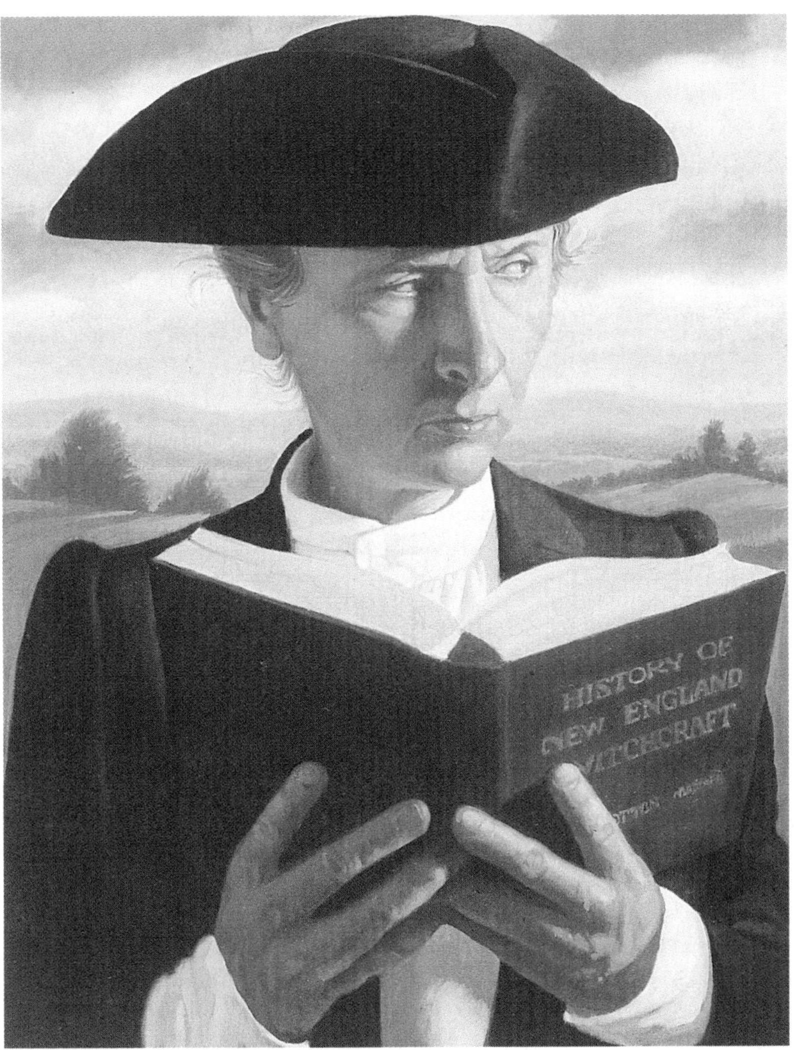

Illustration © 1992 by Michael Garland from *The Legend of Sleepy Hollow.*

Viewing the painting: Which of Ichabod Crane's characteristics are depicted in this painting?

The schoolmaster is generally a man of some importance in the female circle of a rural neighborhood, being considered of vastly superior taste and accomplishments to the rough country swains.[11] Our man was esteemed by the women as a man of great learning, for he had read several books quite through, and was a perfect master of Cotton Mather's[12] *History of New England Witchcraft*, in which, by the way, he most firmly believed. It was often his delight, after his school was dismissed in the afternoon, to stretch himself on the rich bed of clover bordering the little brook that whimpered by his schoolhouse, and there con over old Mather's direful[13] tales.

Another of his sources of fearful pleasure was to pass long winter evenings with the old Dutch wives and listen to their marvelous tales of ghosts and goblins, and haunted fields, and haunted brooks, and haunted bridges, and haunted houses, and particularly of the Headless Horseman, or Galloping Hessian of the Hollow, as they sometimes called him. He would delight them equally by his anecdotes of witchcraft, and would frighten them woefully with speculations upon comets and shooting stars, and with the alarming fact that the world did absolutely turn round, and that they were half the time topsy-turvy!

But if there was a pleasure in all this, it was dearly purchased by the terrors of his walk homewards later. What fearful shapes

11. *Swains* are young men or suitors.

12. *Cotton Mather* (1663–1728) wrote more than 450 books about religion, history, and medicine.

13. To *con over* is to study. *Direful* means "dreadful."

Vocabulary

speculation (spek′ yə lā′ shən) *n.* an opinion or conclusion based on guesswork and shadows beset his path amidst the dim and ghastly glare of a snowy night! And how often was he thrown into complete dismay by some rushing blast, howling among the trees, in the idea that it was the Galloping Hessian on one of his nightly scourings![14]

Among the musical disciples who assembled, one evening in each week, to receive his instructions in psalmody was Katrina Van Tassel, the daughter and only child of a prosperous Dutch farmer. She was a blooming lass of fresh eighteen; plump as a partridge; ripe and melting and rosy-cheeked as one of her father's peaches; and universally famed, not merely as a beauty, but as an heiress. She was a little of a coquette,[15] as might be perceived even in her dress, which was a mixture of ancient and modern fashions, as most suited to set off her charms.

Ichabod Crane had a soft and foolish heart, and it is not to be wondered at that so tempting a morsel soon found favor in his eyes, more especially after he had visited her in her paternal mansion.[16] Old Baltus Van Tassel was a perfect picture of a thriving, contented farmer. His stronghold was situated on the banks of the Hudson, in one of those green, sheltered, fertile nooks, in which the Dutch farmers are so fond of nestling. Close by the farmhouse was a vast barn that might have served for a church, every window and crevice of which seemed bursting forth with the treasures of the farm.

The pedagogue's mouth watered as he looked upon this sumptuous[17] promise of luxurious winter fare. In his devouring mind's eye he pictured to himself every roasting-pig running about him with a pudding in his belly, and an apple in his mouth. The pigeons were snugly put to bed in a comfortable pie and tucked in with a coverlet of crust; the geese were swimming in their own gravy. Not a turkey but he beheld daintily trussed up, with its gizzard under its wing, and, perhaps, a necklace of savory sausages.

As the enraptured[18] Ichabod fancied all this and as he rolled his great green eyes over the fat meadowlands, his heart yearned after the damsel who was to inherit these domains.

When he entered the house, the conquest of his heart was complete. It was one of those spacious farmhouses, with high-ridged but lowly sloping roofs, built in the style handed down from the first Dutch settlers, the low projecting eaves forming a piazza[19] along the front. From this piazza the wondering Ichabod entered the hall, which formed the center of the mansion. Here rows of resplendent pewter[20] ranged on a long dresser; a door left ajar gave him a peep into the best parlor, where the claw-footed chairs and dark mahogany tables shone like mirrors; and a corner cupboard, knowingly left open, displayed immense treasures of old silver and well-mended china.

From the moment that Ichabod laid his eyes upon these regions of delight, the peace of his mind was at an end, and his only

14. *Scourings* are searches.
15. A *coquette* (kō ket′) is a flirt.
16. A *morsel* is a small portion. A *paternal mansion* is a house belonging to a person's father.
17. *Sumptuous* means "costly, showy, and magnificent."
18. *Enraptured* means "carried away by intense joy or delight."
19. A *piazza* (pē az′ ə) is a large covered porch.
20. *Resplendent* (ri splen′ dənt) means "splendid" or "gleaming." *Pewter* is a mixture of tin, lead, and copper.

Vocabulary

perceive (pər sēv′) *v.* to take in or grasp mentally; notice study was how to gain the affections of the peerless[21] daughter of Van Tassel. In this enterprise, however, he had to encounter a host of fearful adversaries[22] of real flesh and blood, the numerous admirers who beset every portal to her heart, keeping a watchful and angry eye upon each other, but ready to fly out in the common cause against any new competitor.

Among these the most formidable was a burly, roaring, roistering blade,[23] of the name of Abraham, or, according to the Dutch abbreviation, Brom Van Brunt. He was broad-shouldered and double-jointed, with short, curly black hair, and a bluff but not unpleasant countenance, having a mingled air of fun and arrogance. From his Herculean[24] frame and great powers of limb, he had received the nickname of "Brom Bones," by which he was universally known. He was famed for great knowledge and skill in horsemanship. He was foremost at all races. He was always ready for either a fight or a frolic, but had more mischief than ill will in his composition; and, with all his overbearing roughness, there was a strong dash of waggish[25] good humor at bottom. He had three or four boon[26] companions, who regarded him as their model, and at the head of whom he scoured the country, attending every scene of feud or merriment for miles round.

This reckless hero had for some time singled out the blooming Katrina for the object of his gallantries, and it was whispered that she did not altogether discourage his hopes. Certain it is, his advances were signals for rival candidates to retire. When his horse was seen tied to Van Tassel's paling,[27] a sure sign that his master was courting within, all other suitors passed by in despair.

Such was the formidable rival with whom Ichabod Crane had to contend, and, considering all things, a stouter[28] man than he would have shrunk from the competition, and a wiser man would have despaired. He had, however, a happy mixture of pliability and perseverance[29] in his nature.

To have taken the field openly against his rivals would have been madness. Ichabod, therefore, made his advances in a quiet and gently insinuating[30] manner. Under cover of his character of singing master, he made frequent visits at the farmhouse.

I profess not to know how women's hearts are wooed and won. To me they have always been matters of riddle and admiration. He who wins a thousand common hearts is entitled to some renown; but he who keeps undisputed sway over the heart of a coquette is indeed a hero. Certain it is, this was not the case with the redoubtable[31] Brom Bones. From the moment Ichabod Crane made his advances, the interests of the former evidently declined. His horse

21. *Peerless* means "without equal; matchless."
22. *A host of fearful adversaries* is a large number of rivals.
23. *Formidable* (for′ mi də bəl) means "causing fear or awe due to size, strength, or power." A *roistering blade* is a lively and attractive young man.
24. *Herculean* (hur′ kyə lē′ ən) means "very strong and muscular," and is taken from the Greek hero *Hercules.*
25. *Waggish* means "humorous" or "friendly."
26. *Boon* means "merry."
27. A *paling* is one of the pickets of a fence.
28. *Stouter* means "braver" or "stronger."
29. *Pliability* is the ability to adjust to changes. *Perseverance* is determination to continue despite difficulty.
30. *Insinuating* means "suggesting indirectly; hinting."
31. Something that is *redoubtable* causes fear or awe and deserves respect.

Vocabulary

renown (ri noun′) *n.* widespread reputation; fame

was no longer seen tied at the palings on Sunday nights, and a deadly feud gradually arose between him and the schoolmaster of Sleepy Hollow.

Brom, who had a degree of rough chivalry in his nature, would have carried matters to open warfare, and have settled their pretensions to the lady according to the mode of the knights-errant of yore[32]—by single combat; but Ichabod was too conscious of the superior might of his adversary to enter the lists[33] against him. He had overheard a boast of Bones, that he would "double the schoolmaster up, and lay him on a shelf of his own schoolhouse"; and he was too wary to give him an opportunity. There was something extremely provoking in this obstinately pacific system; it left Brom no alternative but to play boorish[34] practical jokes upon his rival. Ichabod became the object of whimsical persecution to Bones and his gang of rough-riders. They harried his hitherto peaceful domains;[35] smoked out his singing school, by stopping up the chimney; broke into the schoolhouse at night and turned everything topsy-turvy; so that the poor schoolmaster began to think all the witches in the country held their meetings there.

In this way matters went on for some time, without producing any material effect on the relative situation of the rivals. On a fine autumn afternoon, Ichabod, in pensive mood, sat enthroned on the lofty stool whence he usually watched all the concerns of his little literary realm. His scholars were all busily intent upon their books, or slyly whispering behind them with one eye kept upon the master; and a kind of buzzing stillness reigned throughout the schoolroom. It was suddenly interrupted by the appearance of a man who came clattering up to the school door with an invitation to Ichabod to attend a merry-making, or "quilting frolic," to be held that evening at Mynheer[36] Van Tassel's.

All was now bustle and hubbub in the late quiet schoolroom. The scholars were hurried through their lessons; books were flung aside without being put away on the shelves; inkstands were overturned, benches thrown down; and the whole school was turned loose an hour before the usual time.

The gallant Ichabod now spent at least an extra half-hour brushing up his best and indeed only suit of rusty black, and arranging his locks by a bit of broken looking glass that hung up in the schoolhouse. That he might make his appearance before his mistress in the true style of a cavalier,[37] he borrowed a horse from the farmer with whom he was living and issued forth, like a knight-errant in quest of adventures. But

32. *Chivalry* (shiv′ əl rē) refers to the qualities of a knight, such as honor, courage, skill in battle, and respect for women. Here, *pretensions* are claims. *Knights-errant of yore* are wandering knights of long ago.
33. To *enter the lists* is to compete in a tournament.
34. The *obstinately pacific system* refers to Ichabod's stubborn refusal to compete openly with Brom. *Boorish* means "crude; bad-mannered."
35. Brom and his friends raided the schoolhouse–the one territory that Ichabod controlled *(his domains)* and that had been peaceful up to this time *(hitherto)*.
36. *Mynheer* (mīn hār′) is Dutch for *Mr.* or *Sir.* (The word is sometimes shortened to *Heer.*)
37. A *cavalier* is a gallant knight.

Vocabulary

wary (wār′ ē) *adj.* cautious; on the alert
pensive (pen′ siv) *adj.* thinking deeply, often about something sad

it is proper that I should, in the true spirit of romantic story, give some account of the looks and equipment of my hero and his steed. The animal he bestrode was a broken-down plow horse that had outlived almost everything but his viciousness. He was gaunt[38] and shaggy, with a thin neck and a head like a hammer; his rusty mane and tail were tangled and knotted with burrs. Still, he must have had fire in his day, if we may judge from the name he bore of Gunpowder.

Ichabod was a suitable figure for such a steed. He rode with short stirrups, which brought his knees nearly up to the pommel[39] of the saddle; his sharp elbows stuck out like grasshoppers'. He carried his whip perpendicularly in his hand, and, as his horse jogged on, the motion of his arms was not unlike the flapping of a pair of wings.

It was toward evening that Ichabod arrived at the castle of the Heer Van Tassel, which he found thronged[40] with the pride and flower of the adjacent country. Brom Bones, however, was a hero of the scene, having come to the gathering on his favorite steed, Daredevil, a creature, like himself, full of mettle[41] and mischief, which no one but himself could manage.

I pause to dwell upon the world of charms that burst upon the enraptured gaze of my hero as he entered the state parlor of Van Tassel's mansion. Not those of the lasses, but the ample charms of a genuine Dutch country tea table. There was the doughty doughnut, the tenderer olykoek, and the crisp and crumbling cruller;[42] sweet cakes and shortcakes, ginger cakes and honey cakes, and the whole family of cakes. And then there were apple pies and peach pies and pumpkin pies, besides slices of ham and smoked beef; not to mention broiled shad[43] and roasted chickens.

I want breath and time to discuss this banquet as it deserves, and am too eager to get on with my story. Happily, Ichabod Crane was not in so great a hurry as his historian, but did ample justice to every dainty.

He could not help, too, rolling his large eyes round him as he ate, and chuckling with the possibility that he might one day be lord of all this scene of almost unimaginable luxury and splendor. Then, he thought, how soon he'd turn his back upon the old schoolhouse and kick any itinerant[44] pedagogue out-of-doors that should dare to call him comrade!

And now the sound of the music from the common room, or hall, summoned to the dance. How could the flogger of urchins[45] be otherwise than animated and joyous? The lady of his heart was his partner in the dance, and smiling graciously in reply to all his amorous looks, while Brom Bones, sorely smitten with[46] love and jealousy, sat brooding by himself in one corner.

When the dance was at an end, Ichabod was attracted to a knot of the sager[47] folks, who, with old Van Tassel, sat smoking at one end of the piazza, gossiping over former

38. *Gaunt* means "looking like skin and bones."
39. The *pommel* of a saddle is the part that juts out at the front and top.
40. *Thronged* means "crowded."
41. *Mettle* is spirit and courage.
42. The *doughty* (dō′ tē), *olykoek* (ol′ i kook′), and *cruller* (krul′ ər) are three types of pastries.
43. *Shad* is a kind of fish.
44. *Itinerant* (ī tin′ ər ənt) means "traveling from place to place."
45. A *flogger of urchins* is one who whips children.
46. *Amorous* (am′ ər əs) means "loving; romantic." *Sorely smitten with* means "extremely affected by."
47. *Sager* (sāj′ ər) means "wiser" or "better educated."

times, and drawing out long stories about the war. But all these were nothing to the tales of ghosts and apparitions that succeeded.[48] Many dismal tales were told about funeral trains and mourning cries and wailings heard and seen about the great tree where the unfortunate Major André was taken, and which stood in the neighborhood. The chief part of the stories, however, turned upon the favorite specter of Sleepy Hollow, the Headless Horseman, who had been heard several times of late, patrolling the country, and, it was said, tethered his horse nightly among the graves in the churchyard.

The tale was told of old Brouwer, a disbeliever in ghosts, how he met the horseman returning from his foray into Sleepy Hollow, and was obliged to get up behind him; how they galloped over bush and brake, over hill and swamp, until they reached the bridge, when the horseman suddenly turned into a skeleton, threw old Brouwer into a brook, and sprang away over the treetops with a clap of thunder.

This story was immediately matched by a thrice-marvelous adventure of Brom Bones, who made light of the Galloping Hessian as an arrant jockey. He affirmed[49] that, on returning one night from the neighboring village of Sing Sing, he had been overtaken by this midnight trooper; that he had offered to race with him for a bowl of punch, and should have won it, too, for Daredevil beat the goblin horse all hollow, but, just as they came to the church bridge, the Hessian bolted, and vanished in a flash of fire.

All these tales sank deep in the mind of Ichabod. He repaid them in kind with large extracts[50] from his invaluable author, Cotton Mather, and added many fearful sights which he had seen in his nightly walks about Sleepy Hollow.

The revel now gradually broke up. Ichabod only lingered behind, according to the custom of country lovers, to have a tête-à-tête[51] with the heiress, fully convinced that he was now on the high road to success. What passed at this interview I will not pretend to say, for in fact I do not know. Something, however, must have gone wrong, for he certainly sallied forth, after no very great interval, with an air quite desolate and chopfallen.[52] Without looking to the right or left to notice the scene of rural wealth on which he had so often gloated, he went straight to the stable, and with several hearty cuffs and kicks, roused his steed most uncourteously from the comfortable quarters.

It was the very witching time of night that Ichabod, heavy-hearted and crestfallen, pursued his travel homewards.

All the stories of ghosts and goblins that he had heard in the afternoon now came crowding upon his recollection. He had never felt so lonely and dismal. He was, moreover, approaching the very place where many of the scenes of the ghost stories had been laid. In the center of the road stood an enormous tulip tree. It was connected with the tragical story of the unfortunate André, who had been taken prisoner close by, and was universally known by the name of Major André's Tree.

48. Here, *succeeded* means "followed; came after."
49. *Made light of* means "joked about." *Arrant* (ar′ ənt) means "outright." *Affirmed* means "stated firmly and positively."
50. *Extracts* are passages or images from a book.
51. A *tête-à-tête* (tet′ ə tet′) is a private conversation between two people.
52. *Sallied forth* means "went out briskly." Someone who is *chopfallen* is discouraged or downhearted.

About two hundred yards from the tree a small brook crossed the road, and ran into a marshy and thickly wooded glen, known by the name of Wiley's Swamp. A few rough logs, laid side by side, served for a bridge over this stream. To pass this bridge was the severest trial. It was at this identical spot that the unfortunate André was captured. This has ever since been considered a haunted stream, and fearful are the feelings of the schoolboy who has to pass it alone after dark.

As he approached the stream his heart began to thump. He summoned up, however, all his resolution, gave his horse half a score of kicks in the ribs, and attempted to dash briskly across the bridge. But instead of starting forward, the perverse old animal made a lateral[53] movement, and ran broadside against the fence. Ichabod, whose fears increased with the delay, jerked the reins on the other side and kicked lustily with the opposite foot. It was all in vain. His steed started, it is true, but it was only to plunge to the opposite side of the road into a thicket of brambles and alder bushes. Just at this moment a splashing step by the side of the bridge caught the sensitive ear of Ichabod. In the dark shadow of the grove, on the margin of the brook, he beheld something huge, misshapen, black, and

Illustration © 1992 by Michael Garland from *The Legend of Sleepy Hollow.*

Viewing the painting: How could you explain this picture if you hadn't read the story?

53. *Perverse* means "stubbornly determined to go against what is expected or desired." *Lateral* means "sideways."

towering. It stirred not, but seemed gathered up in the gloom, like some gigantic monster ready to spring upon the traveler.

The hair of the affrighted pedagogue rose upon his head with terror. What was to be done? To turn and fly was now too late; and besides, what chance was there of escaping ghost or goblin, if such it was, which could ride upon the wings of the wind? Summoning up, therefore, a show of courage, he demanded in stammering accents, "Who are you?" He received no reply. He repeated his demand in a still more agitated voice. Still there was no answer. Just then the shadowy object of alarm put itself in motion, and, with a scramble and a bound, stood at once in the middle of the road. Though the night was dark and dismal, yet the form of the unknown might now in some degree be made out. He appeared to be a horseman of large dimensions, and mounted on a black horse of powerful frame. He made no offer of harm or sociability, but kept aloof on one side of the road, jogging along on the blind side of old Gunpowder, who had now got over his fright and waywardness.

Ichabod, who had no relish[54] for this strange midnight companion, and bethought himself of the adventure of Brom Bones with the Galloping Hessian, now quickened his steed, in hopes of leaving him behind. The stranger, however, quickened his horse to an equal pace. Ichabod pulled up and fell into a walk, thinking to lag behind—the other did the same. There was something in the moody and dogged silence of this persistent companion that was mysterious and appalling. It was soon fearfully accounted for. On mounting a rising ground, which brought the figure of his fellow traveler in relief against the sky, gigantic in height, and muffled in a cloak, Ichabod was horror-struck on perceiving that he was headless—but his horror was still more increased on observing that the head, which should have rested on his shoulders, was carried before him on the pommel of the saddle. His terror rose to desperation. He rained a shower of kicks and blows upon Gunpowder, hoping, by a sudden movement, to give his companion the slip—but the specter started full jump with him.

They had now reached the road which turns off to Sleepy Hollow; but Gunpowder, who seemed possessed with a demon, instead of keeping on it, made an opposite turn, and plunged headlong downhill to the left. This road leads through a sandy hollow, and just beyond swells the green knoll on which stands the whitewashed church.

As yet the panic of the steed had given his unskillful rider an apparent advantage in the chase; but just as he had got halfway through the hollow the girths[55] of the saddle gave way, and he felt it slipping from under him. He seized it by the pommel, and endeavored to hold it firm, but in vain; and he had just time to save himself by clasping old Gunpowder round the neck, when the saddle fell to the earth, and he heard it trampled underfoot by his pursuer. The goblin was hard on his

54. *Relish for* means "enjoyment of" or "interest in."

55. *Girths* are straps passed under the horse's belly to hold the saddle on.

Vocabulary

aloof (ə lo͞of′) *adj.* emotionally distant; uninvolved; standoffish haunches; and (unskillful rider that he was!) he had much ado to maintain his seat, sometimes slipping on one side, sometimes on another, and sometimes jolted on the high ridge of his horse's backbone, with a violence that he feared would cleave him asunder.[56]

An opening in the trees now cheered him with the hopes that the church bridge was at hand. He recollected the place where Brom Bones's ghostly competitor had disappeared. "If I can but reach that bridge," thought Ichabod, "I am safe." Just then he heard the black steed panting and blowing close behind him; he even fancied that he felt his hot breath. Another convulsive kick in the ribs, and old Gunpowder sprang upon the bridge; he thundered over the resounding planks; he gained the opposite side; and now Ichabod cast a look behind to see if his pursuer would vanish, according to the rule, in a flash of fire and brimstone.[57] Just then he saw the goblin rising in his stirrups, and in the very act of hurling his head at him. Ichabod endeavored to dodge the horrible missile, but too late. It encountered his cranium with a tremendous crash—he was tumbled headlong into the dust, and Gunpowder, the black steed, and the goblin rider passed by like a whirlwind.

The next morning the old horse was found without his saddle, and with the bridle under his feet, soberly cropping the grass at his master's gate. Ichabod did not make his appearance at breakfast—dinner hour came, but no Ichabod. The boys assembled at the schoolhouse, and strolled idly about the banks of the brook, but no schoolmaster. An inquiry was set on foot, and after diligent investigation they came upon his traces. In one part of the road leading to the church was found the saddle trampled in the dirt. The tracks of horses' hoofs deeply dented in the road, and evidently at furious speed, were traced to the bridge, beyond which, on the bank of a broad part of the brook, where the water ran deep and black, was found the hat of the unfortunate Ichabod, and close beside it a shattered pumpkin.

The brook was searched, but the body of the schoolmaster was not to be discovered. The mysterious event caused much speculation at the church on the following Sunday. Knots of gazers and gossips were collected in the churchyard, at the bridge, and at the spot where the hat and pumpkin had been found. The stories of Brouwer, of Bones, and a whole store of others, were called to mind; and when they had diligently considered them all, and compared them with the symptoms of the present case, they shook their heads, and came to the conclusion that Ichabod had been carried off by the Galloping Hessian. As he was a bachelor, and in nobody's debt, nobody troubled his head any more about him. The school was removed to a different quarter of the Hollow, and another pedagogue reigned in his stead.

It is true, an old farmer, who had been down to New York on a visit several years after, and from whom this account of the ghostly adventure was received, brought home word that Ichabod Crane was still alive; that he had left the neighborhood, partly through fear of the goblin and

56. *Much ado* is great difficulty. To *cleave him asunder* means "to tear him to pieces."

57. *Brimstone* is smelly, yellow smoke. The "flash" would show that the goblin was from hell, which is said to burn with fire and brimstone.

partly in mortification[58] at having been suddenly dismissed by the heiress. Brom Bones, too, who shortly after his rival's disappearance conducted the blooming Katrina in triumph to the altar, was observed to look exceedingly knowing whenever the story of Ichabod was related, and always burst into a hearty laugh at the mention of the pumpkin, which led some to suspect that he knew more about the matter than he chose to tell.

The old country wives, however, who are the best judges of these matters, maintain to this day that Ichabod was spirited away by supernatural means.[59] The bridge became more than ever an object of superstitious awe; the schoolhouse, being deserted, soon fell to decay, and was reported to be haunted by the ghost of the unfortunate pedagogue; and the plowboy, loitering homeward of a still summer evening, has often fancied his voice at a distance, chanting a melancholy psalm tune among the tranquil solitudes[60] of Sleepy Hollow.

58. *Mortification* is great shame or embarrassment.

59. The country wives blamed Crane's disappearance on ghosts or some other unnatural, unearthly methods.

60. *Solitudes* are lonely, isolated places.

Illustration © 1990 by Russ Flint from *The Legend of Sleepy Hollow.*

Viewing the painting: Could this be a modern scene? Why or why not?

Responding to Literature

PERSONAL RESPONSE

What would you do if you thought you were being chased by a ghostly figure? Jot down a few words of advice for Ichabod Crane.

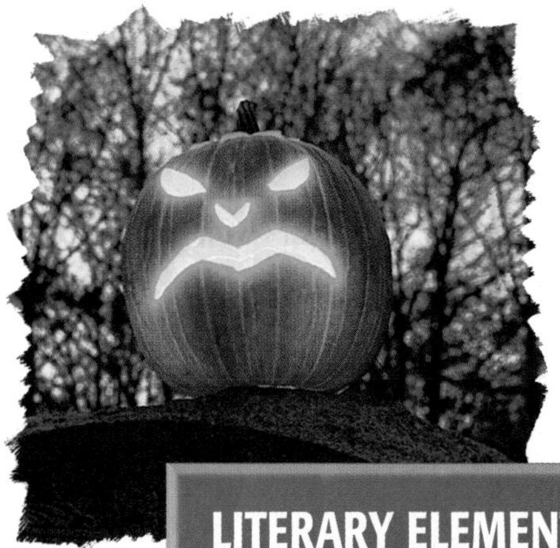

Analyzing Literature

RECALL

1. What does Ichabod Crane look like? Cite details from the story.
2. How does Crane spend his afternoons and evenings?
3. Why does Crane become rivals with Brom Bones?
4. According to the townspeople, what happened to Crane?

INTERPRET

5. Why is Ichabod Crane's physical appearance important in this story?
6. What does Crane's fascination with the supernatural tell us about his character?
7. Why is Crane interested in Katrina? Why might Crane think Katrina would be interested in him? Give several reasons for your answers.
8. What do you suppose really happened to Crane? What in the story supports your answer?

EVALUATE AND CONNECT

9. Think back to the ghostly stories you discussed in the **Focus Activity** on page 815. What elements do they have in common with "The Legend of Sleepy Hollow"? Why do you think writers of scary stories often use so many of the same elements?
10. In your opinion, did Ichabod Crane deserve the fate he received? Why or why not?

LITERARY ELEMENTS

Literary Legend

A **legend** is a type of folktale–a story believed to be based on a historical event. Legends often exaggerate the truth. For example, many legends give characters extraordinary abilities that they did not possess in real life. Many legends were originally oral tales, but most have now been written down. A legend becomes a **literary legend** when a published version of the story is the form that is familiar to most people.

1. What aspects of "The Legend of Sleepy Hollow" might be based in fact?
2. How might the publication of a legend affect the original (oral) story?
3. What other literary legends can you name?

- See **Literary Terms Handbook,** p. R5.

Literature and Writing

Writing About Literature

Point of View "The Legend of Sleepy Hollow" is told from a **third-person point of view,** that is, by a narrator who is not a character in the story. How might this story be different if told from a character's point of view? Imagine you are Katrina or Ichabod or any other character, and rewrite a section of the story from that point of view.

Creative Writing

Urban Legends Have you heard that alligators live in the sewers of New York City? This story is an **urban legend,** a contemporary tale based on events that seem possible, but probably did not occur. With a partner, write an urban legend. Begin with something scary or strange that could happen where you live. Brainstorm ways to exaggerate your tale. Share your legend with the class.

Extending Your Response

Learning for Life

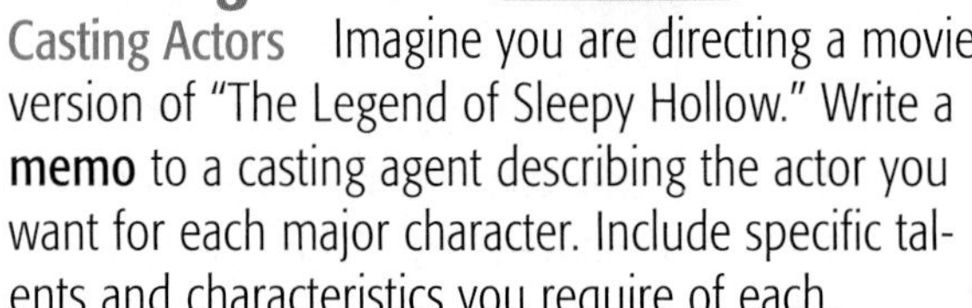

Casting Actors Imagine you are directing a movie version of "The Legend of Sleepy Hollow." Write a **memo** to a casting agent describing the actor you want for each major character. Include specific talents and characteristics you require of each.

interNET CONNECTION

"Legend" on the Web Pay a virtual visit to Sleepy Hollow and Tarrytown. Type the names of these places into a search engine, and visit Web sites to learn more about the region, the legend, and Washington Irving.

Literature Groups

Compare American Legends How does "The Legend of Sleepy Hollow" compare with other American legends, such as those about Johnny Appleseed and Davy Crockett? Brainstorm a list of American legends that includes Irving's story. Discuss how the tales are similar and different. Present your conclusions to the class.

Johnny Appleseed

Reading Further

For strange tales from other places, try:

Wings of a Falcon by Cynthia Voigt

Haunted Waters by Mary Pope Osborne

Save your work for your portfolio.

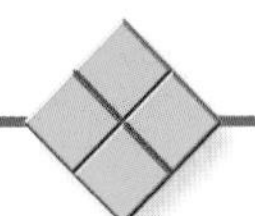

Skill Minilessons

GRAMMAR AND LANGUAGE • VARYING SENTENCE STRUCTURE

Many sentences follow a set pattern:
subject + verb + direct object or predicate noun
(A **direct object** receives the action of the verb. A **predicate noun** follows a linking verb and renames the subject.)
Ichabod Crane [subject] *had* [verb] *a soft and foolish heart* [direct object].
However, you can add rhythm to your writing by rearranging the order of sentence elements so that you don't always start with the subject.
A soft and foolish heart [direct object] *had* [verb] *Ichabod Crane* [subject].

- For more about sentence structure, see **Language Handbook,** pp. R32–R33.

PRACTICE Rewrite the following sentences by changing the order of sentence elements.

1. The schoolhouse was a low building with one large room.
2. Ichabod Crane was a schoolmaster to remember.
3. A dreamy atmosphere hung over the valley where Ichabod Crane lived.
4. Brom Bones brooded, worried by his love.
5. The sad animal Crane rode was a broken-down plow horse.

READING AND THINKING • CAUSE AND EFFECT

In "The Legend of Sleepy Hollow," Washington Irving uses a string of cause-and-effect relationships. For example, Crane's fearful imagination causes him to believe in the story of the Headless Horseman.

PRACTICE Complete each sentence to show the effect of the cause. Then explain in writing how the three effects you named caused the final event in the story.

1. Because Ichabod admires the rich property of Baltus Van Tassel, he _______ .
2. Because Brom Bones loves Katrina, he _______ .
3. Because Ichabod believed in the story of the Headless Horseman, he _______ .

- For more about text structures and cause and effect, see **Reading Handbook,** p. R87.

VOCABULARY • THE LATIN ROOT *SPEC*

The word *speculation* comes from the Latin root *spec,* which means "to see or look at." This root is found in many words, often with a prefix that modifies its meaning. For example, if you *suspect* someone or something, you "look under" the surface. The prefix *sus-* is the same as *sub-* and means "under." The following prefixes have been attached to *spec:*

intro-: inside   *circum-:* around
retro-: back   *pro-:* forward

PRACTICE Use the meaning of *spec* and the prefixes listed to complete each statement.

1. If you are a *circumspect* person, you are
   a. clumsy   c. fast
   b. careful   d. humorous
2. *Introspective* people pay attention to
   a. neighbors   c. feelings
   b. clothing   d. classmates
3. To look at something in *retrospect* is to look
   a. afterwards   c. through a telescope
   b. with regret   d. beforehand

SUSPENSE STORY

What keeps your eyes glued to the pages of a mystery, a horror story, or a spooky tale? Writers of these stories are experts in the art of suspense—the building excitement and anxiety that pulls readers into a story and keeps them hooked until the end. To create this tension and arouse curiosity, writers give special attention to the elements described below.

MODEL: "The Legend of Sleepy Hollow"

CHARACTERS The main characters are described clearly, so that readers learn about their appearance, actions, and thoughts–including their fears. For example, in "The Legend of Sleepy Hollow," readers see that Ichabod Crane's imagination often gets the better of him, especially after a night spent telling ghost stories.

> What fearful shapes and shadows beset his path amidst the dim and ghastly glare of a snowy night! And how often was he thrown into complete dismay by some rushing blast, howling among the trees, in the idea that it was the Galloping Hessian on one of his nightly scourings!

SETTING Every detail about the setting contributes to the feeling of tension, and sometimes, of foreboding.

> . . . a small brook crossed the road, and ran into a marshy and thickly wooded glen, known by the name of Wiley's Swamp. A few rough logs, laid side by side, served for a bridge over this stream. . . .This has . . . been considered a haunted stream, and fearful are the feelings of the schoolboy who has to pass it alone after dark.

CONFLICT AND CLIMAX The conflicts, or problems, that the characters experience lead to the moment of most intense excitement, called the *climax*.

> Just then [Ichabod] saw the goblin rising in his stirrups, and in the very act of hurling his head at him.

ACTIVE READING MODEL

Active Reading Strategies

Tips for Reading a Suspense Story

Suspense stories can keep you reading for hours if you are an active reader. You'll get more out of the story if you talk to yourself as it unfolds. Use the following strategies to help you enjoy the suspense stories in this theme.

• For more about reading strategies, see **Reading Handbook,** pp. R70–R93.

QUESTION

As the plot twists and turns, you may feel like racing ahead in the story to find out what happens. However, be sure you understand details.

Ask Yourself . . . What does this conversation tell about the characters? Why is this background information in the story? What will it tell me that I need to know?

APPLYING THE STRATEGIES

Read the next selection, "The Tell-Tale Heart." As you read, use the **Active Reading Model** notes in the margins to help you enjoy the selection.

PREDICT

Look for clues that suggest what might happen next, and then make predictions about the story's outcome. Later, as you continue to read, verify or adjust your predictions.

Ask Yourself . . . What are the possible outcomes? Which one is most likely? Is this character clever enough or brave enough to find a way out of this dilemma?

RESPOND

Let yourself be carried away by the tension and excitement.

Ask Yourself . . . What would I do in this situation? What advice would I give these characters?

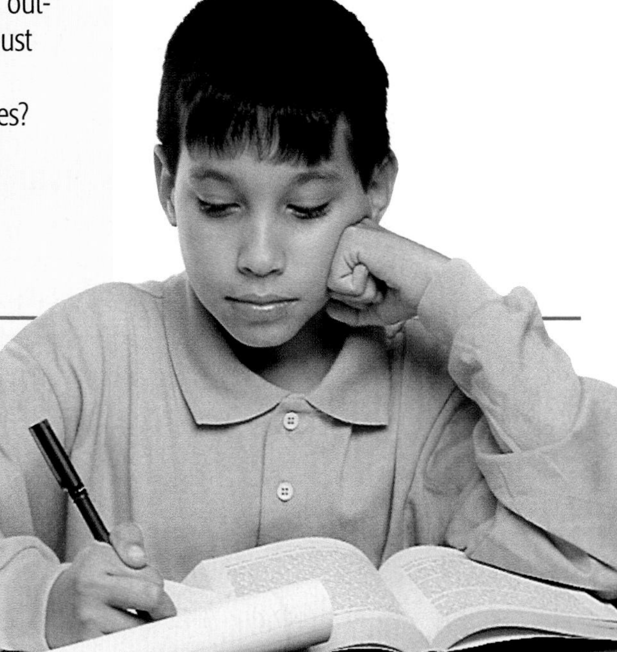

ACTIVE READING MODEL

Before You Read

The Tell-Tale Heart

MEET
EDGAR ALLAN POE

"I was never *really* insane, except on occasions where my heart was touched," Edgar Allan Poe once wrote to his mother-in-law. During his life, Poe was known for writing about mysterious forces, wicked crimes, and death. Unfortunately, his life was as sad as those of most of his characters. He was poor for most of his life. His mother died when he was two, and he was disowned by his foster father. In addition, Poe's wife died when she was only twenty-four.

Edgar Allan Poe was born in 1809 and died in 1849. "The Tell-Tale Heart" was first published in Pioneer *magazine in January 1843.*

FOCUS ACTIVITY

Do we see ourselves as others see us?

FreeWrite

How is the way people view themselves different from the way others view them? Freewrite your answer.

Setting a Purpose

Read this short story to find out what the narrator thinks about himself and the acts he has committed.

BACKGROUND

Did You Know? Poe spent most of his life writing poetry, beginning as a teenager and sacrificing material comforts for twenty years so that he could concentrate on his art. The success he finally found with his poem "The Raven" didn't improve his financial status. The poem was reprinted and parodied everywhere, and Poe was invited to tour the country lecturing and reading his work. However, he was paid less than $15 for the poem, and lecturing paid barely enough to support him. Three years after "The Raven" came out, Poe still could not afford to keep his house warm during his wife's final battle with tuberculosis.

VOCABULARY PREVIEW

acute (ə kūt′) *adj.* sharp and strong or intense; p. 835

vex (veks) *v.* to disturb, annoy, or anger, especially by some small, repeated action; p. 836

stifled (stī′ fəld) *adj.* held back; smothered; p. 837

wane (wān) *v.* to draw to a close; approach an end; p. 839

audacity (ô das′ ə tē) *n.* reckless boldness; daring; p. 840

singularly (sing′ gyə lər lē) *adv.* unusually or remarkably; extraordinarily; p. 841

vehemently (vē′ ə mənt lē) *adv.* strongly; intensely; passionately; p. 841

hypocritical (hip′ ə krit′ i kəl) *adj.* pretending to be what one is not; fake; insincere; p. 841

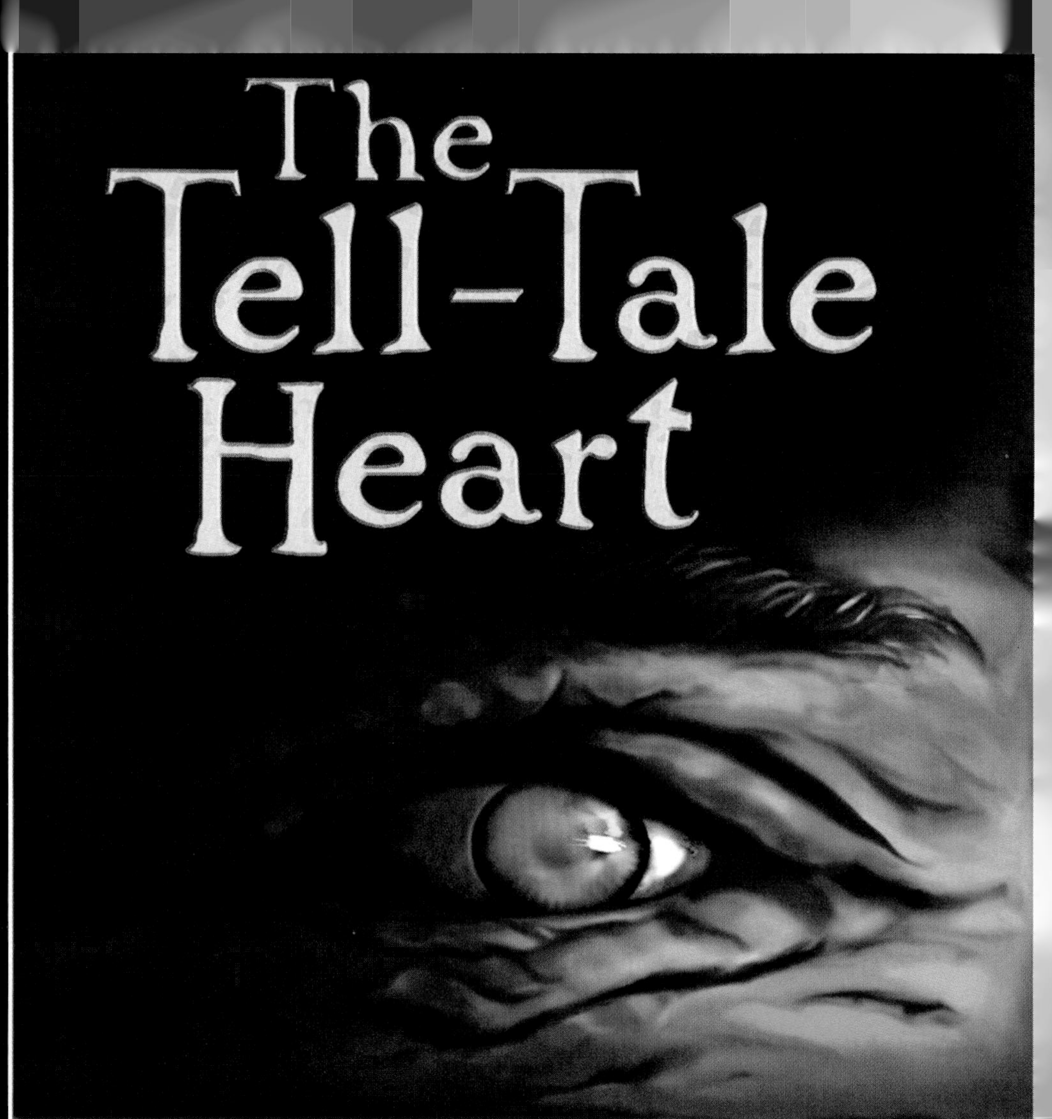

Edgar Allan Poe

TRUE!—NERVOUS—VERY, VERY DREADFULLY NERVOUS I had been and am; but why *will* you say that I am mad? The disease had sharpened my senses—not destroyed—not dulled them. Above all was the sense of hearing acute. I heard all things in the heaven and in the earth. I heard many things in hell. How, then, am I mad? Hearken! and observe how healthily—how calmly I can tell you the whole story.

ACTIVE READING MODEL

ADJUST S

What is unus about the pu tion? What d suggest abou narrator?

acute (ə kūt′) *adj.* sharp and strong or intense

The Tell-Tale Heart

CLARIFY

What is the narrator trying to tell you?

VISUALIZE

Try to picture the movements of this man as he enters the room.

It is impossible to say how first the idea entered my brain; but once conceived, it haunted me day and night. Object there was none. Passion there was none. I loved the old man. He had never wronged me. He had never given me insult. For his gold I had no desire. I think it was his eye! yes, it was this! One of his eyes resembled that of a vulture—a pale blue eye, with a film over it. Whenever it fell upon me, my blood ran cold; and so by degrees—very gradually—I made up my mind to take the life of the old man, and thus rid myself of the eye for ever.

Now this is the point. You fancy me mad. Madmen know nothing. But you should have seen *me*. You should have seen how wisely I proceeded—with what caution—with what foresight—with what dissimulation[1] I went to work! I was never kinder to the old man than during the whole week before I killed him. And every night, about midnight, I turned the latch of his door and opened it—oh, so gently! And then, when I had made an opening sufficient for my head, I put in a dark lantern, all closed, closed, so that no light shone out, and then I thrust in my head. Oh, you would have laughed to see how cunningly I thrust it in! I moved it slowly—very, very slowly, so that I might not disturb the old man's sleep. It took me an hour to place my whole head within the opening so far that I could see him as he lay upon his bed. Ha!—would a madman have been so wise as this? And then, when my head was well in the room, I undid the lantern cautiously—oh, so cautiously—cautiously (for the hinges creaked)—I undid it just so much that a single thin ray fell upon the vulture eye. And this I did for seven long nights—every night just at midnight—but I found the eye always closed; and so it was impossible to do the work; for it was not the old man who vexed me, but his Evil Eye. And every morning, when the day broke, I went boldly into the chamber, and spoke courageously to him, calling him by name in a hearty tone, and inquiring how he had passed the night. So you see he would have been a very profound[2] old man, indeed, to suspect that every night, just at twelve, I looked in upon him while he slept.

Upon the eighth night I was more than usually cautious in opening the door. A watch's minute hand moves more quickly than did mine. Never before that night, had I *felt* the extent of my own powers—of my sagacity.[3] I could scarcely contain my feelings of triumph. To think

1. *Dissimulation* means "the hiding or disguising of one's true feelings and intentions."
2. Here, *profound* means "very thoughtful and wise."
3. *Sagacity* (sə gas′ ə tē) is wisdom and good judgment.

Vocabulary

vex (veks) *v.* to disturb, annoy, or anger, especially by some small, repeated action that there I was, opening the door, little by little, and he not even to dream of my secret deeds or thoughts. I fairly chuckled at the idea; and perhaps he heard me; for he moved on the bed suddenly, as if startled. Now you may think that I drew back—but no. His room was as black as pitch with the thick darkness, (for the shutters were close fastened, through fear of robbers,) and so I knew that he could not see the opening of the door, and I kept pushing it on steadily, steadily.

ACTIVE READING MODEL

I had my head in, and was about to open the lantern, when my thumb slipped upon the tin fastening, and the old man sprang up in the bed, crying out—"Who's there?"

VISUALIZE

Imagine a movie scene showing the narrator's entry into the old man's room.

I kept quite still and said nothing. For a whole hour I did not move a muscle, and in the mean time I did not hear him lie down. He was still sitting up in the bed, listening;—just as I have done, night after night, hearkening to the death watches[4] in the wall.

Presently I heard a slight groan, and I knew it was the groan of mortal terror. It was not a groan of pain or of grief—oh, no!—it was the low stifled sound that arises from the bottom of the soul when overcharged with awe. I knew the sound well. Many a night, just at midnight, when all the world slept, it has welled up from my own bosom, deepening, with its dreadful echo, the terrors that distracted me. I say I knew it well. I knew what the old man felt, and pitied him, although I chuckled at heart. I knew that he had been lying awake ever since the first slight noise, when he had turned in the bed. His fears had been ever since growing upon him. He had been trying to fancy them causeless, but could not. He had been saying to himself—"It is nothing but the wind in the chimney—it is only a mouse crossing the floor," or "it is merely a cricket which has made a single chirp." Yes, he has been trying to comfort himself with these suppositions:[5] but he had found all in vain. *All in vain;* because Death, in approaching him, had stalked with his black shadow before him, and enveloped the victim. And it was the mournful influence of the unperceived shadow that caused him to feel—although he neither saw nor heard—to *feel* the presence of my head within the room.

RESPOND

What effect does this very slow action have on you?

When I had waited a long time, very patiently, without hearing him lie down, I resolved to open a little—a very, very little crevice[6]

4. *Death watches* are beetles that bore into wood, especially of old houses and furniture. Some superstitious people believe that these insects' ticking sounds foretell death.
5. *Suppositions* are things one assumes, or supposes, to be true.
6. A *crevice* (krev′ is) is a crack in or through something.

Vocabulary

stifled (stī′ fəld) *adj.* held back; smothered

Hidden Room of 1,000 Horrors (The Tell-Tale Heart), 1963. Movie still.

Viewing the photograph: How does this photograph add to the horror of the story?

in the lantern. So I opened it—you cannot imagine how stealthily, stealthily—until, at length, a single dim ray, like the thread of the spider, shot from out the crevice and fell upon the vulture eye.

It was open—wide, wide open—and I grew furious as I gazed upon it. I saw it with perfect distinctness—all a dull blue, with a hideous veil over it that chilled the very marrow in my bones; but I could see nothing else of the old man's face or person: for I had directed the ray as if by instinct, precisely upon the damned spot.

PREDICT

Based on the vivid description of the heartbeat, what do you think will happen?

And now have I not told you that what you mistake for madness is but over acuteness of the senses?—now, I say, there came to my ears a low, dull, quick sound, such as a watch makes when enveloped in cotton. I knew *that* sound well, too. It was the beating of the old man's heart. It increased my fury, as the beating of a drum stimulates the soldier into courage.

But even yet I refrained and kept still. I scarcely breathed. I held the lantern motionless. I tried how steadily I could maintain the ray upon the eye. Meantime the hellish tattoo[7] of the heart increased. It grew quicker and quicker, and louder and louder every instant. The old

7. The heart was making a drumming or rapping sound. (This *tattoo* comes from a Dutch word; the other *tattoo,* a design on the skin, comes from the language of Tahiti, a Pacific island.)

man's terror *must* have been extreme! It grew louder, I say, louder every moment!—do you mark me well? I have told you that I am nervous: so I am. And now at the dead hour of the night, amid the dreadful silence of that old house, so strange a noise as this excited me to uncontrollable terror. Yet, for some minutes longer I refrained and stood still. But the beating grew louder, louder! I thought the heart must burst. And now a new anxiety seized me—the sound would be heard by a neighbor! The old man's hour had come! With a loud yell, I threw open the lantern and leaped into the room. He shrieked once—once only. In an instant I dragged him to the floor, and pulled the heavy bed over him. I then smiled gaily, to find the deed so far done. But, for many minutes, the heart beat on with a muffled sound. This, however, did not vex me; it would not be heard through the wall. At length it ceased. The old man was dead. I removed the bed and examined the corpse. Yes, he was stone, stone dead. I placed my hand upon the heart and held it there many minutes. There was no pulsation. He was stone dead. His eye would trouble me no more.

ADJUST SPEED

How might you vary your reading rate in this passage? Why?

If still you think me mad, you will think so no longer when I describe the wise precautions I took for the concealment of the body. The night waned, and I worked hastily, but in silence. First of all I dismembered the corpse. I cut off the head and the arms and the legs.

I then took up three planks from the flooring of the chamber, and deposited all between the scantlings.[8] I then replaced the boards so cleverly, so cunningly, that no human eye—not even *his*—could have detected any thing wrong. There was nothing to wash out—no stain of any kind—no blood-spot whatever. I had been too wary for that. A tub had caught all—ha! ha!

When I had made an end of these labors, it was four o'clock—still dark as midnight. As the bell sounded the hour, there came a knocking at the street door. I went down to open it with a light heart—for what had I *now* to fear? There entered three men, who introduced themselves, with perfect suavity, as officers of the police. A shriek had been heard by a neighbor during the night; suspicion of foul play had been aroused; information had been lodged at the police office, and they (the officers) had been deputed[9] to search the premises.

8. The *scantlings* (more commonly called joists) are the boards that hold up the floor planks.
9. *Suavity* (swäv′ ə tē) is a smooth, polite, gracious manner. The officers were appointed, or *deputed* (di pū′ tid), by a superior officer. (This makes them deputies, in effect, although they probably have other official titles.)

Vocabulary

wane (wān) *v.* to draw to a close; approach an end

ACTIVE READING MODEL

Hidden Room of 1,000 Horrors (The Tell-Tale Heart), 1963. Movie still.

Viewing the photograph: What seems to be tormenting the man in this picture? Compare this realistic image with the illustration of the eye on page 835. Which image best helps you to visualize the story? Why?

I smiled—for *what* had I to fear? I bade the gentlemen welcome. The shriek, I said, was my own in a dream. The old man, I mentioned, was absent in the country. I took my visitors all over the house. I bade them search—search *well.* I led them, at length, to *his* chamber. I showed them his treasures, secure, undisturbed. In the enthusiasm of my confidence, I brought chairs into the room, and desired them *here* to rest from their fatigues, while I myself, in the wild audacity of my perfect triumph, placed my own seat upon the very spot beneath which reposed[10] the corpse of the victim.

PREDICT

What do you think may be indicated when the officers sit down?

The officers were satisfied. My *manner* had convinced them. I was singularly at ease. They sat, and while I answered cheerily, they chatted

10. Here, *reposed* means "lay dead."

Vocabulary

audacity (ô das′ ə tē) *n.* reckless boldness; daring

singularly (sing′ gyə lər lē) *adv.* unusually or remarkably; extraordinarily

ACTIVE READING MODEL

of familiar things. But, ere long, I felt myself getting pale and wished them gone. My head ached, and I fancied a ringing in my ears: but still they sat and still chatted. The ringing became more distinct—it continued and became more distinct: I talked more freely to get rid of the feeling: but it continued and gained definitiveness—until, at length, I found that the noise was *not* within my ears.

No doubt I now grew *very* pale—but I talked more fluently,[11] and with a heightened voice. Yet the sound increased—and what could I do? It was *a low, dull, quick sound—much such a sound as a watch makes when enveloped in cotton*. I gasped for breath—and yet the officers heard it not. I talked more quickly—more vehemently; but the noise steadily increased. I arose and argued about trifles, in a high key and with violent gesticulations;[12] but the noise steadily increased. Why *would* they not be gone? I paced the floor to and fro with heavy strides, as if excited to fury by the observations of the men—but the noise steadily increased. Oh God! what *could* I do? I foamed—I raved—I swore! I swung the chair upon which I had been sitting, and grated it upon the boards, but the noise arose over all and continually increased. It grew louder—louder—*louder!* And still the men chatted pleasantly, and smiled. Was it possible they heard not? Almighty God!—no, no! They heard!—they suspected!—they *knew!*—they were making a mockery of my horror!—this I thought, and this I think. But anything was better than this agony! Anything was more tolerable than this derision![13] I could bear those hypocritical smiles no longer! I felt that I must scream or die!—and now—again!—hark! louder! louder! louder! *louder!*—

"Villains!" I shrieked, "dissemble[14] no more! I admit the deed!—tear up the planks!—here, here!—it is the beating of his hideous heart!"

RESPOND

Imagine this scene being enacted as a movie. How might an audience respond?

11. To speak *fluently* is to do so smoothly and effortlessly.
12. *Trifles* are unimportant things. Bold, expressive gestures are *gesticulations.*
13. *Derision* is scornful mockery or ridicule.
14. Here, *dissemble* means "to disguise one's true thoughts or feelings; act in an insincere way."

Vocabulary

vehemently (vē′ ə mənt lē) *adv.* strongly; intensely; passionately
hypocritical (hip′ ə krit′ i kəl) *adj.* pretending to be what one is not; fake; insincere

ACTIVE READING MODEL

Responding to Literature

PERSONAL RESPONSE

Can you hear the beating of the dead man's heart as you finish the story? What incidents from the story stay in your mind?

Active Reading Response

Which prediction did you make that was supported by evidence later in the story?

Analyzing Literature

RECALL

1. What reason does the narrator give for committing the murder?
2. What does the old man do when he hears the narrator at his bedroom door?
3. Why do the police come to the door?
4. What does the narrator hear while talking to the police officers in the victim's bedroom?

INTERPRET

5. What does the narrator want his audience to understand about him as he talks about his murder plans? Explain.
6. How does the narrator feel about frightening the old man? Support your answer with examples from the story.
7. How does the narrator react when the police first arrive? Why does he behave this way?
8. Why does the narrator confess to his crime?

EVALUATE AND CONNECT

9. Theme Connection How does the author make the narrator a convincing character? Is any of his behavior normal? Explain.
10. Who has the "tell-tale" heart in this story–the narrator or the old man? Defend your choice.

LITERARY ELEMENTS

Mood

The **mood** of a story is the emotional effect it has on a reader. The overall mood of "The Tell-Tale Heart" is one of anxiety and fear. One way Poe achieves this mood is through the rhythm of his language, which mimics a fast, irregular heartbeat. Poe's use of exclamation marks and dashes conveys agitation, as does the narrator's repetition of the word "nervous."

1. Find three other passages in the story in which punctuation and repetition help project a mood.
2. Find a description of the victim that supports the story's overall mood of anxiety and fear.

● See **Literary Terms Handbook,** p. R6.

Extending Your Response

Literature Groups

Unanswered Questions What questions do you still have about this story? With your group, discuss questions such as these: Is the narrator of the story insane, or is he just evil? How do you explain the power that the old man's eye and heartbeat had over the narrator? Why did the narrator continue to hear the old man's heartbeat after he was dead? Share your answers with the rest of the class.

Learning for Life

Presenting an Argument Imagine you are the narrator's defense attorney. Write an argument for why he should not be convicted of murder. Deliver your argument to your classmates.

Writing About Literature

Suspenseful Scene Which scene from this story did you find most gripping or scary? Why did it affect you this way? Write a paragraph or two explaining your answer. Include details and examples from the story to support your answer.

Creative Writing

Police Report Imagine that you are one of the police officers called to the house after a neighbor heard a scream. What facts do you uncover? Write a police report about this case.

Reading Further

If you enjoyed this story, try:
Look for Me by Moonlight by Mary Downing Hahn

Save your work for your portfolio.

Skill Minilesson

VOCABULARY • ANALOGIES

An **analogy** is a type of comparison that is based on the relationships between things or ideas. Analogies are often used on tests to measure how well you can figure things out and how good your vocabulary is. A test will not tell you what kind of relationship is shown by the first pair of words. You'll have to figure that out. Then you'll need to find another pair of words that could be used to illustrate the same relationship.

- For more about analogies, see **Communications Skills Handbook,** pp. R66–R67.

PRACTICE Complete each analogy.

1. cramp : sharp :: ache :
   a. brief c. sudden
   b. dull d. slight
2. loud : quiet :: stifled :
   a. soft c. released
   b. ignored d. touched
3. knock : pound :: vex :
   a. soothe c. scold
   b. torture d. comfort
4. taunt : scorn :: praise :
   a. approval c. disgust
   b. complaint d. care

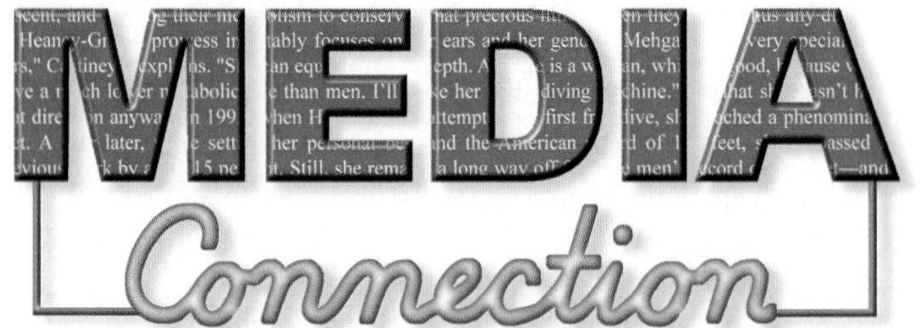

WEB SITE

The word "mystery" probably conjures images of Sherlock Holmes and the board game *Clue* instead of Greek tragedies. See how these elements fit together to give us the mysteries that we enjoy today.

The History of the Mystery

Address: http://www.mysterynet.com/history/

From Poe to the Present

Mystery and crime stories are among the most popular forms of fiction today, and the popularity of the genre is no mystery to millions of readers worldwide.

The fascination with mystery and crime can be traced back to Ancient Greece, where playwrights like Sophocles and Euripides enthralled the local citizenry with their plays combining mystery and drama. In first-century B.C. Rome, Cicero argued passionately in court in defense of accused criminals, captivating Romans with his speeches.

Each April in New York City, the Mystery Writers of America hosts the annual Edgar Allan Poe awards to honor outstanding mystery writers. Their top honor, the Edgar, is shown here.

Mystery and crime stories as we know them today did not emerge until the mid-nineteenth century when Edgar Allan Poe introduced mystery fiction's first fictional detective, Auguste C. Dupin, in his 1841 story, "The Murders in the Rue Morgue." The acknowledged father of the mystery story, Poe continued Dupin's exploits in stories such as "The Mystery of Marie Roget" (1842) and "The Purloined Letter" (1845).

"The Murders in the Rue Morgue" is the most famous example of a mystery style known as the "locked room," in which "a murder victim is found inside an apparently sealed enclosure and the detective's challenge is to discover the murderer's modus operandi" (Crime Classics).

Poe was one of the first to shift the focus of mystery stories from the description of shocking events and eerie setting to a "study of the criminal's mind" (Crime Classics).

As important as his contributions were to the genre, Poe was influenced greatly by the early work of Charles Dickens who,

The History of the Mystery

Address: http://www.mysterynet.com/history/

with his contemporary, Wilkie Collins, made major contributions to the genre as well. The rising literacy rates combined with more leisure time contributed greatly to the popularity of novels in general and mysteries in particular.

In 1878, with the publication of "The Leavenworth Case," Katherine Anne Greene became the first woman to write a detective novel. This novel introduced elements of detection later used to great effect by writers of the English-country-house-murder school, a style that focuses on "members of a closed group, often in a country house or village, who become suspects in a generally bloodless and neat murder solved by a great-detective kind of investigator" (Crime Classics).

Sherlock Holmes, Sir Arthur Conan Doyle's brilliant detective, arrived on the mystery scene in the late nineteenth century in "A Study in Scarlet" (1887). Holmes possessed a singular style unlike any detective seen before. With his distinctive style and his flair for deducing clues, Holmes, with his ever-reliable sidekick, Dr. Watson, quickly became indispensable to mystery readers everywhere.

The 1920s ushered in the Golden Age of mystery fiction. A time of growing prosperity in both England and America, the popularity of mystery fiction was at an all-time high.

During the height of Golden Age fiction's popularity, London publisher Allen Lane came up with an idea that further helped to expand the availability of mysteries to the public. Along with his two brothers, he obtained limited rights to hardcover books written by Dorothy L. Sayers and other mystery writers. Their new paperback line was issued in 1935 with only ten titles and quickly expanded to seventy titles within a year. Penguins, as they were called, were easily accessible to the public due to their much lower cost and availability in department stores, where most of the public shopped at the time. These paperbacks helped to bring mysteries, along with other types of fiction as well, to the public.

Another type of crime fiction, the "police procedural," surfaced in the 1940s, and its style coincided perfectly with the advent of television. As its name implies, it differed from other styles of crime writing because of its realistic portrayal of police methods. The stories were always presented from the point of view of the police, usually in a gritty, realistic style.

Mystery in all its forms will undoubtedly continue to capture the public's imagination, regardless of the medium, well into the future.

Respond

1. How has the mystery developed since its origins in Ancient Greece? In what ways has the mystery story stayed the same?
2. What types of mysteries do you enjoy? Jot down the names of your favorite mystery writers, book titles, television shows, and movies.

Before You Read

The Raven

FOCUS ACTIVITY

Is it easy to forget, even briefly, a time of sorrow?

Journal

Write a few things you might say to help a friend who is mourning the loss of a loved one.

Setting a Purpose

Read to find out whether the narrator is trying to forget something or someone, or if he is trying to remember.

BACKGROUND

The Time and Place "The Raven" may be based on incidents from Edgar Allan Poe's own experiences during his days as a student at the University of Virginia. The setting is the room of a man who is reading an old academic book on a stormy night.

Did You Know? Poe's most famous poem was "The Raven." After its publication in 1845, the poem gained the kind of popularity that a hit song enjoys today. Unlike popular modern songwriters, however, the writer didn't become wealthy.

Poe's death has been as haunted by misfortune as his life was. His family couldn't afford a tombstone for his grave. Years after his death, a tombstone purchased by a distant relative was ready for delivery when it was struck by a train and destroyed. The people of Baltimore raised money for a monument to Poe, who had lived there, but the clay model was destroyed by fire before it could be cast in bronze. A second model was demolished in an earthquake. Finally, in 1875, the bronze sculpture shown on the right was erected in Poe's honor.

Edgar Allan Poe Monument, Baltimore, MD.

The Raven

Edgar Allan Poe

Once upon a midnight dreary, while I pondered, weak and weary,
Over many a quaint and curious volume of forgotten lore°—
While I nodded, nearly napping, suddenly there came a tapping,
As of some one gently rapping, rapping at my chamber door.
"'Tis some visitor," I muttered, "tapping at my chamber door—
Only this and nothing more."

Ah, distinctly I remember it was in the bleak December;
And each separate dying ember° wrought° its ghost upon the floor.
Eagerly I wished the morrow;—vainly I had sought to borrow
From my books surcease° of sorrow—sorrow for the lost Lenore—
For the rare and radiant maiden whom the angels name Lenore—
Nameless *here* for evermore.

---

2 *Lore* means "learning."

8 An *ember* is a glowing fragment of wood in the ashes of a fire. *Wrought* means "worked."

10 *Surcease* means "an end."

And the silken, sad, uncertain rustling of each purple curtain
Thrilled me—filled me with fantastic terrors never felt before;
So that now, to still the beating of my heart, I stood repeating
"'Tis some visitor entreating° entrance at my chamber door—
Some late visitor entreating entrance at my chamber door;—
This it is and nothing more."

Presently my soul grew stronger; hesitating then no longer,
"Sir," said I, "or Madam, truly your forgiveness I implore;°
But the fact is I was napping, and so gently you came rapping,
And so faintly you came tapping, tapping at my chamber door,
That I scarce was sure I heard you"—here I opened wide the door;—
Darkness there and nothing more.

Deep into that darkness peering, long I stood there wondering, fearing,
Doubting, dreaming dreams no mortal ever dared to dream before;
But the silence was unbroken, and the stillness gave no token,
And the only word there spoken was the whispered word, "Lenore!"
This I whispered, and an echo murmured back the word "Lenore!"
Merely this and nothing more.

Back into the chamber turning, all my soul within me burning,
Soon again I heard a tapping somewhat louder than before.
"Surely," said I, "surely that is something at my window lattice;°
Let me see, then, what thereat is, and this mystery explore—
Let my heart be still a moment and this mystery explore;—
'Tis the wind and nothing more!"

---

16 *Entreating* is pleading.
20 To *implore* is to ask earnestly.
33 *Lattice* refers to strips of wood or metal overlapped in a crisscross pattern.

Open here I flung the shutter, when, with many a flirt and flutter
In there stepped a stately Raven of the saintly days of yore.°
Not the least obeisance° made he; not a minute stopped or stayed he;
But, with mien° of lord or lady, perched above my chamber door—
Perched upon a bust° of Pallas° just above my chamber door—
Perched, and sat, and nothing more.

Then this ebony bird beguiling° my sad fancy into smiling,
By the grave and stern decorum° of the countenance° it wore,
"Though thy crest be shorn and shaven, thou," I said, "art sure no craven,°
Ghastly grim and ancient Raven wandering from the Nightly shore—
Tell me what thy lordly name is on the Night's Plutonian shore!"°
Quoth the Raven, "Nevermore."

Much I marvelled this ungainly° fowl to hear discourse° so plainly,
Though its answer little meaning—little relevancy bore;
For we cannot help agreeing that no living human being
Ever yet was blessed with seeing bird above his chamber door—
Bird or beast upon the sculptured bust above his chamber door,
With such name as "Nevermore."

But the Raven, sitting lonely on the placid° bust, spoke only
That one word, as if his soul in that one word he did outpour.
Nothing farther then he uttered—not a feather then he fluttered—
Till I scarcely more than muttered "Other friends have flown before—
On the morrow *he* will leave me, as my hopes have flown before."
Then the bird said "Nevermore."

---

38 *Saintly days of yore* are sacred days of long ago. This refers to the Bible story in which ravens bring food to the prophet Elijah in the wilderness.

39 *Obeisance* (ō bā′ səns) is a polite gesture of respect, such as a bow or curtsy.

40 *Mien* (mēn) means "a way of carrying oneself" or "manner."

41 A *bust* is a statue of the head and shoulders. *Pallas* is another name for Athena, the Greek goddess of wisdom.

43 Someone who is *beguiling* uses charm to influence.

44 *Decorum* (di kôr′ əm) is dignity. *Countenance* is a facial expression.

45 A *craven* is an extremely cowardly person.

47 A *Plutonian shore* refers to darkness, like the edge of death. In Roman mythology, Pluto was god of the dead, whose land of darkness was separated from the land of the living by rivers.

49 *Ungainly* means "awkward-looking." *Discourse* means "to speak or converse."

55 *Placid* means "peaceful."

The Raven. Gustave Doré (1832–1883). Engraving.

Viewing the art: In what ways does this picture match the mood of "The Raven"? Explain.

Startled at the stillness broken by reply so aptly° spoken,
"Doubtless," said I, "what it utters is its only stock and store
Caught from some unhappy master whom unmerciful Disaster
Followed fast and followed faster till his songs one burden bore—
Till the dirges° of his Hope that melancholy burden bore
Of 'Never—nevermore.'"

But the Raven still beguiling all my fancy into smiling,
Straight I wheeled a cushioned seat in front of bird, and bust and door;
Then, upon the velvet sinking, I betook myself to linking
Fancy unto fancy, thinking what this ominous bird of yore—
What this grim, ungainly, ghastly, gaunt, and ominous bird of yore
Meant in croaking "Nevermore."

This I sat engaged in guessing, but no syllable expressing
To the fowl whose fiery eyes now burned into my bosom's core;
This and more I sat divining,° with my head at ease reclining
On the cushion's velvet lining that the lamp-light gloated o'er,
But whose velvet violet lining with the lamp-light gloating o'er,
She shall press, ah, nevermore!

Then, methought, the air grew denser, perfumed from an unseen censer°
Swung by Seraphim° whose foot-falls tinkled on the tufted° floor.
"Wretch," I cried, "thy God hath lent thee—by these angels he hath sent thee
Respite—respite° and nepenthe° from thy memories of Lenore;
Quaff,° oh quaff this kind nepenthe and forget this lost Lenore!"
Quoth the Raven "Nevermore."

---

61 *Aptly* means "appropriately."
65 *Dirges* are slow, mournful songs, often funeral hymns.
75 *Divining* means "guessing."
79 A *censer* is a container for burning incense.
80 *Seraphim* are angels of the highest rank, said to have three pairs of wings. *Tufted* means "carpeted."
82 *Respite* (res′ pit) is a brief period of relief from pain or labor. *Nepenthe* (ni pen′ thē) is a sleeping drug or anything that eases pain or sorrow by bringing forgetfulness.
83 To *quaff* is to drink deeply.

"Prophet!" said I, "thing of evil!—prophet still, if bird or devil!—
Whether Tempter° sent, or whether tempest° tossed thee here ashore,
Desolate yet all undaunted, on this desert land enchanted—
On this home by Horror haunted—tell me truly, I implore—
Is there—*is* there balm in Gilead?°—tell me—tell me, I implore!"
Quoth the Raven "Nevermore."

"Prophet!" said I, "thing of evil!—prophet still, if bird or devil!
By that Heaven that bends above us—by that God we both adore—
Tell this soul with sorrow laden if, within the distant Aidenn,°
It shall clasp a sainted maiden whom the angels name Lenore—
Clasp a rare and radiant maiden whom the angels name Lenore."
Quoth the Raven "Nevermore."

"Be that word our sign of parting, bird or fiend!" I shrieked, upstarting—
"Get thee back into the tempest and the Night's Plutonian shore!
Leave no black plume as a token of that lie thy soul hath spoken!
Leave my loneliness unbroken!—quit the bust above my door!
Take thy beak from out my heart, and take thy form from off my door!"
Quoth the Raven "Nevermore."

And the Raven, never flitting, still is sitting, *still* is sitting
On the pallid° bust of Pallas just above my chamber door;
And his eyes have all the seeming of a demon's that is dreaming,
And the lamp-light o'er him streaming throws his shadow on the floor;
And my soul from out that shadow that lies floating on the floor
Shall be lifted—nevermore!

---

86 Here, *Tempter* is the Devil. A *tempest* is a violent storm.

89 *Balm in Gilead* (gil′ ē əd) means "relief from pain and suffering." In the Bible, the phrase refers to a healing ointment made from a tree in a region of Palestine.

93 *Aidenn* (ā′ den) comes from an Arabic form of *Eden* and means "heaven" or "paradise."

104 *Pallid* (pal′ id) means "pale."

Responding to Literature

PERSONAL RESPONSE

What questions would you like to ask the speaker? What would you ask the raven?

Analyzing Literature

RECALL AND INTERPRET

1. What is the speaker's mood at the beginning of the poem? Why does he feel this way? Explain.
2. When the speaker hears tapping at his door, who does he think it is at first? How does he feel when it turns out to be something else? Include details from the poem in your answers.
3. What is the speaker's first reaction to the raven's presence? What is his reaction by the poem's end? What happens to change his mind?

EVALUATE AND CONNECT

4. What effect might the **repetition** of "Nevermore" have on a reader? Find three other examples of repetition in the poem.
5. Poe said that he broke the mood of "The Raven" at the halfway point, the end of line 54. What effect might this change have on a reader? Support your answer with examples.
6. Do you think the raven knows what it is saying? Or is the speaker reading into it his own thoughts? Explain your answer.

LITERARY ELEMENTS

Allusion

An **allusion** is a reference to a character, place, or situation from another work of art or literature, or from history. For example, the raven in Poe's poem may be an allusion to the bird that served as a messenger for Apollo, the Greek sun god. Also, *ravenous,* meaning "extremely hungry," comes from the word *raven.* That meaning is echoed in the line "Take thy beak from out my heart."

1. What other animal could Poe have used in place of the raven in this poem?
2. Find three other allusions in the poem and research their meanings.

- See **Literary Terms Handbook,** p. R1.

Extending Your Response

Creative Writing

A Poet Speaks Write a short poem inspired by either the mood or the rhyme scheme and rhythm of "The Raven." (For more on **rhyme scheme,** see **Literary Terms Handbook,** page R8.) Rehearse your poem with a partner, and then recite it for the class.

Literature Groups

Nevermore? Reexamine the poem. As a group, identify lines that show how the speaker's attitude toward the dead Lenore changes throughout the poem. Share your conclusions with the class.

Save your work for your portfolio.

COMPARING SELECTIONS

The Tell-Tale Heart and The Raven

COMPARE **SETTINGS**

The settings of "The Tell-Tale Heart" and "The Raven" are important parts of these stories.

1. Compare Poe's use of doors in advancing the plot of the two selections.
2. Why, do you think, is darkness important in each selection?
3. Contrast the presence or absence of sound in the two settings.

COMPARE **TECHNIQUES**

Both "The Tell-Tale Heart" and "The Raven" are stories that rely on horror and fear of the supernatural to capture an audience.

1. What elements in each story create the mood of horror?
2. How is the supernatural used in each story?
3. How is the personality of the narrator in each story important in creating the mood?

COMPARE **EXPERIENCES**

Think about your experience of modern horror stories and films. How are contemporary stories of fear and the supernatural like these tales by Poe? How are they different? With a group, choose a modern story of horror or the supernatural—from a book or a film—and compare it with one of Poe's works. In your comparison, discuss the subject matter, the main character, and the details that create horror or fear for the audience. Share comparisons with another group.

The Raven. Gustave Doré (1832–1883). Engraving.

Interdisciplinary Connection

SCIENCE

The Science of Dreams

While you are sleeping, your mind is working. It is making up stories–often strange and unreal tales–called *dreams.* You dream of being chased through your house by a bear. Or, you are soaring high on the back of a bird, with clouds brushing past you. Some dreams of events or people seem so real that you must remind yourself that you were just dreaming. Perhaps that is what really happened to the narrator of "The Raven" when he saw a raven mysteriously appear in his study.

Scientists have made many discoveries about the way people dream. You probably dream four or five times a night. During dreams, your eyes move back and forth beneath your eyelids, as if you are reading quickly or watching something that is moving back and forth. This is "rapid eye movement," or *REM.* During REM sleep, you also may breathe faster, and certain parts of your body may twitch. Normally, however, most of your muscles are at rest. This is your body's way of keeping you from acting out your dreams.

In the story *Alice in Wonderland,* Lewis Carroll writes a bizarre adventure about Alice, who dreams that she follows a white rabbit down a rabbit hole.

Examining Your Dreams

Researchers believe you are most likely to dream about the day's experiences, but dreams also may reflect wishes and fears. Despite years of study, researchers disagree about the purpose of dreams. Do they merely entertain you during sleep? Do they improve learning? No one knows for sure. Like well-written stories, dreams convey sights, sounds, smells, tastes, and textures that seem real even when you know they are not. Chances are good that if you wake up suddenly–because of a ringing alarm clock or other loud noise–you will recall at least a few details from your dreams. Some writers keep journals of their dreams to help them create stories and reflect on life. It is believed that Edgar Allan Poe used this technique.

ACTIVITY

For a week, keep a journal of some of the more vivid images you remember from your dreams. Write them down as soon as you wake up. Then, choose some images you wouldn't mind sharing and use them to help create a story or poem. If you have difficulty remembering dreams, choose a real event and describe it as if it had been a dream.

Before You Read

The Woman in the Snow

MEET PATRICIA C. MCKISSACK

Patricia C. McKissack's life was shaped by the Civil Rights movement of the 1960s. "That was the period in which African Americans were really looking up . . . and doors were opening—ever so slightly, but still opening." McKissack and her husband, Fred, have cowritten nearly one hundred books, many dealing with African American history. The story "The Woman in the Snow" touches upon changing attitudes toward racial segregation between the 1930s and 1960s.

Patricia C. McKissack was born in Nashville, Tennessee, in 1944. She has also published under her birth name, L'Ann Carwell.

FOCUS ACTIVITY

Do you like stories about supernatural beings? Why might a person believe in any of these beings?

Discuss

Are stories of supernatural beings always scary stories?

Setting a Purpose

Read to experience a story about the supernatural and the changing attitudes on race in the United States.

BACKGROUND

The Time and Place The story takes place in an unnamed town in the American South. The first part after the introduction is set in 1935, during the Depression, when millions of workers were jobless. Then the story changes to 1960.

Did You Know? In 1955 Montgomery, Alabama, like many southern towns, was racially segregated. Although seventy-five percent of the city's bus riders were African American, they had to give up their seats to white riders. When Rosa Parks refused to get up after a long day's work and give her seat to a white man, she was arrested. The Women's Political Caucus swung into action, distributing 35,000 leaflets around the city calling for a bus boycott. The majority of black residents carpooled and walked for an entire year until the U.S. Supreme Court forced the city to integrate the buses.

VOCABULARY PREVIEW

pivotal (piv′ ət əl) *adj.* of central importance; p. 857
plummet (plum′ it) *v.* to fall downward; p. 858
petite (pə tēt′) *adj.* small and slender; little; p. 859
recoil (ri koil′) *v.* to draw back, as in fear; p. 859
pathetically (pə thet′ i kəl ē) *adv.* pitifully; p. 861
careening (kä rēn′ ing) *adj.* tilting or swaying while moving, as if out of control; p. 861
substance (sub′ stəns) *n.* basic material; solid quality; p. 862
console (kən sōl′) *v.* to comfort or cheer someone who is sad or disappointed; p. 863

The Woman in the Snow

Bus in a Snowstorm. John Wesley Hardrick (1891–1968). Oil on board, 20 x 24 in. Indianapolis Museum of Art.

Retold by Patricia C. McKissack

The year-long Montgomery, Alabama, bus boycott in 1955–56 was a pivotal event in the American civil rights movement. Blacks refused to ride the buses until their demand of fair and equal treatment for all fare-paying passengers was met. Today the right to sit anywhere on a public bus may seem a small victory over racism and discrimination.

Vocabulary
pivotal (piv′ ət əl) *adj.* of central importance

But that single issue changed the lives of African Americans everywhere. After the successful boycott in Montgomery, blacks in other cities challenged bus companies, demanding not only the right to sit wherever they chose but also employment opportunities for black bus drivers. Many cities had their own "bus" stories. Some are in history books, but this story is best enjoyed by the fireplace on the night of the first snowfall.

Grady Bishop had just been hired as a driver for Metro Bus Service in 1935. When he put on the gray uniform and boarded his bus, nothing mattered, not his obesity,[1] not his poor education, not growing up the eleventh child of the town drunk. Driving gave him power. And power mattered.

One cold November afternoon Grady clocked in for the three-to-eleven shift. "You've got Hall tonight," Billy, the route manager, said matter-of-factly.[2]

"The Blackbird Express." Grady didn't care who knew about his nickname for the route. "Not again." He turned around, slapping his hat against his leg.

"Try the *Hall Street Express*," Billy corrected Grady, then hurried on, cutting their conversation short. "Snow's predicted. Try to keep on schedule, but if it gets too bad out there, forget it. Come on in."

Grady popped a fresh stick of gum into his mouth. "You're the boss. But tell me. How am I s'posed to stay on schedule? What do those people care about time?"

Most Metro drivers didn't like the Hall Street assignment in the best weather, because the road twisted and turned back on itself like a retreating snake. When slick with ice and snow, it was even more hazardous. But Grady had his own reason for hating the route. The Hall Street Express serviced black domestics[3] who rode out to the fashionable west end in the mornings and back down to the lower east side in the evenings.

"You know I can't stand being a chauffeur for a bunch of colored maids and cooks," he groused.

"Take it or leave it," Billy said, walking away in disgust.

Grady started to say something but thought better of it. He was still on probation,[4] lucky even to have a job, especially during such hard times.

Snow had already begun to fall when Grady pulled out of the garage at 3:01. It fell steadily all afternoon, creating a frosted wonderland on the manicured lawns that lined West Hall. But by nightfall the winding, twisting, and bending street was a driver's nightmare.

The temperature plummeted, too, adding a new challenge to the mounting snow. "Hurry up! Hurry up! I can't wait all day," Grady snapped at the boarding passengers. "Get to the back of the bus," he hustled them on impatiently. "You people know the rules."

The regulars recognized Grady, but except for a few muffled groans they paid

1. *Obesity* (ō bē′ sə tē) is the condition of being extremely overweight.
2. When Billy spoke *matter-of-factly,* he was businesslike, showing little or no emotion.
3. Household workers are often called *domestics.*
4. Here, *on probation* refers to Grady's working for a trial period before being given a permanent job—or let go.

Vocabulary
plummet (plum′ it) *v.* to fall downward

their fares and rode in sullen silence out to the east side loop.

"Auntie! Now, just why are you taking your own good time getting off this bus?" Grady grumbled at the last passenger.

The woman struggled down the wet, slippery steps. At the bottom she looked over her shoulder. Her dark face held no clue of any emotion. "Auntie? Did you really call me *Auntie?*" she said, laughing sarcastically. "Well, well, well! I never knew my brother had a white son." And she hurried away, chuckling.

Grady's face flushed with surprise and anger. He shouted out the door, "Don't get uppity with me! Y'all know *Auntie* is what we call all you old colored women." Furious, he slammed the door against the bitter cold. He shook his head in disgust. "It's a waste of time trying to be nice," he told himself.

But one look out the window made Grady refocus his attention to a more immediate problem. The weather had worsened. He checked his watch. It was a little past nine. Remarkably, he was still on schedule, but that didn't matter. He had decided to close down the route and take the bus in.

That's when his headlights picked up the figure of a woman running in the snow, without a hat, gloves, or boots. Although she'd pulled a shawl over the lightweight jacket and flimsy dress she was wearing, her clothing offered very little protection against the elements.[5] As she pressed forward against the driving snow and wind, Grady saw that the woman was very young, no more than twenty. And she was clutching something close to her body. What was it? Then Grady saw the baby, a small bundle wrapped in a faded pink blanket.

"These people," Grady sighed, opening the door. The woman stumbled up the steps, escaping the wind that mercilessly ripped at her petite frame.

"Look here. I've closed down the route. I'm taking the bus in."

In big gulping sobs the woman laid her story before him. "I need help, please. My husband's gone to Memphis looking for work. Our baby's sick, real sick. She needs to get to the hospital. I know she'll die if I don't get help."

"Well, I got to go by the hospital on the way back to the garage. You can ride that far." Grady nodded for her to pay. The woman looked at the floor. "Well? Pay up and get on to the back of the bus so I can get out of here."

"I—I don't have the fare," she said, quickly adding, "but if you let me ride, I promise to bring it to you in the morning."

"Give an inch, y'all want a mile. You know the rules. No money, no ride!"

"Oh, please!" the young woman cried. "Feel her little head. It's so hot." She held out the baby to him. Grady recoiled.

Desperately the woman looked for something to bargain with. "Here," she said, taking off her wedding ring. "Take this. It's gold. But please don't make me get off this bus."

He opened the door. The winds howled savagely. "Please," the woman begged.

5. Here, *elements* means "the forces of nature; weather."

Vocabulary

petite (pə tēt′) *adj.* small and slender; little
recoil (ri koil′) *v.* to draw back, as in fear

Old Trinity in Winter. Guy Wiggins (1883–1962). Oil on canvas, 24 x 20 in. Private collection.
Viewing the painting: What literary element in the story does this painting emphasize?

"Go on home, now. You young gals get hysterical over a little fever. Nothing. It'll be fine in the morning." As he shut the door the last sounds he heard were the mother's sobs, the baby's wail, and the moaning wind.

Grady dismissed the incident until the next morning, when he read that it had been a record snowfall. His eyes were drawn to a small article about a colored woman and child found frozen to death on Hall Street. No one seemed to know where the woman was going or why. No one but Grady.

"That gal should have done like I told her and gone on home," he said, turning to the comics.

It was exactly one year later, on the anniversary of the record snowstorm, that Grady was assigned the Hall Street Express again. Just as before, a storm heaped several inches of snow onto the city in a matter of hours, making driving extremely hazardous.

By nightfall Grady decided to close the route. But just as he was making the turnaround at the east side loop, his headlight picked up a woman running in the snow—the same woman he'd seen the previous year. Death hadn't altered her desperation. Still holding on to the blanketed baby, the small-framed woman pathetically struggled to reach the bus.

Grady closed his eyes but couldn't keep them shut. She was still coming, but from where? The answer was too horrible to consider, so he chose to let his mind find a more reasonable explanation. From some dark corner of his childhood he heard his father's voice, slurred by alcohol, mocking him. *It ain't the same woman, dummy. You know how they all look alike!*

Grady remembered his father with bitterness and swore at the thought of him. This *was* the same woman, Grady argued with his father's memory, taking no comfort in being right. Grady watched the woman's movements breathlessly as she stepped out of the headlight beam and approached the door. She stood outside the door waiting . . . waiting.

The gray coldness of Fear slipped into the driver's seat. Grady sucked air into his lungs in big gulps, feeling out of control. Fear moved his foot to the gas pedal, careening the bus out into oncoming traffic. Headlights. A truck. Fear made Grady hit the brakes. The back of the bus went into a sliding spin, slamming into a tree. Grady's stomach crushed against the steering wheel, rupturing his liver and spleen.[6] *You've really done it now, lunkhead.* As he drifted into the final darkness, he heard a woman's sobs, a baby wailing—or was it just the wind?

Twenty-five years later, Ray Hammond, a war hero with two years of college, became the first black driver Metro hired. A lot of things had happened during those two and a half decades to pave the way for Ray's new job. The military had integrated its forces

6. To *rupture* is to break or burst open. The *liver* and *spleen,* both located near the stomach, are important internal organs.

Vocabulary

pathetically (pə thet′ i kəl ē) *adv.* pitifully

careening (kä rēn′ ing) *adj.* tilting or swaying while moving, as if out of control during the Korean War. In 1954 the Supreme Court had ruled that segregated[7] schools were unequal. And one by one, unfair laws were being challenged by civil rights groups all over the South. Ray had watched the Montgomery bus boycott with interest, especially the boycott's leader, Dr. Martin Luther King, Jr.

Ray soon found out that progress on the day-to-day level can be painfully slow. Ray was given the Hall Street Express.

"The white drivers call my route the Blackbird Express," Ray told his wife. "I'm the first driver to be given that route as a permanent assignment. The others wouldn't take it."

"What more did you expect?" his wife answered, tying his bow tie. "Just do your best so it'll be easier for the ones who come behind you."

In November, Ray worked the three-to-eleven shift. "Snow's predicted," the route manager barked one afternoon. "Close it down if it gets bad out there, Ray."

The last shift on the Hall Street Express.

Since he was a boy, Ray had heard the story of the haunting of that bus route. Every first snowfall passengers and drivers testified that they'd seen the ghost of Eula Mae Daniels clutching her baby as she ran through the snow.

"Good luck with Eula Mae tonight," one of the drivers said, snickering.

"I didn't know white folk believed in haints,"[8] Ray shot back.

But parked at the east side loop, staring into the swirling snow mixed with ice, Ray felt tingly, as if he were dangerously close to an electrical charge. He'd just made up his mind to close down the route and head back to the garage when he saw her. Every hair on his head stood on end.

He wished her away, but she kept coming. He tried to think, but his thoughts were jumbled and confused. He wanted to look away, but curiosity fixed his gaze on the advancing horror.

Just as the old porch stories had described her, Eula Mae Daniels was a small-framed woman frozen forever in youth. "So young," Ray whispered. "Could be my Carolyn in a few more years." He watched as the ghost came around to the doors. She was out there, waiting in the cold. Ray heard the baby crying. "There but for the grace of God goes one of mine," he said, compassion overruling his fear. "Nobody deserves to be left out in this weather. Ghost or not, she deserves better." And he swung open the doors.

The woman had form but no substance. Ray could see the snow falling *through* her. He pushed fear aside. "Come on, honey, get out of the cold," Ray said, waving her on board.

Eula Mae stood stony still, looking up at Ray with dark, questioning eyes. The driver understood. He'd seen that look before, not from a dead woman but from plenty of his passengers. "It's okay. I'm for

7. In general terms, *integrate* means "to bring parts (or people) together," and *segregate* means the opposite. Military service had long been open to all races, but African Americans were usually trained separately and often assigned to all-black units. In southern states, segregation laws had required that blacks and whites use "separate but equal" public facilities.

8. *Haints* is Ray's way of saying *haunts,* meaning "ghosts."

Vocabulary

substance (sub′ stəns) *n.* basic material; solid quality

Viewing the photograph: This photograph was taken in Montgomery, Alabama, in April 1956. The "EASE THAT SQUEEZE" sign refers to traffic problems, not seating on the bus. What information about the bus boycott does this photo reveal?

real. Ray Hammond, the first Negro to drive for Metro. Come on, now, get on," he coaxed her gently.

Eula Mae moved soundlessly up the steps. She held the infant to her body. Ray couldn't remember ever feeling so cold, not even the Christmas he'd spent in a Korean foxhole.[9] He'd seen so much death, but never anything like this.

The ghost mother consoled her crying baby. Then with her head bowed she told her story in quick bursts of sorrow, just as she had twenty-five years earlier. "My husband is in Memphis looking for work. Our baby is sick. She'll die if I don't get help."

"First off," said Ray. "Hold your head up. You got no cause for shame."

"I don't have any money," she said. "But if you let me ride, I promise to bring it to you tomorrow. I promise."

Ray sighed deeply. "The rule book says no money, no ride. But the book doesn't say a word about a personal loan." He took a handful of change out of his pocket, fished around for a dime, and dropped it into the pay box. "You're all paid up. Now, go sit yourself down while I try to get this bus back to town."

9. A *foxhole* is a pit that soldiers usually dig quickly for cover from enemy fire.

Vocabulary

console (kən sōl′) *v.* to comfort or cheer someone who is sad or disappointed

Eula Mae started to the back of the bus.

"No you don't," Ray stopped her. "You don't have to sit in the back anymore. You can sit right up front."

The ghost woman moved to a seat closer, but still not too close up front. The baby fretted. The young mother comforted her as best she could.

They rode in silence for a while. Ray checked in the rearview mirror every now and then. She gave no reflection, but when he looked over his shoulder, she was there, all right. "Nobody will ever believe this," he mumbled. "*I* don't believe it.

"Things have gotten much better since you've been . . . away," he said, wishing immediately that he hadn't opened his mouth. Still he couldn't—or wouldn't—stop talking.

"I owe this job to a little woman just about your size named Mrs. Rosa Parks. Down in Montgomery, Alabama, one day, Mrs. Parks refused to give up a seat she'd paid for just because she was a colored woman."

Eula Mae sat motionless. There was no way of telling if she had heard or not. Ray kept talking. "Well, they arrested her. So the colored people decided to boycott the buses. Nobody rode for over a year. Walked everywhere, formed car pools, or just didn't go, rather than ride a bus. The man who led the boycott was named Reverend King. Smart man. We're sure to hear more about him in the future. . . . You still with me?" Ray looked around. Yes, she was there. The baby had quieted. It was much warmer on the bus now.

Slowly Ray inched along on the icy road, holding the bus steady, trying to keep the back wheels from racing out of control. "Where was I?" he continued. "Oh yeah, things changed after that Montgomery bus boycott. This job opened up. More changes are on the way. Get this: They got an Irish Catholic[10] running for President. Now, what do you think of that?"

About that time Ray pulled the bus over at Seventeenth Street. The lights at Gale Hospital sent a welcome message to those in need on such a frosty night. "This is it."

Eula Mae raised her head. "You're a kind man," she said. "Thank you."

Ray opened the door. The night air gusted up the steps and nipped at his ankles. Soundlessly, Eula Mae stepped off the bus with her baby.

"Excuse me," Ray called politely. "About the bus fare. No need for you to make a special trip . . . back. Consider it a gift."

He thought he saw Eula Mae Daniels smile as she vanished into the swirling snow, never to be seen again.

10. John F. Kennedy's election made him the first Catholic president, as well as the first president born in the 1900s and the youngest president.

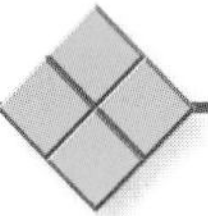

Responding to Literature

PERSONAL RESPONSE

Think about what you discussed for the **Focus Activity** on page 856. Was this story scary? Why or why not?

Analyzing Literature

RECALL

1. What is presented as Grady Bishop's main personality trait?
2. What happens to Grady a year later when he again sees the woman with the baby?
3. What enables Ray Hammond to get a job driving buses?
4. What does Ray do for the woman and baby?

INTERPRET

5. Why, in your opinion, is Grady such an angry person?
6. Why does Grady fear the woman the second time he sees her?
7. What qualities that make Ray a good bus driver also make him the person the ghost has been waiting for?
8. Why, in your opinion, does the woman appear to ride the bus one more time?

EVALUATE AND CONNECT

9. Is it fair to say Grady represents the bad old days and Ray the dawn of equality? Why or why not?
10. What, do you think, would happen if a parent with a sick child tried to board a bus today, but could not afford the fare?

Untitled (513/3), 1982. Gerhard Richter. Oil on canvas, 69.8 x 54.6 cm. Private collection.

LITERARY ELEMENTS

Oral Tradition

Long before people invented writing, they told stories. Stories passed down in this way are part of the **oral tradition** of a society. Since most people long ago spent the daylight hours finding and preparing food, storytelling often took place after dark, around the fire. The flames and shadows made it easy for listeners to believe in the "haints," ghosts, and other beings whose presence could not be explained.

1. The author of "The Woman in the Snow" says, "This story is best enjoyed by the fireplace on the night of the first snowfall." Do you think that sounds engaging? Why or why not?
2. Think back on scary stories you've been told. List three stories you've heard. Was it scarier to hear them than it would be to read them?

- See **Literary Terms Handbook,** p. R7.

Extending Your Response

Personal Writing

A Change for the Better? Ray tells the woman in the snow how much things have improved since she "went away." For example, buses and jobs have been integrated. Do you think the world has improved in your lifetime? Write a couple of paragraphs about how some things have changed in recent times, for either better or worse. You might ask your parents about the changes they've seen in their lifetimes and write a paragraph about those changes.

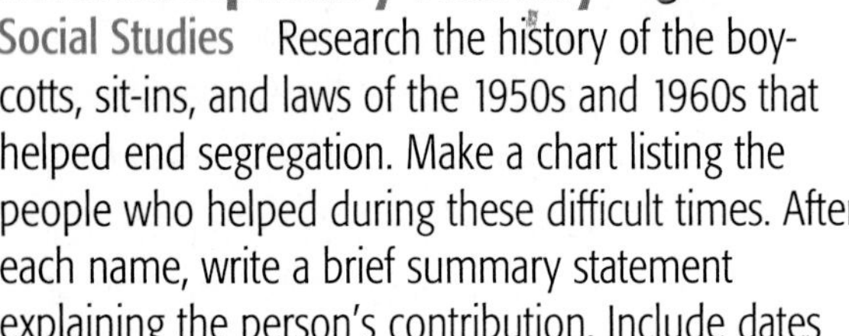

Interdisciplinary Activity

Social Studies Research the history of the boycotts, sit-ins, and laws of the 1950s and 1960s that helped end segregation. Make a chart listing the people who helped during these difficult times. After each name, write a brief summary statement explaining the person's contribution. Include dates and place names when possible.

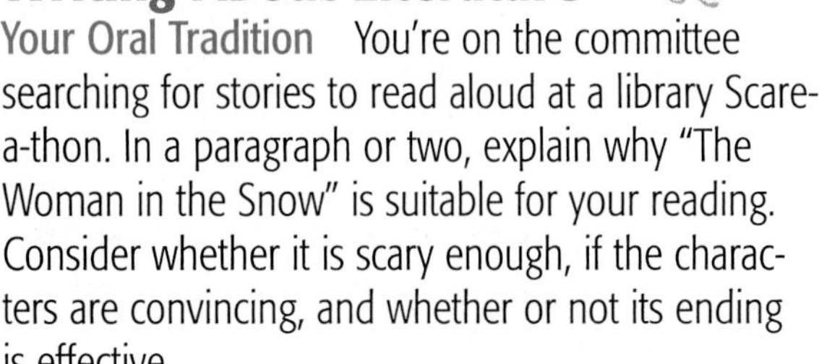

Writing About Literature

Your Oral Tradition You're on the committee searching for stories to read aloud at a library Scare-a-thon. In a paragraph or two, explain why "The Woman in the Snow" is suitable for your reading. Consider whether it is scary enough, if the characters are convincing, and whether or not its ending is effective.

Literature Groups

Compare Drivers There are many differences between the two bus drivers in this story. Divide your group in two to discuss the following statements:

- Each driver gives to others what he has gained from his own life.
- Each driver gets back from life what he gives out to others.

Cite passages from the story to support your opinion.

Save your work for your portfolio.

Skill Minilesson

VOCABULARY • PREFIXES

Eula Mae Daniels tries to *console* her baby. *Console* comes from the Latin prefix *com-,* which means "together," and the Latin word *solari,* which means "to calm or soothe." Ray Hammond has watched her with *compassion. Passion* originally meant "to suffer," so *compassion* is the feeling of "suffering with" another person.

Co-, com-, con-, cor-, and *col-* are different spellings of the same prefix. The spelling differs depending on what letter follows the prefix.

PRACTICE Look for word parts that you recognize in each word on the left. Then use what you know about prefixes and other word parts to match each word to its definition.

1. correlate	a. to blend
2. commix	b. to work together
3. constrain	c. to hold in or back by force
4. correspond	d. to write letters or notes back and forth
5. collaborate	e. to show a connection between

Making and Verifying Predictions

As a skillful reader, you become involved in the action of a story and in the behavior of the characters. You wonder what will happen next. How will this character behave when faced with a problem? To make useful predictions, you use your prior knowledge of the situation and details from the story. For example, what did you think Grady would do when you first read the following passage from "The Woman in the Snow"? What did you know that helped you predict his behavior?

> "I—I don't have the fare," she said, quickly adding, "but if you let me ride, I promise to bring it to you in the morning."

As you continue reading, you check to see if your predictions were correct. You are **verifying predictions.** Did you use your prior knowledge of segregation and racial attitudes? Did you consider Grady's personality and his attitudes?

- For more about making and verifying predictions, see **Reading Handbook,** p. R85.

ACTIVITY

Choose a selection from this book that you would enjoy rereading, or a novel or short story you are reading for pleasure. As you begin to read, watch for clues about the characters, the setting, and the plot. Call on your prior knowledge–your reading or personal experiences that fit into the subject of the story. Then write down your prediction as the plot unfolds. Do this five or six times, and then verify your predictions. Consider these questions:

1. How did you choose when to make your predictions? Did you choose to make a prediction when the action was exciting or when a character needed to make a decision?
2. Were your predictions usually correct?
3. Why were some predictions incorrect? Had you read too quickly? Did you have enough prior knowledge to predict correctly? Did you have a clear understanding of the character's motivations?
4. How did making and verifying predictions improve your reading comprehension?

Using Apostrophes to Show Possession

The apostrophe is used to show possession. Sometimes it is used alone; sometimes it is combined with the letter *s*.

Problem 1 Singular, possessive nouns

Grady Bishops job is driving a bus.

One snowy night, the bus brakes don't work.

Solution Use an apostrophe and an *s* to make a singular noun possessive, even if the noun ends in *-s*.

Grady Bishop's job is driving a bus.

One snowy night, the bus's brakes don't work.

Problem 2 Plural nouns ending in *-s*

The passengers groans are muffled when they recognize Grady.

Solution Add an apostrophe to make the plural noun possessive.

The passengers' groans are muffled when they recognize Grady.

Problem 3 Plural nouns not ending in *-s*

Grady doesn't care at all about peoples needs or difficulties.

Solution If a plural noun does not end in *-s*, add an apostrophe and an *s*.

Grady doesn't care at all about people's needs or difficulties.

Problem 4 Possessive personal pronouns

If a woman needs help, it's not Grady's problem, it's her's.

Solution Omit apostrophes in possessive pronouns, such as *hers*.

If a woman needs help, it's not Grady's problem, it's hers.

- For more about apostrophes, see **Language Handbook,** p. R42.

EXERCISE

Write the possessive form of each word.

a. baby	**c.** driver	**e.** yours	**g.** watch	**i.** brakes
b. folk	**d.** piles	**f.** buses	**h.** address	**j.** children

Before You Read

The Dinner Party

MEET MONA GARDNER

When Mona Gardner wrote a story set in India, she knew her setting well. She lived in India, as well as in Japan, China, Hong Kong, and Bali. In the late 1930s, she traveled all over the Far East as a correspondent for an American newspaper syndicate, reporting on the turmoil that would lead to World War II.

Mona Gardner (1900–1982?) was born in Seattle, Washington. This story first appeared in the Saturday Review of Literature *in 1942.*

FOCUS ACTIVITY

Do men and women handle crises differently? Does one gender react better than the other?

Journal

Describe a time when someone prejudged your ability to handle a tough situation on the basis of your gender.

Setting a Purpose

As you read this story, consider the feelings of the women and men at the dinner party.

BACKGROUND

The Time and Place The time is the early 1900s. The place is India when it was a British colony.

Did You Know? Most societies once had firmly established roles for the men and women of that society. These roles depended largely on tradition, and also on the fact that women, because they bore children, were more likely than men to perform tasks that allowed them to care for children. Because many roles were based on gender, some societies developed beliefs that these roles were only suitable for one gender. In modern times, these beliefs have changed in many cultures. Both men and women have been freed to do work and to pursue hobbies based on their abilities and preferences.

VOCABULARY PREVIEW

naturalist (nach′ ər ə list) *n.* one who studies living things, especially plants or animals, by observing them directly; p. 871

arresting (ə res′ ting) *adj.* demanding the attention; striking; p. 871

sober (sō′ bər) *v.* to make or become serious and quiet; p. 871

forfeit (fôr′ fit) *v.* to lose as a penalty for some error or failure; p. 871

The Dinner Party

Mona Gardner

An Elegant Dinner Party. Jean Beraud (1849–1936). Pencil and watercolor heightened with white, 10 x 13 in. Private collection. Christie's Images.

The country is India. A large dinner party is being given by a colonial official and his wife. The guests are army officers and government attachés[1] and their wives, and an American naturalist.

At one side of the long table a spirited discussion springs up between a young woman and a colonel. The woman insists women have long outgrown the jumping-on-a-chair-at-sight-of-a-mouse era. The colonel says that women haven't the nerve control of men. Several men at the table agree with him.

"A woman's unfailing reaction in any crisis," the colonel says, "is to scream. And while a man may feel like it, yet he has that ounce more of control than a woman has. And that last ounce is what counts!"

The American scientist does not join in the argument, but sits watching the other guests. As he looks, he sees a strange expression come over the face of the hostess. She is staring straight ahead, the muscles of her face contracting slightly. With a small gesture she summons the native boy standing behind her chair. She whispers to him. The boy's eyes widen; he turns quickly and leaves the room. No one else sees this, nor the boy when he puts a bowl of milk on the verandah[2] outside the glass doors.

The American comes to with a start. In India, milk in a bowl means only one thing.

1. *Attachés* (at′ ə shāz′) are assistants to an ambassador or other high official.
2. A *verandah* is a long porch, usually with a roof, along one or more sides of a house.

It is bait for a snake. He realizes there is a cobra in the room.

He looks up at the rafters—the likeliest place—and sees they are bare. Three corners of the room, which he can see by shifting only slightly, are empty. In the fourth corner a group of servants stand, waiting until the next course can be served. The American realizes there is only one place left—under the table.

His first impulse is to jump back and warn the others. But he knows the commotion will frighten the cobra and it will strike. He speaks quickly, the quality of his voice so arresting that it sobers everyone.

"I want to know just what control everyone at this table has. I will count three hundred, and not one of you is to move a single muscle. The persons who move will forfeit 50 rupees.[3] Now! Ready!"

The people sit like stone images while he counts. He is saying ". . . two-hundred and eighty . . ." when, out of the corner of his eye, he sees the cobra emerge and make for the bowl of milk. Screams ring out as he jumps to slam shut the verandah doors.

"You were right, Colonel!" the host says. "A man has just shown us an example of real control."

"Just a minute," the American says, turning to his hostess, "there's one thing I'd like to know. Mrs. Wynnes, how did you know that cobra was in the room?"

A faint smile lights up the woman's face as she replies: "Because it was crawling across my foot."

3. *Rupees* (ro͞o pēz′) are units of money used in India.

Vocabulary

naturalist (nach′ ər ə list) *n.* one who studies living things, especially plants or animals, by observing them directly
arresting (ə res′ ting) *adj.* demanding the attention; striking
sober (sō′ bər) *v.* to make or become serious and quiet
forfeit (fôr′ fit) *v.* to lose as a penalty for some error or failure

Responding to Literature

PERSONAL RESPONSE

What was your reaction to the host's praise of the American scientist? Do you agree that he was "an example of real control"?

Analyzing Literature

RECALL

1. What do the young woman and the colonel argue about?
2. When does the American first realize something is wrong?
3. What does the American do when he sees the snake bait being put on the verandah?
4. Who turns out to have the most control of anyone in this story?

INTERPRET

5. How does the young woman show that she is not free from prejudice?
6. What does the hostess whisper to the servant?
7. Does the American show "that last ounce of control"? Support your answer.
8. What, in your opinion, is the purpose of this story?

EVALUATE AND CONNECT

9. Are any of the characters in this very short story developed fully by the writer? What effect does this kind of characterization have on the story?
10. Review your notes from the **Focus Activity** on page 869. Do you think the colonel's argument could be made today? If so, what response would he be likely to get? What facts would you give to prove or disprove his claim?

LITERARY ELEMENTS

Resolution

Resolution is the part of a plot that reveals or suggests the outcome of a conflict. In the resolution, the main conflict, problem, or disagreement is resolved.

1. What two conflicts form the plot of "The Dinner Party"?
2. What event resolves each conflict?
3. Were the conflicts resolved to your satisfaction? Explain.

- See **Literary Terms Handbook**, p. R8.

Extending Your Response

Writing About Literature

Comparing Characters With a partner, reread the story and make notes on the characteristics shown by the British colonel and the American naturalist. Write a brief comparison of the two.

Learning for Life

Performance Appraisal You are a supervisor at NASA, evaluating applicants for a training program for future astronauts. Evaluate the four main characters in the story: the colonel, the hostess, the young woman, and the American naturalist. In two or three paragraphs, explain why you would or would not consider each person for the program.

Personal Writing

Attitudes and Arguments Why, in your opinion, does the hostess in the story have so little dialogue? If you had been the hostess, would you have responded to the claims made at the start of the story that men had more control of their emotions than women had of theirs? What might you have said after the cobra had been shut out?

Literature Groups

In Our Nature Even the young woman who argues with the colonel agrees that women used to jump on chairs at the sight of a mouse. Is she right? Were women more timid a few generations back? Have they outgrown that? Is it likely that all British military men would share the colonel's ideas? Would all American scientists have the wits to keep everyone sitting quietly? Is it fair to generalize about any group? Discuss these questions within your group.

Save your work for your portfolio.

Skill Minilesson

VOCABULARY • MULTIPLE-MEANING WORDS

Knowing one meaning of a word can sometimes help you figure out another meaning. For example, if a suspected criminal is *arrested,* the person is stopped. An *arresting* sight is one that stops you by demanding your attention.

PRACTICE Use your knowledge to match each underlined word with its definition.

1. a cutting remark	a. mastery
2. a pocket of ignorance	b. inconsistent
3. a command of French	c. small area
4. on the scent of the thief	d. meant to hurt
5. a spotty record of attendance	e. trail of clues

Writing WORKSHOP

Expository Writing: Explaining a Mystery

Mysteries, spine-tingling stories–who can resist them? We love to shiver through chilling tales, and often seek logical explanations for them long afterward. Whether it's a suspenseful television or book plot, an urban legend, or a real-life experience, unraveling a mystery story can be as fun as experiencing it for the first time.

Assignment: Follow the process on these pages to develop your own factual explanation of a mysterious event.

- As you write your explanation, refer to **Writing Handbook,** pp. R50–R55.

The Writing Process

PREWRITING

PREWRITING TIP

If you choose a story from television or film, see the **Listening, Speaking, and Viewing** feature on page 813 for tips on how to examine it.

Choose a Tale

Take a moment to recall mysterious stories that you've heard, read, or seen on film or TV. Talk with friends to jog your memory. Make a list of stories. Then choose one that you find particularly intriguing–or particularly chilling.

Examine the Facts

In a sentence or two, summarize the mysterious or chilling story you've chosen. Then list the facts of

Story:
My brother and I kept hearing spooky voices in our room.

Facts:
*voices came from heater
*voices came only at night
*we lived in a duplex apartment
*our room shared a wall with neighbors
*neighbors worked all day, home only at night

Possible Explanation:
Maybe our neighbors' voices came through the heater duct.

the story, and decide on a reasonable explanation. List as many facts as you can to support your explanation.

Consider Your Audience and Purpose

Plan your draft with your audience and purpose in mind. Your audience will be your classmates and teacher–and perhaps other people. You might submit your essay to your school newspaper. If you focus on a personal experience, you might share your essay with friends or family. Your purpose is to explain, so you'll need to make your train of thought clear. What background information will your readers need?

Plan and Consider

Lay out your facts in an order that makes sense, showing how they lead to your explanation. Add details to support each fact. Then evaluate the scenario you are describing. What conclusions can you draw about it? Do you see it as a coincidence, a mix-up, a hoax, or a genuine mystery–or perhaps as a little of each?

Facts:	**Details:**
We lived in a duplex.	*Neighbors had no kids, knew and liked us.*
Our room shared a wall with neighbors.	*Mom thought sound came from their living room wall.*
Voices came from heater.	*Wall heater; neighbors had similiar one.*
Voices came only at night.	*Sounded faint and metallic; we were so scared!*
Neighbors worked all day, home only at night.	*They got home near our bedtime.*

Explanation: *It was probably our neighbors' voices, distorted and muffled by heater.*

Conclusion: *No one was trying to fool us. Our fears led us to fool ourselves.*

DRAFTING

Drafting Tip

To keep readers' interest, vary the lengths and patterns of your sentences.

Open with Suspense

Start with a summary of the chilling tale or event. You needn't provide your explanation right away. Instead, build suspense by introducing the story as a mystery. Weave facts into your summary, but don't add them up for readers yet.

Explain and Evaluate

Discuss the facts and details of the story, showing how they add up to your explanation. Use your prewriting notes, and make your reasoning clear. To close, present your conclusions about the tale or event you've focused on.

MODEL · DRAFTING

The faint, tinny voices gave my brother and me the creeps. They came from the wall heater in our room, but only when we were in our beds at night. Once, in the dark, before we nodded off to sleep, we heard the spooky voices say our names!

Now, years later, we understand the facts behind the mystery. For one thing, we lived in a duplex.

REVISING

Revising Tip

Does your partner find your reasoning hard to follow? Try adding transitions such as *thus, this shows that, since, because, therefore,* or *so.*

Rework or Rewrite

After a break, return to your draft to map out changes. Use the **Questions for Revising** as a guide. If you have a partner, ask him or her to point out strong points as well as weak points. You might either rework your original or write another draft from scratch.

QUESTIONS FOR REVISING

- ☑ How does my opener create suspense? How might I make it more suspenseful?
- ☑ Where might I add facts or details to strengthen my explanation?
- ☑ How might I vary my sentence patterns to keep readers' interest?
- ☑ How do the facts of the story support my evaluation?

EDITING/PROOFREADING

Before making a final copy, check your grammar and mechanics, making needed corrections. Look for each point mentioned on the **Proofreading Checklist.** Pay special attention to the use of apostrophes, as shown in the **Grammar Link** on page 868.

Grammar Hint

Never use an apostrophe in *its*, the possessive pronoun meaning "belonging to it." *It's*, with an apostrophe, is a contraction of "it is."

It's a perfect day to give the dog its bath.

PROOFREADING CHECKLIST

- ☑ Punctuation, including apostrophes, is correct. (Be sure no apostrophes are used with personal pronouns such as *theirs, yours,* and *its.*)
- ☑ Sentences are complete; there are no fragments or run-ons.
- ☑ All verbs agree with their subjects.
- ☑ Spelling and capitalization are correct.

MODEL • EDITING/PROOFREADING

The scare left it's mark on my little brother. He still keeps the lamp near his bed on all night.

TECHNOLOGY TIP

You and a partner might copy your drafts onto each other's disks and proofread for each other. Be sure you discuss each correction.

PUBLISHING/PRESENTING

Try compiling your class's essays into an anthology with a title such as *Stranger than Fiction.* Work together to arrange essays in an order that makes sense, and to create an introduction, a title page, a table of contents, and a cover. Class members who enjoy art might contribute illustrations.

PRESENTING TIP

You might divide your anthology into sections based on the essays' themes.

Reflecting

Think about the following questions. Write detailed responses in your journal.

- On which part of this assignment did you work hardest? Explain.
- What grade do you think your essay deserves? Why?

Save your work for your portfolio.

Theme Wrap-Up

Responding to the Theme

1. Which selection did you find the scariest? Why?
2. What new thoughts do you have about the following ideas as a result of reading this theme?
   - Our own imaginations can be scarier than fiction.
   - An overactive imagination can cause big trouble for its owner.
   - Some stories reflect our worst fears.
3. Present your theme project to the class.

Analyzing Literature

SUSPENSE

Writers create suspense by making readers wonder what might happen next. Choose two suspenseful scenes from the theme. Explain how each writer creates suspense in the selection.

Evaluate and Set Goals

1. Of the following activities, which did you enjoy the most? Which did you find the most difficult?
   - reading and understanding the selections
   - writing your own pieces
   - analyzing and discussing the selections
   - presenting ideas and projects
   - researching topics
2. How would you assess your work in this theme, using the following scale? Give at least two reasons for your assessment.

   4 = outstanding　　2 = fair
   3 = good　　1 = weak
3. Think about what you found challenging in this theme, and choose a goal to work toward in the future.
   - Record your goal and three steps you will take to try to reach it.
   - Meet with your teacher to review your plan for achieving your goal.

Build Your Portfolio

SELECT

Choose two pieces of work from this theme for your portfolio. Write a note to accompany each choice. Use these questions as a guide.

- ✦ Which do you consider your best work? Why?
- ✦ Which turned out to be most challenging? What did you learn from creating it?

REFLECT

Take some time to review all of the work you have selected for your portfolio. Organize the pieces–by theme or by order of preference, for example. Then prepare a table of contents and an introductory note for your completed portfolio.

Reading on Your Own

If you have enjoyed the literature in this theme, you might also be interested in the following books.

The House of Dies Drear

by Virginia Hamilton The house is old, huge, and guarded by a cross caretaker. In addition, there are supposed to be a buried treasure and a ghost. Thomas and his family discover the history of the house and of their own ancestors as they explore the building's connection with the Underground Railroad.

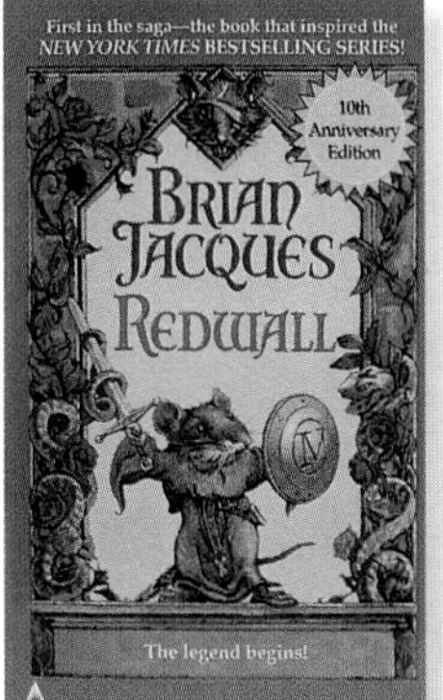

Redwall

by Brian Jacques The creatures living at Redwall Abbey are a peaceful group until the king of vermin declares war against them. Matthias, an apprentice mouse, sets out to find a magic sword that can save Redwall. This is the first book in a series of more than ten tales of quests and fights between good and evil.

Foundation

by Isaac Asimov This book is the first in a series of books that combine science and technology with human strengths and weaknesses. Characters must struggle to achieve their dreams in this classic science fiction novel.

Companions of the Night

by Vivian Vande Velde Sixteen-year-old Kerry is always sensitive to her little brother Ian's tears. As a result, she agrees to make a scary late-night trip to the laundromat to recover Ian's stuffed bear. At the laundromat, Kerry's scary adventure begins.

Standardized Test Practice

Read the following passage. Then read each question on page 881. Decide which is the best answer to each question. Mark the letter for that answer on your paper.

Earth-Shaking Facts

A severe earthquake can be one of the most frightening natural occurrences. An earthquake is just what its name says it is—a quaking, or trembling, of the Earth. It can happen when rock layers move, and the results can be devastating.

The Composition of Earth

The planet Earth is largely composed of rock hidden beneath soil and oceans. This huge ball of rock has three main parts: the core, the mantle, and the crust. The core is a mass of molten metal at the Earth's center. The mantle, which is about 1,800 miles thick, surrounds the core. The crust, a layer about twenty-two miles thick, rings the mantle. Think of Earth as a globe made up of layers, like an onion.

Several types of rock make up the Earth's crust. The rock under the oceans is dense and similar to basalt. The rock beneath the continents is mostly granite, a very hard type of rock. The outer layer of the crust is broken into large pieces called plates. These plates are always moving, but at a very slow pace.

Rock Movements and Energy Waves

At times, the Earth's slowly moving plates collide, and one plate may move under another. Sometimes, moving plates rub against one another as they travel in opposite directions or at different speeds. The energy released by these collisions or by friction moves outward in waves. To experience this type of movement, imagine that you are holding a stick in each hand. You strike them together, hard. The collision of the sticks releases waves of energy. When the energy waves reach your hands, you feel it as a stinging sensation.

When sticks collide in your hands or when an earthquake occurs, waves travel outward in all directions. Some waves caused by the movement of plates travel deep within the Earth and are rarely felt by people. Other waves travel along or near Earth's surface. These are the waves that do visible damage—destroying buildings, collapsing bridges, causing landslides, and tearing up roads.

Earthquakes are complex and powerful. They can be devastating in populated areas of the world. At the same time, their strength and mystery make them fascinating, as well as important, to study.

1 What is the best summary of the passage?

A Earthquakes are rare events in the natural world.

B Earthquakes cause destruction and should be prevented.

C Earthquakes can be understood only by scientists.

D Earthquakes are natural events and there is much to know about them.

2 The author of this passage gives you enough reasons to believe that earthquakes are —

F safe and fun to see

G quiet and dull

H complex and destructive

J pleasant and mild

3 The word <u>sensation</u> in the passage most nearly means —

A feeling

B emotion

C particle

D wave

4 An earthquake is made up of —

F waves of energy

G the Earth's core

H miles of lava and air

J water and heat

5 Which of these statements is a FACT presented in the passage?

A Earthquakes are easy to predict since they are simple to explain.

B The movement of plates on Earth's crust can cause an earthquake.

C Earthquake waves travel in only one direction.

D The crust is 1,700 miles thick.

6 What is the main idea of the section labeled "The Composition of Earth"?

F The upper part of the continents is mostly granite.

G The core is at the center of Earth.

H Earth is made up of three main layers.

J An earthquake can happen at any time and in any place.

Reference Section

Literary Terms Handbook

A

Act A major division of a play. A play may be subdivided into several acts. Most modern plays have one, two, or three acts. *The Diary of Anne Frank,* for example, has two acts. Acts are usually composed of one or more scenes.

See page 710.
See also SCENE.

Alliteration The repetition of consonant sounds, most often at the beginnings of words and syllables. Edgar Allan Poe uses alliteration in the following line from "The Raven":

Doubting, dreaming dreams no mortal ever
dared to dream before. . . .

See pages 294–295, and 506.

Allusion A reference in a work of literature to a well-known character, place, or situation from another work of literature, music, or art, or from history. For example, O. Henry's "The Ransom of Red Chief" contains an allusion to the biblical story of David and Goliath, a tale in which a small and apparently powerless hero overcomes a feared and powerful giant.

See page 853.

Antagonist A person or force that opposes the **protagonist,** or central character, in fiction. The reader is generally meant not to sympathize with the antagonist. In "The Treasure of Lemon Brown," there are several antagonists–for example, the thugs who attack Greg and Lemon Brown and the problems of age and loneliness that attack the elderly musician.

See also CONFLICT, PROTAGONIST.

Anthropomorphism Attributing human characteristics to an animal or object. For example, in the folktale "Talk," the farmer's crops and animals speak to the farmer and to one another.

Assonance The repetition of vowel sounds, especially in a line of poetry. For example, the sound of long *e* is repeated in Margaret Walker's "Sorrow Home."

. . . reared in steam-heated flats

See page 506.
See also ALLITERATION, CONSONANCE.

Author's purpose The intention of the writer–for example, to explain, to tell a story, to persuade, to amuse, or to inform. An author may have more than one purpose. In "The Gettysburg Address," one of Lincoln's purposes was to honor a group of people.

See pages 476 and 646.

Autobiography The story of a person's life written by that person.

See page 196.
See also BIOGRAPHY, MEMOIR.

B

Ballad A short narrative song or poem. Folk ballads, which usually tell of an exciting or dramatic episode, were passed on by word of mouth for generations before being written down. The story of John Henry was passed down primarily in musical form. Literary ballads, which usually have known authors, are written in imitation of folk ballads.

See page 356.
See also NARRATIVE POETRY, ORAL TRADITION.

Biography The account of a person's life written by someone other than the subject. Biographies can be short or book-length.

See also AUTOBIOGRAPHY, MEMOIR.

C

Character A person or other creature in a literary work. A **dynamic character** is one who changes during the story, as does Jim in Kurt Vonnegut's "The Kid Nobody Could Handle." A **static character** remains the same throughout the story, like the crazed narrator of Edgar Allan Poe's "The Tell-Tale Heart."

See pages 23, 46–47, 358, 508, and 832.
See also CHARACTERIZATION.

Characterization The methods a writer uses to develop the personality of a character. In **direct characterization,** the story's narrator makes statements about a character's personality. In **indirect characterization,** a character's personality is revealed through his or her words and actions and through what others think and say about him or her. These techniques are often combined, as in the characterization of the father in Gary Paulsen's "Stop the Sun."

See pages 165, 291, and 692–693.
See also CHARACTER.

Climax The point of greatest interest or suspense in a narrative. Usually the climax comes at the turning point in a story or drama. In "Raymond's Run," by Toni Cade Bambara, the climax occurs as Squeaky races against Gretchen and notices Raymond running on the other side of the fence.

See pages 264, 404, 615, and 832.
See also FALLING ACTION, PLOT, RISING ACTION.

Comedy A type of drama that is humorous and has a happy ending.

See also DRAMA, TRAGEDY.

Conflict The central struggle between opposing forces in a story or play. An **external conflict** is the struggle of a character against an outside force, such as another person, nature, society, or fate. In Yoshiko Uchida's tale "The Wise Old Woman," a man and his mother struggle against the ruler's demands. An **internal conflict** exists within the mind of a character. The man in Uchida's story is torn between loyalty to the ruler and love for his mother.

See pages 247, 358, 561, and 832.
See also ANTAGONIST, PLOT, PROTAGONIST.

Consonance The repetition of identical or similar end or intermediate consonant sounds. The vowel sounds that accompany these repeated consonants usually differ. Shel Silverstein uses consonance in the following line from "Forgotten Language":

Once I understood each word the caterpillar
said, . . .

See page 506.
See also ALLITERATION, ASSONANCE, RHYME, SOUND DEVICES.

D

Description Writing that creates an impression of a setting, a person, an animal, an object, or an event by appealing to one or more of the five senses. In the excerpt from James Herriot's

All Things Bright and Beautiful, the veterinarian provides a strong description of his work with a large patient.

See pages 196 and 444.

Dialect A variation of language spoken by a particular group, or by many people within a geographic region. Dialects differ from standard language. They may contain different structure, sounds, forms, or word meanings. An example of dialect appears in *I Know Why the Caged Bird Sings* by Maya Angelou.

Momma responded with "How you, Sister Flowers?"

See page 207.

Dialogue Conversation between characters in a literary work. These lines from "Golden Glass," by Alma Luz Villanueva, are an example of dialogue in a work of fiction:

"Jason already said he'd bring my food and stuff."

"Where do you plan to shower and go to the bathroom?" Vida wondered.

"With the hose when it's hot and I'll dig holes behind the barn," Ted said so quietly as to seem unspoken.

See pages 157, 692–693, and 728.
See also MONOLOGUE.

Drama A work of literature intended to be performed for an audience. *The Diary of Anne Frank,* by Frances Goodrich and Albert Hackett, is an example of modern drama.

See pages 692–693.
See also STAGE DIRECTIONS.

E

Essay A short piece of nonfiction writing on a single topic. The purpose of the essay is to communicate an idea or opinion. The **formal essay** is serious and impersonal. The **informal essay** may be written in a more conversational style. Anna Quindlen's "Homeless" is an informal essay about the psychological effects of homelessness.

See page 618.

Exaggeration. See HYPERBOLE.

Exposition The author's introduction to the characters, setting, and situation of a story. In the opening paragraphs of "The Battleground," Elsie Singmaster uses exposition to introduce the reader to the background of the story.

See page 522.
See also PLOT.

F

Fable A short, usually simple tale that teaches a moral and sometimes uses animal characters. Morals are often stated directly, often at the end of the fable. In other cases, the moral is understood by the reader, but not stated.

See also THEME.

Falling action In a play or story, the action that follows the climax.

See page 404.
See also PLOT, RISING ACTION.

Fiction Literature in which situations and characters are invented by the writer, such as Robert Cormier's "The Moustache." Two types of fiction are short stories and novels.

See pages 508–509.
See also NONFICTION, NOVEL, SHORT STORY.

Figurative language Language that communicates ideas beyond the literal meanings of words. Figurative language includes elaborate expressions or figures of speech, as opposed to literal language. Although it appears in all kinds of writing, figurative language is especially prominent in poetry.

See also METAPHOR, PERSONIFICATION, SIMILE, SYMBOL.

Figure of speech Language that compares one thing to something that is familiar or that carries a familiar connotation. Simile, metaphor, and personification are examples of figures of speech. In "The Treasure of Lemon Brown," Walter Dean Myers uses a figure of speech by calling Lemon Brown's memories his "treasure."

See also METAPHOR, PERSONIFICATION, SIMILE.

Flashback An interruption in a chronological narrative. A flashback presents readers with scenes from events that occurred earlier than those in the story. Stephen King uses a flashback in the final scene of *Sorry, Right Number.*

Folklore The traditional beliefs, customs, stories, songs, and dances of a culture. Folklore is an oral tradition and is based on the lives of common people.

See also FOLKTALE, LEGEND, MYTH, ORAL TRADITION.

Folktale An anonymous, traditional story passed down orally long before being written down. The author of a folktale is generally anonymous. Folktales include animal stories, trickster tales, fairy tales, myths, legends, and tall tales. "M'su Carencro and Mangeur de Poulet" is a Cajun folktale retold by J. J. Reneaux.

See page 358.
See also LEGEND, MYTH, ORAL TRADITION, TALL TALE.

Foreshadowing The use of clues by the author to prepare readers for events that will happen in a narrative, as in "The Summer of Vietnam" by Barbara Renaud González.

> "Vietnam," he says. The worst answer. The only answer that can make me cry.
> Instead, at night I remember.

See page 141.
See also PLOT, RISING ACTION, SUSPENSE.

Frame story The telling of a story within a story. The frame is the outer story, which usually comes before and follows the inner–and more important–story.

Free verse Poetry that has no fixed pattern of meter, rhyme, line length, or stanza arrangement. "The Pinta, the Nina and the Santa Maria; and many other cargoes of Light," by John Tagliabue, is an example of free verse.

See page 312.
See also METER, RHYME, RHYTHM.

G

Genre An artistic or literary category. Fiction, nonfiction, poetry, and drama are the main literary genres.

H

Haiku Originally a Japanese form of poetry that has three lines and seventeen syllables. The first and third lines have five syllables each; the middle line has seven.

Hero The main character of a literary work, usually a person with admirable qualities. Sally Ann Thunder Ann Whirlwind is the hero of the story by Mary Pope Osborne.

See page 422.
See also PROTAGONIST, TALL TALE.

Historical fiction A novel, play, short story, or narrative poem that sets fictional characters in an earlier historical period and contains accurate details about that time. "The Drummer Boy of Shiloh," by Ray Bradbury, is set during the Civil War.

See page 508.
See also GENRE.

Hyperbole (hī pur′ bə lē) A figure of speech that uses exaggeration to express strong emotion, make a point, or create humor. The following sentence from Langston Hughes's "Thank You, M'am" contains an example of hyperbole:

She was a large woman with a large purse that had everything in it but hammer and nails.

See also FIGURE OF SPEECH.

I

Imagery Language that emphasizes sense impressions that help the reader see, hear, feel, smell, and taste things described in the work. Margaret Walker uses imagery in this passage from "Sorrow Home":

Warm skies and gulf blue streams are in my blood. I belong / with the smell of fresh pine, with the trail of coon, and / the spring growth of wild onion.

See page 109.
See also FIGURATIVE LANGUAGE.

Irony A contrast between what is and what ought to be. **Situational irony** exists when the outcome of a situation is the opposite of what someone has come to expect–for example, the ending of *Sorry, Right Number* by Stephen King. **Verbal irony** exists when a person says one thing and means another–for example, saying "Nice guy!" about someone you dislike.

See pages 124 and 626.

J

Journal An account of day-to-day events or a record of experiences, ideas, or thoughts. A journal may also be called a diary. *Anne Frank: The Diary of a Young Girl* is Anne Frank's account of a short period in her life.

See page 682.
See also NONFICTION.

L

Legend A traditional story handed down orally and believed to be based on history. "The Siege of Courthouse Rock" is a Sioux legend retold by Jenny Leading Cloud.

See pages 416 and 829.
See also FABLE, FOLKLORE, FOLKTALE, MYTH, ORAL TRADITION, TALL TALE.

Limerick A light, usually humorous poem with a regular rhythm pattern and a rhyme scheme of *aabba.*

See also METER, RHYME.

Local color The portrayal of a region's natural and human environment, including the speech and behavior of the inhabitants, usually as a way of adding a realistic flavor to a story. Washington Irving's "The Legend of Sleepy Hollow" uses local color to enhance the tale.

Lyric A verse or poem that can be sung. The words to "I Think Myself Out," by Enid Futterman, are song lyrics.

See also RHYME SCHEME.

Lyric poetry Poems that express thoughts or emotions about a subject. Many of Robert Frost's poems, like "Fire and Ice," are lyric poems.

See page 306.
See also FIGURATIVE LANGUAGE, IMAGERY, METER, RHYME.

M

Memoir A narrative based on an event or person and emphasizing the narrator's personal experience of it. The selection from *All But My Life,* by Gerda Weissmann Klein, is an example of a memoir.

See page 669.
See also AUTOBIOGRAPHY, BIOGRAPHY.

Metaphor A figure of speech that compares seemingly unlike things. In contrast to a **simile,** a metaphor implies the comparison instead of stating it directly; so there is no use of connecting words such as *like* or *as.* There are many metaphors in the "I Have a Dream" speech by Martin Luther King:

Now is the time to rise from the dark and desolate valley of segregation to the sunlit path of racial justice; now is the time to lift our nation from the quicksands of racial injustice to the solid rock of brotherhood.

See pages 295, 393, and 602.
See also FIGURE OF SPEECH, IMAGERY, SIMILE.

Meter A regular pattern of stressed syllables that gives a line of poetry a predictable rhythm. For example, the meter is marked in the following lines from Walt Whitman's poem "O Captain! My Captain!":

The ship has weather'd every rack, the prize we
sought is won:
The port is near, the bells I hear, the people all
exulting.

See pages 294 and 455.
See also RHYTHM.

Monologue A long speech by a character in a play.

See page 761.

Mood The emotional quality or atmosphere of the story. In "If I Forget Thee Oh Earth . . . ," Arthur C. Clarke establishes a nostalgic mood that extends throughout the story.

See pages 183, 692–693, and 842.
See also SETTING.

Myth A traditional story of anonymous origin that explains the beliefs and practices of a people. Myths may tell of extraordinary events from earliest times and may deal with gods, heroes, and supernatural events.

See also FOLKLORE, FOLKTALE, HERO, LEGEND, ORAL TRADITION, TALL TALE.

N

Narration The telling of a sequence of events. "A Mother in Mannville," by Marjorie Kinnan Rawlings, relies heavily on narration to develop the plot.

See pages 175 and 536.
See also NARRATIVE POETRY.

Narrative poetry Verse that tells a story. "The Raven," by Edgar Allan Poe, is a narrative poem.

See page 255.
See also NARRATION.

Narrator The person who tells a story. In fiction, the narrator may be a character in the story. Squeaky, for example, narrates the story in "Raymond's Run" by Toni Cade Bambara.

See pages 35 and 183.
See also POINT OF VIEW.

Nonfiction Writing based mainly on fact, not on imagination. Among the categories of nonfiction are biographies, autobiographies, and essays. For example, *On the Road with Charles Kuralt* is nonfiction.

See also AUTOBIOGRAPHY, BIOGRAPHY, ESSAY, FICTION, JOURNAL.

Novel A book-length fictional narrative. The novel has more space than a short story to develop its plot, characters, setting, and theme.

See also FICTION, SHORT STORY.

O

Onomatopoeia The use of a word or phrase that actually imitates or suggests the sound of what it describes. The following line from Emily Dickinson's "I like to see it lap the miles" contains this example of onomatopoeia:

In horrid, hooting stanza . . .

See also SOUND DEVICES.

Oral tradition Literature that passes by word of mouth from one generation to the next. "Coyote and Wasichu," as edited and retold by Richard Erdoes and Alfonso Ortiz, is an example of a story passed down through the oral tradition.

See page 865.
See also FOLKLORE, FOLKTALE, LEGEND, MYTH.

P

Parallelism The use of a series of words, phrases, or sentences that have similar grammatical form. Parallelism emphasizes the items that are arranged in the similar structures. Note the following example from Robert Cormier's "The Moustache":

"Nana, this is Mike your grandson,
not Mike your husband."

See also REPETITION.

Personification A figure of speech in which a human quality is given to an animal, object, or idea. The speaker in Margaret Walker's poem, "Sorrow Home," personifies the plants of the tropics in the lines:

. . . . The palm tree and banana leaf,
mango and coconut, breadfruit and rubber trees
know me.

See pages 295 and 385.
See also FIGURATIVE LANGUAGE, FIGURE OF SPEECH, METAPHOR.

Plot The sequence of events in a story, novel, or play. The plot begins with **exposition,** which introduces the story's characters, setting, and situation. The **rising action** adds complications to the story's **conflicts,** or problems, leading to the **climax,** or point of greatest interest or suspense. The **falling action** is the logical result of the climax, and the **resolution** presents the final outcome.

See pages 46–47, 375, and 508.
See also CONFLICT, FALLING ACTION, RISING ACTION.

Poetry A type of literature in which language, images, sound, and rhythm are combined to create an emotional effect. Poetry is a compact form of writing that often, but not always, uses rhyme, meter, and figurative language. Other characteristics of some, but not all, poems are a use of metaphor and simile and the division of the work into stanzas.

See pages 294–295.
See also FIGURATIVE LANGUAGE, METAPHOR, METER, RHYME, SIMILE.

Point of view The relationship of the narrator to the story. A story using **first-person point of view** is told by one of the characters, as in "The Raven," by Edgar Allan Poe. The reader sees everything through that character's eyes. In a story with a **limited third-person point of view,** the narrator is outside the story and reveals the thoughts of only one character, but refers to that character as *he* or *she.* In "Stop the Sun," Gary Paulsen uses this point of view. In a story with an **omniscient point of view,** like "Bagged Wolf," by Carol Kendall and Yao-wen Li, the narrator is also outside the story, but can reveal any or all events, thoughts, and actions of the characters, as well as background information important to the story.

See pages 196, 221, and 489.
See also AUTHOR'S PURPOSE.

Props Theater slang (a shortened form of *properties*) for objects and elements of the scenery of a stage play or movie set.

Protagonist The central character in a story, drama, or dramatic poem. Usually the action revolves around the protagonist, who is involved in the main conflict. For example, Grady is the protagonist of Patricia C. McKissack's "The Woman in the Snow."

See ANTAGONIST, CONFLICT.

Pun A humorous play on two or more meanings of the same word, puns often appear in advertising headlines and slogans–for example, "Our hotel rooms give you suite feelings."

R

Refrain A line or lines repeated regularly, usually in a poem or song.

Repetition The recurrence of sounds, words, phrases, lines, or stanzas in a speech or piece of writing. When a line or stanza is repeated in a poem, it is called a refrain. Martin Luther King's speech is famous for his powerful repetition of two phrases:

"I have a dream that . . . ."
"I have a dream today!"

See pages 385 and 499.
See also PARALLELISM, REFRAIN.

Resolution The part of a plot that comes after the falling action. The resolution reveals or suggests the outcome of the conflict.

See page 872.
See also CONFLICT, PLOT.

Rhyme The repetition of identical or similar sounds at the ends of words used close to one another. **End rhyme** occurs at the ends of lines, as in Edgar Allan Poe's "The Raven." **Slant rhyme** occurs when words include sounds that are similar but not identical. Slant rhyme usually involves some variation of **consonance** (the repetition of consonant sounds) or **assonance** (the repetition of vowel sounds). An example of slant rhyme is these lines from May Swenson's "Southbound on the Freeway":

". . . when he passes, winding
among them from behind."

See pages 294 and 462.
See also ASSONANCE, CONSONANCE, REPETITION, RHYME SCHEME.

Rhyme scheme The pattern formed by the end rhyme in a poem. The rhyme scheme is shown by the use of a different letter of the alphabet to name each new rhyme. The famous opening stanza of Henry Wadsworth Longfellow's poem "Paul Revere's Ride" has a rhyme scheme of *aabba.*

Listen, my children, and you shall hear *a*
Of the midnight ride of Paul Revere, *a*
On the eighteenth of April, in Seventy-five; *b*
Hardly a man is now alive *b*
Who remembers that famous day and year. *a*

See also RHYME.

Rhythm The pattern created by the arrangement of stressed syllables, especially in poetry. Rhythm gives poetry a musical quality. Rhythm can be regular, with a predictable pattern or meter, or it can be irregular.

See pages 294 and 688.
See also METER.

Rising action The part of a plot that adds complications to the problems in the story and increases reader interest. In "The Tell-Tale Heart," the suspense increases as the narrator's plans are related.

See page 277.
See also FALLING ACTION, PLOT.

S

Scene A subdivision of an act in a play. Each scene presents action in one place or one situation.

See page 710.
See also ACT.

Science fiction Fiction dealing with the impact of science on societies of the past, present, or future. "If I Forget Thee, Oh Earth . . . ," by Arthur C. Clarke, is science fiction.

See page 596.

Screenplay The script of a film, which, in addition to dialogue and stage directions, usually contains detailed instructions about camera shots and angles. Stephen King's *Sorry, Right Number* is an example of a screenplay.

See page 809.
See also DRAMA, STAGE DIRECTIONS.

Setting The time and place in which the events of a short story, novel, or drama occur. The setting often helps create an atmosphere, or mood.

See pages 46–47, 56, 165, 586, 692–693, and 832.
See also PLOT.

Short story A brief fictional narrative in prose. Elements of the short story include plot, character, setting, point of view, and theme. "The Moustache," by Robert Cormier, is a short story.

See pages 46–47 and 832.
See also CHARACTER, PLOT, POINT OF VIEW, SETTING, THEME.

Simile A figure of speech using *like* or *as* to compare seemingly unlike things. This example of a simile comes from N. Scott Momaday's "New World":

Shadows / withdraw / and lie / away / like smoke.

See pages 295 and 393.
See also FIGURE OF SPEECH.

Sound devices Techniques used to create a sense of rhythm or to emphasize particular sounds. Sound devices include onomatopoeia, alliteration, consonance, assonance, and rhyme.

See also ALLITERATION, ASSONANCE, CONSONANCE, ONOMATOPOEIA, RHYTHM.

Speaker The voice in a poem, like the narrator in a work of fiction. The speaker's tone may communicate an attitude toward the subject of the poem. For example, the speaker of Henry Wadsworth Longfellow's "Paul Revere's Ride" adopts the tone of a public speaker addressing an audience:

Listen, my children, and you shall hear
Of the midnight ride of Paul Revere . . .

See pages 470 and 632.
See also TONE.

Stage directions In a drama, instructions that describe the appearance and actions of characters, as well as sets, costumes, and lighting. Examples of stage directions can be found in *The Diary of Anne Frank,* by Frances Goodrich and Albert Hackett, and in *Sorry, Right Number,* by Stephen King.

See pages 692–693 and 742.

Stanza A group of lines forming a unit in a poem. Stanzas are, in effect, the paragraphs of a poem.

See page 570.

Stereotype A character who is not developed as an individual, but who shows traits and mannerisms supposedly shared by all members of a group.

See page 42.

Style The author's choice and arrangement of words and sentences in a literary work. Style can reveal an author's purpose in writing and attitude toward his or her subject and audience. In "The Dinner Party," the author uses an unexciting, matter-of-fact style to support the calm attitude of the story's hero.

See pages 73, 358, and 639.
See also AUTHOR'S PURPOSE, GENRE.

Suspense A feeling of curiosity, uncertainty, or even dread about what is going to happen next. Writers increase the level of suspense in a story by giving readers clues to what might happen. In "The Tell-Tale Heart," Edgar Allan Poe builds suspense by gradually revealing the narrator's insanity.

See pages 347 and 832.
See also PLOT, RISING ACTION.

Symbol Any object, person, place, or experience that stands for something else because of a resemblance or association. In "The Black Walnut Tree," by Mary Oliver, the tree is a symbol of a family's success in overcoming hard times.

See pages 87 and 300.

T

Tall tale An imaginative tale of adventures or amazing feats of North American folk heroes. The tales take place in realistic local settings. Carl Sandburg's *The People, Yes* identifies the heroes of various tall tales.

See page 366.
See also FOLKLORE, FOLKTALE, HERO, LEGEND, MYTH, ORAL TRADITION.

Theme The main idea of a story, poem, novel, or play. Some works have a stated theme. More frequently, works have a theme that is not stated but is revealed gradually through other elements such as plot, character, setting, point of view, symbol, and irony.

See pages 14, 46–47, 320, and 358.

Title The name of a literary work.

See page 380.

Tone The attitude of the narrator toward a subject. The tone may be eerie, threatening, serious, or light, for example. In "Mother and Daughter," by Gary Soto, the tone is humorous.

See page 68.

Tragedy A play in which a main character suffers a downfall. The tone of a tragedy is serious, and the ending is usually an unhappy one. In plays written before the nineteenth century, the main character is often a person of dignified or heroic stature. The character's downfall may result from outside forces or from a weakness within the character, which is known as a **tragic flaw.**

See page 773.

U

Understatement Language that makes something seem less important than it really is. In *On the Road with Charles Kuralt,* the writer observes: "Times couldn't have been very easy in Gnaw Bone, Indiana." The reader realizes things must have been extremely difficult if citizens had to gnaw on bones to survive.

V

Voice An author's distinctive style, or the particular speech patterns of a character in a story. The voice of the narrator in *On the Road with Charles Kuralt* is the voice of a person who observes and enjoys words and places.

See also AUTHOR'S PURPOSE, STYLE, TONE.

Language Handbook

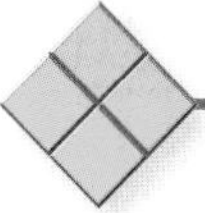

Troubleshooter

Use the Troubleshooter to help you recognize and correct common writing errors.

Sentence Fragment

A sentence fragment does not express a complete thought. It might be missing a subject, a predicate, or both.

Problem: A fragment that lacks a subject

David was hungry. Hadn't eaten all day. *frag*

Solution: Add a subject to the fragment to make a complete sentence.

David was hungry. He hadn't eaten all day.

Problem: A fragment that lacks a predicate

Someone had taken her seat. A tall man. *frag*

Solution: Add a predicate to make the sentence complete.

Someone had taken her seat. A tall man was sitting there.

Problem: A fragment that lacks both a subject and a predicate

We found the kitten. In the garage. *frag*

Solution: Combine the fragment with another sentence.

We found the kitten in the garage.

Rule of Thumb

It is acceptable to use fragments when talking with friends or writing personal letters. Some writers use fragments to produce special effects in stories or dialogue. Use complete sentences, however, in writing for school or business.

LANGUAGE HANDBOOK

Run-on Sentence

A run-on sentence is two or more sentences incorrectly written as one sentence.

Problem: Two main clauses separated only by a comma

They put up the tent in a hurry, night was falling. *run-on*

Solution A: Replace the comma with a period or other end mark, and begin the new sentence with a capital letter.

They put up the tent in a hurry. Night was falling.

Solution B: Place a semicolon between the main clauses.

They put up the tent in a hurry; night was falling.

Problem: Two main clauses with no punctuation between them

I loved the movie my sister hated it. *run-on*

Solution A: Separate the main clauses with a period or other end mark, and begin the second sentence with a capital letter.

I loved the movie. My sister hated it.

Solution B: Add a comma and a coordinating conjunction between the main clauses.

I loved the movie, but my sister hated it.

Problem: Two main clauses with no comma before the coordinating conjunction

Kristie was moving and her classmates would miss her. *run-on*

Solution: Add a comma before the coordinating conjunction.

Kristie was moving, and her classmates would miss her.

Lack of Subject-Verb Agreement

A singular subject calls for a singular form of the verb. A plural subject calls for a plural form of the verb.

Problem: A subject that is separated from the verb by an intervening prepositional phrase

A bowl of cherries are on the table. *agr*

Solution: Ignore a prepositional phrase that comes between a subject and a verb. Make sure that the verb agrees with the subject of the sentence. The object of the preposition is never the subject.

A bowl of cherries is on the table.

Problem: A sentence that begins with *here* or *there*

There goes my brothers. *agr*

Here is Andy and Fatima. *agr*

Solution: The subject is never *here* or *there.* In sentences that begin with *here* or *there,* look for the subject *after* the verb. The verb must agree with the subject.

There go my brothers.

Here are Andy and Fatima.

Problem: An indefinite pronoun as the subject

Either of the sisters walk the dog at night. *agr*

Some of the clothing are too small. *agr*

Some of the clothes is too small. *agr*

Solution: Some indefinite pronouns are singular, some are plural, and some can be either singular or plural, depending upon the noun they refer to. Determine whether the indefinite pronoun is singular or plural, and make sure that the verb agrees with it.

Either of the sisters walks the dog.

Some of the clothing is too small.

Some of the clothes are too small.

Problem: A compound subject that is joined by *and*

Joe and Eric shares a room. *agr*

The author and illustrator are Virginia Clay. *agr*

Solution A: If the parts of the compound subject do not belong to one unit or if they refer to different people or things, use a plural verb.

Joe and Eric share a room.

Solution B: If the parts of the compound subject belong to one unit or if both parts refer to the same person or thing, use a singular verb.

The author and illustrator is Virginia Clay.

Rule of Thumb

If the subject can be replaced by *he, she,* or *it,* use a singular verb. If *they* can replace the subject, use a plural verb.

Problem: A compound subject that is joined by *or* or *nor*

Either a skunk or two raccoons visits our porch each night. *agr*

Neither the stars nor the moon are visible. *agr*

Solution: Make the verb agree with the subject that is closer to it.

Either a skunk or two raccoons visit our porch each night.

Neither the stars nor the moon is visible.

Incorrect Verb Tense or Form

Verbs have different tenses to indicate when the action takes place.

Problem: An incorrect or missing verb ending

I ask you the same question yesterday. *tense*

We have never hike this far before. *tense*

Solution: Add *-ed* or *-d* to a regular verb to form the past tense and the past participle.

I asked you the same question yesterday.

We have never hiked this far before.

Problem: An improperly formed irregular verb

He payed for the groceries. *tense*

The vine had creeped up the wall. *tense*

Solution: Use the correct past or past-participle form of an irregular verb. These forms vary; memorize them, or look them up.

He paid for the groceries.

The vine had crept up the wall.

Problem: Confusion between the past form and the past participle.

She has swam half a mile. *tense*

I seen that movie last week. *tense*

Solution A: Use the past-participle form of an irregular verb, not the past form, when you use the auxiliary verb *have.*

She has swum half a mile.

Solution B: When you do not use the auxiliary verb *have,* use the past form, not the past participle.

I saw that movie last week.

LANGUAGE HANDBOOK

Incorrect Use of Pronouns

The noun that a pronoun refers to is called its antecedent. A pronoun must refer to its antecedent clearly. Subject pronouns refer to subjects in a sentence. Object pronouns refer to objects in a sentence.

Problem: A pronoun that can refer to more than one antecedent

Kenny went to see Tom because he was lonely. *ant*

Solution: Rewrite the sentence, substituting a noun for the pronoun.

Kenny went to see Tom because Tom was lonely.

Problem: Personal pronouns as subjects

Hassan and him are good friends. *pro*

Us and our teacher planned the project. *pro*

Solution: Use a subject pronoun as the subject part of a sentence.

Hassan and he are good friends.

We and our teacher planned the project.

Problem: Personal pronouns as objects

Mom sent Lanny and I a postcard. *pro*

I'm going swimming with he and his cousin. *pro*

Solution: Use an object pronoun as the object of a verb or preposition.

Mom sent Lanny and me a postcard.

I'm going swimming with him and his cousin.

Rule of Thumb

People often choose the wrong form of a pronoun when the pronoun is part of a compound subject or object. Saying the sentence with only the pronoun as the subject or object will often make the correct choice clear. For example, change *Mom sent Lanny and I a postcard* to *Mom sent I a postcard.* The pronoun *I* sounds wrong and should be changed to *me.*

Incorrect Use of Adjectives

Some adjectives have irregular forms: comparative forms for comparing two things and superlative forms for comparing more than two things.

Problem: Incorrect use of *good, better, best*

He's more good at music than art. *adj*

They're the goodest athletes in the school. *adj*

Solution: The comparative and superlative forms of *good* are *better* and *best.* Do not use *more* or *most* or the endings *-er* or *-est* with *good.*

He's better at music than art.

They're the best athletes in the school.

Problem: Incorrect use of *bad, worse, worst*

Of everyone who lost, she felt the most bad. *adj*

The news was badder than we'd expected. *adj*

Solution: Do not use *more* or *most* or the endings *-er* or *-est* with *bad.*

Of everyone who lost, she felt the worst.

The news was worse than we'd expected.

Problem: Incorrect use of comparative adjectives

In spring the days grow more warmer. *adj*

Solution: Do not use both *-er* and *more* at the same time.

In spring the days grow warmer.

Problem: Incorrect use of superlative adjectives

Today Ted ran most fastest. *adj*

Solution: Do not use both *-est* and *most* at the same time.

Today Ted ran fastest.

Incorrect Use of Commas

Commas signal a pause between parts of a sentence and help to clarify meaning.

Problem: Missing commas in a series of three or more items

Kathryn drew a monkey a snake and a parrot. *com*

He ran down the sidewalk up the front steps and into the building. *com*

Solution: When there are three or more items in a series, use a comma after each one, including the item that precedes the conjunction.

Kathryn drew a monkey, a snake, and a parrot.

He ran down the sidewalk, up the front steps, and into the building.

Problem: Missing commas with direct quotations

"Remember" said Mr. Hu "to bring some ideas to class." *com*

Solution: The first part of an interrupted quotation ends with a comma followed by quotation marks. The interrupting words are also followed by a comma.

"Remember," said Mr. Hu, "to bring some ideas to class."

Problem: Missing commas with nonessential appositives

Chantelle Peron an eighth grader will speak at the assembly. *com*

Solution: Determine whether the appositive is truly not essential to the meaning of the sentence. If it is not essential, set off the appositive with commas.

Chantelle Peron, an eighth grader, will speak at the assembly.

Problem: Missing commas with nonessential adjective clauses

This story which I enjoyed very much is about a flood. *com*

Solution: Determine whether the clause is essential to the meaning of the sentence. If it is not essential, set off the clause with commas.

This story, which I enjoyed very much, is about a flood.

Problem: Missing commas with introductory adverb clauses

Although Jean-Paul felt shy^ he tried to be friendly. *com*

Solution: Place a comma after an introductory adverb clause.

Although Jean-Paul felt shy, he tried to be friendly.

Incorrect Use of Apostrophes

An apostrophe shows possession. It can also indicate the missing letters in a contraction.

Problem: Singular possessive nouns

(James) sweatshirt is in the hall. *poss*

The (cats) cry woke me up. *poss*

Solution: Use an apostrophe and an *s* to form the possessive of a singular noun, even one that ends in *-s*.

James's sweatshirt is in the hall.

The cat's cry woke me up.

Problem: Plural possessive nouns ending in *-s*

The (birds) tails help them control their flight. *poss*

Solution: Use an apostrophe alone to form the possessive of a plural noun that ends in *-s*.

The birds' tails help them control their flight.

Problem: Plural possessive nouns not ending in *-s*

The (mens) gym needs new equipment. *poss*

Solution: Use an apostrophe and an *s* to form the possessive of a plural noun that does not end in *-s*.

The men's gym needs new equipment.

Problem: Possessive personal pronouns

That ball is your's; this one is our's. *poss*

Solution: Do not use an apostrophe with any of the possessive personal pronouns.

That ball is yours; this one is ours.

Problem: Confusion between *its* and *it's*

That plant is losing it's leaves, and its brand new! *poss*

Solution: Do not use an apostrophe to form the possessive of *it.* Use an apostrophe to form the contraction of *it is.*

That plant is losing its leaves, and it's brand new!

Incorrect Capitalization

Proper nouns, proper adjectives, and the first words of sentences always begin with a capital letter.

Problem: Words referring to ethnic groups, nationalities, and languages

The menu at the brazilian restaurant was written in the portuguese language. *cap*

Solution: Capitalize proper nouns and adjectives that refer to ethnic groups, nationalities, and languages.

The menu at the Brazilian restaurant was written in the Portuguese language.

Problem: The first word of a direct quotation

She said, "we have a surprise for you." *cap*

Solution: Capitalize the first word in a direct quotation that is a complete sentence. A direct quotation gives the speaker's exact words.

She said, "We have a surprise for you."

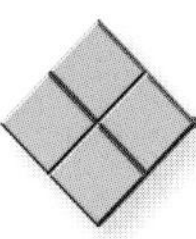

Troublesome Words

Use this section to learn the correct use of easily confused or misused words and expressions.

accept, except *Accept* means "to receive." *Except* means "other than."	He would not **accept** the money. Everyone **except** Alisha is here.
affect, effect *Affect* is a verb meaning "to cause a change in" or "to influence." *Effect* as a noun means "result." As a verb, *effect* means "to bring about or accomplish."	A rainy day can **affect** your mood. Praise has a good **effect** on most people. Advances in medicine will **effect** a healthier society.
a lot *A lot* is two words. It means "a large amount or number," but its meaning is vague; avoid using it in formal writing.	I collected **a lot** of shells. [vague] I collected dozens of shells. [more precise]
all ready, already *All ready* means "completely prepared." *Already* means "before" or "by this time."	She is **all ready** for the big day. I've **already** seen that movie.
all together, altogether *All together* means "in a group." *Altogether* means "completely."	The books cost $9.98 **all together.** Soon the sun disappeared **altogether.**
amount, number Use *amount* with nouns that cannot be counted. Use *number* with nouns that can be counted.	There was a small **amount** of milk in the carton. We found a large **number** of coins in the jar.

bad, badly *Bad* is sometimes used as a predicate adjective. Use *bad* after a linking verb. *Badly* is an adverb. Use *badly* to modify an action verb.	I feel **bad.** I did **badly** on the test.
beside, besides *Beside* means "next to." *Besides* means "in addition to."	Sit here **beside** me. **Besides** skating, baseball is my favorite sport.
between, among Use *between* for two people or things. Use *among* when talking about groups of three or more.	The debate was **between** Sheila and Todd. The bread was shared **among** five people.
bring, take *Bring* means "to carry from a distant place to a closer place." *Take* means "to carry from a nearby place to a more distant one."	Please **bring** me a towel. **Take** this note to your parents.
can, may *Can* indicates ability. *May* expresses permission or possibility.	I **can** swim twenty laps. When the work is done, you **may** rest.
choose, chose *Choose* means "to select." *Chose* means "selected."	Everyone must **choose** a partner. Nadine **chose** yesterday's menu.
doesn't, don't *Doesn't* is the contraction of *does not. Don't* is the contraction of *do not.* Use *doesn't* with a singular subject. Use *don't* with a plural subject.	He **doesn't** understand. They **don't** understand.
farther, further *Farther* refers to physical distance. *Further* refers to time or degree.	Tyler ran **farther** than Nadia. Snow usually begins **further** into the winter. I'll need to think about this **further.**

fewer, less

Use *fewer* in comparisons with nouns that can be counted. Use *less* in comparisons with nouns that cannot be counted.

Fewer students are absent today than yesterday.

There was **less** rain last summer than this one.

formally, formerly

Formally is the adverb form of *formal.* *Formerly* means "in times past."

He bowed **formally.**

The teacher was **formerly** a dancer.

good, well

Good is often used as an adjective meaning "pleasing" or "able." *Well* may be used as an adverb telling how ably something is done or as an adjective meaning "in good health."

Cara is a **good** skater.

She skates **well.**

Because he had a cold, he did not feel **well.**

in, into

In means "inside." *Into* indicates movement from outside to a point within.

The sweater is **in** the drawer.

Put the coin **into** the slot.

its, it's

Its is the possessive form of *it.* *It's* is the contraction of *it is.*

The earth turns on **its** axis.

Ecologists believe **it's** important to recycle.

lay, lie

Lay means "to put" or "to place." *Lie* means "to recline" or "to be positioned."

You can **lay** the blanket on the grass.

I'll **lie** here in the shade.

Rule of Thumb

Be careful not to confuse the present-tense and past-tense forms of *lie* and *lay. Lie* is in the present tense; its past-tense form is *lay. Lay* can also be a present-tense verb; its past-tense form is *laid.*

Then I **lay** in the shade.
I **laid** the blanket on the grass.

learn, teach

Learn means "to receive knowledge." *Teach* means "to give knowledge."

Children **learn** foreign languages easily.

I can **teach** you how to skate.

leave, let

Leave means "to go away." *Let* means "to allow."

They will **leave** at noon.

Let her go where she wishes.

like, as

Use *like,* a preposition, to introduce a prepositional phrase. Use *as,* a subordinating conjunction, to introduce a subordinate clause. Many authorities believe that *like* should not be used to introduce a clause.

The kite soared **like** a bird.

He won first prize, **as** we expected.

Rule of Thumb

As can be a preposition in some cases–for example, *He worked as a carpenter.*

loose, lose

Loose means "not firmly attached." *Lose* means "to misplace" or "to fail to win."

One of her teeth was **loose.**

Don't **lose** this key.

We can't **lose** this game.

many, much

Use *many* with nouns that can be counted. Use *much* with nouns that cannot be counted.

Many flowers were in bloom.

Much applause greeted the band.

of, off

Of is a preposition used to indicate direction, origin, or material. *Off* is the opposite of "on."

The bank is south **of** the park.

Have you read the poems **of** Emily Dickinson?

Please turn **off** the light.

precede, proceed

Precede means "to go or come before." *Proceed* means "to continue."

January **precedes** February.

Finish one task and **proceed** to the next.

quiet, quite

Quiet means "silent" or "motionless." *Quite* means "completely" or "entirely."

At night the street is **quiet.**

The sneakers didn't **quite** fit.

raise, rise

Raise means "to cause to move upward." *Rise* means "to move upward."

They **raise** the flag each morning.

The sun is starting to **rise.**

reason . . . is that, because

Both terms are used to state a reason. Do not use them together in a sentence.

The **reason** I can't go **is that** I have to babysit.

I can't go **because** I have to babysit.

set, sit

Set means "to place" or "to put." *Sit* means "to place oneself in a seated position."

Set the box on the table.

Sit here and rest.

than, then

Than introduces the second part of a comparison. *Then* means "at that time."

Oranges are sweeter **than** grapefruit.

I ate lunch, and **then** I read.

their, they're, there

Their is the possessive form of *they. They're* is the contraction of *they are. There* means "at" or "in that place."

They look like **their** mother.

The winners are tired, but **they're** happy.

Stay **there** until I call you.

theirs, there's

Theirs means "that or those belonging to them." *There's* is the contraction of *there is.*

Our cat is black, and **theirs** is gray.

There's a storm coming.

to, too, two

To means "in the direction of." *Too* means "also" or "excessively." *Two* is the number after one.

Pass the ball **to** Mario.

We were **too** excited to sleep.

She scored **two** points.

where at

Do not use *at* after *where* to ask *at what place?*

Where is the bus stop? [not *Where is the bus stop at?*]

who, whom

Use *who* for subjects. Use *whom* for objects.

Who got the highest grade?

Whom did you see? [direct obj.]

To **whom** should I address this letter? [obj. of a prep.]

Rule of Thumb

When speaking informally, people often use *who* instead of *whom* in sentences like *Who did you see?* In writing and formal speech, distinguish between *who* and *whom.*

who's, whose

Who's is the contraction of *who is. Whose* is the possessive form of *who.*

Who's hungry?

I don't know **whose** hat this is.

your, you're

Your is the possessive form of *you. You're* is the contraction of *you are.*

Tell us about **your** trip.

You're older than he is.

Grammar Glossary

This glossary will help you quickly locate information on parts of speech and sentence structure.

A

Abstract noun. *See* Noun.

Action verb. *See* Verb.

Active voice. *See* Voice.

Adjective A word that modifies a noun or pronoun. An adjective can provide information about size, shape, color, texture, feeling, sound, smell, number, or condition. Adjectives appear in various positions in a sentence. (We hoped for *cool, sunny* weather. The weather was *cool* and *sunny.*)

Many adjectives have different forms to indicate **degree of comparison.** *(light, lighter, lightest)*

The **comparative degree** compares two persons or things. *(bigger, lovelier, more important)*

The **superlative degree** compares more than two persons or things. *(biggest, loveliest, most important)*

Sometimes **pronouns** are used as adjectives. **Possessive adjectives** are possessive pronouns that answer the question *Which one? (my, your, her, his, its, our, their)*

Demonstrative adjectives are pronouns that answer the question *Which one? How many?* (*This* story is exaggerated.)

A **predicate adjective** follows a linking verb and describes the subject by telling what it is like. (That tree looks *old.*)

A **noun** used as an adjective answers the question *What kind?* or *Which one?* (*guitar* string, *science* lesson) A **proper adjective** is formed from a proper noun and begins with a capital letter. Proper adjectives are often created by using the following suffixes: *-an, -ian, -n, -ese,* and *-ish.* (Ital*ian*)

Adjective clause. *See* Clause.

Adverb A word that modifies, or describes, a verb, an adjective, or another adverb by making its meaning more specific. Adverbs answer the questions *How? When? Where?* and *To what extent?* When modifying a verb, an adverb may appear in various positions in a sentence. (Ann spoke *gently* to Claude. *Quickly,* she told him the news.) When modifying an adjective or another adverb, an adverb appears directly before the modified word. (We were *very* excited about the discovery.) The negatives *no, not,* and the contraction *-n't* are adverbs. (I could wait *no* longer.) Other negative words, such as *nowhere* and *never,* can function as adverbs of time, place, and degree. (She has *never* visited us.)

Some adverbs have different forms to indicate **degree of comparison.** *(loud, louder, loudest, sweetly, more sweetly, most sweetly)*

The **comparative** form of an adverb compares two actions.

The **superlative** form compares three or more actions. Some adverbs do not form the comparative and superlative in the regular manner. *(badly, worse, worst)*

Adverb clause. *See* Clause.

Antecedent. *See* Pronoun.

Appositive A noun or a pronoun that is placed next to another noun or pronoun to identify it or add information about it. (Her sister *Beth* is in ninth grade.)

Appositive phrase. *See* Phrase.

Article The adjective *a, an,* or *the.*

A and *an* are **indefinite articles,** which refer to one of a general group of persons, places, things, or ideas. (He bought *a* book.)

The is a **definite article,** which identifies a specific person, place, thing, or idea. (He found *the* book helpful.)

B

Base form. *See* Verb tense.

C

Clause A group of words that has a subject and a predicate and that is used as part of a sentence. Clauses fall into two categories: main clauses and subordinate clauses.

A **main clause** has a subject and a predicate and can stand alone as a sentence. There must be at least one main clause in every sentence. (Samantha turned on the radio, and everyone began to dance.)

A **subordinate clause** has a subject and a predicate, but it cannot stand alone as a sentence. A subordinate clause makes sense only when attached to a main clause. Many subordinate clauses begin with subordinating conjunctions or relative pronouns. (He hadn't seen them *since he was a baby.*) The chart on this page shows the types of subordinate clauses.

Collective noun. *See* Noun.

Common noun. *See* Noun.

Comparative degree. *See* Adjective; Adverb.

Complement A word or phrase that completes the meaning of a verb. Three kinds of complements are direct objects, indirect objects, and subject complements.

A **direct object** answers the question *What?* or *Whom?* after an action verb. (She threw the *ball.* He saw *Sarah.*)

An **indirect object** answers the question *To whom? For whom? To what?* or *For what?* after an action verb. (He gave *Sarah* a mitt.)

A **subject complement** follows a subject and a linking verb. It identifies or describes a subject. The two kinds of subject complements are *predicate nouns* and *predicate adjectives.*

A **predicate noun** (also called a **predicate nominative**) is a noun that follows a linking verb and defines the

Types of Subordinate Clauses			
Clause	**Function**	**Example**	**Begins with . . .**
Adjective clause	Modifies a noun or pronoun in the main clause	I'm reading a book *that I can't put down.*	A relative pronoun, such as *that, which, who, whom,* or *whose*
Adverb clause	Modifies the verb in the main clause	I didn't see him *until I turned around.*	A subordinating conjunction, such as *after, although, because, if, since,* or *until*
Noun clause	Acts as a subject, an object, or a predicate nominative in the main clause	*Whoever scores the most points* wins.	Words such as *how, that, what, whatever, when, where, which, who, whom, whoever, whose,* and *why*

subject by telling what it is. (The flowers were *roses.*)

A **predicate adjective** is an adjective that follows a linking verb and describes the subject by telling what it is like. (The roses were *beautiful.* They smelled *sweet.*)

Complete predicate. *See* Predicate.

Complete subject. *See* Subject.

Complex sentence. *See* Sentence.

Compound noun. *See* Noun.

Compound predicate. *See* Predicate.

Compound preposition. *See* Preposition.

Compound sentence. *See* Sentence.

Compound subject. *See* Subject.

Concrete noun. *See* Noun.

Conjunction A word that joins single words or groups of words.

A **coordinating conjunction** *(and, but, or, nor, for, yet)* joins words or groups of words that are equal in grammatical importance. (I needed some milk, *but* the store was closed.)

Correlative conjunctions *(both . . . and, just as . . . so, not only . . . but also, either . . . or, neither . . . nor)* work in pairs to join words or phrases of equal importance. (I was at home *both* Saturday *and* Sunday.)

A **subordinating conjunction** *(after, although, because, before, if, in order that, since, than, though, until, when, while)* joins a subordinate idea or clause to a main clause. (She arrived *after* the show had begun.)

A **conjunctive adverb** is used to clarify the relationship between main clauses in a sentence. Conjunctive adverbs can replace *and (also, besides, furthermore, moreover)* or *but (however, nevertheless, still);* state a result *(consequently, therefore, so, thus);* or state equality *(equally, likewise, similarly).* (March is a cold month; *however,* some mild days do occur.)

Coordinating conjunction. *See* Conjunction.

Correlative conjunction. *See* Conjunction.

D

Declarative sentence. *See* Sentence.

Definite article. *See* Article.

Demonstrative adjective. *See* Adjective.

Demonstrative pronoun. *See* Pronoun.

Direct object. *See* Complement.

E F G

Exclamatory sentence. *See* Sentence.

Future perfect tense. *See* Verb tense.

Future tense. *See* Verb tense.

Gerund A verb form that ends in *-ing* and is used as a noun. A gerund may function as a subject, an object of a verb, or the object of a preposition. (*Singing* always made Keisha happy. No one could keep her from *singing.*)

Gerund phrase. *See* Phrase.

H

Helping verb A verb that helps the main verb tell about an action or make a statement. (They *had been* sleeping.) The forms of *be* and *have* are the most common helping, or **auxiliary**, verbs. *(am, is, are, was, were, being, been; has, have, had, having)* Other helping verbs are *can, could; do, does, did; may, might; must; shall, should; will, would.*

I

Imperative sentence. *See* Sentence.

Indefinite article. *See* Article.

Indefinite pronoun. *See* Pronoun.

Indirect object. *See* Complement.

Infinitive A verb form that begins with the word *to* and functions as a noun, an adjective, or an adverb. (David wanted *to swim.*)

Infinitive phrase. *See* Phrase.

Intensive pronoun. *See* Pronoun.

Interjection A word or phrase that expresses strong feeling. An interjection has no grammatical connection to other words in a sentence. Commas follow mild ones; exclamation points follow stronger ones. (*Well,* here we are. *Aha!* I found it.)

Interrogative pronoun. *See* Pronoun.

Interrogative sentence. *See* Sentence.

Intransitive verb. *See* Verb.

Inverted order In a sentence written in inverted order, the predicate comes before the subject. Some sentences are written in inverted order for emphasis. (Back and forth *swung the hammock.*) The subject generally follows the predicate in a sentence that begins with *there* or *here.* (*There* is a new girl in the class. *Here* stands the monument.) Questions, or interrogative sentences, are generally written in inverted order. Questions that begin with *who* or *what* follow normal word order.

Irregular verb. *See* Verb tense.

Linking verb. *See* Verb.

Main clause. *See* Clause.

Noun A word that names a person, a place, a thing, or an idea. The chart on this page shows the main types of nouns.

Noun clause. *See* Clause.

Number A noun, pronoun, or verb is **singular** in number if it refers to one; **plural** if it refers to more than one.

Objective pronoun. *See* Pronoun.

Order of subject and predicate. *See* Inverted order.

Participial phrase. *See* Phrase.

Types of Nouns

Noun	Function	Examples
Abstract	Names an idea, a quality, or a characteristic	honesty, fear
Collective	Names a group of things or people	audience, set
Common	Names a general type of person, place, thing, or idea	pilot, kitchen, cabinet, suspense
Compound	Is made up of two or more words	shoelace, home run
Concrete	Names things that you can see or touch	book, house, lamp
Possessive	Shows possession, ownership, or the relationship between two nouns	*Don's* notebook
Predicate	Follows a linking verb and gives information about the subject	Sondra became the class *president.*
Proper	Names a particular person, place, thing, or idea	Michael Jordan, Sugar Bowl, Stanley Cup, Communism

Participle A verb form that can function as an adjective. Present participles always end in *-ing.* (The *burning* sand hurt her feet.) Although past participles often end in *-ed,* they can take other forms as well. (He tried to repair the *broken* table.)

Passive voice. *See* Voice.

Past perfect tense. *See* Verb tense.

Past tense. *See* Verb tense.

Personal pronoun. *See* Pronoun.

Phrase A group of words that acts in a sentence as a single part of speech.

An **appositive phrase** is an appositive along with any modifiers. If not essential to the meaning of the sentence, an appositive phrase is set off by commas. (He brought her a gift, *a bouquet of wildflowers,* on her birthday.)

A **gerund phrase** includes a gerund and any complements and modifiers needed to complete its meaning. (*Climbing steep hills* builds strong muscles.)

An **infinitive phrase** includes the infinitive and any complements and modifiers. (In the evening I like *to curl up with a book.*)

A **participial phrase** contains a participle and any modifiers necessary to complete its meaning. (*Gliding over the frozen pond,* the skater felt at peace with the world.)

A **prepositional phrase** begins with a preposition and ends with a noun or a pronoun called the object of the preposition. A prepositional phrase can function as an adjective, modifying a noun or a pronoun. (We found an album *of old photographs.*) A prepositional phrase may also function as an adverb when it modifies a verb, an adverb, or an adjective. (Donny plays *in a band.*)

A **verb phrase** consists of one or more auxiliary verbs followed by a main verb. (The campers *should have followed* the trail more closely.)

Possessive noun. *See* Noun.

Possessive pronoun. *See* Pronoun.

Predicate The verb or verb phrase and any modifiers that tell what the subject of a sentence does, has, is, or is like.

A **simple predicate** is a verb or verb phrase that tells something about the subject. (Snowflakes *melted.*)

A **complete predicate** includes the simple predicate and any words that modify or complete it. (Melting snowflakes *formed a puddle on the windowsill.*)

A **compound predicate** has two or more verbs or verb phrases that are joined by a conjunction and share the same subject. (James *heard* but *misunderstood* the question.)

Predicate adjective. *See* Complement; Adjective.

Predicate noun. *See* Complement; Noun.

Preposition A word that shows the relationship of a noun or pronoun to some other word in the sentence. Prepositions include *about, above, across, among, as, behind, below, beyond, but, by, down, during, except, for, from, into, like, near, of, on, outside, over, since, through, to, under, until, with.* (We walked *along* the river.)

A **compound preposition** is made up of more than one word. Compound prepositions include *according to, across from, ahead of, as to, because of, by means of, in addition to, in spite of,* and *on account of.* (They sat *across from* each other.)

Prepositional phrase. *See* Phrase.

Present perfect tense. *See* Verb tense.

Present tense. *See* Verb tense.

Progressive form. *See* Verb tense.

Pronoun A word that takes the place of one or more nouns and the words that describe those nouns.

The word or group of words that a pronoun refers to is called its **antecedent**. (In the following sentence, *Carla* is the antecedent of *she: Carla went shopping because she needed new sneakers.*)

A **demonstrative pronoun** points out specific persons, places, things, or ideas. *(this, that, these, those)*

An **indefinite pronoun** refers to persons, places, or things in a more general way than a noun does. *(all, another, any, both, each, either, everything, few, many, most, much, neither, nobody, none, one, several, some)*

An **intensive pronoun** adds emphasis to another noun or pronoun. If an intensive pronoun is omitted, the meaning of the sentence will be the same. (I *myself* would rather stay home.)

An **interrogative pronoun** is used to form questions. *(who, whom, whose, what, which)*

A **personal pronoun** refers to a specific person or thing. Personal pronouns have three cases called nominative, possessive, and objective. The case depends on the function of the pronoun in the sentence. The chart on this page shows the case forms of the various personal pronouns.

A **reflexive pronoun** reflects back to a noun or pronoun used earlier in the sentence, indicating that the same person or thing is involved. (Louise taught *herself* to play the piano.)

A **relative pronoun** is used to begin a subordinate clause. *(who, whose, whomever, that, what, whom, whoever)*

Proper adjective. *See* Adjective.

Proper noun. *See* Noun.

R

Reflexive pronoun. *See* Pronoun.

Regular verb. *See* Verb tense.

Relative pronoun. *See* Pronoun.

S

Sentence A group of words expressing a complete thought. Every sentence has a subject and a predicate. Sentences can be classified by function or by structure. The chart on the next page shows the categories by function; the following subentries describe the categories by structure. *See also* Clause; Predicate; Subject.

A **simple sentence** has only one main clause and no subordinate clauses. (Wendy hiked.) A simple sentence may contain a compound subject, a compound predi-

Personal Pronouns

Case	Singular Pronouns	Plural Pronouns	Function in Sentence
Nominative	I, you, she, he, it	we, you, they	subject or predicate nominative
Objective	me, you, her, him, it	us, you, them	direct object, indirect object, or object of a preposition
Possessive	my, mine, your, yours, her, hers, his, its	our, ours, your, yours, their, theirs	replacement for the possessive form of a noun

Types of Sentences			
Sentence Type	**Function**	**Ends with . . .**	**Examples**
Declarative sentence	Makes a statement	A period	The village postponed the fireworks.
Exclamatory sentence	Expresses strong emotion	An exclamation point	Don't stop for anything!
Imperative sentence	Gives a command or makes a request	A period or an exclamation point	Be sure to attend the concert.
Interrogative sentence	Asks a question	A question mark	Has everyone eaten lunch?

cate, or both. (Wendy and Jane hiked. Wendy swam and hiked. Wendy and Jane swam and hiked.) The subject and the predicate can be expanded with adjectives, adverbs, prepositional phrases, appositives, and verbal phrases. As long as the sentence has only one main clause, however, it remains a simple sentence. (Joseph and Fabienne, my new neighbors, recently moved to the United States from Haiti and plan to settle here.)

A **compound sentence** has two or more main clauses. Each main clause of a compound sentence has its own subject and predicate, and these main clauses are usually joined by a comma and a coordinating conjunction. (The day was warm and muggy, but the breeze was refreshing.) Semicolons may also be used to join the main clauses in a compound sentence. (Water poured from the sky; the drought was over.)

A **complex sentence** has one main clause and one or more subordinate clauses. (He laughed when he saw them.)

Simple predicate. *See* Predicate.

Simple sentence. *See* Sentence.

Simple subject. *See* Subject.

Subject The key noun or pronoun that tells whom or what the sentence is about.

A **simple subject** is the main noun or pronoun. (*Snowflakes* drifted down.)

A **complete subject** includes the simple subject and any words that modify it. (*Big, fluffy snowflakes* drifted down.)

A **compound subject** has two or more simple subjects that are joined by a conjunction. The subjects share the same verb. (Either *Tatiana* or *Sean* usually scores highest.)

Subordinate clause. *See* Clause.

Subordinating conjunction. *See* Conjunction.

Superlative degree. *See* Adjective; Adverb.

Tense. *See* Verb tense.

Transitive verb. *See* Verb.

Verb A word that expresses an action or a state of being and is necessary to make a statement. *(move, feels, said)*

An **action verb** tells what someone or something does. Action verbs can express either physical or mental action. (We *walked* through the park. I *had forgotten* his name.)

A **transitive verb** is an action verb that is followed by a direct object–a word or words that answer the question *What?* or *Whom?* (She *ate* the bread.)

An **intransitive verb** is an action verb that is *not* followed by a direct object. (She *ate* quickly.) A dictionary will indicate whether a verb is transitive or intransitive.

A **linking verb** links, or joins, the subject of a sentence with a word or expression that identifies or describes the subject. (He *is* the winner.) A linking verb does not show action. The most commonly used linking verb is *be* in all its forms. *(am, is, are, was, were, will be, been, being)* Other linking verbs are *appear, become, feel, grow, look, remain, seem, sound, smell, stay,* and *taste.*

Verb phrase. *See* Phrase.

Verb tense The tense of a verb indicates when the action or state of being occurs. All verb tenses are formed from the four principal parts of a verb: a **base form** *(drive)* used for **present tense** and used with *will* or *shall* for **future tense**; a **present participle** *(driving);* a **simple past form** *(drove);* and a **past participle** *(driven).*

A **regular verb** forms its simple past and past participle by adding *-ed* to the base form. *(open, opened, opened)*

An **irregular verb** forms its past and past participle in some other way. *(speak, spoke, spoken)*

The **present perfect tense** expresses an action or condition that occurred at some indefinite time in the past. This tense also shows an action or condition that began in the past and continues into the present. (Edward *has presented* his report. I *have lived* here for four years.)

The **past perfect tense** indicates that one past action or condition began *and* ended before another past action started. (They *had pitched* their tents before the rain started.)

The **future perfect tense** indicates that one future action or condition will begin *and* end before another future event starts. Use *will have* or *shall have* with the past participle of a verb. (By tomorrow you *will have finished* that book.)

Each of the six tenses has a **progressive form** that expresses a continuing action. To make the progressive forms, use the appropriate tense of the verb *be* with the present participle of the main verb. (Rita *is listening.*)

Verbal. *See* Gerund; Infinitive; Participle.

Voice The voice of a verb shows whether the subject performs the action or receives the action of a verb.

The **active voice** occurs when the subject of the sentence performs the action. (Erica *painted* that picture.)

The **passive voice** occurs when the subject receives the action of the verb. (That picture *was painted* by Erica.)

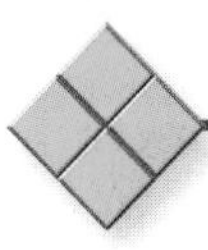

Mechanics

This section will help you use correct capitalization, punctuation, and abbreviations in your writing.

Capitalization

Capitalizing Sentences, Quotations, and Salutations	
Rule	**Example**
A capital letter appears at the beginning of a sentence.	**W**e had won. **E**veryone screamed and yelled.
A capital letter marks the beginning of a direct quotation that is a complete sentence.	Justin said, "**W**e're safe for now."
When a quoted sentence is interrupted by explanatory words, such as *she said,* do not begin the second part of the sentence with a capital letter.	"We're safe," Justin said, "**f**or now."
When the second part of a quotation is a new sentence, put a period after the explanatory words, and begin the new part with a capital letter.	"We're safe for now," Justin said. "**L**et's get some sleep."
Do not capitalize an indirect quotation.	Justin said that **w**e were safe for now.
Capitalize the first word in the salutation and closing of a letter. Capitalize the title and name of the person addressed.	**D**ear **M**r. **A**lfonso: **V**ery truly yours,

Capitalizing Names and Titles of People	
Rule	**Example**
Capitalize the names of people and the initials that stand for their names.	**A**nthony **C**ruz **G. J. B**uchard
Capitalize a title or an abbreviation of a title when it comes before a person's name or when it is used in direct address.	**P**resident Lincoln "We need better housing for the poor, **G**overnor."

Rule	Example
Do not capitalize a title that follows or is a substitute for a person's name.	Margaret Reilly was elected **m**ayor. He asked to speak to the **m**ayor.
Capitalize the names and abbreviations of academic degrees that follow a person's name. Capitalize *Jr.* and *Sr.*	Donna Teshima, **M.D.** Lawrence Palmer **J**r.
Capitalize words that show family relationships when used as titles or as substitutes for a person's name.	We visited **A**unt Anne. He gave **G**randpa a ride.
Do not capitalize words that show family relationships when they follow a possessive noun or pronoun.	We visited Diego's **a**unt. He gave my **g**randpa a ride.
Always capitalize the pronoun *I*.	After **I** eat, **I**'m going for a bike ride.

Capitalizing Names of Places	
Rule	**Example**
Rule of Thumb Do not capitalize articles and prepositions in proper nouns. Gulf **o**f Mexico Lake **o**f **t**he Woods	
Capitalize the names of cities, counties, states, countries, and continents.	**M**inneapolis **F**airfield **C**ounty **A**laska **P**eople's **R**epublic of **C**hina
Capitalize the names of bodies of water and other geographical features.	**I**ndian **O**cean **C**ape **F**ear **M**ount **E**verest
Capitalize the names of sections of a country and regions of the world.	the **M**idwest the **M**iddle **E**ast
Capitalize compass points when they refer to a specific section of a country.	the **N**orthwest the **S**outh

Rule	Example
Do not capitalize compass points when they indicate direction.	New Mexico is **s**outh of Colorado.
Do not capitalize adjectives made from words indicating direction.	**n**orthern Montana
Capitalize the names of streets and highways.	**S**oldier's **F**ield **R**oad
Capitalize the names of buildings, bridges, monuments, and other structures.	**P**eachtree **C**enter **B**uilding **B**ear **M**ountain **B**ridge

Capitalizing Other Proper Nouns and Adjectives	
Rule	**Example**
Capitalize the names of clubs, organizations, businesses, institutions, and political parties.	**I**deal **C**omputer **S**ervices **C**itizens for **C**lean **A**ir
Capitalize brand names but not the nouns following them.	**E**agle bicycles
Capitalize the names of days of the week, months, and holidays.	**M**onday **F**ebruary **I**ndependence **D**ay
Do not capitalize the names of seasons.	**w**inter, **s**pring, **s**ummer, **f**all
Capitalize the first word, the last word, and all important words in the title of a book, play, short story, poem, essay, article, film, television series, song, magazine, newspaper, and chapter of a book.	***T**he **D**iary of **A**nne **F**rank* "**H**ow to **P**aint with **W**atercolors"
Capitalize the names of ethnic groups, nationalities, and languages.	**P**eruvian **A**rab **S**wahili
Capitalize proper adjectives that are formed from the names of ethnic groups and nationalities.	**E**nglish sheepdog **V**ietnamese restaurant

Punctuation

Using the Period and Other End Marks

Rule	Example
Use a period at the end of a declarative sentence.	Tim was reading a magazine.
Use a period at the end of an imperative sentence that does not express strong feeling.	Please pass the juice.
Use a question mark at the end of an interrogative sentence.	What time is it?
Use an exclamation point at the end of an exclamatory sentence or a strong imperative.	What a great idea! Call an ambulance!
Use an exclamation point at the end of an interjection that expresses strong emotion.	Ouch! This bush has thorns.

Using Commas

Rule	Example
Use commas to separate three or more items in a series.	She got dressed, ate breakfast, and ran to catch the bus.
Use a comma to show a pause after an introductory word and to set off names used in direct address.	No, I don't agree with you. Tell me, Derek, how do you feel?
Use a comma after two or more introductory prepositional phrases or when the comma is needed to make the meaning clear. A comma is not needed after a single, short prepositional phrase, but it is acceptable to use one.	By the end of the next century, this town will be a big city. From the strong, people count on leadership. (comma needed to prevent misreading) After the rain the air smelled clean. (no comma needed)
Use a comma after an introductory participle and an introductory participial phrase.	Splashing and shrieking, the children played in the pool.

Rule	Example
Use commas to set off words that interrupt the flow of thought in a sentence.	Kevin, unlike his brother, enjoys arts and crafts.
Use a comma after conjunctive adverbs such as *however, moreover, furthermore, nevertheless,* and *therefore.*	The governor has increased employment; furthermore, he has reduced taxes.
Use commas to set off an appositive if it is not essential to the meaning of a sentence.	My dog, a large collie, always sleeps on my bed.
Use a comma before *and, or,* or *but* when it joins main clauses.	Rebecca searched for the trail, but night was falling.
Use a comma after an introductory adverb clause.	Because the snow was so deep, school was canceled.
In most cases, do not use a comma with an adverb clause that comes at the end of a sentence.	School was canceled because the snow was so deep.
Use a comma or a pair of commas to set off an adjective clause that is not essential to the meaning of a sentence.	Nadia, who is thirteen years old, created a documentary video.
Do not use a comma or pair of commas to set off an essential clause from the rest of the sentence.	Students **who are thirteen or older** can join the video club.
Use commas before and after the year when it is used with both the month and the day. If only the month and the year are given, do not use a comma.	July 4, 1776, is an important day in U.S. history. In November 1998 they moved to Canada.
Use commas before and after the name of a state or a country when it is used with the name of a city. Do not use a comma after the state if it is used with a ZIP code.	She flew to Dallas, Texas, last week. The address is 25 Porter Street, Largo, FL 34640.
Use commas or a pair of commas to set off an abbreviated title or degree following a person's name.	Joy Isaac, Ph.D., will speak on the future of genetics.
Use a comma or commas to set off *too* when *too* means "also."	Luis is coming with us, too. The birds, too, were enjoying the sunshine.

Rule	Example
Use a comma or commas to set off a direct quotation.	He said, "Call me if you need some help." "Call me," he said, "if you need some help."
Use a comma after the salutation of a friendly letter and after the closing of both a friendly and a business letter.	Dear Grandpa, Love, Truly yours,
Use a comma when necessary to prevent mis-reading of a sentence.	After the spring, rain is unusual here.

Using Semicolons and Colons	
Rule	**Example**
Use a semicolon to join the parts of a com-pound sentence when a coordinating conjunc-tion, such as *and, or, nor,* or *but,* is not used.	I looked in the drawer; it was empty.
Use a semicolon to join parts of a compound sentence when the main clauses are long and are subdivided by commas. Use a semicolon even if these clauses are already joined by a coordinating conjunction.	Ashley leaped, grabbed a branch, and hoisted herself up; but the water, gray and swirling, was rising rapidly.
Use a semicolon to separate main clauses joined by a conjunctive adverb. Be sure to use a comma after the conjunctive adverb.	His work had been outstanding; therefore, he was given a raise.
Use a colon to introduce a list of items that ends a sentence. Use a phrase such as *these, the following,* or *as follows* to signal that a list is coming.	Be sure to bring the following: a swimsuit, a towel, sunscreen, and sunglasses.
Do not use a colon to introduce a list preceded by a verb or preposition.	Be sure to bring a swimsuit, a towel, sun-screen, and sunglasses. (No colon is used after *bring.*)
Use a colon to separate the hour and the min-utes when you write the time of day.	Meet me at 12:30.
Use a colon after the salutation of a business letter.	Dear Ms. Kendall:

Using Quotation Marks and Italics	
Rule	**Example**
Use quotation marks before and after a direct quotation.	"He's wearing a green tee shirt," I said.
Use quotation marks with both parts of a divided quotation.	"I knew his name," I said, "but I've forgot-ten it."
Use a comma or commas to separate a phrase such as *she said* from the quotation itself. Place the comma that precedes the phrase inside the closing quotation marks.	"Let's get pizza," she said, "and then rent a movie."
Place a period that ends a quotation inside the closing quotation marks.	He said, "Mom is at work."
Place a question mark or an exclamation point inside the quotation marks when it is part of the quotation.	Julie asked, "What causes the colors of the sunset?"
Place a question mark or an exclamation point outside the quotation marks when it is part of the entire sentence.	How nice of him to say "You go first"!
Use quotation marks for the title of a short story, essay, poem, song, magazine or newspa-per article, or book chapter.	short story: "Thank You, M'am" poem: "Thirteen Ways of Looking at a Blackbird" article: "Kids Clean Up the City"
Use italics or underlining for the title of a book, play, film, television series, magazine, news-paper, or work of art.	book: *All Things Bright and Beautiful* magazine: *People* painting: *The Starry Night*
Use italics or underlining for the names of ships, trains, airplanes, and spacecraft.	ship: *Titanic* train: *Orient Express* spacecraft: *Challenger*

Using Apostrophes

Rule	Example
Use an apostrophe and an *s* (*'s*) to form the possessive of a singular noun.	my father**'s** car Charles**'s** helmet
Use an apostrophe and an *s* (*'s*) to form the possessive of a plural noun that does not end in *-s*.	the geese**'s** wings the children**'s** room

Rule of Thumb

If a thing is jointly owned by two or more individuals, only the last name needs an apostrophe: *Rob and Sarah's dog.* If the ownership is not joint, each name needs an apostrophe: *Amanda's and Bernadette's mothers.*

Rule	Example
Use an apostrophe alone to form the possessive of a plural noun that ends in *-s*.	three boy**s'** seats the Miller**s'** apartment
Use an apostrophe and an *s* (*'s*) to form the possessive of an indefinite pronoun.	someone**'s** jacket anyone**'s** name
Do not use an apostrophe in a possessive pronoun.	The cat cleaned **its** paws. My home is **yours.** The computer is **hers.**
Use an apostrophe to replace letters that have been omitted in a contraction.	it + is = it**'s** can + not = ca**n't** I + have = I**'ve**
Use an apostrophe to form the plural of letters, figures, and words when they are used as themselves.	Write three *7***'s.** The word is spelled with two *m***'s.** The sentence contains three *and***'s.**
Use an apostrophe to show missing numbers in a year.	the fall of **'97**

Using Hyphens, Dashes, and Parentheses	
Rule	**Example**
Use a hyphen to show the division of a word at the end of a line. Always divide the word between its syllables. **Rule of Thumb** One-letter divisions are not permissible. Do not divide proper nouns.	Consult a dictionary for correct di- vision of syllables.
Use a hyphen in compound numbers.	forty-five
Use a hyphen in a fraction that is used as a modifier. Do not use a hyphen in a fraction used as a noun.	We expect a one-third increase in enrollment. Add about one third of the flour.
Use a hyphen or hyphens in certain compound nouns.	merry-go-round great-grandmother
Hyphenate a compound modifier only when it precedes the word it modifies.	I enjoy a well-written story. The story was well written.
Use a hyphen after the prefixes *all-*, *ex-*, and *self-* when they are joined to any noun or adjective.	all-star ex-president self-conscious
Use a hyphen to separate any prefix from a word that begins with a capital letter.	un-American mid-December
Use a dash or dashes to show a sudden break or change in thought or speech.	I found my old skates—they didn't fit me anymore—and donated them to the thrift shop.
Use parentheses to set off words that define or helpfully explain a word in the sentence.	The puma **(**also known as the mountain lion or cougar**)** is one of the big cats of the Americas.

Abbreviations	
Rule	**Example**
Abbreviate the titles *Mr., Mrs., Ms.,* and *Dr.* before a person's name. Also abbreviate any professional or academic degree that follows a name. The titles *Jr.* and *Sr.* are *not* preceded by a comma.	George Ryan **Sr.** Raquel Sanchez, **Ph.D.**
Use capital letters and no periods with abbreviations that are pronounced letter by letter or as words. Exceptions are *U.S.* and *Washington, D.C.,* which do use periods.	**NOW** National Organization for Women **AHL** American Hockey League
With exact times use *A.M.* (ante meridiem, "before noon") and *P.M.* (post meridiem, "after noon"). For years use *B.C.* (before Christ) and, sometimes, *A.D.* (anno Domini, "in the year of the lord," after Christ).	9:30 **A.M.** 1:55 **P.M.** 2000 **B.C.** **A.D.** 350
Abbreviate days and months only in charts and lists.	Project Deadlines Outline **Sept.** 30 First draft **Oct.** 30 Final report **Nov.** 15
In scientific writing abbreviate units of measure. Use periods with English units but not with metric units.	inch(es) **in.** yard(s) **yd.** meter(s) **m** milliliter(s) **ml**
On envelopes only, abbreviate street names and state names. In general text, spell out street names and state names.	Ms. Denise Pitkin 29 Gould **St.** Lake Oswego, **OR** 97034 Denise lives on Gould **Street** in Lake Oswego, **Oregon.**

Writing Numbers	
Rule	**Example**
In charts and tables, always write numbers as numerals. Other rules apply to numbers not in charts or tables.	Student Test Scores Student / Test **1** / Test **2** / Test **3** Lai, W. / **82** / **89** / **94** Ostos, A. / **88** / **90** / **87**
Spell out numbers that you write in one or two words.	This year I will turn **fourteen** and my mom will turn **forty-two.**
Use numerals for numbers of more than two words.	The necklace had **136** beads.
Spell out any number that begins a sentence, or reword the sentence so that it does not begin with a number.	**Three hundred twenty** people signed the petition. The petition was signed by **320** people.
Write very large numbers as a numeral followed by the word *million* or *billion.*	The sun is about **93 million** miles from Earth.
If related numbers appear in the same sentence, use all numerals.	There were **249** students in the school, and only **7** were absent.
Spell out ordinal numbers (*first, second,* and so forth).	He was the **eighth** winner of the annual award.
Use words to express the time of day unless you are writing the exact time or using the abbreviation *A.M.* or *P.M.*	Be at my house by **two o'clock.** The movie begins at **4:40.** He exercises at about **8:00 A.M.**
Use numerals to express dates, house and street numbers, apartment and room numbers, telephone numbers, page numbers, amounts of money of more than two words, and percentages. Write out the word *percent.*	November **11, 1952** page **7** **60** percent **one** dollar **ten** cents **$1.10**

Spelling

The following basic rules, examples, and exceptions will help you master the spellings of many words.

ie and *ei*

Many writers find the rules for certain combinations of letters, like *ie* and *ei,* difficult to remember. One helpful learning strategy is to develop a rhyme to remember a rule. Look at the following rhyme for the *ie* and *ei* rule.

Rule	Examples
Put *i* before *e,*	piece, field, relief
except after *c*	perceive, deceit, conceive
or when sounded like *a,*	eighty, veil, freight
as in *neighbor* and *weigh.*	

Exceptions The words *seize, leisure, weird, height, either, foreign, protein,* and *species* do not follow the rule.

-cede, -ceed, and *-sede*

Because various combinations of letters in English are sometimes pronounced the same way, it is often easy to make slight spelling errors. With the exceptions below, spell the *sēd* sounds at the end of words as *-cede:* precede, accede, intercede.

Exceptions One word uses *-sede* to spell the final *sēd* sounds: supersede.

Three words use *-ceed* to spell the final *sēd* sounds: proceed, exceed, succeed.

Unstressed vowels

Notice the vowel sound in the second syllable of the word *his-to-ry.* This is the unstressed vowel sound; dictionary respellings use the schwa symbol (ə) to indicate it. Because any of several vowels can be used to spell this sound, you might find yourself uncertain about which vowel to use. To spell words with unstressed vowels, try thinking of a related word in which the syllable containing the vowel sound is stressed.

Unknown Spelling	Related Word	Correct Spelling
hist_ry	hist**o**ric	history
occup_nt	occup**a**tion	occupant
pot_nt	pot**e**ntial	potent
or_gin	or**i**ginal	origin

Adding prefixes

When adding a prefix to a word, keep the original spelling of the word. If the prefix forms a double letter, keep both letters.

inter + national = international
un + necessary = unnecessary
re + elect = reelect

Suffixes and the silent e

Many English words end in a silent letter *e.* Sometimes the *e* is dropped when a suffix is added. When adding a suffix that begins with a consonant to a word that ends in silent *e,* keep the *e.*

excite + ment = excitement
shame + ful = shameful

Common Exceptions awe + ful = awful; judge + ment = judgment

When adding a suffix that begins with a vowel or *y* to a word that ends in silent *e,* usually drop the *e.*

scare + y = scary
complete + ion = completion

Common Exception mile + age = mileage

When adding a suffix that begins with *a* or *o* to a word that ends in *ce* or *ge,* keep the *e* so the word will retain the soft *c* or *g* sound.

notice + able = noticeable
courage + ous = courageous

When adding a suffix that begins with a vowel other than *e* to a word that ends in *ee* or *oe,* keep the *e.*

canoe + able = canoeable
agree + ing = agreeing

Suffixes and the final *y*

When adding a suffix to a word that ends in a consonant + *y*, change the *y* to *i* unless the suffix begins with *i*. Keep the *y* in a word that ends in a vowel + *y*.

apply + ed = applied
destroy + ed = destroyed
apply + ing = applying
destroy + ing = destroying

Doubling the final consonant

Double the final consonant in words that end in a single consonant preceded by a vowel if the word is one syllable. Double the consonant if the word has an accent on the last syllable that remains after the suffix is added, or if it is a word made up of a prefix and a one-syllable word.

grin + ing = grinning
refer + al = referral
remop + ed = remopped
plan + er = planner
repel + ent = repellent
unplug + ing = unplugging

Do not double the final consonant if the accent is not on the last syllable, or if the accent shifts when the suffix is added. Also do not double the final consonant if it is preceded by two vowels or by another consonant. If the word ends in a consonant and the suffix begins with a consonant, do not double the final consonant.

counsel + ing = counseling
prefer + ence = preference
commit + ment = commitment
melt + ed = melted
treat + ing = treating
travel + ing = traveling

Adding *-ly* and *-ness*

When adding *-ly* to a word that ends in a single *l*, keep the *l*, but when the word ends in a double *l*, drop one *l*. When adding *-ness* to a word that ends in *n*, keep the *n*.

ideal + ly = ideally
full + ly = fully
thin + ness = thinness
real + ly = really
dull + ly = dully
open + ness = openness

Forming compound words

When joining a word that ends in a consonant to a word that begins with a consonant, keep both consonants.

air + plane = airplane
post + card = postcard
ball + park = ballpark
suit + case = suitcase

Forming plurals

English words form plurals in many ways. Most nouns simply add *-s.* The following chart shows other ways of forming plural nouns and some common exceptions to the pattern.

GENERAL RULES FOR FORMING PLURALS		
If a Word Ends in	**Rule**	**Example**
ch, s, sh, x, z	add *-es*	watch, watches
a consonant + *y*	change *y* to *i* and add *-es*	berry, berries
a vowel + *y* or *o*	add *-s*	video, videos monkey, monkeys
a consonant + *o* common exceptions	generally add *-es* but sometimes add *-s*	potato, potatoes solo, solos
f or *ff* common exceptions	add *-s* change *f* to *v* and add *-es*	cuff, cuffs loaf, loaves
lf	change *f* to *v* and add *-es*	elf, elves
fe	change *f* to *v* and add *-s*	wife, wives

A few plurals are exceptions to the rules in the previous chart, but they are easy to remember. The following chart lists these plurals and some examples.

SPECIAL RULES FOR FORMING PLURALS	
Rule	**Example**
To form the plural of proper names and one-word compound nouns, follow the general rules for plurals.	Marino, Marinos Burch, Burches wristwatch, wristwatches
To form the plural of hyphenated compound nouns or compound nouns of more than one word, make the most important word plural.	sister-in-law, sisters-in-law half-moon, half-moons maid of honor, maids of honor
Some nouns have unusual plural forms.	foot, feet mouse, mice child, children
Some nouns have the same singular and plural forms.	moose deer scissors

The Writing Process

The writing process consists of five stages, from choosing a topic to presenting a finished piece of writing. These stages are *prewriting, drafting, revising, editing/proofreading,* and *publishing/presenting.* You do not need to follow them in a strict order but can move back and forth among them as your ideas develop. For example, before revising your first draft, you might present it to a friend for feedback, or you might go back to prewriting and gather more information about your topic.

The Writing Process

Prewriting

In the prewriting stage, you explore topic ideas, choose a topic, gather information, and begin to organize your material.

Exploring ideas

Ask yourself the following questions before you begin:

- What is my general purpose? An assignment? A personal reason?
- What audience do I have in mind? Classmates? The general public?
- What do my purpose and audience determine about the length of my paper? the kinds of topics that are appropriate? the tone and language of my writing (formal or informal; serious or light; objective or personal)?

Once you have given some thought to these questions, the following techniques can help you find a topic to write about.

- Scan your memory for interesting, funny, or moving personal experiences.
- Flip through a variety of magazines and newspapers.
- Browse through a library catalog.
- Brainstorm for topics with a group of classmates.

Choosing a topic

When you have several possible topics in mind, ask yourself these questions about each one:

- Does it fulfill my assignment or my own purpose for writing?
- Is it appropriate for the length of paper I plan to write? Would I need to narrow or broaden this topic?
- Do I know enough about this topic, or can I find enough information?

Gathering information

How you gather your information will depend upon the kind of paper you are writing.

If you are writing a personal essay, try one or both of the following techniques.

Freewriting Set a time limit of ten minutes, and write down everything that comes to mind on your topic. You might want to list your thoughts and images under general headings or make a cluster diagram.

Discussion Talk about your topic with other people. Take notes on your ideas as they come to you.

If you are writing a report or a persuasive essay, you will probably need to locate pertinent factual information and take notes.

Use library resources, such as books, magazines, newspapers, documentary and informational videos, and the Internet.

Interview people knowledgeable about your topic, such as teachers and other professionals, members of organizations, hobbyists, people from a pertinent country or culture, or people who lived through an era important to your topic.

Organizing your material

Determine the main points, subtopics, or events you will be writing about, and choose a general order in which to present them.

Sometimes the best order will be obvious. For example, a biography usually calls for chronological order; a persuasive essay often begins or ends with the most important point; a description of a place may lend itself to spatial order, such as from near to far or from low to high. For other kinds of writing, such as science reports, you will need to experiment to find the best order.

After deciding on the general order, make a rough outline. It can be as simple as a list or include headings and subheadings.

Drafting

In the drafting stage, use your notes and outline to write a rough version of your paper. Drafting is an opportunity to explore and develop your ideas.

Tips for drafting

- You might want to write your draft very quickly, capturing the rapid flow of your ideas, or you might wish to work slowly, rethinking and revising as you write. Choose the approach that works best for you.
- Whether you work quickly or slowly, don't focus on details. Concentrate on developing the main ideas. At this stage, just circle or list minor points that need more work.
- Keep your purpose in mind, and use your outline as a guide. If part of your outline doesn't work, omit it. If better ideas occur to you as you write, feel free to change your direction.

Revising

In the revising stage, evaluate your draft and look for ways to improve and refine it. Before you revise, put your draft aside for a while; then reread it carefully. At this point you might benefit from a peer review of your writing.

Peer review

Discuss your writing with another student, called a peer reviewer. You may want to direct the responses of your peer reviewer in specific ways:

- Have readers tell you what they have read in their own words. If you do not hear your ideas restated, you should revise for clarity.
- Ask readers to tell you what parts of your writing they liked best and why. You may want to expand those elements when you revise.
- Discuss the ideas in your writing with your readers. Have them share their own ideas about the topic. Include any new insights you gain in your revision.

Tips for revising

Ask yourself the following questions:

- Does my writing have an introduction, a body, and a conclusion?
- Is my writing appropriate for my audience?
- Is the order of my information and ideas logical and effective?
- Have I developed my ideas clearly and with enough detail?

- Do all of my details support my main idea? Are any of them irrelevant or confusing?
- Is my information accurate?
- Have I chosen the best, most precise words?
- Have I achieved my purpose?

Editing/Proofreading

The editing stage is the time to polish your revised draft, proofread it for errors in grammar and spelling, and make a clean copy of it. Use the checklist below, then use the proofreading checklist found on page R140 or on the inside back cover of this book.

Editing for style

Use the following checklist:

- ☑ **Have I avoided clichés?**
- ☑ **Have I avoided wordiness?**
- ☑ **Is the tone of my writing appropriate to my purpose?**
- ☑ **Have I made clear connections between ideas?**
- ☑ **Do my sentences and paragraphs flow smoothly?**

Publishing/Presenting

There are many opportunities for presenting school writing projects or your independent writing to an audience. Consider some of the following suggestions:

- Give or send your writing to a friend or relative.
- Present it orally to your class.
- Submit it to a local newspaper.
- Submit it to the newsletter of an appropriate organization.
- Submit it to a magazine that accepts writing by young people.
- Send it to a group of people via E-mail.
- Post it on an electronic bulletin board.
- Join or form a writers group at your school, library, or youth center, and read one another's works.

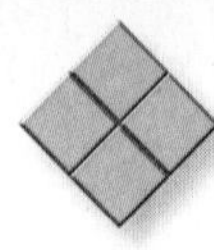

Writing Modes

Writing is often identified as being one of four types, or modes: expository, descriptive, narrative, or persuasive.

Expository Writing

Expository writing informs and explains. The most familiar form of expository writing is the essay. Other examples of expository writing include instructions, newspaper or magazine articles, and textbooks. The chart below lists four types of expository writing.

- ☑ **Does my opening contain attention-getting details or questions to hook the reader?**
- ☑ **Are my explanations complete, clear, and accurate?**
- ☑ **Have I included interesting examples? facts? statistics? quotations from experts?**
- ☑ **Have I presented information in a logical order?**
- ☑ **Have I defined any unfamiliar terms?**
- ☑ **Have I made any comparisons clear and logical?**
- ☑ **Does my conclusion bring my writing to a satisfactory close?**

Type	Introduction	Body	Sample Questions
Definition	Identify the item you are defining, and clearly state your purpose for writing.	Supply details to give readers a clear uderstanding of the item you are defining.	What is the Internet?
Compare and contrast	Identify the objects you are comparing and your purpose for making the comparison.	List the similarities and differences among the subjects. Organize by subject or feature.	How is the government of Canada like and unlike that of the United States?
Process	State the process you are explaining and its importance.	Describe the process step by step.	How are animated cartoons made?
Cause and effect	Write a topic sentence that makes the cause-and-effect relationship clear.	Use a pattern of cause-to-effect or effect-to-cause. Use transition words like *as a result, therefore,* and *because.*	Why did the *Titanic* sink?

Descriptive Writing

When you write a description, your goal is to communicate a vivid impression of a person, place, or thing. You will need to observe, remember, or imagine your subject carefully, and then select details and organize your ideas. Descriptive writing is found in travel brochures, in advertisements, and often in combination with narrative writing.

- ☑ **Have I used sensory details that capture the mood or feeling of the subject being described?**
- ☑ **Have I used vivid and precise language?**
- ☑ **Have I shown a scene rather than told about it?**
- ☑ **Have I included appropriate metaphors, similes, and other figures of speech?**
- ☑ **Have I organized details in a logical way?**
- ☑ **Are my transitions smooth and clear?**
- ☑ **Have I chosen words with the appropriate connotation as well as denotation?**

Narrative Writing

When you write a narrative, you are telling a story. If the story recounts true events that happened to real people, it is nonfiction. If it springs from your imagination, it is fiction. Fiction and nonfiction narratives share the same basic elements: setting, characters, and action.

- ☑ **Have I introduced the characters and the setting in sufficient detail?**
- ☑ **Have I presented a conflict or sequence of events?**
- ☑ **If the order of events is not chronological, can the reader follow the order easily?**
- ☑ **Have I told the story from a consistent point of view?**
- ☑ **Is there a satisfactory conclusion?**

Persuasive Writing

The purpose of persuasive writing is to convince an audience to think or act in a particular way. Effective persuasive writing presents an opinion and backs it up with sound reasons.

- ☑ **Have I taken into account the values and interests of my audience?**
- ☑ **Have I stated my position clearly?**
- ☑ **Have I arranged my arguments from strongest to weakest or from weakest to strongest?**
- ☑ **Have I backed up my position with facts, statistics, and examples?**
- ☑ **Have I avoided highly emotional language?**
- ☑ **Have I concluded with a summary of my argument, a strong appeal, or a call to action?**

Research Report Writing

When you write a research report, you explore a topic by gathering factual information from several different sources. Through your research, you develop a point of view or draw a conclusion, which becomes the thesis of your report.

Selecting a Topic

Because a research report usually takes several weeks to research and write, your choice of topic is especially important. Follow these guidelines:

- Brainstorm a list of questions about a subject you would like to explore. Choose one that is neither too narrow nor too broad for the length of your paper. Use that question as your topic.
- Be sure your topic genuinely interests you.
- Be sure you can find information from several different sources on your topic.

Doing Research

As you gather information, make sure each source you use is reliable. Check publication dates of books and articles to see how up-to-date the information is. If you interview someone for information, be sure that person is an expert in the field or has firsthand knowledge.

Making Source Cards

In a research report, you must document the sources of your information. To keep track of your sources, write the author, title, publication information, and location of each source on a separate index card. Give each source card a number, and write it in the upper right-hand corner. These cards will be useful for preparing a list of works cited.

Compiling Note Cards

As you find material on your topic, record each piece of information on a separate note card. The following suggestions will help you take notes efficiently and avoid plagiarizing, that is, presenting someone else's words or ideas as your own.

- If the passage is lengthy, write the main points and summarize the details.
- If the information is presented in only a sentence or two, paraphrase, or restate it in your own words.
- If the author's wording is especially effective, you might want to use the passage as a quotation. Copy the exact words, and put them in quotation marks.

Include the information shown in this sample note card.

Sample Note Card

7 — **Write the source number from your source card.**

Write a key word or phrase that tells you what the information is about. — ***Physical problems***

Some former gymnasts, now in their twenties, have the bone density of 90-year-olds. p. 26 — **Write the number of the page or pages on which you found the information.**

Developing Your Thesis

As you begin researching and learning about your topic, think about the overall point you want to make. Write down a thesis statement, and keep it in mind as you continue your research to determine what information is and is not relevant. However, be prepared to change your thesis if the information you find does not support it.

Writing an Outline

When you have gathered information from several sources, use your note cards to write an outline. First, group together note cards that contain related information. Use the topic of each group as a main heading in your outline. Under each main heading, write subheadings that show the kinds of information you will provide. Write your thesis statement at the beginning of your outline.

Sample Outline

Many people are beginning to wonder if the price of success for female Olympic gymnasts is worth the sacrifice.

I. Changes in gymnastics since 1972
   A. Effect of Olga Korbut
   B. Age of athletes
   C. Need to be small and thin
II. Injuries
   A. Daily strain on the body
   B. Accidents
III. Emotional pressure
   A. Time spent training
   B. Pressures from parents and coach
   C. Rigid scoring system

The thesis statement identifies your topic and the overall point you will make.

Label main headings with Roman numerals.

Label subheadings with capital letters.

Documenting Your Information

You can avoid plagiarism by documenting, or showing the source of, information you use in your paper. Only information that can be found in several widely available sources does not need to be documented.

To document a piece of information, place a brief reference in parentheses just before the end punctuation in the sentence that contains the information.

The chart below shows how works are documented, or cited.

Type	Explanation	Example
Author cited in text	Page number in parentheses	According to Brown . . . (172).
Book with one author	Name of author followed by page number(s)	(Downing 15)
Book with more than one author	Include names of both authors	(Charbonneau and Lander 56)
Books with more than three authors	Add the abbreviation *et al.* after the first author's name	(Johnson et al. 104)

Bibliography or Works Cited

At the end of your paper, list all the sources that you documented in parentheses. Arrange them alphabetically by the author's last name, as shown below. If all your sources are print media (books, magazines, newspapers), label your list *Bibliography.* If you used other media, such as on-line articles, videotapes, or interviews, label your list *Works Cited.*

Works Cited

On-line article: "Cleopatra VII THEA PHILOPATOR." Britannica Online. Vers. 98.1.1 Mar. 1998. Encyclopaedia Britannica. 23 Dec. 1998 <http://www.eb.com:180>.

Magazine article: Holland, Barbara. "Cleopatra: What Kind of Woman Was She, Anyway?" Smithsonian Feb. 1997: 57–64.

Book with two authors: Hoobler, Dorothy, and Thomas Hoobler. Cleopatra. New York: Chelsea House Publishers, 1988.

Book with one author: Nardo, Don. The Importance of Cleopatra. San Diego: Lucent Books, 1994.

Interview: Provost, Eliza. Interview. 28 October, 1998.

Indent all but the first line of each item.

Include page numbers for a magazine article but not for a book, unless the book is a collection of essays by different authors.

Business Writing

Writing a Business Letter

Two standard formats for business letters are block style and modified block style. In block style all the elements line up at the left margin. There are no paragraph indents. In modified block style, the heading and closing begin just right of the center and paragraphs are indented.

The following business letter uses modified block style.

46 Brendan Street
Kingwood, TX 77345
March 11, 1999

In the heading, write your address and the date on separate lines.

Ms. Carolyn Vincenti
Town Center Building, Suite 7B
1 Cross Boulevard
Kingwood, TX 77345

In the inside address, the name and address of the person to whom the letter is sent are written on separate lines.

Dear Ms. Vincenti:

The greeting is followed by a colon.

In my social studies class at Haley Middle School, we are doing projects on careers, and I have chosen newspaper reporting as my topic. I have read many of your articles in the *Kingwood Monitor* and would be very interested in talking with you about your job.

In James's introduction, he lets Ms. Vincenti know who he is and why he is writing.

Would it be possible for me to meet with you for a brief interview sometime in the next two weeks? I could come to the Town Center building any weekday after three o'clock. You can reach me at the address above or call me at 555-8947.

In the body of his letter, James provides details concerning his request.

I look forward to hearing from you. Learning about your work as a reporter would be very valuable to me and my classmates. Thank you for your time and interest.

James concludes by restating his purpose and thanking Ms. Vincenti.

Sincerely,
James Yuan
James Yuan

The closing is *Sincerely, Sincerely yours,* or *Yours truly* followed by a comma and both the signature and printed name of the letter writer.

Besides requesting an interview, an effective business letter can serve other purposes. The following are a few of them:

Purpose	Example
To request information	An animal psychologist has a radio program on a local station. You write to ask how to train your dog not to bark at night.
To make a complaint	You have had your new computer repaired twice in six months. You write to the manufacturer to express your disappointment with the product.
To express an opinion	The city council member for your district has proposed building a new youth center. You write to her to express your support.

Writing a Memo

A memorandum, or memo, is a brief, efficient way of communicating information to another person or group of people. It begins with a header that provides basic information. A memo does not have a formal closing.

TO: Hiking Club members
FROM: Mike Nguyen
SUBJECT: Saturday outing
DATE: October 5, 1999

If you plan to participate in our next outing, please be at the front entrance of the school on Saturday, October 10, at 10:00 A.M. Wear or bring the following:

sturdy, rubber-soled shoes
long pants
sweater or sweatshirt
notebook and pencil
lunch, including a beverage

Using a Computer for Writing

Using a computer to write offers advantages at every stage of the writing process.

Prewriting

A computer can help you gather and organize ideas and information.

Brainstorming

While brainstorming for topics or details, you can dim the computer screen and do "invisible writing." Some writers find that this technique allows their ideas to flow more freely.

Researching

CD-ROMs are disks that store large amounts of text, graphics, and sounds. If your computer has a CD-ROM player, you can use a CD-ROM encyclopedia to find not only text and pictures, but also sound, animated cartoons or graphics, and live-action video clips.

If you have a modem and are connected with an on-line service, you can access material from an on-line encyclopedia or magazine.

Outlining

Some word-processing programs offer an outlining feature that automatically indents headings and uses different type styles for main headings and subheadings.

Drafting/Revising

Most word-processing programs make it easy to do the following:

- *insert* new text at any point in your document
- *delete* or *copy* text
- *move* text from one position to another
- *undo* a change you just made
- *save* each draft or revision of your document
- *print* copies of your work-in-progress for others to read

Editing/Proofreading

You can edit and proofread directly on the computer. If you prefer, you can mark your changes on a printout, or hard copy, of your document and then input the changes on screen. Either way, the following word-processing features are helpful.

- Grammar checker The computer finds possible errors in grammar and suggests revisions.
- Spelling checker The computer finds misspellings and suggests corrections.
- Thesaurus If you want to replace an inappropriate or overused word, you can highlight the word and the computer will suggest synonyms.
- Search and replace If you want to change or correct something that occurs several times in your document, the computer can instantly make the change throughout the document.

Rule of Thumb: The grammar checker, spelling checker, and thesaurus cannot replace your own careful reading and judgment. Because English grammar is so complex, the suggestions that the grammar checker makes may not be appropriate. Spelling is easier for a computer to monitor, but the spelling checker will not tell you that you have typed *brake* when you meant *break,* for example, because both are valid words. The thesaurus may offer you several synonyms for a word, but you need to consider the connotations of each before deciding which, if any, fits your context.

Presenting

The computer allows you to enhance the readability, attractiveness, and visual interest of your document in many ways.

Formatting your text

The computer gives you a variety of options for the layout and appearance of your text. You can easily add or change the following elements.

- margin width and number of columns
- type size and style
- page numbering
- header or footer (information such as a title that appears at the top or bottom of every page)

Visual aids

Some word-processing programs have graphic functions that allow you to create graphs, charts, and diagrams.

Study and Test-Taking Skills

Study Skills

Use this section to learn skills for studying effectively.

Taking notes in class

The notes you take while listening in class will help you understand and remember what you hear. Follow these guidelines:

- Take down only the main ideas and key details.
- Listen for transitions and signal words.
- Use numerals, abbreviations, and symbols for speed.

Using study time effectively

Follow these guidelines:

- Review your assignments and due dates. Write the due dates in a calendar.
- Break down your long-term goals into smaller tasks.
- Study at the same time and in the same place each day.
- Begin study time with your most difficult assignment.
- Take a short break after reaching each goal.
- Try a variety of study methods, including reading, summarizing, developing your own graphic aids (such as clusters), and discussing material with a study partner.

Taking Classroom Tests

Use this section to learn strategies for taking classroom tests.

Preparing for a test

Use these tips to prepare for a test:

- Find out what information the test will cover.
- Make a study schedule. Include time for reviewing your class notes, homework, quizzes, and textbook.
- As you study, jot down questions that might be on the test.
- If you have difficulty answering them, look up the information.
- Once you know the material fairly well, study with another student or group of students. Pool your study questions and take turns answering them.

Taking objective tests

An objective test is a test of factual information. The questions are generally either right or wrong; there is no difference of opinion. At the beginning of an objective test, scan the number of items. Then budget your time.

Multiple-choice items Multiple-choice items include an incomplete sentence or a question and three or four responses. Use these tips for answering multiple-choice questions.

- Read each item carefully to know what information you are looking for.
- Read all choices before answering. Sometimes an answer may seem correct, but a choice that follows it may be better.
- Be careful about choosing answers that contain absolute words, such as *always, never, all,* or *none.* Since most statements have exceptions, absolute statements are often incorrect.

Example:

Which of the following statements is true of mammals and only of mammals?

a. They have four limbs.
b. They drink their mother's milk.
c. They are warm-blooded.
d. They have backbones.

Not *all* mammals have four limbs; not *only* mammals are warm-blooded or have backbones. All and only mammals drink their mother's milk. The correct answer is *b.*

Answering essay questions

Essay questions usually require an answer of at least one paragraph. Use the following guidelines:

- Read the question carefully. If permitted, underline key words.
- Plan your time to allow for revision.
- Jot down key ideas to include in your answer.
- Develop a thesis statement and a rough outline.
- Provide several supporting details for each main idea.
- In your conclusion summarize what you have shown.

Key Verbs in Essay Questions	
Argue	Give your opinion and give reasons that support your opinion.
Compare and contrast	Discuss likenesses and differences.
Define	Give details that show exactly what something is like.
Demonstrate (also illustrate, show)	Give examples to support a point.
Describe	Present a picture with words.
Discuss	Show detailed information on a particular subject.
Explain	Give reasons.
Identify	Give specific characteristics.
List (also outline, trace)	Give details, give steps in order, give a time sequence.
Summarize	Give a short overview of the most important ideas or events.

Taking Standardized Tests

Standardized tests are given to groups of students around the country. Use this section to learn strategies for taking standardized tests.

Tips for taking standardized tests

Use the following tips for taking standardized tests.

- Most standardized tests are graded electronically. Make sure you understand how to mark your answer sheet, and be careful to avoid stray marks that might be misread.
- If points are not subtracted for incorrect answers, try to give an answer for every item, even if you are only guessing.
- If you can't answer a question quickly, move on to the next item. You can go back to the unanswered questions later if you have time.

Reading comprehension A reading-comprehension item includes a written passage and questions about the passage. The questions will ask you to identify the main idea or draw conclusions from the information.

Vocabulary Vocabulary items may ask you to choose a word that best completes a sentence, or they may ask you to select a definition of a word in a sentence. Using what you know about context clues, root words, and prefixes will help you make the right choice.

Analogies Analogy items test your understanding of the relationships between things or ideas. On standardized tests, analogies are written in an abbreviated format, as shown below.

man : woman :: buck : doe

The symbol : means "is to"; the symbol :: means "as."

This chart shows some word relationships you might find in analogy tests.

Relationship	Definition	Example
Synonyms	Two words have a similar meaning.	huge : gigantic :: scared : afraid
Antonyms	Two words have opposite meanings.	bright : dull :: far : near
Use	Words name a user and something used.	farmer : tractor :: writer : pen
Cause-effect	Words name a cause and its effect.	tickle : laugh :: polish : shine
Category	Words name a category and an item in it.	fish : tuna :: building : house
Description	Words name an item and a characteristic of it.	knife : sharp :: joke : funny

Grammar, usage, and mechanics Standardized tests measure your understanding of correct grammar, usage, and mechanics, usually by asking you to identify the section of a sentence that contains an error. Look for errors in grammar, usage, spelling, capitalization, and punctuation.

Listening, Speaking, and Viewing Skills

Listening Effectively

By improving your listening skills, you can increase your ability to understand and remember what you hear.

Tips for effective listening

Use these tips to sharpen your listening skills.

- Clear your mind of distractions, and concentrate on the speaker's words. Identify the main points or ideas. If you will need to use the information later, take notes.
- If you don't understand something, ask a question. Asking questions right away helps avoid confusion later on.
- If the information is important and you are the only listener, repeat the information back to the speaker to make sure you have understood correctly.
- If you have taken notes, review them as soon as possible after the speaker has finished; fill in information you may have left out.

Listening critically

As you listen, it is important to evaluate what you are hearing. Ask yourself these questions:

- Is the information accurate? What experience or education does the speaker have? What are his or her sources of information?
- Are the ideas logical and reasonable? Does the speaker back them up with sound facts, reasons, and examples?
- Is the speaker biased? Does he or she want something from me, such as my money or my vote? If so, could the information be exaggerated, distorted, or incomplete?

Interpreting nonverbal clues

Understanding nonverbal clues is part of effective listening. Nonverbal clues are everything you may notice about a speaker *except* what the speaker says. As you listen, ask yourself these questions:

- Where and how is the speaker standing?
- Are some words spoken more loudly than others?

- Does the speaker make eye contact?
- Does he or she smile or look angry?
- What message is sent by the speaker's gestures and facial expression?

Speaking Effectively

Use this section to improve your speaking skills in both formal and informal situations.

Speaking informally

Most of your oral communication is informal. When you speak casually with your friends, family, and neighbors, you use informal speech. Human relationships depend on this routine but effective form of communication.

- Be courteous. Listen until the other person has finished speaking. Do not interrupt.
- Speak in a relaxed and spontaneous manner.
- Make eye contact with your listeners.
- Do not monopolize a conversation. Let others have a chance to speak.
- When telling a story, show enthusiasm. Act out the parts and draw in your audience.
- When giving an announcement or directions, speak clearly and slowly. Check that your listeners understand the information.

Giving a formal speech

Unlike informal speaking, giving a formal speech involves considerable thought and planning. Delivering a speech in front of a live audience is the last stage of a five-stage process that is similar to the writing process. Like an essay or report, a formal speech has an introduction, a thesis statement, supporting facts and details, and a conclusion. The success of your speech will depend as much on the way you present it as on its content. Keep the following tips in mind as you practice and present your speech:

- Speak clearly and at a normal pace.
- Vary the volume and pitch of your voice according to what you are saying, as you do in normal speech.
- Pause after making an important point or after giving your audience a lot of information.
- Use hand gestures to emphasize important points and to help convey information. Be sure the gestures you use feel natural to you.
- Make eye contact with people in different parts of the audience.

Working in Groups

Use this section to learn how to work cooperatively with people in a group.

Roles in groups

Groups accomplish their goals most efficiently by assigning different roles to their members. The chart below shows three basic roles and the responsibilities of each.

Group Member	Responsibilities
Chairperson	Announces each discussion topic; keeps the discussion focused; moves the group toward a decision
Recorder	Writes down all ideas; reads ideas to be reviewed; records final decisions
Participants	Contribute and defend ideas; voice constructive criticism; vote on decisions

Group procedures

Once roles have been assigned, the group works toward its goal in an orderly way.

- The group sets an agenda, a list of things to be done or discussed.
- The chairperson announces the topic at hand.
- Participants contribute ideas and discuss the pros and cons of each.
- After sufficient discussion, the chairperson may ask the recorder to read the suggestions.
- The chairperson gives each participant a last chance to present his or her ideas.
- The chairperson calls for a vote and announces the decision.
- The recorder writes down the decision.

Sometimes the group needs more time to generate and think about ideas. In this case, the meeting might end without a decision but with everyone clearly understanding his or her responsibilities for the next meeting.

Viewing Effectively

Information is as likely to be transmitted through visual images as through the spoken or written word. Sharpening your visual perceptions can help you understand and analyze movies, videos, television programs, and advertisements.

Viewing to understand

Images that are prominent in a film may be symbols of a theme or an idea the director wants to convey. Images from nature such as a river, a snake, or a storm, are often used as symbols. So are colors, such as yellow for warmth or green for growth.

Facial expressions, gestures, posture, and clothing can be clues to the feelings and motives of characters in a drama. Clothing and hairstyles are also clues to the historical setting.

Viewing critically

Critical viewing means thinking about what you see while watching a TV program, newscast, film, or video. It requires paying attention to what you hear and see, and deciding whether information is true, false, or exaggerated. If the information *seems* to be true, try to determine whether it is based on a fact or an opinion.

Fact versus opinion A fact is something that can be proved or disproved. An opinion is what someone *believes* is true. Opinions are based on feelings and experiences, but cannot be proved.

Television commercials, political speeches, and even the evening news contain both facts and opinions. They use emotional words and actions to persuade the viewer to agree with a particular point of view. They may also use faulty reasoning, such as linking the wrong cause and effect. Think through what is being said. The speaker may seem sincere, but do his or her reasons make sense? Are the reasons based on facts or on unfair generalizations?

Commercials contain both obvious and hidden messages. The obvious message is the spoken words of the commercial. The hidden message comes across in *how* the message is presented. Look carefully at commercials to see whether a product is really worth buying.

The Reading Process

As reading materials get more difficult, you'll need to use a variety of active reading strategies to understand texts.

This handbook is designed to help you find and use the tools you'll need before, during, and after reading.

Word Identification

Word identification skills are necessary building blocks for understanding what you read. They prepare you to deal with unknown words you'll encounter.

Look before, at, and after a new word. Use the other words and sentences around an unknown word to help you make an educated guess about what that word might be. Think about the following questions as you try to read new words.

- Can I sound this new word out?
- Can I figure this new word out from its place in the sentence?
- What other word would make sense in this sentence?

Using letter-sound cues

One way to figure out a new word is to try to sound it out. Use the following tips when sounding out new words:

- Look at the beginning of the word. What letter or group of letters makes up the beginning sound or syllable of the word?

  Example: In the word *magnificent, mag* rhymes with *bag.*

- Look at the end of the word. What letter or group of letters makes up the ending sound or syllable?

  Example: In the word *magnificent, cent* is a word you know.

- Look at the middle of the word. Is there a word you already know inside the new word? What vowel or vowel pattern is represented in each syllable?

  Example: In the word *magnificent,* the syllables *ni* and *fi* have the same vowel sound as the word *it.*

Now try pronouncing the whole word: *mag ni fi cent.*

Using language structure cues

Word order, or **syntax,** helps you make sense of a sentence, so looking at the position of a new word in a sentence can help you identify a word. For instance, look at the following nonsense sentence:

The drazzy lurds miffled the bonkee blams.

Your experience with English sentence patterns and parts of speech tells you that the action word, or verb, in this sentence is *miffled.* Who did the *miffling?*–the *lurds.* What kind of *lurds* were they?–*drazzy.* Whom did they *miffle?*–the *blams.* What kind of blams were they?–*bonkee.* Even though you do not know word meanings in the nonsense sentence, you can make some sense of the entire sentence by using syntax.

Use the order of words in a sentence to help you figure out parts of speech. Then use that knowledge to identify new words and their meanings.

Using context clues

When you read on your own, you can often figure out the meaning of a new word by looking at its **context,** the other words and sentences that surround it. For instance, look at the following example:

Mr. Hargrove was very upset at first. However, my offer to pay for his broken window seemed to ***mollify*** *him.*

You can guess from the first sentence that *mollify* is a word that means something different than being upset. If you guessed that it means to *calm someone down,* you have successfully used context clues to find meaning.

Tips for Using Context

- Look before, at, and after the unknown word for
  - –a synonym or definition of the unknown word in a sentence.
    The ***flotilla,*** *a* ***small group of ships,*** *could be seen in the harbor.*
  - –a clue to what the word is like or not like.
    Unlike *her* ***punctual*** *sister, Susan was always* ***late.***
  - –a general topic associated with the word.
    The ***cooking*** *teacher discussed the best way to* ***poach*** *the fish.*
  - –a description or action associated with the word.
    He used the ***mulching*** *tool to* ***dig*** *up the garden.*
- Connect what you know with what the author has written.
- Predict a possible meaning and apply the meaning in the sentence.
- Try again if your guess does not make sense.

Using word parts to read new words

Noticing word parts can help you sound out and understand unknown words. Look at some of the following word parts:

- **Roots** The base part of a word is called its root. If you know a root within a new word, start from there to sound out the rest of the word. *(insecurity)*
- **Plurals** Many times nouns are changed from singular to plural by adding *-s* , *-es,* or *-ies. (dogs, buses, babies)*
- **Comparative endings** Used for adjectives and adverbs, *-er* or *-est* added to a word forms a comparison. *(stronger, strongest)*
- **Inflectional endings** Other endings, such as *-ing* or *-ed* can be important parts of both the meaning and pronunciation of a word *(walk, walked, walking)*.
- **Prefixes** These syllables, added to the beginning of words, change the meaning of the words. For example, *un-* means "not," so *unnecessary* means "not necessary."
- **Suffixes** Added to the end of a word, a suffix changes its meaning. For example, *-less* means "without" or "lacking," so *useless* means "without use."

Using reference materials

When looking at or around an unknown word does not help you identify it, dictionaries, glossaries, thesauruses, and other reference sources can be useful tools. References provide derivations and spellings as well as pronunciations.

A **dictionary** provides the pronunciation and literal meaning or meanings of a word. It also gives other forms of the word, its part of speech, alternative spellings, examples, synonyms, origins, and other useful information. Look at the dictionary entry below to see what valuable information it provides.

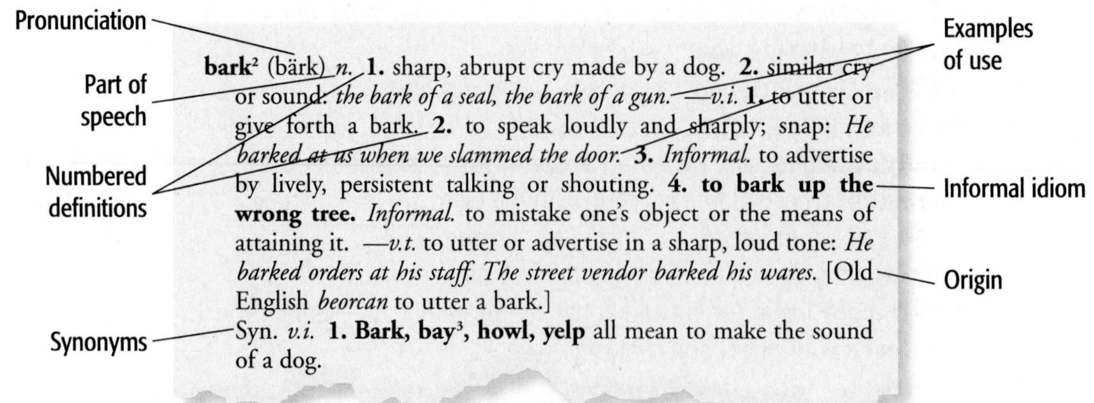

bark[2] (bärk) *n.* **1.** sharp, abrupt cry made by a dog. **2.** similar cry or sound: *the bark of a seal, the bark of a gun.* —*v.i.* **1.** to utter or give forth a bark. **2.** to speak loudly and sharply; snap: *He barked at us when we slammed the door.* **3.** *Informal.* to advertise by lively, persistent talking or shouting. **4. to bark up the wrong tree.** *Informal.* to mistake one's object or the means of attaining it. —*v.t.* to utter or advertise in a sharp, loud tone: *He barked orders at his staff. The street vendor barked his wares.* [Old English *beorcan* to utter a bark.]
Syn. *v.i.* **1. Bark, bay**[3]**, howl, yelp** all mean to make the sound of a dog.

A **glossary** is a condensed dictionary within a specific text. It provides an alphabetical listing of words used within that text, together with their definitions and other information necessary to understand the word as it appears in the text. Look at the example below.

A

abash [ə bash′] *v.* to make embarrassed and ashamed.

abet [ə bet′] *v.* to approve of, encourage, or help.
– **abettor,** *n.*

abject [ab′jekt, ab jekt′] *adj.* having lost one's spirit and self-respect; wretched.

abrasion [ə brā′zhən] *n.* a scraping.

abscond [ab skond′] *v.* to run off quickly and secretly.

absolve [ab zolv′, -solv′] *v.* to set free from responsibility or blame.

abut [ə but′] *v.* to be next to; border on.

abyss [ə bis′] *n.* a bottomless depth.

A **thesaurus** is a dictionary of synonyms and antonyms, and can be especially useful for choosing precise, descriptive language. Some thesauruses are available on CD-ROM and on the Internet.

Reading Fluency

Becoming an accomplished reader is like learning a sports skill or a musical instrument: the more you practice, the better you'll get. The more you read aloud, the less attention you will need to pay to sounding words out and the more attention you can give to understanding the meaning in a selection.

Tips for Becoming a Fluent Reader

- Develop a good sight vocabulary.
- Practice reading out loud on independent level materials.
- Begin with a short, interesting passage.
- Reread the same passage out loud at least three times.
- As your reading sounds smoother, move on to a longer or slightly more difficult passage.

Reading in appropriate level materials

How do you decide if something is too easy, too hard, or just right for you to read? If you want to develop into a smooth, fluent reader, it is important to read regularly in materials that are easy for you. However, it is also important to grow as a strategic reader, and to do that, you will want to read materials that are challenging but manageable.

To decide what level of reading material is right for each reading task, look at the following chart:

Reading level	Definition/Criteria	When to use
Independent level	No more than 5 difficult words per 100 words read	On your own, anytime To practice smooth reading
Instructional level	No more than 10 difficult words per 100 words read	With support from teacher, parent, or other more experienced reader To challenge yourself
Beyond instructional level	More than 10 difficult words per 100 words read	As material read to you by someone else To develop new vocabulary through listening

Adjusting reading rate—skimming, scanning, and careful reading

Adjust your reading speed to suit your purposes and the task you face. When you read something for enjoyment, you might read quickly. If you want to refresh your memory of a passage or get a quick impression of new material, skim the selection. **Skimming** is reading quickly over a piece of writing to find its main idea or to get a general overview of it. When you need to find a particular piece or type of information, scan the selection. In **scanning,** you run your eyes quickly over the material, looking only for key words or phrases that have to do with the information you seek.

When you read a chapter of a textbook filled with new concepts, when you follow complex written directions, or when you study for a test, read slowly, take notes, make a graphic organizer, and even reread passages in order to remember them later.

Look at the following models.

The sun was almost down as Stacy climbed the steps of the sagging old porch. She had to push aside some cobwebs to get to the doorbell. As her hand went up, the door mysteriously opened slowly and with an ominous creaking sound. Stacy poked her head inside to see if anyone was there. A candle was burning on a table in the corner. Suddenly she saw a gray figure glide up the staircase. Maybe the kids were right about this old house!

Green plants make food by a process called photosynthesis. In this process, energy from light is combined with water and carbon dioxide to make food. Light is absorbed by a green substance in leaves called chlorophyll. This substance is stored in bodies called chloroplasts. In each chloroplast, the light causes carbon dioxide to mix with the hydrogen atoms in water to make sugar. From this sugar, plants make food.

Which paragraph could you read more quickly? Why? What would you do to be sure you remembered the information in each paragraph?

Reading aloud

There are various reasons for reading out loud. Oral reading can make any writer's work come to life. A readers theater, a dialogue or monologue, and other enactments allow you to convey meaning with your voice and can be very enjoyable ways of sharing a memorable selection. Reading a complicated paragraph aloud can also be a powerful aid to understanding. Here are some suggestions for reading aloud:

- First, read the selection silently a number of times.
- Think about the best way to make the main ideas understandable to your listeners.
- Use pauses to separate complete thoughts, and be sure you observe all punctuation marks.
- Read carefully and clearly. Vary your speed and volume to reflect the important ideas in a passage.
- Use a lively voice. Emphasize important words and phrases to make the meaning clear.
- Practice difficult words and phrases until you've mastered them.
- Practice in front of another person if possible, or use a tape recorder to hear how you sound.

Reading silently

When you read silently for any length of time, be sure to avoid any distractions or interruptions.

Tips for Sustained Silent Reading

- Be sure you're comfortable, but not too comfortable.
- Check your concentration regularly by asking yourself questions about the selection.
- Summarize what you've read from time to time.
- Use a study guide or story map (see page R94) to help you keep focused through difficult passages.
- Make a graphic organizer, if necessary, to understand and remember important concepts or a sequence of events.
- Take regular breaks when you need them.

TRY THE STRATEGIES

With a partner, choose a selection from your text and look it over. Read the selection silently, adjusting your speed to the difficulty of the text. When both of you are finished, take turns asking questions to check your comprehension. Finally, choose a small section of the passage and take turns reading it aloud. Exchange suggestions about your oral reading.

Reading a Variety of Texts

Whether you read for education or entertainment, reading a variety of texts will improve your skills as a strategic reader. Throughout this textbook, you've read examples of both classic and contemporary writing. From "The Tell-Tale Heart" to "On the Road with Charles Kuralt," you have seen how a wide variety of selections broadens your knowledge and deepens your appreciation of people and cultures.

Reading varied sources

Strategic readers take advantage of a variety of sources for information and for entertainment. For instance, to create a detailed and interesting portrait of a famous person from your hometown or state, you might refer to sources like those listed below:

- **Textbooks** provide a basic foundation of information.
- **Letters, memos, speeches, newspapers,** and **magazines** add personal perspectives not available in other sources.
- **Databases, library indexes,** and **Internet sites** often supply interesting information.

- **Novels, poems, plays,** and **anthologies,** or collections of literature, provide excellent opportunities to read for pleasure as well as to explore the ideas of a writer in a particular time.

Reading for various purposes

Active reading begins with thinking about a reason for reading. You may find that you have more than one purpose or that your purposes overlap. For instance, you might read to enjoy an intense and thrilling mystery and, at the same time, discover how police detectives work. The reading strategies you use to guide you through a text will depend on your purposes.

When your purpose for reading is

- **to be informed,** read slowly, take notes, construct a graphic organizer, reread, and review difficult sections.
- **to be entertained,** read at a faster rate.
- **to appreciate a writer's craft,** read simply to enjoy how well others write.
- **to discover models for your own writing,** look at other writers' works to help stimulate your own ideas.
- **to take action,** be sure you understand all facts, directions, and instructions.

TRY THE STRATEGIES

Choose a topic that interests you, and read about it in at least three different sources. Decide on some sort of action to take as a result of your reading. You may write a short report, give a speech, demonstrate how something works, or try to persuade your classmates to believe or do something. Make a short presentation to your class, explaining your purpose for reading and the value of each of your sources.

Vocabulary Development

Having a good vocabulary means more than just knowing the meanings of isolated words. It means knowing the larger concepts that surround those words. The very best way to build a good vocabulary is to read widely, listen carefully, and participate actively in discussions where new words and concepts are used.

Listening

Books that may be just a little too hard for you to read on your own are often excellent choices as selections to be read aloud to you. They provide a good way to learn new vocabulary. "Read alouds" also give you a model for your own future oral reading. As you hear new words, try to pay attention to their context, or other words and thoughts surrounding the unknown words. Try to guess at what meaning would make sense for new words. Many times you will guess accurately if you pay careful attention.

Using experience and prior knowledge

Because of your life experiences, you know certain things and understand the meanings of certain words and ideas. Those experiences, called **prior knowledge,** help you determine word meanings. For instance, if you have had experience using computers, you'll understand the following sentence:

She needed to clean her mouse in order to make her cursor move more smoothly.

Sometimes you'll need to look beyond the exact meaning of words in a selection.

- Idioms An expression that has a meaning apart from the literal meaning of the words is called an idiom. If someone has *pulled the wool over your eyes,* it means that he or she has fooled you. When someone is *pulling your leg,* he or she is joking with you. In each case, combine the words with your own prior knowledge to interpret what the expression really means.
- Multiple meanings Words can have more than one meaning, so check the context to be sure the meaning you have chosen makes sense.
  We may have to ***fire*** *that crew if they can't put out the* ***fire.***
  Will you ***check*** *to see if my* ***check*** *is in the mail?*
- Figurative language Writers sometimes make comparisons by using figurative language, such as similes and metaphors. A **simile** uses *like* or *as* to compare two unlike things, while a **metaphor** compares two unlike things without using *like* or *as.*
  Simile: *Sleep covered him* ***like*** *a soft, heavy blanket.*
  Metaphor: *Her mood was a dark cloud that shadowed the room.*
- Analogies A comparison based on the relationship between two things or ideas is called an analogy. Analogies sometimes are written like this: *fish : gills :: human : lungs.* To understand the analogy, try turning it into short identical sentences. For instance, *A fish breathes with gills. A human breathes with lungs.*

Clarifying meanings with reference aids

Sometimes meanings of words and phrases can remain unclear even after using context, drawing on your personal background, and listening carefully. In that case, look to other reference aids to help clarify the meanings and usage of difficult terms.

- **Thesauruses** and books of synonyms can clarify a word by listing other words that have similar meanings. Be sure to notice what part of speech a word is, so you can determine how to use it in a sentence.
- **Dictionaries** will often be able to clear up word meanings because they provide a variety of definitions for a word and examples of each definition in a sentence. You can often find the meaning of idioms by looking in a dictionary under the main word in the phrase. Look at the idioms listed under the entry word *fire.*

between two fires. under physical or verbal attack from both sides.
on fire. **a.** burning; ignited. **b.** inflamed or overwhelmed with intense emotional feeling; eager; zealous; passionate.
to catch fire. to become ignited; begin to burn.
to go through fire and water. to experience or endure great danger, hardships, or trials.
to hang fire. **a.** to fail or be slow to discharge: *The artillery hung fire, and the enemy got through the line.* **b.** to be slow in acting; hesitate. **c.** to be delayed: *The deal hung fire for several weeks.*
to lay a fire. to arrange material so that it may be burned.
to open fire. **a.** to begin to shoot: *They opened fire on the enemy.* **b.** to begin; commence.
to play with fire. to do or meddle with something dangerous or risky.
to set fire to. to cause to burn; ignite.

- **Computer software** will often include reference materials that can clarify meanings and usage for difficult words.

Using word parts and origins to determine meaning

Another way to determine the meaning of a word is to take the word itself apart. If you understand the meaning of the **base,** or **root** part of a word and also know the meanings of key syllables added to the beginning or end of the base, you can often figure out what a word means.

Word Part	Definition	Example
Root or base	the most basic part of a word	*ced* means "go"
Prefix	a syllable used before a root word to add to or change its meaning	*pre-* means "before" *precede* means "go before"
Suffix	a syllable used after a root word to add to or change its meaning	*-ous* means "full of" *joyous* means "full of joy"

Word origins English contains many words based on roots from ancient languages like Greek and Latin. Having some knowledge of word derivations in either of these languages can help you determine meanings, pronunciations, and spellings in English.

Root	Meaning	Example
astro (Greek)	star	astronaut, astronomy, asterisk
ped (Latin)	foot	pedal, pedestrian
vid (Latin)	see	video, evidence
hydr (Greek)	water	hydrant, dehydrate

Affixes These syllables are added either to the beginning or end of a word. For example, the word *unusually* is made up of the root *usual* and the affixes *un-* and *-ly.* The prefix *un-* means "not." The suffix *-ly* means "in a particular manner." If you put them together, *unusually* means "not in the usual manner."

Using word meanings across subjects

Have you ever learned a new word and then noticed it in many different places and across many different subjects? The word may not mean exactly the same thing in each place, but you can often use what you know about a word meaning to help you interpret its meaning in a different context. Look at the following example from two different subjects:

Social studies: *One major **product** manufactured in the South is cotton cloth.*

Math: *After you multiply those two numbers, explain how you arrived at the **product**.*

You may know that a product is something manufactured by a company. In math, a product is a number that results from multiplying two other numbers together. In both situations, a product is the result of something.

Listening to news stories and current events is a good way to increase your vocabulary. Actively discuss ideas as well as new vocabulary that you hear in news reports. Friends, teachers, and parents will have their own ideas about the subtle meanings of words, so careful listening will add to your vocabulary development. Look at the model on the next page. Can you figure out the meaning of the italicized word in the first sentence of the following news report?

The U.S. Customs Department announced today that its agents *confiscated* dozens of stolen computers near the U.S.-Canadian border. The computers were found in a large unmarked truck that had initially been stopped for speeding. Agents hope to use the computers as evidence in the case.

What strategies did you use to determine that *confiscated* means "seized"? How could you use the word in another context?

TRY THE STRATEGIES

Find a science or social studies textbook that includes a list of key vocabulary at the beginning of a chapter. Use prior knowledge or word parts and origins to predict what the words might mean. Then read the passages where the words are located and use syntax or context to check or further refine the meanings you predicted.

Determining connotation and denotation

Determining special meanings of words is an important aid to understanding. Look at these two examples of ways to distinguish between word meanings:

- **Denotation** A denotation expresses the literal, or dictionary meaning of a word. A word may have more than one denotation, but all of its denotations will be listed in the dictionary.
- **Connotation** When a word has an emotion or an underlying value that accompanies its dictionary meaning, it has a connotation. You may say that flowers have a *fragrance,* but that garbage has a *stench.* Both words mean "smell," but the connotation of *fragrance* is pleasant, while the word *stench* connotes something unpleasant.

Understanding historical influences of words

In addition to giving you word spellings, pronunciations, and meanings, a dictionary will give you the historical background of a word. Many English words have Greek, Latin, or Anglo-Saxon origins. The Earl of Sandwich used to enjoy eating meat between two pieces of bread. Can you guess how we have used that historical influence to add to our English vocabulary? It's also easy to see why Janus, the Roman god of beginnings, gave his name to the first month of the year.

Comprehension

The main job in reading is to comprehend, or understand, what you have read. Using the best strategies at the right times will help you improve your comprehension and make your reading interesting and fun.

Previewing

Before you begin to read, it's helpful to **preview** a selection.

- **Look** at the title and the illustrations and other images that are included.
- **Read** the headings, subheadings, and anything in bold letters.
- **Skim** the passage; that is, take a quick look at the whole thing.
- **Decide** what the author's purpose might be for writing.
- **Predict** what the selection will be about.
- **Set a purpose** for your own reading.

Using knowledge and experience to understand

When you use your own knowledge and experience and combine it with the words on a page, you create meaning in a selection. Drawing on this personal background is called **activating prior knowledge.** To expand and extend your prior knowledge, share it in lively classroom discussions. Ask yourself questions like these as you start to read:

- What do I know about this topic?
- Have I been to places similar to the setting described by this writer?
- What experiences have I had that compare with what I am reading?
- What characters from life or literature remind me of the characters or narrator in the selection?

Establishing and adjusting purposes for reading

Think about these possible purposes that you might have for reading:

- to find out something
- to understand a process or an idea
- to interpret a writer's work and create meaning in a passage
- to enjoy a selection or be entertained by a story
- to solve problems or to perform a task

Each purpose allows for different active reading strategies. To find information for a report, you might skim an entire passage until you find the section you're looking for and then read more slowly. To understand new information, you might read slowly from beginning to end, or even reread passages that are unclear. To simply enjoy a piece of good writing, you may allow yourself to read quickly or slow yourself down to appreciate something beautifully written.

Whatever your purposes are as you move through a selection, it's important to be able to adjust those purposes as well as your strategies to get the most out of your reading.

Making and verifying predictions

As you read, take educated guesses about story events and outcomes. **Make predictions** before and during your reading. Using your prior knowledge and the information you have gathered in your preview, predict what you will learn or what might happen in a selection. Whether your original prediction is precisely accurate does not matter, but careful predictions and later **verifications** or **adjustments,** based on your reading, increase your understanding of a selection.

Monitoring and modifying reading strategies

No matter what your purposes for reading, your most important task is to understand what you have read. Ask yourself questions as you move through a passage. Monitor or check your understanding using the following strategies:

- **Summarize** what you read by answering who, what, where, why, and when.
- **Clarify** what you don't understand by careful rereading.
- **Question** important ideas and story elements.
- **Predict** what will happen next.
- **Evaluate** what you have read so far.

Tips for Monitoring Understanding

- **Reread.** If silently rereading a passage several times does not help to clear it up, try reading it aloud.
- **Map out the main thoughts or ideas.** A graphic organizer can help get your thoughts on track. (See page R93.)
- **Look for context clues.** Often a writer will include an example or a definition of a difficult word in the surrounding sentences.
- **Ask questions.** Teachers, parents, and other classmates can shed light on difficult written passages if you let them.
- **Write comments** as well as questions on another piece of paper for later review or discussion.
- **Use reference aids.** Dictionaries, glossaries, thesauruses, and encyclopedias–electronic or print–provide easy access to most information.

Visualizing

Creating pictures in your mind as you read is a powerful aid to understanding. According to your imagination and the text, what do characters look like? What does the setting look like? Can you picture the steps in a process when you read nonfiction? If you can visualize what you read, selections will be more vivid, and you'll recall them better later on. Be sure, though, that what you picture is accurately based on information from the text.

TRY THE STRATEGIES

During a time when your teacher is reading aloud to you, either from a piece of fiction or nonfiction, try sketching what you're hearing. If the selection is fiction, draw a character, setting, or action based on text description. If the selection is nonfiction, see if you can draw the steps in a process or make a small diagram of a place or thing described. Compare your sketch with a partner's and talk about similarities and differences. Go back to the text to adjust or verify your information.

Constructing graphic organizers

Graphic organizers help you draw a picture of what you're reading so you can sort ideas out, clear up difficult passages, and remember important ideas in a selection. Look at the following examples of good graphic organizers and notice how they are used.

Web You can show a main idea and supporting details by using a web. Put the main idea in the middle circle and the supporting details in the surrounding circles. Notice how you might include other circles branching off from the detail circles. Use those for further information about your details.

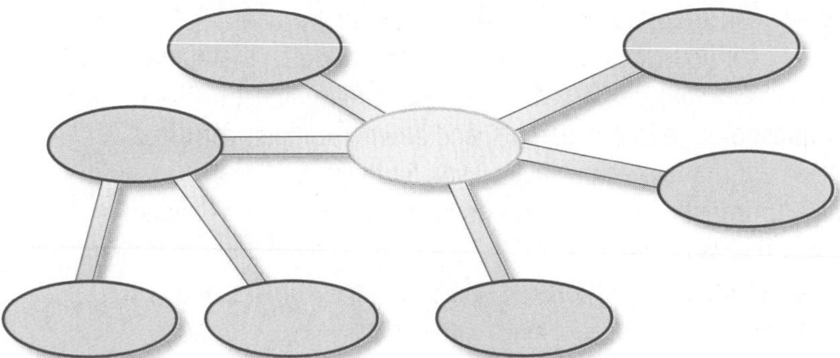

Flow chart When you want to keep track of events in a time order or show a cause-and-effect relationship between events, use a flow chart. Arrange your ideas or events in the boxes, putting them in their logical order. Then draw arrows between the boxes to show how one idea or event flows into another.

Venn diagram To look at the similarities and differences between two ideas, characters, or events, use a Venn diagram. The outer portions of each circle will show how two items contrast or are different. Use the overlapping portion of the circles to show how they are the same.

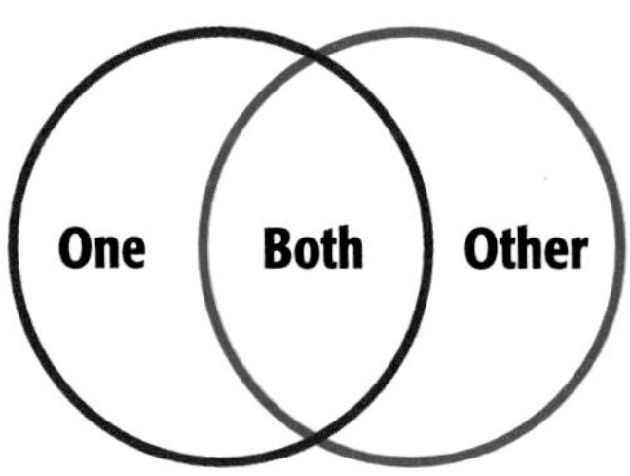

Using text structures

Writers organize their ideas in a variety of ways, depending on their topic and their purpose for writing. When you find that pattern of organization or **text structure** within a selection, it's easier to locate and recall a writer's ideas. Here are four examples of ways that writers structure or organize text:

Kind of Organization	Purpose	Clues
Comparison and contrast	To determine similarities and differences	Words and phrases such as *similarly, on the other hand, in contrast to, but, however*
Cause and effect	To explore the reasons for something and to examine the results of events or actions	Words and phrases such as *so, because, as a result*
Chronological order	To present events in time order	Words and phrases such as *first, next, then, later, finally*
Problem/Solution	To examine how conflicts or obstacles are overcome	Words and phrases such as *need, attempt, help, obstruction*

READING HANDBOOK

To find the text structure of a passage, look for **signal words and phrases** that contain clues about how the writer has organized ideas. Read the two models below.

In order to organize his science project, Jamie **first** needed to determine how many specimens he would use in his control group and again in his test group. **Then** he would have to order some cockroaches, arrange for the delivery of the glass cases where the little critters would live for two months, and find out how much and what they would eat. **After he did that**, Jamie sat down with his plans for the project to determine what he intended to prove.

Signal words and phrases

Jon listened carefully as the woman interviewed on the nightly news telecast explained how that particular day had been the best and the worst day of her life. **On the one hand,** the tornado that tore through her tiny community left her nothing but a concrete slab to call home. Everything her family had worked for was gone. **On the other hand,** she and her husband and their daughter were safe. The young mother's face was full of tiny cuts and bruises, **but** she smiled continuously at the little girl who played on her lap. **In contrast to** the reporter's worried expression and concerned questions, both husband and wife expressed how lucky they felt. As the interview ended, Jon knew he had found a wonderful subject for his Thanksgiving narrative essay.

Signal words and phrases

What is the basic text structure of the first model? of the second? Explain how you determined your answers.

Determining main ideas and supporting details

The most important idea in a paragraph or passage is called the **main idea.** The examples or ideas that further explain the main idea are called **supporting details.** Some main ideas are clearly stated in sentences within a passage. Other times, without directly stating a main idea, an author will suggest it by providing a variety of clues.

Many times the main idea will be the first sentence of a paragraph, but not always. A main idea might be anywhere, even in the last sentence in a passage.

A selection can have a number of main ideas in it. Each paragraph might contain a main idea, as in most nonfiction, or entire passages can have a main idea, as in both fiction and nonfiction.

When you need to find the main idea, ask yourself these questions:

- What is each sentence about?
- Is there one sentence that tells about the whole passage or that is more important than the others?
- If the main idea is not directly stated, what main idea do the supporting details point out?

Finding the main ideas will help you understand a selection. Look at the following model.

Main idea — **Many of the animals that live on the ocean floor have found a way to cope with the darkness—they are luminous.** Some species of fish are hosts to bacteria that glow in the dark. When they eat the bacteria, the hosts' bodies glow from the bacteria inside them. One species of fish in the Indian Ocean has these bacteria in spots under each eye. The fish's eyes seem to glow in the dark. However, when the fish is threatened, it can raise black folds of skin that hide the light. The bathysphere fish seems to have lights in its teeth to attract food, while the hatchet fish glows with lights that only look like teeth. These lights seem to scare away other fish. — Supporting details

Sequencing

The order in which thoughts are arranged is called **sequence.** A good sequence is one that is logical, given the ideas in a selection. Here are three common forms of sequencing:

- Chronological order–time order
- Spatial order–the order in which things would be arranged within a certain space
- Order of importance–going from most important to least important or the other way around

Recognizing the sequence of something is very important when you have to follow directions. If you fail to follow steps in a certain order, you may not be able to accomplish your task.

Paraphrasing

Retelling something using your own words is **paraphrasing.** You might paraphrase just the main ideas of a selection, or you might retell an entire story in your own words. Paraphrasing is a useful strategy for reviewing and for checking comprehension.

Original text: *The Four Corners area of Colorado, Utah, New Mexico, and Arizona is home to a multitude of ancient dwellings.*

Paraphrase: *In the area where Colorado, Utah, New Mexico, and Arizona meet, you can find many very old homes.*

Summarizing

When you **summarize,** you relate the main ideas of a selection in a logical sequence and in your own words, combining three skills in one. To create a good summary, include all the main ideas and only essential supporting details.

A good summary can be easily understood by someone who has not read the whole text or selection. Look at the following model and summary:

The Dead Sea is not dead. It is not a sea, either. Even though the water of the Dead Sea is too salty for fish and other animals to live there, some microscopic organisms that use the sun to photosynthesize, and others from which petroleum can be made make the waters of the Dead Sea their home. This body of water is not a sea but is instead a salt lake. It has the lowest elevation of any place on earth. The water contains more salt and other minerals than any other body of water.

Summary: The Dead Sea, a salt lake, is the saltiest body of water in the world, and is also the lowest place on earth. Even though fish and other animals cannot live there, microscopic plants call the Dead Sea home.

TRY THE STRATEGIES

Read "I Have a Dream" on page 494 of this book. On separate paper, list the main ideas in the selection. Under each main idea, list the supporting details that explain it. Use this information to write a one-paragraph summary of what you have read.

Drawing and supporting inferences

Writers don't always directly state what they want you to understand in a selection. By providing clues and interesting details, they suggest certain information. Whenever you combine those clues with your own background and knowledge, you are drawing an inference. An **inference** involves using your reason and experience to come up with an idea, based on what an author implies or suggests. The following active reading behaviors are examples of drawing an inference:

- Inferring You infer when you use context clues and your own knowledge to figure out what an author is suggesting.
- Predicting When you guess what a story will be about or what will happen next, you are predicting.
- Drawing conclusions A conclusion is a general statement you can make and explain with reasoning or with supporting details from a selection.
- Generalizing When you draw an inference that can apply to more than one item or group, you are making a generalization.
- Classifying When you recognize something as fitting into a category, you classify it.

Finding similarities and differences across texts

As your reading takes you across a variety of sources, compare and contrast the things you've read. When you look for similarities and differences in your reading selections, you'll gain a better understanding of all the material you've read. Ask yourself in what ways sources might be alike or different. What is included in one selection that might be left out of another? Why might that be?

Here are some of the ways you can compare and contrast writers' works:

- Scope Take a broad look at each entire selection. How would you compare the time periods covered? How much information is given in each nonfiction selection? How many characters and settings are involved in fiction pieces?
- Treatment Look at how each writer presents important ideas. Who tells the story? Is the narrator's attitude serious or funny? How would you compare the writers' purposes? styles?
- Organization Compare selections in terms of how writers arrange their thoughts. Is a writer using **chronological order? comparison and contrast? cause and effect? problem and solution?**

When you look for similarities and differences in what you've read, you'll learn to read more critically and get more out of each selection.

Distinguishing fact from opinion

When deciding whether to believe what a writer has written, you need to distinguish between fact and opinion. A **fact** is a statement that can be proved with supporting information. An **opinion,** on the other hand, is what a writer believes, based on his or her personal viewpoint. Writers can support their opinions with facts, but an opinion is something that cannot be proved. Look at the following examples of fact and opinion:

Fact: *Two students in our school scored higher on national tests than any other students in our district.*
Opinion: *Everyone knows that our school has the smartest students in the district.*

When interpreting anything you read, be sure that you distinguish between statements of fact and opinion.

Answering questions

How do you decide where to look for answers to questions about selections you've read? Look at the chart below to help you decide.

Type of question	What is it?	Example	How to find the answer
Literal	Has a definite answer	What color was Snow White's hair?	Look for direct statement in text.
Interpretive	Answer based on text and prior knowledge	Why was Snow White a threat to the queen?	Use text information and/or prior knowledge.
Open-ended	No right or wrong answer	Is Snow White a role model for today's children?	Use personal background and feelings.

You may find different types of questions on a test.

Tips for Answering Test Questions

- True or false questions If any part of a true or false question is false, the correct answer is "false."
- Short answer Use complete sentences so your responses will be clear. Try to put your thoughts in a logical sequence.
- Multiple choice First read all the responses. Eliminate the answers you know are incorrect. Choose the best answer from the remaining responses.

Representing text information

After you've read in various sources, you may need to reproduce what you have learned in a visual way, perhaps to present it to your class or to show the teacher that you have understood it.

- **Outlines** An outline is helpful if you are organizing information to present a report. Roman numerals, together with upper- and lower-case letters show the basic structure of the report. Look at this sample model of a topic outline.

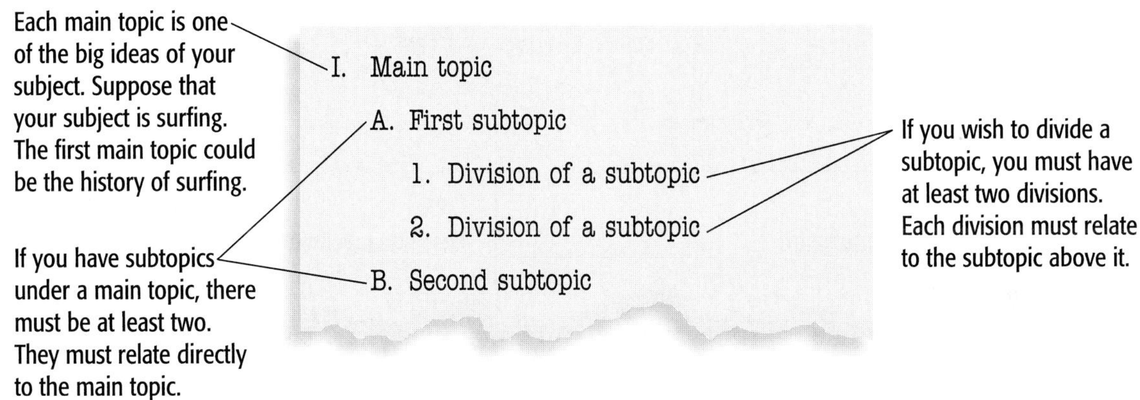

Each main topic is one of the big ideas of your subject. Suppose that your subject is surfing. The first main topic could be the history of surfing.
I. Main topic
A. First subtopic
1. Division of a subtopic
2. Division of a subtopic
B. Second subtopic
If you have subtopics under a main topic, there must be at least two. They must relate directly to the main topic.
If you wish to divide a subtopic, you must have at least two divisions. Each division must relate to the subtopic above it.

- **Time lines** A time line shows the chronological order of events over a period of time. Look at the example below.

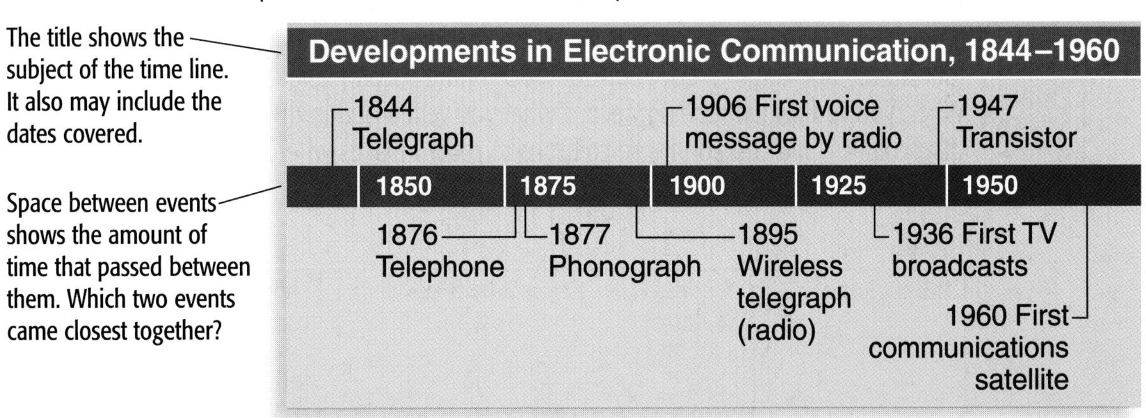

- **Graphic organizers** Word webs, flow charts, Venn diagrams, and other kinds of graphic organizers can help you present information in a visual way.

Using study strategies

If you're preparing for a quiz or test or getting ready for a class presentation, you'll want to use a study strategy that helps you organize and remember the material you've read. Here are some useful strategies:

- Using story maps A story map can help you sort out important literary elements in works of fiction. Look at the model below to see how a story map works as a tool for review.

STORY MAP

Characters	**Setting**
Plot Conflict (problem)	**Plot** Resolution (solution)

- Using KWL KWL is a good way to keep track of what you are learning when you read informational text. Make three columns on a page. Label the first column *What I **K**now,* the second column *What I **W**ant to Know,* and the third column *What I **L**earned.* Before you begin reading, list the things you already know about a topic in the first column. List your questions in the second column. When you've finished reading, record what you've learned in the third column. You can add more columns to record places where you found information and places to look for more.

KWL

What I Know	**What I Want to Know**	**What I Learned**	**Where I Got Information**
			Where I Can Get More

- Using SQ3R A useful study strategy for studying subject areas like science or social studies is SQ3R. It stands for **s**urvey, **q**uestion, **r**ead, **r**ecord, and **r**eview. Here's how it works:
  1. **Survey** Take a quick look over the entire selection you need to study. Notice anything boldfaced. Look at any headings, subheadings, or pictures.
  2. **Question** Think of a number of questions you'll want to answer as you read.
  3. **Read** Read the selection carefully. Vary your reading rate as you encounter easy or difficult passages.
  4. **Record** Take notes about important ideas. Record your comments and any additional questions that come up as you read.
  5. **Review** When you've finished reading, go back over the text once again to be sure you've understood important ideas.
- Creating and using study guides Your teacher may provide you with a guide to focus your attention on important vocabulary and ideas. You can also create your own guide by using end-of-chapter questions to focus your reading.

TRY THE STRATEGIES

Select a chapter from your social studies or science text. Use SQ3R as you read the material. Have a classmate quiz you by using end-of-chapter questions to see how well you remember what you studied.

Literary Response

Whenever you share your thoughts and feelings about something you've read, you are responding to text. You have your own learning style, so you will want to respond in ways that are comfortable for you. Some students learn best when speaking and writing, while others enjoy moving around or creating something artistic.

Tips for Responding to and Interpreting Literature

- **Discuss** what you have read, and share your views in active classroom discussions or at home.
- **Keep a journal** about what you read. Record your thoughts and feelings as well as questions you might have about a selection.
- **Take part in dramatizations, oral interpretations,** and **readers theater.** These activities can allow you to present characters through actions and dialogue and allow you to use your voice, facial expressions, and body language to convey meaning.
- **Tape record or videotape** your oral readings or dramatizations.

Supporting responses and interpretations

Whether you respond with your mind or with your emotions, you need to support your responses by going back to the text itself. Make sure you provide details from the author's work to back up your thoughts and feelings. It is not enough to say, "I really liked the main character." You must show what you liked about him or her. Look for specific descriptions and information. Ask yourself questions like these:

- What is interesting about this story's setting?
- What do I like or dislike about this character?
- How is the overall theme or idea expressed?
- What specific details account for my views about this selection?
- How have my own experiences and prior knowledge influenced my feelings in this selection?

Identifying the purpose of a text

Authors have a variety of reasons for writing. They may simply want to **entertain** you. They may want to **inform** you about a topic. They may feel the need to **express** thoughts and emotions through a narrative or biographical essay. They also may want to **influence** your thinking and **persuade** you to believe something or act in a certain way. How can you tell what a writer's purpose is? To identify the purposes of different types of texts, use the following tips:

Tips for identifying the purpose of a text

- **Look at word choices.** Authors select words according to their connotations, which carry emotional or implied meanings, as well as their denotations, or dictionary meanings.
- **Consider the intended audience.** Most selections are written with an audience in mind. A speech at a pep rally might have a different purpose than one given before student council members.
- **Look at the structure of the text.** By figuring out if a writer has used chronological order, comparison-and-contrast structure, or perhaps cause-and-effect structure, you can help determine his or her purpose.

Comparing elements across genres

Have you ever seen a movie or a television program that was based on a book you read? How were they similar? How were they different? Sometimes scenes are left out of the movie in order to make the story fit into a particular time frame. Some characters in movies are not represented precisely as they are described in books. As you look to see how the same story may vary across cultures or genres, look at similarities and differences in the following story elements:

- Characters Are all characters represented? Are some characters combined?
- Settings Is the setting presented similarly in each work? What differences affect the story as a whole?
- Plot How is the plot adjusted to fit the strengths and limitations of the genre?
- Themes or ideas Are important ideas well developed?
- Author's point of view Does the author's attitude affect how the story is told?
- Author's purpose Why is the author telling this story?
- Author's style What format and word choices are used?

Analyzing inductive and deductive reasoning

As you think about works you've read, ask yourself whether the reasoning behind an author's ideas is logical. Here are two kinds of logical reasoning writers use.

Inductive reasoning When you consider a certain number of examples a writer gives you, or if you can see a particular number of cases to illustrate a point or an idea, you may be able to arrive at a **generalization**–a conclusion or general statement–by using **inductive reasoning.** For example, if the tulips your class planted on the north side of your school building did not grow, there is never any grass on that side of the building, and a tree planted there last year still has no leaves, you can inductively reason that the north side of buildings may not be the best place to plant things. This logic moves from the specific to the general.

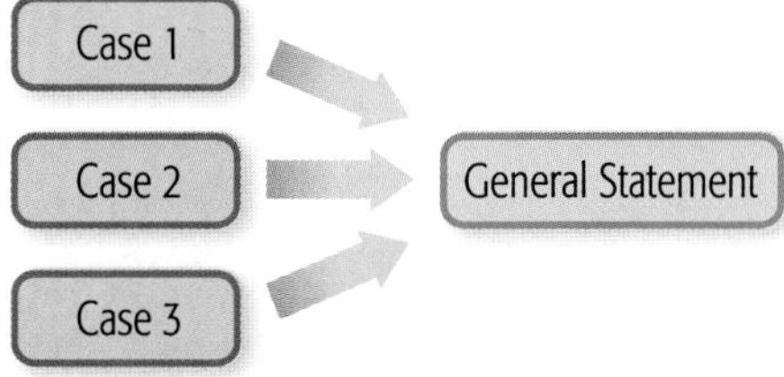

Deductive reasoning When you take a general statement and apply it through reasoning to a number of specific situations, you are using **deductive reasoning.** For example, you know that plants do not grow well in shady areas. Therefore, you can deductively reason that it might not be wise to plant tulips or expect grass or trees to grow on the shady side of the building. This logic moves from the general to the specific.

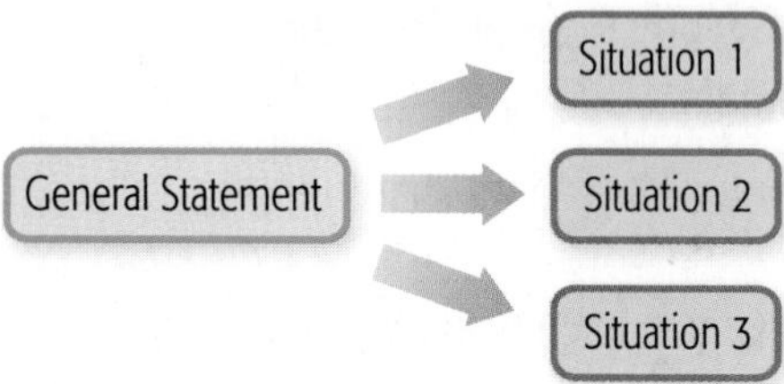

Inquiry and Research

Asking and answering questions is at the heart of being an active reader. As you read in a variety of sources, you will think of new questions or revise the ones you started with to take into account new information. When you ask important questions and carefully research thorough answers, you will draw conclusions about your topic, and in the best situations, the process will lead you to other interesting questions and areas for further study.

Forming and revising questions

Finding an interesting and relevant question or topic is a very important first step in doing research and deserves your careful attention.

Tips for Asking Research Questions

- Think of a question or topic that interests you.
- Choose a question that helps you focus your investigation on one main idea.
- Be sure the question is not too broad or too narrow.
  Too broad: *How can people preserve the environment?*
  Better: *What changes in waste management law have been made in my state within the last five years?*

Using text organizers

Once you've found an interesting question to investigate, the next step is to locate and then organize information you find. Textbooks, references, magazines, and other sources use a variety of ways to help you find what you need quickly and efficiently.

- **Tables of contents** Look at a table of contents first to see whether a resource offers information you need.

- Indexes An index is an alphabetical listing of significant topics covered in a book. It is in the back of a book.
- Headings and subheadings Headings often identify the information that follows.
- Graphic features Photos, diagrams, maps, charts, graphs, and other graphic features can convey a large amount of information at a glance.

Using multiple sources for research

Any research you do will be more interesting and balanced when you include different types of sources. Each source will provide a different slant to your topic. To find the most recent information, it may be necessary to use sources other than books. The following are some helpful resources for conducting research:

- Print resources: textbooks, magazines, reference books, and other specialized references
- Nonprint information: films, videos, and recorded interviews
- Electronic texts: CD-ROM encyclopedias and the Internet
- Experts: people who are specialists on the topic you've chosen

Interpreting graphic aids

When you're researching a topic, be sure to read and interpret the graphic aids included. **Graphic aids** let you see information at a glance.

Reading a map Maps are flat representations of land. A **compass rose** allows you to determine direction. A **legend** explains the map's symbols, and a **scale** shows you how the size of the map relates to the actual distances covered. Look at the map below.

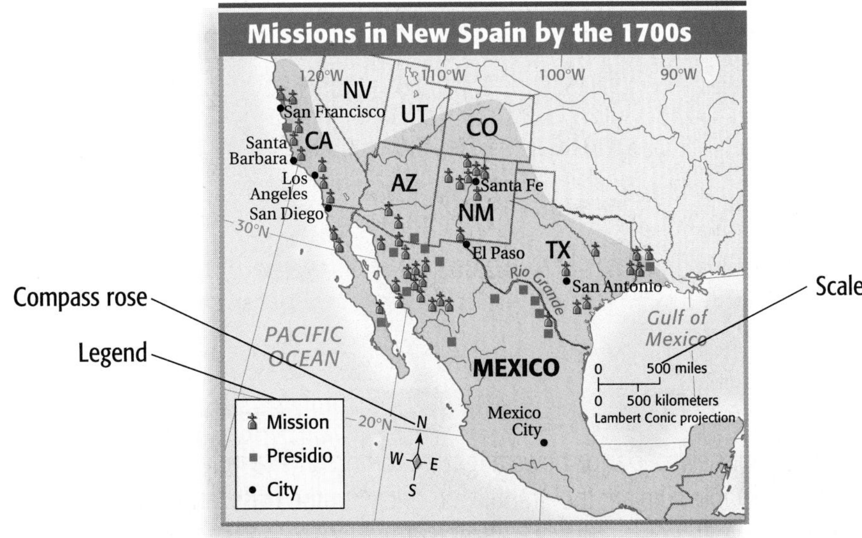

Reading a graph You can see how two or more things relate in a graph. Graphs can use circles, dots, bars, or lines. Look at the title and the labels on the bar graph below. Can you interpret the information?

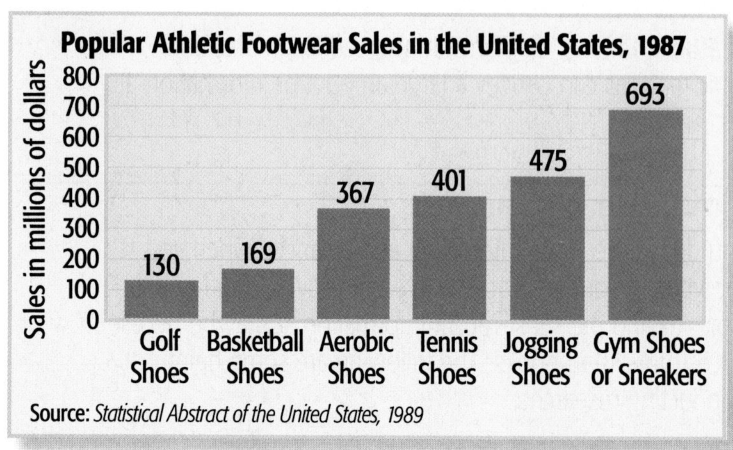

Source: *Statistical Abstract of the United States, 1989*

Reading a table A table allows you to group numbers or facts together and put them into categories so you can compare what is in each category. Look at the table below. Read the title first. You are looking at populations of the largest U.S. cities. Now read the labels at the top of each column. The information in the first two columns shows you the cities compared and their current size ranking. You can read across rows to find information about one city, or you can compare the five largest cities with one another in any given year. What other information can you gather from this table?

Population of Largest U.S. Cities

Rank	City	1950	1960	1970	1980	1990
1	New York City	7,891,984	7,781,984	7,895,563	7,071,639	7,322,564
2	Los Angeles	1,970,358	2,479,015	2,811,801	2,966,850	3,485,398
3	Chicago	3,620,962	3,550,404	3,369,357	3,005,072	2,783,726
4	Houston	596,163	938,219	1,233,535	1,595,138	1,630,553
5	Philadelphia	2,071,605	2,002,512	1,949,996	1,688,210	1,585,577

Source: *U.S. Bureau of the Census*

TRY THE STRATEGIES

Look in a current newspaper or newsmagazine to find an example of a chart, graph, or table. Explain the graphic aid briefly to the class, and analyze the information presented.

Organizing information

Now that you've read about your research topic in a variety of sources, how will you put it all together? Here are some suggestions:

- **Record** information on note cards. Use a new card for each main idea or important piece of information.
- **Summarize** information before you write it on a card. That way you'll have the main ideas in your own words.
- **Outline ideas** by putting your note cards in order and creating a written outline so you can see how subtopics and supporting information will fit under the main ideas.
- **Make a table or graph** to compare items or categories of information.

Tips for Charting Information

- Decide what information you want your audience to see at a glance.
- Decide what kind of table or graph will best show the information.
- Choose a title for your graphic aid. and label the categories horizontally and vertically.
- Check the accuracy of your information; plot it out carefully.
- Use different colors, if possible, to distinguish between items.

Producing projects and reports

How should you present the information you've gathered? Before you decide, think about these questions:

- How can I briefly and clearly convey important information? What would best capture the attention of my audience?
- What graphic aids can I use to illustrate my main ideas?
- What pattern of organization would suit this information? chronological order? comparison and contrast? cause and effect?
- Would an illustration or a cartoon help to make a certain point?

When considering a format to use for your report, you might consider a **written** or an **oral report,** a **debate,** an **interview,** or a **dramatic** or **video presentation.**

Drawing conclusions and asking further questions

You will certainly form opinions about your topic after you've finished your research. A **conclusion** is a general statement that you'll make about what you have learned. Remember that you started your research with an important question, so your answer to that question may help to form your conclusion. In the best situations, a conclusion will lead you to other interesting questions and areas for further reading.

Read the following excerpts and the conclusion that follows. Then look at the question for further research.

> *Project Mercury*, initiated in 1958 and completed in 1963, was the United States' first human-in-space program. It was designed to further knowledge about humanity's capabilities in space. . . . The *Gemini* spacecraft, twice as large as the *Mercury* capsule, accommodated two astronauts. *Apollo* was the designation for the United States' effort to land a person on the Moon and return that person safely to Earth. The goal was successfully accomplished with *Apollo 11* on July 20, 1969, culminating eight years of rehearsal and centuries of dreaming. . . . *Project Skylab* was designed to demonstrate that humans can work and live in space for prolonged periods without ill effects.

> In a historic moment, Mission Commander Robert Cabana and Russian Cosmonaut/Mission Specialist Sergei Krikalev swung open the hatch between the Endeavour and the First Element of the International Space Station at 1:15 CST, Thursday, December 10, 1998. . . . International Space Station flight controllers at Mission Control, Houston and at the Russian Mission Control Center in Korolev, outside Moscow, will spend the next five months monitoring the station's systems. . . . The International Space Station continues the largest scientific cooperative program in history, drawing on the resources and scientific expertise of 16 nations.

Conclusion: Space exploration has become more advanced in the past thirty years, involving the scientific cooperation of a number of countries around the world.

Question for further research: What advances in space exploration does NASA hope to accomplish in the next thirty years?

Tips for Drawing Conclusions

- Don't try to twist the facts to support your ideas.
- Don't make statements that go beyond the facts you've gathered.
- Recognize that your conclusions might be different than you originally thought.
- Be sure to record accurately where you got your information.
- Never present ideas that aren't yours as your own.

Glossary

This glossary lists the vocabulary words found in the selections in this book. The definition given is for the word as it is used in the selection; you may wish to consult a dictionary for other meanings of these words. The key below is a guide to the pronunciation symbols used in each entry.

a	at	**ō**	hope	**ng**	sing
ā	ape	**ô**	fork, all	**th**	thin
ä	father	**oo**	wood, put	**<u>th</u>**	this
e	end	**o͞o**	fool	**zh**	treasure
ē	me	**oi**	oil	**ə**	ago, taken, pencil, lemon, circus
i	it	**ou**	out	**′**	indicates primary stress
ī	ice	**u**	up	**′**	indicates secondary stress
o	hot	**ū**	use		

A

abyss (ə bis′) *n.* an extremely deep hole; p. 411

acute (ə kūt′) *adj.* sharp and strong or intense; p. 835

adept (ə dept′) *adj.* highly skilled; masterful; p. 243

adolescence (ad′ əl es′ əns) *n.* the period or process of growing from youth to adulthood; teenage years; p. 624

advocate (ad′ və kit) *n.* one who publicly supports or urges; p. 272

aggravating (ag′ rə vāt ing) *adj.* irritating; annoying; p. 718

aggression (ə gresh′ ən) *n.* the habit or practice of launching attacks; p. 21

aghast (ə gast′) *adj.* filled with fear or horror; p. 276

agonize (ag′ ə nīz′) *v.* to suffer greatly; struggle painfully; p. 625

alight (ə līt′) *v.* to come down after flight; land; p. 413

aloof (ə lo͞of′) *adj.* emotionally distant; uninvolved; standoffish; p. 823

alternative (ôl tur′ nə tiv) *n.* another choice; p. 106

amiable (ā′ mē ə bəl) *adj.* friendly, good-natured; p. 801

anguish (ang′ gwish) *n.* extreme suffering; p. 594

angular (ang′ gyə lər) *adj.* bony and lean; p. 51

anomalous (ə nom′ ə ləs) *adj.* not following the usual or regular; abnormal; p. 192

anonymous (ə non′ ə məs) *adj.* having no known name or origin; lacking qualities that make one different; p. 40

appalled (ə pôld′) *adj.* shocked; horrified; p. 148

apparition (ap′ ə rish′ ən) *n.* ghostly vision; p. 817

apprehension (ap′ ri hen′ shən) *n.* fear of what may happen; dread; p. 749

aromatic (ar′ ə mat′ ik) *adj.* having a pleasant smell or special, delicate flavor; p. 242

arresting (ə res′ ting) *adj.* demanding the attention; striking; p. 871

arrogant (ar′ ə gənt) *adj.* full of self-importance; too proud; p. 147

askew (ə skū′) *adv.* in a twisted way; crookedly; p. 439

audacity (ô das′ ə tē) *n.* reckless boldness; daring; p. 840

awed (ôd) *adj.* filled with wonder combined with respect; p. 84

B

ban (ban) *v.* to forbid; outlaw; prohibit; p. 677

banish (ban′ ish) *v.* to force a person to leave a country or community; p. 259

baptism (bap′ tiz′ əm) *n.* a ceremony in which a person is cleansed of sin and becomes a member of a Christian religion; p. 71

barren (bar′ ən) *adj.* bare; empty; dull or uninteresting; p. 164

barter (bär′ tər) *v.* to trade goods for goods; p. 274

bedraggled (bi drag′ əld) *adj.* wet, dirty, and rumpled; untidy; p. 666

benediction (ben′ ə dik′ shən) *n.* a divine blessing or the condition of being blessed; p. 440

benevolence (bə nev′ ə ləns) *n.* kindliness; generosity; p. 271

bewilderment (bi wil′ dər mənt) *n.* deep confusion; p. 262

bland (bland) *adj.* dull and uninteresting; p. 808

bleak (blēk) *adj.* cheerless; depressing; p. 488

blithely (blīth′ lē) *adv.* in a lighthearted way; cheerfully; p. 20

bravado (brə vä′ dō) *n.* a false show of bravery; pretended courage; p. 152

brazenly (brā′ zən lē) *adv.* in a boldly rude manner; p. 21

C

cajole (kə jōl′) *v.* to persuade, especially by soothing words; coax; p. 486

capitulate (kə pich′ ə lāt′) *v.* to stop resisting; surrender; p. 666

careening (kä rēn′ ing) *adj.* tilting or swaying while moving, as if out of control; p. 861

catastrophic (kat′ əs trof′ ik) *adj.* disastrous; p. 104

chasm (kaz′ əm) *n.* a deep hole or crack, as in the earth's surface; p. 807

chronic (kron′ ik) *adj.* lasting a long time or returning repeatedly; p. 284

collective (kə lek′ tiv) *adj.* having to do with a group of persons or things; common; shared; p. 205

commence (kə mens′) *v.* to begin; start; p. 9

commend (kə mend′) *v.* to express approval of; p. 262

communion (kə mūn′ yən) *n.* closeness to, and sympathy with, another through sharing feelings or thoughts; p. 52

compelling (kəm pel′ ing) *adj.* impressive and forceful; p. 630

competently (kom′ pət ənt lē) *adv.* capably; p. 202

complex (kom′ pleks) *n.* an exaggerated concern or fear; an overwhelming idea or feeling; p. 284

comply (kəm plī′) *v.* to obey or go along with a request; p. 343

comprehend (kom′ pri hend′) *v.* to grasp mentally; understand fully; p. 596

conceive (kən sēv′) *v.* to form; imagine; p. 473

concoct (kon kokt′) *v.* to make or put together, using skill and intelligence; p. 53

conscientious (kon′ shē en′ shəs) *adj.* guided by one's conscience; showing careful attention to what is right and wrong; p. 818

consecrate (kon′ sə krāt′) *v.* to make, declare, or honor as holy; p. 474

console (kən sōl′) *v.* to comfort or cheer someone who is sad or disappointed; p. 863

conspicuous (kən spik′ ū əs) *adj.* easily seen; apparent; p. 701

conspiratorial (kən spir′ ə tôr′ ē əl) *adj.* joining or acting together, especially to carry out some secret or evil deed or for a hidden or illegal purpose; p. 287

constitute (kon′ stə to͞ot′) *v.* to form; make up; compose; p. 625

convey (kən vā′) *v.* to express; communicate; p. 30

corroded (kə rōd′ əd) *adj.* eaten away by degrees, by gnawing or chemical action; p. 245

covet (kuv′ it) *v.* to desire strongly; wish for longingly; p. 513

cower (kou′ ər) *v.* to shrink away as in fear or shame; p. 131

craggy (krag′ ē) *adj.* rugged, uneven, and worn; p. 285

crevice (krev′ is) *n.* a narrow crack; p. 574

cringe (krinj) *v.* to draw back, as from fear or dislike; p. 217

crouch (krouch) *v.* to stoop or bend, especially with knees bent; p. 558

crux (kruks) *n.* the most important point or part; p. 41

curt (kurt) *adj.* so brief or short as to seem rude; p. 242

D

decree (di krē′) *v.* to set forth an official rule, order, or decision; dictate; p. 259

decry (di krī′) *v.* to criticize openly; p. 343

default (di fôlt′) *v.* to fail to do as required; p. 495

dejected (di jek′ tid) *adj.* sad; depressed; in low spirits; p. 793

demean (di mēn′) *v.* to degrade; disgrace; p. 664

desolate (des′ ə lit) *adj.* without comfort; p. 495

detract (di trakt′) *v.* to take something away; lessen; p. 474

diligence (dil′ ə jəns) *n.* great attention, care, and effort; p. 513

discern (di surn′) *v.* to detect or recognize; identify; p. 21

disclose (dis klōz′) *v.* to make known; reveal; p. 486

discord (dis′ kôrd) *n.* disagreement; conflict; p. 498

discrimination (dis krim′ ə nā′ shən) *n.* unfair treatment, especially as a result of policies directed against minority groups; p. 495

disembark (dis′ im bärk′) *v.* to get off of a train, airplane, ship, or other vehicle; p. 644

disgruntled (dis grunt′ əld) *adj.* displeased; p. 744

disheveled (di shev′ əld) *adj.* untidy or rumpled; p. 483

disperse (dis purs′) *v.* to go off in different directions; p. 592

distinct (dis tingkt′) *adj.* clearly heard, seen, or felt; p. 174

diverse (di vurs′) *adj.* noticeably different; varied; p. 630

diversion (di vur′ zhən) *n.* something that draws the attention away; distraction; p. 148

docile (dos′ əl) *adj.* easily managed, trained, or taught; p. 103

doggedly (dô′ gid lē) *adv.* stubbornly; firmly; p. 514

dominant (dom′ ə nənt) *adj.* having the greatest power or force; controlling; p. 817

dote (dōt) *v.* to show extreme affection; p. 341

drone (drōn) *v.* to talk in a dull, monotonous tone or make a steady, low, humming sound; p. 170

dry (drī) *adj.* not interesting; dull; boring; p. 608

dumbfounded (dum′ found′ əd) *adj.* made speechless with amazement; astonished; p. 400

E

eerie (ēr′ ē) *adj.* weird, especially in a frightening way; p. 10

elaborate (i lab′ ər it) *adj.* complicated and fancy; p. 240

eloquence (el′ ə kwəns) *n.* speech or writing that is expressive, effective, and stirring; p. 485

embodiment (em bod′ ē mənt) *n.* the bodily form of an idea or quality; visible form; p. 664

emit (i mit′) *v.* to utter; send forth, or give out, as a sound; p. 341

emphatically (em fat′ i kəl ē) *adv.* very definitely; clearly; p. 643

emulate (em′ yə lāt′) *v.* to imitate; p. 28

encounter (en koun′ tər) *v.* to meet unexpectedly or casually; p. 215

enfeebled (en fē′ bəld) *adj.* lacking force, strength, or effectiveness; weakened; p. 40

engulf (en gulf′) *v.* to swallow up; overwhelm; p. 219

enhance (en hans′) *v.* to make greater; p. 676

enmity (en′ mə tē) *n.* the bitter hatred between enemies; ill will; p. 412

exalt (ig zôlt′) *v.* to raise in status, dignity, power; glorify; p. 498

extinguish (iks ting′ gwish) *v.* to put out; end; destroy; p. 624

F

forage (fôr′ ij) *v.* to hunt or search about for food or needed supplies; p. 364

ford (fôrd) *n.* a shallow place where a river or stream may be crossed on foot; p. 384

foreboding (fôr bō′ ding) *n.* a feeling that something evil is going to happen; p. 748

forfeit (fôr′ fit) *v.* to lose as a penalty for some error or failure; p. 871

founder (foun′ dər) *v.* to break down, collapse, or fail; p. 611

frail (frāl) *adj.* lacking in strength; weak; p. 162

frenzy (fren′ zē) *n.* a state of great excitement or deep disturbance; p. 762

frustration (frus trā′ shən) *n.* disappointment or irritation at being kept from doing or achieving something; p. 107

furtive (fur′ tiv) *adj.* secret; shifty; sly; p. 152

futility (fū til′ ə tē) *n.* uselessness; hopelessness; p. 155

G

gaudily (gô′ də lē) *adv.* in a way that is bright and showy to the point of being in bad taste; p. 241

gloat (glōt) *v.* to feel or express pleasure or satisfaction in one's own success or achievement, especially in a triumphant or slightly nasty way; p. 63

gravely (grāv′ lē) *adv.* very seriously; p. 275

grimace (grim′ əs) *n.* a twisting of the face, as in pain or displeasure; p. 664

H

haggle (hag′ əl) *v.* to bargain, especially about price or the terms of an agreement; p. 373

haughtily (hô′ tə lē) *adv.* in a way that shows too much pride in oneself and great scorn for others; p. 259

heft (heft) *v.* to lift up; p. 245

humility (hū mil′ ə tē) *n.* the quality of being humble or modest; p. 32

hypocritical (hip′ ə krit′ i kəl) *adj.* pretending to be what one is not; fake; insincere; p. 841

hysteria (his ter′ ē ə) *n.* great, uncontrollable terror, panic, or other strong emotion; p. 54

I

illiteracy (i lit′ ər ə sē) *n.* the inability to read or write; p. 205

immortality (im′ ôr tal′ ə tē) *n.* the state of living or lasting forever; p. 440

impaired (im pārd′) *adj.* lessened in quality; damaged; p. 135

impel (im pel′) *v.* to drive to action; cause; p. 190

impending (im pen′ ding) *adj.* about to occur; p. 806

impromptu (im promp′ to͞o) *adj.* made or done on the spur of the moment, without preparation; p. 6

impudent (im′ pyə dənt) *adj.* boldly discourteous; p. 346

impulse (im′ puls) *n.* an internal force that causes one to act without thinking about it; p. 215

incentive (in sen′ tiv) *n.* that which urges to action, especially a promised reward for working harder; p. 483

incompatible (in′ kəm pat′ ə bəl) *adj.* not capable of existing or working together in harmony; conflicting; p. 644

incomprehensible (in′ kom prē hen′ sə bəl) *adj.* not understandable; p. 483
incur (in kur′) *v.* to acquire (something undesirable); bring upon oneself; p. 31
indifference (in dif′ ər əns) *n.* a lack of feeling, concern, or care; p. 20
indignantly (in dig′ nənt lē) *adv.* with dignified anger in response to an insult or injustice; p. 718
inert (i nurt′) *adj.* without power to move or act; lifeless; p. 613
inevitably (i nev′ ə tə blē) *adv.* in a way that cannot be avoided or prevented; p. 667
inextricably (in eks′ tri kə blē) *adv.* in a way that cannot be separated; p. 496
infinite (in′ fə nit) *adj.* boundless; limitless; extremely great; p. 105
inflict (in flikt′) *v.* to force (something unwelcome) on someone; p. 33
inhibition (in′ hə bish′ ən) *n.* a restraint on one's urges; p. 105
insight (in′ sīt) *n.* an understanding of the inner character or hidden nature of something; p. 598
insolence (in′ sə ləns) *n.* deliberate rudeness; disrespect; p. 578
instinctive (in stingk′ tiv) *adj.* rising from an impulse or natural tendency; not learned; p. 189
integrity (in teg′ rə tē) *n.* moral uprightness; honesty; p. 187
intellectual (int′ əl ek′ cho͞o əl) *adj.* appealing to or involving intelligence or mental ability; p. 130
intently (in tent′ lē) *adv.* in a firmly focused way; with concentration; p. 8
intercession (in′ tər sesh′ ən) *n.* a request, appeal, or prayer in the interest of another or others; p. 400
interim (in′ tər im) *n.* the time between events; meantime; p. 804
interminable (in tur′ mi nə bəl) *adj.* lasting, or seeming to last, forever; endless; p. 518
intimate (in′ tə mit) *adj.* closely associated; p. 189
intolerant (in tol′ ər ənt) *adj.* unwilling to put up with; not accepting; p. 205
intricate (in′ tri kit) *adj.* full of complicated detail; p. 31
intuition (in′ to͞o ish′ ən) *n.* an ability to know things without having to reason them out; p. 755
invariably (in vār′ ē ə blē) *adv.* constantly; always; p. 131
invigorating (in vig′ ə rāt ing) *adj.* energizing; refreshing; p. 666
involuntary (in vol′ ən ter′ ē) *adj.* not done willingly; p. 8

J

joviality (jō′ vē al′ ə tē) *n.* hearty, good-natured humor; p. 21
jubilation (jo͞o′ bə lā′ shən) *n.* great joy and excitement; p. 736
jut (jut) *v.* to extend outward or upward from a surface; bulge; p. 415

L

laboriously (lə bôr′ ē əs lē) *adv.* with great effort; p. 171
laden (lād′ən) *adj.* loaded; weighed down; burdened; p. 173
lapse (laps) *v.* to slip, drift, or fall (into); p. 286
legacy (leg′ ə sē) *n.* anything handed down from an ancestor or from the past; p. 40
legitimately (li jit′ ə mit lē) *adv.* in a way that follows the rules; legally; p. 441
liable (lī′ ə bəl) *adj.* likely; apt; p. 555
loathe (lō<u>th</u>) *v.* to regard with extreme disgust; hate; p. 709
loom (lo͞om) *v.* to appear or come into view in a way that seems very large and, often, threatening; p. 271
lucid (lo͞o′ sid) *adj.* mentally alert; clear-headed; p. 286
lunacy (lo͞o′ nə sē) *n.* insanity; senseless conduct; folly; p. 514

lurch (lurch) *v.* to move suddenly in a jerky and uneven manner; p. 67

lurk (lurk) *v.* to lie hidden or move about in a sneaky way; p. 631

M

maladjustment (mal′ ə just′ mənt) *n.* poor adjustment to conditions or requirements; p. 220

malice (mal′ is) *n.* a desire to harm another; ill will; p. 104

manifest (man′ ə fest′) *adj.* obvious; clear; plain; evident; p. 644

meager (mē′ gər) *adj.* not enough in amount or quantity; insufficient; p. 64

melancholy (mel′ ən kol′ ē) *adj.* sadly thoughtful; p. 676

meticulous (mi tik′ yə ləs) *adj.* showing great concern about details; p. 55

minimal (min′ ə məl) *adj.* smallest or least possible; very small; p. 529

modest (mod′ ist) *adj.* tending to avoid praise or credit; humble; bashful; p. 532

mutely (mūt′ lē) *adv.* without speaking; silently; p. 443

N

naive (nä ēv′) *adj.* innocent to the ways of the world; p. 32

naturalist (nach′ ər ə list) *n.* one who studies living things, especially plants or animals, by observing them directly; p. 871

O

obliged (ə blījd′) *adj.* forced, bound, or required; p. 361

obligingly (ə blī′ jing lē) *adv.* helpfully; agreeably; p. 220

obscure (əb skyoor′) *v.* to hide; p. 134

obviously (ob′ vē əs lē) *adv.* in a way that is easily seen or understood; clearly; p. 560

ominous (om′ ə nəs) *adj.* threatening harm or evil; p. 11

onslaught (ôn′ slôt′) *n.* a forceful or destructive attack; assault; p. 747

opportunist (op′ ər to͞o′ nist) *n.* one who takes advantage of every opportunity, regardless of consequences; p. 127

P

pact (pakt) *n.* an agreement; deal; pledge; p. 413

painstakingly (pānz′ tā′ king lē) *adv.* in a way requiring close, careful labor or attention; p. 30

palatable (pal′ ə tə bəl) *adj.* agreeable to the taste, mind, or feelings; acceptable; p. 345

pandemonium (pan′ də mō′ nē əm) *n.* wild disorder and uproar; p. 765

paramount (par′ ə mount′) *adj.* above all others in influence or importance; supreme; p. 630

pathetically (pə thet′ i kəl ē) *adv.* pitifully; p. 861

patriarch (pā′ trē ärk′) *n.* the male head of a family; p. 173

pauper (pô′ pər) *n.* a very poor person, especially one supported by public charity; p. 638

pensive (pen′ siv) *adj.* thinking deeply, often about something sad; p. 822

perceive (pər sēv′) *v.* to take in or grasp mentally; notice; p. 820

peremptory (pə remp′ tər ē) *adj.* allowing no refusal; p. 342

perennial (pə ren′ ē əl) *adj.* lasting for a long time; p. 595

persistently (pər sis′ tənt lē) *adv.* repeatedly; p. 200

perturb (pər turb′) *v.* to disturb greatly; p. 680

petite (pə tēt′) *adj.* small and slender; little; p. 859

pious (pī′ əs) *adj.* having either genuine or pretended religious devotion; p. 583

pitch (pich) *n.* an often high-pressure sales presentation; p. 242

pivotal (piv′ ət əl) *adj.* of central importance; p. 857

placid (plas′ id) *adj.* calm or peaceful; p. 106
plight (plīt) *n.* an unfortunate or dangerous situation; p. 274
plummet (plum′ it) *v.* to fall downward; p. 858
poise (poiz) *n.* relaxed and self-controlled dignity in manner; p. 760
ponder (pon′ dər) *v.* to think over carefully; p. 680
potential (pə ten′ shəl) *n.* possibility of success; p. 241
prejudice (prej′ ə dis) *n.* an opinion formed without considering all sides of a question; p. 679
prestigious (pre sti′ jəs) *adj.* having widely recognized importance and influence; impressive; p. 625
presumably (pri zo͞o′ mə blē) *adv.* supposedly; probably; p. 805
pretense (prē′ tens) *n.* a false show or appearance, especially for the purpose of deceiving; falseness; p. 289
priceless (prīs′ lis) *adj.* of greater value than can be measured; p. 373
primly (prim′ lē) *adv.* in a formal, proper way; p. 170
prodigious (prə dij′ əs) *adj.* enormous; p. 498
prodigy (prod′ ə jē) *n.* an extraordinarily gifted or talented person, especially a child; p. 555
prominent (prom′ ə nənt) *adj.* widely known; p. 338
proposition (prop′ ə zish′ ən) *n.* a suggestion or plan; proposal; p. 473
prowess (prou′ is) *n.* great ability or skill; p. 269
proximity (prok sim′ ə tē) *n.* closeness in space, time, order, or degree; nearness; p. 644
purged (purjd) *adj.* cleansed of whatever is unclean; p. 591

Q

quaint (kwānt) *adj.* charming in an old-fashioned way; pleasingly unusual or odd; p. 638
quest (kwest) *n.* a search made to achieve a goal; p. 151

R

recoil (ri koil′) *v.* to draw back, as in fear; p. 859
redeemed (ri dēmd′) *adj.* gotten or won back; recovered; p. 625
refined (ri fīnd′) *adj.* free from coarseness or crudeness; showing good taste and manners; p. 201
refrain (ri frān′) *v.* to hold oneself back; restrain oneself; p. 384
regally (rē′ gəl lē) *adv.* in a grand, dignified manner, as if done by a king or queen; royally; p. 287
remorse (ri môrs′) *n.* a deep, painful feeling of guilt or sorrow for wrongdoing; p. 153
renegade (ren′ ə gād′) *n.* one who abandons or turns against a group, cause, or allegiance; traitor; p. 344
renovate (ren′ ə vāt′) *v.* to make like new; p. 173
renown (ri noun′) *n.* widespread reputation; fame; p. 821
repress (ri pres′) *v.* to hold back or keep under control; restrain; p. 514
reproach (ri prōch′) *v.* to scold or blame; p. 401
reputation (rep′ yə tā′ shən) *n.* what people generally think about the character of a person or thing; good name; p. 555
resolutely (rez′ ə lo͞ot′ lē) *adv.* determinedly; p. 219
resolve (ri zolv′) *n.* steady determination; firmness of purpose; p. 631
revel (rev′ əl) *v.* to take great pleasure; p. 644
revert (ri vurt′) *v.* to return to an earlier condition, behavior, or belief; p. 667
revive (ri vīv′) *v.* to come back to consciousness; show new life, strength, or freshness; p. 373
righteousness (rī′ chəs nəs) *n.* the condition of being right, moral, just, or legal; p. 519

S

sacred (sā′ krid) *adj.* holy; deserving of great respect; p. 85
sagely (sāj′ lē) *adv.* very wisely; p. 276

savor (sā′ vər) *v.* to take great delight in; p. 191
scavenger (skav′ in jər) *n.* an animal, such as a hyena or vulture, that feeds on dead, decaying plants or animals; p. 272
scour (skour) *v.* to rub energetically in order to clean, wash, or brighten; p. 597
scowling (skou′ ling) *n.* a facial expression of anger or disapproval; angry frown; p. 384
serene (sə rēn′) *adj.* calm; peaceful; undisturbed; p. 290
serenity (sə ren′ ə tē) *n.* calmness; peacefulness; p. 485
servile (sur′ vil) *adj.* like a servant; too humble; p. 218
sheathe (shē<u>th</u>) *v.* to enclose in a case or covering; p. 54
sheepishly (shē′ pish lē) *adv.* in an awkwardly embarrassed way; bashfully; p. 81
sheer (shēr) *adj.* very steep; straight up or down; p. 410
simultaneously (sī′ məl tā′ nē əs lē) *adv.* at the same time; p. 20
singularly (sing′ gyə lər lē) *adv.* unusually or remarkably; extraordinarily; p. 841
skirmish (skur′ mish) *n.* a brief or minor conflict; p. 583
slither (sli<u>th</u>′ ər) *v.* to move along with a sliding or gliding motion, as a snake; p. 52
slung (slung) *adj.* hung or thrown loosely; p. 161
smug (smug) *adj.* overly pleased with oneself; too self-satisfied; p. 20
sober (sō′ bər) *v.* to make or become serious and quiet; p. 871
solemn (sol′ əm) *adj.* serious; p. 439
sophisticated (sə fis′ tə kā′ tid) *adj.* having or showing knowledge or experience of the world; p. 65
specific (spi sif′ ik) *adj.* entirely clear and definite; p. 603
speculation (spek′ yə lā′ shən) *n.* an opinion or conclusion based on guesswork; p. 819
stately (stāt′ lē) *adv.* noble; dignified; majestic; p. 79
steadfastly (sted′ fast′ lē) *adv.* faithfully; steadily; p. 593
stealthily (stel′ thə lē) *adv.* in a secret or sneaky manner; p. 762
stifled (stī′ fəld) *adj.* held back; smothered; p. 837
stimulus (stim′ yə ləs) *n.* something that causes a response; p. 135
strenuous (stren′ ū əs) *adj.* very active; energetic; p. 800
subdued (səb do͞od′) *adj.* quiet and downcast; p. 725
subsequently (sub′ sə kwənt lē) *adv.* at a later time; p. 21
substance (sub′ stəns) *n.* basic material; solid quality; p. 862
subterfuge (sub′ tər fūj′) *n.* a trick or other method used to escape or conceal something; deception; p. 188
subtle (sut′ əl) *adj.* not open or direct; not obvious; p. 243
suffused (sə fūzd′) *adj.* spread through or over, as with light, color, emotion, or quality; p. 186
sullen (sul′ ən) *adj.* stubbornly withdrawn or gloomy because of bad humor; sulky; p. 485
summit (sum′ it) *n.* the highest point or part; peak; p. 415
summon (sum′ ən) *v.* to send for or request the presence of, especially with authority; p. 263
superficial (so͞o′ pər fish′ əl) *adj.* lacking deep meaning; shallow; unimportant or unnecessary; p. 677
syndrome (sin′ drōm′) *n.* a group of symptoms that, together, indicate a certain disease; p. 608

T

tamale (tə mä′ lē) *n.* cornmeal, meat, and red peppers in corn husks, cooked by steaming or roasting; p. 71
tangible (tan′ jə bəl) *adj.* able to be seen, touched, or felt; real; p. 129
taunt (tôt) *v.* to make fun of in a scornful, insulting way; p. 64
taut (tôt) *adj.* tense; tight; p. 199

tempest (tem′ pist) *n.* a violent windstorm, usually accompanied by rain, hail, snow, or thunder; p. 530

tentatively (ten′ tə tiv lē) *adv.* hesitantly; uncertainly; p. 6

tirade (tī rād′) *n.* a long angry or scolding speech; p. 67

tranquillity (trang kwil′ ə tē) *n.* the state or quality of being calm and free from disturbance; quietness; p. 681

transition (tran zish′ ən) *n.* passage from one position, condition, or activity to another; change; shift; p. 576

tremor (trem′ ər) *n.* a shaking or trembling movement; p. 8

tribulation (trib′ yə lā′ shən) *n.* great misery or distress; p. 496

U

unabashed (un′ ə basht′) *adj.* not ashamed or self-conscious; bold; p. 706

uncomprehendingly (un kom′ pri hend′ ing lē) *adv.* without understanding; p. 106

unnerving (un nurv′ ing) *adj.* causing nervousness or upset; disturbing; p. 147

unrestrained (un′ ri strānd′) *adj.* not held in check or under control; p. 216

unseemly (un sēm′ lē) *adj.* not proper to the time or place; not in good taste; p. 80

unsound (un sound′) *adj.* not accurate or sensible; p. 372

unwavering (un wā′ vər ing) *adj.* unchanging; not shifting or moving; steady; p. 592

V

vain (vān) *adj.* 1. unsuccessful; useless; p. 485 2. overly concerned with or proud of one's appearance, abilities, or accomplishments; conceited; p. 636

valiant (val′ yənt) *adj.* brave; courageous; p. 582

valid (val′ id) *adj.* well-supported by facts; true; p. 204

vehemently (vē′ ə mənt lē) *adv.* strongly; intensely; passionately; p. 841

vex (veks) *v.* to disturb, annoy, or anger, especially by some small, repeated action; p. 836

vibrant (vī′ brənt) *adj.* full of life and energy; p. 402

vile (vīl) *adj.* very bad; unpleasant; foul; p. 715

virtue (vur′ cho͞o) *n.* a good quality or admirable trait; p. 584

vividly (viv′ id lē) *adv.* clearly; intensely; p. 52

W

wallow (wol′ ō) *v.* to become or remain helpless; p. 497

wan (won) *adj.* pale or weak, indicating illness or weariness; p. 515

wane (wān) *v.* to draw to a close; approach an end; p. 839

wary (wār′ ē) *adj.* cautious; on the alert; p. 822

waver (wā′ vər) *v.* to become uncertain; falter; p. 681

wretchedness (rech′ id nəs) *n.* great unhappiness or deep distress; p. 521

Spanish Glossary

A

abyss/abismo *s.* hueco muy profundo; p. 411
acute/agudo *adj.* fuerte o intenso; p. 835
adept/versado *adj.* experto; muy capacitado; p. 243
adolescence/adolescencia *s.* período o proceso de crecimiento de la juventud a la edad adulta; pubertad; p. 624
advocate/defensor *s.* el que apoya públicamente una causa; p. 272
aggravating/exasperante *adj.* irritante; molesto; p. 718
aggression/agresión *s.* acción de atacar; p. 21
aghast/espantado *adj.* lleno de miedo o terror; p. 276
agonize/agonizar *v.* sufrir mucho; pensar en algo con gran dolor o preocupación; p. 625
alight/aterrizar *v.* tocar tierra después de un vuelo; p. 413
aloof/retraído *adj.* emocionalmente distante; reservado; p. 823
alternative/alternativa *s.* otra posibilidad; p. 106
amiable/amigable *adj.* amistoso; amable; cordial; p. 801
anguish/angustia *s.* gran sufrimiento; p. 594
angular/angular *adj.* huesudo y flaco; p. 51
anomalous/anómalo *adj.* que no es usual ni regular; anormal; p. 192
anonymous/anónimo *adj.* que no tiene nombre u origen; que carece de cualidades que lo distinguen; p. 40
appalled/pasmado *adj.* horrorizado; sobresaltado; impresionado; p. 148
apparition/aparición *s.* visión fantasmal; p. 817
apprehension/aprensión *s.* miedo de lo que pueda ocurrir; temor; p. 749
aromatic/aromático *adj.* que tiene un olor agradable o un sabor especial y delicado; p. 242
arresting/llamativo *adj.* que llama la atención; impresionante; p. 871
arrogant/arrogante *adj.* lleno de vanidad; presumido; p. 147
askew/oblicuamente *adv.* de modo torcido; p. 439
audacity/audacia *s.* osadía; atrevimiento; p. 840
awed/admirado *adj.* que siente asombro y respeto a la vez; p. 84

B

ban/censurar *v.* prohibir; desaprobar; p. 677
banish/desterrar *v.* obligar a una persona a abandonar su país o comunidad; deportar; p. 259
baptism/bautismo *s.* ceremonia en la que se limpia de pecado a una persona e ingresa a la religión cristiana; p. 71
barren/árido *adj.* vacío; tedioso o falto de interés; p. 164
barter/trocar *v.* intercambiar objetos; canjear; p. 274
bedraggled/mugriento *adj.* mojado, sucio y arrugado; desgreñado; p. 666
benediction/bendición *s.* gracia divina o acto de ser bendecido; p. 440
benevolence/benevolencia *s.* amabilidad; generosidad; p. 271
bewilderment/estupefacción *s.* gran confusión; p. 262
bland/insulso *adj.* soso; insípido; aburridor; p. 808
bleak/desolado *adj.* triste; deprimente; p. 488
blithely/despreocupadamente *adv.* de un modo tranquilo y alegre; p. 20
bravado/bravuconería *s.* falsa demostración de valentía; coraje fingido; p. 152

brazenly/descaradamente *adv.* de un modo atrevido y rudo; p. 21

C

cajole/persuadir *v.* convencer con promesas o palabras amables; halagar; p. 486

capitulate/capitular *v.* rendirse; dejar de resistirse; p. 666

careening/tambaleante *adj.* que se inclina o se ladea mientras se mueve, como si estuviera fuera de control; p. 861

catastrophic/catastrófico *adj.* desastroso; p. 104

chasm/grieta *s.* hueco o abertura profunda, como en la superficie terrestre; p. 807

chronic/crónico *adj.* que dura mucho tiempo o que se repite continuamente; p. 284

collective/colectivo *adj.* que tiene que ver con un grupo de personas o cosas; común; compartido; p. 205

commence/comenzar *v.* empezar; iniciar; p. 9

commend/ensalzar *v.* aprobar; alabar; p. 262

communion/comunión *s.* cercanía y entendimiento entre dos personas; p. 52

compelling/irresistible *adj.* importante; impresionante y convincente; p. 630

competently/competentemente *adv.* capazmente; hábilmente; p. 202

complex/complejo *s.* preocupación o miedo exagerado; idea o sentimiento obsesivo; perturbación; p. 284

comply/acatar *v.* obedecer o cumplir una solicitud; p. 343

comprehend/comprender *v.* captar mentalmente; entender por completo; p. 596

conceive/concebir *v.* formar; imaginar; p. 473

concoct/confeccionar *v.* hacer o fabricar con habilidad e ingenio; p. 53

conscientious/concienzudo *adj.* que actúa guiado por la conciencia; que se interesa por lo que es bueno y malo; p. 818

consecrate/consagrar *v.* declarar o tratar como sagrado; p. 474

console/consolar *v.* calmar o animar a alguien que está triste o desilusionado; p. 863

conspicuous/conspicuo *adj.* sobresaliente; aparente; p. 701

conspiratorial/de conspirador *adj.* que obra en conjunto, especialmente para llevar a cabo un acto secreto, incorrecto o ilegal; p. 287

constitute/constituir *v.* formar; crear; p. 625

convey/transmitir *v.* expresar; comunicar; p. 30

corroded/corroído *adj.* carcomido o consumido mediante una acción química; p. 245

covet/codiciar *v.* desear con fuerza; anhelar; p. 513

cower/encogerse *v.* agacharse, como cuando se tiene miedo o vergüenza; p. 131

craggy/escabroso *adj.* abrupto, áspero y desgastado; p. 285

crevice/grieta *s.* hendedura estrecha; p. 217

cringe/contraerse *v.* encogerse o retirarse, como cuando se siente miedo o desagrado; p. 217

crouch/acuclillarse *v.* agacharse o encogerse, especialmente con las rodillas dobladas; p. 558

crux/punto crucial *s.* punto o parte más importante; p. 41

curt/lacónico *adj.* tan corto o breve que parece descortés; p. 242

D

decree/decretar *v.* dar una regla, orden o decisión oficial; dictaminar; p. 259

decry/desaprobar *v.* criticar abiertamente; p. 343

default/incumplir *v.* fallar; dejar de hacer algo solicitado; p. 495

dejected/abatido *adj.* triste; deprimido; desanimado; p. 793

demean/degradar *v.* rebajar; deshonrar; p. 664

desolate/desolado *adj.* que no se puede consolar; p. 495

detract/quitar *v.* reducir mérito o valor; desvirtuar; p. 474

diligence/diligencia *s.* gran atención, cuidado y esfuerzo; p. 513

discern/discernir *v.* detectar o reconocer; identificar; p. 21

disclose/divulgar *v.* revelar; dar a conocer; publicar; p. 486

discord/discordia *s.* desacuerdo; conflicto; p. 498

discrimination/discriminación *s.* trato injusto, especialmente como resultado de políticas contra grupos minoritarios; p. 495

disembark/desembarcar *v.* bajarse de un tren, avión, barco u otro vehículo; p. 644

disgruntled/descontento *adj.* malhumorado; p. 744

disheveled/desaliñado *adj.* desarreglado; p. 483

disperse/dispersar *v.* ir en diferentes direcciones; p. 592

distinct/claro *adj.* que se puede escuchar, ver o sentir claramente; p. 174

diverse/diverso *adj.* patentemente diferente; variado; p. 630

diversion/distracción *s.* algo que distrae o aparta la atención; p. 148

docile/dócil *adj.* fácil de manejar, entrenar o enseñar; p. 103

doggedly/tenazmente *adv.* tercamente; firmemente; p. 514

dominant/dominante *adj.* que tiene el mayor poder o fuerza; aquél que controla; p. 817

dote/adorar *v.* demostrar inmenso afecto; p. 341

drone/hablar monótonamente *v.* hablar con tono soso; hacer un sonido bajo y constante, como un zumbido; p. 170

dry/árido *adj.* que no es interesante; aburridor; p. 608

dumbfounded/sin habla *adj.* que queda mudo por el asombro; pasmado; p. 400

E

eerie/misterioso *adj.* raro, especialmente de un modo que causa miedo; p. 10

elaborate/elaborado *adj.* complicado; hecho con mucho esmero; p. 240

eloquence/elocuencia *s.* acto de hablar o escribir de modo expresivo, efectivo y conmovedor; p. 485

embodiment/encarnación *s.* representación de una idea o cualidad; forma visible; p. 664

emit/emitir *v.* pronunciar; enviar o hacer un sonido; p. 341

emphatically/enfáticamente *adv.* muy definidamente; claramente; p. 643

emulate/emular *v.* imitar; p. 28

encounter/encontrarse *v.* tener una reunión inesperada; ver a alguien casualmente; p. 215

enfeebled/debilitado *adj.* que carece de fuerza, vigor o efectividad; p. 40

engulf/absorber *v.* tragar; sumir; p. 219

enhance/realzar *v.* aumentar; intensificar; p. 676

enmity/enemistad *s.* odio entre enemigos; hostilidad; p. 412

exalt/exaltar *v.* elevar en condición, dignidad o poder; glorificar; p. 498

extinguish/extinguir *v.* apagar; terminar; destruir; p. 624

F

forage/forrajear *v.* cazar o buscar alimento o suministros; p. 364

ford/vado *s.* lugar poco profundo de un río o quebrada que se puede atravesar a pie; p. 384

foreboding/presentimiento *s.* sensación de que algo malo está por ocurrir; p. 748

forfeit/perder *v.* dejar de tener una cosa o derecho como castigo; confiscar; p. 871

founder/fallar *v.* desbaratarse; caer; irse a pique; p. 611

frail/frágil *adj.* que no tiene fuerza; débil; p. 162

frenzy/frenesí *s.* estado de gran emoción o profunda alteración; p. 762

frustration/frustración *s.* desilusión o irritación por no poder hacer o alcanzar algo; p. 107

furtive/furtivo *adj.* secreto; engañoso; p. 152

futility/futilidad *s.* insignificancia; algo que es inútil o no vale la pena; p. 155

G

gaudily/ostentosamente *adv.* de un modo muy llamativo, al punto de ser de mal gusto; p. 241

gloat/vanagloriarse *v.* sentir o expresar placer o satisfacción por un éxito o logro, particularmente de un modo triunfante o malicioso; p. 63

gravely/gravemente *adv.* muy seriamente; p. 275

grimace/mueca *s.* gesto de la cara, como cuando se siente dolor o fastidio; p. 664

H

haggle/regatear *v.* pedir rebaja de un precio o discutir los términos de un acuerdo; p. 373

haughtily/altivamente *adv.* de un modo que muestra demasiado orgullo propio y desprecio por otros; p. 259

heft/levantar *v.* alzar; p. 245

humility/humildad *s.* cualidad de ser humilde o modesto; p. 32

hypocritical/hipócrita *adj.* que aparenta ser lo que no es; solapado; falso; p. 841

hysteria/histeria *s.* gran terror, furia u otra emoción muy fuerte e incontrolable; p. 54

I

illiteracy/analfabetismo *s.* no saber leer ni escribir; p. 205

immortality/inmortalidad *s.* capacidad de vivir o durar por siempre; p. 440

impaired/deteriorado *adj.* rebajado en calidad; dañado; p. 135

impel/impeler *v.* impulsar; motivar; causar; p. 190

impending/inminente *adj.* que está por ocurrir; p. 806

impromptu/impremeditado *adj.* que se hace de manera espontánea y sin preparación; p. 6

impudent/impudente *adj.* descarado; atrevido; p. 346

impulse/impulso *s.* fuerza interna que nos hace actuar sin pensarlo; p. 215

incentive/incentivo *s.* algo que motiva una acción, especialmente la recompensa que se promete por un esfuerzo o trabajo; p. 483

incompatible/incompatible *adj.* que no es capaz de existir o actuar conjuntamente y en armonía; contrario; p. 644

incomprehensible/incomprensible *adj.* imposible de entender; p. 483

incur/incurrir *v.* adquirir una obligación o algo indeseable; contraer una deuda; p. 31

indifference/indiferencia *s.* falta de sentimiento, preocupación o interés; p. 20

indignantly/indignadamente *adv.* de modo que demuestra rabia debido a un insulto o injusticia; p. 718

inert/inerte *adj.* que no se puede mover o actuar; sin vida; p. 613

inevitably/inevitablemente *adv.* que no se puede evitar o prevenir; p. 667

inextricably/inextricablemente *adv.* de un modo que no se puede separar; p. 496

infinite/infinito *adj.* sin límites; extremadamente grande; p. 105

inflict/infligir *v.* imponer algo que no se desea; p. 33

inhibition/inhibición *s.* acto de contener un impulso o deseo; p. 105

insight/perspicacia *s.* comprensión de la condición o naturaleza oculta de algo; visión; p. 598

insolence/insolencia *s.* atrevimiento; descortesía; p. 578

instinctive/instintivo *adj.* que surge de un impulso o tendencia natural; que no se ha aprendido; p. 189

integrity/integridad *s.* rectitud moral; honestidad; p. 187

intellectual/intelectual *adj.* referente a la inteligencia o habilidad mental; p. 130

intently/resueltamente *adv.* con concentración y firmeza; p. 8

intercession/intercesión *s.* solicitud, llamado u oración en bien de otros; p. 400

interim/ínterin *s.* tiempo entre dos sucesos; mientras tanto; p. 804
interminable/interminable *adj.* que dura o parece durar por siempre; eterno; p. 518
intimate/íntimo *adj.* muy cercano; allegado; p. 189
intolerant/intolerante *adj.* que no acepta o cede; p. 205
intricate/intrincado *adj.* con muchos detalles complicados; p. 31
intuition/intuición *s.* habilidad de saber algo sin tener que razonarlo; p. 755
invariably/invariablemente *adv.* de modo constante; siempre; p. 131
invigorating/vigorizador *adj.* tonificante; fortalecedor; refrescante; p. 666
involuntary/involuntariamente *adj.* sin intención o voluntad; p. 8

J

joviality/jovialidad *s.* buen humor; alegría; p. 21
jubilation/júbilo *s.* gran alegría y emoción; p. 736
jut/sobresalir *v.* proyectar fuera de una superficie; p. 415

L

laboriously/laboriosamente *adv.* con gran esfuerzo; p. 171
laden/cargado *adj.* repleto; atiborrado; p. 173
lapse/deslizarse *v.* caer o resbalarse; p. 286
legacy/legado *s.* algo que se recibe de un antepasado o del pasado; p. 40
legitimately/legítimamente *adv.* de un modo que sigue las reglas; legalmente; p. 441
liable/propenso *adj.* que tiene tendencia a; predispuesto; p. 555
loathe/abominar *v.* odiar; detestar; p. 709
loom/vislumbrarse *v.* asomarse o hacerse presente de un modo que parece muy grande y a menudo amenazador; p. 271
lucid/lúcido *adj.* mentalmente alerta; sagaz; p. 286
lunacy/disparate *s.* locura; conducta absurda; p. 514
lurch/tambalearse *v.* moverse repentinamente de modo abrupto y sin equilibrio; dar tumbos; p. 67
lurk/acechar *v.* ocultarse o moverse furtivamente; estar latente; p. 631

M

maladjustment/inadaptación *s.* que no se ajusta bien a las condiciones o los requisitos; p. 220
malice/malicia *s.* deseo de lastimar u ofender a alguien; p. 104
manifest/manifiesto *adj.* obvio; claro; preciso; evidente; p. 644
meager/exiguo *adj.* que no es suficiente en cantidad o volumen; insuficiente; p. 64
melancholy/melancólico *adj.* nostálgico; pensativo y triste; p. 676
meticulous/meticuloso *adj.* que se preocupa mucho por los detalles; p. 55
minimal/mínimo *adj.* lo más pequeño o lo menos posible; muy pequeño; p. 529
modest/modesto *adj.* que no desea elogios; humilde; sencillo; p. 532
mutely/mudamente *adv.* sin hablar; silenciosamente; p. 443

N

naive/ingenuo *adj.* inocente de las realidades de la vida; p. 32
naturalist/naturalista *s.* quien estudia los seres vivos, especialmente plantas y animales, mediante observación directa; p. 871

O

obliged/obligado *adj.* forzado, comprometido o impulsado a hacer algo; p. 36

obligingly/servicialmente *adv.* que muestra deseos de ser útil o servir; cortésmente; p. 220

obscure/ocultar *v.* esconder; disimular; p. 134

obviously/obviamente *adv.* de un modo que se puede ver o entender fácilmente; claramente; p. 560

ominous/ominoso *adj.* siniestro; nefasto; amenazador; p. 11

onslaught/embestida *s.* ataque furioso o destructivo; asalto; p. 747

opportunist/oportunista *s.* alguien que se aprovecha de cualquier oportunidad sin importarle las consecuencias; p. 127

P

pact/pacto *s.* acuerdo; convenio; p. 413

painstakingly/esmeradamente *adv.* de un modo que requiere gran cuidado o atención; p. 30

palatable/apetecible *adj.* agradable al gusto, la mente o los sentimientos; apetitoso; p. 345

pandemonium/pandemonio *s.* gran desorden o disturbio; p. 765

paramount/supremo *adj.* por encima de todos los demás en influencia o importancia; superior; p. 630

pathetically/patéticamente *adv.* trágicamente; conmovedoramente; p. 861

patriarch/patriarca *s.* líder masculino de una familia; anciano respetable; p. 173

pauper/indigente *s.* persona muy pobre que suele vivir de la caridad pública; p. 638

pensive/pensativo *adj.* que está callado y dedicado a pensar, a menudo cosas tristes; p. 822

perceive/percibir *v.* captar mentalmente; notar; p. 820

peremptory/perentorio *adj.* que no permite negativa; urgente; p. 342

perennial/perenne *adj.* que dura por largo tiempo; p. 595

persistently/persistentemente *adv.* repetidamente; p. 200

perturb/perturbar *v.* molestar; inquietar; turbar; p. 680

petite/menudo *adj.* de estatura baja y delgado; pequeño; p. 859

pious/piadoso *adj.* que demuestra devoción religiosa real o fingida; p. 583

pitch/plática de propaganda *s.* presentación de ventas con presión; p. 242

pivotal/fundamental *adj.* de importancia central; p. 857

placid/plácido *adj.* calmado o pacífico; p. 106

plight/aprieto *s.* situación difícil o peligrosa; p. 274

plummet/desplomarse *v.* caer verticalmente; p. 858

poise/aplomo *s.* actitud serena y controlada; p. 760

ponder/ponderar *v.* pensar algo cuidadosamente; p. 680

potential/potencial *s.* posibilidad de éxito; p. 241

prejudice/prejuicio *s.* opinión que se tiene de algo sin considerar todos los aspectos; p. 679

prestigious/prestigioso *adj.* que goza de importancia e influencia; notable; p. 625

presumably/presumiblemente *adv.* supuestamente; probablemente; p. 805

pretense/simulación *s.* demostración o apariencia falsa, especialmente con el propósito de engañar; falsedad; p. 289

priceless/incalculable *adj.* de tanto valor que no se puede calcular; p. 170

primly/remilgadamente *adv.* de un modo muy formal; p. 170

prodigious/prodigioso *adj.* enorme; vasto; p. 498

prodigy/prodigio *s.* persona extraordinariamente talentosa o inteligente, en particular un niño; p. 555

prominent/prominente *adj.* ampliamente conocido; p. 338

proposition/proposición *s.* sugerencia o plan; propuesta; p. 473

prowess/habilidad *s.* gran pericia o destreza; p. 269

proximity/proximidad *s.* cercanía en espacio, tiempo, orden o grado; p. 644

purged/purgado *adj.* limpio o purificado de cualquier suciedad; p. 591

Q

quaint/pintoresco *adj.* con un encanto antiguo; raro o peculiar de modo placentero; p. 638

quest/búsqueda *s.* intento de alcanzar una meta; p. 151

R

recoil/recular *v.* retroceder, como cuando se siente miedo; p. 859

redeemed/redimido *adj.* rescatado; recuperado; p. 625

refined/refinado *adj.* libre de aspereza; que muestra buen gusto y educación; p. 201

refrain/refrenarse *v.* abstenerse de hacer algo; restringirse; p. 384

regally/fastuosamente *adv.* de un modo grandioso; digno de un rey o una reina; majestuosamente; p. 287

remorse/remordimiento *s.* sentimiento de culpa o arrepentimiento; p. 153

renegade/renegado *s.* el que abandona o le da la espalda a un grupo, causa o alianza; traidor; p. 344

renovate/renovar *v.* modernizar; volver como nuevo; p. 173

renown/renombre *s.* amplia reputación; fama; p. 821

repress/reprimir *v.* mantener bajo control; oprimir; p. 514

reproach/reprochar *v.* regañar o culpar; p. 401

reputation/reputación *s.* opinión general sobre la condición de una persona o cosa; buen nombre; p. 555

resolutely/resueltamente *adv.* con determinación; p. 219

resolve/resolución *s.* determinación fija; firmeza al actuar; p. 631

revel/deleitarse *v.* recrearse; hacer algo con placer; p. 644

revert/revertir *v.* volver a una condición, comportamiento o creencia anterior; p. 667

revive/revivir *v.* recuperar la conciencia; mostrar nueva vida, fuerza o frescura; p. 373

righteousness/rectitud *s.* comportamiento recto, justo o legal; p. 519

S

sacred/sagrado *adj.* bendito; que merece gran respeto; p. 85

sagely/sabiamente *adv.* muy sensatamente; p. 276

savor/saborear *v.* deleitarse con algo; p. 191

scavenger/carroñero *s.* animal que se alimenta de carroña, como por ejemplo las hienas o buitres que se alimentan de plantas o animales muertos y en descomposición; p. 272

scour/frotar *v.* restregar con fuerza para limpiar, lavar o brillar; p. 597

scowling/ceño fruncido *s.* expresión facial de rabia o desacuerdo; p. 384

serene/sereno *adj.* calmado; pacífico; tranquilo; p. 290

serenity/serenidad *s.* calma; tranquilidad; p. 485

servile/servil *adj.* que sirve humildemente; p. 218

sheathe/enfundar *v.* meter en un forro o cubierta; p. 54

sheepishly/tímidamente *adv.* de modo que demuestra timidez o vergüenza; p. 81

sheer/escarpado *adj.* muy empinado; perpendicular; p. 410

simultaneously/simultáneamente *adv.* al mismo tiempo; p. 20

singularly/singularmente *adv.* de modo único o especial; extraordinariamente; p. 841

skirmish/pleito *s.* conflicto leve o de poca duración; escaramuza; p. 538

slither/culebrear *v.* deslizarse o escurrirse por el suelo como una serpiente; p. 52

slung/tirar *v.* lanzar o arrojar; p. 161
smug/presumido *adj.* demasiado vanidoso; p. 20
sober/calmarse *v.* adquirir una actitud seria y callada; p. 871
solemn/solemne *adj.* serio; p. 439
sophisticated/sofisticado *adj.* que tiene o demuestra conocimiento o experiencia del mundo; p. 65
specific/específico *adj.* muy claro y definido; p. 603
speculation/especulación *s.* opinión o conclusión basada en una suposición; p. 819
stately/solemnemente *adv.* de modo noble, digno o majestuoso; p. 79
steadfastly/constantemente *adv.* resueltamente; con determinación; p. 593
stealthily/clandestinamente *adv.* de un modo secreto o furtivo; p. 762
stifled/reprimido *adj.* frenado; oprimido; p. 837
stimulus/estímulo *s.* algo que causa una respuesta; p. 135
strenuous/vigoroso *adj.* muy activo; lleno de energía; p. 800
subdued/sometido *adj.* callado y abatido; p. 725
subsequently/posteriormente *adv.* después; más adelante; p. 21
substance/sustancia *s.* material básico; solidez; p. 862
subterfuge/subterfugio *s.* truco o método usado para escapar o esconder algo; evasiva; p. 188
subtle/sutil *adj.* que no es abierto o directo; que no es obvio; p. 243
suffused/bañado *adj.* cubierto de luz, color, emoción o cualidad; p. 186
sullen/malhumorado *adj.* retraído o taciturno debido al mal humor; hosco; p. 485
summit/cumbre *s.* punto o parte más alta; cima; p. 425
summon/convocar *v.* solicitar la presencia de alguien, a menudo con autoridad; p. 263
superficial/superficial *adj.* sin un significado profundo; vacío; que no tiene importancia o no es necesario; p. 677
syndrome/síndrome *s.* grupo de síntomas que, en conjunto, definen cierta enfermedad; p. 608

T

tamale/tamal *s.* mezcla de diversos ingredientes envueltos en hojas de maíz que se cocina al vapor o a la brasa; p. 71
tangible/tangible *adj.* que se puede ver, tocar o sentir; real; p. 129
taunt/mofarse *v.* burlarse de modo despreciable o insultante; p. 129
taut/tirante *adj.* tenso; estirado; p. 199
tempest/tempestad *s.* fuerte ventarrón, por lo común acompañado de lluvia, granizo, nieve o truenos; p. 530
tentatively/tentativamente *adv.* que no es definitivo; inciertamente; p. 6
tirade/diatriba *s.* discurso largo, furioso o lleno de críticas; p. 67
tranquillity/tranquilidad *s.* estado o cualidad de mantener la calma; quietud; p. 681
transition/transición *s.* paso de una posición, condición o actividad a otra; cambio; p. 576
tremor/temblor *s.* estremecimiento o sacudida; p. 8
tribulation/tribulación *s.* gran problema o pena; p. 496

U

unabashed/desenvuelto *adj.* que no demuestra timidez; atrevido; p. 706
uncomprehendingly/incomprensiblemente *adv.* de modo que no se entiende; p. 106
unnerving/inquietante *adj.* que causa inquietud o molestia; angustioso; p. 147
unrestrained/desenfrenado *adj.* que no se controla; p. 216
unseemly/impropio *adj.* que no es apropiado para el momento o lugar; que no es de buen gusto; p. 80
unsound/falso *adj.* que no es correcto o preciso; p. 372

unwavering/firme *adj.* constante; que no cambia ni se mueve; p. 592

V

vain/vano *adj.* inútil; ineficaz; p. 485
valiant/valiente *adj.* que demuestra valor; p. 582
valid/válido *adj.* respaldado por los hechos; verdadero; p. 204
vehemently/vehementemente *adv.* intensamente; apasionadamente; p. 841
vex/fastidiar *v.* molestar o enfurecer, especialmente mediante una acción repetitiva y tonta; p. 836
vibrant/vibrante *adj.* lleno de vida y energía; p. 402
vile/vil *adj.* muy malo; abominable; perverso; p. 715
virtue/virtud *s.* buena cualidad o rasgo admirable; p. 584
vividly/vívidamente *adv.* claramente; intensamente; p. 52

W

wallow/quedar desvalido *v.* quedar indefenso; p. 497
wan/lánguido *adj.* pálido o débil, como resultado de una enfermedad o gran cansancio; p. 515
wane/declinar *v.* llegar al fin; menguar; p. 839
wary/cauteloso *adj.* cuidadoso; alerta; p. 822
waver/vacilar *v.* dudar; p. 681
wretchedness/desdicha *s.* gran tristeza o profunda pena; p. 521

Index of Skills

Boldface page references indicate an extensive treatment of the topic.

References beginning with R refer to handbook pages.

Literary Concepts

Reading and Thinking

Grammar and Language

Vocabulary

Writing

Listening, Speaking, and Viewing

Research and Study Skills

Media and Technology

Life Skills

Interdisciplinary Studies

Index of Authors and Titles

K

L

M

N

O

P

Q

R

S

T

Index of Art and Artists

Acknowledgments

(Continued from page iv)

Literature

Theme 1

"The Treasure of Lemon Brown" by Walter Dean Myers. © 1983, Walter Dean Myers. Originally appeared in *Boys' Life.* Reprinted by permission of the author.

"My Two Dads" by Marie G. Lee, reprinted by permission of the author. "My Two Dads" first appeared in the *Brown Alumni Monthly.*

"A Dictionary of Japanese-American Terms" by R. A. Sasaki, from *Into the Fire,* copyright © 1996 by The Greenfield Review Press. Reprinted by permission of the author.

"Homeless" from *Living Out Loud* by Anna Quindlan. Copyright © 1987 by Anna Quindlan. Reprinted by permission of Random House, Inc.

"Homeless Children Write Book About Homelessness" Copyright © NPR® 1993. The news report by NPR's Howard Berkes was originally broadcast on National Public Radio's "Weekend Edition® Saturday" on December 25, 1993, and is used with the permission of National Public Radio, Inc. Any unauthorized duplication is strictly prohibited.

"The Farmer and His Sons" from *Anno's Aesop* by Mitsumasa Anno. Copyright © 1989 by Mitsumasa Anno. Reprinted by permission of Orchard Books, New York.

"Golden Glass" by Alma Luz Villanueva. Reprinted by permission of the author.

"Mother and Daughter" from *Baseball in April and Other Stories,* copyright © 1990 by Gary Soto, reprinted by permission of Harcourt Brace & Company.

"Chanclas" from *The House on Mango Street.* Copyright © 1984 by Sandra Cisneros. Published by Vintage Books, a division of Random House, Inc., and in hardcover by Alfred A. Knopf, Inc. Reprinted by permission of Susan Bergholz Literary Services, New York. All rights reserved.

"Real Indians Eat Jell-O" by Laurie Carlson. Reprinted by permission of the author.

"The Medicine Bag" by Virginia Driving Hawk Sneve, from *Boys' Life,* March 1975. Reprinted by permission of the author.

Theme 2

"All in a Day's Work" Copyright © 1973, 1974 by James Herriot, from *All Things Bright and Beautiful* by James Herriot. Reprinted by permission of Harold Ober Associates Incorporated. Copyright © 1973, 1974 by James Herriot, from *All Things Bright and Beautiful* by James Herriot. Reprinted by permission of St. Martin's Press Incorporated.

"Flowers for Algernon" by Daniel Keyes. Copyright © 1959, 1987 by Daniel Keyes. Reprinted by permission of the author.

"The Kid Nobody Could Handle," from *Welcome to the Monkey House* by Kurt Vonnegut Jr. Copyright © 1961 by Kurt Vonnegut Jr. Used by permission of Delacorte Press/Seymour Lawrence, a division of Bantam Doubleday Dell Publishing Group, Inc.

"You Gotta Be" Words and Music by Des'ree, Additional Music by Ashley Ingram. Copyright © 1994 Sony Music Publishing, U.K. and Careers-BMG Music Publishing Inc. All rights on behalf of Sony Music Publishing U.K. administered by Sony/ATV Music Publishing, 8 Music Square West, Nashville, TN 37203. All rights reserved. Used by permission.

"Thank You Ma'am" by Langston Hughes. Copyright © 1958 by Langston Hughes. Copyright renewed 1986 by George Houston Bass. Reprinted by permission of Harold Ober Associates Incorporated.

"The Journey" from *Days of Plenty, Days of Want* by Patricia Preciado Martin. (University of Arizona Press, 1999). Originally published in *La Confluencia,* 1980. Reprinted by permission of the author.

"Knoxville, Tennessee" from *Black Feeling, Black Talk, Black Judgment* by Nikki Giovanni. Copyright © 1968, 1970 by Nikki Giovanni. By permission of William Morrow & Company, Inc.

"Legacies" from *My House* by Nikki Giovanni. Copyright © 1972 by Nikki Giovanni. By permission of William Morrow & Company, Inc.

"A Mother in Mannville" reprinted with the permission of Scribner, a division of Simon & Schuster from *When the Whippoorwill* by Marjorie Kinnan Rawlings. Copyright 1936, 1940 by Marjorie Kinnan Rawlings; copyrights renewed © 1964, 1968 by Norton Baskin.

Excerpt from *I Know Why the Caged Bird Sings* by Maya Angelou. Copyright © 1969 by Maya Angelou. Reprinted by permission of Random House, Inc.

Excerpt from "Maya's Way: Maya Angelou's Zest for Life Continues to Fuel Her Creative Fire" by Patti Thorn. Reprinted with permission from the Rocky Mountain News.

Theme 3

"In the Middle of a Pitch" by Bill Meissner. From *Hitting Into the Wind,* Random House, 1994, Southern Methodist University paperback, 1997. Reprinted by permission of the author.

"The Wise Old Woman" from *Sea of Gold,* copyright © 1965 by Yoshiko Uchida. Courtesy of the Bancroft Library, University of California, Berkeley.

"Bagged Wolf" from *Sweet and Sour: Tales From China.* Copyright © 1980 by Carol Kendall and Yao-wen Li. Reprinted by permission of Bodley Head.
"Bagged Wolf" from *Sweet and Sour: Tales From China.* Copyright © 1980 by Carol Kendall and Yao-wen Li. Reprinted by permission of Clarion Books/Houghton Mifflin Co. All rights reserved.

"The Moustache" from *Eight Plus One: Stories by Robert Cormier* by Robert Cormier. Copyright © 1975 by Robert Cormier. Reprinted by permission of Pantheon Books, a division of Random House, Inc.

"The Black Walnut Tree" from *Twelve Moons* by Mary Oliver. Copyright © 1978 by Mary Oliver. First appeared in *The Ohio Review.* By permission of Little, Brown & Company.

"Fire and Ice" and "Dust of Snow" from *The Poetry of Robert Frost,* edited by Edward Connery Lathem, copyright 1951 by Robert Frost, copyright 1923, © 1969 by Henry Holt and Company, Inc. Reprinted by permission of Henry Holt and Company, Inc.

"Between What I See and What I Say . . ./Entre Lo Que Veo y Digo . . ." by Octavio Paz, from *Collected Poems 1957–1987.* Copyright © 1986 by Octavio Paz and Eliot Weinberger. Reprinted by permission of New Directions Publishing Corp.

"Identity" by Julio Noboa Polanco. Reprinted by permission of the author.

"the lesson of the moth," from *Archy and Mehitabel* by Don Marquis. Copyright 1927 by Doubleday, a division of Bantam Doubleday Dell Publishing Group, Inc. Used by permission of Doubleday, a division of Bantam Doubleday Dell Publishing Group, Inc.

"Going to the EXTREME: Young daredevils zip into mainstream" by Karen Thomas. Copyright © 1997, USA Today. Reprinted with permission.

Theme 4

"John Henry" from *A Natural Man: The True Story of John Henry* by Steve Sanfield. Reprinted by permission of David R. Godine, Publisher, Inc. Copyright © 1986 by Steve Sanfield.

Excerpt from *The People, Yes* by Carl Sandburg, copyright © 1936 by Harcourt Brace & Company and renewed 1964 by Carl Sandburg, reprinted by permission of the publisher.

"Sally Ann Thunder Ann Whirlwind" from *American Tall Tales* by Mary Pope Osborne. Text copyright © 1991 by Mary Pope Osborne. Reprinted by permission of Alfred A. Knopf, Inc.

"Lazy Peter and His Three-Cornered Hat" from *The Three Wishes: A Collection of Puerto Rican Folktales,* copyright © 1969 by Ricardo E. Alegria. Reprinted by permission of the author.

"M'su Carencro and Mangeur de Poulet" from *Cajun Folktales* by J. J. Reneaux (August House, 1992). Copyright © 1992 by J. J. Reneaux. Reprinted by permission of August House, Inc.

"Talk" from *The Cow-Tail Switch and Other West African Stories* by Harold Courlander and George Herzog, copyright © 1947 by Henry Holt and Company, Inc., © 1975 by Harold Courlander. Reprinted by permission of Henry Holt and Company, Inc.

"The People Could Fly" from *The People Could Fly* by Virginia Hamilton. Text copyright © 1985 by Virginia Hamilton. Reprinted by permission of Alfred A. Knopf, Inc.

"The Souls in Purgatory" by Guadalupe Baca-Vaughn. Reprinted by permission of the author.

"Spotted Eagle & Black Crow" from *The Sound of Flutes* by Richard Erdoes. Copyright © 1976 by Richard Erdoes. Reprinted by permission of Pantheon Books, a division of Random House, Inc.

"The Siege of Courthouse Rock" from *American Indian Myths and Legends* by Richard Erdoes and Alfonso Ortiz, editors. Copyright © 1984 by Richard Erdoes and Alfonso Ortiz, editors. Reprinted by permission of Pantheon Books, a division of Random House, Inc.

"Chicoria" from *Cuentos: Tales from the Hispanic Southwest* retold in English by Rudolfo A. Anaya. Copyright © 1980 by The Museum of New Mexico Press. Reprinted by permission of the publisher.

"Coyote and Wasichu" from *American Indian Myths and Legends* by Richard Erdoes and Alfonso Ortiz, editors. Copyright © 1984 by Richard Erdoes and Alfonso Ortiz. Reprinted by permission of Pantheon Books, a division of Random House, Inc.

"Pet survives trip on the wild side: plucky poodle returns alive after dog-napping by coyotes" by Guy Kelly. Reprinted with the permission of the Rocky Mountain News.

Theme 5

"The Drummer Boy of Shiloh" by Ray Bradbury. Reprinted by permission of Don Congdon Associates, Inc. Copyright © 1960 by the Curtis Publishing Co., renewed 1988 by Ray Bradbury.

"Author Says Paul Revere's Midnight Ride Not a Solitary One" Copyright © NPR® 1994. The news report by NPR's Robert Siegel was originally broadcast on National Public Radio's "All Things Considered®" on April 18, 1994, and is used with the permission of National Public Radio, Inc. Any unauthorized duplication is strictly prohibited.

"The Pinta, the Nina, and the Santa Maria and many other cargoes of light" by John Tagliabue, reprinted from *Prairie Schooner* by permission of the University of Nebraska Press. Copyright © 1963 University of Nebraska Press. Copyright © renewed 1991 University of Nebraska Press.

"The Other Pioneers" by Roberto Felix Salazar. *The LULAC National,* July 1939. Reprinted by permission of the League of United Latin American Citizens.

"Traveling the Long Road to Freedom, One Step at a Time" by Donovan Webster, from *Smithsonian* October 1996. Reprinted by permission of the author.

Excerpt from *Harriet Tubman: Conductor on the Underground Railroad* by Ann Petry. Reprinted by permission of Russell & Volkening as agents for the author. Copyright © 1955 by Ann Petry, renewed in 1983 by Ann Petry.

"I Have a Dream" reprinted by arrangement with The Heirs to the Estate of Martin Luther King, Jr., c/o Writers House, Inc. as agent for the proprietor. Copyright © 1968 by the Estate of Martin Luther King.

"Sorrow Home" from *This Is My Century: New and Collected Poems.* Copyright © 1989 by Margaret Walker Alexander. Reprinted by permission of the University of Georgia Press.

"Sit-Ins" from *This Is My Century: New and Collected Poems.* Copyright © 1989 by Margaret Walker Alexander. Reprinted by permission of the University of Georgia Press.

"Almost in America" from *Letters from Rifka* by Karen Hesse, © 1992 by Karen Hesse. Reprinted by permission of Henry Holt and Company, Inc.

Theme 6

"Raymond's Run" from *Gorilla, My Love* by Toni Cade Bambara Copyright © 1970 by Toni Cade Bambara. Reprinted by permission of Random House, Inc.

Excerpt from "Fast Finisher" by Joe Henderson, reprinted by permission of Runner's World Magazine. Copyrighted 1996, Rodale Press, Inc. All rights reserved.

"Forgotten Language" from *Where the Sidewalk Ends* by Shel Silverstein. Copyright © 1974 by Evil Eye Music, Inc. Used by permissions of HarperCollins Publishers.

"New World" copyright © N. Scott Momaday, from *In the Presence of the Sun,* St. Martin's Press, 1992. Reprinted by permission of the author.

"Thank You in Arabic" from *Going Where I'm Coming From.* Copyright © 1995 by Naomi Shihab Nye. Reprinted by permission of the author.

Excerpts from EarthView Survey, Copyright © 1998 National 4-H Council. Reprinted by permission.

"If I Forget Thee, Oh Earth" by Sir Arthur C. Clarke. Reprinted by permission of the author and the author's agents, Scovil Chichak Galen Literary Agency, Inc.

Poem #585 reprinted by permission of the publishers and the trustees of Amherst College from *The Poems of Emily Dickinson,* Thomas H. Johnson, ed., Cambridge, Mass.: The Belknap Press of Harvard University Press, Copyright © 1951, 1955, 1979, 1983 by the President and Fellows of Harvard College.

"Southbound on the Freeway" reprinted with the permission of Simon & Schuster Books for Young Readers, an imprint of Simon & Schuster Children's Publishing Division from *The Complete Poems to Solve* by May Swenson. Copyright © 1993 The Literary Estate of May Swenson. First appeared in the *New Yorker,* 2/16/63.

"Stop the Sun" copyright © 1986 by Gary Paulsen, from *Boys' Life,* January 1986. Reprinted by permission.

"The Summer of Vietnam" copyright © 1992 by Barbara Renaud Gonzalez. First published in *New Chicana/Chicano Writing,* University of Arizona Press. Reprinted by permission of Susan Bergholz Literary Services, New York. All rights reserved.

"Americans All" from *Paper Trail* by Michael Dorris. Copyright © 1994 by Michael Dorris. Reprinted by permission of HarperCollins Publishers, Inc.

Theme 7

Excerpts from *All But My Life* by Gerda Klein. Copyright © 1957 and copyright renewed 1995 by Gerda Weissmann Klein. Reprinted by permission of Hill & Wang, a division of Farrar, Straus & Giroux, Inc.

Excerpt from *Anne Frank: The Diary of a Young Girl* by Anne Frank. Copyright © 1952 by Otto H. Frank. Used by permission of Doubleday, a division of Bantam Doubleday Dell Publishing Group, Inc.

Excerpt from the Anne Frank House Web site (www.annefrank.nl/), reprinted by permission of the Anne Frank Center, New York.

"The Anne Frank House: Amsterdam" by Joan LaBombard from *The Counting of Grains,* 1990, San Diego Poets Press. This poem first appeared in *Yankee* magazine, September 1988. Reprinted by permission of the author.

The Diary of Anne Frank by Frances Goodrich and Albert Hackett. Copyright © 1954, 1956 as an unpublished work. Copyright © 1956 by Albert Hackett, Frances Goodrich Hackett and Otto Frank. Reprinted by permission of Random House, Inc.

Lyric excerpts of "I Think Myself Out." Lyrics by Enid Futterman, Music by Michael Cohen. Copyright © 1985 by Enid Futterman and Michael Cohen. The arrangement copyright © 1996 by Enid Futterman and Michael Cohen. Jem Associates and Williamson Music owners of publication and allied rights throughout the world (all rights administered by Williamson Music). International Copyright Secured. All Rights Reserved. Used by Permission.

Theme 8

"Sorry, Right Number" by Stephen King. Reprinted by permission of Stephen King, c/o Arthur B. Green & Co.

Excerpt from "American Gothic," *ABC Nightline,* December 10, 1997. Special thanks to ABC News Nightline for permission to reprint.

"The Woman in the Snow" from *The Dark Thirty* by Patricia McKissack. Text copyright © 1992 by Patricia McKissack. Reprinted by permission of Alfred A. Knopf, Inc.

"The Dinner Party" by Mona Gardner, copyright © 1942, 1970 by *Saturday Review,* reprinted by permission of Bill Berger Associates, Inc.

Excerpt from "The History of the Mystery" MysteryNet.com, copyright © 1996, 1999 Newfront Productions. Reprinted by permission.

Maps

Ortelius Design, Inc.

Photography

Abbreviation key: **AH**=Aaron Haupt; **AR**=Art Resource, New York; **BAL**=Bridgeman Art Library, London/New York; **CB**=Corbis-Bettmann; **CI**=Christie's Images; **FMWPC**= Frank & Marie-Therese Wood Print Collection, Alexandria VA; **LPBC/AH**=book provided by Little Professor Book Company. Photo by AH; **LOC**=Library of Congress; **PR**=Photo Researchers; **SIS**=Stock Illustration Source; **SS**=SuperStock; **TSI**=Tony Stone Images; **TSM**=The Stock Market.

Cover (baseball mitt)Geoff Butler, (painting)*Strike,* 1949. Jacob Lawrence. Tempera on Masonite, 20 x 24 in. The Howard University Gallery of Art, Washington DC; **vii** (t to b)CI, Anna Belle Lee Washington/SS, Daniel Cox/Natural Exposures, CI, AR, NASA, Anne Frank House & Museum, Amsterdam, Christopher Johnson/Stock Boston; **viii** (t)Peter Menzel/MATERIAL WORLD, (b)Amanita Pictures; **ix** SS; **x** Amanita Pictures; **xi** (t, bl)Corbis, (br)China Pictorial Photo Service; **xii** Daniel J. Cox/Natural Exposures; **xiii** Kactus Foto, Santiago, Chile/SS; **xiv** (t)First Image, (b)Movie Still Archives; **xv** Dane Tilghman; **xvi** (l)Amanita Pictures, (r)Private collection/Christian Pierre/SS; **xvii** Jeffrey Hall; **xviii** Dave G. Houser/Corbis; **xix** (t)Francisco Cruz/SS, (b)The Kobal Collection; **xx** Illustrated by Russ Flint; **xxi** (l)courtesy Mystery Writers of America, (r)First Image; **xxii** Illustrated by Gustave Dore; **xxx–1** Peter Menzel/MATERIAL WORLD; **2** Universal Press Syndicate; **3** Amanita Pictures; **4** courtesy Harper Collins Publishers; **5** Lee MARhall/FPG; **7** National Museum of American Art, Washington DC/AR (1967.59.748); **11** Private collection/Gil Mayers/SS; **13** Amanita Pictures; **14** First Image; **15** CI/SS; **17** ©1998 Separate Cinema Archive; **18** Courtesy Karl Jacoby; **19** Courtesy Katie Butler; **20–21** Matt Meadows; **22** (t)Matt Meadows, (b)D.J. Ball/TSI; **23** Alain Evrard/PR; **26** Rob Leri; **27** David and Jeanne Carlson, from *American Scene Painting, California 1930s and 1940s* by R.L. Westphal; **29** Courtesy Allen Say; **31** Doug Martin; **32** David Forbert/SS; **33** The E. Gene Crain Collection; **36** Tom Tracy/TSI; **38** (t)courtesy Random House, (c)Joyce Ravid, (b)Doug Martin; **39** Amanita Pictures, (inset)Doug Martin; **40** First Image; **42** Charles Gupton/Stock Boston; **46** Amanita Pictures; **49** Geoff Butler; **50** (l)courtesy Alma Luz Villanueva, (r)Geoff Butler; **51** Suzanne Murphy/FPG; **53** Private collection/David Nevins/SS; **56** H. Armstrong Roberts; **59** AH; **61** (t)courtesy Carolyn Soto, (b)First Image; **62** Courtesy Yreina D. Cervantez; **66** Courtesy El Museo del Barrio, gift of Joanne Blanco; **68** Amanita Pictures; **70** (t)AP/Wide World Photo, (b)Amanita Pictures; **71** (t)AH, (b)Matt Meadows; **72** AH; **74** Courtesy El Museo del Barrio, gift of Joann Blanco; **76** Amanita Pictures; **77** Courtesy Virginia Driving Hawk Sneve; **79** Kam Mak/SIS; **80** Doug Martin; **82** CI; **84** AR/Werner Forman Archive/British Museum, London; **85** David Schultz/TSI; **87** Amanita Pictures; **88** From the David T. Vernon Collection of Native

American Indian Center, Colter Bay Indian Arts Museum, Grand Teton National Park WY. Photographers John Oldenkamp and Cynthia Sabransky; **95** (t)AH, (b)Geoff Butler; **98–99** SS; **100** Universal Press Syndicate; **101** Matt Meadows; **102** AP/Wide World Photos; **103** CI; **104** Mark Torso; **106** Rob Talbot/TSI; **107** Amanita Pictures; **108** AH; **109** USDA; **110** AH; **112** Courtesy Daniel Keys; **115** Bob Daemmrich/Stock Boston; **116** Movie Still Archives; **119, 121** Archive Photo; **122 through 125** Amanita Pictures; **128** Doug Martin; **129** Amanita Pictures; **131** PhotoFest; **134** Diana Ong/SS; **135** ©Kodansha Ltd. 1986; **139** Collection of Prince Sadruddin Aga Khan, Geneva; **141** Matt Meadows; **145** Les Stone/Sygma; **146–147** AH; **149** Giraudon/AR; **152** Doug Martin; **154** CB; **156** Courtesy Tam Van Tran; **157** Amanita Pictures; **158** AH; **159** Ron Davis/Shooting Star; **160** (t)Schomburg Center for Research in Black Culture, The New York Public Library, Astor, Lenox and Tilden Foundation, (b)Amanita Pictures; **161** Gift of Helen Farr Sloan, ©1998 Board of Trustees, National Gallery of Art, Washington DC; **162** Hampton University Museum, Hampton VA; **164** Amanita Pictures; **166** National Gallery of Art, Washington DC; **168** Courtesy Patricia P. Martin; **169, 170–171** Chuck Place; **172** Photograph: James O. Milmoe. Courtesy The Anschutz Collection; **173** Chuck Place; **174** (t)Chuck Place, (b)Jeffrey Dunn/Stock Boston; **175, 176, 177** Geoff Butler; **180** Judie Burstein/Globe Photos; **181** Anna Belle Lee Washington/SS; **182** Courtesy Loïs Mailou Jones; **184** Archive Photos; **185** (t)W. Cody/Corbis Los Angeles, (b)Amanita Pictures; **186** Keith Turpie; **187–188** CI; **189** Amanita Pictures; **190** William J. Weber; **191** Thomas R. Fletcher/Stock Boston; **192** Amanita Pictures; **193** Lambert/Archive Photos; **197** Geoff Butler; **198** Yoham Kahana/Shooting Star; **199** Courtesy Mary-Anne Martin/Fine Art, New York; **200** Hyacinth Manning-Carner/SS; **202** Amanita Pictures; **203** NY State Historical Association, Cooperstown, photo by Richard Walker; **206** John Kaprielian/PR; **207** Amanita Pictures; **209** Doug Martin; **210** Paul Fetters/Matrix; **212** AP/Wide World Photo; **213** Amanita Pictures; **215** AH; **216** Ganjay M. Marathe/Dinodia Picture Agency; **217** ©1998 Richard Estes/licensed by VAGA, New York, NY/courtesy of the Marlborough Galleries, New York.; **221** First Image; **224** Amanita Pictures; **227** Bob Daemmrich/Stock Boston; **231** (br)Geoff Butler, (others)LPBC/AH; **234–235** Corbis Media; **237** CI/SS; **238** Jim Altobell; **239** Courtesy ACA Galleries, New York and John Dobbs; **243** Bret Wills; **244** Walker Art Center, Minneapolis MN; **246** Gregory Thorp; **247** Glencoe photo; **251** (t)Glencoe photo, (b)Doug Martin; **252** Photo courtesy the Archives of the American Illustrators Gallery, New York. ©by Asap of Holderness NH 03245 USA; **254** Museum of the City of New York; **256** Photo courtesy the Archives of the American Illustrators Gallery, New York. ©by Asap of Holderness NH 03245 USA; **257** National Baseball Library, Cooperstown NY; **258** Glencoe photo; **259** Asian Art Museum of San Francisco, The Avery Brundage Collection (B76 D3); **261** ©The British Art Museum; **264** Doug Martin; **266** Photofest; **268** Courtesy of Chu-tsing Li; **269** Daniel J. Cox/Natural Exposures; **270** By courtesy of The Board of Trustees of The Victoria & Albert Museum, London/BAL/SS; **273** Dallas Museum of Art, Foundation for the Arts Collection, gift of James H. and Lillian Clark Foundation. Mondrian/Holtzman Trust; **276** CI; **277** China Pictorial Photo Service; **281** (l)Beth Bergman, (r)AH; **282** AH; **285** Edmundson Collection, Des Moines Art Center. Photograph: Michael Tropea, Chicago; **286** Doug Martin; **288** SIS; **291** Doug Martin; **292** Stephen Rose/TSI; **295** First Image; **297** Geoff Butler; **298** (t)Barbara Savage Cheresh, (b)CI; **299** Amanita Pictures; **300** Doug Martin; **301** First Image; **302** (t)CB, (b)Alden Blackington, courtesy Dartmouth College Library; **303** Flint Institute of Arts. Gift of the Viola E. Bray Charitable Trust (67.29); **304–305** CI; **306** Doug Martin; **307** A & F Michler/Peter Arnold, Inc.; **309** CB; **310, 311, 312** CI; **316** (t)Clem Spalding, (bl)Paul Thompson/FPG, (br)Ed Frascino, courtesy University Press of New England; **317** SS; **318** Jack Novak/SS; **320** Roger K. Burnard; **323** Rudi VonBriel; **325** Bob Daemmrich/Stock Boston; **329** (br)Geoff Butler, (others)LPBC/AH; **332** Kactus Foto, Santiago, Chile/SS; **334** Universal Press Syndicate; **335** First Image; **336** Universal Press Syndicate; **337** CB; **338–339** AH; **340** CI; **347** Geoff Butler; **348** Everett Collection; **350** (l)CB, (r)Amanita Pictures; **351** Matt Meadows; **353** From *The Legend of John Henry* by Terry Small. Copyright ©1994 by Terry Small. Used by permission of Bantam Doubleday Dell Books for Young Readers; **357** Doug Martin; **359** Geoff Butler; **360** Paul Conklin; **365** Michael McCurdy, courtesy Alfred A. Knopf; **366–367** S. Michael Bisceglie/Animals Animals; **370** Glencoe photo; **371** AH; **374** Collection of Ileana Font, Mirama, Puerto Rico; **375** Amanita Pictures; **377** Courtesy J.J. Reneaux; **378** Courtesy Saulo Moreno; **380** Roger K. Burnard; **382** (t)Herbert Cohen, (b)courtesy IN University; **383** Photo: Claude Postel/©C.A.A.C.–The Pigozzi Collection, Geneva; **384** AH; **385** Geoff Butler; **386** Saulo Moreno; **388** (t)Ron Rovtar, (b)Photo by Earlie Hudnell, Jr./Artcetera; **389** Courtesy Leo & Diana Dillon; **391** Photo courtesy the Wyeth Collection; **394** Chase Swift/Corbis Los Angeles; **397** CB; **398** (l)courtesy Carlos G. Vaughn, (r)Richard B. Levine; **399** CI; **400** Chuck Place; **401** AH; **402** Instituto Nacional de Bellas Artes Direccion de Asuntos Juridicon; **404** Nicolas Sapieha/AR; **407** Photo by Christopher G. Knight; **408** Richard Erdoes; **409** Courtesy Jerry Ingram; **411** Mark Newman/SS; **413** CI; **414** (t)Natural History Museum, Smithsonian Institution, (b)Grant Heilman; **416** University of NE Lincoln, Christlieb Collection. Photograph by Roger Bruhn; **418** (t)Glencoe photo, (bl)Glencoe photo, (br)courtesy Mindy Dwyer; **419** Museum of TX Tech University, Lubbock TX; **421** Courtesy the San Antonio Museum of Art; **422** AH; **423** Movie Still Archive; **430** (br)Geoff Butler, (others)LPBC/AH; **434–435** Dane Tilghman; **436** Universal Press Syndicate; **438** Ralph Merlino/Shooting Star; **439** LOC; **441** Larry Sherer/High Impact; **442–443** First Image; **444** NY Historical Society; **448** (t)CB, (b)Museum of Fine Art, Boston. Gift by subscription and Francis Bartlett Fund.; **449** Arthur Hoppock Hearn Fund, 1950, The Metropolitan Museum of Art, New York (50.117); **452** SS; **454** Doug Martin; **455** Tom Brass/Stock Boston; **458** FPG; **459** Photo by Thomas Kosa; **460–461** Larry Sherer/High Impact; **463** FMWPC; **466** (t)Phyllis Graber Jensen, (b)Photo by Frank Lerner, ©1975 Time-Life Books. Courtesy The Showers-Brown Collection, The Star of The Republic Museum TX; **467** National Maritime Museum; **468** The Nelson-Atkins Museum of Art, Kansas City MO. Gift of Mr. and Mrs. Robert B. Fizzell through the Friends of Art; **470** Panhandle-Plains Historical Museum; **472** (t)LOC, (c)David Noble/FPG, (b)FPG; **473** Amanita Pictures; **474** Collection of Mr. & Mrs. Robert L. Sharpe; **475** AR; **476** Lance Nelson/TSM; **478** Wayne Sorce; **479** (l)AP/Wide World Photos, (r)Amanita Pictures; **480** National Museum of American Art, Washington DC/AR; **482** CB; **487** National Portrait Gallery, Smithsonian Institution/AR; **488** National Museum of American Art, Washington DC/AR; **492** (l)Corbis, (r)courtesy Frances Foster, (border)AH; **493** (l)Bob Adelman/Magnum Photos, (r)Corbis; **494** *The King Mural* by Don Miller ©District of Columbia Public Library; **497** FPG; **499** FMWPC; **500** AH; **503** (t)Nancy Crampton, (b)UPI/CB; **504** Grant Heilman; **505** AP/Wide World Photos; **506** Matt Meadows; **508** National Archives; **509** Geoff Butler; **510** (l)Adams County Historical Society, (r)LOC; **511** LOC; **512** US Army Military Historical Institute; **515** National Archives (#111-B-357); **516** AH; **520** From the original painting by Mort Kunstler, *The Gettysburg Address* ©1987 Mort Kunstler, Inc.; **523** Randy O'Rouke/TSM; **526** (l)courtesy Scholastic, Inc., (r)Amanita Pictures; **527** Tim Courlas; **528** North Wind Picture Archives; **531** LOC; **532** Amanita Pictures; **535** Photography Collection, Miriam and Ira D. Wallach Division of Art, Prints and Photographs, The New York Public Library. Astor, Lenox and Tilden Foundations.; **536** Amanita Pictures; **541** Doug Martin; **545** AH, (br)Geoff Butler; **548** Christian Pierre/SS; **551** Scala/AR (K52827); **552** ©1998 Bill Gaskins; **553** Courtesy Robin Holder; **554–556, 557–558** AH; **559** David Madison; **560** AH; **561–562** Amanita Pictures; **564** Barbara Shaw Photography; **566** (tl)Nancy Crampton, (bl)AP/Wide World, (r)Doug Martin; **569** Linda Lomehaftewa; **570** Photograph ©1998 The Museum of Modern Art, New York. Gift of Mr. And Mrs. Stanley B. Resor; **571** Courtesy N. Scott Momaday; **573** Gerardo Somoza/Outline; **574** AH; **575** (t)AH, (b)Paola Koch/PR; **576** Lawrence Migdale/Stock Boston; **579** Jim Harrison/Stock Boston;

585 (t)illustration by Nancy Carpenter, courtesy Simon & Schuster, (b)Glencoe photo; **586** Holt Studios International/PR; **590** Dana Fineman; **591–597** NASA; **598** (tl)Amherst College Library, (bl)CB, (r)Jeff Clark; **599** The Harry T. Peters Collection, Museum of the City of New York; **601** O.K. Harris Works of Art, New York; **602** John Holcroft/SS; **606** (l)Ruth Wright Paulsen, (r)courtesy US Army Center of Military History; **607** Courtesy H. Avery Chenowith and the US Marine Corps Art Collection.; **609** Lucia Gallery, New York/T.F. Chen/SS; **612** Ernest Manewal/FPG; **615** Jeffrey Hall; **619** Thomas R. Fletcher/Stock Boston; **621** Geoff Butler; **622** (l)courtesy Barbara Gonzalez, (r)Warren Motts Photographic Center; **623** Hubertus Kanus/PR; **624** G. Randall/FPG; **626** Kulik Photographic; **628** (t)courtesy University of North TX Press, (b)FMWPC; **629** CI; **630** Joseph Nettis/PR; **632** Jeffrey S. Hall; **634** (l)CBS/Archive Photos, (r)AH; **635** David Frazier PhotoLibrary; **636** Joseph Sohm, ChromoSohm, Inc./Corbis; **637** (t)Geoff Butler, (b)UPI/CB; **639** Doug Wilson/Black Star; **642** (t)Miriam Berkely, (b)Lawrence Manning/Corbis Los Angeles; **643–645** National Museum of American Art/AR; **646** Jim Cummins/FPG; **650** Karen Thomas/Stock Boston; **651** (t)Bob Daemmrich/Stock Boston, (tc)Doug Martin, (bl)Doug Martin, (br)Jerry Berndt/Stock Boston; **655** AH, (br)Geoff Butler; **658–659** Dave G. Houser/Corbis; **660** CB; **661** AH; **662** Carl Cox; **663** Jon Love/The Image Bank, (inset)courtesy HBO Pictures; **665** Jeffrey Hall; **667** Wide World Photo; **668** Courtesy HBO Pictures; **669** Amanita Pictures; **674** (l)Wide World Photo, (r)Anne Frank House & Museum, Amsterdam; **675 through 681** Anne Frank House & Museum, Amsterdam; **682** Archive Photos/Foto International; **684** Anne Frank House & Museum, Amsterdam; **685** (t)Everett Collection, (b)Anne Frank House & Museum, Amsterdam; **686** (t)courtesy San Diego Poets Press, (b)Anne Frank House & Museum, Amsterdam; **687** Randy Wells/TSI; **689** Office of War Documentation, Amsterdam; **693** Seattle Children's Theatre/photo Fred Andrews; **695** Geoff Butler; **696** UPI/CB; **697** The Kobal Collection; **702 through 727** PhotoFest; **728** Amanita Pictures; **732, 738, 741** PhotoFest; **742** Amanita Pictures; **745 through 750** PhotoFest; **754** Archive Photo/Foto International; **759 through 771** PhotoFest; **773** Doug Martin; **774** Anne Frank House & Museum, Amsterdam; **776** Doug Martin; **779** Glencoe photo; **783** (br)Geoff Butler, (others)LPBC/AH; **786–787** Francisco Cruz/SS; **788** ©1996 Los Angeles Times Syndicate; **789** Movie Still Archives; **790** (l)Ted Thai/Sygma, (r)The Kobal Collection; **791** Frank Saragnese/FPG; **792 through 796** AH; **797** (t)AH, (b)Diana Ong/SS; **798** AH; **799** (t)AH, (b)Edward Holub/Photonica; **800 through 803** AH; **804** (t)AH, (b)K. Shimauchi/Photonica; **805** AH; **806** (t)AH, (b)Barnaby Hall/Photonica; **807–808** AH; **809** Christopher Johnson/Stock Boston; **810** AH; **815** FMWPC; **816–817** Illustrated by Russ Flint, from the book *The Legend of Sleepy Hollow;* **819, 825** Illustration ©1992 by Michael Garland from *The Legend of Sleepy Hollow.* Published by Boyds Mills Press, Inc. Reprinted by permission; **828** Illustrated by Russ Flint, from the book *The Legend of Sleepy Hollow;* **829** Randy O'Rouke/TSM; **830** Kimberly Bulcken Root; **833** Geoff Butler; **834** FMWPC; **838** Movie Still Archives; **840** Everett Collection; **842** Amanita Pictures; **843** AH; **844** Courtesy Mystery Writers of America; **846** Larry Sherer/High Impact; **847** Tom Ulrich/TSI; **850** Mary Evans Picture Library; **854** Illustration Gustave Doré; **855** Illustration by Peter Weevers; **856** Courtesy Dial Books; **857** Collection of George and Terry Gray, photograph ©1996 Indianapolis Museum of Art; **859** AH; **860** CI; **863** (t)AP/Wide World Photo, (b)AH; **865–870** CI; **872** Joe McDonald/Tom Stack & Associates; **873** NASA; **879** (br)Geoff Butler, (others)LPBC/AH.

Editing/Proofreading Checklist

Use this proofreading checklist to help you check for errors in your writing, and use the proofreading symbols in the chart below to mark places that need corrections.

- ☑ **Have I avoided run-on sentences and sentence fragments and punctuated sentences correctly?**
- ☑ **Have I used every word correctly, including plurals, possessives, and frequently confused words?**
- ☑ **Do verbs and subjects agree? Are verb tenses correct?**
- ☑ **Do pronouns refer clearly to their antecedents and agree with them in person, number, and gender?**
- ☑ **Have I used adverb and adjective forms and modifying phrases correctly?**
- ☑ **Have I spelled every word correctly, and checked the unfamiliar ones in a dictionary?**

Proofreading Symbols		
⊙	Lieut⊙Brown	Insert a period.
∧	No one came∧(to) the party.	Insert a letter or a word.
≡	I enjoyed paris.	Capitalize a letter.
/	The Class ran a bake sale.	Make a capital letter lowercase.
⁀ ‿	The campers are home sick.	Close up a space.
(sp)	They visited (N.Y.) (sp)	Spell out.
∧ ;	Sue, please come; I need your help.	Insert a comma or a semicolon.
∩∪	He enjoyed feild day.	Transpose the position of letters or words.
#	alltogether	Insert a space.
℘	We went to to Boston.	Delete letters or words.
∨ ∨ ∨	She asked "Whos coming?"	Insert quotation marks or an apostrophe.
/ = /	mid January	Insert a hyphen.
¶	"Where?" asked Karl. ¶"Over there," said Ray.	Begin a new paragraph.